RPG II AND RPG III PROGRAMMING

Second Edition

RPG II AND RPG III PROGRAMMING

Carl Feingold C.P.A., C.D.P.
West Los Angeles College, Emeritus

Howard Eulencamp
*Los Angeles Valley College, Instructor
Los Angeles Community College District,
Supervising Systems & Programming
Analyst*

Steve Gonsoski
*West Los Angeles College, Instructor
Los Angeles Community College District,
Senior Programmer Analyst*

Wm. C. Brown Publishers
Dubuque, Iowa

Book Team
Developmental Editor *Beth Kundert*
Designer *K. Wayne Harms*
Visuals Processor *Joyce E. Watters*

wcb
Chairman of the Board *Wm. C. Brown*
President and Chief Executive Officer *Mark C. Falb*

wcb
Wm. C. Brown Publishers, College Division
President *G. Franklin Lewis*
Vice President, Editor-in-Chief *George Wm. Bergquist*
Vice President, Director of Production *Beverly Kolz*
Vice President, National Sales Manager *Bob McLaughlin*
Director of Marketing *Thomas E. Doran*
Marketing Communications Manager *Edward Bartell*
Marketing Information Systems Manager *Craig S. Marty*
Marketing Manager *Craig S. Marty*
Production Editorial Manager *Colleen A. Yonda*
Production Editorial Manager *Julie A. Kennedy*
Publishing Services Manager *Karen J. Slaght*
Manager of Visuals and Design *Faye M. Schilling*

Copyright © 1982, 1989 by Wm. C. Brown Publishers. All rights reserved

Library of Congress Catalog Card Number: 88-71392

ISBN 0-697-00991-2

No part of this publication may be reproduced, stored in a retrieval system, or transmitted, in any form or by any means, electronic, mechanical, photocopying, recording, or otherwise, without the prior written permission of the publisher.

Printed in the United States of America by Wm. C. Brown Publishers
2460 Kerper Boulevard, Dubuque, IA 52001

10 9 8 7 6 5 4 3 2 1

Contents

Preface xi

1 Introduction to Basic RPG Concepts 1

Programs and Programming Languages 2
  Source Programs 2
  Source Programs to Object Programs 3
    Saving and Executing Object Programs 3
    Basic Compilation and Execution Operations 3
  Summary 4
Building Blocks of Data Processing 6
  Record Layout 7
  Printer Spacing Chart 9
  Summary 11
Specification Forms 11
RPG Basic Cycle 12
RPG Logic Cycle 15
  Basic Data-Processing Logic 16
  Indicators 17
  RPG Logic Related to Indicators 17

2 Input and Output Processing 26

Describing Data 27
RPG Basic Logic Cycle 27
  Data Movement within the Cycle 27
Writing Specifications for Input and Output Operations 27
Control Specifications 28
Describing Files 29
  File Description Specifications 31
    Filename 31
    File Use 32
    File Designation 32
    Record Size 33
    Overflow Indicators 33
    Program Cycle Operations 34
    RPG Specifications 34
    Using Overflow and 1P Indicators Together 35
    Device Designation 36
  Summary 36

Line Counter Specifications 36
  Filename 38
  Specifications 38
Describing Input Records 39
  Input Specifications 40
    Filename 40
    Specifying Record Type Sequence 40
    Specifying Record Identifying Indicators 41
  Specifying Record Identification Codes 45
  Describing Fields 47
    Describing Fields within Records 47
    Field Location 47
    Type of Data 47
    Field Name 48
  Summary 49
Describing Output Records 50
  Output Specifications 52
    Filename 53
    Record Type 54
    Field name 55
    Field Location 56
  Printed Reports 56
    Spacing 56
    Skipping 57
  Editing 58
  *PLACE 58
  First Page Indicator 60
    Program Cycle Operations 60
    RPG Specifications 61
  Summary 64
  Heading Output 65
    Constants 65
    1P Indicator and Type 65
    Spacing and Skipping 65
Writing the First Program 66
  Common Entries 66
    Keying Instructions 66
    Page Number 66
    Line Number 66
    Form Type 67
    Comments 67
    Program Identification 68

Calculation Operations 80

Logic Cycle 81
Purpose of Calculations 82

  Operations 82
  Data 83
  Conditions 83
  Order 84
  Tests 84
Writing Specifications for Calculation Operations 84
  Arithmetic Operations 84
    Describing Type of Operations 85
    Describing Use of Data 85
    Describing Result Field 87
    Testing Results of Arithmetic Operations 88
    Move Remainder (MVR) 90
    Coding Arithmetic Operations— Summary 90
    Calculation Notes 92
  Compare Operations 92
    Rules for Numeric Constants 93
    Rules for Alphameric Constants 93
    Coding Compare Operations— Summary 94
Using Indicators to Control Calculations and Output 97
  Resulting Indicators 97
    RPG Specifications 99
  Last Record Indicator (LR) 100
    Program Cycle Operations 100
    RPG Specifications 103
Editing 104
  Edit Codes 104
    Edit Code Z (Zero Suppress) 105
    Edit Code Y (Date Field Edit) 105
  Edit Words 107
    Floating $ 107
    Asterisk Fill 108
Reserved Fields 110
  PAGE 110
  User Date 110
    UDATE 111
    UMONTH, UDAY, UYEAR 111
    Notes on Coding PAGE and UDATE 111

Summary 113
   Indicators 113
   Calculations 116
   Heading Output 116
   Detail Output 116
   Total Output 116
   Constants 116
   Edit 116
RPG III Enhancements 116
   Calculations 116

4 Control Level Operations 132

Control Breaks 133
   Levels of Control and Indicators 133
   Subtotals and Totals 136
Basic RPG Logic 136
   Program Cycle Operations 136
Coding a Listing Program with Level Control 137
   Control Level Terminology 137
   RPG Logic 139
   Control Level Indicators 139
   RPG Specifications 140
   Control Level Coding 140
      Assignment of Level Indicators 140
      Output Coding with Level Indicators 144
Using the Blank After Specifications 145
Group Indication 146
Control Level—Summary 147
   RPG Logic Cycle 147
   Indicators L1–L9 147
   Specifications 147
   Blank After Coding 150
   Group Indication 150

5 Program Control of Operations 171

Controlling Operations in an RPG Program 172
Control of Output 172
   Calculation Time Output (EXCPT Operation) 172
      Conditioning the Use of EXCPT Operation 174
      Fetch Overflow 174
      Overflow Printing with EXCPT Operation 175
Control of Calculations 180
   Setting Indicators On and Off (SETON and SETOF) 180
   Branching and Looping 182
      Bypassing Calculations 183
      Go To (GOTO) 187
      Tag (TAG) 187
      GOTO Operation—Summary 188
   Movement of Data Calculations 189

Zero and Add (Z-ADD) 189
Zero and Subtract (Z-SUB) 191
MOVE Operation (MOVE and MOVEL) 191
   Moving Data 191
   Specifications for Moving Data 192
   Data Movement—Summary 193
Subroutines 194
   Coding Subroutines 195
   Subroutine Operations Codes 200
   Begin Subroutine (BEGSR) 200
   End Subroutine (ENDSR) 200
   Execute Subroutine (EXSR) 200
   Subroutine Rules—Summary 200
   Subroutine—Summary 201
RPG III Enhancements 201
   EXCPT Name 201
   Move (MOVE) 203
   Move Left (MOVEL) 203
   Simplified Subroutines 203
   Compare and Branch (CABxx) 204
   Structured Programming Operations 205
      Do (DO) 206
      Do Until (DOUxx) 207
      Do While (DOWxx) 207
      If/Then (IFxx) 208
      And (ANDxx) 208
      Or (ORxx) 210
      Else (ELSE) 210
      End (END) 210

6 Table Handling 229

Tables 232
   Forming Tables 234
   Table Files 234
      Arguments and Functions 234
      Table Records and Entries 234
      Table Sequence 234
      Table Loading 235
      Retrieving Entries 235
      Table Updating 235
Describing Table-Input Records 235
   Number of Table-Input Records Required for a Table 235
   Number of Entries on a Table-Input Record 235
   Describing Table-Input Records with Extension Specifications 235
      Assigning Table Names 236

      Number of Table Entries per Table-Input Record 236
      Number of Table Entries per Table 238
      Length of Entry 238
      Packed or Binary Field 239
      Entries with Decimal Positions 240
      Sequence of Table Entries 240
      Positions 46–47 240
      Comments 240
      Program Identification 240
      Summary 240
Loading Tables 240
   Compile Time Tables 241
      Changing Compile Time Tables 241
      Loading Compile Time Tables 242
   Preexecution Time Tables 242
      Changing Preexecution Time Tables 242
      Loading Preexecution Time Tables 242
      Specifications for Preexecution Time Tables 242
Coding the Table Lookup Operation (LOKUP)—Single Table 243
   Operation of a Table Lookup (LOKUP) 244
Related Tables 245
   Two-Table Search 246
   Designing Table-Input Records for Two Tables 247
      Alternating Entries on One Record 247
      Describing Two Tables with Extension Specifications 248
   Coding the Table Lookup Operation (LOKUP) 249
Using Table Data in Calculations and Output 249
   Conditioning Operations on the Basis of a Table Lookup 249
      Searching for Low, High, or Equal Conditions 251
      Sequence of Tables 252
   Moving Data in a Table Entry 254
   Modifying the Content of a Table 255
      Making Temporary Changes to Table Data 255
      Making Permanent Changes to Table Data 257
      Short Tables for Adding New Table Entries 257
   Output of an Entire Table 258

7 Arrays 285

When to Use an Array Instead of a Table 286
Specifying an Array 286
    Defining an Array 286
Array Loading 288
    Loading at Compile/Preexecution Time 288
    Loading Arrays during RPG Program Execution 290
        Array Information in One Record 290
        Array Information in More Than One Record 293
        Modifying the Content of Arrays 293
Updating Arrays 293
Using Arrays 299
    Array Name and Index 299
    Referencing an Array in Calculations 299
    Array-to-Array Calculations 301
    Array Calculations 302
        Adding All Elements within an Array (XFOOT) 304
Lookup of an Array (LOKUP) 304
    Searching an Array for a Particular Element 304
    Starting the Search at a Particular Element 305
    Determining if a Search Is Successful 308
    Referencing an Element That Satisfies a Search 308
    Searching an Array for More Than One Element 309
    Output during an Array Search 311
Output of an Entire Array 311
    Specifying Output with Extension Specifications 311
    Specifying Output with Output Specifications 312
Accumulating Groups of Totals 315
Referencing Individual Elements of an Array 318
    Indexing an Array 318
        Specifying an Index That Does Not Change 318
        Specifying an Index That Can Be Changed 318
        Output of Individual Elements of an Array 318
        Referencing Only Part of a Field 318
Move Array (MOVEA) 323
RPG III Enhancements 327
    Move Array (MOVEA) 327
    Sort Array (SORTA) 327
        *IN 328
        *INxx 328

8 Disk Processing 347

Direct Access (Mass Storage Devices) 348
Terminology 349
    Direct Access Storage Device (DASD) 349
    File 349
    Record 349
    Key 350
    Volume 350
Data Files 350
    Sequential Files 350
    Indexed Files 351
    Direct Files 351
Processing Techniques 351
    Sequential Processing 351
    Random Processing 351
Data File Organization 354
    Sequential Organization 354
    Indexed Organization 354
    Direct Organization 355
    Disk File Organization—Summary 355
        Sequential Organization 355
        Indexed Organization 355
        Direct Organization 355
Sequential File Organization 356
    Creating a Sequential File 356
    Maintaining a Sequential File 363
        Adding Records 363
        Tagging Records for Deletion 373
        Updating Records 373
        Reorganizing a File 373
Indexed File Organization 382
    Creating an Indexed File 382
        Creating an Ordered Indexed File 382
        Creating an Unordered Indexed File 382
Maintaining an Indexed File 388
    Updating Records 388
        Updating Records Sequentially by Key 388
        Updating Records Randomly by Key 388
    CHAIN Operation 388
    Adding Records 394
        Adding Records Randomly by Key Using Chaining 396
        Adding Records Randomly by Key without Chaining 400
        Adding Records Sequentially by Key 401
    Tagging Records for Deletion 405
    Reorganizing a File 405
Other Ways to Process Indexed Files 405
    Processing an Indexed File Consecutively 405
    Processing an Indexed File Randomly by Relative Record Number 405
Direct File Organization 405
    Creating a Direct File 406
Record Address Files (RAF) 406
    Processing within Limits 406
    Processing Using Record Address File Key 408
        Files Containing Record Key Limits 409
        Creating a File with Record Key Limits 410
        Processing Sequentially within Limits 410
        File Description Specifications 410
        Extension Specifications 412

9 Multifile Batch Processing 428

Application Design Considerations 429
Primary Files 429
Secondary Files 429
    Processing Multiple Sequential Files 429
Multifile Processing 430
    Match Fields 430
Checking Sequence of Records within a File 432
    File Containing Only One Record Type 432
    File Containing More Than One Record Type 432
    Same Match Fields for All Record Types 434
Matching Records 435
    Matching Record Technique 438
    Matching Record Indicator 440
    Matching Comparisons 440
    Order of Processing Multiple File Records 440
    Processing Matching Records—Two or More Files 441
    Rules for Specifying Matching Records on Input Specifications 442
    Matching Fields 442
    Matching Record Entries on Calculation Specifications 442
    Matching Field Entries on Output Specifications 442
    One Record Type in Each File 444
    When All Records in One File Have Been Processed 444

Use of Match Fields and
Control Fields in the Same
File 446
End-of-File Processing 449
Alternating the Order of
Processing Files (FORCE) 449
   Specifying the Next File to
   Process 451
Read (READ) 457
   Processing Full Procedural or
   Demand Files (READ) 457
Chaining 461
   Chain (CHAIN) 464
   Random Processing 468
Field Record Relation 471
   OR Relationship 472
     Use with Control Fields 474
     Use with Matching
     Fields 474
     Use with Chaining
     Fields 474
     Use with External Indicators
     and Selective Processing 475

10 Other RPG Statements 498

Move Zone Operations 499
   Altering the Structure of
   Characters 499
   How Move Zone Operations
   Work 499
   Coding a Move Zone
   Operation 500
   Differences in the Move Zone
   Operations 500
     *Move from High-Order
     Zone to High-Order Zone
     (MHHZO)* 502
     *Move from Low-Order
     Zone to High-Order Zone
     (MLHZO)* 502
     *Move from High-Order
     Zone to Low-Order Zone
     (MHLZO)* 502
     *Move from Low-Order
     Zone to Low-Order Zone
     (MLLZO)* 502
Test Numeric (TESTN) 502
Test Zone (TESTZ) 504
Bit Operations 507
   Set Bit On (BITON) 507
   Set Bit Off (BITOF) 509
   Test Bit (TESTB) 510
Look Ahead 514
Writing Specifications for Look
Ahead 514
Look Ahead Fields—
Summary 514
Display Information
(DSPLY) 519
Zoned, Packed, and Binary
Formats 520
   Zoned (Unpacked)
   Format 520
   Packed Decimal Format 522
   Binary Format 523

11 RPG III and the IBM System/38 552

RPG III Rationale 553
RPG III Improvements (IBM
System/38) 553
   Hardware 553
   Software 553
   Technique 554
RPG III Language
Enhancements 554
   Source Entry Utility
   (SEU) 554
     *SEU Sequence
     Number* 554
     *Source Diagnostic Error
     Notation* 554
     SEU Summary 554
   Externally Described Data
   (CPF) 555
   Data Description Specification
   (DDS) 556
   Full Procedural File
   Specifications 557
   File Operations 558
     *Random Retrieval from a
     File on RECNO or Key
     Value (CHAIN)* 558
     *Delete Record
     (DELET)* 558
     *Execute Format
     (EXFMT)* 558
     *Read A Record
     (READ)* 558
     *Read Next Modified
     Record (READC)* 558
     *Read Equal Key
     (READE)* 560
     *Read Prior Key
     (READP)* 560
     *Set Greater Than
     (SETGT)* 560
     *Set Greater Than or Equal
     To (SETLL)* 560
     *Modify Existing Record
     (UPDAT)* 560
     *Create New Records
     (WRITE)* 560
   File Control Operations 561
     *Force End Of Data
     (FEOD)* 561
     *Open File for Processing
     (OPEN)* 561
     *Close File for Processing
     (CLOSE)* 561
   Work Station Support 561
     Externally Described
     WORKSTN Files 562
     Processing an Externally
     Described WORKSTN
     File 562
     Command Key
     Indicators 563
     Work Station Subfile
     Operations 563
   Processing WORKSTN
   Files 565
     Program Described
     WORKSTN Files 566
       Input Files 566
       Output Files 566
       Combined Files 566

12 RPG III Features 577

Interprogram Functions 578
   CALL/RETRN
   Function 578
   SPECIAL File with PLIST
   Operation 580
Data Structures 580
   Multiple Occurrence Data
   Structures 580
   File Information Data
   Structures (INFDS) 581
Calculation Modifications 584
   Compare and Branch
   (CABxx) 584
   Short Form of Arithmetic
   Operations 584
   Calculation Time Output
   (EXCPT) 584
   Sort Array (SORTA) 584
   Indicators Referenced as Data
   (*IN, *INxx, *IN,xx) 584
   Field Definition (DEFN) 584
   Relative End-Positions (40–43)
   on Output Specifications 585
   Figurative Constants 586
   Time (TIME) 586
   Shutdown (SHTDN) 588
   User-Defined Edit Codes
   (5–9) 588
   Dynamic Space/Skip Function
   (PRTCTL) 588
   Display Function
   (DSPLY) 588
   Improved Relative File
   Support 588
   Table File Replacement 590
   Default Control
   Specification 590
New Compilation Listing
Functions 590
   Cross-Reference Listing 590
   Text Descriptions from Data
   Description
   Specifications 590
   Resulting Indicator
   Usage 590
   /EJECT Specifications 590
   /SPACE Specifications 590
   Nesting Indication 591
   Last Update Indication 591
Enhanced Debug Facilities 592
   System Debug Facility 592
   Formatted Dump 592
   Debug Function
   (DEBUG) 592
   Program Dump
   (DUMP) 592
   Create RPG Program
   (CRTRPGPGM) 592
   Check Reconciliation System 592

Appendixes 605

A DEBUG Function 606

B Detailed RPG II Object Program Logic 613

C Reference Tables—RPG II 617
Program Indicators—Summary 617
Operation Codes—Summary 618
Valid Indicators 619

D The Programmer's Job 620

E Summary Charts—RPG III 632
Operation Codes—Summary 632
RPG III Restrictions—Summary 633

F RPG III Enhancements 634

G Problems for Term Assignment 639

H Indexed and Direct Files 658

I Input Data for Chapter 2–10 Problems 676

J Input Data for Appendix G Problems 684

Glossary 689

Index 699

Preface

It is the function of a computer to accept and to process information to produce a certain result. In accomplishing this outcome, the computer needs more than just the input; it requires a complete set of instructions (a program) telling it which information in the input records to use, what to do with this information, and how the output is to look. The purpose of this text is to provide the information needed to perform these tasks in RPG II and RPG III programming. A programming background is not necessary. Whereas an equal facility in other programming languages would require considerable experience, a user can become proficient in RPG programming after writing only a few programs.

The RPG programming language is a highly flexible problem-solving language that provides programming solutions to a wide variety of data-processing problems. RPG is a convenient means of preparing reports from information available in such computer-readable forms as disk, diskette, and magnetic tape, or directly from terminals. Also, it is a means of establishing and updating files as well as preparing reports.

Persons with no previous knowledge of computers or programming will find the text useful. Those already knowledgeable in a programming language, but who wish to take advantage of the easy report writing and file capabilities of RPG, will also benefit from this text. RPG programming topics are approached and organized according to their normal use in data-processing jobs and are supported with examples where appropriate. This edition incorporates the modifications to the RPG language made by RPG III. Chapters will discuss the differences between RPG II and RPG III in separate sections called RPG III Enhancements. Chapters 11 and 12 are devoted exclusively to RPG III.

The text is designed to allow the user to write programs early in the course. The large number of illustrated examples will help the student progress from problem definition to problem solution.

Chapter 1 is an introduction to data processing and provides a foundation for the programming effort. Students who have completed an introductory course in data processing will find this chapter to be a helpful review of the basic concepts of data processing. Those who have had no previous exposure to data processing will find necessary and basic information for writing programs in chapter 1.

Chapter 2 introduces the basic RPG II programming cycle and logic. Features and advantages of the RPG cycle are explained. The fundamental importance of indicators to RPG II programming is discussed; input and output processing are emphasized. The necessary coding for file description, input, and output specifications is described in sufficient detail for the student to write input and output processing problems.

Chapter 3 combines listing with calculations to cover the basic elements of writing RPG II programs. Both arithmetic and compare operations are presented through discussion and illustrative examples. The important phases of arithmetic operations and the testing of results of arithmetic operations are examined.

Chapter 4 looks at the many facets of control level programming. Control level programming includes the accumulation of subtotals and the printing of both detail and total lines under controlled conditions. The relationship of control fields, control groups, and control breaks is shown.

Chapter 5 shows the ways in which the program may be changed according to the needs of the programmer to accommodate conditions encountered in the processing. Subroutines are introduced. The RPG III enhancements included in this chapter look into the structured concepts of DOs, IFs, and CABs.

Chapter 6 deals with one of the most important subjects of RPG II—table handling. RPG II has some of the simplest methods of handling tables that any programming language can offer. Coverage of the basic concepts of table handling should give the student an adequate foundation for learning to program tables.

Chapter 7 discusses the functions of arrays, explaining what an array is and how it differs from a table. Array loading, updating arrays, and using arrays are explained. RPG III enhancements include the treatment of indicators such as the array *IN.

Chapter 8 explains the use of mass storage devices, concentrating on disk storage as the most popular mass storage device currently in use. Important points of disk storage including the popular methods of data organization on disk are discussed and illustrated. Basic terms used in disk processing are presented to give the student an understanding of their use in programming disk storage devices. Creating and maintaining disk data files are among the topics covered.

Chapter 9 discusses data-processing applications involving the processing of different files from diverse physical media. Application design considerations and matching records techniques are presented. Primary, secondary, and sequential files are explained as are the techniques for checking the sequence of files containing one or more records. Chaining records and field record relationship techniques are also explained. Chapter 10 deals with such RPG II statements as move zone operations, test numeric operations, test zone operations, bit operations, and the display operation.

Chapter 11 discusses RPG III and the IBM System/38, a complementary environment offering a new interactive future for RPG. Chapter 12 looks at RPG III features and provides an illustrative RPG III program for discussion.

Provided with each chapter are sets of problems and questions for review.

The appendixes offer additional programming information or provide the data related to programming problem assignments.

We would like to thank Hagai Payes, RPG III Data Processing Consultant, for his technical assistance; Doug Arter, department chairman of the Los Angeles Valley College, Computer Science Department, for his support; Tom Sommers, Ray Mullins, James Hampton, and Tim McMains of Los Angeles Valley College for their cooperation in the operation and maintenance of the IBM PCs, minicomputers, and assorted mainframes. Numerous uploads, downloads, executions, and printings went into the writing and testing of the approximately seventy-five programs incorporated in the illustrative programs and programming problems of the text.

We would also like to express our appreciation to John Stout and staff of Wm. C. Brown Publishers for providing the original typeset manuscript in computer-readable format, a procedure that immensely facilitated the production of this revision.

We express our gratitude to IBM for permitting us to use forms and other materials.

Introduction to Basic RPG Concepts

1

Outline

Programs and Programming
    Languages
Source Programs
Source Programs to Object
    Programs
    Saving and Executing Object
    Programs
    Basic Compilation
    and Execution Operations
Summary

Building Blocks of Data Processing
    Record Layout
    Printer Spacing Chart
    Summary
Specification Forms
RPG Basic Cycle
RPG Logic Cycle
    Basic Data Processing Logic
    Indicators
    RPG Logic Related to Indicators

Data processing is a planned series of actions and operations upon information, using various types of data-processing equipment to achieve desired results. All of the necessary devices and procedures used in the operation constitute a data-processing system.

Programs and Programming Languages

Data-processing systems do only what they are told. It might seem as though these systems require more information to do a job than you would need to do the same job. But remember, a data-processing system cannot think. Consequently, it must be given explicit instructions for even the simplest of tasks.

Systems require three basic informational elements in performing any job:

1. **Input**—information to work with
2. **Processing**—instructions telling what to do with the information
3. **Output**—instructions describing the expected results

In data-processing terms, input is the information entered into the system, processing is what the system does with the input, and output is the result of the processing. Instructions must be written to tell the system what to do at each of these stages in the processing. This set of instructions is called a **program.**

To communicate with the system, the system's language or one that can be translated into that language must be used. The system's language is called **machine language.** Machine language is made up of binary data, consisting of ones and zeroes. These data have a specific meaning to the system and, when interpreted by the system, cause it to perform a desired function.

Because machine language is so different from the language we use daily, it is extremely difficult to write programs with it. For this reason, programming languages have been created to allow the programmer to use familiar words and symbols for writing instructions.

The RPG programming language is composed of letters, numbers, and symbols which, when put together, form an instruction (express a thought). When creating instructions in the RPG language, certain rules must be followed, just as you would when constructing a sentence in English. These rules are called the syntax of RPG. Information concerning these rules will be found later in the text.

The programmer writes a set of instructions called a **source program.** (See Figure 1.1.) This source program is translated by a utility program called a **compiler,** producing a machine language program called an **object program.** The object program is used to process the job and may be used over and over again to do the same job.

Source Programs

Any written program must describe the input, processing, and output requirements of the job. For example, one instruction might direct the system to read an input record, another might specify that two numbers be added, and another might tell the system to print a line on the printer. Because all jobs are not the same, a different set of instructions (or **program**) must be provided for each job to be done.

Program instructions are given on a variety of RPG **specification forms.** (See Figure 1.10.) These forms have been specially designed to help the programmer write instructions according to the rules of RPG language. The act of writing instructions on these forms is called **coding;** the entries made on these forms are called specifications.

Each form supplies different information depending upon the particular input, processing, and output requirements of the job. For example, the programmer would have to describe what the input data is like and specify the device (e.g., a disk unit) that will read it. The programmer must also describe how the input data is to be processed. This description includes what operations (e.g., add or subtract) must be performed on the data. Finally the programmer must specify what kind of output is desired (e.g., a printed report), what information must be included in the output, and how that information is to be arranged.

After the specification forms have been coded the coded information can be put into the system. Since the system cannot read the coded forms the specifications must be put into a format that the system can read. The specifications can be keyed onto a diskette or keyed directly into the system, depending on the environment.

Figure 1.1 Programmer functions

```
1.  Define the system devices you will be using.
2.  Define the INPUT.
3.  Define the PROCESSING.
4.  Define the OUTPUT.
```

Source Programs to Object Programs

To restate, a system understands only machine language and cannot directly execute a coded program like the RPG programming language. The program written in RPG (the source program) must be translated into machine language (the object program) by a compiler. Compilers are supplied by computer manufacturers for particular computer systems. A compiler performs three functions:

1. It produces a source program listing, a printout of all symbolic instructions as entered by the programmer.
2. It produces a listing of syntax errors (language rule violations) or compiler diagnostics.
3. It produces a machine language equivalent of the source program known as an object module.

The RPG compilation of a source program is performed using the specifications supplied by the programmer. If specification errors are found that preclude completion of compilation, processing is suspended and a printout of appropriate messages is given. Compilation may in other cases continue to completion even though errors are found that would prohibit successful object program execution. Certain omissions from specifications can be tolerated, although the compiler may insert standard values and processes into the object program by default. The occurrence of syntax errors is noted in the printed record of the compilation. The programmer must re-edit the source program until the syntax errors are eliminated.

Saving and Executing Object Programs

The RPG compiler may be directed to place an object program in a permanent file. These object programs may be incorporated into the programmer's program library for subsequent use. Another option is to execute a compiled object program immediately. In such a case, job control instructions (JCL) are given to the system and the inputs needed are made available to the file devices. Specific device assignments can be made at this time as required.

Before any attempt is made to fill out the specification forms, a thorough analysis must be made of all procedures to be used for processing the data. These include describing the format of the source data and determining how the data is to be processed in developing the finished report. System flowcharts should be drawn to show the flow of data through the system. (See Figure 1.2.)

Basic Compilation and Execution Operations

Using the RPG compiler to create an object program involves the following steps (see Figure 1.3):

1. The programmer must evaluate the program through the preparation of Input Layout forms, Printer Spacing Chart, flowcharts, analysis sheets, input/output requirements, and processing requirements.
2. The programmer must provide the coding—information for the RPG compiler in the form of specification sheets.
3. The coded information must be keyed from these specification sheets onto disk or diskettes.
4. Keyed information (the source program), together with the compiler job control language instructions, is fed to an input device for compiling the source program into a machine language program (the object program).

Figure 1.2 System flowcharts—examples

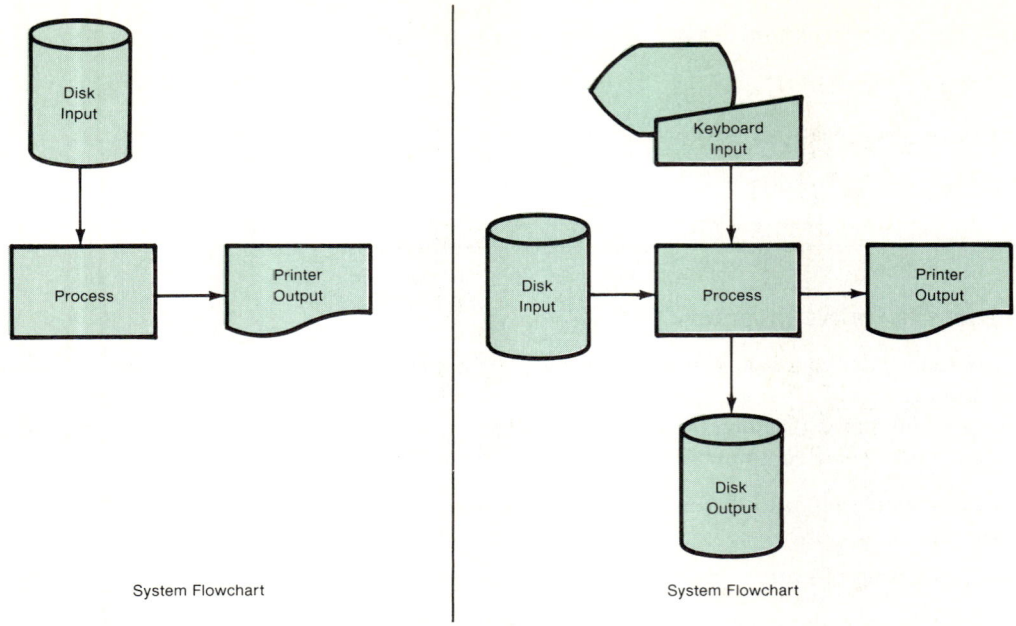

5. The compiler translates the source program into an object module.
6. The object program is loaded into the computer.
7. The input files are read in for the preparation of the desired output and files.

Summary
1. Details for coding disk or diskette output might come from the record layout. Details might come from the Printer Spacing Chart if output is printed. Or, details for output coding might come from both record layout and Printer Spacing Chart.
2. Information on documents needs to be transferred to RPG coding sheets in order for the RPG compiler to translate the source coding into an executable load member. The original coding is not executable.
3. Information that has been transferred to coding sheets could then be called source or original coding. The coding must then be keyed to disk or diskette. It will then be called a **source program** or, if it is in a library, it will be called a **source member.** Now the coding can be read by the system, but cannot yet be executed. The next step, then, is to make the program executable. That process is called compiling, or **compilation.** The source program is translated by RPG from the coding form to an executable form called a **load program,** or **load member.** Now the program is ready to produce a final report or listing.
4. Once in an executable form, the code may be loaded into the processing unit. The data may now be processed to produce the desired result.
5. Terms
    a. *Source code*—the original code on the RPG sheets transferred from the supporting documents.
    b. *Compiler*—the program that translates the source coding into a load member so that it may be executed.
    c. *Load member*—the translated, executable form of program.
    d. *Execute*—to run the program in order to produce the desired results. (See Figure 1.4.)

Figure 1.3 Basic compilation and execution operation

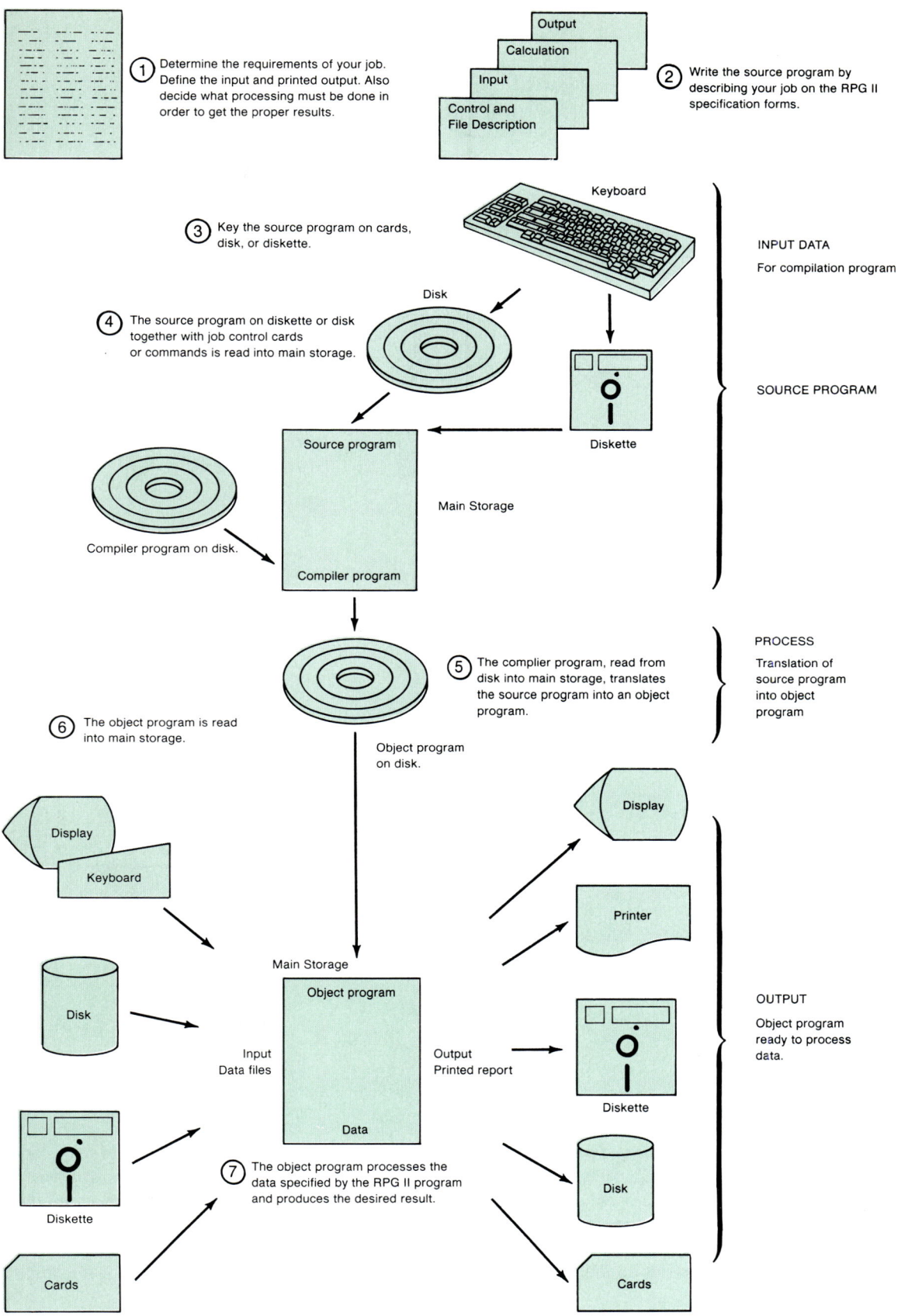

Introduction to Basic RPG Concepts

Figure 1.4 Compilation and execution of RPG programs

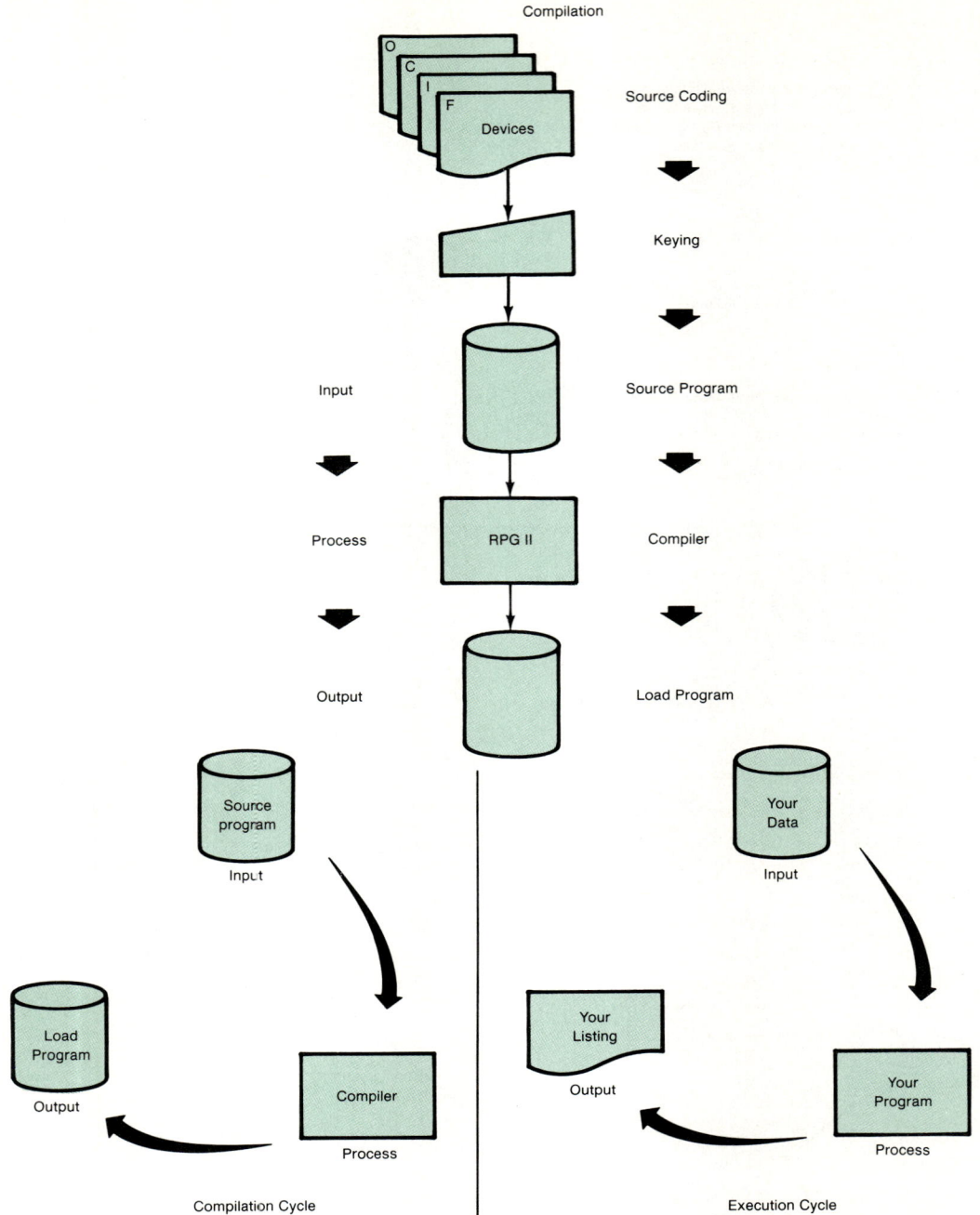

Building Blocks of Data Processing

A logical unit of information is a field. A **field** is a data element within a record. Fields may contain **alphabetic** (characters A–Z, #, $, and @), **numeric** (characters 0–9), or **alphameric** (both alphabetic and numeric) data; they may contain one character or many characters. Examples of fields are employee name, rate of pay, and number of exemptions.

All fields related to a given employee constitute the employee record. A **record** is the major entry of a file and usually carries an identification value and a number of additional elements of information.

Figure 1.5 Fields, records, files—examples

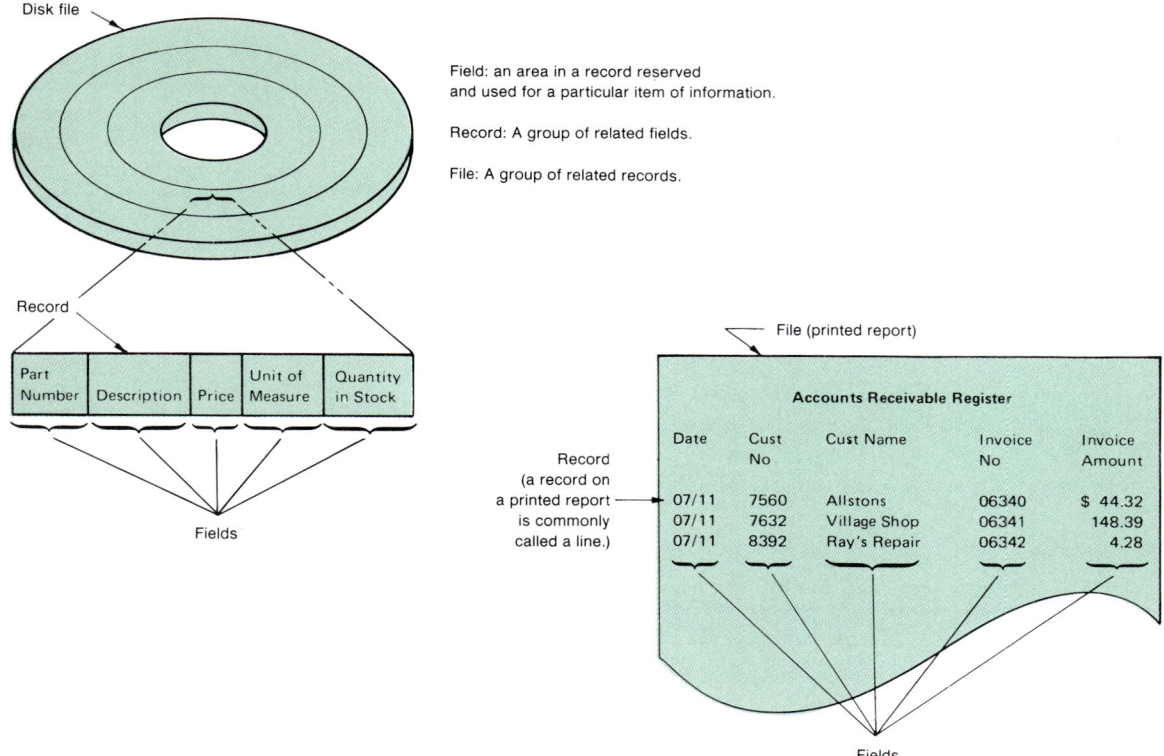

There may be different types of records based on the number and order of fields. For example, all the master data make up an employee master record; any new transactions for an employee are the employee transaction record and would be used to update the employee master record.

All related records for employees constitute a file. A **file** is an aggregation of data organized for a consistent purpose. Master files and transaction files contain their appropriate records. If the files can be found on a disk, they are disk files; if the files are on a printer, they are printer files. Examples of files are inventory files, employee files, accounts payable files, and equipment characteristic files. (See Figure 1.5.)

File devices are the computer peripherals used for input and output.

Record Layout

The Record Layout form helps to define the record and fields of the file in more detail. This form provides the following information:

1. Field locations within the record. It also specifies the starting and ending positions of the field.

2. Length of field.

3. Type of field—alphabetic or numeric. A field such as a name field is obviously alphabetic. If type of field is in question, an *A* or *N* placed below the field will identify it.

4. Number of decimal positions associated with a numeric field. Note that the decimal is never written on the input record itself, but its position is indicated by an arrow.

5. Field names. These may be used in referring to particular pieces of information. (See Figures 1.6 and 1.7.)

Introduction to Basic RPG Concepts

Figure 1.6 Record layout

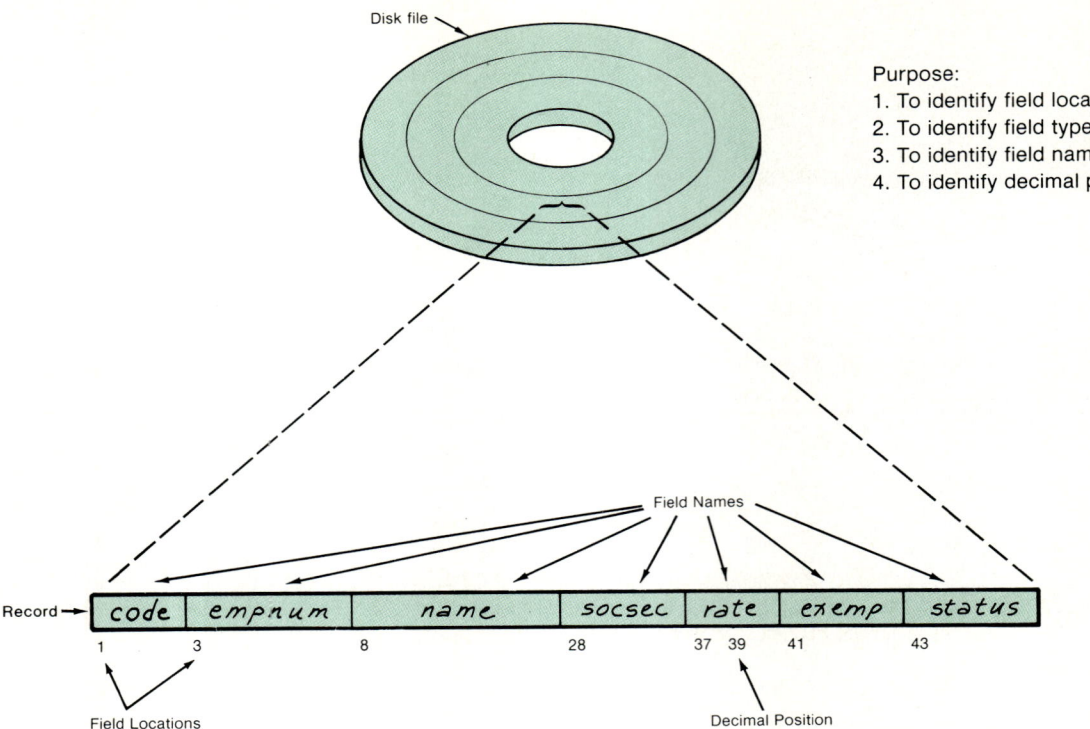

Figure 1.7 Record layout form—example

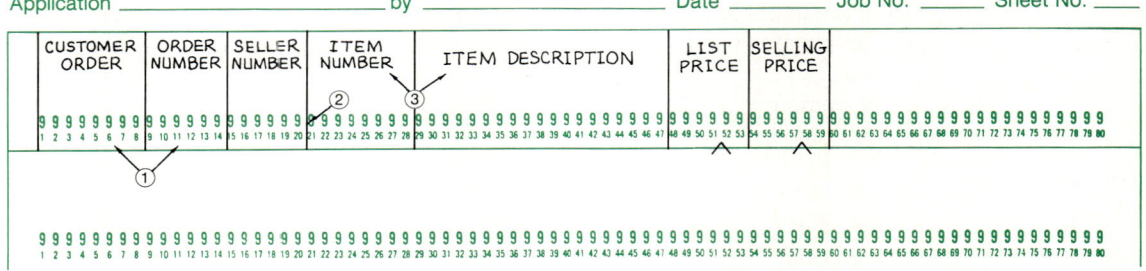

Notes on the Coding

The record layout form shows what records in a file look like. This form is filled out at the time a file is designed. It shows what fields are in the record (1) and the exact location and length of each (2). It may also show field names and explain what kind of data is in each field (3).

Figure 1.8 Printer spacing chart—example

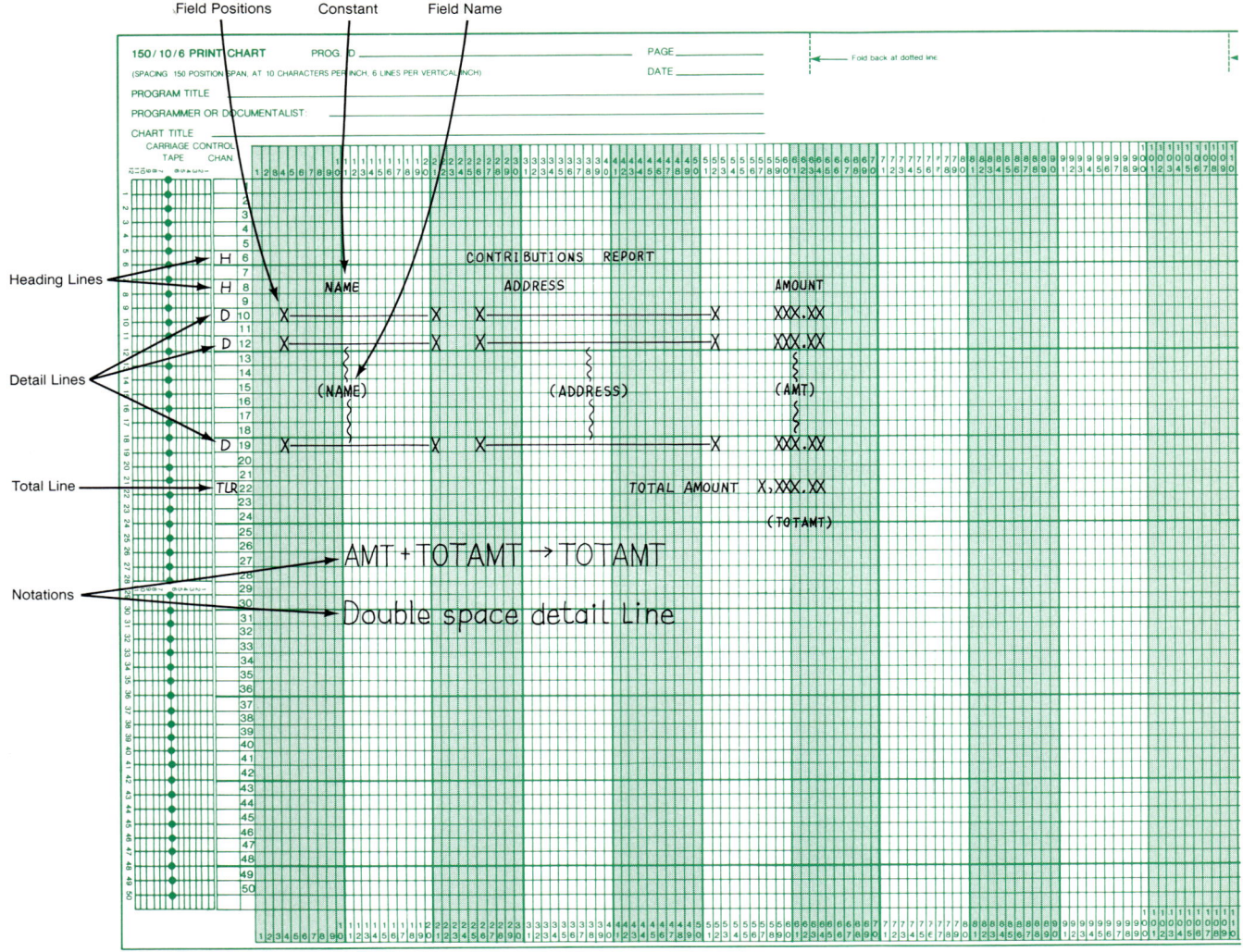

Purpose:
1. To describe the design of the printed report.
2. To specify spacing, constants, field positions, and field names.
3. To note calculations and comments.

Printer Spacing Chart

Before writing the specification sheets, the programmer should create a worksheet for the printer. This is a form used to represent visually specific operations. (See Figure 1.8.) When output is to be a printed report, it is helpful to lay out the report on the Printer Spacing Chart. The Printer Spacing Chart serves as a guide, making it much easier to prepare output specifications.

The design of the report is shown on the Printer Spacing Chart through the arrangement of information. Information such as constants, field names, and field positions is entered on appropriate heading, detail, and total lines. These three types of lines correspond to the heading, detail, and total records made up of fields and constants. Together, these records make up the file of records to be printed.

The Printer Spacing Chart provides the programmer with the following information (see Figure 1.8):

1. Format of the desired headings.
2. Number of print positions necessary for output, including such editing symbols as commas, periods, and dollar signs.

3. Number of characters in each field and whether characters are alphabetic, numeric, or alphameric. Fields are shown as xx.xx or X————X, with the field name below in parentheses ( ).
4. Punctuation is shown as it will appear on the report and occupies an actual print position. Punctuation does not take a position on the input record layout. Instead, the implied position of the decimal point is indicated with an arrow.
5. Constants (data that do not change) are shown as they will appear, one character per print position.
6. Total lines and different levels of totals desired.
7. Vertical spacing of the print line.
8. Any special skipping.
9. Any zero suppression desired.
10. Any control codes.
11. Notations on the bottom of the form serve two purposes:
    a. Special instructions for spacing the report.
    b. Calculation information for arriving at some of the fields represented on the Printer Spacing Chart.

A **heading line** identifies the report and the columns of information in the report. A **detail line** indicates where information from individual records is to be printed. A **total line** indicates where a total is to be printed.

Constant is the name given to words, numerals, and characters that are entered as they are to appear in the report. Constants do not change during the execution of the program. Each field must be named and entered on the Printer Spacing Chart. Field names are enclosed in parentheses on the Printer Spacing Chart to indicate that they do not appear on the printed report. The field has specific positions assigned to it; the field name does not.

Planning vertical spacing of a printed report is much like planning the spacing for a typewritten report. For example, if you type on line 3, and want the next line of type to be on line 6, you need to triple-space to get two blank lines between line 3 and line 6. Count the lines on a Printer Spacing Chart in the same way.

1. Heading lines
   a. The letter *H* precedes the line number.
   b. Heading lines are written out as they are to appear on the report, one letter in each position.
   c. Use the vertical spacing of the report design.
2. Detail lines
   a. The letter *D* precedes the line number.
   b. Variable fields are indicated with an *X* in each field position.
   c. A decimal point or a comma and other editing symbols are inserted in numeric fields where appropriate.
   d. Each variable field is represented by a field name in parentheses.
   e. Use the vertical spacing of the report design. (Include at least two detail lines to indicate the spaces.)
   f. Use constant fields if appropriate.
3. Total lines
   a. The letter *T* precedes the line number.
   b. Fields are indicated with *X*s in the needed positions.
   c. A decimal point or a comma and other editing symbols can be inserted in numeric fields where appropriate.
   d. Represent each variable field by a field name or names in parentheses.
   e. Use constant fields if appropriate.
   f. Use the vertical spacing of the report design.
4. Notations
   a. Describe the operations to be performed.
   b. Specify directions for the program.
   c. May be indicated anywhere on the Printer Spacing Chart.

Summary

1. The Record Layout form is used to define the input data fields for a program. It specifies the field name, position in the record, decimal position, if any, and whether the field is alphabetic, numeric, or both.
2. The system flowchart helps to define the peripheral devices and how they will be used. It provides an overview of the program.
3. A Printer Spacing Chart may have three types of lines: heading, detail, and total. These correspond to the three types of records that could be written on the printer.
4. The notations at the bottom of the Printer Spacing Chart provide instructions to the programmer about special spacing requirements and any calculations that will need to be performed on the fields for the output. Each variable field used must be given a name so that it can be referenced in the program. Names are usually assigned at the same time the spacing chart is prepared, since the names should be close to the fields for easy identification. Names are assigned by the programmer and should be similar to the actual field names to be referenced.
    a. *H* indicates a heading line.
    b. *D* indicates a detail line.
    c. *TL* indicates a total line. If more than one type of total is desired, the characters following the *TL* indicate those total levels.
5. Terms
    a. *Field*—a logical unit of information.
    b. *Record*—a collection of related fields.
    c. *File*—a collection of related records.

Specification Forms

After the requirements of the desired report have been evaluated, the programmer must provide information to the RPG compiler. This is accomplished through the preparation of specification forms. (See Figure 1.9.)

Figure 1.9   Preparing specification forms

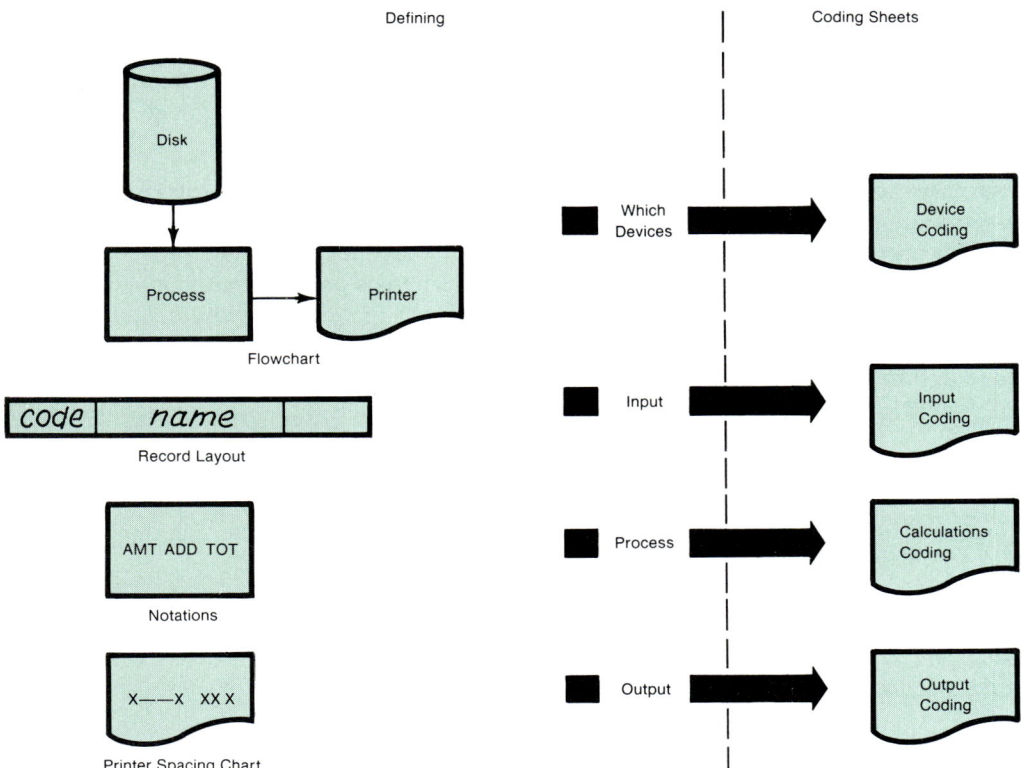

The programmer must prepare specifications that describe the input to the object program, the calculations needed, and the output desired. Specialized forms simplify this task. The entries on these forms are entered onto disk or diskettes and are subsequently read by the RPG compiler. (See Figure 1.4.) The compiler examines these entries for correctness and cross-consistency. If errors are found, diagnostic messages are printed to assist in making corrections. The specifications are processed as completely as possible even when the detected errors will preclude successful execution of the object program. It should be noted that a successful compilation (no **syntax** errors) does not guarantee correct execution (as, for example, when program logic errors exist).

Seven types of specification forms are available for use in the three logical specification areas of input, calculation, and output. (See Figure 1.10.) Forms are used in various combinations depending upon the characteristics of the problem at hand.

1. **Control specifications.** Some systems require control specifications. The control line appears at the top of the Control and File Description sheet. Control specifications give the compiler information about the system and tell whether any special RPG functions are desired.

2. **File description specifications.** This form describes all files to be used by the object program as well as the devices to be used. It describes the environment for the particular job.

3. **Extension specifications.** This form is used when table or array files, record address files, or chaining files are part of the problem.

4. **Line counter specifications.** This form is used when printing cannot be done within the standard vertical print formatting conventions.

5. **Input specifications.** This form is used to describe input files such as record layouts or record fields. The programmer describes the input available to the object program in terms of files, records, fields, and devices for processing data. The programmer's description of input need only be complete enough to allow selection of necessary records and fields. Records and fields not pertinent to desired processing need not be described.

6. **Calculation specifications.** This form is used to describe the nature of the processing: arithmetic operations, data movements, comparisons, table lookup, or indicator settings. In the calculation specifications the user describes the conditions under which each calculation is to be performed. Examples of conditions are the presence or absence of a record identifying code, a specified control level, a positive result of a previous calculation, or the occurrence of the last record of a file. The calculations include arithmetic, moving fields, making comparisons, selecting the next processing sequence (including using internal and external subroutines), defining internal subroutines, setting indicators for later reference, table or array lookup, and chaining (retrieving a record during calculation). The particular requirements of each calculation operation are also specified.

7. **Output specifications.** This form is used to describe how the finished report is to look. The output specifications describe the files, records, fields, and devices used for output from the program. The conditions that must be met for output to be produced are included. For files to be updated, output specifications supplement the file descriptions provided in the input specifications. For new output files, the output specifications supply their record organization and field positions. For printed reports, the editing desired for fields is described. Editing includes such functions as zero suppression, insertion of floating dollar signs, insertion of credit balance symbols, and printing numeric fields with commas.

RPG Basic Cycle

Three critical parts of coding in RPG language are the specifications, the logic cycle, and the indicators.

The specifications describe the files, records, and fields for the program. They tell specifically what to do.

The RPG logic cycle determines when a function is performed and handles the routine matters of moving data and turning some indicators on and off.

Indicators control whether or not a function takes place.

Figure 1.10 Specification sheets

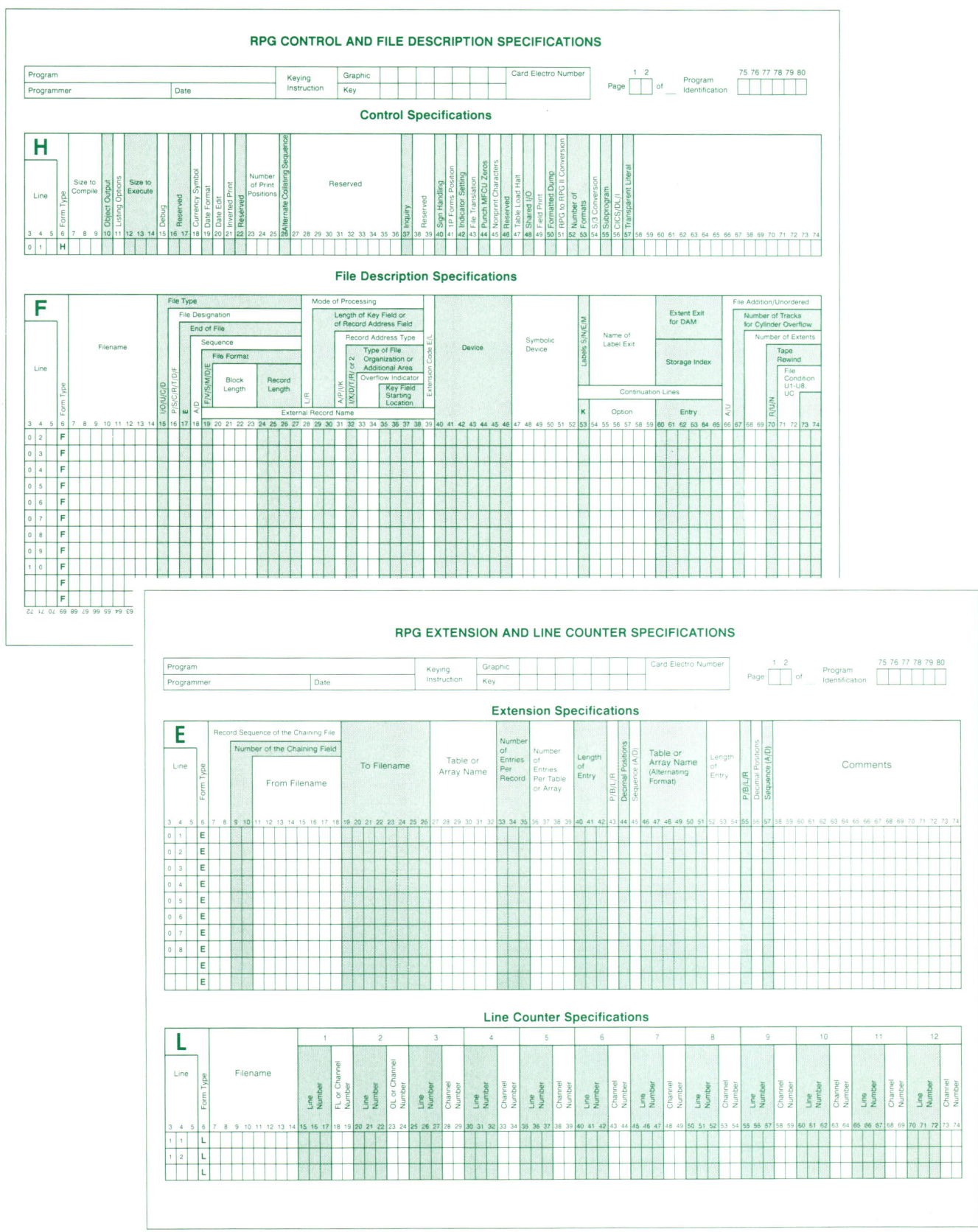

Figure 1.10 continued

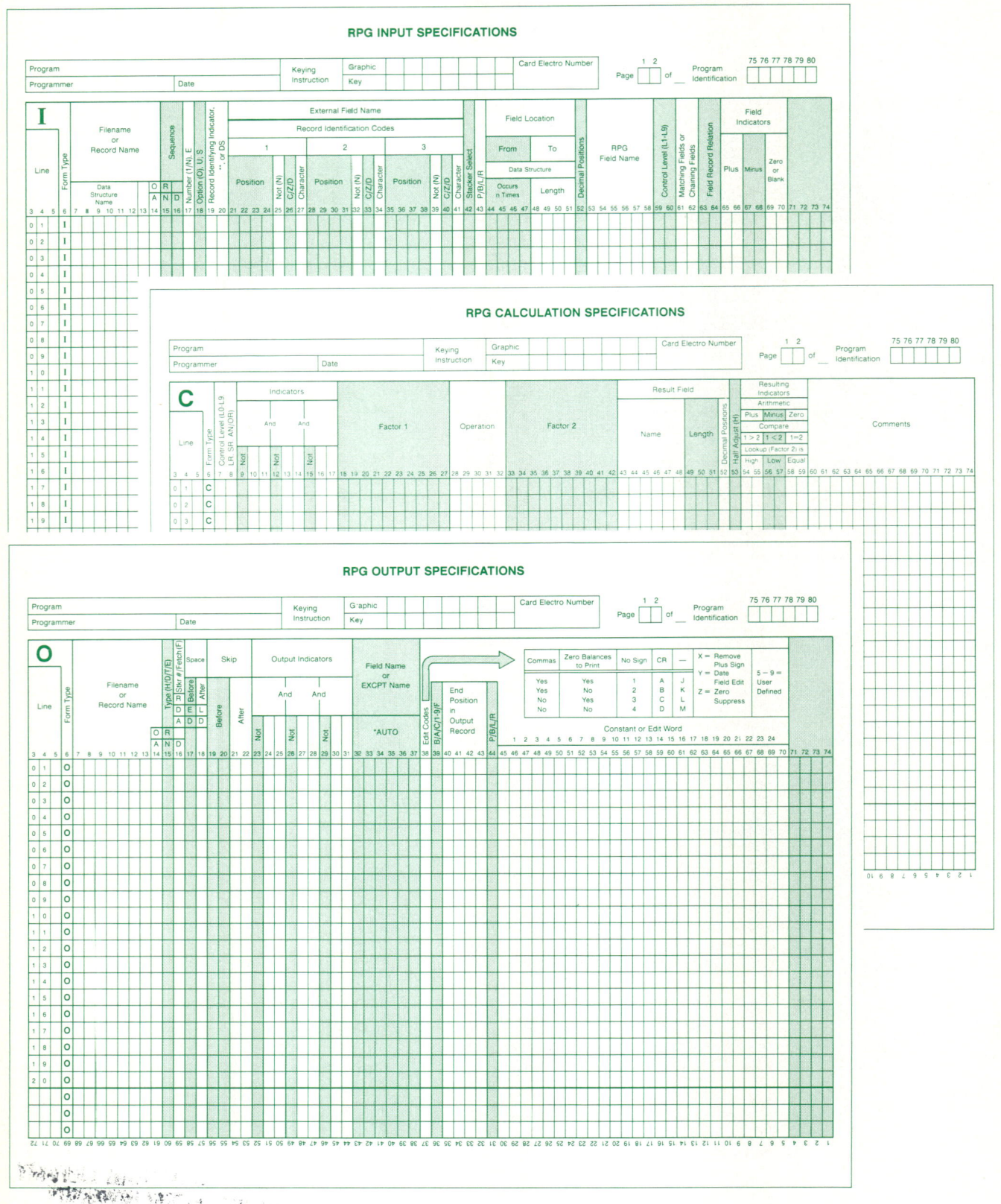

14   RPG II and RPG III Programming

Figure 1.11 Overview of the RPG logic cycle

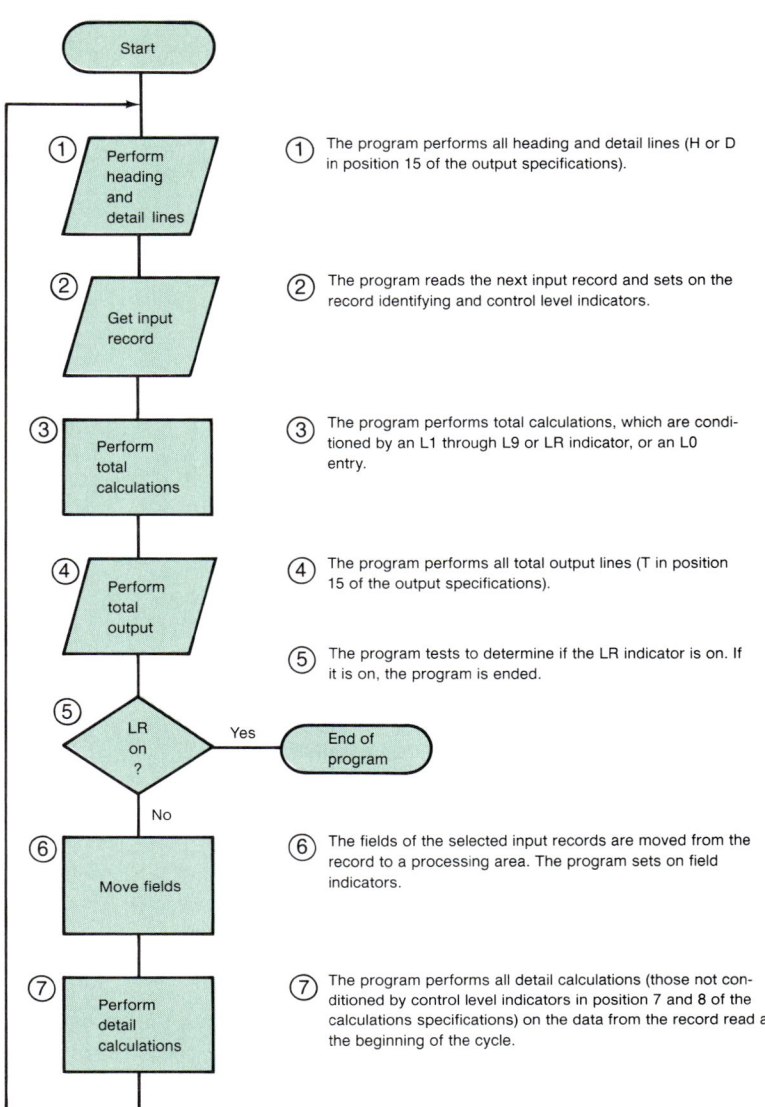

RPG Logic Cycle

Jobs must be performed in a particular order and systems must do their jobs in a particular order. The logical order for the job is supplied by the RPG compiler and/or the programmer coding.

It is important to know the order of the operations in the RPG program cycle since this enables the programmer to write specifications that make correct use of the cycle. (See Figure 1.11.) By knowing the order in which the operations in the cycle are performed, the program can be organized in an efficient manner and unnecessary coding can be eliminated.

Figure 1.12 RPG logic

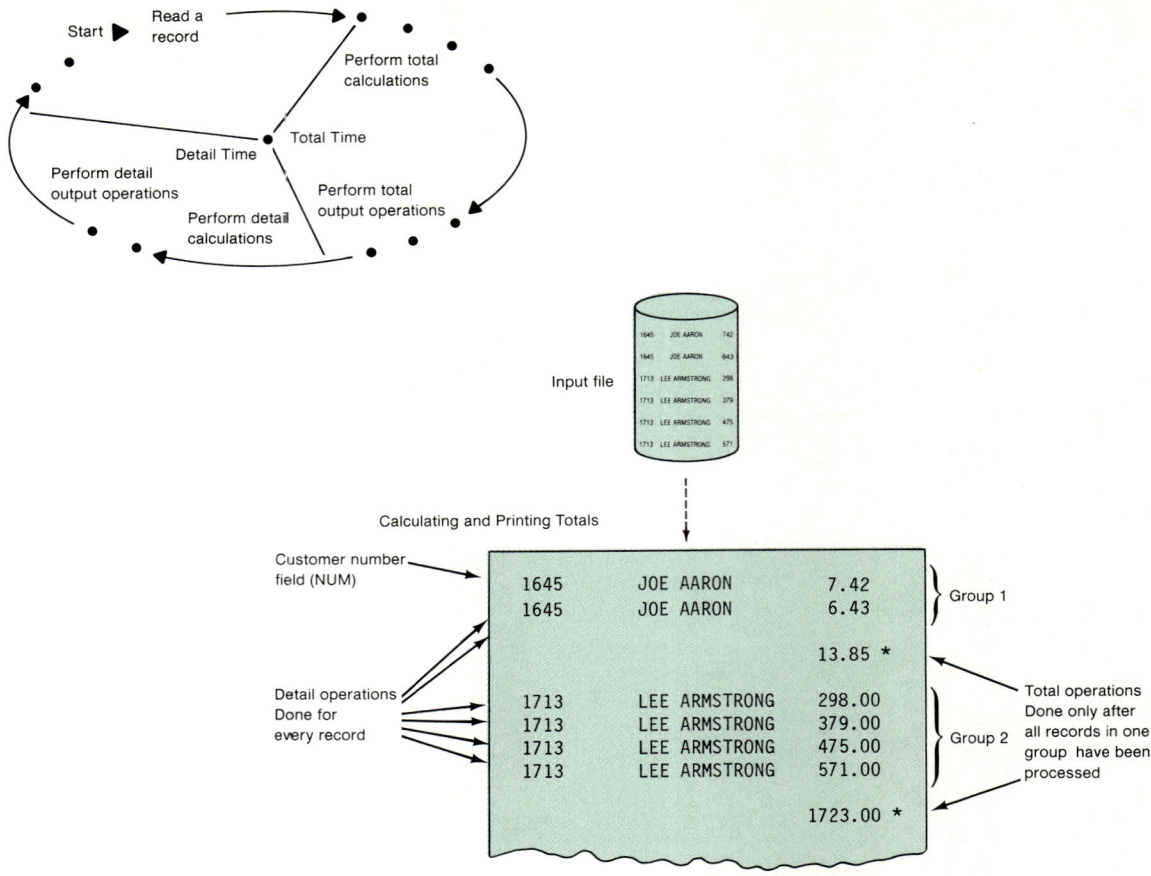

Basic Data-Processing Logic

All records in a file of input records are not typically read at once. Most computers are not large enough to store and work with information from all records at the same time. Therefore, the records are read one at a time.

RPG logic uses three-step logic. (See Figure 1.12.) A record is read, the necessary calculations are performed, and output operations are done. The term **program cycle** refers to all operations performed from the time one record is read until the next record is read. One program cycle is therefore one revolution around the program logic circle shown in Figure 1.12. Since one program cycle (one revolution) is needed for each record read, many program cycles are required for every job.

RPG logic is an extended version of this three-step logic. It calls for calculations and output operations to be done at two different times in one program cycle. These two times have been given the names detail time and total time. **Total time,** as the name suggests, is the time in which total operations are done on the data accumulated from a group of related records. **Detail time** is the time in which operations are performed for individual records. Detail operations are done for every record read, but total operations are done only after a certain group of records are read.

The RPG compiler supplies the program with the logic framework that enables it to do detail and total operations. However, it is the programmer who determines on the specification sheets when total operations should be done, which calculation and output operations should be done at detail time, and which are to be done at total time. The only way to tell the program what to do in certain operations is through the use of indicators.

Indicators

The RPG program uses switch-like signals called indicators to tell it when a particular situation occurs. **Indicators** permit the programmer to control the logic of the program. The programmer must know how to indicate when (and which) actions are to be performed.

RPG logic is built around these indicators whose status (on or off) affects the sequence of the program's operations. RPG logic is set up to test the status of various indicators at specific times. By testing the indicators, the program knows what to do next.

RPG logic is designed to take care of all types of jobs. The logic must be understood before specifications making correct use of that logic can be written.

RPG Logic Related to Indicators

As stated, RPG logic is built around indicators. In the specification forms, indicators tell the program what to do and when to do it. Although indicators are used, normally the program does not set them. Some operation codes permit indicators to turn on and off by themselves with the compiler determining the logic needed to control the setting of indicators.

Indicators are set to signal various conditions occurring during the execution of the program. In addition to setting indicators, RPG logic also causes tests to be made for various indicators at certain times in the program cycle. Specific operations are performed as a result of these tests.

It is easy to mistake an indicator that is on for one that is off, and vice versa. It is extremely important to know when the indicators are on and when they are off in the program cycle. Many programs fail just because the programmer did not understand RPG logic concerning indicators.

Each indicator, the time at which it is set, and the time at which it may be tested will be introduced as its function becomes important to the general discussion of the RPG programming process. (See Figures 1.13 and 1.14.)

Figure 1.13 Indicators documentation

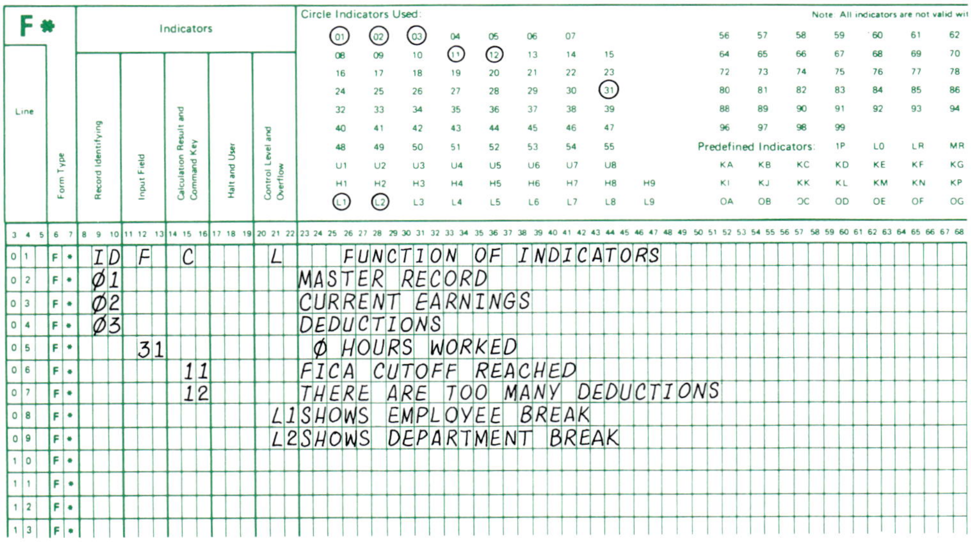

Indicators—show what kind of indicator it is.

Function of Indicators—to describe the purpose of the indicator.

Circle Indicators Used—to avoid using an indicator more than once.

Introduction to Basic RPG Concepts

Illustrative Program

Simple Listing: Stock Inventory Report

Job Definition

A detail printed report, titled Stock Inventory Report, is to be produced from a file of records arranged in ascending numerical order (using the material number). On hand cost will be calculated for each record. A date record is the first record in the file.

Input

The stock input record has the following layout:

Positions	Type	Field Description	
7–09	Numeric	Material number	(xxx)
12–16	Numeric	Stock number	(xxxxx)
19–23	Numeric	Unit cost	(xxx.xx)
26–49	Alpha	Item description	
70–73	Numeric	Quantity on hand	(xxxx)
74–74	Alpha	Code	(Letter *M*)

The date input record has the following layout:

Positions	Type	Field Description	
1–06	Numeric	Date	(mmddyy)
74–74	Alpha	Code	(Letter *D*)

Processing

For each record, multiply the unit cost and quantity on hand to calculate the on hand cost. Round this cost to the nearest whole dollar. Calculate total on hand cost for each group of records.

Output

The report will have six columns of information: material number, stock number, description, unit cost, quantity on hand, and on hand cost. Print a column heading over each of these columns. Double space detail lines; position total lines three spaces ahead of the next group.

This Printer Spacing Chart shows how the report is formatted:

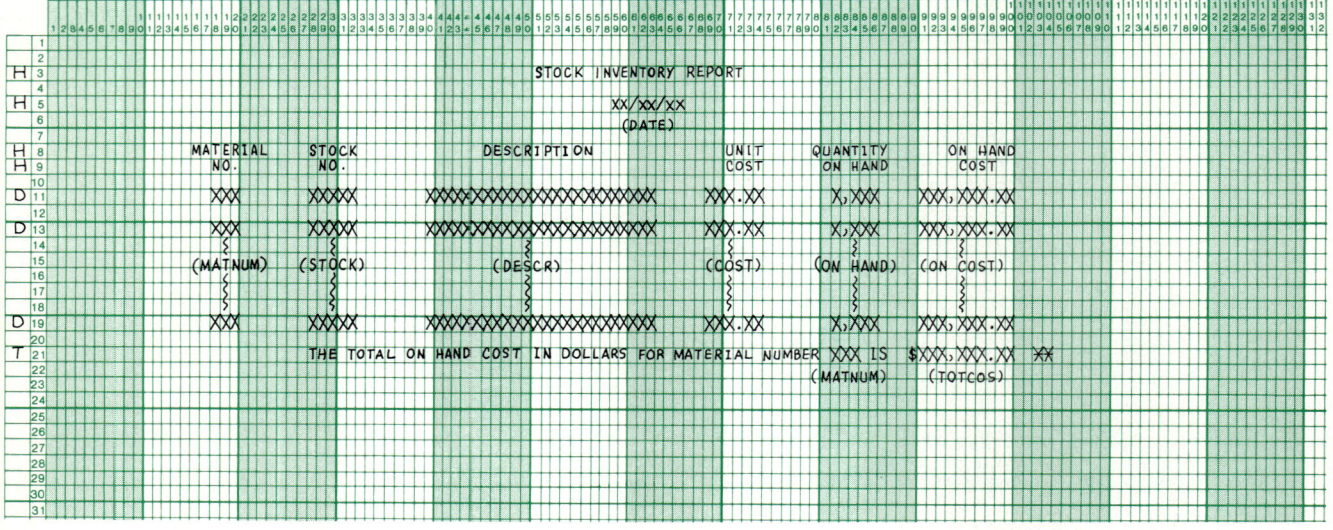

Coding sheets for Stock Inventory Report problem:

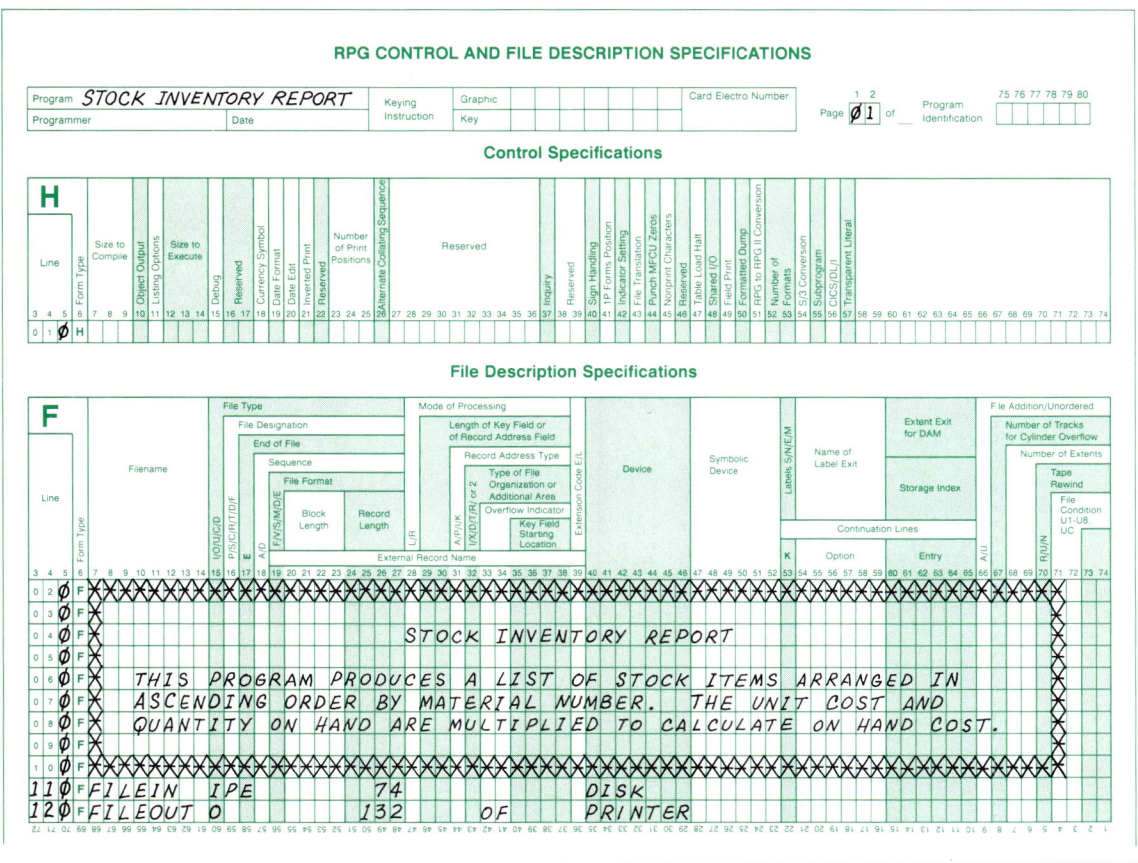
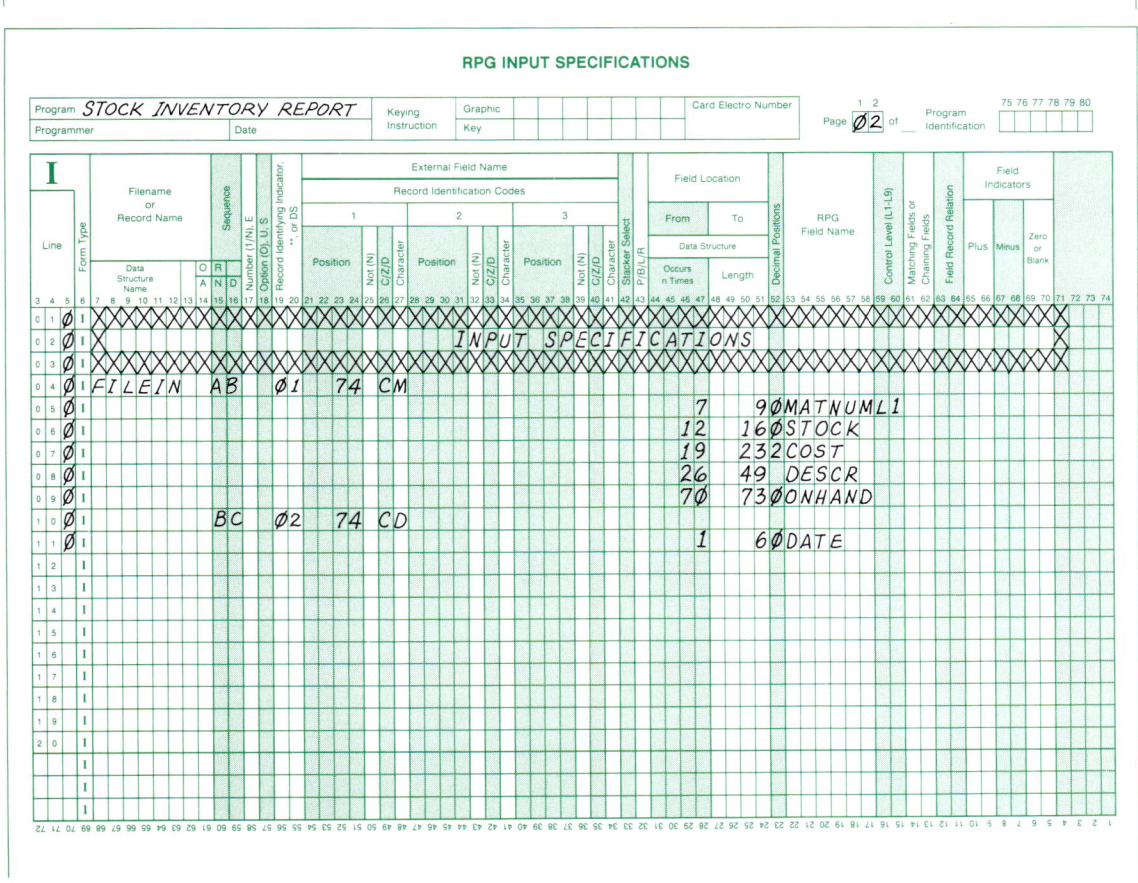

Introduction to Basic RPG Concepts 19

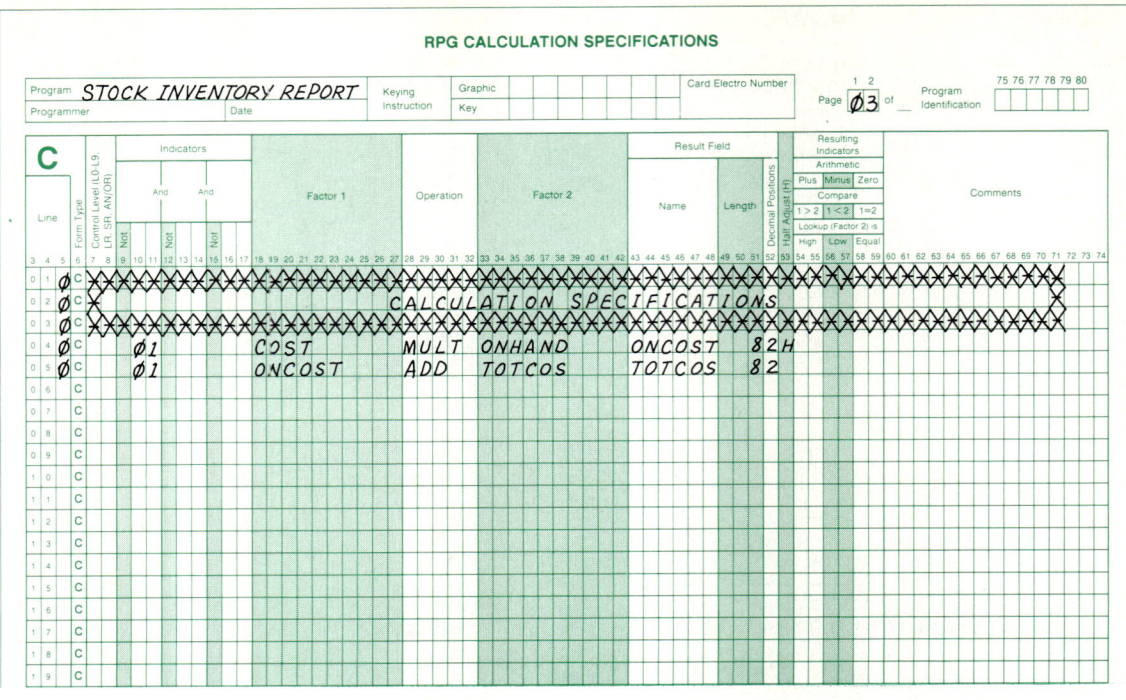

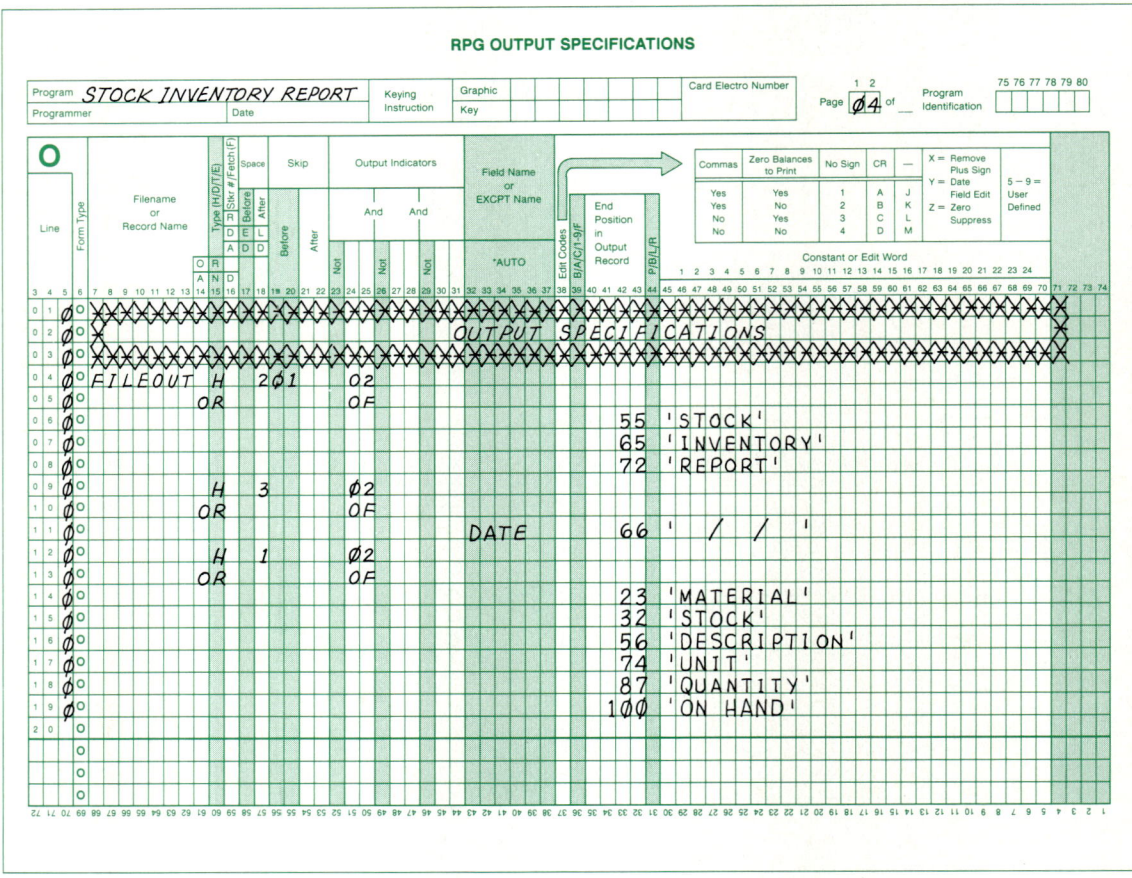

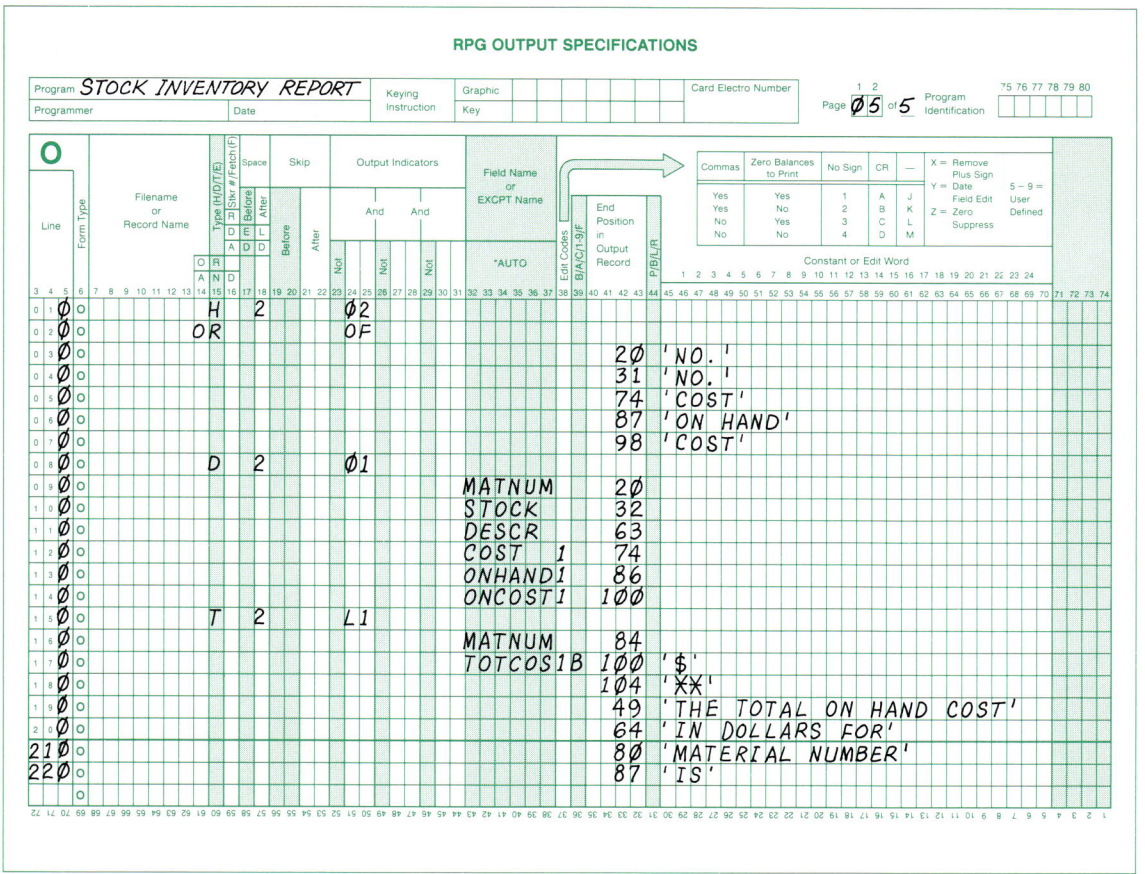

The source listing is as follows:

```
 1     01010H
 2   * 01020F****************************************************************
 3   * 01030F*                                                               *
 4   * 01040F*                 STOCK INVENTORY REPORT                        *
 5   * 01050F*                                                               *
 6   * 01060F*   THIS PROGRAM PRODUCES A LIST OF STOCK ITEMS ARRANGED IN     *
 7   * 01070F*   ASCENDING ORDER BY MATERIAL NUMBER.  THE UNIT COST AND      *
 8   * 01080F*   QUANTITY ON HAND ARE MULTIPLIED TO CALCULATE ON HAND COST.  *
 9   * 01090F*                                                               *
10   * 01100F****************************************************************
11     01110FFILEIN   IPE F      74           DISK
12     01120FFILEOUT  O  F     132     OF     PRINTER
13   * 02010I****************************************************************
14   * 02020I*                 INPUT SPECIFICATIONS                          *
15   * 02030I****************************************************************
16     02040IFILEIN   AB  01   74 CM
17     02050I                                      7   90MATNUML1
18     02060I                                     12  160STOCK
19     02070I                                     19  232COST
20     02080I                                     26   49 DESCR
21     02090I                                     70  730ONHAND
22     02100I         BC  02   74 CD
23     02110I                                      1   60DATE
24   * 03010C****************************************************************
25   * 03020C*                 CALCULATION SPECIFICATIONS                    *
26   * 03030C****************************************************************
27     03040C   01        COST      MULT ONHAND    ONCOST  82H
28     03050C   01        ONCOST    ADD  TOTCOS    TOTCOS  82
29   * 04010O****************************************************************
30   * 04020O*                 OUTPUT SPECIFICATIONS                         *
31   * 04030O****************************************************************
32     04040OFILEOUT  H  201       02
33     04050O            OR        OF
34     04060O                                  55 'STOCK'
35     04070O                                  65 'INVENTORY'
36     04080O                                  72 'REPORT'
```

Introduction to Basic RPG Concepts

```
37  040900      H 3      02
38  041000      OR       OF
39  041100                         DATE          66 '  /  / '
40  041200      H 1      02
41  041300      OR       OF
42  041400                                       23 'MATERIAL'
43  041500                                       32 'STOCK'
44  041600                                       56 'DESCRIPTION'
45  041700                                       74 'UNIT'
46  041800                                       87 'QUANTITY'
47  041900                                      100 'ON HAND'
48  050100      H 2      02
49  050200      OR       OF
50  050300                                       20 'NO.'
51  050400                                       31 'NO.'
52  050500                                       74 'COST'
53  050600                                       87 'ON HAND'
54  050700                                       98 'COST'
55  050800      D 2      01
56  050900                         MATNUM        20
57  051000                         STOCK         32
58  051100                         DESCR         63
59  051200                         COST  1       74
60  051300                         ONHAND1       86
61  051400                         ONCOST1      100
62  051500      T 2      L1
63  051600                         MATNUM        84
64  051700                         TOTCOS1B 100 '$'
65  051800                                      104 '**'
66  051900                                       49 'THE TOTAL ON HAND COST'
67  052000                                       64 'IN DOLLARS FOR'
68  052100                                       80 'MATERIAL NUMBER'
69  052200                                       87 'IS'
```

A Stock Inventory Report is to be printed as follows:

```
                         STOCK INVENTORY REPORT

                               10/01/87


MATERIAL    STOCK           DESCRIPTION           UNIT    QUANTITY    ON HAND
  NO.        NO.                                  COST    ON HAND      COST

  025       96543     CARBORUNDUM WHEELS          10.25     4,646     47,621.50

            THE TOTAL ON HAND COST IN DOLLARS FOR MATERIAL NUMBER 025 IS   $47,621.50 **

  222       01598     STAINLESS RODS               8.59       934      8,023.06

  222       09346     HI GRADE CARBON              4.82        52        250.64

  222       11632     CARBON STEEL                 5.96     1,598      9,524.08

            THE TOTAL ON HAND COST IN DOLLARS FOR MATERIAL NUMBER 222 IS   $17,797.78 **

  331       11723     STAINLESS PINS               9.17        52        476.84

  331       11725     STAINLESS TUBING             1.15       915      1,052.25

  331       11899     STAINLESS FITTINGS          15.67     1,792     28,080.64

            THE TOTAL ON HAND COST IN DOLLARS FOR MATERIAL NUMBER 331 IS   $29,609.73 **

  712       62549     HEX STOCK TITANIUM         100.48        89      8,942.72

  712       65342     TITANIUM BARS               95.89        85      8,150.65

  712       72359     STEEL PLATE                 11.86        98      1,162.28

  712       81192     FLAT ROLLED STEEL SHEETS    15.92     1,139     18,132.88

            THE TOTAL ON HAND COST IN DOLLARS FOR MATERIAL NUMBER 712 IS   $36,388.53 **

  995       81536     STEEL FLANGE                 4.80     1,985      9,528.00

  995       45678     ALLIGATOR PUMPS            965.43     9,999     53,334.57

            THE TOTAL ON HAND COST IN DOLLARS FOR MATERIAL NUMBER 995 IS   $62,862.57 **
```

RPG II and RPG III Programming

Questions for Review

1. What are the main parts of a data-processing system?
2. Briefly describe the main parts of a data-processing system and their main functions.
3. Name the three basic elements that must be part of every job and give a brief description of each.
4. What is a program?
5. What is meant by the term machine language?
6. What is a source program, a compiler, and an object program?
7. Differentiate between coding and specifications.
8. What are the three main functions the compiler performs?
9. Must a program be compiled each time it is used or may the object module be saved?
10. Briefly, what are the basic operations involved in writing RPG programs?
11. What is a field, a record, and a file?
12. What are file devices?
13. What is a record layout and how does it help to define the record and fields of the file in more detail?
14. What information does the Printer Spacing Chart provide?
15. What are heading, detail, and total lines?
16. Why are specifications forms used?
17. Briefly, what are the main functions of the seven specifications forms used in RPG programming?
18. Why is it important to know the order of the operations in the RPG program cycle?
19. What is a program cycle?
20. What is meant by detail time and total time?
21. What are indicators and what is their function?

Problems

Problem 1

Prepare a Printer Spacing Chart for the following. Be sure that the heading is properly centered and leave five spaces between each column.

```
              CUSTOMER NAME AND ADDRESS LISTING

    NAME              STREET ADDRESS         CITY          STATE      ZIP

    ARTSON       H V  123 WOOD LANE          DES MOINES    CALIF.     93465

    BELBOR       G T  784 GRAND DRIVE        SEMMDALE      VA.        17427

    BEIGHT       L P  NEW SPRING BLVD        HERR          MD.        25672

    CALIPHANDER  A C  23 STRETCH BLVD        MITTAK        ALA.       37690

    DIERR        D T  1 MADISON ROAD         HEAROLD       N.M.       76903
```

The input data has the following format:

NAME & INITIALS	ADDRESS	CITY	STATE	ZIP
99999999999999	999999999999999	9999999999999	9999999	99999999999
1-14	15-29	30-42	43-49	50-60

Problem 2

Prepare a Printer Spacing Chart for the following. Be sure that the heading is properly centered and leave five spaces between each column.

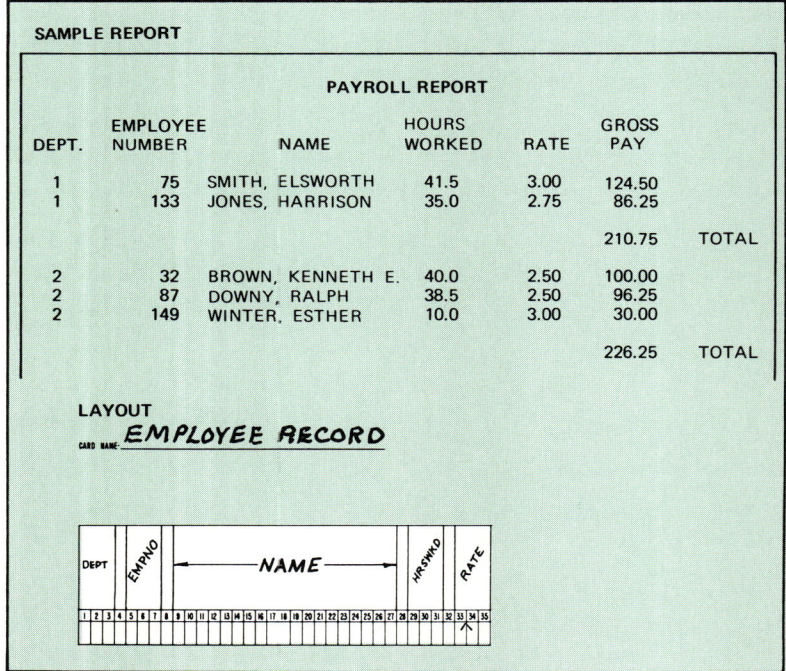

Problem 3

Create a spacing chart plan using the following description of a report:

The report contains five column headings: item number, selling price, cost, profit, and percent profit. The spacing is triple from the heading to the first detail line and double for all detail lines. Item number is a four-position field and is to be zero suppressed. The fields for selling price, cost, and profit have five positions with two decimals. The percent profit field is four positions with three decimals. Edit these fields with zero suppression. To calculate profit, subtract cost from selling price. To calculate percent profit, divide profit by cost and round the answer to three decimal places.

Problem 4

In the following illustration, indicate the functions that are performed at each step in the RPG logic cycle.

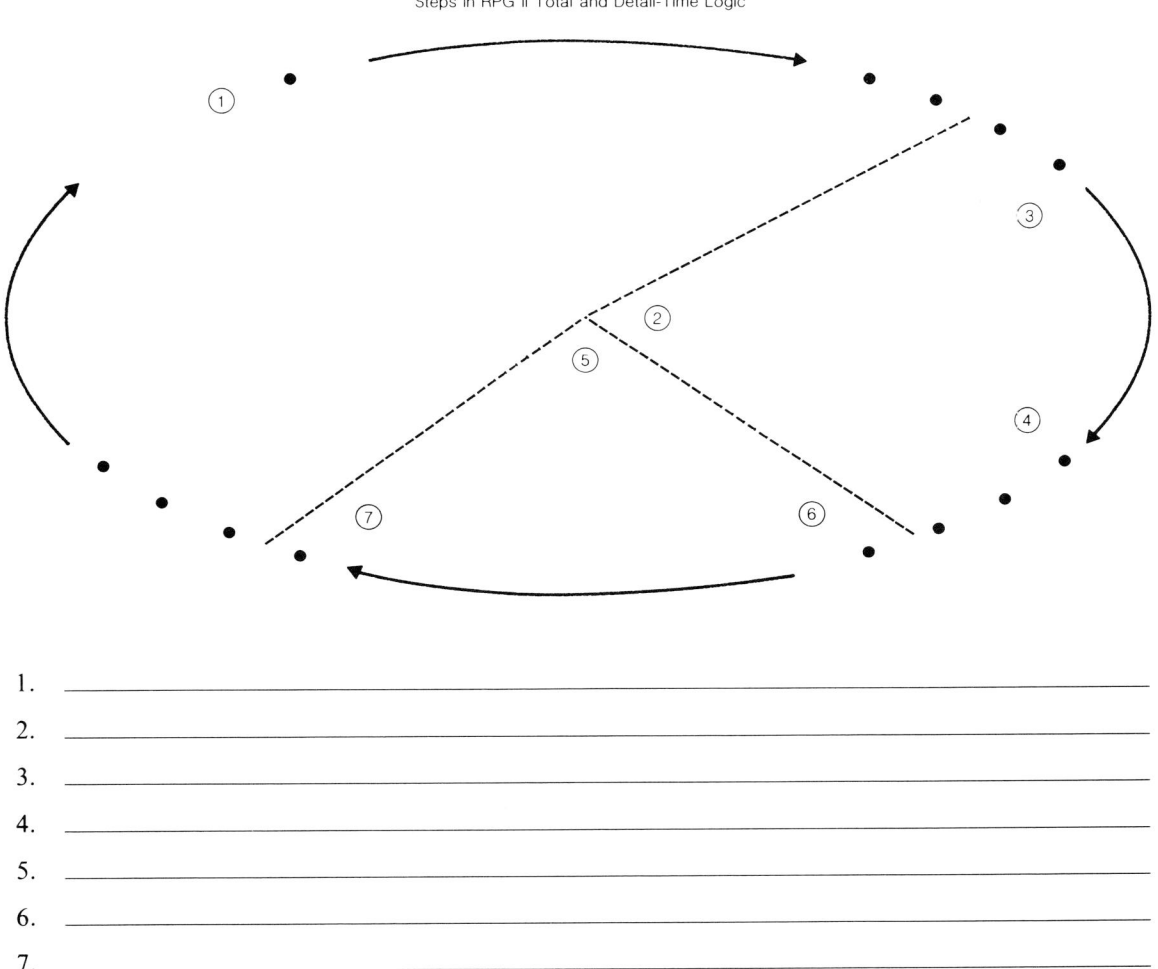

Steps in RPG II Total and Detail-Time Logic

1. _____
2. _____
3. _____
4. _____
5. _____
6. _____
7. _____

2 Input and Output Processing

Outline

Describing Data
RPG Basic Logic Cycle
    Data Movement within the Cycle
Writing Specifications for Input
        and Output Operations
Control Specifications
Describing Files
    File Description Specifications
        Filename
        File Use
        File Designation
        Record Size
        Overflow Indicators
        Program Cycle Operations
        RPG Specifications
        Using Overflow Indicator
            and 1P Indicators Together
        Device Designation
    Summary
Line Counter Specifications
    Filename
    Specifications
Describing Input Records
    Input Specifications
        Filename
        Specifying Record Type
            Sequence
        Specifying Record Identifying
            Indicators
        Specifying Record Identification
            Codes
        Describing Fields
        Describing Fields within
            Records
        Field Location
        Type of Data
        Field Name
    Summary

Describing Output Records
    Output Specifications
        Filename
        Record Type
        Field Name
        Field Location
    Printed Reports
        Spacing
        Skipping
    Editing
    *PLACE
    First Page Indicator
        Program Cycle Operations
        RPG Specifications
    Summary
    Heading Output
        Constants
        1P Indicator and Type
        Spacing and Skipping
Writing the First Program
    Common Entries
    Keying Instructions
        Page Number
        Line Number
        Form Type
        Comments
        Program Identification

Figure 2.1   Simplified RPG logic cycle

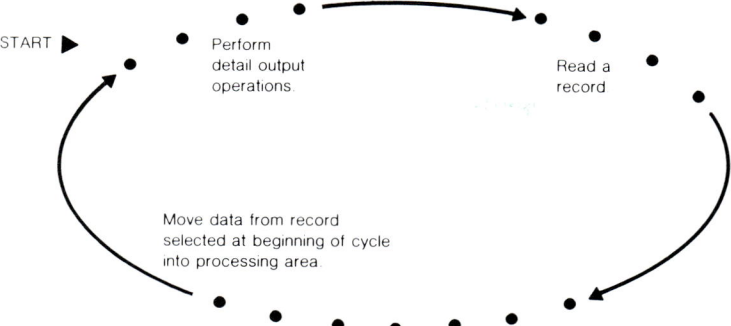

Describing Data

In RPG programming, as in all data-processing operations, the programmer is concerned with the manipulation of all the data. Object programs read in data, change data organization and format, create new data through combination and calculating functions, and write out data in files and printed form. Data is always organized in files; files are made up of records; records are made up of fields.

Data read in by an input device must be transferred to the computer's processing unit before it can be used. Moving data is a mandatory operation that is performed in exactly the same manner for every job; hence, the compiler automatically supplies the instructions to move data.

The area of the program to which the most care must be given by the programmer is the description of the data. Most errors in RPG usage result from either incorrect use or imprecise description of the data fields with which most of the calculation operations deal.

RPG Basic Logic Cycle

In RPG programming, certain entries are coded on the input or output specifications. The fixed logic cycle of RPG will determine exactly when the coding will be executed. The cycle assists programming by handling some of the routine activities such as reading records and moving data. (See Figure 2.1.)

Data Movement within the Cycle

Initially, a record is read into the input/output (I/O) area from the file designated as *I* on the file description specifications. Next, the record is identified according to input specifications.

After the record is read into the I/O area and identified, the data are moved from the I/O area to the fields. This separation into fields is done according to the coding on the input specifications. Fields must be separated by individual names so that specific processing may be coded for them. In calculations the programmer may need to work with certain fields in performing the output. The fields may be in a different order from that found in the input record.

Once the data has been moved from the I/O area to the fields, the detail calculations or detail output may be performed using these fields. (See Figure 2.2.) For output, the processing is reversed. The fields are moved back to the I/O area to the output record. The positions of the fields in the output record are coded on the output specifications.

The basic logic cycle performs the routine tasks of moving data, but the programmer provides the "specifics" through coding.

Writing Specifications for Input and Output Operations

One of the simplest jobs that can be done on a system is to read information from an input record, then output that same information in the form of a printed report, but perform no calculations.

Figure 2.2 Input data movement within cycle

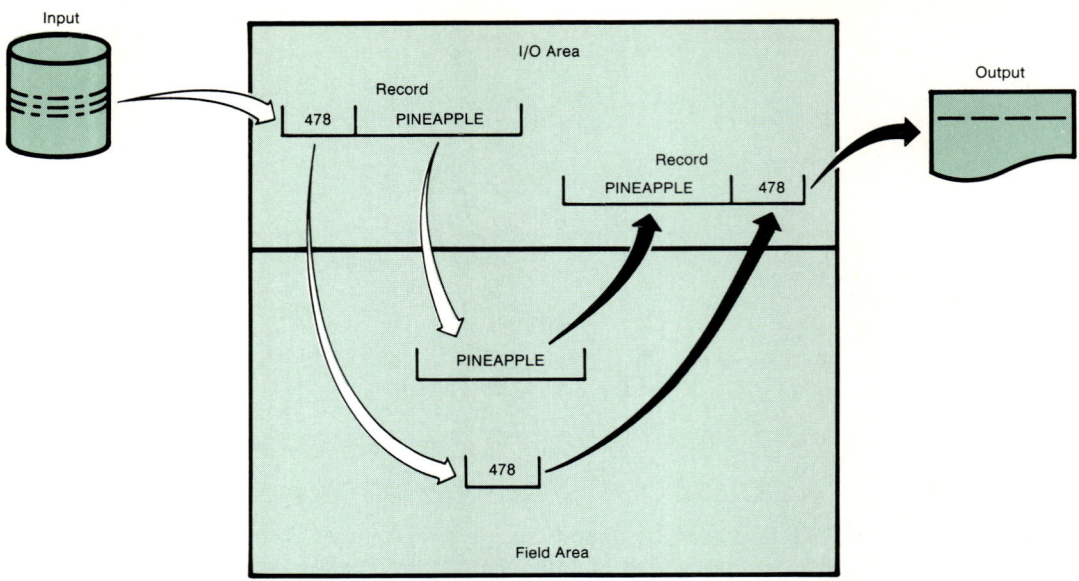

Control Specifications (H Specification)

Form H is used to provide information about the job and to describe the system to the RPG compiler. (See Figure 2.3.) The H form may be optional. When omitted, standard default values are assumed; however, when present, it precedes other source language statements. (See Figure 2.4.)

The H, or header, specification is associated more with the execution of the program than with the logic of the coding. The header specification is used primarily to supply the name of the program in its executable form and to specify special options during compilation or execution.

The main function of the H specification is to assign a unique name to the program so that it can be identified when it is time to execute the program.

The name assigned may be from 1–6 characters, must begin with an alphabetic character, and must contain no embedded blanks or special characters. A common approach to naming is to establish a group for the program names with the first two or three characters (e.g., PAY101, PAY134, PAY780).

Figure 2.3 Control card specifications

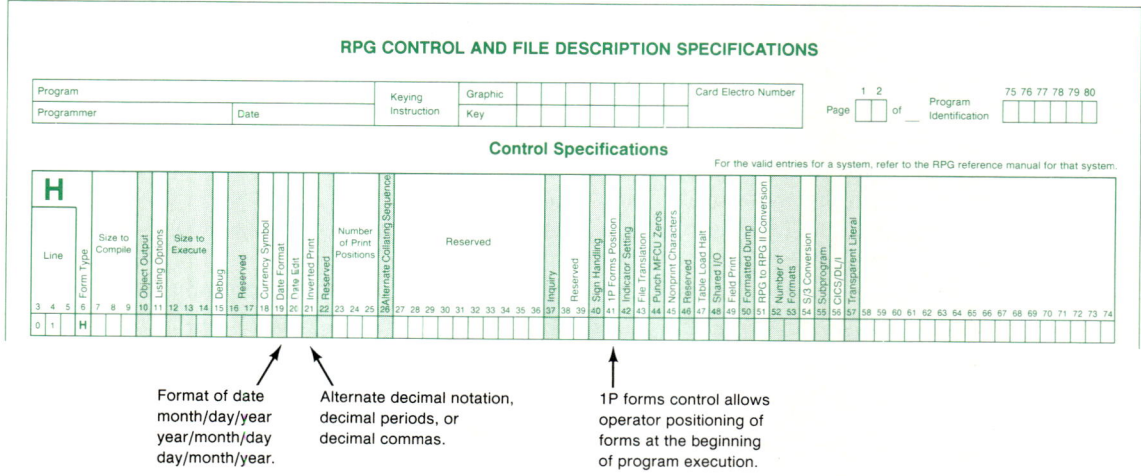

28 RPG II and RPG III Programming

Figure 2.4 Header card (control card) specifications

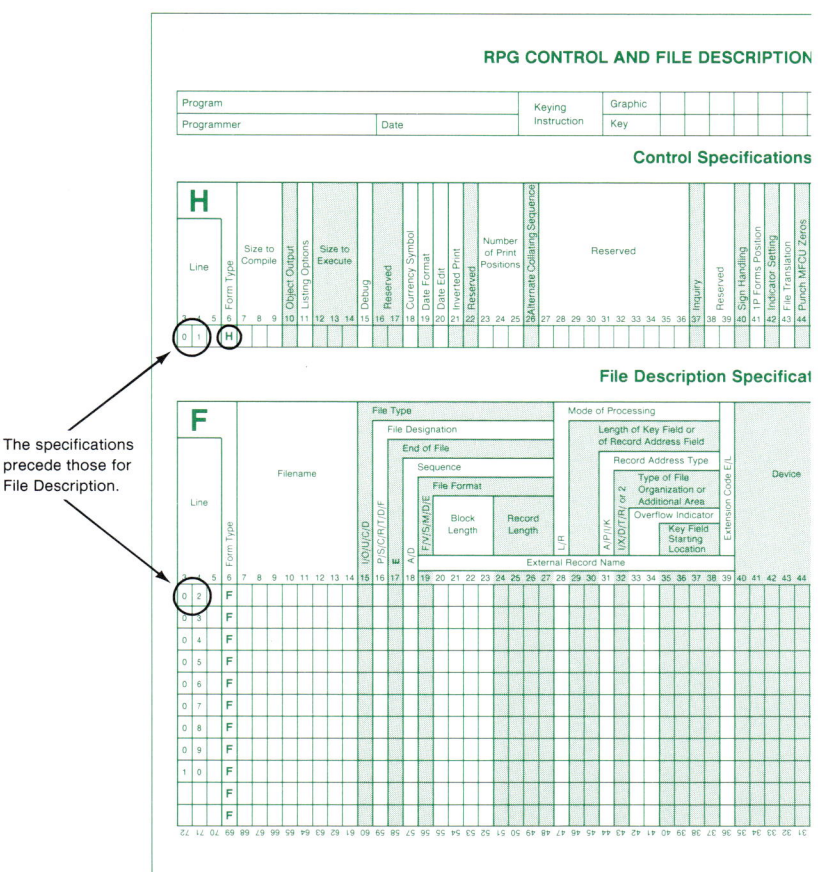

The H specifications may contain special compilation and execution options. The following are types of entries that may be included:

1. Position 10 for the format of the executable program
2. Position 11 for a complete or partial listing of the program
3. Positions 12–14 for the storage size of the system when the program executes
4. Position 15 to activate DEBUG feature

Actual entries are discussed later in this text and in the RPG reference manuals. At present it is sufficient to understand that this specification is capable of providing unique information about a program and about its compilation and execution phases.

Describing Files

The File Description Specifications form is used to describe all the files used by the program. (See Figure 2.5.) Included in this information are the names of the files, the device used with the files, and information on how the files are to be used. Every file used in the job must be described on a separate line. Many simple jobs require only one input file and one output file.

Files are described using a specifications form organized and labeled in a way that informs and prompts the programmer regarding the detailed entries necessary for each class of file. File Description Specifications forms are used to describe all the files used by the program. (See Figure 2.6.) Each file is assigned a unique name for future reference. Entries indicate whether the file is input or output.

Figure 2.5 File description specifications

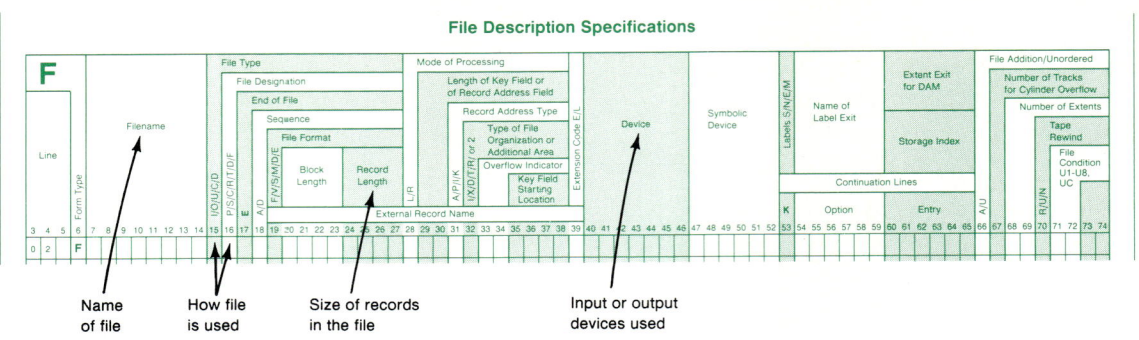

Figure 2.6 File description specifications—purposes

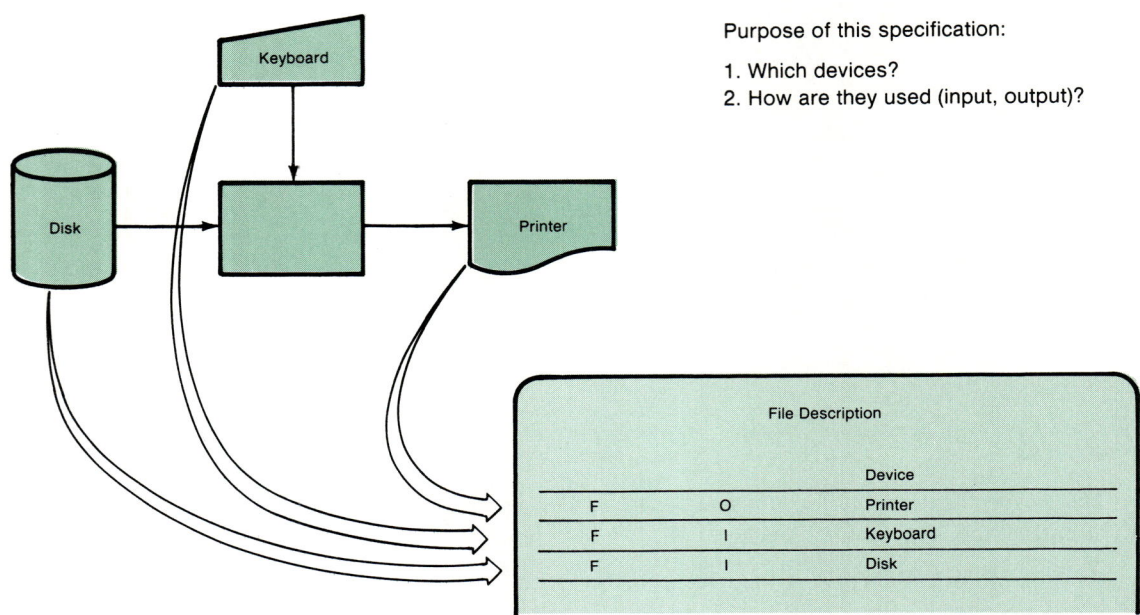

Various entries are made, depending upon the class of the file, to enable the compiler to provide correct instructions for file handling to the computer. These entries include such information as whether the file is to be checked for an end-of-file condition, the sequence of the file (if ordered), whether the file contains fixed length or variable length records, and the length of the blocks and records of the file. The kind of input/output device for the file is also entered; examples of such devices include disk, printer, magnetic tape, or work station (console).

For printer files, an (overflow) indicator may be designated that will be turned on later by the object program to test whether a certain print line position has been reached on the page. This is helpful in vertical format control. A Line Counter form (L specification) may be used. This form is used to assign form length and the number of lines the programmer wishes to print upon a page.

Each file used in the program must be described on a separate line of the File Description form. (See Figure 2.7.)

Figure 2.7 File description specifications—example

Purpose:
1. To name each file.
2. To indicate whether a file is Input, Output, or Combined (both input and output).
3. To designate input files as Primary or Secondary.
4. To indicate the record and block length of each file.
5. To tell the computer on which device the particular file will be read or written at execution time.

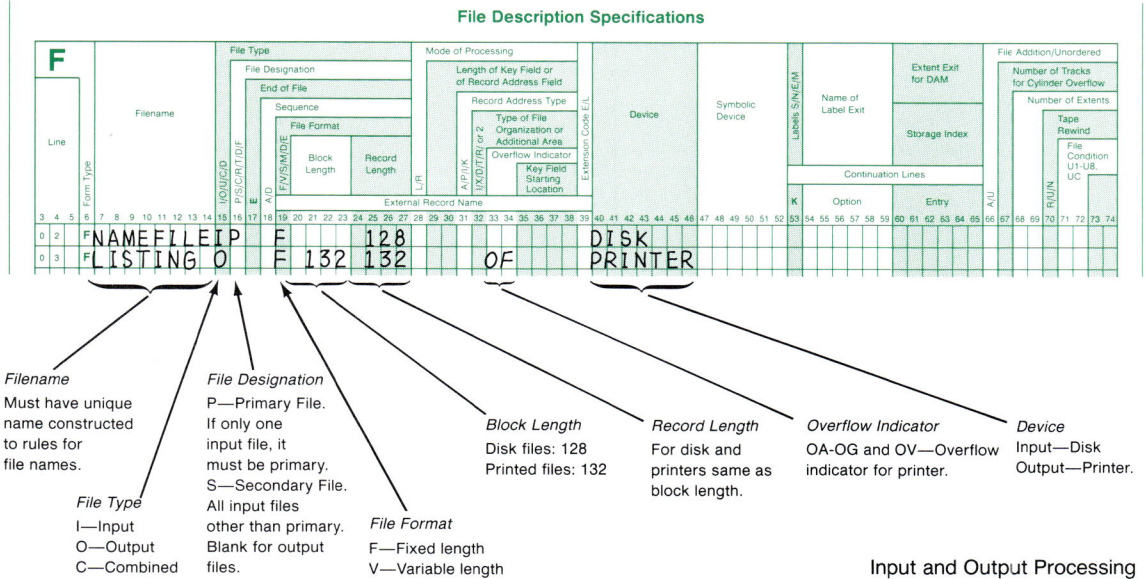

Input and Output Processing

File Description Specifications (F Specification)

The file description specifications describe what and how devices are being used in the job. In other words, file description specifications define the environment for a particular job. The system flowchart provides the outline for the entries that must be made on the file description specifications, including device names (e.g., CRT, disk, printer) and how they are used (input or output).

Filename (Positions 7–14)
Every file used in a job must be named. The name provides the user and the compiler with a means of identifying the file. During compilation, the compiler associates the filename with other characteristics of the file. Thus, the file may be referred to by the name throughout the program, and the compiler knows exactly which file is being referenced.

The compiler, however, recognizes the filenames only if they conform to the following rules:

1. A filename must be 1–8 characters long.

2. The first character of a filename must be alphabetic. (IBM considers the alphabet to consist of the letters *A–Z* and special characters *@, $,* and *#*. This is an IBM extension, not necessarily allowable on all machines.) The remaining characters in the name can be either alphabetic or numeric.

3. Blanks must not appear between characters in the filename.

4. A filename must be unique. No two files used in a program can have the same name. A filename may be used for no other purpose than as the name of a file.

5. The filename must begin in position 7 on the specifications form.

It is a good practice to assign meaningful filenames. Meaningful names indicate something about the file, such as the type of records in the file or the use of the file. For example, the abbreviation CUSTCHG might be assigned to an input file consisting of records for all customers having charge accounts. (See Figure 2.8.)

Figure 2.8 Filename—examples

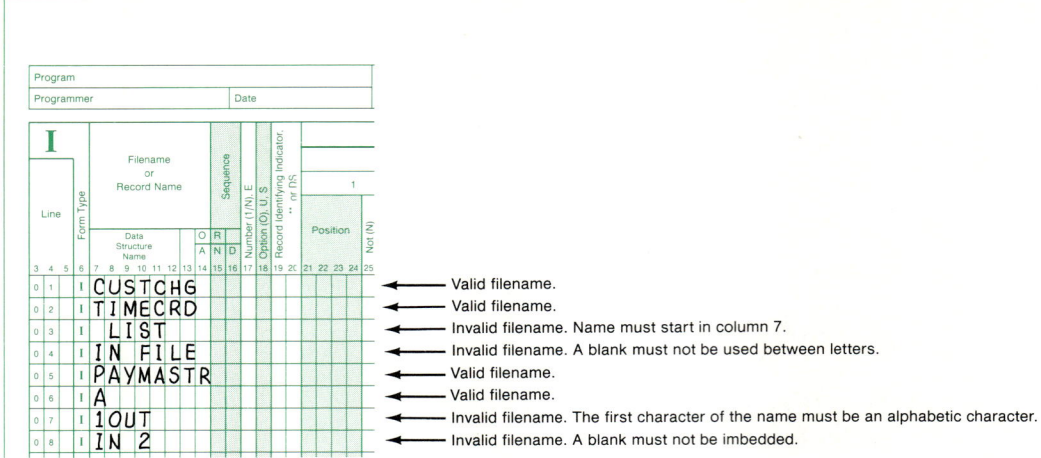

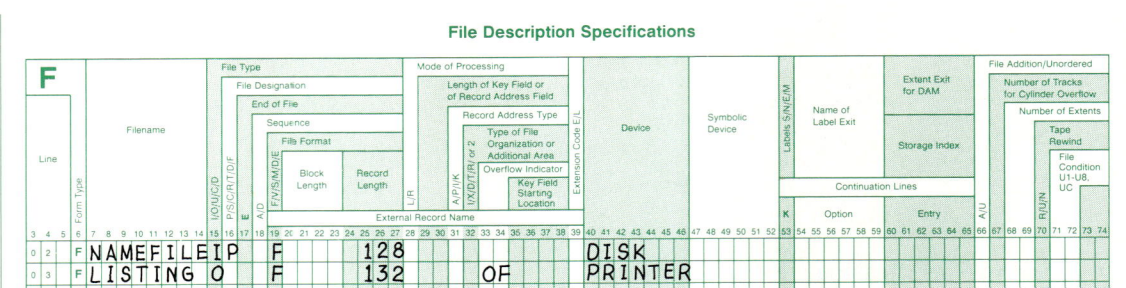

Figure 2.9 File type—examples

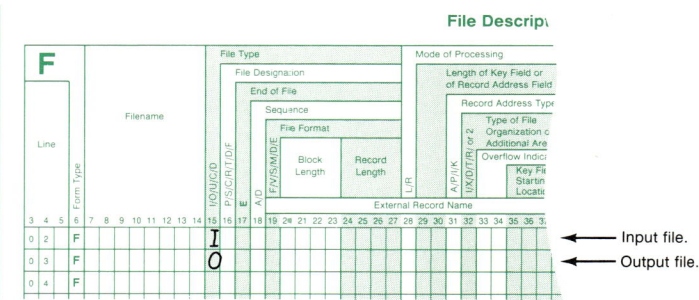

File Use (Position 15)

Each file used in the program must have its use described. Files can be either input files or output files. If records are read from a file, the file is an input file. If a new file is created during the job, the new file is an output file. (Files have other uses, but these will be discussed later in the text.)

File use can be specified by placing either an *I* (input) or an *O* (output) in position 15. Every file must have an entry under file type to help identify its use. (See Figure 2.9.)

File Designation (Position 16)

Position 16 is used to explain more about the use of input files. Every input file and combined file must be designated as primary (*P*) or secondary (*S*). A primary file is the file that is read first so there is

32   RPG II and RPG III Programming

Figure 2.10 Record length—examples

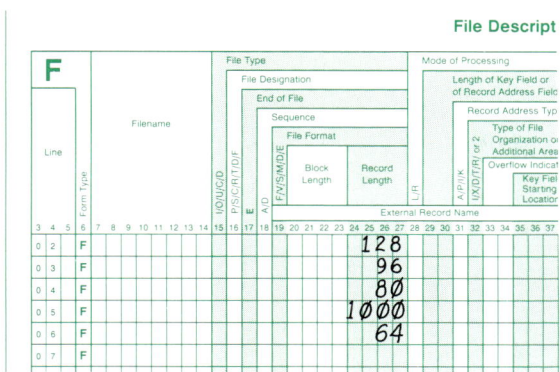

only one primary file in any program; all other input files are secondary. Other types of file designations will be discussed later in the text.

Record Size (Positions 24–27)
When describing files, the character length of records in the file must be specified. Record length is entered in positions 24–27, with the last digit specified in column 27. (See Figure 2.10.)

The record length specification provides two pieces of information:

1. It tells the compiler how much storage to set aside for a record (input or output).

2. It specifies how many characters must be read to get a complete input record.

The size of records (lines) on the printer is also easy to determine. Printed records are limited by the number of print positions in a line of the particular printer being used.

A record size smaller than actual printer size may be specified. If this is done, the programmer must be certain that none of the lines to be printed are longer than the length specified. Otherwise the RPG compiler will generate error messages requiring that the program be corrected and recompiled.

The computer must be told the length of the records it has to process. If the wrong record length entry is made for a file, an error condition will occur during execution of the program.

Other information may be required in positions 28–32 and 35–38 to describe how the input file is to be stored on the specific device.

Overflow Indicators (OA–OG, OV) (Positions 33–34)
Overflow indicators are used to signal the end of a printed page. (See Figure 2.11.) One indicator can be assigned to each printer file; this indicator will turn on when the overflow line is exceeded. The overflow line is exceeded when the last normal printing position, or line, on a page is reached. These indicators are assigned in positions 33–34 of the file specifications. Lines that are to be printed at the end of one page or the beginning of another are conditioned by the overflow indicator.

The following are functions of overflow indicators:

1. To print headings on every page except the first page of a report. (The 1P indicator allows headings to be printed on the first page.)

2. To control where printing begins and ends on a page.

3. To advance forms from one page to the next (provided a skip is specified on the output form).

Overflow can be handled either automatically by the system or through specifications coding using the line counter. Printing always occurs on the first predetermined line of a form and ends with the last predetermined line, with overflow occurring after the last line is printed. Forms then advance to the first predetermined line of the new page. Heading lines can be printed on the first page if 1P is used.

If the programmer does not wish overflow handled automatically, the programmer can specify with overflow indicators on the coding forms how it is to be handled.

Input and Output Processing 33

Figure 2.11 Overflow handling

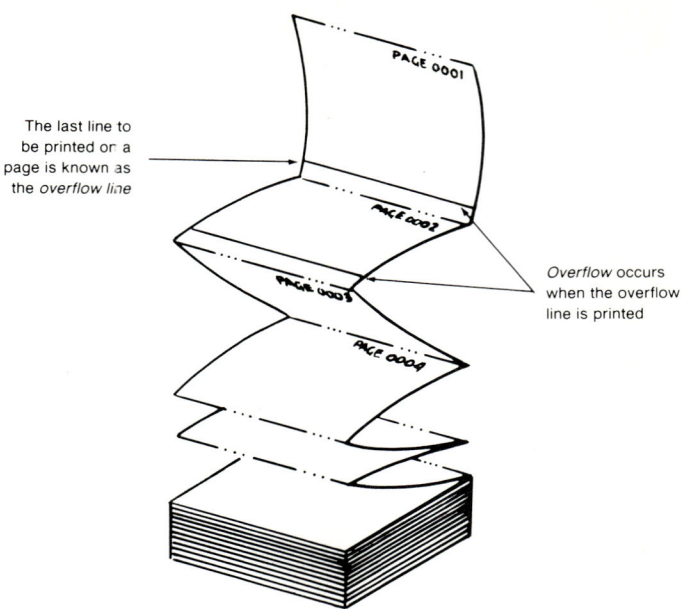

Printers use continuous forms (a series of pages divided by perforations). Overflow handling refers to the means of advancing forms from one page to the next.

Program Cycle Operations

The program sets on the programmer-assigned overflow indicator whenever the overflow line is exceeded. By setting the overflow indicator on, the program remembers that overflow has occurred. Overflow indicators can be set on at one of two times: (1) at detail time when a detail record prints on the overflow line or (2) at total time when a total record prints on the overflow line. Notice that the only time a check is made to see if the overflow indicator is on is immediately following total output. If the overflow indicator is on, overflow operations are performed in the following sequence. (See Figure 2.12.)

1. Print any total lines conditioned by the overflow indicator.

2. Skip to a new page, provided a skip was specified on a line conditioned by the overflow indicator.

3. Print all heading and detail lines conditioned by the overflow indicator. If multiple detail or total lines are to be printed in a single cycle, printing may continue past the designated overflow line. This is because all detail and total printing for a single cycle is completed before overflow operations occur.

RPG Specifications

There are eight overflow indicators: seven designated by the letters OA–OG and OV. Any one of these indicators may be entered in positions 33–34 on the File Description Specifications form. If more than one printer file is involved in the job, however, a different overflow indicator must be specified for each file.

The overflow indicator specified for a file on the File Description Specifications form must also be specified on the Output Specifications form for that file. (See Figure 2.13.)

Besides specifying the overflow indicator, it must be specified that the forms should advance. This is accomplished by placing a skip specification in positions 19–20 on the Output Specifications form.

If no skip specification for advancing forms is made in a heading line conditioned by the overflow indicator the forms will not advance to a new page when overflow occurs.

Spacing past the overflow line causes the overflow indicator to be turned on; skipping to a new page turns the indicator off.

Figure 2.12 RPG logic for overflow indicator

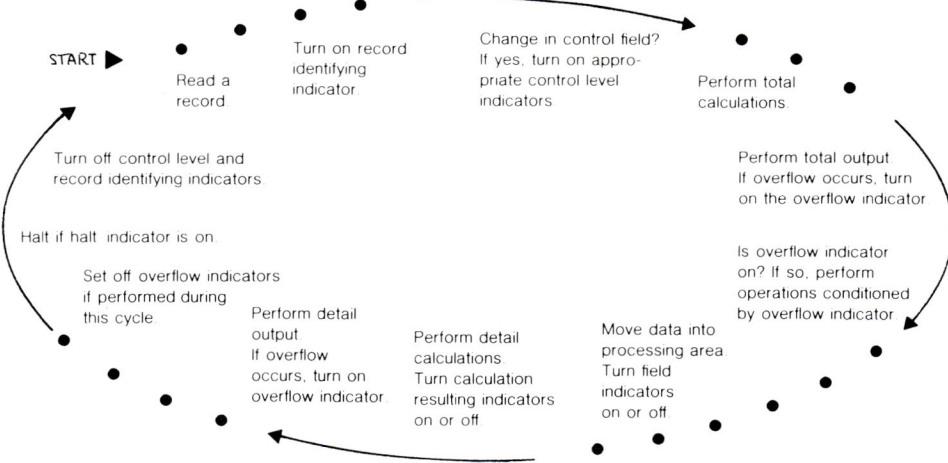

Figure 2.13 Using overflow and 1P indicators together—example

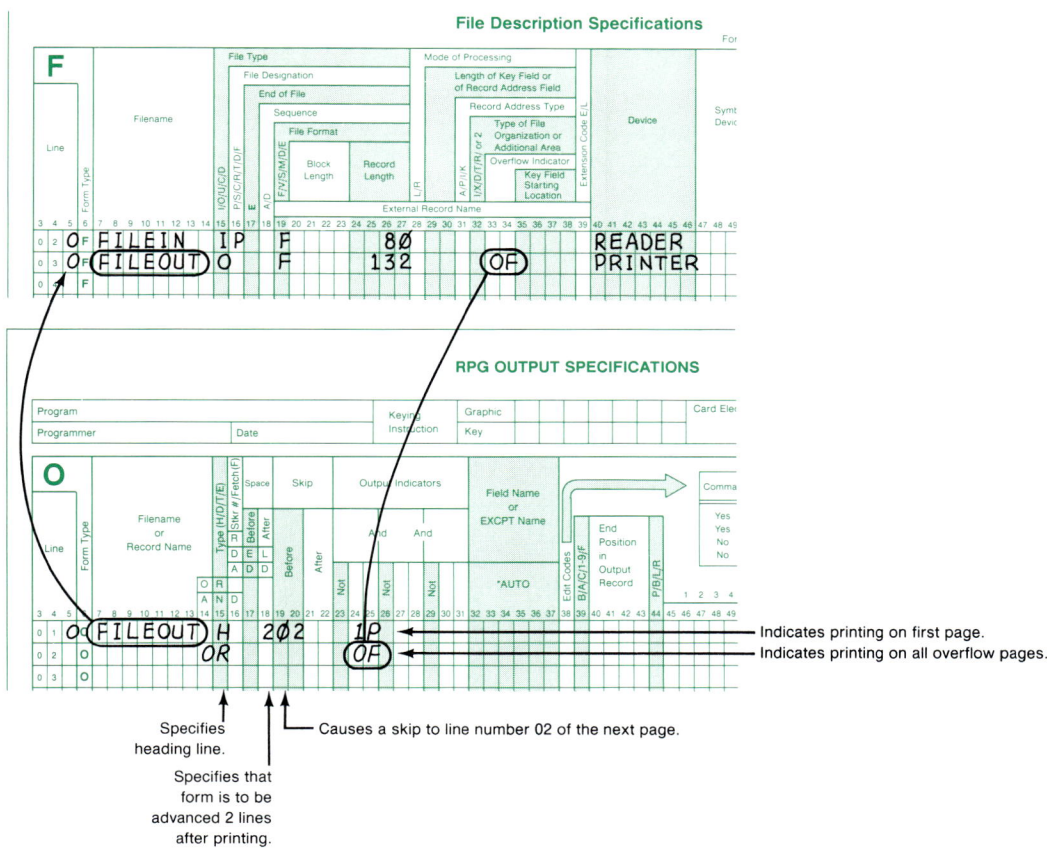

Using Overflow and 1P Indicators Together

The overflow indicator is most often used with other indicators. One of the most important uses of the overflow indicator is with the 1P indicator although 1P and overflow indicators cannot both be on at the same time.

If headings are desired on all pages of a report, both the 1P and the overflow indicators are used. 1P causes headings to be printed on the first page; the overflow indicators cause them to print on all succeeding pages. If a record is to be printed under one or the other of the conditions (when either 1P or overflow indicator is on) an OR relationship should be specified. (See Figure 2.13.)

Input and Output Processing   35

Device Designation (Positions 40-52)

The devices used for job input and output must be specified. Types of devices (e.g., printer, disk, work station, etc.) depend upon the characteristics of the job, the system used, and the devices available.

To indicate the device used for the name file, enter the RPG code name for that device in positions 40-52. The name must begin in position 40. *Note:* Code names differ for each system. The RPG reference manual for a particular system will provide the code names that are applicable.

During compilation, the compiler associates the file name with the device name. When the file name is used on the rest of the program, the system will know which device to use.

Summary

The file description coding is an important beginning to RPG programming. It describes the devices that will be used and how they will be used. Another important function of the file description coding is the guide to the rest of the coding that it provides.

The records in the files designated as input (those having an *I* in column 15 of the file description specifications) must be further described on the input specifications. (These specifications give detail about the records and the fields in the records.)

The records in the files designated as output (those having an *O* in column 15 of the file description specifications) must be further described on the line counter specifications (if included) and the output specifications.

Line Counter Specifications

The Line Counter Specifications form is used for all output files that have had an *L* encoded in position 39 of the File Description Specifications form. (See Figure 2.14.) This form helps define top of page, bottom of page, and overflow line.

The overflow indicator and its coding will take care of headings on pages other than the first. Line counter specifications are required only if the form length or the overflow line differs from system defaults.

The following coding is necessary for line counter specifications. (See Figure 2.15.)

1. The File Description Specifications form must be coded with an *L* in position 39 to indicate that the Line Counter Specifications form will be used. (The Line Counter Specifications form can only be used with printer output files.)

2. The file name on the line counter specifications must be defined as the printer file on the file description specifications.

3. The values for the form length and overflow line should correspond to the actual page and form design.

4. The remainder of the form is not used.

5. The line counter specifications will directly follow the file description specifications (providing there is no extension specification) during the compiling of the program. (See Figure 2.14.)

The Line Counter Specifications sheet and the overflow indicator may be used separately since they are independent of each other. When the programmer wishes to control the arrangement of the printing on a page, the Line Counter Specifications sheet is used to describe the page to the computer. The entries on this form will indicate where on the page the printing will end. (See Figure 2.14.)

Two types of print control functions can be performed. First, an RPG forms-overflow condition can be sensed on any designated line on the page. This means that the overflow indicator (OA–OG or OV) specified for the file printer will be turned on automatically when the paper form print line associated with the *OL* entry has been reached. The overflow indicator may be used subsequently as a condition for printing of totals and page numbers, skipping to a new page, printing of headers, and performing calculations.

The second type of function performed under line control is to skip the paper form to the print line position associated with the designated line number. The skip occurs before or after the printing of a line for which the line number is entered on the Output Specifications form. The line number entered

Figure 2.14 Overflow described by the programmer—example

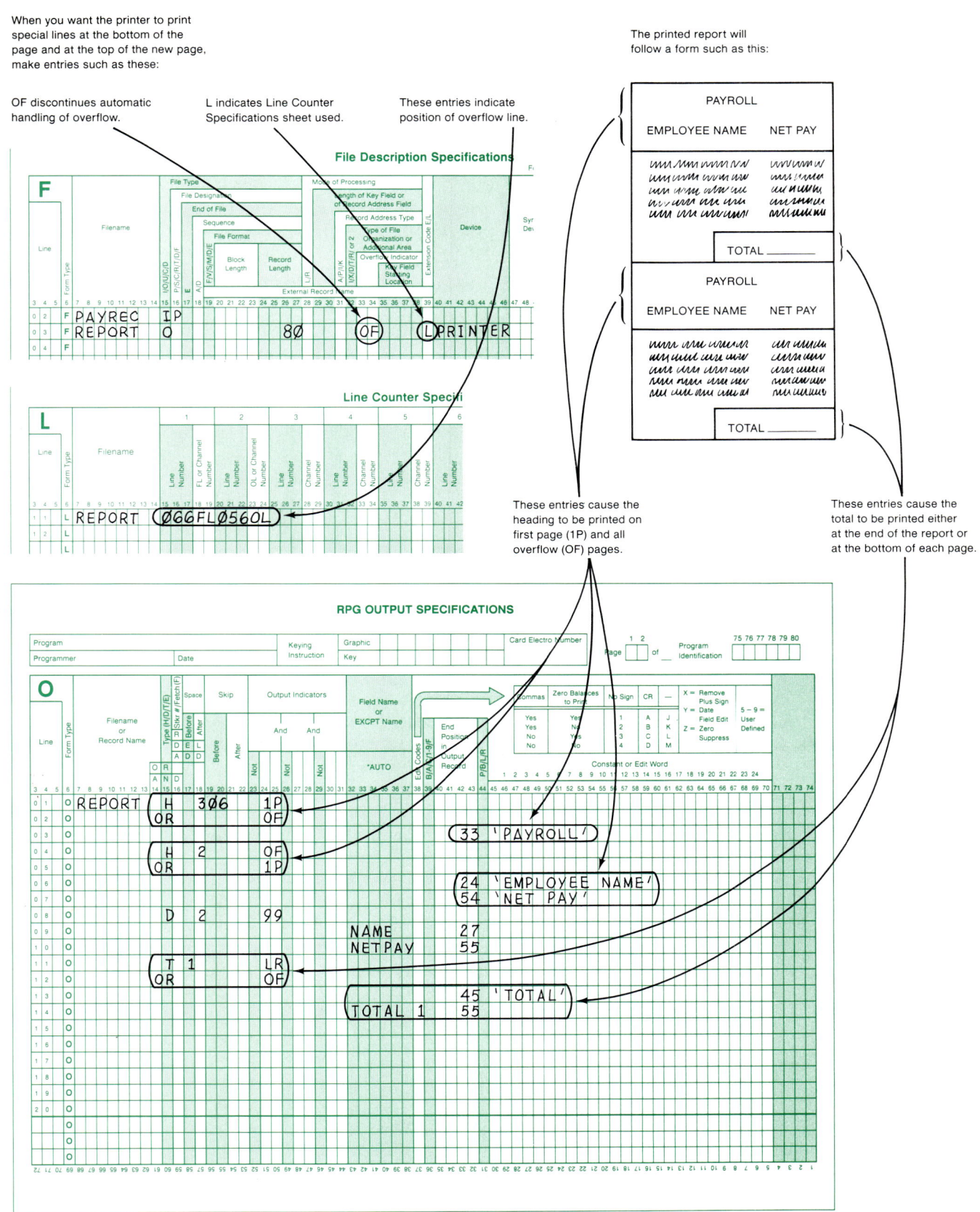

Input and Output Processing 37

Figure 2.15 Line counter specifications—summary

Purpose:
To specify where on the page or form the printing is to end.

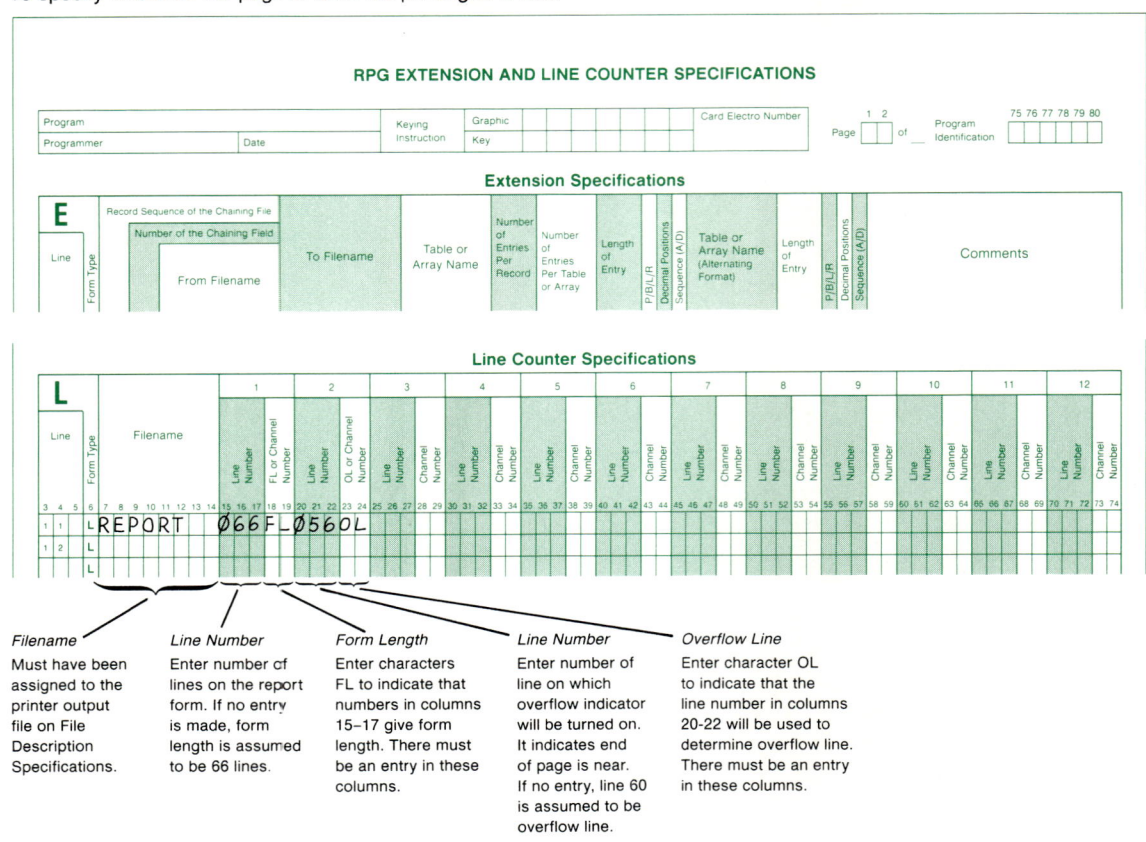

in positions 19–20 causes a skip before; the number entered in positions 21–22 creates a skip after the printed line. This function is especially useful for highly formatted reports and partially preprinted form stock, such as check blanks or Internal Revenue Service reports. (See Figure 2.14.)

Filename

The filename given on the line counter specifications must be the same filename assigned to the output file for that entry on the File Description Specifications Form.

Specifications

Line counter specifications are found on the bottom section of the Extension and Line Counter Specifications form and are used exclusively for defining the number of lines to be printed on each page.

Only a printer filename can be used in filename positions 7–14. Positions 15–24 contain the entries for report formatting.

In positions 15–17 enter the number of available lines.

In positions 18–19 put the letters *FL* to show that the previous specifications have a form length.

In positions 20–22 enter the number of the overflow line when the programmer wants the overflow indicator to be turned on.

In positions 23–24 enter the letters *OL* to show that the previous specification was the overflow line.

Positions 25–74 are not used. (See Figure 2.15.)

Figure 2.16 Input Specifications form

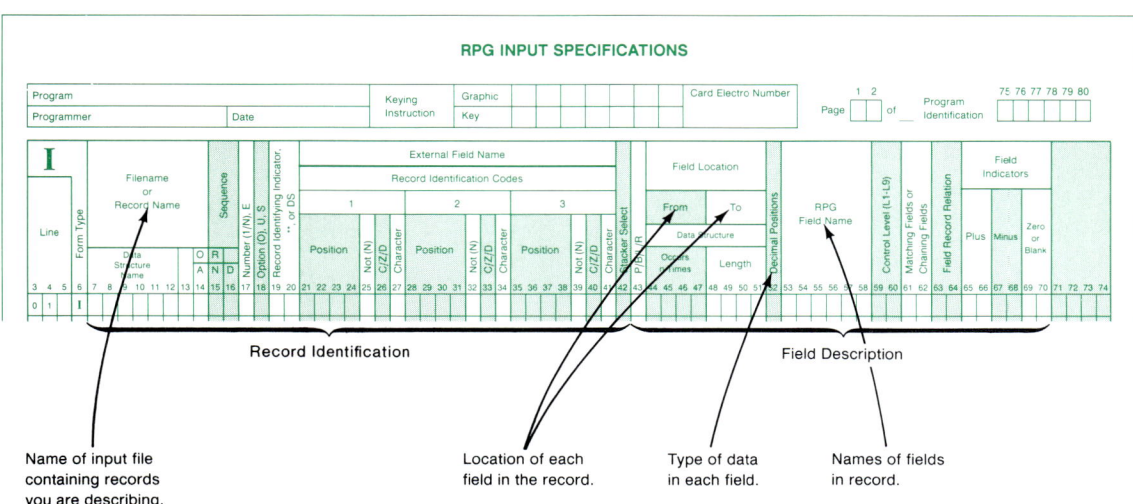

Describing Input Records

Besides describing files, the records within files must also be described. The compiler needs this information to create an object program that will read records properly. Input records are described on the Input Specifications form. (See Figure 2.16.) Information needed to describe the record in a file includes the name of the file containing the record, the name of each field in the record, and the location of each field in the record. The Record Layout form may be used to help describe input records. This form shows the location and length of all fields in the record. (See Figures 2.17 and 2.18.)

Figure 2.17 Describing input records

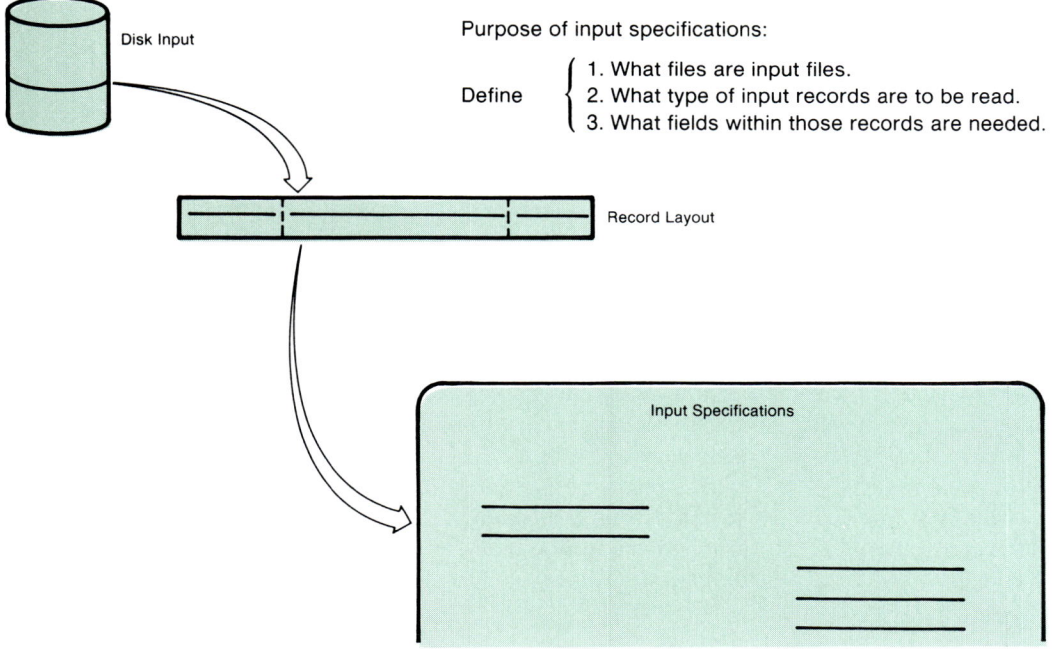

Input and Output Processing 39

Figure 2.18 Describing input fields

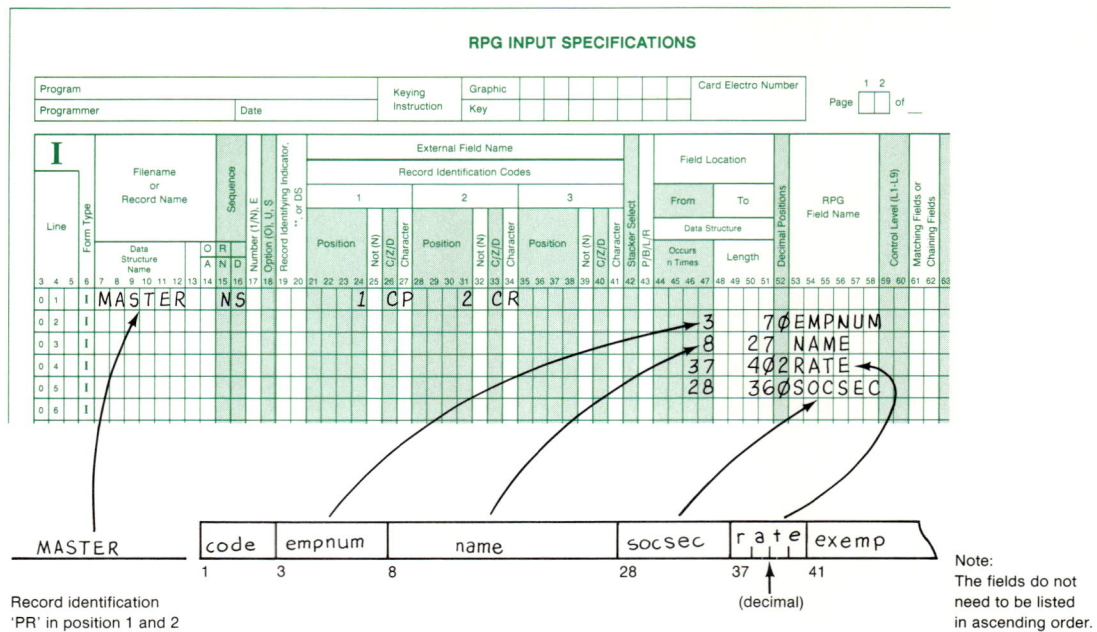

Input Specifications

The Input Specifications form will be used to describe the contents of the input files, the records, and the fields of records to be used in the program. The files to be coded on the Input Specifications form are the ones that are coded *I* on the File Description Specifications form. The detail information needed for Input Specifications will come from the record layouts. These specifications may be divided into two categories. (See Figure 2.16.)

1. File and record type identification (positions 7–42). These specifications describe the input record and its relationship to other records in the file.

2. Field description entries (positions 43–70). These specifications describe fields in the records.

These two sets of specifications are written on the Input Specifications form. The field description entries must start at least one line lower than file and record type identification entries.

Filename (Positions 7–14)
To tell the compiler which records are being described, the name of the file containing these records is entered in positions 7–14. This name must be the same (and spelled the same) as the one assigned to the input file on the File Description Specifications form. (See Figure 2.19.)

Specifying Record Type Sequence (Positions 15–16)
The sequence entry tells the computer whether or not it has to check the sequence of record types within a file. Sometimes records must be in a particular order within a record type group, but at other times the order makes no difference. When records need not be in a particular order, enter two alphabetic characters in positions 15–16. Different alphabetic characters can be used for each record.

If a check for sequence is to be made, a numeric entry is entered that assigns a special sequence to different record types in a file. Entries must also be made in positions 17–18.

The entries in position 17 have the following functions:

Entry	Explanation
blank	Record types are not sequenced (positions 15–16 have alphabetic entries).
1	Only one group of this type is present in the sequenced group.
N	One or more records of this type may be present in the sequenced group.

Figure 2.19 Filename—example

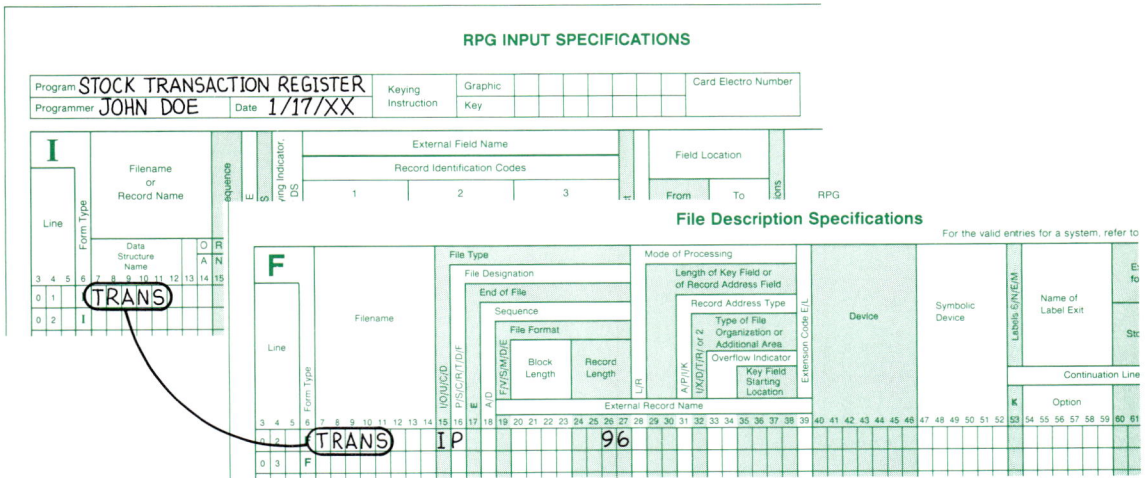

The entries in position 18 have the following functions:

Entry	Explanation
blank	Record type must be present (if sequence checking is specified).
O	Option (record type may or may not be present).

Note: Entries in positions 17 and 18 need be made only if there is a numeric entry in positions 15–16.

Positions 15–16 should have an entry for every record type specified. If there is only one record type per file, the entry should be alphabetic. If the programmer fails to use a sequence entry, the compiler prints a message saying that no entry was made in positions 15–16.

Specifying Record Identifying Indicators (Positions 19–20)

RPG processing of records requires a means of knowing when a record has been input and is available for processing. To provide for this, an entry is made assigning a unique number indicator to each record type. When this record is encountered during input, the assigned indicator is turned on and available. A record identifying indicator is set on right after a record is read and is set off before the next record is read. An indicator in either an on or off state may be called out as a condition for calculating or output processing. Even for files having one record type, an indicator code should be entered on the specifications form.

A record identifying indicator may be specified in positions 19–20 for each record. Record identifying indicators are numbered 01–99. A different number is used for each record type.

A record identifying indicator is specified on the same line as the identification code. All fields for the records are then listed, starting one line below the identification code and identifying indicator. The filename need be specified only once; it is placed on the specification line describing the first record in the file.

After reading a record, the program checks the identification codes to determine which record it has read. When it finds a match between the codes on the record and the codes stored from the Input Specifications form, it turns on the record identifying indicator associated with that record. This is the program's way of remembering which record it has read.

Record identifying indicators can be used to condition calculations, output records, or output fields. In this way, the program performs the operations for each different record type. (See Figures 2.20 and 2.21.)

When record identifying indicators are used to condition calculations and output operations, the programmer can be assured that these operations will be done only for the appropriate records. If indicators are not used, operations will be done for all records.

Input and Output Processing

Figure 2.20 Order of record types within a group—example

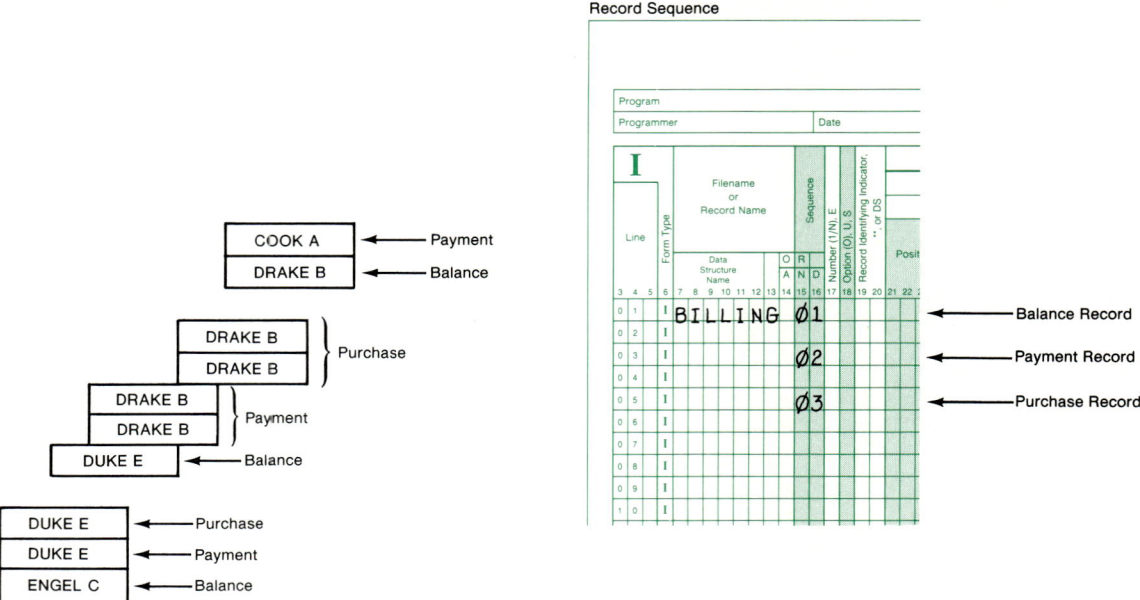

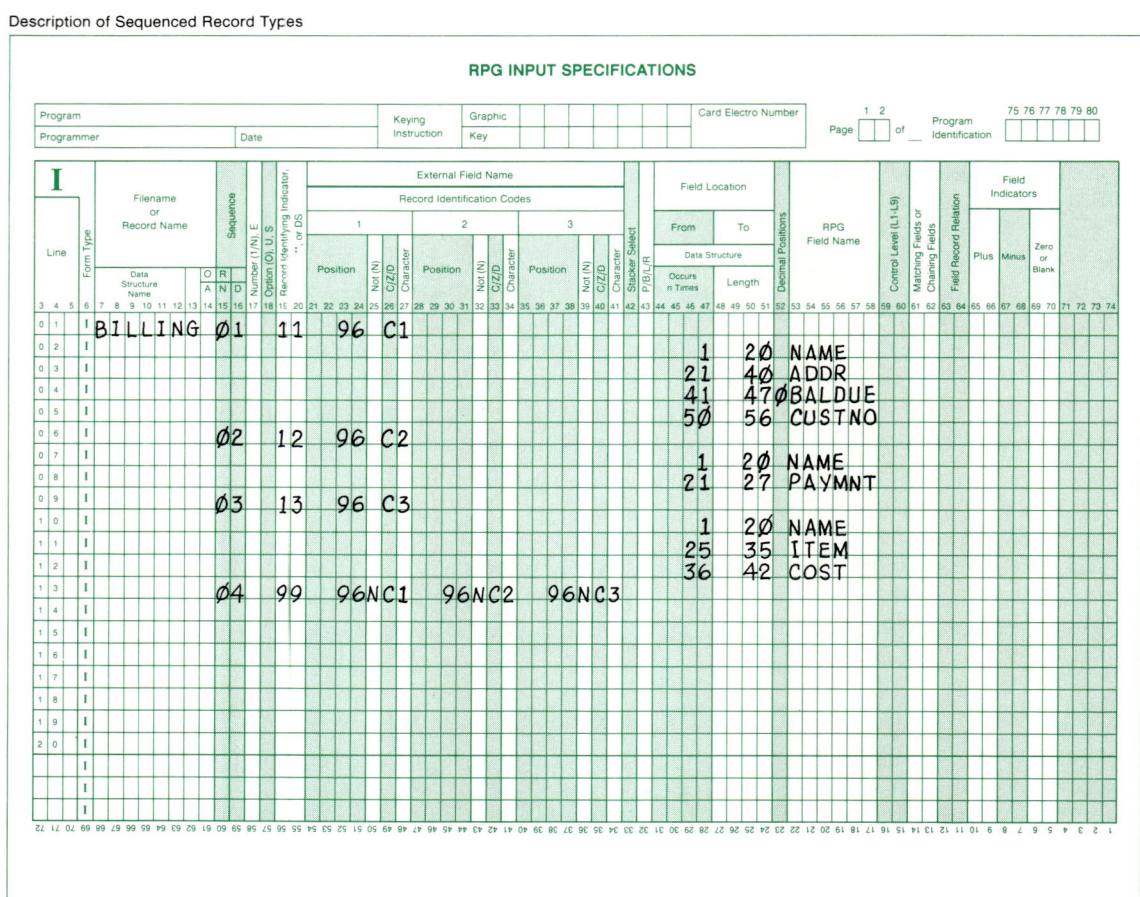

Figure 2.20 continued

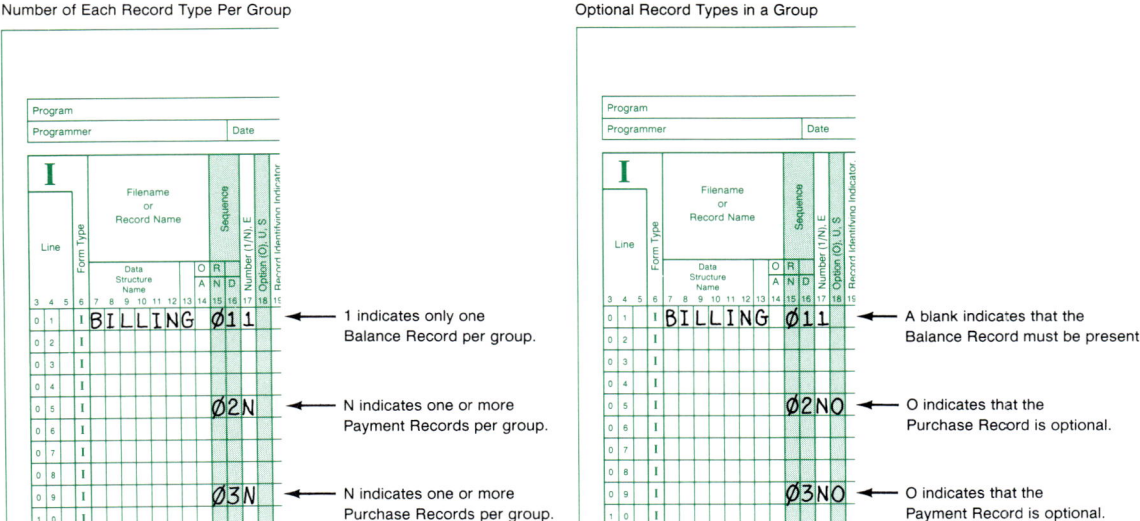

Notes on the Coding

Many data processing jobs require the use of several kinds of information. Sometimes this information must be in a special order to produce the correct results.

In this example, to do an end-of-month billing job the programmer needs several kinds of information. For each account the programmer must know:

1. The balance forward at the beginning of the month
2. Payments made during the month
3. Purchases made during the month

To get the amount due, subtract payments made from the balance forward and then add new purchases to that amount.

Information concerning balance forward, payments, and purchases is usually on more than one record. Payments are usually recorded as they are received. Purchases are recorded as they are made. The balance forward is also kept on a separate record.

Thus, to do the billing job, three different types of records are necessary for each account. Furthermore, these records must be read in a special order. The balance forward must come first. The payment and purchase records can be in any order; it makes no difference whether the programmer subtracts all payments first, adds all receipts first, or adds receipts and subtracts payments in any order. However, the programmer must decide on the order of these records for the job and keep them in that order for the duration of the job, since the computer will always expect them in a certain order.

Figure 2.21 Uses of record identifying indicators—example

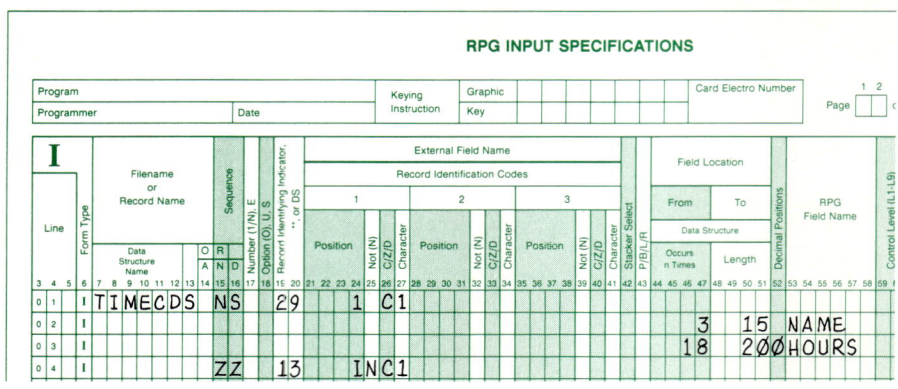

Record identifying indicator is turned on when record is read. Invalid records (without a "1" in column 1) turn on indicator 13.

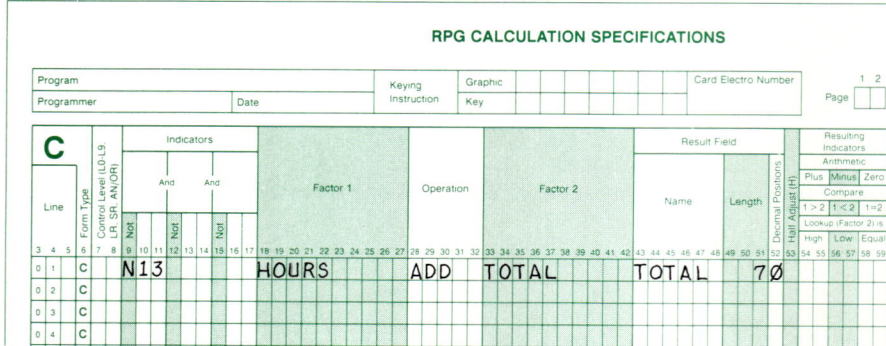

Exclude invalid records from calculations.

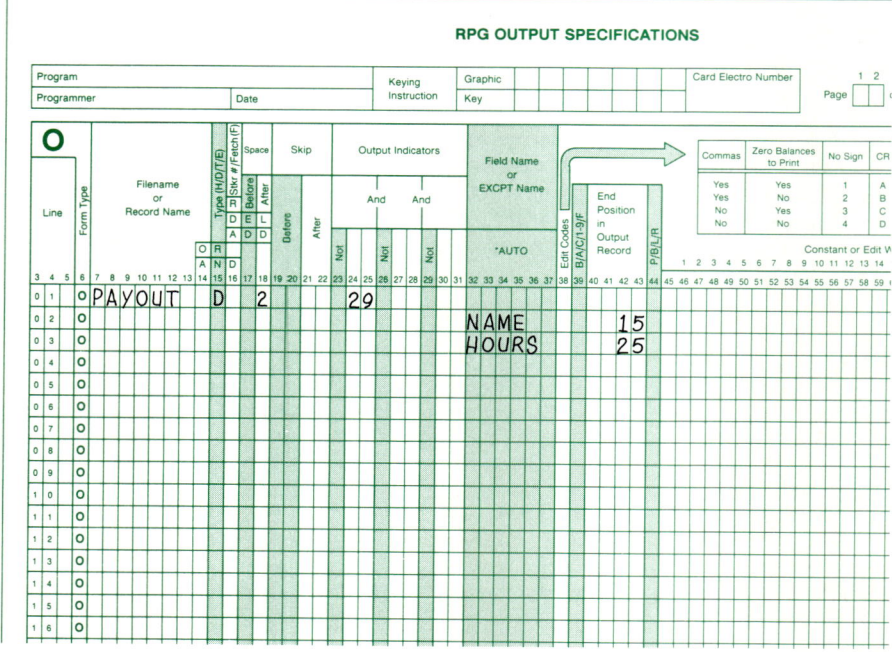

If 29 is on, then print out fields NAME and HOURS.

Figure 2.22 Input specifications—record identification

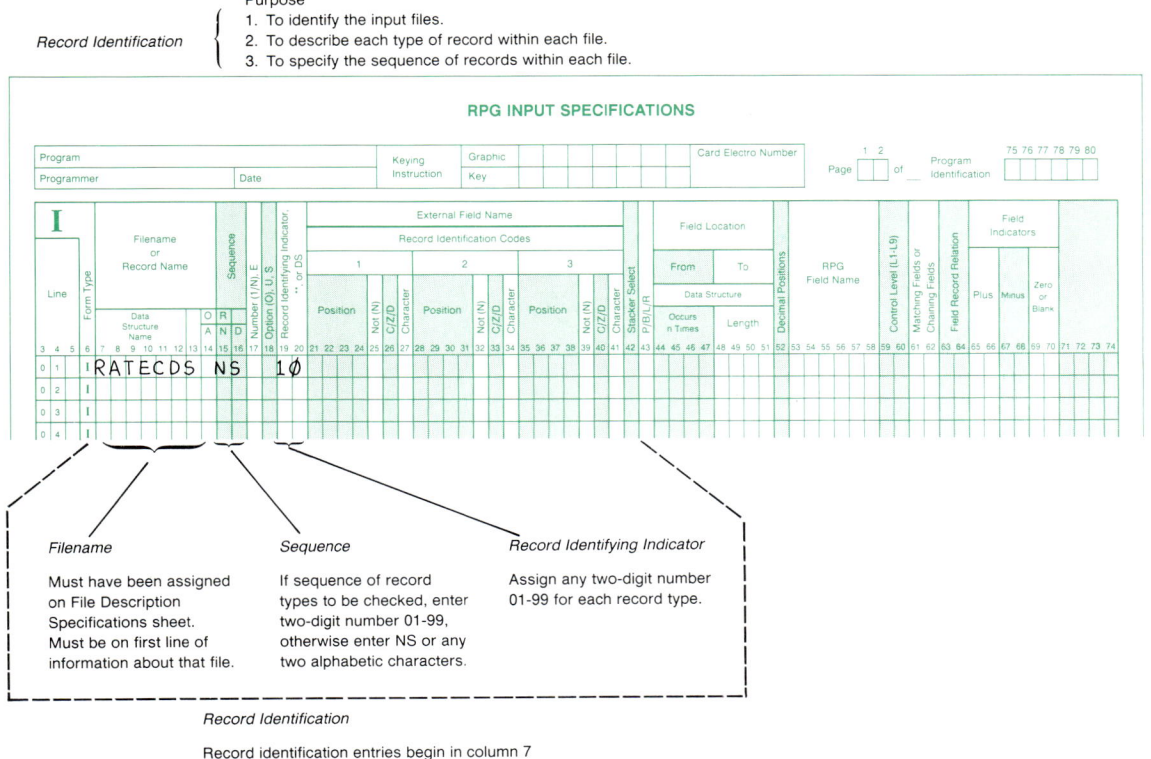

Record identification entries begin in column 7
There may be no entries to the right of column 42.

Record identifying indicators should be assigned even when there is only one record type in the file. If this is not done, the compiler prints a message specifying that record identifying indicators have not been assigned. (See Figure 2.22.)

The record identifying indicator should also be used to condition detail output records. This prevents detail lines from being written on the first cycle. If the detail line is not conditioned by a record identifying indicator, any constants specified on the detail line will be printed even though the first record is not read.

In cases where there are multiple record types, it is sometimes advisable to assign a catchall record identifying indicator to find records that do not meet any of the provided criteria (i.e., invalid records). This indicator can be used to condition error messages on output or to avoid inclusion in inappropriate calculations. (See Figures 2.20 and 2.21.)

Specifying Record Identification Codes (Positions 21–41)

RPG identifies record types by examining a character position or positions within the record. (See Figure 2.23.) These positions must contain characters, digit codes, or zone codes unique for each record type or a stated character, digit, or zone code must not be present. The particular code or code combination for each record type of each input file is inserted on the Input Specifications form within the position(s) in which the code(s) may be examined.

When creating records, an identification code should be included in each record. For example, to identify an item transaction record, a *T* may be placed somewhere in the record. Any combination of letters and numbers for the code may be used, and they may be placed anywhere in any record position.

When describing the record on the Input Specifications form, positions 21–41 are used to describe the record's identification codes and the location of the code in the record.

Input and Output Processing

Figure 2.23 Record identifying indicator—example

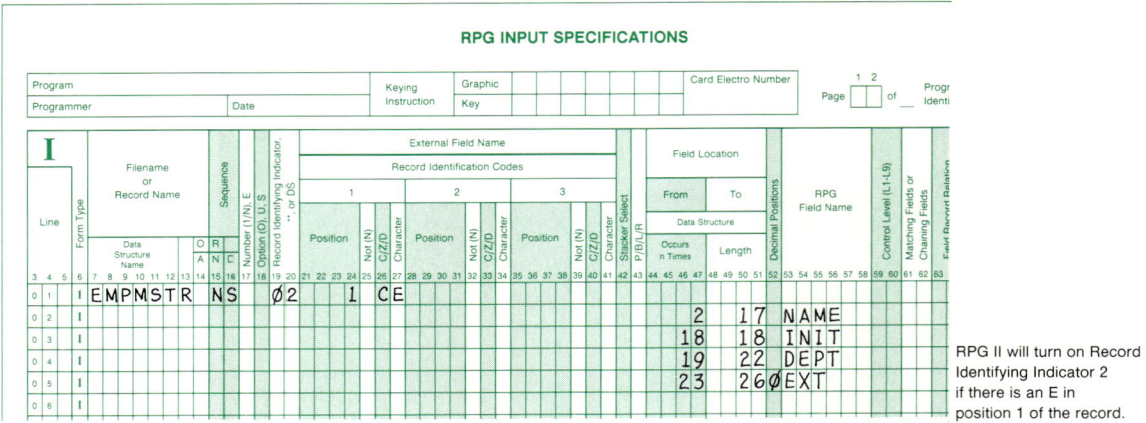

The conditions will be codes that were designed into the record. The following entries may be made in positions 21–41, for one, two, or three separate codes. These entries are "anded," meaning that all must be present for the record identifying indicator to be turned on.

1. The position of the code in the record (columns 21–24, 28–31, 35–38 with the rightmost digit in columns 24, 31, and 38).
2. Whether to check for a character, zone code, or digit code (columns 26, 33, and 40).
3. The actual character to check for in the record (columns 27, 34, and 41).
4. Whether an OR condition exists. If so, two lines are used and the coding for the field definition will be on the line following the last OR condition.
5. Whether an AND condition exists. If more than three codes are checked for, the additional codes are written on the following line, together with the field definitions.

The record identifying indicator is turned off by RPG at the end of the logic cycle. This occurs after the indicator has been used to control the calculations or output. (See Figure 2.24.)

Figure 2.24 Record identifying indicators—examples

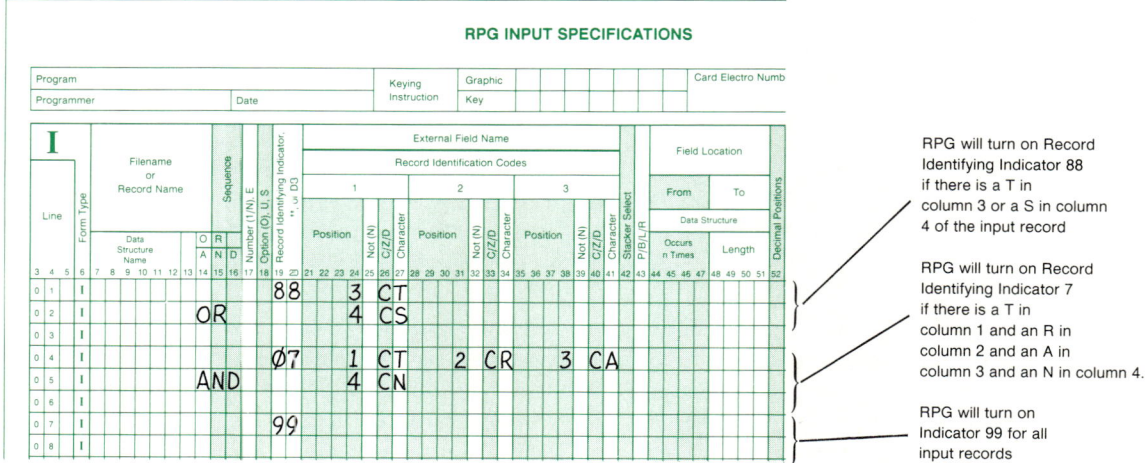

46 RPG II and RPG III Programming

Describing Fields

Data fields for each input record are described with respect to the record in which the individual field occurs. Each field used in a program must be completely defined once; later reference to fields for calculation or output purposes are by name only, and the field description need not be repeated.

A data field of an input record is described by the assignment and entry of a unique name, the entry of the beginning and ending position in the record, and the indication of whether the field is alphameric or numeric.

Several other entries are made for input data fields, depending upon the uses of the field in input processing. Other entries include the indication of the number of decimal positions for numeric fields.

Each type of record in the input file must be described. This description includes the names of all fields used from the record, the location of the fields, and the type of data in the fields.

When describing fields from each record type in the input file, a unique name must be given to each field of every record type. If, however, two or more record types contain identical fields, the same name may be assigned to the fields of each record type. Only one storage area would be assigned for the same field from several record types because the information in the field for each type is the same.

Field description requires more than a simple listing of the fields in each record because the RPG compiler needs to know which fields are in each type of record as well as which record it is reading. The compiler identifies records through record identification codes and record identifying indicators.

Describing Fields within Records

Each record within a file contains one or more fields of data. Entries on Input Specifications forms are designed to tell the computer (*a*) where these fields are in the record, (*b*) what type of information they contain, and (*c*) what name is used to refer to them. Each line of specifications describing each field of the record is written on a separate line.

Field Location (Positions 44–51)

After a field name is assigned, the location of the field within the record must be specified. This enables the compiler to associate the field name with the right information. To describe the field location, the position in the record at which the field begins and ends must be specified. The starting position (From) is specified in positions 44–47; the ending position (To) is specified in positions 48–51. (See Figure 2.25.) When a field is only one character long, the starting and ending position entries are the same. Entries must be made in both the From and To columns for every field. Although there are four positions under From and To, only one or two digits need to be entered in each position. Digits should be right-justified; that is, they should be entered in the right-hand positions, leaving the left-hand positions blank.

The compiler determines the field length on the basis of the From and To entries. The compiler needs field lengths to determine how many storage positions to allow for each field. If the specified field locations indicate a field length of six, the compiler will allow six positions in storage for that field.

Type of Data (Position 52)

To complete the description of the input fields, the compiler checks position 52. (See Figure 2.25.) This position indicates whether data in each field is alphameric or numeric. If position 52 is blank, the compiler assumes the field to be alphameric. A numeric field (a field containing numeric data only) must

Figure 2.25 Type of data—example

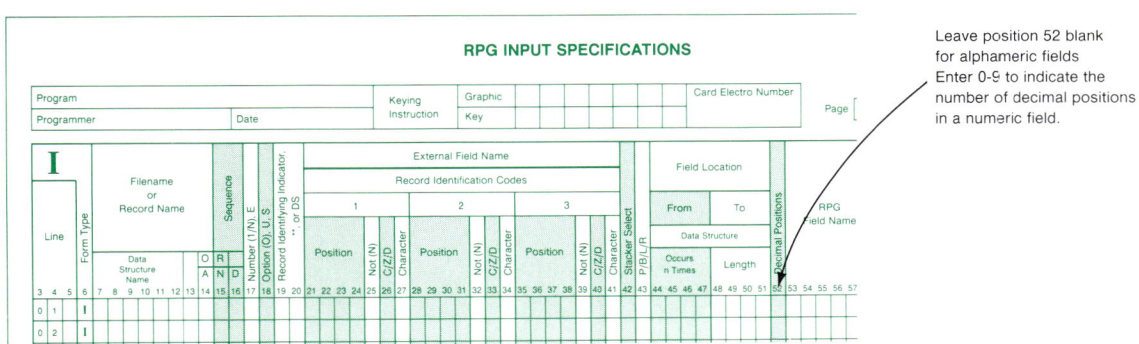

Input and Output Processing 47

have an entry in position 52 to tell the computer that the field is numeric. Only numeric fields may be specified for calculations with a maximum of fifteen digits. In numeric fields, the number in position 52 indicates the number of decimal positions (digits to the right of the decimal point) in the field.

The decimal positions entry is necessary because (*a*) decimal points are not stored in the record and (*b*) that information tells the computer to automatically align the decimal points of any data resulting from calculations on that field.

Although decimal points are not included in fields, they must be considered if correct calculations are to be performed and output data is to appear in the correct format. Specifying the number of decimal positions in a numeric field provides the compiler with the information necessary to produce an object program capable of handling numeric data with decimals. An integer is specified by using 0 (zero) in position 52.

Remember, any field used in arithmetic operations (add, subtract, multiply, or divide) must be specified as numeric.

Field Name (Positions 53–58)

The field name is used throughout the program to identify a field. Once it has been described on the input specifications, only its name need be used in the program. (See Figure 2.26.)

Only the field described on the input specifications will be read by the computer. A record could have several fields; for example, a record may contain the fields NAME, ADDR, TELNO, AGE, HEIGHT, and WEIGHT. This is the form in which the field names would be entered on the specifications sheets. However, if only NAME, ADDR, and TELNO are required for a certain program, only those fields need be described on input specifications. When the computer reads the record, the fields AGE, HEIGHT, and WEIGHT will be ignored.

To identify individual fields in the record, each field must be given a unique name. From the information placed on the File Description Specifications form, the compiler determines the storage area for each input record. The field names supplied on the Input Specifications form tell the compiler to divide this storage area into smaller sections so that each can be addressed separately.

The rules for forming field names are as follows:

1. The field name must be from 1–6 characters long.

Figure 2.26 Assigning field names

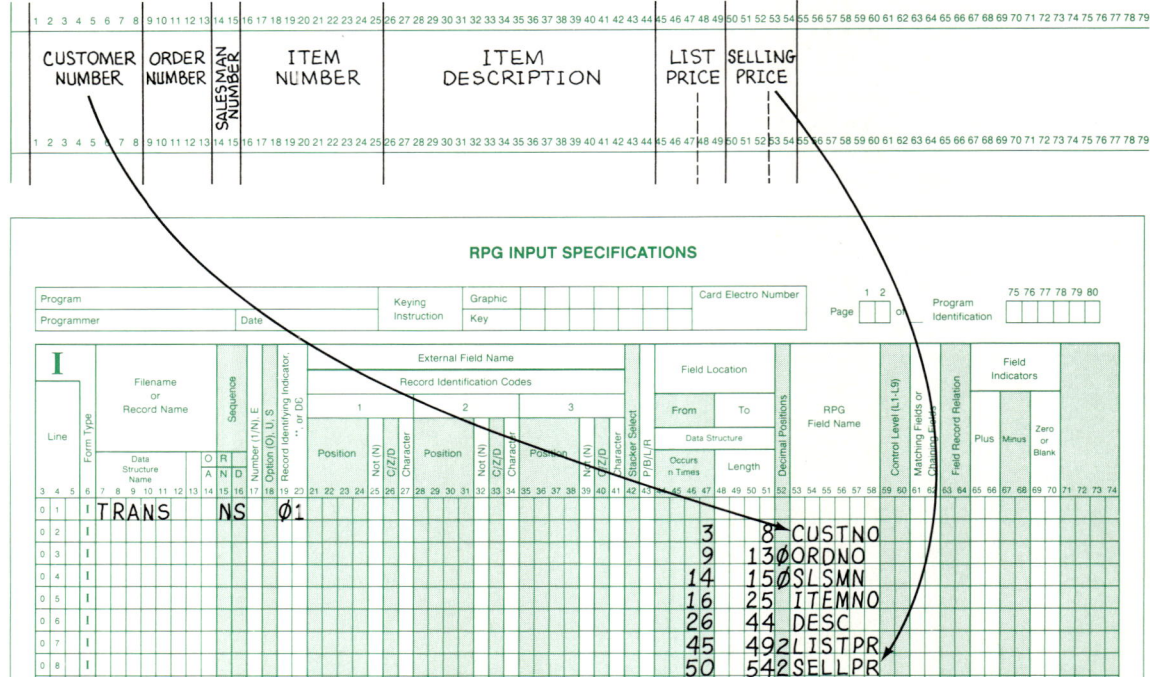

48   RPG II and RPG III Programming

2. The first character must be alphabetic. Remaining characters can be either alphabetic or numeric. (IBM includes the special characters $, @, and # as alphabetic.)

3. Blanks must not be placed between characters in a field name.

4. The field name must begin in position 53 on the Input Specifications form.

It is good practice to assign meaningful names. For example, a field containing customer numbers would be more meaningful if it were called CUSTNO rather than FIELDA. CUSTNO indicates something about the data in the field.

Enter field names starting one line below the record identification lines, using a separate line for each field. Be sure to name every field that contains information necessary for the job. If all fields of a record are required, name them all; if only a few fields are needed, name only those that will be needed for the job. The entire record is read regardless of the number of fields used from that record; however, only information in fields named is used.

Summary

The input specifications will be used to describe the input files, records, and fields. (See Figure 2.27.) The files to be coded on the input specifications are the ones that are coded *I* on the file description specifications. The detail information needed for the input specifications will come from the record layouts.

Figure 2.27 Summary—input specifications

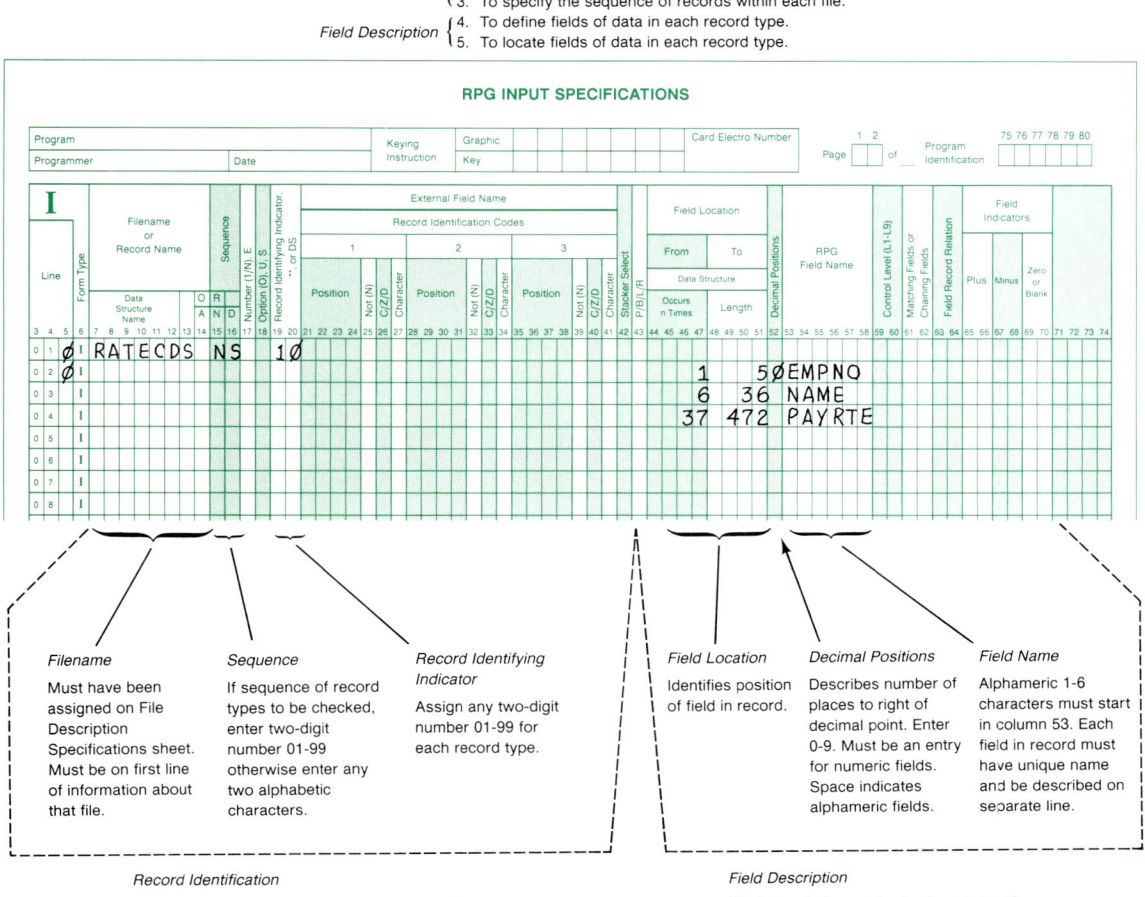

Input and Output Processing

Some RPG rules for input specifications are as follows.

A. *File Coding*
   1. Filename starts in column 7
   2. Filename must have been previously defined on the File Description Specifications form
B. *Record Coding*
   1. Identifies record types by codes
   2. Sequences records (if any)
   3. Is found on the same line as filename
C. *Field Coding*
   1. Gives each field description on a separate line
   2. Lists From and To positions from the record layout
   3. Contains decimal positions, if numeric (even if zero)
      a. Blank indicates alphameric field
      b. Zero (*0*) indicates integer field
      c. Nonzero digit (1–9) indicates number of digits to right of decimal point
   4. Field names are left-justified
      a. 1–6 characters
      b. No embedded blanks
      c. First character alphabetic, others alphabetic or numeric

Describing Output Records

Output records are described on the Output Specifications form. Information needed includes the name of the file containing the output record, the name of each field in the record, and where each field is to be placed in the record. (See Figure 2.28.)

For a printed report, additional entries describing the format of the report are necessary; that is, the desired spacing and punctuation must be indicated. The Printer Spacing Chart and Record Layout form are useful when writing output specifications. The Record Layout form shows the organization of the fields in a record; the Printer Spacing Chart shows the format of the printed records. (See Figure 2.29.)

In the case of output records, the file that is to contain the record is named in the Output Specifications form. For printer files, the record type is also entered. There are four record types: header, detail, total, and exception. Also in the case of printer files, the desired line-spacing and form-skipping instructions are entered. (See Figure 2.30.)

Figure 2.28 Output Specifications form

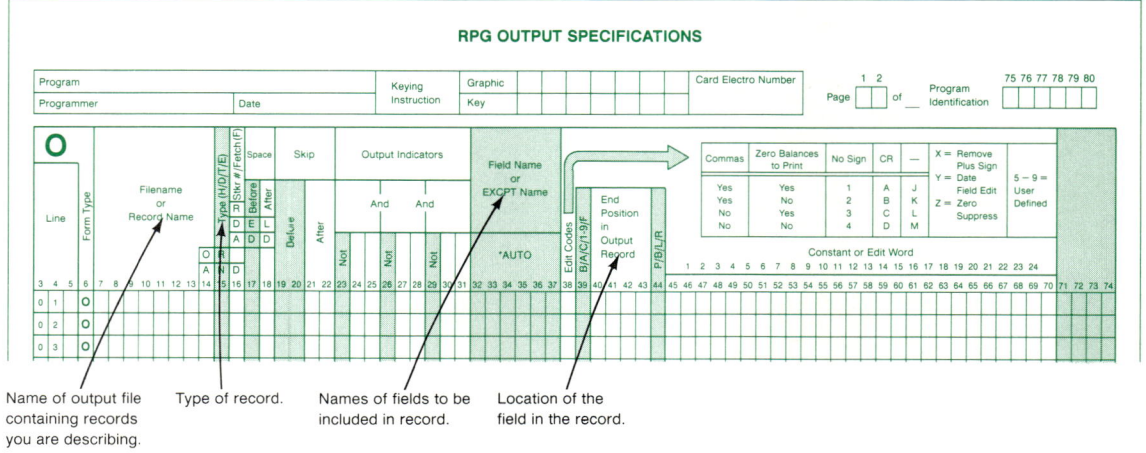

Figure 2.29   Describing output records

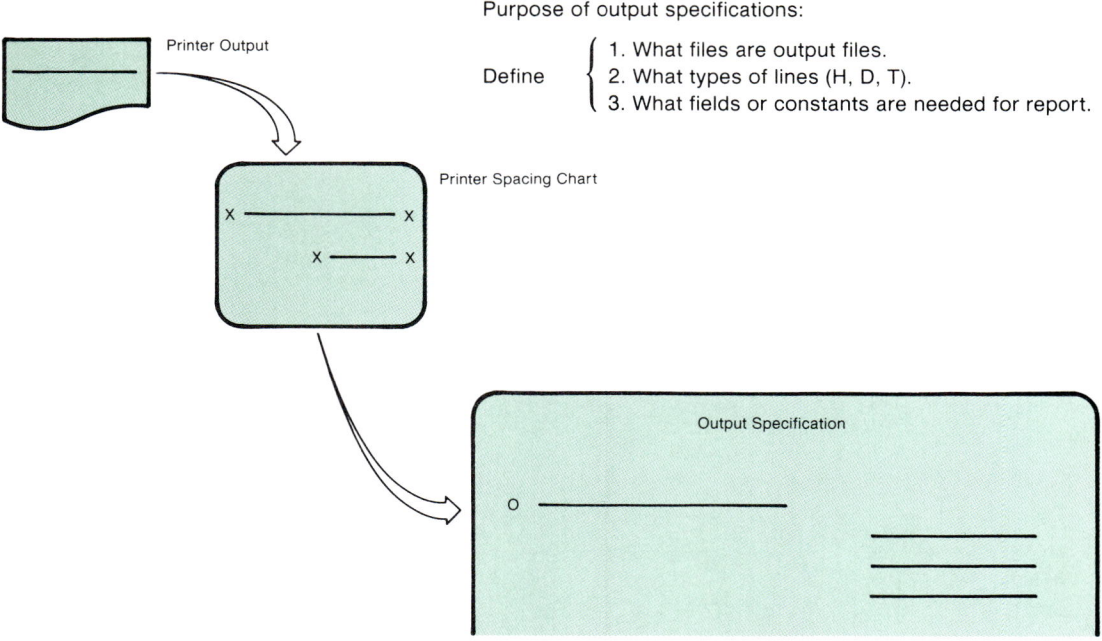

Figure 2.30   Describing output fields

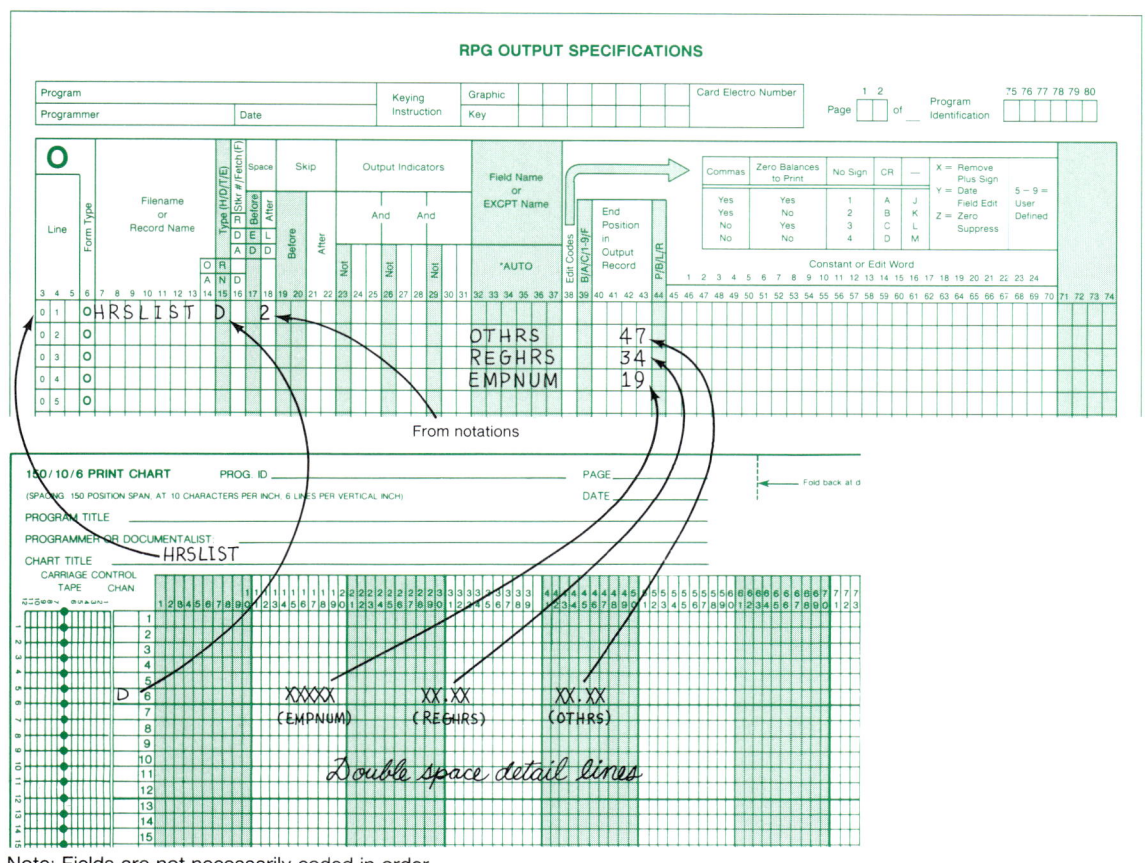

Note: Fields are not necessarily coded in order.

Input and Output Processing

Figure 2.31 Indicators—example

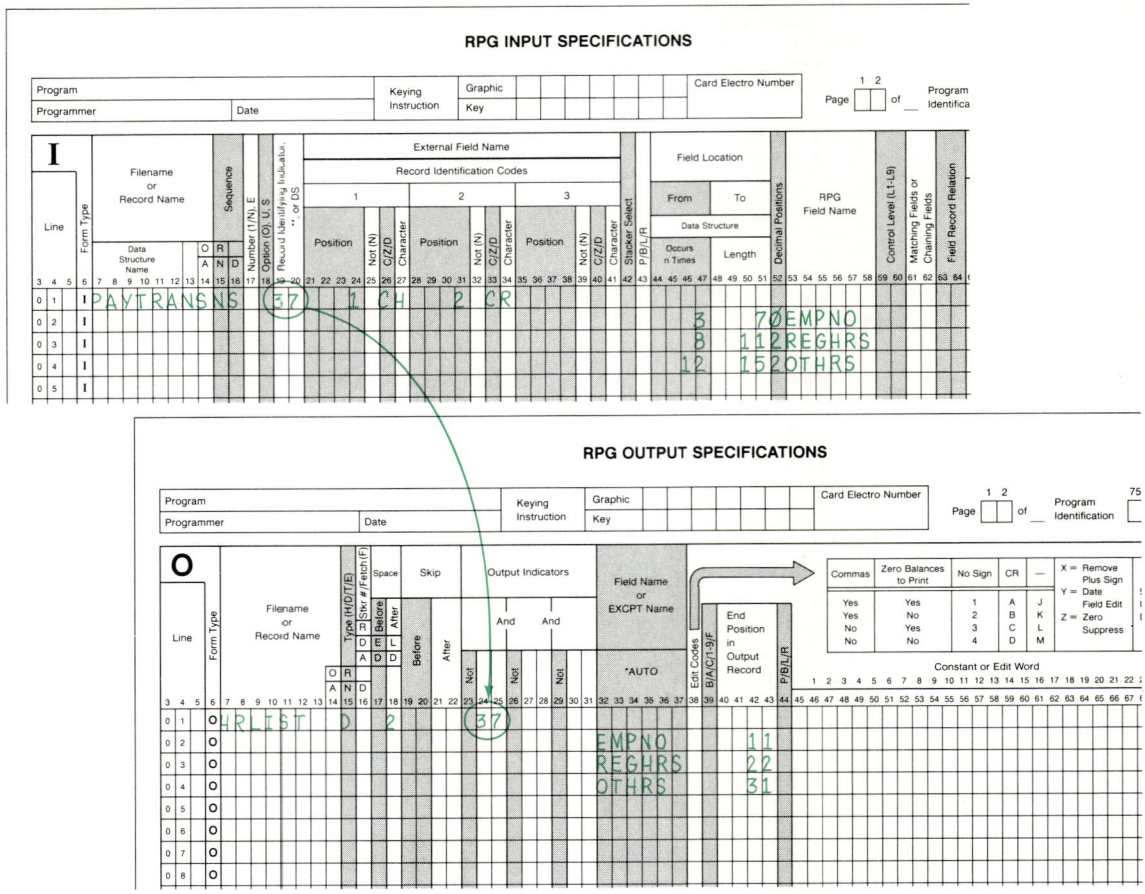

The conditions under which the records should be printed or written to other files are specified for all output records. Conditions are stated in terms of indicators that are turned on when a specified input record type is identified. (See Figure 2.31.) One or more conditions may be required for output to occur. Also, output may be conditioned by an indicator for which an off status is specified. Indicators other than record identifying indicators (01–99) are the halt indicators (H0–H9), control level indicators (L1–L9), external indicators (U1–U8), the first page indicator (1P), the matching indicator (MR), the last record or end-of-job indicator (LR), and the forms overflow indicators (OA–OG and OV).

The indicators assigned show the results of RPG functions. These are set as a result of designated record type but may also be set, if specified, as a result of calculation operations. Some of the other indicators may be turned on or off by means of the calculation operations SETON or SETOF.

In any case, the various indicators are available for defining the conditions for output of a record and are entered on the output form for that purpose. The programmer should keep careful notes of the indicators selected and assigned, their significance, and the use to be made of them in the preparation of the program specifications. By careful notation, the programmer avoids inconsistent and conflicting indicator assignments. Failure to reference assigned resulting indicators and failure to define the indicators that are referred to will result in error conditions reported by the compiler.

Output Specifications

The output specifications will be used to describe the output files, types of lines (records), and fields. The fields to be described are coded *O* on the File Description Specifications form. The detail information needed for the output specifications will come from the Printer Spacing Chart or the Record Layout form if output is on disk. If the output is displayed on a cathode ray tube (CRT), the information comes from a screen layout form.

Figure 2.32 Output Specifications form

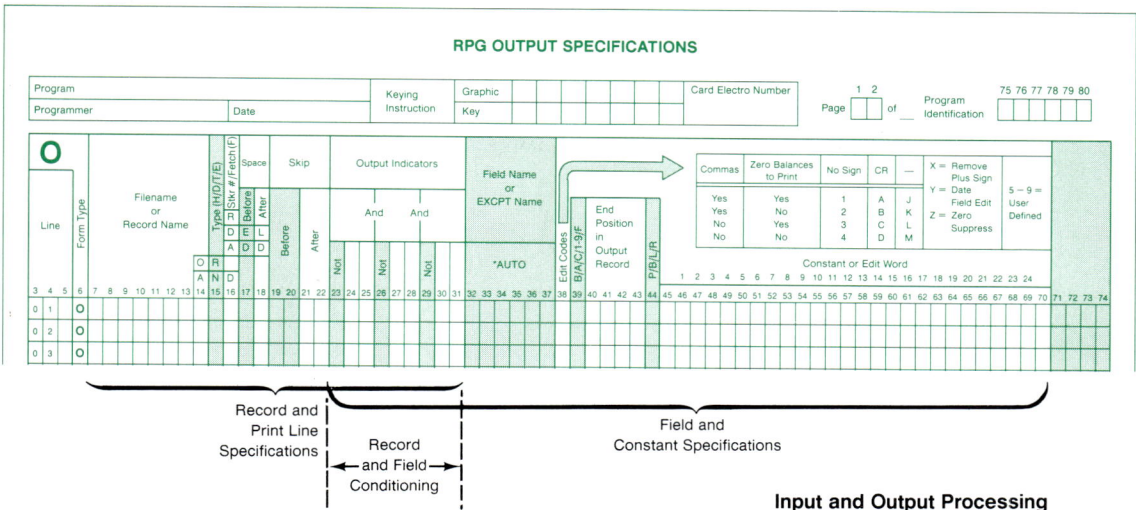

If printed output is to be produced, the computer must be told when to print, what to print, and where to print. The layout of the report shown on the Printer Spacing Chart provides this information. This report is put in coded form on the Output Specifications form.

Output specifications describe output records. These specifications are divided into two general categories. (See Figure 2.32.)

1. Record description entries (positions 7–31), which describe the output file records to be written
2. Field description entries (positions 32–74), which indicate the position and the format of data in the output record

The field description entries begin one line lower than the record description entries.

Filename (Positions 7–14)

The output record to be created and the device needed to create the record is indicated by entering the filename in positions 7–14. Make sure the name entered is the same (and spelled exactly the same) as the name entered on the File Description Specifications form for the output file. (See Figure 2.33.)

Figure 2.33 Filename—example

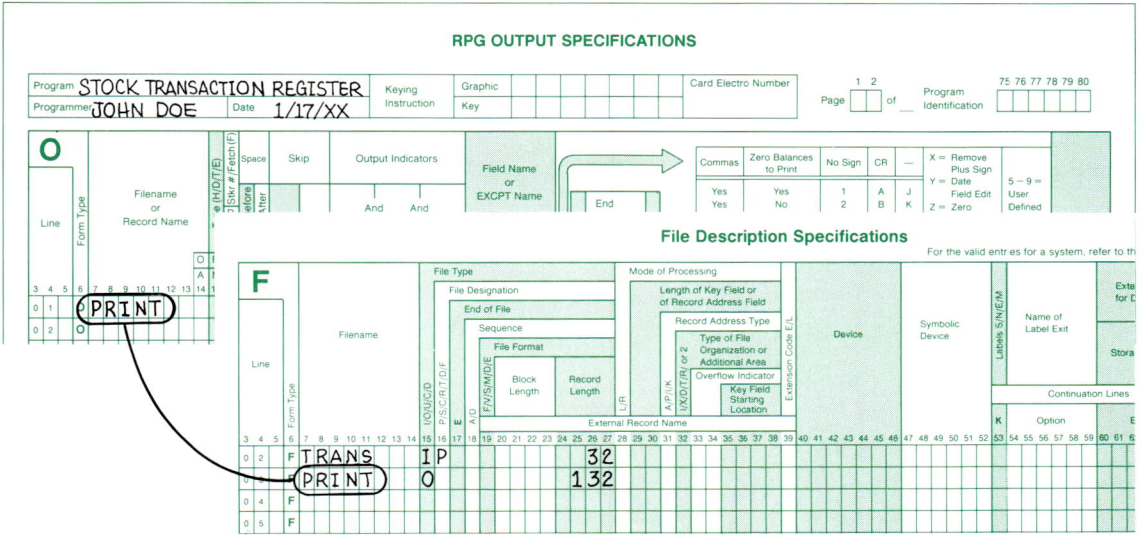

Input and Output Processing

Figure 2.34 Record types—examples

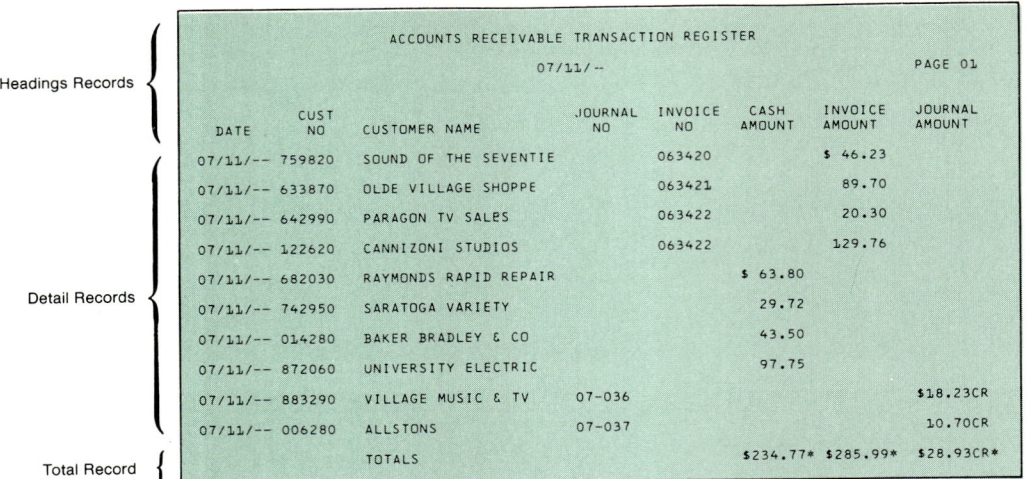

Record Type (Position 15)

Four different types of records can be specified on the Output Specifications form. These are heading (*H*), detail (*D*), exceptions (*E*), and total (*T*) records. The types *H, D,* and *T* are usually found in all printed reports.

Heading records (*H*) are printed at the top of each page. Heading records include report titles, column headings, or any other information needed to identify the kinds of information found in the report.

Detail records (*D*) contain information about an individual item. Information in a detail record is often taken directly from an input record and/or some calculated fields.

Total records (*T*) are written after a group of detail records. An *L* is usually placed after the *T* with a character indicating the control level. (Control levels are discussed in chapter 4.) Total records usually contain data that are the product of calculations on information in a group of detail records. (See Figure 2.34.)

The exception type will be explained later in the text. To specify record type, an appropriate entry is placed in column 15. If the Printer Spacing Chart has been properly filled out it contains record type information. (See Figure 2.35.)

Figure 2.35 Specifying record types

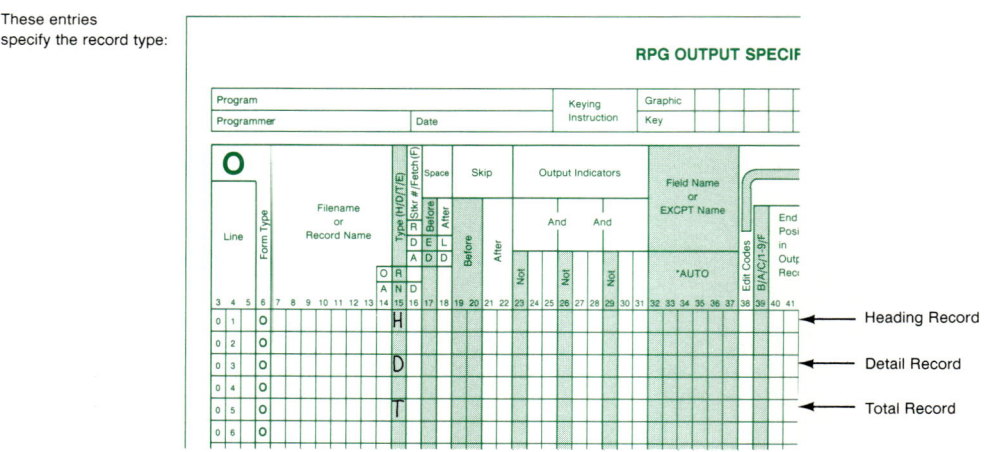

Figure 2.35 continued

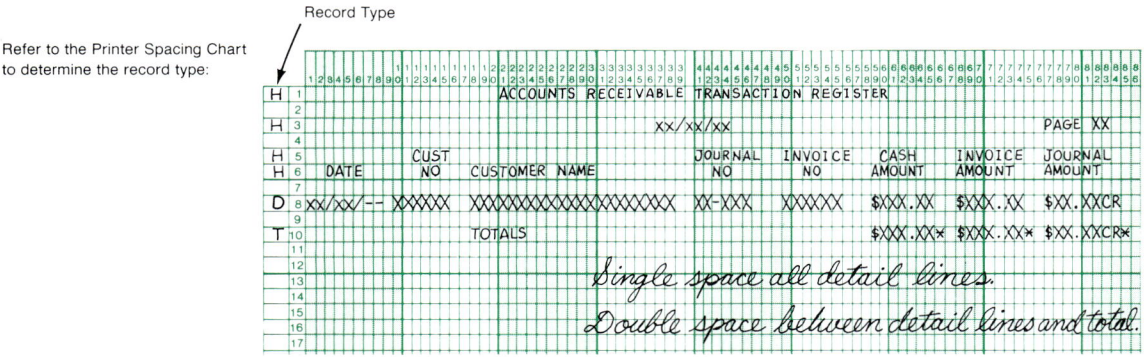

Figure 2.36 Assigning field names

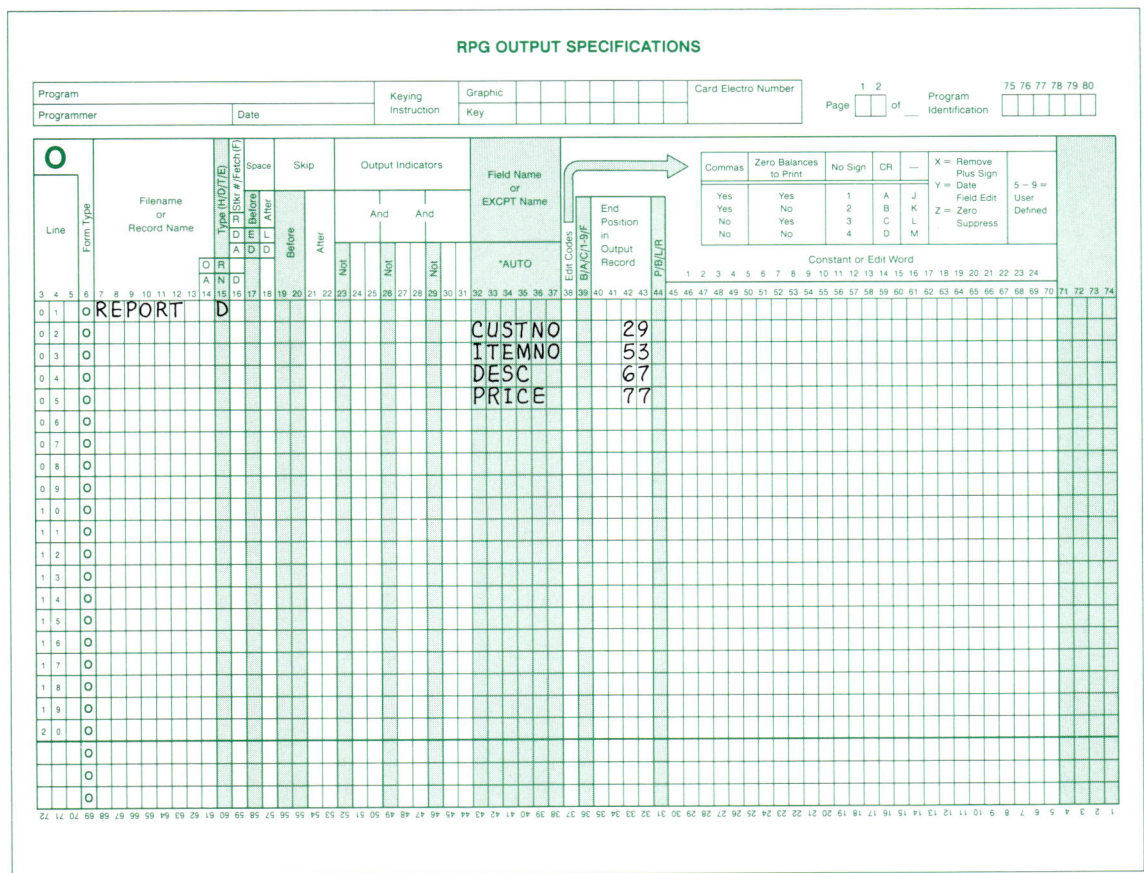

Field Name (Positions 32–37)
To specify the information to be placed in each output record, each variable field to be included must be named. These fields are specified in positions 32–37 on separate lines of the Output Specifications form. The list of fields is begun one line below the record description entries. (See Figure 2.36.)

When listing the fields, the name previously given to a field must be entered (for example, a field named on the Input Specifications form). If the name entered on the Output Specifications form is not the one previously used, the compiler will not know what information is being referred to.

Input and Output Processing

Figure 2.37 Field locations

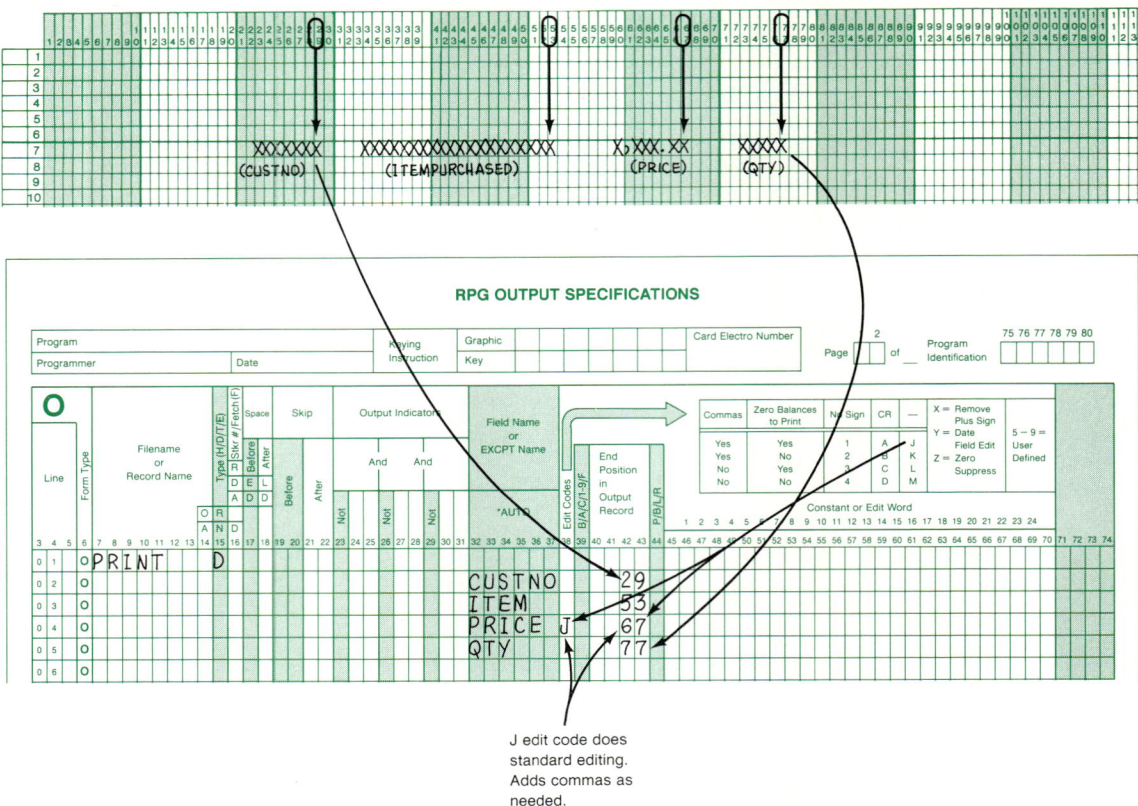

J edit code does standard editing. Adds commas as needed.

Field names are used to create the output record in the output storage area. Information is placed in the storage area one field at a time in the desired list on the Output Specifications form.

Constant information may also be specified on the output form.

Field Location (Positions 40–43)
Fields are specified for placement in the output record with an entry in positions 40–43 (under the heading End Position in the output record). This entry must designate the exact position of the last character in a field in the output storage area at the time the record is created. This placement of this entry is easily determined from either the Printer Spacing Chart or the Record Layout form. (See Figure 2.37.)

Printed Reports

When output is a printed report, additional entries are needed on the Output Specifications form to make the report easy to read. Information must be neatly arranged in rows and columns with adequate space between items in the same line.

Spacing (Positions 17–18)
The field location entries (positions 40–43) control the space between fields; positions 17–18 (Space) control the space between lines. The space columns can be used to specify no space or for up to three spaces between lines. (See Figure 2.38.)

The printer will single-, double-, or triple-space between lines if the numbers 1, 2, or 3 are entered in the appropriate positions. If a number is entered in position 17 (Space Before), the printer spaces before printing on the line. If a number is entered in position 18 (Space After), the printer spaces after printing the line. Numbers may be entered in both positions 17 and 18. For example, by specifying three spaces before printing and three spaces after, five blank lines will appear between printed lines. The printer spaces three lines after printing a line, then spaces three lines before printing the next line. Thus the next printed line is six lines beyond the last line printed.

Figure 2.38 Spacing—example

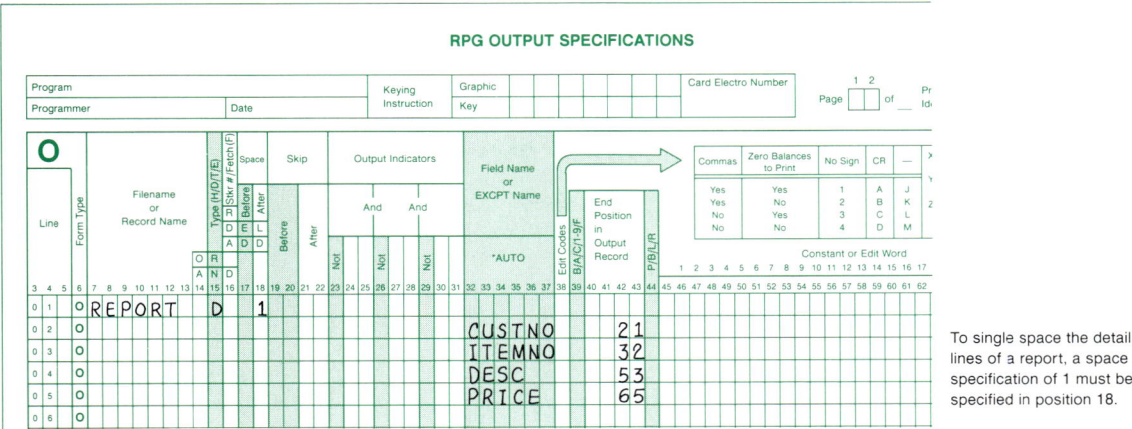

Skipping (Positions 19-22)

The skip positions are used to advance the printer to a specific line on a page. The space entry moves the printer up to three lines; the skip entry moves the printer to a specified line.

Entries in skip positions 19-22 can be used both to control spacing between lines and to control printing on the first and last lines on a page. A skip can be made before or after a line is printed. This is indicated by coding the skip in either positions 19-20 (Skip Before) or 21-22 (Skip After). The entry place in these positions depends on the type of printer being used. (See Figure 2.39.)

The Skip Before entry (positions 19-20) tells the printer on which line to print. The first printing line is indicated by 01 in positions 19-20; very often this first printed line is line 6 on a page. This entry is frequently used to begin printing on a new page. Every time the printer receives a Skip Before instruction, it automatically skips to that line, if it has not already reached it. However, if the computer receives an instruction to Skip Before to line 12 when it has just printed on line 17, then it will skip to line 12 on a new page before printing the next line.

Normally a heading line requires a Skip Before entry. However, it is more efficient to use Space After or Skip After instructions for all other lines. This is because the printer will space or skip to the correct position for the next line as soon as one line has been printed and while data to be printed on the next line is being processed. Unless it is told to which line to skip before it prints the first line of a report, the printer will continue printing without skipping at all.

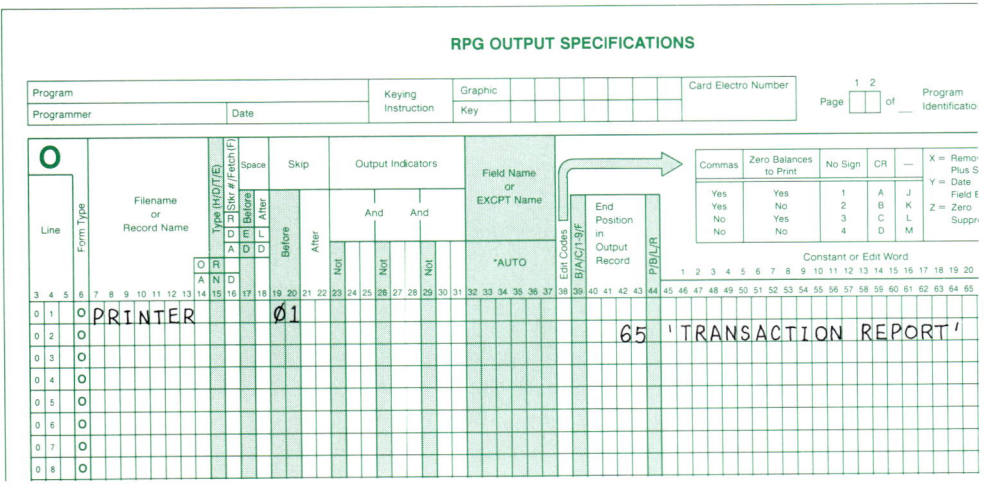

Input and Output Processing

Figure 2.40 *PLACE entry—example

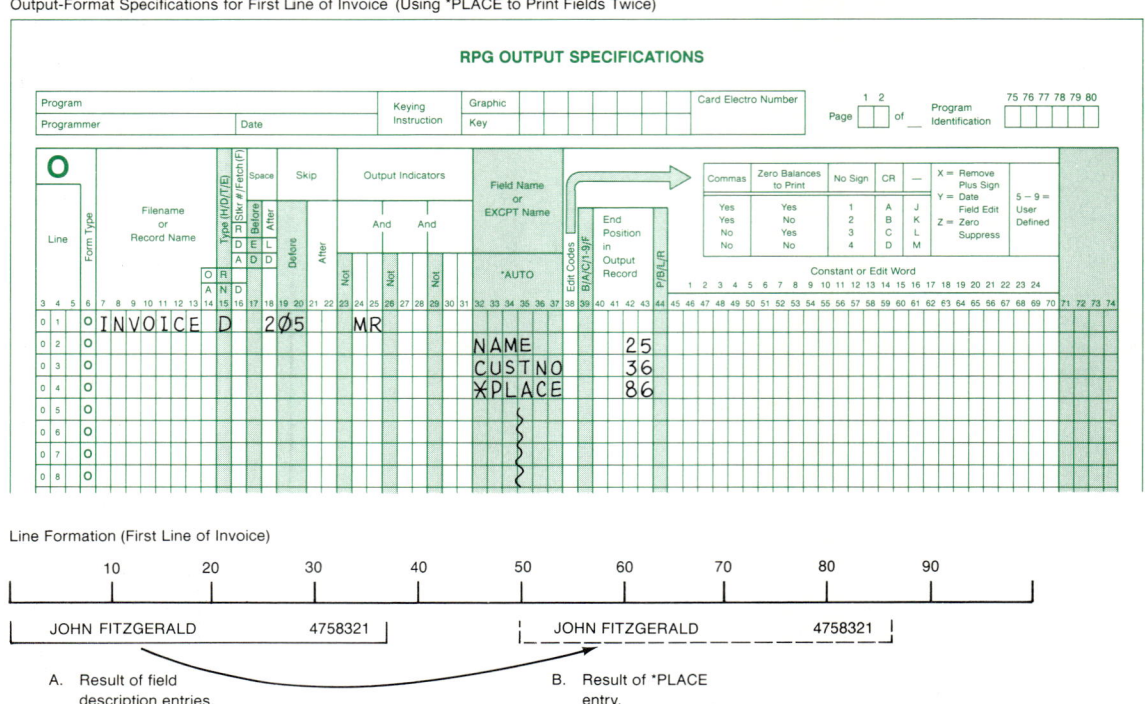

A. Result of field description entries.

B. Result of *PLACE entry.

Editing

Editing is a means of punctuating numeric fields by adding decimal points, commas, and negative signs. Editing can also suppress the printing of leading zeroes (e.g., the first two digits in the number 00149 are called leading zeros).

When a numeric field is read into storage, it contains no decimal point or commas. When an unedited field is printed, it appears exactly as it is found in storage. A large number that is printed without commas or decimal points is hard to read. Furthermore, an unedited field may not be meaningful when printed because of the way the system stores negative numbers.

The system uses the last digit in a numeric field to indicate the sign (plus or minus) of a number. If the field is negative, the system combines a minus sign with the last digit. When a negative number is printed in unedited form, the combination of the digit and sign appears as a letter. For example, minus 6349 prints as 634R. On the other hand, a positive field has no sign; a numeric field that does not have a negative sign is assumed to be positive. A positive field, therefore, prints normally. Positive 6349 would print as 6349.

The compiler can provide instructions for editing in a number of ways. All that needs to be done is to enter an edit code in position 38 or to enter an edit word in positions 45–70 of the Output Specifications form. Many codes are available and they will be discussed in detail in chapter 3.

Note: When a field is to be edited, characters are often added to it. When printed, the edited field requires more space than it did on the input records or in storage. When specifying the end position for an edited field, always take into account the spaces that will be needed for adding punctuation. The Printer Spacing Chart shows the amount of space needed for edited fields.

*PLACE

*PLACE is a special RPG function that can be used to accomplish duplicate printing with less coding. The specification *PLACE tells the compiler to duplicate the part of the line specified and to place the duplicated information in a different position on the same line. *PLACE means a special function is to be performed. This specification should not be used as a field name because the RPG compiler will assume the preceding field should be duplicated. When using *PLACE, the programmer must first

Figure 2.41 *PLACE entry—example

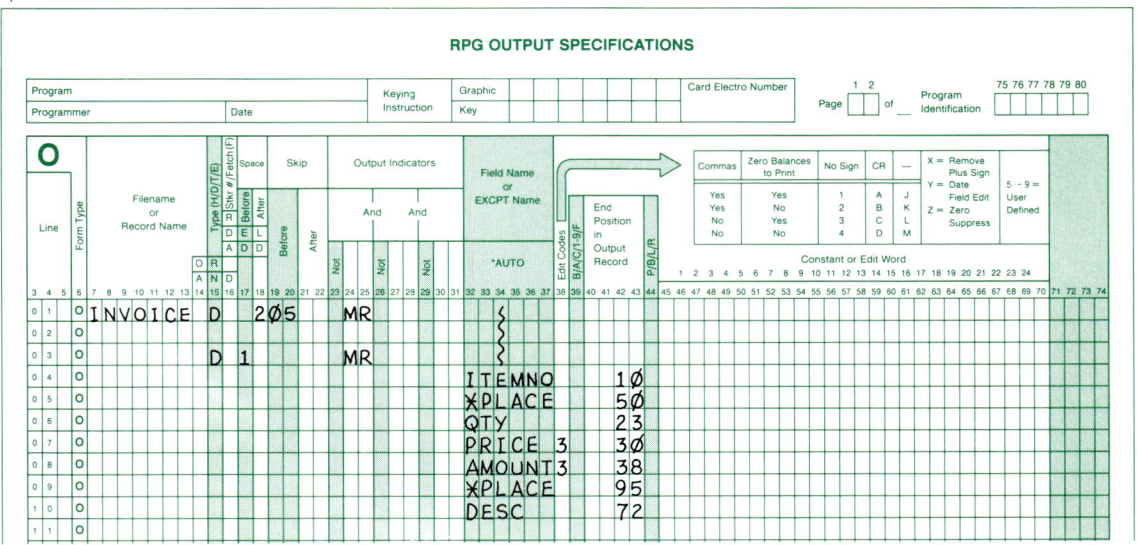

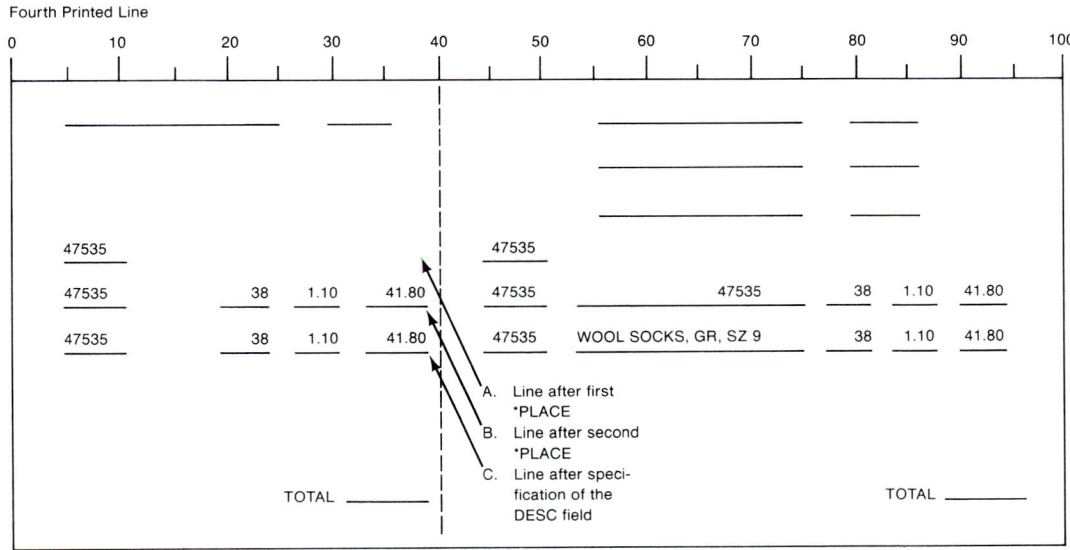

define all fields that are to be duplicated for each record. The end position for each field is given as usual. Then *PLACE is entered on the line below the fields that are to be duplicated. (See Figure 2.40.)

The compiler does not know where to print unless an end position is specified for the *PLACE entry. When specifying this end position, the programmer must know where the fields are to be printed. The amount of space needed for the printing of *all* characters to be duplicated must be considered. The end position specified must always allow room for the printing of duplicated fields.

*PLACE operates in the same way as normal field names. The order in which operations associated with *PLACE are performed is that of the sequence in which *PLACE is specified on the Output Specifications form in relation to other output entries.

The *PLACE specification duplicates not only letters and numerals, but blank spaces. It will duplicate all the characters (including blanks) from the start position to the end position specified for a field. These duplicated characters are then placed so that they end in the end position specified for the *PLACE entry. (See Figure 2.41.)

Input and Output Processing

Figure 2.42 *PLACE entry—examples

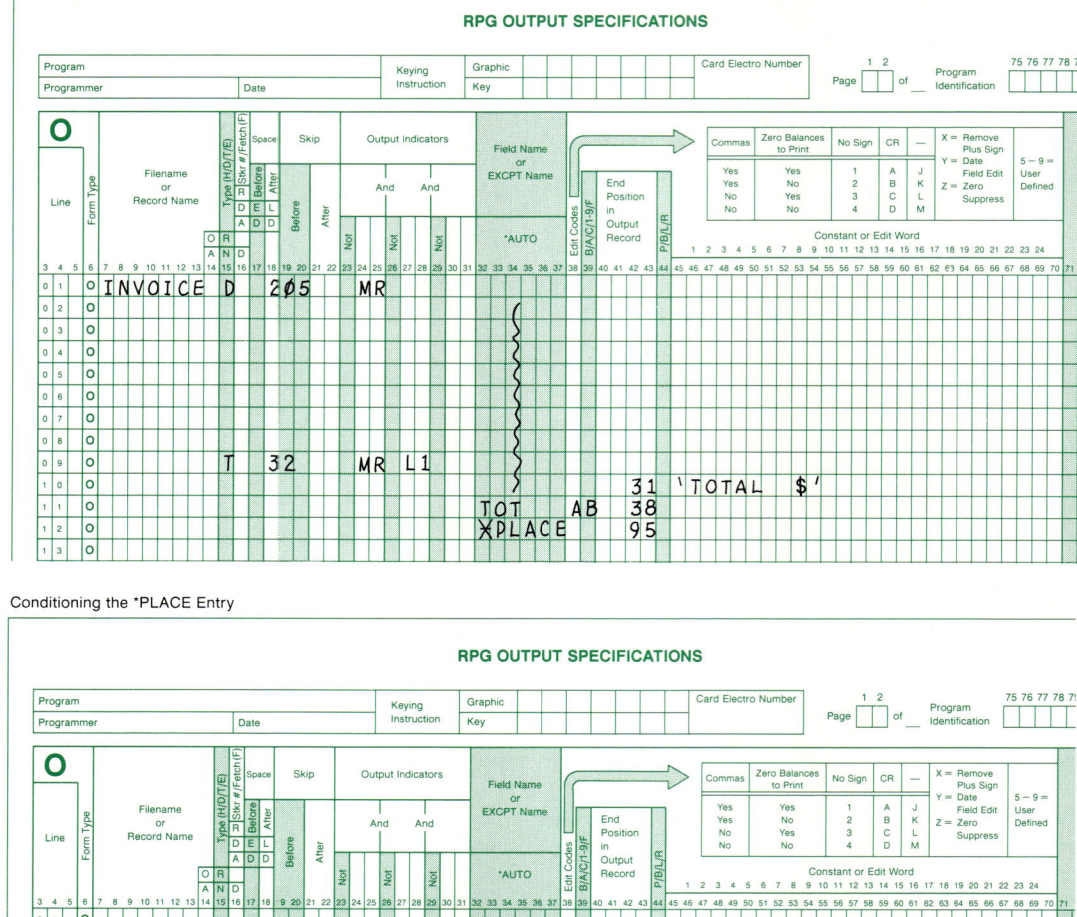

*PLACE can duplicate constants as well as fields. The same specifications are used for both. (See Figure 2.42.)

*PLACE can be used to print the same field several times in the line. This is done by entering *PLACE with the end position once for each time the fields are to be duplicated. If the field is to be duplicated twice, two *PLACE entries are needed. (See Figure 2.43.)

First Page Indicator

The first page (1P) indicator is used on the Output Specifications form to specify the headings to be printed on the first page of a report. (See Figure 2.44.) Headings, usually printed at the top of the page, include such things as report titles or column names.

Program Cycle Operations
One operation in the program cycle is concerned with the 1P indicator. The 1P indicator is automatically set on at the beginning of every job. Consequently, the first operation of the system is to print any output records conditioned by 1P (or not conditioned by any other indicator). Once this has happened the 1P indicator is turned off, the first record is read, and the program cycle operations are then executed in order.

Figure 2.43 *PLACE entry—example

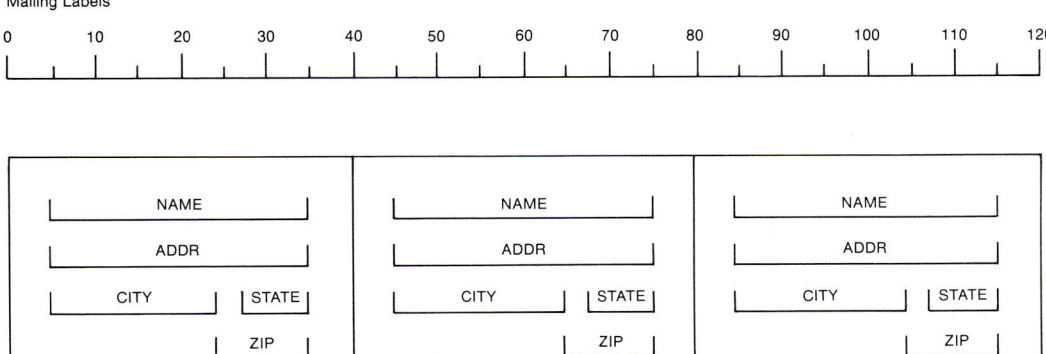

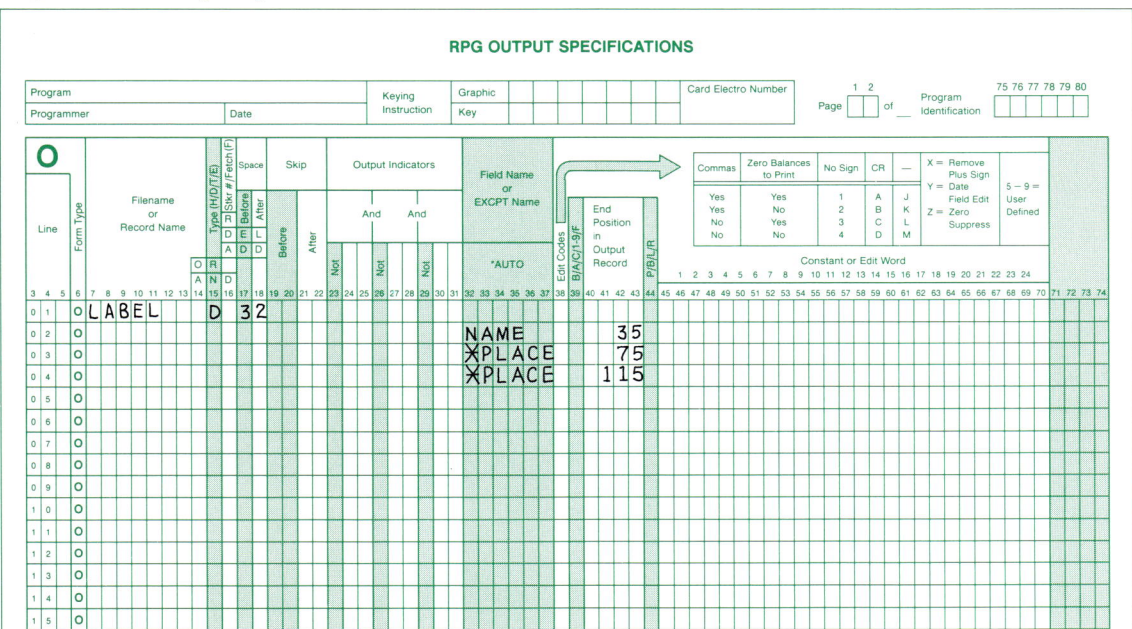

Headings conditioned by 1P are printed only once—at the beginning of the first page of the report. Any heading records that are not conditioned by 1P are handled in the same way as detail records. This means that they can be printed in every cycle along with detail records.

RPG Specifications

Heading information to be printed on the first page of a report is specified by using constants (actual information instead of field names). Constants for headings must be specified according to these rules:

1. Constants must be entered in positions 45–70 of the Output Specifications form.

2. Constants can contain any of the characters in the data character set.

3. Constants must be enclosed in apostrophes. (The beginning apostrophe is always entered in position 45.)

4. Two variables, date and page number, can be printed by using the system-supplied field names.

5. No field name can be used on the same line as a constant.

6. An end-position entry must be made for every constant. (See Figure 2.45.)

Figure 2.44 First-page coding—example

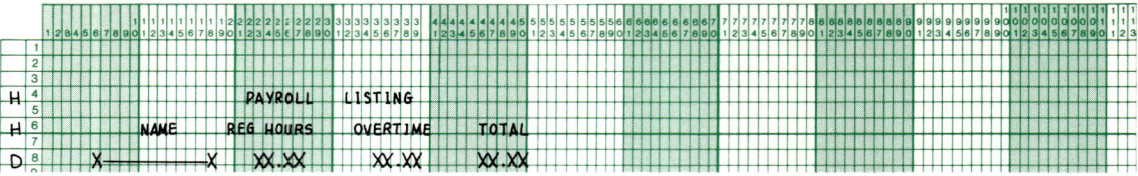

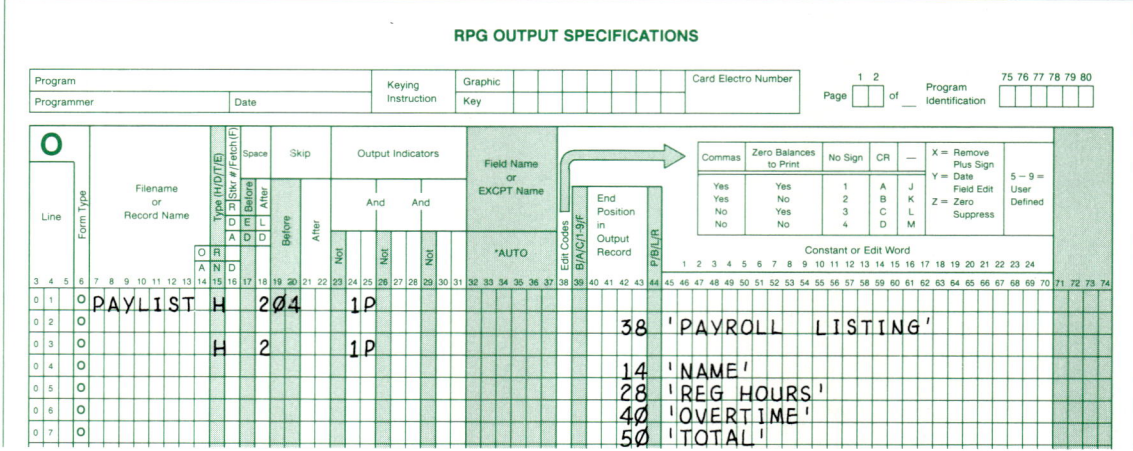

Reading this output coding:

On the file named PAYLIST, if the 1P indicator is on—skip to line 04 BEFORE printing the heading PAYROLL LISTING. Take 2 spaces after you print it (we are now on line 06).

If 1P is still on print out another heading (the second H) using the constants NAME, REG HOURS, OVERTIME, and TOTAL in the ending positions designated. After printing this heading take 2 more spaces so you will be on line 08 and ready to print the D line.

Note that the TYPE, FILENAME, and INDICATORS are on one line and the constants are each on separate lines.

Figure 2.45 Constants—examples

62   RPG II and RPG III Programming

Headings too long to specify on one line of the Output Specifications form can be split and placed on separate lines. However, an end position must be given for each part. (See Figure 2.46.)

Heading lines should be specified first on the Output Specifications form. It is best to specify the record types in this order: heading, detail, and total. (See Figure 2.47.)

Figure 2.46 Heading specification—examples

The heading shown in the printer spacing chart takes 28 positions. A constant containing a maximum of 24 characters can be specified on one specification line. Because the entire heading cannot be specified on one line, it must be broked into parts. The examples given show three different ways to specify this heading.

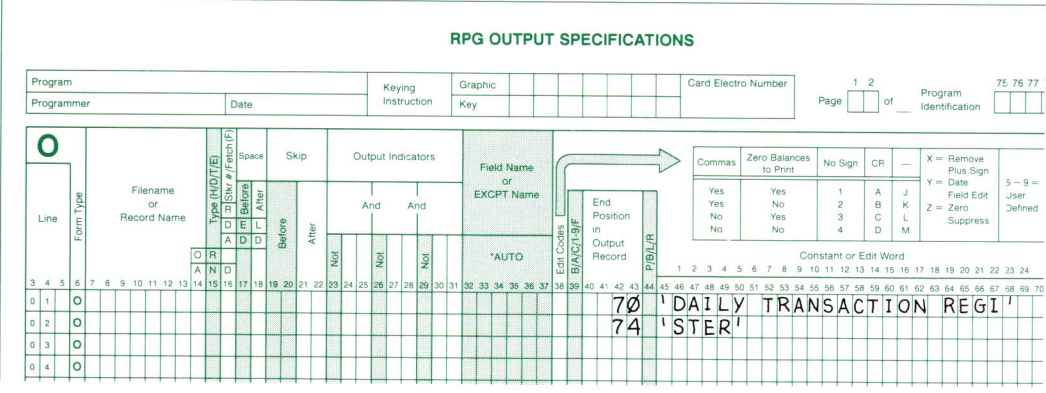

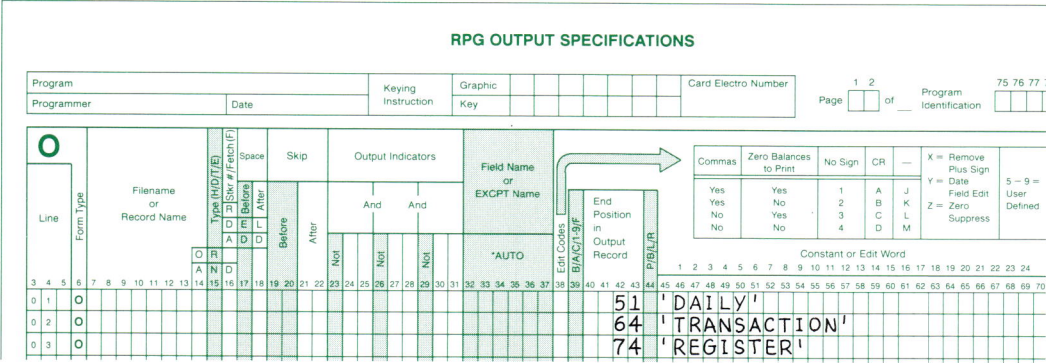

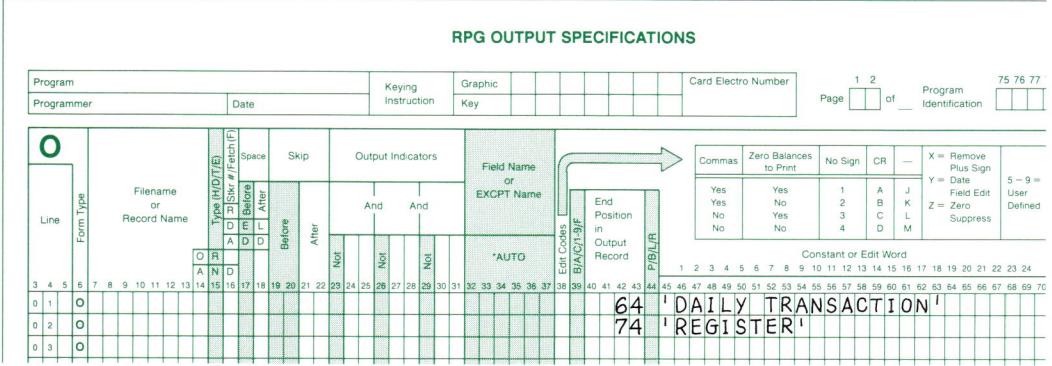

Figure 2.47 Coding heading and detail lines

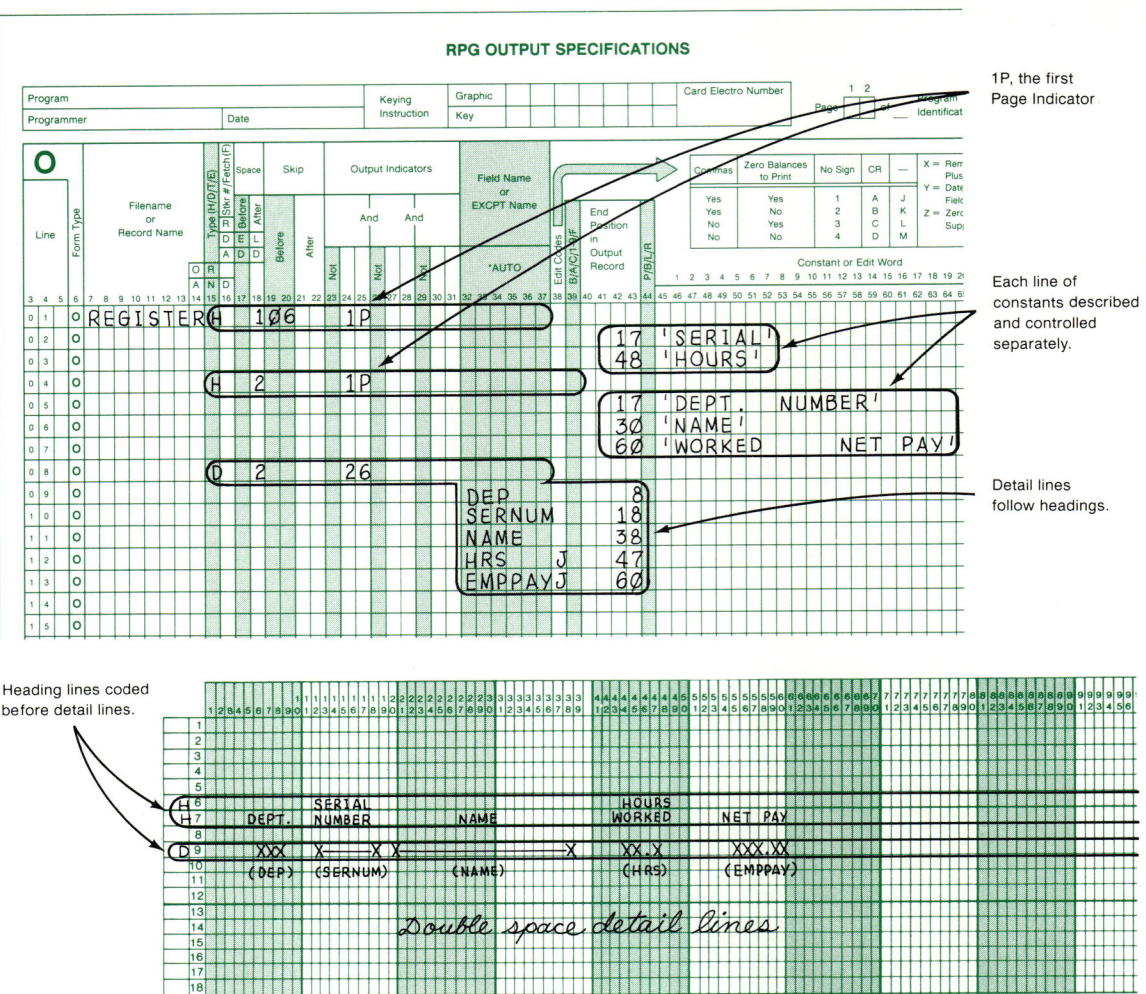

Summary

The output specifications will be used to describe the output files, types of lines (records), and fields. The files to be described are the ones coded *O* on the File Description Specifications form. The detail information needed for the output specifications will come from the Printer Spacing Chart or the Record Layout form if output is to be on disk. If the output is displayed on a cathode ray tube (CRT), the detail information will come from the screen layout form.

Following are some RPG rules for output specifications (see Figure 2.48):

A. *File Coding*
   1. Filename starts in column 7
   2. Filename must have been previously defined on the File Description Specifications form
B. *Record Coding* (type *H, D,* or *T*)
   1. *H, D,* or *T* from the Printer Spacing Chart
   2. Spacing for this line (0, 1, 2, 3 lines, before or after printing)
   3. Skipping for this line (advancing to a specific line number, before or after printing)
C. *Field Coding*
   1. Each field description is on a separate line
   2. End position is from the spacing chart
   3. Field names are left-justified and must have been previously defined
   4. Editing/punctuating numeric fields by adding commas, decimal points, etc.
   5. Constants used for printing heading (data that do not change)

Figure 2.48 Output Specifications form

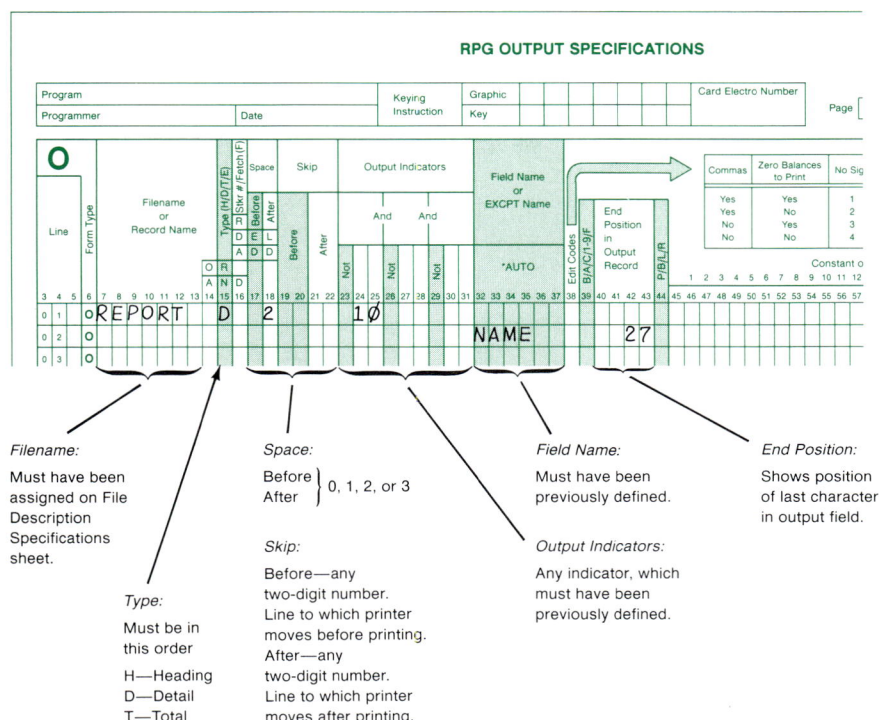

After completing this chapter, the programmer should be able to code a complete RPG program for a simple listing (one requiring no calculations). Using supporting documentation, such as flowchart, Record Layout form, and Printer Spacing Chart, code the solution to the problem on a blank specifications sheet. If a computer is available, compile and execute the program. Coding should include the correct use of indicators and proper headings. Use previous examples as a reference.

Heading Output

Headings on the first page of reports using the 1P indicator are printed before the RPG cycle ever reads a record. These headings must then be specified as constants. The constants are coded on the Output Specifications form using the Printer Spacing Chart as a guide.

Constants

Constants must be enclosed in quotes starting at position 45 and be placed on a line separate from the filename and the type. Constants may be coded individually or may be grouped together if the ending position of two constants together is used. Be certain that the appropriate number of blank positions appears in these constants.

1P Indicator and Type

The 1P indicator is used to control the heading output. The *H* in column 15 tells RPG that a heading record or line is to be written. If there are two records, there will be two *H* entries, each with its own 1P indicator and constants for that record or line. After the first line is printed, RPG will check for more headings; 1P is still on so the second line will be printed.

Spacing and Skipping

It may be necessary to position the form to a particular line on the first page. Use the space and skip entries.

Figure 2.49 Keying instructions—examples

Program		Keying Instruction	Graphic	Ø	O	2	Z		Card Electro Number
Programmer	Date		Key	N	A	N	A		

Writing the First Program

The specification forms are designed to minimize programmer error. The position headings name the information to be entered and show the encoding alternatives whenever possible. The programmer's primary responsibility is to be precise in making the entries.

Name spelling must be consistent throughout the specifications. For example, EMPLNR is interpreted by the compiler as a different name than EMPLNO or EMPNR, even though the meaning and mnemonic value may be the same. Quantitative entries, such as record and field sizes and field positions, must be exact. Errors in these kinds of entries usually can be avoided if the file and report layouts show the exact sizes of records and the sizes and positions of fields. The rules for justification of entries as defined for each entry position of the specification forms must be observed.

Common Entries

Following is a discussion of the types of entries common to all specification forms.

Keying Instructions

Keying instructions are provided to avoid confusion in interpreting certain characters. For example, the digit *0* (zero) can be confused with the letter *O*; the numeral 2 and the letter *Z* may also cause problems. The graphic line will identify the actual character used, while the key will be labeled *A* (alphabetic) or *N* (numeric). Any identifying code may be used to clearly distinguish between the characters. (See Figure 2.49.)

Page Number (Positions 1–2)

The page number, assigned in positions 1 and 2, is to be consistent with the order in which the specifications are submitted to the compiler for the preparation of the object program. Following is the order in which specifications must be submitted:

- Header (Control) Specifications
- File Description Specifications
- Extension Specifications
- Line Counter Specifications
- Input Specifications
- Calculation Specifications
- Output Specifications

If more than one page is needed for any form type, the page number should be consistent with the order of pages within that type.

Line Number (Positions 3–5)

The line number, found in positions 3–5, is partially preprinted on the majority of lines of each form. The line number is completed by entering a zero in column 5. Thus, lines are numbered by tens on each specification page. This is a helpful convention in that the programmer may insert new lines in the sequence without having to renumber. These new lines can be placed on the unnumbered lines at the bottom of the form and given a line number not ending in zero. For example, three lines could be inserted between lines 070 and 080 by numbering the insertions 071, 072, 073, or 072, 074, and 076. The latter way of numbering allows for further insertions. (See Figure 2.50.)

The page and line numbers and their sequence are checked by the compiler, and an out-of-sequence condition will be indicated where it is found. The out-of-sequence condition will not halt compilation, however. The numbers are printed on the source program listing with notations for out-of-sequence indications, if any. Page and line may be used as a finder or cross-reference number to locate a particular item in the source program for change or correction.

Figure 2.50 Line number and comments encoding

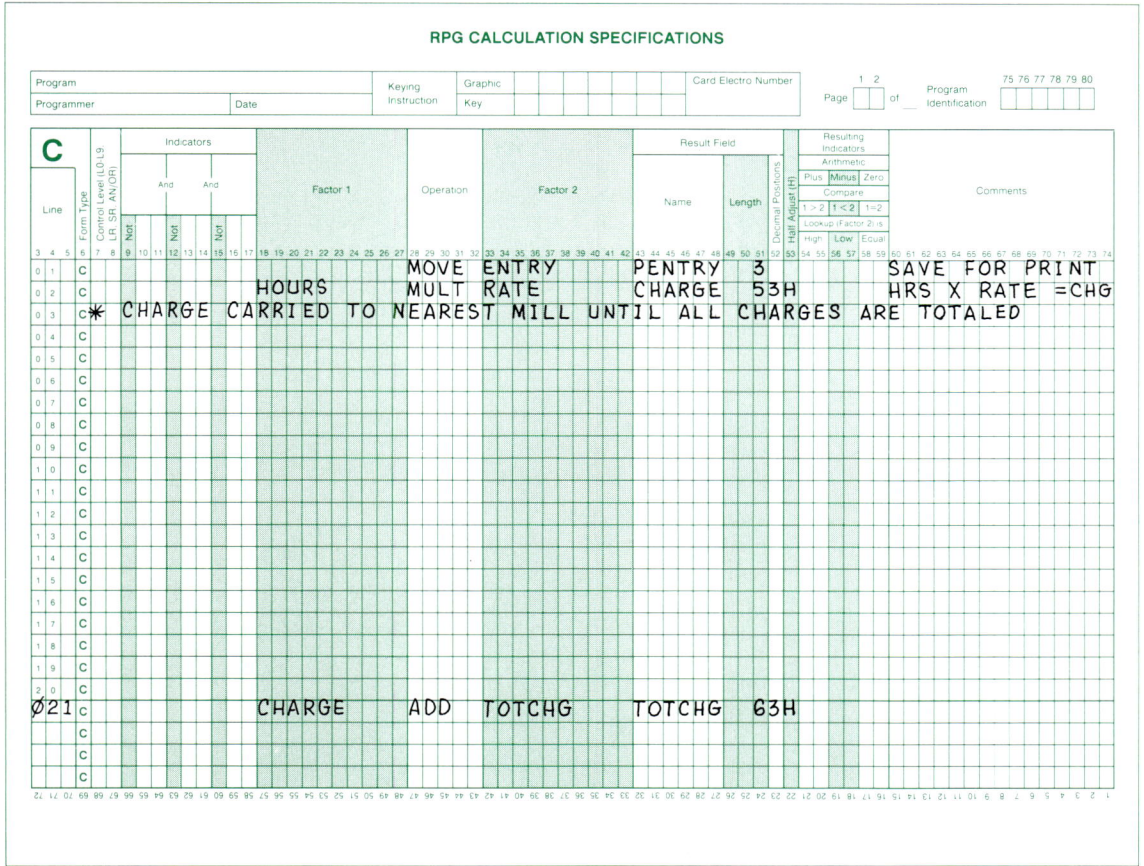

Form Type (Position 6)
The form type in position 6 is preprinted on each type of form and consists of the initial character of the name of each specification area. These are:

H   Header (Control)
F   File Description
E   Extension
L   Line Counter
I   Input
C   Calculation
O   Output

Any entry with coding in position 6 other than that mentioned above will be bypassed, and a diagnostic message will be printed on the source program listing. Also, any entry missing a code in position 6 will generate numerous diagnostic messages.

Comments
The extension and calculation specification forms provide a space on each entry line that may be used for a brief comment or note as the specification is prepared. Such entries may either explain the reasons for the other entries in that line or tell what object program actions should result. The programmer may often find it helpful to enter notes and comments for keeping track of the position in a logical sequence of entries and improving the readability of the specification for later reference or understanding by others.

An additional capability for entry of comments is available on all form types. This capability is exercised by entering an asterisk (*) in position 7 of any form line. All positions beyond the asterisk in position 7 may then be used for comment or note entries. Comment entries are not processed by the compiler, but instead are printed on the source program listing.

Program Identification (Positions 75-80)

Columns 75–80 are used primarily when source input is on cards, and are generally left blank in cardless environments.

The program identification positions are the same on all specification forms for a particular RPG program. Any unique entry is permissible. Normally, the identifying number or code assigned by the programmer is consistent with the program identification scheme of the host installation. This field has no effect on the compiling process.

Illustrative Program

Simple Listing: Returned Check Register

Job Definition
A report is to be printed listing all returned checks designating them as either regular or special.

Input
The input file has the following layout:

Position	Field Description
1–05	Check number
6–10	Check amount (xxx.xx)
11–21	Last name
22–22	Initial
23–23	Code

Output
This Printer Spacing Chart shows how the report is formatted:

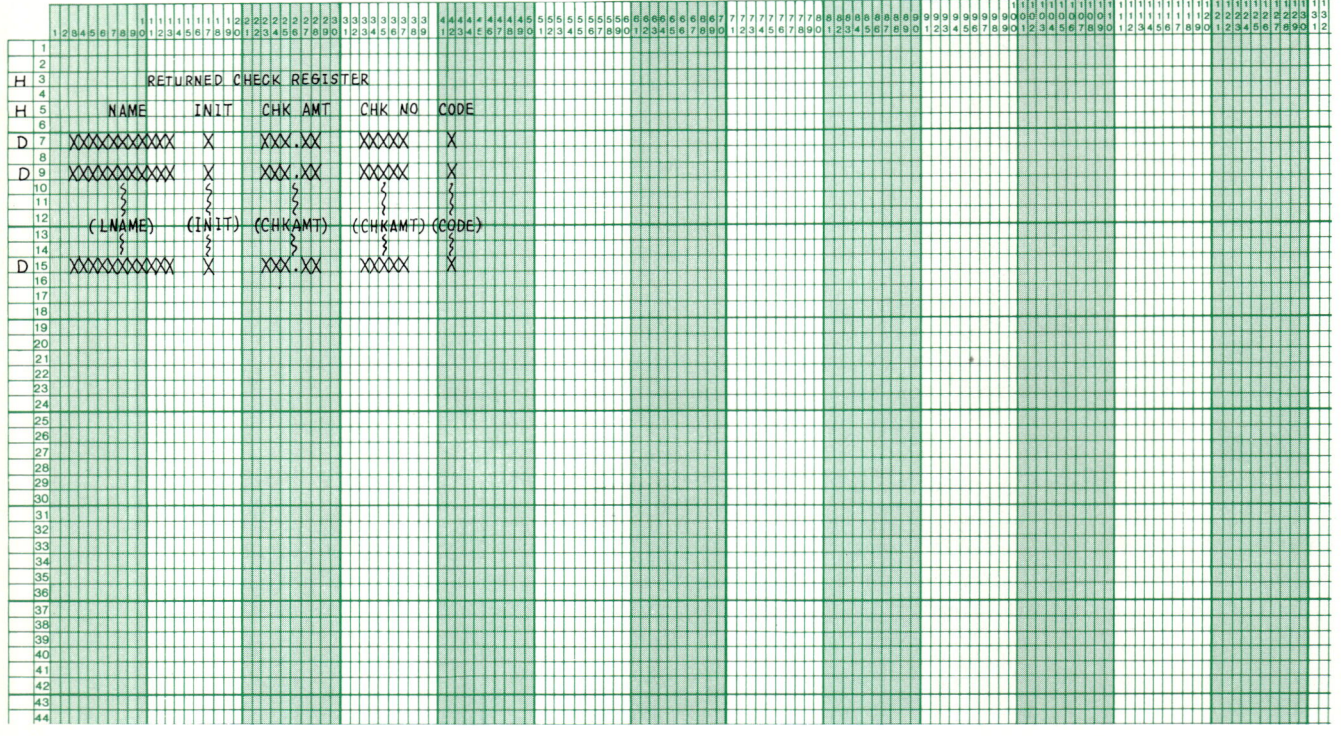

Coding sheets for Returned Check Register problem:

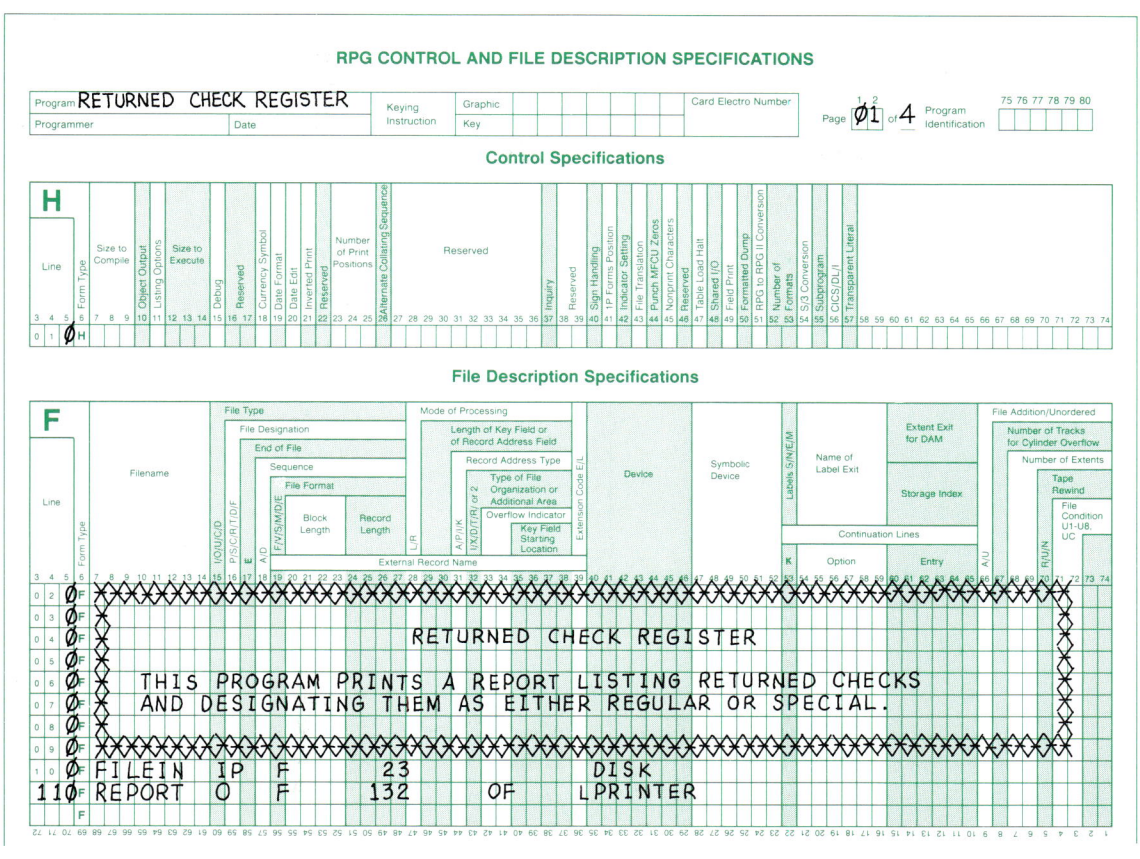

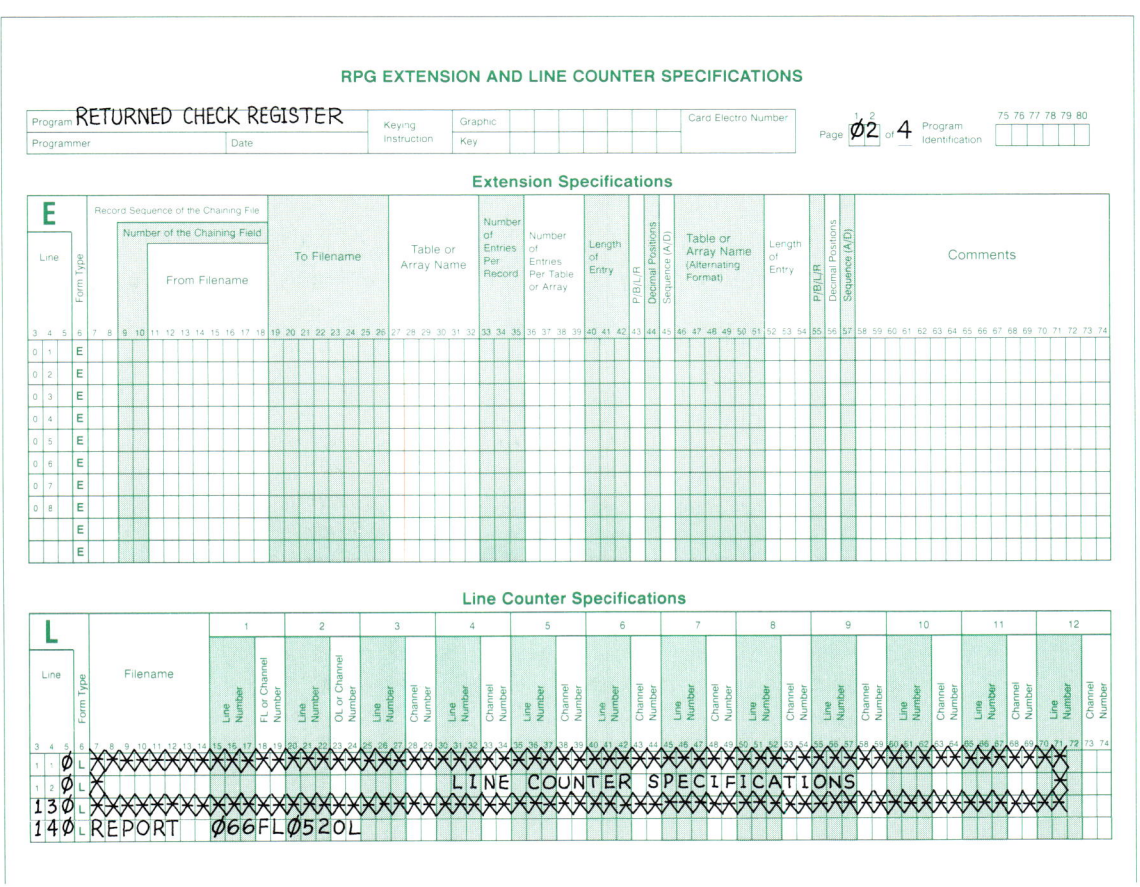

Input and Output Processing

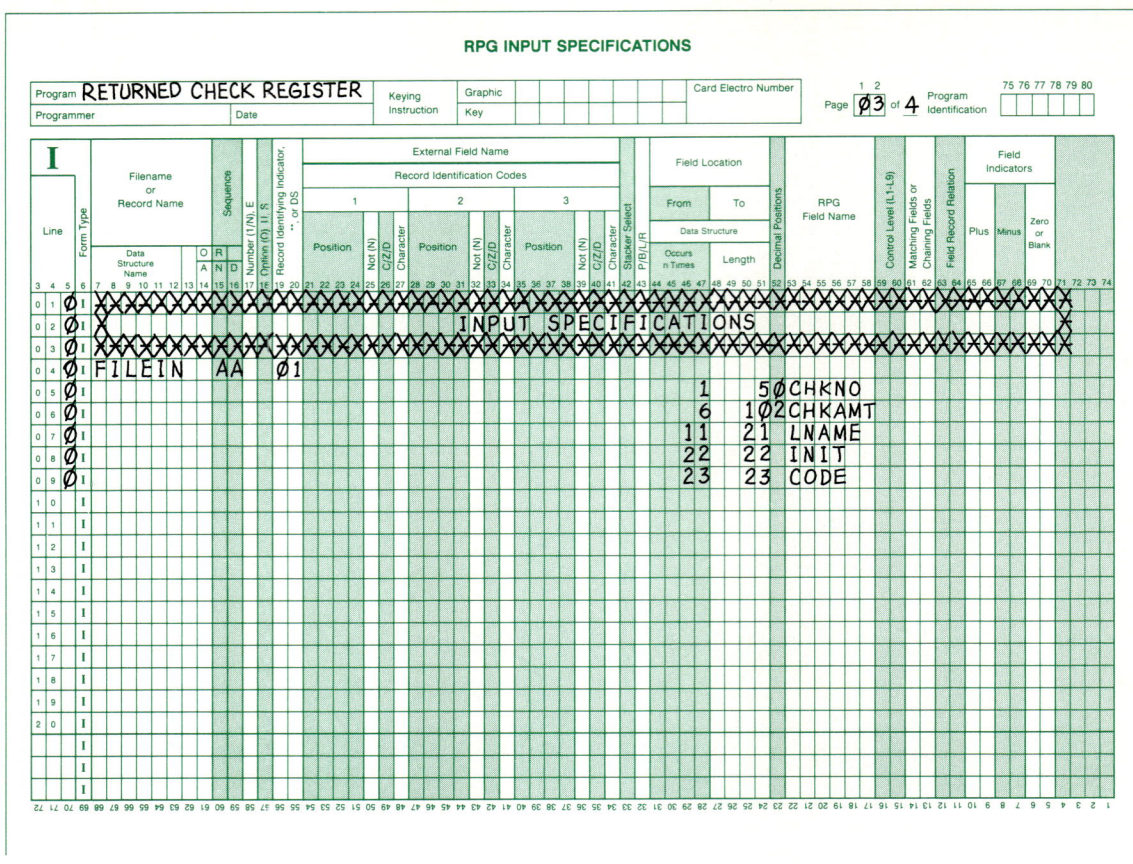
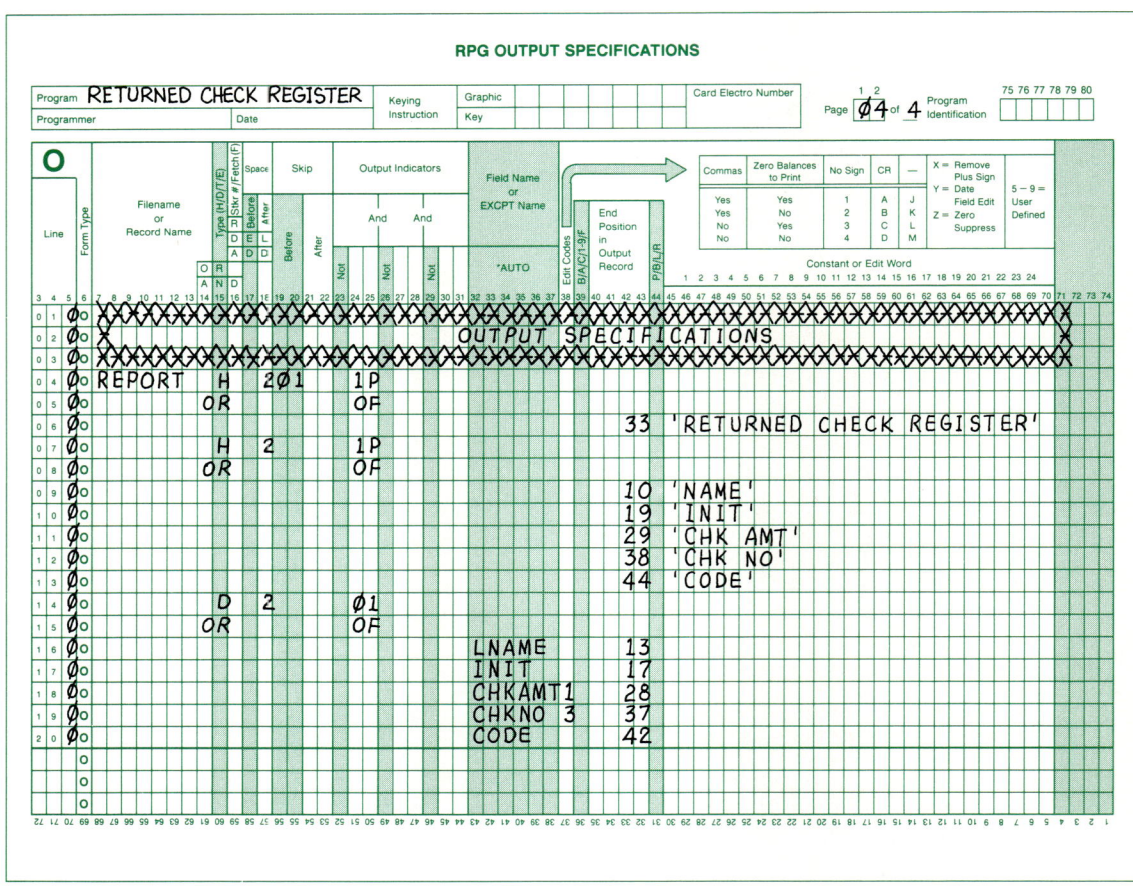

The source listing is as follows:

```
 1    01010H
 2  * 01020F*************************************************************
 3  * 01030F*                                                            *
 4  * 01040F*                  RETURNED CHECK REGISTER                   *
 5  * 01050F*                                                            *
 6  * 01060F*    THIS PROGRAM PRINTS A REPORT LISTING RETURNED CHECKS    *
 7  * 01070F*    AND DESIGNATING THEM AS EITHER REGULAR OR SPECIAL.      *
 8  * 01080F*                                                            *
 9  * 01090F*************************************************************
10    01100FFILEIN   IP  F      23            DISK
11    01110FREPORT   O   F     132        OF  LPRINTER
12  * 02010L*************************************************************
13  * 02020L*                 LINE COUNTER SPECIFICATIONS                *
14  * 02030L*************************************************************
15    02040LREPORT   066FL0520L
16  * 03010I*************************************************************
17  * 03020I*                    INPUT SPECIFICATIONS                    *
18  * 03030I*************************************************************
19    03040IFILEIN   AA  01
20    03050I                                         1   50CHKNO
21    03060I                                         6  102CHKAMT
22    03070I                                        11   21 LNAME
23    03080I                                        22   22 INIT
24    03090I                                        23   23 CODE
25  * 04010O*************************************************************
26  * 04020O*                   OUTPUT SPECIFICATIONS                    *
27  * 04030O*************************************************************
28    04040OREPORT   H  201   1P
29    04050O           OR     OF
30    04060O                                    33 'RETURNED CHECK REGISTER'
31    04070O         H   2    1P
32    04080O           OR     OF
33    04090O                                    10 'NAME'
34    04100O                                    19 'INIT'
35    04110O                                    29 'CHK AMT'
36    04120O                                    38 'CHK NO'
37    04130O                                    44 'CODE'
38    04140O         D   2    01
39    04150O           OR     OF
40    04160O                         LNAME      13
41    04170O                         INIT       17
42    04180O                         CHKAMT1    28
43    04190O                         CHKNO  3   37
44    04200O                         CODE       42
```

A Returned Check Register is to be printed as follows:

```
         RETURNED CHECK REGISTER

     NAME       INIT   CHK AMT   CHK NO   CODE

   HOLMES        A       97.50    1567      R

   FRANKLIN      B       55.10    1569      R

   STEVENS       S       73.50    1570      R

   WALKER        F      127.75    1571      S

   JONES         D       33.00    1573      R

   ROSEMAN       B       18.75    1574      S

   MORGAN        R       47.50    1577      S

   GREEN         H      108.15    1578      R

   MITCHELL      T       74.00    1579      R

   PENNY         J       29.00    1582      R

   MORGAN        R      144.50    1583      S

   CRAIG         A       82.50    1588      R

   WARD          M      119.75    1590      R
```

Illustrative Program

Line Counter Specification: Transaction Register

Job Definition

Print a report listing all items sold during a week. The selling of an item is known as a transaction, so the report is titled *Transaction Register*.

During the week, a transaction file is created. At end of each day, transaction records are keyed from information obtained from order forms during the day. To get the printed transaction report, list the information from all input records on the printed report.

Input

Sales transaction file consisting of 42-byte records, the format of which is shown on this Record Layout form:

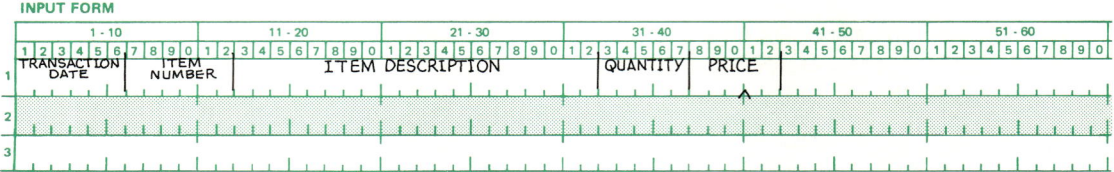

Output

This Printer Spacing Chart shows how the report is formatted:

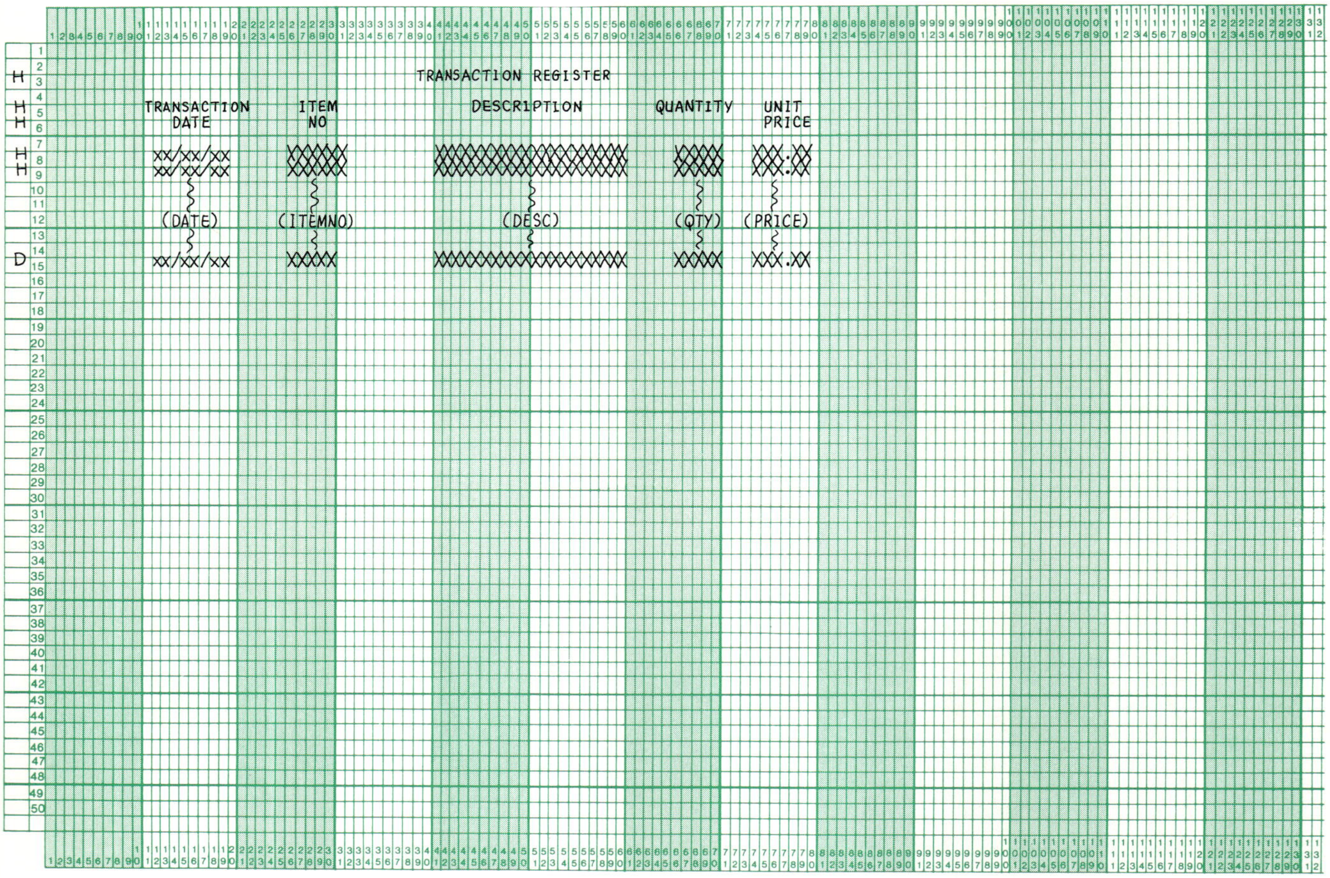

Coding sheets for Transaction Register problem:

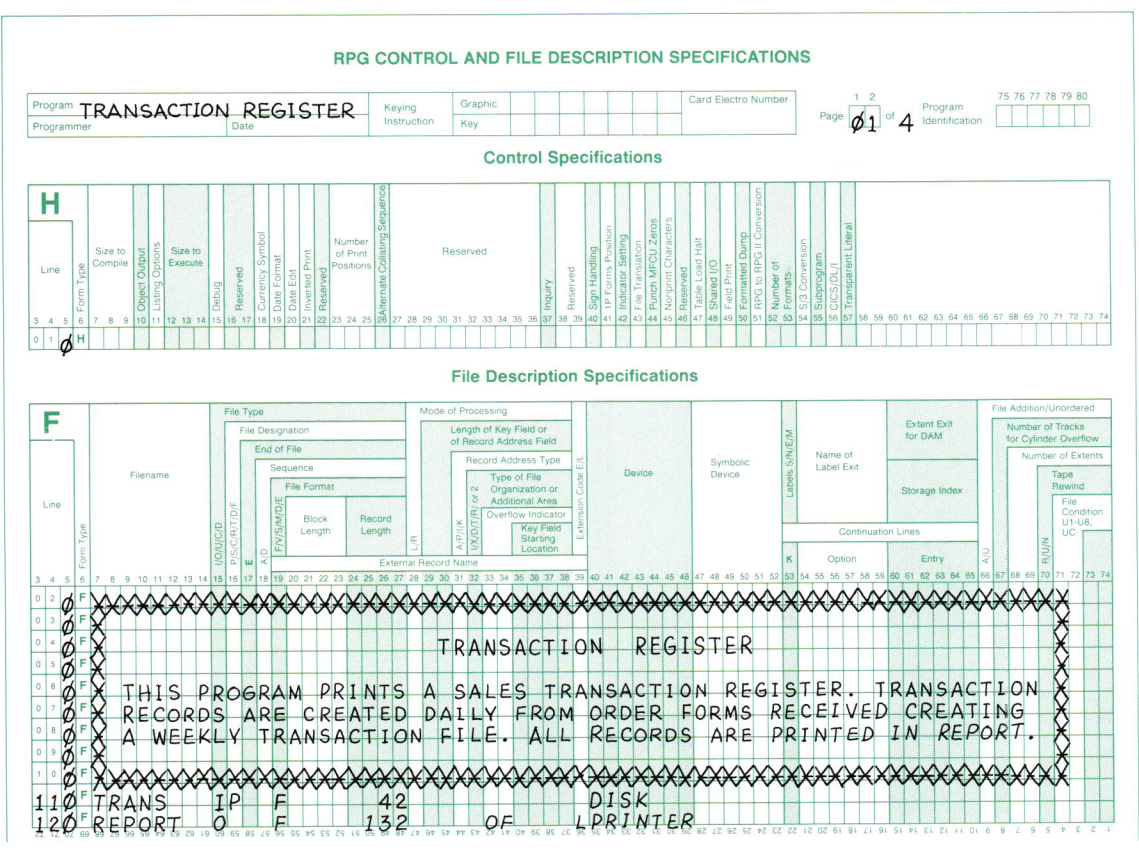

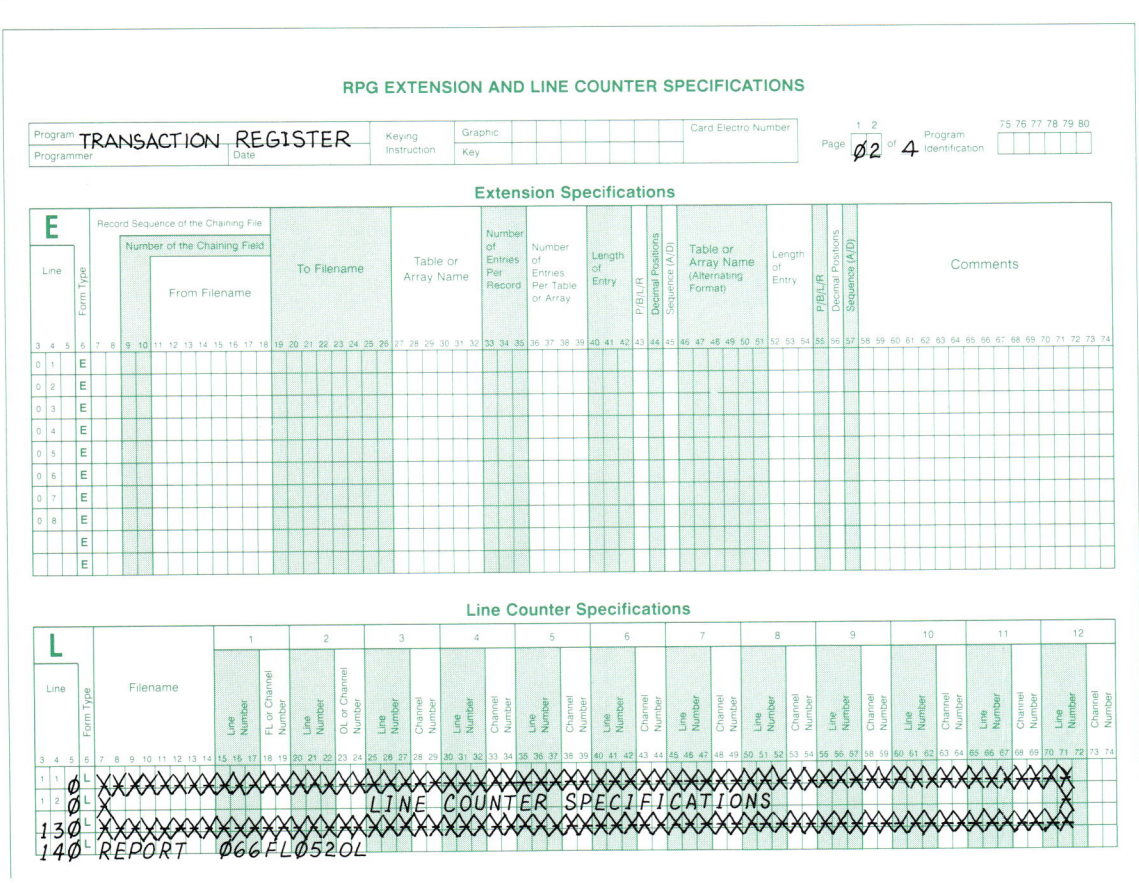

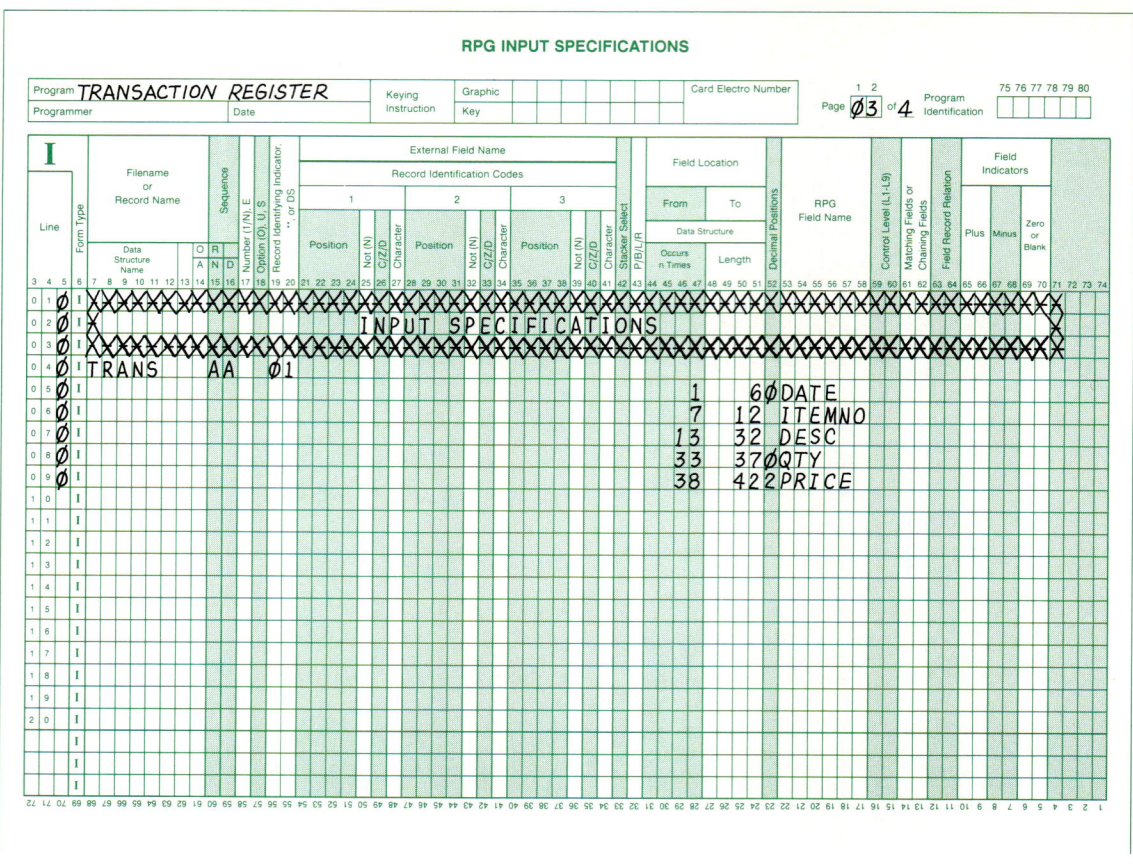
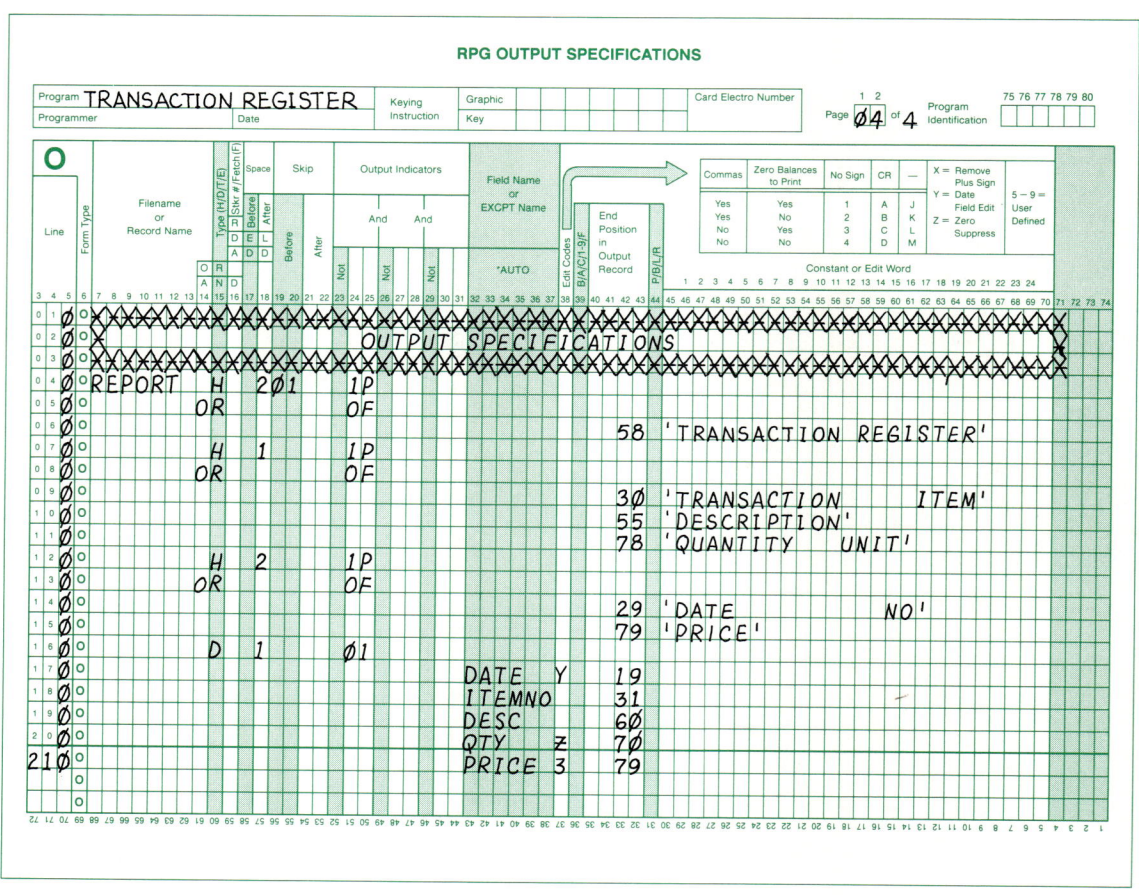

The source listing is as follows:

```
 1    01010H
 2  * 01020F******************************************************
 3  * 01030F*                                                     *
 4  * 01040F*              TRANSACTION   REGISTER                 *
 5  * 01050F*                                                     *
 6  * 01060F* THIS PROGRAM PRINTS A SALES TRANSACTION REGISTER. TRANSACTION *
 7  * 01070F* RECORDS ARE CREATED DAILY FROM ORDER FORMS RECEIVED CREATING  *
 8  * 01080F* A WEEKLY TRANSACTION FILE. ALL RECORDS ARE PRINTED IN REPORT. *
 9  * 01090F*                                                     *
10  * 01100F******************************************************
11    01110FTRANS    IP  F       42           DISK
12    01120FREPORT   O   F      132     OF    LPRINTER
13  * 02010L******************************************************
14  * 02020L*              LINE COUNTER SPECIFICATIONS            *
15  * 02030L******************************************************
16    02040LREPORT   066FL052OL
17  * 03010I******************************************************
18  * 03020I*                 INPUT SPECIFICATIONS                *
19  * 03030I******************************************************
20    03040ITRANS    AA  01
21    03050I                                     1   60DATE
22    03060I                                     7   12 ITEMNO
23    03070I                                    13   32 DESC
24    03080I                                    33  370QTY
25    03090I                                    38  422PRICE
26  * 04010O******************************************************
27  * 04020O*                OUTPUT SPECIFICATIONS                *
28  * 04030O******************************************************
29    04040OREPORT   H  201      1P
30    04050O         OR          OF
31    04060O                                     58 'TRANSACTION REGISTER'
32    04070O         H   1       1P
33    04080O         OR          OF
34    04090O                                     30 'TRANSACTION    ITEM'
35    04100O                                     55 'DESCRIPTION'
36    04110O                                     78 'QUANTITY    UNIT'
37    04120O         H   2       1P
38    04130O         OR          OF
39    04140O                                     29 'DATE           NO'
40    04150O                                     79 'PRICE'
41    04160O         D   1      01
42    04170O                             DATE  Y  19
43    04180O                             ITEMNO   31
44    04190O                             DESC     60
45    04200O                             QTY   Z  70
46    04210O                             PRICE 3  79
```

A Transaction Register is to be printed as follows:

```
                         TRANSACTION REGISTER

TRANSACTION       ITEM         DESCRIPTION           QUANTITY      UNIT
   DATE           NO                                               PRICE

 9/23/87         413010     CH001 BOX 100A FLUSH        10         4.90
 9/23/87         412146     CH148 BREAKER 15A          100          .89
 9/23/87         411116     1500 TWIN SOCKET B         500         1.12
 9/24/87         503029     MOTOR 1/2 HP 60 CYC          2       146.78
 9/24/87         317802     TERMINAL CLIP              100         5.12
 9/24/87         326917     TERMINAL BAR               100         4.12
 9/24/87         411121     1506 SOCKT ADAPT BRN       400          .19
 9/25/87         412997     CH173 BREAKER 30A           60         1.15
 9/25/87         413088     CH176 BREAKER 60A           40         1.15
 9/25/87         411174     C151 SIL SWITCH BRN        200         1.16
 9/25/87         413090     CH005 BR BOX 150A           10         4.98
 9/25/87         718326     FC803 FUSE 15A             200          .32
```

Questions for Review

1. Why is the programmer concerned with the manipulation of data in RPG programming?
2. How is data organized?
3. List the steps involved in the RPG basic cycle.
4. What is the Control Specifications form used for?
5. What are the main functions of the File Description Specifications form?
6. What are filenames and what are the rules for their formation?
7. How is the file use specified on the File Description Specifications form?
8. How is a file designated?
9. How is a record length specified and what is its main purpose?
10. What is an overflow indicator and what are its uses?
11. List the sequence of operations performed when the overflow indicator is on.
12. How are the overflow and 1P indicators used together?
13. How are the devices used specified?
14. How are input records described?
15. Briefly describe the two main categories of information on the Input Specifications form.
16. What is the main purpose of filenames in the Input Specifications form?
17. What is the importance of specifying the record type sequence?
18. What is the purpose of the record identifying indicator and how is it specified?
19. How are record identifying indicators used?
20. When is a record identifying indicator turned on and turned off?
21. What is a record identification code and how is it specified?
22. What is an OR condition and an AND condition, and how are they specified?
23. How are data fields within records described?
24. What is the main purpose of a field name?
25. What are the rules for forming field names?
26. Why must a field location be specified and how is it described?
27. How does the compiler determine whether the data in each field is alphameric or numeric?
28. How are output records described?
29. How are output conditions specified on the output form?
30. What are Output Specifications forms used for?
31. What are the two general categories of output specifications?
32. Describe three different types of records that can be specified on the Output Specifications form.
33. What are the field names in the output specifications used for?
34. What are the additional entries required for printed reports?
35. How is editing accomplished in RPG programs?
36. How is the 1P indicator set on and off within the program cycle?

37. How are constants specified for headings?

38. What is the main function of the *PLACE operation and how is it used?

Problems

Problem 1

Code the necessary file description, input specifications, and output specifications based on the following information. Create your own data names and use the system device names of your installation.

INPUT FORM

1-10	11-20	21-30	31-40	41-50	51-60	61-70
LAST NAME	FIRST NAME		STREET ADDRESS	CITY	ST	ZIP

(with MIDDLE INITIAL marked at column 31)

[Printer spacing chart showing "UNFORMATTED LIST" heading and three detail lines of X's representing the record]

Output is as follows:

```
            UNFORMATTED LIST

GOLDMAN         STEVEN      J1445 MAIN ST VAN NUYS   CA914010001
ANDONAEGUI      NICOLA      X425 HARVARD   L. A.     CA900380010
LEWIS           VICTORIA    Q3444 VICTORY  BURBANK   CA914110004
SHERMAN         HAROLD      R777 SUNSET STRIP L. A.  CA900270003
```

Problem 2

Use the flowchart, Record Layout form, and Printer Spacing Chart to help you write an RPG program that will print a report listing all employees hired during the current calendar year.

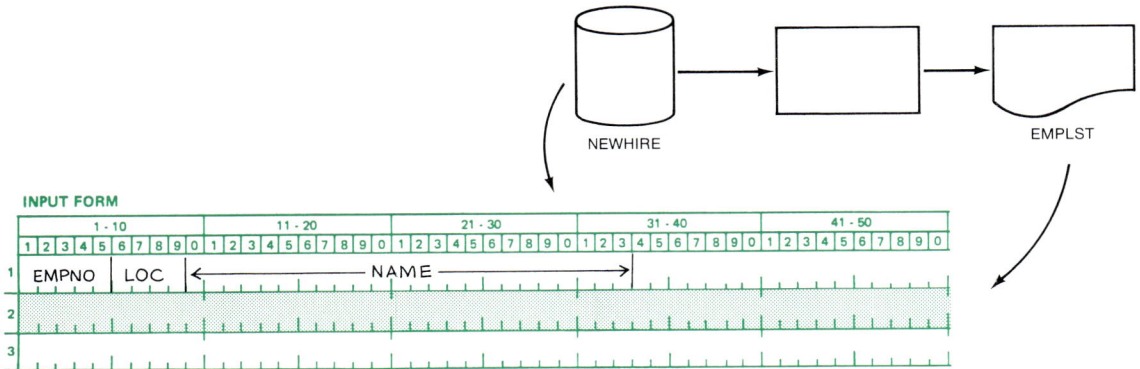

Input and Output Processing 77

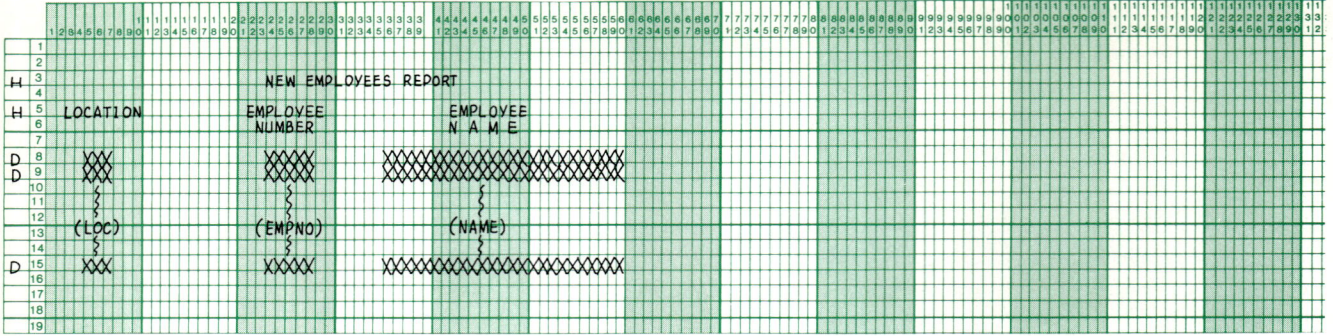

Output is as follows:

```
                        NEW EMPLOYEES REPORT

        LOCATION        EMPLOYEE            EMPLOYEE
                         NUMBER             N A M E

          SWA            68832           ROBERT  JONES
          SWA            68322           JACK    SMITH
          STH            78832           HENRY   KAHN
          TTH            79876           MARGARET KAISER
          STH            68325           JUSTIN  KRAMER
```

Problem 3

A sales analysis report is to be prepared as shown in the Printer Spacing Chart below.
The fields on the input file records are arranged as follows:

Position	Field Description
1–02	Salesman number
3–08	Amount of sale (two decimal positions)
9–23	Customer name
30–30	Area

Using these input specifications, code the file description, input specifications, and output specifications for this job. Choose your own file and field names.

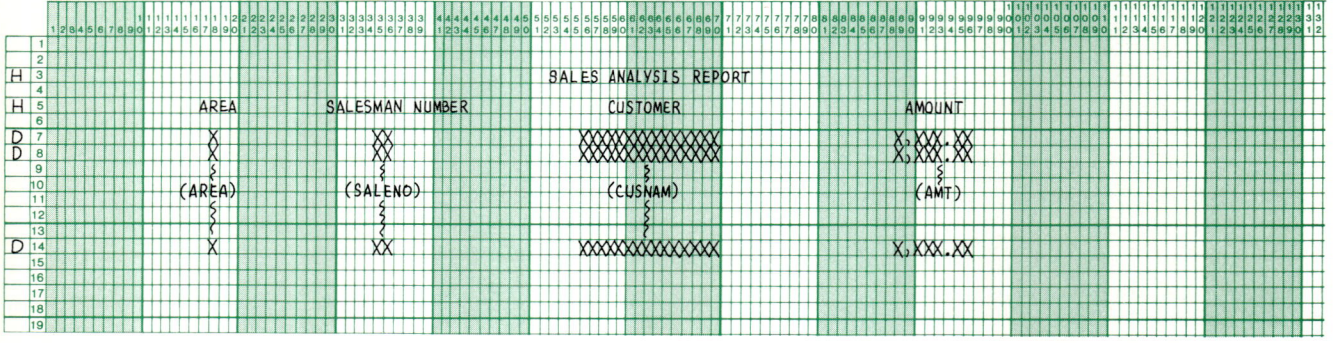

Output is as follows:

```
                             SALES ANALYSIS REPORT

         AREA       SALESMAN NUMBER       CUSTOMER            AMOUNT

          A              01             STEVEN LEWIS           398.64
          A              02             DAVID MAIN              24.91
          C              03             MICHAEL MELTON       9,641.11
          D              04             JEAN MYERS             499.23
          F              05             HAROLD OWENS         1,239.41
```

RPG II and RPG III Programming

Problem 4

A report is to be prepared listing quarterly earnings and the social security tax on those earnings. The report is to be prepared based upon the information in the Printer Spacing Chart below.

The fields on the input file QTRFILE are as follows:

Positions	Field Description	Format
1–09	Social security number	
10–30	Name	
31–35	Social security tax	(xxx.xx)
36–41	Quarterly amount	(xxxx.xx)

Using these input specifications, code the file description, input specifications, and output specifications for this job. The output file is called SSLIST. Use the field names on the Printer Spacing Chart.

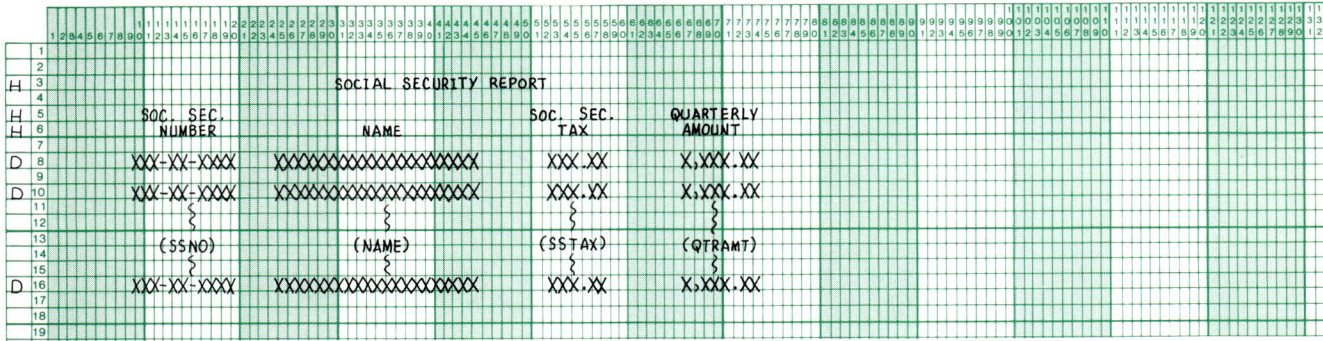

Output is as follows:

```
          SOCIAL SECURITY REPORT

SOC. SEC.                    SOC. SEC.    QUARTERLY
 NUMBER        N A M E         TAX         AMOUNT

502-12-6934   RON PATTERSON    313.67      627.34

419-63-8319   THOMAS PATRICK   123.46      246.92

214-90-6184   MARIA PEREZ       62.43      124.86

436-70-4125   LEE RICHARDSON     9.79       19.58

383-80-7581   JOHN SANDERS      47.74       95.48
```

3 Calculation Operations

Outline

Logic Cycle
Purpose of Calculations
  Operations
  Data
  Conditions
  Order
  Tests
Writing Specifications for Calculation
    Operations
  Arithmetic Operations
    Describing Type of Operations
    Describing Use of Data
    Describing Result Field
    Result Field Length
    Decimal Positions
    Half-adjusting Results
    (Rounding)
    Testing Results of Arithmetic
      Operations
    Move Remainder (MVR)
    Coding Arithmetic Operations—
      Summary
    Calculation Notes
  Compare Operations
    Rules for Numeric Constants
    Rules for Alphameric Constants
    Coding Compare Operations—
      Summary
Using Indicators to Control
    Calculations and Output
  Resulting Indicators
    RPG Specifications
  Last Record Indicator (LR)
    Program Cycle Operations
    RPG Specifications

Editing
  Edit Codes
    Edit Code Z (Zero Suppress)
    Edit Code Y (Date Field Edit)
  Edit Words
    Floating $
    Asterisk Fill
Reserved Fields
  PAGE
  User Date
    UDATE
    UMONTH, UDAY, UYEAR
    Notes on Coding PAGE
      and UDATE
  Summary
    Indicators
    Calculations
    Heading Output
    Detail Output
    Total Output
    Constants
    Edit
RPG III Enhancements
  Calculations

Figure 3.1 Expanded RPG logic cycle

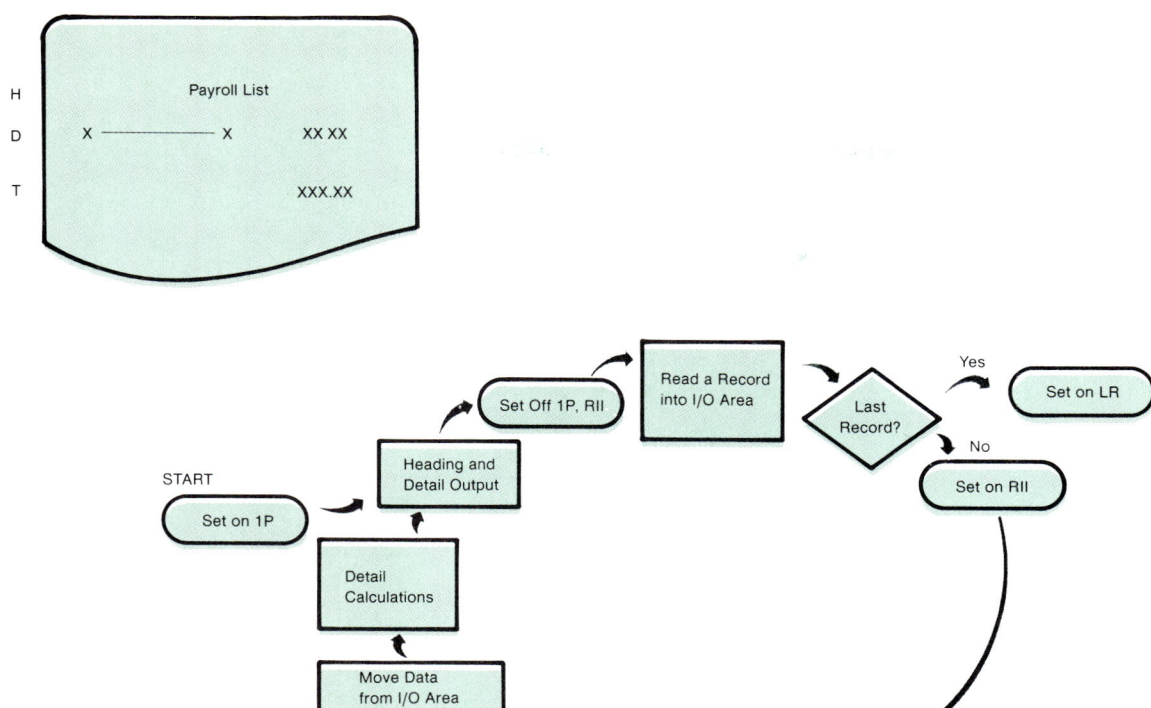

Legend

RII—Record Identifying Indicator
LR—Last Record Indicator
1P—First Page Indicator

The text has so far dealt only with programs that will read an input record and print a detail line with appropriate headings. Most programming applications are more complicated than that. Most require calculations on data and print totals at the end of the report. These operations require some expansion on the RPG logic cycle. This chapter will present the expanded cycle, introduce some new indicators, and demonstrate programs using headings, calculations, and final totals.

Logic Cycle

The RPG logic cycle starts at the time the 1P indicator turns on. This indicator controls the printing of headings on the first pages of reports.

Just before the first record is read in the logic cycle, the 1P indicator is automatically turned off by RPG. Since the indicator is on for just one cycle and no records are read during that cycle, the printing is limited to constants or special reserved fields such as date or the page number.

The 1P indicator causes the headings on the first page to print. The cycle is repeated using the record identifying indicator to control the detail output. After that the program needs to be brought to an end. To end the cycle and print any final totals an indicator is used to signal the end of the report.

The last record indicator (LR) signifies that the last record has been read and processed. (See Figure 3.1.) This indicator may then be used for any end-of-report totals. The coding of the LR indicator is similar to that of output entries. It is usually associated with the *E* entry in position 17 of the File Description Specifications form of one or more input files. (See Figures 3.2 and 3.3.)

Figure 3.2 Indicators—examples

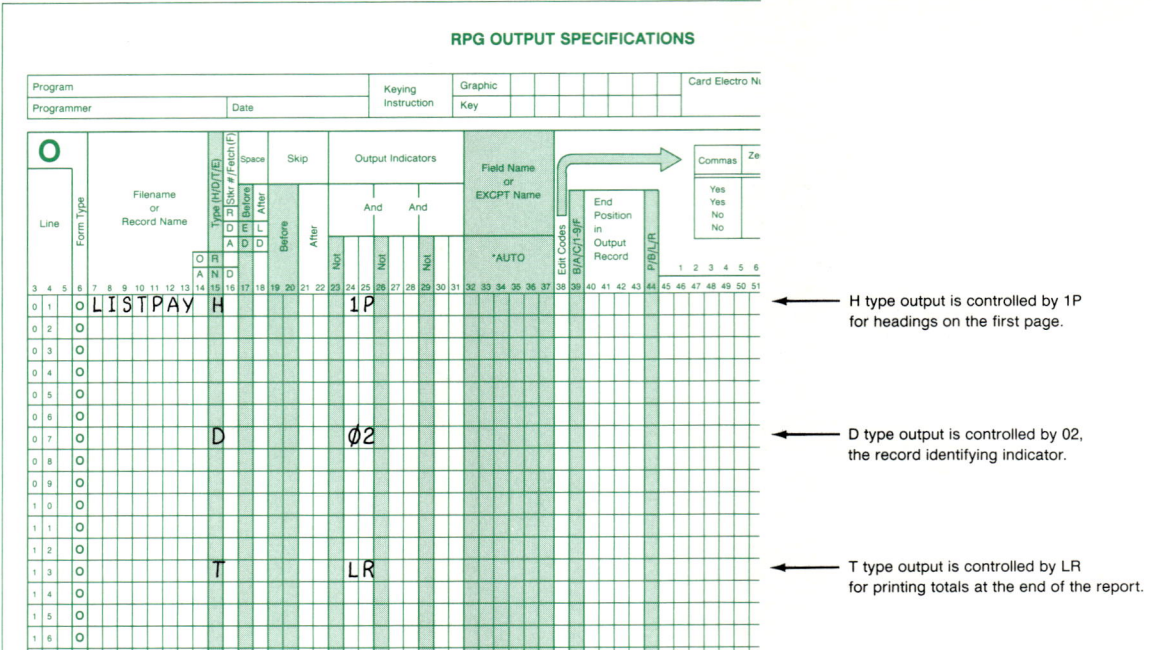

Figure 3.3 Indicator summary

Indicator	Assigned	Turned on by	Turned off by	Usage
RII	Input	Conditions of codes in the record	RPG II at the end of cycle	Detail processing detail output
1P	In the cycle	RPG II	RPG II at the end of cycle	First page headings
LR	In the cycle	After the last record has been processed	RPG II	Last record processing and output

Legend

RII—Record Identifying Indicator   1P—First Page Indicator   LR—Last Record Indicator

Purpose of Calculations

Most programs require that some arithmetic or logical operations be performed on the data in order to produce meaningful output reports. Details of these operations are spelled out in the flowchart or the narrative part of the problem statement.

The problem of the programmer is to translate the notations or narrative on the calculation specifications according to RPG syntax rules. The purpose of the Calculation Specifications form is to tell

1. Which *operations* are to be performed on the data
2. The *conditions* that must exist for those operations to be carried out
3. The *order* of the operations
4. The *tests* to be performed on the results of the operations

Operations

Arithmetic operations (such as add, subtract, multiply, and divide) and logical operations to compare information all have to be coded. Each of the operations is coded with an abbreviated, mnemonic, RPG name (ADD, SUBtract, MULTiply, DIVide). (See Figure 3.4.)

Figure 3.4 Calculations specifications—purposes

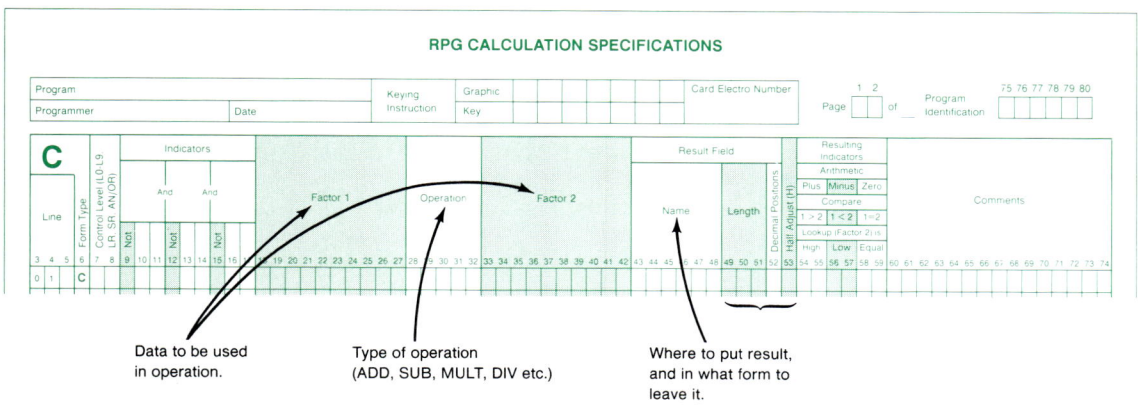

Figure 3.5 Data—examples

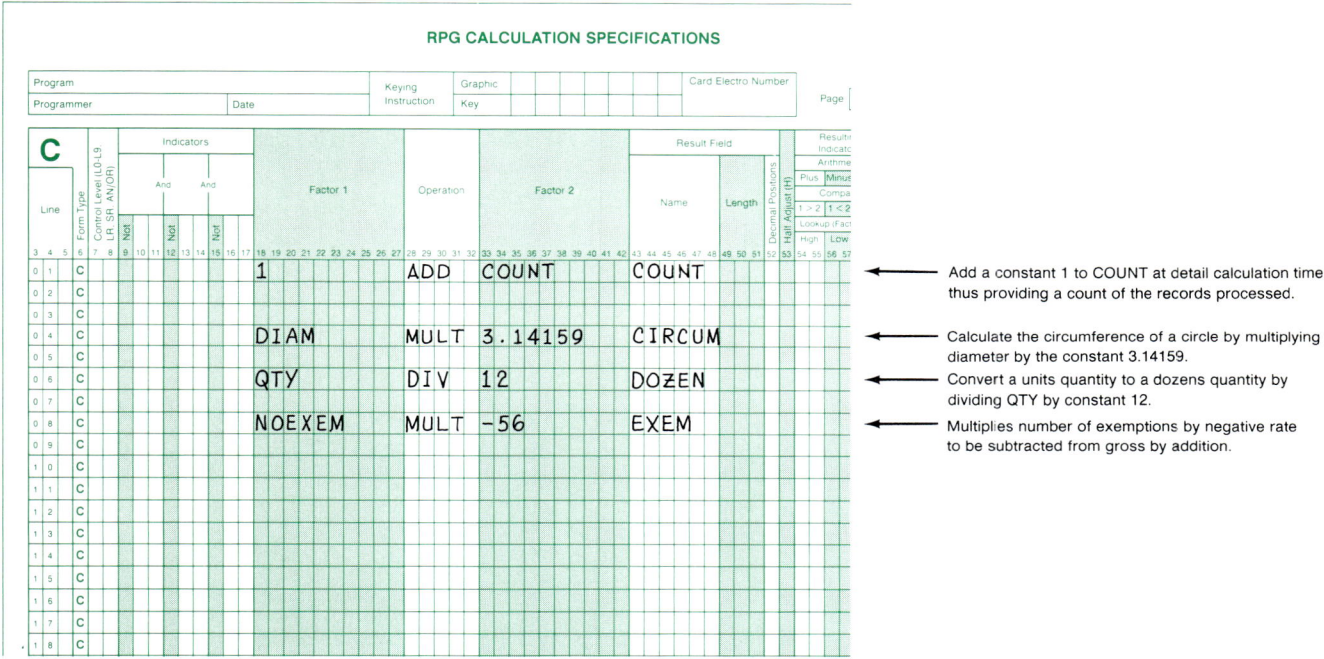

- Add a constant 1 to COUNT at detail calculation time, thus providing a count of the records processed.
- Calculate the circumference of a circle by multiplying diameter by the constant 3.14159.
- Convert a units quantity to a dozens quantity by dividing QTY by constant 12.
- Multiplies number of exemptions by negative rate to be subtracted from gross by addition.

Data

Two types of data are specified on the Calculation Specifications form: fields and literals.

Fields like those read and defined on input may be used in either factor 1, factor 2, or the result field.

Literals are information, as opposed to a field name that represents information. To ADD 1 TO TOTAL, simply enter 1 as factor 1. This is a **numeric literal.** (See Figure 3.5.)

To compare a field to RED, enter 'RED' as a factor in the calculation. Alphabetic literals must be enclosed in single quotes to distinguish them from field names.

Conditions

Indicators will be used to control if an operation should be performed. If the record identifying indicator is set to 23 when there is a *D* in position 1 of the record, then 23 will be used on the Calculation Specifications form; that operation will be performed only if 23 is on. A calculation may have several indicators to condition it or may involve no indicators.

Figure 3.6 Calculation specifications—example

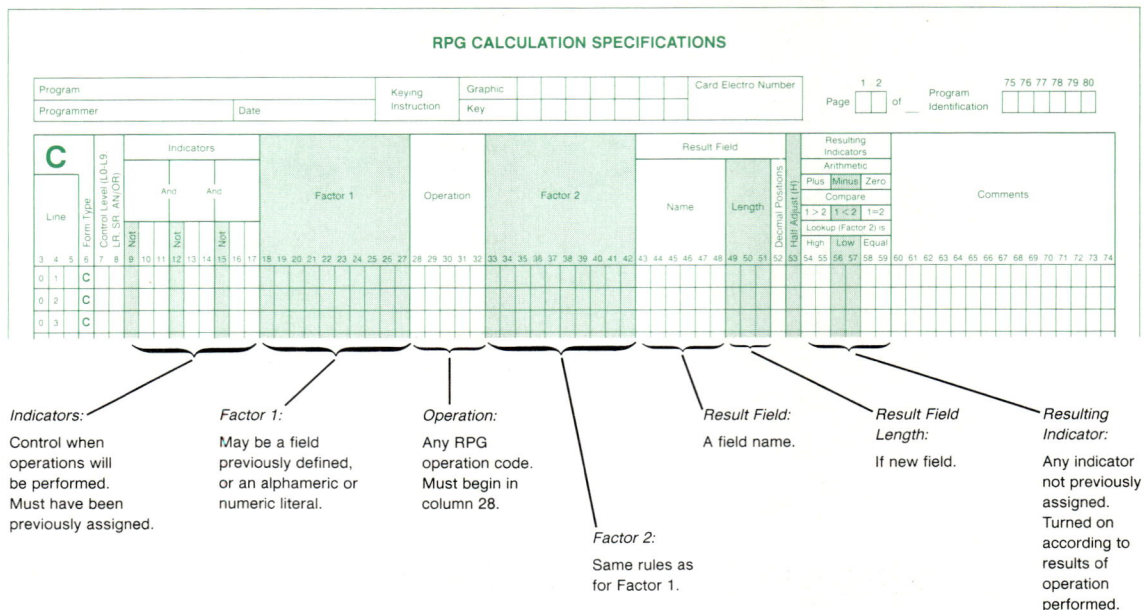

Indicators:
Control when operations will be performed. Must have been previously assigned.

Factor 1:
May be a field previously defined, or an alphameric or numeric literal.

Operation:
Any RPG operation code. Must begin in column 28.

Factor 2:
Same rules as for Factor 1.

Result Field:
A field name.

Result Field Length:
If new field.

Resulting Indicator:
Any indicator not previously assigned. Turned on according to results of operation performed.

Order

The sequence in which the calculations are coded will be the order in which they will be performed. Each line of codes designates a separate operation. After the calculation specifications are completed, they should be read to ensure that the proper order for accomplishing the desired results has been established.

Tests

The results of operations may have to be checked once they have been performed. Is one factor greater than the other? Is NETPAY a negative item? Resulting indicators are used to test the results of operations.

Writing Specifications for Calculation Operations

Most jobs require some processing. RPG processing can include calculating, comparing, moving, or changing data. (See Figure 3.6.)

Arithmetic Operations

Arithmetic operations are used frequently in preparing reports and updating files. Sales quantities must be extended by unit price and products must be summed for such printed outputs as invoices and sales records. Addition and subtraction functions are needed for file posting.

RPG provides the facilities for adding two fields together or for subtracting one from another and storing the results. A constant or literal value may be specified as one of the factors. For instance, to count a number of transactions, a literal value of one (coded as 1) may be added to a field called COUNT and the results may be returned to COUNT for each transaction. Modified addition and subtraction operations are available to set a field to zero before adding and subtracting.

Multiplication and division operations can be specified for fields or a field and a literal. The result can be stored in a designated field, which may be the same as one of the factors. A field may be multiplied by itself for squaring. The remainder of a division operation may be preserved for further calculations.

If necessary, automatic decimal point alignment is performed for arithmetic operations. The sign of the result field is determined by the rules of algebra. Operations are available to remove or change signs of the fields, thus making possible the use of absolute values.

The Calculation Specifications form is used to describe the operations to be performed on the data. Needed information for specifications includes the type of operation to be done, the field(s) or constant to be used in the calculation, and the location where the result of the calculation is to be placed.

One operation is specified on each line. In each program cycle the processing steps are performed in the order specified on the form. If calculations must be done in a particular order, operations must be listed in that order.

Describing Type of Operations (Positions 28-32)

Type of calculation is indicated by the operation code entry in positions 28–32 on the Calculation Specifications form.

Following are four of the most common operation codes:

Add (ADD)—this operation causes factor 2 to be added to factor 1. The sum is placed in the result field. Factor 1 and factor 2 are not changed by the operation unless one of them is the result field.

Subtract (SUB)—this operation causes factor 2 to be subtracted from factor 1. The difference is placed in the result field. Factor 1 and factor 2 are not changed by the operation unless one of them is the result field.

Multiply (MULT)—this operation causes factor 1 to be multiplied by factor 2. The product is then placed in the result field. Factor 1 and factor 2 are not changed unless one of them is the result field. When a field is used (such as a factor) that is described as a result field, the result field must be large enough to hold the product.

Divide (DIV)—this operation causes factor 1 to be divided by factor 2. The quotient is placed in the result field. Factor 1 and factor 2 are not changed unless one of them is the result field. Division by zero is invalid. (See Figure 3.7.)

Describing Use of Data (Positions 18-27, 33-42)

After the type of operation has been specified, the data to be used must be identified. If ADD is specified, the system must be told what to add. This is done by naming the fields to be used in positions 18–27 (factor 1) and 33–42 (factor 2).

Instead of naming a field in factor 1 or factor 2, a constant can be entered. (Constant and literal are interchangeable terms.) That is, the actual data may be entered instead of a field containing the data. For example, 700 (actual data) may be entered as factor 1 or factor 2. AMOUNT would be the name of a field containing the data.

Constants can be either numeric or alphameric. Only numeric constants are used in a calculation operation. The rules for using numeric constants are as follows:

1. Constants can contain up to ten digits using the digits 0–9.

2. Constants can have a sign and decimal point. The sign, if used, must be the leftmost character. The decimal point, if used, must be shown as part of the constant (e.g., 35.74).

3. The first character of the constant must be placed in the leftmost position of the factor field.

4. Constants cannot contain imbedded blanks.

The contents of a field can change during the execution of the program, but the constants do not. If the same number is to be added, multiplied, subtracted, or divided during every program cycle, a constant may be used.

To the compiler, a constant is like a field name. During compilation, the compiler checks factor 1 and factor 2 for constants. If there are any, the compiler assigns a storage location for the constant and gives instructions to the computer to put the appropriate constant in that location at the beginning of job execution. (See Figure 3.5.)

When fields are entered in factor 1 and factor 2, their order must be considered because the specified operation may affect the result.

Figure 3.7 Arithmetic operations—example

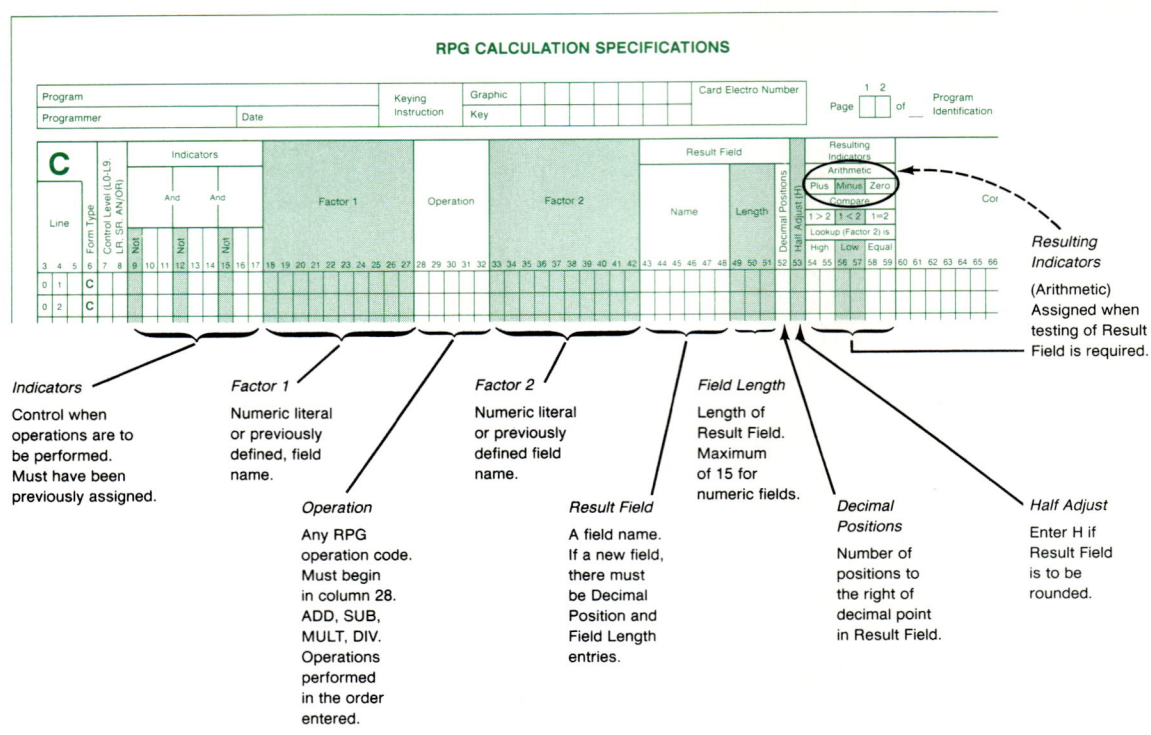

Indicators
Control when operations are to be performed. Must have been previously assigned.

Factor 1
Numeric literal or previously defined, field name.

Operation
Any RPG operation code. Must begin in column 28. ADD, SUB, MULT, DIV. Operations performed in the order entered.

Factor 2
Numeric literal or previously defined field name.

Result Field
A field name. If a new field, there must be Decimal Position and Field Length entries.

Field Length
Length of Result Field. Maximum of 15 for numeric fields.

Decimal Positions
Number of positions to the right of decimal point in Result Field.

Half Adjust
Enter H if Result Field is to be rounded.

Resulting Indicators
(Arithmetic) Assigned when testing of Result Field is required.

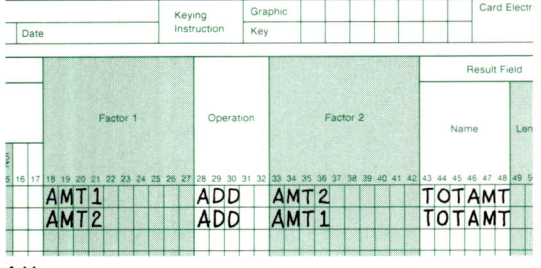

Add

Factor 2 is added to Factor 1 and the sum placed in the Result Field.

Either line adds the two amount fields. The order of the fields makes no difference in addition.

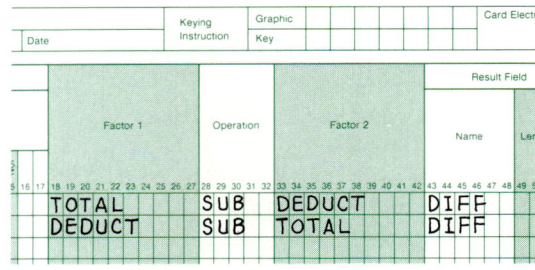

Subtract

Factor 2 is subtracted from Factor 1 and the difference placed in the Result Field.

The order of Factor 1 and Factor 2 in subtract operations is important. The bottom line would not produce the desired result.

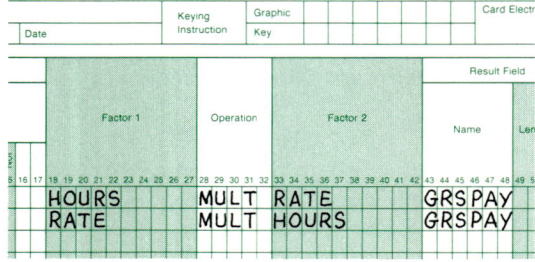

Multiply

Factor 1 is multiplied by Factor 2 and the product placed in the Result Field.

Either line multiplies the hours and rate to obtain the gross pay. The order of the fields makes no difference in multiplication.

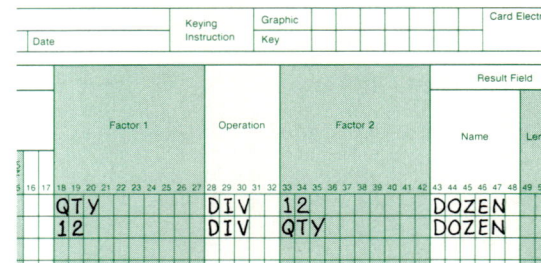

Divide

Factor 1 is divided by Factor 2 and the quotient is placed in the Result Field Factor 2 cannot be zero.

The order of the fields in divide operations is important. The bottom line will not convert a units quantity to dozens.

86   RPG II and RPG III Programming

Figure 3.8 Result field—examples

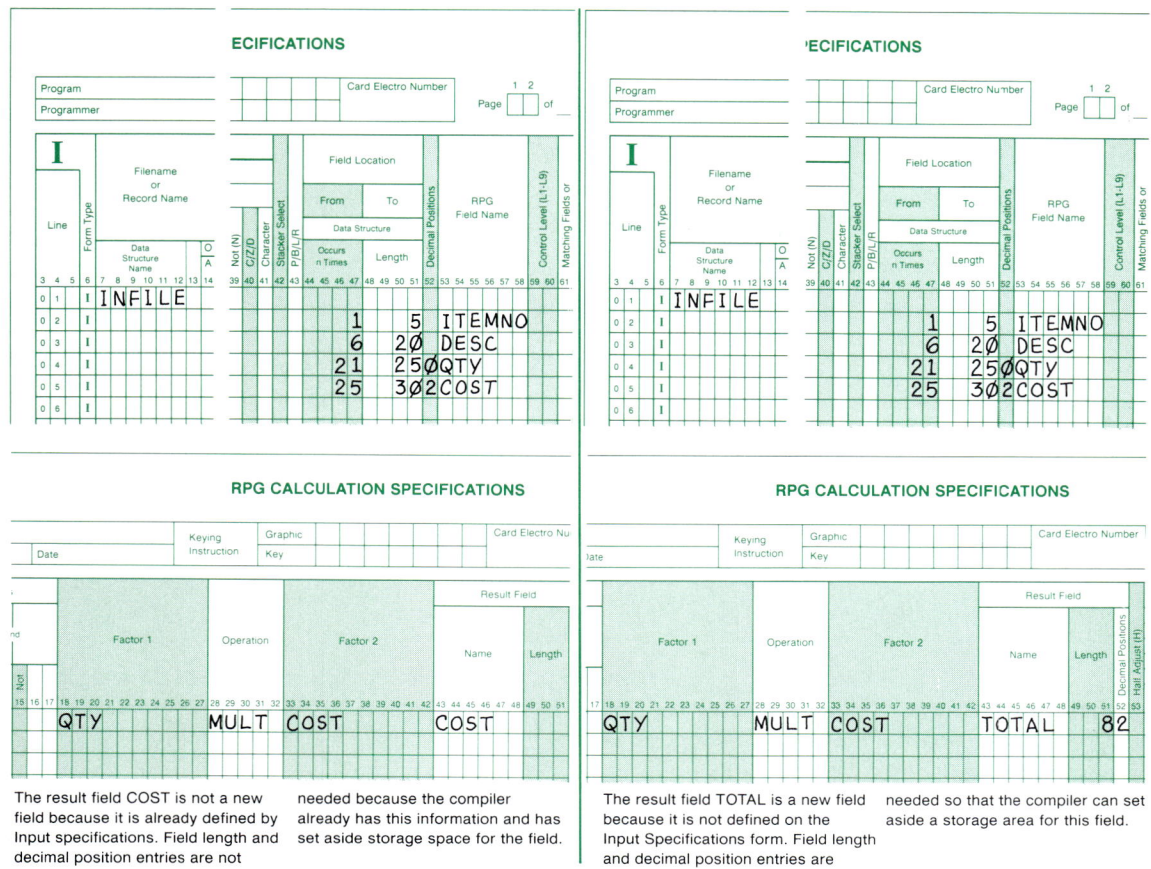

Describing Result Field (Positions 43-48)

The storage location of the result of a calculation is specified in positions 43-48 (the result field). The name entered in the result field can be the name of a field already defined on the input or calculation specifications or can be given a new field name.

A new name for a result field is not needed in the following two situations:

1. The contents of an input field are no longer required in the program and field is the correct size.

2. The contents of an input field or result field already defined on the Calculation Specifications form are to be replaced with a new value.

If a new field is named, the **field length** (positions 49-51) and decimal position (position 52) must be specified so that the compiler can assign adequate storage for the new field. (See Figure 3.8.)

Result Field Length (Positions 49-51)

The result field first named (on either input or calculation specifications) must be sufficiently large to hold the executed results. The length of the fields involved in the operation must always be considered. For example, if a two-position field is to be added to a three-position field, the largest result possible must be determined.

```
 999
  99
----
1098
```

The four digits in this result indicate that a result field length of at least four must be specified.

Calculations 87

Figure 3.9 Half-adjusting—example

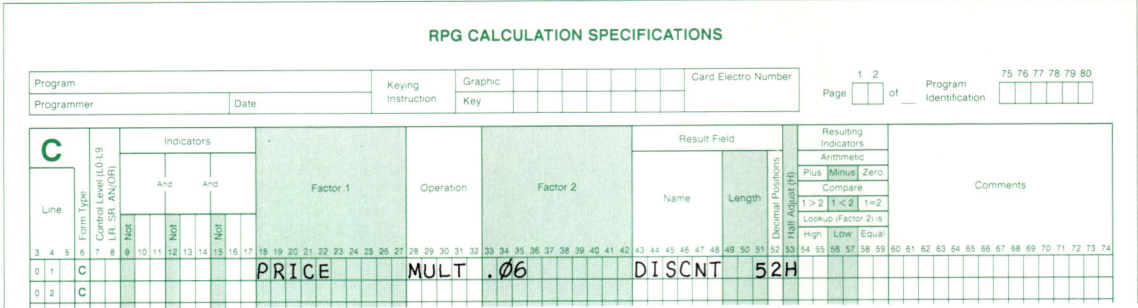

In this example, DISCNT is half-adjusted. The entry in position 52 (Decimal Positions) indicates the number of digits to be retained after half-adjusting is completed. In this case, two digits are required. The multiplication and half-adjusting would be done like this:

```
    74.98  ← Assumed value of PRICE.
 ×    .06  ← Constant representing 6% discount rate.
   4.4988  ← Result which must be half-adjusted to 2 places.
   1       ← 1 is added to 9 because 8 is greater than 4.
   4.50̸8̸8̸  ← Slashed digits are dropped since only two decimal positions are required.
```

If this calculation would occur many times in the program, as in a running total, a result field length larger than four would probably be needed. It is up to the programmer to determine the largest field length needed; failure to specify a large enough result field can mean a loss of data.

Field length and decimal positions entries are made once and only once for each field, on the input and calculation specifications. A field may not have its decimal characteristics modified by redefining its field length and decimal positions in the calculations. (See Figure 3.8.)

Decimal Positions (Position 52)

For a new result field, an entry must be placed in position 52. If the new field is to be numeric but contains no digits to the right of the decimal point, enter a zero. Remember, this entry indicates the type of field (numeric or alphameric) as well as the decimal position. If the result field is not specified as numeric, the compiler will not provide instructions for the calculation operation.

Half-adjusting Results (Rounding) (Position 53)

In RPG, the process of rounding results is called **half-adjusting.** When the digit to the right of the last digit to be retained is greater than 4, 1 is added to the last digit. For example, the number 4.56258 rounded to four decimal positions becomes 4.5626. The same number rounded to two decimal positions is 4.56.

Half-adjusting is accomplished internally by algebraically adding 5 (-5 if the field is negative) one position to the right of the last specified digit in the result field. After this addition, all digits to the right of the rounded digit are truncated.

To half-adjust any calculation result, an *H* is placed in position 53 of the Calculation Specifications form on the same line as the calculation. (See Figure 3.9.)

Testing Results of Arithmetic Operations (Positions 54–59)

The results of an arithmetic operation (ADD, SUB, MULT, DIV) can be tested for plus, minus, or zero by entering resulting indicators in the appropriate positions on the Calculation Specifications form. (See Figure 3.10.)

1. A resulting indicator entered in positions 54–55 turns on the indicator if the result field is positive (plus).

2. A resulting indicator entered in positions 56–57 turns on the indicator if the result field is negative (minus).

Figure 3.10 Resulting indicators

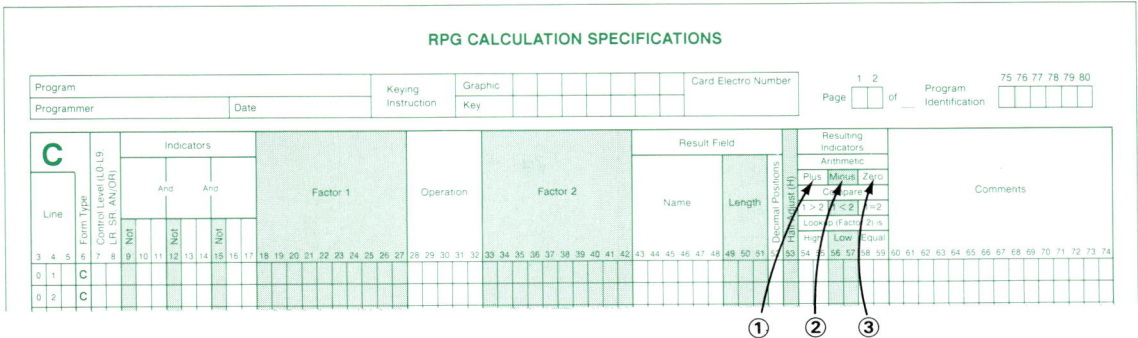

1. A resulting indicator entered in positions 54–55 tells the system to determine if the result field is positive (plus).
2. A resulting indicator entered in positions 56–57 tells the system to determine if the result field is negative (minus).
3. A resulting indicator entered in positions 58–59 tells the system to determine if the result field is zero.

The indicated tests are performed each time the operation is executed. However, the assigned indicator is set only if the field satisfies the condition tested. If indicator 90 is entered in positions 54–55 to test the result field for plus, indicator 90 would be set only if the result field were plus. If the condition is not met, the indicator is set off.

3. A resulting indicator entered in positions 58–59 turns on the indicator if the result field is zero.

The indicated tests are performed each time the operation is executed. However, the assigned indicator is set on only if the field satisfies the condition tested. If indicator 90 is entered in positions 54–55 to test the result field for plus, indicator 90 would be set on only if the result field were plus. If the condition is not met, the indicator is set off.

When testing for more than one condition, the same or different indicators may be used in these positions. If the intention is to do different operations for each of the three conditions, enter a different resulting indicator to test for each condition. (See Figure 3.11.)

If the intention is to do the same operation when the result field meets either one or two conditions (plus or zero, minus or zero) the same indicator may be used to test for both conditions. (See Figure 3.12.)

Figure 3.11 Resulting indicators—examples

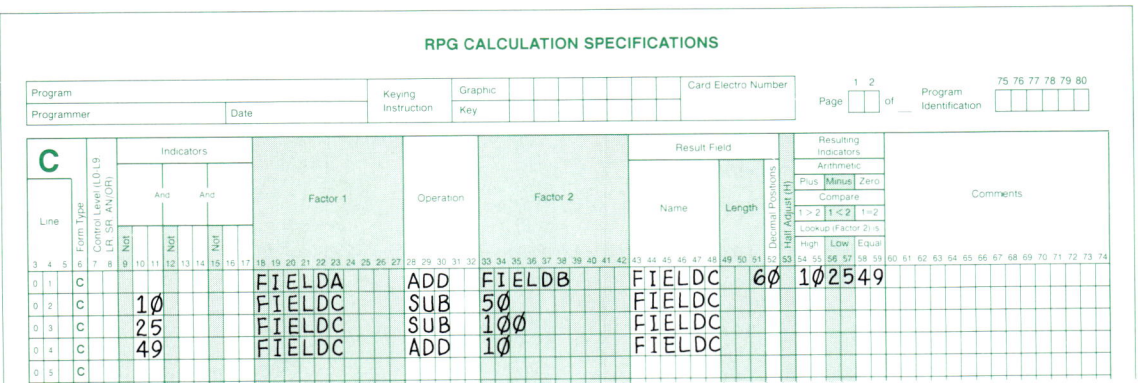

Notes on the Coding

FIELDC is tested for all three conditions. if the field is positive, indicator 10 is set on and the operation on line 02 is performed. If the field is negative, indicator 25 is set on and the operation on line 03 is done. If the field is zero, indicator 49 is set on and the operation on line 04 is done.

Calculations

Figure 3.12 Arithmetic operations—examples

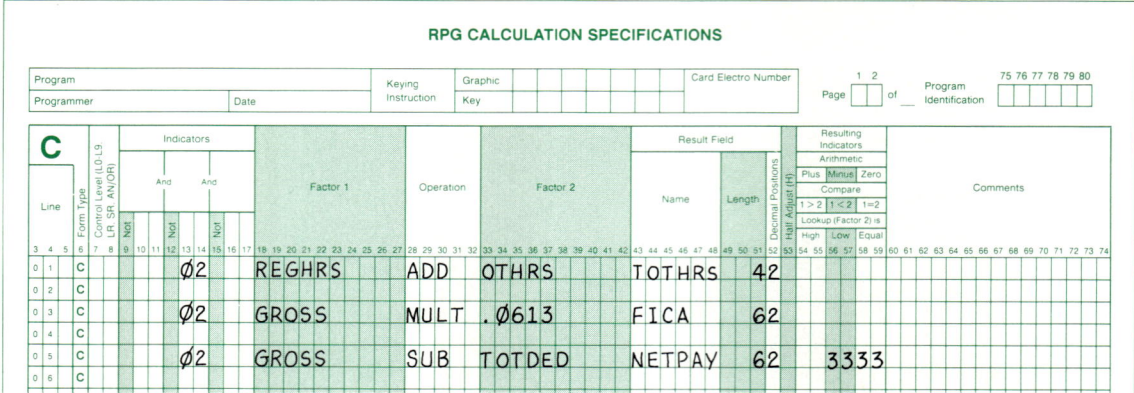

Notes on the Coding

Line 01: **REGHRS** could have been factor 2 and **OTHRS** could have been factor 1 without affecting the operation. When this operation is performed, **REGHRS** will be added to **OTHRS** and the sum will <u>replace</u> whatever is in the field **TOTHRS**. It does not accumulate all the **TOTHRS**. We will have another method to do that.

Line 03: Again factors 1 and 2 could be reversed. When this operation is performed, the product of **GROSS** and .0613 will replace whatever is in the field **FICA**.

Line 05: In this coding the factors could <u>not</u> be reversed. After this operation is performed, the difference between **GROSS** and **TOTDED** will be in the field **NETPAY**. Then RPG will check this result field to see if it is **MINUS** or **ZERO**. If either of these conditions are met, indicator 33 turns on.

Move Remainder (MVR)

The Move Remainder (MVR) operation moves the remainder from the previous divide operation to a separate field named under the result field. Factor 1 and factor 2 must not be used. *This operation must immediately follow the divide operation and should be conditioned by the same indicators.* Any remainder resulting from a divide is lost unless the Move Remainder operation is specified as the next operation. If Move Remainder is the next operation, the result of the divide operation cannot be half-adjusted (rounded). The maximum length of the remainder is fifteen, including decimal positions. The number of significant decimal positions is the greater of the following possibilities:

1. The number of positions in factor 1 of the previous divide operation
2. The sum of the decimal positions in factor 2 and the result field of the previous divide operation

The maximum whole number positions in the remainder is equal to the whole number positions in factor 2 of the previous divide operation. (See Figures 3.13 and 3.14.)

Coding Arithmetic Operations—Summary

The following are the rules for coding arithmetic operations:

Indicators (positions 9–17)—must have been previously assigned; they control when the operation is to be performed.

Factor 1 (positions 18–27)—any previously defined field name or numeric literal (constant).

Operation (positions 28–32)—RPG operation code (ADD, SUB, MULT, DIV) must begin in position 28; operations are performed in the order entered.

Factor 2 (positions 33–42)—any previously defined field name or numeric literal.

Result field (positions 43–48)—field name used to store results of the operation. It may be a new field that was not read in on input. If it is a new field, there must be decimal position and field length entries.

Figure 3.13 MOVE REMAINDER—example

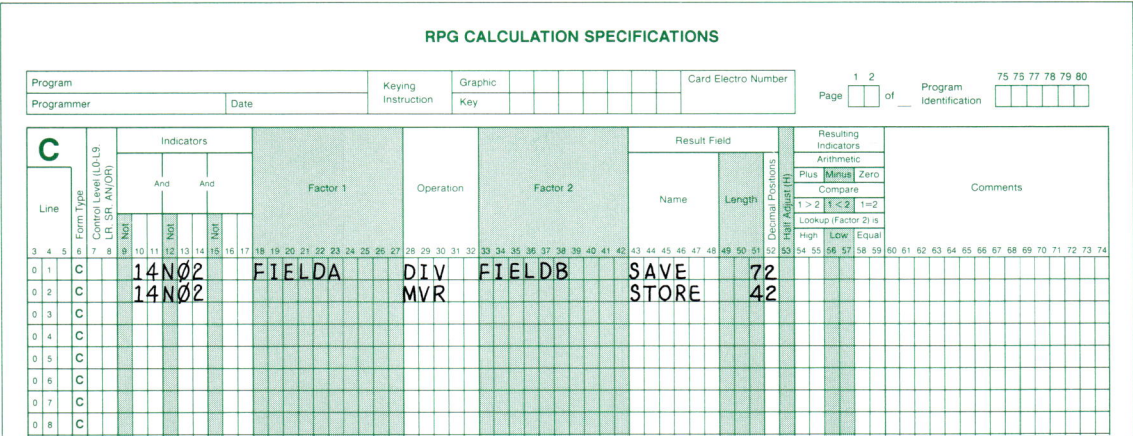

Figure 3.14 MOVE REMAINDER—examples

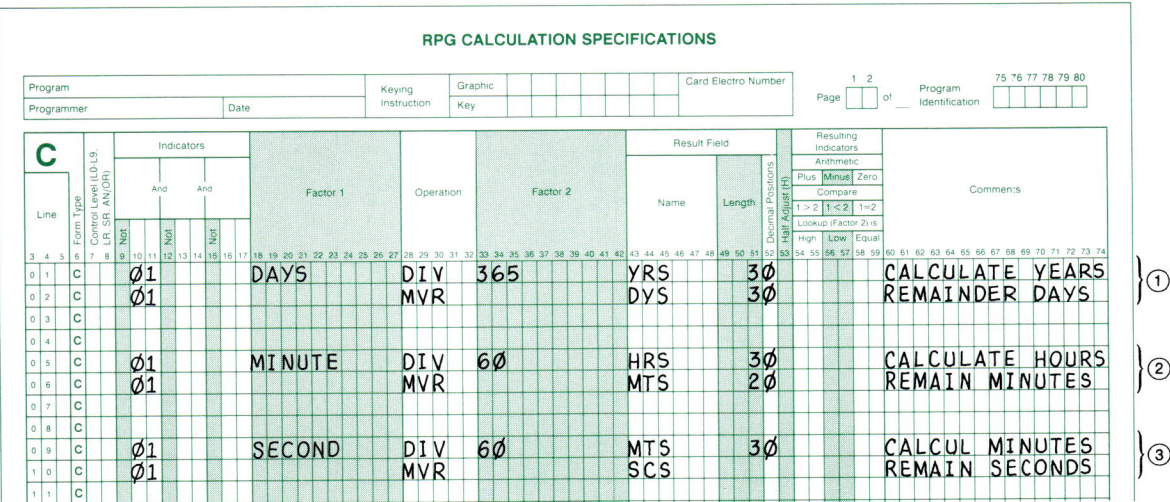

Notes on the Coding

1. Converting days into years and days
2. Converting minutes into hours and minutes
3. Converting seconds into minutes and seconds

Field length (positions 49–51)—length of the result field. Maximum of fifteen for numeric fields. If it is a new field, RPG must know its length. The field must be large enough for all calculations to be performed. The Printer Spacing Chart will aid in defining this field.

Decimal positions (position 52)—number of positions to the right of the decimal point in the result field. Since these are arithmetic operations, the fields will be numeric and must have an entry in this position.

Half-adjust (position 53)—enter *H* if the result field is to be rounded.

Resulting indicators (positions 54–59)—assigned to a result field. If an indicator is coded in these positions with an arithmetic operation, then RPG will test if the result field is plus, minus, or zero after the operation. (See Figure 3.15.)

Calculations 91

Figure 3.15   Arithmetic operations—example

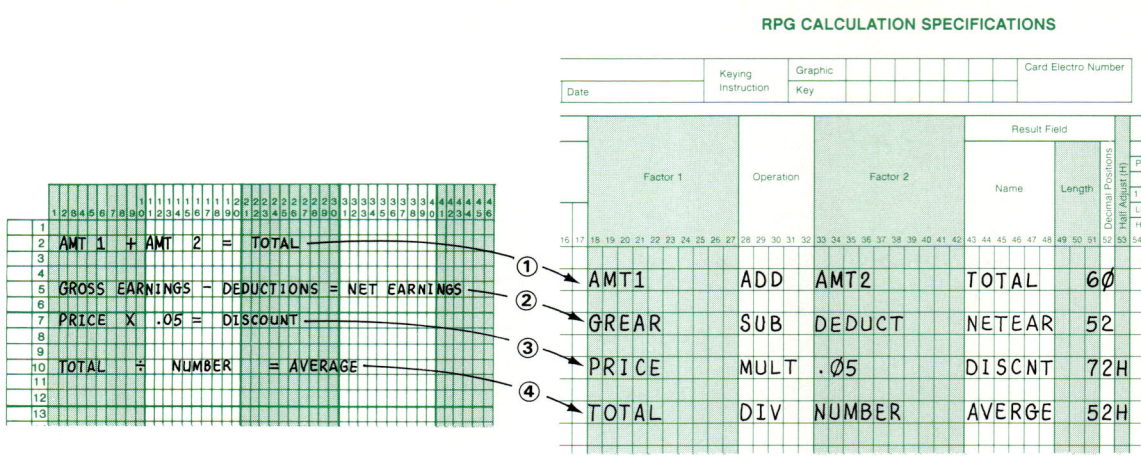

① Add (ADD)
This operation causes Factor 2 to be added to Factor 1. The sum is placed in the Result Field Factor 1 and Factor 2 are not changed by the operation.

② Subtract (SUB)
This operation causes Factor 2 to be subtracted from Factor 1. The difference is placed in the Result Field Factor 1 and Factor 2 are not changed by the operation.

③ Multiply (MULT)
This operation causes Factor 1 to be multiplied by Factor 2. The product is then placed in the Result Field Factor 1 and Factor 2 are not changed. When you use (as a factor) a field which is described as a Result Field, you must be sure the Result Field is large enough to hold the product.

④ Divide (DIV)
This operation causes Factor 1 to be divided by Factor 2. The quotient is placed in the Result Field Factor 1 and Factor 2 are not changed. Division by zero is invalid.

Calculation Notes

Arithmetic operations can be performed only on numeric fields or constants. The result field must also be numeric. The following is true for arithmetic operations in which all three fields are used:

1. Factor 1, factor 2, and the result field may all be different fields.
2. Factor 1, factor 2, and the result field may all be the same field.
3. Factor 1 and factor 2 may be the same field but different from the result field.
4. Either factor 1 or factor 2 may be the same as the result field.

The length of any field involved in arithmetic operations cannot exceed fifteen characters. Any data stored in the result field replace the data that was there previously. (See Figure 3.15.)

Compare Operations

In many jobs, it is necessary to know whether a field is greater than, smaller than, or equal to another field. RPG language has an operation code COMP, which allows the programmer to compare fields. The compare operation requires entries in factor 1, operation, factor 2, and resulting indicator fields. (See Figure 3.16.)

When compared, factor 1 and factor 2 can be in one of three relationships:

1. Factor 1 greater than factor 2
2. Factor 1 less than factor 2
3. Factor 1 equal to factor 2

Figure 3.16 Compare operations

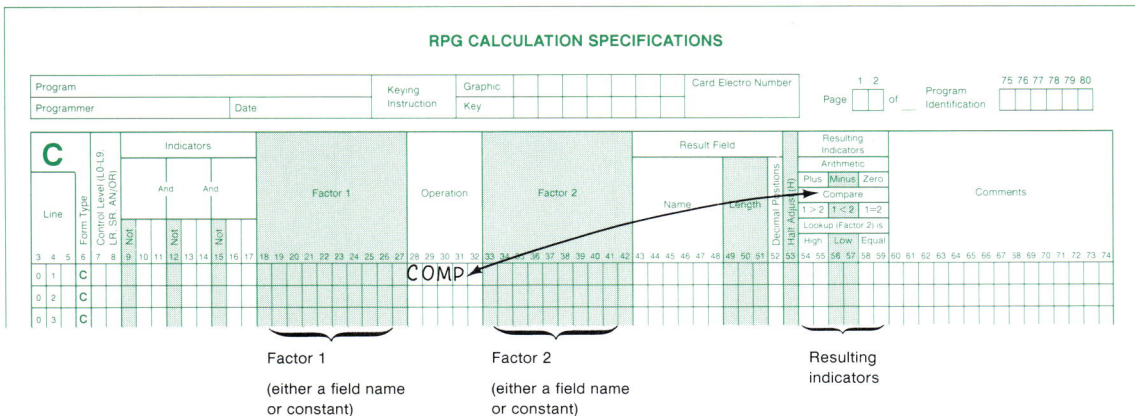

A test should be made to check for one, two, or all three of these relationships by entering indicators in the appropriate positions.

1. Resulting indicator in positions 54–55 turns on the indicator if factor 1 is greater than factor 2
2. Resulting indicator in positions 56–57 turns on the indicator if factor 1 is less than factor 2
3. Resulting indicator in positions 58–59 turns on the indicator if factor 1 is the same as factor 2

The specified test is made each time the COMP operation is executed. However, the resulting indicator is set on only when the proper relationship exists. If indicator 50 is entered in positions 54–55 to test whether factor 1 is greater than factor 2, indicator 50 can be set only when factor 1 is greater than factor 2. If the relationship does not exist, the indicator is set off.

When testing for more than one condition, the same or different indicators in these positions may be used. If a different operation is to be done for each of the three conditions, enter a different resulting condition to test for each condition on the Calculation Specifications form.

If the same operation is desired when either one of two conditions exists (factor 1 is greater than factor 2 or factor 1 equals factor 2), the same indicator can be used to test for both conditions on the Calculation Specifications form.

Numeric constants must be used in arithmetic calculation operations. In a COMP operation, however, constants can be either alphameric or numeric. Rules for using alphameric constants as factor 1 or factor 2 are a little different from those for using numeric constants.

Rules for Numeric Constants
1. A numeric constant can be any combination of the digits 0–9. Decimal points and signs can also be included.
2. The maximum length of a numeric constant is ten characters, including sign and decimal point.
3. Numeric constants must not be enclosed in apostrophes (').

Rules for Alphameric Constants
1. An alphameric constant can be any combination of characters (letters, digits, and special characters). Blanks are also valid.
2. The maximum length of an alphameric constant is eight characters.
3. Alphameric constants must be enclosed in apostrophes (').

When the COMP operation codes are used, numeric fields or constants, or alphameric fields or constants, can be compared to an alphameric field or constant. (See Figures 3.17, 3.18, and 3.19.)

Figure 3.17 Compare operations—example

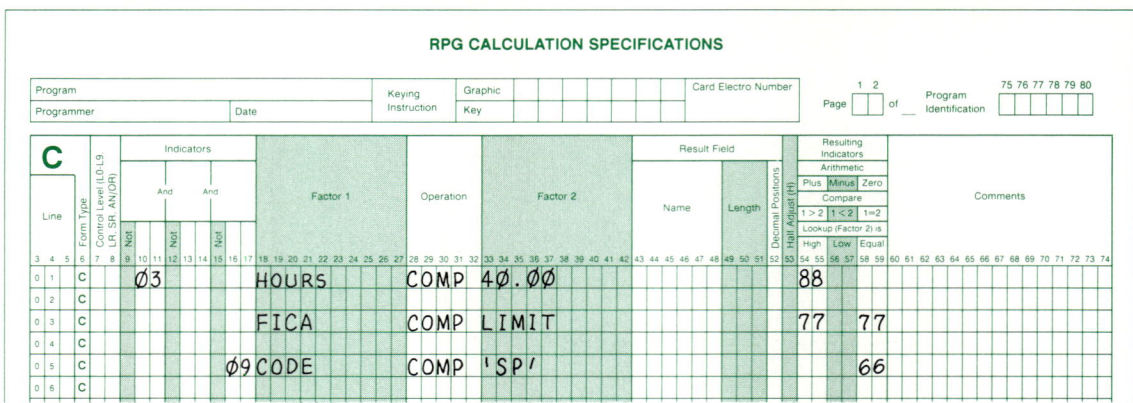

Notes on the Coding

Line 01: The 03 could have been in any one of the three positions without affecting the operation. If 03 is not on, the operation is not performed. Note that the decimal point is in the constant, so we will compare to 40.00 not 4000.

Line 03: Since there were no conditions, there are no entries in columns 9 to 17. The 03 above it has no effect; it is only conditioning the first comparison.

Line 05: The **'SP'** was an alphameric constant, so it must be enclosed in quotation marks. Again, the 09 could have been coded in any one of the three positions (10-11, 13-14, or 16-17).

Figure 3.18 Compare operation—example

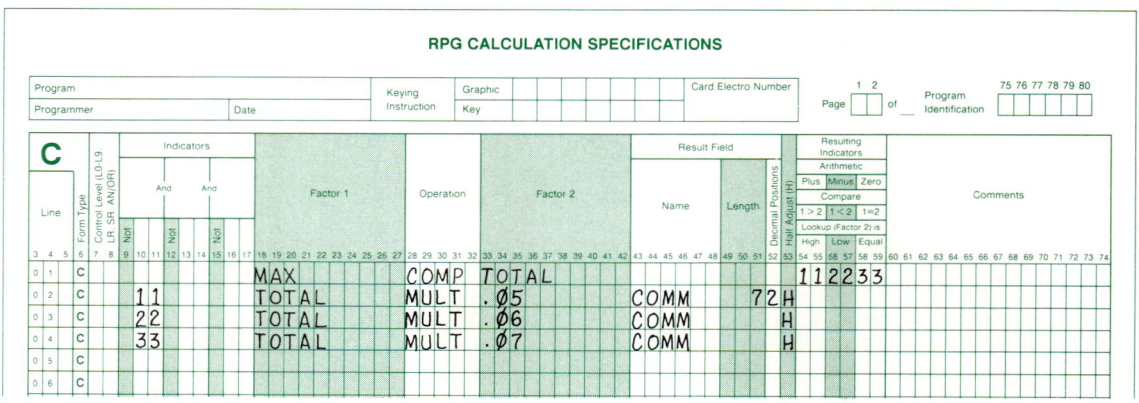

Notes on the Coding

In this operation, the contents of the field **MAX** is compared to the contents of the field **TOTAL**. If **MAX** is greater than **TOTAL**, indicator 11 is set on and the operation on line 02 is done. If **MAX** is less than **TOTAL**, indicator 22 is set on and the operation on line 03 is done. If **MAX** is equal to **TOTAL**, indicator 33 is set on and the operation on line 04 is done. Only the resulting indicator for the condition that is true is set on. The other resulting indicators are set off.

Coding Compare Operations—Summary

In processing the records from a file, decisions may have to be made about the value of certain fields. The compare operation COMP allows the comparison of one field against another field or against a constant.

The following are the rules for coding the COMP operation:

Indicators (positions 9–17)—must have been previously assigned and control when an operation is to be performed.

Figure 3.19 Compare operation—example

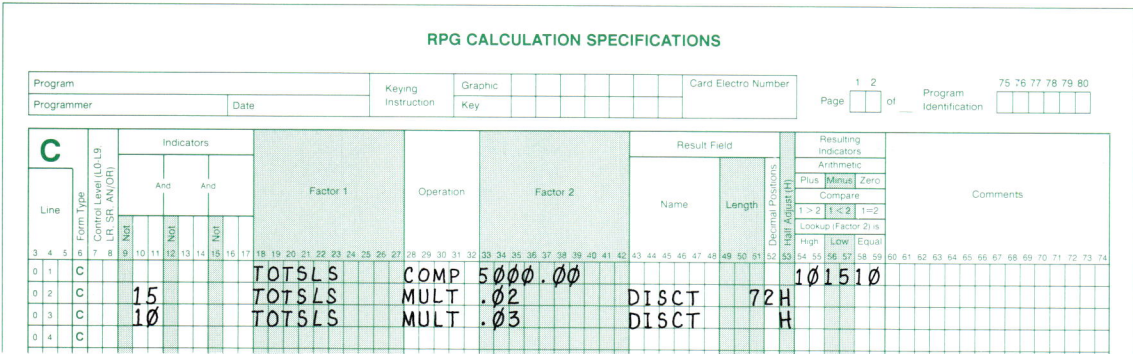

Notes on the Coding

These operations are used for finding the amount of discount to give customers. A customer who purchases goods worth $5000.00 or more receives a 3 percent discount, but one who purchases goods worth less than $5000.00 receives only a 2 percent discount. **TOTSLS** is first compared to $5000.00. If **TOTSLS** is less than $5000.00, indicator 15 is set on and the operations on line 02 are performed (2 percent discount is calculated). However, if **TOTSLS** is either equal to or greater than $5000.00, indicator 10 set on and the operation on line 03 is performed (3 percent discount is calculated).

Factor 1 (positions 18–27)—can be any previously defined field name; a numeric or alphabetic literal. Alphabetic literals are enclosed in apostrophes. All entries must be left-justified.

Operation (positions 28–32)—COMP must be left-justified. Compares factor 1 with factor 2.

Factor 2 (positions 33–42)—same as factor 1.

Resulting indicators—high (positions 54–55)—turned on if factor 1 is greater than factor 2.

Resulting indicators—low (positions 56–57)—turned on if factor 1 is less than factor 2.

Resulting indicators—equal (positions 58–59)—turned on if factor 1 equals factor 2. (See Figure 3.20.)

Figure 3.20 Compare operations—summary

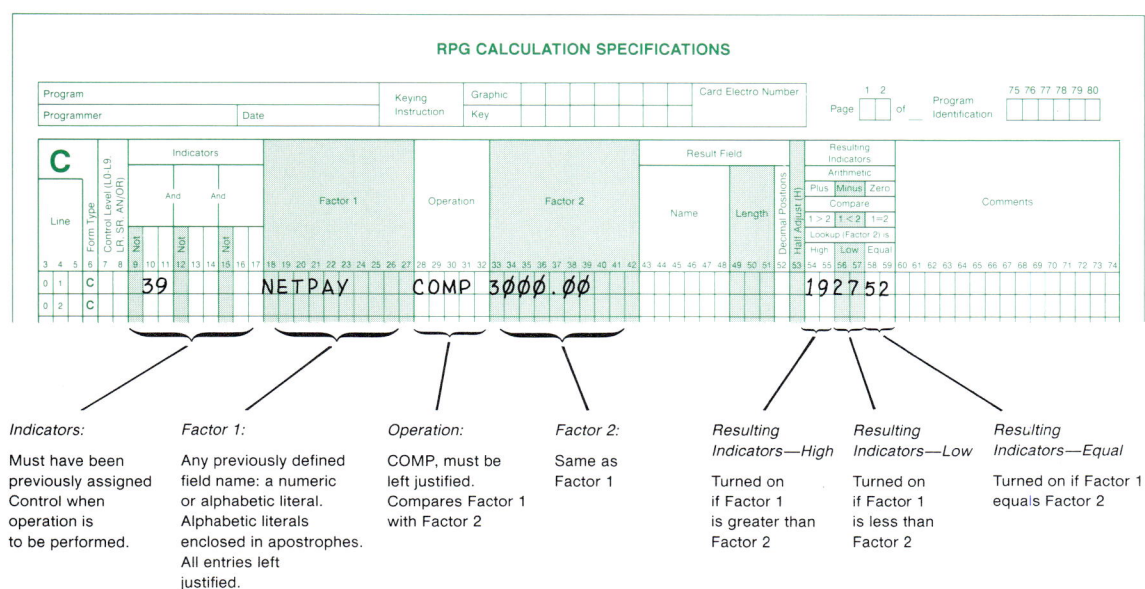

Calculations   95

Figure 3.21 Assignment and use of indicators

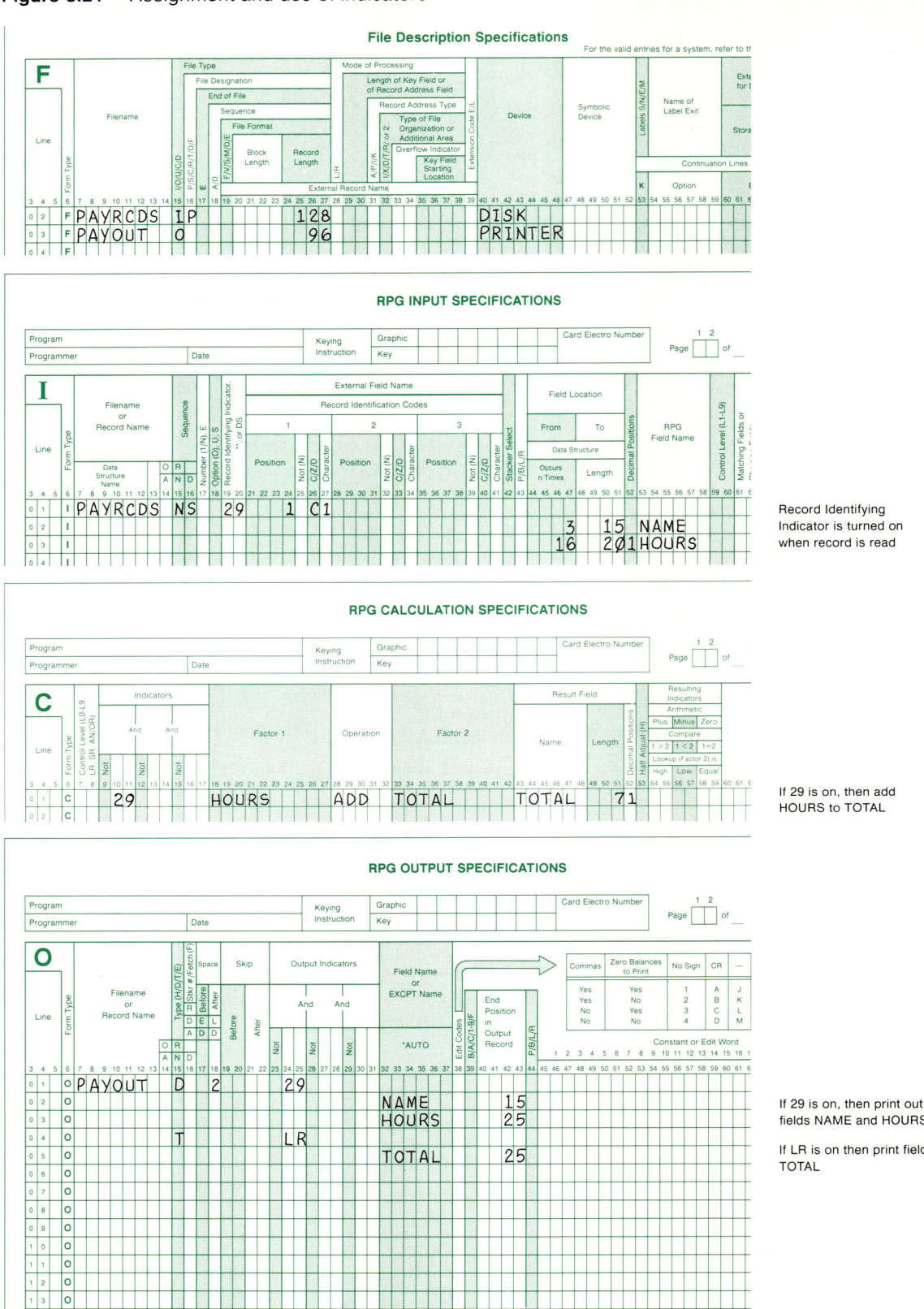

Using Indicators to Control Calculations and Output

On the Calculation and Output Specifications forms, all the calculations and outputs to be done on the job are described. Sometimes all calculations and output operations must be performed on every program cycle. More often, however, the operations are to be performed only when a certain record is read or if a certain condition exists as a result of a calculation. (See Figure 3.21.)

In positions 7–17 (indicators) of the Calculation Specifications form and positions 23–31 (output indicators) of the Output Specifications form, conditions are specified when certain calculations and output operations are to be done.

Resulting Indicators (01–99)

Sometimes the decision to do a certain operation is based on the result of a previous operation. Resulting indicators are turned on based upon the result of a calculation operation. Any operation that is dependent upon the result of the calculation can be conditioned by a resulting indicator. Resulting indicators tell which operations are to be done and under what conditions they are to be done. (See Figures 3.22 and 3.23.) Resulting indicators can be used to determine such things as whether a result is larger, smaller, or equal to a predetermined number and whether a certain result is plus, minus, or zero.

Resulting indicators may be turned on or off at either detail or total calculation time. An indicator that is set as a result of the calculation operation retains this setting until the next time a calculation is done for which the same indicator is a resulting indicator and the condition is not satisfied. (See Figure 3.24.)

A resulting indicator may change status in the same cycle. This happens when a single indicator is assigned to signal the result of both a total and a detail calculation. The total calculation could turn it off and the detail calculation could turn it on, or vice versa.

Figure 3.22 Resulting indicator—usage

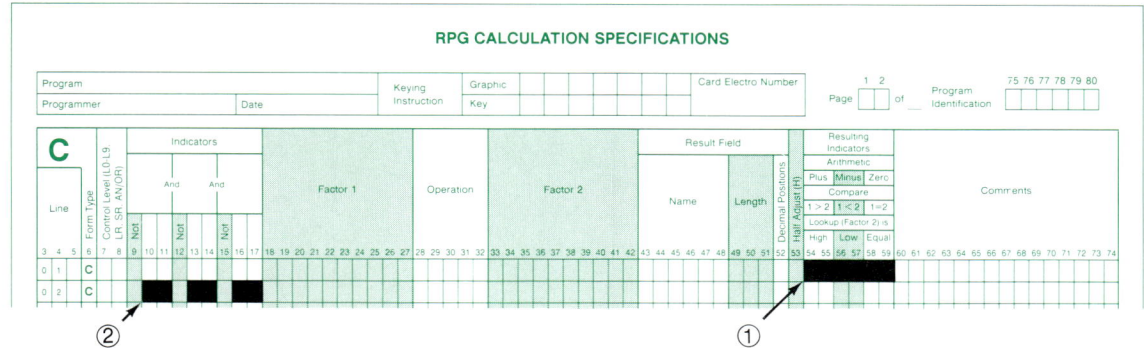

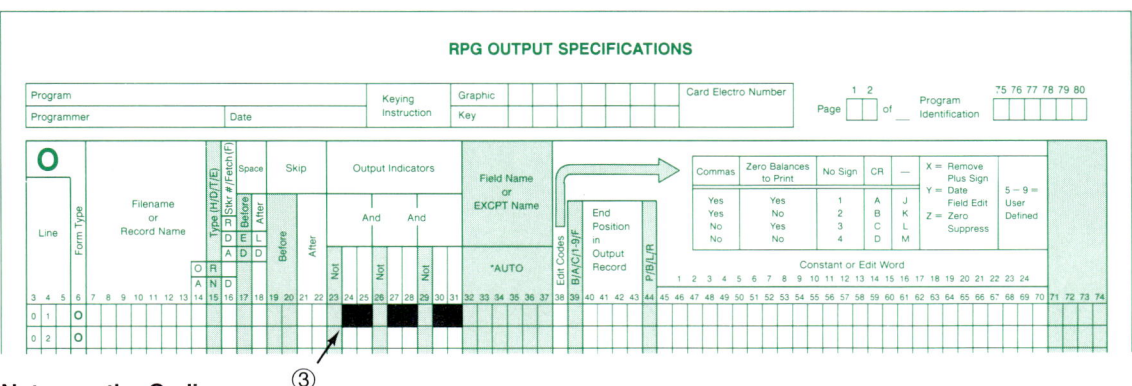

Notes on the Coding

Resulting indicators are assigned at (1), then used to condition calculation operations at (2) and output operations at (3).

Calculations 97

Figure 3.23 Resulting indicator—example

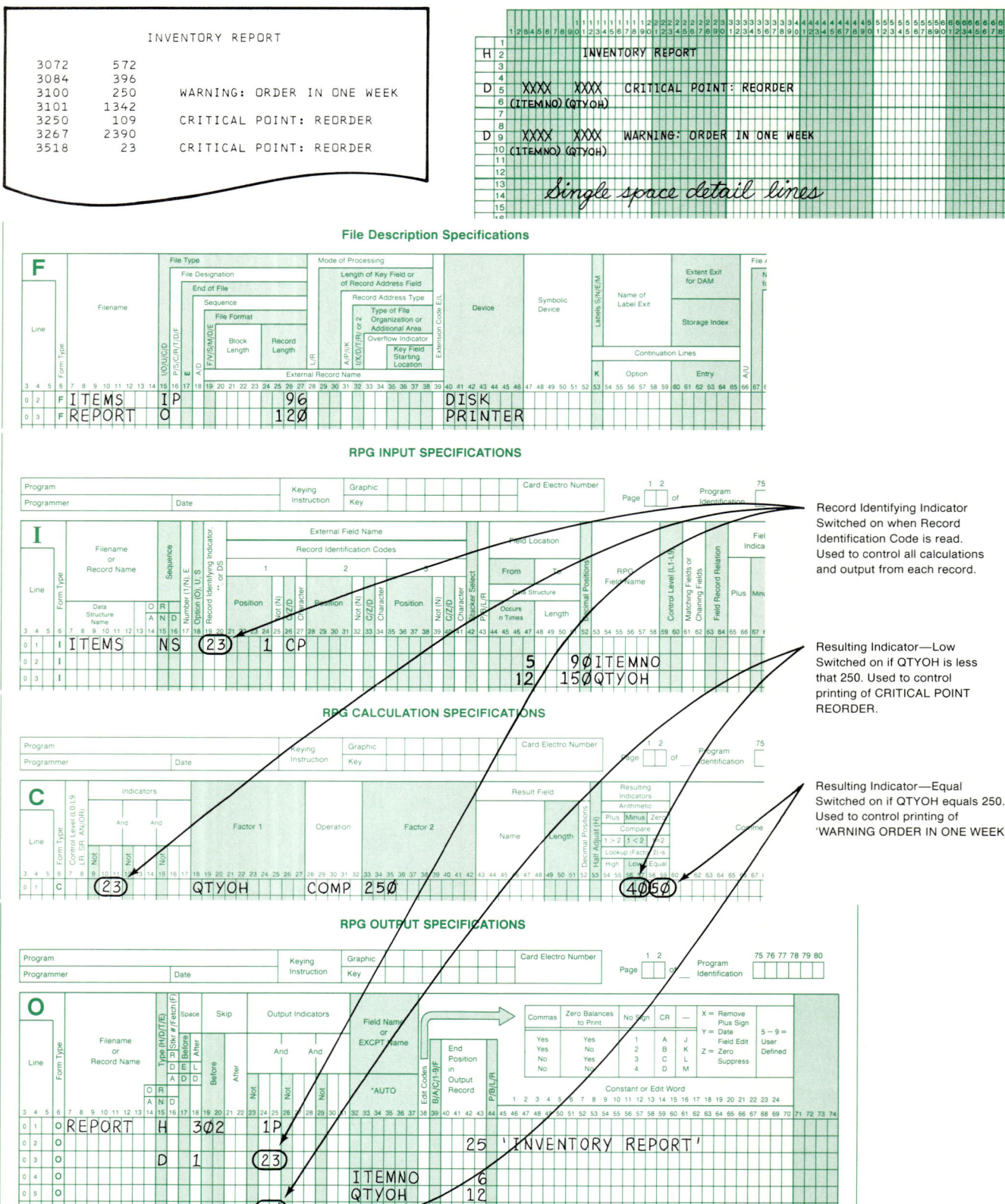

98 RPG II and RPG III Programming

Figure 3.24 Resulting indicator specifications

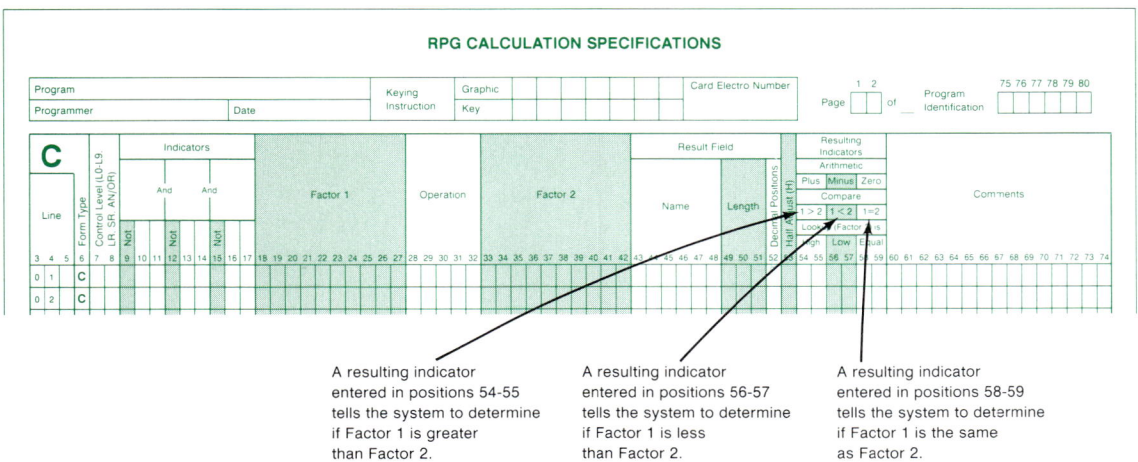

The use of resulting indicators can be demonstrated using the example of an inventory job that determines whether an item needs to be reordered. After inventory is taken, the quantity on hand is reordered for each item below a certain level. If the quantity on hand is 100 or less, reorder should be immediate. If the quantity is more than 100, the item need not be reordered at this time. A list of all items is printed. All items to be reordered are indicated with a double asterisk.

A programmer may use the SETON or SETOF commands to turn indicators ON or OFF, as with resulting indicators. (See Figures 3.25 and 3.26.) Settings change only when a calculation or compare operation is performed or when indicators are set off intentionally. For example, if a resulting indicator is set on by a detail calculation, it retains this setting until either the next time it is used as a resulting indicator or it is intentionally set off.

RPG Specifications

The type of operation used to check the result field depends on the type of result being checked. If the programmer wishes to determine whether the result field is larger, smaller, or equal to a certain number, a compare (COMP) operation must be used. If the programmer wants to determine whether the result field is plus, minus, or zero, an arithmetic operation (ADD, SUB, MULT, or DIV) must be used. Resulting indicators 01–99 can be specified on the Calculation Specifications form.

Figure 3.25 Setting indicators

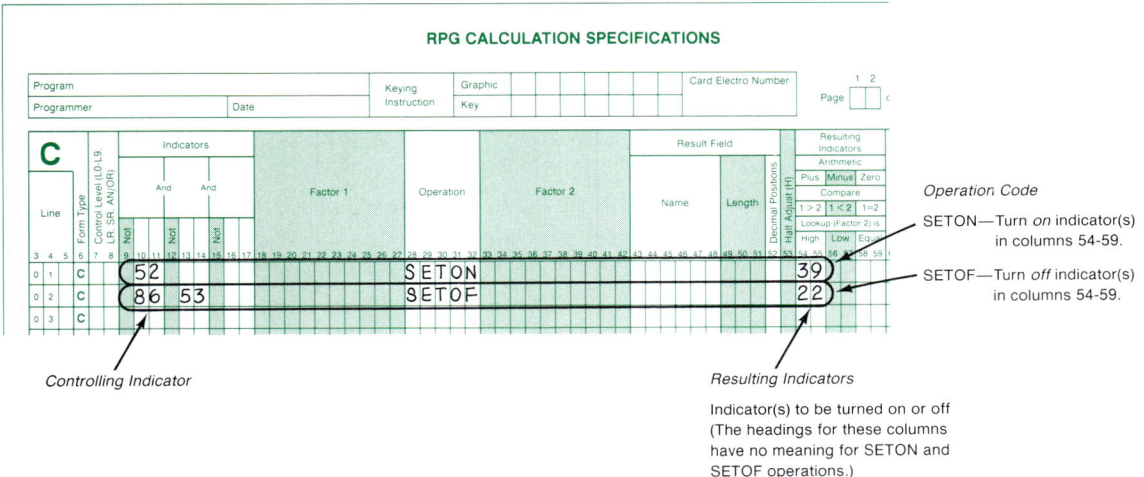

Calculations 99

Figure 3.26 Use of SETON to replace indicators

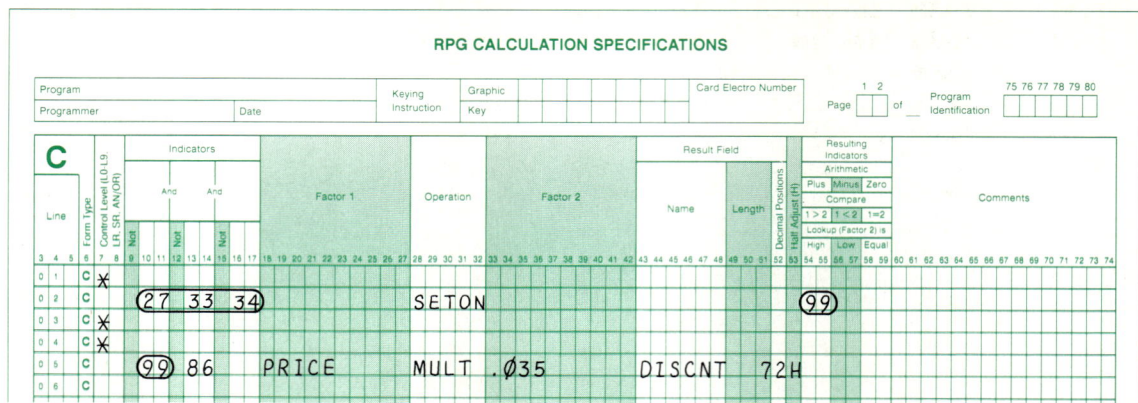

This calculation: PRICE × .035 = DISCOUNT is to be performed when these indicator conditions exist: 27 and 33 and 34 and 86.

Procedure:

1. Replace three indicators with one new one.
2. Use the new indicator in an AND relationship with the fourth to control the calculation.

Resulting indicators and record identifying indicators are used in the same way to condition calculation and output specifications. The same entry should not be used as both a resulting indicator and a record identifying indicator. (See Figure 3.27.)

Last Record Indicator (LR)

The **last record indicator** (LR) is associated with end-of-job procedures. The program tests LR to indicate that the last data record has been read and that end-of-job processing is to take place. (See Figure 3.28.)

The last record indicator is a little different from other indicators. When the end-of-file record is read, the LR indicator is turned on (if an *E* was specified for that particular input file on the File Description form, if more than one input file was used). Since the end-of-file record has no data in it, detail operations need not be performed. RPG logic is set up so that total operations, not detail operations, are done when LR is on. The program ends at that point.

When the last record indicator is turned on, all control level indicators are turned on also. Thus, the total operations, conditioned by L1–L9 and LR, are performed on both calculations and output.

Use of the last record indicator is optional. When LR is not used in specifications, the computer automatically supplies end-of-job instructions. If the LR indicator is used, certain operations are indicated, such as printing a total count of all records.

Program Cycle Operations

Each data file should have an end-of-file record; RPG is set to sense an end-of-file record containing identifying information indicating the end of the data file.

When a record is read, the program checks to see if all the records in a file have been processed. If all records in all files have been processed, the program sets on all control level indicators L1–L9. (Control level indicators L1–L9 are explained in chapter 4.) The program also sets on the LR indicator to indicate that all records have been processed. All total operations (those conditioned by LR and L1–L9) are performed. After total operations have been done, the program checks to see if LR is on. If it is, processing stops. (See Figure 3.29.)

Figure 3.27 Inventory job specifications using resulting indicators

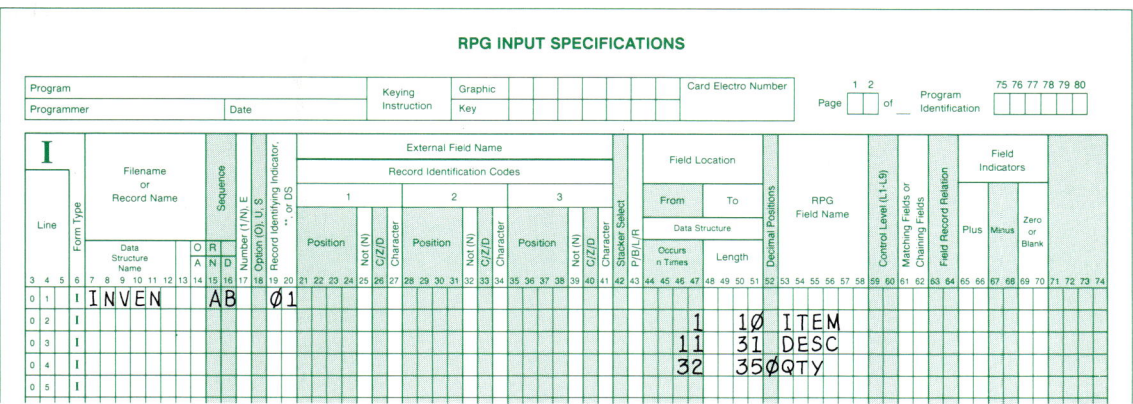

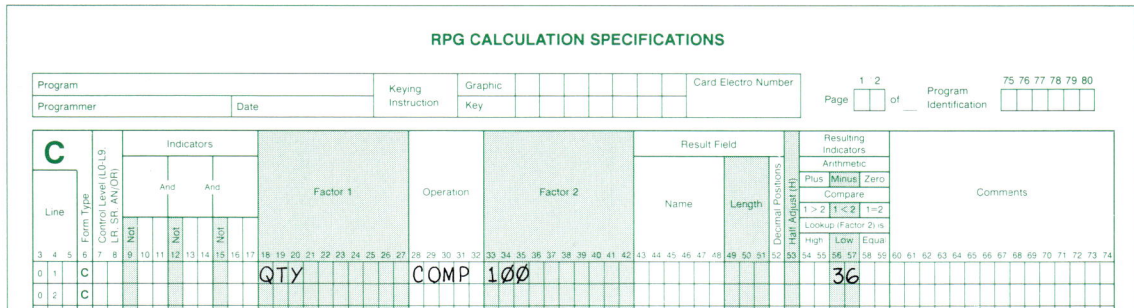

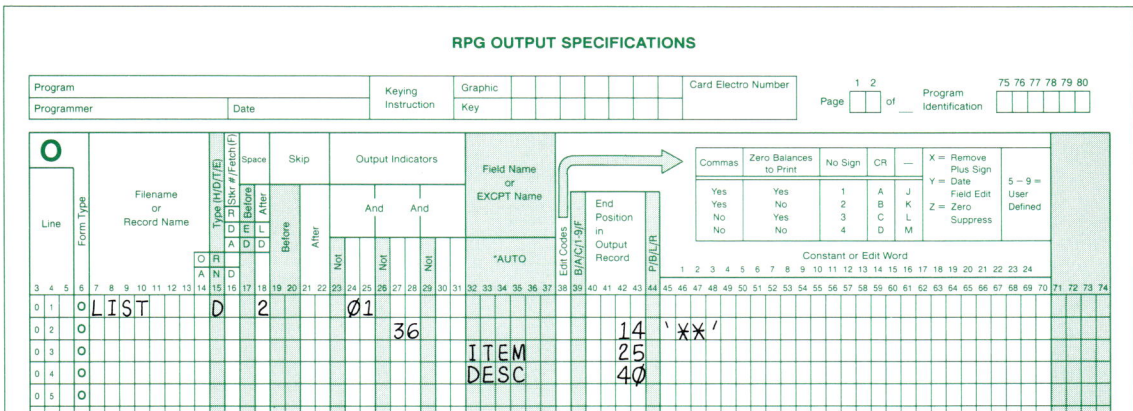

Notes on the Coding

The use of resulting indicators is demonstrated by an inventory job that determines whether an item needs to be reordered. After inventory is taken, the quality on hand is recorded for each item. If the quantity on hand is 100 or less, reorder should be immediate. If the quantity on hand is over 100, the item need not be reordered at this time. A list of all items is printed. All items to be reordered are indicated with a double asterisk. The program above shows the specifications for the job. Use these specifications to help you follow the program cycle that follows.

Calculations 101

Figure 3.28 Last record (LR) indicator specification

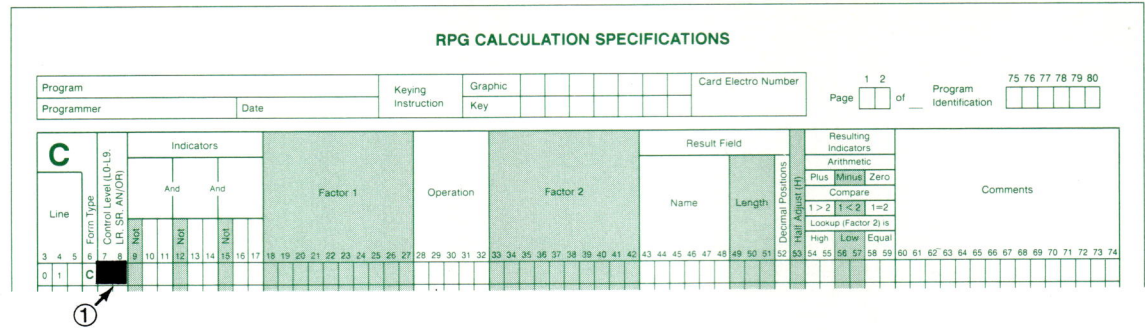

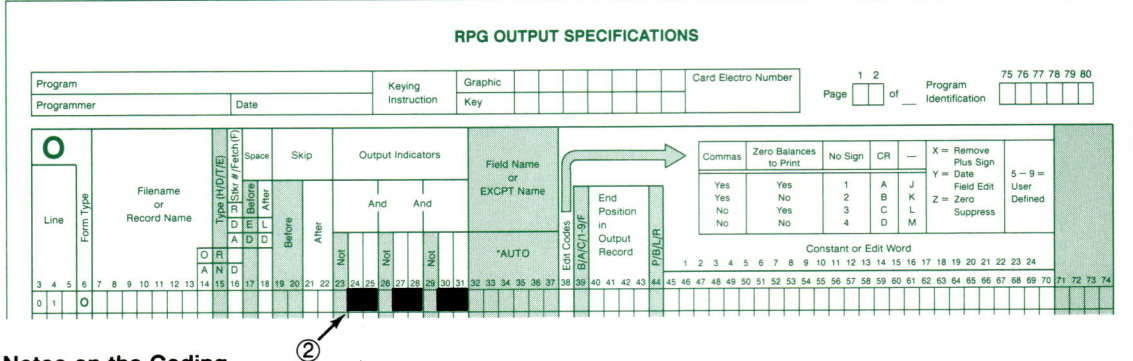

Notes on the Coding

The LR indicator is specified at (1) to tell the system which calculations are to be done after the last record is processed. The LR indicator is specified at (2) to tell the system which output operations are to be done after the last record is processed.

Figure 3.29 Total lines conditioned by LR

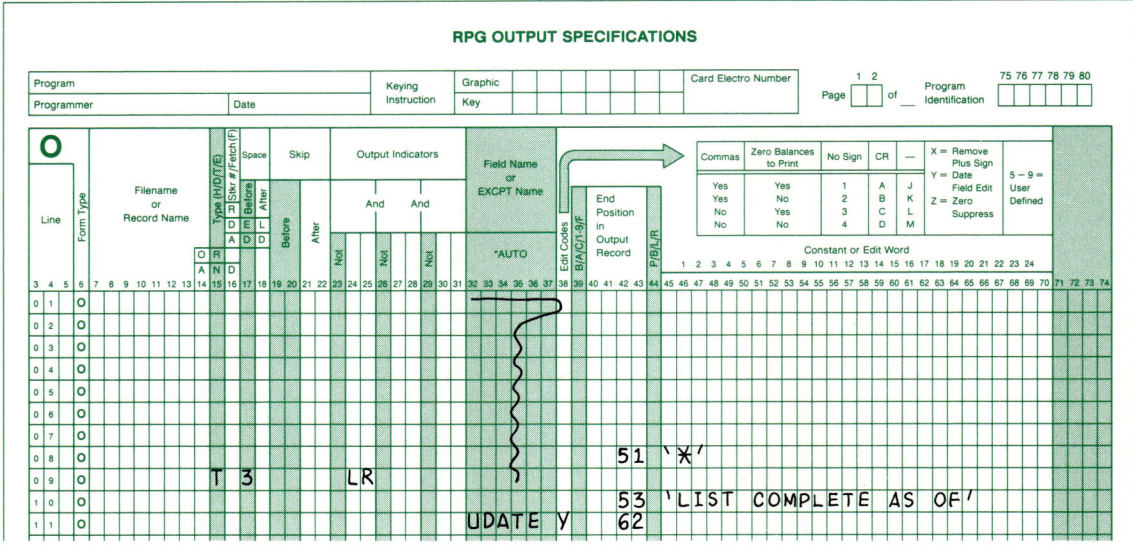

Notes on the Coding

A last record (LR) indicator can be used to condition all operations done at the end of the job. These usually include the calculating of totals for all records and/or writing summary information. Suppose the group printing job that found total charges for each customer required the statement List Complete as of (date job was run). Since this is to print out after all records have been processed, it is conditioned by LR. The following Output Specifications show the conditioned output message followed by the program cycle illustrating the LR indicator.

102   RPG II and RPG III Programming

Figure 3.29 continued

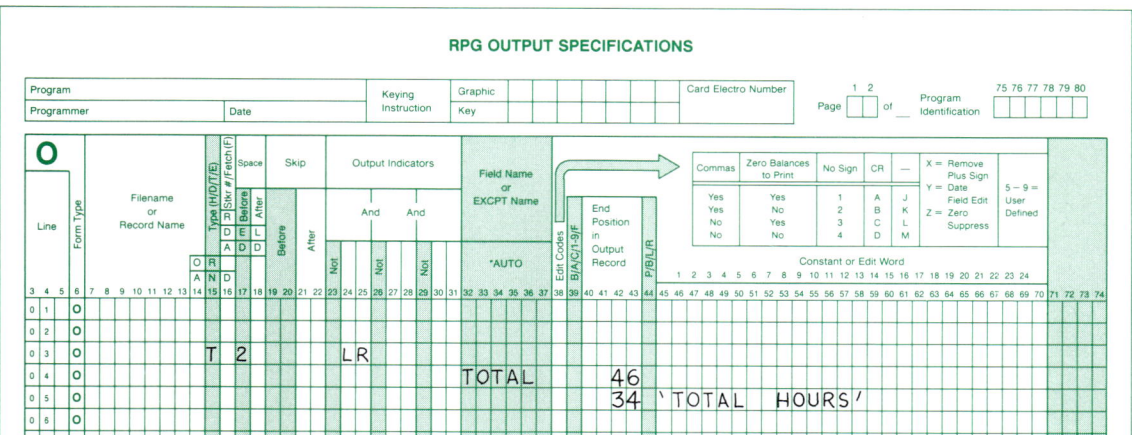

Notes on the Coding

The field TOTAL and the constant TOTAL HOURS will print when the LR indicator is on. This indicator will only be on after the detail records are all read so that the total will be available when it is needed.

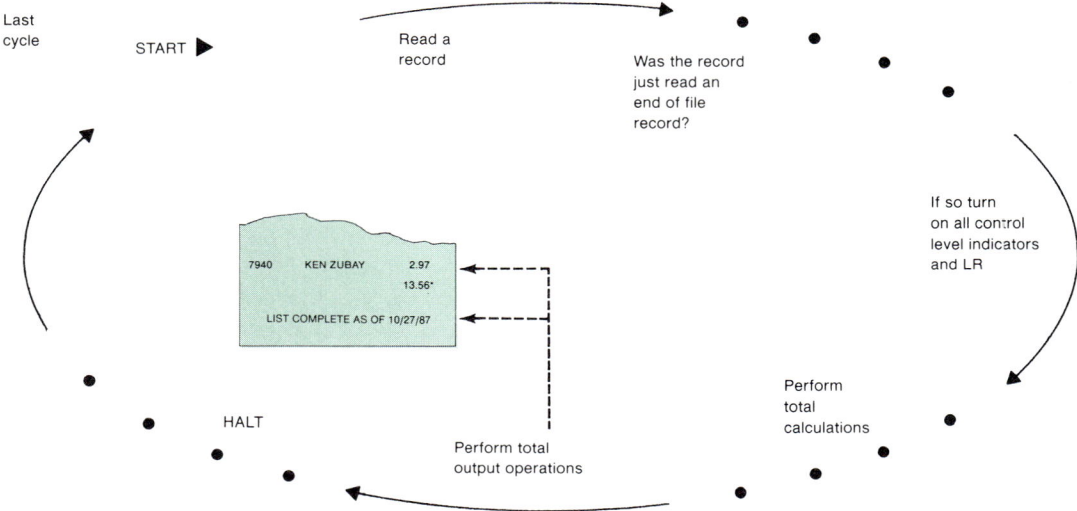

RPG Specifications

The LR indicator is specified with an LR on the calculation specifications or output specifications. This entry specifies which operations are to be done after the last record is processed.

The LR indicator can cause final totals to be printed at the end of a report. The printing of the final totals or any other data at the end of the report is controlled by the LR indicator. The value of the field, however, accumulates at every detail time—every time the record identifying indicator is on. This is an important part of working with indicators. One indicator may be used to do the job of accumulating and another to control the output of the total. Constants can also be printed on the total cycle. (See Figures 3.29 and 3.30.)

Calculations   103

Figure 3.30 Indicator summary

INDICATOR	ASSIGNED	TURNED on BY	TURNED off BY	USAGE
RII	Input	Conditions of codes in the record	RPG at the end of the cycle	Detail Processing detail output
1P	In the cycle	RPG	RPG at the end of cycle	First page headings
LR	In the cycle	After the last record has been processed	End of job	Last record processing and output
Resulting	Calculation (Compare) (Arithmetic)	Conditions met High, low, equal plus, minus	The next test	Calculations Output records or fields

Editing

RPG provides the flexibility required for printing a variety of reports. It allows the programmer to specify how a printed field is to be punctuated. Editing, as this type of punctuation is called, can be specified on the Output Specifications form in two ways—by means of edit codes and edit words.

Edit Codes

Potentially, all numeric data fields could need commas, decimal points, or credit symbols. Numeric fields are read in unedited (without commas or decimal points) and contain only a definition of the number of decimal positions assigned on the input or calculation specifications. Thus the field must be edited to be more readable when printed.

The Output Specifications form has the edit codes printed on it in the form of a table. It consists of three main parts: a description of the type of editing required, the edit code to use, and three special edit codes. (See Figure 3.31.)

In choosing an edit code, the table is used to assess the requirements of the job, asking such questions as: Should commas be printed? Should zero balances be printed? Is the field negative? If so, what sign should be printed? After these questions are answered, the appropriate edit code is selected.

Figure 3.31 Edit codes

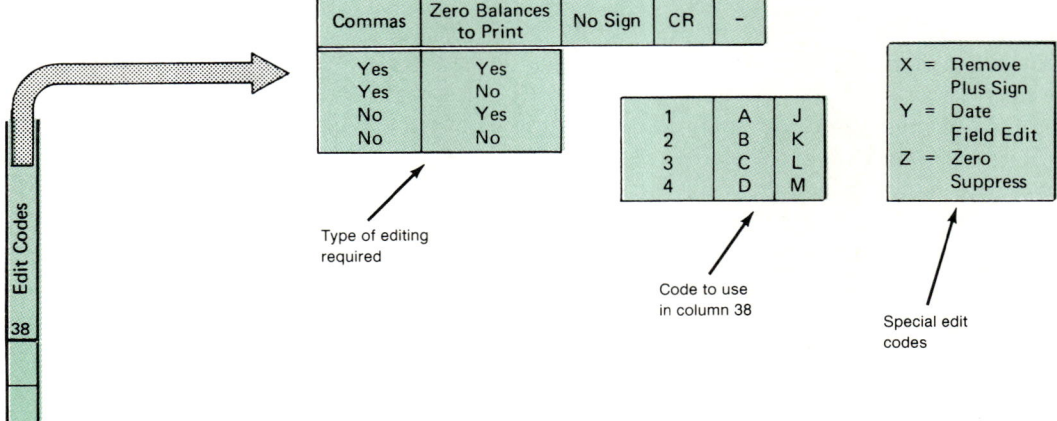

104   RPG II and RPG III Programming

Figure 3.32 Edit codes

Edit Code	Commas	Decimal Point	Sign For Negative Balance			Zero Suppress	Print Out On Zero Balance
			No Sign	CR	– (Minus)		
1	Yes	Yes	No Sign			Yes	.00 or 0
2	Yes	Yes	No Sign			Yes	Blanks
3		Yes	No Sign			Yes	.00 or 0
4		Yes	No Sign			Yes	Blanks
A	Yes	Yes		CR		Yes	.00 or 0
B	Yes	Yes		CR		Yes	Blanks
C		Yes		CR		Yes	.00 or 0
D		Yes		CR		Yes	Blanks
J	Yes	Yes			–	Yes	.00 or 0
K	Yes	Yes			–	Yes	Blanks
L		Yes			–	Yes	.00 or 0
M		Yes			–	Yes	Blanks
X[1]							
Y[2]						Yes	
Z[3]						Yes	

[1] The X code removes the plus sign of the field.
[2] The Y code is used for date fields. It suppresses only the leftmost zero and puts slashes in a three to six digit field according to the following pattern:
   nn/n
   nn/nn
   nn/nn/n
   nn/nn/nn
[3] The Z code removes signs and suppresses zeros.

Note: The edit codes shown in the first column are used in position 38 of the Output Specifications form to punctuate the field named on the same line. Only numeric fields can be edited. The decimal point is automatically inserted in the correct position.

The two basic coding rules of editing are that the field to be punctuated be defined as numeric and that the edit code be entered on the same line as the field in position 38.

The correct edit code can be determined by analyzing the Printer Spacing Chart requirements and asking the following questions (see Figure 3.32):

Are commas to be printed if the field is greater than three whole numbers?

If the field to be edited is zero, is .00 to print?

If the value of a field is negative, which symbol should print—none, CR, or –?

On the basis of the answers to these three questions, one code is selected and entered in position 38 beside the field to be edited. Each of these codes will automatically suppress the leading zeros and place the decimal point according to any previous definition on Input or Calculation Specifications forms.

Edit Code Z (Zero Suppress)
The Z edit code is used to edit a numeric field with no decimal positions. Z causes leading zeros to be suppressed. It does not insert any punctuation.

Edit Code Y (Date Field Edit)
The Y edit code is used to punctuate date fields according to the number of digits in the data. The Y code will punctuate the date field with slashes between month, day, and year. (See Figures 3.33 and 3.34.)

Figure 3.33 Examples of editing

Edit Codes					
Field length and digits	1769532	02	00	000	041345
Field characteristics	Positive Number—Two Decimal Positions	Negative Number—Two Decimal Positions	Zero—Two Decimal Positions	Zero—No Decimal Positions	Positive Number—Three Decimal Positions
1	17,695.32	.02	.00	0	41.345
2	17,695.32	.02			41.345
3	17695.32	.02	.00	0	41.345
4	17695.32	.02			41.345
A	17,695.32	.02CR	.00	0	41.345
B	17,695.32	.02CR			41.345
C	17695.32	.02CR	.00	0	41.345
D	17695.32	.02CR			41.345
J	17,695.32	.02–	.00	0	41.345
K	17,695.32	.02–			41.345
L	17695.32	.02–	.00	0	41.345
M	17695.32	.02–			41.345
X	1769532	OK	00	000	041345
Y	Must be used with a 3 to 6-digit field.			0/0	4/13/45
Z	1769532	2			41345

Note:

This table shows the effects of editing on five different fields. It illustrates what will be printed by using each edit code on the fields.

Figure 3.34 Edit code—examples

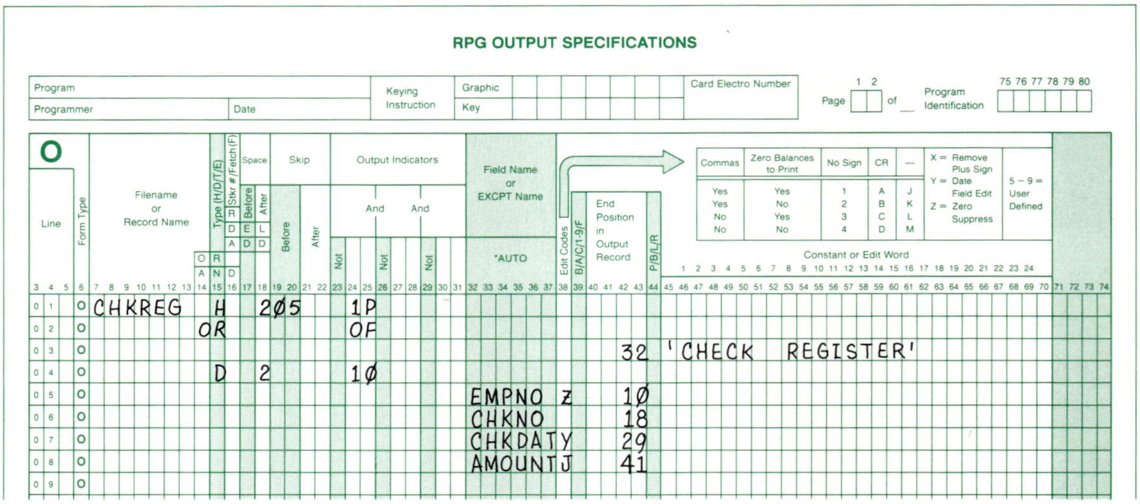

Notes on the Coding

EMPNO will print without leading zeros.

CHKNO is not edited. This means that check number 1 will print 00001 if it is a five-digit field. This is not wrong; it is your preference.

CHKDAT will be edited with slashes between month, day, and year.

AMOUNT will be edited with commas, zero balances will print, and a minus sign will print if the field happens to be negative. The decimal point will be placed according to the field's definition on the Input or Calculation Specifications.

Figure 3.35 Edit word—date—example

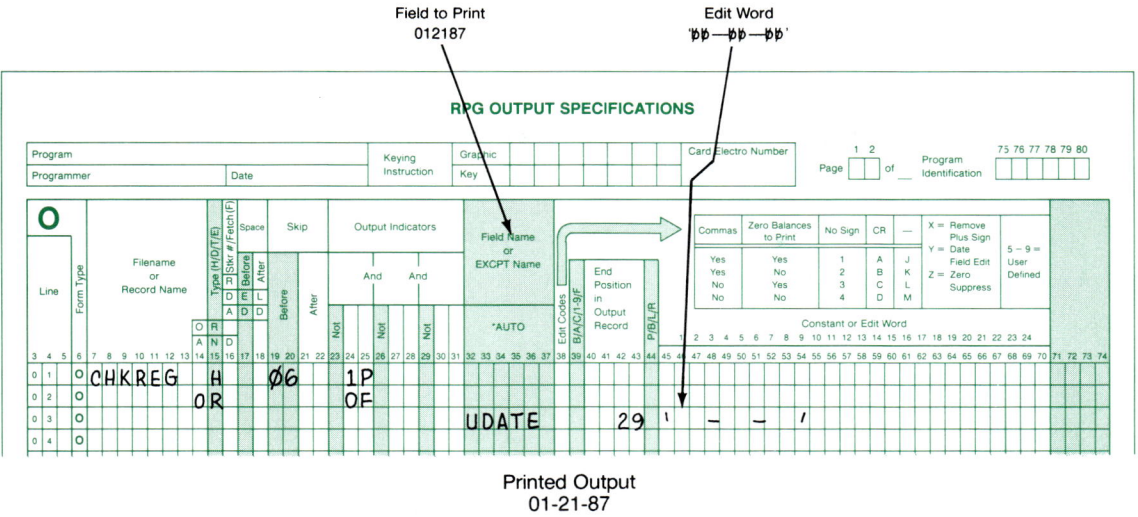

Figure 3.36 Edit words—telephone number and social security number—example

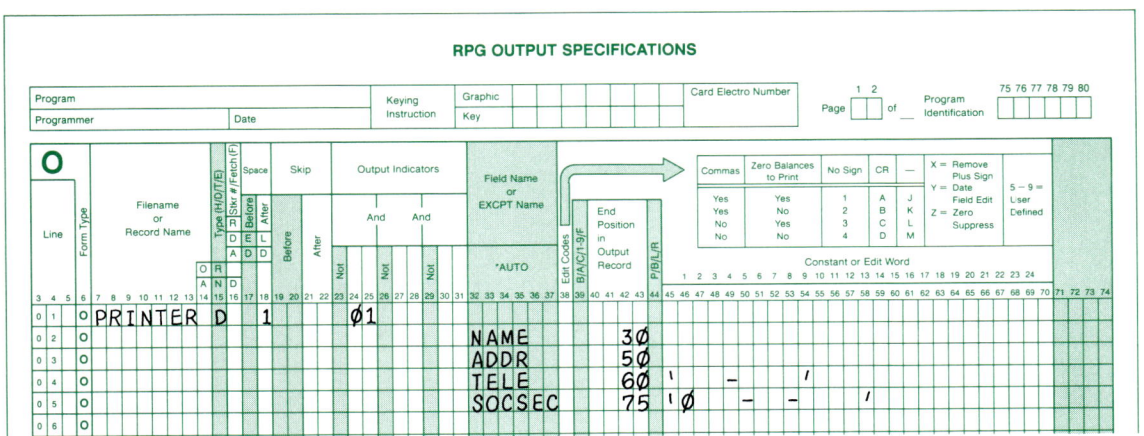

Edit Words

As a general rule, the edit codes will take care of the necessary punctuation of numeric fields. Like most rules, however, there are exceptions. If some special editing is desired, such as the dollar sign or dashes instead of slashes in the date, the edit codes will not do the job. An edit word may then be used. The edit word is coded like a constant, and is enclosed in quotes and on the same line as the field to be edited.

Think of the edit word as a mask with blank spots for the information in the field and characters in place where the editing requires. (See Figures 3.35 and 3.36.) If an edit word is used, an edit code may not be used. It is one or the other; and if the edit code will do the job, it is the one to use. Again, there are exceptions. Two are the floating dollar sign and the asterisk fill.

Floating $

Sometimes a user may want to have a dollar sign ($) appear in front of the first significant digit in a field. Payroll checks are a good case in point. The sign used in such cases is called a **floating dollar sign.** Where it is used, the edit code and the edit word are both used to control the punctuation of the field.

Calculations 107

Figure 3.37 Fixed and floating dollar signs—examples

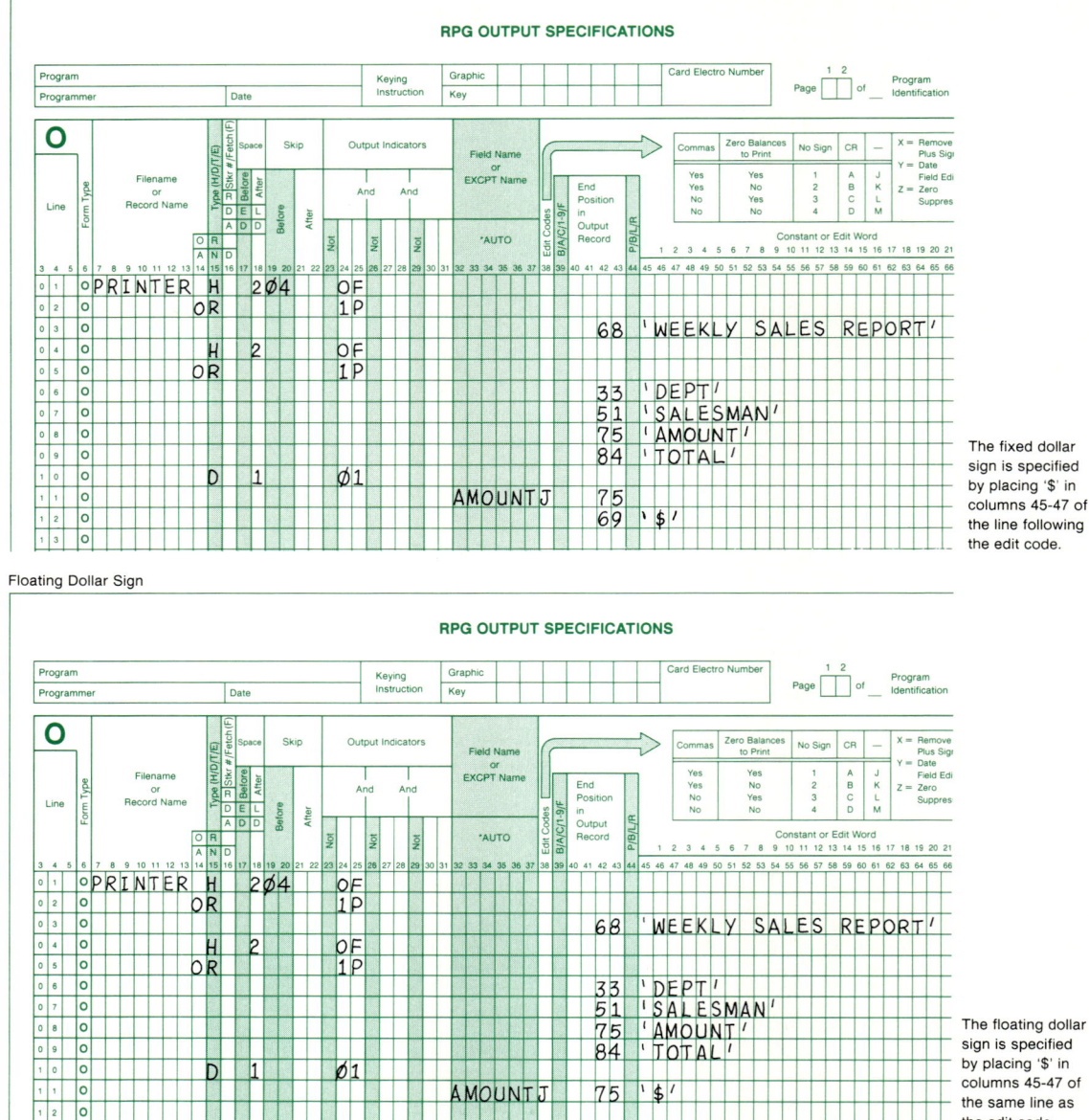

The floating dollar sign ensures that a dollar sign will print just before the first number in the amount as shown in the following:

$12,397.65 $25.00 $347.87

To code the floating dollar sign, a '$' (including the single quotation marks) is entered in positions 45–47 of the same line as the field next to which it is to be printed. (See Figure 3.37.)

Asterisk Fill

The other exception to the use of the edit code and edit word together concerns check protection. Instead of a floating dollar sign, the leading zero positions of the field are filled with asterisks when the field is written. Again, the edit code and edit word appear on the same line of code. An asterisk ('*') enclosed in single quotation marks is entered in positions 45–47 of the line containing the edit code. (See Figures 3.38 and 3.39.)

Figure 3.38 Asterisk fill—example

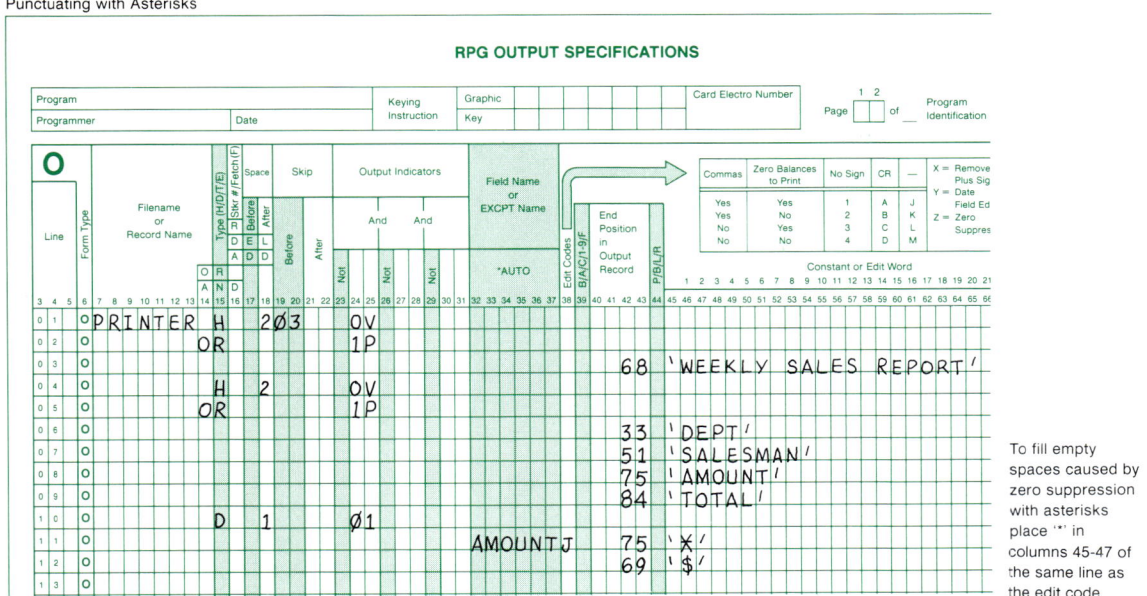

To fill empty spaces caused by zero suppression with asterisks place '*' in columns 45-47 of the same line as the edit code

Figure 3.39 Floating dollar sign and asterisk fill—examples

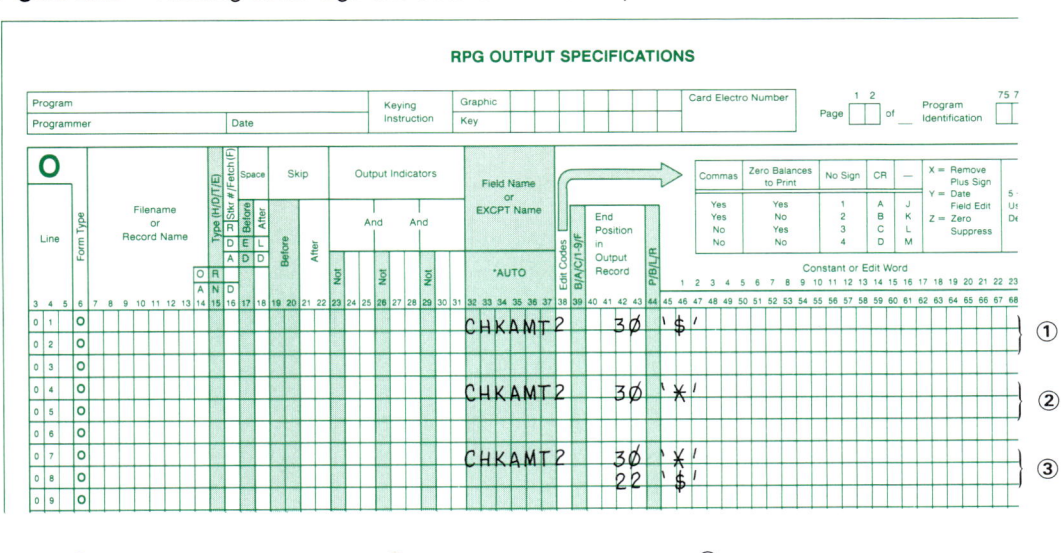

① Using the edit word '$' with an edit code will cause the field CHKAMT to be punctuated and have the $ float in front of the most significant digit. The fields would print as follows.

$4.98
$1,927.00
$88.50

② Using the asterisk fill '*' edit word for the same field will cause the field to be punctuated and have the * fill any leading zeros of the field as follows.

****4.98
1,927.00
***88.50

③ In the last example the same asterisk fill will take place as above. The '$' is not an edit word but is a constant like others you have coded since there is no field on the same line with it. It will print

$****4.98
$1,927.00
$***88.50

Calculations   109

Figure 3.40 Reserved word PAGE—examples

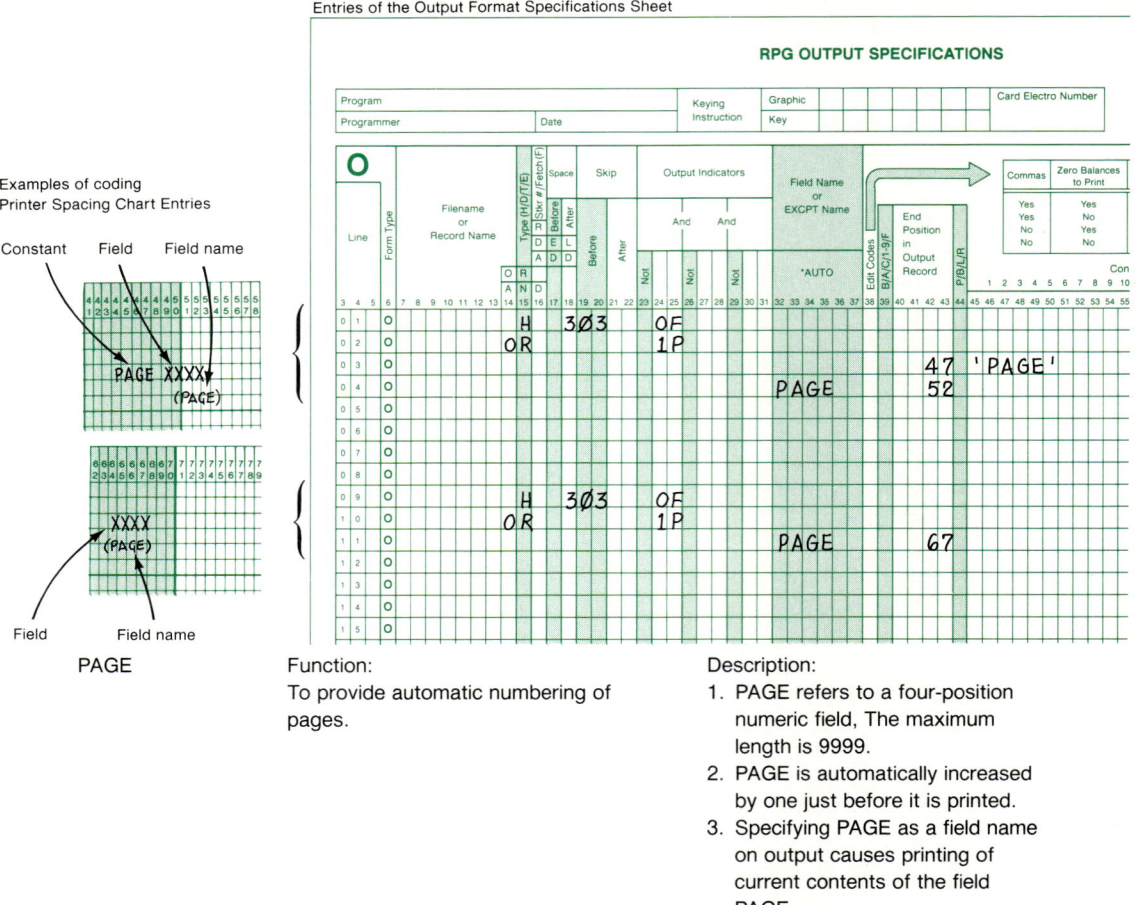

Function:
To provide automatic numbering of pages.

Description:
1. PAGE refers to a four-position numeric field, The maximum length is 9999.
2. PAGE is automatically increased by one just before it is printed.
3. Specifying PAGE as a field name on output causes printing of current contents of the field PAGE.

Reserved Fields

Two special reserved fields enable the user to print the page number and current date on the reports. These two special fields (reserved words) are built into the RPG language. They are coded as fields on the Output Specifications form, but are defined internally by RPG. Since they are reserved fields, they should not be used as field names.

PAGE

The special field name for automatic page numbering is PAGE. Note that the field name PAGE is the reserved word. If the programmer wishes to print the constant 'PAGE' on a report, it is coded in the same manner as any constant. When the actual page number prints, any leading zeros can be suppressed by the use of the Z edit code. (See Figure 3.40.)

The eight possible PAGE entries (PAGE, PAGE1, PAGE2, PAGE3, PAGE4, PAGE5, PAGE6, and PAGE7) may be needed to produce different types of output pages or to number pages for different printer files.

User Date

The user date special words (UDATE, UMONTH, UDAY, UYEAR) allow the programmer to supply a date for the program at execution time. The user date special words access the system date.

UDATE

RPG uses the reserved word UDATE to represent the user's date. This field contains the current date and so allows reports to be dated without reading in a date each time.

UDATE, when specified in positions 32–37 of the output specifications, prints a six-character numeric date field in one of three formats. (The most common of these formats is *mmddyy* using the slash (/) for the edit code Y.)

Use positions 19–20 of the control specifications to specify the date format and the editing to be done. If positions 19–20 are blank, the date format is determined from the content of position 21 (i.e., the program defaults to the month, date, year format and uses "/" as the edit symbol for UDATE unless position 21 contains a *D, I,* or *J* for non-US formats).

		Control Specifications	
Format	**Actual**	**Position 19**	**Position 20**
month/day/year	12/25/86	blank or M	/
year/month/day	86.12.25	Y	.
day/month/year	25 12 86	D	&
month/day/year	11 17 87	blank or M	&
year/month/day	87-11-17	Y	—
day/month/year	17/11/87	D	/

UMONTH, UDAY, UYEAR

UMONTH, UDAY, and UYEAR, when specified in positions 32–37 of the output specifications, print a two-character numeric date field. Use UMONTH to print the month only, UDAY to print the day only, and UYEAR to print the year only.

UDATE can be edited when it is written if Y is specified in position 38 of the output specifications. The control specification entry in position 20 determines the separator character to be inserted (e.g., 12/31/86 or 12.25.86).

UMONTH, UDAY, UYEAR cannot be edited with the Y edit code in position 38 of the output specification.

UDATE, UMONTH, UDAY, and UYEAR can be used as factor 1 or factor 2 of the calculation specifications.

UDATE, UMONTH, UDAY, and UYEAR cannot appear as the result field in a calculation or as an input field.

Blank After (*B* in position 39 of the output specification) cannot be used with UDATE, UMONTH, UDAY, and UYEAR.

If the field itself is six positions long but the Printer Spacing Chart shows punctuation of the field with slashes, the edit code Y should be used to make the date more readable. This type of editing should be written along with the contents of the field UDATE. (See Figure 3.41.)

Notes on Coding PAGE and UDATE

Both reserved words PAGE and UDATE are coded as fields in positions 32–37 of the Output Specifications form.

The Y edit code will punctuate the date field UDATE with slashes between month, day, and year.

The reserved word PAGE may be coded alone or with the constant 'PAGE' depending on the printer spacing requirements. However, each statement must be coded on a separate line. (See Figure 3.41.)

Figure 3.41 Reserved words—UDATE and PAGE—example

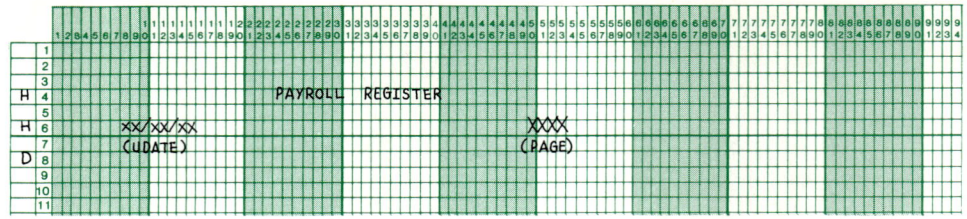

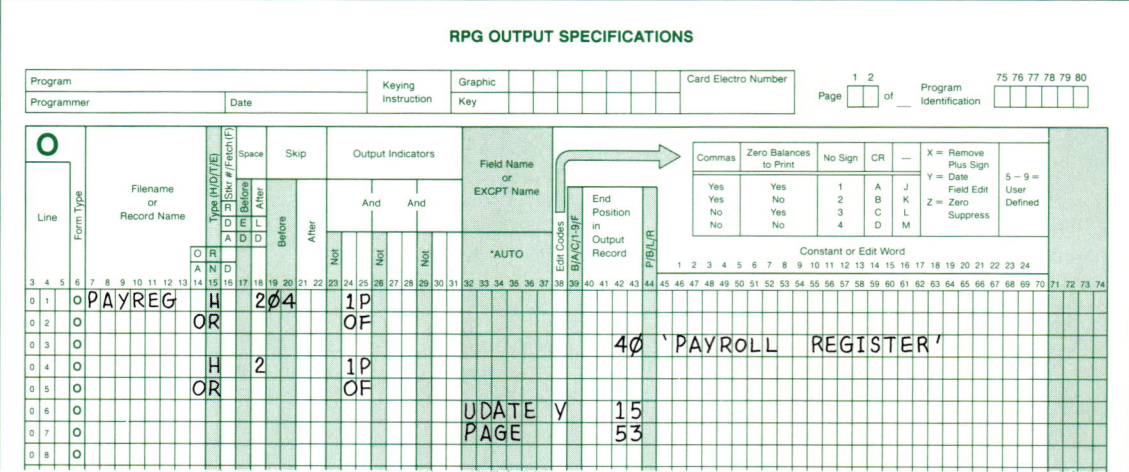

Notes on the Coding

Both reserved words are coded as fields in positions 32 to 37.

The Y edit code will punctuate the date field UDATE with slashes between day, month, and year.

The reserved word PAGE may be coded alone or with the constant PAGE, depending on the Printer Spacing Chart requirements.

Figure 3.41 continued

Examples of coding
Printer Spacing Chart Entries

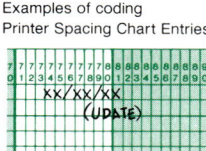

Entries on the Output-Format Specifications Sheet?

[RPG Output Specifications form with the following entries:
- Line 01: O FORM H 203 OF
- Line 02: O OR 1P
- Line 03: O 48 'INVENTORY SUMMARY'
- Line 04: O UDATE 81]

UDATE   Function: Description:
         To make the current data available   1. UDATE is a six-position
         for printing and/or calculations   numeric date field.
         without reading it into the program.   2. UDATE is set up in storage
                                                        prior to the execution
                                                        of the program.
                                                     3. Specifying UDATE as a
                                                        field name on output
                                                        causes printing of the
                                                        current contents of the
                                                        field UDATE.
                                                     4. The Edit Code Y causes
                                                        slashes to separate the
                                                        numbers in the date,
                                                        xx/xx/xx (any data field).

Summary

The following summarizes the relationships of record identifying indicators to the conditioning calculations and to the resultant indicators used to define the printed output.

Indicators

Record identifying indicators assigned on the Input Specifications form are used first to control the calculations and then to control the detail output.

Resulting indicators control the detail output. Depending on the condition set in the compare operation, one constant or another or neither constant may be printed as a result of an indicator's position. If indicator 66 is on, one constant may be printed; if indicator 77 is on, another may be printed. If neither is on, then no message prints. The indicator is on the same line as the field or constant not on the line with *D* (position 15 of output specifications). (See Figure 3.42.)

The 1P indicator, on at the beginning of the program until the first record is read, is used along with the overflow indicator to cause headings to be printed.

The LR indicator, used to print total lines, is automatically set on when an end-of-file condition is reached.

Calculations   113

Figure 3.42 Sample program illustrating listings with calculations

Problem Definition

Write a program to list all employees who have 25 or more years of service with the company. The report should include:

All appropriate headings.

The detail lines should be double-spaced. If anyone has over 30 years, indicate that with a message on that detail line.

The total line should have the count of the number of employees with over 25 years and the constant. It may be printed anywhere after the last detail line.

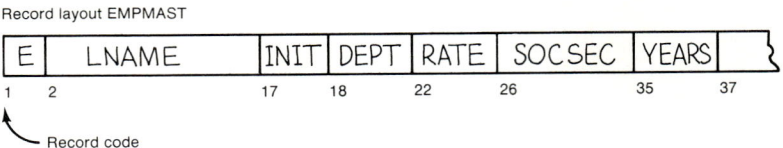

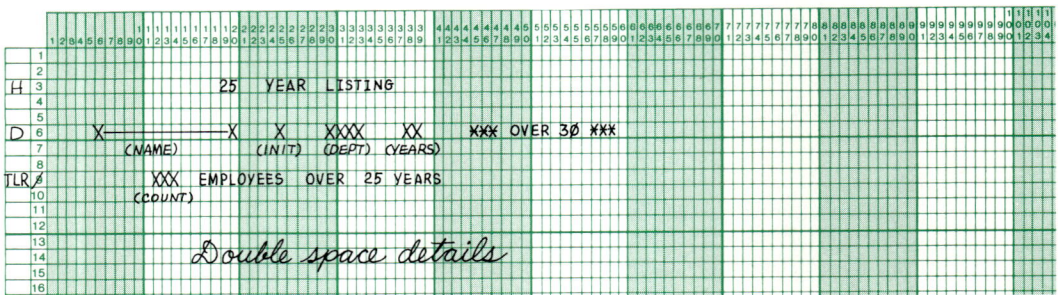

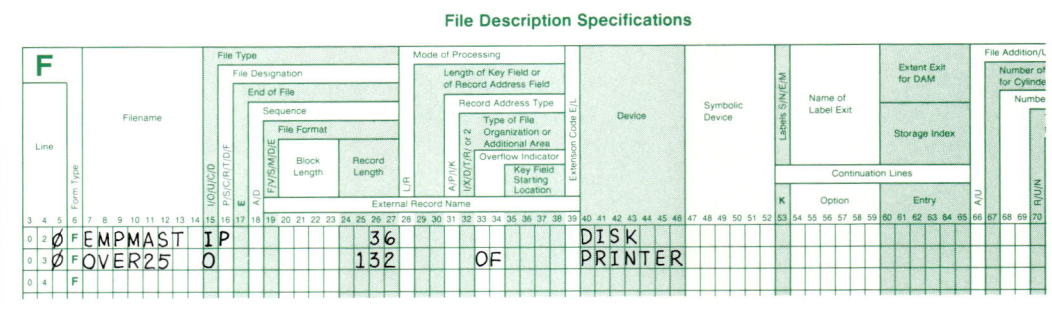

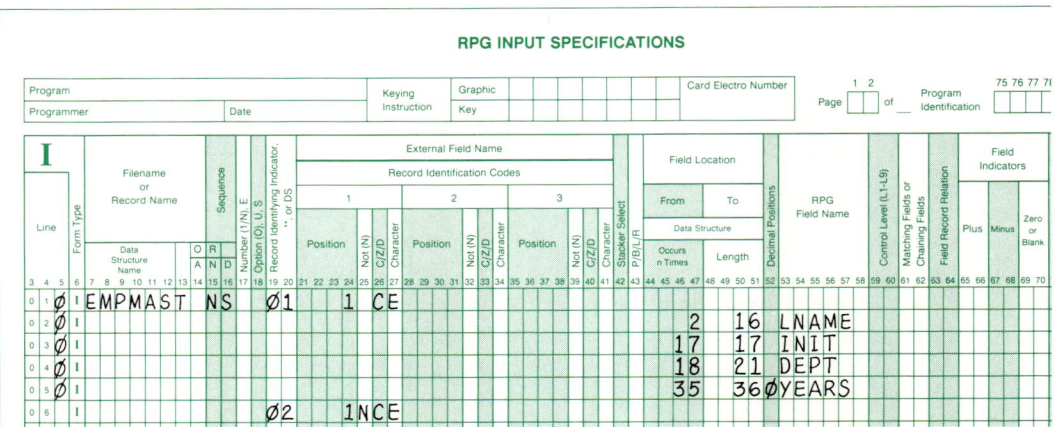

114 RPG II and RPG III Programming

Figure 3.42 continued

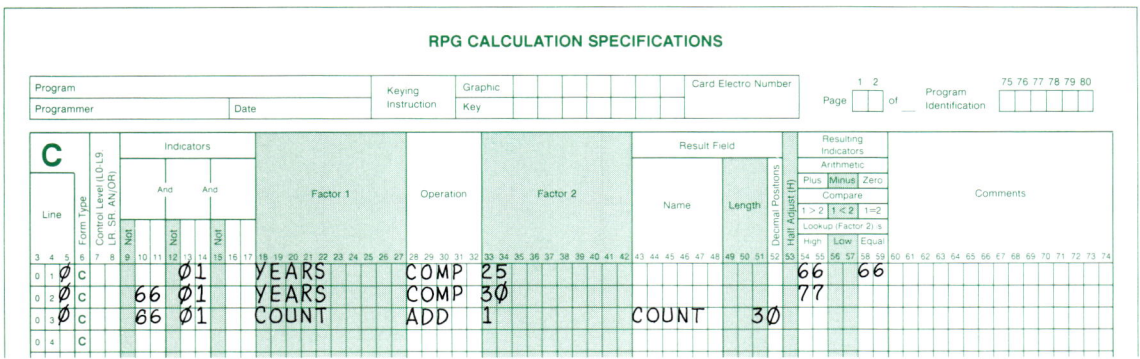

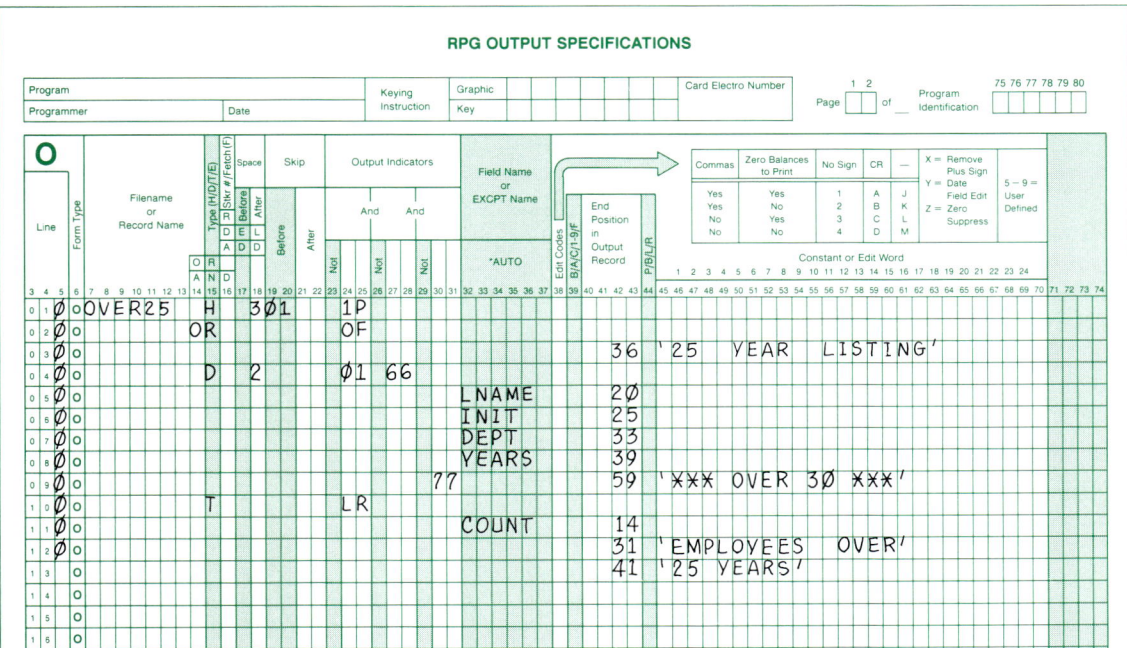

Notes on the Coding

File Description Specifications: These entries are coded from the file specifications and the system designation device names.

Input Specifications: Any indicator from 01 to 99 may be used for the record identifying indicator; record and file coding are on separate lines from the field coding. Note that only the fields required on the output are coded on the input. There was no need to use the RATE and SOCSEC, so they are not described.

Calculation Specifications: The record identifying indicator is used to control each of the calculations. A different indicator (66) is used for the comparison for over 24 years service. If someone has over 24 years, it must be checked to see if it is over 30. Another indicator is used for this comparison. Note that we only want to count those employees who have over 24 years, so we use both the 01 and 66 to do that addition. This will be an accumulating addition, since the result field is also one of the factors.

Output Specifications: The heading is controlled by the 1P and overflow (OF) indicators. The forms coding will start on the first printing line (channel 01) with 3 spaces after. The detail lines are controlled by 01 and 66, since we only want to print those employees with over 24 years, NOT all employees. However, the message *** OVER 30 *** should print only for those with over 30 years, so the 77 is coded on the same line with the constant. The total lines are controlled by LR. There is no space entry required, since the last detail line will take two spaces after it prints. Note the field count is printed using LR, but the accumulating took place using 01 and 66. If a constant will not fit into the columns 46 to 70, break it into two or more lines—each with their own ending positions.

Calculations 115

Calculations

Calculations are the arithmetic and logical operations performed upon the data. In order to perform calculations, the programmer must specify the following:

1. The *operations* to be performed (i.e., ADD, SUB, MULT, DIV, COMP)
2. The *conditions* that must exist before those operations can be carried out (i.e., the indicators used to condition the operation, if any)
3. The *order* of the operations (Operations are carried out sequentially, in the order of coding.)
4. The *tests* to be performed on the data (i.e., COMPare operations and resultant indicators)

Heading Output

Heading output is associated with 1P or the overflow indicators OA–OG and OV. The indicator 1P is on only until the first record is read; then it is turned off. Heading lines generally skip (positions 19–20 of the output specifications) to a new page, then space (positions 17–18 of the output specifications) for succeeding heading lines.

Detail Output

Detail output is conditioned by the record identifying indicator. Detail lines do not skip (positions 19–20 of the output specifications); they space (positions 17–18 of output specifications) between lines.

Total Output

In addition to the output of headings at the top of the report and of detail lines with fields and constants, the tools are now available to print totals and constants at the end of the report. The indicator that controls total printing on the last page is LR.

Constants

Constants are not just for headings; they may be used for detail or total output also. Each field name and each constant must appear on separate lines. If there are multiple constants, there must be some control to determine when they will print. Indicators must be conditioned so that these constants will print at the proper time.

Edit

The edit codes are used with numeric fields only. To determine which code to enter, the Printer Spacing Chart should be checked. The matrix of edit codes on the Output Specifications form should be used with the code entered in position 38.

When an edit code will not provide the exact type of punctuation required (e.g., telephone and social security numbers), then an edit word should be used. Edit words are coded like a constant on the same line as the field to be edited. Spaces in the field (to be filled by data) are left blank and the unique characters, which punctuate the data, are entered in their proper places.

The two special edit words ($ or *) may be used in conjunction with an edit code for check protection with the floating dollar sign or asterisk fill, respectively.

The reserved words PAGE and UDATE will allow page numbering and printing of the current date on each page of the report. According to RPG language specification, both must be coded as fields on the Output Specifications form.

RPG III Enhancements

Following are the RPG III language additions to the material presented in this chapter.

Calculations

A shorter format for the arithmetic operations ADD, SUB, MULT, and DIV is provided in RPG III. (The same functionality is provided in RPG II for the IBM System/34 and the IBM System/36.) The shorter format permits factor 1 or factor 2 to be omitted when either factor will repeat as the result field. (See Figure 3.43.)

Figure 3.43 RPG III calculation entries

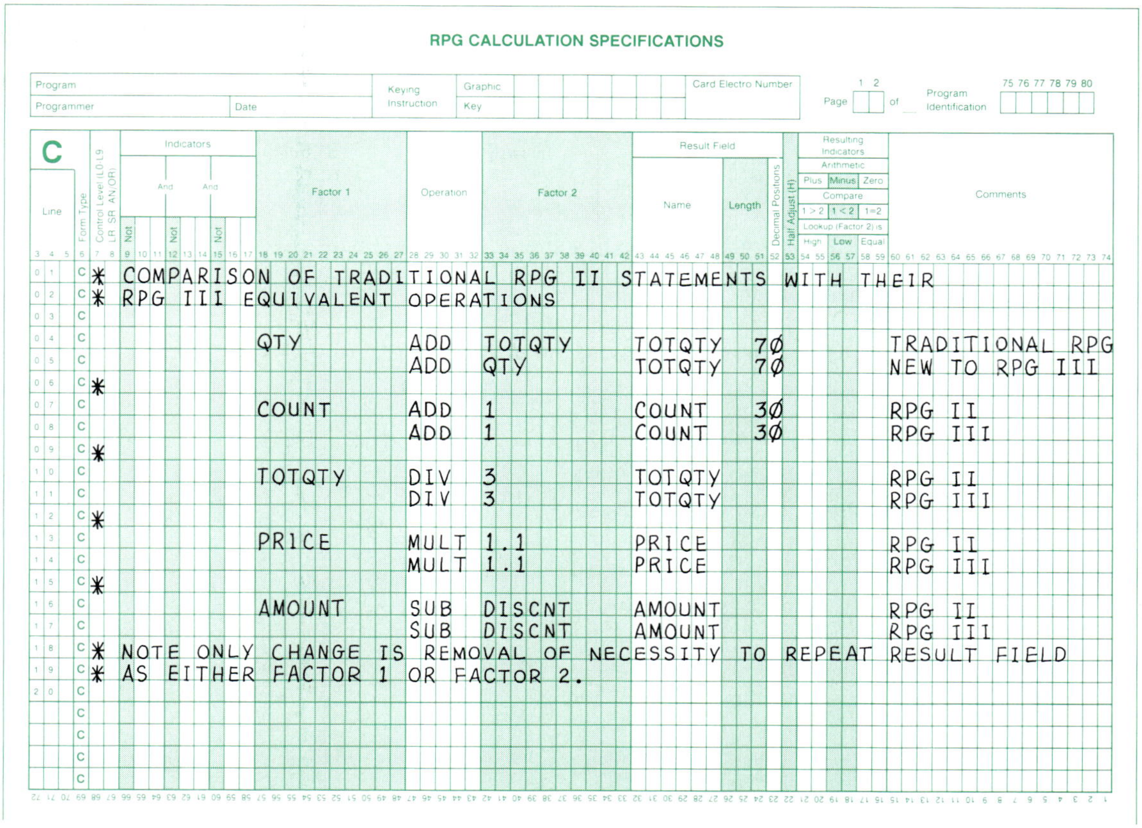

RPG CALCULATION SPECIFICATIONS

Program | Keying Instruction | Graphic | Key | Card Electro Number | Page of | Program Identification
Programmer | Date

```
0 1 C* COMPARISON OF TRADITIONAL RPG II STATEMENTS WITH THEIR
0 2 C* RPG III EQUIVALENT OPERATIONS
0 3 C
0 4 C     QTY       ADD  TOTQTY    TOTQTY  7Ø     TRADITIONAL RPG
0 5 C               ADD  QTY       TOTQTY  7Ø     NEW TO RPG III
0 6 C*
0 7 C     COUNT     ADD  1         COUNT   3Ø     RPG II
0 8 C               ADD  1         COUNT   3Ø     RPG III
0 9 C*
1 0 C     TOTQTY    DIV  3         TOTQTY         RPG II
1 1 C               DIV  3         TOTQTY         RPG III
1 2 C*
1 3 C     PRICE     MULT 1.1       PRICE          RPG II
1 4 C               MULT 1.1       PRICE          RPG III
1 5 C*
1 6 C     AMOUNT    SUB  DISCNT    AMOUNT         RPG II
1 7 C               SUB  DISCNT    AMOUNT         RPG III
1 8 C* NOTE ONLY CHANGE IS REMOVAL OF NECESSITY TO REPEAT RESULT FIELD
1 9 C* AS EITHER FACTOR 1 OR FACTOR 2.
2 0 C
```

Following is an example of **accumulation.** QTY is added to TOTQTY.

	Factor 1	Operation	Factor 2	Result Field
RPG II	QTY	ADD	TOTQTY	TOTQTY
RPG III		ADD	QTY	TOTQTY

This special case of accumulation is known as incrementation. 1 is added to COUNT.

	Factor 1	Operation	Factor 2	Result Field
RPG 11	COUNT	ADD	1	COUNT
RPG III		ADD	1	COUNT

TOTQTY is divided by three.

	Factor 1	Operation	Factor 2	Result Field
RPG II	TOTQTY	DIV	3	TOTQTY
RPG III		DIV	3	TOTQTY

Price is raised 10%. PRICE is multiplied by 1.1.

	Factor 1	Operation	Factor 2	Result Field
RPG II	PRICE	MULT	1.1	PRICE
RPG III		MULT	1.1	PRICE

DISCNT is subtracted from AMOUNT.

	Factor 1	Operation	Factor 2	Result Field
RPG II	AMOUNT	SUB	DISCNT	AMOUNT
RPG III		SUB	DISCNT	AMOUNT

This capability not only reduces coding requirements, but improves program readability in that the intention of the instruction is more clearly conveyed.

Illustrative Program

Accumulating Final Totals: Deduction Register

Job Definition
Print a report listing the deductions for employees for the week and accumulate the totals for each class of deduction.

Input
Deduction file consists of 38-byte records including the following fields:

Positions	Field Description	
1–01	Code	
2–06	Employee number	
7–21	Name	
22–25	Health plan	(XX.XX)
26–29	Dues	(XX.XX)
30–33	Bonds	(XX.XX)
34–38	Gross pay	(XXX.XX)

Processing
Final totals for health plan, dues, and bond deductions.

Output
This Printer Spacing Chart shows how the report is formatted:

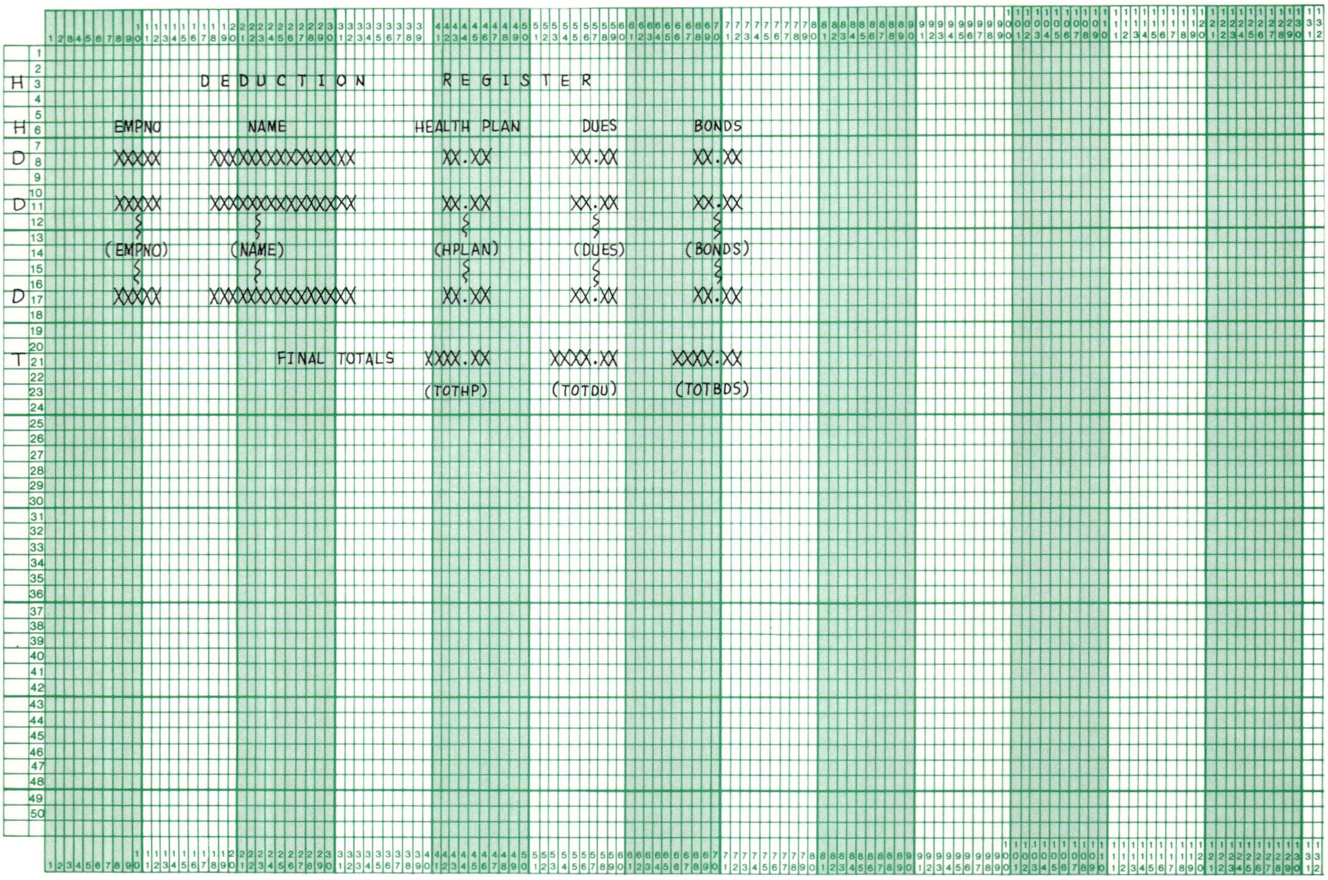

```
          EMPNO    NAME              HEALTH PLAN    DUES      BONDS
H         DEDUCTION REGISTER
H         EMPNO    NAME              HEALTH PLAN    DUES      BONDS
D         XXXX     XXXXXXXXXXXXXXX   XX.XX          XX.XX     XX.XX
D         XXXX     XXXXXXXXXXXXXXX   XX.XX          XX.XX     XX.XX
          (EMPNO)  (NAME)            (HPLAN)        (DUES)    (BONDS)
D         XXXX     XXXXXXXXXXXXXXX   XX.XX          XX.XX     XX.XX
T                  FINAL TOTALS      XXXX.XX        XXXX.XX   XXXX.XX
                                     (TOTHP)        (TOTDU)   (TOTBDS)
```

Coding sheets for Deduction Register Report problem:

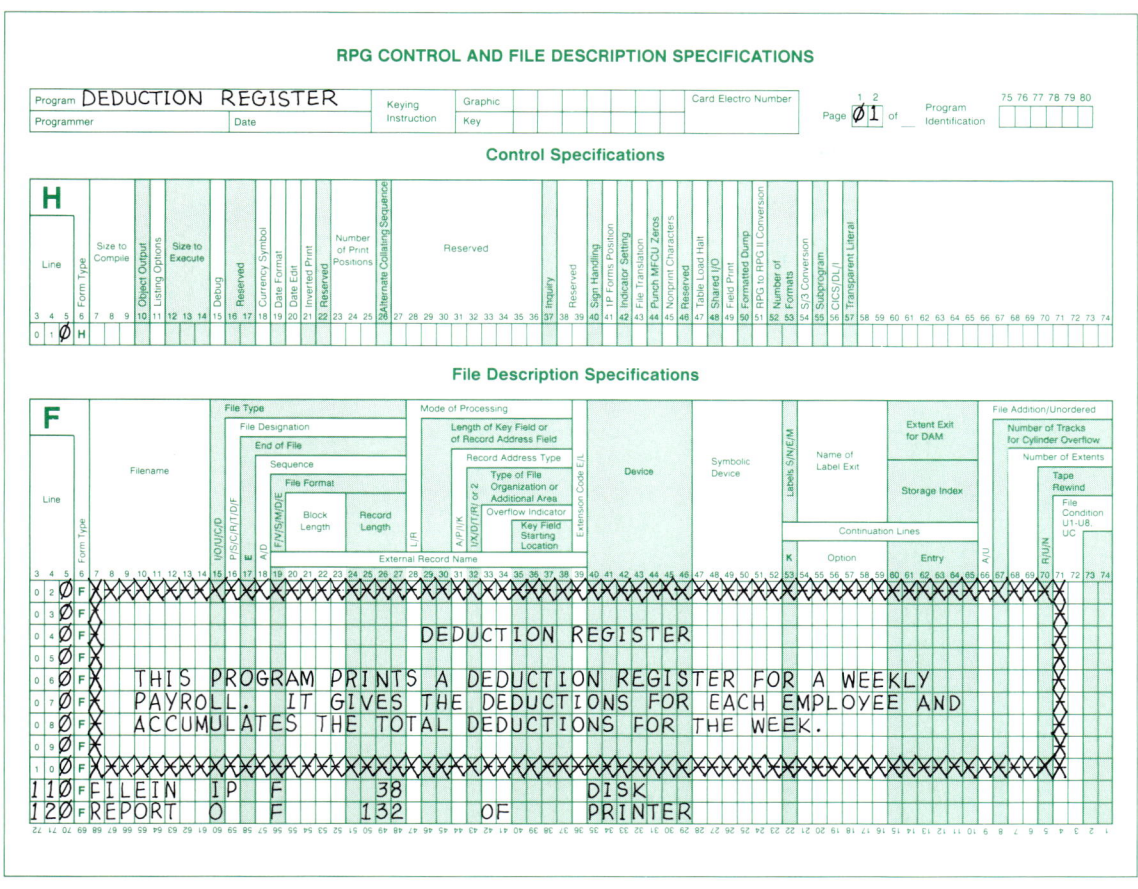

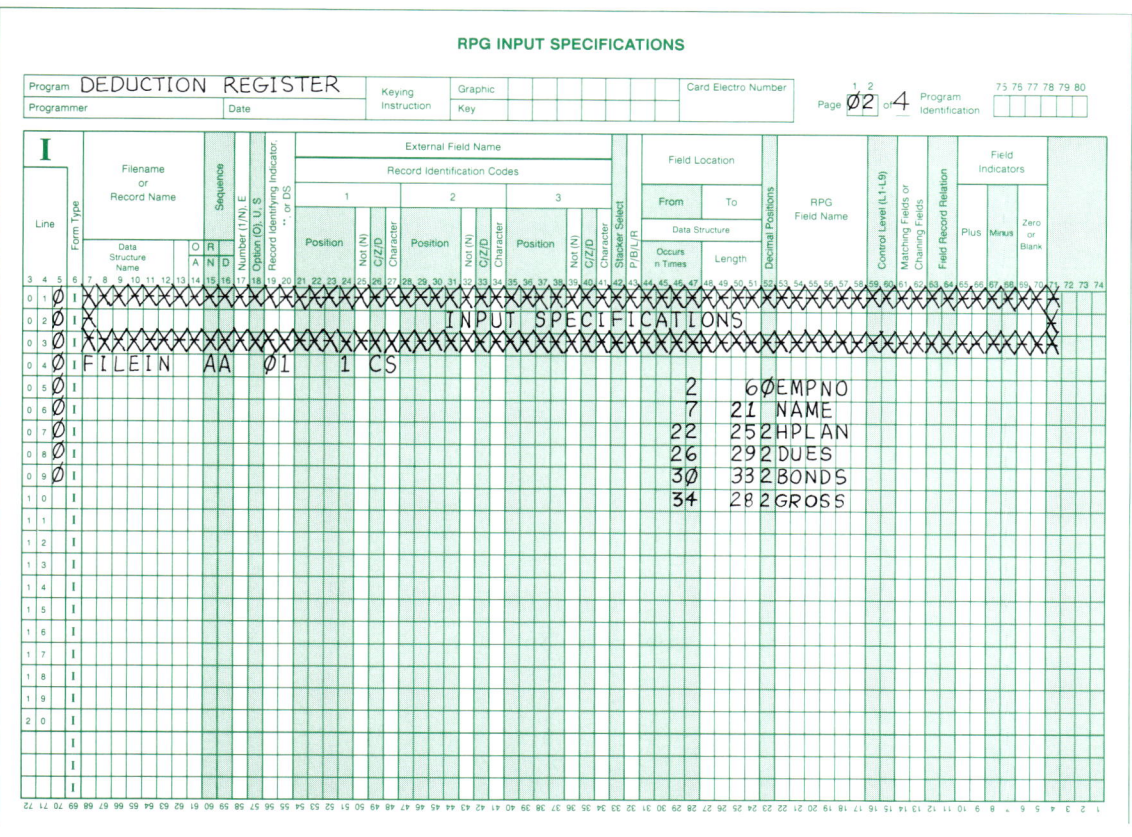

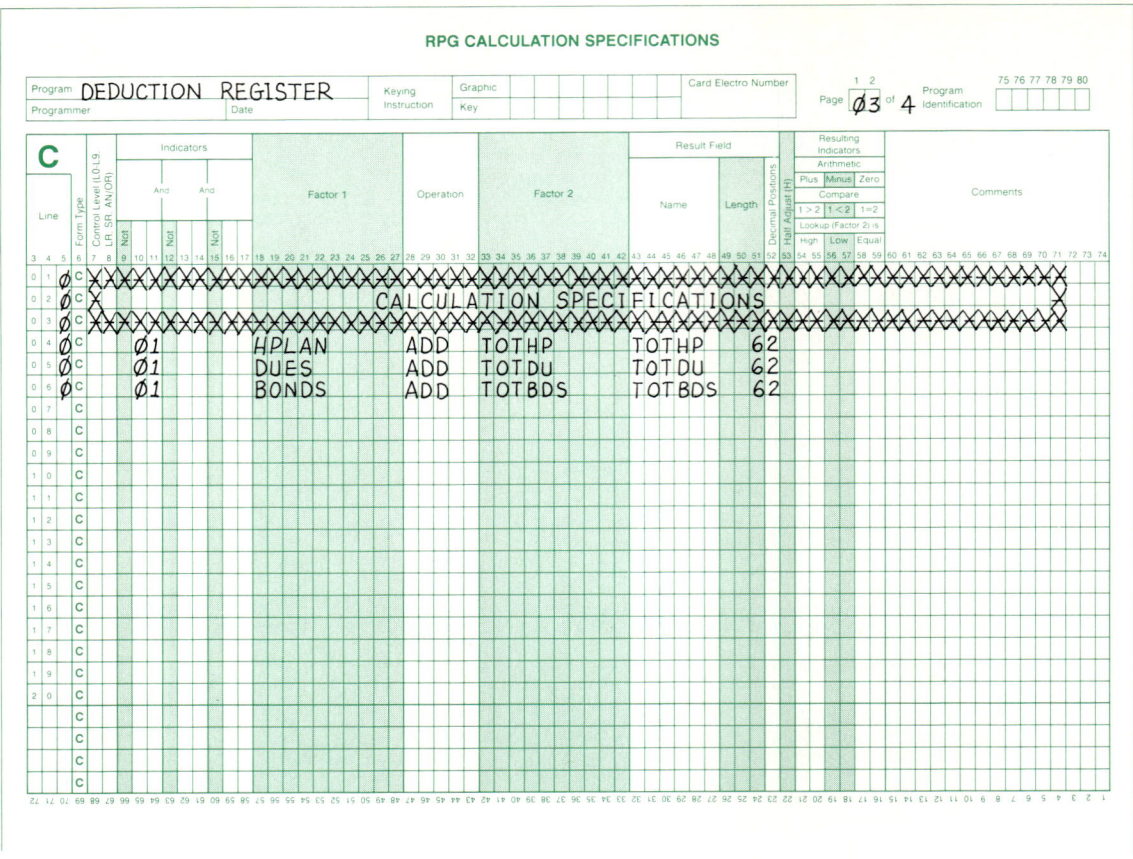

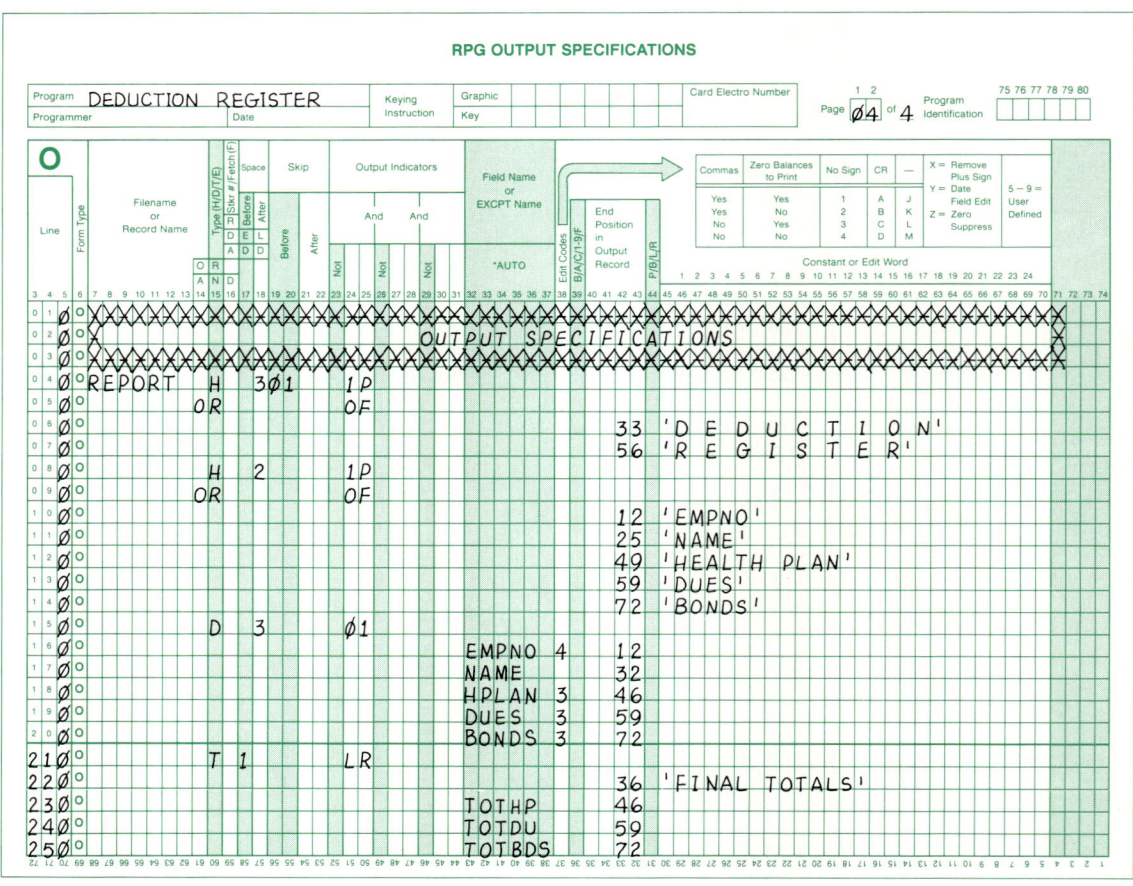

The source listing is as follows:

```
 1   01010H
 2 * 01020F****************************************************************
 3 * 01030F*                                                               *
 4 * 01040F*                     DEDUCTION REGISTER                        *
 5 * 01050F*                                                               *
 6 * 01060F*  THIS PROGRAM PRINTS A DEDUCTION REGISTER FOR A WEEKLY        *
 7 * 01070F*  PAYROLL. THE PROGRAM PRINTS THE PAYROLL DEDUCTION FOR EACH   *
 8 * 01080F*  EMPLOYEE AND ACCUMULATES THE TOTAL DEDUCTIONS FOR THE WEEK.  *
 9 * 01090F*                                                               *
10 * 01100F****************************************************************
11   01110FFILEIN   IP  F      38           DISK
12   01120FREPORT   O   F     132        OF PRINTER
13 * 02010I****************************************************************
14 * 02020I*                    INPUT SPECIFICATIONS                       *
15 * 02030I****************************************************************
16   02040IFILEIN   AA  01   1 CS
17   02050I                                          1   1 CD
18   02060I                                          2  60EMPNO
19   02070I                                          7  21 NAME
20   02080I                                         22  252HPLAN
21   02090I                                         26  292DUES
22   02100I                                         30  332BONDS
23   02110I                                         34  382GROSS
24 * 03010C****************************************************************
25 * 03020C*                   CALCULATION SPECIFICATIONS                  *
26 * 03030C****************************************************************
27   03040C   01       HPLAN     ADD  TOTHP     TOTHP   52
28   03050C   01       DUES      ADD  TOTDU     TOTDU   52
29   03060C   01       BONDS     ADD  TOTBDS    TOTBDS  52
30 * 04010O****************************************************************
31 * 04020O*                    OUTPUT SPECIFICATIONS                      *
32 * 04030O****************************************************************
33   04040OREPORT   H  301           1P
34   04050O         OR               OF
35   04060O                                     33 'D E D U C T I O N'
36   04070O                                     56 'R E G I S T E R'
37   04080O         H  2             1P
38   04090O         OR               OF
39   04100O                                     12 'EMPNO'
40   04110O                                     25 'NAME'
41   04120O                                     49 'HEALTH PLAN'
42   04130O                                     59 'DUES'
43   04140O                                     72 'BONDS'
44   04150O         D  3             01
45   04160O                              EMPNO  4   12
46   04170O                              NAME       32
47   04180O                              HPLAN  3   46
48   04190O                              DUES   3   59
49   04200O                              BONDS  3   72
50   04210O         T  1             LR
51   04220O                                     36 'FINAL TOTALS'
52   04230O                              TOTHP  3   46
53   04240O                              TOTDU  3   59
54   04250O                              TOTBDS3    72
```

The Deduction Register is to be printed as follows:

```
                  D E D U C T I O N         R E G I S T E R

     EMPNO       NAME            HEALTH PLAN      DUES         BONDS

     14283    PAUL BROWN            18.75        15.00         25.00

     14284    ROB BAXTER             4.50         5.00         10.00

     14291    JORDAN COOLEY          4.00         5.00         10.00

     14293    JIM DAVIS              9.50        10.00         25.00

     14296    TOM FITCH              5.00         5.00           .00

     14298    GLEN GREENBARG         5.00         5.00          5.00

     14305    JAY GORDON            15.75        10.00         10.00

     14306    GEORGE HALL           10.00        15.00         25.00

     14307    MARK JONES            20.00         5.00         25.00

     14308    VICTORIA LEWIS         7.50         5.00          5.00

     14310    ROGER RAGAINS         10.00        10.00         10.00

     14312    MIKE TAKAMI           15.00        15.00         25.00


                        FINAL TOTALS  125.00       105.00        175.00
```

Illustrative Program

Simple Calculations Accumulating Final Totals: Transaction Register

Job Definition

Print a report listing all sales transactions for a week. This report is similar to the transaction report found in chapter 2 except that this report contains the sales amount per item and the final total of all sales items for the week. Sales amount (the quantity sold multiplied by item price) is not found in the input record and must, therefore, be calculated. If quantity is greater than or equal to 100, give a 10 percent discount (i.e., multiply sales amount by .9).

Input

Sales transaction file consisting of 42-byte records. The format of input records is shown on this Record Layout form:

Processing

    Multiply quantity times unit price to find sales amount.
    Compare quantity to 100.
    If quantity is greater than or equal to 100, multiply sales amount by .9.
    Find final total for weekly item sales.

Output
This Printer Spacing Chart shows how the report is formatted:

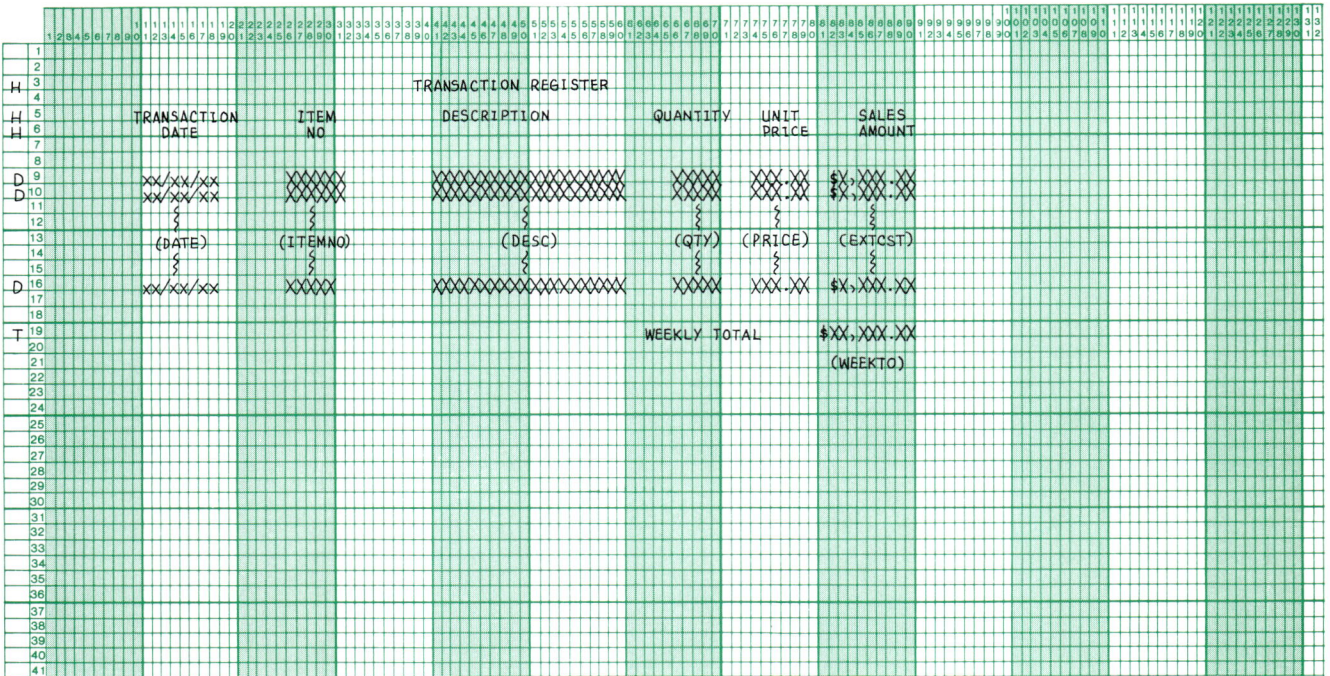

Coding sheets for Transaction Register problem:

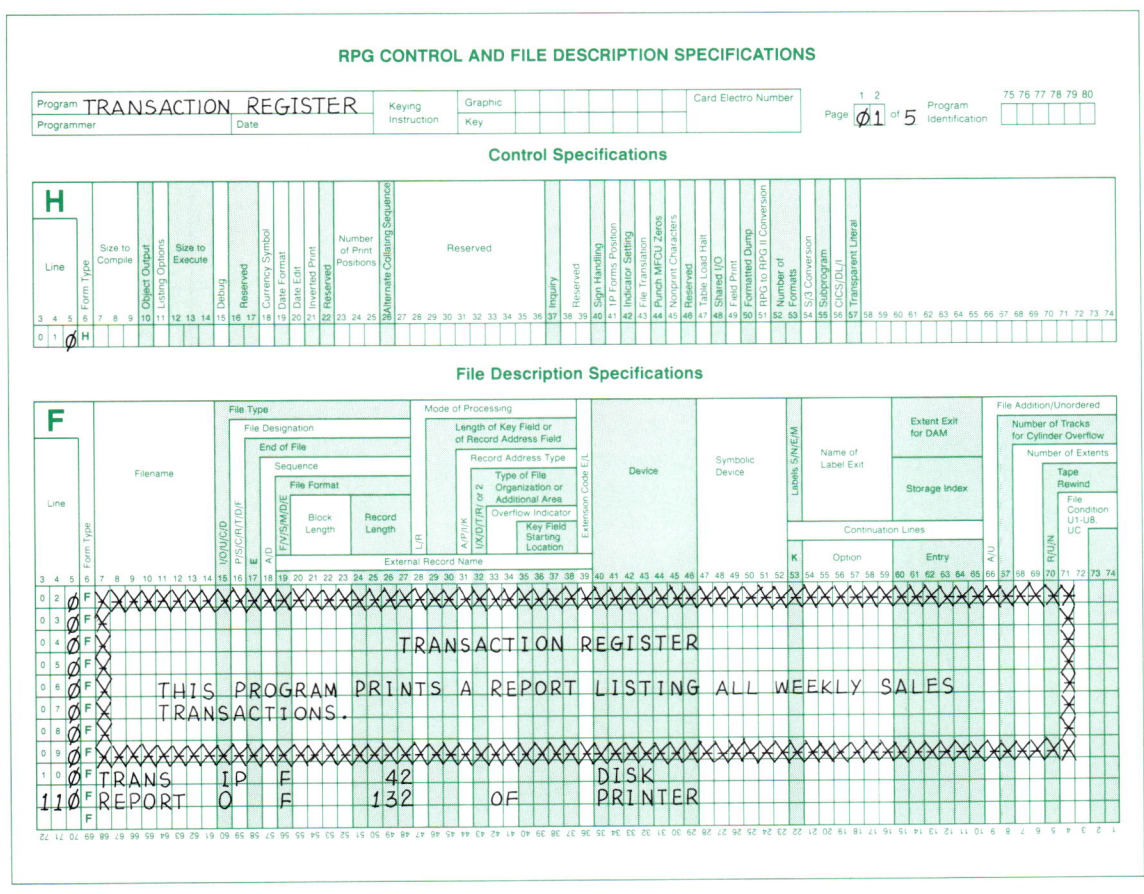

Calculations   123

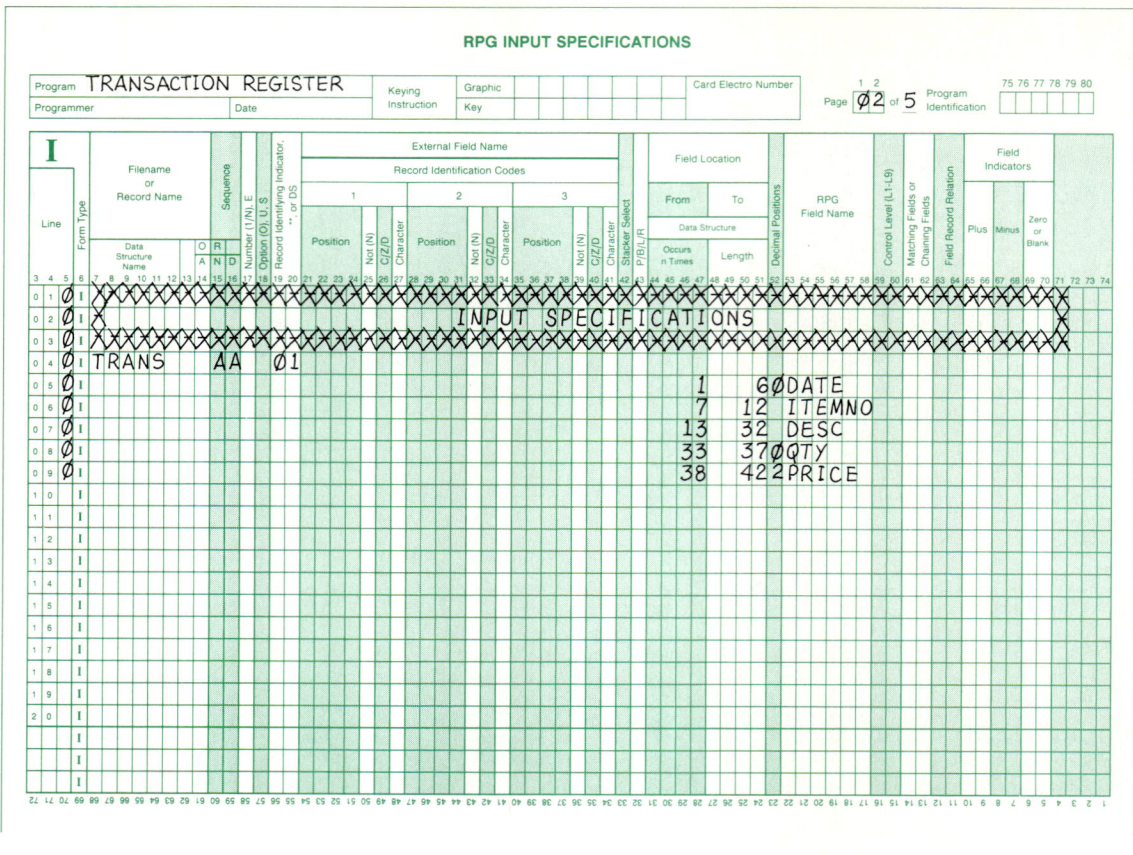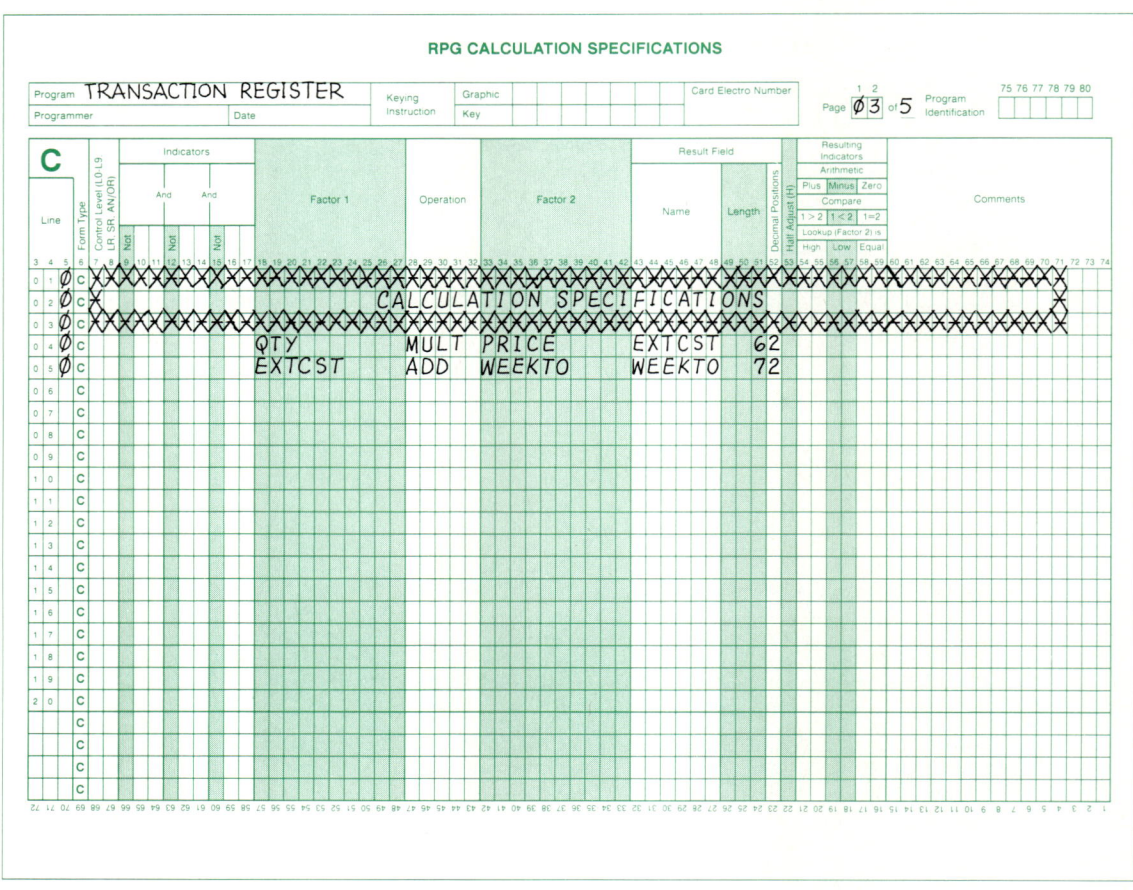

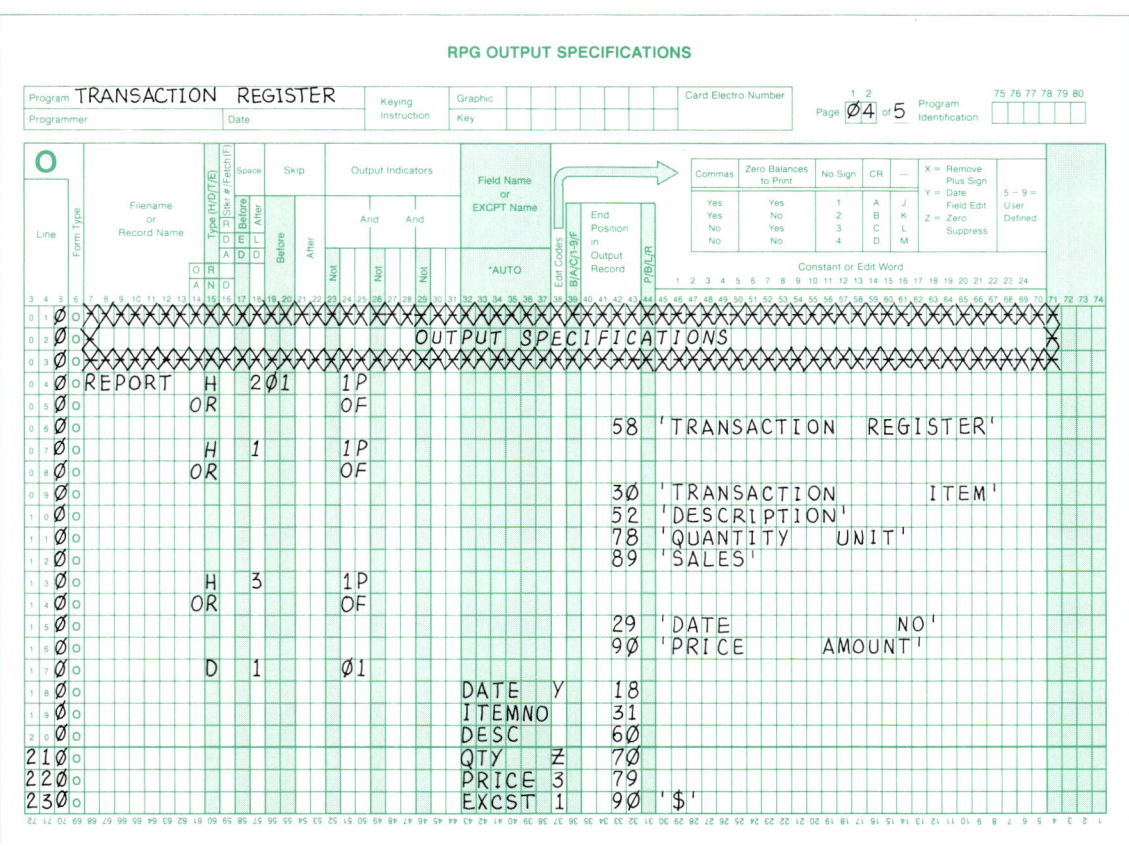
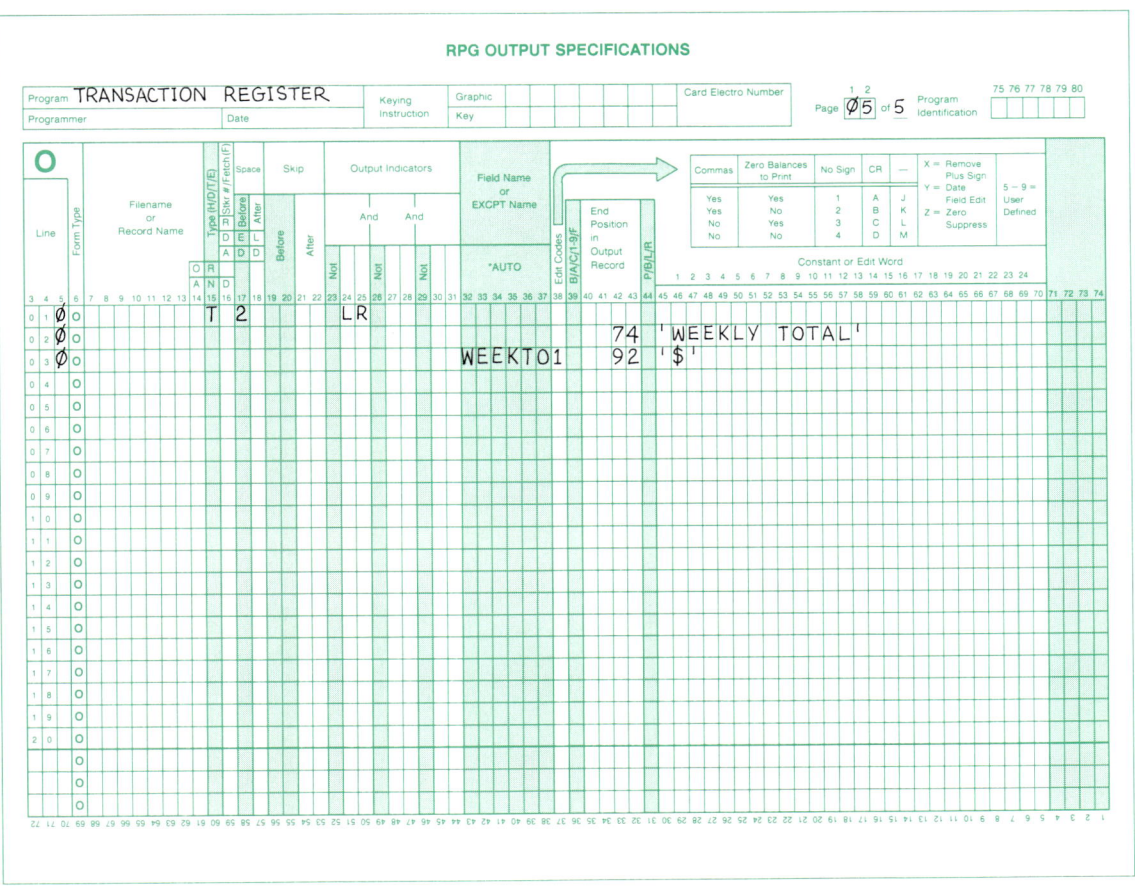

Calculations

The source listing is as follows:

```
 1     01010H
 2   * 01020F*************************************************************
 3   * 01030F*                                                            *
 4   * 01040F*               TRANSACTION REGISTER                         *
 5   * 01050F*                                                            *
 6   * 01060F*    THIS PROGRAM PRINTS A REPORT LISTING ALL WEEKLY SALES   *
 7   * 01070F     TRANSACTIONS.                                           *
 8   * 01080F*                                                            *
 9   * 01090F*************************************************************
10     01100FTRANS    IP  F      42           DISK
11     01110FREPORT   O   F     132       OF  PRINTER
12   * 02010I*************************************************************
13   * 02020I*                  INPUT SPECIFICATIONS                      *
14   * 02030I*************************************************************
15     02040ITRANS    AA  01
16     02050I                                        1   60DATE
17     02060I                                        7   12 ITEMNO
18     02070I                                       13   32 DESC
19     02080I                                       33  370QTY
20     02090I                                       38  422PRICE
21   * 03010C*************************************************************
22   * 03020C*                CALCULATION SPECIFICATIONS                  *
23   * 03030C*************************************************************
24     03040C           QTY       MULT PRICE     EXTCST   62
25     03050C           EXTCST    ADD  WEEKTO    WEEKTO   72
26   * 040100***********************************************************
27   * 040200*                  OUTPUT SPECIFICATIONS                    *
28   * 040300***********************************************************
29     040400OREPORT   H  201      1P
30     040500       OR              OF
31     040600                                      58 'TRANSACTION  REGISTER'
32     040700        H   1          1P
33     040800       OR              OF
34     040900                                      30 'TRANSACTION     ITEM'
35     041000                                      52 'DESCRIPTION'
36     041100                                      78 'QUANTITY    UNIT'
37     041200                                      89 'SALES'
38     041300        H   3          1P
39     041400       OR              OF
40     041500                                      29 'DATE          NO'
41     041600                                      90 'PRICE     AMOUNT'
42     041700        D   1          01
43     041800                            DATE  Y   18
44     041900                            ITEMNO    31
45     042000                            DESC      60
46     042100                            QTY   Z   70
47     042200                            PRICE 3   79
48     042300                            EXTCST1   90 '$'
49     050100        T   2          LR
50     050200                                      74 'WEEKLY TOTAL'
51     050300                            WEEKTO1   90 '$'
```

A Transaction Register Report is to be printed as follows:

```
                          TRANSACTION  REGISTER

TRANSACTION     ITEM       DESCRIPTION           QUANTITY    UNIT       SALES
   DATE          NO                                          PRICE      AMOUNT


  9/23/87      413010      CH001 BOX 100A FLUSH     10        4.90      $49.00
  9/23/87      412146      CH148 BREAKER 15A       100         .89      $89.00
  9/23/87      411116      1500 TWIN SOCKET B      500        1.12     $560.00
  9/24/87      503029      MOTOR 1/2 HP 60 CYC       2      146.78     $293.56
  9/24/87      317802      TERMINAL CLIP           100        5.12     $512.00
  9/24/87      326917      TERMINAL BAR            100        4.12     $412.00
  9/24/87      411121      1506 SOCKT ADAPT BRN    400         .19      $76.00
  9/25/87      412997      CH173 BREAKER 30A        60        1.15      $69.00
  9/25/87      413088      CH176 BREAKER 60A        40        1.15      $46.00
  9/25/87      411174      C151 SIL SWITCH BRN     200        1.16     $232.00
  9/25/87      413090      CH005 BR BOX 150A        10        4.98      $49.80
  9/25/87      718326      FC803 FUSE 15A          200         .32      $64.00

                                         WEEKLY TOTAL       $2,452.36
```

RPG II and RPG III Programming

Questions for Review

1. Briefly explain the steps in the logic cycle of the RPG program.
2. What problems face the RPG programmer in calculation operations?
3. What is the purpose of the Calculation Specifications form?
4. Describe the two types of data specified on the Calculation Specifications form.
5. What are conditions in Calculation Specifications forms?
6. How is the order of operations specified?
7. What are tests used for?
8. What facilities are provided by RPG for arithmetic operations?
9. Describe two formats recording comments in the Calculation Specifications form.
10. Why is the sequence of operations important?
11. Briefly describe the add, subtract, multiply, and divide operations.
12. What are the rules for using numeric constants?
13. In what situation will a new name not be needed for a result field?
14. What is the RPG programmer's responsibility in the use of result fields?
15. How are decimal positions and half-adjusting results treated in RPG?
16. How are results of arithmetic operations tested?
17. What are the three compare relationships and how can they be tested?
18. What are the rules for numeric constants? For alphameric constants?
19. How are resulting indicators used in the compare operations?
20. At what times in a program are resulting indicators turned on?
21. How do the compare and arithmetic operations differ in checking the result field?
22. What is the last record indicator and how does it differ from other indicators?
23. What is meant by editing?
24. What are edit codes and how do they appear on the Output Specifications form?
25. What are the coding rules necessary to accomplish editing?
26. What are edit words and when are they used?
27. What are the PAGE and UDATE fields and how are they used?
28. How are constants and indicators used on detail output?
29. How are constants and indicators used on total output?
30. What is the function of the Move Remainder (MVR) instruction and when is it used?

Problems

Problem 1

Code the necessary file description, input, calculation, and output specifications for the following:

General Description
Prepare a Billings Register report.

Input
A file called ACCOUNTS; the record layout is shown below.

Calculations
Payments are to be compared with charges. If payments are less than charges, the message BILL is to be printed.

Output
The printed report is called BILLINGS REGISTER. If payments are less than charges, print the message BILL on that detail line. The Printer Spacing Chart for the Billings Register Report is shown below.

Use your own names for files and other fields not defined on the Record Layout form or Printer Spacing Chart.

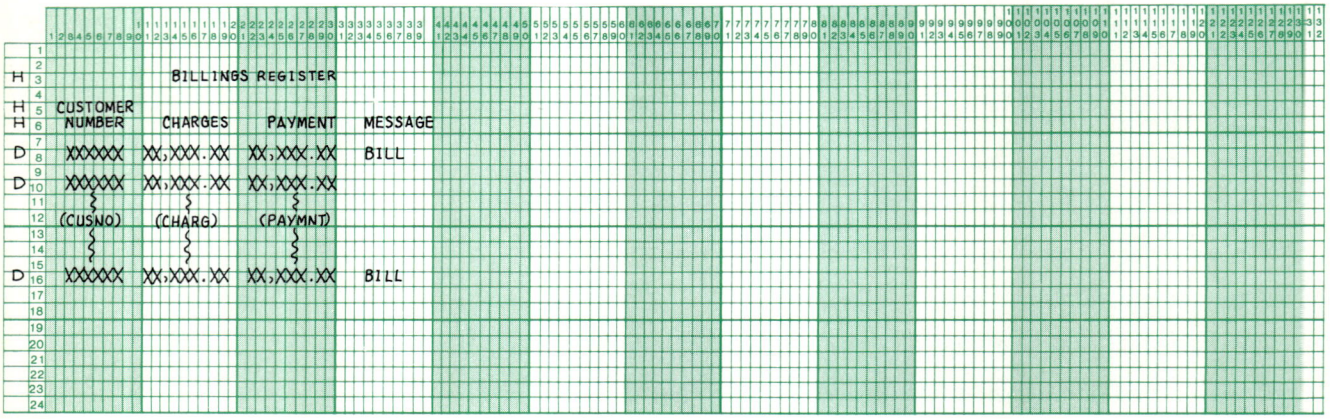

Output is as follows:

```
         BILLINGS REGISTER
CUSTOMER
 NUMBER     CHARGES     PAYMENT     MESSAGE

 245231      530.42      400.00     BILL

 246134    5,000.01    4,000.00     BILL

 251416      466.67      500.00

 319874    2,500.25      500.00     BILL

 431942   50,500.50   75,000.00
```

128 RPG II and RPG III Programming

Problem 2

Use the flowchart, Record Layout form, and Printer Spacing Chart to help write an RPG program responsible for printing a report listing information associated with employee hours worked during a particular pay period. Accumulate totals of the regular hours and overtime hours, and print them at the end of the report.

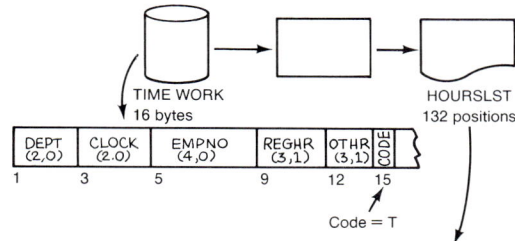

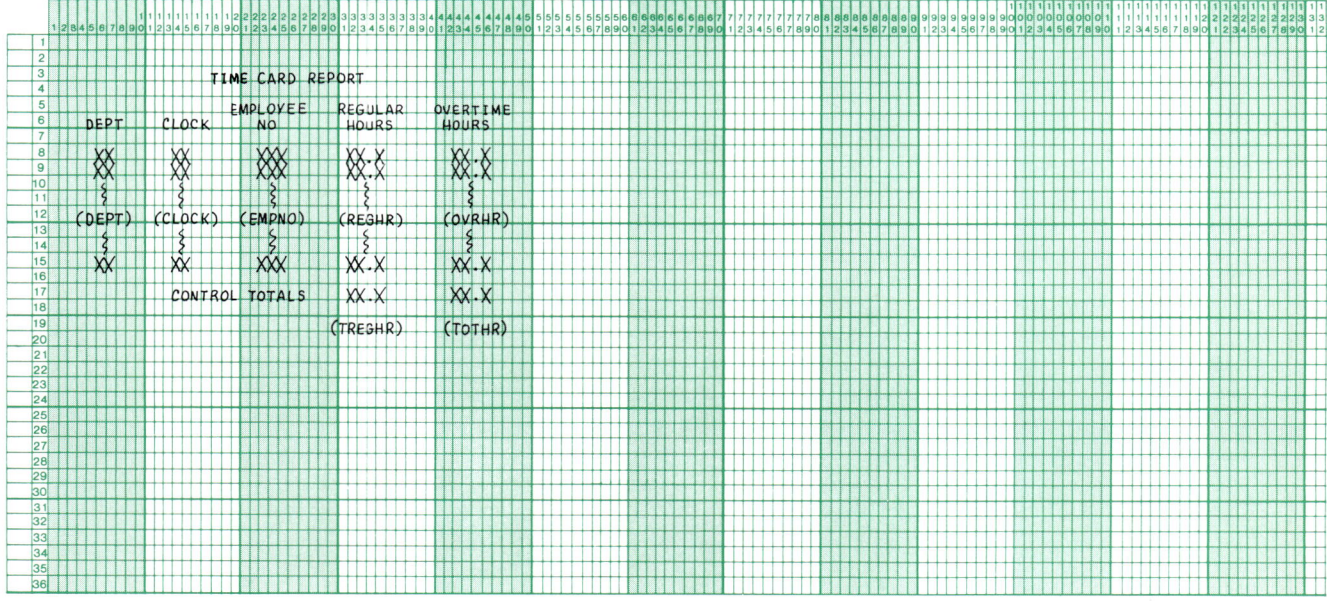

Output is as follows:

```
              TIME CARD REPORT

                    EMPLOYEE   REGULAR   OVERTIME
DEPT     CLOCK         NO       HOURS     HOURS

 55       04          7214      40.0       4.0
 55       04          7392      35.5        .0
 55       09          7419      40.0      10.5
 74       09          4193      15.0        .0
 74       15          3284      20.5        .0
 99       15          1272      40.0      15.0
 99       15          1438      35.0        .0
 99       30          5277      40.0        .0

        CONTROL TOTALS         266.0      29.5
```

Problem 3

Code the necessary file description, input, calculation, and output specifications for the following:

General Description

A Monthly Commissions report is to be produced from an input file.

Calculations 129

Input
A file called SLSCDS; each record contains data on one transaction. The record layout is shown below.

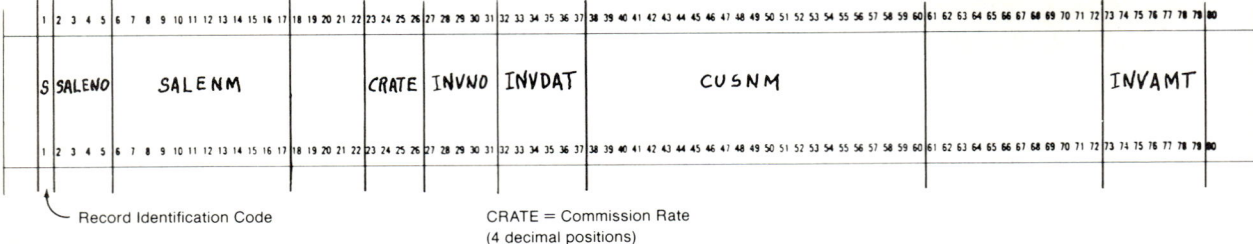

Calculations
For each record, invoice amount is multiplied by commission rate to give commission amount. A final total is printed at the end of the report.

Output
A printed report called COMREP is to be printed. The Printer Spacing Chart is shown below.

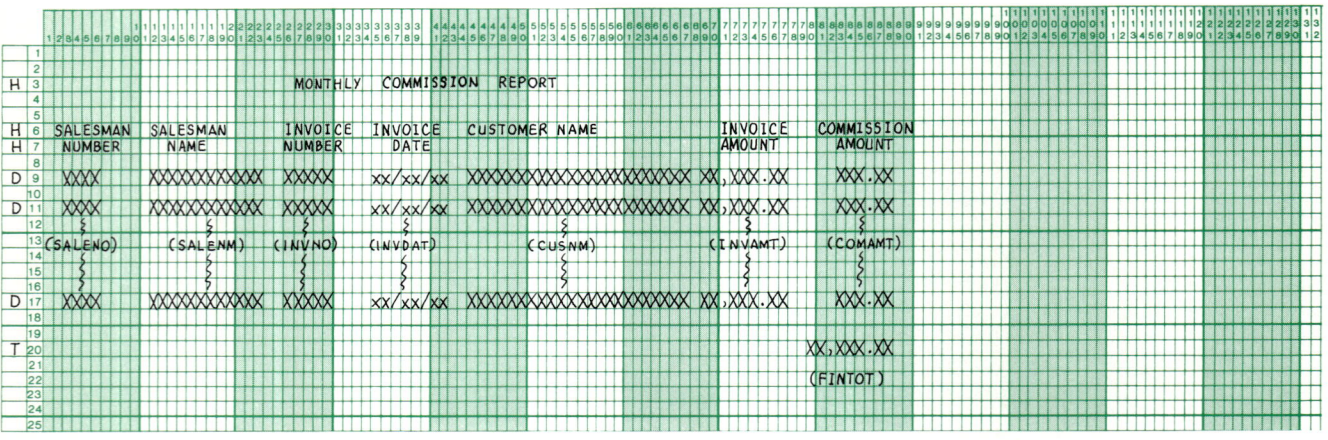

Output is as follows:

```
                      MONTHLY   COMMISSION   REPORT

SALESMAN   SALESMAN      INVOICE   INVOICE   CUSTOMER NAME         INVOICE     COMMISSION
NUMBER     NAME          NUMBER    DATE                            AMOUNT      AMOUNT

  1552     JOHN HOFFMAN   38164    4/19/87   PAUL FRIEDMAN          3,050.04       15.86

  1631     RICHARD KING   74719    9/23/87   BARBARA SMITH          3,050.04       43.62

  1679     LARRY HAM      54257    1/10/87   JOSEPH BURK           19,468.32       99.96

  1741     PAULA LONDON   61906    8/20/87   HERBERT HOWARD            34.19        3.53

  1832     ED GRIFFEN     72393    9/30/87   RON MARTINEZ             727.34      174.13

                                                                                  337.10
```

Problem 4

At each stop they make, drivers working for a fuel oil company record beginning and ending meter readings and the number of gallons of oil delivered to the customer. Later, the account number, meter readings, and gallons delivered are entered into the computer.

All regular customers are charged $3.00 per gallon. However, hospital and government agencies receive a 2 percent discount. The code to show which customers receive a discount is located in the account field. If the last digit is 0, no discount is given; if the last digit is 5, the discount is given.

Write the File Description Specifications, Calculation Specifications, and Output Specifications forms to do the following:

1. Check the driver's calculations to determine gallons delivered to each account. Subtract the beginning meter reading from the ending meter reading.

2. Calculate the amount charged to each account (AMOUNT).

3. Find the total number of gallons sold for the day (TOTALG) and total amount charged (TOTALA).

4. Print a report listing daily transactions and totals. If there is an error in the driver's calculations, print the account number, code, and the message: 'CALCULATION ERROR'.

The input specifications and the Printer Spacing Chart for the job are as follows:

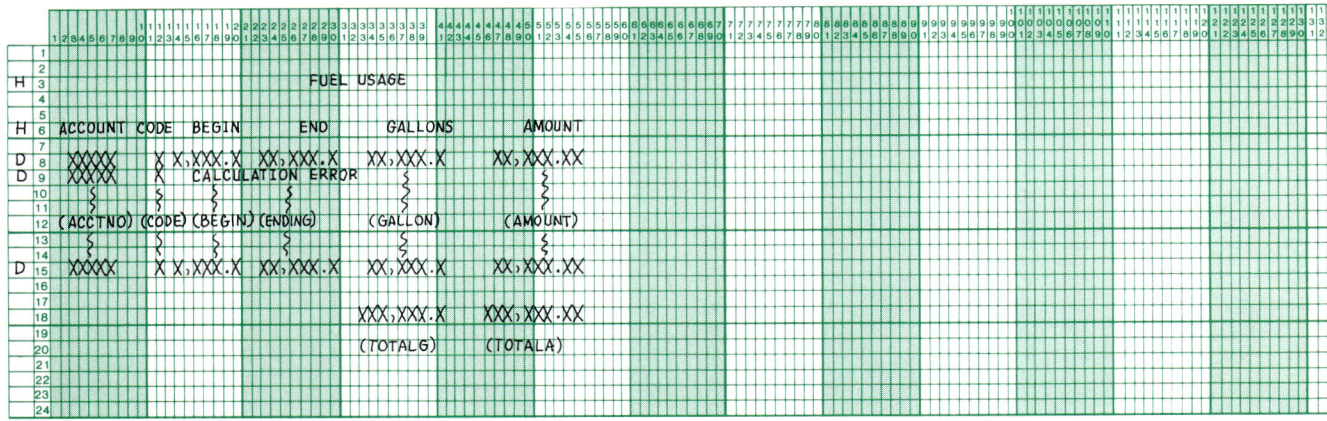

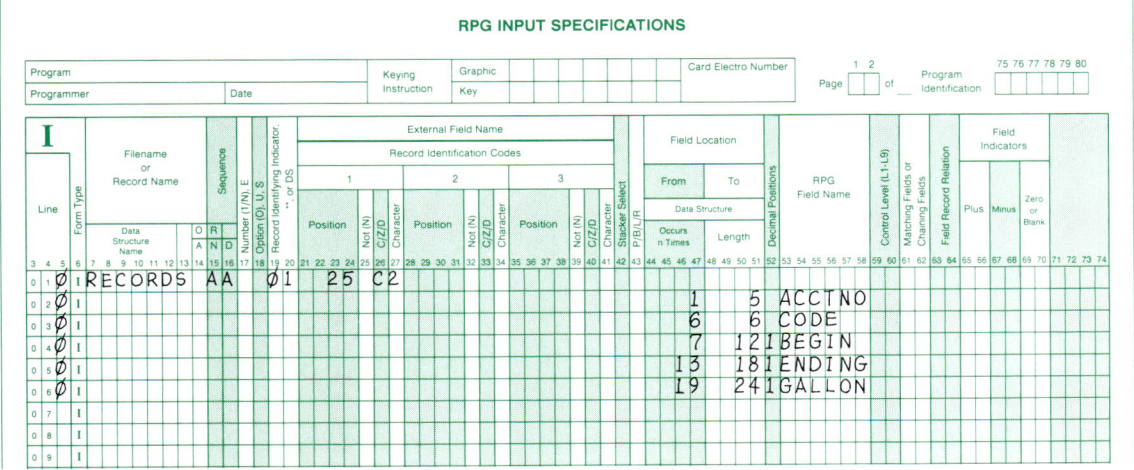

Output is as follows:

```
               FUEL USAGE

ACCOUNT CODE  BEGIN      END      GALLONS    AMOUNT

13255    0    120.0      140.0     20.0       60.00
14162    5    145.0      153.0      8.0       23.52
14510    5    CALCULATION ERROR
16783    0    180.0      235.0     55.0      165.00
18532    0    CALCULATION ERROR

                                   83.0      248.52
```

Calculations   131

4 Control Level Operations

Outline

Control Breaks
   Levels of Controls and Indicators
   Subtotals and Totals
Basic RPG Logic
   Program Cycle Operations
Coding a Listing Program
     with Level Control
   Control Level Terminology
   RPG Logic
   Control Level Indicators
   RPG Specifications
   Control Level Coding
     Assignment of Level Indicators
     Output Coding with Level
       Indicators

Using the Blank After Specifications
Group Indication
Control Level—Summary
   RPG Logic Cycle
   Indicators L1–L9
   Specifications
   Blank After Coding
   Group Indication

Figure 4.1 Report with group totals

```
                           MONTHLY COMMISSION REPORT

SALESMAN    SALESMAN    INVOICE    INVOICE                              INVOICE      COMMISSION
NUMBER      NAME        NUMBER     DATE       CUSTOMER NAME             AMOUNT       AMOUNT

3296        SMITH, J    19899      11/03/87   JACOBS & HARRIS INC       8,387.70     419.39
                         9948      11/05/87   WRING-WELL WASHERS           48.95       2.45
                        10385      11/10/87   ROLLS-CANARDLY INC        1,382.25      69.11
                                                                                     490.95

3621        WALTERS, M  18333      11/05/87   FLUORIDE WELLS INC        2,189.27     109.46
                        18137      11/08/87   COOL-AIR INC                785.83      39.29
                        12845      11/10/87   LOS ESPANOLAS S A           892.75      44.64
                        13899      11/10/87   ICE MANUFACTURERS INC        99.50       4.98
                        12387      11/12/87   JERRY CONTRACTORS INC     1,083.25      54.16
                        10534      11/13/87   SEASHELL DISTRIBUTORS       684.49      34.22
                         8052      11/16/87   FRANCE HILL RESEARCH         34.56       1.73
                        18232      11/23/87   NATIONAL TEA COMPANY        947.62      64.22
                        15305      11/26/87   ASHTON MACHINE COMPANY    1,284.38      64.22
                                                                                     416.92
```

Control Breaks

Many accounting and management information processing activities require control breaks. Files are logically subdivided based on values of fields within data records of those files. Such files are usually sequenced on those values. All records having the same value are therefore in the same logical subdivision. When the value changes, a new group of records becomes available. (See Figure 4.1.) A change in a controlling data value is called a **control break.** The control break may be detected by the object program and cause processing commensurate with the end of a group. Examples of further processing include the printing of subtotals, skipping to a new page, or reinitializing fields for the next file subdivision.

Inventory valuation is an example of an application requiring control break detection and processing. The inventory file is ordered by stock number within warehouse number. The value of each item in the first warehouse is calculated and printed as a detail record. A subtotal of the value of all items in the warehouse is accumulated. When a record with a new warehouse number is input, the current warehouse subtotal is printed and the subtotal accumulator field is added to a company total field that is set to zero at the beginning of the run. The subtotal accumulator field is then reset to zero to start accumulation for the next warehouse. The printer is advanced to a new page and the headings printed. Then the calculation of stock item values is begun for the next warehouse. Each time the warehouse number changes, a control break occurs. (See Figure 4.2.)

Levels of Control and Indicators

In practical applications, many levels of control may be required. An example is a sales report derived from a file of sales records sequenced on (1) product code, (2) sales account, (3) sales office, (4) geographic district, (5) region, and (6) subsidiary company within the corporation. The sales records are details reflecting individual sales; the individual sales are never printed.

The lowest level of detail for a product code is the total sales figure for a time period. Consequently, in this particular example, six levels of control are required. The problem is accommodated by assigning

Figure 4.2 Inventory valuation—example

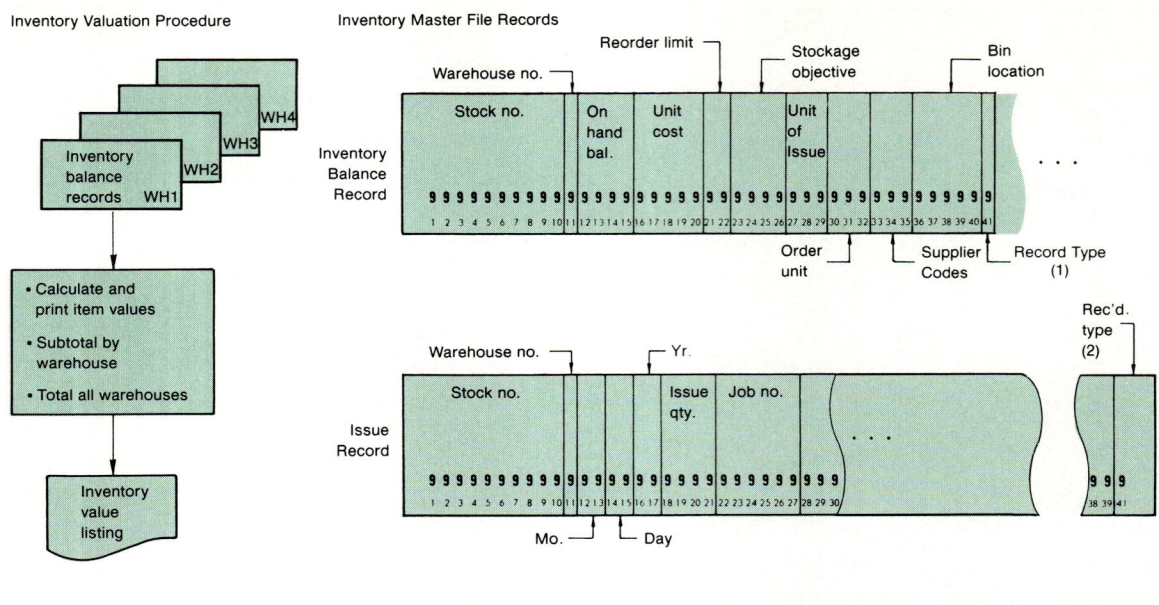

the level indicators L1–L6 to the input fields containing the data elements numbered 1–6, respectively. A change in the data field from record to record at any level causes the indicator at that level to be turned on, as well as all indicators at lower levels of control. The level indicators are used to condition the printing of output lines appropriate to the level of control break.

It is desirable for any print line in a report of this type to be readily identifiable as to the new level of control break that has occurred to cause printing. Also, it may be easy to distinguish between details, totals, and levels of subtotals. Several techniques are commonly used to make these distinctions. The lowest level of print line is usually unidentified. The next higher level may be indicated by appending two asterisks. That pattern is maintained throughout. For reports with more than three or four control levels the approach of using an increasing succession of asterisks (or similar character) may be unsatisfactory because the reader may have to stop to count too often. Also, the format restrictions of reports having high information density on a page may preclude appending a sufficient number of asterisks.

Such situations may be remedied by the use of captions, such as ACCT TOTAL or DEPT TOTAL, which are inserted in the output record before printing. (See Figure 4.3.)

Figure 4.3 Control levels—examples

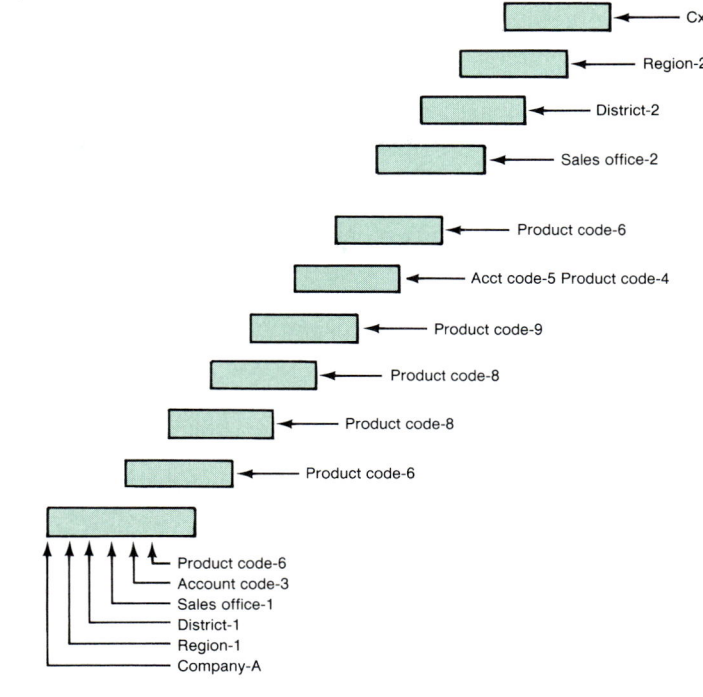

Record Format

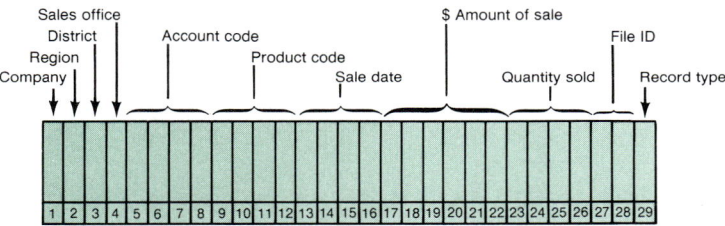

Sales Report			June 1987				Page 1
Co.	Reg.	Dist.	Ofc.	Acct.	Prod.	Qty.	Amt.
1	1	1	1	5	4	20	400.00
					7	10	360.00
							760.00*
				9	5	5	55.00
							.
							1040.20**
			3	29	4	10	200.00
							.
							37690.00
		6	2	49	3	50	600.00
							.
		Eastern Region Total					604862.16
	2	1	3	1096	2	45	90.00
							.
							1064.40*
							8420.60**
							79160.70
		Western Region Total					205370.20
		Company Z Total					580400.60
		Corporate Total					1,943,604.20

Control Level Operations

Subtotals and Totals

From the preceding discussion it is apparent that many common reports require accumulation of subtotals at various control levels, and that major totals are required at the highest control levels. By referencing control level indicators as conditions for totaling operations, these requirements may be readily met within the structure of RPG. For detail record processing, the desired quantitative fields are accumulated by summing into a result field for the first control level. When a control break occurs at the first control level, the result (accumulator) field for that level is added into the result field for the second control level. The first level subtotal is then output in a print line with an appropriate indicator.

A convenient feature of RPG is that the user may specify that the first control level subtotal field be reset to zero after it has been used as a data source for printing or for other output. The reset to zero (or to blanks for alphameric fields) may be specified for any output field at any level of control. Reset to zero is necessary to allow accumulation of a new subtotal for the control level until the next control break.

For higher-level control breaks, the contents of all subordinate-level subtotal accumulator fields must be added successively into the next higher control level subtotal accumulator. The subtotal at the level where the control break has occurred is also added into the next higher level accumulator field. The RPG object program then prints (for output) the subtotals for all subordinate levels and for the level where the control break has occurred. Appropriate level indicators should be shown. All subtotal accumulator fields should be reset to zero after being used as a data source for output.

The performance of an RPG program can be controlled in many ways. The basic elements of controlling calculations and output, especially the concept of RPG object program cycle and the use of indicators to condition specifications, have already been discussed. This chapter supplements those basic concepts by presenting topics related to level control programming.

On the Calculations and Output Specifications forms, all calculations and output to be done on a particular job are described. Sometimes all the calculations and output operations must be performed on every program cycle. More often, however, it is necessary to perform operations under certain conditions. For example, some calculation may need to be performed or some output produced only when a control break occurs.

Basic RPG Logic

Calculation and output operations are performed at two different times in one program cycle. The names detail and total have been assigned to the times at which calculation and output operations are performed. Total time, as the name suggests, is the time in which total operations are done on data accumulated from a group of related records. Detail time is the time in which operations are performed for individual records. *Detail operations are done for every record read, but total operations are done only after a certain group of records are read.* (See Figure 4.4.)

Program Cycle Operations

A system can perform calculations and output operations at two different times in one cycle—at detail time and at total time. Total operations associated with control level indicators are not done in every cycle; they are done during the cycle in which the control field changes.

After a record is read, the program determines whether the control field in the record just read is different from the control field in the previous record. If it is, a control break occurs and the control level specified is set on. When the indicator is on, it means that all records in the control group have been read and total operations can be performed. Control level indicators remain on throughout the detail calculations and the output processing of the record that caused the control break. They are then set off before the next record is read.

Detail operations for the record that causes the control break are done only after total operations for previous records have been performed. The control level indicator assigned to the field that caused the control break remains on so that the first record of the group may be identified with that indicator. The record that caused the control break is not processed before the total operations are done because that would cause the information from that record to be included with information from records in the previous group, causing that total to then be in error.

Figure 4.4 RPG logic cycle with level control

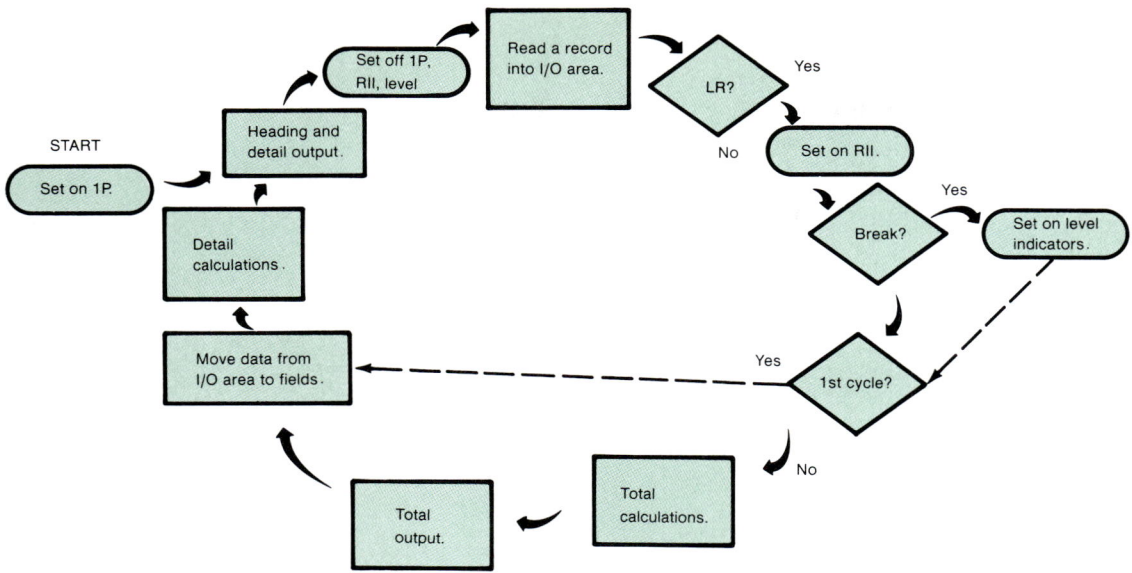

According to RPG logic, after a record is read, the program checks to see whether information in the control fields of the record selected differs from the control field information in the previous record. (The program always saves the control field information for such a comparison.) If there has been a change, the proper control level indicator (the one assigned by the programmer) is turned on. This means that all records from one group have been read. All total operations can then be performed. Control level indicators are always turned off just before the next record is read.

During the step between total and detail time the data from the record read at the beginning of the cycle is moved to a processing area and is made available for use in calculations and output. Data from this record is not available at total time. Total operations are performed only on data accumulated from previous records. Detail operations on the record that caused the control level indicator to be turned on are done only after total operations for previous records are finished. (See Figure 4.5.)

To prevent the data from the first record in a new control group from being accumulated in the totals for the previous group, total operations are done before detail operations. (See Figure 4.6.)

Coding a Listing Program with Level Control

The RPG coding rules have so far permitted us to program a report that has headings, detail lines, and a total at the end. If totals are required before the end of the report, level control programming is necessary. To write programs that will provide totals after a group of records as well as at the end of the report, it is necessary to have some additional understanding of coding, of the use of indicators for control, and of the expanded RPG logic cycle.

Control Level Terminology

In order to process records as a group the records must be organized and have a control field in each record. This will enable the computer to first print all detail total information for the group before beginning the details for the next group.

All records with the same control field are called a **control group.** The **control field** is a field common to all records that is used to identify the control breaks according to which special calculations and/or output are to be performed. The control field is a field designed into the record for some special purpose. The control field might be a department number, an account number, or a salesman number, for instance. All records for a control group are grouped together so that the detail information from each may be processed and accumulated together for totals.

Figure 4.5 Illustration of detail and total time

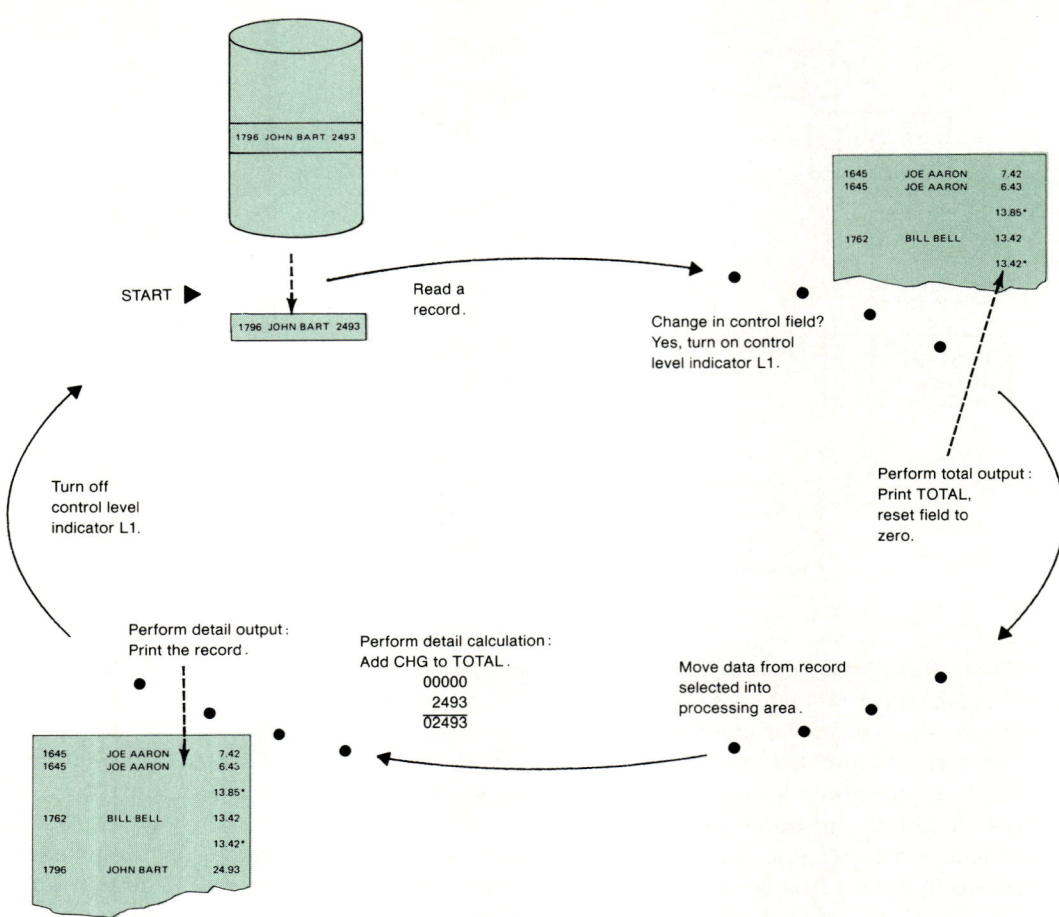

Figure 4.6 Program cycle operations for the control level indicators

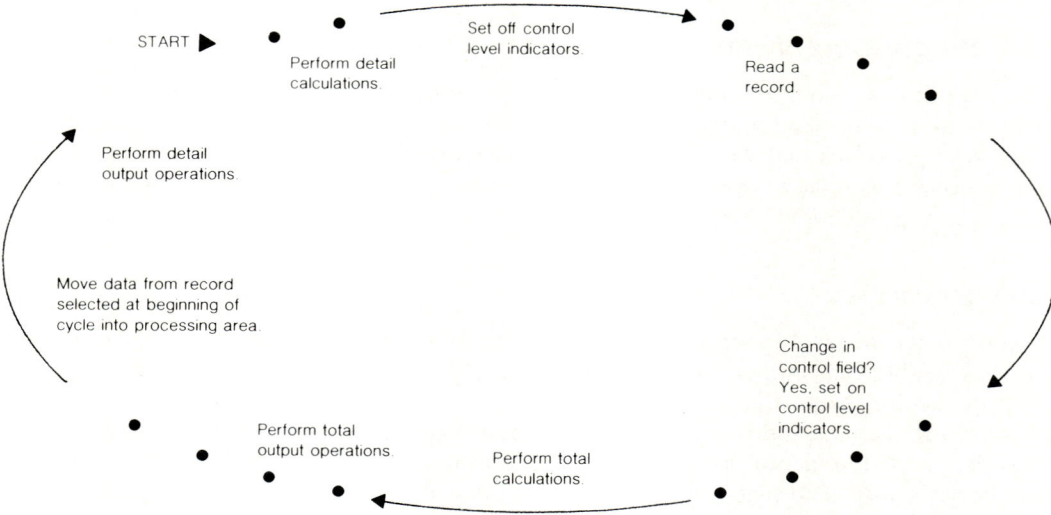

138   RPG II and RPG III Programming

Figure 4.7 Relationship between control field, control break, and control group

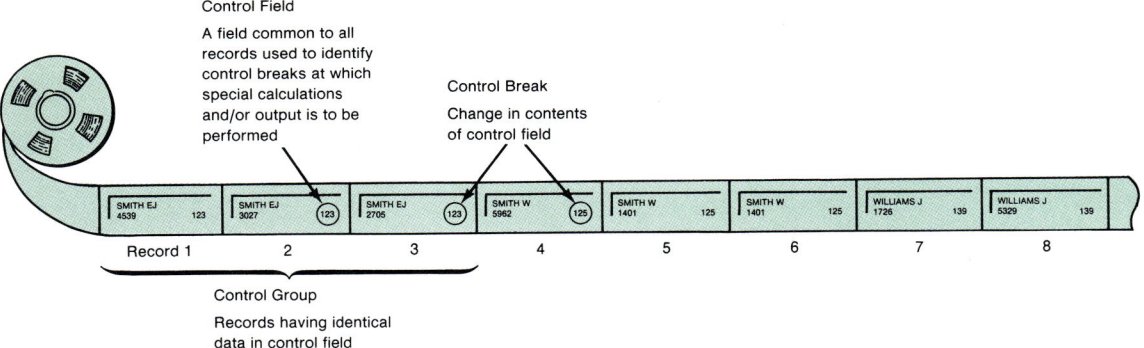

Whenever a control field changes from one group to another it is called a control break. A control break is any change in the content of a control field. The change is recognized before any totals are printed. (See Figure 4.7.)

RPG Logic

RPG will check the field(s) designated as control fields on the Input Specifications form. If it finds any change in the content of a field (indicating a control break), RPG will then set on the control level indicator specified on the Input Specifications form. After checking to see if there is a difference between this record and the previous one, RPG will then see if this is the first cycle.

Since the first record is different from no record, a control break occurs. No totals are read, however, so the total blocks are bypassed and the data are moved directly from the I/O area to the fields.

If it is not the first cycle, RPG will attempt to do the total calculations and the total output.

The record that causes the control break is the first record of the new group. This means that all the detail processing for the previous group is complete. Therefore, before the data is moved to fields for this new group, the totals for the prior group must be completed. That is why the total calculations and total output occur where they do.

Control Level Indicators

The special indicators in RPG that are assigned to control levels are called **control level indicators.** The programmer has to tell the computer which fields are control fields, which control level indicators to turn on when a control break occurs, and what calculations and output are required at that time. All calculations or outputs controlled by L indicators will be performed before those controlled by record identifying indicators.

Control level indicators are used when it is necessary to calculate and print totals. Nine different indicators can be used (L1–L9), allowing as many as nine different levels of totals in the same program. The control level indicators tell the program two things:

1. When totals should be calculated
2. Which calculations and output operations are total operations

A control level indicator is placed in positions 59–60 next to the input field specified on the Input Specifications form. From this location the control level indicator determines when totals should be calculated and printed. This input field is known as the control field. Whenever the content of this control field changes, a control break occurs. A control break turns on the control level indicator assigned to the control field, as well as all lower control level indicators. The system performs all calculations and output operations (total operations) that are conditioned by these control level indicators. If a control break causes L3 to be turned on, L1 and L2 are also turned on. This allows control over several levels of totals and subtotals. Examples are daily, weekly, and monthly totals.

When the output operations controlled by LR have been performed, the program is finished. An LR control break causes all lower-level control breaks to take place.

Figure 4.8 Control level coding

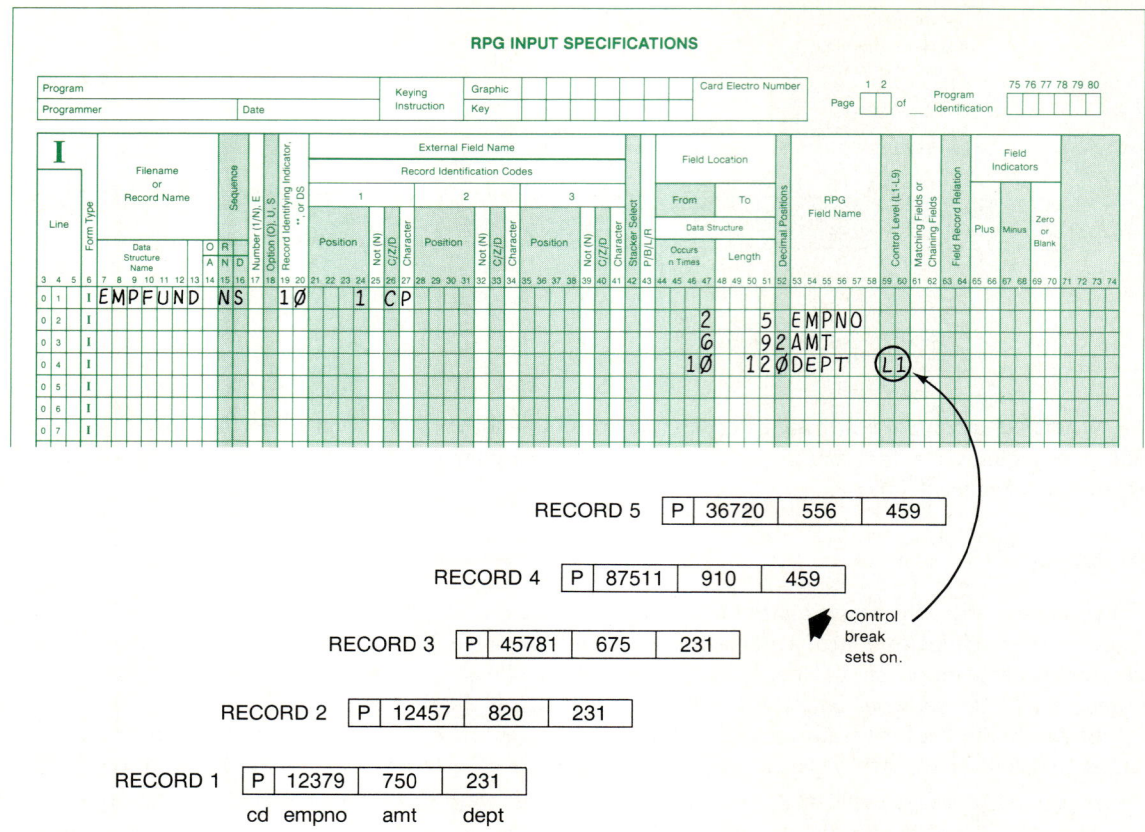

Note: The field to which you assign a control level indicator becomes the control field.

RPG Specifications

To specify a field as a control field, a control level indicator (L1–L9) is assigned to an input field in positions 59–60 on the Input Specifications form. (See Figure 4.8.) To specify which operations are total operations, the same control level indicator is assigned in positions 7–8 on the Calculation Specifications form and in positions 24–25, 27–28, or 30–31 on the Output Specifications form. (See Figure 4.9.) Control level indicators are not used in the output specifications to indicate detail and total records. Rather, a *T* is used in position 15 to indicate a total output operation and an *H* or a *D* is used to indicate an operation done at detail time.

Up to three different indicators may be specified on a line of the Output Specifications form. If only one indicator is being used, it may be entered in any one of the three positions. The control level indicators may be used to condition either an output record or only particular fields within an output record. The L1–L9 indicators may also be used at detail time for controlled printing.

Control Level Coding

Control level coded reports provide an organized format that is under the control of the programmer.

Assignment of Level Indicators

The RPG cycle will check for a control break and set on the appropriate level indicator, but the programmer must assign both the field to be checked and the indicator to be turned on. The control fields are assigned on the Input Specifications form.

There are nine control level indicators, L1–L9.

The control level indicator is assigned beside the field that has been designated as the control field.

Figure 4.9 Assignment and use of control level indicators

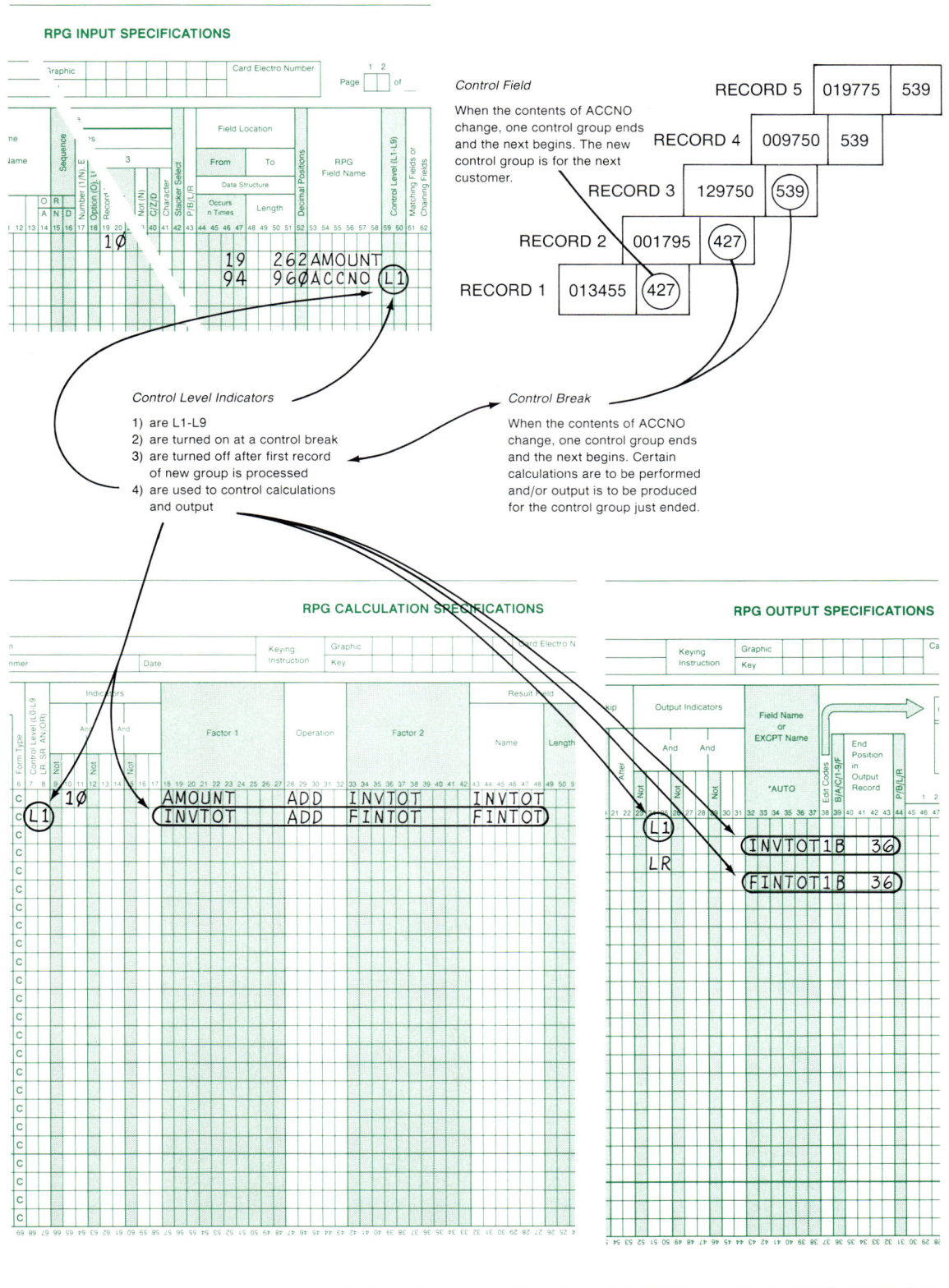

Control Level Operations 141

Figure 4.10 Control level indicators—specifications

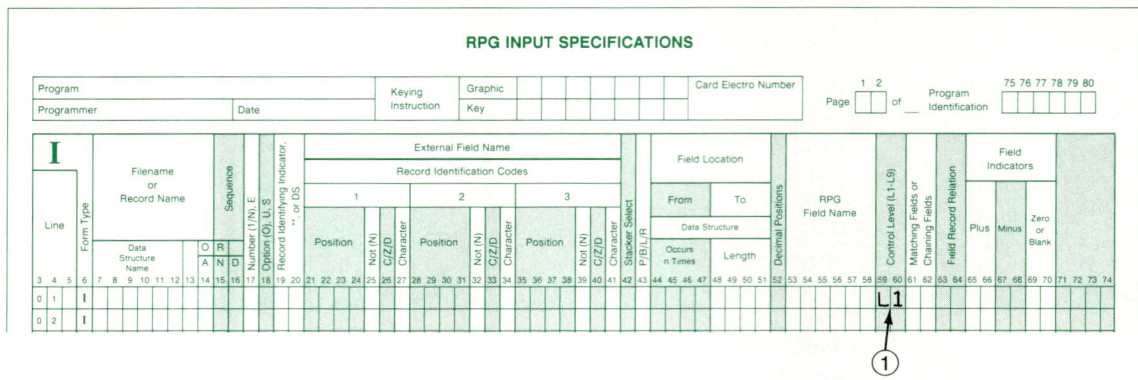

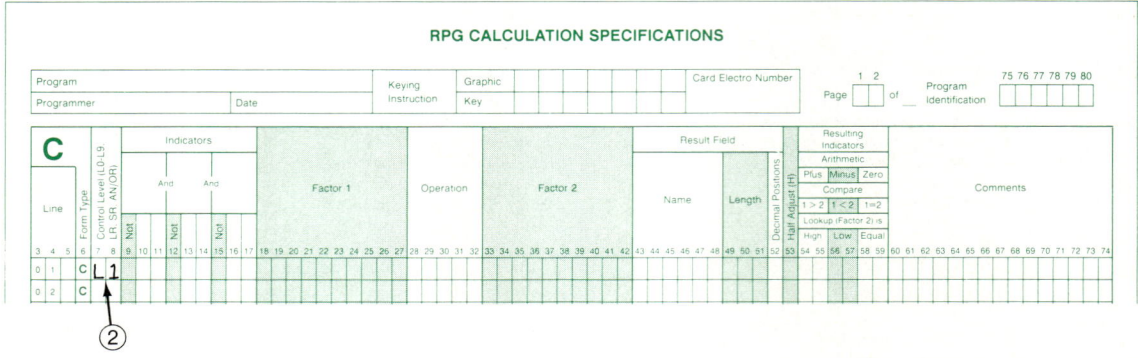

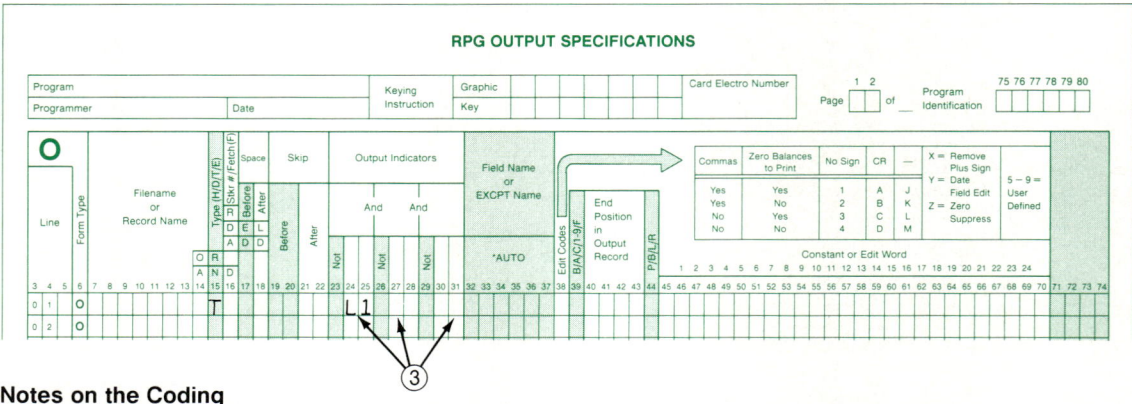

Notes on the Coding

Control level indicators are specified at (1) to tell the computer when total operations are to be done. They are used at (2) to tell which operations are total calculations. They are used in any of the positions indicated by (3) with a T in position 15 to tell which lines are total lines.

The field is described on the Input Specifications form; like any other field it is described by means of location, field name, and decimal positions. The only additional coding for a control field is the specification of a control level indicator beside the field in positions 59–60. (See Figures 4.10 and 4.11.)

Early in the RPG cycle a check is made for a control break. When there is a difference between the control field in the record just read and the one before it, the assigned level indicator is turned on.

The indicator is on for the remainder of the cycle. This means it may be used during total calculations, total output, detail calculations, and detail output. Control level indicators are turned off automatically at the end of the RPG cycle.

If more than one level of totals is required, more than one control level indicator is used. Suppose the programmer needs totals by departments, and departments are within branches, and branches are

Figure 4.11 Control level indicator assignment—example

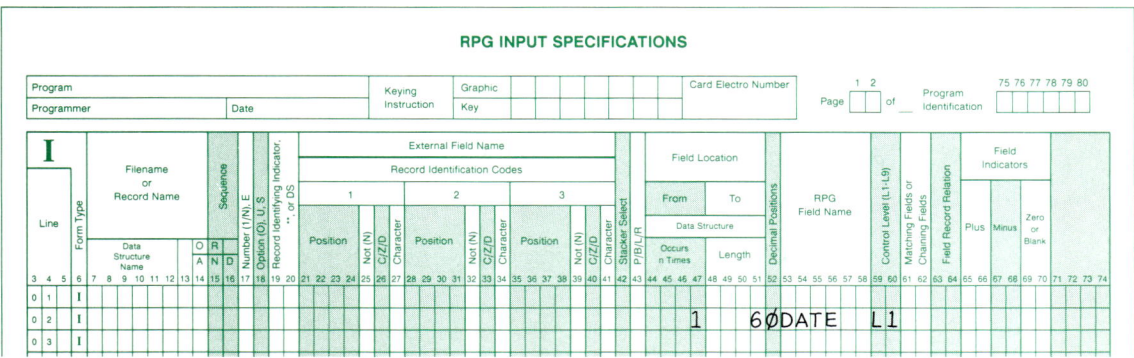

Notes on the Coding

L1, assigned on the same specification line as the date field, tells the system to use DATE as the control field.

within districts, and a total at the end of all districts may be needed. The following control level indicators might be assigned:

Department might be assigned L1.
Branch might be assigned L2.
District might be assigned L3.
Final might be assigned LR.

The first field is the least significant field; the last field is the most significant field. *The higher the control level number, the more significant the field.* Proper coding will assure that totals are printed in the correct order. (See Figure 4.12.)

Figure 4.12 Detail and total calculations—examples

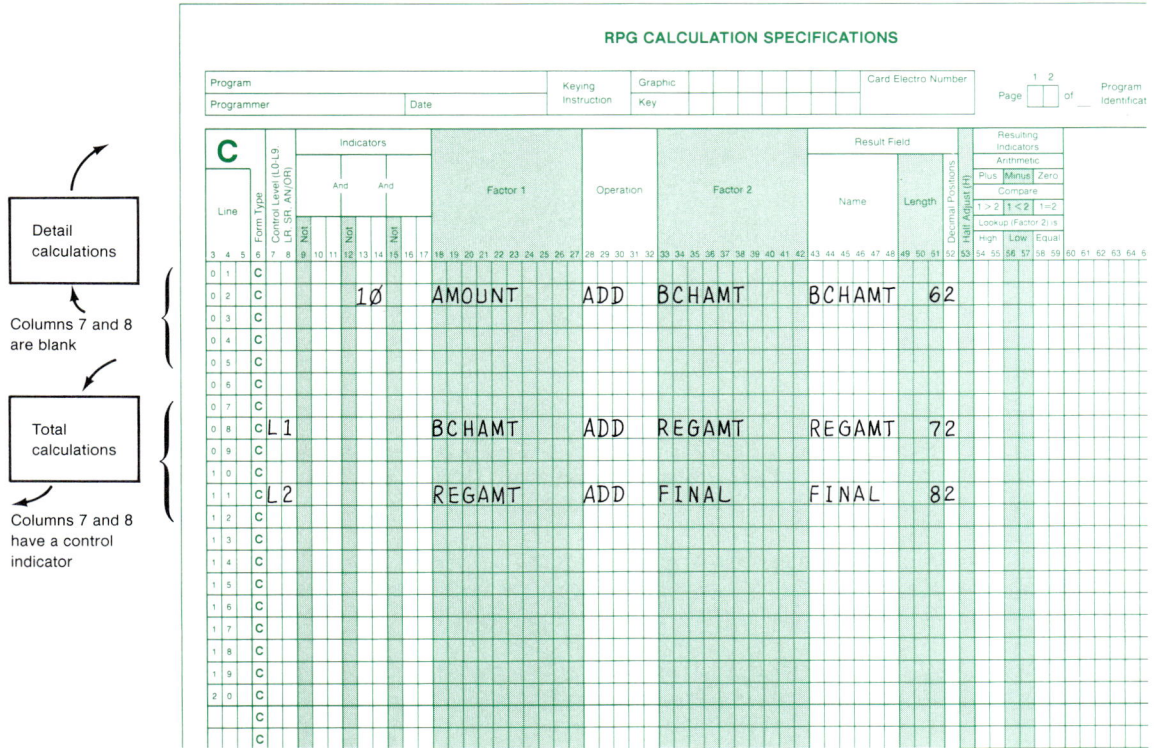

Control Level Operations   143

Output Coding with Level Indicators

Coding *H, D,* or *T* in position 15 on the Output Specifications form tells RPG what type of output record is needed and what time in the cycle to perform that output. Following are some of the rules associated with control level indicators on the output specifications:

1. The output should be coded in the order *H, D, T*.

2. The total output should be in the order of the lowest level first, followed by the next level, and so on, to LR coding (if required).

Figure 4.13 Control level coding—example

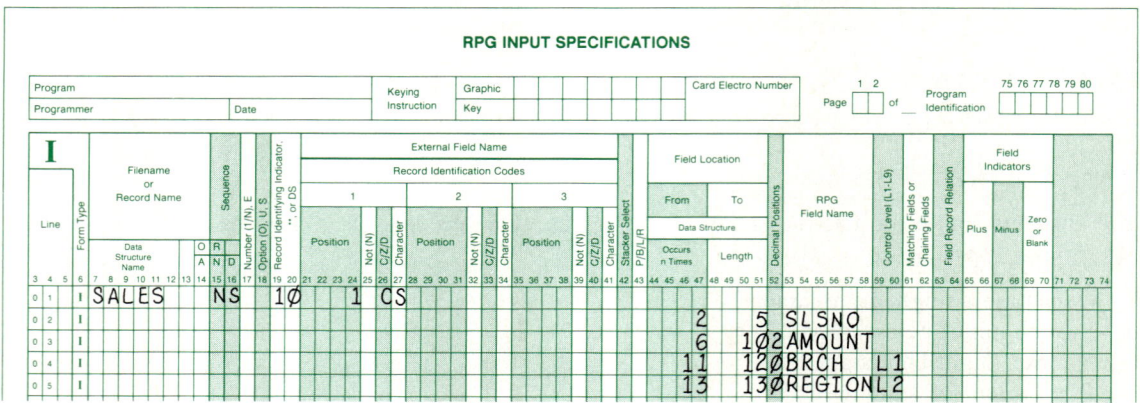

Notes on the Coding

Since there are several branches within any region, the BRCH is the least significant control field and should be assigned the lowest control indicator—L1.

The next level of control is the REGION; it is assigned the next control level indicator—L2.

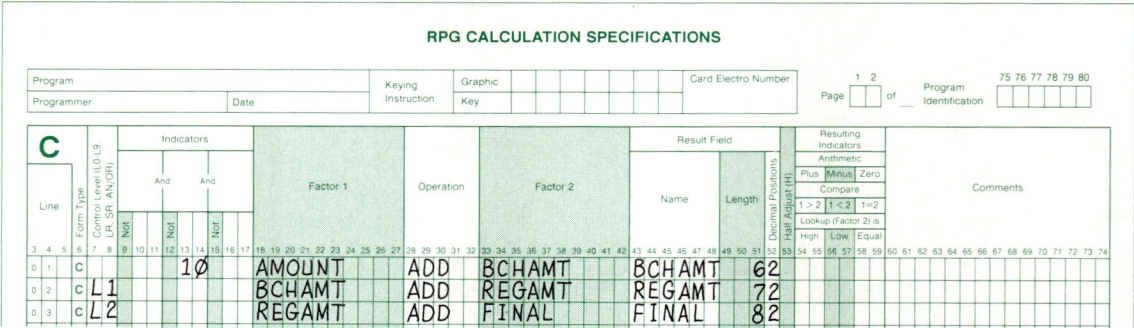

Notes on the Coding

Line 01: the field AMOUNT will be added to BCHAMT at Detail time every time record identifying indicator 10 is on. This is an accumulating addition, since the result field is the same as one of the factors. While BCHAMT is accumulating for each detail cycle, it will not be printed until the end of the group—until L1 control break.

Line 02: The field BCHAMT is accumulated into the field REGAMT at Total time when the L1 indicator is on. This calculation is saving the accumulated BCHAMT, which makes up part of the REGAMT. The BCHAMT is about to be printed at L1, but the REGAMT will not print until the L2 control break—at the end of the region.

Line 03: The field REGAMT is accumulated into the field FINAL at Total time when the L2 indicator is on. The calculation is saving the several REGAMTs for the final total, which will be printed at LR.

Figure 4.13 continued

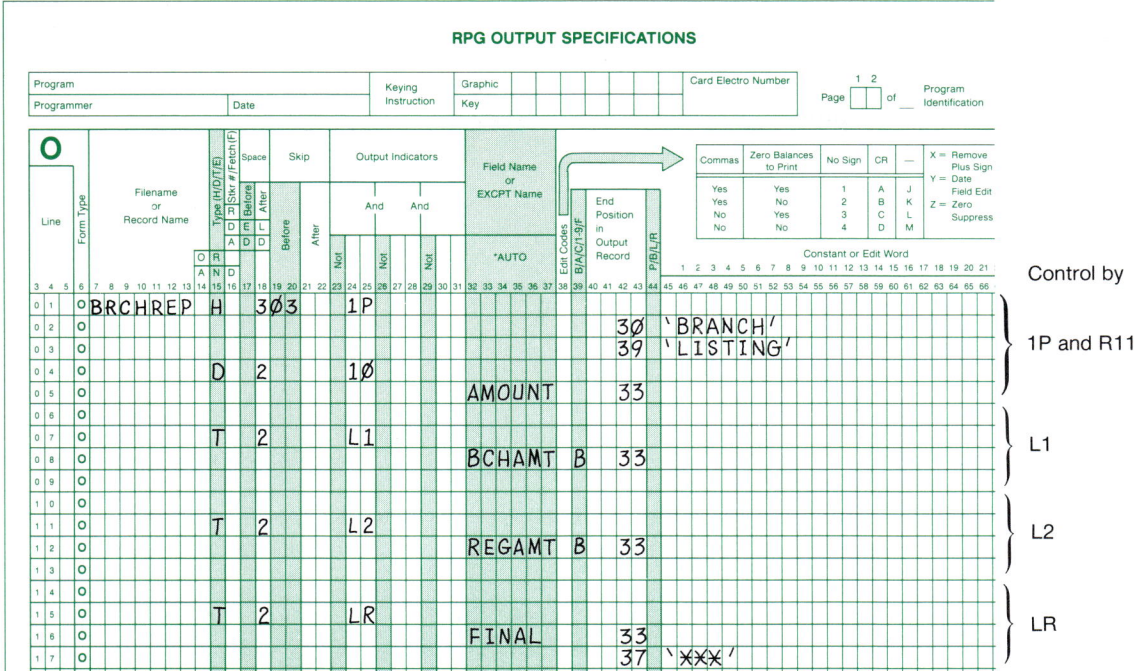

Notes on the Coding

The Output should be coded in the order H, D, T.

The Total Output should be in the order of the lowest level first, followed by the next level, and so on to LR coding (if required).

For Total coding, the T by itself or the L1 by itself are not enough. The T and a level indicator must be coded.

After the totals are written out, such as BCHAMT or REGAMT, the Detail Calculations in that same cycle are continuing to accumulate into those fields unless something is done about it. To "clear," or set the field to zeros in order to be ready for the next group of records. A B is entered in column 39 to BLANK-AFTER OUTPUT. It provides a way to zero the fields after they have been written. If the field need not be blanked, as on the Final total, the entry is omitted.

3. For total coding, the *T* by itself or the *L*1 by itself is not enough. Both the *T* and the *L* level indicators must be coded.

4. Detail calculations will continue to accumulate into those fields unless the fields are reinitialized to zero. This "blanking" or "zeroing out" must be done in order for the field to be ready for the next group of records. A *B* is placed in position 39 of the Output Specifications form to provide the clearing function. The *B* stands for **blank after** output. It provides a way to zero the fields after they have been output. (See Figure 4.13.)

Using the Blank After Specifications

In RPG, fields in storage can be set to blanks (in the case of alphameric fields) or zeros (in the case of numeric fields) after they have been written out. This is done by entering a *B* in position 39 of the Output Specifications form.

The blank after is a particularly useful feature when doing total operations. It allows the programmer to use the same field over and over for accumulating and printing totals. For example, a numeric field can be used to accumulate totals for a particular group of records. After the records are accumulated and printed for that group, the same numeric field can be used to accumulate the totals for the next group of records. To do this, place a *B* in position 39 of the Output Specifications form for

Control Level Operations 145

Figure 4.14 Printed report of all items in stock

CLASS	ITEM NO	DESCRIPTION	ON HAND
00124	7657352	SWEATER, V-NK, SZ 32	10
00124	63241B1	SWEATER, V-NK, SZ 34	16
00124	43151CK	CARDIGAN, SZ 36	17
.	.	.	
00124	76738K2	CARDIGAN, SZ 40	8
00125	54321K4	T-SHIRT, WH, SZ 30	11
00125	56422K4	T-SHIRT, WH, SZ 32	14
00125	57381J4	T-SHIRT, WH, SZ 40	15
00125	58324B1	T-SHIRT, WH, SZ 42	8
.	.	.	
00125	57421C2	T-SHIRT, BK, SZ 46	12
00126	67341B3	WOOL SOCKS, BL 10	11

the total field. If a *B* is not placed in position 39, the totals for the second group of records will be added to the totals for the first group of records.

Note: A word of caution in the use of the blank after is that this specification can wipe out a variable used as a constant as quickly as it can be used to zero out an intermediate total.

Group Indication

The preparation of detail reports is a job basic to any data-processing installation. Detail reports consist of one line of printing for each record read; a transaction listing is a good example. (See Figure 4.14.)

Because product classes are repeated for each line, the report is cluttered and hard to read. The same report grouped by class is much easier to read. (See Figure 4.15.) Here all items from one class are listed together, with headings used on each page to identify the information. Since all items on one

Figure 4.15 Report group—indicated by product class

PAGE 0001

CLASS	ITEM NO	DESCRIPTION	ON HAND
00124	46732J1	SWEATER, V-NK, SZ 32	10
	63241B1	SWEATER, V-NK, SZ 34	16
	43151CK	CARDIGAN, SZ 36	17

PAGE 0002

CLASS	ITEM NO	DESCRIPTION	ON HAND
00125	54321K4	T-SHIRT, WH, SZ 30	11
	56422K4	T-SHIRT, WH, SZ 32	14
	57381J4	T-SHIRT, WH, SZ 40	15
	58324B1	T-SHIRT, WH, SZ 42	–8

PAGE 0003

CLASS	ITEM NO	DESCRIPTION	ON HAND
00126	67341B3	WOOL SOCKS, BL 10	11
	67432B3	WOOL SOCKS, GR 10	9

page apply to the same class, the class is printed only once. Such a report is referred to as a group-indicated report. Group indication is the printing of control information on one line per group. (See Figure 4.16.)

Control Level—Summary

RPG Logic Cycle

A check for a control break has been added to the logic cycle. If a control break is found, the assigned level indicator is turned on by RPG. Two new processing blocks are then added—total calculations for end-of-group operations and total output for writing group totals.

These new processing points in the cycle occur before moving data from the I/O areas to the field. The record that causes the control break is the first record of a new group; all processing of the previous group must be completed before any action on the new one takes place.

Indicators L1–L9

The control level indicators are assigned on the Input Specifications form and are placed beside the fields designated as control fields. If more than one level of control is needed indicators are assigned based on the significance of the fields (from lowest to highest, L1–L9). Because these indicators turn off at the end of the cycle, they may be used at total as well as at detail time of the cycle when the control breaks occur.

Specifications

All detail activity is coded before all total activity on the calculations and output specifications. When coding more than one level, code the lowest (L1) first, L2 next, and so on, until LR processing takes place.

1. RPG recognizes a control break when the control field in the record is different from the previous record.

Figure 4.16 Control level coding—example

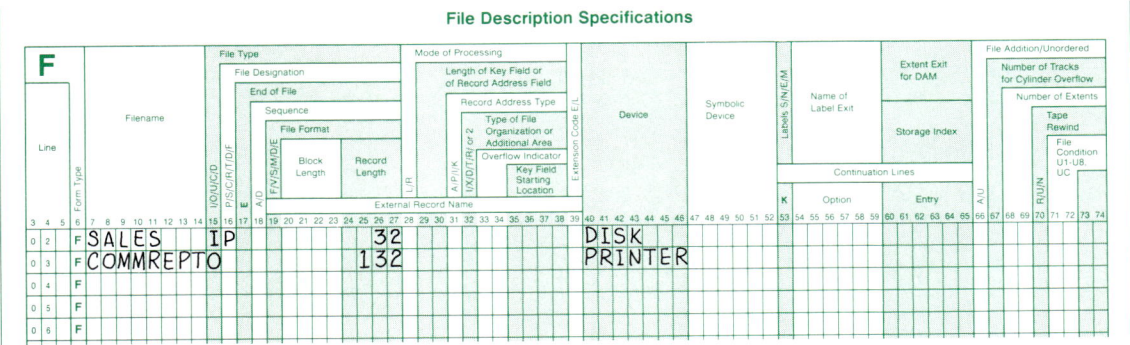

Notes on the Coding

While the File Description Specifications do not have a unique place in the RPG cycle, they do play an important part in determining the environment for the entire program. This includes what devices will be used and how they will be used in this program.

In this example, SALES is the Input Primary file on DISK. Each of the records in this file will have 32 bytes. This is the file that is read when the RPG cycle says, "Read a record into the I/O area."

The file named COMMREPT is the output for this program. The PRINTER has 132 print positions for the output records. When the RPG cycle is at Total or Detail Output time, data will be directed to the device designated as Output.

Figure 4.16 continued

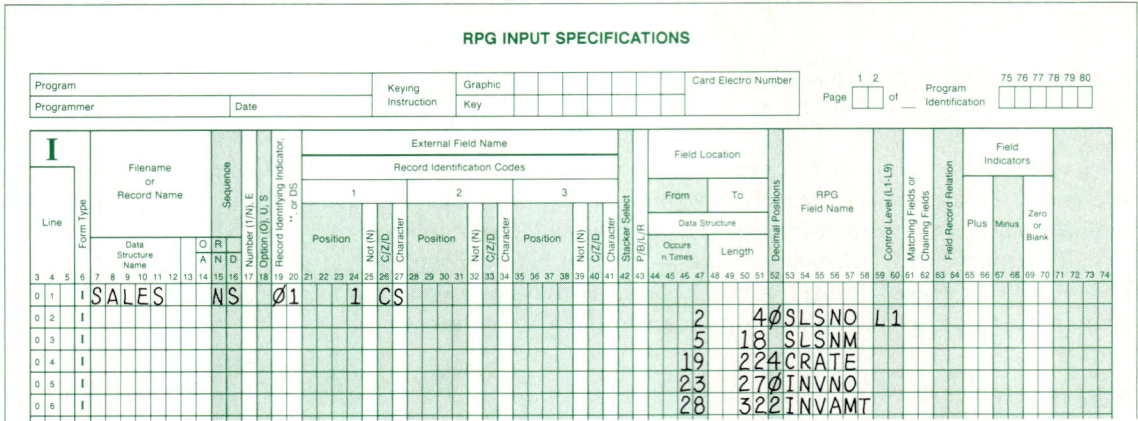

Notes on the Coding

The Input Specifications serve multiple purposes in any RPG program. In this example, the coding is:

Turn on record identifying indicator 01 if there is an S in position 1 of the record. This happens when the RPG cycle states, "Turn on the record identifying indicator."

When it is time to check for a control break, RPG will compare the field SLSNO in this record with the previous record. If they are different, the L1 indicator turns on. SLSNO is the control field, since you will have several records for any salesman and you need the total of their commissions on these records.

At "move data from the I/O area to the fields," the data in the I/O area is separated according to the locations and names specified on these Input Specifications. Decimal positions will be very important for the calculations involving the commission.

Note that while the field CRATE is not printed on the report, it is still required for the calculation and must be read and defined on the input.

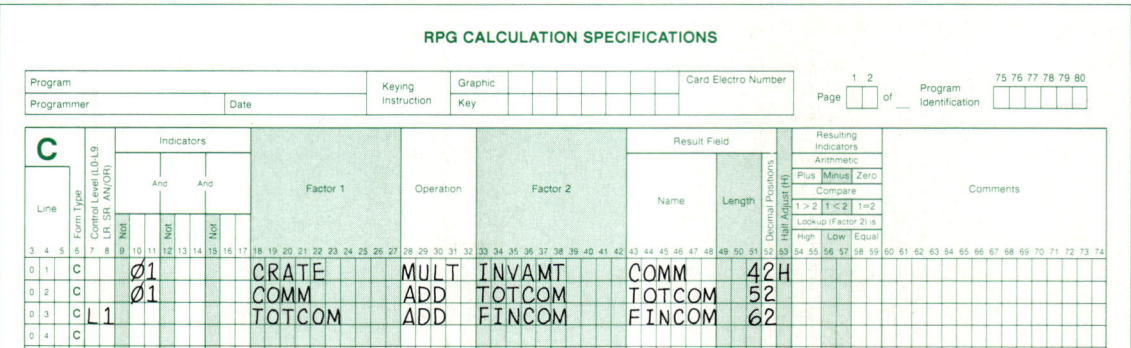

Notes on the Coding

At detail calculation time in the cycle, if indicator 01 is on, multiply the CRATE by the INVAMT to get the COMM. Since the commission is a new field, it must be defined. Use the Printer Spacing Chart for the size. The "half-adjust" entry is optional if you want to round up to two decimals. This operation must come before the accumulation of the TOTCOM.

Again at detail time in the cycle. If indicator 01 is on, accumulate the COMM, which was just computed into the field TOTCOM. This is a new field also and must be defined. Even though the field TOTCOM will not print until L1 total time, it must be accumulated each detail cycle as it is computed. If you wait until a control break to do this calculation, you will miss all the detail records and their calculation of COMM. Why doesn't the first calculation accumulate the commission? Because the field COMM is not one of the factors.

Finally, at total time in the cycle, If L1 is on, accumulate the TOTCOM for each individual salesman into the final total FINCOM, which will print at the end of the report. You are saving this value, since it is about to be printed at Total Output and will be coded to BLANK-AFTER.

RPG II and RPG III Programming

Figure 4.16 continued

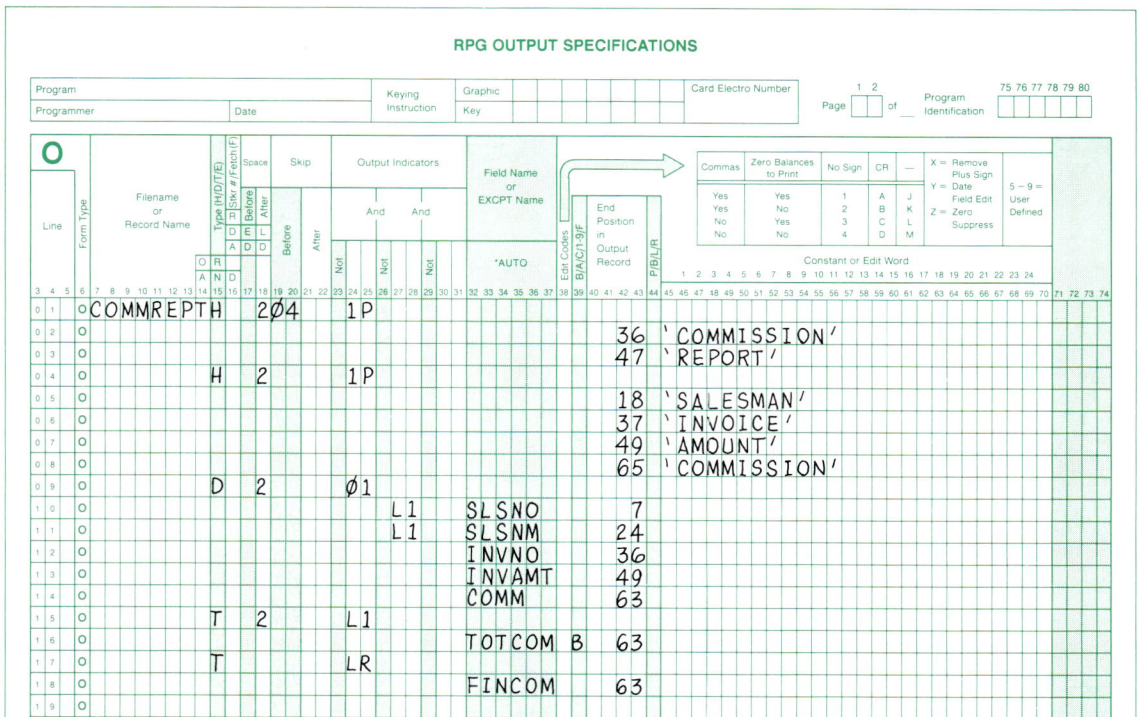

Notes on the Coding

At the start of the RPG cycle, after the 1P indicator turns on, skip to Channel 04 of the form and write out the first heading line with two spaces after it is written. Since 1P is still on, write a second heading line (another H in position 15) and take two more spaces after that line is written. The next type of output is D, but that 01 indicator will not be on until after you read a record and identify it.

At detail time of the cycle, if the 01 indicator is on, write out the fields INVNO, INVAMT, and COMM. If it is the first record of a new group (L1 on at detail time), also write out SLSNO and SLSNM. That last use of the level indicators at detail time enables you to get a "group-indicated" report.

The program will continue to write these detail lines every time the 01 indicator is on at detail time of the cycle. The headings cannot print again, since the 1P indicator is off for the rest of the cycle; the totals will not print until a control break occurs and the L1 indicator is turned on.

Note that L1 is assigned only to the SLSNO for recognizing a control break. However, it may be used for both SLSNO and SLSNM to control printing.

2. The control level indicators turn off automatically just before a new record is read into the I/O area. The record identifying indicator is turned off at this time.

3. Total output is for end-of-group totals or for the totals printed at last record time. The detail output is for the individual records, which print under control of the record identifying indicator.

4. A check for the first cycle must be done because the first record causes a control break. The first cycle differs from the previous record, since there was no previous record. Total processing is bypassed on the first cycle.

5. The total blocks precede the movement of data because total processing is for the last group. The record that caused the control break is the first record of the new group, and the processing is delayed until the total for the last one is finished.

Control Level Operations 149

Figure 4.17 Indicator summary

Indicator	Assigned	Turned on by	Turned off by	Usage
RII	Input	Conditions of codes in the record	RPG II at the end of cycle	Detail processing detail output
1P	In the cycle	RPG II	RPG II at the end of cycle	First page headings
LR	In the cycle	After the last record has been processed	RPG II	Last record processing and output
Resulting	Calculations (compare) (arithmetic)	Conditions met —high low equal —plus minus zero	The next test	Calculations output records of fields
Level	Input	Control break	RPG II at the end of cycle	Detail and total calculations and output

Blank After Coding

Detail accumulations will continue to be added to previous accumulation throughout the program unless the fields are cleared to zero. A *B* is placed in position 39 of the Output Specifications form to perform the clearing function. This blank after feature is particularly useful when doing total operations because it allows the programmer to use the same field over and over for accumulating and printing totals.

Group Indication

Group indication is the printing of control information on one line per group. This permits the listing of all items of one group of common information only once. Because the common information is printed only once for each group, the report is not cluttered and hard to read. (See Figure 4.15.)

Illustrative Program

Control Levels—Group Indication: Transaction Register

Job Definition
Print a weekly sales transaction report that lists daily transactions, total sales for the day, and total sales for the week. The report is similar to the one created in chapter 3. The only difference is the addition of control levels and group indication.

Input
This consists of a sales transaction file consisting of 42-byte records. Records are arranged in ascending order by date. The format of the input records is shown on this Record Layout form:

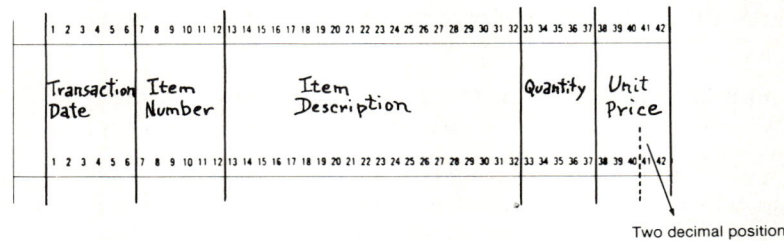

Two decimal positions

150   RPG II and RPG III Programming

Processing
  Multiply quantity times unit price to find sales amount.
  Accumulate sales amount to find total item sales per day.
  Accumulate total daily sales to find total weekly sales.

Output
This Printer Spacing Chart shows how the report is formatted:

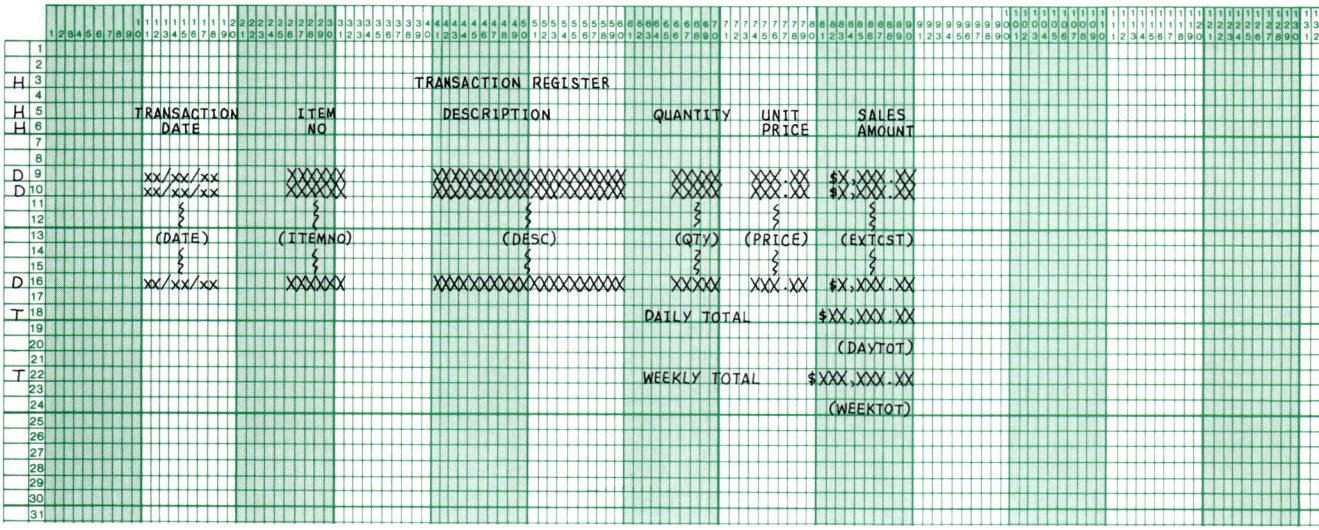

Coding sheets for Transaction Register problem:

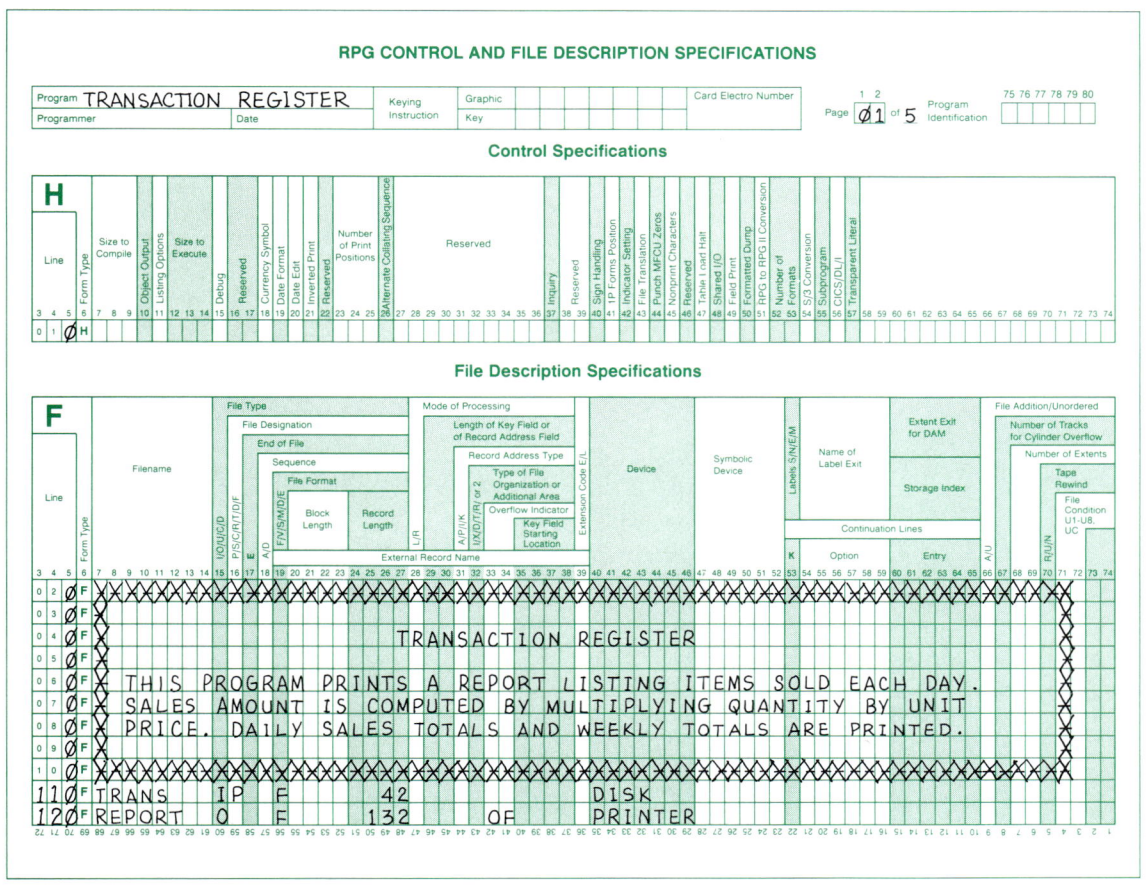

Control Level Operations 151

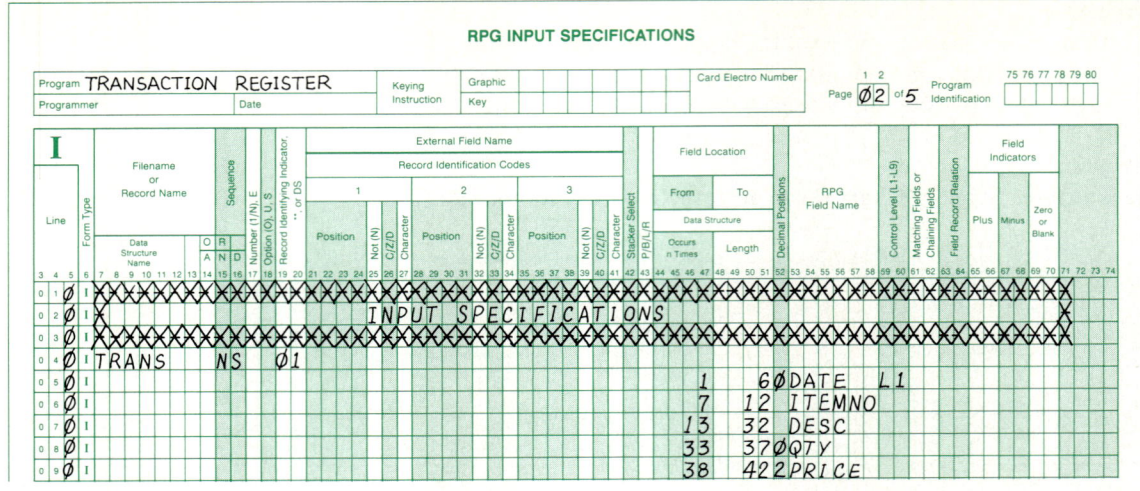
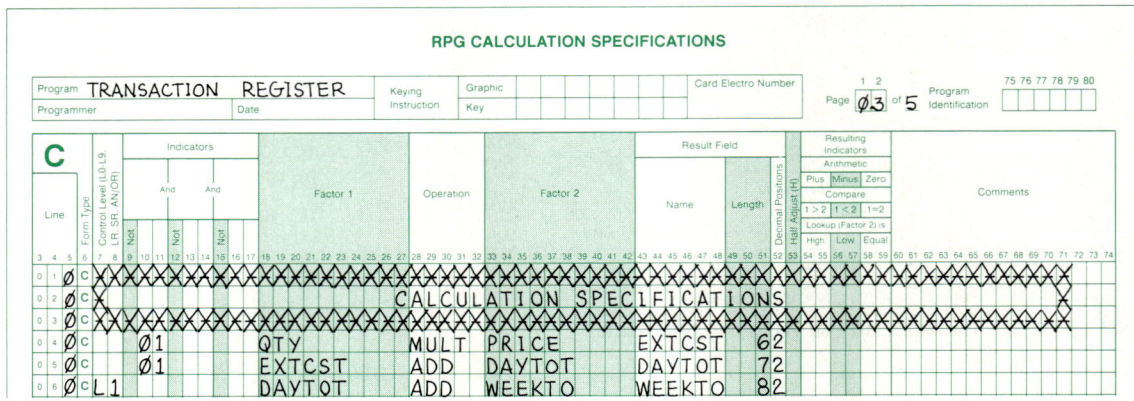
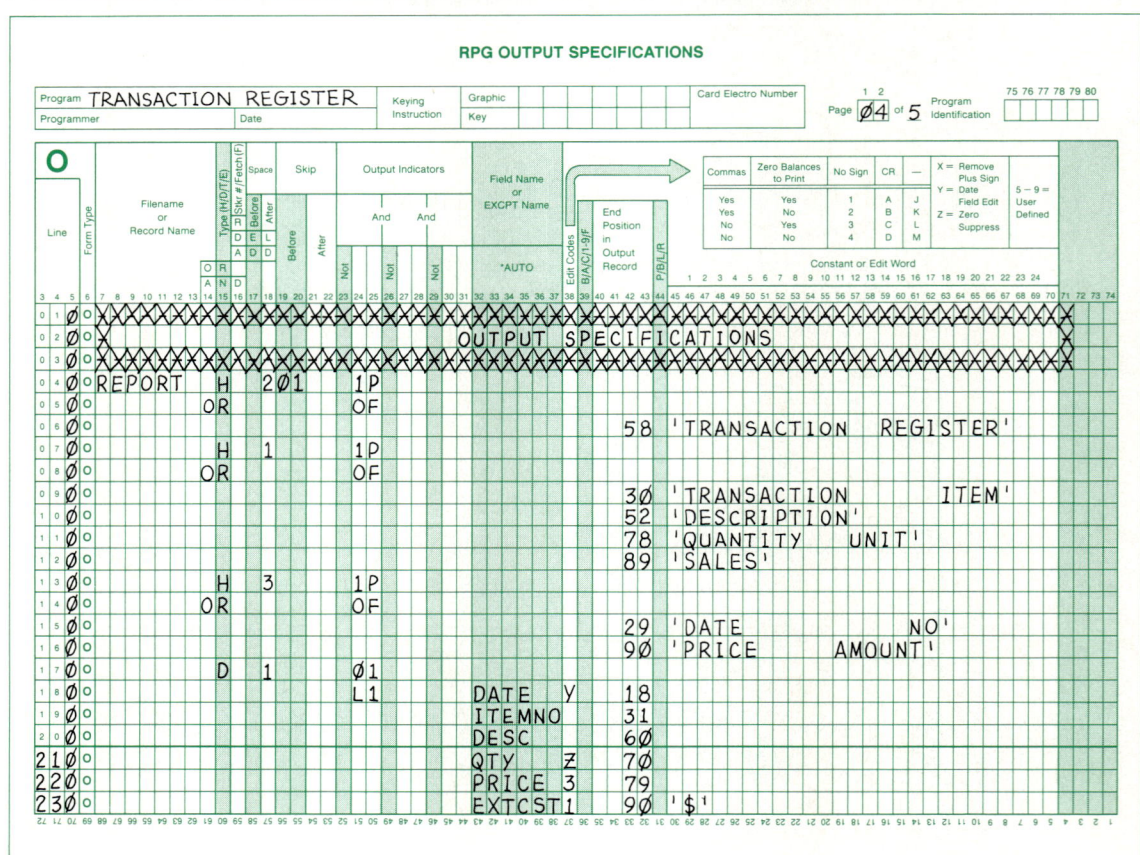

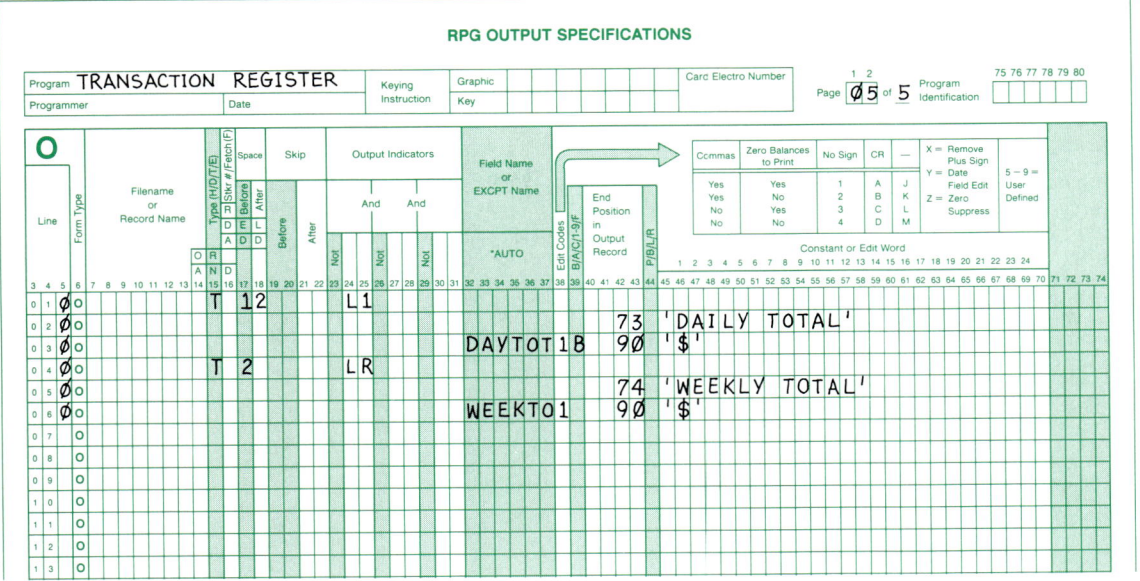

The source listing is as follows:

```
 1    01010H
 2  * 01020F************************************************************
 3  * 01030F*                                                          *
 4  * 01040F*              TRANSACTION REGISTER                        *
 5  * 01050F*                                                          *
 6  * 01060F* THIS PROGRAM PRINTS A REPORT LISTING ITEMS SOLD EACH DAY. *
 7  * 01070F* SALES AMOUNT IS COMPUTED BY MULTIPLYING QUANTITY BY UNIT  *
 8  * 01080F* PRICE. DAILY SALES TOTALS AND WEEKLY TOTALS ARE PRINTED.  *
 9  * 01090F*                                                          *
10  * 01100F************************************************************
11    01110FTRANS    IP  F      42            DISK
12    01120FREPORT   O   F     132     OF     PRINTER
13  * 02010I************************************************************
14  * 02020I*              INPUT SPECIFICATIONS                        *
15  * 02030I************************************************************
16    02040ITRANS    NS  01
17    02050I                                        1   60DATE     L1
18    02060I                                        7   12 ITEMNO
19    02070I                                       13   32 DESC
20    02080I                                       33   370QTY
21    02090I                                       38   422PRICE
22  * 03010C************************************************************
23  * 03020C*              CALCULATION SPECIFICATIONS                  *
24  * 03030C************************************************************
25    03040C    01      QTY       MULT PRICE     EXTCST   62
26    03050C    01      EXTCST    ADD  DAYTOT    DAYTOT   72
27    03060CL1          DAYTOT    ADD  WEEKTO    WEEKTO   82
28  * 04010O************************************************************
29  * 04020O*              OUTPUT SPECIFICATIONS                       *
30  * 04030O************************************************************
31    04040OREPORT   H  201   1P
32    04050O         OR       OF
33    04060O                                   58 'TRANSACTION   REGISTER'
34    04070O         H    1   1P
35    04080O         OR       OF
36    04090O                                   30 'TRANSACTION     ITEM'
37    04100O                                   52 'DESCRIPTION'
38    04110O                                   78 'QUANTITY   UNIT'
39    04120O                                   89 'SALES'
40    04130O         H    3   1P
41    04140O         OR       OF
42    04150O                                   29 'DATE          NO'
43    04160O                                   90 'PRICE     AMOUNT'
44    04170O         D    1   01
45    04180O                   L1   DATE   Y   18
46    04190O                        ITEMNO     31
47    04200O                        DESC       60
48    04210O                        QTY    Z   70
49    04220O                        PRICE  3   79
50    04230O                        EXTCST1    90 '$'
51    05010O         T   12   L1
52    05020O                                   73 'DAILY TOTAL'
53    05030O                        DAYTOT1B   90 '$'
54    05040O         T    2   LR
55    05050O                                   74 'WEEKLY TOTAL'
56    05060O                        WEEKTO1    90 '$'
```

A Transaction Register is to be printed as follows:

```
                              TRANSACTION   REGISTER

 TRANSACTION    ITEM         DESCRIPTION          QUANTITY    UNIT       SALES
    DATE         NO                                           PRICE      AMOUNT

   9/23/87      413010       CH001 BOX 100A FLUSH      10      4.90      $49.00
                412146       CH148 BREAKER 15A        100       .89      $89.00
                411116       1500 TWIN SOCKET B       500      1.12     $560.00
                                                  DAILY TOTAL           $698.00

   9/24/87      503029       MOTOR 1/2 HP 60 CYC       2     146.78     $293.56
                317802       TERMINAL CLIP           100       5.12     $512.00
                326917       TERMINAL BAR            100       4.12     $412.00
                411121       1506 SOCKT ADAPT BRN    400        .19      $76.00
                                                  DAILY TOTAL         $1,293.56

   9/25/87      412997       CH173 BREAKER 30A        60       1.15      $69.00
                413088       CH176 BREAKER 60A        40       1.15      $46.00
                411174       C151 SIL SWITCH BRN     200       1.16     $232.00
                413090       CH005 BR BOX 150A        10       4.98      $49.80
                718326       FC803 FUSE 15A          200        .32      $64.00
                                                  DAILY TOTAL           $460.80


                                                  WEEKLY TOTAL        $2,452.36
```

Illustrative Program

Control Levels—Group Indication: Daily Sales Register

Job Definition
Print a daily sales register that uses two different types of records. The sales are accumulated by day, and the daily sales are accumulated for the entire week. The total number of sales is accumulated.

Input
Two types of records are used for input.

Record Type	Positions	Field Designation	
Date	1–3	Month	
	4–5	Day	
	6–6	Code (character -)	
Sales	6–8	Salesman number	
	9–10	Entry day	
	11–15	Customer number	
	51–57	Sales amount	(XXXXX.XX)

Processing
    Print the "Week of" and page number at the top of each page.
    Accumulate the total sales for each day.
    Accumulate the total daily sales to find the total sales overall.
    Count each sales record.

Output
The Printer Spacing Chart shows how the report is formatted:

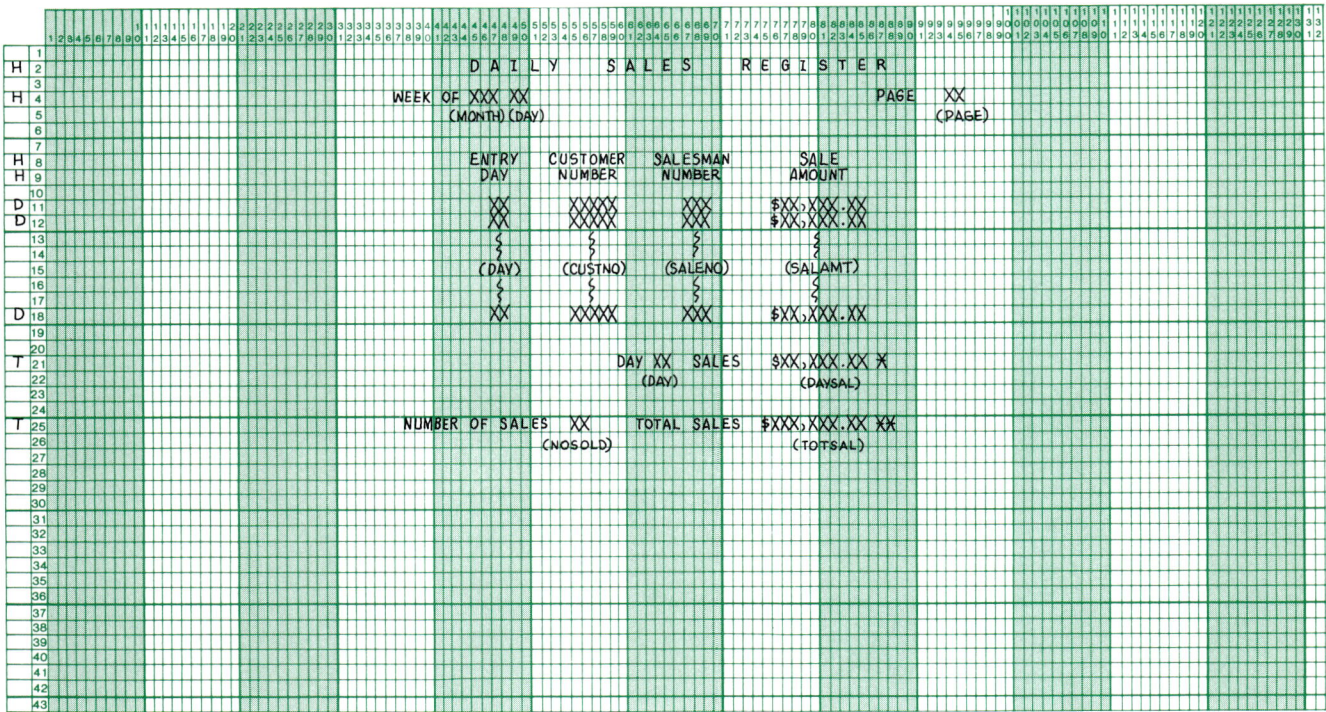

Coding sheets for Daily Sales Register problem:

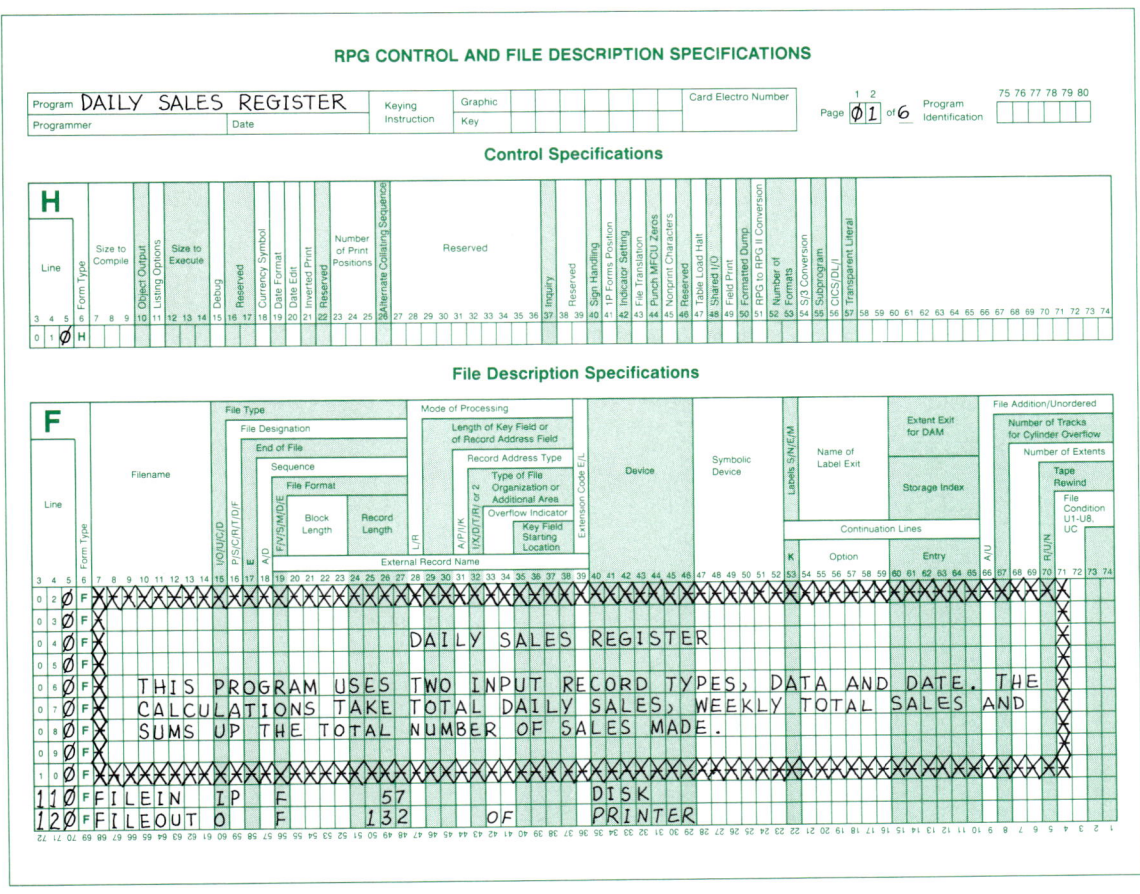

Control Level Operations 155

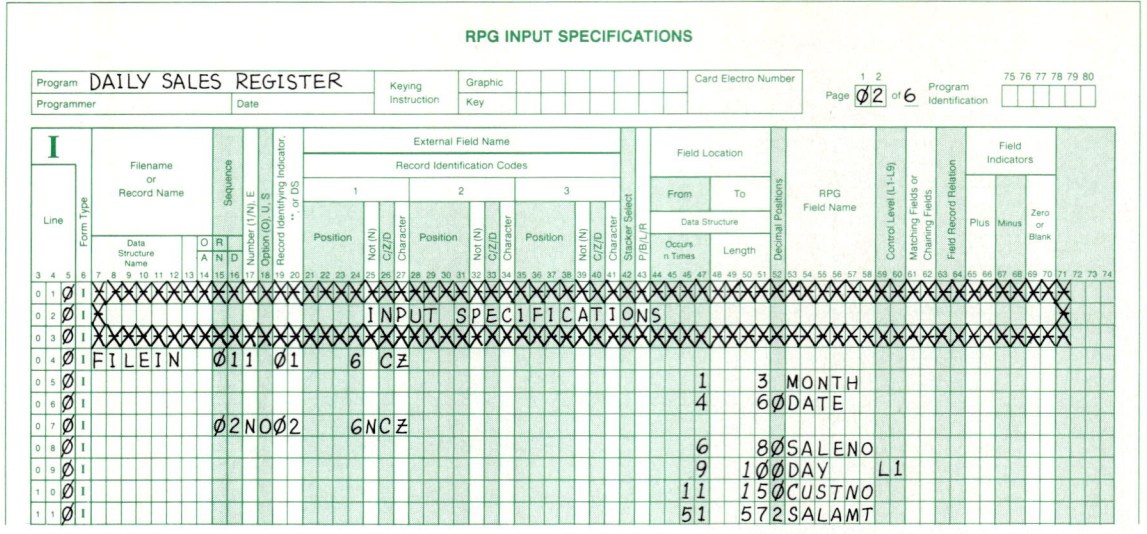
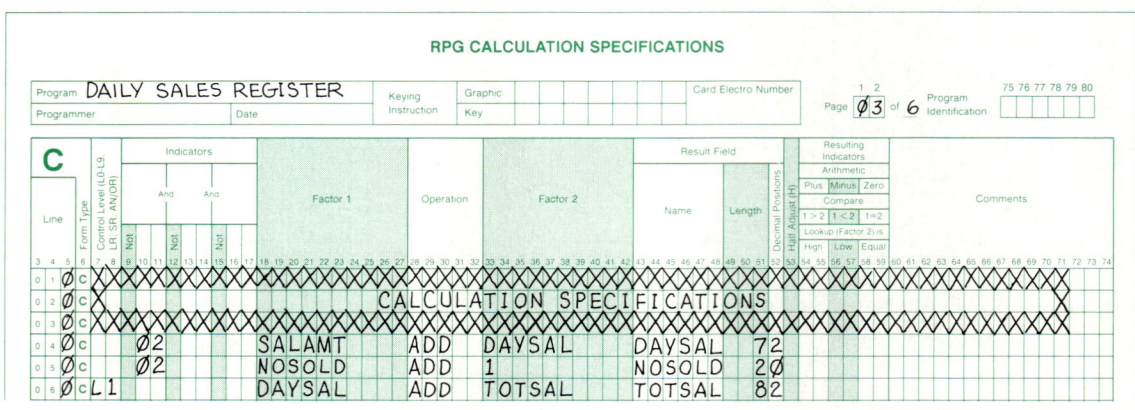
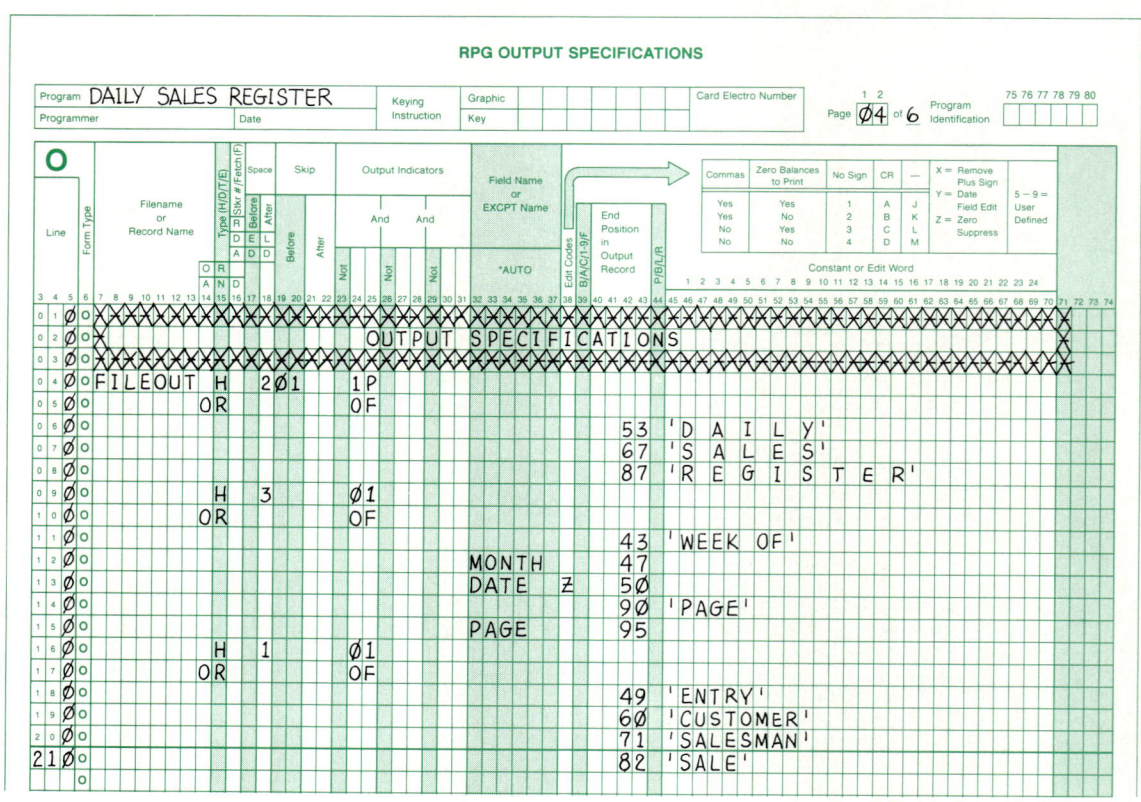

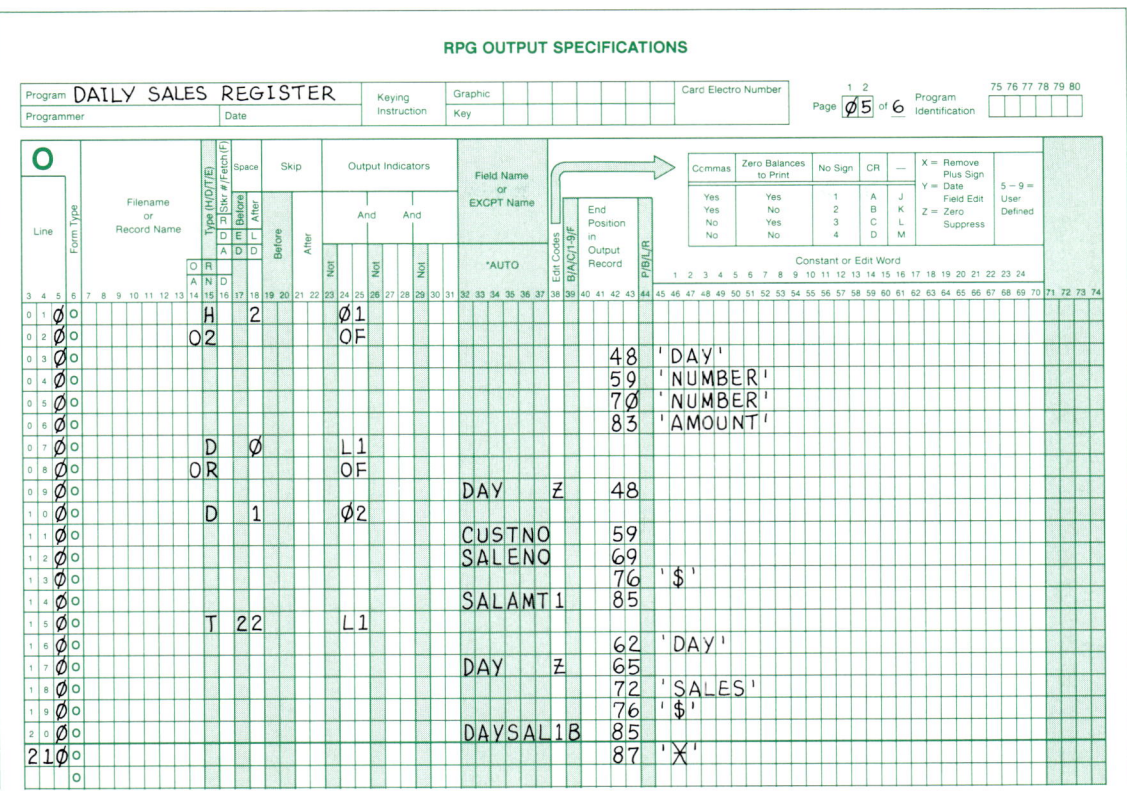
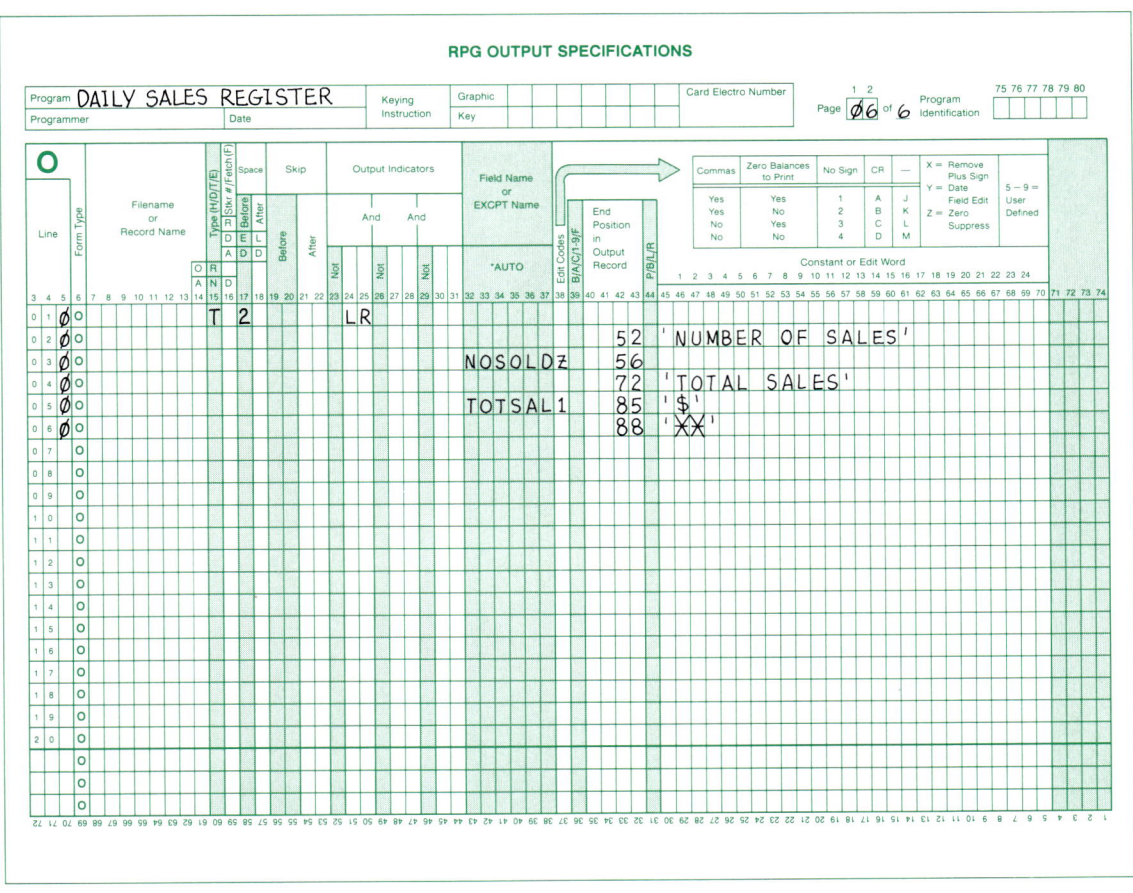

Control Level Operations

The source listing is as follows:

```
 1     01010H
 2   * 01020F****************************************************************
 3   * 01030F*                                                              *
 4   * 01040F*                   DAILY SALES REGISTER                       *
 5   * 01050F*                                                              *
 6   * 01060F*  THIS PROGRAM USES TWO INPUT RECORD TYPES, DATA AND DATE. THE*
 7   * 01070F*  CALCULATIONS TAKE TOTAL DAILY SALES, WEEKLY TOTAL SALES AND *
 8   * 01080F*  SUMS UP THE TOTAL NUMBER OF SALES MADE.                     *
 9   * 01090F*                                                              *
10   * 01100F****************************************************************
11     01110FFILEIN  IP  F      57         DISK
12     01120FFILEOUT O   F     132    OF   PRINTER
13   * 02010I****************************************************************
14   * 02020I*               INPUT SPECIFICATIONS                           *
15   * 02030I****************************************************************
16     02040IFILEIN   011 01   6 CZ
17     02050I                                         1   3 MONTH
18     02060I                                         4  50DATE
19     02070I          02N002  6NCZ
20     02080I                                         6  80SALENO
21     02090I                                         9 100DAY      L1
22     02100I                                        11 150CUSTNO
23     02110I                                        51 572SALAMT
24   * 03010C****************************************************************
25   * 03020C*             CALCULATION SPECIFICATIONS                       *
26   * 03030C****************************************************************
27     03040C    02      SALAMT    ADD  DAYSAL    DAYSAL   72
28     03050C    02      NOSOLD    ADD  1         NOSOLD   20
29     03060CL1          DAYSAL    ADD  TOTSAL    TOTSAL   82
30   * 04010O****************************************************************
31   * 04020O*              OUTPUT SPECIFICATIONS                           *
32   * 04030O****************************************************************
33     04040OFILEOUT H  201     1P
34     04050O        OR         OF
35     04060O                                        53 'D A I L Y'
36     04070O                                        67 'S A L E S'
37     04080O                                        87 'R E G I S T E R'
38     04090O         H  3      01
39     04100O        OR         OF
40     04110O                                        43 'WEEK OF'
41     04120O                           MONTH        47
42     04130O                           DATE   Z     50
43     04140O                                        90 'PAGE'
44     04150O                           PAGE         95
45     04160O         H  1      01
46     04170O        OR         OF
47     04180O                                        49 'ENTRY'
48     04190O                                        60 'CUSTOMER'
49     04200O                                        71 'SALESMAN'
50     04210O                                        82 'SALE'
51     05010O         H  2      01
52     05020O        OR         OF
53     05030O                                        48 'DAY'
54     05040O                                        59 'NUMBER'
55     05050O                                        70 'NUMBER'
56     05060O                                        83 'AMOUNT'
57     05070O         D  0      L1
58     05080O        OR         OF
59     05090O                           DAY    Z     48
60     05100O         D  1      02
61     05110O                           CUSTNO       59
62     05120O                           SALENO       69
63     05130O                                        76 '$'
64     05140O                           SALAMT1      85
65     05150O         T 22      L1
66     05160O                                        62 'DAY'
67     05170O                           DAY    Z     65
68     05180O                                        72 'SALES'
69     05190O                                        76 '$'
70     05200O                           DAYSAL1B     85
71     05210O                                        87 '*'
72     06010O         T  2      LR
73     06020O                                        52 'NUMBER OF SALES'
74     06030O                           NOSOLDZ      56
75     06040O                                        72 'TOTAL SALES'
76     06050O                           TOTSAL1      85 '$'
77     06060O                                        88 '**'
```

A Daily Sales Register is printed as follows:

```
           D A I L Y    S A L E S    R E G I S T E R
WEEK OF AUG  3                                       PAGE 0001

     ENTRY   CUSTOMER   SALESMAN       SALE
      DAY    NUMBER     NUMBER        AMOUNT

       3     08257      071        $  1,189.90
             11243      079        $    168.06
             29031      079        $     63.00
             29964      079        $  1,294.86
             79992      095        $     87.74
             85486      125        $     20.25

                     DAY  3  SALES  $  2,823.81 *

       4     01179      002        $70,711.29
             02865      037        $12,716.92
             09002      001        $    842.17
             13605      001        $  3,092.72
             27654      009        $    217.90
             32007      022        $    429.65
             65952      016        $    223.35
             99003      058        $  4,000.00

                     DAY  4  SALES  $92,234.00 *

       5     00390      092        $     27.00
             05006      056        $    897.00
             12125      181        $    371.98
             20239      145        $     18.16

                     DAY  5  SALES  $  1,314.14 *

       6     00106      100        $  1,494.73
             00298      024        $  2,020.60

                     DAY  6  SALES  $  3,515.33 *

       7     00256      003        $     79.53
             00321      005        $    590.10
             00652      008        $     95.18
             18569      090        $    421.15
             20106      132        $    706.42
             20902      027        $     55.80
             25452      060        $  2,166.96
             40764      043        $  1,914.35

                     DAY  7  SALES  $  6,029.49 *

  NUMBER OF SALES  28    TOTAL SALES  $105,916.77 **
```

Illustrative Program

Multiple Control Levels: Hospital Patient Report

Job Definition
Print a report indicating the various patient totals for cities and counties within each state of the United States. An overall total is indicated for the entire United States.

Input
A record containing the number of patients is entered for each hospital of the United States. The records are sorted as follows: major = state, intermediate = county, and minor = city.

The following are the fields for each record:

Positions	Field Designation
1–6	Date
7–8	State
9–11	County
12–14	City
15–18	Hospital number
70–75	Number of patients

Processing
Accumulate the total number of patients for each city.
Accumulate the city patient totals to find the county totals.
Accumulate the county patient totals to find the state totals.
Accumulate the state patient totals to find the United States total.

Output
The Printer Spacing Chart shows how the report is formatted:

```
                    HOSPITAL PATIENT REPORT                          PAGE XXX
                                                                         (PAGE)
       STATE      COUNTY            CITY           NUMBER OF PATIENTS

        XX      XXXXXXXXXXXX     XXXXXXXXXXXX         XXX,XXX
        XX      XXXXXXXXXXXX     XXXXXXXXXXXX         XXX,XXX
         ?           ?                ?                  ?
       (STATE)    (COUNTY)         (CITY)            (CTYTOT)
         ?           ?                ?                  ?
        XX      XXXXXXXXXXXX     XXXXXXXXXXXX         XXX,XXX
                              COUNTY TOTAL            XXX,XXX *    (COTYTO)
                              STATE TOTAL           X,XXX,XXX *    (STATTO)
                              UNITED STATES TOTAL  XX,XXX,XXX **   (USTOT)
```

160   RPG II and RPG III Programming

Coding sheets for Hospital Patient Report problem:

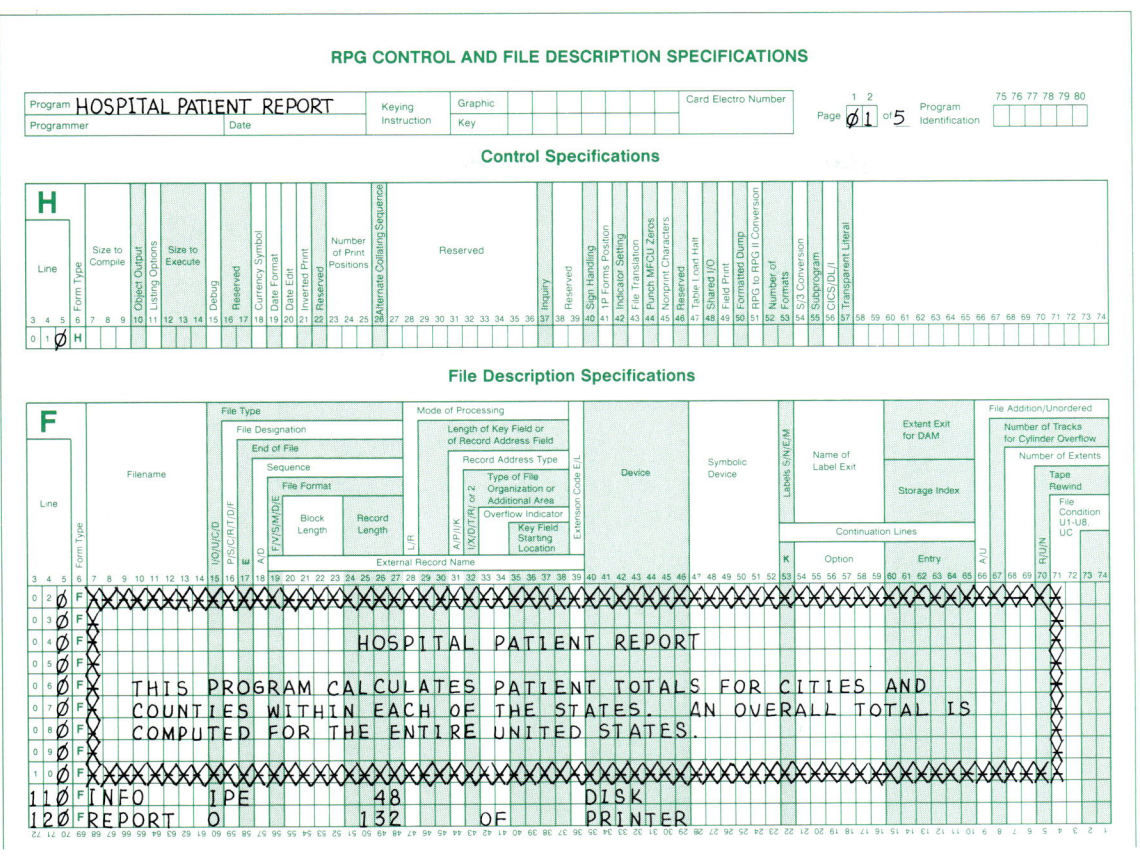
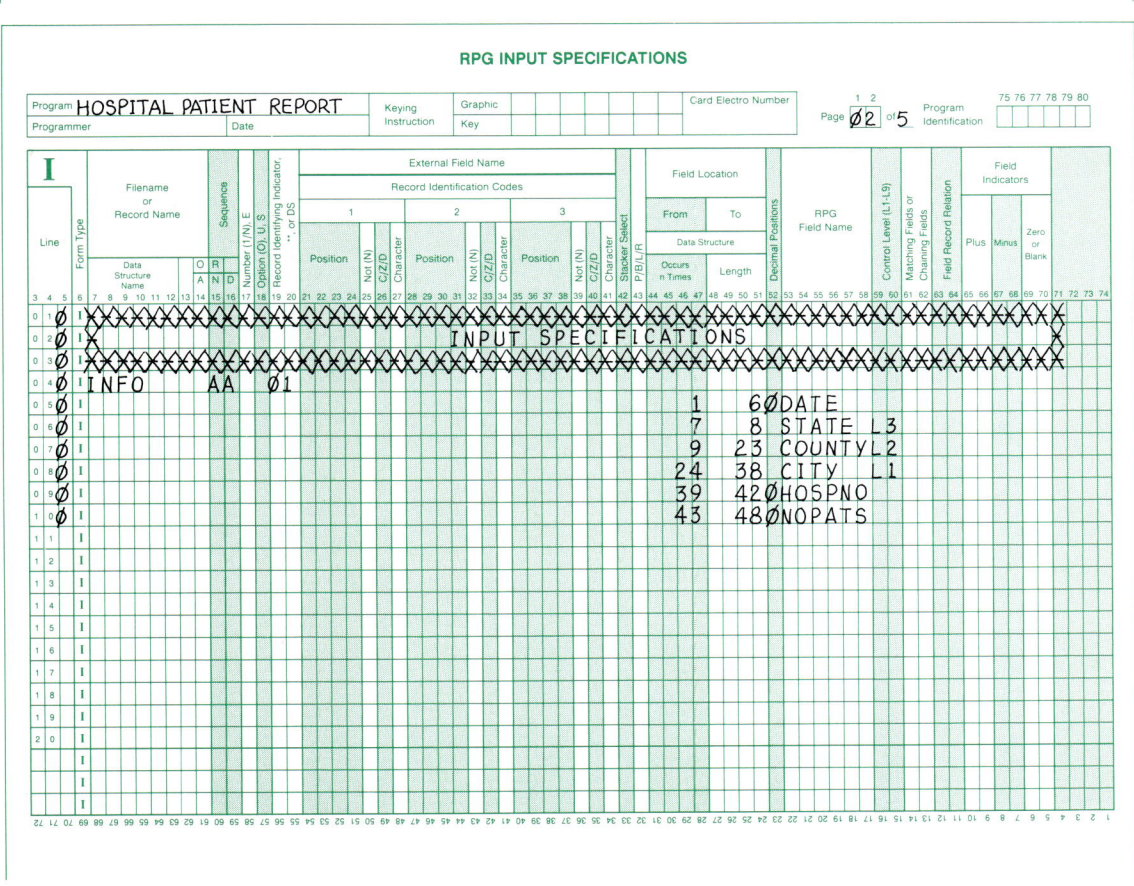

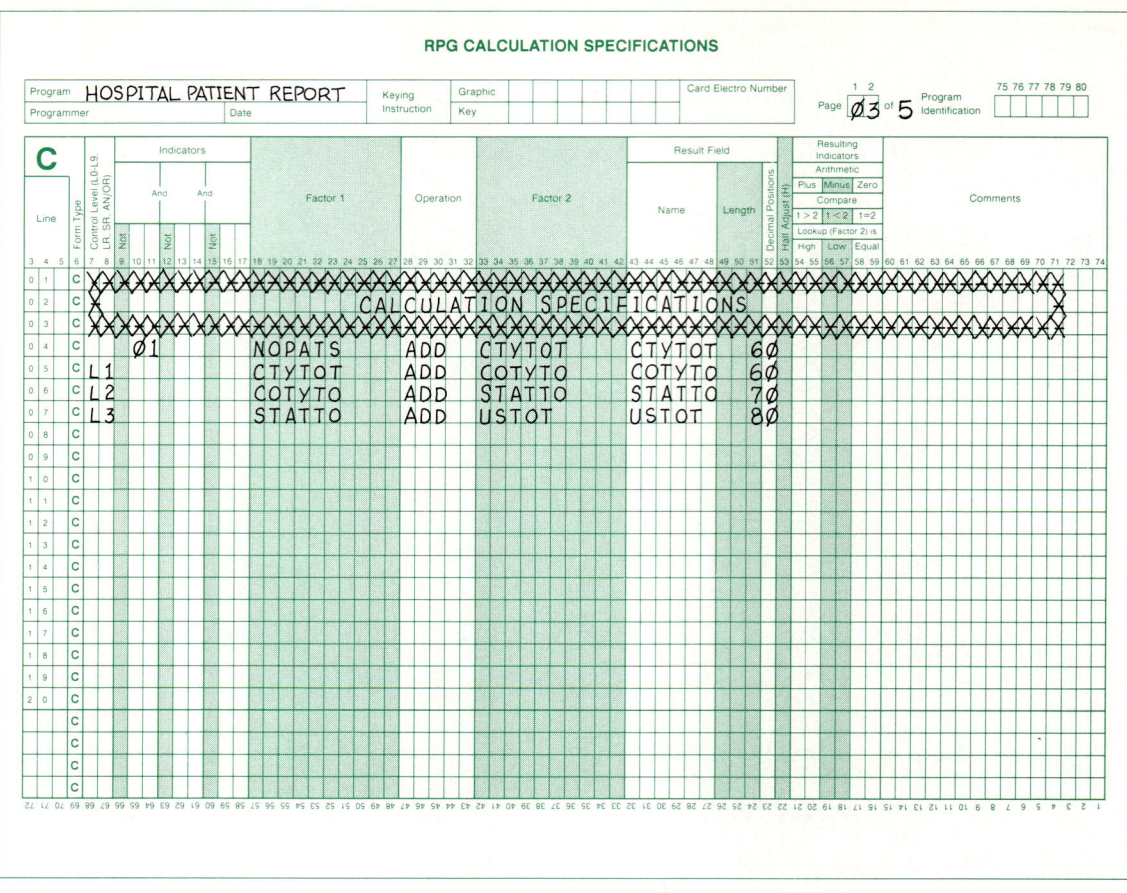
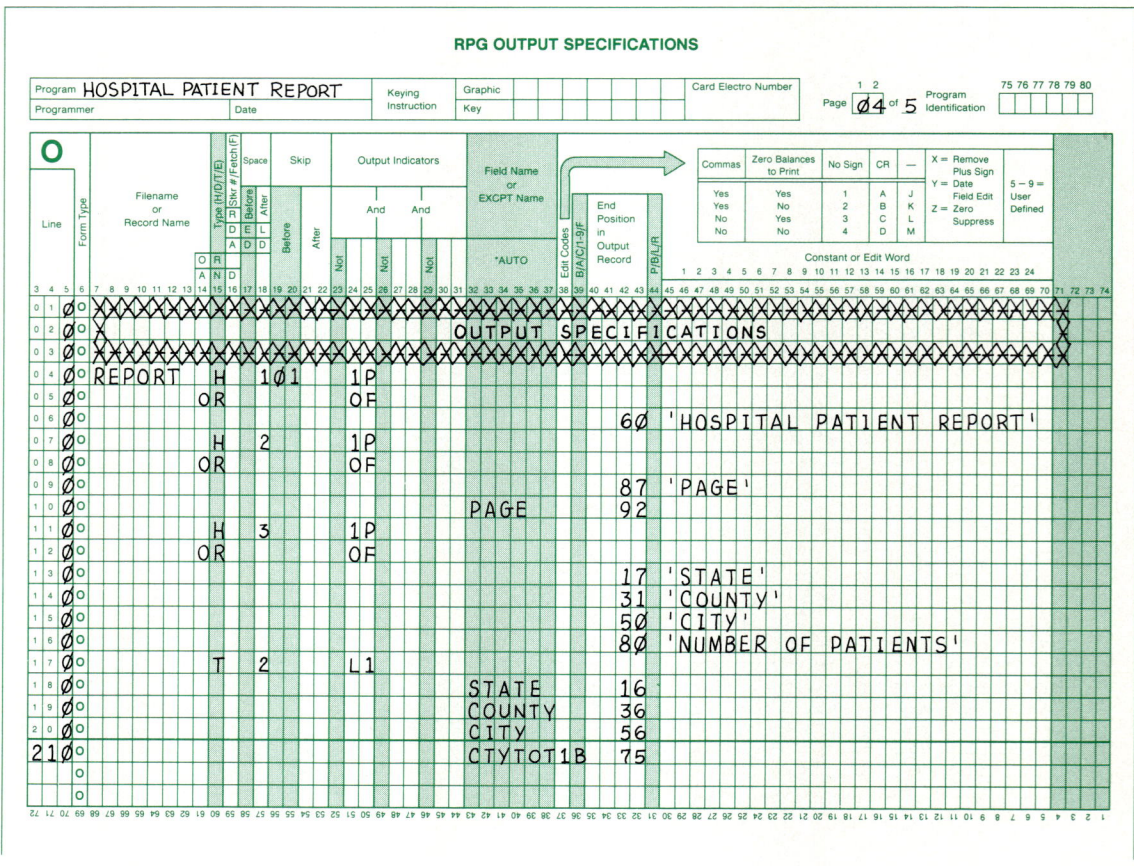

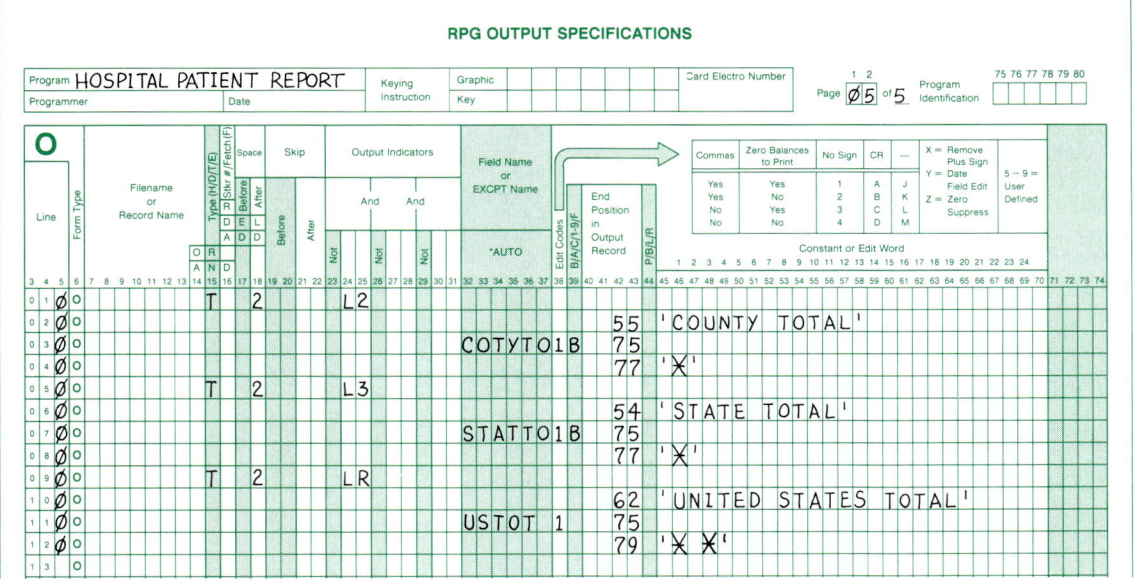

The source listing is as follows:

```
 1     01010H
 2   * 01020F********************************************************
 3   * 01030F*                                                      *
 4   * 01040F*              HOSPITAL PATIENT REPORT                 *
 5   * 01050F*                                                      *
 6   * 01060F* THIS PROGRAM CALCULATES PATIENT TOTALS FOR CITIES AND*
 7   * 01070F* COUNTIES WITHIN EACH OF THE STATES.  AN OVERALL TOTAL IS*
 8   * 01080F* COMPUTED FOR THE ENTIRE UNITED STATES.               *
 9   * 01090F*                                                      *
10   * 01100F********************************************************
11     01110FINFO    IPE         48           DISK
12     01120FREPORT  O          132        OF PRINTER
13   * 02010I********************************************************
14   * 02020I*              INPUT SPECIFICATIONS                    *
15   * 02030I********************************************************
16     02040IINFO    AA  01
17     02050I                                    1   60DATE
18     02060I                                    7    8 STATE  L3
19     02070I                                    9   23 COUNTYL2
20     02080I                                   24   38 CITY   L1
21     02090I                                   39   420HOSPNO
22     02100I                                   43   480NOPATS
23   * 03010C********************************************************
24   * 03020C*            CALCULATION SPECIFICATIONS                *
25   * 03030C********************************************************
26     03040C   01       NOPATS    ADD  CTYTOT    CTYTOT   60
27     03050CL1          CTYTOT    ADD  COTYTO    COTYTO   60
28     03060CL2          COTYTO    ADD  STATTO    STATTO   70
29     03070CL3          STATTO    ADD  USTOT     USTOT    80
30   * 04010O********************************************************
31   * 04020O*              OUTPUT SPECIFICATIONS                   *
32   * 04030O********************************************************
33     04040OREPORT  H  101       1P
34     04050O            OR             OF
35     04060O                                         60 'HOSPITAL PATIENT REPORT'
36     04070O         H  2         1P
37     04080O            OR             OF
38     04090O                                         87 'PAGE'
39     04100O                             PAGE        92
40     04110O         H  3         1P
41     04120O            OR             OF
42     04130O                                         17 'STATE'
43     04140O                                         31 'COUNTY'
44     04150O                                         50 'CITY'
45     04160O                                         80 'NUMBER OF PATIENTS'
46     04170O         T  2        L1
47     04180O                             STATE       16
48     04190O                             COUNTY      36
49     04200O                             CITY        56
50     04210O                             CTYTOT1B    75
51     05010O         T  2        L2
52     05020O                                         55 'COUNTY TOTAL'
53     05030O                             COTYTO1B    75
54     05040O                                         77 '*'
55     05050O         T  2        L3
56     05060O                                         54 'STATE TOTAL'
57     05070O                             STATTO1B    75
58     05080O                                         77 '*'
59     05090O         T  2        LR
60     05100O                                         62 'UNITED STATES TOTAL'
61     05110O                             USTOT 1     75
62     05120O                                         79 '* *'
```

Control Level Operations

A Hospital Patient Report is to be printed as follows:

```
                       HOSPITAL PATIENT REPORT
                                                                        PAGE 0001
   STATE      COUNTY            CITY         NUMBER OF PATIENTS

    CA      SAN DIEGO        SANTEE              542
                             COUNTY TOTAL        542 *
    CA      VENTURA          OXNARD              321
                             COUNTY TOTAL        321 *
                             STATE TOTAL         863 *
    DE      KENT             DOVER             1,406
    DE      KENT             LEBANON           1,984
                             COUNTY TOTAL      3,390 *
                             STATE TOTAL       3,390 *
    FL      TAMPA            PENSACOLA         2,727
                             COUNTY TOTAL      2,727 *
                             STATE TOTAL       2,727 *
    IL      MCLEAN           BLOOMINGTON       2,686
    IL      MCLEAN           NORMAL              400
                             COUNTY TOTAL      3,086 *
                             STATE TOTAL       3,086 *
    MD      BALTIMORE        BACTIMONE           731
    MD      BALTIMORE        CATONSVILLE       4,104
    MD      BALTIMORE        PIKESVILLE        1,001
                             COUNTY TOTAL      5,836 *
    MD      HOWARD           WORTHINGTON         231
                             COUNTY TOTAL        231 *
    MD      ANNE ARUNDEL     GLEN BURNIE       1,462
                             COUNTY TOTAL      1,462 *
                             STATE TOTAL       7,529 *
    NE      SOMSERSET        MADISON           2,184
                             COUNTY TOTAL      2,184 *
                             STATE TOTAL       2,184 *


                       HOSPITAL PATIENT REPORT
                                                                        PAGE 0002
   STATE      COUNTY            CITY         NUMBER OF PATIENTS

    WA      GILLESPIE        FREDRICKBERG      2,034
                             COUNTY TOTAL      2,034 *
    WA      GEILLESPIE       KERRVILLE         4,752
                             COUNTY TOTAL      4,752 *
    WA      TRAVIS           AUSTIN            3,335
    WA      TRAVIS           GEORGETOWN        2,829
                             COUNTY TOTAL      6,164 *
                             STATE TOTAL      12,950 *

                         UNITED STATES TOTAL  32,729 * *
```

Questions for Review

1. What is a control break?
2. What are levels of control and how are they indicated?
3. How is the accumulation of subtotals and totals related to control levels?
4. Why is it important to reset an accumulator to zero?
5. When are detail and total operations performed in the basic RPG cycle?
6. Briefly explain the program cycle operations at detail time and total time.
7. What is a control group? A control field?
8. What is the RPG logic as it relates to control breaks?
9. What are control level indicators and how are they used in RPG programs?
10. What does a control break do?
11. How are output operations conditioned by LR performed?
12. What is the additional coding required on the Output Specifications form for control levels?
13. In what sequence are control level indicators assigned?
14. How is output coding accomplished with control level indicators?
15. What is the blank after specification and how is it useful in total operations?
16. What is group indication and how is it specified in RPG programs?

Problems

Problem 1

Use the flowchart, record layout, and Printer Spacing Chart to write an RPG program that prepares a report totaling the hours for a given job. Different employees work on several jobs during the week and submit their time and number along with the job identification. All of these records have been grouped by job number for this report.

    Calculations should include the accumulation of total hours for each job and a count of the number of active jobs.

The output report should follow the Printer Spacing Chart; the job number should print only for the first record of a group that is group indicated.

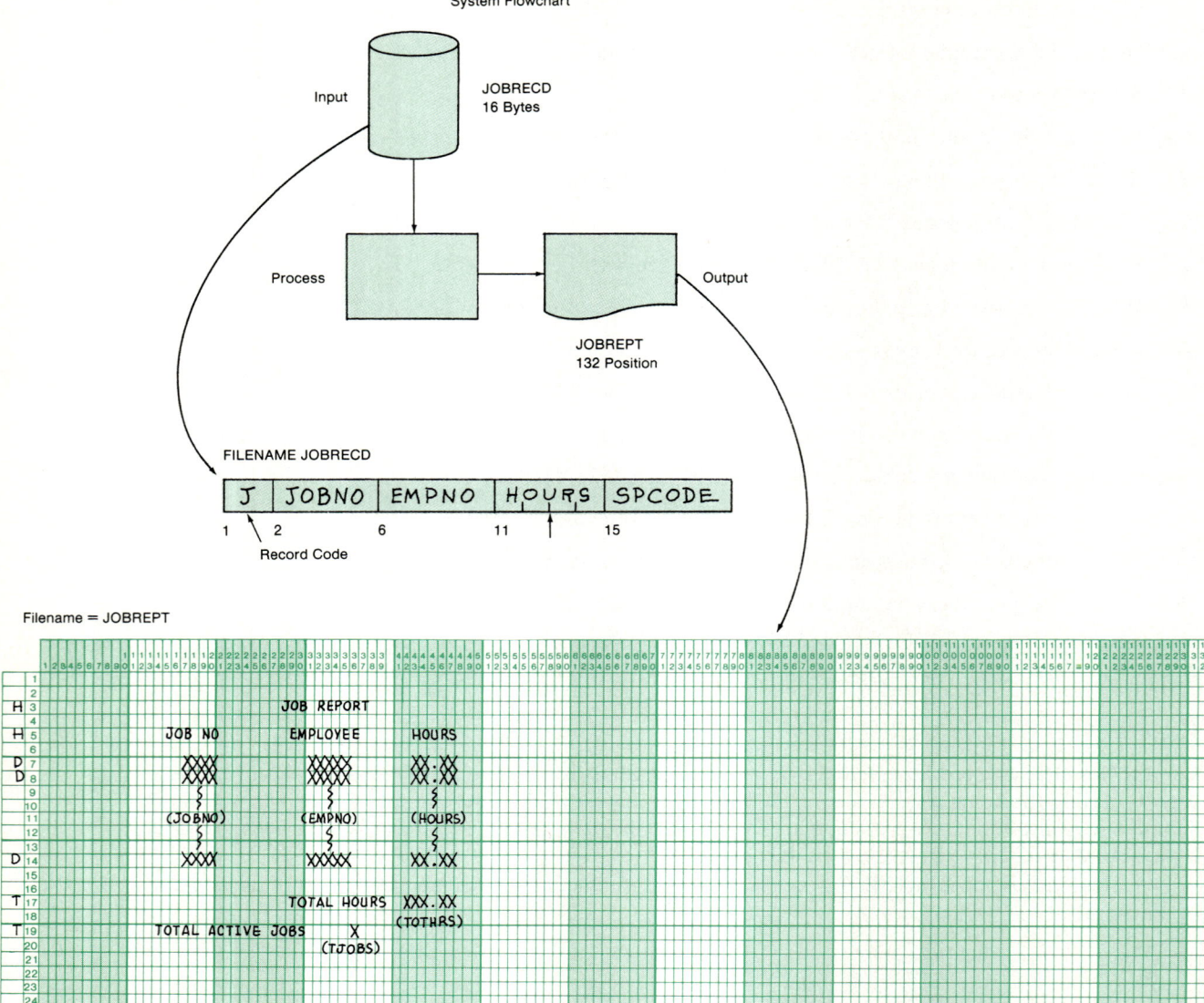

Output is as follows:

```
                    JOB REPORT
    JOB NO        EMPLOYEE      HOURS

     0281           68312       12.50
     0281           59478       30.00

                   TOTAL HOURS  42.50

     0283           67129       15.50
     0283           70049       42.30

                   TOTAL HOURS  57.80

     0285           71312       40.30

                   TOTAL HOURS  40.30

    TOTAL ACTIVE JOBS       5
```

Problem 2

Using the following flowchart, Record Layout form, and the Printer Spacing Chart, write an RPG program that will print a directory of employee telephone numbers. The records are grouped by location so that a count of the number of employees in a given location can be printed. A printout of the total number of phone numbers listed in the entire directory is also required. The location description should be printed only once for any given location.

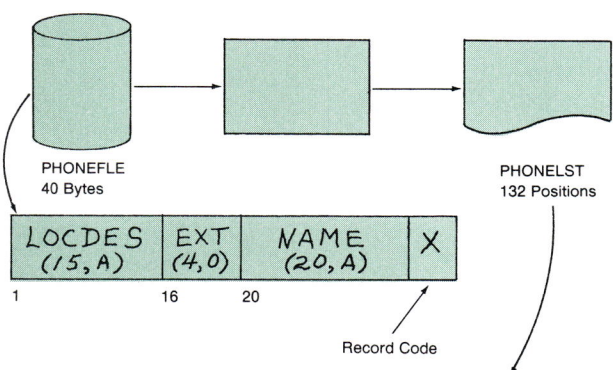

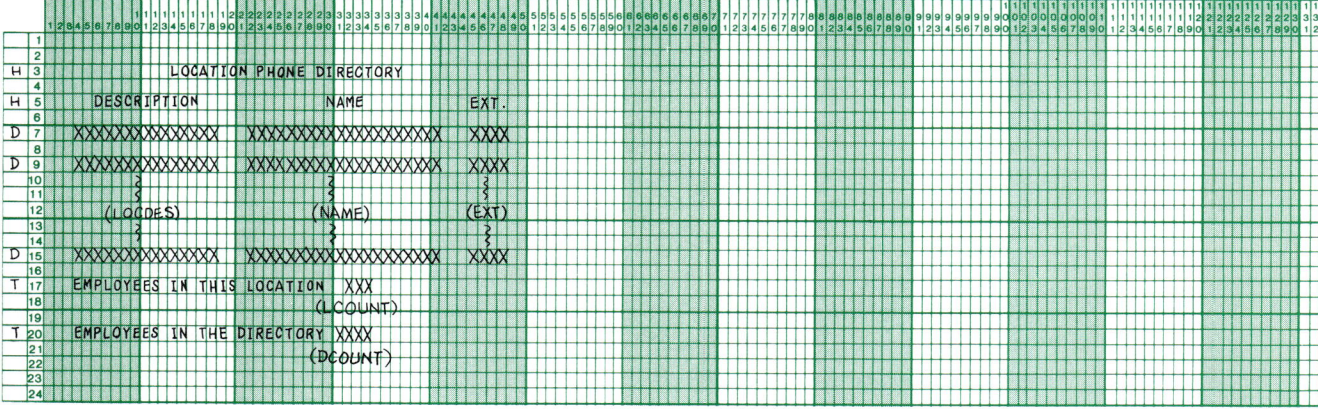

Output is as follows:

```
            LOCATION PHONE DIRECTORY
     DESCRIPTION          NAME            EXT.
     LOAN DEPARTMENT    BILL BROOKS       2701
                        JOHN CALDWELL     2680
                        DAVID HAMILTON    2712
     EMPLOYEES IN THIS LOCATION    3

     PAYROLL SECTION    BENNY BROWN       4014
                        ROBERT CARLSON    4238
                        LARRY HOOPER      4115
                        JOHN JOHNSON      4229
     EMPLOYEES IN THIS LOCATION    4

     EMPLOYEES IN THE DIRECTORY    7
```

Control Level Operations 167

Problem 3

Code the necessary file descriptions, input specifications, calculation specifications, and output specifications for the following:

General Description

Prepare a Sales Analysis report.

Input

This is a file called SLSRCS. The record layout follows.

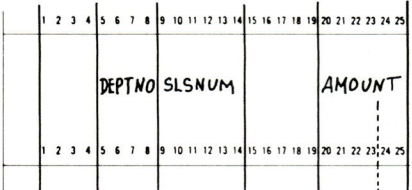

Calculations

Accumulate total sales for each salesman. For each department, accumulate total sales. Accumulate a final total for all departments.

$$\text{AMOUNT} + \text{SLSAMT} = \text{SLSAMT}$$
$$\text{SLSAMT} + \text{DEPAMT} = \text{DEPAMT}$$
$$\text{DEPAMT} + \text{FINTOT} = \text{FINTOT}$$

Output

A printed report called SLSRPT is to be output. The report is to be group-indicated by department and by salesman. Print * beside each salesman total, ** beside each department total, and *** beside the final total. Print the current date and page number on each page. Print the column headings DEPARTMENT, SALESMAN NO., and AMOUNT on each page.

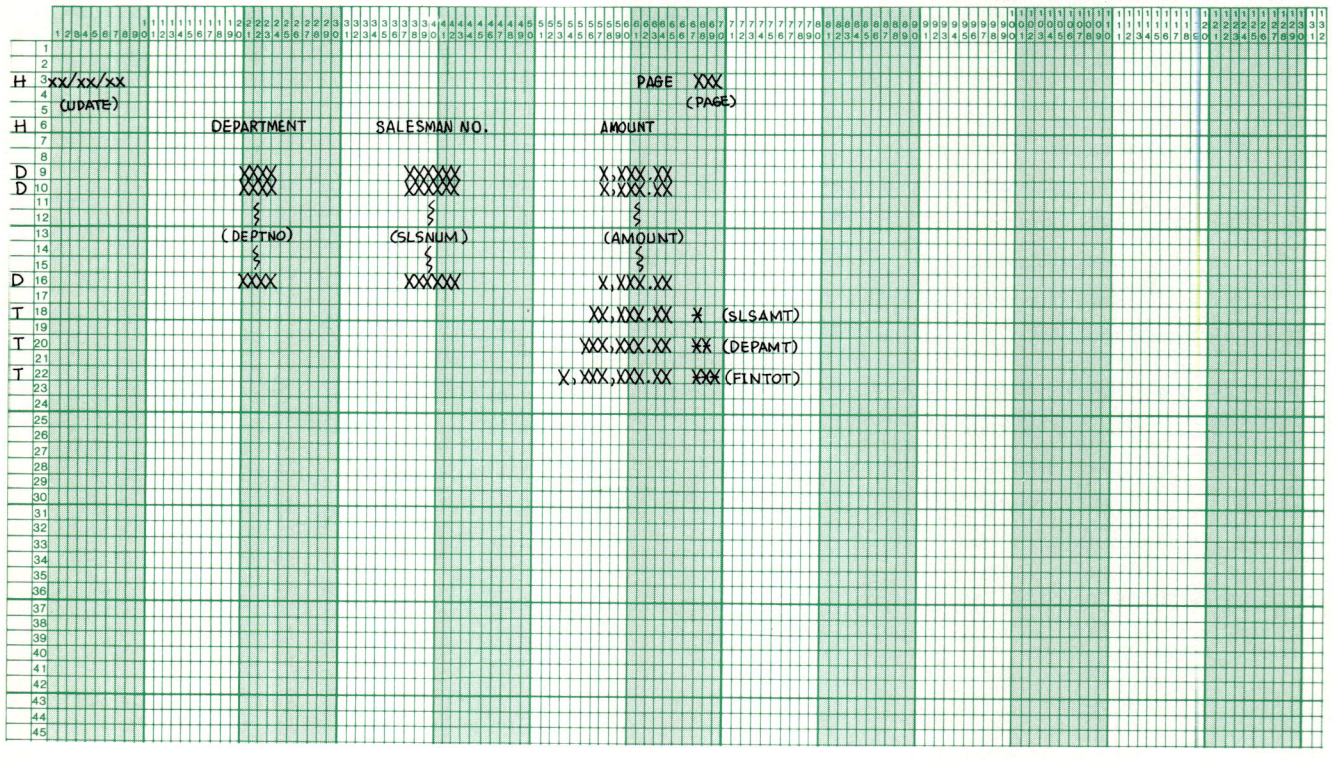

Output is as follows:

```
2/28/87                                              PAGE    1

           DEPARTMENT      SALESMAN NO.        AMOUNT

              1002           791245           1,962.80
                                              2,531.05
                                                822.71

                                              5,316.56  *

                             789449           3,488.49
                                                901.52

                                              4,390.01  *

                                              9,706.57  **

              1050           691248             399.23
                                             11,053.98
                                                 20.75

                                              1,473.96  *

                             729231           6,531.14
                                              8,601.52
                                                853.20
                                                 85.01

                                             16,070.87  *

                             798882           5,149.80

                                              5,149.80  *

                                             22,694.63  **

                                             32,401.20  ***
```

Problem 4

An invoice billing is to be prepared according to the output sample.

Input
The input file consists of 47-byte records with the following fields:

Positions	Field	Format
1–5	Product number	(XXXXX)
6–11	Quantity	(XXXXXX)
12–17	Unit price	(XXX.XXX)
38–42	Description	
43–47	Invoice number	(XXXXX)

Processing
All answer fields should be rounded to two decimal places.

1. Compute sales amount = quantity × unit price.
2. All sales amounts are to be totaled for the same invoice number.
3. Compute discount amount and net amount due as follows:
    a. When total sales exceed $1,000, allow a 3 percent discount.
    b. When total sales are $1,000 or less, allow a 2 percent discount.
    c. Subtract discount amount from total sales amount to arrive at net amount due.
4. Customer number, customer name, and invoice number are to be group-indicated.
5. The billing is to be printed in the output format shown below.

Output

The output format is as follows:

CUST NO.	CUSTOMER NAME	INVOICE NO.	PROD. NO.	QUANTITY	UNIT PRICE	DESCRIPTION		SALES AMOUNT
00246	ACME HDWE CO., INC	24681	12345	651	4.751	HAMMER-BALL PEEN	EA	3,092.90
			24762	13	246.953	BOILER-STEAM	EA	3,210.39
			47672	11	189.752	WASHING MACHINE	EA	2,087.27
			67302	821	4.875	NAILS-STEEL WIRE	LB	4,002.38
						TOTAL SALES		12,392.94 *
						DISCOUNT ALLOWED		371.79
						NET AMOUNT DUE		12,021.15 **
12481	E.C. MORGAN CO.	24682	15762	671	.752	LAG SCREWS	DZ	504.59
			38576	76	1.065	CLIPS-FILE	GR	80.94
			69251	52	6.521	PAINT	GL	339.09
						TOTAL SALES		924.62 *
						DISCOUNT ALLOWED		18.49
						NET AMOUNT DUE		906.13 **
28762	WILLIAMS TOOL CO.	24683	07603	1,105	.151	NUTS HEX 1/8	DZ	166.86
			07603	1,105	.151	NUTS HEX 1/8	DZ	166.86
			39827	37	264.721	GRADERS	EA	9,794.68
						TOTAL SALES		10,128.40 *
						DISCOUNT ALLOWED		303.85

Program Control of Operations

5

Outline

Controlling Operations in an RPG Program
Control of Output
   Calculation Time Output (EXCPT Operation)
   Conditioning the Use of EXCPT Operation
   Fetch Overflow
   Overflow Printing with EXCPT Operation
Control of Calculations
   Setting Indicators On and Off (SETON and SETOF)
   Branching and Looping
     Bypassing Calculations
     Go To (GOTO)
     Tag (TAG)
     GOTO Operation—Summary
   Movement of Data Calculations
     Zero and Add (Z-ADD)
     Zero and Subtract (Z-SUB)
     MOVE Operation (MOVE and MOVEL)
     Moving Data
     Specifications for Moving Data
     Data Movement—Summary
     Zero and Add (Z-ADD)
     Move (MOVE)
     Move Left (MOVEL)
Subroutines
   Coding Subroutines
   Subroutine Operation Codes
   Begin Subroutine (BEGSR)
   End Subroutine (ENDSR)
   Execute Subroutine (EXSR)
   Subroutine Rules—Summary
   Subroutine—Summary

RPG III Enhancements
   EXCPT Name
   Move (MOVE)
   Move Left (MOVEL)
   Simplified Subroutines
   Compare and Branch (CABxx)
   Structured Programming Operations
     Do (DO)
     Do Until (DOUxx)
     Do While (DOWxx)
     If/Then (IFxx)
     And (ANDxx)
     Or (ORxx)
     Else (ELSE)
     End (END)

Controlling Operations in an RPG Program

There are many ways to control the performance of RPG operations. The concept of the RPG program cycle and the use of indicators to condition specifications have already been discussed; these are the basic elements of controlling calculations and output. This chapter builds upon those basic concepts by presenting topics on improving the performance of the RPG programs and doing more complex jobs.

The Calculations and Output Specification forms describe all the calculations and output. Sometimes all calculations and output operations must be performed on every program cycle. More often, however, only certain operations are needed for specific cycles.

Control of Output

Normally the generated RPG program includes instructions that read in data *prior* to processing. Likewise, RPG provides instructions to write or print records *after* the calculations are performed.

For some data-processing problems, it may be necessary to read in one or more records or to produce output records *during* calculation steps.

Following are two operations that can alter the normal generated RPG calculations in order to perform output functions:

EXCPT—allows records to be written at the time calculations are being done.

Fetch overflow—allows the alteration of basic RPG overflow logic.

Calculation Time Output (EXCPT Operation)

The RPG special operation code EXCPT allows the user to write as many records during one program cycle as are required. This operation makes it possible for records to be written at the time calculations are being done. This is used primarily when a variable number of similar or identical records (either detail or total) are to be written in one program. (Normally, only the exact number of records specified in the Output Specifications form are written to a file in one program cycle.) For example, EXCPT might be used to produce a variable number of identical mailing labels, to write out the contents of a table, or to produce a number of records containing the same information. (See Figure 5.1.)

When the EXCPT operation is used, EXCPT is entered in positions 28–32; positions 7–17 may have entries but all other positions must be blank. The line or lines to be written during calculation time are indicated by an *E* in position 15 of the Output Specifications form. Exception lines may not be used in a combined file.

Typically, a record is written at either detail or total output time. When using EXCPT, records can be put out during detail or total calculation time. Each time the operation code EXCPT is used, specified records are written immediately. For example, if eight EXCPT operation codes are used in succession, an exception output cycle will occur eight times. The records produced will be identical if the data fields between the EXCPT operation codes in the exception records are not altered on the Calculation Specifications form.

When the EXCPT operation code is used, records to be output during calculation time must be specified. These records are identified by an *E* in position 15 of the Output Specifications form. Only those output lines identified by an *E* will be output during an exception output cycle. (See Figure 5.2.)

EXCPT can be used with magnetic media, such as tape or disk, as well as with printed output. The code operates in the same manner in all cases. Each time the EXCPT code is encountered, output lines identified by an *E* in position 15 are executed (if they are conditioned properly).

Only output files may have EXCPT records specified: EXCPT cannot be used for combined files.

Figure 5.1 EXCPT operation (producing variable number of identical records)

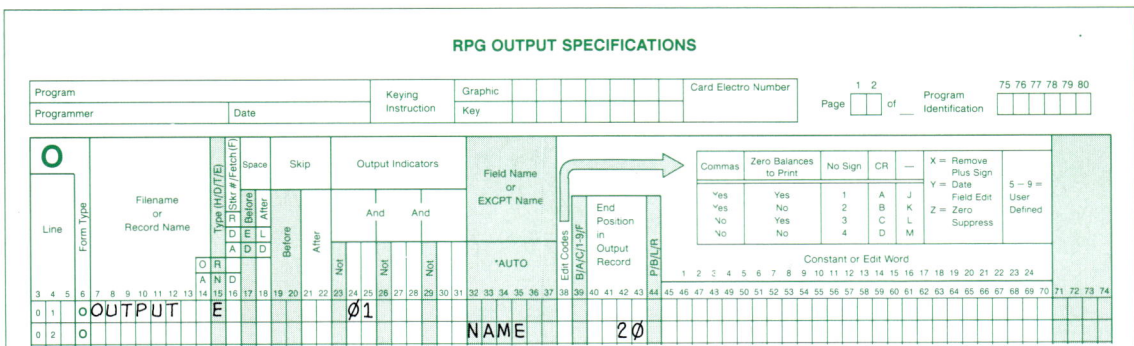

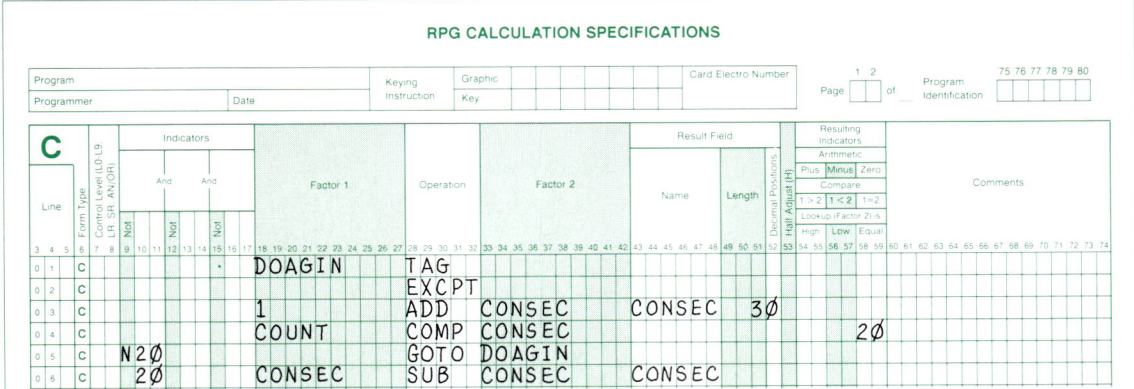

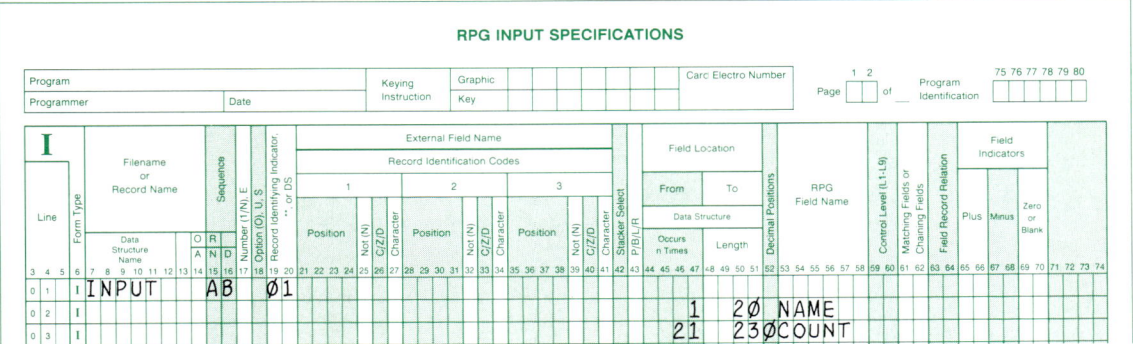

Notes on the Coding

The figure above shows the use of the EXCPT operation to produce a variable number of records having the same information.

Records in the input file have two fields, NAME and COUNT. The NAME field is to be entered into a certain number of records. The number is indicated in the COUNT field. Every time the operation code EXCPT is performed, the exception record indicated by the E in position 15 of the Output Specifications form is written.

The field CONSEC is used to keep track of the number of records written. Each time an exception record is written, 1 is added to CONSEC. CONSEC is then compared with COUNT, the field that tells how many records should be written. If they are not equal (indicator 20 is not on), a branch is taken back to DOAGIN. Another record is written. One is added to CONSEC and CONSEC is compared to COUNT.

If these fields are now equal, another input record is read. If not, the same operations are repeated.

Whenever CONSEC equals COUNT, enough records have been written, and CONSEC is subtracted from itself, making it zero. The last operation is necessary so that an accurate count can be kept for the next record.

Program Control of Operations 173

Figure 5.2 EXCPT operation code used with exception records

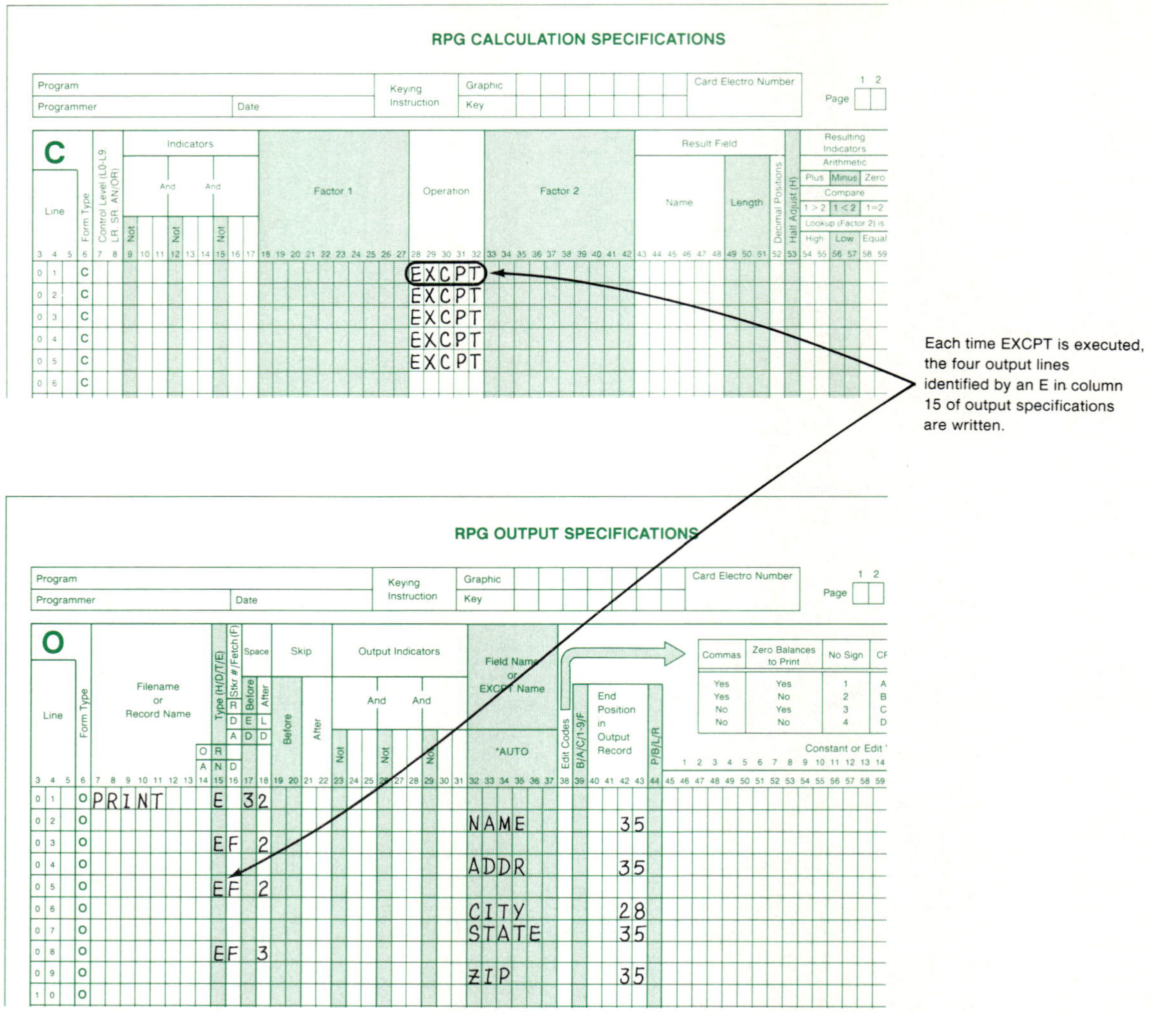

[RPG Calculation Specifications form showing lines 01-06 with C form type, and EXCPT operation code entered in the Operation field (positions 28-32) on lines 01-05, with the first EXCPT circled]

*[RPG Output Specifications form showing:
- Line 01: PRINT, Type E, positions 32
- Line 02: (blank)
- Line 03: Type EF, space 2, NAME in position 35
- Line 04: (blank)
- Line 05: Type EF, space 2, ADDR in position 35
- Line 06: (blank)
- Line 07: CITY in position 28, STATE in position 35
- Line 08: Type EF, space 3
- Line 09: ZIP in position 35]*

Each time EXCPT is executed, the four output lines identified by an E in column 15 of output specifications are written.

Conditioning the Use of EXCPT Operation

An EXCPT operation may be conditioned in two ways: (1) on the Calculation Specifications form and (2) on the Output Specifications form.

The EXCPT operation can be conditioned on the Calculation Specifications form in the same way that other operations are conditioned. An indicator used on the Calculation Specifications form controls the printing of all EXCPT records. (See Figure 5.3.) Individual EXCPT records are controlled by indicators specified in positions 23–31 of the Output Specifications form. These indicators are used for EXCPT records in the same way that they are used for all other records.

Restriction: Overflow indicators cannot be used to condition an EXCPT line. This means that an EXCPT record cannot be a record that is printed only when the end of the page has been reached.

Remember, EXCPT lines are exceptions; they print at calculation time only—not at output time. Therefore, they cannot possibly print when other overflow lines are printed.

Fetch Overflow

An EXCPT line may be printed on the overflow line. If it is, the overflow indicator will be turned on as usual. EXCPT lines can even fetch overflow by placing an *F* in position 16 of any exception line. If the overflow indicator is on when the EXCPT line with an *F* in position 16 is reached, all lines conditioned by the overflow indicator will print before the exception line.

Figure 5.3 Conditioning the use of EXCPT operation

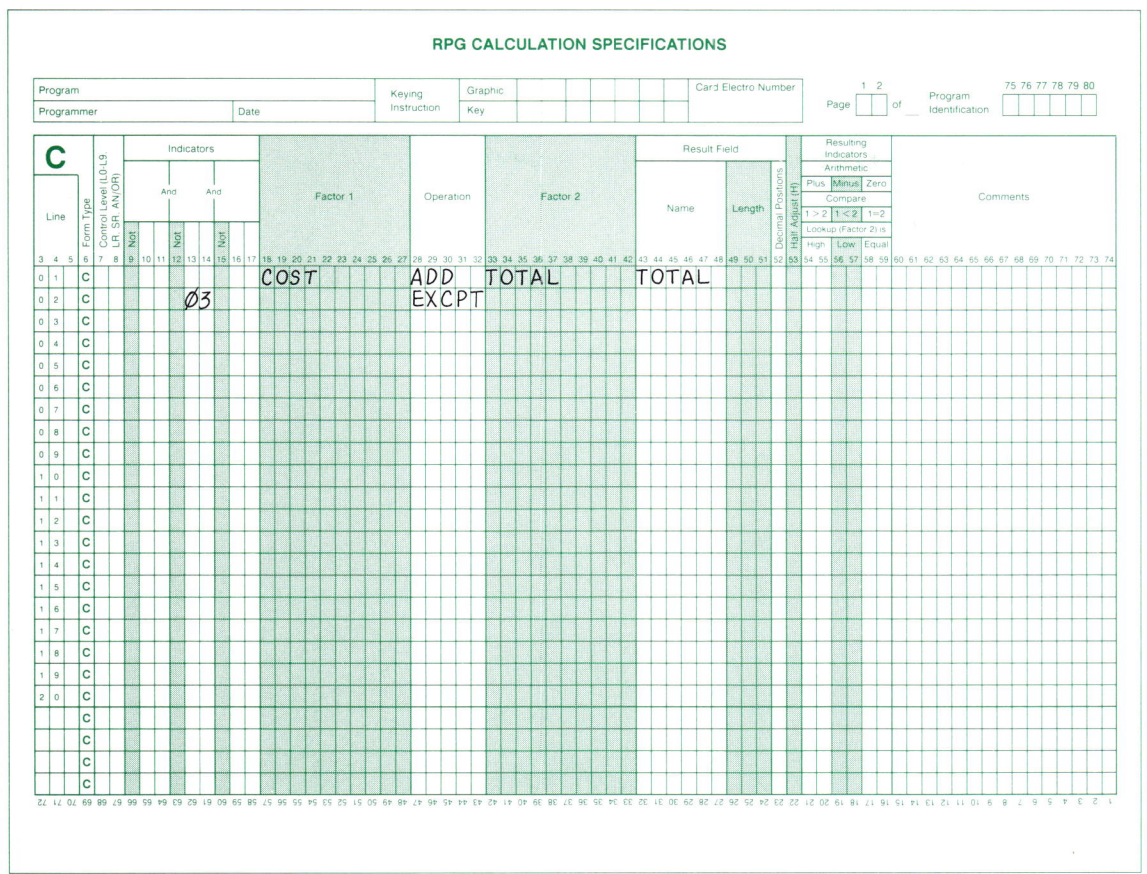

Overflow Printing with EXCPT Operation

Overflow conditions cannot condition an exception line, but they can condition fields within an exception line. The use of the EXCPT operation code causes only exception lines to be printed during calculation time. If the overflow line is sensed when an exception line is printed, the overflow indicator turns on as usual. Overflow processing, however, does not occur until another exception line conditioned to print (with fetch overflow specified) is encountered.

The actual overflow output lines (totals and/or headings) must be coded as H, D, or T types. The use of fetch overflow will cause the H, D, or T overflow output lines to be printed if the overflow indicator is on. The overflow output lines are printed before the line on which fetch overflow is specified. The user may also force overflow by issuing a SETON of the appropriate overflow indicator. This must occur before EXCPT operation code and fetch overflow must have been specified. (See Figure 5.4.)

Fetch overflow allows the basic RPG overflow logic to be changed. Forms can be made to advance to the next page at the time total or detail records are printed instead of waiting for the usual time.

During the regular program cycle, the RPG program tests only once to see if the overflow indicator is on; this occurs immediately after total output. By using fetch overflow specifications, the computer can be told to check if the overflow indicator is on before it prints total, detail, or exception records. This instruction to check is given by entering an *F* in position 16 of the Output Specifications form for any detail, total, or exception record. When an *F* is encountered, a test is made before that line is to be printed. (See Figure 5.5.)

Program Control of Operations

Figure 5.4 Overflow printing: setting the overflow indicator

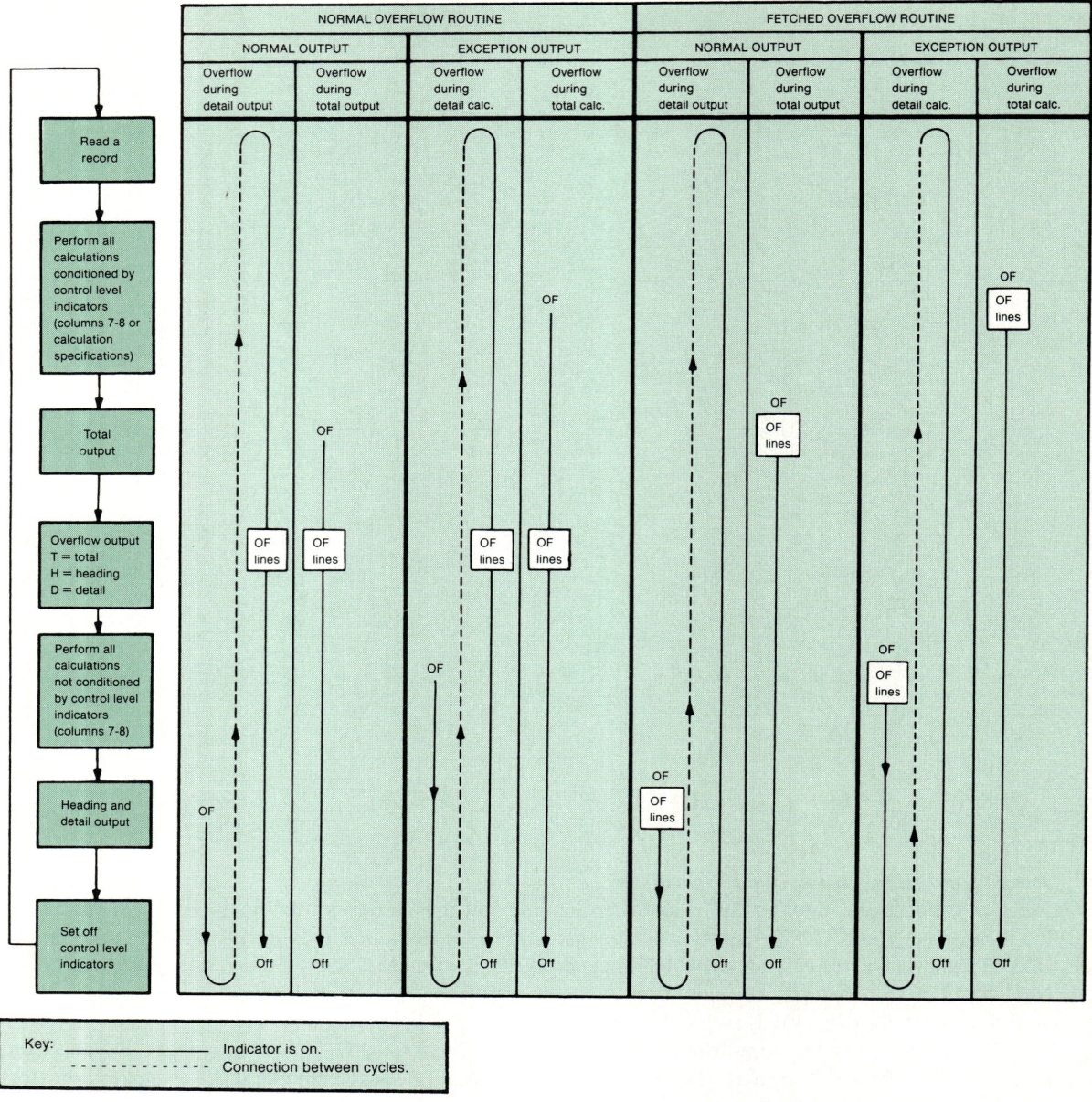

When the overflow line is reached during the regular program cycle, the remaining detail lines, total lines, and total overflow lines (lines conditioned by the overflow indicators) are printed on the page even after overflow has occurred. Therefore, enough room must be left between the overflow lines and the actual end of the page to accommodate all these lines that are yet to print. (See Figure 5.6.)

However, a number of problems can arise when this is done. For example, if a different number of detail or total lines can be printed each time, enough room may not have been allowed between the overflow line and the end of the page to take care of all total lines that will print before the forms advance. Therefore, printing is done on the perforation. (See Figure 5.7.) The programmer may also have to allow so much room between the overflow line and the end of that page that often only half a page is used.

Figure 5.5 Fetch overflow specifications

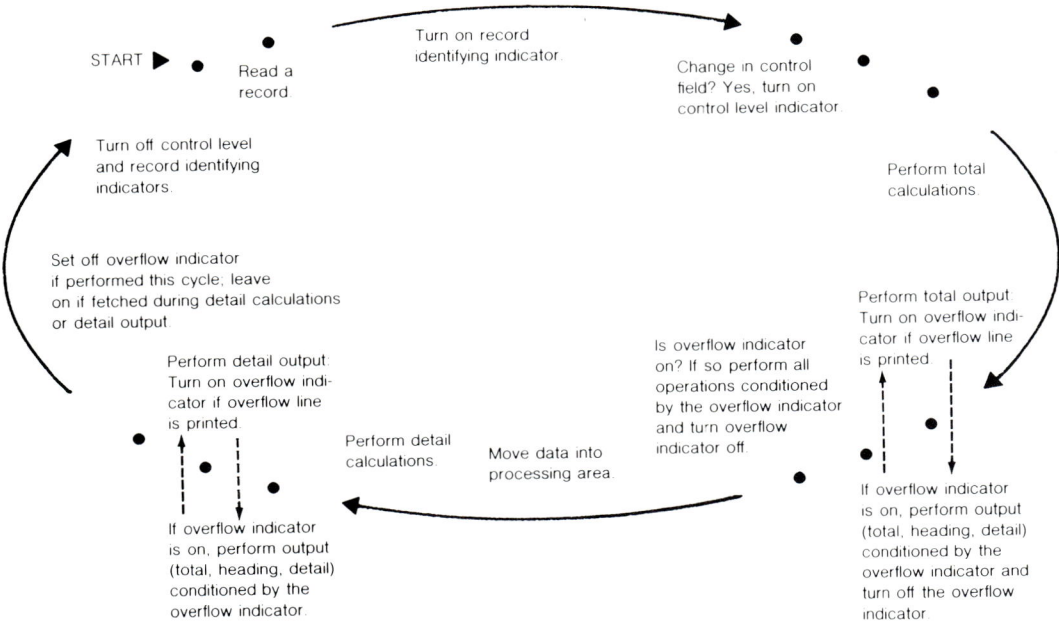

Figure 5.6 Logic for fetch overflow

Program Control of Operations 177

Figure 5.7 Printing over the perforation

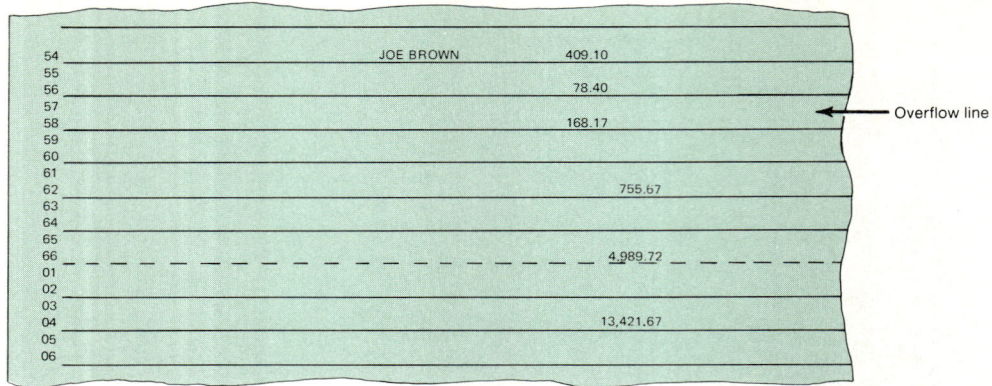

When the detail line was printed on the overflow line, all total lines were also printed before the forms advanced. As a result, printing occurred over the perforation onto the next page.

A solution to these problems may be to call for printing of overflow lines and a forms advance any time after the overflow line has been reached. Causing overflow lines to be printed ahead of the usual time is known as the **fetch overflow.** Overflow created in this way produces the following results:

1. All total lines conditioned by the overflow indicator are printed.

2. Forms advance to a new page when a skip to the first line has been specified in a line conditioned by an overflow indicator.

3. Heading and detail lines conditioned by the overflow indicator are printed.

4. The line that fetched overflow is printed.

5. Any detail and/or total lines left to be printed for that program cycle are printed. (See Figure 5.8.)

Figure 5.8 Printing total records on the overflow page

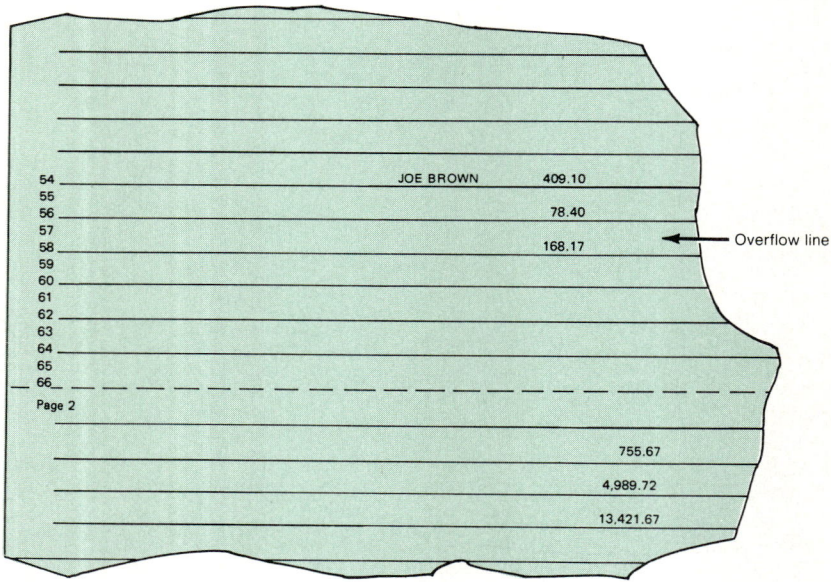

What records should most logically be printed on an overflow page? The answer is probably all those records that printed on or over the perforation. By specifying an F in column 16 of the first total specification, the program checks to see if the overflow indicator is on. If it is on at this time, forms will advance before total records are printed. Specifying an F in column 16 of the first total specifications will cause all total records to be printed on an overflow page.

Figure 5.9 Uses of fetch overflow

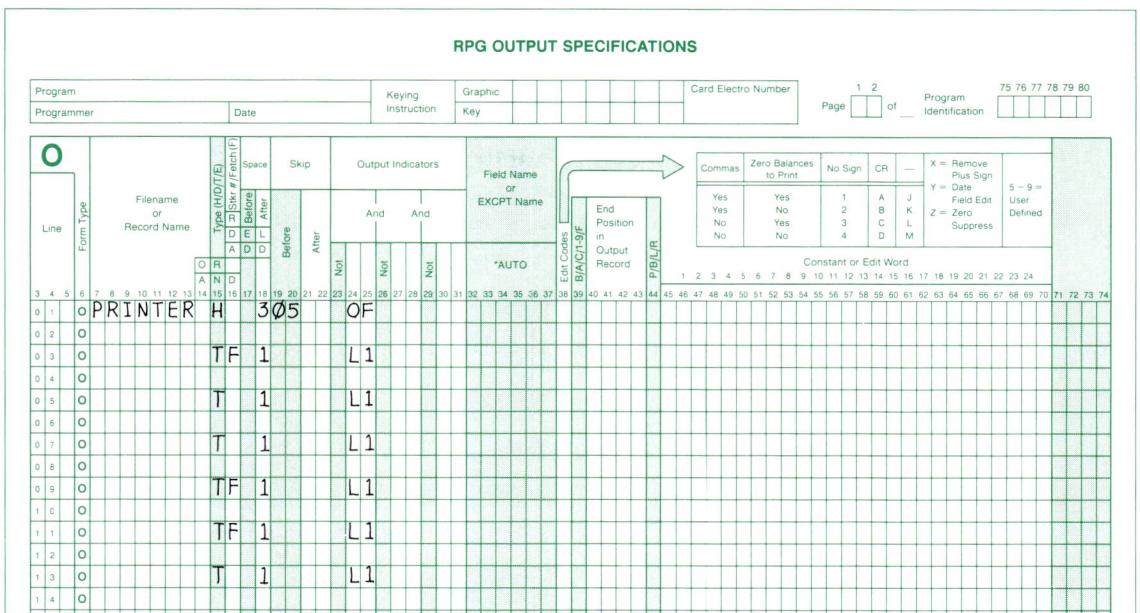

Notes on the Coding

The above figure shows the use of a fetched overflow routine (F in column 16).

The total lines 03, 09, and 11 can fetch the overflow routine. They do this, however, only if the overflow line has been sensed prior to the printing of one of these lines.

If the overflow indicator is turned on before the output line specified in line 03 is printed and if control level indicator L1 is on, forms advance to the new page as specified by the skip entry in the heading line. The heading line and all total lines are printed on the new page.

If, however, the printing of the line specified in 03 caused the overflow indicator to turn on, the following happens:

1. The line specified in 05 prints on the same page.

2. The line specified in 07 prints on the same page.

3. The line specified in 09 fetches an overflow (F in column 16) and causes the heading line and all total lines (09, 11, and 13) to print on a new page.

For the printer file, an *F* in position 16 on the Output Specifications form specifies that the overflow routine will be fetched. An *F* can be specified for any total, detail, or exception line except those conditioned by an overflow indicator.

Fetch overflow routine should be used when (1) a particular line, when printed, could cause an overflow and (2) if an overflow occurred, there would not be enough room left on the page to print the remaining detail and/or total output lines plus lines conditioned by the overflow indicator.

Specifying an *F* in position 16 of an output line causes that line to be printed on an overflow condition, but only after all specified overflow lines have been printed. Thus, use of fetch overflow allows specified overflow lines (e.g., headings) to be printed during detail or total time.

When the system encounters an *F* in position 16 of an output line, it checks to see if the output associated with that line will trigger an overflow condition. If an overflow condition is encountered, the system delays the output for that line until the lines conditioned by overflow (e.g., totals and/or headings with overflow indicators in positions 23–31) have all been output. (See Figures 5.4 and 5.9.)

Control of Calculations

Following are some of the operations that allow the user to control the indicators and/or the order of calculations.

SETON and *SETOF*—allow the user to control the indicators.

GOTO and *TAG*—allow the user to control the order of calculations. These operations are used whenever the programmer wishes to bypass certain calculations that are not needed in this RPG cycle. These operations also allow the user to repeat the calculations (or portions of the calculations) several times in the RPG cycle.

MOVE and *Z-ADD*—allow the user to control the movement of data fields during calculations.

BEGSR and *ENDSR*—subroutines that are sets of calculation steps. These steps may be performed following any other calculation.

Setting Indicators On and Off (SETON and SETOF)

Coding programs with multiple functions may require some additional control of the indicators. So far, indicators have been turned on by the RPG fixed logic or the conditions coded on specification forms. Using the operation codes SETON and SETOF, indicators may be turned on or off directly on the Calculations Specifications form. (See Figure 5.10.)

The SETON and SETOF instructions should be used when it is necessary to take control of the indicators in the program. It is the programmer's method of remembering conditions or overriding what

Figure 5.10 Setting indicators—examples

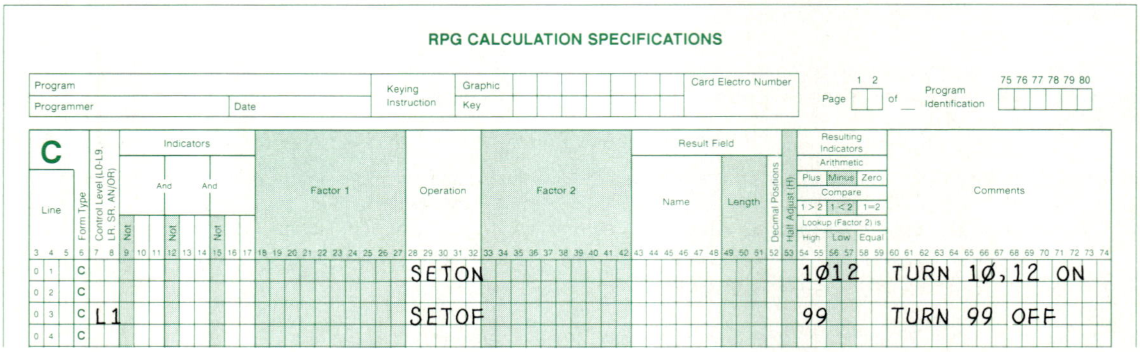

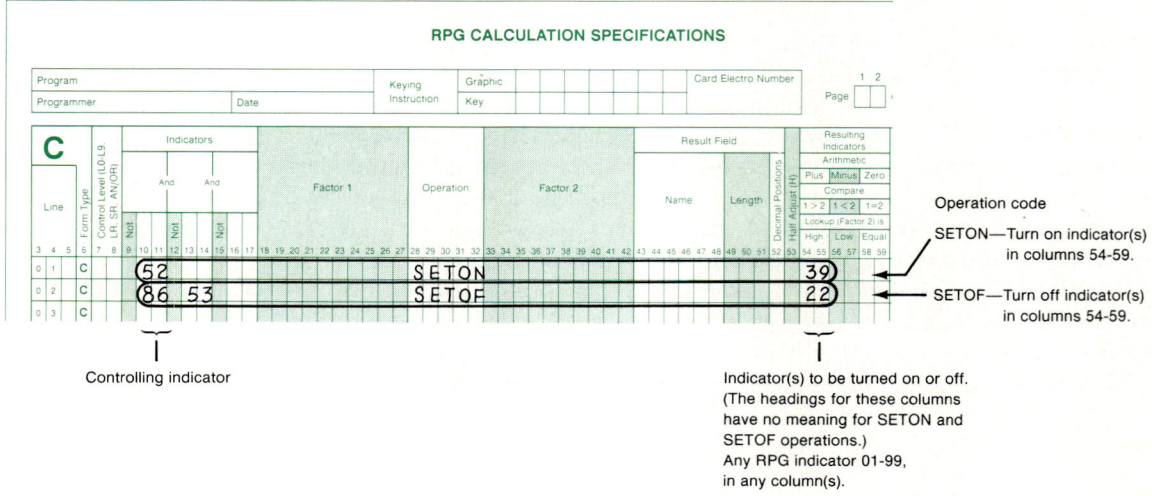

Figure 5.11 Setting indicators

180 RPG II and RPG III Programming

Figure 5.12 Use of SETON to remember conditions existing during detail calculations

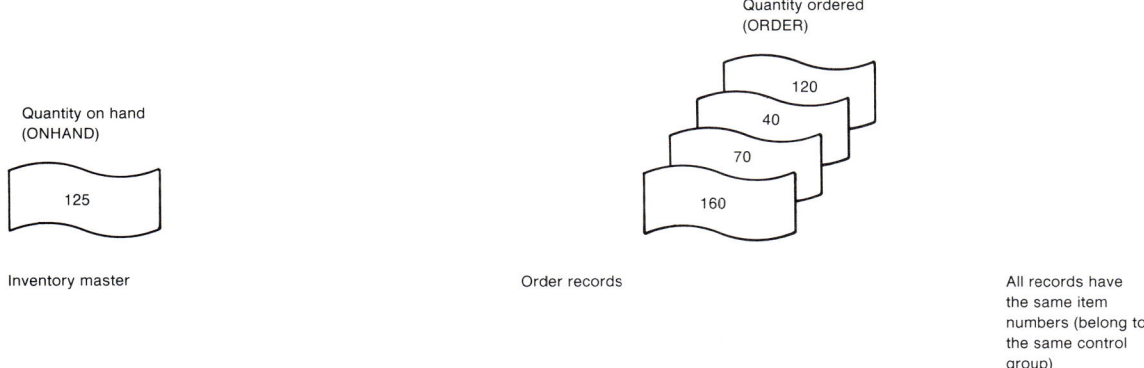

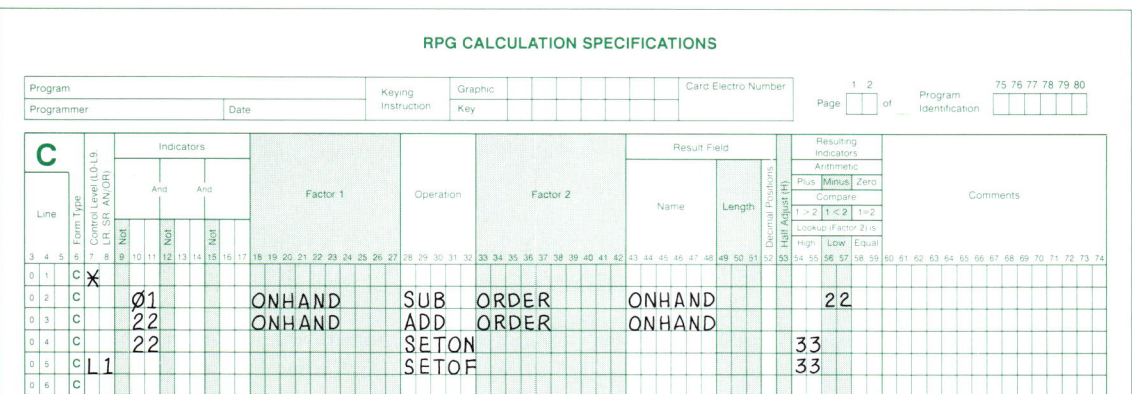

RPG might do with indicators (See Figure 5.11.) Following are typical uses of the SETON and SETOF operations:

1. The SETON can be used to remember a record. The record's identifying indicator will turn off at the end of the cycle. (See Figure 5.12.) To remember if that type of record has been read, another indicator is SETON. This indicator will remain on until it is set off, unless it was used as a resulting indicator elsewhere in the program.

2. Use SETON to represent several different conditions in the program. (See Figure 5.13.) Different error-condition indicators can be set on to signify that an error exists.

3. Since these indicators are SETON by the programmer in the program, it is also the responsibility of the programmer to turn them off. Each SETOF instruction can turn off up to three different indicators.

4. If four or more indicators are to be replaced, then an AN(d) coding entry can be made. This is valuable if later operations are to be conditioned by the four indicators.

Note: In both OR and AN(d) coding, the SETON instruction is on the last line of conditioning indicators.

In general, any indicator turned on by a SETON instruction will stay on until a SETOF instruction is received or until the program ends. It is sometimes necessary, however, to SETON an indicator that is also used as a field indicator or as a record identifying indicator. In these cases, the indicator remains on until there is a change in record type or in the status of the field, or until a SETOF instruction is given. Indicators that have been set on for one record may not be required for the next. Therefore, care must be taken to ensure that indicators that are set on are set off before detail calculations for the next record. Indicators can be arranged to be set off at (a) the end of the calculations for the record that set them on or (b) the beginning of the calculation for the next record.

Program Control of Operations 181

Figure 5.13 Use of SETON to replace indicators

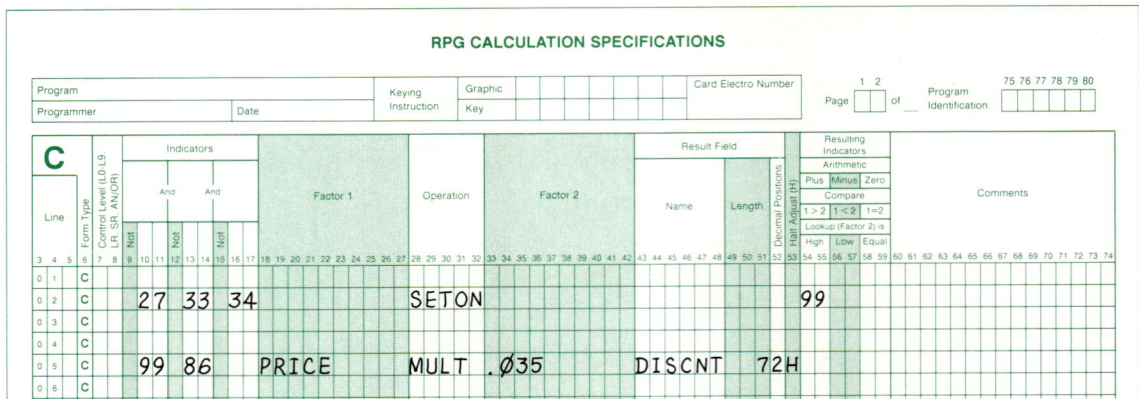

This calculation: PRICE × .035 = DISCOUNT is to be performed when these indicator conditions exist: 27 and 33 and 34 and 86.

Procedure:
1. Replace three indicators with one new one.
2. Use the new indicator in an AND relationship with the fourth to control the calculation.

If calculation must be conditioned by more than three indicators in an AN(d) relationship, the SETON operation can be used. The SETON instruction may also be used to "remember" certain conditions that existed during detail calculations.

In summary, these operation codes are used to control indicators in the program. They are used to remember records, to remember conditions, and to replace several indicators. SETON causes any indicators in positions 54–59 to be turned on, while SETOF causes any indicators in positions 54–59 to be turned off. (See Figure 5.14.)

Branching and Looping

The computer usually works through the calculations in the order in which they are entered on the Calculation Specifications form. However, RPG allows the programmer to make use of a very important technique on the Calculation Specifications form. This technique is called branching. **Branching** occurs when the computer stops following calculations in the order entered and branches past some of them. The branch may move backward or forward through the calculations. For example, in a billing application, interest may be payable on overdue balances. For fully paid up accounts, the computer can be told to branch forward past the interest calculations.

An example of backward branching is found in the calculation of compound interest. The program is set up to calculate interest for one year. At the end of this set of calculations, it is branched back to repeat the set. This creates a loop of calculations. The program will continue looping until the interest is calculated for the required number of years.

Operations are normally performed in the order that they appear on the Calculations Specifications form. There may be times, however, when it is necessary to alter that sequence of the operations as, for example, when the programmer wishes to

1. Skip several operations when certain conditions occur
2. Perform certain operations for several, but not all, record types
3. Perform several operations over and over again

Figure 5.14 SETON and SETOF—examples

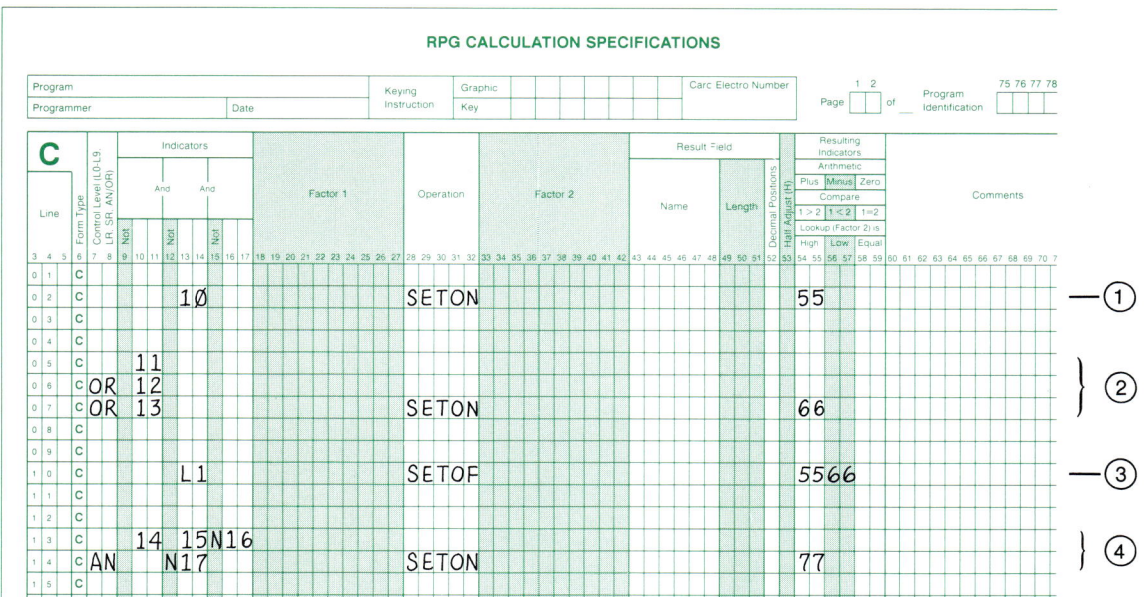

Notes on the Coding

1. The SETON is used to remember a record. The record's identifying indicator (10) will turn off at the end of the cycle.

2. The SETON is used to remember several different indicators.

3. The SETOF will turn off indicators 55 and 66 at detail time if the L1 indicator is on (the first record of a new group.)

4. The SETON is used to replace four or more indicators with the use of the AN coding entry.

   Note: On both the OR and AN coding, the SETON instruction is on the last line of the conditioning indicators.

Additional Notes on the Coding

A key point to remember in using the SETON and SETOF operation codes is that you are responsible for the indicators. If the programmer turns one on, then the indicator stays on until the programmer turns it off.

The AN and OR coding shown with the SETON is not restricted to this operation code. The programmer might have coded a COMP or ADD instruction if 11 or 12 or 13 were on.

Note in the fourth example that the programmer may code an indicator as not on N16, N17 for example.

Bypassing Calculations

Operations that have bypassed the use of indicators have not yet been discussed. For each calculation conditioned by an indicator, a check is made to see whether the condition set by the indicator has been satisfied. (When several sequential operations are conditioned by the same indicator(s), the test is only made on the first operation.) If the conditions have been satisfied, the operation is performed. Calculations are bypassed or omitted when conditions are satisfied. When bypassing calculations in this way, the program has to check the conditions set for each of the operations to determine whether or not to do them. This requires time and storage space inside the computer.

Another way to bypass calculations is to branch around them. With the latter method, the indicator setting for each operation is not checked. When the branch is taken around operations, the operations are just skipped. (See Figure 5.15.)

Program Control of Operations   183

Figure 5.15 Bypassing calculations by branching

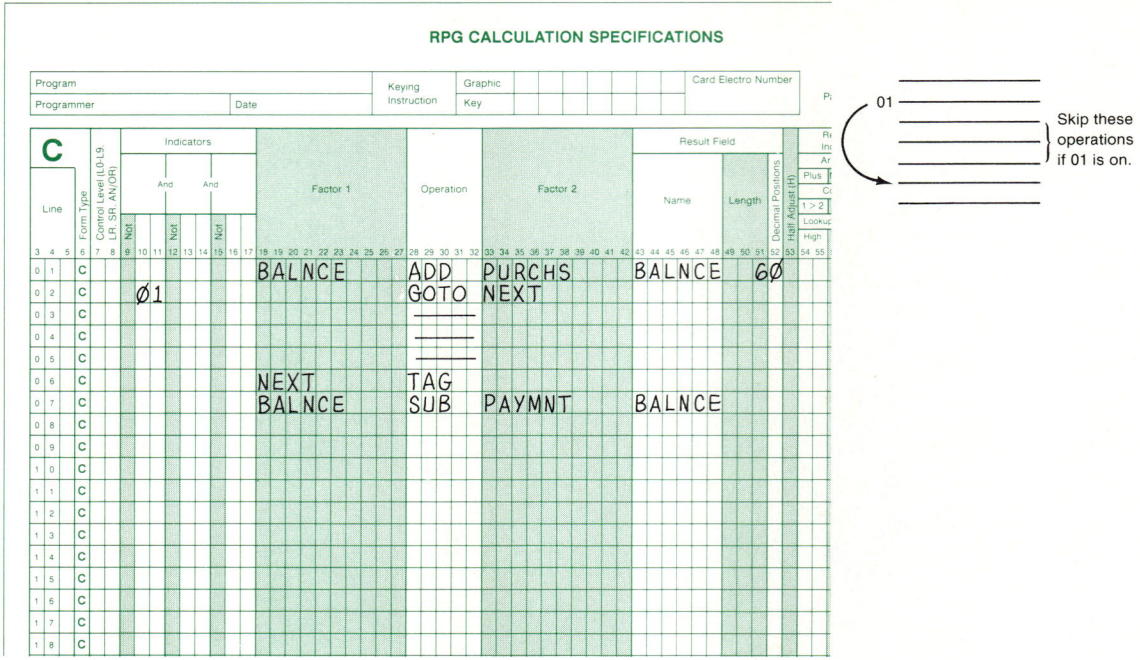

Two operations are used for branching—GOTO and TAG. GOTO is the code that causes a branch to another spot in the calculations. The TAG operation gives the name and location of the spot to which the GOTO operation branches. GOTO causes a branch; the TAG code does nothing but act as a name tag.

GOTO signals a branch to the spot name in factor 2. This name must also appear in the TAG statement, where it is entered in factor 1. The rules for forming a name for GOTO and TAG are the same as those for forming any field name.

A GOTO statement can be conditioned by an indicator, but a TAG cannot (with the exception of control level indicators, positions 7–8). When a GOTO is not conditioned, a branch occurs in every program cycle. There are many situations in which branching will help to write more efficient and effective programs. The following are examples:

When doing different operations for different record types, a record identifying indicator can be used to show what operations should be done for each record type. In such situations, a branch can be made directly to the set of calculations that should be done for the record type just read. When these calculations are done, a branch can be made to the end of all calculations. This eliminates checking operations to see if a set of calculations should be done for the record type being processed. (See Figure 5.16.)

When doing a matching record job that requires that all calculations be done only when records match, all specifications can be conditioned by MR (the matching record indicator). Otherwise, GOTO and TAG can be used to branch around all calculations when records do not match. (See Figure 5.17.) Branching is an easy way to bypass all calculations that should not be performed because of an error. (See Figure 5.18.)

Branching to different points in the program may be accomplished by using a number of GOTO and TAG operation codes. A branch may be made from one detail calculation to another detail calculation, or from one total calculation to another total calculation. However, a branch from a detail to a total calculation or vice versa is not permitted.

A GOTO statement may be used to branch backward in order to repeat statements that have already been done. Doing the same statements over and over again in a program cycle is called looping. The statements done several times in one cycle, plus the branching statement, make up the loop. (See Figure 5.19.)

Figure 5.16 Doing different operations for different record types

Operations Performed for Different Record Types

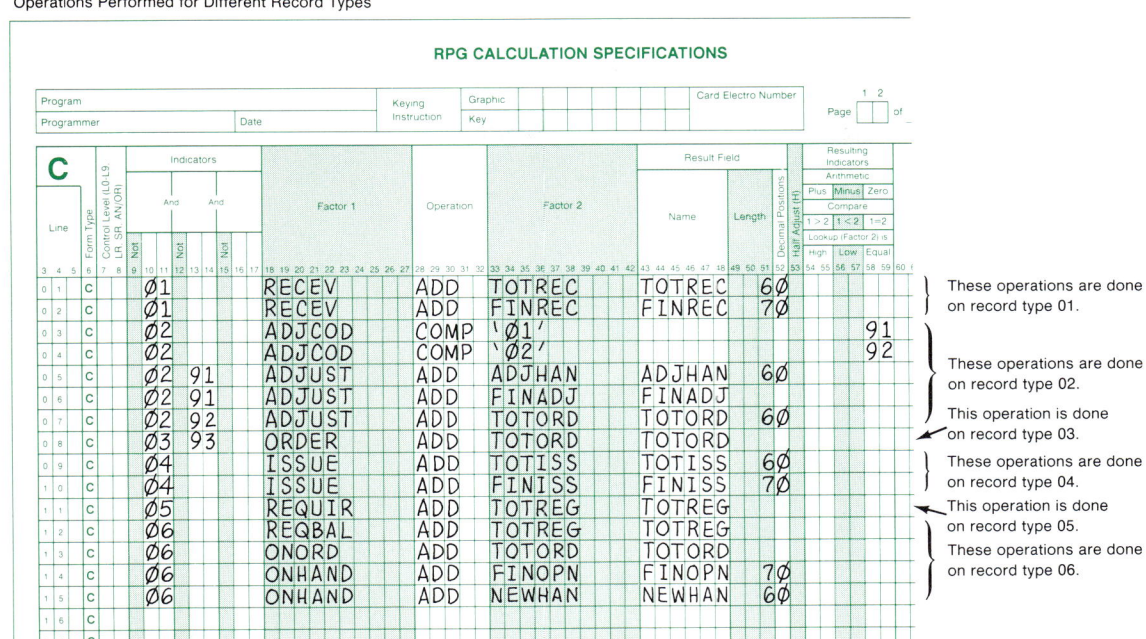

Recommended Branching Structure

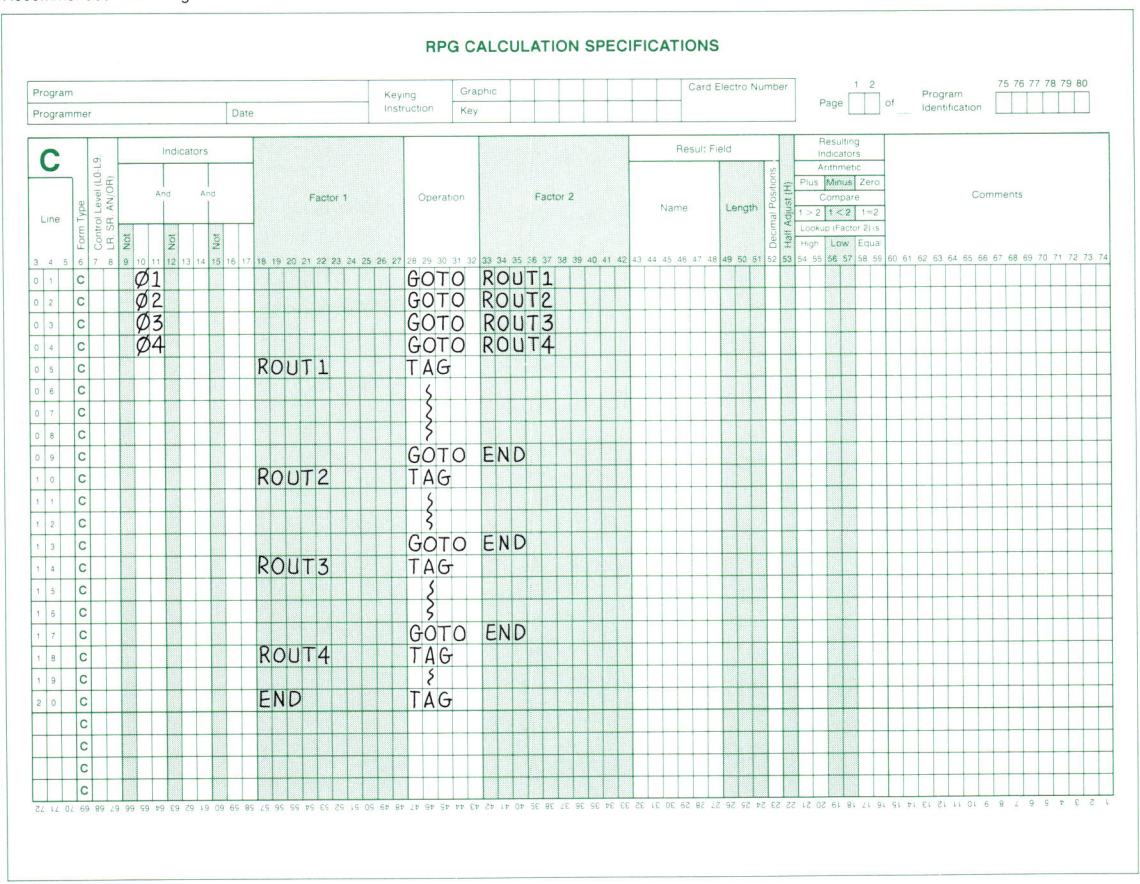

Program Control of Operations 185

Figure 5.17 Branching in a matching records job

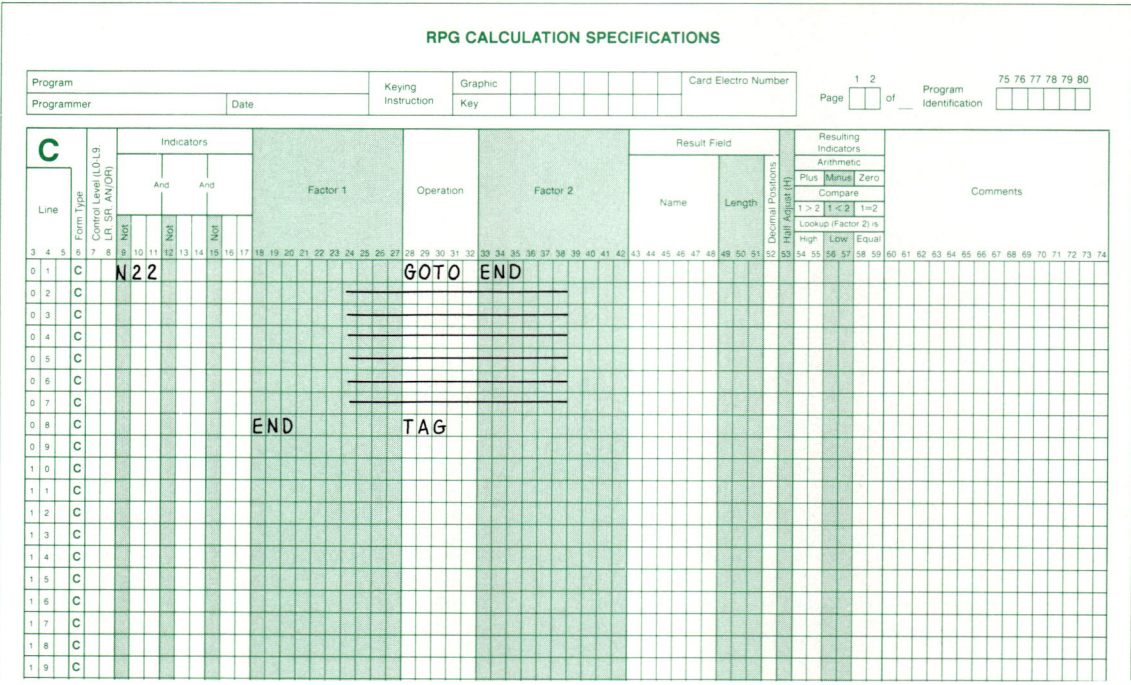

Figure 5.18 Branching when an error occurs

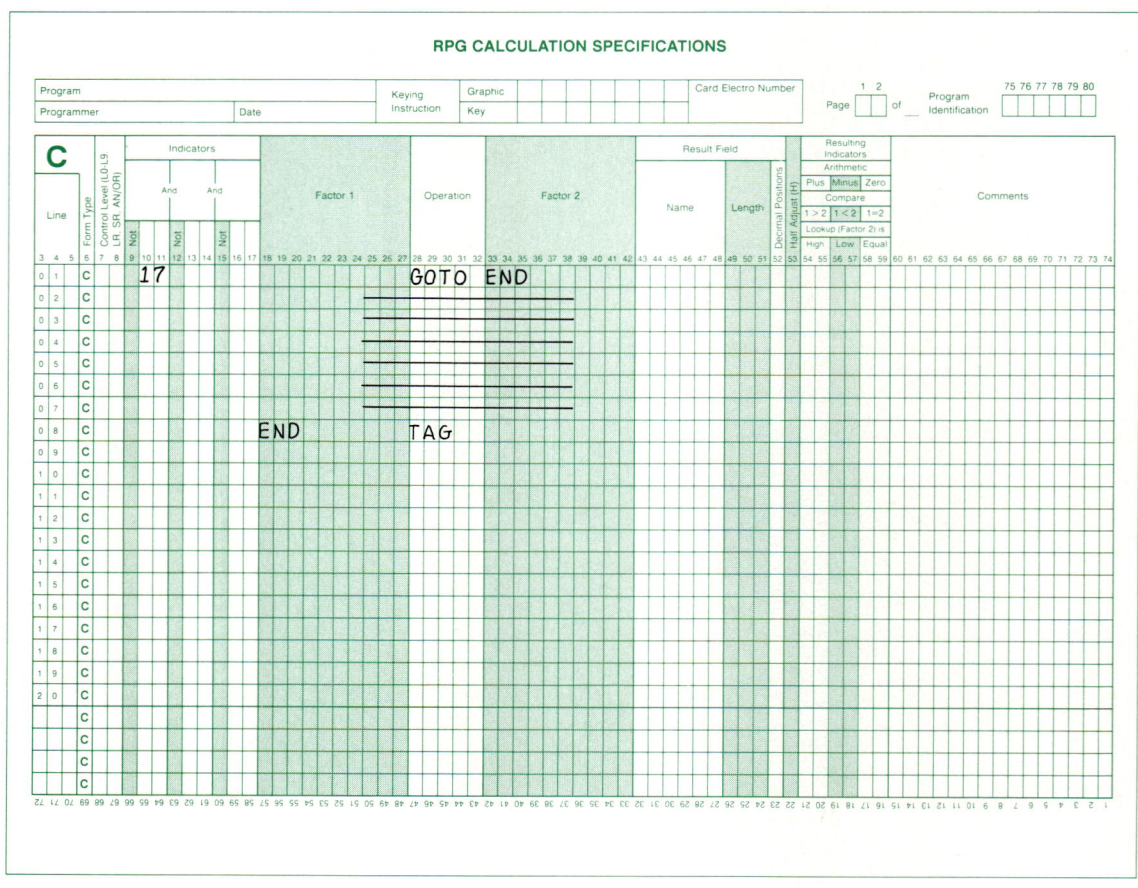

Figure 5.19 Loops—example

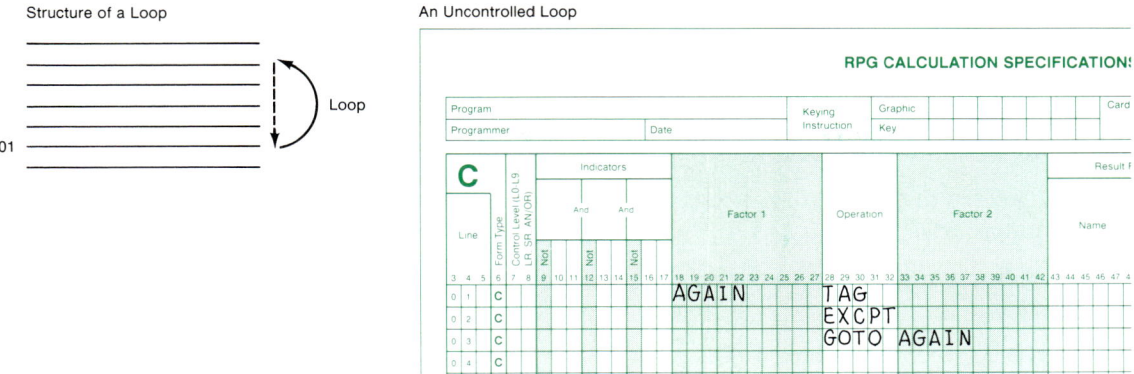

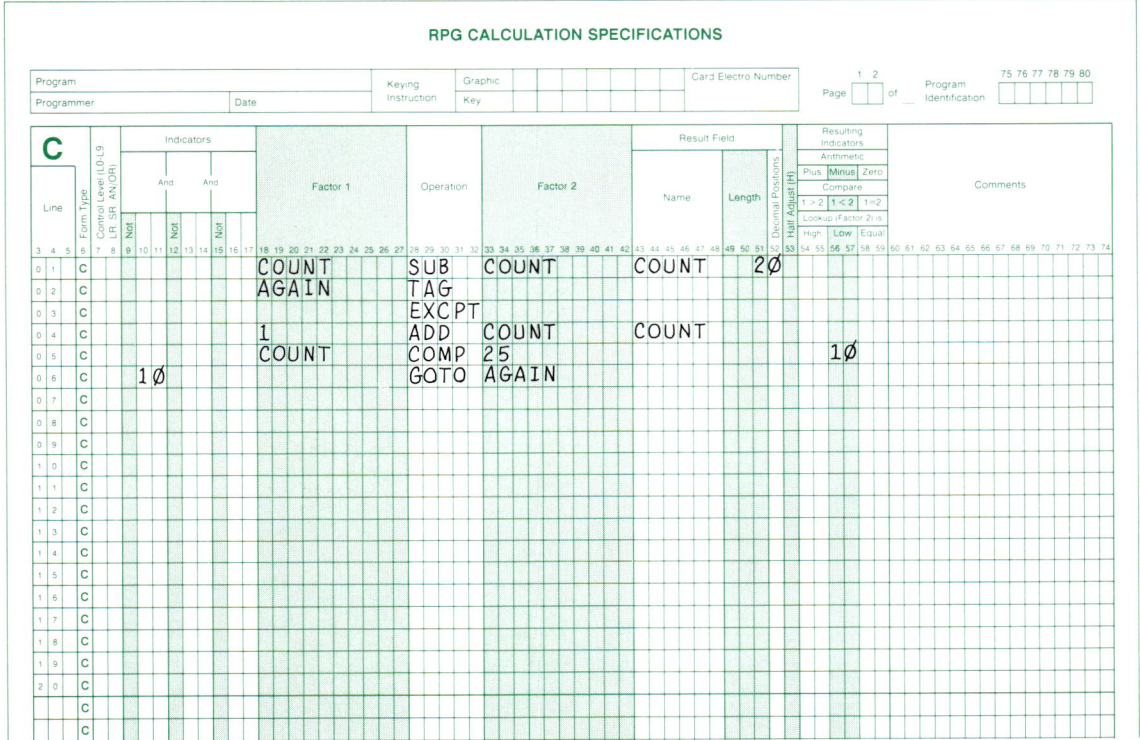

Go To (GOTO)
The GOTO operation instructs the program to skip other types of instructions. A branch may be made to an earlier line or to a later specification line. A skip cannot be made from a calculation that is not conditioned by a control level indicator (positions 7–8) to one that is, or vice versa. Nor can a branch be made from a calculation within a subroutine to a calculation outside of the subroutine, or vice versa.

Factor 2 must contain the name of the point to which the branch is to be made. Factor 1 and the result field are not used by this operation. The GOTO operation may be conditioned by any indicator. If it is not conditioned, the operation is always performed.

Tag (TAG)
The TAG operation code names the point to which the branch is being made in the GOTO operation. Factor 1 contains this label and the name must begin in position 18. This same label may not be used for more than one TAG instruction.

Program Control of Operations 187

Factor 2 and the result field are not used. No indicators may be entered in positions 9–17 for a TAG instruction. Control level indicators must be used, however, if branching is to occur at total time. If branching is to occur *every* time, control level indicator L0 must be used.

GOTO Operation—Summary

The GOTO and TAG operation codes may be used to give calculations more flexibility as the programs start to involve multiple functions (See Figure 5.20.)

They may be used to branch around certain calculations or to loop back and repeat certain operations. (See Figure 5.21.)

If a looping function is coded, make sure that there is a provision within the loop to branch out. (See Figure 5.22.)

For each GOTO, there must be a TAG.

Many GOTOs may branch to the same TAG.

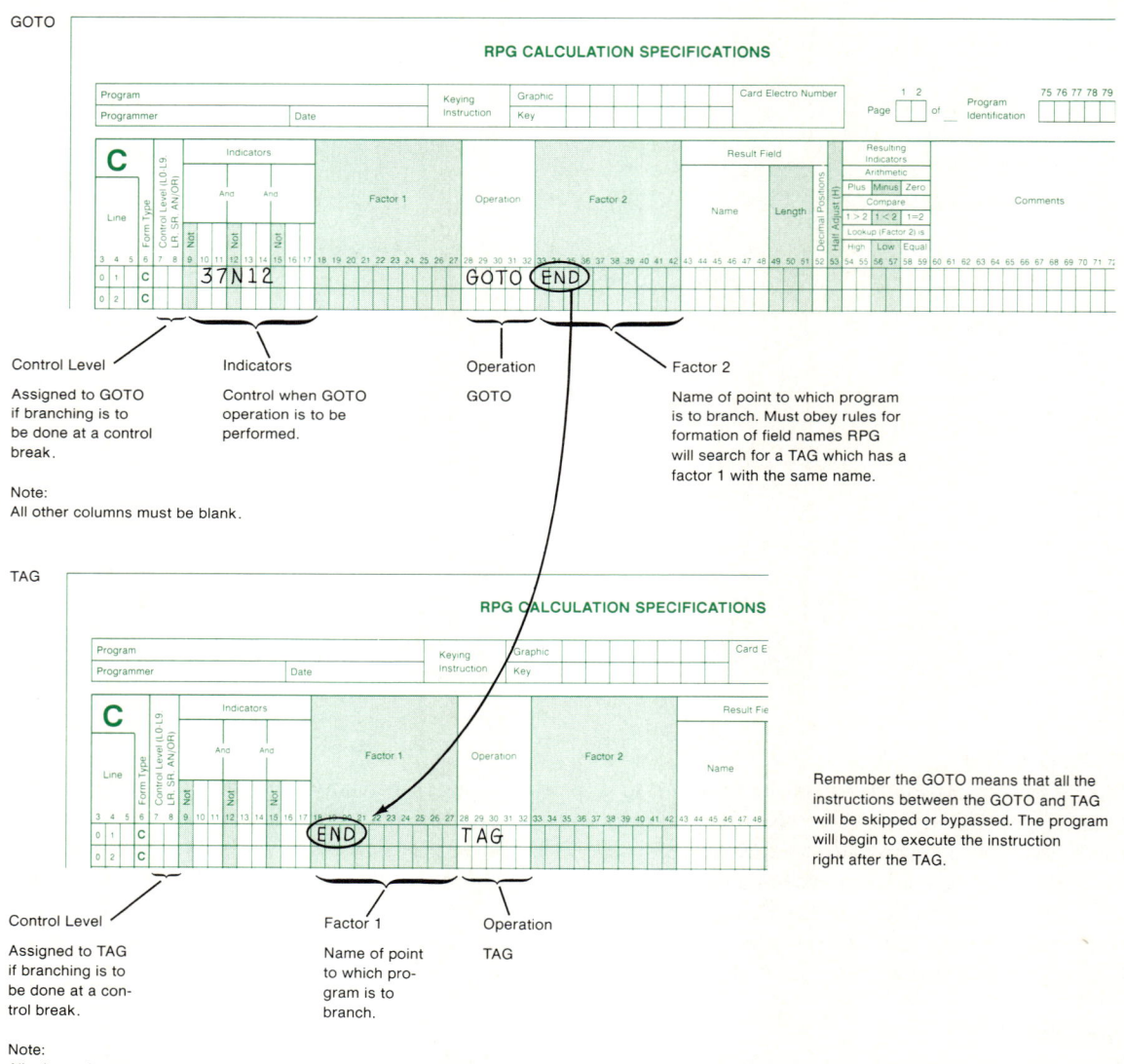

Figure 5.20 GOTO and TAG operation codes—examples

188 RPG II and RPG III Programming

Figure 5.21 GOTO operation—examples

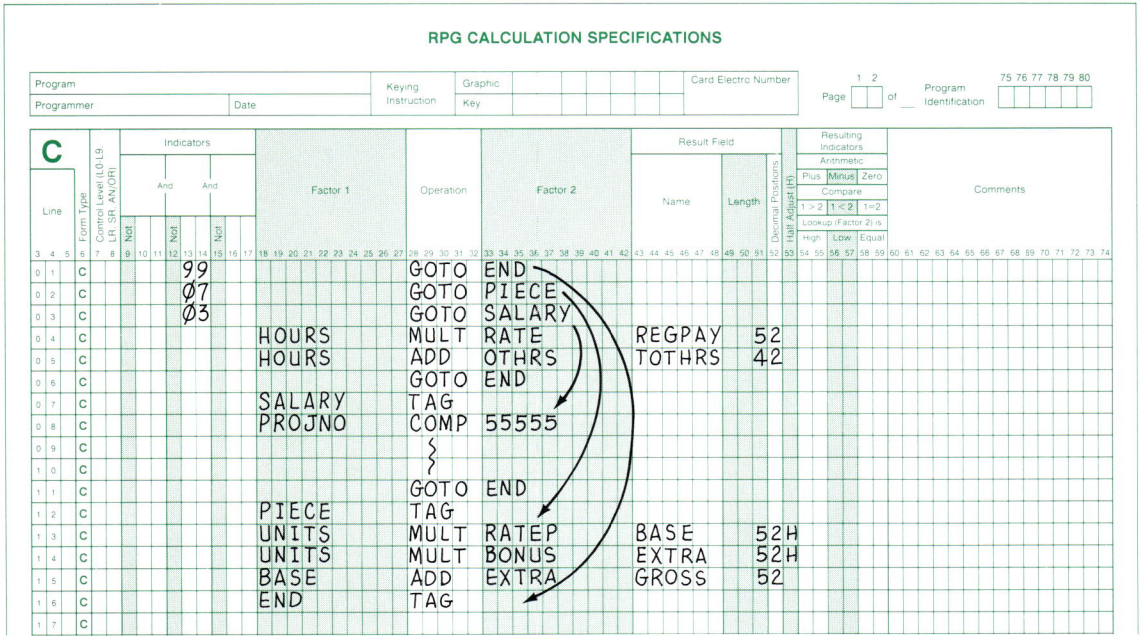

Notes on the Coding

If 99 is on, all calculations are bypassed.

If 07 is on, RPG skips to the PIECE TAG, and then performs those calculations.

If 03 is on, RPG skips to the SALARY TAG, performs the salary operations, and then skips to the END TAG.

If none of the above occur, it must be an hourly record. Those operations are done, and the RPG skips to the END TAG.

Using this approach to code the calculations, the programmer should be able to:

1. Develop the program in modules
2. Save processing time when the program executes.

NOTE: There may be multiple GOTOs to the same TAG.

If there are detail and total calculations in the program, the GOTO *may not* go from one to the other. The GOTO and TAG may only be used within detail or within total calculations.

These operations are used when it is necessary to control the sequence of operations.

Movement of Data Calculations

Because the programs involve multiple functions, the programmer may need to manipulate data fields. The operation codes that allow the programmer to move data on the Calculation Specifications form are Z-ADD, Z-SUB, and the MOVE operation codes.

Zero and Add (Z-ADD)

The Z-ADD is an arithmetic operation that works with numeric fields. It moves data from factor 2 to the result field as follows:

1. It replaces the value of the result field with the value of factor 2.
2. Nothing happens to factor 2.
3. Factor 1 is always blank.

Program Control of Operations   189

Figure 5.22 GOTO loop—example

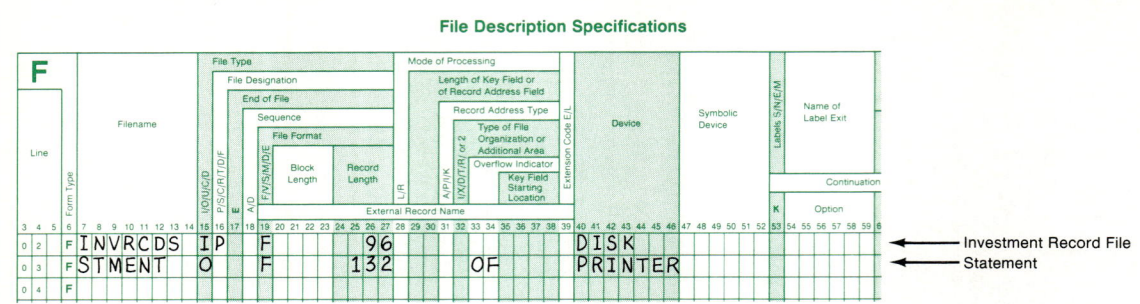

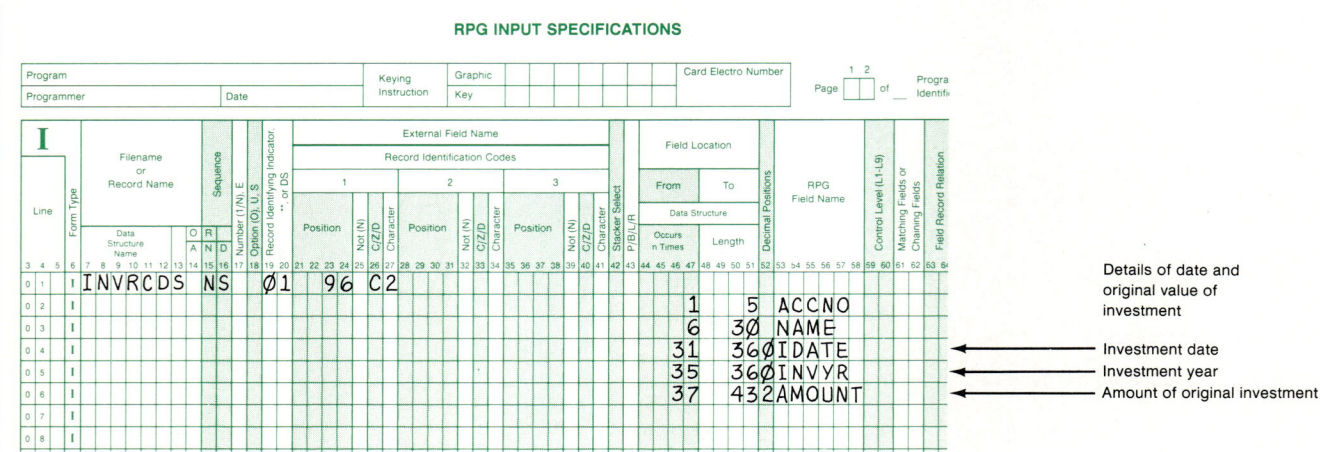

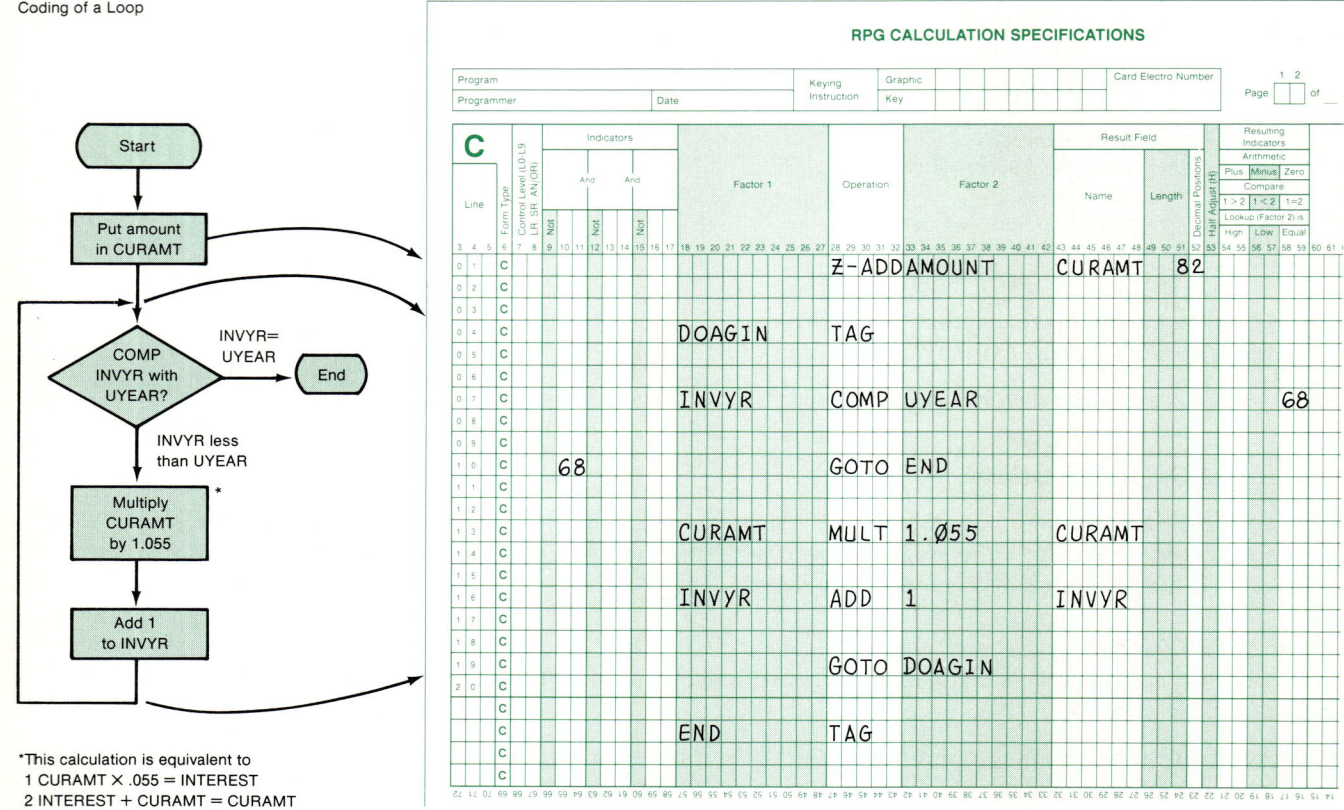

*This calculation is equivalent to
1 CURAMT × .055 = INTEREST
2 INTEREST + CURAMT = CURAMT

Figure 5.23 Z-add operation—example

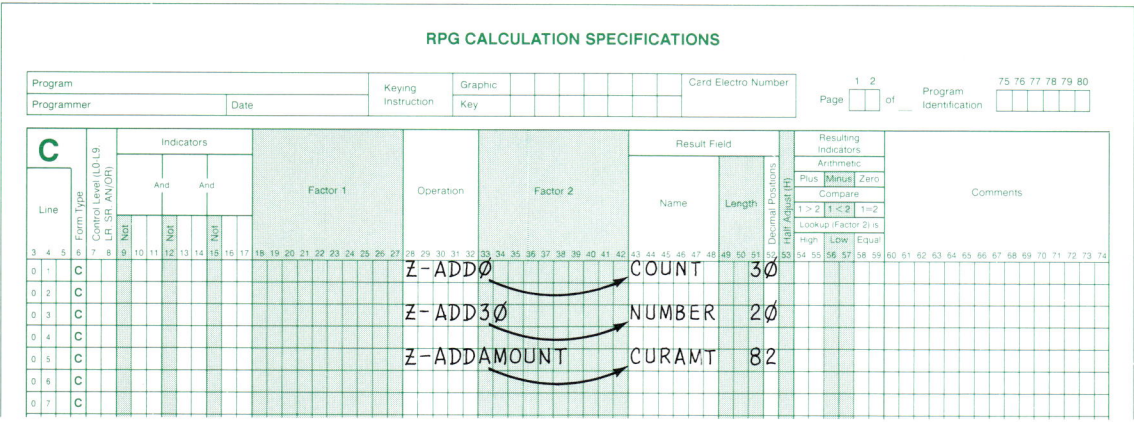

Notes on the Coding

Line 01: Z-ADD sets the result field to zero and then adds factor 2; after the operation, COUNT will be zero.

Line 02: Z-ADD sets an initial value in a field; after the operation, NUMBER will be 30.

Line 03: Z-ADD moves the value of a field to another field so both the original and a new amount may be available for output. After the operation, AMOUNT and CURAMT will be the same.

The Z-ADD instruction may be used when the programmer needs to set a field to zero, place a initial value in a field, or move the values of one field to another. Z-ADD instruction eliminates any problems that may arise from having sending and receiving fields of different sizes. (See Figure 5.23.)

Zero and Subtract (Z-SUB)

The Z-SUB instruction is an arithmetic operation that works with numeric fields. Factor 2 is subtracted from a field of zeros and the difference is placed in the result field. This actally places the negative value of factor 2 in the result field. Factor 1 is not used. (See Figure 5.24.)

Z-SUB can be used to reverse the sign in a field. A positive value can be made negative and a negative value can be made positive.

MOVE Operation (MOVE and MOVEL)

Where the Z-ADD operation works with numeric data, the MOVE operation is used with either alphabetic or numeric data. There are actually two MOVE operation codes—MOVE, which is move from the right; and MOVEL, which is move from the left.

The key point to remember about the MOVE or MOVEL is that the operation stops whenever there is nothing more to move or when there is not any more room to move the data. This is critical when the result field is relatively long since there will be some data left over from the previous value of the field.

Moving Data

A program can be instructed to manipulate data in many different ways. It can cause data to be added, subtracted, multiplied, compared, tested, or divided. Data can also be caused to move. When data is moved, a copy of data in one field is transferred to another field. In the process of transfer, it may or may not be changed, depending upon the specifications.

Data may be moved for many reasons including:

1. To save information from a field
2. To separate one field into two or more parts
3. To change a numeric field to an alphameric field or vice versa

Program Control of Operations

Figure 5.24 Zero and subtract—example

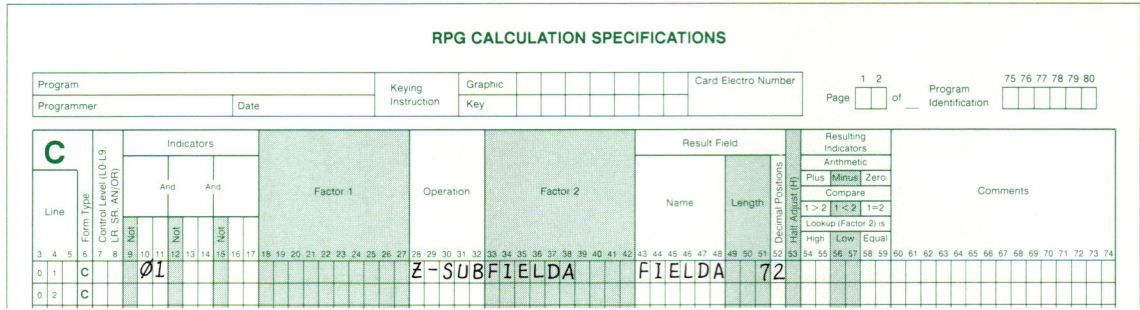

Note on the Coding

FIELDA can be made a positive or negative value in the result field depending upon the original value in factor 2.

Specifications for Moving Data

RPG allows the programmer to move the contents of one field and place it in another. RPG has two move operations codes—MOVE and MOVEL.

The MOVE operation causes the content of the field in factor 2 to be copied into the right-hand end of the result field. In general, the MOVE operation continues either until the result field is filled or until all of factor 2 has been copied. (See Figure 5.25.)

The MOVEL operation causes the content of the field in factor 2 to be copied into the left-hand end of the result field. As with the MOVE operation, the MOVEL operation continues either until the result field is filled or until all of factor 2 has been copied. (See Figure 5.26.)

Figure 5.25 MOVE operation—examples

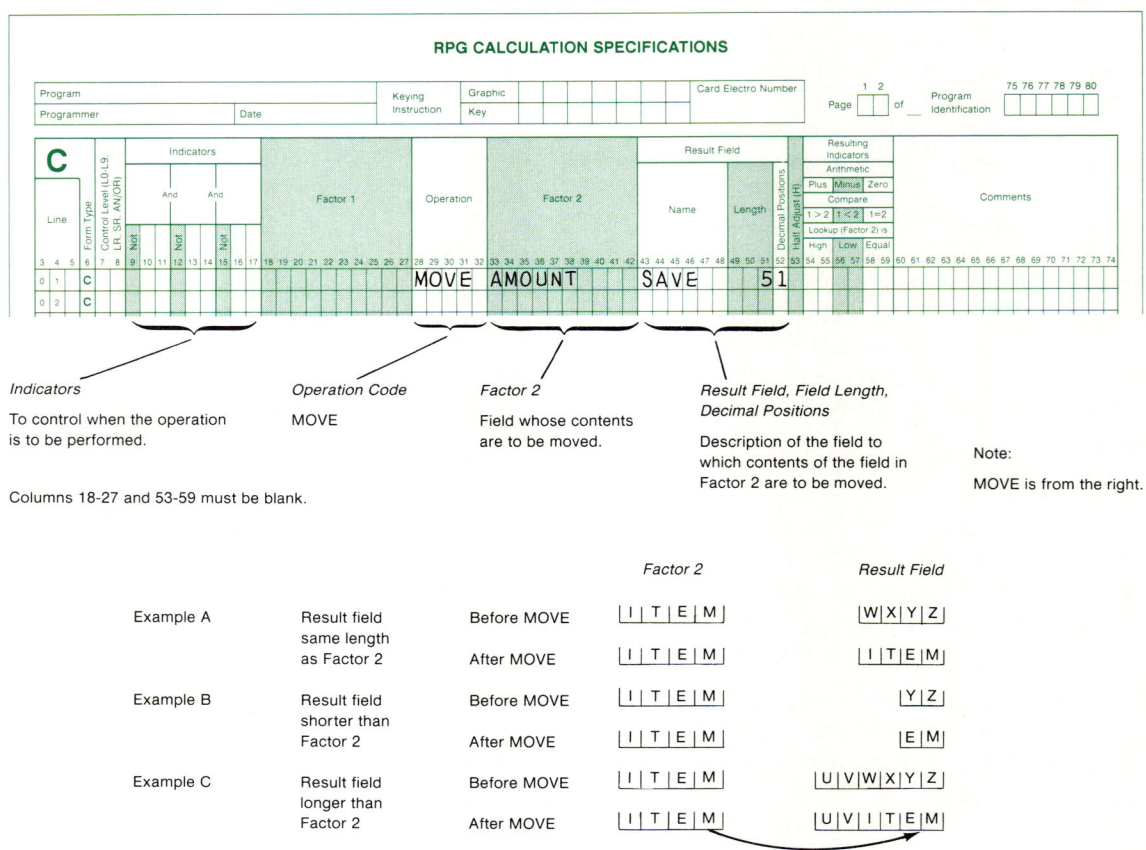

192   RPG II and RPG III Programming

Figure 5.26 MOVEL operation—examples

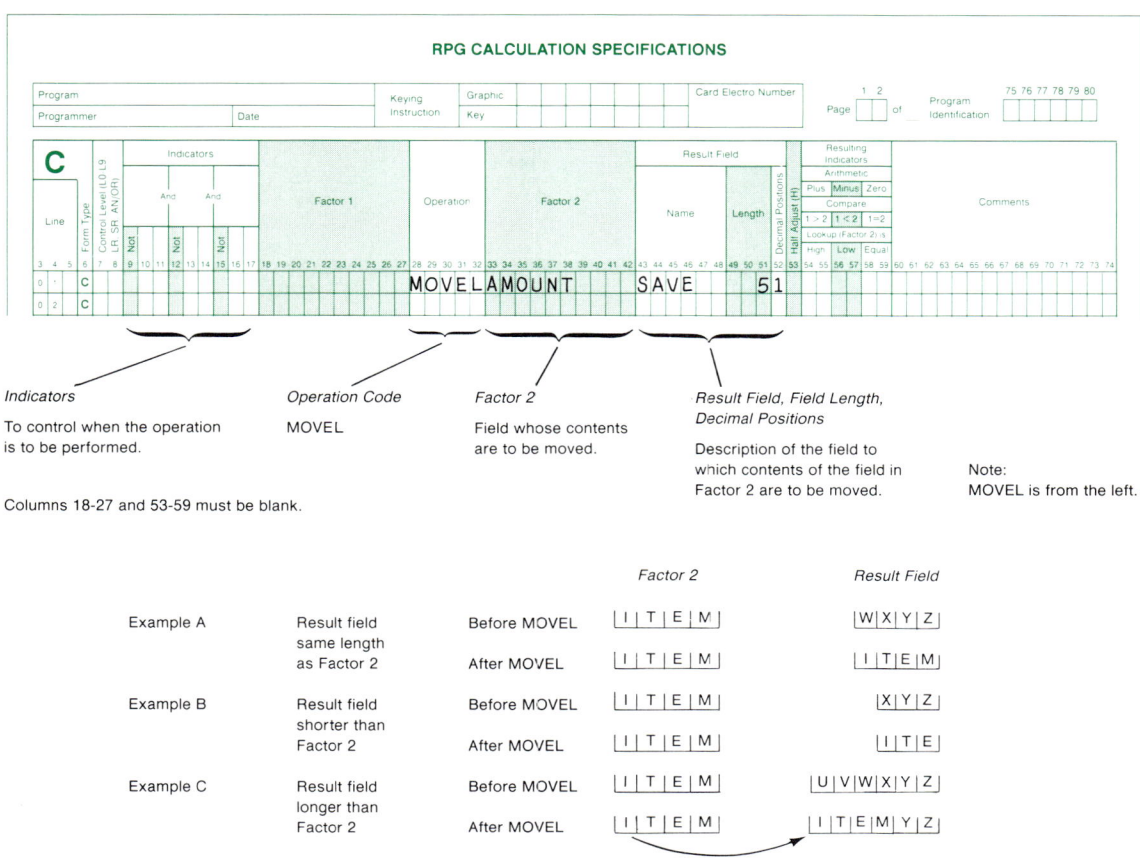

Factor 2 and the result field are always used for both operations. Factor 2 may be either a fie or a constant. Any conditioning indicators may be used; however, factor 1 and resulting indicators may not be specified.

If the result field is the same length as factor 2, all characters in factor 2 are transferred. If the result field is shorter than factor 2, only the number of characters needed to fill the result field are transferred. On the other hand, if the result field is longer than factor 2, all characters in factor 2 are moved to the *rightmost* positions of the result field. The excess leftmost characters of the result field remain unchanged.

The MOVEL operation is just the reverse of the MOVE operation. It moves a copy of the characters starting from the leftmost positions of factor 2 into the *leftmost* positions of the result field. (See Figure 5.27.)

Move operations move part or all of factor 2 to the result field. Factor 2 remains unchanged. Factor 1 is not used in any move operations; it must always be blank and no resulting indicators may be used. Numeric fields may be changed to alphameric fields by move operations and vice versa. To change a numeric field to an alphameric field, place the name of the numeric field in factor 2 and use an alphameric result field. To change an alphameric field to a numeric field, place the name of the alphameric field in factor 2 and use a numeric result field.

Data Movement—Summary

Zero and Add (Z-ADD)
This operation causes factor 2 to be added to a field of zeros and the sum to be placed in the result field.

Move (MOVE)
The MOVE operation causes characters from factor 2 to be moved to the rightmost positions in the result field. Moving starts with the rightmost character. If factor 2 is longer than the result field, the

Program Control of Operations   193

Figure 5.27 MOVE operations—examples

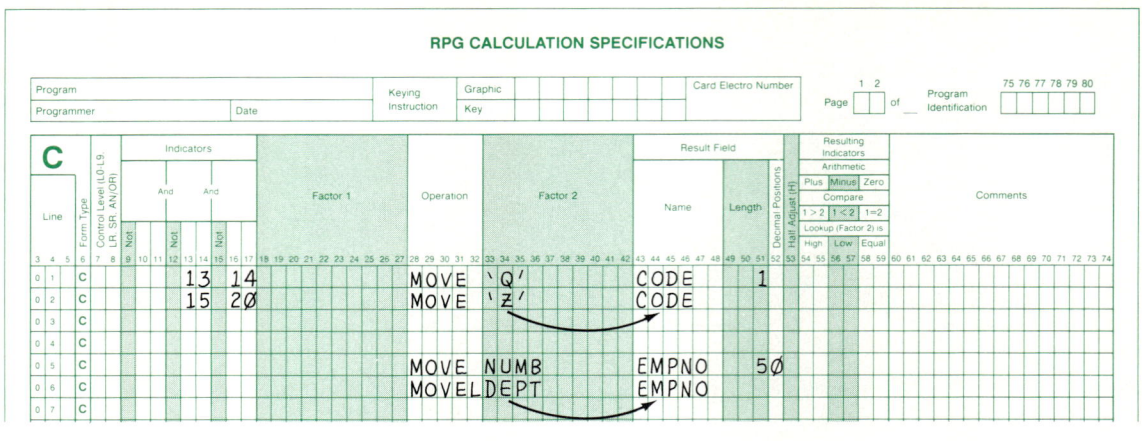

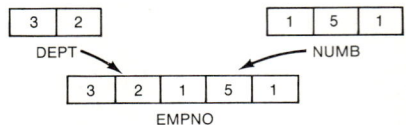

Notes on the Coding

1. Based on certain indicator conditions, it may be necessary to move a unique code into a field for later output to the disk. Note the quotes for the alphabetic field.

2. If two separate fields need to be put together for another operation, the MOVE and MOVEL can do it. Remember, the move stops when there is nothing more to be moved.

excess leftmost characters of factor 2 are not moved. If the result field is longer than factor 2, the characters to the left of the data just moved are unchanged. (See Figure 5.28.)

Move Left (MOVEL)
The MOVEL operation causes characters from factor 2 to be moved to the leftmost positions in the result field. Moving starts with the leftmost character. If factor 2 is longer than the result field, the excess rightmost characters of factor 2 are not moved. If the result field is longer than factor 2, the characters to the right of the data just moved are unchanged.

Subroutines

A subroutine is part of another main routine and is a routine performed over and over again. A program is called a routine because the instructions in a program are done repeatedly (as a program cycle). A **subroutine** is a group of instructions in the main program that may be done several times throughout one program cycle.

It is sometimes necessary to write a program that calls for the same operations to be performed at several different times. Instead of writing these instructions each time they are needed, it is easier and less time consuming if they can be written just once and referred to as they are needed. This can be accomplished by writing a subroutine, consisting only of those operations that need to take place at several points in the program.

The same sequence of operations might be required in several different programs. Instead of writing these specifications in each program, the operations can be coded once in a subroutine. This subroutine can then be included in as many programs as necessary.

Subroutines can be used to

1. Eliminate duplicate coding by performing the same calculations several times in the same program cycle or in several different programs
2. Reduce the storage requirements of RPG programs

Figure 5.28 Control of calculations—examples

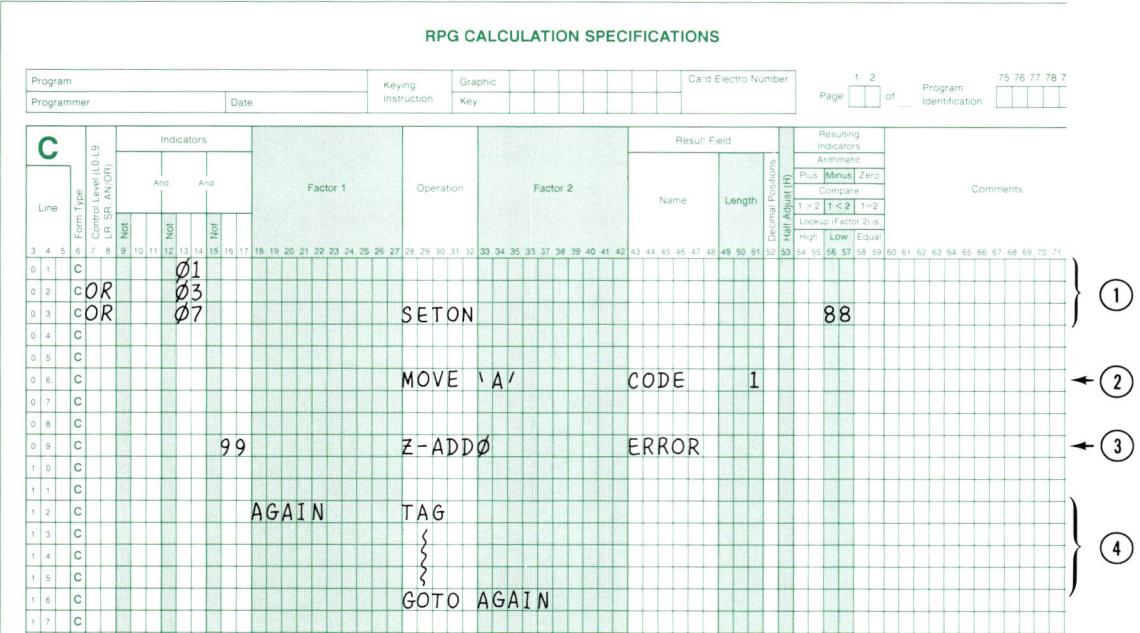

Notes on the Coding

1. The SETON must be coded on the last line of the 07 indicator. The 88 could have been in any of the positions 54 to 59.

2. Don't forget that the alphabetic literal must be enclosed in quotes.

3. The field ERROR will be set to zero only if indicator 99 is on. The field should have a field length if it was not previously defined. Remember the Z-ADD works with numeric fields only.

4. The programmer might have coded any operations between GOTO and the TAG. Certainly one of them should be another GOTO to get out of the loop.

Coding Subroutines

Subroutines are coded and used on the Calculation Specifications form. They are entered after all other calculation operations. Every subroutine must have a name, but no two subroutines used in the same program may have the same name.

The name of the subroutine is entered in factor 1, and is placed on the same line as the operation code BEGSR. The subroutine name may be from one to six characters long and must begin in position 18 with an alphabetic character. The remaining characters can be any combination of alphabetic or numeric characters but can contain no special characters. Blanks may not appear between characters in the name.

Each specification line within the subroutine (except AN(d) or OR lines) must have SR in positions 7–8 to identify it as a subroutine line. (This is optional in RPG III and is becoming optional in all IBM machines.) The last statement of the subroutine is indicated by the operation code ENDSR. (See Figure 5.29.) Factor 1 of the ENDSR statement may contain a name. The name indicates the point to which a GOTO within the subroutine can branch. (See Figure 5.30.)

The subroutine, even though specified last on the Calculation Specifications form, may be performed at any point in the calculation operations. (Detail and total time operations may not be combined in the same subroutine.) Whenever the subroutine is used, enter the operation code EXSR (execute subroutine). The name of the subroutine to be used must also be entered as factor 2. Using the EXSR operation is known as calling a subroutine.

The operation code EXSR causes the operations in the subroutine named in factor 2 to be performed. After all calculation operations in the subroutine are done, the operation following the EXSR is performed.

Program Control of Operations 195

Figure 5.29 Structure of a subroutine

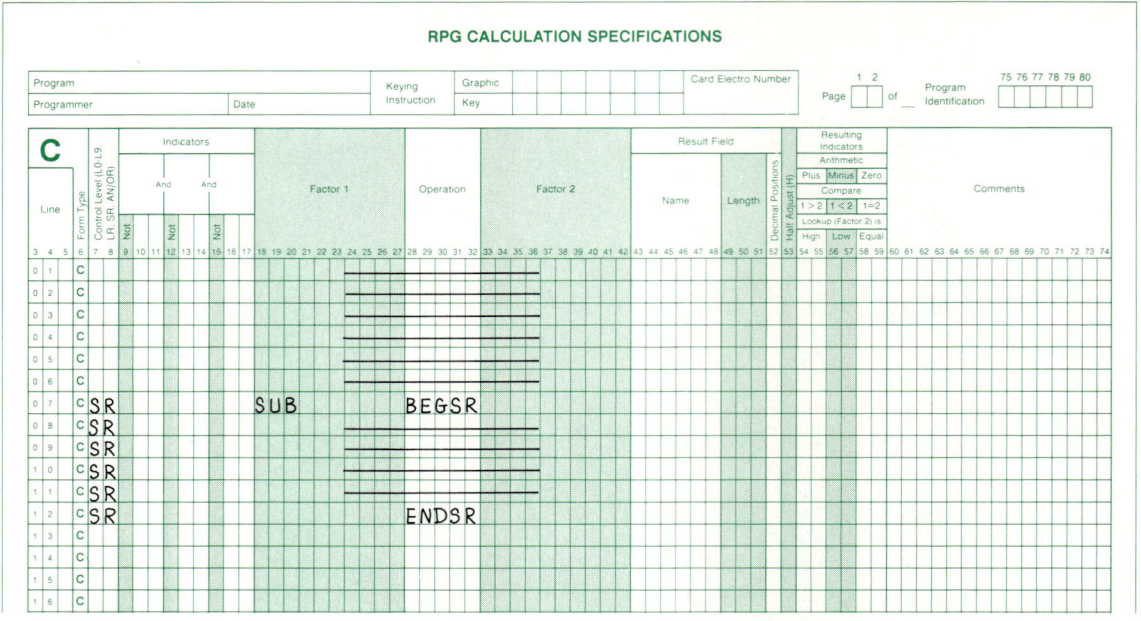

Figure 5.30 Branching subroutine—example

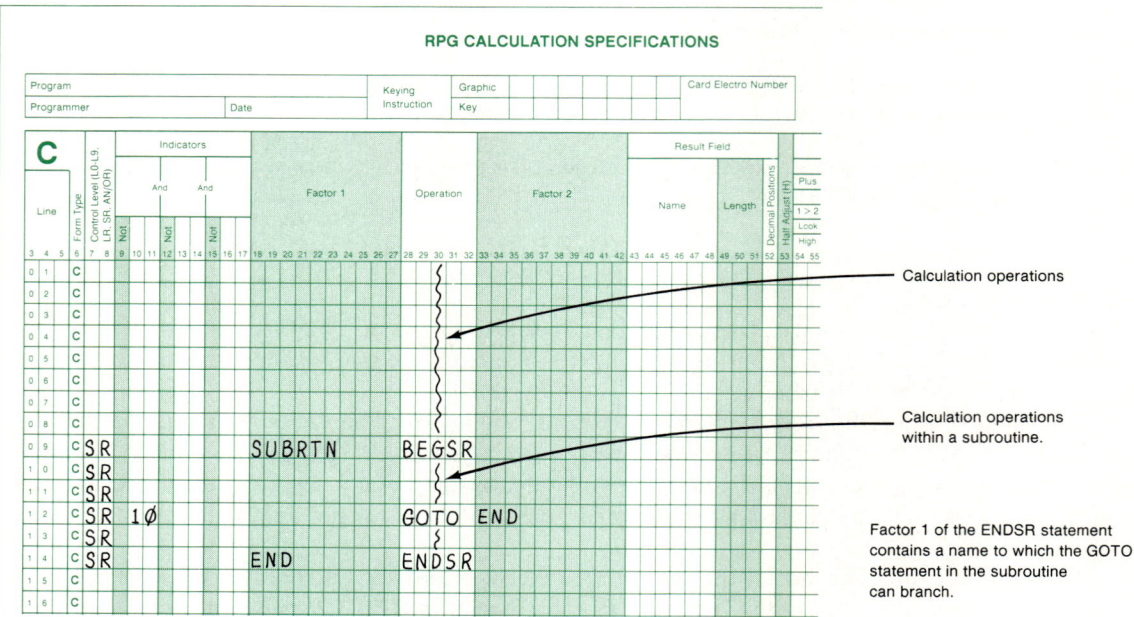

Indicators may be used with **EXSR** code to condition when the subroutine should be executed. Any valid indicator may be used in positions 7–17. If no indicators are used, the subroutine is always executed.

Any RPG operation may be performed within a subroutine. Operations within the subroutine may be conditioned by any valid indicator in positions 9–17. Since SR must appear in positions 7–8, control level indicators cannot be used in these positions.

This means that individual operations within the subroutine cannot be conditioned by a control level indicator used in positions 7–8. However, entire subroutines can be conditioned by control level indicators. This can be done by using the control level indicator with the EXSR operation.

Fields used in the subroutine may be defined either inside or outside the subroutine. In either case, fields can be used by both the main routine and the subroutine. Subroutines can be used in the main program as the programmer wishes. However, a subroutine may not be written within a subroutine. This means that within one subroutine, there may be an EXSR operation, but a subroutine cannot call itself and cannot call the subroutine that called it.

Subroutines need not be defined in the order in which they are used. However, each subroutine must have a different name and a BEGSR and ENDSR operation code.

If the same fields can be used by both the subroutine and main routine, the fields may be defined in either routine. The characteristics of the field must be the same in both routines, however. The fields defined in a subroutine must be defined in a general way so that they apply to all situations for which a subroutine is used. For example, if DISTA is used as the field name in a subroutine to calculate district sales, the information will always be taken from DISTA field when calculating commission. However, if the routine is to be used to handle information from both DISTB and DISTC fields, the use of the specific field limits the subroutine to one situation. Using a general field DIST will allow the subroutine to calculate district sales for all districts. (See Figure 5.31.)

Figure 5.31 Sales commission job using subroutines

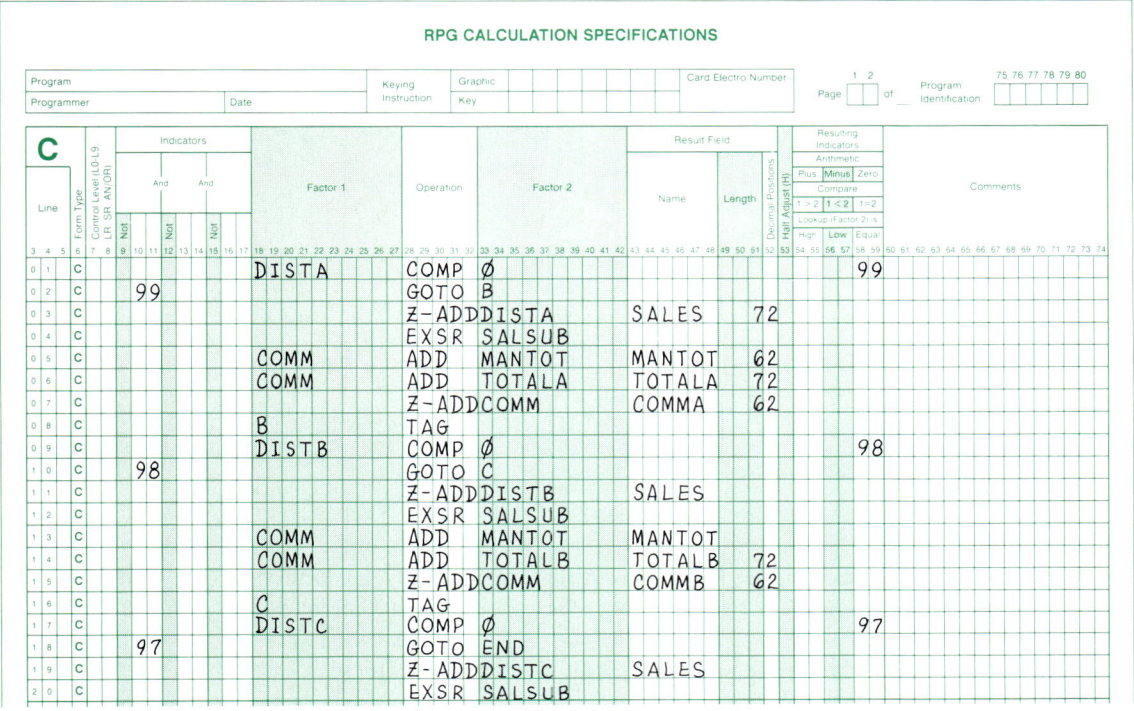

Program Control of Operations 197

Figure 5.31 continued

RPG CALCULATION SPECIFICATIONS

Line	Form Type	Control Level	Ind Not	And Not	And Not	Factor 1	Operation	Factor 2	Result Name	Length	Dec	H	Hi	Lo	Eq	Comments
01	C					COMM	ADD	MANTOT	MANTOT							
02	C					COMM	ADD	TOTALC	TOTALC	72						
03	C						Z-ADD	COMM	COMMC	62						
04	C					END	TAG									
05	C	SR				SALSUB	BEGSR									
06	C	SR				SALES	COMP	1000.00							1010	
07	C	SR	10			SALES	MULT	.03	COMM	62		H				
08	C	SR	10				GOTO	FINISH								
09	C	SR				SALES	COMP	5000.00					12	11	11	
10	C	SR	11			SALES	SUB	1000.00	OVER	62						
11	C	SR	11			OVER	MULT	.02	COMM			H				
12	C	SR	11			30.00	ADD	COMM	COMM							
13	C	SR	11				GOTO	FINISH								
14	C	SR	12			SALES	SUB	5000.00	OVER							
15	C	SR	12			OVER	MULT	.01	COMM			H				
16	C	SR	12			110.00	ADD	COMM	COMM							
17	C	SR				FINISH	ENDSR									

RPG OUTPUT SPECIFICATIONS

Line	Form Type	Filename or Record Name	Type	Stk/Fet	Space Before	Space After	Skip Before	Skip After	Output Indicators	Field Name or EXCPT Name	Edit Codes	End Position	P/B/L/R	Constant or Edit Word
01	O	REPORT	H		110		1P							
02	O											68		'COMMISSION REPORT'
03	O		H		311		1P							
04	O	OR						OV						
05	O											35		'SALESMAN'
06	O											55		'DIST A'
07	O											65		'DIST B'
08	O											75		'DIST C'
09	O											110		'TOTAL'
10	O		D		2		01							
11	O									NAME		45		
12	O									COMMA	1B	55		
13	O									COMMB	1B	65		
14	O									COMMC	1B	75		
15	O									MANTOT	1B	110		
16	O		T					LR						
17	O									TOTALA	1	55		
18	O									TOTALB	1	65		
19	O									TOTALC	1	75		
20	O													

When a GOTO statement is used in a subroutine, a branch may be made only to another statement in the same subroutine. A GOTO branch cannot be made to a statement within a subroutine from outside the subroutine. (See Figure 5.32.)

If it is necessary to perform the same operations in many different programs, the same outline may be used to eliminate duplicate coding in each program. The operations are coded once and the subroutine is used along with the main program deck.

Figure 5.32 Branching within a subroutine

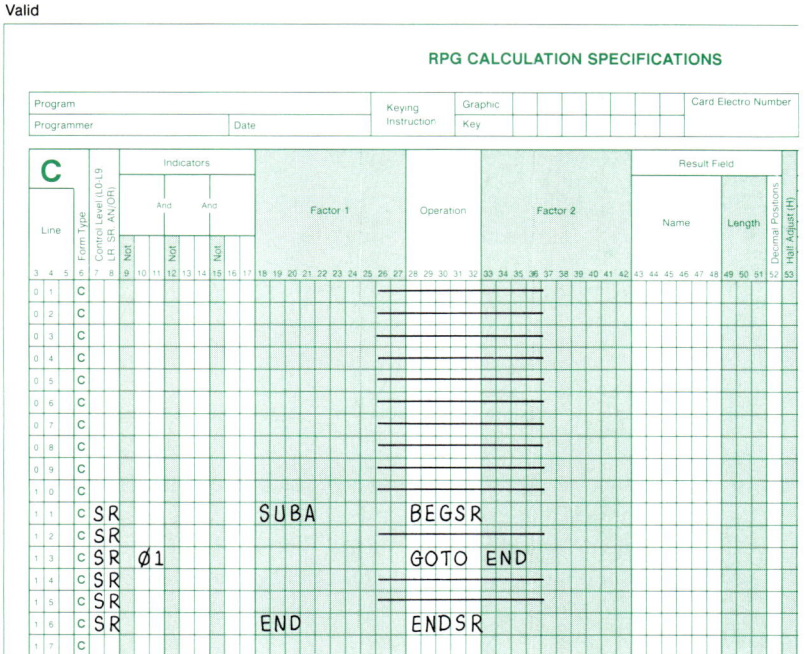

Program Control of Operations

If the subroutine is to be used in several different programs

1. The correct name of the subroutine must be placed in factor 2 when the subroutine is called in the main program using the EXSR operation code.
2. All fields that will be used by both the subroutine and the main routine must have the same name in each routine.

Subroutine Operation Codes

Subroutine operation codes are used only for subroutines. Subroutine operation codes must be written in specification lines following all detail and total calculations. Subroutine lines are usually identified by an *SR* in positons 7–8.

Begin Subroutine (BEGSR)

The BEGSR operation code serves as the beginning point of the subroutine. Factor 1 must contain the name of the subroutine.

End Subroutine (ENDSR)

The ENDSR operation code must be the last statement of the subroutine. It serves to define the end of the subroutine. Factor 1 may contain a name. This name then serves as a point to which the programmer can branch by a GOTO statement within the subroutine. The ENDSR operation ends the subroutine and automatically causes a branch back to the next statement after EXSR operation.

Execute Subroutine (EXSR)

The EXSR operation causes all the operations in the subroutine to be performed. EXSR may appear anywhere in the program. Whenever it appears, the subroutine is executed. After all operations in the subroutine are done, the operation in the line following the EXSR operation is performed.

This operation may be conditioned by an indicator, meaning the subroutine is executed only when all conditions are satisfied. Factor 2 must contain the name of the subroutine that is to be executed. This same name must appear on a BEGSR instruction.

Subroutine Rules—Summary

1. Any operation code that can be used in calculations can be used in a subroutine with the exceptions of BEGSR and ENDSR.
2. All arithmetic, compare and testing, move, lookup, EXSR, and branching operations may be used in the subroutines.
3. A branch may be made only to another statement in the subroutine when using the GOTO statement.
4. A branch may be made to the ENDSR statement if a name is put in factor 1 of the ENDSR statement.
5. No branch may be made to a statement outside the subroutine.
6. A branch may not be made to a TAG statement within the subroutine from a GOTO statement outside of the subroutine.
7. A subroutine may not be coded within another subroutine. However, one subroutine can call another subroutine. This means that within one subroutine, there may be an EXSR statement. A subroutine, however, cannot call itself and cannot call the subroutine that called it.
8. Any indicators that are valid in positions 9–17 can be used to condition an operation within a subroutine. That operation will only be performed when the conditions established by the indicators are satisfied. The BEGSR and ENDSR operations, however, cannot be conditioned by any indicator.
9. If the EXSR statement is conditioned by an indicator, the entire subroutine will be performed only when conditions for the EXSR statement are met.

10. Control level indicators cannot be used to condition statements within a subroutine since SR must appear in positions 7–8. The indicators used in the EXSR statement determine whether the entire subroutine is performed at detail time or total time.

Subroutine—Summary

RPG provides a special facility for handling subroutines. A subroutine is a set of calculation steps that may be performed following any other calculation.

The following are the steps in describing an RPG subroutine:

1. Enter the letters SR in positions 7–8 on every line containing a subroutine step.

2. Enter a unique name as factor 1 and the operation code BEGSR (begin subroutine) as the first entry in the series.

3. Code the calculations to be performed in the subroutines in the order needed to solve that part of the program.

4. Enter the operation code ENDSR (end subroutine) on the line following the last calculation.

5. If a GOTO operation in a subroutine is used to bypass all remaining calculations in that subroutine, it may be directed to the ENDSR step by specifying a label as factor 1 in the ENDSR step and by using the same label in the GOTO step.

6. Each subroutine must have a unique name.

7. Subroutines must appear last in the set of all calculations for a job.

8. To use a subroutine during either detail time or total time calculations, specify in factor 2 both the operation EXSR (execute subroutine) and the name of the subroutine as factor 2.

9. When the EXSR operation is encountered, the program branches to the designated subroutine, performs the calculations in it, and automatically returns to the next step in the main program to continue normal activity.

RPG III Enhancements

Significant changes to the language features taught in this chapter have been made for RPG III.

The manner in which exception time output is handled has been altered. The very term "exception time" has become a misnomer, since exception time becomes "regular" time output controlled by a programmer in RPG III. This is consistent with the more general movement of the language toward full procedural files. (See Chapter 11.)

Changes to operation codes have been made, as well. Some are enhanced. MOVE and MOVEL are improved to provide resultant indicators.

The subroutine syntax of RPG III is simplified.

COMP and GOTO are combined in CABxx. This introduces various other operation codes using the GT, LT (greater than, less than) concept of comparison in conjunction with the concept of a branch to a label (TAG). (The greater than/less than concept of comparison does not exclude the use of indicators.)

Structured programming is introduced and is heavily supported with the new verbs DO, DOUxx, DOWxx, IFxx, ELSE, and END, which are its building blocks.

EXCPT Name

RPG III, with its continued emphasis on programmer-controlled input/output and its associated deemphasis of the logic cycle, stresses the EXCPT operation code and makes certain enhancements of the verb. The EXCPT name, indicated in positions 32–37 of the output specification of an exception record (and an *E* in position 15), can be used to identify a record or records to be written when the EXCPT is executed with the EXCPT name as factor 2. (See Figure 5.33.)

Figure 5.33 EXCPT records written during calculations

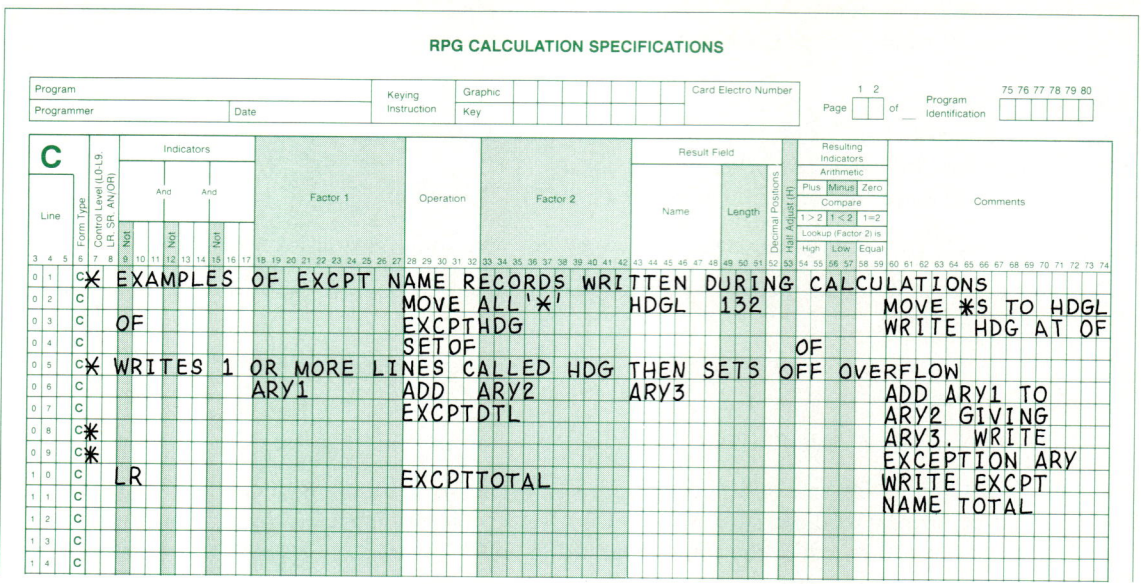

Figure 5.34 EXCPT name records

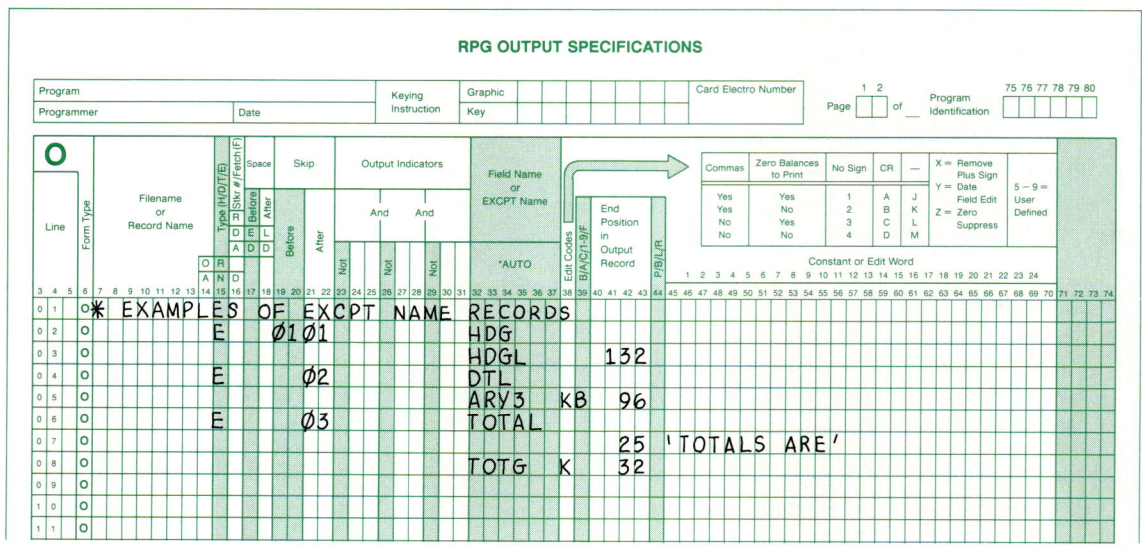

Having multiple output lines with same EXCPT name would permit three (or more) lines to be associated with each other (e.g., mailing label applications). Note that although only exception records (not heading, detail, or total lines) may have EXCPT names, it is possible to design multiple exception lines with the name and function of HDG, multiple exception lines with the name and function of DTL, and multiple exception lines with the name and function of TOTAL. (See Figure 5.34.)

By the careful exercise of programming logic, one can write multiple lines of any type through the expanded logic of the EXCPT operation code with its associated EXCPT name.

Remember the following when specifying the EXCPT operation:

The exception records to be written during calculation time are indicated by an *E* in position 15 of the output specifications. An EXCPT name, which is the same name as is specified as factor 2 of an EXCPT operation, can be specified in positions 32–37 of exception records.

Only exception records—not heading, detail, or total records—can contain an EXCPT name.

Figure 5.35 SR not in columns 7 and 8—example of MOVE with resultant indicators

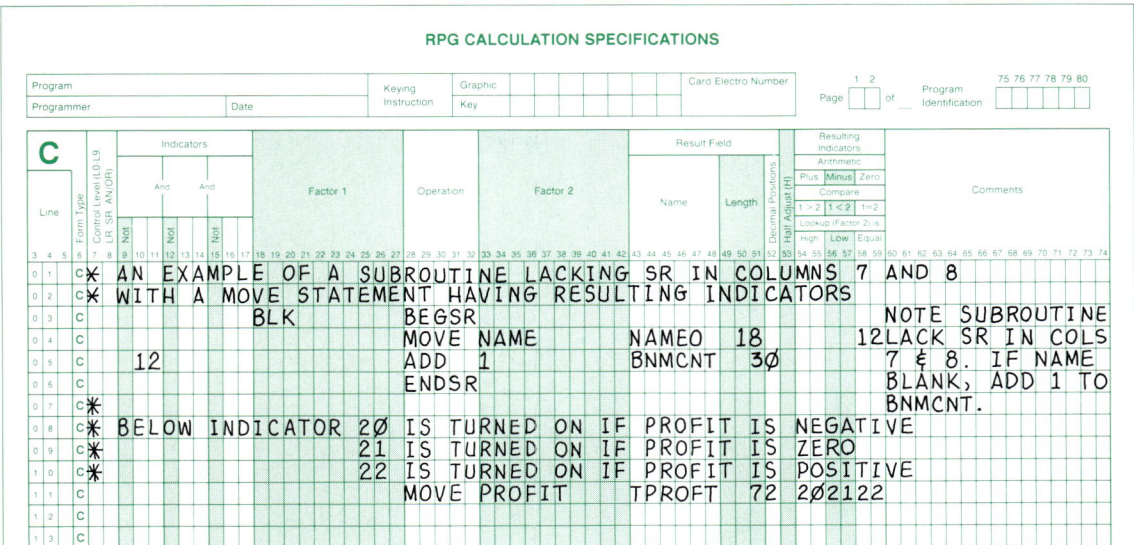

When the EXCPT operation with a name in factor 2 executes and if the test for conditioning indicators is met, only those exception records of the same EXCPT name are checked and written.

When factor 2 is blank, only those exception records with no name in positions 32–37 are checked and written, if the test for conditioning indicators is met.

Any exception records that are conditioned only by an overflow indicator will not be written, even though the overflow indicator is on. Overflow output of exception records follows the rules of the RPG cycle and fetch overflow.

Move (MOVE)

RPG III permits resulting indicators to be set during the MOVE operation. Thus blank or missing alphameric fields as well as negative, positive, or zero numeric fields can be detected during their manipulation.

When resulting indicators are specified for MOVE operations, the result field determines which indicator is set on. If the result field is alphameric, only one resulting indicator (positions 58–59) can be specified. This indicator is set on if the result field is all blanks. When the result field is numeric, all three resulting indicator positions may be used. (See Figure 5.35.)

Resulting indicators cannot be specified if the result field is an array.

Move Left (MOVEL)

As with MOVE, RPG III permits the MOVEL operation code to have resultant indicators. The rules are the same, except that the sign of the rightmost character of factor 2 is converted and used as the sign of the result field, whether or not the rightmost character was included in the move operation.

Likewise, as with MOVE, resulting indicators cannot be specified if the result field is an array.

Simplified Subroutines

Coding the characters *SR* in positions 7–8 of the calculation specifications in order to specify lines of a subroutine has been made optional. Thus blanks in these positions are acceptable to RPG III. A subroutine and the operations which comprise it are defined by the BEGSR and ENDSR statements, alone. (See Figure 5.35.)

Program Control of Operations

Figure 5.36 CABxx—examples

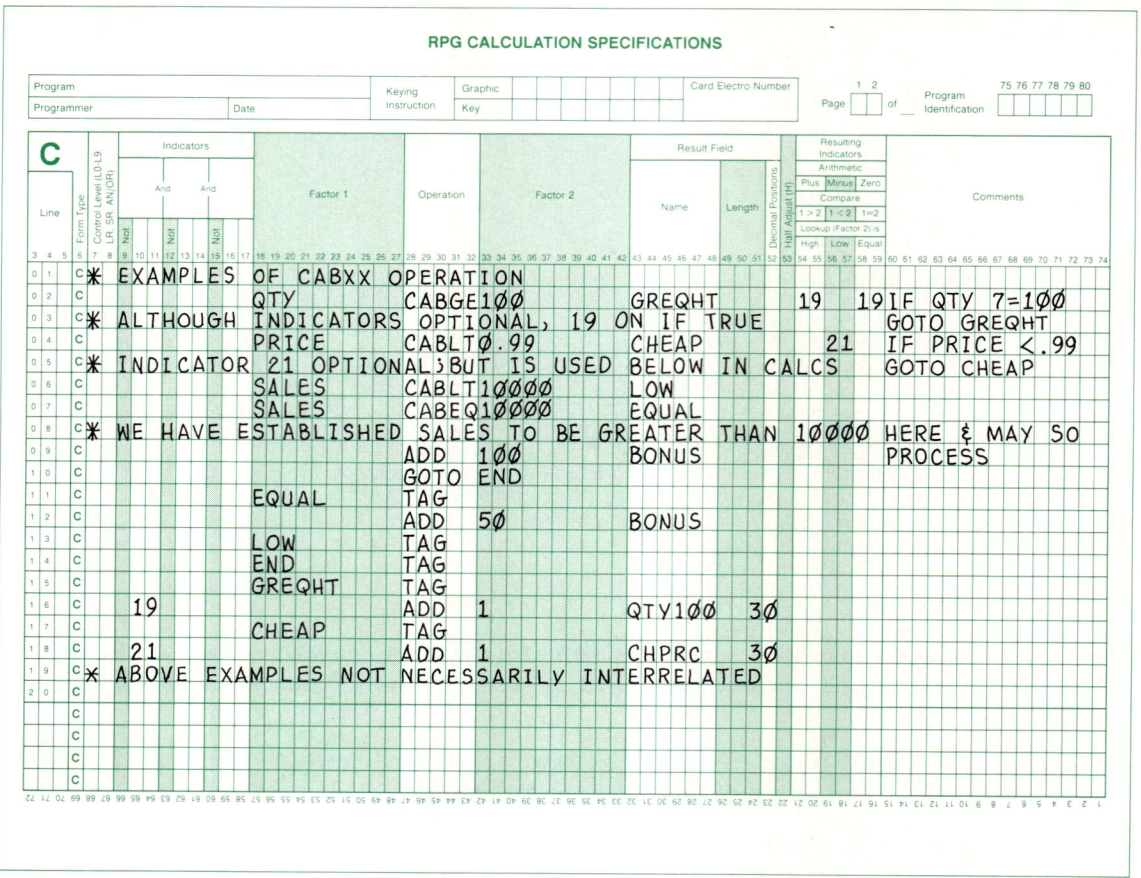

Compare And Branch (CABxx)

The CABxx operation compares factor 1 with factor 2. If the result of the operation agrees with the xx portion of the operation, the program does a GOTO to the TAG specified in the result field. The xx can mean any of the folowing:

xx	Meaning
GT	Factor 1 is greater than factor 2.
LT	Factor 1 is less than factor 2.
EQ	Factor 1 is equal to factor 2.
NE	Factor 1 does not equal factor 2.
GE	Factor 1 is greater than or equal to factor 2.
LE	Factor 1 is less than or equal to factor 2.
blanks	A GOTO to the TAG specified in the result field is executed independently of the compare.

    The tag name specified in the result field must be associated with a unique TAG operation and must not be the name of a file, record, field, or subroutine in the same program.

    Resulting indicators are optional except when xx is blank. When xx is blank, at least one resulting indicator must be specified. When specified, the resulting indicators are set to reflect the results of the compare. (See Figure 5.36.)

Structured Programming Operations

RPG III emphasizes structured programming concepts. Rather than simplify the GOTO, a more likely mission of the RPG III authors would be to eliminate it entirely. To this end, RPG III introduces certain innovations into its structured programming operations. Following are those operations:

DO (Do) The DO operation allows the execution of a group of calculations one or more times based upon a variable's starting value. The operation causes the named variable to grow by a series of stated or implied increments until a limit value is reached. The starting value is placed in factor 1 of the DO operation. This value is incremented by a value specified in factor 2 of the associated END operation. Incrementation continues until the limit specified as factor 2 of the DO operation is reached.

DOUxx (Do Until) The DOUxx operation allows the execution of a group of calculations one or more times based upon the results of comparing factor 1 and factor 2 *until* the xx condition is met.

DOWxx (Do While) The DOWxx operation allows the execution of a group of calculations one or more times based upon the results of comparing factor 1 and factor 2 *while* the xx condition is true.

IFxx (If/Then) The IFxx operation allows the execution of a group of calculations based upon the results of comparing factor 1 and factor 2.

ANDxx (And) RPG III includes two additional operations, ANDxx and ORxx, which lend the quality of "nested ifs" to IFxx. ANDxx can also be used with DOUxx and DOWxx to create the structured concepts DO WHILE X = 7 AND Y = 9, or DO UNTIL NAME = "JONES" AND BDATE > 340824.

ORxx (OR) ORxx, as with ANDxx, enhances the structured capabilities of RPG III. The six logical operators: GT, LT, GE, LE, EQ, and NE all apply to ANDxx, ORxx, DOWxx, DOUxx, IFxx, and CABxx. ORxx permits complex logic such as DO WHILE NAME = "SMITH" or AGE < 50.

ELSE (Else Do) The ELSE operation optionally goes with an IFxx operation and identifies a group of instructions to be executed if the IFxx comparison should fail. ELSE shares an END statement with the IFxx statement. If an IFxx operation has an ELSE operation, the END statement goes at the end of the ELSE group of operations.

END (End) The END statement goes with DO, DOWxx, DOUxx, IFxx, and ELSE statements, denoting the end of a block of operations; factor 2 is blank except for DO END statement which contains a loop increment.

These structured programming enhancements still make heavy use of the implicit comparison (a characteristic of structured programming constructs). The xx of DOWxx, DOUxx, IFxx, ANDxx, and ORxx have the same values as they have in the CABxx operation. The values for xx can be any of the following:

xx	Meaning
GT	Factor 1 is greater than factor 2.
LT	Factor 1 is less than factor 2.
EQ	Factor 1 is equal to factor 2.
NE	Factor 1 does not equal factor 2.
GE	Factor 1 is greater than or equal to factor 2.
LE	Factor 1 is less than or equal to factor 2.

Figure 5.37 DO, DOUxx, DOWxx—examples

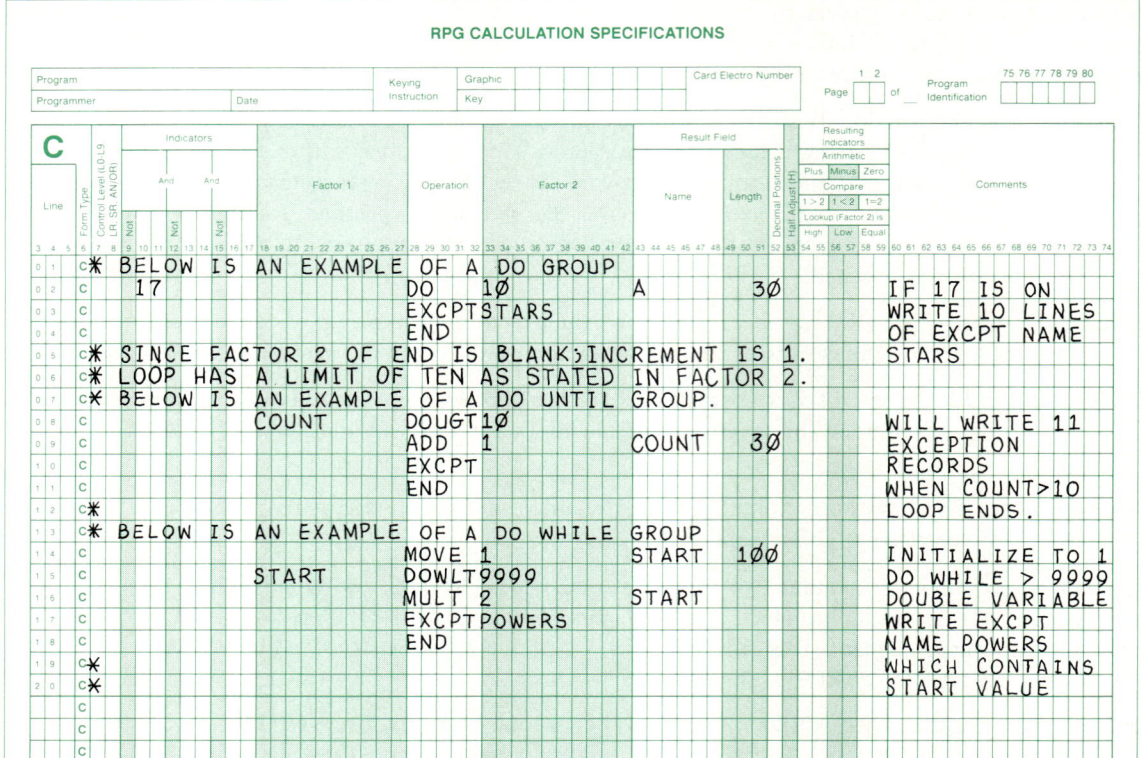

Do (DO)

The DO operation allows a group of calculation operations (a **do-group**) to be performed repeatedly. Factor 1 can be a numeric literal (of integer value) or a numeric field name with zero decimal positions and contains the starting value for the control of the DO operation.

Factor 2 can be a numeric literal (likewise of integer value) or a numeric field name with zero decimal positions and contains the limit value. The result field can be a numeric field name that contains the current index value. If factor 1 is not specified, the starting value is 1. If factor 2 is not specified, the limit value is 1.

If the result field is not specified, the compiler generates a field to be used as the index field. Factor 2 of the END statement associated with the do-group contains the explicit increment added to the index. When this field is blank, the increment defaults to 1. A DO operation and an associated END operation form a do-group. Figure 5.37 contains an example of the DO operation.

The DO operation functions in the following manner:

1. A test is made for conditioning indicators on the DO statement line. If the conditions are met, the do-group is performed. If the conditions are not met, control passes to the next executable statement following the associated END statement, bypassing the instructions in the do-group.

2. If the test for conditioning indicators on the DO statement is met, the starting value (factor 1 of the DO operation) is placed in the index (result field of the DO operation).

3. The index value (result field of the DO operation) is compared with the limit value (factor 2 of the DO operation). If the index value is greater than the limit value, control passes to the operation immediately following the associated END statement, bypassing the operations in the do-group.

4. If the index value (result field of the DO operation) is less than or equal to the limit value (factor 2 of the DO operation), the calculation operations between the DO statement and its associated END statement are performed.

5. A test is made for conditioning indicators on the associated END statement. If the conditions are not met, control passes to the calculation operation immediately following the associated END statement (ending the loop regardless of indices, tests, and limits).

6. If the test for conditioning indicators on the associated END statement is met, the increment (factor 2 of the associated END statement) is added to the index (result field of the DO statement) and control passes to step 3.

Things to remember when specifying the DO operation:

1. The loop index, increment, limit value, and indicators can be modified within the loop to affect the termination of the do-group.

2. A do-group cannot span both detail and total calculations.

3. Branching into do-groups will produce undesirable and relatively unpredictable results. Branching out of do-groups remains an acceptable means of ending lookups and remains the responsibility of the programmer to control.

Do Until (DOUxx)

The DOUxx operation allows a group of calculations (a do-group) to be performed one or more times (but always at least once) until a certain relationship, specified by xx, exists between factor 1 and factor 2. This gives the effect of a loop (without a GOTO) and a test for that loop's termination. A DOUxx operation and its associated END statement form a do-group. The interpretation of xx is the same as for CABxx.

Conditioning indicators can be used to determine if the initial DOUxx comparison should be made. The DOUxx comparison determines if the remainder of the do-group should be performed. Factor 1 and factor 2 must contain either an alphameric or numeric literal or a field name. The factor 1 and the factor 2 entries must be of the same data type—both alphameric or both numeric. The comparison of factor 1 and factor 2 is the same as for CABxx. Figure 5.37 contains an example of the DOUxx operation.

The DOUxx operation functions in the following manner:

1. A test is made for conditioning indicators on the DOUxx statement line. If the conditions are met, the do-group is performed. If the conditions are not met, control passes to the next executable statement following the associated END statement, bypassing the group.

2. A test is made for conditioning indicators on the associated END statement. If the conditions are not met, control passes to the calculation operation immediately following the associated END statement and the loop is ended.

3. If the test for conditioning indicators on the associated END statement is such that the END statement is executed, factor 1 and factor 2 of the DOUxx operation are compared to determine whether the relationship specified by xx exists. If the relationship expressed by xx is false, the do-group is performed.

4. The do-group continues executing until the relationship specified by xx is true. Control then passes to the operation immediately following the END statement associated with the do-group, bypassing the operations comprising the do-group.

Do While (DOWxx)

The DOWxx operation allows a group of calculations (a do-group) to be performed zero, one, or more times, while a certain relationship, specified by xx, exists between factor 1 and factor 2. A DOWxx operation and its associated END statement form a do-group. The interpretation of xx is the same as for CABxx and DOUxx.

Conditioning indicators can be used to determine whether the do-group should be performed. (More accurately, indicators determine whether the initial test is to be made that will, in turn, determine if the do-group will be performed.) Factor 1 and factor 2 must contain either an alphameric or numeric literal or a field name. The factor 1 and the factor 2 entries must be of the same data type—both alphameric or both numeric. The comparison of factor 1 and factor 2 is the same as for CABxx and DOUxx. Figure 5.37 contains an example of the DOWxx operation.

The DOWxx operation functions in the following manner:

1. A test is made for conditioning indicators on the DOWxx statement line. If the conditions are met, the DOWxx operation compares factor 1 to factor 2 to determine whether the relationship in xx exists. If the conditions are not met, control passes to the next executable statement following the associated END statement, bypassing the operations of the do-group.

2. If the relationship expressed by xx is false, control passes to the next executable calculation operation immediately following the associated END statement, ignoring the statements of the do-group. If the relationship expressed by xx is true, the do-group is performed.

3. If the test for conditioning indicators on the associated END statement is such that the END statement is executed, control is passed to the DOWxx statement. If the test for conditioning indicators on the associated END statement is such that the END statement is not executed, control is passed to the calculation operation immediately following the associated END statement, thereby ending the loop.

4. The do-group continues executing until the relationship specified by xx is false. Control then passes to the operation immediately following the END statement associated with the do-group, without executing the group's instructions.

If/Then (IFxx)

The IFxx operation allows a group of calculations to be performed if a certain relationship, specified by xx (in the same manner as CABxx, DOWxx, and DOUxx), exists between factor 1 and factor 2. The major difference between IFxx and the DOs is the repeated iterations performed by the DOs.

Conditioning indicators can be used to determine whether or not the if-group should be executed (i.e., whether the initial test should be made). Factor 1 and factor 2 must contain either an alphameric or numeric field literal or a field name. The factor 1 and factor 2 entries must be of the same data type—both alphameric or both numeric.

If the relationship between factor 1 and factor 2 expressed by xx does not exist, control passes to the calculation operation immediately following the associated END statement, bypassing the statements comprising the IFxx group. However, if the relationship between factor 1 and factor 2 does not exist, and an ELSE operation is specified for and associated with the IFxx operation, control passes to the first executable statement following the ELSE statement. (See Figure 5.38.)

Conditioning indicators on the associated END statement *must* be blank.

An END statement must be used to close an IFxx group. If an IFxx statement is followed by an ELSE statement, an END statement is needed after the ELSE statement. An END statement may not be used after the IFxx group. (See Figure 5.38.)

And (ANDxx)

The IFxx operation allows a group of calculations to be performed if a certain relationship, specified by xx (in the same manner as CABxx, DOWxx, and DOUxx), exists between factor 1 and factor 2. ANDxx permits a second (or more) condition to be tested. ANDxx can be used with DOUxx or DOWxx, also. (See Figure 5.39.)

Conditioning indicators can be used to determine whether or not the if/and-group should be executed (i.e., whether the initial test should be made). Factor 1 and factor 2 must contain either an alphameric or numeric field literal or a field name. The factor 1 and factor 2 entries must be of the same data type—both alphameric or both numeric. In an "anded" condition, both the IF comparison and the AND comparison must be true for the if/and-group to be executed.

If the relationships expressed by xx in both the IFxx statement and the ANDxx do not exist between the respective factors 1 and 2, control passes to the calculation operation immediately following the associated END statement, bypassing the statements comprising the if/and-group. However, if the relationships between the respective factors 1 and factors 2 do not exist, and an ELSE operation is specified for and associated with the IFxx and the ANDxx operation, control passes to the first executable statement following the ELSE statement.

Conditioning indicators on the associated END statement *must* be blank.

Figure 5.38 IFxx—examples

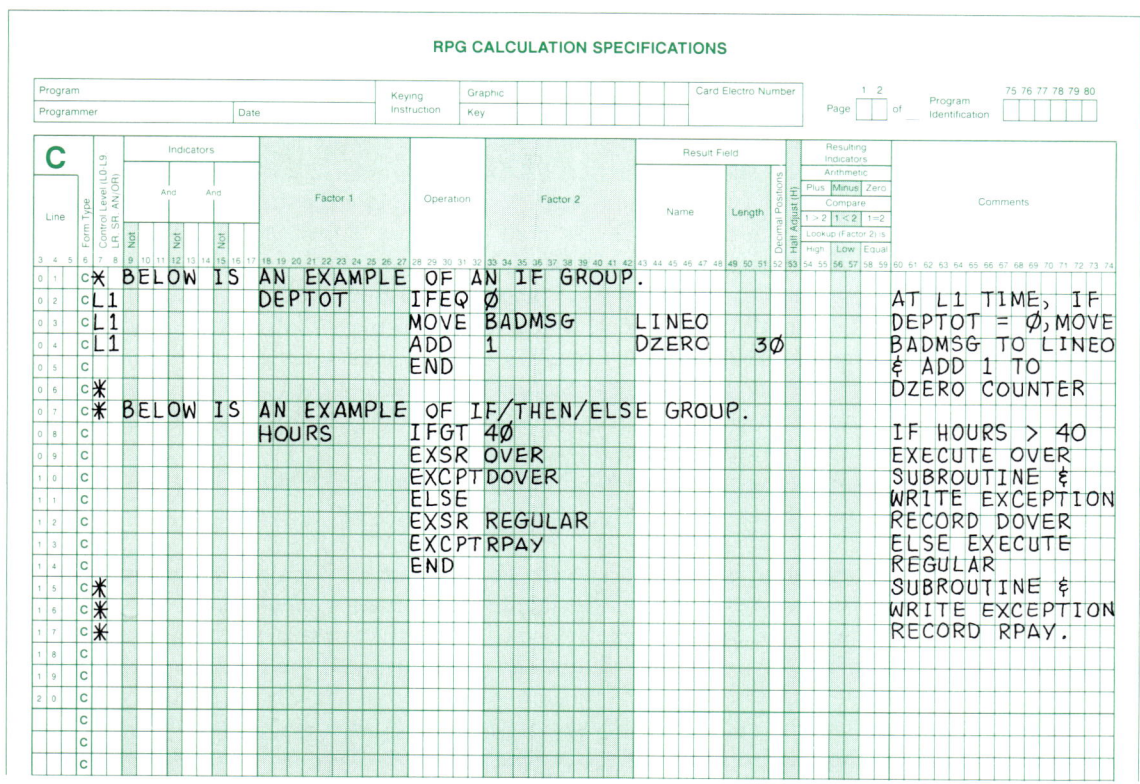

Figure 5.39 ANDxx and ORxx—examples

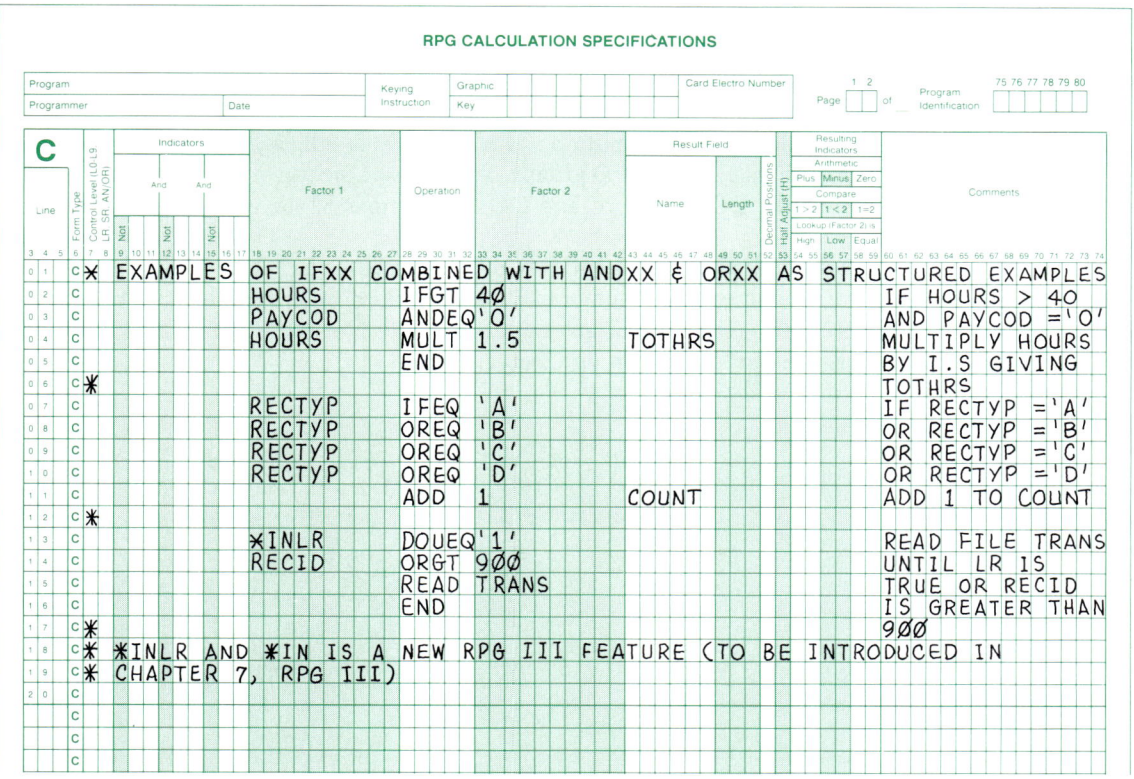

Program Control of Operations

Or (ORxx)

The IFxx operation allows a group of calculations to be performed if a certain relationship, specified by xx (in the same manner as CABxx, DOWxx, and DOUxx), exists between factor 1 and factor 2. ORxx permits a second (or more) condition to be tested. ORxx can be used with DOUxx or DOWxx, also. (See figure 5.39.)

Conditioning indicators can be used to determine whether or not the if/or-group should be executed (i.e., whether the initial test should be made). Factor 1 and factor 2 must contain either an alphameric or numeric field literal or a field name. The factor 1 and factor 2 entries must be of the same data type—both alphameric or both numeric. In an "ored" condition, either the IF comparison or the OR comparison must be true for the if/or-group to be executed.

If the relationships expressed by xx do not exist between the respective factors 1 and factors 2 in either the IFxx statement or the ORxx statement, control passes to the calculation operation immediately following the associated END statement, bypassing the statements comprising the if/or-group. However, if the relationships between the respective factors 1 and 2 do not exist, and an ELSE operation is specified for and associated with the IFxx and the ORxx operation, control passes to the first executable statement following the ELSE statement.

Conditioning indicators on the associated END statement *must* be blank.

Else (ELSE)

The nonexecutable ELSE operation is optional with the IFxx operation. An alternate block of code is specified for execution if the comparison of the associated IFxx operation should prove false. ELSE is specified immediately following the calculations performed if the IFxx comparison expressed by xx is met. ELSE is followed immediately by the calculations to be performed if the conditions expressed by xx are not met.

The control level entry positions (positions 7–8) can be blank or can contain L0–L9 or LR to group the statement within the appropriate section of the program.

An IFxx operation cannot span detail and total time (cannot both have entries such as L1 in positions 7–8 of one calculation operation and have blanks in other calculation operations).

Conditioning indicator entries (positions 9–17) are not permitted. An END operation must be used to close the IFxx/ELSE group. (See Figure 5.38.)

End (END)

The END operation specifies the end of a DO, DOWxx, DOUxx, or IFxx/ELSE group and is thus used to signal the end of a block of code.

The use of conditioning indicators is significant with the various do-groups, and is prohibited in the cases of the IFxx/END or IFxx/ELSE/END groups. To see about the use of conditioning indicators with END statements, review the DO, DOWxx, and DOUxx sections of the text. (See Figures 5.37, 5.38, and 5.39.)

The use of factor 2 is prohibited except in the case of a DO operation. Factor 2 is the value of the increment of the DO operation and can be a numeric; a nonzero literal with zero decimal positions; or a numeric, integer, or field name of similar characteristics. If factor 2 of the END statement of a DO operation is not specified, the increment has an implied value of 1.

Illustrative Program

Subroutines—Compare: Class Grades

Job Definition
Print a report listing all the students in a class and their grades on three exams plus the final exam. A subroutine is to be used to calculate the average points for each student in determining their final grades. The average points for the class are to be calculated, also.

Input
A record is created for each student with the following information:

Positions	Field Description
1–09	Social security number
10–15	Date (mm/dd/yy)
21–40	Student name
41–45	Course
51–54	Ticket number
59–61	Exam 1
64–66	Exam 2
69–71	Exam 3
74–76	Final exam

Processing
1. Use the following method to create a subroutine for calculating the average points for each student:
    a. Find the average grade of exams 1, 2, and 3.
    b. Add the average grade for those three exams to the final exam point total.
    c. Divide by 2 the total obtained to calculate the average number of points earned.
2. Post the letter grade based on the following:

Average Points	Grade
90–100	A
80–89	B
70–79	C
60–69	D
0–59	F

3. Calculate the average points for class.
4. List each student per the output format given.

Output
This Printer Spacing Chart shows how the report is formatted:

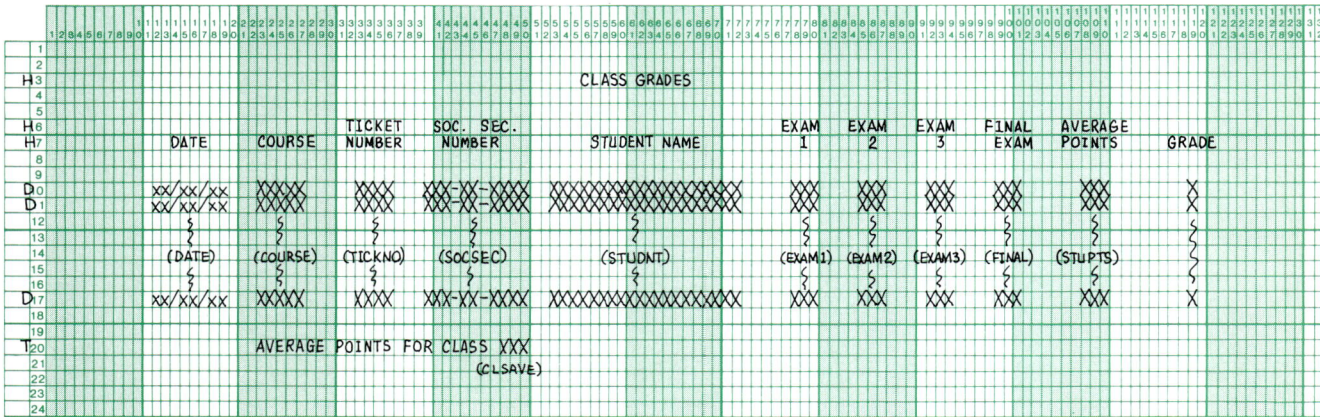

Coding sheets for Class Grades Report problem:

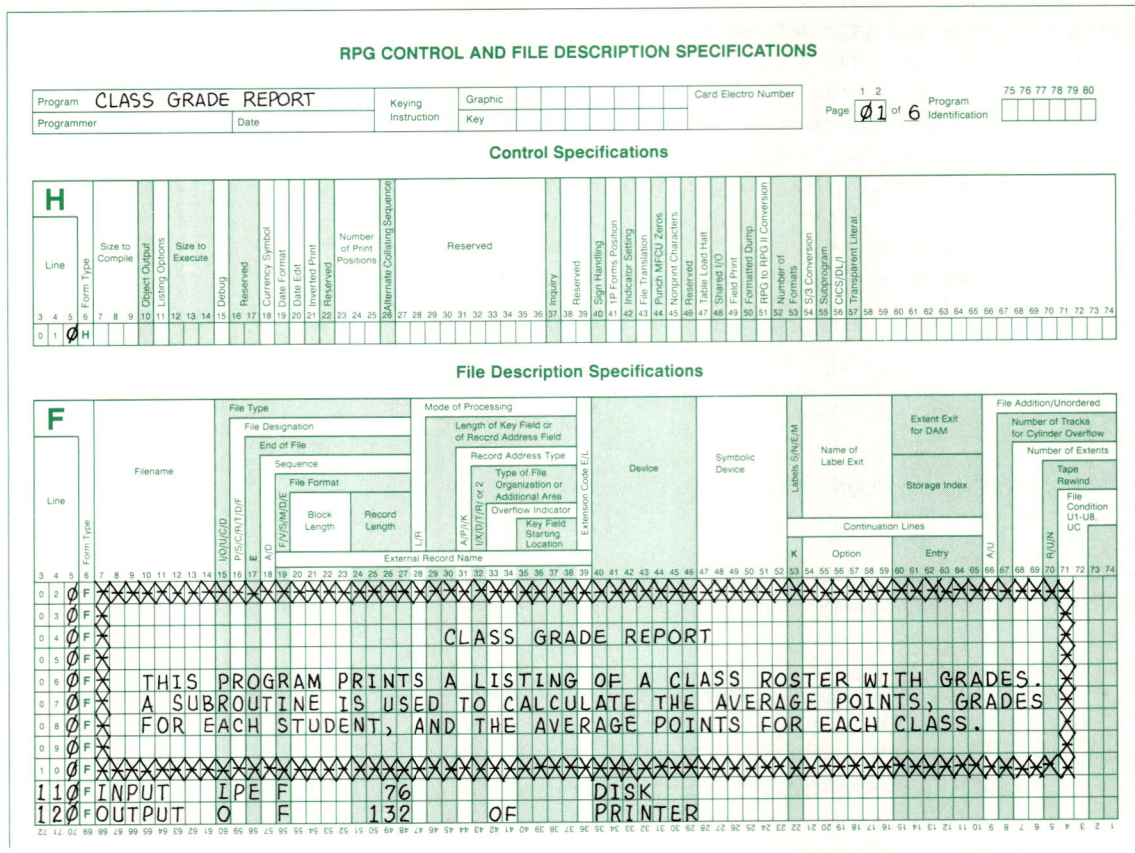

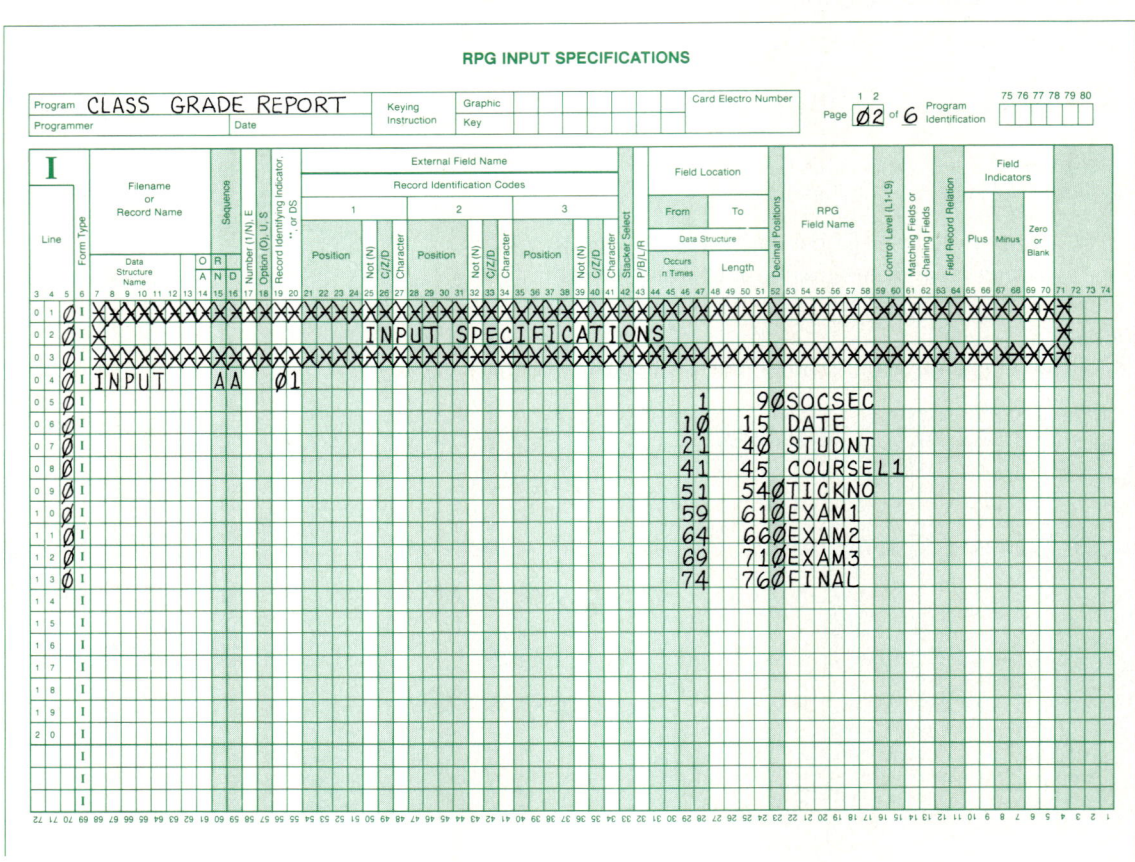

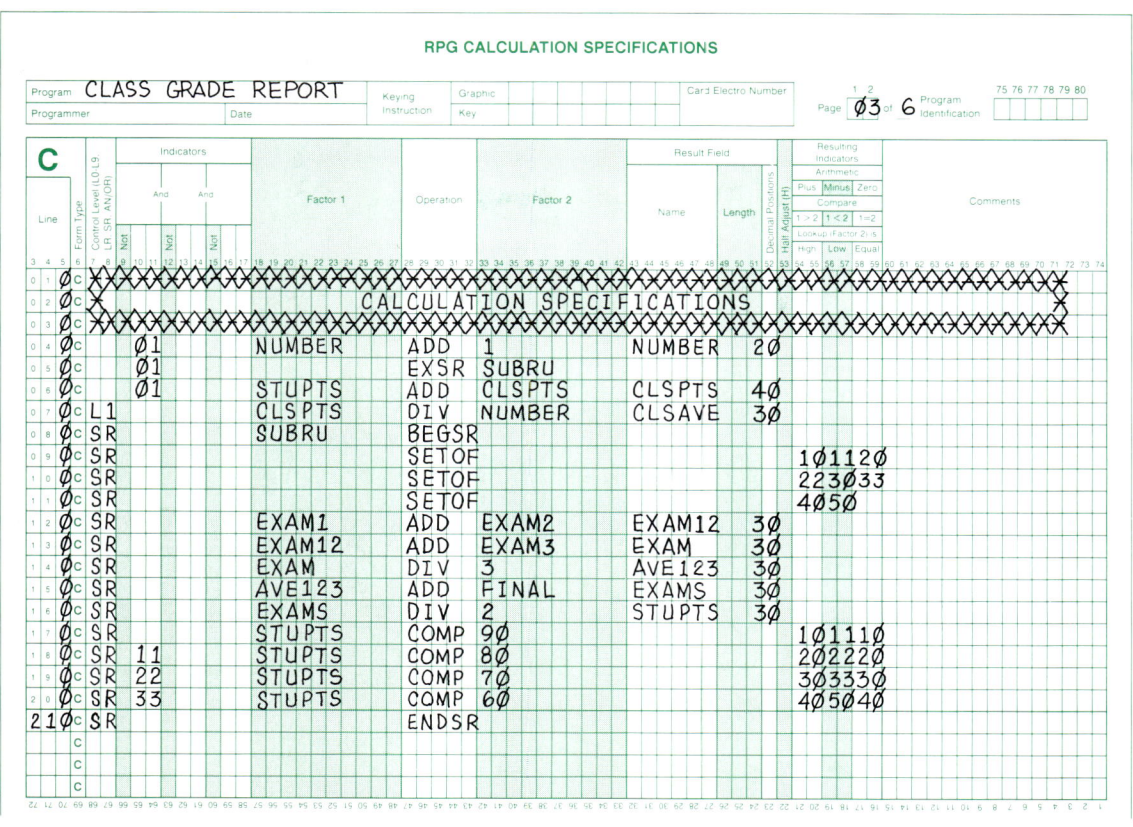

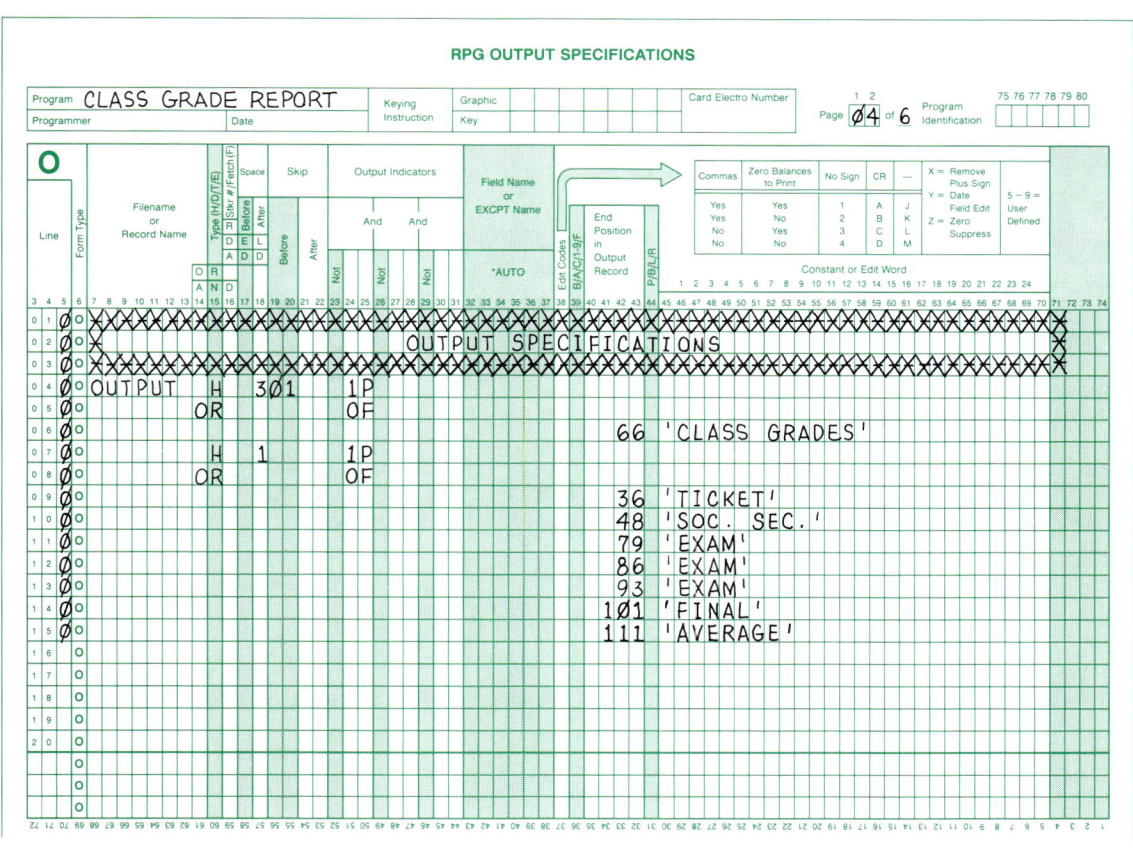

Program Control of Operations 213

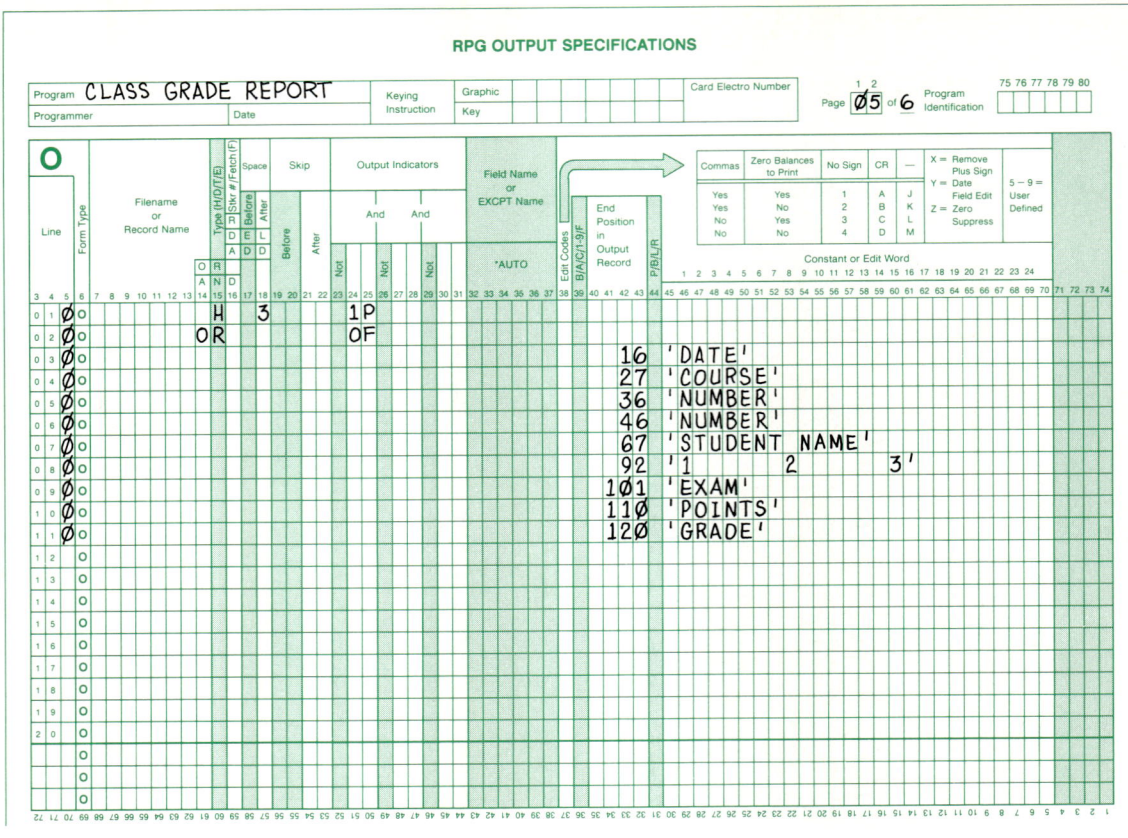
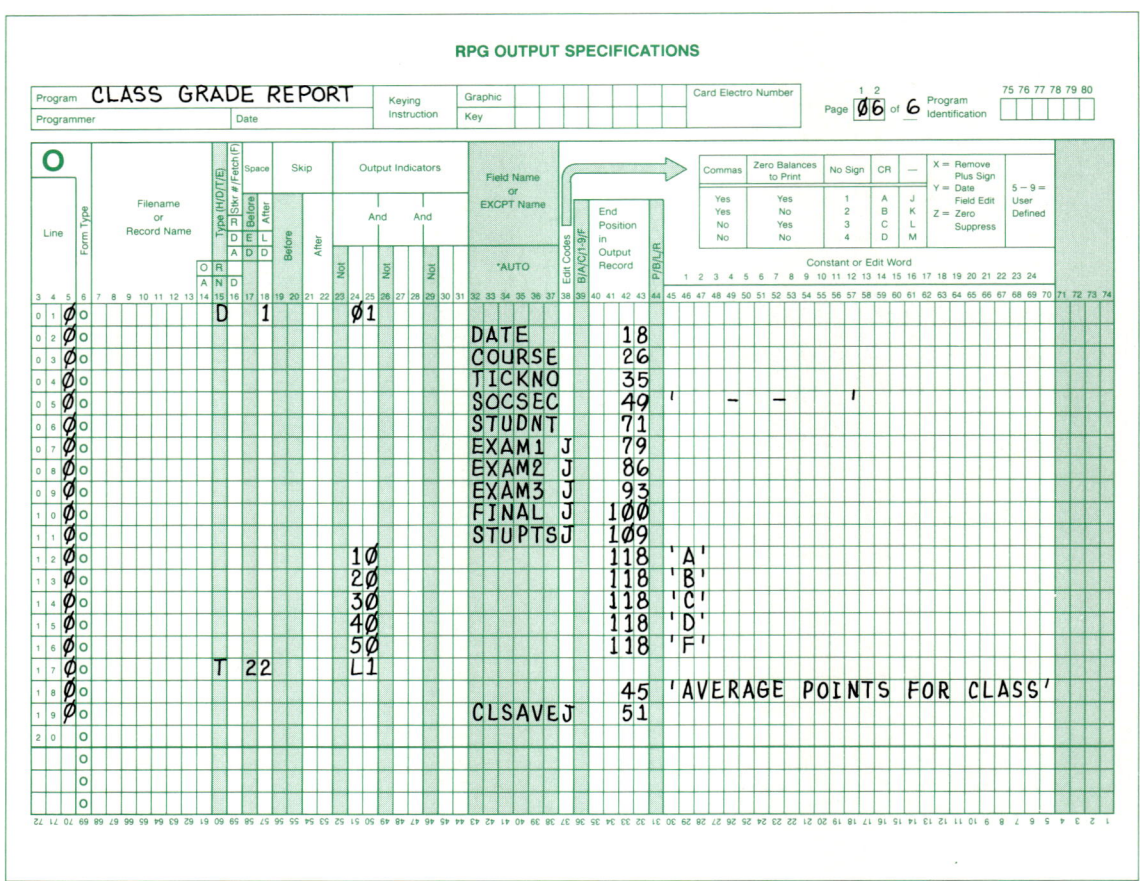

The source listing is as follows:

```
 1    01010H
 2  * 01020F****************************************************************
 3  * 01030F*                                                                *
 4  * 01040F*                    CLASS GRADE REPORT                          *
 5  * 01050F*                                                                *
 6  * 01060F*  THIS PROGRAM PRINTS A LISTING OF A CLASS ROSTER WITH GRADES.  *
 7  * 01070F*  A SUBROUTINE IS USED TO CALCULATE THE AVERAGE POINTS, GRADES  *
 8  * 01080F*  FOR EACH STUDENT, AND THE AVERAGE POINTS FOR EACH CLASS.      *
 9  * 01090F*                                                                *
10  * 01100F****************************************************************
11    01110FINPUT    IPE F     76           DISK
12    01120FOUTPUT   O  F    132         OF PRINTER
13  * 02010I****************************************************************
14  * 02020I*                  INPUT SPECIFICATIONS                          *
15  * 02030I****************************************************************
16    02040IINPUT     AA  01
17    02050I                                        1   90SOCSEC
18    02060I                                       10   15 DATE
19    02070I                                       21   40 STUDNT
20    02080I                                       41   45 COURSEL1
21    02090I                                       51  540TICKNO
22    02100I                                       59  610EXAM1
23    02110I                                       64  660EXAM2
24    02120I                                       69  710EXAM3
25    02130I                                       74  760FINAL
26  * 03010C****************************************************************
27  * 03020C*                CALCULATION SPECIFICATIONS                      *
28  * 03030C****************************************************************
29    03040C   01        NUMBER  ADD  1         NUMBER  20
30    03050C   01                EXSR SUBRU
31    03060C   01        STUPTS  ADD  CLSPTS    CLSPTS  40
32    03070CL1           CLSPTS  DIV  NUMBER    CLSAVE  30
33    03080CSR           SUBRU   BEGSR
34    03090CSR                   SETOF                            101120
35    03100CSR                   SETOF                            223033
36    03110CSR                   SETOF                            4050
37    03120CSR           EXAM1   ADD  EXAM2     EXAM12  30
38    03130CSR           EXAM12  ADD  EXAM3     EXAM    30
39    03140CSR           EXAM    DIV  3         AVE123  30
40    03150CSR           AVE123  ADD  FINAL     EXAMS   30
41    03160CSR           EXAMS   DIV  2         STUPTS  30
42    03170CSR           STUPTS  COMP 90                          101110
43    03180CSR 11        STUPTS  COMP 80                          202220
44    03190CSR 22        STUPTS  COMP 70                          303330
45    03200CSR 33        STUPTS  COMP 60                          405040
46    03210CSR                   ENDSR
47  * 04010O****************************************************************
48  * 04020O*                  OUTPUT SPECIFICATIONS                         *
49  * 04030O****************************************************************
50    04040OOUTPUT   H  301     1P
51    04050O         OR         OF
52    04060O                                     66 'CLASS GRADES'
53    04070O         H    1     1P
54    04080O         OR         OF
55    04090O                                     36 'TICKET'
56    04100O                                     48 'SOC. SEC.'
57    04110O                                     79 'EXAM'
58    04120O                                     86 'EXAM'
59    04130O                                     93 'EXAM'
60    04140O                                    101 'FINAL'
61    04150O                                    111 'AVERAGE'
62    05010O         H    3     1P
63    05020O         OR         OF
64    05030O                                     16 'DATE'
65    05040O                                     27 'COURSE'
66    05050O                                     36 'NUMBER'
67    05060O                                     46 'NUMBER'
68    05070O                                     67 'STUDENT NAME'
69    05080O                                     92 '1       2       3'
70    05090O                                    101 'EXAM'
71    05100O                                    110 'POINTS'
72    05110O                                    120 'GRADE'
73    06010O         D    1      01
74    06020O                         DATE       18
75    06030O                         COURSE     26
76    06040O                         TICKNO     35
77    06050O                         SOCSEC     49 ' - - '
78    06060O                         STUDNT     71
79    06070O                         EXAM1  J   79
80    06080O                         EXAM2  J   86
81    06090O                         EXAM3  J   93
82    06100O                         FINAL  J  100
83    06110O                         STUPTSJ   109
84    06120O                   10               118 'A'
85    06130O                   20               118 'B'
86    06140O                   30               118 'C'
87    06150O                   40               118 'D'
88    06160O                   50               118 'F'
89    06170O         T   22     L1
90    06180O                                     45 'AVERAGE POINTS FOR CLASS'
91    06190O                         CLSAVEJ    49
```

A Class Grade Report is to be printed as follows:

CLASS GRADES

DATE	COURSE	TICKET NUMBER	SOC. SEC. NUMBER	STUDENT NAME	EXAM 1	EXAM 2	EXAM 3	FINAL EXAM	AVERAGE POINTS
FALL87	BDP1	0144	568-08-1002	ABE, LYNNE G	76	80	78	82	80
FALL87	BDP1	0144	556-98-3021	AKAGI, SUSAN S	99	100	99	98	98
FALL87	BDP1	0144	259-16-6428	BELL, ERNEST	54	89	84	79	77
FALL87	BDP1	0144	557-98-4804	BLACKWELL, GLEN L	57	54	64	58	58
FALL87	BDP1	0144	556-94-2447	CHATMAN, CARLA E	64	89	84	80	79
FALL87	BDP1	0144	111-30-9013	DINIZ, FRANCISCO J	64	79	75	75	73
FALL87	BDP1	0144	330-52-8528	HODGES, MICHAEL A	65	80	74	79	76
FALL87	BDP1	0144	565-96-4105	JOHNSON, DENISE N	56	84	86	90	82
FALL87	BDP1	0144	556-13-8842	JOHNSON, NIMROD J	66	67	49	70	65
FALL87	BDP1	0144	547-60-8757	LEWIS, BRIAN	77	97	84	80	83
FALL87	BDP1	0144	551-06-7605	LEWIS, TONY	45	58	62	69	62
FALL87	BDP1	0144	560-66-7910	MCKEE, JEFFREY	58	85	75	69	70
FALL87	BDP1	0144	435-52-4734	PIGGEE, HAROLD	64	79	76	83	78
FALL87	BDP1	0144	556-96-4996	POWELL, BOBBIE J	66	70	68	76	72
FALL87	BDP1	0144	573-02-1310	SANFORD, MICHAEL M	49	85	77	89	79
FALL87	BDP1	0144	558-34-6964	SORENSON, JAMES	61	98	95	100	92
FALL87	BDP1	0144	555-04-8482	STRIPLING, PHIL M	52	71	48	66	61
FALL87	BDP1	0144	570-98-0908	TAKAYAMA, GARY M	81	90	98	92	90
		AVERAGE POINTS FOR CLASS		76					
FALL87	BDP3	3018	551-04-6479	TOGIA, SEMURANA	48	55	64	61	58
FALL87	BDP3	3018	562-90-5490	TOOLEYU, KARLA A	79	77	69	75	75
FALL87	BDP3	3018	563-96-1025	TRAVIS, HIRAM J	70	86	87	88	84
FALL87	BDP3	3018	572-92-5201	WAGGONER, LARRY	75	97	86	95	90
FALL87	BDP3	3018	546-72-7068	WALL, MICHAEL G	100	97	97	100	99
FALL87	BDP3	3018	571-70-5632	WINGERT, JOESPH	68	81	80	84	80
		AVERAGE POINTS FOR CLASS		77					

Illustrative Program

Subroutines—EXCPT Depreciation Schedule

Job Definition
Print a depreciation schedule based on the straight-line, the double-declining balance, and sum-of-year's digits methods of depreciating various assets. The depreciation schedule is to be printed for each asset, giving the annual depreciation and the current book value until the limit is reached under each method.

Input
A record is created for each asset with the following information:

Positions	Field Description
1–08	Serial number
9–28	Name of asset
29–36	Cost (XXX,XXX.XX)
37–42	Scrap value (X,XXX.XX)
43–44	Estimated life (years)
45–46	Limit (years)

Processing

The depreciation schedule is to be prepared using subroutines for each method based on the following information.

Assume the following are example sets of facts to be used for determining depreciation by applying the three depreciation methods where Cost=6000, Scrap Value=1680, and Estimated Life=8 years.

1. *Straight-line method.* The factor used in computing the annual depreciation is (Cost − Scrap Value) ÷ Estimated Life = Annual Depreciation. The annual depreciation remains the same for the life of the asset. For example:

    6000 (Cost) − 1680 (Scrap Value) = 4320 (Depreciation)
    4320 (Depreciation) ÷ 8 (Estimated Life in Years) = 540 (Annual Depreciation)

2. *Double-declining balance method.* In this method, the rate of depreciation is determined by dividing 100% by the estimated life. This rate is then doubled and applied to the original cost, resulting in the first year's depreciation. Each succeeding year's depreciation is determined by subtracting the accumulated depreciation from the original cost and then applying the rate to the (declined) balance. Scrap value is not considered.

    For example, 8 (Estimated Life) divided into 100 percent equals 12.5 percent. This rate, doubled, equals 25 percent.

    1st year: 6000 (Cost) × .25 (Rate) = 1500 (Annual Depreciation)
    2nd year: 6000 (Cost) − 1500 (Accumulated Depreciation) = 4500 (Declined Balance)
    4500 (Declined Balance) × .25 (Rate) = 1125 (Annual Depreciation)

    The process is repeated for the life of the asset.

3. *Sum-of-year's digits method.* The following steps are used in determining the annual depreciation using this method:

    a. Add the digits of the number of years in the estimated life.
    b. The first year's depreciation is obtained by creating a fraction of the number of the year and the sum of the digits.

    The numerator is the number of the year (in reverse sequence, with the highest number first) and the denominator is the sum of the digits. The sum of the digits may be determined by using the following formula:

    $$\frac{N(N+1)}{2} \quad N = \text{number of years in estimated life}$$

    For example:

    6000 (Cost) − 1680 (Scrap Value) = 4320 (Depreciation)

    Formula for determining sum-of-year's digits:

    $$\frac{N(N+1)}{2} \quad \frac{8 \times (8+1)}{2} = 36$$

    First year's depreciation: 8 ÷ 36 × 4320 = 960
    Second year's depreciation: 7 ÷ 36 × 4320 = 840
    Third year's depreciation: 6 ÷ 36 × 4320 = 720
    *
    *
    *
    Eighth year's depreciation: 1 ÷ 36 × 4320 = 120

4. *Book value.* For each method, the book value of the asset at the end of the period is obtained by subtracting the accumulated depreciation from the original cost.

5. *Limit.* Each year's depreciation is to be printed until the limit is reached.

6. *Printing.* Each asset is to be printed on a separate sheet.

Output
This Printer Spacing Chart shows how the report is formatted.

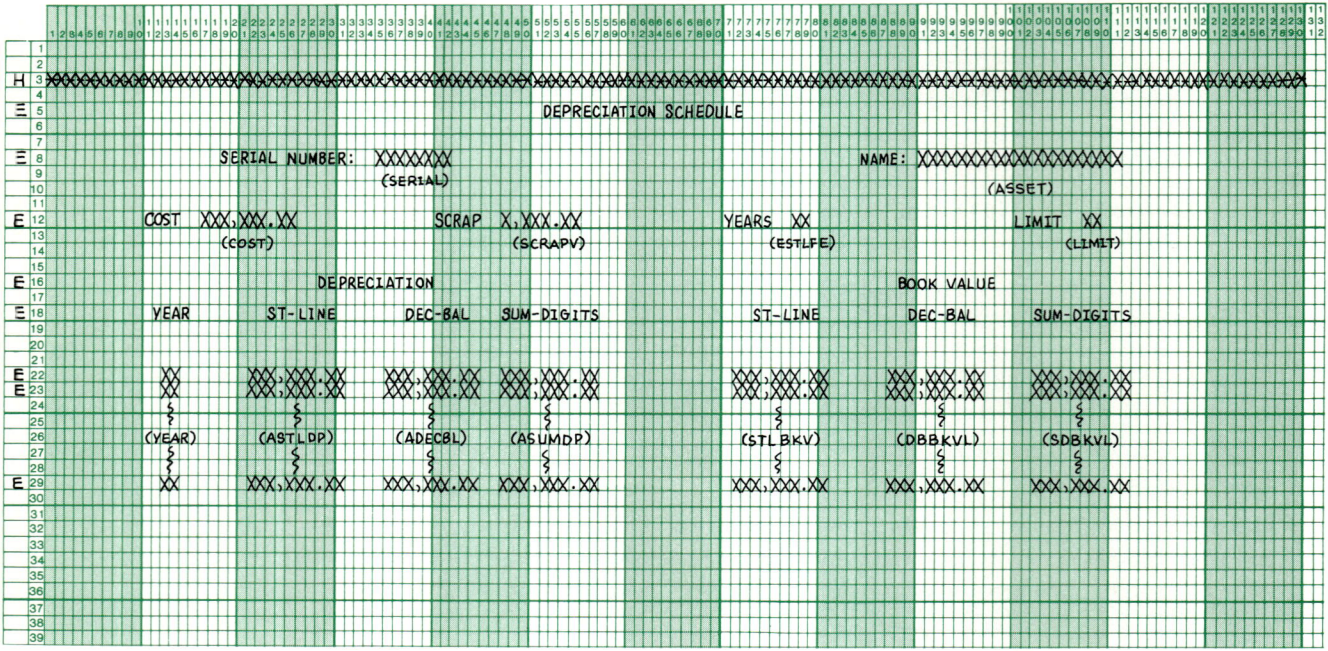

Coding Sheets for Depreciation Schedule problem:

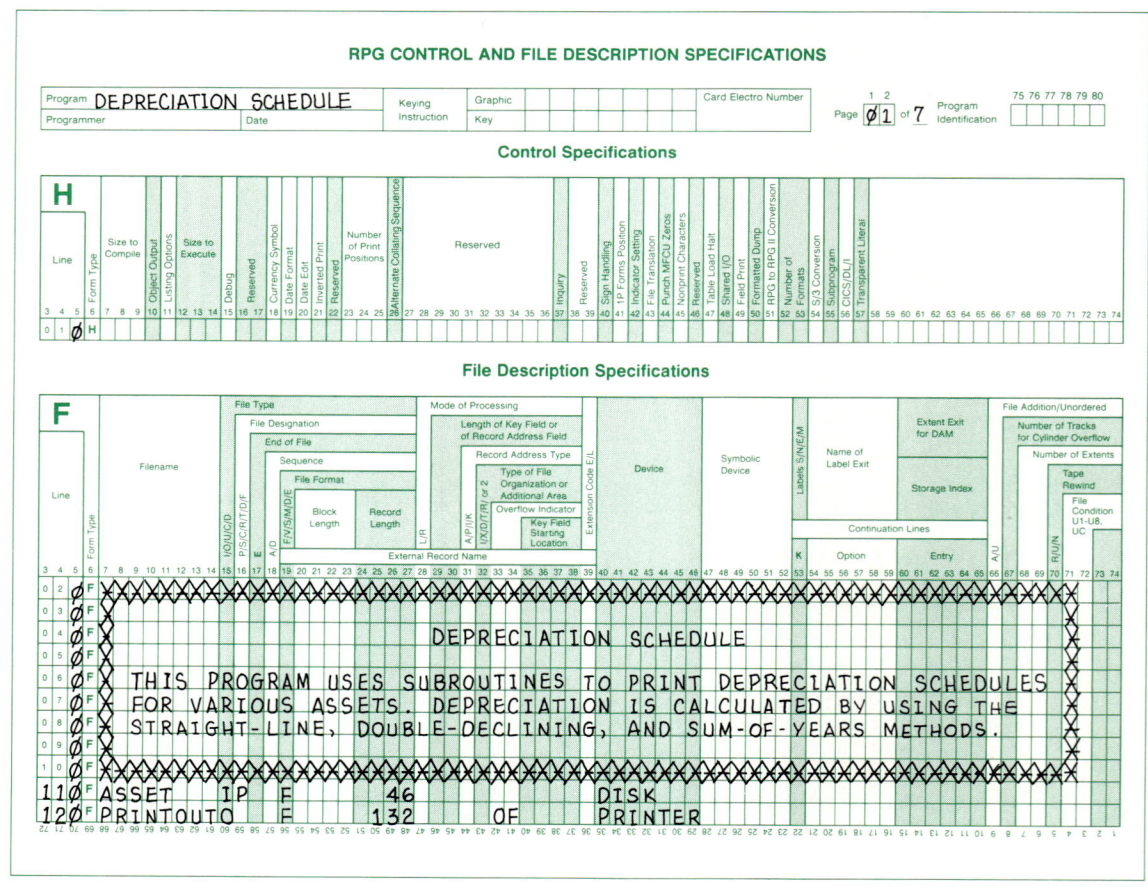

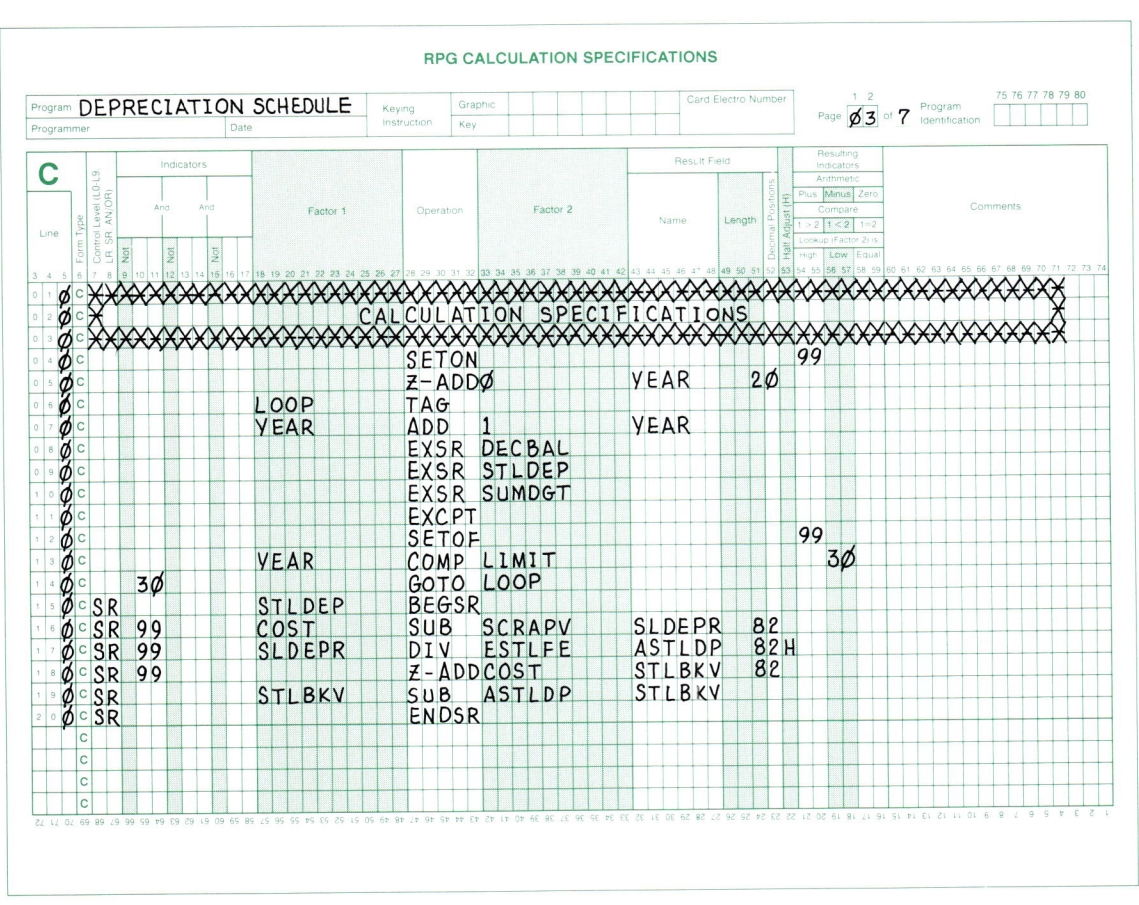

Program Control of Operations

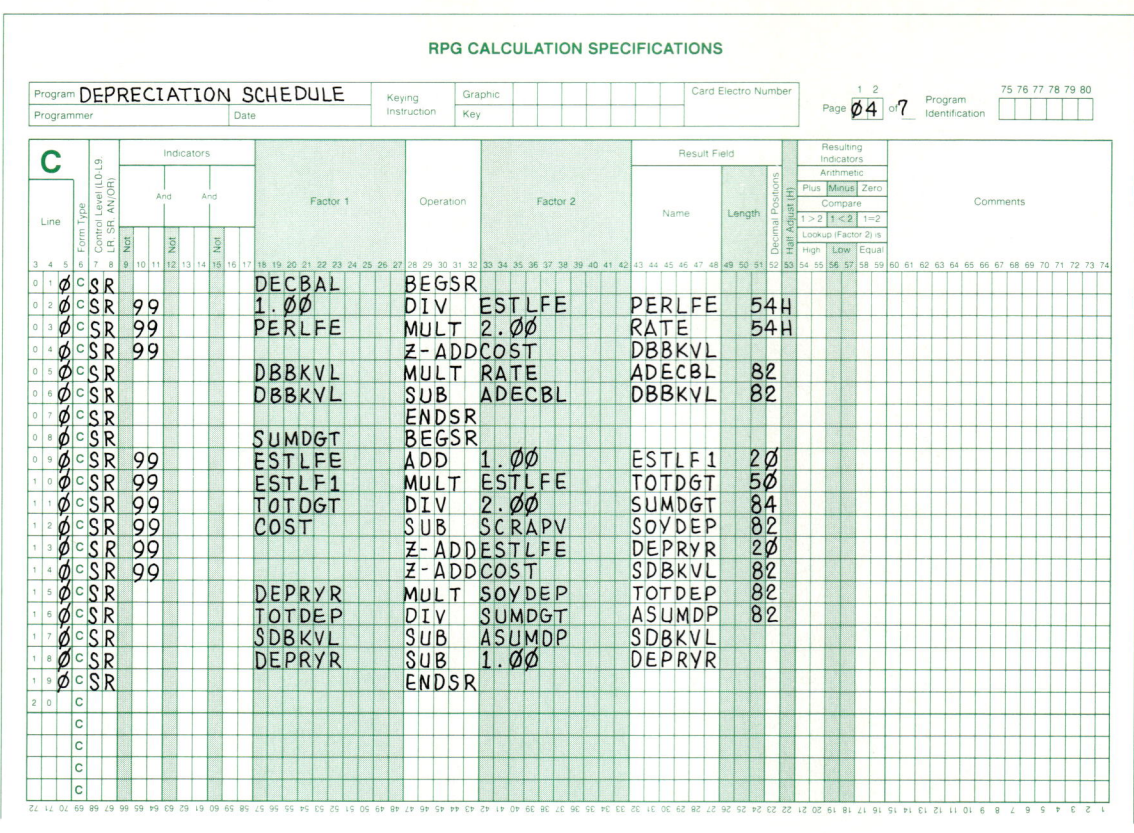
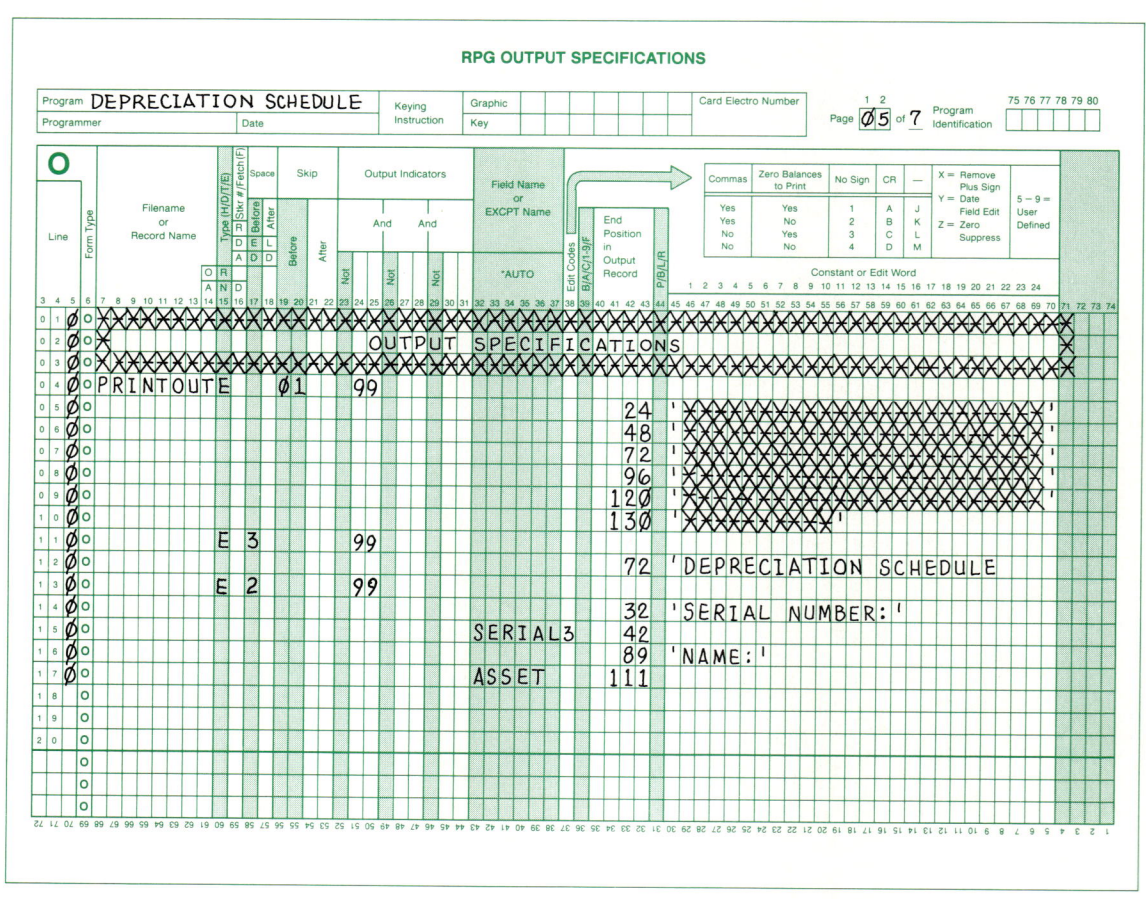

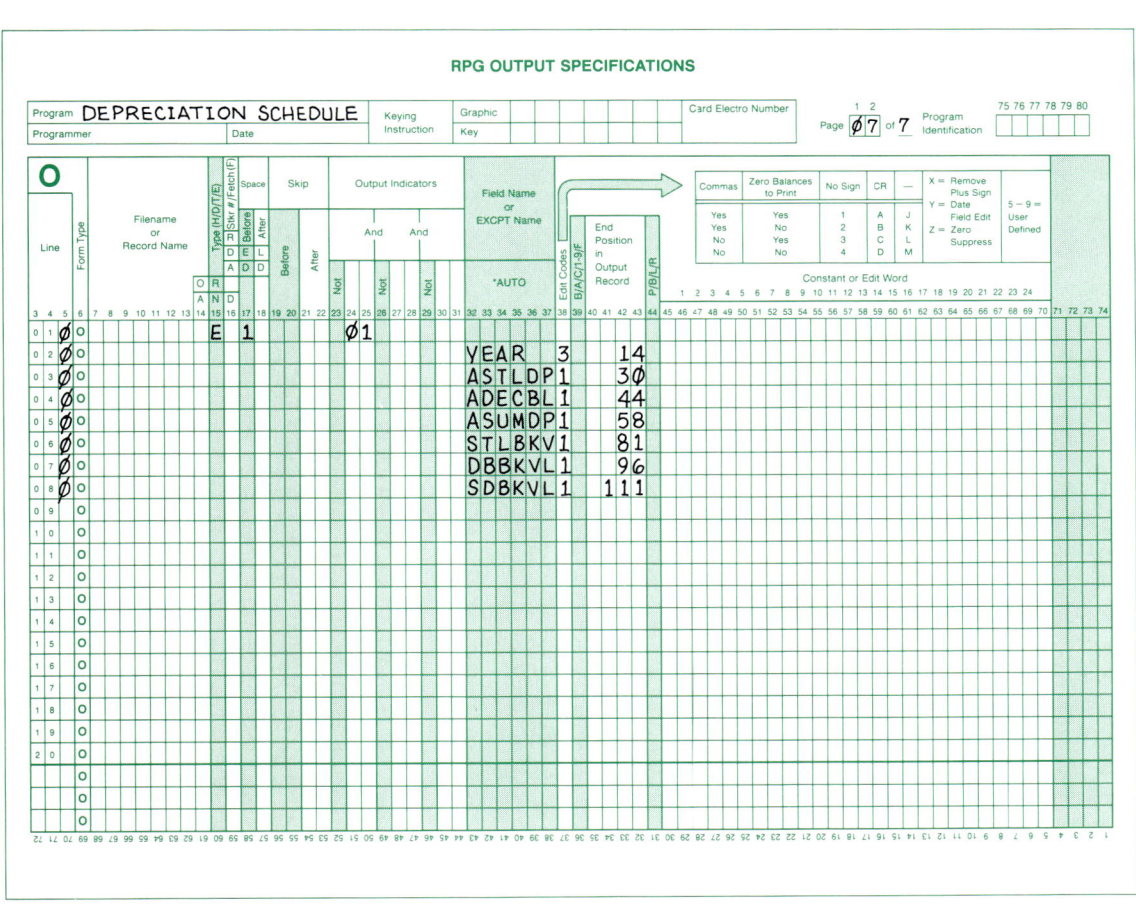

The source listing is as follows:

```
 1   01010H
 2 * 01020F****************************************************************
 3 * 01030F*                                                               *
 4 * 01040F*                  DEPRECIATION SCHEDULE                        *
 5 * 01050F*                                                               *
 6 * 01060F* THIS PROGRAM USES SUBROUTINES TO PRINT DEPRECIATION SCHEDULES *
 7 * 01070F* FOR VARIOUS ASSETS. DEPRECIATION IS CALCULATED BY USING THE   *
 8 * 01080F* STAIGHT-LINE, DOUBLE-DECLINING, AND SUM-OF-YEARS METHODS.     *
 9 * 01090F*                                                               *
10 * 01100****************************************************************
11   01110FASSET   IP  F      46            DISK
12   01120FPRINTOUTO   F     132         OF PRINTER
13 * 02010I****************************************************************
14 * 02020I*                  INPUT SPECIFICATIONS                         *
15 * 02030I****************************************************************
16   02040IASSET    AA  01
17   02050I                                        1    80SERIAL
18   02060I                                        9    28 ASSET
19   02070I                                       29   362COST
20   02080I                                       37   422SCRAPV
21   02090I                                       43   440ESTLFE
22   02100I                                       45   460LIMIT
23 * 03010C****************************************************************
24 * 03020C*                  CALCULATION SPECIFICATIONS                   *
25 * 03030C****************************************************************
26   03040C   01                 SETON                              50
27   03050C   01                 Z-ADD0         YEAR    20
28   03060C            LOOP      TAG
29   03070C   01       YEAR      ADD  1         YEAR    20
30   03080C   01                 EXSR DECBAL
31   03090C   01                 EXSR STLDEP
32   03100C   01                 EXSR SUMDGT
33   03110C   01                 EXCPT
34   03120C   01                 SETOF                              50
35   03130C   01       YEAR      COMP LIMIT                         30
36   03140C      30              GOTO LOOP
37   03150CSR          STLDEP    BEGSR
38   03160CSR 50       COST      SUB  SCRAPV    SLDEPR  82
39   03170CSR 50       SLDEPR    DIV  ESTLFE    ASTLDP  82H
40   03180CSR 50                 Z-ADDCOST      STLBKV  82
41   03190CSR          STLBKV    SUB  ASTLDP    STLBKV  82
42   03200CSR                    ENDSR
43   04010CSR          DECBAL    BEGSR
44   04020CSR 50       1.00      DIV  ESTLFE    PERLFE  54H
45   04030CSR 50       PERLFE    MULT 2.00      RATE    54H
46   04040CSR 50                 Z-ADDCOST      DBBKVL  82
47   04050CSR          DBBKVL    MULT RATE      ADECBL  82
48   04060CSR          DBBKVL    SUB  ADECBL    DBBKVL  82
49   04070CSR                    ENDSR
50   04080CSR          SUMDGT    BEGSR
51   04090CSR 50       ESTLFE    ADD  1.00      ESTLF1  20
52   04100CSR 50       ESTLF1    MULT ESTLFE    TOTDGT  50
53   04110CSR 50       TOTDGT    DIV  2.00      SUMDGT  84
54   04120CSR 50       COST      SUB  SCRAPV    SOYDEP  82
55   04130CSR 50                 Z-ADDESTLFE    DEPRYR  20
56   04140CSR 50                 Z-ADDCOST      SDBKVL  82
57   04150CSR          DEPRYR    MULT SOYDEP    TOTDEP  82
58   04160CSR          TOTDEP    DIV  SUMDGT    ASUMDP  82
59   04170CSR          SDBKVL    SUB  ASUMDP    SDBKVL  82
60   04180CSR          DEPRYR    SUB  1.00      DEPRYR  20
61   04190CSR                    ENDSR
62 * 05010O****************************************************************
63 * 05020O*                  OUTPUT SPECIFICATIONS                        *
64 * 05030O****************************************************************
65   05040OPRINTOUTE   01  50
66   05050O                                       24 '************************'
67   05060O                                       48 '************************'
68   05070O                                       72 '************************'
69   05080O                                       96 '************************'
70   05090O                                      120 '************************'
71   05100O                                      130 '**********'
72   05110O       E  3       50
73   05120O                                       72 'DEPRECIATION SCHEDULE'
74   05130O       E  2       50
75   05140O                                       32 'SERIAL NUMBER:'
76   05150O                           SERIAL3     42
77   05160O                                       89 'NAME:'
78   05170O                           ASSET      111
79   06010O       E 21       50
80   06020O                                       14 'COST'
81   06030O                           COST   1    26
82   06040O                                       45 'SCRAP'
83   06050O                           SCRAPV1     55
84   06060O                                       75 'YEARS'
85   06070O                           ESTLFE3     79
86   06080O                                      105 'LIMIT'
87   06090O                           LIMIT 3    109
88   06100O       E 31       50
89   06110O                                       40 'DEPRECIATION'
90   06120O                                       98 'BOOK VALUE'
```

```
 91    061300        E  13      50
 92    061400                                   15  'YEAR'
 93    061500                                   30  'ST-LINE'
 94    061600                                   44  'DEC-BAL'
 95    061700                                   57  'SUM-DIGITS'
 96    061800                                   80  'ST-LINE'
 97    061900                                   96  'DEC-BAL'
 98    062000                                  112  'SUM-DIGITS'
 99    070100        E   1      01
100    070200                       YEAR    3   14
101    070300                       ASTLDP1     30
102    070400                       ADECBL1     44
103    070500                       ASUMDP1     58
104    070600                       STLBKV1     81
105    070700                       DBBKVL1     96
106    070800                       SDBKVL1    111
```

A Depreciation Schedule is to be printed as follows:

****

DEPRECIATION SCHEDULE

SERIAL NUMBER: 6578094   NAME: LOADER

COST   6,000.00   SCRAP   1,680.00   YEARS   8   LIMIT   5

	DEPRECIATION			BOOK VALUE		
YEAR	ST-LINE	DEC-BAL	SUM-DIGITS	ST-LINE	DEC-BAL	SUM-DIGITS
1	540.00	1,500.00	960.00	5,460.00	4,500.00	5,040.00
2	540.00	1,125.00	840.00	4,920.00	3,375.00	4,200.00
3	540.00	843.75	720.00	4,380.00	2,531.25	3,480.00
4	540.00	632.81	600.00	3,840.00	1,898.44	2,880.00
5	540.00	474.61	480.00	3,300.00	1,423.83	2,400.00

****

DEPRECIATION SCHEDULE

SERIAL NUMBER: 7840795   NAME: DISPLAY CASES

COST   3,200.00   SCRAP   500.00   YEARS   10   LIMIT   3

	DEPRECIATION			BOOK VALUE		
YEAR	ST-LINE	DEC-BAL	SUM-DIGITS	ST-LINE	DEC-BAL	SUM-DIGITS
1	270.00	640.00	490.90	2,930.00	2,560.00	2,709.10
2	270.00	512.00	441.81	2,660.00	2,048.00	2,267.29
3	270.00	409.60	392.72	2,390.00	1,638.40	1,874.57

****

DEPRECIATION SCHEDULE

SERIAL NUMBER: 14756438   NAME: FURNITURE

COST   6,050.00   SCRAP   500.00   YEARS   12   LIMIT   5

	DEPRECIATION			BOOK VALUE		
YEAR	ST-LINE	DEC-BAL	SUM-DIGITS	ST-LINE	DEC-BAL	SUM-DIGITS
1	462.50	1,007.93	853.84	5,587.50	5,042.07	5,196.16
2	462.50	840.00	782.69	5,125.00	4,202.07	4,413.47
3	462.50	700.06	711.53	4,662.50	3,502.01	3,701.94
4	462.50	583.43	640.38	4,200.00	2,918.58	3,061.56
5	462.50	486.23	569.23	3,737.50	2,432.35	2,492.33

```
**************************************************************************************

                              DEPRECIATION SCHEDULE
            SERIAL NUMBER:  38926042                           NAME:  AUTO

      COST   16,010.00        SCRAP  1,500.00      YEARS  7           LIMIT  7


                    DEPRECIATION                          BOOK VALUE

      YEAR    ST-LINE    DEC-BAL    SUM-DIGITS     ST-LINE    DEC-BAL    SUM-DIGITS


        1    2,072.86   4,575.65   3,627.50      13,937.14  11,434.35  12,382.50
        2    2,072.86   3,267.93   3,109.28      11,864.28   8,166.42   9,273.22
        3    2,072.86   2,333.96   2,591.07       9,791.42   5,832.46   6,682.15
        4    2,072.86   1,666.91   2,072.85       7,718.56   4,165.55   4,609.30
        5    2,072.86   1,190.51   1,554.64       5,645.70   2,975.04   3,054.66
        6    2,072.86     850.26   1,036.42       3,572.84   2,124.78   2,018.24
        7    2,072.86     607.26     518.21       1,499.98   1,517.52   1,500.03
```

Questions for Review

1. What is sometimes problematic about the RPG generated program instructions?

2. What are some operations that alter the normal generated RPG calculations in performing input/output functions and what are the main functions of each?

3. How is fetch overflow used?

4. What is the most common problem of normal overflow operations? How does fetch overflow solve this problem?

5. What are the events that occur in fetch overflow?

6. When should fetch overflow be used?

7. What is the EXCPT operation and how is it used?

8. How may the EXCPT operation be conditioned?

9. How may the EXCPT operation be used with overflow printing?

10. What is the main purpose of SETON and SETOF instructions and when should they be used?

11. What are some typical uses of SETON and SETOF instructions?

12. What is meant by branching?

13. How does the computer bypass calculations using indicators?

14. What advantage is there in using branch operations to bypass calculations compared to using indicators?

15. What are two operations used for branching and what is the main function of each?

16. Briefly, what are situations in which branching will help write more efficient and effective programs?

17. What is the operation and purpose of the Z-ADD instructions?

18. What are the main reasons for moving data?

19. What is the basic difference between the MOVE and MOVEL operations?

20. What is a subroutine and how is it normally used in RPG programs?

21. How are subroutines coded?

22. How is a subroutine called?

23. What is the function of the zero and subtract instruction and in what situations is it used?

Problems

Problem 1

Write a program that will print a salary table of monthly, yearly, daily, and hourly wages. The values to be entered are the initial monthly salary, the monthly limit of the table, and the monthly salary increments. For example, assume the values 800, 1200, and 50 are entered as input. The monthly initial value is 800, 1200 is the monthly limit of the table, and 50 is the monthly salary increments.

Input

Positions	Field Description
1–05	Monthly salary (initial)
6–10	Monthly salary (limit of the table)
11–15	Monthly salary (increments)

Processing

1. Compute the yearly, weekly, daily, and hourly salaries based on the monthly rate.
2. Assume a five-day week and an eight-hour day.
3. The output is to be printed according to the format shown in the Printer Spacing Chart below.

Output

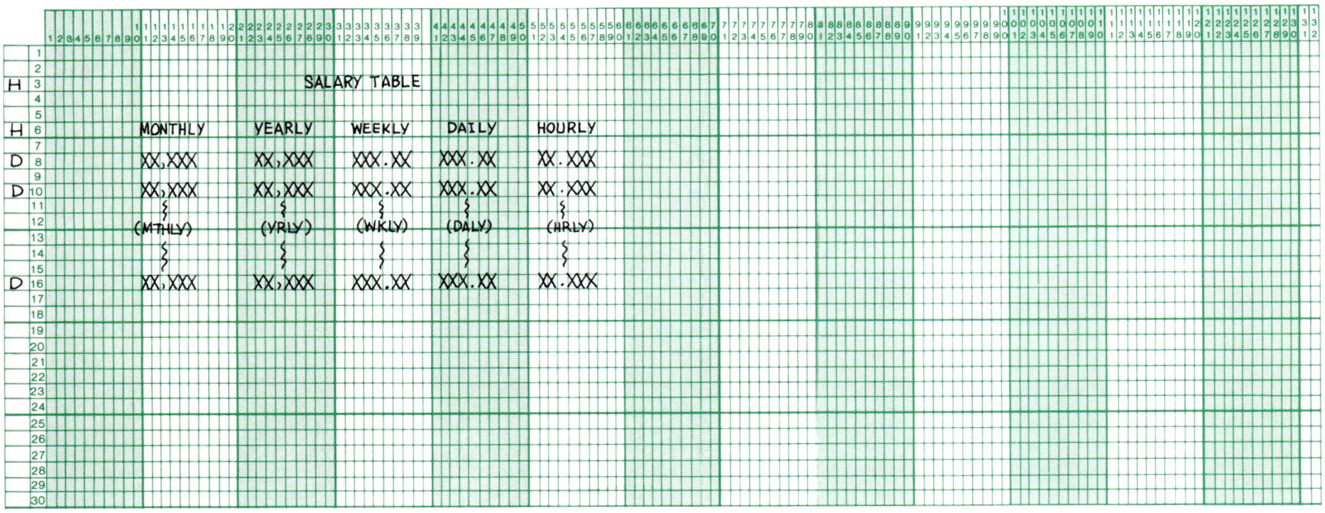

Output is as follows:

SALARY TABLE

MONTHLY	YEARLY	WEEKLY	DAILY	HOURLY
800	9,600	184.62	36.92	4.615
850	10,200	196.15	39.23	4.904
900	10,800	207.69	41.54	5.193
950	11,400	219.23	43.85	5.481
1,000	12,000	230.77	46.15	5.769
1,050	12,600	242.31	48.46	6.058
1,100	13,200	253.85	50.77	6.346
1,150	13,800	265.38	53.08	6.635
1,200	14,400	276.92	55.38	6.923

Problem 2

Code the necessary file description, input specifications, calculations specifications, and output specifications based on the following information.

Input

The input record is a 20-byte record containing the following information:

Positions	Field Description
1–05	Quantity
10–14	List price (XXX.XX) (two decimal positions)
20–20	Code

Calculations

Calculations are performed according to the following flowchart:

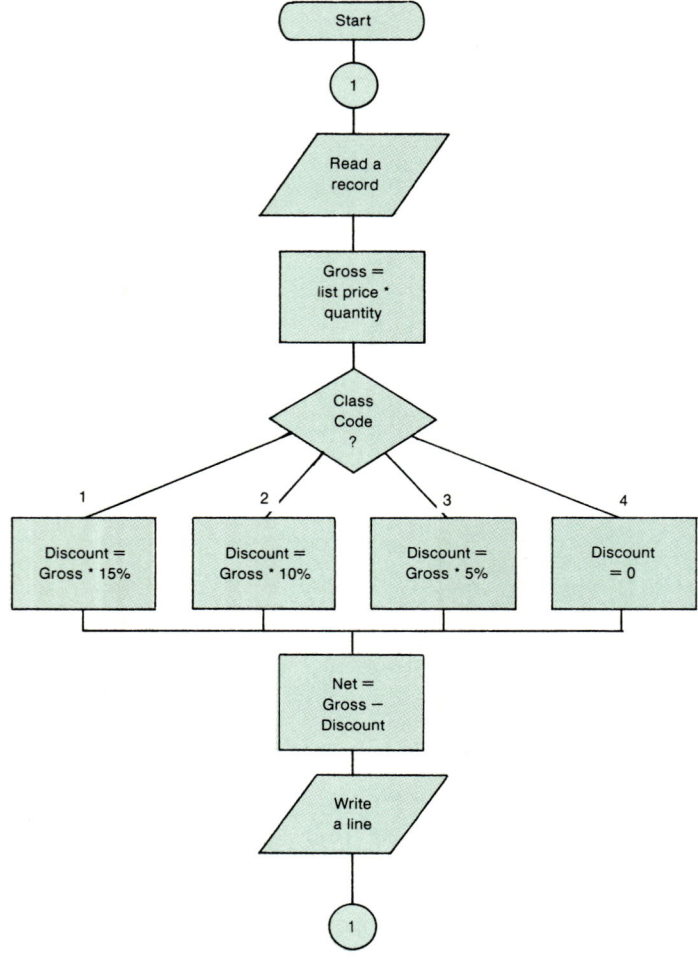

Output

Prepare a Printer Spacing Chart, leaving five spaces between each field and including both input and calculated fields. Be sure to include all necessary headings. Use your own data names where necessary. Use subroutines in your calculations.

Output is as follows:

```
                              DISCOUNT REPORT

QUANTITY     LIST PR.      CODE        GROSS       DISCOUNT         NET


      50        50.00         1       2,500.00       375.00       2,125.00

     750        25.00         4      18,750.00          .00      18,750.00

   1,500        15.30         3      22,950.00     1,147.50      21,802.50

  12,000         9.63         2     115,560.00    11,556.00     104,004.00

     500         1.20         2         600.00        60.00         540.00
```

Problem 3

A payroll file consists of records containing the following information:

Positions	Field Description	
1–03	Department	
04–08	Number	
09–17	Social security number	
18–22	Gross pay	(XXXX.XX)
23–27	Withholding tax	(XXX.XX)
28–32	Social security tax	(XXX.XX)
53–56	Deduction 1	(XX.XX)
57–60	Deduction 2	(XX.XX)
61–64	Decuction 3	(XX.XX)
65–68	Deduction 4	(XX.XX)

The net pay is to be computed using the following formula:

$$\text{NET} = \text{GROSS} - \text{WITHTAX} - \text{SSTAX} - D1 - D2 - D3 - D4$$

All deductions are to be taken from gross pay unless doing so causes the net pay amount to become zero or negative in value. If that happens, add back the last deduction, print an exception record on a special report, and bypass all further calculations for that record. Include messsages on the exception report indicating which, if any, deductions were taken.

Prepare a Printer Spacing Chart to represent heading and detail lines of the exception record report. Include the UDATE and PAGE fields on the heading lines.

Create your own data names where needed; indicate the necessary heading lines on the Printer Spacing Chart. In the output, include all information from the input, the net pay, and any necessary messages.

Output is as follows:

```
         3/07/87                    PAYROLL  DEDUCTION  EXCESSES                          PAGE   1


DEPT. NO.   SOC. SEC. NO.   GROSS   WITH. TX.   FICA    DED 1   DED 2   DED 3   DED 4

  50  1600   564-49-1212   941.62    594.16    219.41   92.11   97.48   97.48     .00   ACTUAL PAY IS  35.94   INCLUDING D1

  62  2300   581-01-0334   877.77    587.70     58.97   81.99   94.19   94.19    9.28   ACTUAL PAY IS  54.92   INCLUDING D1, D2

  62  4400   495-14-9142    94.82     81.48      8.24    5.19    2.43    2.43    5.19   ACTUAL PAY IS   5.10   NO DEDUCTIONS TAKEN
```

Problem 4

The area in which all salespeople work is divided into three districts—A, B, and C. Some work only in one district, while others may work in parts of two or more districts.

The input file contains a record for each salesperson as shown. The amounts in the district fields indicate the total weekly sales made by individuals in each district. If the salesperson did not work in a district or made no sales in that district, the field contains zeros.

Input

Positions	Field Description	Format
1–25	Salesperson name	
26–32	District A	(XXXXX.XX)
33–39	District B	(XXXXX.XX)
40–46	District C	(XXXXX.XX)

Processing

1. Prepare a report showing the commissions earned in each district by each salesman.
2. Accumulate the total commission for each salesman and for each district.
3. The percentage of commission is as follows:
    a. 3 percent of gross sales $.01–$1,000, plus
    b. 2 percent of gross sales $1,000.01–$5,000, plus
    c. 1 percent of gross sales over $5,000
4. Create a subroutine to calculate the commission.

Output

The desired output provides two pieces of information following the Printer Spacing Chart:

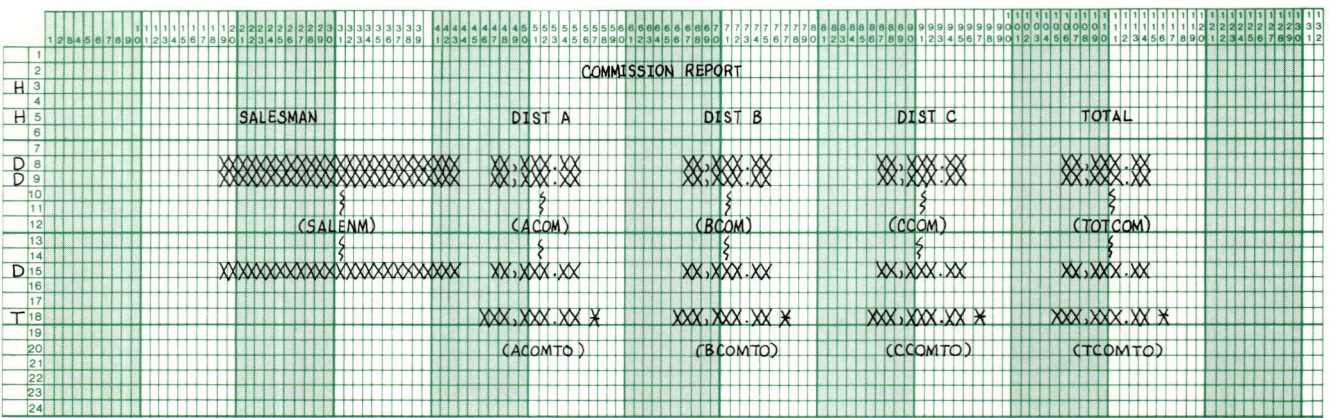

1. Total commission earned by each salesman by district, and the total for all districts
2. Total commissions paid to all salesmen for each district.

Output is as follows:

```
                       COMMISSION REPORT

          SALESMAN             DIST A          DIST B          DIST C


         JANE DOE                28.52          120.00             .00
         HENRY HINES              34.00           16.67          135.00
         JOSEPH LEWIS             13.80             .00           12.60
         WALTER REID              41.85           44.41          151.79
         JACK SMITH              139.29          886.29          711.23


                                257.46 *      1,067.37 *      1,010.62 *
```

Table Handling

6

Outline

Tables
    Forming Tables
    Table Files
        Arguments and Functions
        Table Records and Entries
        Table Sequence
        Table Loading
        Retrieving Entries
        Table Updating
    Describing Table-Input Records
        Number of Table-Input Records Required for a Table
        Number of Entries on a Table-Input Record
        Describing Table-Input Records with Extension Specifications
        Assigning Table Names
        Number of Table Entries per Table-Input Record
        Number of Table Entries per Table
        Length of Entry
        Packed or Binary Field
        Entries with Decimal Positions
        Sequence of Table Entries
        Positions 46–47
        Comments
        Program Identification
        Summary
    Loading Tables
        Compile Time Tables
            Changing Compile Time Tables
            Loading Compile Time Tables
        Preexecution Time Tables
            Changing Preexecution Time Tables
            Loading Preexecution Time Tables
            Specifications for Preexecution Time Tables

Coding the Table Lookup Operation (LOKUP)—Single Table
Operation of a Table Lookup (LOKUP)
Related Tables
    Two-Table Search
    Designing Table-Input Records for Two Tables
    Alternating Entries on One Record
    Describing Two Tables with Extension Specifications
    Coding the Table Lookup Operation (LOKUP)
Using Table Data in Calculations and Output
    Conditioning Operations on the Basis of a Table Lookup
    Searching for Low, High, or Equal Conditions
    Sequence of Tables
Moving Data in a Table Entry
Modifying the Content of a Table
    Making Temporary Changes to Table Data
    Making Permanent Changes to Table Data
    Short Tables for Adding New Table Entries
Output of an Entire Table

Figure 6.1 Tables—examples

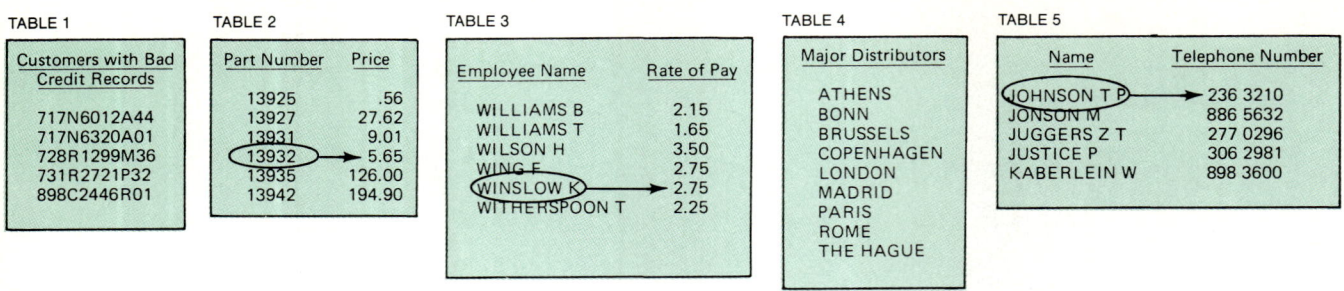

In table 2, a reference to Part Number 13932 locates the corresponding Price 5.65, relative position 4.

In table 3, a reference to the Employee Name Winslow K locates the corresponding Rate of Pay 2.75, relative position 5.

In table 5, a reference to Name Johnson TP locates the corresponding Telephone Number 236 3210, relative position 1.

If you wish to make a telephone call, you must first know the number. Imagine trying to obtain the number if no telephone directories or directory services were available. Many objectives of data processing are similar to this; therefore, programming requires that similar items and types of information be grouped and organized so that they can be referenced easily and quickly.

A **table** is a collection of related items organized in such a way that each item of information can be referenced by its position within that collection. A telephone directory consists of two tables of information—a name list arranged alphabetically, and a number list arranged in no apparent order. Each telephone number, however, occupies a position in the number list corresponding to the position of a particular name in the name list. (It is not the contents, but the relative position in the table—e.g., the seventh entry in both tables.)

Each item within a table is called a table element. Each name in a telephone directory is an element of the name table; each number is an element of the telephone number table. (See Figure 6.1.)

To find Ken Adams' telephone number, you would look through a list of names to locate KEN ADAMS. This procedure of checking of the elements of a table one at a time to find a particular entry is called searching a table. The name KEN ADAMS is the **search word** and is known as the **argument**. The matching entry is the corresponding telephone number known as the **function**. (See Figure 6.2.)

Figure 6.2 Searching a table

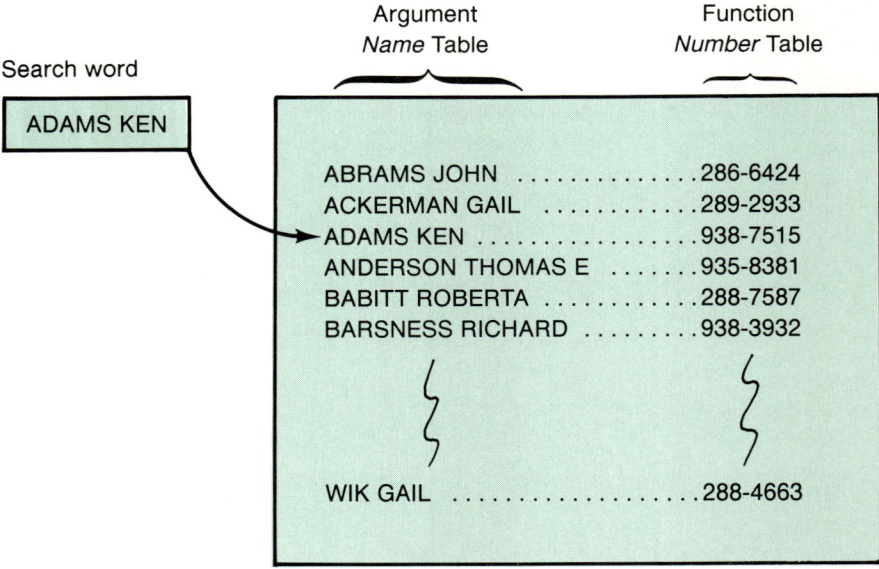

230   RPG II and RPG III Programming

Even though two related tables are used, as in the case of a telephone directory, only one table (the name table) is actually searched. When the search condition has been satisfied, the data in the corresponding element of the second table (the number table) becomes available. Thus, the first table is used as a means of locating data in the second table.

A telephone directory is an example of tables containing organized information that are referenced over and over again in our daily lives. Likewise, tables are used to organize data in data-processing jobs that must be referenced repeatedly.

For example, assume that a customer has purchased various items from a company sales catalog. The sales file would contain records showing customers' account numbers, the items ordered (each identified by a code), and the number of each item ordered by each customer.

The company keeps an inventory file of data about each item carried in stock. A separate record is maintained for each item code, the quantity on hand, and the unit cost of each item. (See Figure 6.3.)

Before any item is shipped, it is necessary to determine whether that item is still in stock. A clerk might have to spend a great deal of time looking up each item ordered to see if it is in the inventory file. The same item is likely to be ordered by many customers; thus, the inventory file records would have to be referenced over and over again.

RPG can search for the data in much less time by performing a table lookup function. A table would be set up in storage listing all the available items.

A field in the sales record tells the program which item to look up. The table will be checked against every sales record read into the computer to see if the record matches some table entry. (See Figure 6.3.)

Figure 6.3 Searching a table for a particular data item

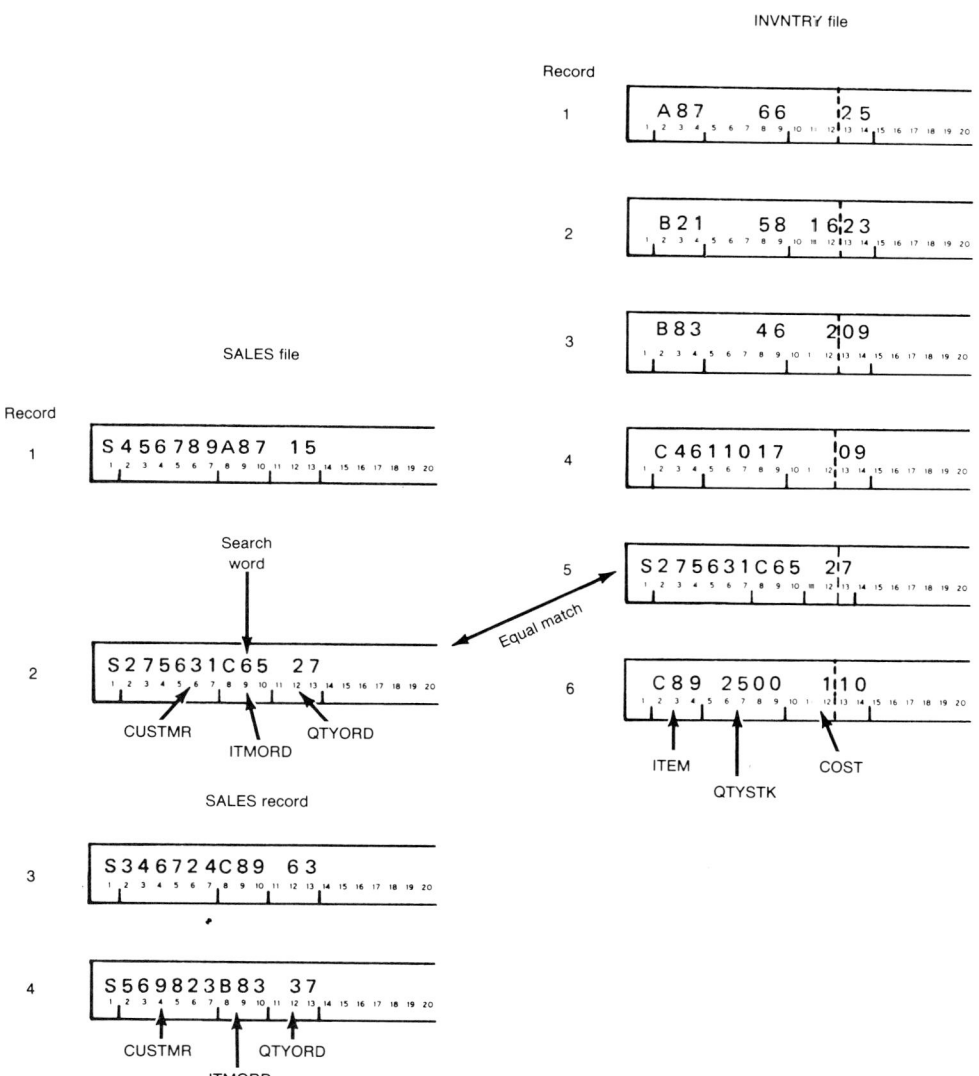

Table Handling

Besides the ability to search quickly for data, table lookup can often reduce the number of RPG specifications needed to perform a job. To do this, the table needs to be set up and defined and the lookup operation to be performed needs to be specified.

Tables

Tables are systematically arranged sets of information that are more limited in scope than other files. Examples are tables of freight rates, withholding percentages, prices, and conversion coefficients. Tables are used in computer programs much as they are used by clerks in manual systems. The document (or record) being processed provides a piece of information (e.g., an item stock number). The known information is then used to obtain another piece of information from a table either by search or by lookup. Thus, the item stock number might be used to look up the item price in a table that contains the prices of all stock numbers.

Another use of tables is to verify information, rather than require that some other data be retrieved. For example, an input account code may be used to search a table containing all active account codes to determine whether or not the input code is valid.

Figure 6.4 Table usage—example

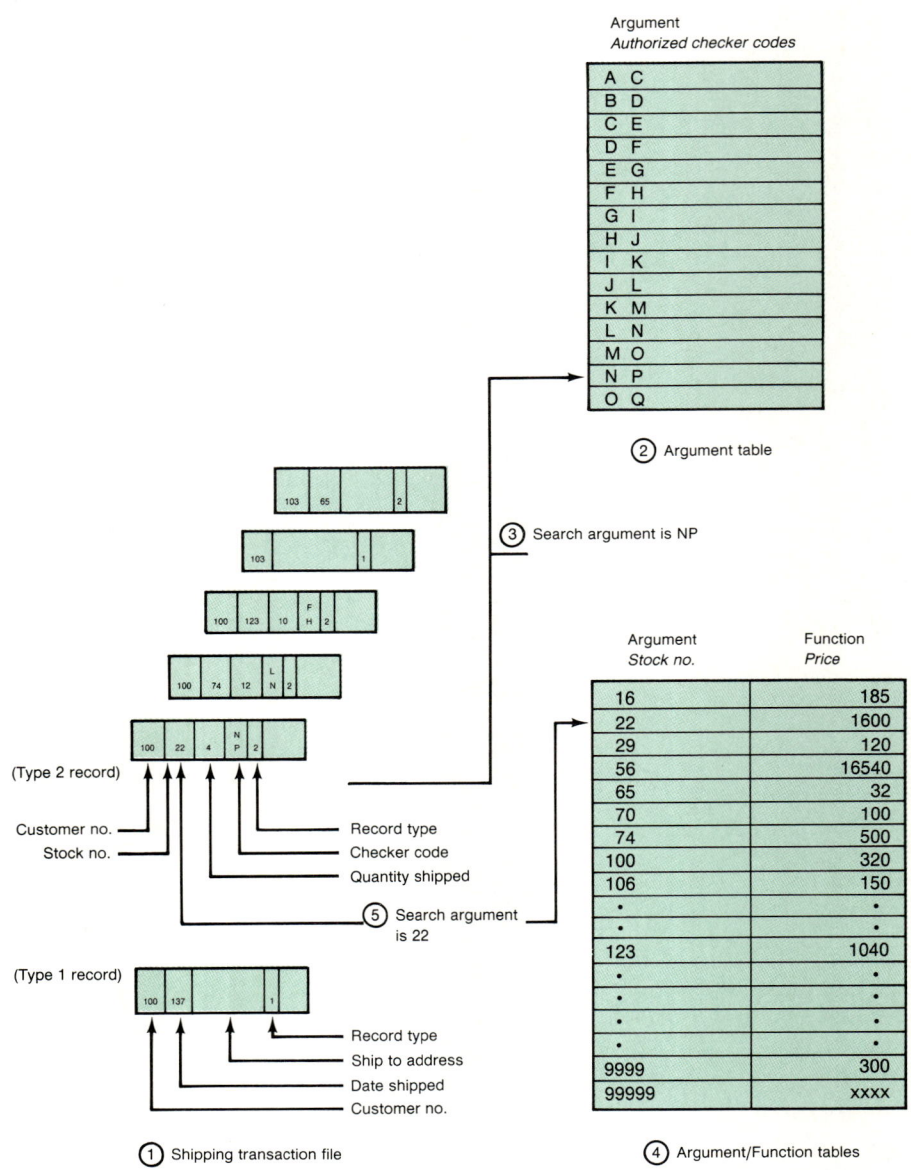

Figure 6.4 continued

Notes

The above figure shows examples of table usage.

A shipping transaction file (1) is sequenced by stock number within record type within customer number.

There is a type 1 record for each customer and a variable number of type 2 records.

The type 1 record shows the date of shipment and the address to which a shipment is made.

Each type 2 record shows a stock number for each item shipped, the quantity shipped, and a code assigned by a checker to each line item.

Line items are checked randomly by different checkers to control errors in both order makeup and shipping dock pilferage. The checker's codes are regenerated in a random pattern and are reassigned each processing cycle for code integrity. The current authorized codes are in an argument table (2).

During processing of each line item transaction, the checker code is validated by searching the table of current authorized codes (3), using the value from the transaction record as the search argument. Transactions without a valid checker code are returned to the shipping dock supervisor for rechecking of the order.

Item stock numbers and associated item prices are maintained in associated argument and function tables (4). The stock number from the type 2 transaction record is used to obtain the item price from the price table (5). The price is then used in extending the item quantity to produce line item price.

A record for the line item is output for invoicing.

A third use of tables is for updating. Entries may be changed during processing and then be returned to their proper places in the table. An example of updating might be the substitution of new prices in a price table. Another example might be the posting of sales transactions to a summary table of departmental sales activity.

The advantage of using a table format over a standard sequential file arrangement is that the table is compact and may be completely contained in computer memory for random processing. Any member of the entire set of entries comprising the table may be retrieved for use either once or repeatedly during the course of processing by a program.

The entries in a table may be arguments, functions, pairs of arguments and functions, or pairs of functions and arguments. The arguments in a table are the values against which a search argument is compared when a lookup of table data is performed. A table of arguments may be used alone, as in the validation example mentioned previously. More commonly, however, a table of arguments has one or more associated function tables. A function table may be read into the computer together with the arguments table as a set of alternating (paired) entries or the tables may be read in separately.

To retrieve or access a function, the associated argument table is searched using a search argument and designated search criteria. When the argument entry that meets the criteria is found, its relative entry position in the argument table is noted. The desired function then becomes available in the same relative entry position in the function table. (See Figure 6.4.)

Although tables are commonly used in combination with the processing of other files, they may be processed alone to produce a report or to update a table. Consider the processing of an employee hourly pay rate table to be updated by a cost-of-living increase formula for all employees. The pay rate tables are in an unordered function table that is accessed by reference to an associated argument table of employee category codes in ascending sequence.

The first search argument is a program constant or literal value that is used to retrieve the first argument and function from the tables. The retrieval pay rate entry is updated by the increase formula and is restored to its original place in the function table. The retrieved argument is used in accessing the next higher entry in the argument table and its associated function from the function table.

The process is continued successively for each entry in the table until there are no more entries. The update function table is written in the file for future reference.

Forming Tables

Tables used by the program may be formed by using word processors or text editors to create files on disk. Although punched cards are presently obsolete, they were once used widely as a table input medium. Tables may also be formed by the computer program and may be output to any sequential file medium. They have the same format structure rules whether on disk, tape, or cards. The primary difference for files formed on punched cards is that the fixed card size limits the entries that may be contained in a table file record.

Table Files

The complete set of entries comprising a table is considered a sequentially organized file, although the table entries may or may not be in sequence within the table. The entries do have strict positional relationships, however, and must be treated in a sequential fashion when being input or output. A table file must have a unique name.

Several table files may be assigned to the same device if necessary. Thus, several table files may be input from magnetic tape or disk.

Table files are read in before any other files are processed. They are input in the same format in which they are specified on the extension specifications.

Arguments and Functions

All arguments and functions of a table must be of the same length and must be either all alphameric or all numeric. If they are numeric and contain mixed numbers, they must all have the same number of places to the right of the decimal.

Table Records and Entries

For more efficient use of file media, table entries may be grouped into records. Table entries are arguments, functions, or pairs (arguments/functions or functions/arguments). For long entries, grouping may not be desirable; however, tables with relatively long entries are uncommon. If the programmer expects a table to require frequent resorting, the record should be defined as having only one entry and the table file should be set up to contain just a single record. This is for convenience of maintenence.

Table file records must contain only an integral number of entries. An argument, function, or pair may not be split across a record boundary. All records of a given table file must contain the same number of entries, except the last record may have fewer entries if the last entry of the table does not fill the last record.

Table Sequence

The entries in an argument table may be in ascending order, descending order, or no specific order. The entries in a function table are usually unordered and hold only a positional relationship to the entries in an associated argument table. Whenever possible, argument entries should be arranged in ascending or descending order for greatest efficiency in accessing.

An unordered table may be searched only for a case of equality with the search argument. An ordered table, on the other hand, may be searched under five different criteria with respect to the search argument. Those criteria are

1. Table argument *equal to* search argument
2. Table argument *greater than* search argument
3. Table argument *less than* search argument
4. Table argument *greater than or equal to* search argument
5. Table argument *less than or equal to* search argument

Even though only the equal-to criterion is used with an unordered table, the searching process is performed more efficiently by the object program if the table is in ascending or descending order and if it is specified as such. The table argument that most closely matches the search argument and that satisfies the search criterion is the result of the search, no matter what kind of table search it happens to be. If the search criterion specified is the equal condition, the first table argument that is equal to the search argument is the result. However, consider the example of searching with a less-than condition and a search argument of 25 in a table containing 30, 20, 10 entries (descending sequence). This search will produce 20 as a result, 20 being the closest argument less than 25. The result argument determines the function (and argument) made available in the table hold areas. In searching tables, alphameric arguments are compared logically; numeric arguments are compared algebraically.

Table Loading

Table data can be loaded into the computer at two different points—at the time the source program is being compiled (compile time) or at the beginning of the object program execution (execution time).

Usually a large table is loaded at execution time from a file of records into a tape, a disk, or main storage. The table should be loaded and read before the actual processing of data begins.

Tables may be stored permanently on disk and tapes, accessed by the program, and brought into main storage as needed. Deletions and additions to these tables can be made by a separate computer run prior to the processing routine.

Regardless of the method employed for loading tables, all elements to be loaded into a table must have the same length and format. Each table must have a unique name, but may or may not be sequentially organized in the type of lookup operation to be performed. A table may be filled with fewer (but not more) entries than specified. The last item in a table should specify the end of the data. Usually a blank item or an all-zero field is a test for an end-of-table condition.

Retrieving Entries

To use table data in a search, the name of the arguments table or function table is used. This procedure effectively retrieves the table data for the table holding area.

Table Updating

Table entries in the table holding area are changed by using the name of the argument or function table. The argument table is searched using a search argument; then the entry to be inserted or added is placed in a holding area.

Describing Table-Input Records

Data used to create a table must be obtained from table-input records. These records can be taken from keyboard, magnetic tape, or disk. These records are read by the computer and entries are placed side by side in storage to form a table.

Number of Table-Input Records Required for a Table

The number of records required for the table data depends on the number of entries to be recorded on each record.

Number of Entries on a Table-Input Record

Table-input records may either contain one entry or a number of entries. The point to remember is that all table-input records for a single table except the last one must contain the same number of entries.

The use of one entry per record is convenient if the entries need to be arranged in a particular order. Then adding or deleting entries requires merely the addition or removal of a record. Otherwise, it would be necessary to re-create all of the records from the point of change to the end of the table. If, however, the entries need not be in a particular order, then including a number of entries in each record reduces the number of records required.

Describing Table-Input Records with Extension Specifications

When the table layout has been completed, it must be described to the computer. The computer must be told the length of the items, the number of decimal positions they contain, and the number of items per record.

Once the table-input records have been designed, they have to be described to the RPG compiler program. Ordinarily the data on input records are described by entering the data on the Input Specifications form. However, data on table-input records are described by coding extension specifications on

Figure 6.5 Extension Specifications form

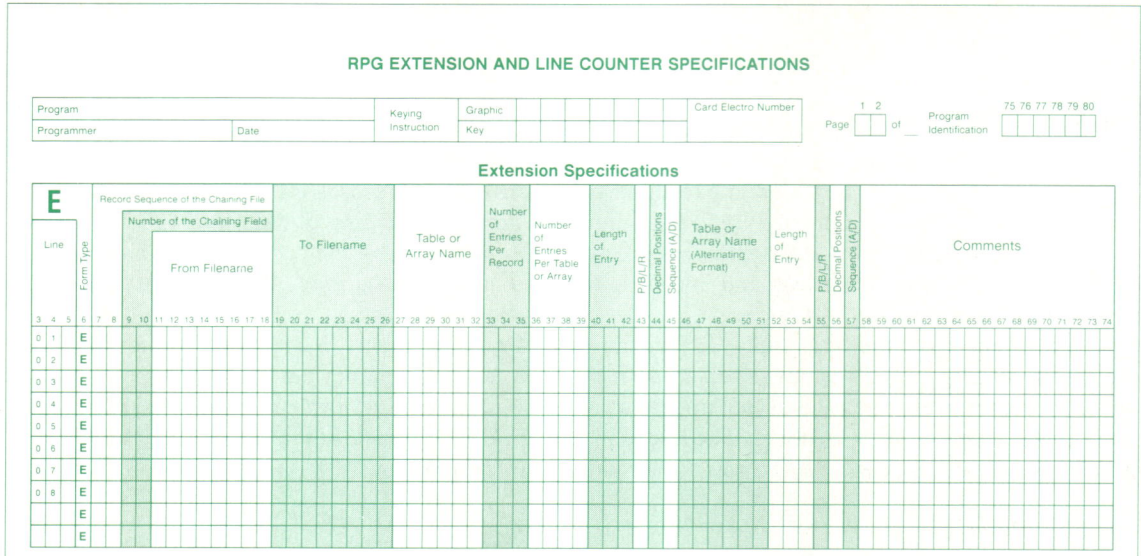

the upper half of the Extension and Line Counter Specifications form. Hereafter, the upper portion of the form will be referred to as the Extension form and the lower portion as the Line Counter form. (See Figure 6.5.)

The extension specifications provide the following information about each table to be used:

1. Name of each table (positions 27–32)
2. Number of entries per table-input record (positions 33–35)
3. Number of table entries per table (positions 36–39)
4. Length of each entry (positions 40–42)
5. Whether packed or binary data are contained in the table (position 43)
6. Number of decimal positions in each numeric entry (position 44)
7. Sequence of entries, if any (position 45)
8. Alternating entries (positions 46–57)
9. Comments (positions 58–74)
10. Program ID (positions 75–80)

Each type of entry will be discussed in turn in the following paragraphs. The From filename (positions 11–18), the To filename (positions 19–26), and the entries in positions 46–57 will be discussed later in this section.

Assigning Table Names (Positions 27–32)

Every table used in a program must be assigned a name four to six characters in length. The table name may be any combination of alphabetic characters and numbers; however, the first three characters of the name must be TAB.

The general rules for naming tables are the same as those for naming fields. A specific rule for assigning a table name that distinguishes it from the assignment of a field name is that the table name must begin with the characters TAB. (See Figure 6.6.)

If possible, it is helpful to assign meaningful table names. For example, the assigned table name TABITM gives an indication of the type of data contained in the table. (In this example, TABITM represents item codes.)

When a single table is used, the table name is entered in positions 27–32 of the Extension form.

Number of Table Entries per Table-Input Record (Positions 33–35)

The number of entries in each table-input record is specified in positions 33–35. This tells the compiler program to expect that all table-input records will contain a specified number of entries with the exception of the last record, which may contain fewer entries. (See Figure 6.7.)

236 RPG II and RPG III Programming

Figure 6.6 Table names—examples

Which of the following table names are not acceptable and why?

TABA
TAB C
TB1@3
TAB$2
15ABCD
TABSTATE
*TAB

TAB C and *TAB are not acceptable, as table names cannot contain blanks or special characters, such as the *.

TAB$2, on the other hand, is an acceptable table name, since $ is one of the three special characters that can be considered an alphabetic character (the other two characters are # and @).

15ABCD and TB1@3 are invalid because they do not begin with the alphabetic characters TAB.

TABSTATE contains more than six characters, therefore it cannot be an acceptable table name.

TABA and TAB$2 are the only two valid table names shown above.

Figure 6.7 Describing table input records—example

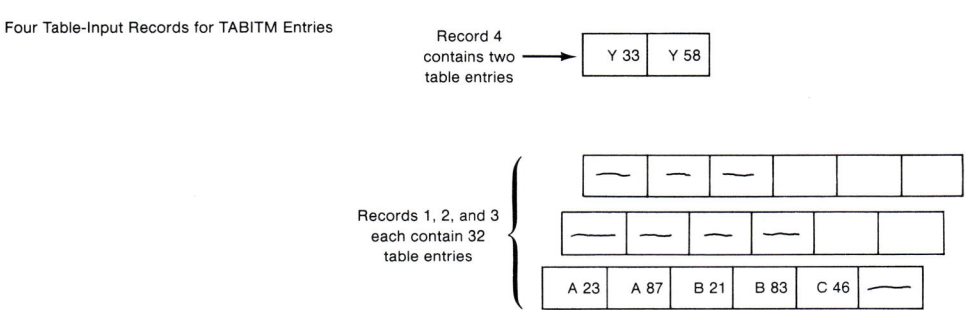

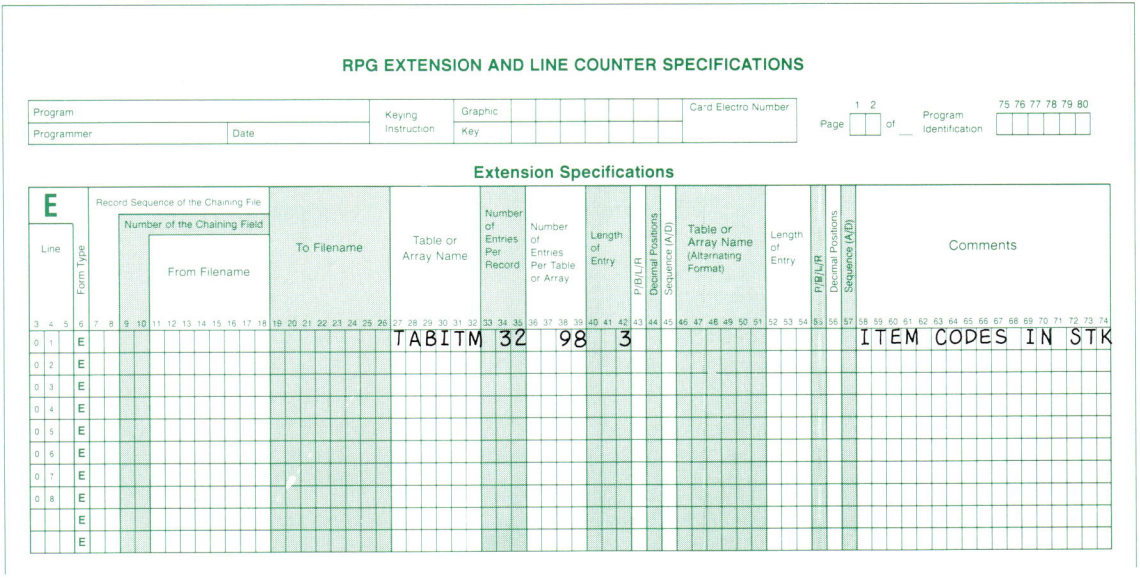

Table Handling   237

Figure 6.8 Table entries—examples

TABPRT Part number	TABAMT* Price
001	127.62
002	198.32
003	000.27
004	000.01
005	001.98
009	003.79
010	005.67
014	002.33
026	014.67
045	029.33
096	029.34
097	000.05
098	000.09
099	001.19
100	002.22
101	126.73
110	596.74
115	393.75
126	697.75
137	001.92

If this data is loaded, TABPRT and TABAMT will be full (20 entries fill the table)

TABPRT Part number	TABAMT* Price
001	127.62
002	198.32
003	000.27
004	000.01
005	001.98

If this data is loaded, TABPRT and TABAMT will not be full

Table Entries (Number Per Table)

RPG EXTENSION AND LINE COUNTER SPECIFICATIONS

Extension Specifications

```
TABPRT  12  20  3 0
TABAMT  12  20  5 2
```

This entry indicates that TABPRT and TABAMT may both have a maximum of 20 entries

*Decimals are for illustration only.

When two related tables are described, each table-input record must contain the corresponding items from each table written in alternating form. These two alternating table items are considered as one entry. The number entered must end in position 35. Corresponding items from related tables (each pair of alternating entries) must be on the same record. If there is room, comments may be entered on table-input records in the positions following table entries.

Number of Table Entries per Table (Positions 36–39)

Positions 36–39 indicate the maximum number of table items that can be contained in an entire table named. This number may apply to one table or to two alternating tables, but any number entered in these positions must end in position 39. If alternating tables are described, corresponding table entries are considered as one entry.

If the table is full, this entry gives the exact number of items it contains. However, if the table is not full, the entry gives the number of items that can be put into it. A table that is not full is known as a short table. (See Figure 6.8.)

Since the number of items for two related tables must be the same, the entry in these positions also gives the number of items in a second table (positions 46–51).

Length of Entry (Positions 40–42)

The length of each table entry is indicated in positions 40–42, with the number ending in position 42. It is only possible to specify one length. Therefore, this means that all entries in the table must be of the same length.

All table items must contain the same number of characters. It is almost impossible, however, for every item to be of the same length. To remedy this, zeros or blanks are added at the beginning of numeric items in creating tables in order to make them the same length; blanks are added to alphameric items. For alphameric items, blanks may be added either before or after the item. (See Figure 6.9.)

For instance, the programmer may wish to make a table containing the months of the year. The solution to the length problem here is a simple one—all entries are made the length of the longest entry. The word September contains the most characters; therefore, each entry is nine characters long. To make June an entry with a length of nine, five blanks are placed after the letter *E*. Inserting extra blanks to lengthen data entries is referred to as padding with blanks. If the table entries were numbers instead of letters, the short entries would be padded with zeros.

Padding a table with blanks should not be confused with spacing entries on a record. No blanks occur *between* entries. Blanks can, however, be made a part of an entry in order to make all entries the same length. (See Figure 6.10.)

Figure 6.9 Length entries—examples

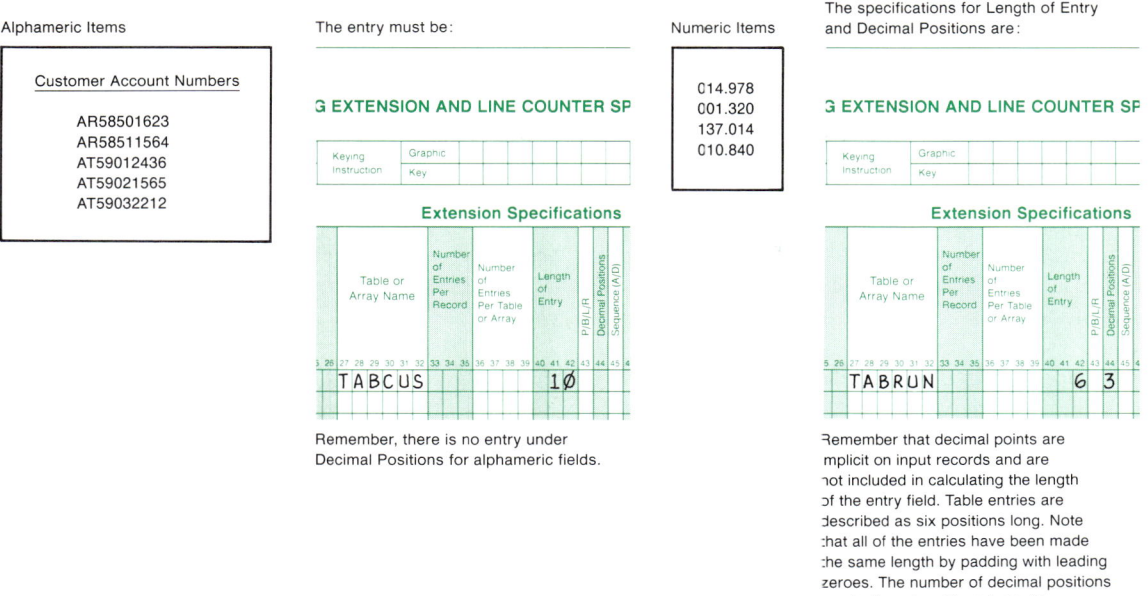

Figure 6.10 Padding table items—examples

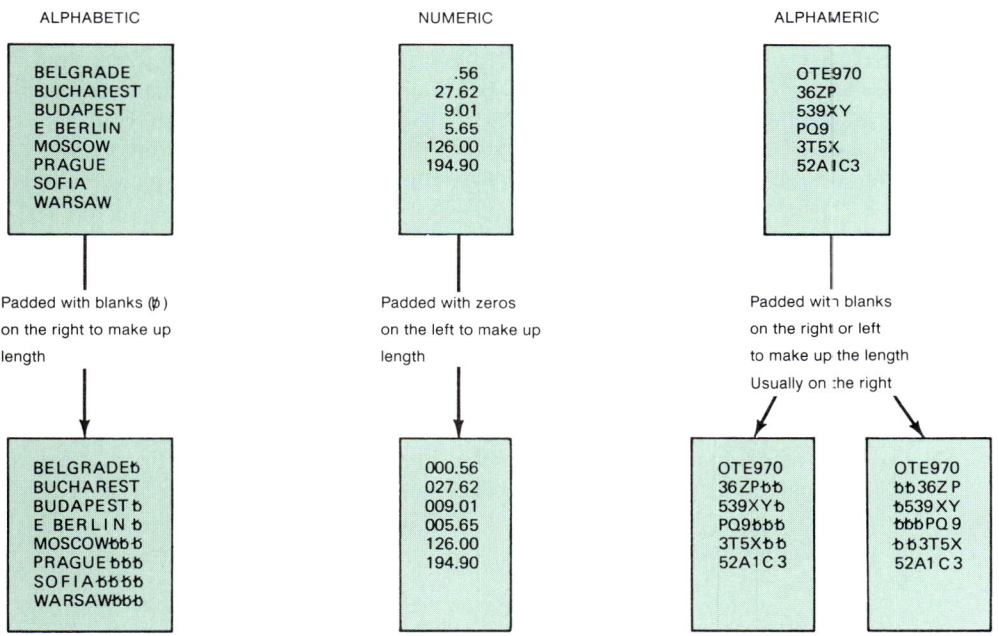

Packed or Binary Field (Position 43)

An entry must be made in position 43 if the data for the table is in packed decimal (P) or binary (B) format. This entry applies only to numeric tables. For numeric tables in packed decimal format, the unpacked decimal length of the entries must be entered in positions 40–42 (length of entry). For numeric tables in binary format, enter the number of bytes required in storage for the binary field. For a two-position binary field, the decimal number stored there can be one to four digits in length. The entry in positions 40–42, in this case, is 4. For a four-position binary field, the decimal number can be up to nine digits; therefore, the entry is 9.

This entry must be left blank to accommodate information in decimal format. More detailed information on packed and binary formats will be found in chapter 10.

Table Handling 239

Entries with Decimal Positions (Position 44)
When the entries of a table are numeric, it is necessary to specify in position 44 the number of decimal positions (0–9) in each entry. Even if a numeric entry contains no decimal positions, a *0* must still be entered to indicate numeric data. When decimal positions are not specified (position 44 is left blank), RPG considers the table entries to be alphameric.

If two alternating tables are described in one file, the specifications in this position apply to the table containing the item that appears first on the record.

Sequence of Table Entries (Position 45)
If the table entries are in ascending or descending order, an *A* or *D* is entered under table sequence (position 45). Note that if a table is to be in sequence, the entry is made on the Extension form. For input files other than table files, the sequence entry is always made on the File Description Specifications form.

Position 45 is used to describe the sequence (ascending or descending) of the data in a table. When an entry is made in position 45, the table is checked for the specified sequence. If a preexecution time table is out of sequence, an error occurs and the program halts immediately. The program can be restarted from the point where it stopped if it is not necessary to correct the out-of-sequence condition. However, if the programmer wishes to correct the out-of-sequence condition, the program execution must be restarted from the beginning. (Some systems require the table to be ordered and specified as such before the program can be executed.)

Ascending order means that the table items are entered starting with the lowest data item (according to the collating sequence) and proceeding to the highest. Descending order means that the table items are entered starting with the highest data item and proceeding to the lowest.

If alternating tables are described in one file, the entry in position 45 applies to the table containing the item that appears first on the record.

If the programmer is searching a table for an item (LOKUP) and wishes to know if the item is high or low compared to the search word, the table must be in either ascending or descending order. When a specific sequence is specified, RPG checks the data in a table to verify that sequence. In checking for sequence, an equal condition is considered valid. This allows the programmer to pad the beginning of a table with zeros or blanks, or to pad the end of the table with 9s (assuming ascending sequence).

Positions 46-57
These positions are used only when describing a second table entered in alternating format with the table named in positions 27–32. All the fields in this section have the same significance and require the same entries as the fields with corresponding titles in positions 27–45.

Comments (Positions 58-74)
Any information may be entered in positions 58–74. The comments should help the programmer understand or remember what is being done in each specification line. Comments are not instructions to the RPG program; they serve only as means of documenting the program.

Program Identification (Positions 75-80)
Positions 75–80 are used for program identification.

Summary
Figure 6.11 summarizes the description of table-input records on the extension specification.

Loading Tables

Table data can be loaded into the computer at two different points in time—at the time the RPG source program is compiled (compile time tables) or at the beginning of the RPG object program execution (preexecution time tables). In compile time tables, the actual table data are included as a part of the RPG source program. During the process of compilation, these tables are stored with the program for future use. Preexecution time tables are created just before they are needed, and are stored in the computer as a file. A preexecution time table is defined in the same manner on the Extension form, but must also be described as an input file on the File Description Specifications form.

Figure 6.11 Extension specifications for simple tables—summary

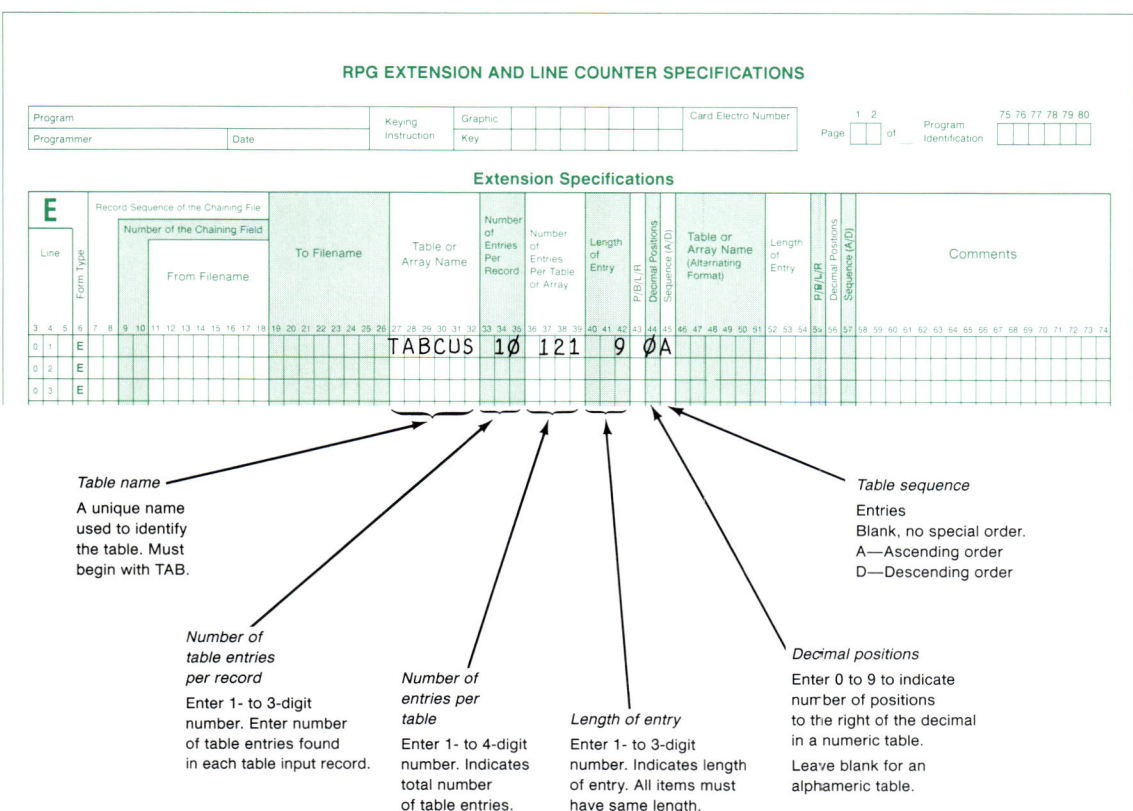

How often the programmer wishes to make permanent changes to the data in the table usually dictates the time to load the tables. The choice should be made as the job is planned since the decision may affect the design of the table-input records and the specification entries required. Furthermore, the process of loading table-input records can differ depending on the type of table used.

Compile Time Tables

Tables loaded at the same time as the RPG source program are referred to as **compile time tables.** Compile time tables are appended as part of the source program using a word processor or text editor. (The IBM System/38 uses source entry utility, commonly known as SEU.) In other words, the table file is compiled (or translated into the machine or object program) along with the RPG source program. In this way, the table data are actually part of the object program. Every time the particular object program is run, the table(s) is brought into storage at the same time as the program.

Changing Compile Time Tables

Temporary changes to data in a compile time table for testing purposes are made as easily as for any other table. Calculation specifications that have been previously coded in the program can modify any of the table elements.

Making permanent changes to a compile time table or adding new entries in a short compile time table requires recompiling the RPG source program along with the new or changed table input records. The object program produced then contains the current table data. Of course, this process of recompilation requires extra time.

Loading Compile Time Tables

A table to be compiled with the program should follow the RPG source program. There should be a record immediately before the table containing a double asterisk (**) in positions 1–2. Position 3 must be blank, but the remaining positions may be used for such comments as the table name. If more than one table is to be compiled, a ** record should be placed before each table. Furthermore, the compile time tables must be loaded in the same order as they are described on the Extension form.

Preexecution Time Tables

In general, if a table is to be permanently modified a number of times, it is better to create a preexecution time table. Such a table file is not compiled with the RPG source program. Instead, only the source program is compiled or translated into the object program. Once the object program has been loaded into the computer to be executed, the table file is loaded separately. Like any other input data file, table files are used *by* the object program rather than being a part *of* the program.

Changing Preexecution Time Tables

Modifying a preexecution time table takes much less time and effort than changing a compile time table. Modifying the content of the table permanently (whether a short table or a full table) can be done easily by inserting and deleting change records. In any event, only the table file is changed. Since there is no need to make changes in the RPG object program, it is unnecessary to recompile the entire program.

Loading Preexecution Time Tables

Preexecution time tables are similar to any other input data files in that the RPG object program uses the files when the program is executed. However, unlike other data files, preexecution time tables are read completely before operations involving the tables are done. The ** record that precedes each compile time table is not used for preexecution time tables.

If both preexecution time table files and other input data files are to be used by the program, all tables are loaded before the data files.

Specifications for Preexecution Time Tables

Since a preexecution time table is a separate file to be used by the program, the entire file of table-input records must be defined on the file descriptions just as any other file must be defined. This specification is not required for compile time tables because records are not used as a file; instead compile time table data becomes part of the object program.

The preexecution time table must be described as an input file on the File Description Specification form and must include these entries:

1. A filename different from the table name. This filename should be assigned to the preexecution table file (positions 7–14).

2. An *I* in position 15. This distinguishes the file as an input file.

3. A *T* in position 16. This indicates a table file.

4. An *E* in position 39. This indicates that the records in the table file are further described on the Extension form.

These particular entries are combined with the others necessary for describing files on the File Description Specifications form.

Ordinarily, if an input file is to be in a particular sequence, an entry (*A* or *D*) is made in position 18 of the File Description Specifications form. However, when specifying a sequence for table files, the sequence positions (45 and 57) on the Extension form must be used, rather than the sequence position on the file descriptions.

The filename assigned on the File Description Specifications form is also entered under the From filename (positions 11–18) on the Extension form. For compile time tables, no entry is made in positions 11–18. Because no file description specifications are made, no filename is assigned to compile time table records. (See Figure 6.12.)

Figure 6.12 Defining a preexecution time table file

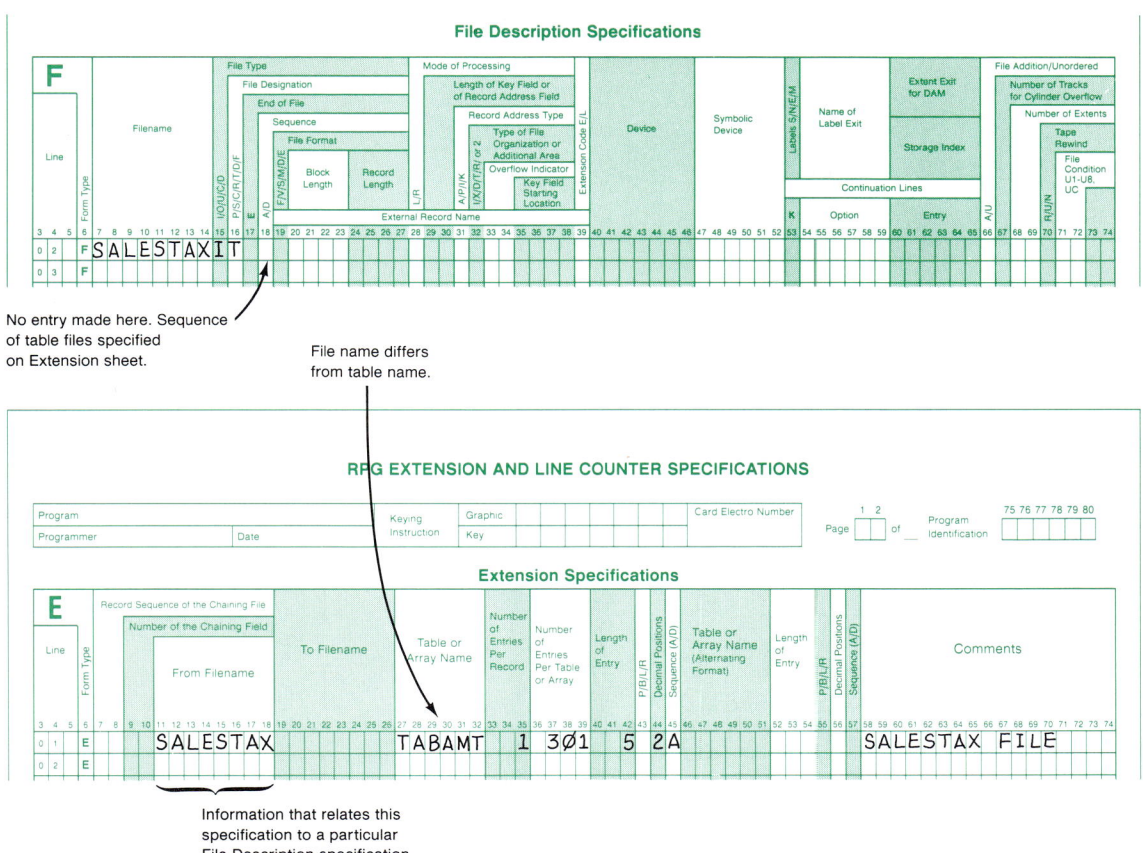

Coding the Table Lookup Operation (LOKUP)—Single Table

Once the table input records have been described, RPG can be told to search a table by coding the LOKUP operation on the Calculations Specifications form. A single search is used to determine whether or not a given value is in the table. This involves specifying:

1. The LOKUP operation code
2. The name of the table to be searched
3. The data being searched for
4. Conditions that must be satisfied for a successful search

The operation code LOKUP is entered in positions 28–32 of the Calculations Specifications form. This operation code causes a search to be made for a particular item in the table named in factor 2. Thus, the name of the table being searched is entered under factor 2 (positions 33–42) beginning in position 33. Remember that the table being searched must have been previously described on the Extension form.

Factor 1 (positions 18–27) contains the field name of the data used for comparison during the table search. (See Figure 6.13.) The search data and the table entries must have the same length, the same number of decimal positions, and the same format (alphameric or numeric).

In a search for a matching item, an equal condition must be satisfied. To determine if the search was successful, a resulting indicator must be assigned for the lookup. This indicator will turn on when (and if) the equal condition is satisfied.

Table Handling 243

Figure 6.13 The LOKUP operation code—example

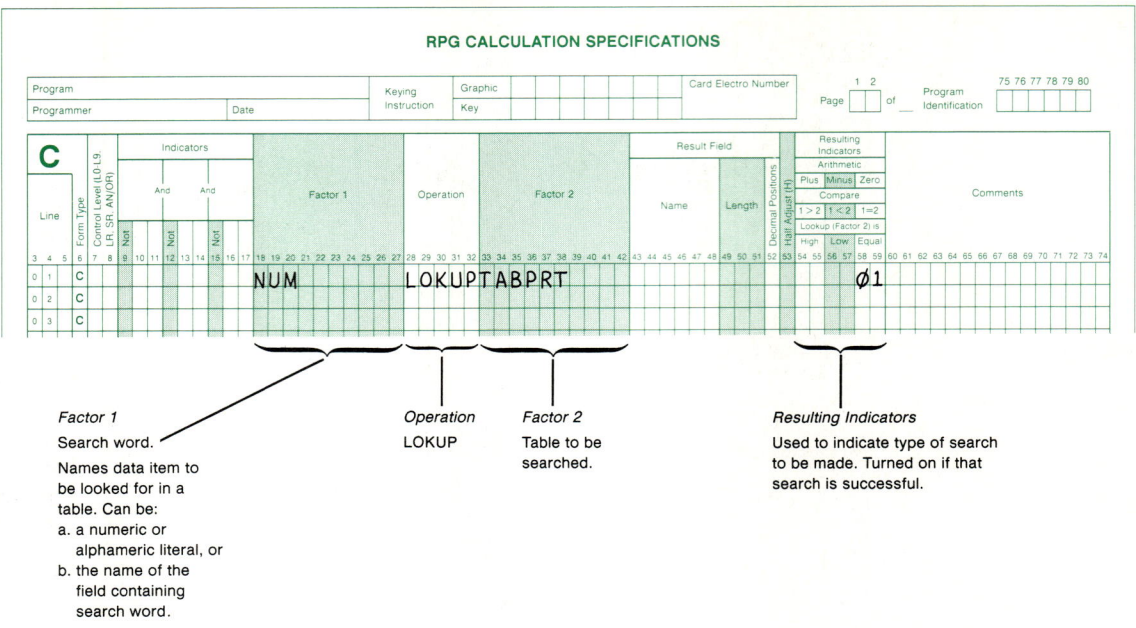

Operation of a Table Lookup (LOKUP)

Following is the sequence of steps performed in a table lookup:

1. A search field value is compared against the first table entry.

2. If the table entry is what is being searched from, the table value is made available for processing and output.

3. If the first table entry is not what is being searched for, the program compares the search value against the next table value. Step 2 is repeated.

4. If the search produces no acceptable table entry and the entire table has been searched, the lookup operation is complete.

In order to describe the table lookup activity, the following steps must be taken:

1. Describe the tables to be used by making entries on the Extension form (and the File Description Specifications form, if needed).

2. Describe the input field (or constant) that contains (or is) the searching value.

3. Describe the LOKUP (table lookup) operation including:
   a. The search field or constant as factor 1
   b. LOKUP as the operation
   c. The table to be searched as factor 2
   d. Another table that contains corresponding values as the result field (optional)
   e. At least one resulting indicator in positions 54–59

A resulting indicator is used to test the lookup operation for certain conditions. (See Figure 6.14.)

    Normally the reason for doing a table lookup operation is to use the value found in the corresponding table (the one in the result field) for additional calculations. If no search table entry (the factor 2 table) satisfies the problem requirement, the programmer may wish to bypass all further calculations or to stop the computer run altogether. One reason for stopping the run is that if the table data, the search field data, or the constant are wrong, the operator should probably rerun the job after corrections are made. Otherwise, if the job continues, all output may be garbage.

    To stop the computer, the programmer uses a special halt indicator. When a halt indicator is turned on, processing continues for all remaining steps including output for that record; then the computer

Figure 6.14 Single-table search—example

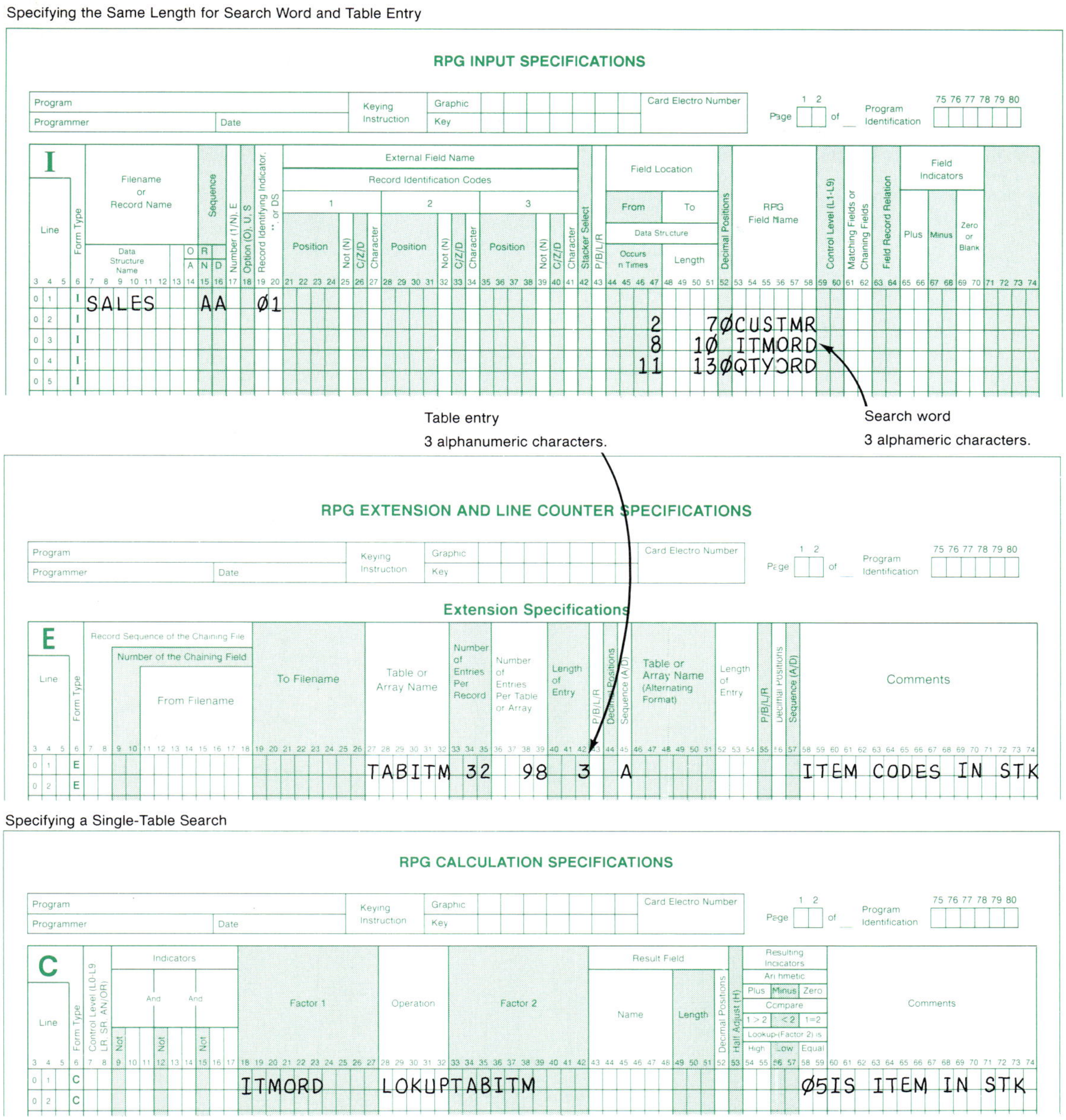

Specifying the Same Length for Search Word and Table Entry

[RPG Input Specifications form showing:]
- Line 01: SALES AA 01
- Line 02: 2 70 CUSTMR
- Line 03: 8 10 ITMORD
- Line 04: 11 130 QTYORD

Table entry — 3 alphanumeric characters.
Search word — 3 alphameric characters.

[RPG Extension and Line Counter Specifications form showing:]
- Line 01: TAB ITM 32 98 3 A ITEM CODES IN STK

Specifying a Single-Table Search

[RPG Calculation Specifications form showing:]
- Line 01: ITMORD LOKUP TABITM 05 IS ITEM IN STK

stops. If a GOTO instruction is used, all further processing will be bypassed, but the machine will not stop running. By including the SETON instruction and any one of the halt indicators (H1–H9), the machine will stop after both processing and output for that record have been completed. At that point the operator becomes aware that something has gone wrong in the program. The programmer must provide a set of instructions to the operator in this situation to complete the job with the error either noted or removed until the error can be corrected. Any action on the part of the operator (including restarting the machine) automatically turns off the halt indicator.

Related Tables

Related tables are frequently used for such information as name and telephone number; invoice amount and discount rate; and employee number and rate of pay. Related tables are, in fact, two simple tables—the data in the second being directly related to the data in the first. If the programmer wishes to know

Table Handling   245

Figure 6.15 Related tables—examples

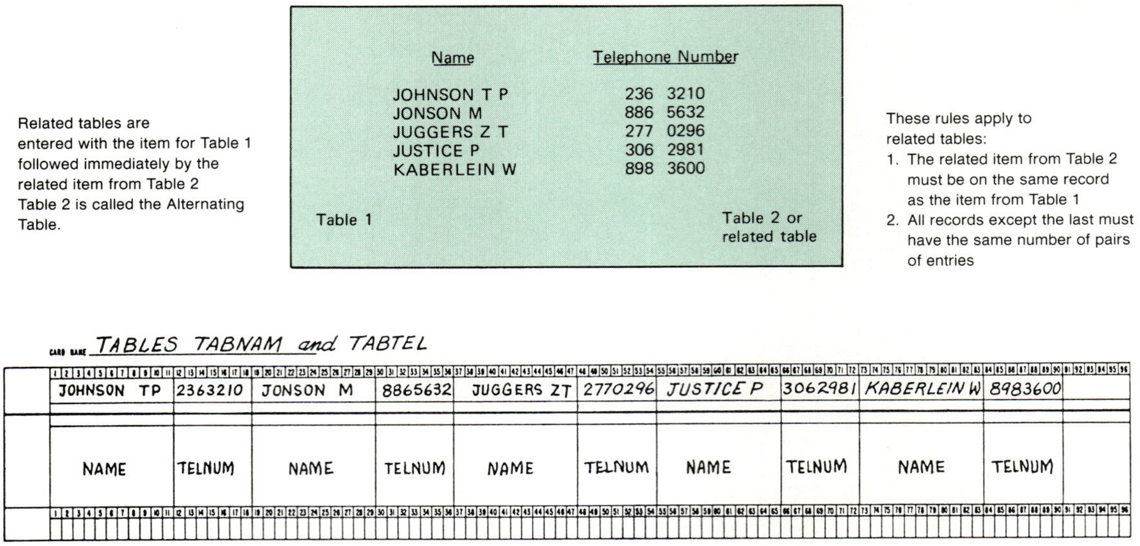

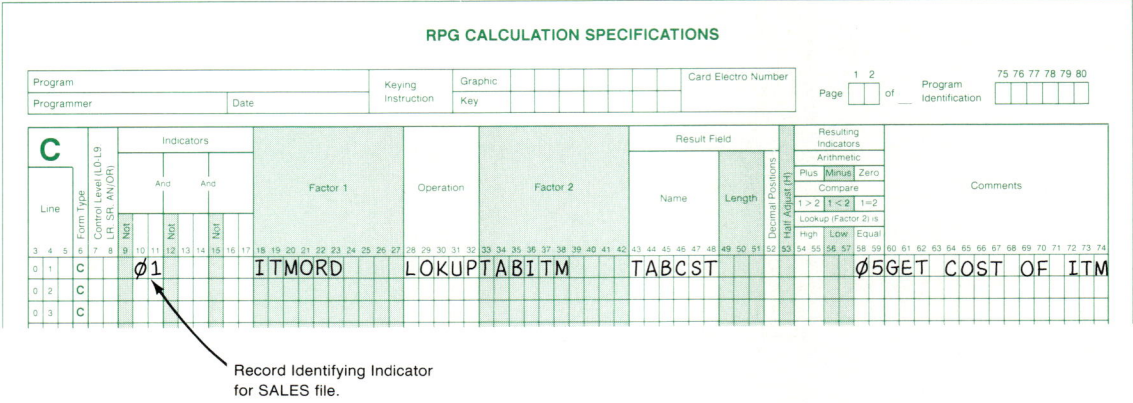

Related tables are entered with the item for Table 1 followed immediately by the related item from Table 2. Table 2 is called the Alternating Table.

These rules apply to related tables:
1. The related item from Table 2 must be on the same record as the item from Table 1
2. All records except the last must have the same number of pairs of entries

Figure 6.16 Specifying a two-table search

the telephone number of Jaggers T M, a search is made of table 1 (name) until Jaggers T M is found. The data required is the telephone number (table 2). This procedure is used many times with a telephone directory. RPG works in the same way. (See Figure 6.15.)

Two-Table Search

A single table can be searched merely to see if certain information (an item code) is in the table. However, more information is typically needed in a search. For example, when orders are shipped, bills must be sent to each customer for the amount of the order. Before RPG can print the bills, it must calculate the amount each customer owes. To do this, the unit cost of each item must be determined. (See Figure 6.16.) The unit cost of an item is then multiplied by the number ordered to give the total amount due from a customer for that type of item.

When two related tables are used, only one table is actually searched. When the search condition (an equal or any other condition) has been satisfied, the data in the corresponding position or element of the second table (related table) become available. Thus, the first table is used as a means of locating data in the second table. (See Figure 6.17.) In a telephone directory, the name is used as a means of locating the telephone number.

Figure 6.17 Related tables usage—example

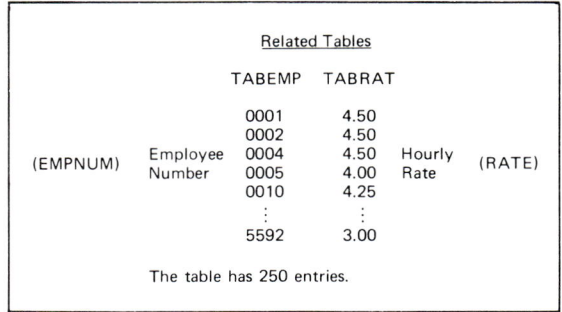
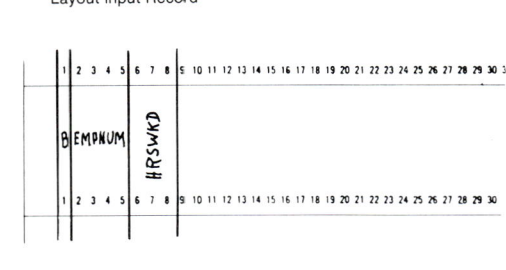
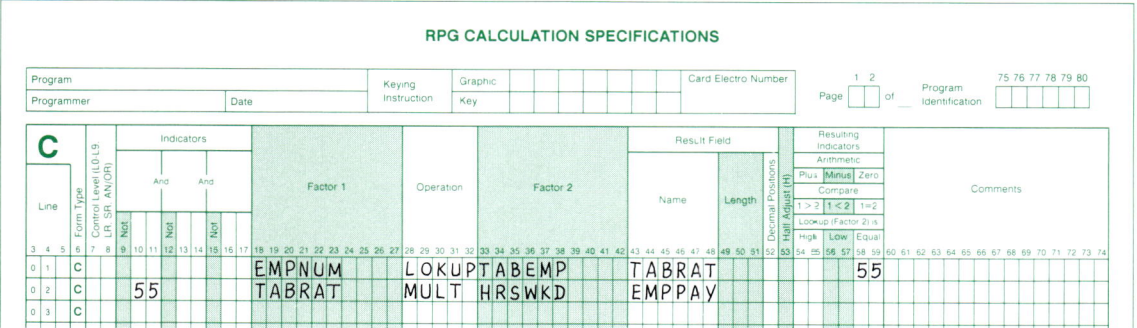

Notes on the Coding

This program is used to compute the pay due to employees.

The information above is used to make the entries on the Calculation Specifications form that will supply the figures for the amount of pay due.

The operation code LOKUP is used in the same manner as a simple table. For related tables, the result field contains the name of the table from which data are to be taken. If the search is successful, the item corresponding to the search word is made available by using the name specified in the result field as a field name.

Designing Table-Input Records for Two Tables

Following are two similar, but distinctly different, methods for designing table-input records for two tables.

Alternating Entries on One Record

A method of designing table-input records allows the programmer to use only one table-input file for both tables. This method tends to save record space and usually reduces the number of RPG specifications needed to describe the table-input records. Entries from the first table are alternated with entries from the second table. The records are then referred to as alternating format table-input records.

When using the alternating format, every record in the table-input file must begin with the same type of table entry. The number of entries put on an alternating format table-input record is up to the programmer. The programmer may put on as many pairs of related entries as the record can contain. All records except the last must contain the same number of entries.

All entries for a single table must be alike; that is, entries must all be alphameric or all be numeric. However, the entries for an alphameric table and the entries for a numeric table can both be on the same table-input record when using an alternating format. (See Figure 6.18.)

Although each table-input record contains entries from both tables, two separate tables are created in storage from these records. The RPG compiler knows that two tables, rather than one, are to be set up because of the way the records are described on the Extension forms.

Figure 6.18 Alternating format table-input records

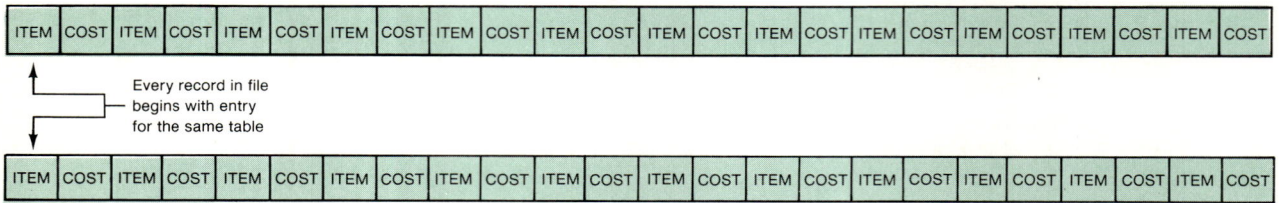

Single table — Input file
Entries for TABITM and TABCST
in alternating format

Figure 6.19 Describing separate table-input records

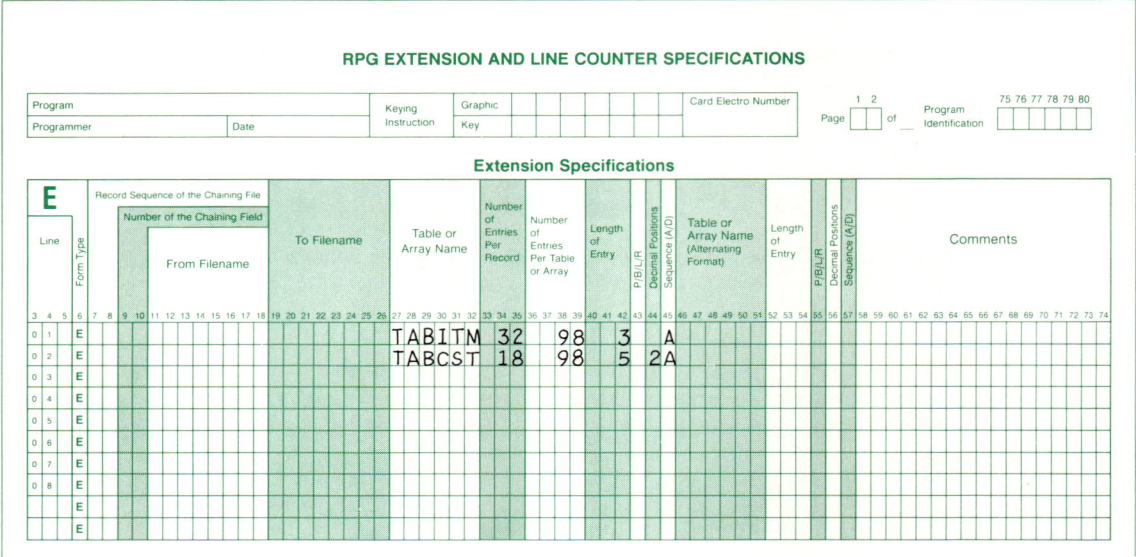

Describing Two Tables with Extension Specifications

When two related tables are used in a job, the programmer has the choice of designing two table-input files (one for each table) or only one table-input file consisting of alternating format table-input record.

If the programmer decides to set up two separate table-input files, each table will need to have its own set of input records; a separate line of extension specifications is needed for each table. (See Figure 6.19.)

When the alternating format is used, only one extension line is coded. Since one line is coded for each set of input records, the second table of the alternating format record must be entered on the same extension line as the first table. Any table may be coded as either the argument or the function.

Remember that two separate tables are created, even if the alternating format is used. Therefore, unique names must be specified for both tables on the Extension form. The table whose entry appears first on a table-input record is named in positions 27–32. The name of the alternating table is entered in positions 46–51 of the same line. The alternating table is always the table whose entry is the second one in a pair of related entries. If table entries are entered from a separate file, an entry in positions 11–18 is required. (See Figure 6.20.)

Figure 6.20 Describing alternating format table-input records

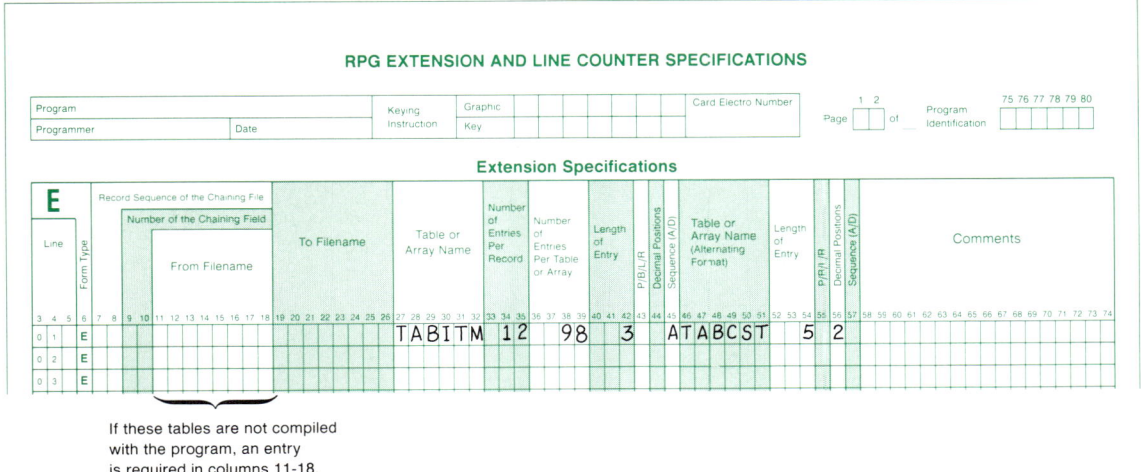

Notice that number of entries per record (positions 33–35) and number of entries per table (positions 36–39) do not have corresponding specifications for alternating tables. Since the number of entries per record and number of entries per table must be the same for each of the alternating tables, separate specifications are not needed for the second table.

The length of table entry (positions 52–54), however, must be indicated since it may be different for the two tables. The decimal positions (position 56) and sequence entry (position 57) of the alternating tables may differ.

Coding the Table Lookup Operation (LOKUP)

After both tables have been set up, a table may be searched to find the element that contains the matching item (search word). One table is used to point to the equivalent entry in another table. This simple lookup procedure is coded with the same calculation specifications as those used with the single-table search. The field name that contains the search code is entered under factor 1; the LOKUP operation is specified in positions 28–32; and the name of the table being searched is entered under factor 2. If an equal match is found in searching the table, the appropriate resulting indicator as specified in positions 58–59 is turned on.

If the second table is also referenced, additional specifications must be entered on the same line of the Calculation Specifications form. The name of the table from which the data are to be made available is entered as the result field (positions 43–48). When (and if) the equal search is satisfied, the corresponding data looked up in the second table are made available. Field length and decimal positions are not necessary inclusions on the Calculation Specifications form (positions 49–52), as these fields have been previously described on the Extension form. (See Figure 6.21.) However, if these specifications are entered again on the Calculation Specifications form, the numbers must agree with those on the Extension form.

Using Table Data in Calculations and Output

A table lookup is performed because the programmer wishes the information referenced to be used in a particular way. For some jobs, this referenced data may be used in calculations. At other times, this data may be used for output.

Conditioning Operations on the Basis of a Table Lookup

Certain calculations and output specifications may or may not be performed, depending on the results of a table lookup. Conditioning indicators are used in making these determinations. (See Figure 6.22.)

Figure 6.21 Two-table search—example

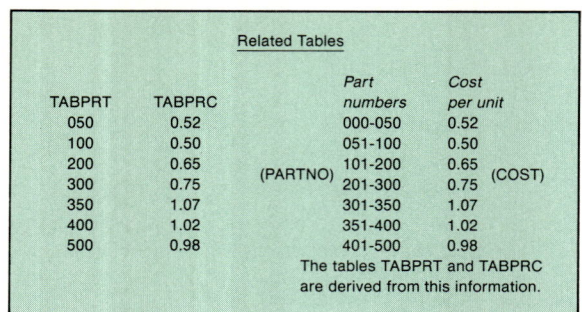
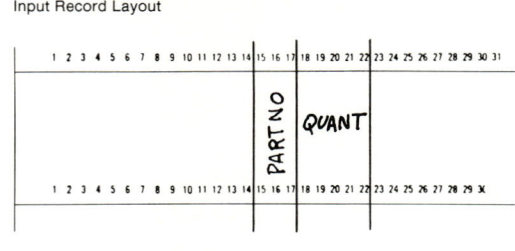

Entry for the Lookup Operation

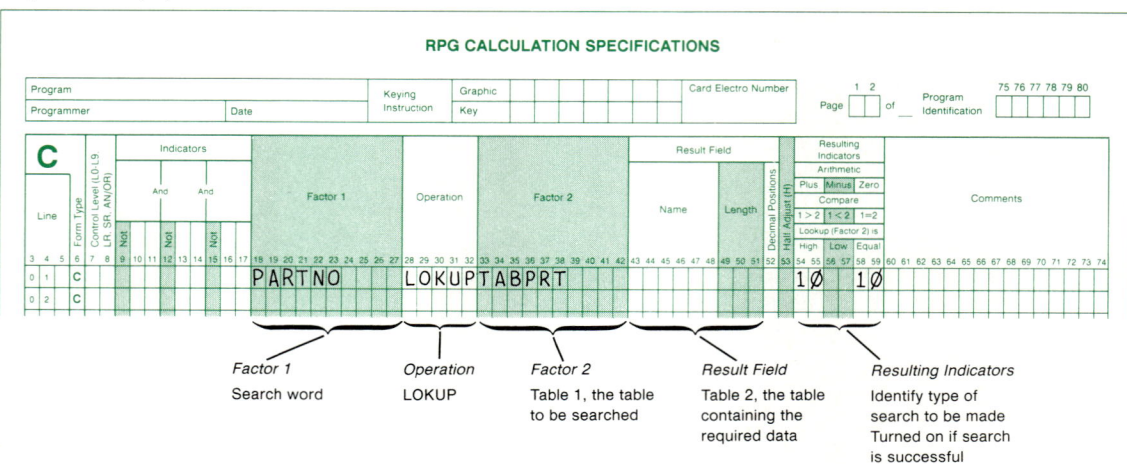

Figure 6.22 Conditioning operations based on table lookup

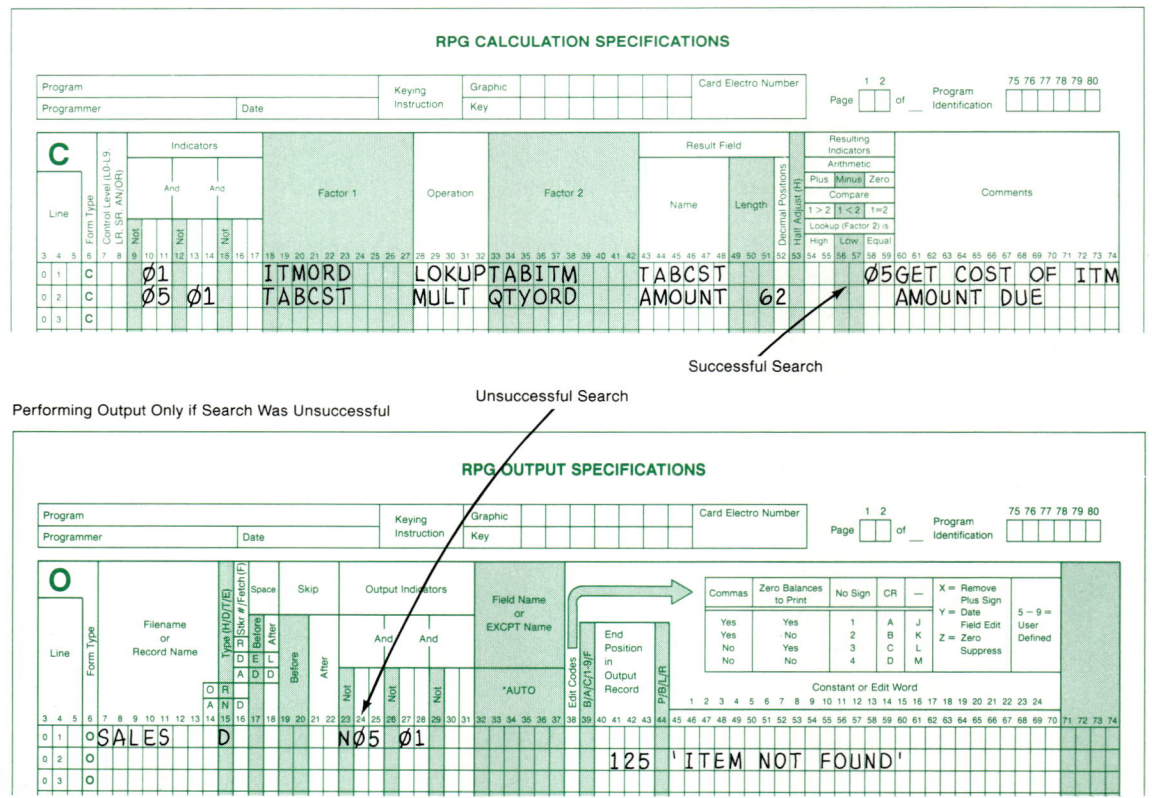

Searching for Low, High, or Equal Conditions

Up to this point, table lookup operations have involved only a search for an equal condition. However, in some cases, it may be necessary to have a search word that is less than or greater than an entry in the table being searched. The table to be searched must be organized in a specified sequence, and a resulting indicator must be used to indicate what condition is to be satisfied for a successful search. To specify that a LOKUP is to retrieve a table element higher (greater) than the search word, a resulting indicator must be entered in positions 54–55 (Lookup High) of the Calculation Specifications form.

A table can also be searched to locate any entry that is lower in value than the search word. In such a case, the table is searched for an entry that is lower (less) than, yet closest in value to, the search word. A search for a low condition is specified in the same way as a search for a high condition, except that the resulting indicator is entered in positions 56–57, rather than 54–55.

In coding a table lookup, either one or two conditions may be specified. A particular search may be considered successful if it satisfies

1. An equal condition only (see Figure 6.23)
2. A high condition only
3. A low condition only
4. Either a high or an equal condition (see Figure 6.24)
5. Either a low or an equal condition (see Figure 6.25)

A search for either a low or a high condition (for the same LOKUP operation) is not specified since the majority of items in the table will satisfy one of the two conditions. The condition(s) to be satisfied can depend on the type of data in the table, the data used as the search word, and the sequence of the data within the table. (See Figure 6.26.)

Figure 6.23 Searching for equal condition

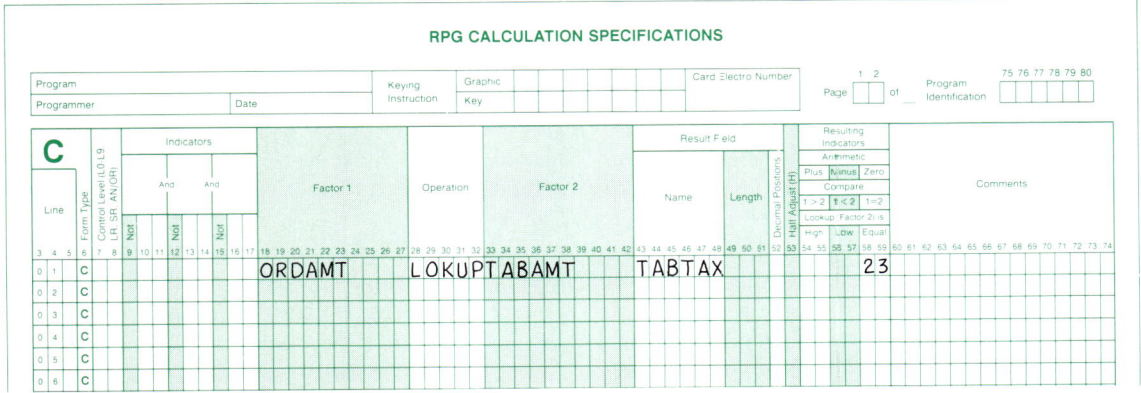

Figure 6.24 Searching for high or equal condition

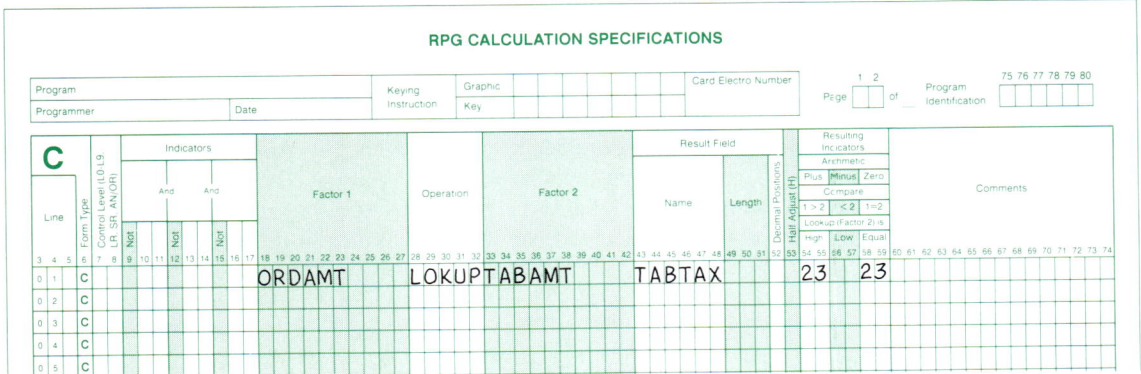

Table Handling

Figure 6.25 Resulting indicators—LOKUP operation code—examples

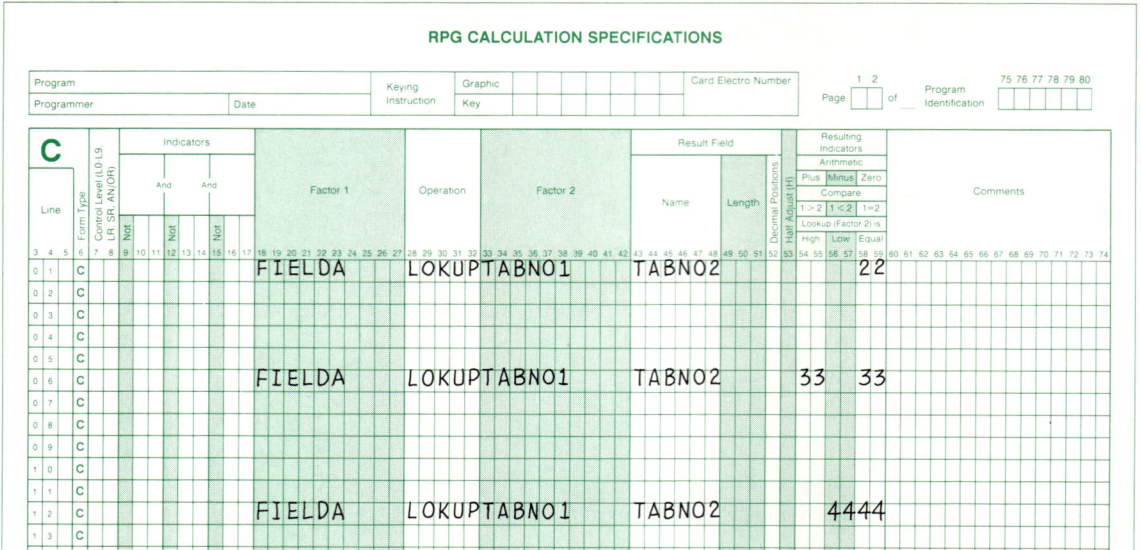

Notes on the Coding

These specifications demonstrate the use of resulting indicators in a lookup operation.

If a table item is found in TABNO1 that is equal to the data item in FIELDA, turn on indicator 22.

When a table item is found in TABNO1 that is equal to or higher than the data item in FIELDA, turn on indicator 33.

When a table item is found in TABNO1 that is equal to or lower than the data item in FIELDA, turn on indicator 44.

Sequence of Tables

A table search for an equal condition only can be performed with the table entries in any order. Starting at the beginning of the table the table elements are checked, one at a time, until an equal entry is found or the end of the table is reached, whichever occurs first.

When searching for high or low conditions, table entries must be in either ascending or descending sequence. This is because the program must select the entry that is higher or lower than, yet closest in value to, the search word. With the table entries in sequence, the program can determine where in the sequence the search word value would appear if it were in the table. (See Figure 6.27.) For example, if table elements 2-4-6-9-11 are in ascending sequence, a search word of 7 naturally comes between elements 6 and 9. Thus, element 6 satisfies the low condition, while element 9 satisfies the high condition (closest in value and yet higher than the search word). Likewise, if the table is in descending sequence 11-9-6-4-2, the search word 7 comes between 9 and 6. Regardless of the sequence (A or D), 9 satisfies the high condition, while 6 satisfies the low condition.

If the table elements are not in sequence (e.g., 2-4-11-9-6), the LOKUP might retrieve the wrong element. Elements are checked one at a time from the beginning of the table. A search word for a low condition would incorrectly retrieve 2 because it is the first element that satisfies the low condition. While the element 6 is actually closer in value to the search word, it would not be made available. Likewise, a search word for a high condition would retrieve the element 11 because it is the first entry encountered after element 4 that is greater than the search word. Element 9, which is closer in value, yet higher than the search word, would not be retrieved since the table is not in sequence.

The sequence of a table is specified by entering an *A* or a *D* under table sequence (positions 45 and 57) on the Extension form. (See Figure 6.28.) When an entry is made in a sequence position, the RPG program will check the table entries to ensure they are in the appropriate order (ascending or descending) when loaded.

Generally, table entries are arranged in ascending order if a sequence is necessary. For certain jobs, however, a descending order is more suitable. For example, if entries with higher values will be

Figure 6.26 Table search and output—example

Output from a Table Lookup

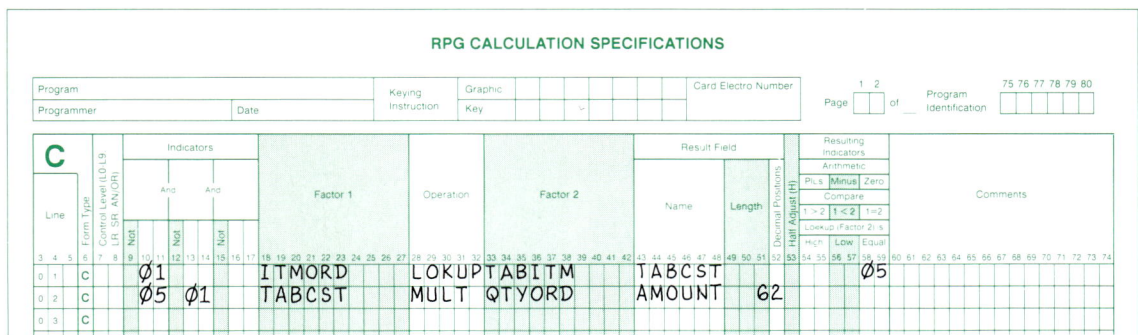

Referencing Looked-up Table Data

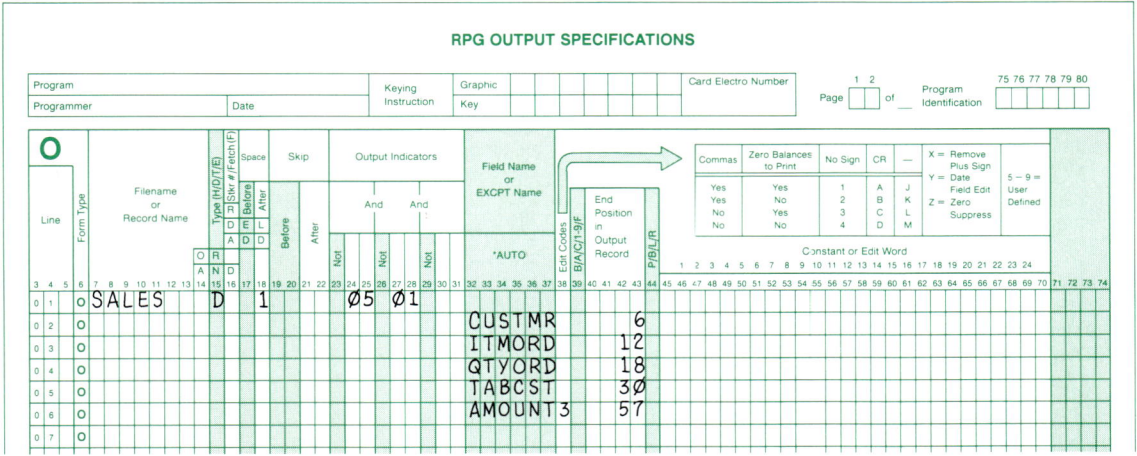

Notes on the Coding

TABITM contains the codes of all items carried in stock.

The related table, TABCST, contains the unit cost for each item.

A SALES file contains the records of customer orders, providing the customer number, code for the item ordered, and the quantity ordered.

The purpose of the job is to calculate the amount each customer owes and to print the information on a report. The report is to contain information from the SALES record (item ordered, quantity ordered), data looked up from TABCST (unit cost), and data from calculations (total amount due).

Table Handling 253

Figure 6.27 Two related tables for determining sales tax—example

TABAMT	TABTAX	TABAMT	TABTAX	TABAMT	TABTAX	TABAMT	TABTAX	TABAMT	TABTAX	TABAMT	TABTAX
.16	.00	16.83	.50	33.49	1.00	50.16	1.50	66.83	2.00	83.49	2.50
.49	.01	17.16	.51	33.83	1.01	50.49	1.51	67.16	2.01	83.83	2.51
.83	.02	17.49	.52	34.16	1.02	50.83	1.52	67.49	2.02	84.16	2.52
1.16	.03	17.83	.53	34.49	1.03	51.16	1.53	67.83	2.03	84.49	2.53
1.49	.04	18.16	.54	34.83	1.04	51.49	1.54	68.16	2.04	84.83	2.54
1.83	.05	18.49	.55	35.16	1.05	51.83	1.55	68.49	2.05	85.16	2.55
2.16	.06	18.83	.56	35.49	1.06	52.16	1.56	68.83	2.06	85.49	2.56
2.49	.07	19.16	.57	35.83	1.07	52.49	1.57	69.16	2.07	86.83	2.57
2.83	.08	19.49	.58	36.16	1.08	52.83	1.58	69.49	2.08	87.16	2.58
3.16	.09	19.83	.59	36.49	1.09	53.16	1.59	69.83	2.09	87.49	2.59
3.49	.10	20.16	.60	36.83	1.10	53.49	1.60	70.16	2.10	87.83	2.60
3.83	.11	20.49	.61	37.16	1.11	53.83	1.61	70.49	2.11	88.16	2.61
4.16	.12	20.83	.62	37.49	1.12	54.16	1.62	70.83	2.12	88.49	2.62
4.49	.13	21.16	.63	37.83	1.13	54.49	1.63	71.16	2.13	88.83	2.63
4.83	.14	21.49	.64	38.16	1.14	54.83	1.64	71.49	2.14	89.16	2.64
5.16	.15	21.83	.65	38.49	1.15	55.16	1.65	71.83	2.15	89.49	2.65
5.49	.16	22.16	.66	38.83	1.16	55.49	1.66	72.16	2.16	89.83	2.66
5.83	.17	22.49	.67	39.16	1.17	55.83	1.67	72.49	2.17	90.16	2.67
6.16	.18	22.83	.68	39.49	1.18	56.16	1.68	72.83	2.18	90.49	2.68
6.49	.19	23.16	.69	39.83	1.19	56.49	1.69	73.16	2.19	90.83	2.69
6.83	.20	23.49	.70	40.16	1.20	56.83	1.70	73.49	2.20	91.16	2.70
7.16	.21	23.83	.71	40.49	1.21	57.16	1.71	73.83	2.21	91.49	2.71
7.49	.22	24.16	.72	40.83	1.22	57.49	1.72	74.16	2.22	91.83	2.72
7.83	.23	24.49	.73	41.16	1.23	57.83	1.73	74.49	2.23	92.16	2.73
8.16	.24	24.83	.74	41.49	1.24	58.16	1.74	74.83	2.24	92.49	2.74
8.49	.25	25.16	.75	41.83	1.25	58.49	1.75	75.16	2.25	92.83	2.75
8.83	.26	25.49	.76	42.16	1.26	58.83	1.76	75.49	2.26	93.16	2.76
9.16	.27	25.83	.77	42.49	1.27	59.16	1.77	75.83	2.27	93.49	2.77
9.49	.28	26.16	.78	42.83	1.28	59.49	1.78	76.16	2.28	93.83	2.78
9.83	.29	26.49	.79	43.16	1.29	59.83	1.79	76.49	2.29	94.16	2.79
10.16	.30	26.83	.80	43.49	1.30	60.16	1.80	76.83	2.30	94.49	2.80
10.49	.31	27.16	.81	43.83	1.31	60.49	1.81	77.16	2.31	94.83	2.81
10.83	.32	27.49	.82	44.16	1.32	60.83	1.82	77.49	2.32	95.16	2.82
11.16	.33	27.83	.83	44.49	1.33	61.16	1.83	77.83	2.33	95.49	2.83
11.49	.34	28.16	.84	44.83	1.34	61.49	1.84	78.16	2.34	94.83	2.84
11.83	.35	28.49	.85	45.16	1.35	61.83	1.85	78.49	2.35	95.16	2.85
12.16	.36	28.83	.86	45.49	1.36	62.16	1.86	78.83	2.36	95.49	2.86
12.49	.37	29.16	.87	45.83	1.37	62.49	1.87	79.16	2.37	95.83	2.87
12.83	.38	29.49	.88	46.16	1.38	62.83	1.88	79.49	2.38	96.16	2.88
13.16	.39	29.83	.89	46.49	1.39	63.16	1.89	79.83	2.39	96.49	2.89
13.49	.40	30.16	.90	46.83	1.40	63.49	1.90	80.16	2.40	96.83	2.90
13.83	.41	30.49	.91	47.16	1.41	63.83	1.91	80.49	2.41	97.16	2.91
14.16	.42	30.83	.92	47.49	1.42	64.16	1.92	80.83	2.42	97.49	2.92
14.49	.43	31.16	.93	47.83	1.43	64.49	1.93	81.16	2.43	97.83	2.93
14.83	.44	31.49	.94	48.16	1.44	64.83	1.94	81.49	2.44	98.16	2.94
15.16	.45	31.83	.95	48.49	1.45	65.16	1.95	81.83	2.45	98.49	2.95
15.49	.46	32.16	.96	48.83	1.46	65.49	1.96	82.16	2.46	98.83	2.96
15.83	.47	32.49	.97	49.16	1.47	65.83	1.97	82.49	2.47	99.16	2.97
16.16	.48	32.83	.98	49.49	1.48	66.16	1.98	82.83	2.48	99.49	2.98
16.49	.49	33.16	.99	49.83	1.49	66.49	1.99	83.16	2.49	99.83	2.99
										100.16	3.00

referenced more often than entries with lower values, the amount of time required to search a table will be decreased by placing such entries at the beginning of the table (highest to lowest). Table entries to be in descending order are designated by entering a *D* in positions 45 and 57 rather than an *A*.

The fact that a table is to be in sequence can affect the design of the table-input record. In general, table-input records containing one entry per record (or a pair of entries if alternating format is used) are most desirable for sequence tables. In this way, when a sequenced table is to be updated with additions or deletions, the changed records can simply be inserted or removed.

Moving Data in a Table Entry

Suppose it is necessary to use a table to look up data from a related table. One table contains codes for all items carried in stock, while another table contains information about each of the items.

Figure 6.28 Specifying sequence of table entries

Line	Form Type		Table or Array Name	Number of Entries Per Record	Number of Entries Per Table or Array	Length of Entry	P/B/L/R	Decimal Positions	Sequence (A/D)	Table or Array Name (Alternating Format)	Length of Entry	P/B/L/R	Decimal Positions	Sequence (A/D)	Comments
01	E		TABAMT	1	301	5		2	A	TABTAX	3		2	A	
02	E														
03	E														
04	E														
05	E														
06	E														
07	E														

A table entry may contain more than one field of information. For example, each entry in TAB123 contains a fifteen-character item description, followed by a four-digit unit cost with two decimal positions, and a three-digit quantity in stock. A pair of related tables would be TABCOD, which contains a four-digit item number used for lookup, and TAB123, which contains information about each item.

Following a successful search, the entire looked-up entry may be used in calculations and output by merely specifying the table name. If the table name TAB123 is specified on the Output Specifications form, the description, cost, and quantity will all be output without any intervening spaces between fields of the item. The data items will be run together, just as they appear in the table entry.

If a table entry contains several fields of data, only part of the table entry may be needed for a particular job. For example, to do a billing operation, only the item description and cost from TAB123 may be needed. To reference only part of an entry, the data in TAB123 entry must be separated after a successful search. This is done by moving data from TAB123 into smaller, separate fields, which can then be used in calculations and output. (See Figure 6.29.)

Modifying the Content of a Table

At some point the programmer may wish to make changes in the data contained in a table. These changes may be temporary, for a particular run; or they may be permanent, so that every time a job is run that references that table, the program uses the changed table data.

Making Temporary Changes to Table Data

Temporary changes to the entries in a table can be made by way of calculation specifications that are actually a part of the RPG program. For example, two tables provides the item code and unit price for each part. If the price of a part is changed for a particular run, the programmer must necessarily change the entry for that part in the unit price table.

On a successful search, the unit price for that part is made available from the corresponding entry in the unit price table. This information is available for the table under result field.

By using the name of the table referenced in the result field of a LOKUP in any operation other than LOKUP, the programmer is actually referring to the table entry last looked up.

The use of a table name as the result field of a calculation operation is one means of modifying the content of that table. (See Figure 6.30.) Since the changes are indicated by specification entries, they must be planned while the programmer is still writing the RPG specifications. Otherwise, the instructions could not become part of the object program.

It is important to note that any changes made to a table during execution of the program are changes that will exist for that run only unless additional specifications are made that indicate a permanent change. Thus, the next time the program is run, the original data will be used. (See Figure 6.31.)

Figure 6.29 Isolating parts of table entries—examples

Table Entries of More Than One Data Field

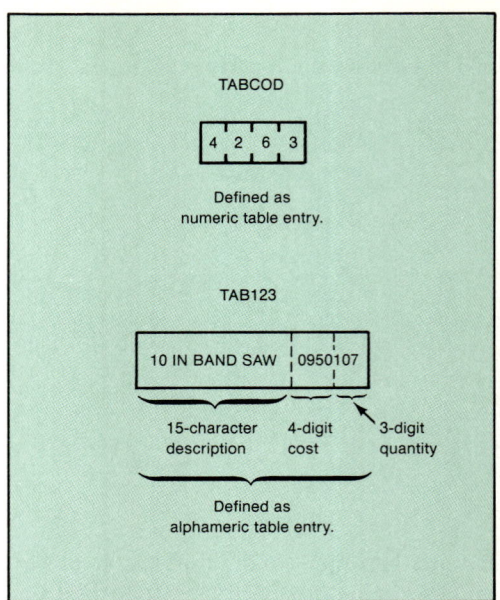

Isolating Part of a Table Entry

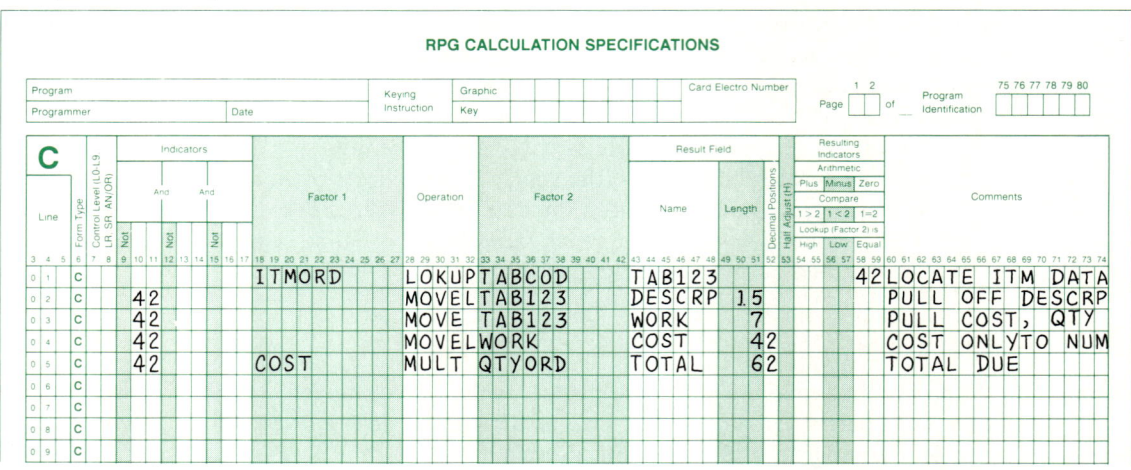

Figure 6.30 Modifying a table temporarily

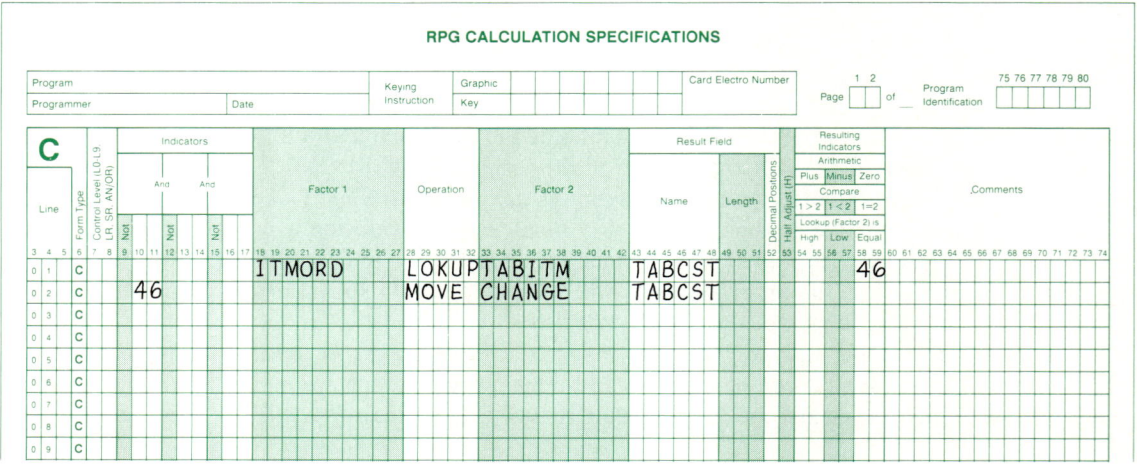

Figure 6.31 Changing table data during calculations

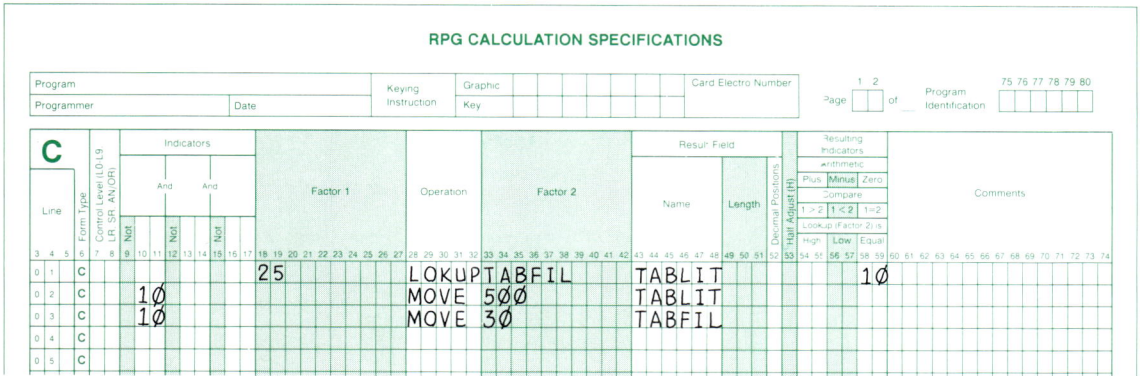

Notes on the Coding

All elements in TABFIL, which contains 25, are to be changed to 30.

The corresponding elements in TABLIT are to be changed to 500.

The search word is the constant 25.

On each program cycle, when a match is found in the table TABFIL, the entry from TABFIL and its corresponding entry in TABLIT become available for change.

The number 500 is then moved into the TABLIT element and the number 30 is moved into TABFIL.

Making Permanent Changes to Table Data

Whether the content of a table must be permanently changed generally depends on the type of data contained in the table. For example, a table used to keep inventory records will undoubtedly change quite often. Assume that a company uses a table to hold the quantity on hand for each part manufactured. Every time the company manufactures more of a particular part or sells (and delivers) a part, the quantity on hand for that part must be increased or decreased accordingly.

The only way to make a permanent change to the data in a table is to change the table-input records. If the data is changed as a result of calculation specifications performed during a run, the changed data can be output. In this way, the output can be used as table-input records for the next run.

Short Tables for Adding New Table Entries

Rather than change data already stored in a table, the programmer may wish instead to add additional data to an existing table. For example, assume that a company wants to keep a list of employee numbers and hourly wages in two tables. At the present time, there are 46 employees on the company payroll; thus, there will be 46 entries in each table. However, it is known that the number of employees may increase to somewhere between 90 and 100. Therefore, it will be necessary to add entries to the table as new employees are hired.

At the time the table-input records are set up, the programmer must describe them on the Extension form. This means that the number of entries per table must be specified. If only 46 entries per table are specified, it will be necessary to code new extension specifications every time the number of table entries changes. Since the extension specifications are compiled and become part of the object program, it will be necessary to recompile the program to make such a change.

If it is known beforehand that the size of the table will increase, a short table can initially be built. In a short table, only some of the table entries contain actual table data. The program fills the unused entries with blanks. The storage required for the unused table entries will not be available to hold any other data. (See Figure 6.32.)

As new employees are hired, the new table entries can be added by inserting additional table input records. The original extension specifications will correctly describe the table. These specifications merely indicate the maximum number of entries allowed for each table. (See Figure 6.33.)

Whether the RPG source program and the table-input records must be recompiled depends on which method was originally selected for loading the table.

Figure 6.32 Adding entries to a short table

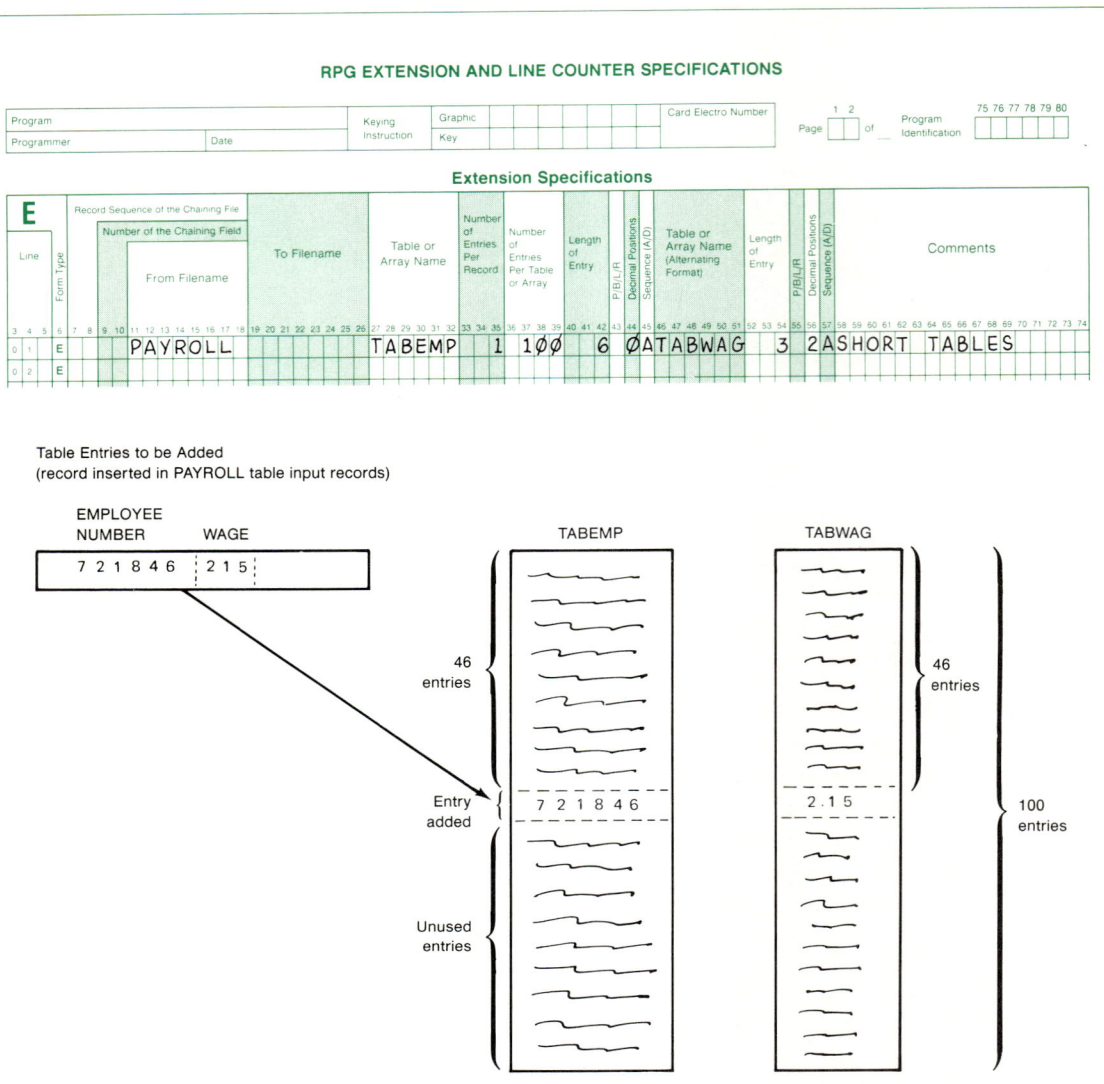

Output of an Entire Table

For various reasons, the programmer may want output of an entire table. Perhaps a listing of the table entries is needed to determine if any changes should be made. If the program updates a table, the programmer may wish to output all the entries to be used as table input the next time the program is run.

An entire table can be output only at the end of the job, that is, after all other output has been completed (LR on). Even if the table is a short table, all entries are put out, including those that are unused (containing blanks or zeros).

It is easy to specify that an entire table be output at the end of a job. Just as for any type of output, the output file must be given a name and assigned to an output device on the File Description Specifications form. However, no output specifications are necessary for end-of-job table output. Merely specify the name of the output file in the To file name (positions 19–26) of the Extension form on the same line as the description of the table-input records. The table will be put out automatically at the end of the job in the same format as the table-input records, that is, one output record per table-input record. (See Figure 6.34.) For this reason, the table output may be difficult to read if one entry runs into another on the input record.

Figure 6.33 Adding table entries to a short table—example

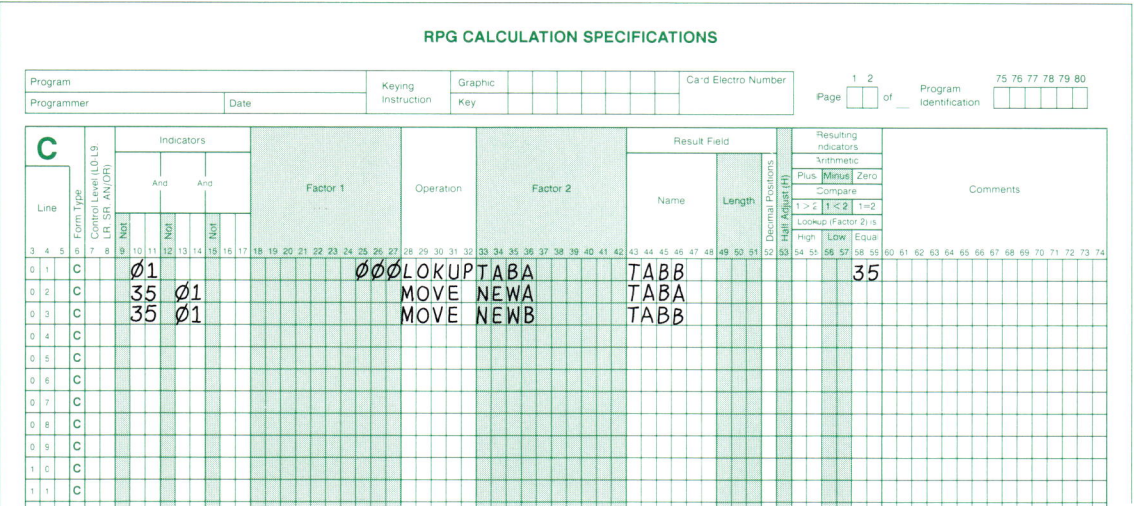

Notes on the Coding

The LOKUP operation is conditioned by indicator 01. Indicator 01 is on when a record is read containing information in the fields NEWA and NEWB. These fields are to be added to the short tables TABA and TABB respectively.

To get the entry in the correct place in the table, a search is made to find the first empty entry. Unfilled entries are filled with zeros. Thus, the search word used is 000.

When the first 000 entry is found (indicator 35 turns on), NEWA and NEWB become part of the related tables TABA and TABB. These entries are temporary unless they are written on table records.

Figure 6.34 Specifications for output of entire table at end of job

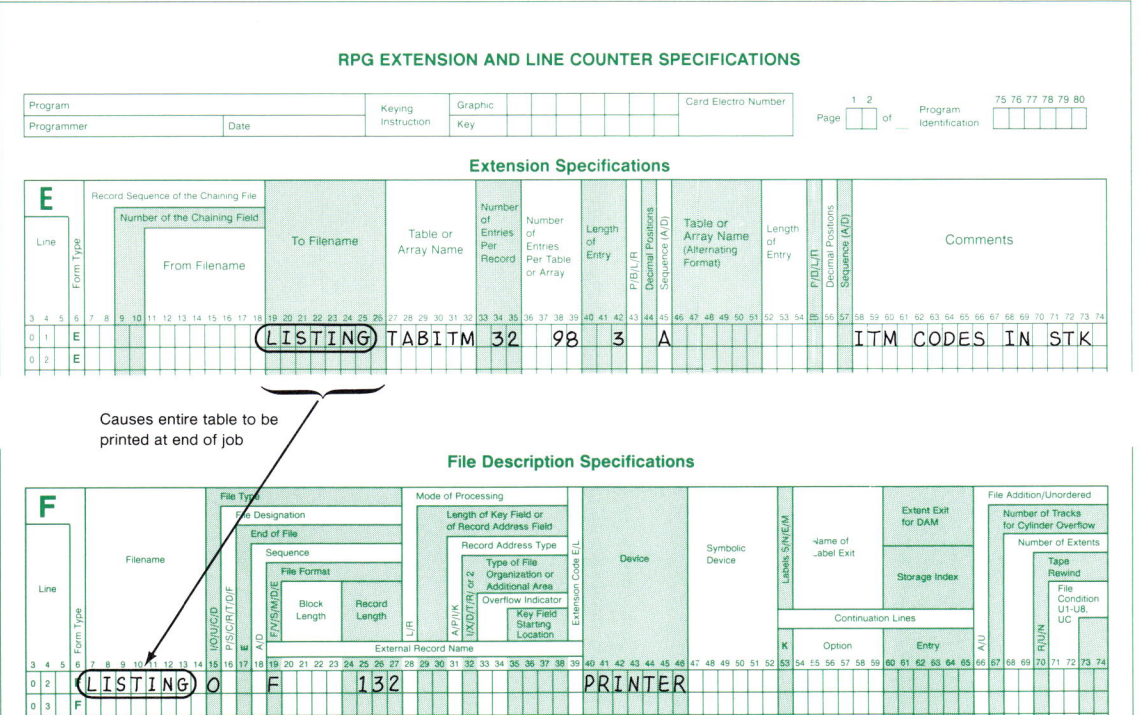

Table Handling 259

Although the format of the output and input records will be the same, the output data may not be exactly the same as the input data. This is because table entries are put out as they are at the end of a job. Thus, if the program has changed or updated any table entries, the modified data will be put out, not the original data. (See Figures 6.35, 6.36, and 6.37.)

Figure 6.35 Operations using tables—examples

Line	Form Type	Control Level	Not	Ind1	Not	Ind2	Not	Ind3	Factor 1	Operation	Factor 2	Result Name	Length	Dec	H	Hi	Lo	Eq	Comments
01	0C								STKNO	LOKUP	TABSN	TABCST				10			FIND COST
02	0C			10					TABCST	MULT	QTY	EXTCST	62	H					EXTEND COST×QTY
03	0C			10					EXTCST	LOKUP	TABAMT	TABPCT				11		11	FIND DISCT PCT
04	0C			21						MOVE	TABPCT	DISPCT	22						SAVE DISCT PCT
05	0C*																		
06	0C								CUSTNO	LOKUP	TABCUS	TABKEY				15			FIND CUSFIL KEY
07	0C		N	15						EXCPT									INVALID CUSTNO
08	0C			15					TABKEY	CHAIN	CUSFIL								GET CUST RECORD
09	0C*																		
10	0C								9999	LOKUP	TABCUS	TABKEY				20			FIND EMPTY NTRY
11	0C			20						Z-ADD	NEWCUS	TABCUS							ADD NEWCUS
12	0C			20						MOVE	CUSKEY	TABKEY							ADD NEW TABKEY
13	0C								400000	LOKUP	TABAMT	TABPCT				19		19	FIND COST AMT
14	0C			19						Z-ADD	390000	TABAMT							REPL COST AMT
15	0C			19						MOVE	NEWPCT	TABPCT							REPL PCT
16	0C*																		
17	0C								OLDCUS	LOKUP	TABCUS					30			FIND CUST
18	0C			30						MOVE	9999	TABCUS							DELETE CUST
19	0C		N	30						EXCPT									INVALID CUSTNO
20	C																		

Figure 6.35 continued

Notes on the Coding

Line   Meaning

010   Stock number (STKNO) is used in an equal search of an argument table of stock numbers (TABSN) to retrieve an item cost from the function table TABCST. Indicator 10 is set on when the search is successful.

020   The item cost from the function table holding area is multiplied by QTY to give an extended cost (EXTCST).

030   EXTCST is used as the argument in a high or equal search of an argument table (TABAMT) to find a discount percentage in a function table (TABPCT).

040   The entry in the TABPCT holding area is moved to a field (DISPCT) for later use.

060   A customer number (CUSTNO) is the argument in an equal search of a customer table (TABCUS) to find the key to the customer's record in a function table (TABKEY). If found, indicator 15 is set on; if not found, indicator 15 is set off.

070   If the customer filekey is not found (N15), an exception record is output.

080   If it is found, the entry in the TABKEY holding area is used in a CHAIN operation to get the customer record from an indexed sequential file (CUSFIL). (The CHAIN operation and indexed sequential file are explained later in the text.)

100   The numeric literal 9999 is used in searching for an empty entry position in TABCUS and TABKEY.

110   A new customer number (NEWCUS) replaces the dummy entry in TABCUS.

120   A customer key (CUSKEY) replaces the dummy entry in TABKEY.

130   A numeric literal 400000 (representing $4000.00) is used as the argument in a high or equal search of TABAMT and the associated function table TABPCT.

140   A numeric literal 390000 (representing $3900.00) replaces the cost amount limit in the TABAMT holding area.

150   A new percentage field (NEWPCT) replaces the percentage in the TABPCT holding area.

170   An old customer is used in an equal search of TABCUS. If it is found, indicator 30 is set on; if it is not found, indicator 30 is set off.

180   If the number was found, a numeric literal 9999 (a dummy padding entry) replaces the old customer number in the TABCUS holding area.

190   If the number was not found (N30) an exception record is output.

NOTE: Whenever a value is placed in a table holding area, the same value also replaces the corresponding specific entry in that table.

Figure 6.36 Payroll specifications—table example

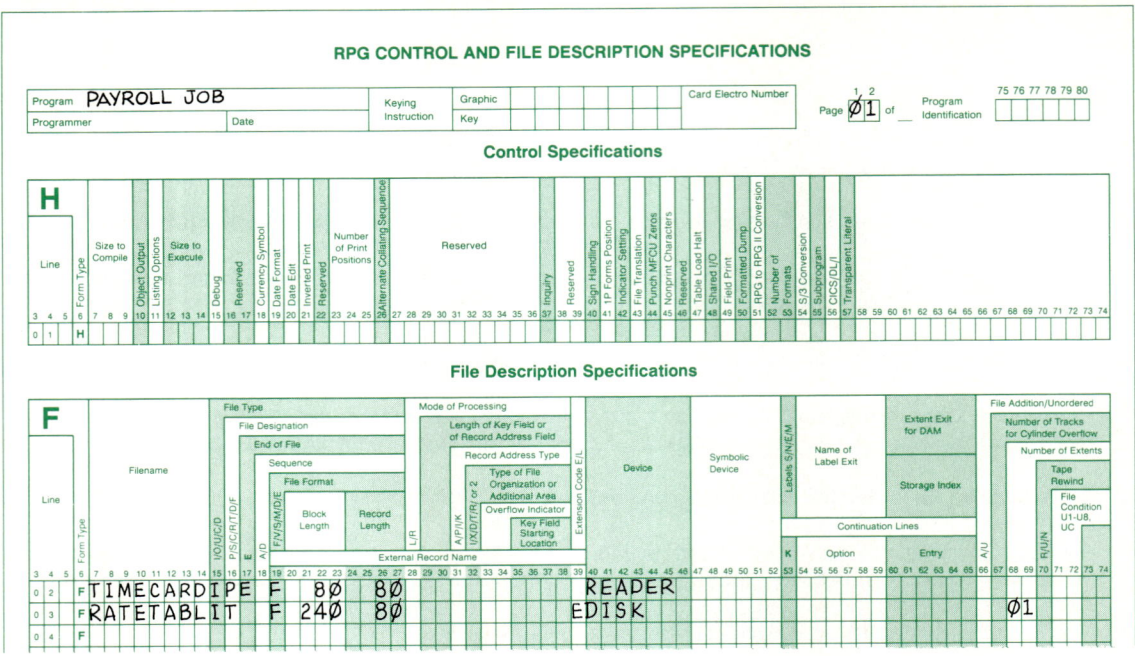

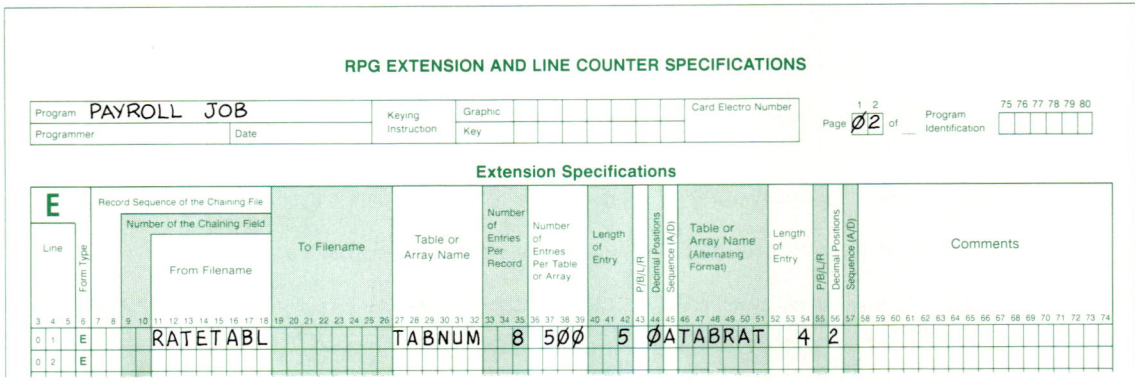

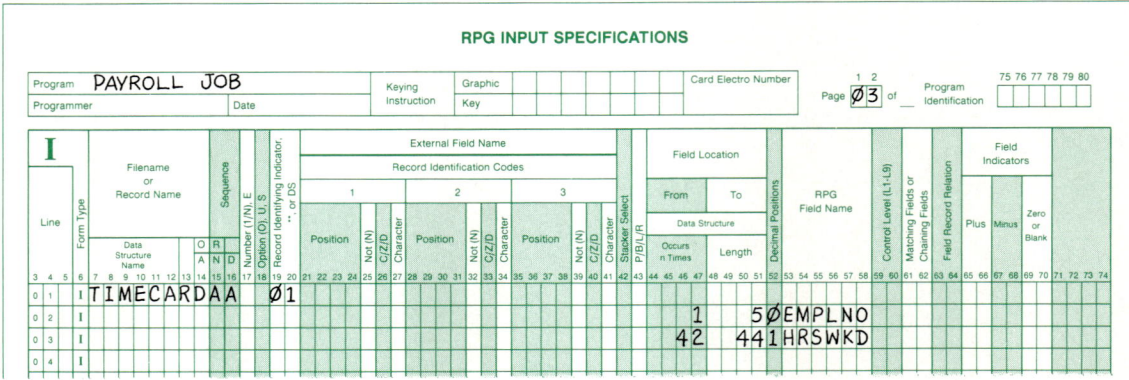

Figure 6.36 continued

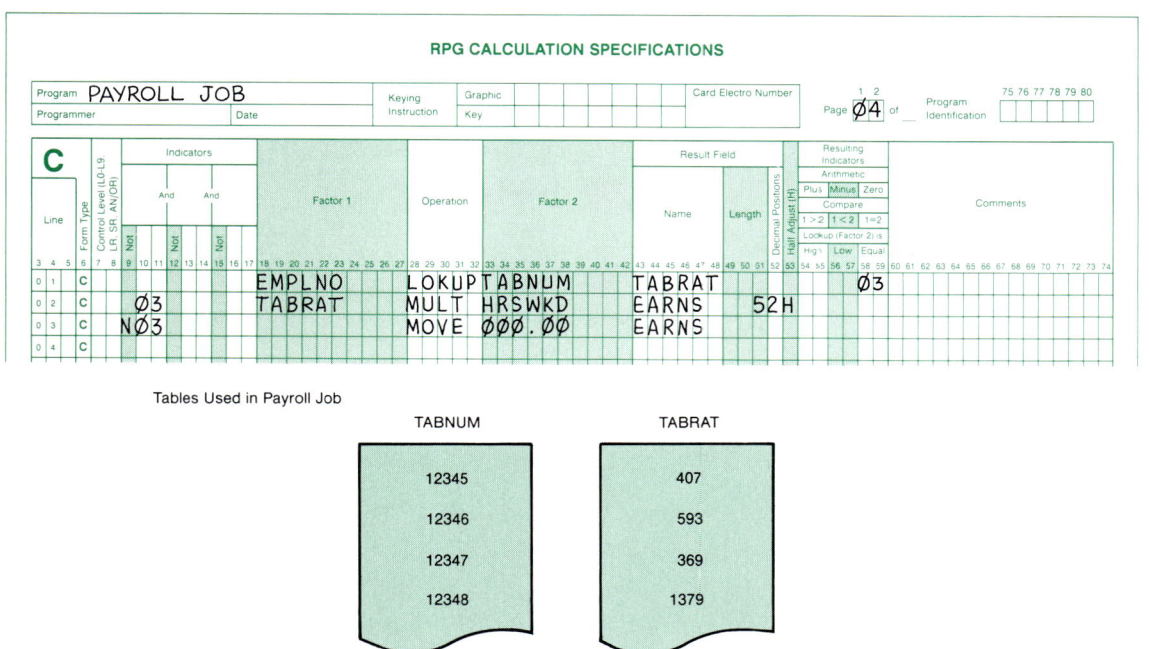

Tables Used in Payroll Job

Example of Using Tables

A payroll job requires two related tables. TABNUM is the search table, containing employee numbers. TABRAT is the related table, containing employee salary rates. After an employee's rate has been found, the rate is multiplied by the number of hours worked. The result is the amount earned.

The table entries are organized in alternating format on the input records. On line 01 of the Extension form, the table searched is called TABNUM. There are eight entries in each input record and 500 entries in the table. Each table entry is five positions long and contains no decimal positions. The table is in ascending sequence. The related table is called TABRAT. Each entry is four positions long and contains two decimal positions.

Line 01 of the Calculation form causes the employee number (EMPNUM) to be used as the search word for the data contained in TABNUM (the search table). Indicator 03 is turned on when the program finds an entry in TABNUM that is equal to the search word.

Line 02 of the Calculation form is performed when indicator 03 is on. The rate for the employee, taken from the related table TABRAT, is multiplied by the number of hours worked (HRSWKD). The result is stored in the field EARNS, which is five positions with two decimal positions. The result is half-adjusted.

When the search word does not find an equal entry in TABNUM (indicator 03 is not on), line 03 is performed. The literal 000.00 is then moved to the field EARNS, indicating that the employee does not have an entry in the table.

Table Handling

Figure 6.37 Table lookup—example

Problem

Print a list of items as ordered by customers. The list is to look like the sample report. One set of table data contains fifty item number entries, one for each item that is for sale. A second set of table data contains fifty corresponding cost entries. Here is a partial list of table data from both of them.

Table of Items	Table of Costs
12354	2.50
22615	7.79
74002	9.85
33675	.25

Input records contain the item number and the quantity sold. In order to print the report, it is necessary to look up the unit price for the item and then multiply by the quantity to find out the amount of the sale.

Report

```
                        SALES

  ITEM NUMBER    QUANTITY    UNIT PRICE    SALE PRICE

     22615         100          7.79         799.00
     33675          50           .25          12.50
     12354         740          2.50        1,850.00
```

When table data is used to solve a problem, we need to describe the table or tables being used and to describe any calculations and/or output associated with this data. Tables are described on an Extension Specifications sheet. A table lookup operation (LOKUP) is used on the Calculation sheet to search one table in order to find a corresponding table value in the order. After a desired value is found, it may be used for additional calculations and/or output.

Figure 6.37 continued

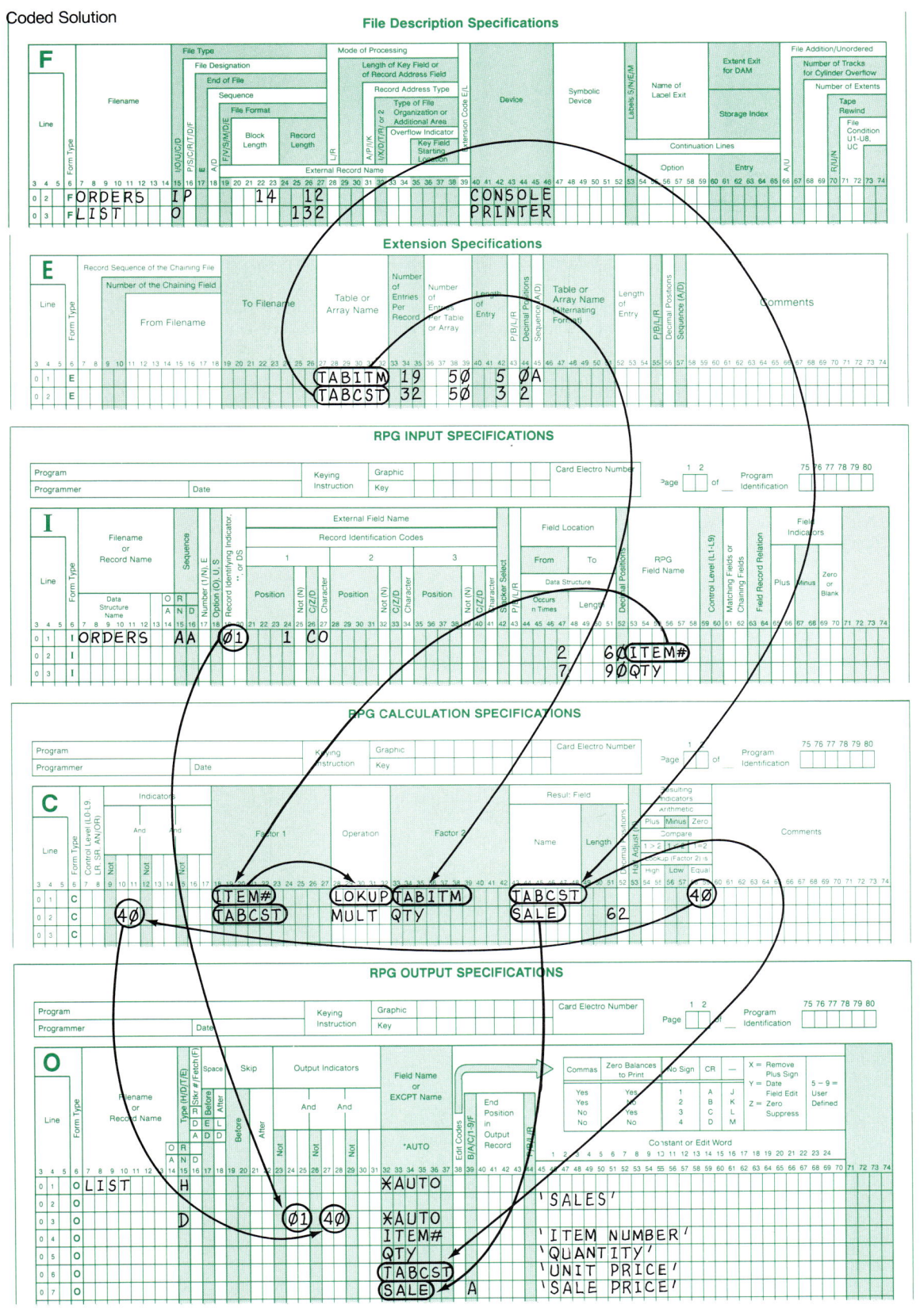

Table Handling 265

Figure 6.37 continued

Notes on the Coding

File Description: Two files are described.

Extension: Two tables (TABITM and TABCST) are described.

Input: The keyed record and its fields (ITEM# and QTY) are described.

Calculation: Use an input field (ITEM#) as factor 1, specify the table lookup operation (LOKUP), the table to be searched (TABITM) as factor 2, the table containing corresponding unit prices (TABCST) as the result field, and assign an unused indicator for the desired search condition.

In our example, we are searching for an equal condition, so indicator 40 was assigned positions 58 and 59.

The second calculation (multiply unit price by number of items) is to be done when a desired table entry is found, so it is controlled by indicator 40. The cost value in the corresponding table (TABCST) is multiplied by the quantity (QTY) to determine the sales price (SALE) of the item we keyed as input (ITEM#).

Output: Four fields are to be printed when the unit price is found for the keyed item.

NOTE: *Auto Report:* A function of the RPG program that simplifies the defining of formats for printed reports and allows the inclusion of previously written statements in new programs. Auto report uses simplified specifications and standard RPG specifications to generate a complete RPG source program.

Auto report includes the function *AUTO to simplify the use of report page headings, column headings, positioning of data fields from left to right, and certain calculations for the accumulation of totals.

*AUTO is available as a special feature on most compilers.

Illustrative Program

Alternating Tables—Table Lookup: Tax Deduction Report

Job Definition
Print a report listing the name of the taxpayer with the proper tax deduction based on the table for miles driven during the year.

Input
A record is entered for each taxpayer with the following information:

Positions	Field Designation
1–09	Social security number
10–29	Name
36–41	Mileage driven

Processing
Set up a compile time table for the tax deductions based on the following information:

State Gasoline Tax Table

Nonbusiness Miles Driven	Tax Rate (in dollars)
Under 3,000	12
3,000–3,499	19
3,500–3,999	22
4,000–4,499	25
4,500–4,999	28
5,000–5,499	30
5,500–5,999	33
6,000–6,499	36
6,500–6,999	39
7,000–7,499	42
7,500–7,999	45
8,000–8,499	48
8,500–8,999	51
9,000–9,499	53
9,500–9,999	56
10,000–10,999	61
11,000–11,999	67
12,000–12,999	72
13,000–13,999	78
14,000–14,999	84
15,000–15,999	90
16,000–16,999	95
17,000–17,999	101
18,000–18,999	107
19,000–19,999	113
20,000 miles*	116

*For over 20,000 miles, use table amounts for total miles driven. (For example, for 25,000 miles, add the deduction for 5,000 miles to the deduction for 20,000 miles.)

Using the table above, determine the tax deduction for the number of miles driven.
Perform a table lookup to determine the tax deduction based on the number of miles driven.

Output
This Printer Spacing Chart shows how the report is formatted:

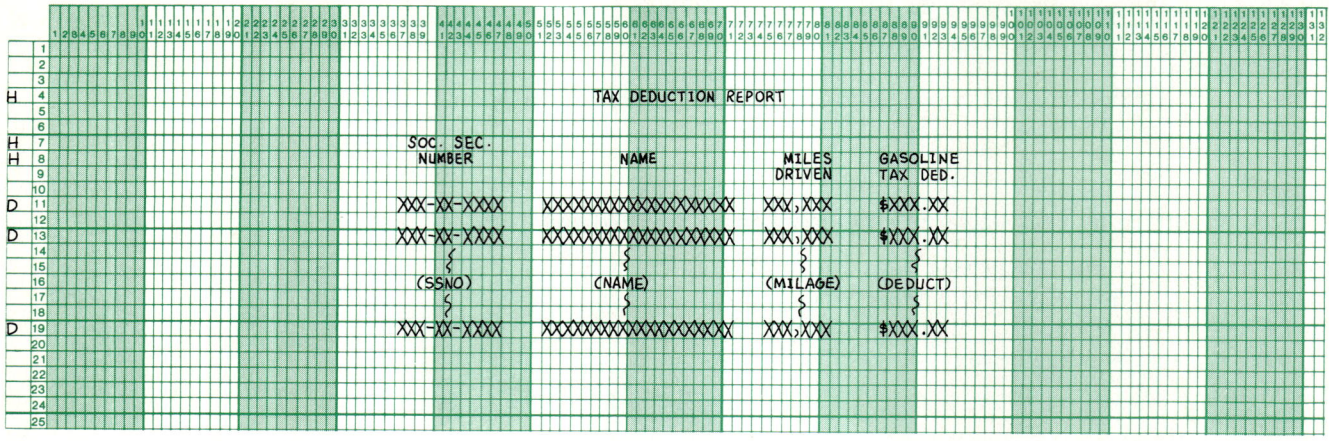

Coding sheets for Tax Deduction Report:

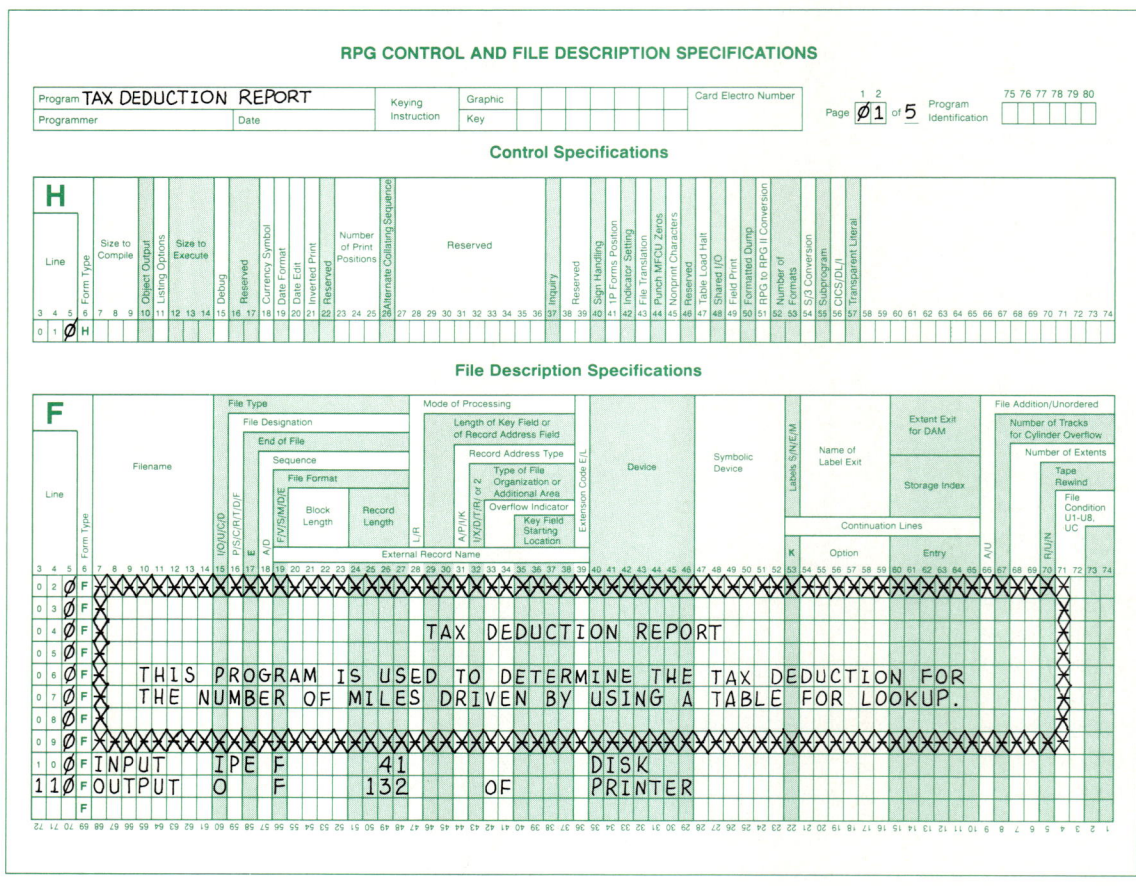

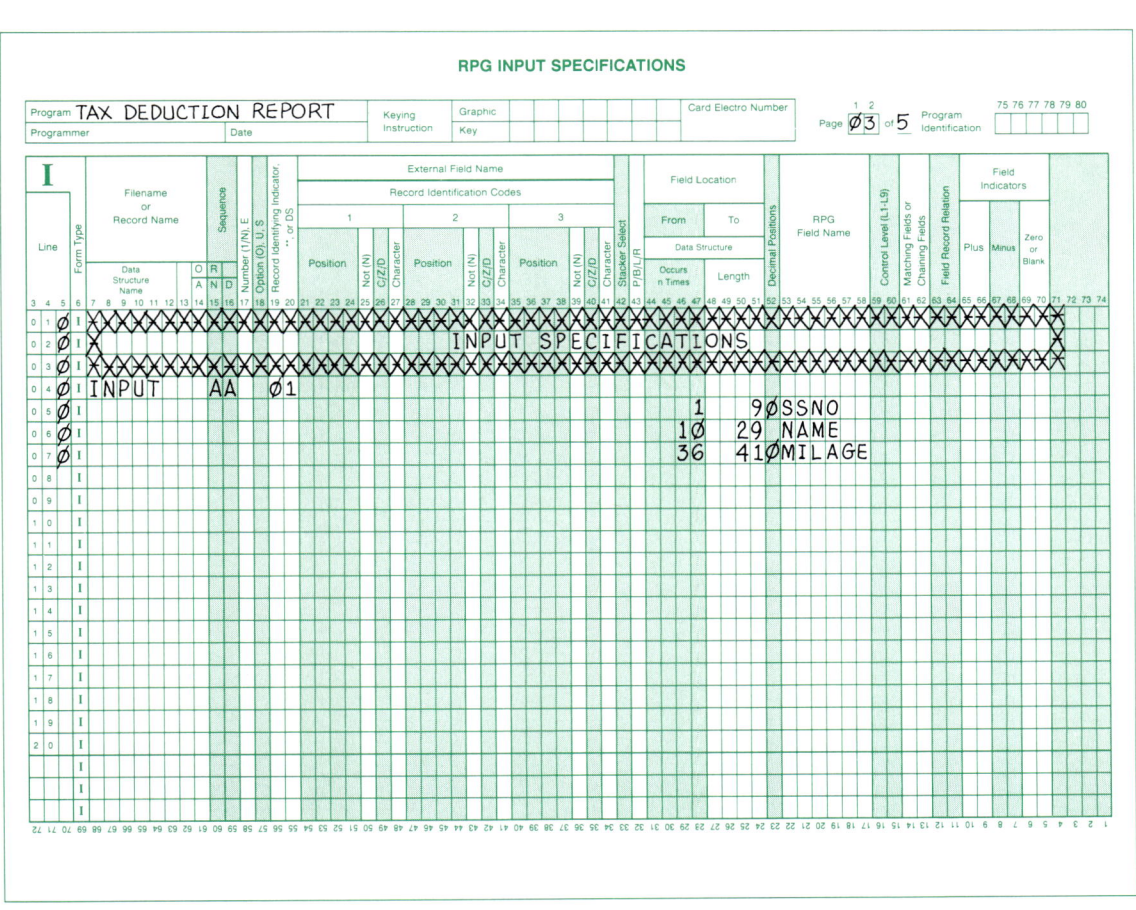

Table Handling 269

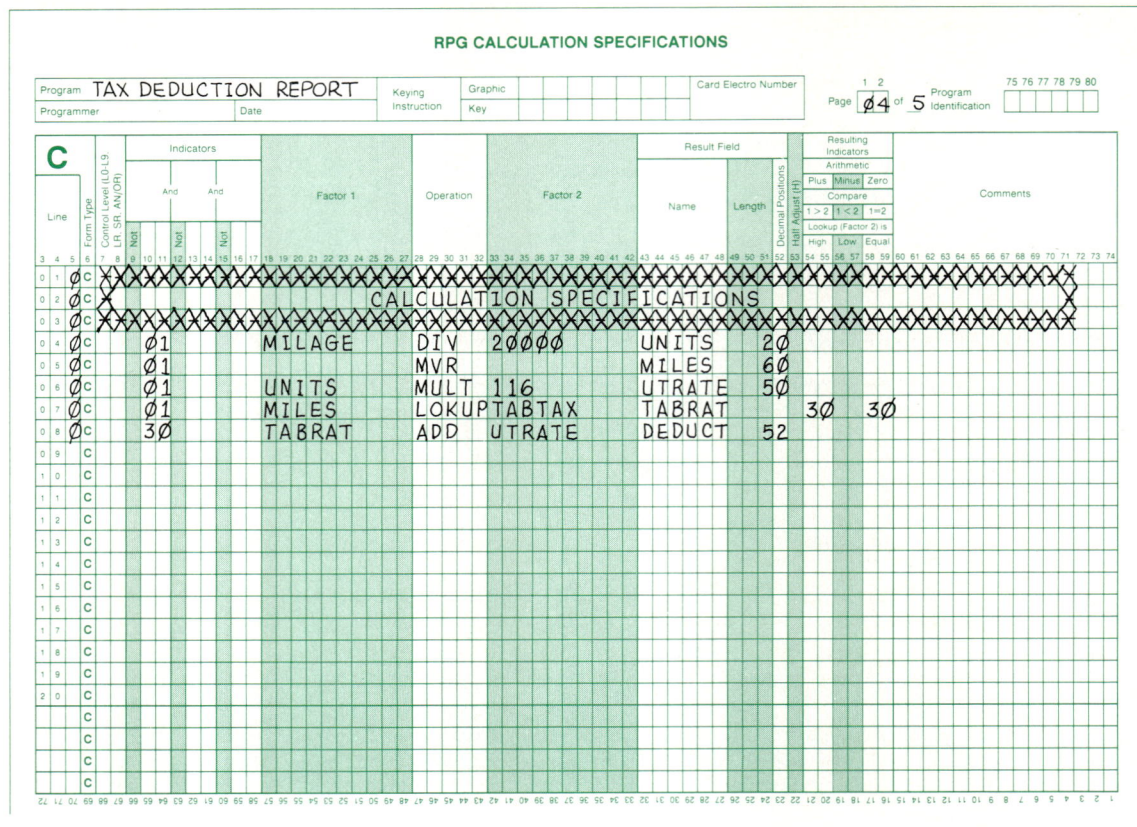

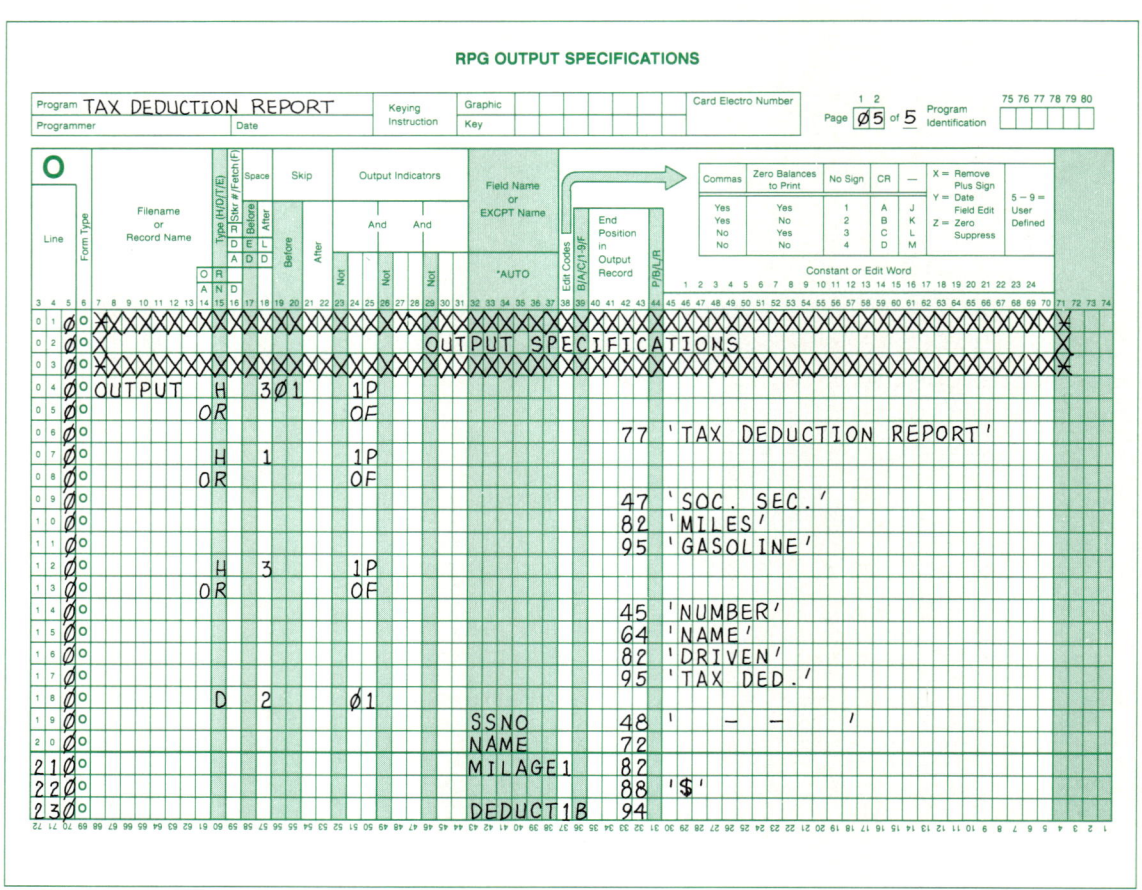

The source listing is as follows:

```
 1     01010H
 2   * 01020F***********************************************************
 3   * 01030F*                                                         *
 4   * 01040F*              TAX DEDUCTION REPORT                       *
 5   * 01050F*                                                         *
 6   * 01060F*  THIS PROGRAM IS USED TO DETERMINE THE TAX DEDUCTION FOR*
 7   * 01070F*  THE NUMBER OF MILES DRIVEN BY USING A TABLE FOR LOOKUP.*
 8   * 01080F*                                                         *
 9   * 01090F***********************************************************
10     01100FINPUT   IPE F      41           DISK
11     01110FOUTPUT  O   F     132     OF    PRINTER
12   * 02010E***********************************************************
13   * 02020E*                EXTENSION SPECIFICATIONS                 *
14   * 02030E***********************************************************
15     02040E              TABTAX  1  26   6 0ATABRAT      3 0A
16   * 03010I***********************************************************
17   * 03020I*                  INPUT SPECIFICATIONS                   *
18   * 03030I***********************************************************
19     03040IINPUT    AA 01
20     03050I                                        1   90SSNO
21     03060I                                       10   29 NAME
22     03070I                                       36   410MILAGE
23   * 04010C***********************************************************
24   * 04020C*                CALCULATION SPECIFICATIONS                *
25   * 04030C***********************************************************
26     04040C    01      MILAGE    DIV  20000    UNITS    20
27     04050C    01                MVR           MILES    60
28     04060C    01      UNITS     MULT 116      UTRATE   50
29     04070C    01      MILES     LOKUPTABTAX   TABRAT       30 30
30     04080C    30      TABRAT    ADD  UTRATE   DEDUCT   52
31   * 05010O***********************************************************
32   * 05020O*                 OUTPUT SPECIFICATIONS                   *
33   * 05030O***********************************************************
34     05040OOUTPUT   H  301   1P
35     050500         OR        OF
36     050600                                  77 'TAX DEDUCTION REPORT'
37     050700         H   1    1P
38     050800         OR        OF
39     050900                                  47 'SOC. SEC.'
40     051000                                  82 'MILES'
41     051100                                  95 'GASOLINE'
42     051200         H   3    1P
43     051300         OR        OF
44     051400                                  45 'NUMBER'
45     051500                                  64 'NAME'
46     051600                                  64 'DRIVEN'
47     051700                                  95 'TAX DED.'
48     051800         D   2     01
49     051900                         SSNO     48 '  -  -   '
50     052000                         NAME     72
51     052100                         MILAGE1  82
52     052200                                  88 '$'
53     052300                         DEDUCT1B 94
54     ** COMPILE TIME TABLES
55     003000012
56     003499019
57     003999022
58     004499025
59     004999028
60     005499030
61     005999033
62     006499036
63     006999039
64     007499042
65     007999045
66     008499048
67     008999051
68     009499053
69     009999056
70     010999061
71     011999067
72     012999072
73     013999078
74     014999084
75     015999090
76     016999095
77     017999101
78     018999107
79     019999113
80     999999116
81     /*
```

A Tax Deduction Report is to be printed as follows:

```
                         TAX DEDUCTION REPORT

    SOC. SEC.                         MILES      GASOLINE
    NUMBER         DRIVEN                        TAX DED.

    556-98-3021    BELL, ERNEST        75,362    $438.00
    556-94-2447    CHATMAN, CARLA E    13,471    $ 78.00
    111-30-9013    DINIZ, FRANCISCO J   6,314    $ 36.00
    330-52-8528    HODGES, MICHAEL A   36,293    $211.00
    556-13-8842    JOHNSON, NIMROD J   17,954    $101.00
    560-66-7910    LEWIS, RODNEY       27,901    $161.00
    556-96-4996    LEWIS, MICHAEL     104,727    $608.00
    573-02-1310    SANFORD, MICHAEL M     400    $ 12.00
    573-98-9084    TAKAYAMA, GARY M    13,017    $ 78.00
    563-96-2106    TRAVIS, HIRAM S      8,520    $ 51.00
    573-93-5201    WAGGONER, LARRY     18,791    $107.00
    574-70-2075    WINGERT, JOSEPH R   12,001    $ 72.00
```

Illustrative Program

Alternating Tables—Multiple Control Levels: Monthly Sales and Commission Report

Job Definition
Commissions are paid to salespeople based upon the number of units sold. The unit commission varies with the product sold, and the total commission is based upon the number of units of each particular product sold. Sales are determined by the number of units sold times the individual product selling price.

Prepare a report showing the total sales and commissions earned for each salesman and each territory, as well as a final total of all sales and commissions.

Input
A table is to be set up as follows:

Product	Commission Rate	Selling Price
1	$ .10	$ 16.00
2	$ .20	$ 30.00
3	$ .30	$ 43.00
4	$ .40	$ 60.00
5	$ .50	$ 75.00

The input record contains the following fields:

Positions	Field Designation
1–02	Territory number
3–05	Salesman number
6–11	Date
12–30	Name
31–35	Units sold
36–36	Product number

Processing
Set up two alternating tables for commissions and sales for each product. Calculate the commissions earned by multiplying the units sold by the appropriate rate.

Calculate the sales by multiplying the units sold by the appropriate selling price.

Prepare a report that will show the total number of units sold, total sales, and total commissions earned for each product for each salesperson.

Show a total for each territory for the same fields as above.

Show a final total of all fields at the end of the report.

Output
This Printer Spacing Chart shows how the report is formatted:

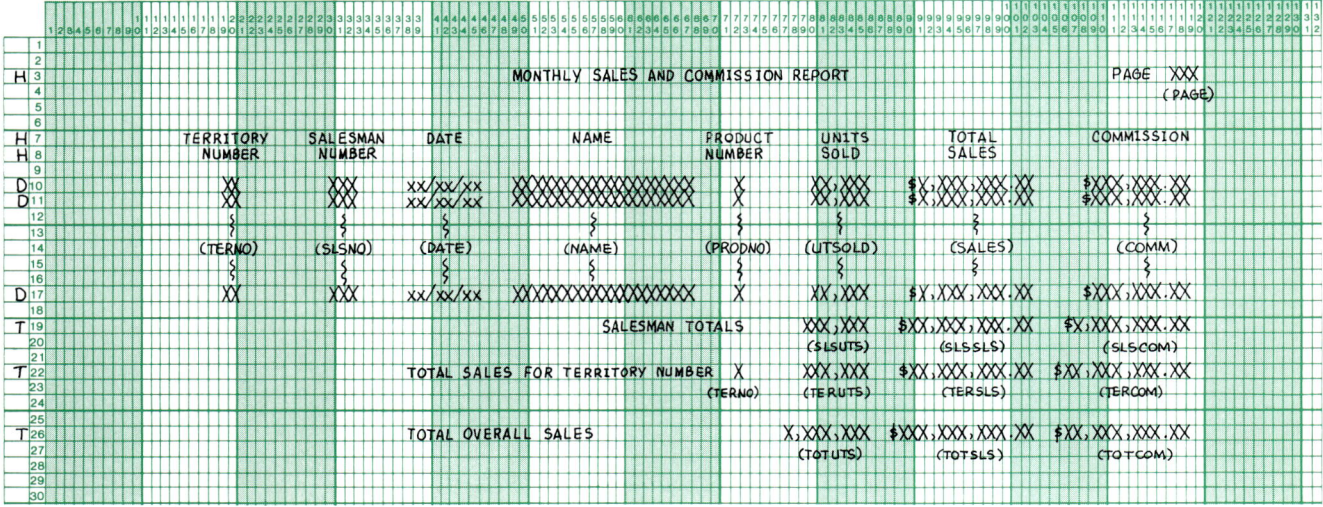

Coding sheets for Monthly Sales and Commission Report problem:

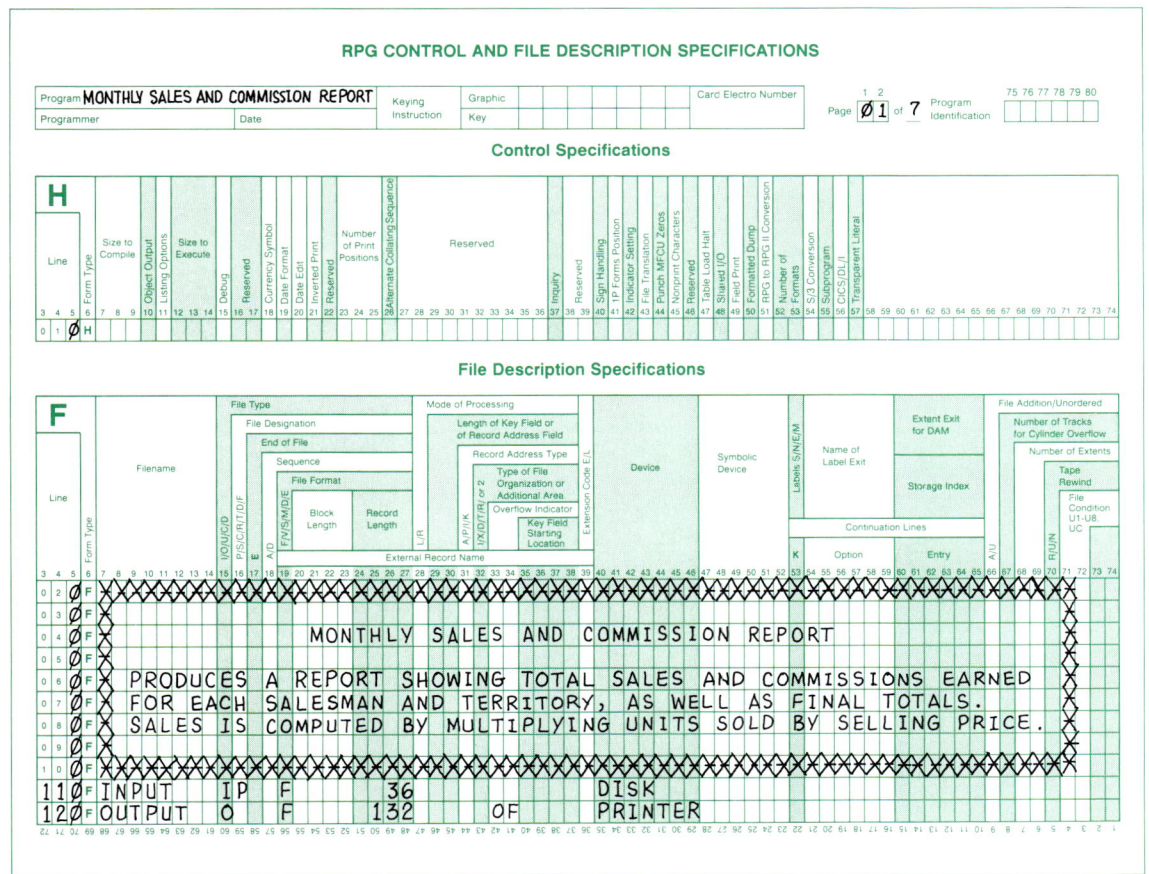

Table Handling 273

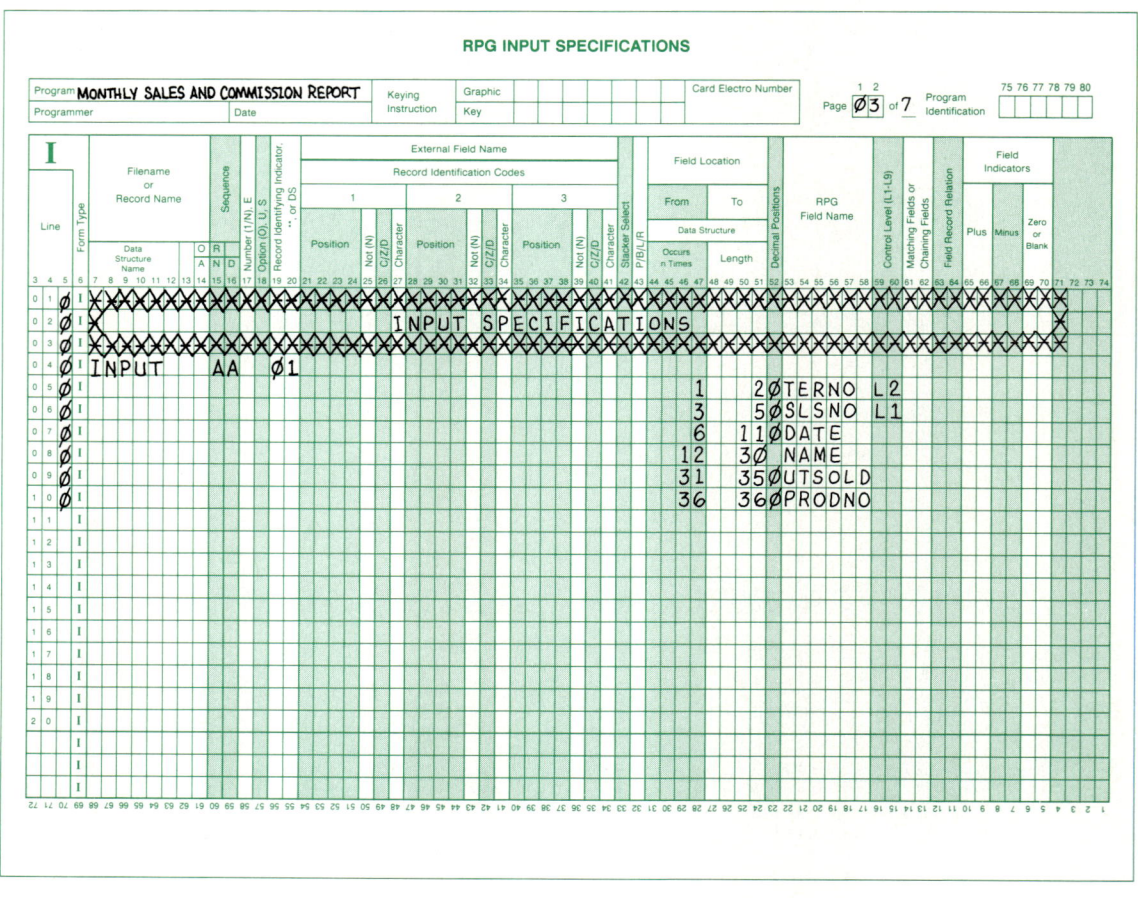

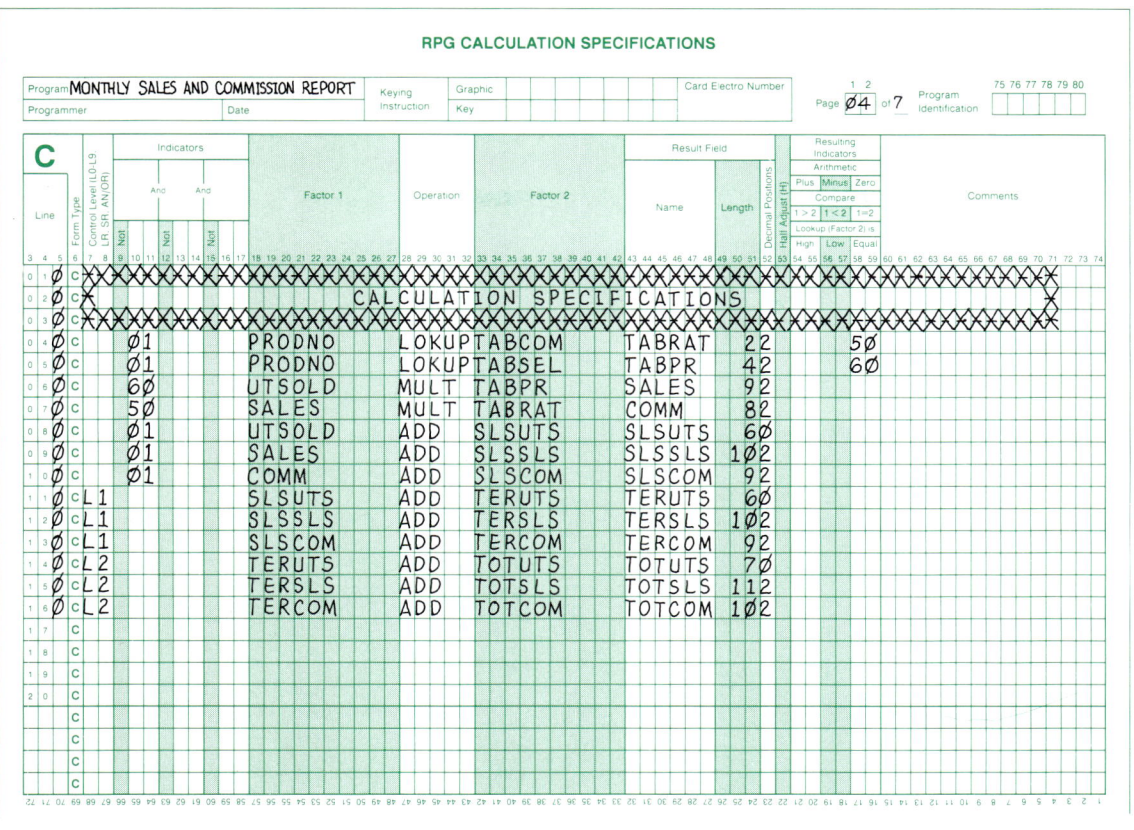

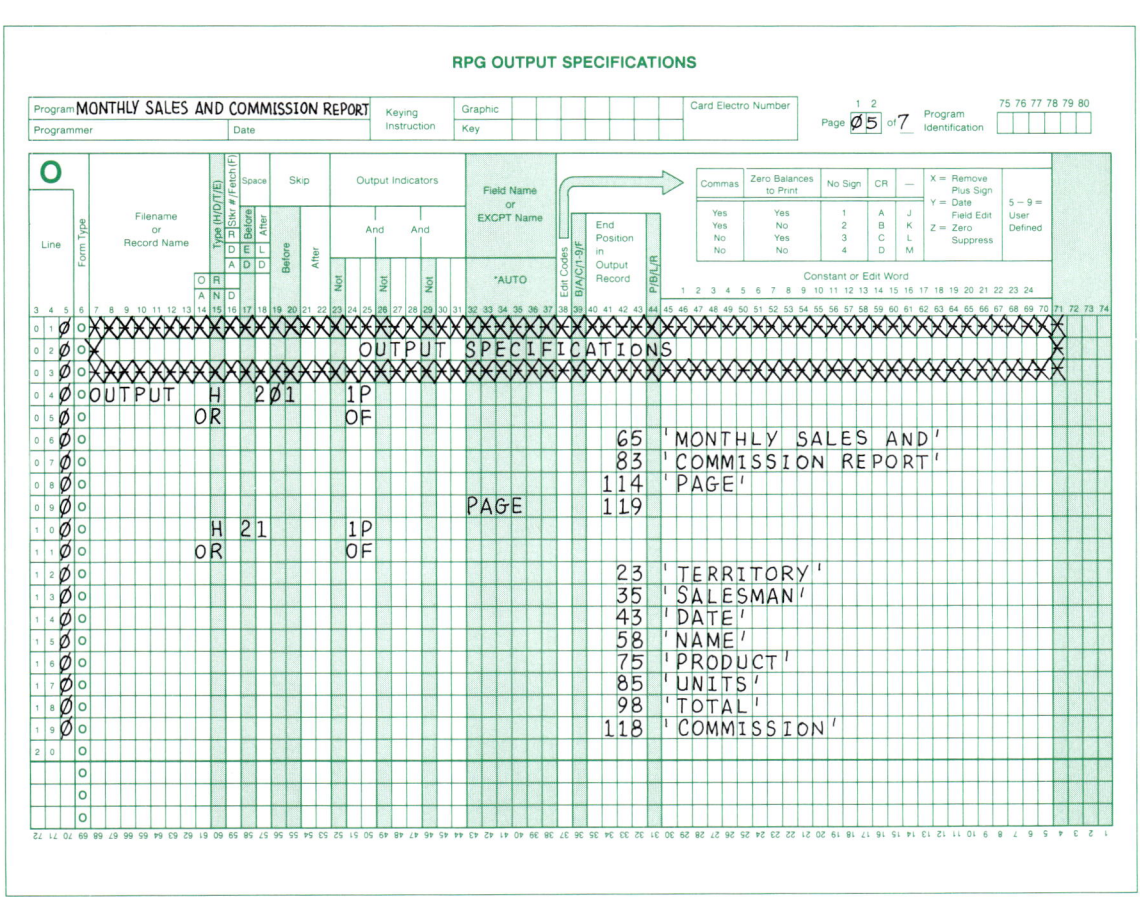

Table Handling

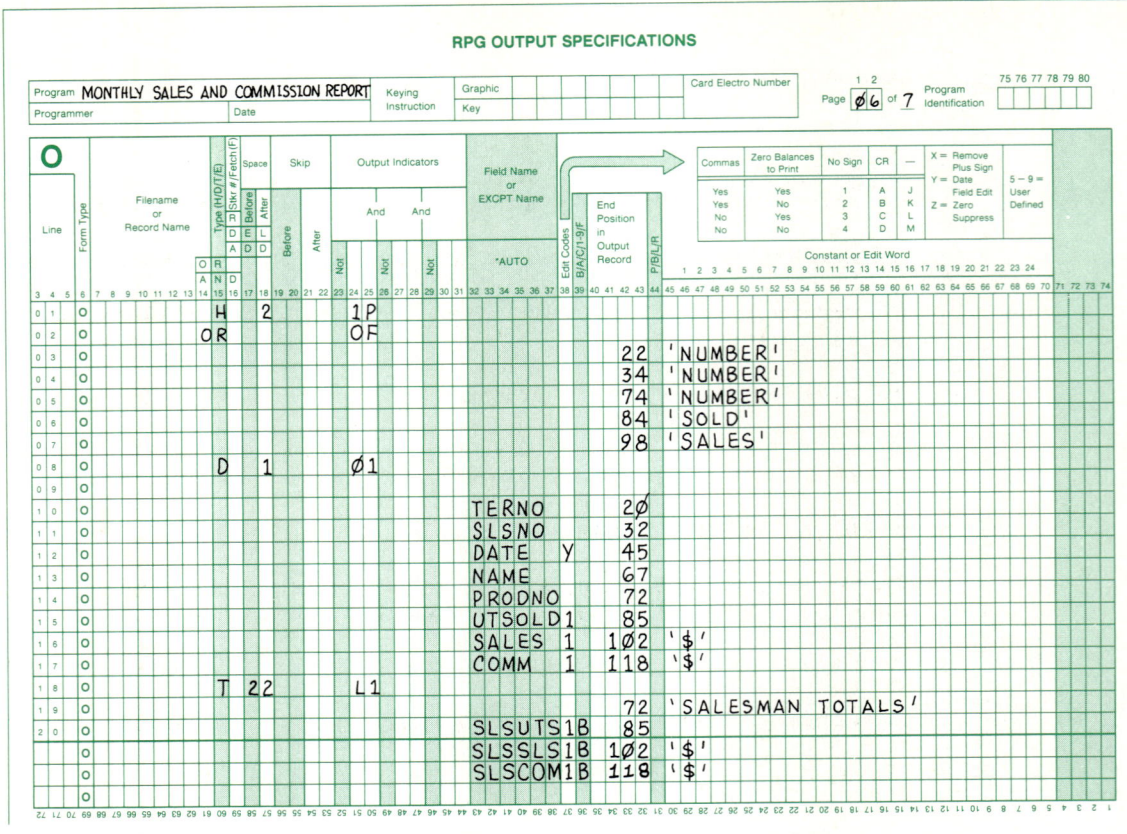
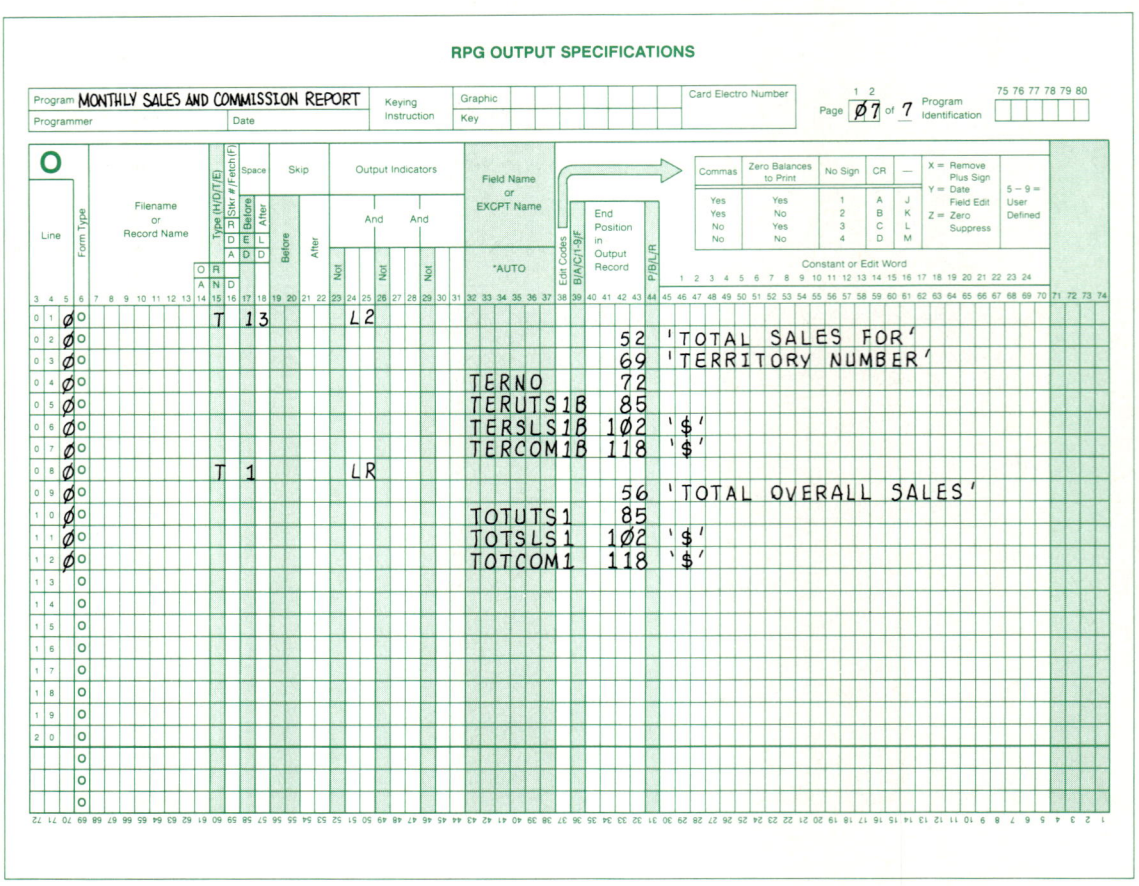

The source listing is as follows:

```
 1    01010H
 2  * 01020F****************************************************************
 3  * 01030F*                                                              *
 4  * 01040F*            MONTHLY SALES AND COMMISSION REPORT               *
 5  * 01050F*                                                              *
 6  * 01060F* PRODUCES A REPORT SHOWING TOTAL SALES AND COMMISSIONS EARNED *
 7  * 01070F* FOR EACH SALESMAN AND TERRITORY, AS WELL AS FINAL TOTALS.    *
 8  * 01080F* SALES IS COMPUTED BY MULTIPLYING UNITS SOLD BY SELLING PRICE.*
 9  * 01090F*                                                              *
10  * 01100F****************************************************************
11    01110FINPUT   IP  F      36           DISK
12    01120FOUTPUT  O   F     132    OF     PRINTER
13  * 02010E****************************************************************
14  * 02020E*                  EXTENSION SPECIFICATIONS                    *
15  * 02030E****************************************************************
16    02040E                   TABCOM  5   5  1 0ATABRAT  2 2
17    02050E                   TABSEL  5   5  1 0ATABPR   4 2
18  * 03010I****************************************************************
19  * 03020I*                   INPUT SPECIFICATIONS                       *
20  * 03030I****************************************************************
21    03040IINPUT   AA  01
22    03050I                                        1   20TERNO L2
23    03060I                                        3   50SLSNO L1
24    03070I                                        6  110DATE
25    03080I                                       12   30 NAME
26    03090I                                       31  350UTSOLD
27    03100I                                       36  360PRODNO
28  * 04010C****************************************************************
29  * 04020C*                CALCULATION SPECIFICATIONS                    *
30  * 04030C****************************************************************
31    04040C      01       PRODNO    LOKUPTABCOM    TABRAT  22   50
32    04050C      01       PRODNO    LOKUPTABSEL    TABPR   42   60
33    04060C      60       UTSOLD    MULT TABPR     SALES   92
34    04070C      50       SALES     MULT TABRAT    COMM    82
35    04080C      01       UTSOLD    ADD  SLSUTS    SLSUTS  60
36    04090C      01       SALES     ADD  SLSSLS    SLSSLS 102
37    04100C      01       COMM      ADD  SLSCOM    SLSCOM  92
38    04110CL1             SLSUTS    ADD  TERUTS    TERUTS  60
39    04120CL1             SLSSLS    ADD  TERSLS    TERSLS 102
40    04130CL1             SLSCOM    ADD  TERCOM    TERCOM  92
41    04140CL2             TERUTS    ADD  TOTUTS    TOTUTS  70
42    04150CL2             TERSLS    ADD  TOTSLS    TOTSLS 112
43    04160CL2             TERCOM    ADD  TOTCOM    TOTCOM 102
44  * 05010O****************************************************************
45  * 05020O*                   OUTPUT SPECIFICATIONS                      *
46  * 05030O****************************************************************
47    05040OOUTPUT  H  201    1P
48    05050O        OR        OF
49    05060O                                      65 'MONTHLY SALES AND'
50    05070O                                      83 'COMMISSION REPORT'
51    05080O                                     114 'PAGE'
52    05090O                             PAGE    119
53    05100O        H   21    1P
54    05110O        OR        OF
55    05120O                                      23 'TERRITORY'
56    05130O                                      35 'SALESMAN'
57    05140O                                      43 'DATE'
58    05150O                                      58 'NAME'
59    05160O                                      75 'PRODUCT'
60    05170O                                      85 'UNITS'
61    05180O                                      98 'TOTAL'
62    05190O                                     118 'COMMISSION'
63    06010O        H    2    1P
64    06020O        OR        OF
65    06030O                                      22 'NUMBER'
66    06040O                                      34 'NUMBER'
67    06050O                                      74 'NUMBER'
68    06060O                                      84 'SOLD'
69    06070O                                      98 'SALES'
70    06080O        D    1    01
71    06090O                             TERNO    20
72    06100O                             SLSNO    32
73    06110O                             DATE  Y  45
74    06120O                             NAME     67
75    06130O                             PRODNO   72
76    06140O                             UTSOLD1  85
77    06150O                             SALES 1 102 '$'
78    06160O                             COMM  1 118 '$'
79    06170O        T   22    L1
80    06180O                                      72 'SALESMAN TOTALS'
81    06190O                             SLSUTS1B 85
82    06200O                             SLSSLS1B 102 '$'
83    06210O                             SLSCOM1B 118 '$'
84    07010O        T   13    L2
```

```
85    070200                                    52 'TOTAL SALES FOR'
86    070300                                    69 'TERRITORY NUMBER'
87    070400                       TERNO    Z   72
88    070500                       TERUTS1B     85
89    070600                       TERSLS1B    102 '$'
90    070700                       TERCOM1B    118 '$'
91    070800        T 1     LR
92    070900                                    56 'TOTAL OVERALL SALES'
93    071000                       TOTUTS1      85
94    071100                       TOTSLS1     102 '$'
95    071200                       TOTCOM1     118 '$'
96    ** compile time tables
97    110220330440550
98    **
99    116002300034300460005750O
100   /*
```

A Monthly Sales and Commission Report is to be printed as follows:

```
                              MONTHLY SALES AND COMMISSION REPORT                                    PAGE 0001


TERRITORY   SALESMAN    DATE        NAME            PRODUCT     UNITS       TOTAL           COMMISSION
NUMBER      NUMBER                                  NUMBER      SOLD        SALES

  10          111      9/03/87   JONES, HENRY          1          100        $1,600.00          $160.00
  10          111      9/10/87   JONES, HENRY          2        2,301       $69,030.00       $13,806.00
  10          111      9/17/87   JONES, HENRY          3           60        $2,580.00          $774.00
  10          111      9/24/87   JONES, HENRY          4       20,502    $1,230,120.00      $492,048.00

                                 SALESMAN TOTALS              22,963    $1,303,330.00      $506,788.00

  10          222      9/01/87   LEWIS, CELINE         1           55          $880.00           $88.00
  10          222      9/14/87   LEWIS, CELINE         2           70        $2,100.00          $420.00
  10          222      9/22/87   LEWIS, CELINE         3          800       $34,400.00       $10,320.00

                                 SALESMAN TOTALS                 925       $37,380.00       $10,828.00

                    TOTAL SALES FOR TERRITORY NUMBER 10       23,888    $1,340,710.00      $517,616.00

  24          350      9/10/87   JOHNSTON, HOWARD      1          100        $1,600.00          $160.00
  24          350      9/24/87   JOHNSTON, HOWARD      2          100        $3,000.00          $600.00

                                 SALESMAN TOTALS                 200        $4,600.00          $760.00

  24          565      9/10/87   MONTGOMERY, DAN       3          100        $4,300.00        $1,290.00
  24          565      9/18/87   MONTGOMERY, DAN       4          100        $6,000.00        $2,400.00

                                 SALESMAN TOTALS                 200       $10,300.00        $3,690.00

                    TOTAL SALES FOR TERRITORY NUMBER 24          400       $14,900.00        $4,450.00


                    TOTAL OVERALL SALES                       24,288    $1,355,610.00      $522,066.00
```

Questions for Review

1. What is a table?
2. What is a table element?
3. What are the three main uses of tables?
4. What are arguments and functions?
5. How may tables be formed?
6. What is a table file?
7. How are arguments and functions used in tables?
8. What is the rule regarding the number of entries in table file records?
9. When should entries in a table have a specified sequence?
10. What are the two different times in the course of a job that table data may be loaded into the computer?
11. How are data retrieved from the table?
12. How are tables updated?
13. What entries are required on the Extension form to describe table-input records?
14. What are the rules for assigning table names?
15. How are two related tables described?
16. What are the rules related to the number of table entries?
17. What are the rules relative to length of entries?
18. What entries are required in the decimal positions and sequence positions?
19. For what purposes are comments used?
20. What is the principal advantage of compile time tables and how are they changed?
21. How is a compile time table loaded?
22. Why is it desirable to use preexecution time tables?
23. How are preexecution time tables loaded?
24. How are the specifications written for preexecution time tables?
25. What is a table lookup operation and how is it coded?
26. Briefly describe the operation of the table lookup.
27. What are the necessary steps in describing the table lookup operation?
28. How does one stop the computer operation?
29. What are related tables and how are they used?
30. What is a two-table search?
31. How are alternating entries coded on one record?
32. Must all entries in alternating format be in the same form?
33. How are two record tables on the Extension form coded?
34. How is the table coded for sequential tables?
35. How are table data used in calculations and output?

36. What conditions may be searched for in a table lookup operation?
37. Why is the sequence of tables important?
38. How may table entries be moved?
39. How may temporary changes to table data be made?
40. How may permanent changes to table data be made?
41. What is a short table and for what is it used?
42. How may an entire table be output?

Problems

Problem 1

Two related tables contain the name and telephone number of subscribers to a certain system of purchasing. Set up two related tables so that a search can be made using the name as the search argument and the telephone number as the function. There are ten subscribers.

The output should be a listing including the name of the subscriber and the telephone number. An indication should be made if the subscriber is not in the table.

The table record is as follows:

Positions	Field Description
1–11	Name
12–18	Telephone number
19–29	Name
30–36	Telephone number
37–47	Name
48–54	Telephone number
55–65	Name
66–72	Telephone number

The input record contains only one field.

| 1–11 | Name |

The output form is to be as follows:

Name	Telephone Number
JOHNSON T P	236–3210
JONSON M	886–5632
JUGGERS Z T	277–0296
JUSTICE P	306–2981
KABERLEIN W	898–3600

The area code is the same for all.

Requirements

Code the necessary file description specifications, extension specifications, input specifications, calculation specifications, and output specifications on the appropriate forms.

Output is as follows:

```
        PHONE LIST

    NAME            TELEPHONE NUMBER
JOHNSON T P         236-3210
JONSON M            886-5632
JUGGERS Z T         277-0296
JUSTICE P           306-2981
KAMBERLEIN          SUBSCRIBER NOT IN TABLE
```

Problem 2

To compute the weekly pay for each employee, the rate of pay as found in the table TABPAY is multiplied by the number of hours worked (a three-position field with one decimal position). The weekly pay amount is a five-position field with two decimals after rounding.

Using the specifications below, code the necessary file description specifications, extension specifications, input specifications, calculation specifications, and output specifications on the appropriate forms.

TABEMP	TABPAY
1062	5.25
1063	6.25
1064	5.40
1065	4.50
1066	5.50
1067	4.75
1068	6.50
1069	4.50
1070	5.00
1071	8.00

Input

Positions	Field Description
1–04	Employee number
35–37	Hours (XX.X)

Calculations

Perform a search of the table using employee number as the search word. After a successful search, perform the necessary calculations.

Output

Leave five positions between each field. Output the employee number, hours worked, rate of pay, and gross pay. Output is as follows:

EMPLOYEE NUMBER	HOURS WORKED	RATE OF PAY	GROSS PAY
1062	15.5	5.25	81.38
1065	32.5	4.50	146.25
1066	40.0	5.50	220.00
1068	5.0	6.50	32.50
1071	25.0	8.00	200.00

Problem 3

To compute the correct amount of an invoice, the amount of tax must be added to the purchase price. To do this, a table is set up as follows and the correct tax is added to the purchase price.

Tax is calculated at $ .06 per $1.00 and each fraction over $1.00 is based on the following rates. (There is no tax on any amount under $1.00.)

Fraction over $1.00	Rate
.01–.19	$ .01
.20–.39	.02
.40–.59	.03
.60–.79	.04
.80–.99	.05

Input

Positions	Field Description
1–05	Customer number
10–14	Purchase price (XXX.XX)

Calculations

Search the table for correct amount. Add this amount to purchase price to determine total price.

Output

Print a report showing the customer number, purchase price, tax, and total price. Leave five spaces between each field. Be sure to include the proper headings.

Code the necessary file description specifications, extension specifications, input specifications, calculation specifications, and output specifications on the appropriate forms.

Output is as follows:

CUSTOMER NUMBER	PURCHASE PRICE	TAX	TOTAL PRICE
10865	1.49	.19	1.68
12850	.52	.00	.52
22560	1.68	.20	1.88
25647	1.21	.08	1.29
26841	1.85	.21	2.06
36875	123.56	7.51	131.07
47250	258.63	15.62	274.25
78250	653.24	39.20	692.44

Problem 4

To perform invoice billing, a corporation processes an input record as follows:

Positions	Field Description
3–06	Customer Number
7–11	Item
12–14	Weight (XX.X)
15–19	Cost (XXX.XX)

According to company policy, merchandise is delivered by truck unless a customer requests delivery by parcel post. To date, the following fifteen customers (by number) have requested parcel post service:

174	2109	596	1157	1475
195	169	456	1366	377
2105	2733	1100	290	1977

The customer always pays parcel post charges. The charge is made in accordance with the weight of the ordered item as follows (assume that no order weighs more than thirty pounds):

Weight in Pounds	Postal Charges	Weight in Pounds	Postal Charges	Weight in Pounds	Postal Charges
1	$ 0.45	11	$ 0.65	21	$ 0.85
2	.50	12	.70	22	.90
3	.55	13	.70	23	.90
4	.55	14	.75	24	.95
5	.55	15	.75	25	.95
6	.55	16	.75	26	.95
7	.60	17	.80	27	1.00
8	.60	18	.80	28	1.00
9	.65	19	.85	29	1.05
10	.65	20	.85	30	1.05

Note: Any fraction of a pound over the weight shown is assigned the next higher rate.

To produce invoices, the billing program must do the following:

1. Determine if a customer has requested parcel post delivery.

2. If so, determine how much postage is required for the weight ordered.

3. Print the amount of postage on the output report.

    These functions can be best performed by setting up three tables:

    A table of customers who have requested parcel post delivery
    Two related tables of weights and postal rates

    Your job is to

1. Design table input records for the three tables. The table of customers requiring parcel post service should be created as a preexecution time short table to allow for frequent additions and deletions. A table of twenty-four entries should be sufficient for containing additions. The weight and postal rate tables should be loaded at compile time since they will not be modified.

2. Define and describe the tables with File Description and Extension Specifications forms.

3. Code the LOKUP operation(s) on a Calculation Specifications form to determine how much postage is due, if any.

4. Code the Output Specifications form to print the customer number, item, weight, cost, postage, and total cost. Leave five spaces between each field. Be sure to include the proper headings.

Output is as follows:

CUSTOMER NUMBER	ITEM	WEIGHT	COST	POSTAGE	TOTAL COST
2105	55741	24.2	25.00	2.70	27.70
100	57882	10.0	700.30	.00	700.30
290	24502	19.1	570.95	2.30	573.25
502	86512	35.0	23.04	.00	23.04
1977	51202	14.8	450.00	2.01	452.01

Arrays

7

Outline

When to Use an Array Instead of
   a Table
Specifying an Array
   Defining an Array
Array Loading
   Loading at Compile/Preexecution
      Time
   Loading Arrays during RPG
      Program Execution
     Array Information in One
       Record
     Array Information in More
       Than One Record
     Modifying the Content of Arrays
Updating Arrays
Using Arrays
   Array Name and Index
   Referencing an Array in
      Calculations
   Array-to-Array Calculations
   Array Calculations
     Adding All Elements within
      an Array (XFOOT)
Lookup of an Array (LOKUP)
   Searching an Array for
      a Particular Element
   Starting the Search at
      a Particular Element
   Determining if a Search
      Is Successful
   Referencing an Element
      That Satisfies a Search
   Searching an Array for More
      Than One Element
   Output during an Array Search

Output of an Entire Array
   Specifying Output
      with Extension
      Specifications
   Specifying Output
      with Output Specifications
Accumulating Groups of Totals
Referencing Individual Elements
   of an Array
   Indexing an Array
     Specifying an Index That
      Does Not Change
     Specifying an Index That
      Can Be Changed
   Output of Individual Elements
     of an Array
   Referencing Only Part of
     a Field
Move Array (MOVEA)
RPG III Enhancements
   Move Array (MOVEA)
   Sort Array (SORTA)
   *IN
   *INxx

Figure 7.1 Twelve-element numeric array

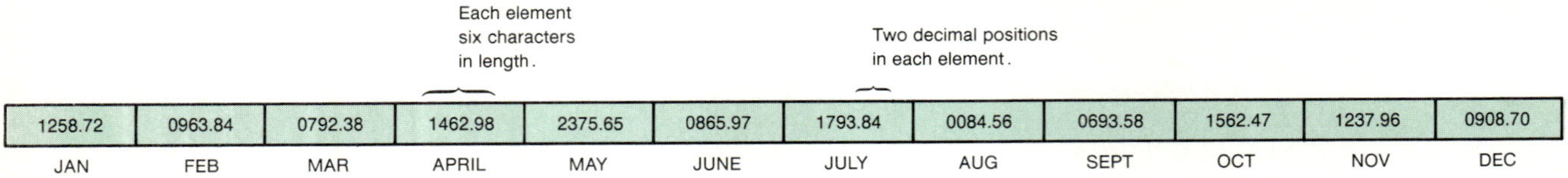

Each element six characters in length.

Two decimal positions in each element.

1258.72	0963.84	0792.38	1462.98	2375.65	0865.97	1793.84	0084.56	0693.58	1562.47	1237.96	0908.70
JAN	FEB	MAR	APRIL	MAY	JUNE	JULY	AUG	SEPT	OCT	NOV	DEC

An **array** is a continuous series of data fields stored side by side so they can be referenced as a group. In an array, each individual data field is called an **element.** Each element of the array has the same characteristics; that is, each element contains data in the same format (alphameric or numeric), of the same length, and with the same number of decimal positions. (See Figure 7.1.)

An array is very similar to a table. Both arrays and tables are set up by coding extension specifications. The type of data that can be put in an array are the same as can be put in a table. The data can be keyed in by the operator to tape or disk. The data can be loaded into an array at compilation time or just before execution time. An array can also be built from data extracted from normal input files or from data produced during the program as a result of calculations. The way data are arranged in storage is the same for tables and arrays—one element of the data immediately follows another. However, the uses of tables and arrays differ considerably.

When to Use an Array Instead of a Table

In most cases, tables contain constant data such as tax rates, shipping instructions, or discount rates. The constant data are then used for calculations or printing with variable transaction data. Arrays are generally used for variable data and for totals used independently of the variable transaction data. Tables are used largely for looking up values. Arrays are useful for accommodating totals and intermediary values created during calculations and for using with elements referenced by subscripts (indices) rather than pointed at by LOKUP.

An appropriate example of a compile time table is a table of the state abbreviations. The state code abbreviations serves as a good example of table application because it is used for LOKUP and because it is compiled rather than read in due to the relative unchangeability of the data.

An example of an array might be counters for type 1 records, type 2 records, and type 3 records, where record type is an index. Arrays should be used instead of tables when it is necessary to reference all elements at one time. Arrays can reduce the number of RPG specifications that need to be coded for such a job as well as the time required to reference the entries. Arrays should also be used to reference a data item directly within a group of items, thus eliminating the necessity of doing a lookup based on a search word.

Specifying an Array

An array is a bank of data elements that can be accessed, moved, manipulated, and modified as needed. The two principal operations involving arrays are XFOOT, used to sum the elements; and LOKUP, used to search an array for a specified field of data. However, before any array can be summed or searched, it must be fully specified.

Specifying an array requires four operational steps:

1. Defining the array format so that the appropriate space can be reserved in storage
2. Loading the data into the array (i.e., filling the array)
3. Updating the array as necessary
4. Outputting the array

Defining an Array

An array can be set up by coding extension specifications in much the same way as specifications are coded for tables. Coding on the Extension form varies slightly, depending on when the data are to be

Figure 7.2 Defining arrays

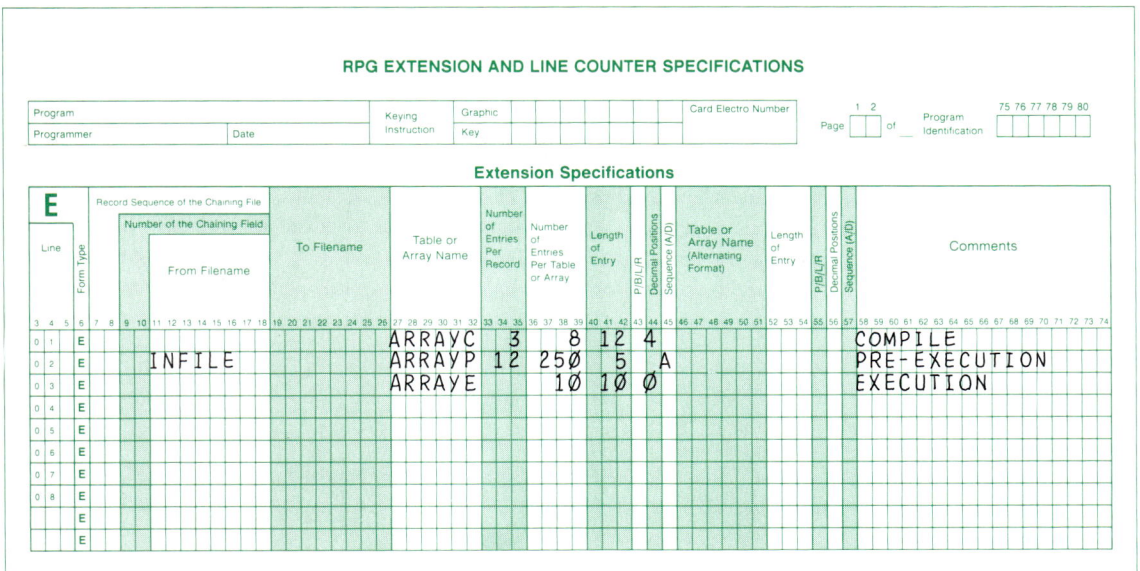

read into the array, that is, set up by the RPG compiler. Array data can be stored in the array at three different times:

1. At compile time. The array records follow immediately and are compiled with the source program.

2. At preexecution time. The array records are read like any other data files except all are read before any processing is done.

3. At execution time. The array is loaded from information in input records or data generated by calculations. (See Figure 7.2.)

The following Extension form entries are used to define and describe arrays:

From filename (positions 11–18). Preexecution time arrays are read from an input file similar to other data files. The name of the file containing the array must be entered in positions 11–18. This file must be designated as a table file in position 16 of the File Description form. A table file is read completely and data are loaded into the array before execution of the program begins. The same file can be named in these positions for more than one array.

To filename (positions 19–26). If an entire array is to be written to an output file at the end of the job, the name of the output file is entered in positions 19–26. Output of execution time arrays is not allowed.

Table or array name (positions 27–32). All arrays used in the program must be assigned a name of six characters or less, which is entered in positions 27–32. The rules for naming arrays are similar to those for naming tables—an array name can consist of any combination of alphabetic characters and numbers. However, while the first character must be an alphabetic character, an array name cannot begin with the letters TAB. The compiler uses TAB to distinguish between an array and a table. *Warning:* The array name chosen should leave room for both punctuation and a subscript for indexing. (Indexing will be discussed later in the text.)

Number of entries per record (positions 33–35). For compile time and preexecution time arrays, enter the number of array elements in each input record. These positions must be left blank in execution time arrays.

Number of entries per table or array (positions 36–39). These positions are used to enter the number of elements in the array (from 1–9999). This number should be entered so that the last digit falls in position 39.

Arrays 287

Length of entry (positions 40–42). The length of each element (number of characters, including blanks) should be specified in positions 40–42, with the number ending in position 42. The length must be the same for every element in the array.

Packed/binary (position 43). Programmers may specify that the array is in packed decimal or binary format.

Decimal positions (position 44). If the elements in an array are numeric, the number (0–9) of digits to the right of the decimal point should be entered in position 44. Even if no decimal positions are present, a zero must be specified if the elements are to be considered numeric. A blank in position 44 indicates that the elements are to contain alphameric data. Remember, however, that if arithmetic operations are to be performed on the elements, the array must be defined as numeric.

Sequence (position 45). If the array data is in sequence, enter *A* (ascending) or *D* (descending) in position 45. Sequence is not checked for execution time arrays, but this position must contain an entry if high or low lookup is used.

Alternating arrays (positions 46–57). Positions 46–57 are used if two related arrays are set up in an alternating format on input records. Alternating arrays cannot be described with execution time arrays.

The extension specifications reserve the appropriate space in storage for the array. How data are actually stored in the array will be made part of a later discussion.

Array Loading

Arrays can be filled (loaded) with data at compile time, run time, or during the RPG program execution. (See Figure 7.3.) All elements to be loaded into an array must have the same length, format, and number of decimal positions, if numeric. Alphameric elements must not exceed 256 characters and numeric entries must not exceed 15 digits. Binary entries are limited to 9 digits. Each array must have a unique name and may or may not be sequentially organized on the type of lookup to be performed. (See Figure 7.4.)

Loading at Compile/Preexecution Time

Arrays are filled from magnetic media at compile/preexecution time; they may be read from one or several devices. The input records must have the following characteristics:

1. Records may not contain incomplete entries. Elements may not be split between two records.

2. The first array entry for each record must begin in position 1 of the record.

Figure 7.3 Loading arrays (tables) from disk

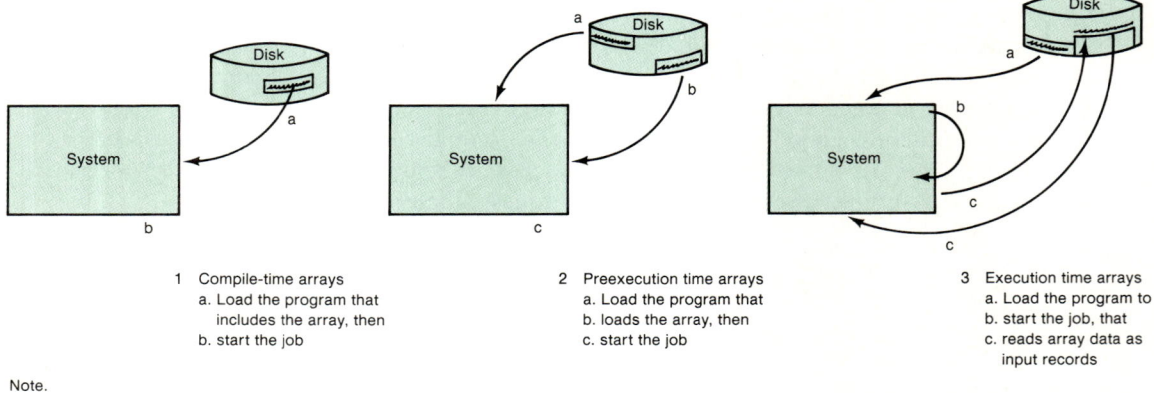

Figure 7.4 Array loading with input specifications

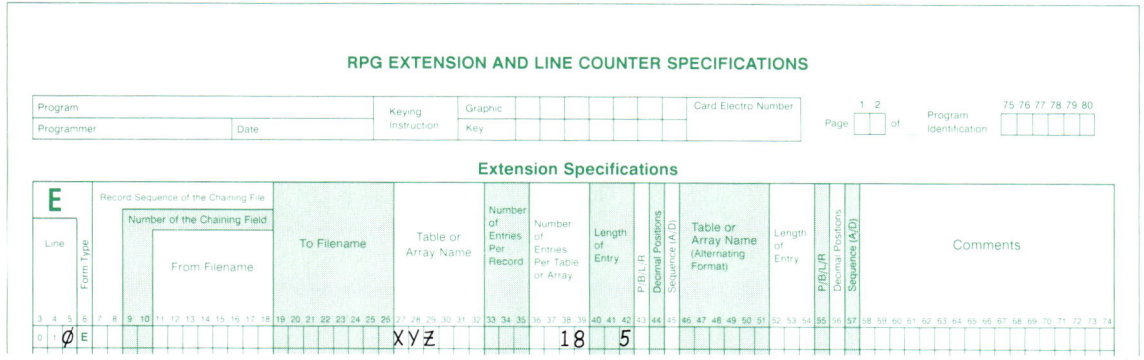

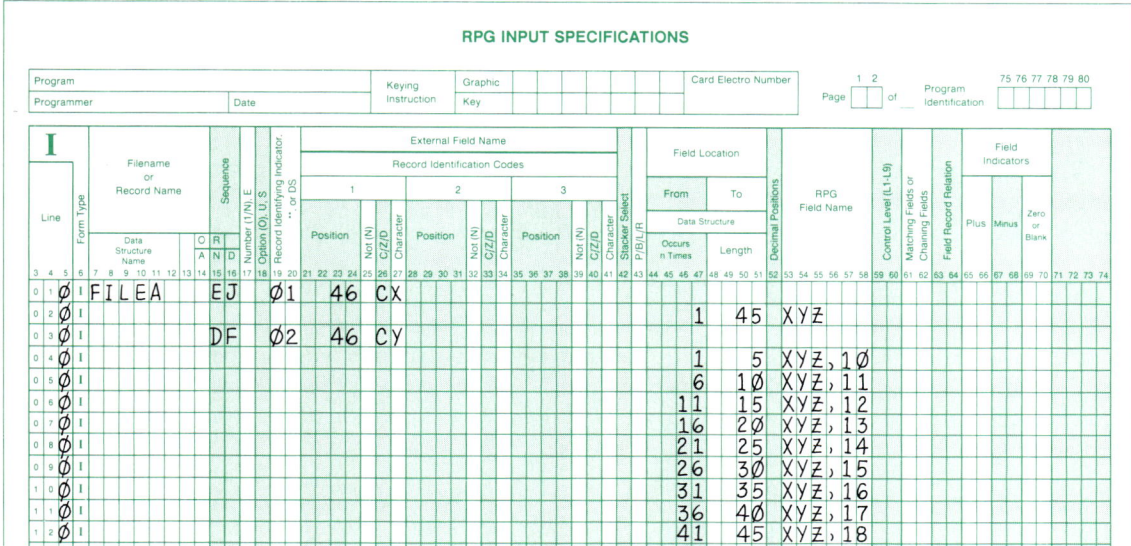

Notes on the Coding

Array XYZ is specified as having eighteen elements (entries), each five characters long.

Note syntax of individual array elements, the array name separated from the subscript by a comma.

On the first record type, array elements are consecutive and, therefore, loaded into the array by means of a single input specification line (see line 020).

Since array elements from the record type defined on line 030 are either not consecutive or defined on several records, they are individually specified by field, location, array name, and index on line 040 to 120.

3. All records must be of fixed length and contain the same number of array entries except the last record, which may contain fewer than the preceding records.

4. No blanks between array elements are permitted. However, each array loaded at compile time must be preceded by a record containing only two asterisks (**) in positions 1 and 2, and a blank in position 3.

5. When alternating arrays are loaded, each record must begin with an entry for the first array and end with an entry for the second array.

6. Records must be in a sequentially organized file.

An array may be filled with fewer, but not more, entries than specified. Arrays loaded at run time can be in any format desired (alphameric, unpacked, packed, or binary).

Arrays 289

Array entries loaded at compile time must be in unpacked format and must follow file translation and collating sequence records. Arrays loaded at run time must be followed by an end-of-file indication; the record may not contain blank entries if a sequence is specified. In this case, the last entry must be the highest number in the sequence for an array in ascending sequence, and the lowest for an array in descending sequence. (See Figures 7.5 and 7.6.)

Sequence is checked if sequence is specified. Sequence must be specified if high or low indicators for a lookup operation are specified.

Loading Arrays during RPG Program Execution

Arrays can be loaded during RPG program execution either from an input file or from the results of calculations or moves performed on such file input. When calculation specifications are executed, the fields are moved to fill arrays.

If an array is loaded from information in input records (execution time array), that information must be described on the Input Specifications form. How the entries are made depends on whether the array information is contained in one or more than one record. Any type of array (compile time, preexecution time, or execution time) can be described on the Input Specifications form.

Execution time arrays are not checked for sequence, but position 45 (sequence) must contain an entry if high or low LOKUP is used.

The array name (positions 27–31), the number of entries per array (positions 36–39), and the decimal length of each array element (positions 40–42) are defined on the Extension form. An execution time array must not have an entry in positions 11–26, 33–35, 43, and 46–57 on the Extension form.

Array Information in One Record

If all of the array information is in one record, it can occupy consecutive positions in the record or be scattered throughout the record. If the array elements are consecutive on the input record, they may be loaded with a single input specification. (See Figure 7.7.) If the array elements are scattered throughout the record, they may be defined and loaded one at a time, one to a specification, or one to a specification line. (See Figure 7.8.)

Figure 7.5 Arrangement of input for compile time tables

```
         1         2         3         4         5         6         7         8
12345678901234567890123456789012345678901234567890123456789012345678901234567890
000100H
.
.
(RPG Source Program)
.
0407900                         ZIP       131
0408000* END OF PROGRAM
** compile time table for branch lookup
100RESED110VANNU120NORTH130PACOI140BURBA
150CHATS160CANOG170GLEND180ENCIN190GRANA
200MOORP210CAMAR220VALEN230TUJUN240SUNLA
250ARLET260SUNVA270LOSFE280ECHOP290WOODL
300REDLA310RIVER320DIAMO330BAKER340SANFR
/*
** compile time month array
JANJANUARY   FEBFEBRUARY  MARMARCH     APRAPRIL
MAYMAY       JUNJUNE      JULJULY      AUGAUGUST
SEPSEPTEMBEROCTOCTOBER    NOVNOVEMBER  DECDECEMBER
/*
```

Figure 7.6 Loading preexecution time arrays—example

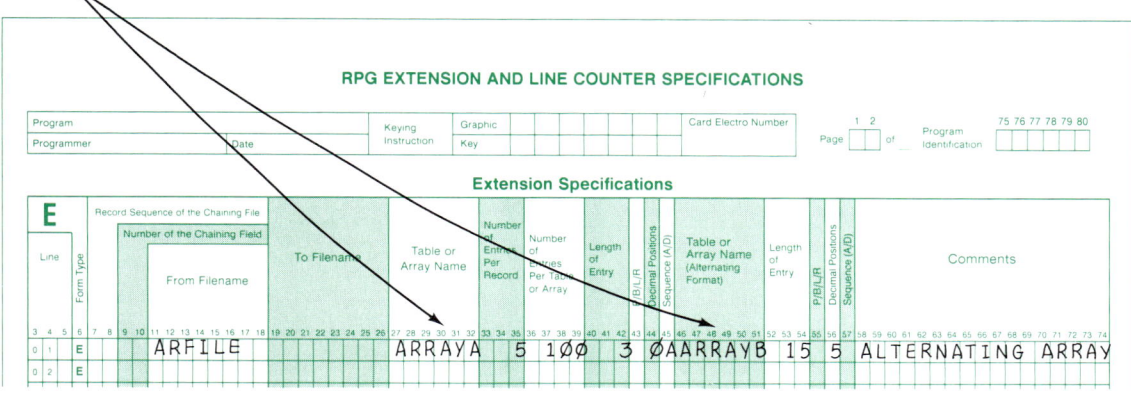

Arrays 291

Figure 7.7 Loading execution time array with consecutive elements—example

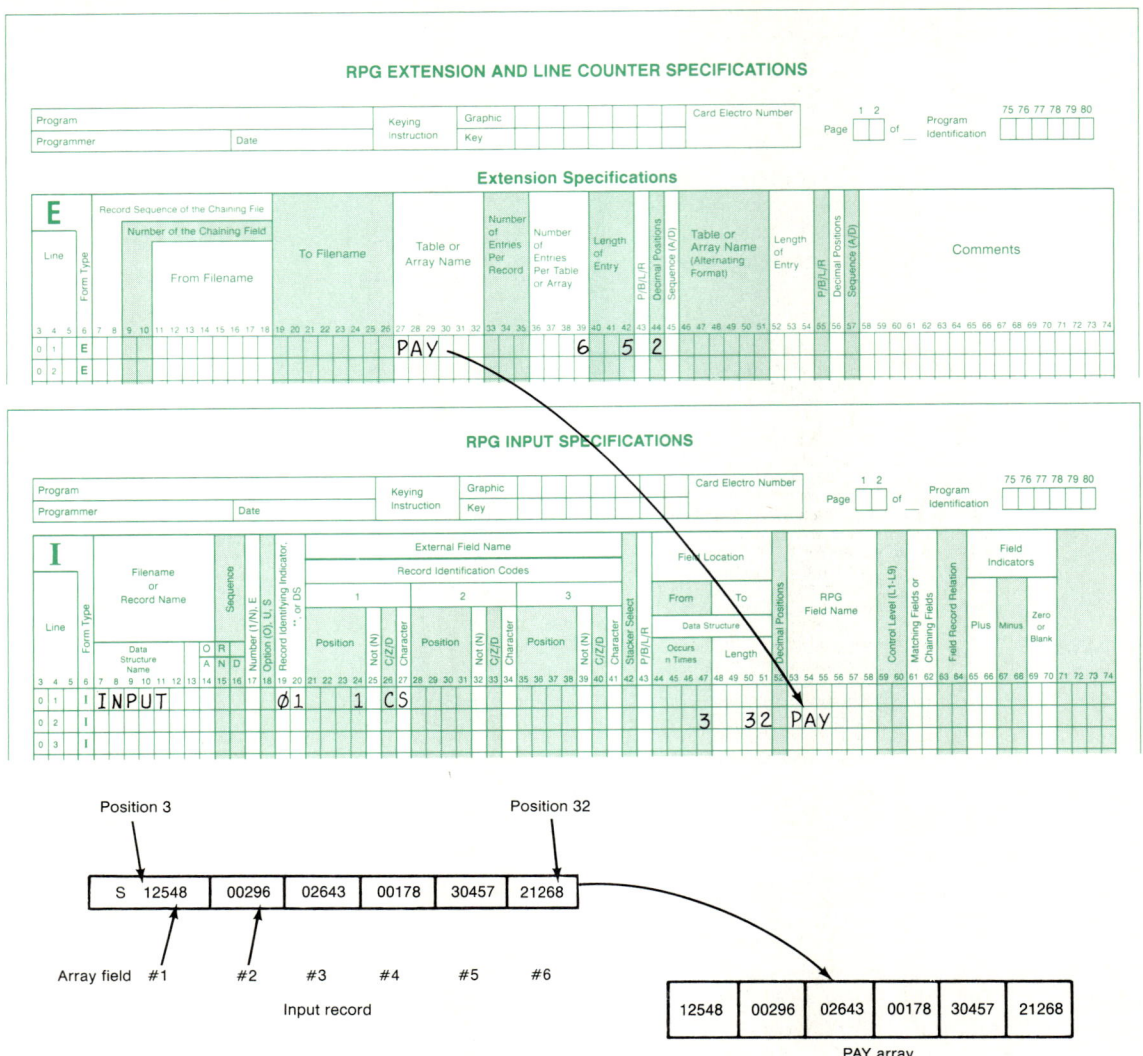

Figure 7.8 Loading array data from scattered fields by means of input specifications—example

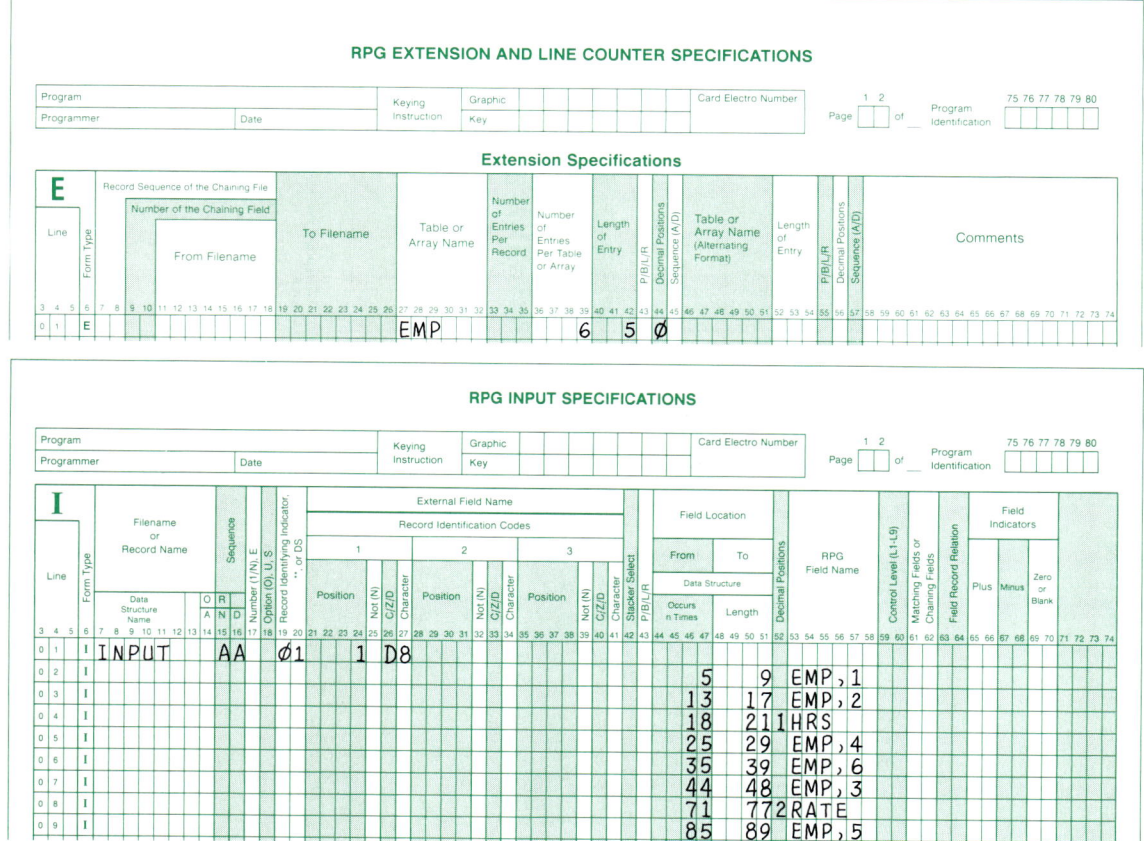

Array Information in More Than One Record

If the array information is in two or more records, many methods may be used to introduce the array to the system. The primary method used will depend on the size of the array and whether the array information is all together in the input records.

RPG program processes one record at a time. The entire array cannot be processed until all of the records containing array information have been read and the information has been moved into the array fields. It may, therefore, be necessary to suppress calculation and output operations until the entire array has been read into the system. (See Figure 7.9.)

Modifying the Content of Arrays

The content of arrays can be modified in the same manner as the content of tables is modified. Entries can be added to arrays by simply writing additional entries on the input records before program execution. However, entries can also be added during execution of the program. The entries added can be created by calculation operations or read from an input record. (See Figures 7.10 and 7.11.)

Updating Arrays

Arithmetic, move, or blanking operations are used to change either an entire array or a single-array element, as indicated in the result field of the Calculation Specifications or under field name in the Output Specifications form. (See Figure 7.12.) Blanking an array or a single-array element is done using the Blank After entry in the Output Specifications form (position 39). The entire array is blanked if the array is specified without an index as the field name; only the array element is blanked if the index is specified (separated from the array name with a comma).

Arrays 293

Figure 7.9 Loading array data consecutive on more than one record—example

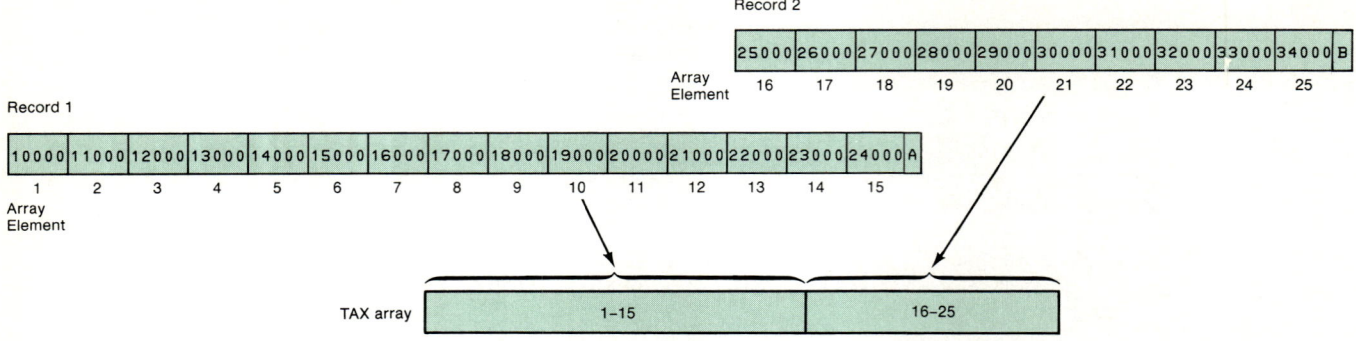
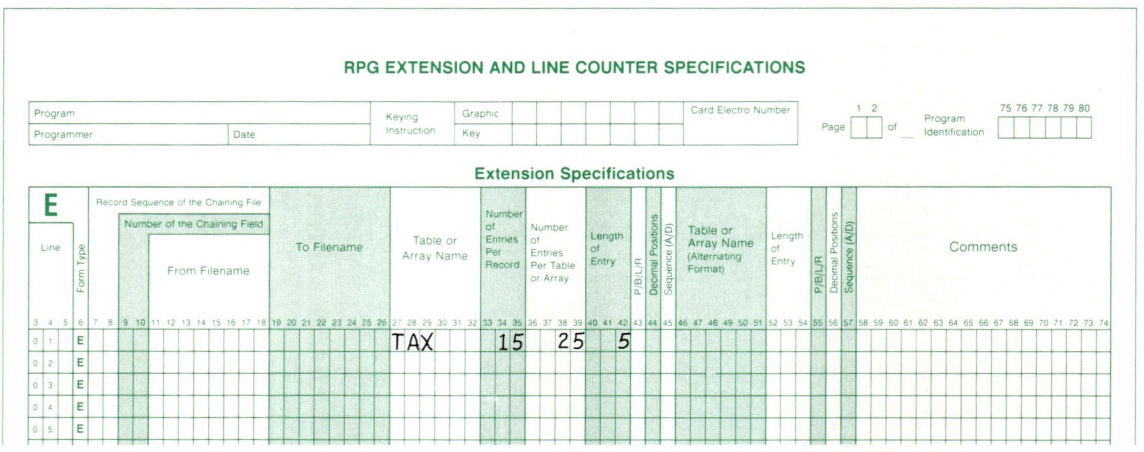
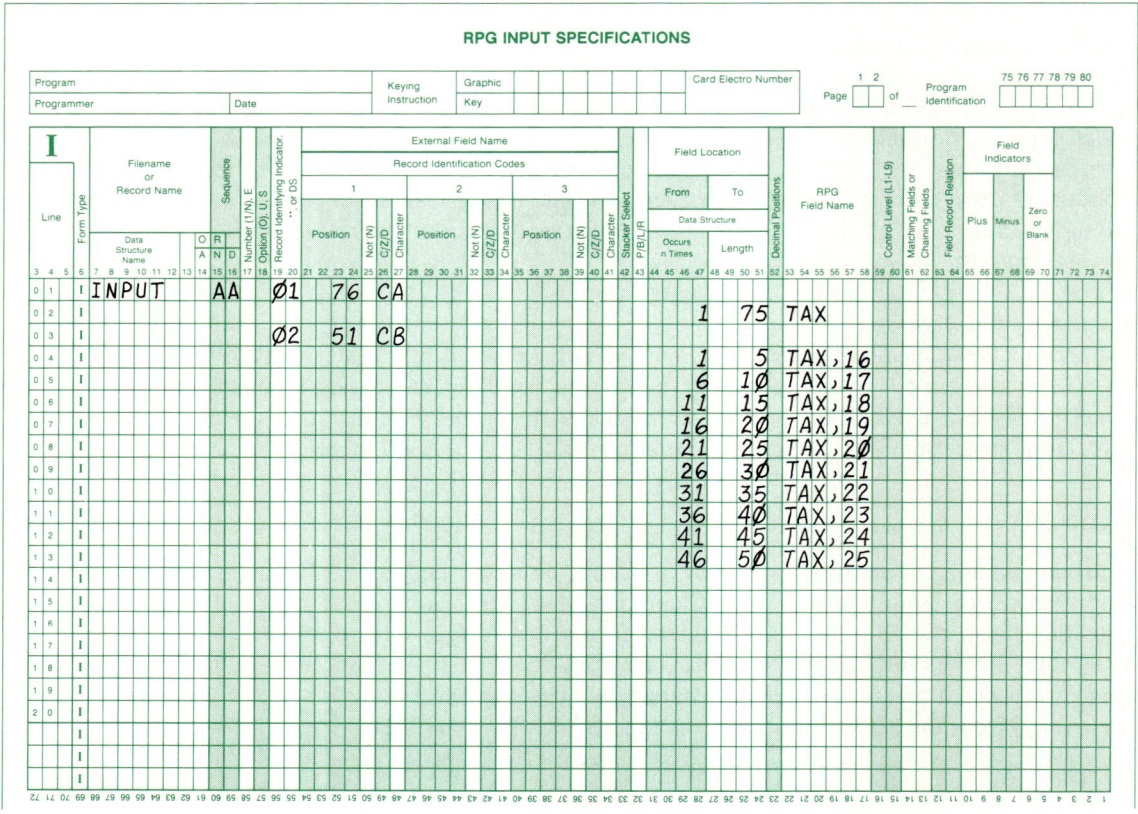

294   RPG II and RPG III Programming

Figure 7.10 Modify contents of array—example

It is important to note that when data is stored in an array by specifying the array name as the field name, the information is placed at the beginning of the array. Thus, the 80 positions of data from this first input record are stored in elements 1-19 of the array.

```
         1         2         3         4         5         6         7         8
12345678901234567890123456789012345678901234567890123456789012345678901234567890

    (INPUT, a sequential file)

10001099900000000000011999000000000000012999000000000000000000000000000000013999
20001499900000000000015999000000000000016999000000000000000000000000000000017999
30001899900000000000019999000000000000020999000000000000000000000000000000021999
40002299900000000000023999000000000000024999000000000000000000000000000000025999
50002699900000000000027999000000000000028999000000000000000000000000000000029999
60003099900000000000031999000000000000000000000000000000000000000000000000000000
/*

    (ARA, an array)

1099911999129991399914999159991699917999189991999920999219992299923999249992599
926999279992899929999309993199
```

NOTE: Although the data is scattered on six input records, as shown above, and the array data is not consecutive, the four fields on each of the first five records are in the same format on each record. The remaining two fields on the sixth record are in the same format as the first two fields on all other records.

Describing One Set of Array, Input Fields for Several Records

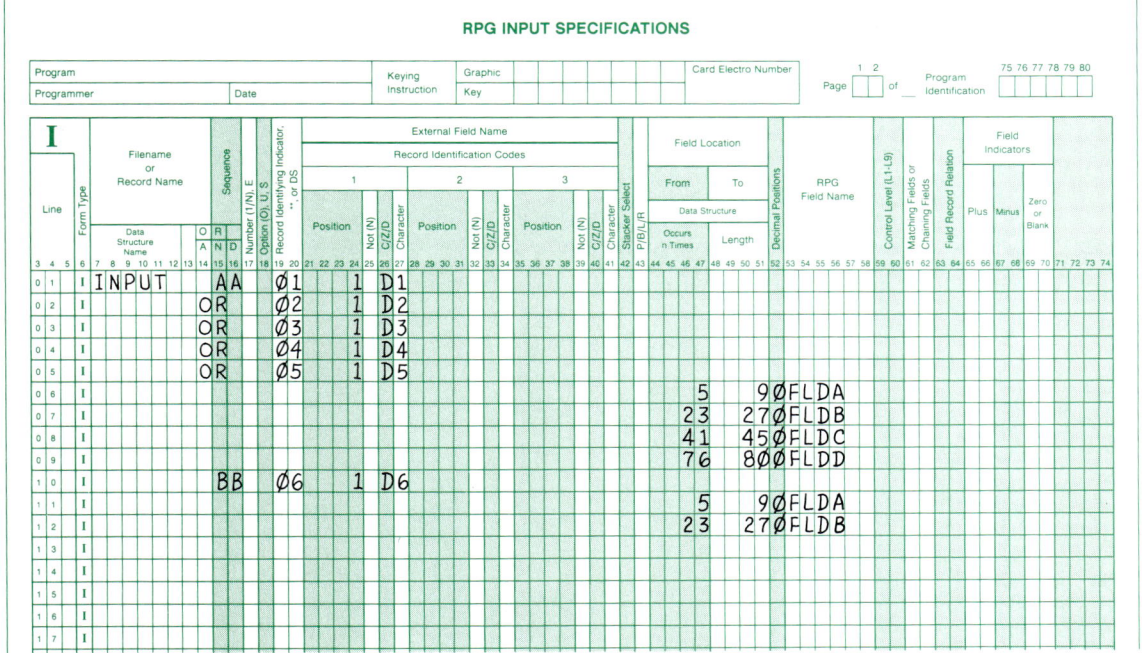

Figure 7.10 continued

Using the Same MOVE for Fields From Several Records

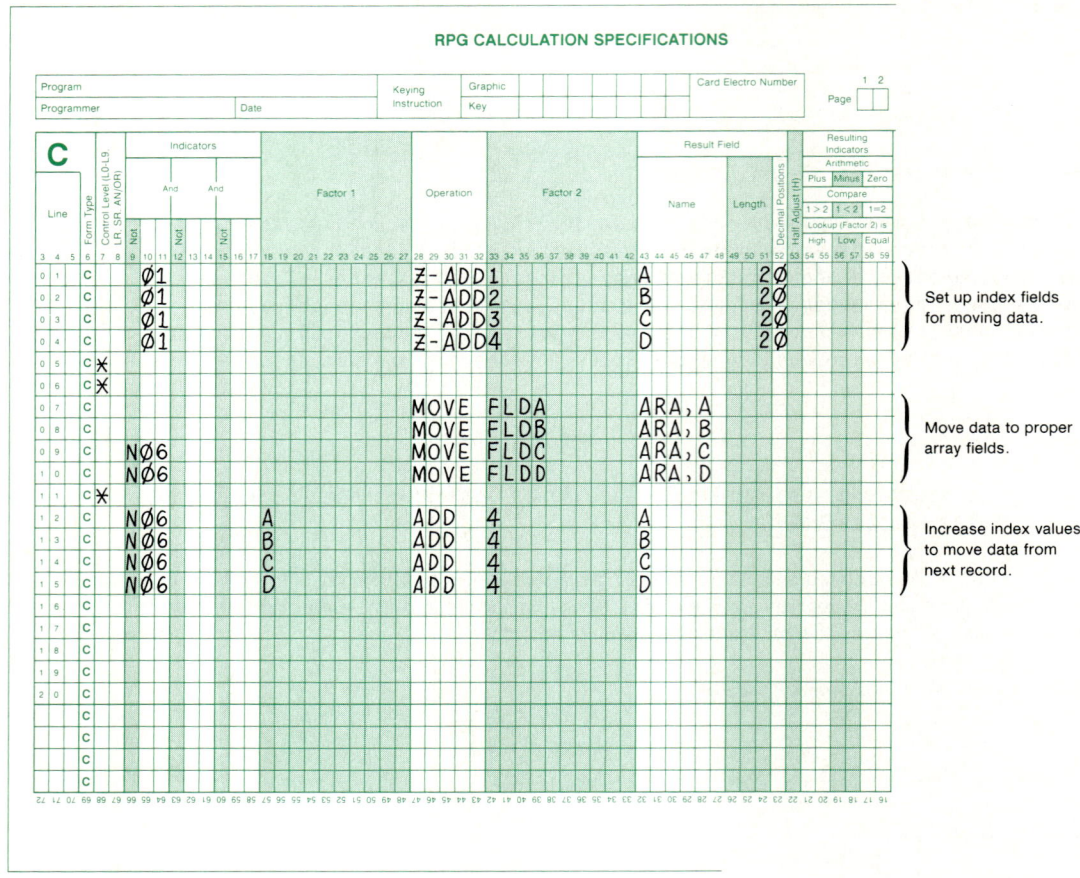

Figure 7.11 Use of calculation specifications to fill an array

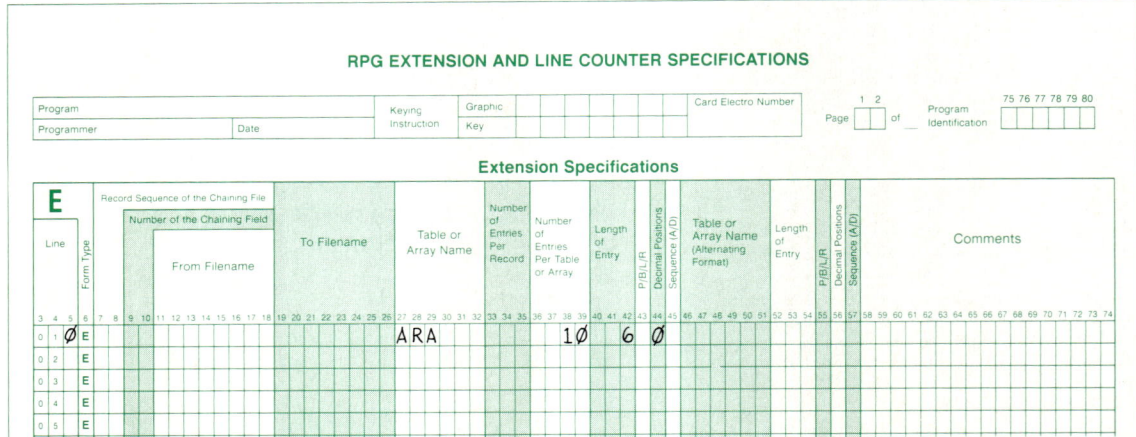

Figure 7.11 continued

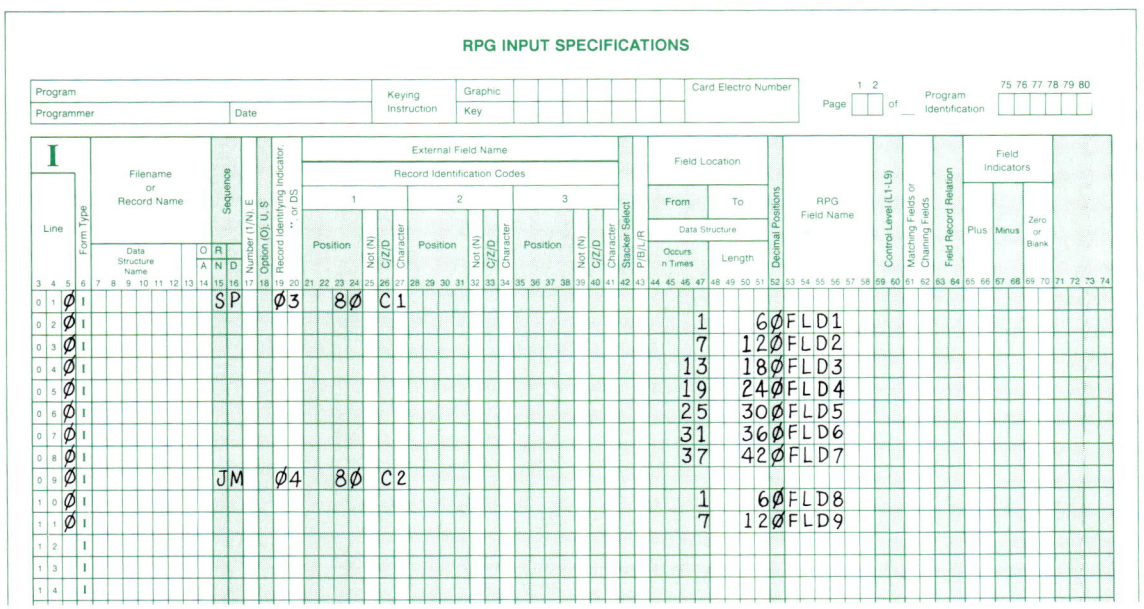

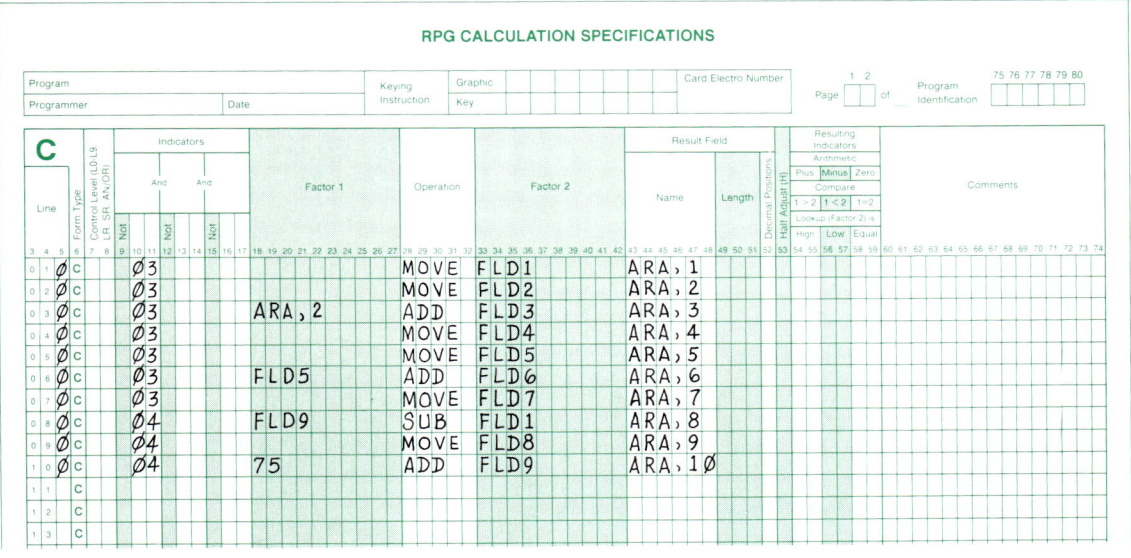

Arrays 297

Figure 7.12 Updating arrays

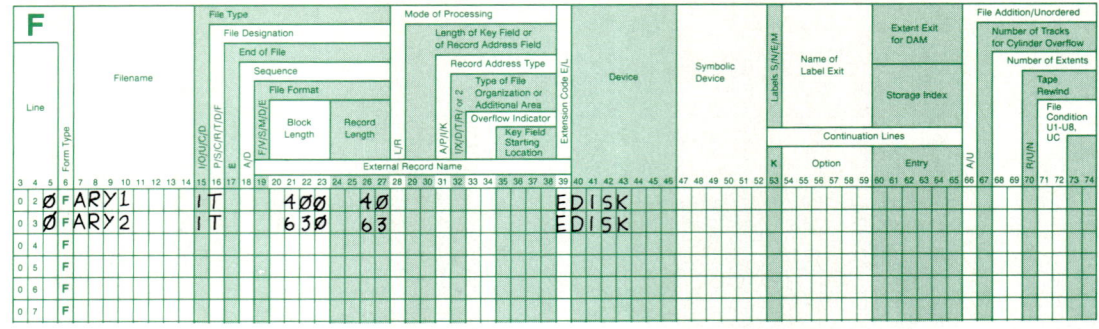

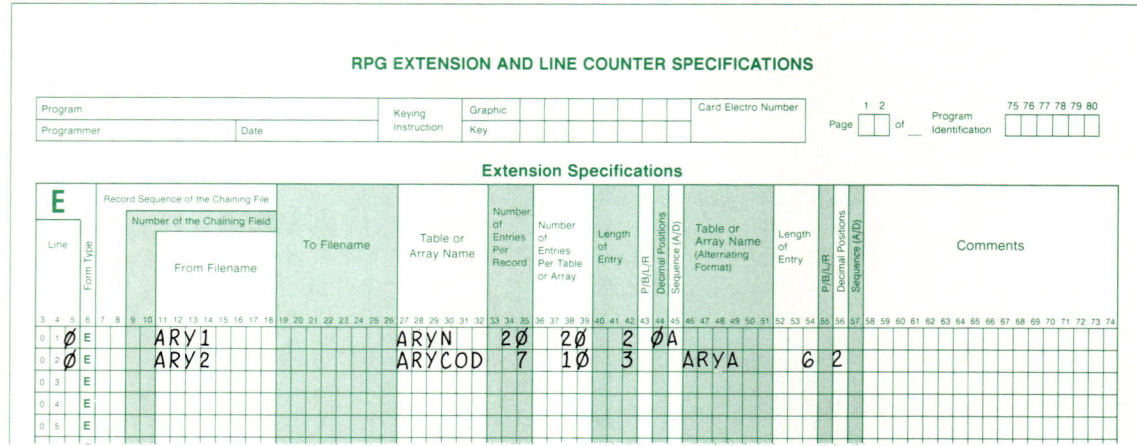

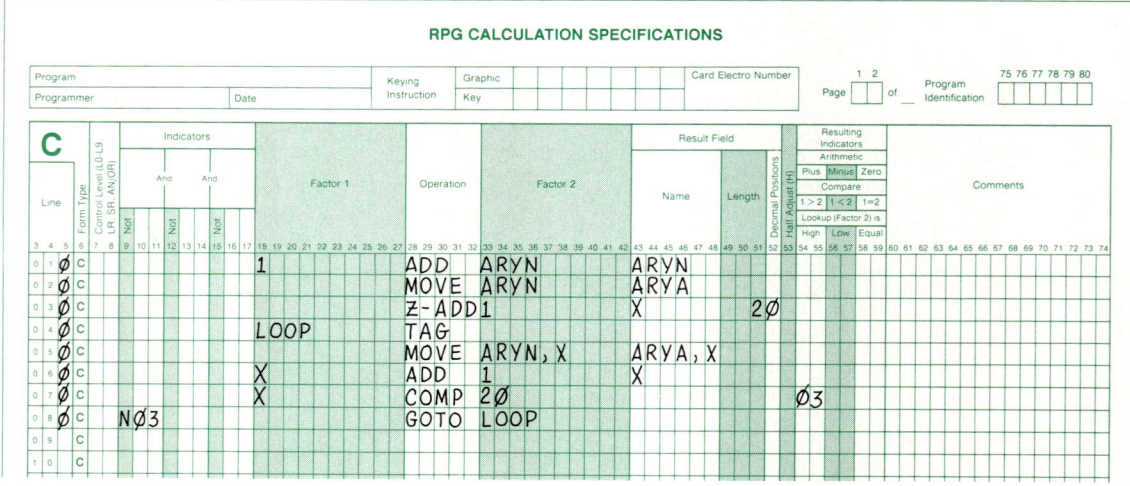

Notes on the Coding

Calculation line 010 adds one to every element of array ARYN. The absence of an index causes all twenty elements of array ARYN to be incremented by factor 1.

Calculation line 020 is also an array operation. The twenty elements in array ARYN are moved to the corresponding elements in array ARYA.

Calculation lines 030 through 080 perform the same operation. Array element X of array ARYN is moved to array element X of array ARYA. This operation is executed for values of X from 1-20.

Figure 7.13 Referencing a particular element of an array—examples

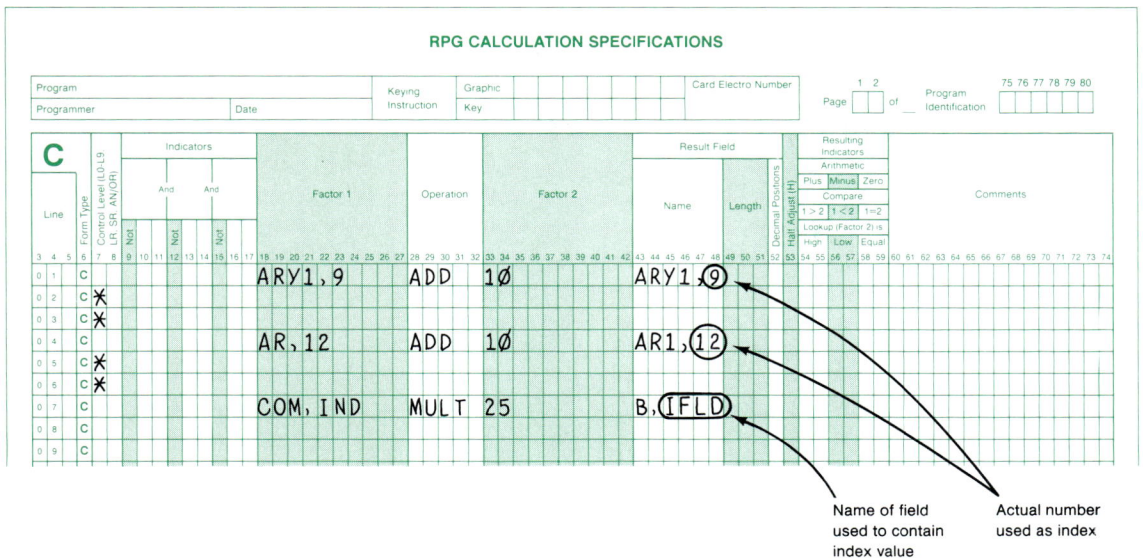

Using Arrays

Arrays can be used in input, output, or calculations specifications. The elements in an array can be referenced individually or the array can be referenced as a whole. Individual elements are referenced by an array name plus an index. The array name alone references the entire array.

Array Name and Index

The array name must begin either in position 27 or in position 46 of the Extension form and must be a valid RPG name. The length of the array name depends on the way in which the array is being used. The array name and index can be from one to six characters long (unless it is specified only in factor 1 or factor 2 of calculation specifications, in which case it can be up to ten characters long). The array name must be a valid RPG name that does not begin with the letters TAB. The array name must begin with an alphabetic entry. The array name is used by itself only when referencing the entire array.

If individual elements of the array are to be referenced, the array name will require an index. An index may be a numeric field with zero decimal positions or a literal. (See Figure 7.13.) A comma must separate the array name and the index. The array name, together with comma and index entry, is limited in length to six positions (on input and output specifications, or in the result field of the calculation specifications). The index must not be zero, negative, or greater than the number of elements in the array.

Referencing an Array in Calculations

An entire array or individual elements in an array can be referenced using calculation specifications. (See Figure 7.14.) Individual elements are processed as normal fields. If an array field is to be used as a result field, the array name with comma and index cannot exceed six characters.

To reference an entire array, the array name is used without an index. (See Figure 7.15.) When **XFOOT** or **LOKUP** operations are used, factor 1 and factor 2 cannot be an array name unless the result field is also an array name.

The following rules apply when using array names without an index in calculations:

1. When the factors and the result field are all arrays with the same number of elements, the operation is performed using each element in sequence starting with the first element from every array until all elements in each of the arrays have been processed. If the arrays do not have the same number of entries, the operation ends when the last element of the array with the fewest elements has been processed.

Figure 7.14 Referencing individual array elements in calculations—example

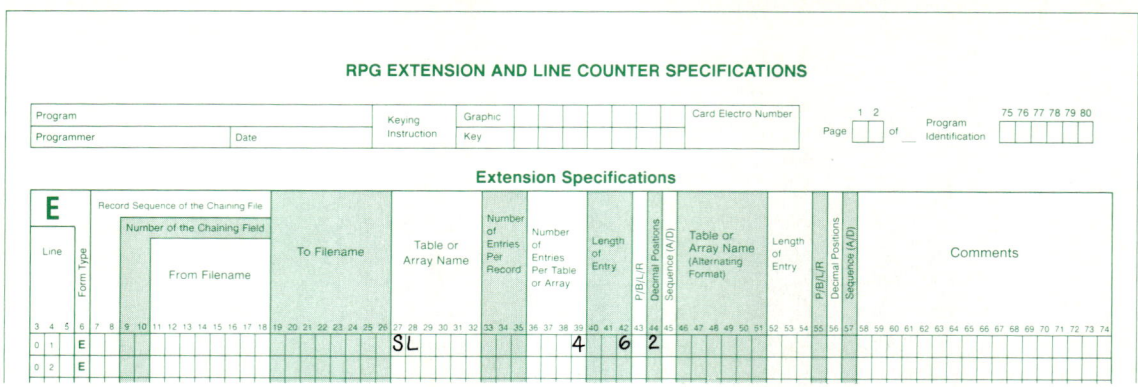

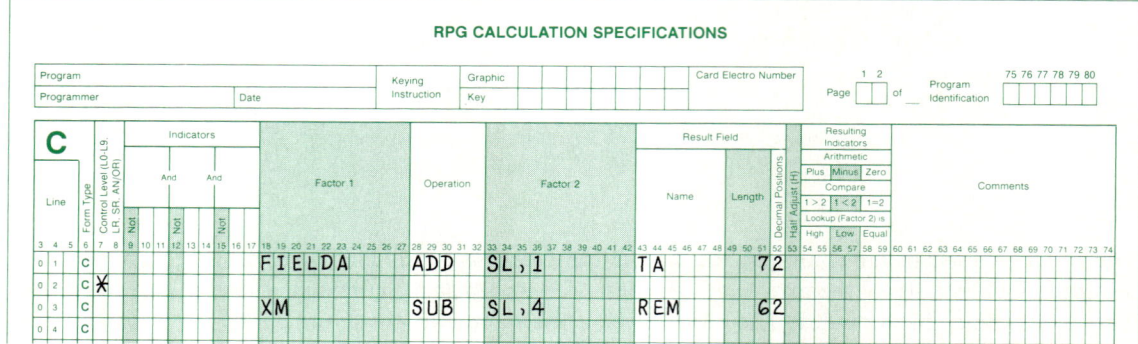

Notes on the Coding

The array named SL contains four numeric entries, each being six positions long with two decimals.

Line 01 of the Calculations form describes the addition of a field FIELDA to SL,1, the data in the first entry in the array SL. The sum is placed in the field TA.

Line 03 of the Calculations form describes the subtraction of SL,4, the fourth element of the array SL, from the field XM, with the differences being placed in the field REM.

2. When one of the factors is a field or constant and the other is an array, and the result field is an array, the operation is performed once for every element in the shorter array. The same field or constant is used in all of the operations.

3. If an operation code uses factor 2 only (such as Z-ADD) and the result field is an array, the operation is performed once for every element in the array. The same field or constant is used in all of the operations. An exception is the MOVEA operation, which moves the field into the array without regard to the elements.

4. Resulting indicators (positions 54–59) cannot be used because multiple operations have to be performed. Exceptions are XFOOT and LOKUP, which allow for resulting indicators.

To illustrate the process of referencing all items in an array, assume that a company employs twelve sales clerks whose daily sales are recorded. Field 1 of the record contains sales for clerk 1, field 2 contains sales for clerk 2, and so on. A different sales record is kept for each day of sales. In addition to a daily amount, the company wishes to gather a monthly sales total for each clerk. Therefore, at the end of the month the daily sales amount for each clerk must be accumulated. An array called MONTH, made up of twelve elements, can be set up to contain the monthly totals. The monthly sales record is read and each clerk's total placed in the appropriate array element. Another element called DAY can be set up to contain the twelve sales amounts for any particular day. In this way, as the sales records for each day are read into the computer, the twelve fields of data are placed into the array called DAY.

Figure 7.15   Referencing all items of an array—example

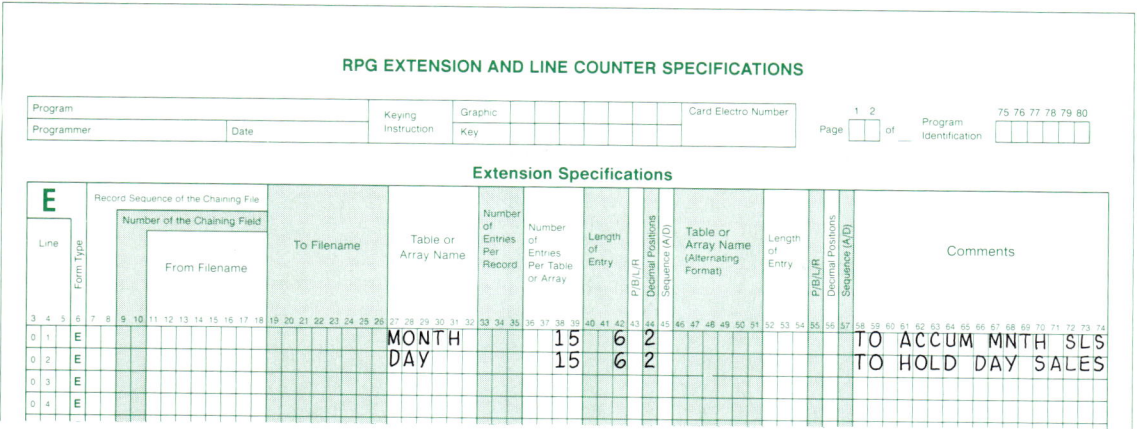

Array-to-Array Calculations

Once the first sales record is read in and the data stored in an array, the twelve elements of DAY are added to the elements of MONTH. In other words, element 1 of DAY is added to element 1 of MONTH, element 2 of DAY is added to element 2 of MONTH, and so on.

The twelve accumulated sales amounts (results of the addition) are stored in MONTH. Then another sales record is read into the DAY array. The new DAY fields are added again to the accumulated totals in MONTH (accumulated totals can be stored on tape or disk), called in at processing time. Updated totals are then written back on tape or disk. (See Figure 7.16.)

This method is similar to using two tables in taking an entry from one table and adding it to another table. However, performing the operations for tables requires more instruction than using arrays to do the job.

With tables, each element (e.g., sales amount for each clerk) must be referenced separately. First, a table lookup must be performed to find the appropriate sales amount from the DAY table. Since the programmer does not know the amount of each sale for each clerk, when a related sales clerk entry is found, the corresponding sales items in the DAY table are made available. Next, the corresponding element of the MONTH table must be looked up. At this point, associated table entries will finally correspond. An additional operation would be required in order to add the two entries, thus arriving at the totals for one sales clerk. The entire procedure must be repeated eleven times to accumulate the totals for the other sales clerks.

For certain types of applications such as this the positional type of table lookup processing offers decided advantages over the conventional factor lookup processing.

Another way in which calculations can be performed on an entire array is by adding (or multiplying, etc.) the same values to each element in the array. For example, suppose that the sales clerks are to receive a 10 percent commission on their total sales to be paid at the end of the month. After all the daily sales have accumulated into the MONTH array, each of the twelve elements in MONTH can be multiplied by .10. These commission amounts can then be placed in another twelve-element array called COMMIS.

Figure 7.16 Adding arrays—example

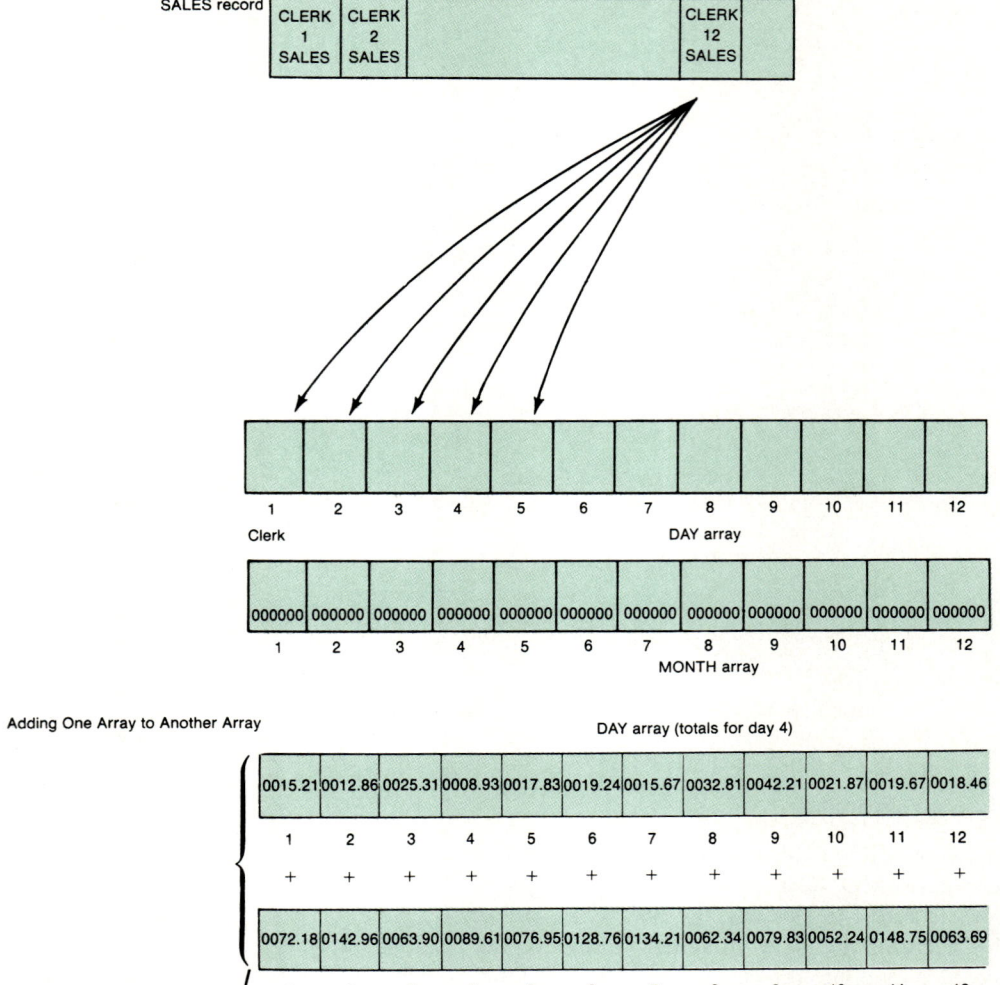

Individual items in an array can be referenced by their position relative to the beginning of the array. A result can be placed in every element of an array.

Array Calculations

The end uses of an array are either to obtain the sum of its elements or to retrieve certain data fields among its elements. (See Figure 7.17.) An array is referenced by the array name followed by a comma and element's index—either an integer constant or the name of a numeric field with no decimal positions. Name, comma, and index together must not exceed six characters, except when specified as factor 1 or factor 2 on the Calculation Specifications form, in which case it can be ten characters long. The index

Figure 7.17 Calculating totals with arrays—examples

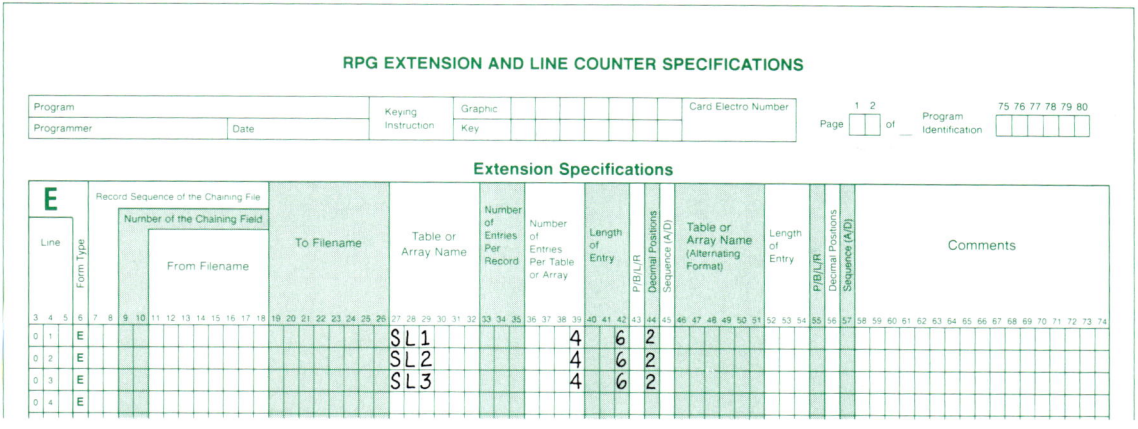
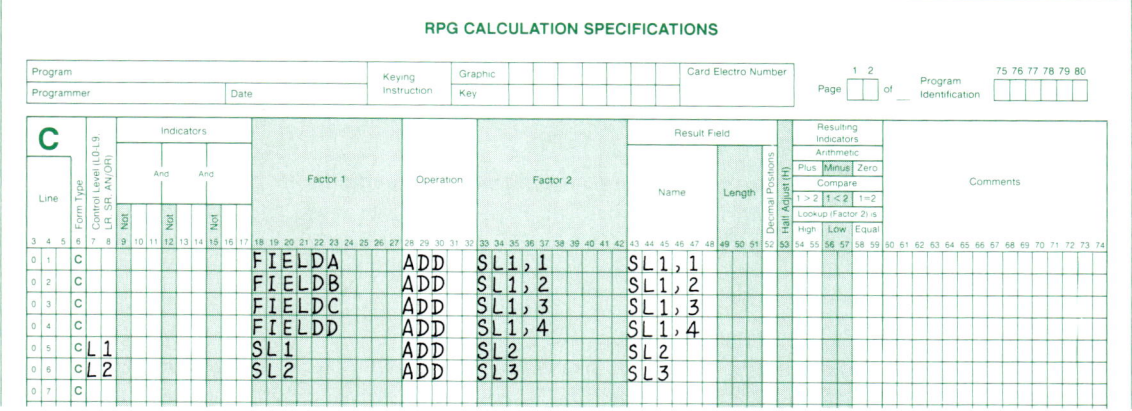
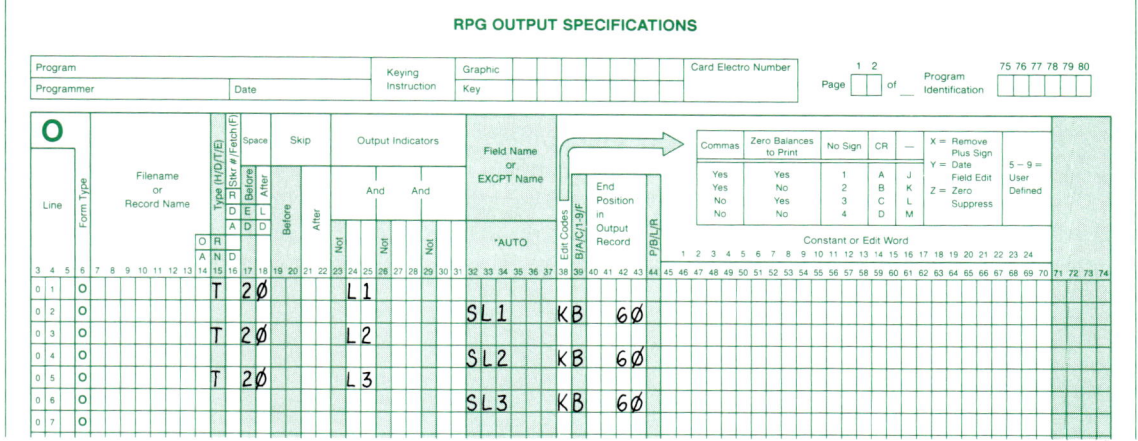

Notes on the Coding

These specifications perform the function of tabulating three levels of totals. The fields FIELDA, FIELDB, FIELDC, and FIELDD are added, as they are read from input records, to the first-level totals SL1,1, SL1,2, SL1,3, and SL1,4.

These first-level totals are added at the time of an L1 control break to corresponding totals SL2,1, SL2,2, SL2,3, and SL2,4.

Similarly, at an L2 control break, the second-level totals are added to corresponding third-level totals SL3,1, SL3,2, SL3,3, and SL3,4.

In addition, as control breaks occur, L1, L2, and L3 total output is performed; total fields are zeros after they are written on the output device.

Arrays   303

Figure 7.18 Adding all elements of an array—example

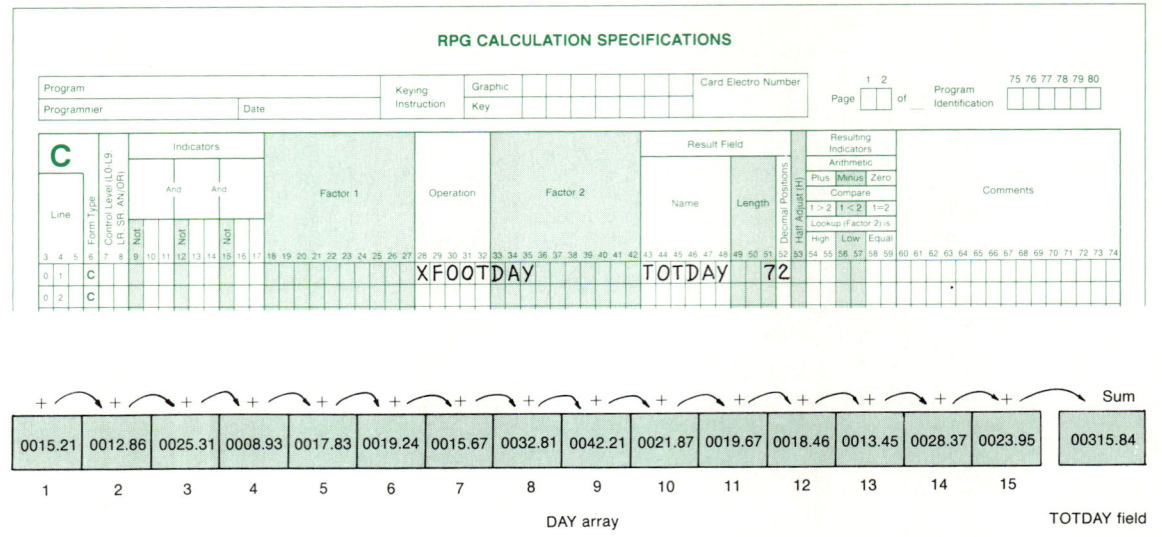

must be an integer value from 1 to *n*, where *n* is the number of elements in the array. Any number greater than *n* cannot be used as an index. When an element is referenced, it is processed as a field except when it is used as factor 2, when the referenced array serves as the start for the search in a LOKUP operation.

Adding All Elements within an Array (XFOOT)

The XFOOT operation code tells the computer to sum the contents of every element named in factor 2 in the array. Factor 1 is left blank since the XFOOT operation involves only the values in one array. The sum of the array elements is then placed in the single field named in the result field. (See Figure 7.18.)

In all other types of array calculations, multiple results are produced in accordance with the number of elements in an array. An XFOOT operation, however, yields just one result—the total of all elements. For this reason, XFOOT is the only operation referencing an entire array that specifies a single field rather than an array name in the result field. Furthermore, since there is only one result, a resulting indicator may be assigned in positions 54–59 to determine if the sum is plus, minus, or zero.

The XFOOT operation is used only on arrays with numeric elements. The result field can be half-adjusted and resulting indicators may be used. If the result field is an element belonging to the same array used in factor 2, the value of the element prior to the XFOOT operation is used in arriving at a total.

Lookup of an Array (LOKUP)

Searching an Array for a Particular Element

An array can be searched to determine if a particular element of data is stored in the array. Actually, the array lookup is coded and performed in a way very similar to a single-table lookup. On the Calculation Specifications form, the following should be specified:

1. The search word to be used
2. The LOKUP operation code
3. The array to be searched
4. The condition that must be satisfied
5. The resulting indicator that turns on if the condition is met (See Figure 7.19.)

Figure 7.19 Searching an array for a particular element—example

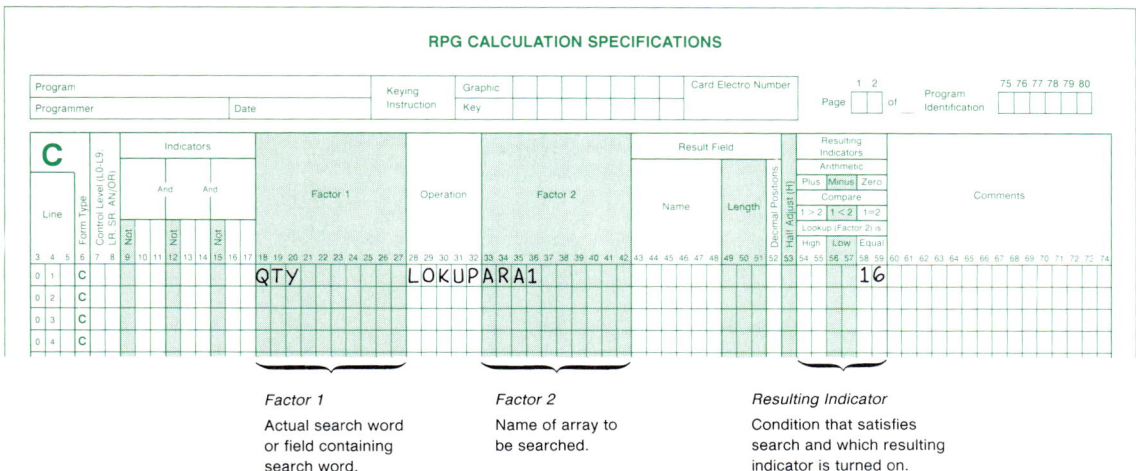

Factor 1 is the search argument and factor 2 designates the array to be searched. The resulting indicator field specifies the condition that must be satisfied, that is, the type of lookup to be performed. The search will be for a value that is next higher, next lower, or equal to the value entered under the appropriate heading in the resulting indicator field. The result field is not used for array LOKUP.

The array lookup continues, one element at a time, until the search condition is satisfied or until the end of the array is reached, whichever occurs first. As is the case for table lookups, array elements must be in sequence (*A* or *D*) if the search is for either a low or a high condition. (See Figure 7.20.)

Although array and table searches are similar, it is an important difference that the programmer be aware that the array lookup is similar to a single-table lookup, not a two-table lookup. Only one array is specified in the lookup operation. Any element referenced as a result of a successful search can only be from the array actually searched. In other words, the array cannot be searched to make available an element from another array, as happens when two related tables are used in a lookup operation. For this reason, no result field is specified in an array lookup operation. In a table lookup, the element found is implied and a reference to the table name, alternating table name, or related table name will produce that element in a calculation or output operation. In an array lookup, the subscript is modified to the value of the element number and another array can be referenced using that index in a manner similar to related tables. Indeed, a reference to the array name (like a table name) refers to *all* elements of the array, not the one looked up.

Starting the Search at a Particular Element

Another important difference between table and array searches is the location of the start of the search. In a table search, only the name of the table to be searched can be specified as factor 2 of the lookup operation. As a result, a table search always begins at the first table element. Likewise, if only an array name is specified as factor 2 of a lookup operation, the search automatically begins at the first element of the named array.

With arrays, however, there is the capability of beginning an array search at any element specified. Under factor 2, the array name followed by a comma and an index can be specified. The index, whether an actual number or the name of a field containing a number, points to the array element where the search is to begin. (See Figure 7.21.)

In a large array, where it is known that the value being sought is not in a particular section of the array, search time can be greatly decreased by beginning the lookup at a particular element. (See Figure 7.22.)

Arrays   305

Figure 7.20 LOKUP operation with array—example

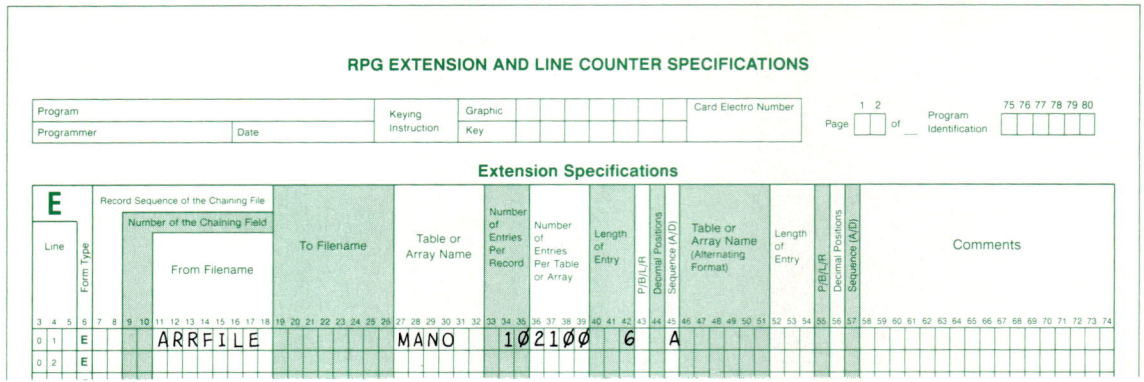

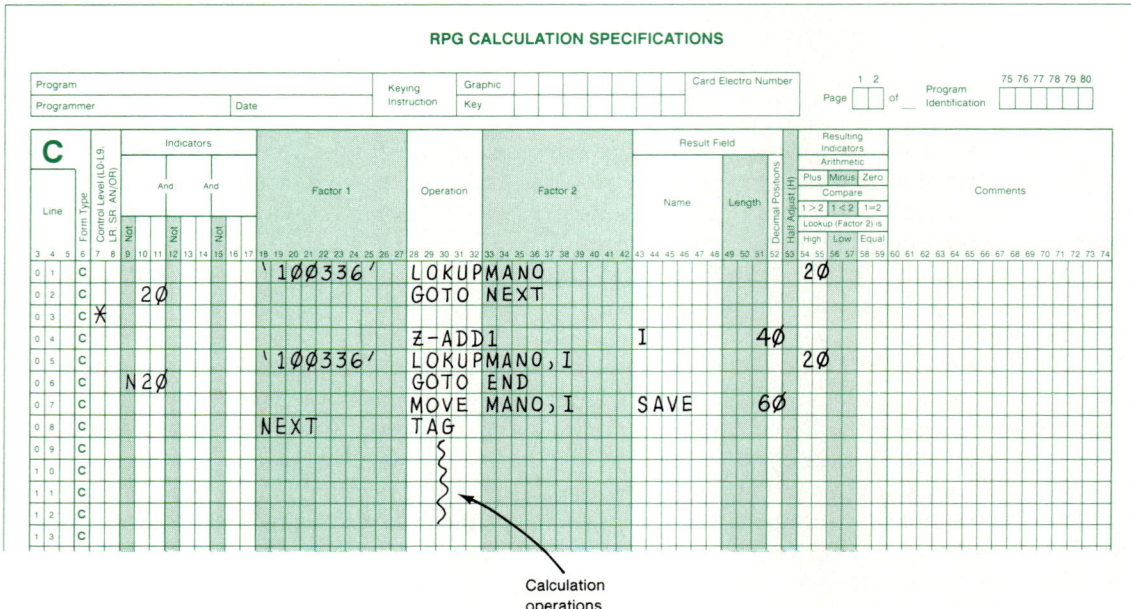

Calculation operations

Notes on the Coding

The above program shows two LOKUPs performed on an array. MANO, a 2100-element array of employee numbers, is read in at preexecution time from file ARRFILE, with six 10-position elements per record; the array elements are in ascending order.

Line 01 of the Calculation form shows a LOKUP of array MANO with the object of finding the element nearest to but higher in sequence than the search word '100336'. If this desired element is found in the array, indicator 20 turns on and the GOTO in line 02 is performed. Notice that the result of this LOKUP indicates only whether or not the desired element exists in the array.

Line 05 of the Calculation form shows essentially the same LOKUP operation—indicator 20 will turn on when the first element higher in sequence than '100326' is found. Note, however, that in this LOKUP operation, the array MANO is indexed by the field I. This index field was set to 1 in line 04 so the LOKUP will begin at the first element of MANO. If the desired element is found, the number of this element (not its contents) is placed in the field I. In this way, the actual element that satisfied the LOKUP can be used in subsequent calculation operations, as in line 07. If no element is found to satisfy the LOKUP, the field 1 would be reset to 1.

Figure 7.21 Array lookup—starting at a particular array item—example

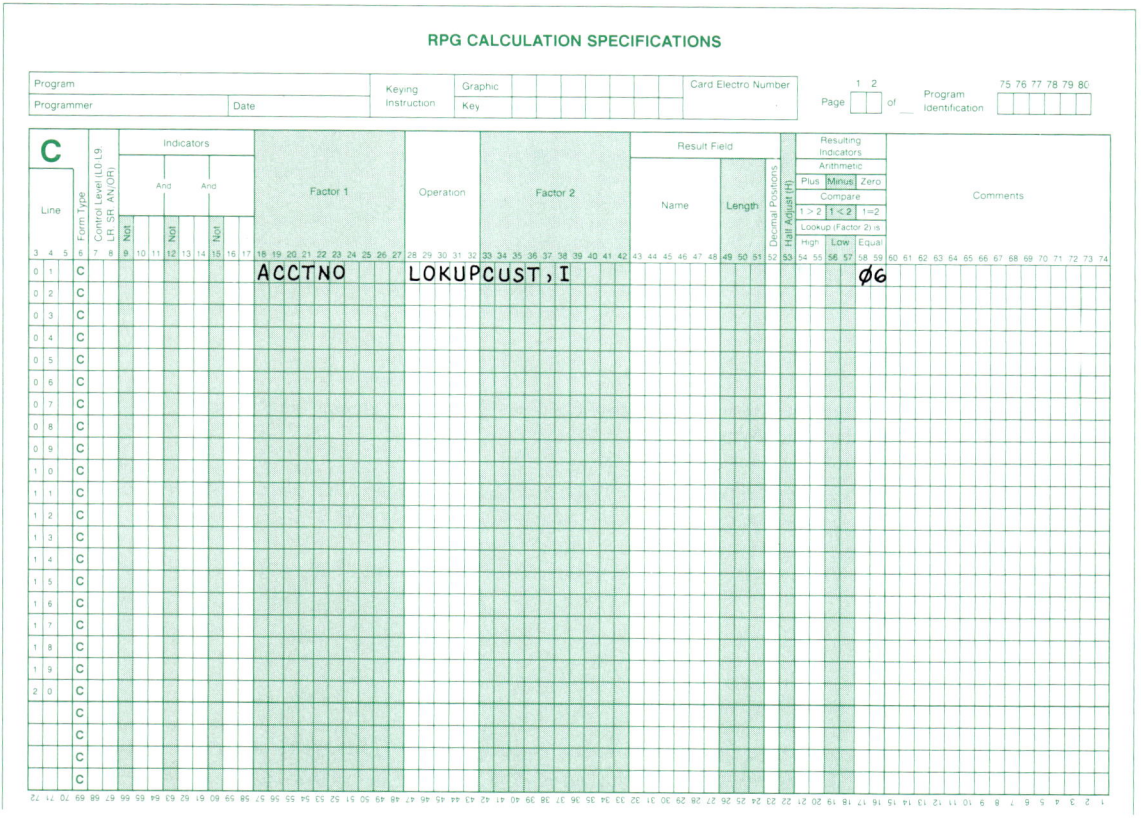

Figure 7.22 Starting an array search at a particular element—example

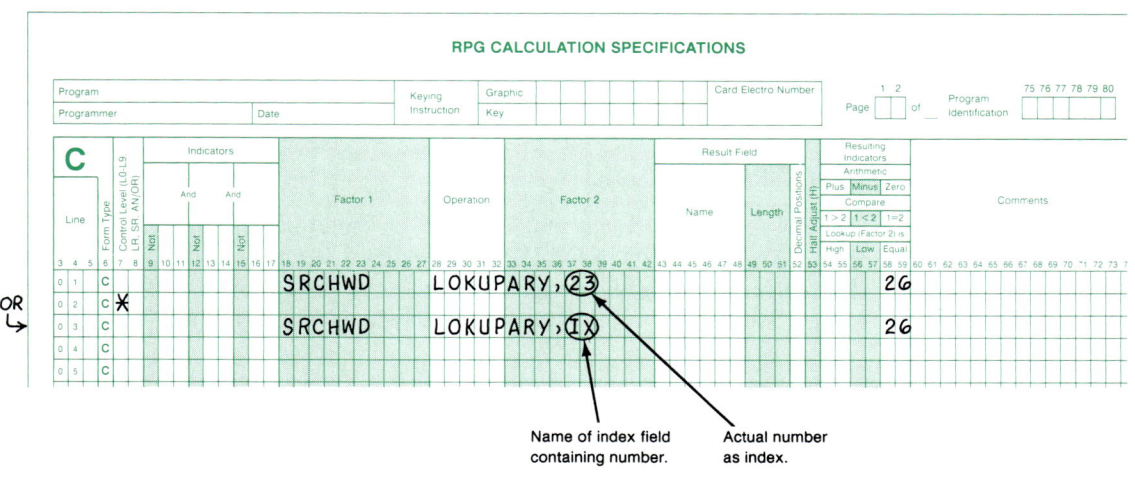

Arrays 307

Figure 7.23 Determining success of search only—example

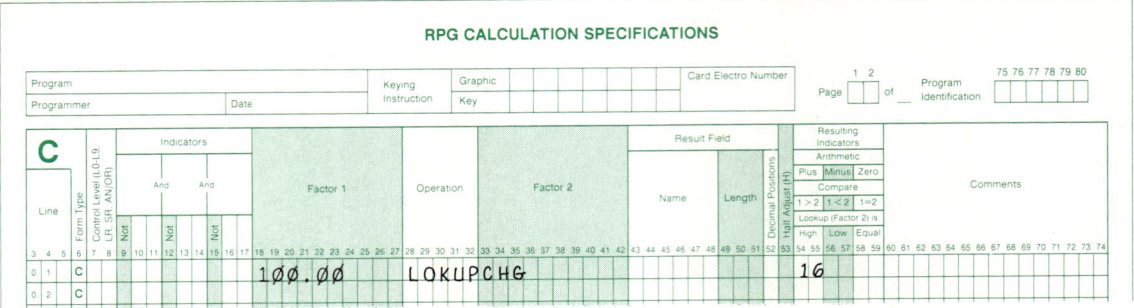

Notes on the Coding

Assume the programmer wishes to check for amounts over $100. If the programmer only wants to determine if there are any elements containing a greater amount, the search can be coded as above.

If indicator 16 is on, indicating a successful search, a message can be printed stating that there is a charge over $100. Otherwise, if indicator 16 is off, a message can be printed stating all charges are under $100.

With the LOKUP specification shown, however, the programmer would have no way of knowing how many elements satisfied the search condition.

Determining if a Search Is Successful

Before the lookup is performed, the index field value is determined. The array search then begins at the element number specified. The array lookup continues, one element at a time, until the search condition is satisfied or the end of the array has been reached, whichever occurs first. If an index field is specified, the number of the array element that first satisfies the search condition is stored in the index field. However, if the end of the array is reached and none of the elements satisfies the search, a *1* is placed in the index field. In any case, if an actual number rather than an index field is specified as the index, the actual index is not changed to reflect the success of the search.

The success of a search is determined according to whether the resulting indicator assigned has been turned on or off. If the resulting indicator is off and the index field has been specified, the index field should contain the value 1—the result of an unsuccessful search. If the first field of an array satisfied the search condition, the index would also contain the value 1; however, in such a case, the resulting indicator would be on. (See Figure 7.23.)

Referencing an Element That Satisfies a Search

After a successful search, the data from the element that satisfied the condition can be used only if the array name with an index field is specified in the LOKUP specifications. If an index field is specified, the number of the field that satisfied the search is stored in the index field. Therefore, the array name with the index field specified in a subsequent calculation or output specification refers to the element that satisfied the search.

If no index field is available (array name specified alone or with a numeric index), the number of the element cannot be determined and so its data cannot be referenced. The only determination that can be made is whether or not one of the elements contains the data for which the search was made. This type of LOKUP is used to determine if a specified element is present in the array or a specified condition was satisfied. The particular element that satisfied the search cannot be obtained in this case because the array name was given without an index field.

The ability to reference a data item that satisfies a search is one of the major differences between array lookup and table lookup. During a table lookup when a field is found that satisfies the search, the table name alone refers to the data item that satisfied the search. Following a lookup for an array, specifying an array name alone refers to the entire array, rather than a particular element of the array. The only way an individual array element can be referenced is to specify the array name with an index field.

Figure 7.24 Determining which array element satisfied the search—example

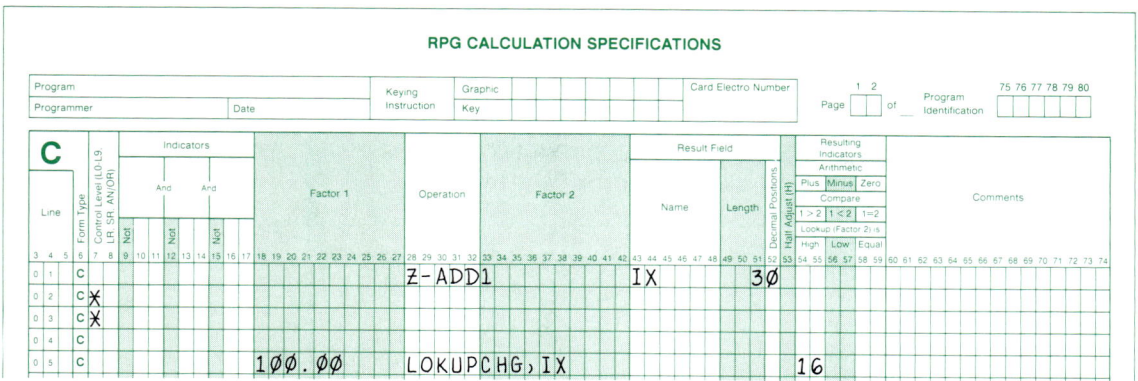

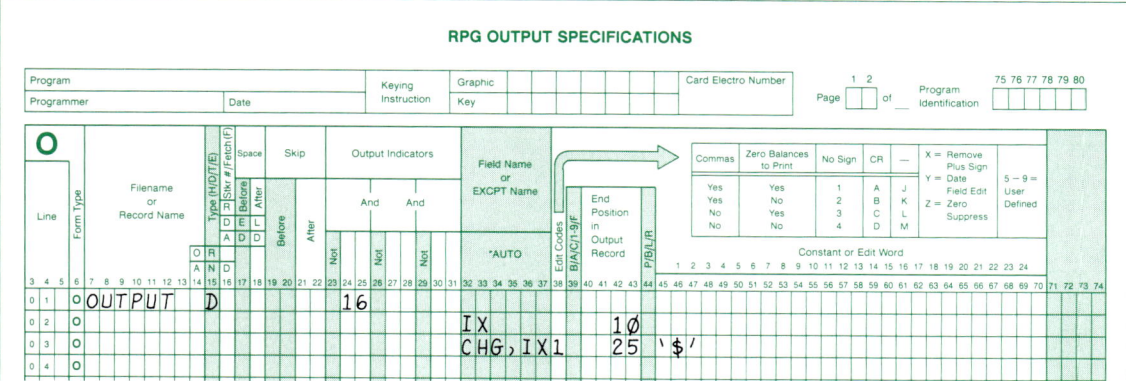

Notes on the Coding

If it is necessary to know which element satisfied the search or, perhaps, how much over $100 the amount is, the array lookup should be coded with an index field.

The index field can be preset to contain the value of 1, so the search begins at the first element of the array. If the search is satisfied, IX will contain the number of the first element over $100 and the resulting indicator will be turned on.

The contents of IX can be printed to indicate which element satisfied the search. The actual contents of that element can be printed by specifying the array name with the index field.

Elements in the array to be searched must have the same total field length and format as the search argument. Decimal alignment is not performed. If an index is specified, it may refer to the name of a numeric field or to a numeric constant. Processing of a lookup operation where the array to be searched is indexed by a numeric constant differs from that for a numeric field index in that the index remains unchanged and, therefore, cannot be retained for future use. As in the search of a nonindexed array, the LOKUP operation serves only to determine if a given element satisfying the search condition is present in the array. The advantage of an indexed over a nonindexed array is that search time can be reduced if it is known that the searched-for element is in a later section of the array.

In a successful search, the actual value found is not retained. Only the element number that can be used for referencing the desired value in other calculations or output is kept. (See Figure 7.24.)

Searching an Array for More Than One Element

An array LOKUP operation is complete when the first element satisfying the search condition is found. If the programmer wishes to find all elements that satisfy the condition, additional specifications causing the program to loop back in calculations must be coded. Repeat the lookup operation from the point where the search was successful.

Arrays 309

Figure 7.25 If more than one array element satisfies the search condition—example

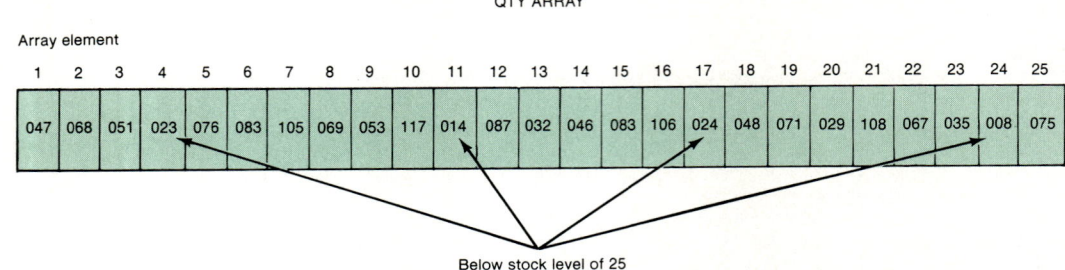

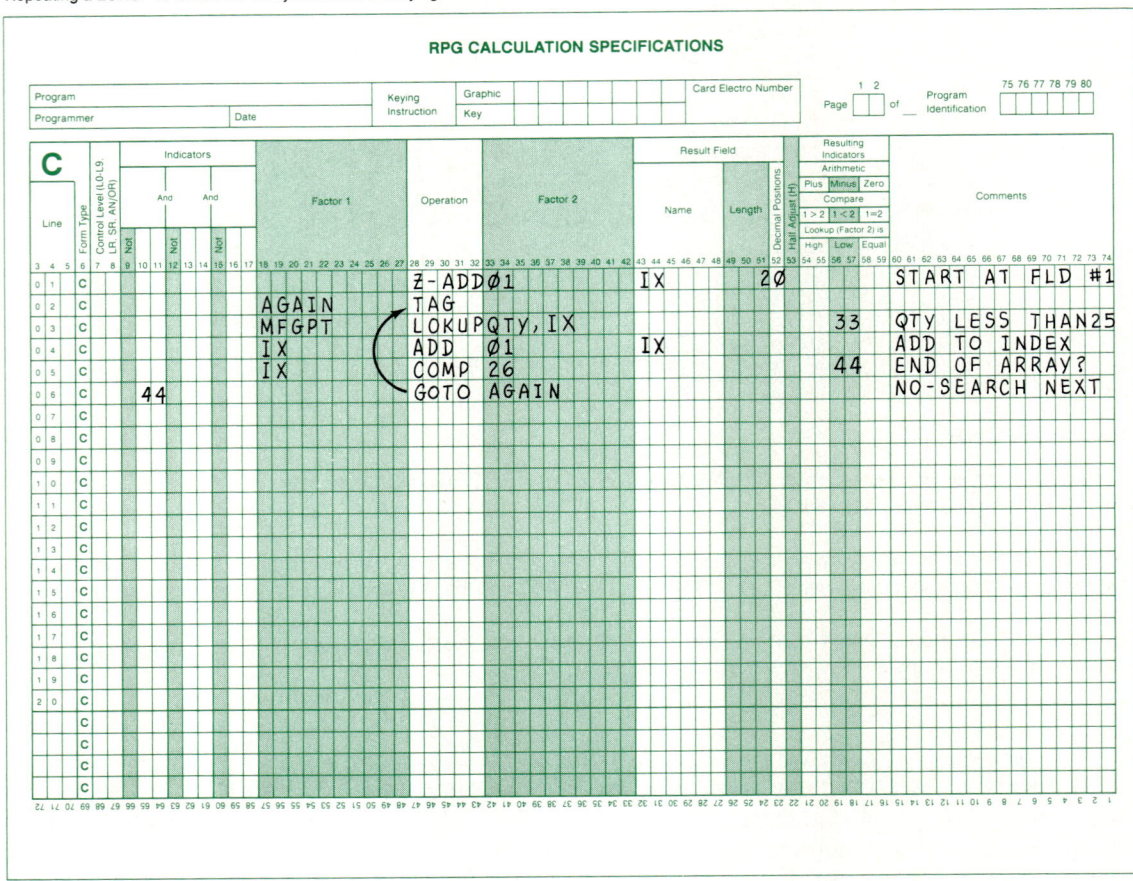

To locate more than one element satisfying the same search condition, the LOKUP must be repeated within a single program cycle. Not only must the LOKUP be repeated but the search must also begin at the point where the previous search ended. The LOKUP can be repeated by using the GOTO and TAG operations. To make sure the repeated search begins where the last search left off, the array name must be specified with an index field in the LOKUP specification. The content of the index field is then updated after each successful search to indicate at which array element the next search should begin. (See Figure 7.25.)

Figure 7.26 Output of array element as it is located in the search—example

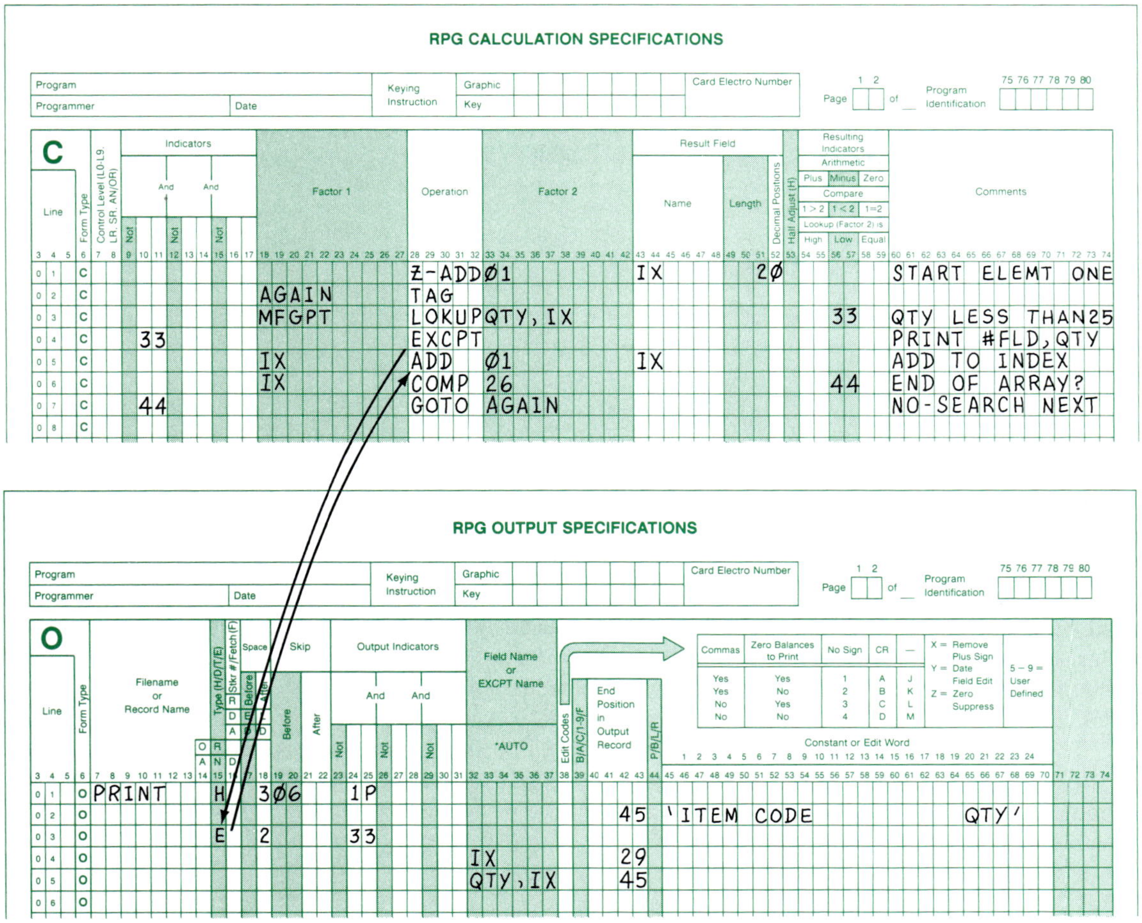

RPG CALCULATION SPECIFICATIONS

Line	Factor 1	Operation	Factor 2	Result Field	Length	Resulting Indicators (Hi/Lo/Eq)	Comments
01		Z-ADD	01	IX	20		START ELEMT ONE
02	AGAIN	TAG					
03	MFGPT	LOKUP	QTY,IX			33	QTY LESS THAN 25
04	33	EXCPT					PRINT #FLD,QTY
05	IX	ADD	01	IX			ADD TO INDEX
06	IX	COMP	26			44	END OF ARRAY?
07	44	GOTO	AGAIN				NO-SEARCH NEXT

RPG OUTPUT SPECIFICATIONS

Line	Filename/Record Name	Type	Space Before	Space After	Output Indicators	Field Name or EXCPT Name	End Position	Constant or Edit Word
01	PRINT	H	3	06	1P			
02							45	'ITEM CODE QTY'
03		E	2		33			
04						IX	29	
05						QTY,IX	45	

Output during an Array Search

In order to print each item located in an array search, output must be done before the content of the index field is changed. Since output specifications are not performed until all calculations are done and since the program in a looped search will continue to look for items to satisfy the search word, normal output would be invalid. The EXCPT operation can be used to cause all items satisfying the search condition to be output as they are found. First, the data in the index field are output; that output is followed by the content of the array element that satisfied the search. After the execution output has been performed, the program continues with the calculation specifications. (See Figure 7.26.)

Output of an Entire Array

It is sometimes necessary to have an entire array written to disk or printed out. Perhaps the programmer wants to look at the content of the array at some point during the program run or at the end of the run. Or, the programmer may want to have array elements put out in order to use them as input for another program. Output of an entire array can be specified in two ways—with extension specifications or with output specifications.

Specifying Output with Extension Specifications

Like tables, compile time arrays and preexecution time arrays can be written out at the end of the job by entering the name of the output file under the To Filename (positions 19–26) heading on the Extension form. The output file must be named on the File Description form, but no output specifications are necessary. The entire array, including unused elements (blanks or zeros), is put out.

The array is put out automatically at the end of the job in the same format as the array input records—one output record per array input record. This may make the array output difficult to read if one entry runs into another on the input record.

Although the format of the output and input records is the same, the data output may not be exactly the same as the data input. The program can change or update array entries, causing modified data instead of the original data to be put out.

Specifying Output with Output Specifications

The second method of specifying output of an entire array is with output specifications. On the Output Specifications form, the array name is specified under field name (positions 32–37). All elements within the named array are printed or written on the indicated output file. All types of arrays—compile, preexecution, and execution—can be put out using output specifications.

Any output conditioning indicators specified in positions 23–31 of the Output Specifications form determine when during the program the array elements will be output. If no indicators are specified, the entire array is output every time a record is processed. Indicators can be specified to put out array data during detail cycles or total time. For example, array data can be put out at total time by customer or inventory item to be used as input for subsequent update runs.

RPG determines (by the end–position specified in positions 40–43 of the Output Specifications form) where the array data are to be placed on the output file. The array elements are put out so that the last element of the named array ends in the position indicated. Note, however, that if all elements cannot be put out on one output record, the array elements must be referenced separately on the Output Specifications form. Output of individual elements will be discussed in a later section of this chapter.

The output of an entire array by means of output specifications requires only one specification. An entire array can be printed or written to disk at any time during the run or at the end of the job, depending on the way in which the output specifications are conditioned. Again, this is possible during the run only if a single output record can contain the entire array. (See Figure 7.27.)

How the data elements are to appear on the output record must be specified. Alphameric elements appear on the output record just as they appear in storage; however, numeric elements may be edited or unedited. If no editing is specified, the elements are written just as they appear in storage, with the last element ending in the end position of the output file. In other words, one element will immediately follow another with no punctuation and no blanks between elements.

Usually, printed array output is easier to read and has a cleaner appearance if edit codes or edit words are used to punctuate the data and to insert spaces between elements. If disk output is desired and the array output records are to be used as input the next time the job is run, editing is usually not specified. This way the elements will be in the appropriate format to be used as input.

Editing affects the position that is specified as the end-position of the output record. If each element in a five-element array contains seven characters, thirty-five positions would be necessary to output the entire array in unedited form. On the other hand, if punctuation and blanks are inserted for each element, the number of positions required increases. When specifying an end-position, enough positions must be allowed to output all edited elements.

Whether or not editing is specified, when output of an entire array is performed every element of that array is put out in the same format. If an edit code or edit word is specified, every element is edited in the same way. Since all elements of an array contain the same type of information, the programmer typically would want all the elements to be punctuated in the same way. If, however, one element must be edited differently from another element in the same array, the elements must be put out separately. This would require individual referencing of the elements of the array.

When an edit code is specified in position 38 of the Output Specifications form, every element of the name array will be punctuated accordingly. Furthermore, any edit code specified for an entire array also causes two blank spaces to be inserted between each element. The insertion of blanks is taken into consideration by the program so that the last element ends in the position specified. (See Figure 7.28.)

Figure 7.27 Output of an entire array—example

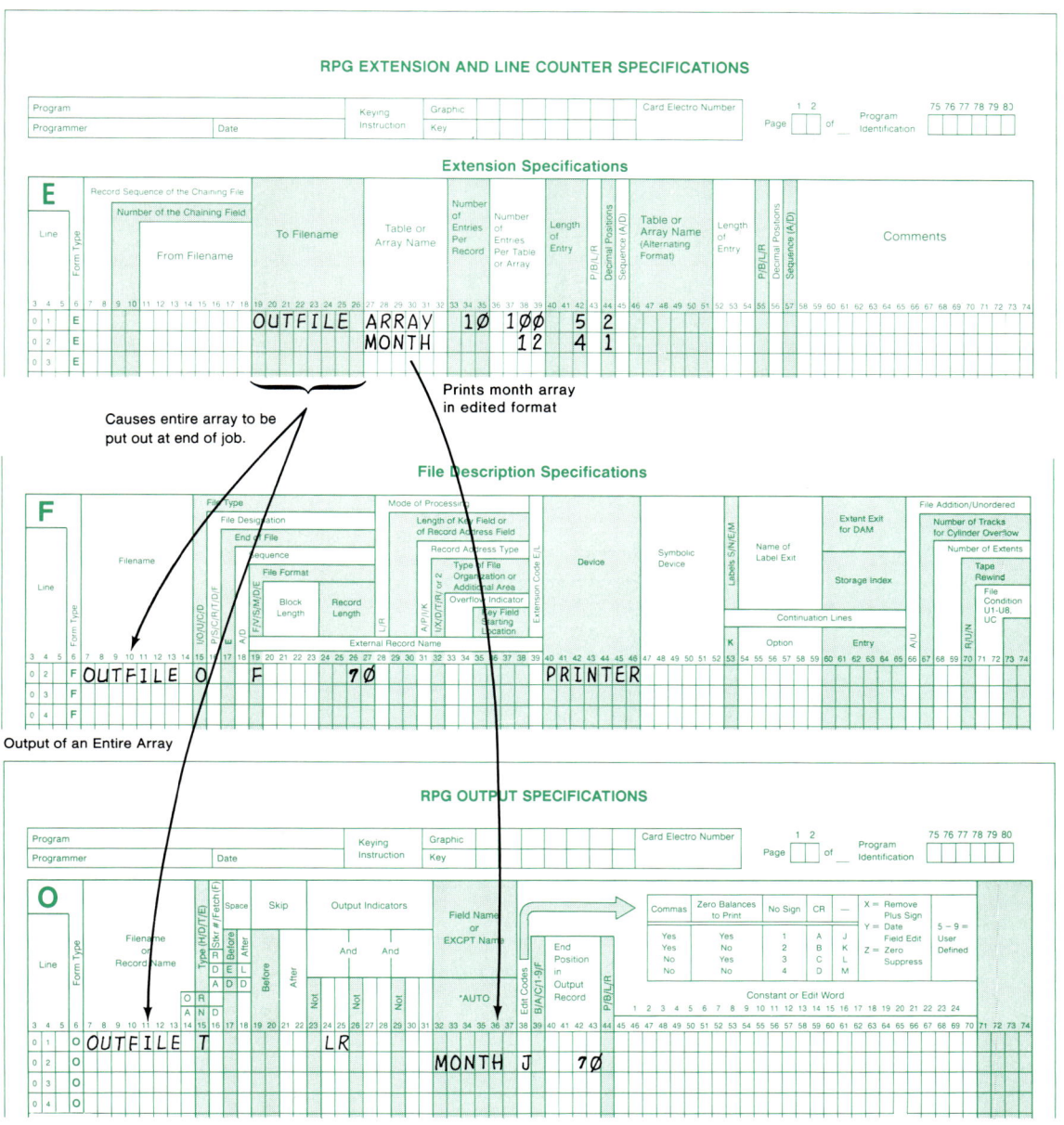

If no edit code specifies exactly how the array fields are to be edited, an edit word may be used to specify the punctuation desired. In this way, the programmer can edit array elements with dollar signs, zero suppression, blanks, constant words, or any combination of punctuation desired. When edit words are used, all punctuation must be specified. Unlike edit codes, edit words do not cause two blanks to be automatically inserted in the output record before each array element. Any extra blanks that are to appear must be indicated in the edit word by an ampersand (&). The two blanks are specified to be printed as part of every element. Thus, the second blank following the last element will be the character in the end position. An additional two positions must have been allowed for each element. (See Figure 7.29.)

Figure 7.28 Output of an entire array with edit codes—example

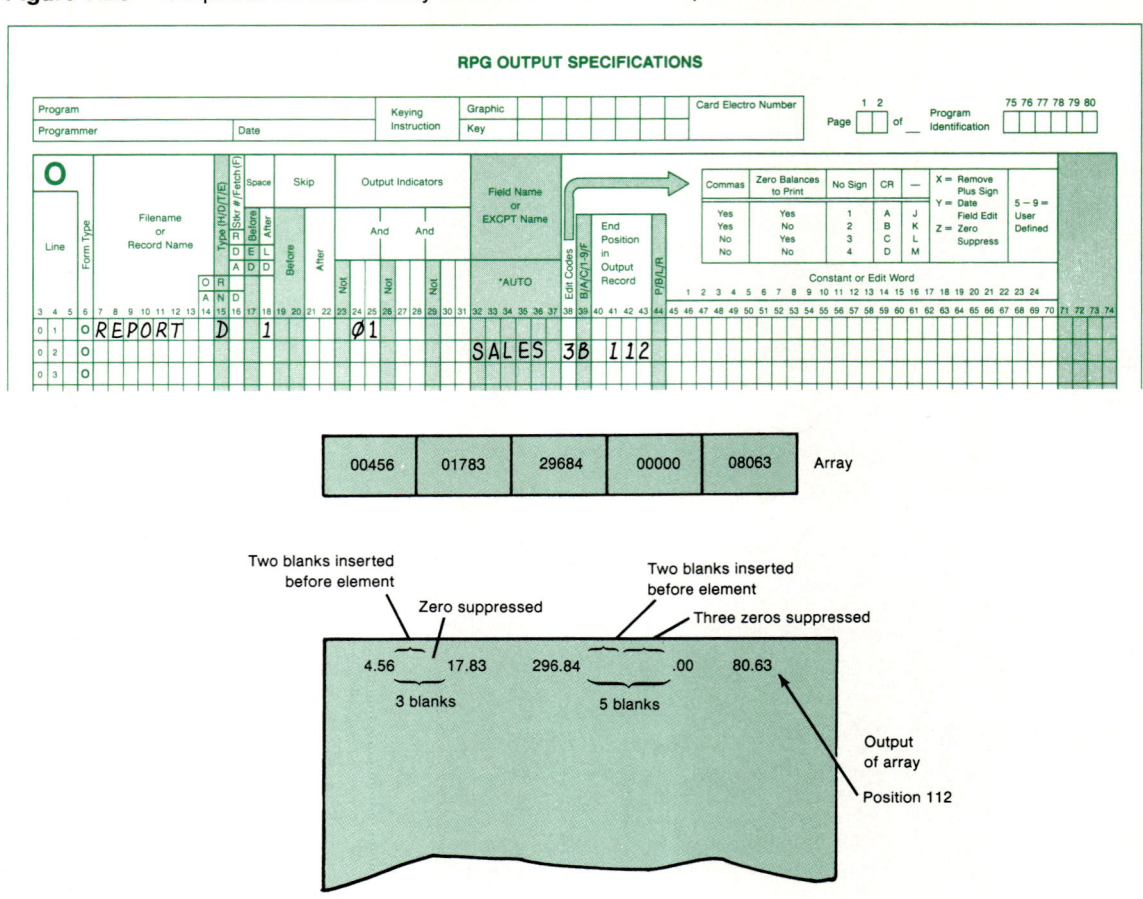

Figure 7.29 Editing an entire array with edit words—example

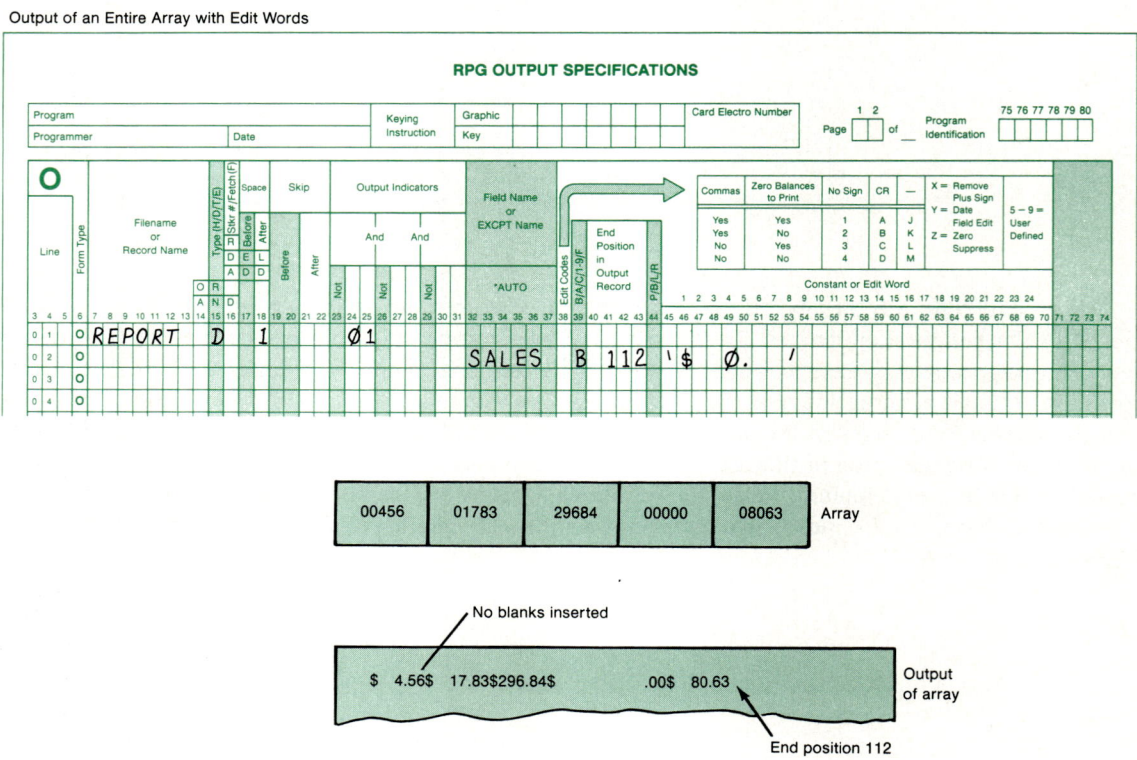

314 RPG II and RPG III Programming

Figure 7.29 continued

Editing Every Element of an Array

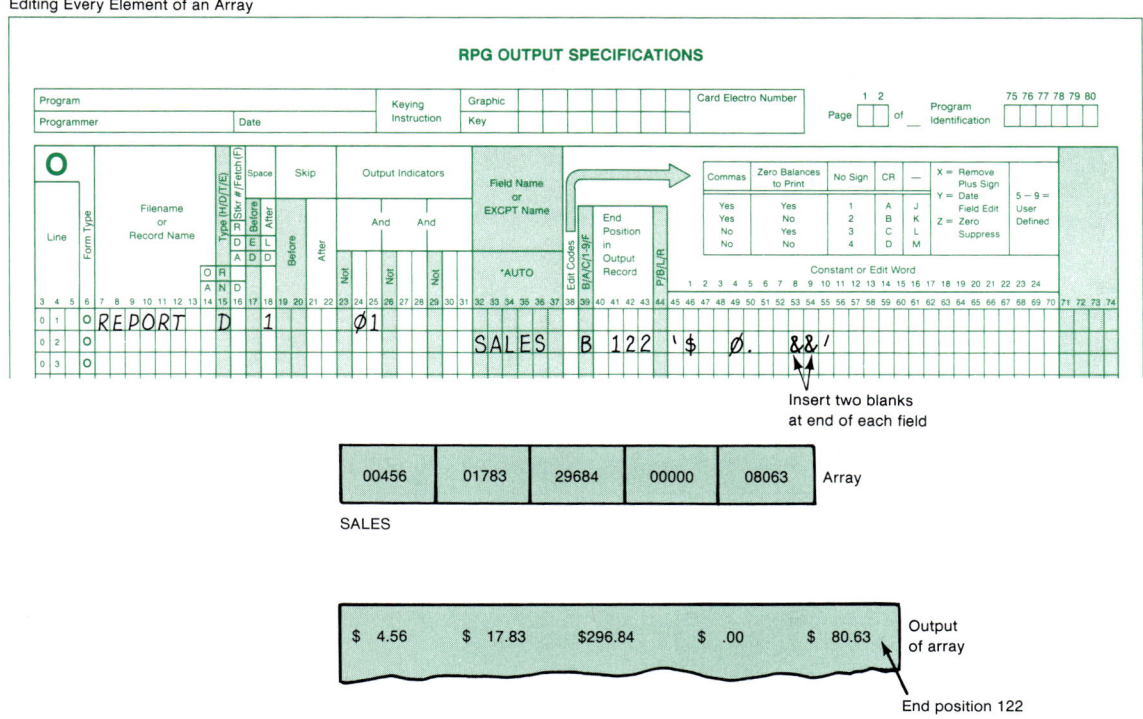

Accumulating Groups of Totals

Arrays can be used to accumulate a total. One of the most common uses of arrays is accumulating more than one group of totals. Such a procedure is called rolling of totals. One total is used to obtain a greater total, which is then used to calculate an even larger total, and so on. Each total is rolled into the next total.

For example, suppose that a company has two regions and that these regions are divided into three branches; each branch is made up of three to six stores. Company sales data are recorded via a CRT. For each store there is a separate record providing the twelve sales amounts for each month of the year. The sales records are organized so that stores are grouped within a branch; branches are grouped within a region. A sales report must be produced showing the monthly sales for each store, for each branch, for all branches within a region, and for both regions (the total monthly sales of the entire company).

To produce the report, four arrays of twelve elements each should be set up. The first array will hold the twelve sales amounts entered from the sales record. The other three arrays will accumulate the necessary totals for each branch, each region, and the entire company.

In general, this job should accumulate store totals into the branch array, branch totals into the region array, and region totals into the total array. Thus, the specifications must perform two functions:

1. Add all elements in one array to all elements of another array
2. Print all elements in each array

For the program to produce the correct totals, the programmer must specify that one array is to be added to another array and printed. To do this, the two fields that identify a record with a particular branch and region should be specified as control fields. A change in the branch (or region) control fields will cause a control break, indicating that the records for all stores in a particular branch (or region) have been processed. (See Figure 7.30.)

Figure 7.30 Accumulation and output of group totals using arrays—example

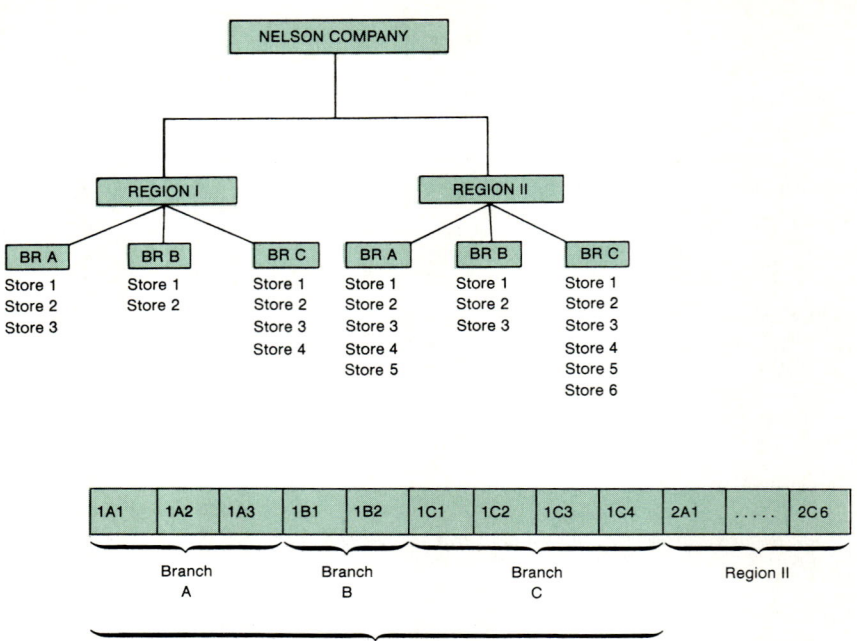

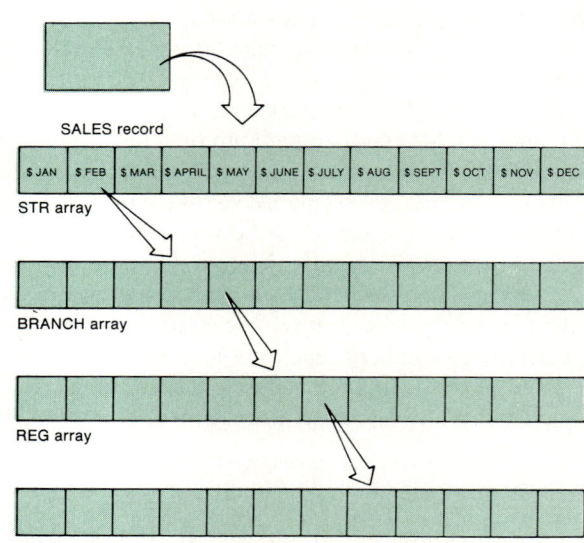

Figure 7.30 continued

Identifying Groups by Assigning Control Level Indicators

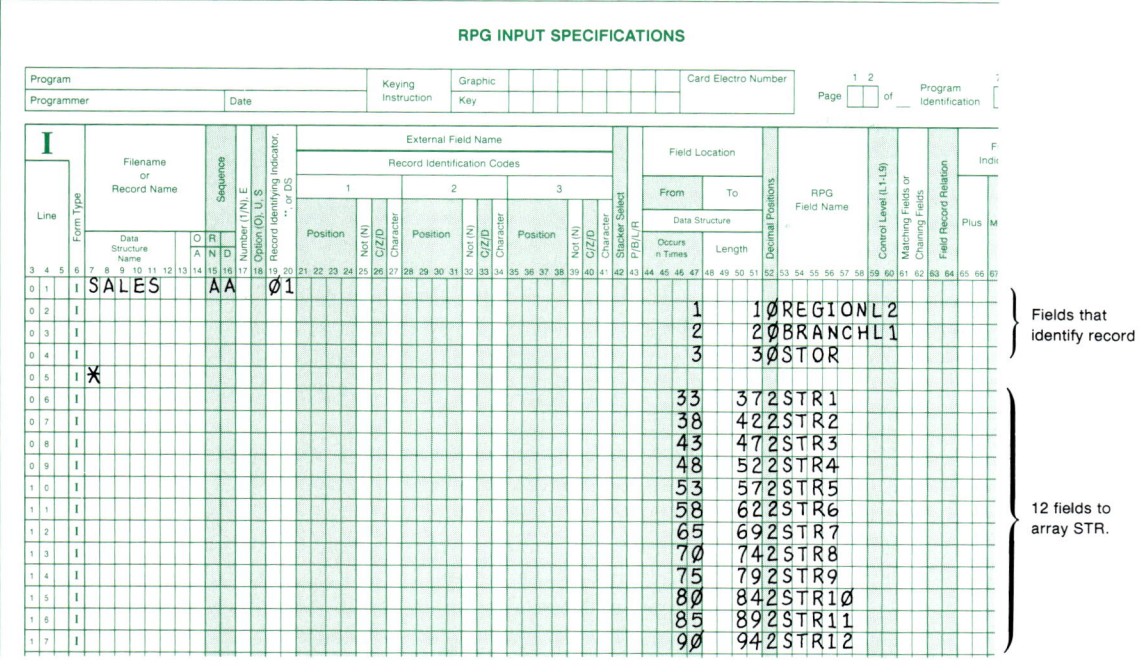

Accumulation and Output of Group Totals Using Arrays

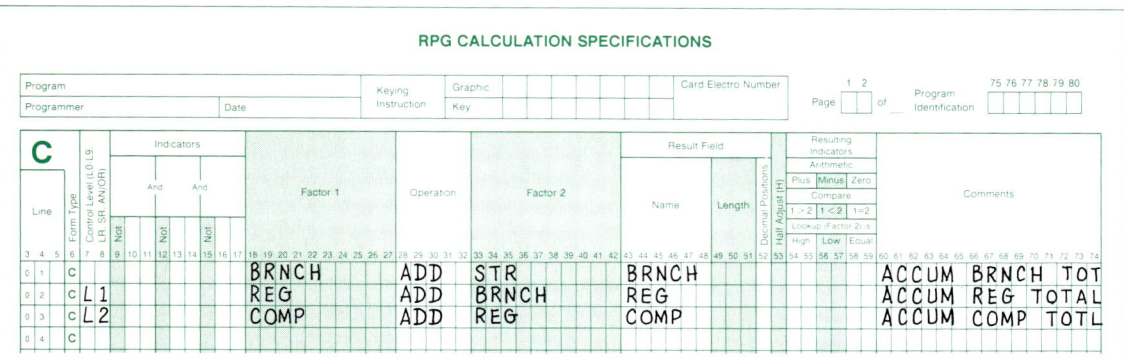

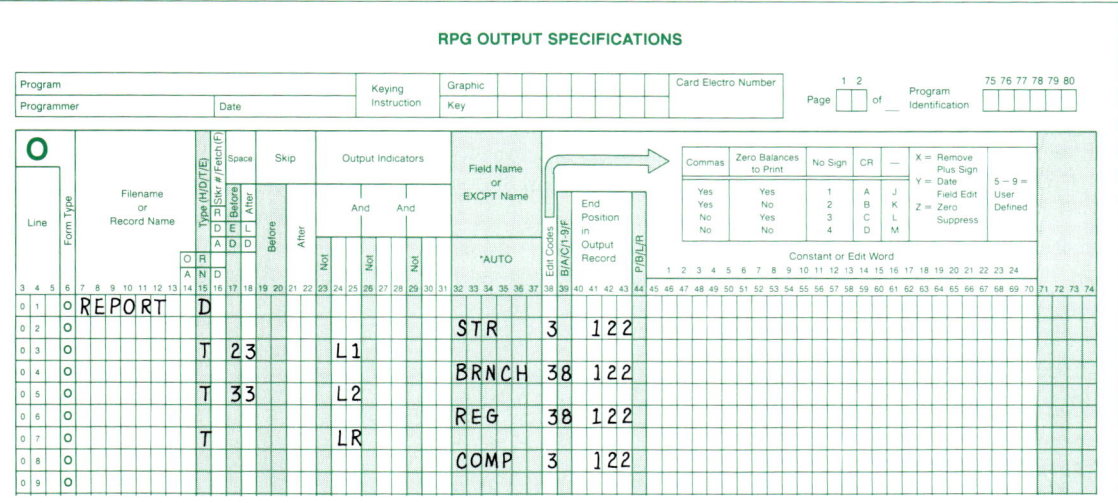

Arrays 317

Referencing Individual Elements of an Array

In addition to referencing all elements of an array, individual array elements can be used in calculations or output. Take, for example, an array in which each element contains the quantity in stock of a particular part manufactured by the company. Element 1 contains the quantity in stock for part 1, element 2 contains the quantity in stock for part 2, and so on. When a shipment of ordered parts is received, the quantity in stock must be updated to reflect the current inventory. This means that only particular elements of the array should be referenced (added to).

Indexing an Array

If a calculation or output specification contains an array name, alone, that specification is automatically performed for every element of the array. To reference only a single element of an array, that element must be identified for the RPG program. This is done by placing a comma after the array name followed by an index pointing to the particular element. This index can be either the actual number of the element to be referenced or the name of a field containing the number of the element to be used. (See Figure 7.31.)

The name used to refer to an array cannot exceed six characters in length. When referencing individual fields, both the array name and an index must be given. Therefore, the array name, plus the comma, plus the index cannot be more than six characters long. The name used to refer to an individual array element may be anywhere from one to six characters in length unless the name (with index) used to refer to an individual array element is specified *only* as factor 1 or factor 2 on the Calculation Specifications form. In this case, the array name, plus the comma, plus the index may be as long as ten characters. However, the array name portion of the reference cannot exceed six characters.

Specifying an Index That Does Not Change
If it is known exactly which element is to be used in a calculation or output operation and the specification is to reference the same element in every program cycle of the job, a constant may be used as an index. (See Figure 7.31.)

Specifying an Index That Can Be Changed
On the other hand, if the array element will vary when a particular specification is performed, the index should be a field name rather than an actual number. In this way, the number stored in the index field can be changed during the program to indicate which array element is to be referenced. (See Figure 7.32.)

Output of Individual Elements of an Array
To output individual elements of an array, the same output specifications are coded as the normal fields. The only difference is that the array name followed by a comma and an index must be specified under field name on the Output Specifications form. The index then points to the particular element to be put out. (See Figure 7.33.)

Thus, referencing individual array elements for output is the same as referencing them for calculations. If the same element is to be put out every time the output specifications are performed, an actual number can be used as an index. Otherwise, if different elements are to be put out individually, a field containing the changing index value should be specified. In any case, the array element (array name, plus comma, plus index) on the Output Specifications form cannot exceed six characters in length.

Edit codes and edit words can be used to punctuate individual numeric array elements. If an entire array is to be put out but elements require different punctuation, each element and its editing should be specified individually. Editing to be done on an individual array element is specified and performed just as it is for any other element. This means that if an edit code is specified for an individual array element, two blanks are *not* automatically inserted before the element, as is the case when an entire array is to be put out. Furthermore, although any type of output can be edited, editing is generally not specified for an array element to be written on a disk for use as input to another run. Only printed output should be edited.

Referencing Only Part of a Field
When a field is referenced in a specification, all characters within that field are used in the calculations or output. However, the programmer may wish to reference only some of the data stored in a field. For

Figure 7.31 Specifying a number as an index—example

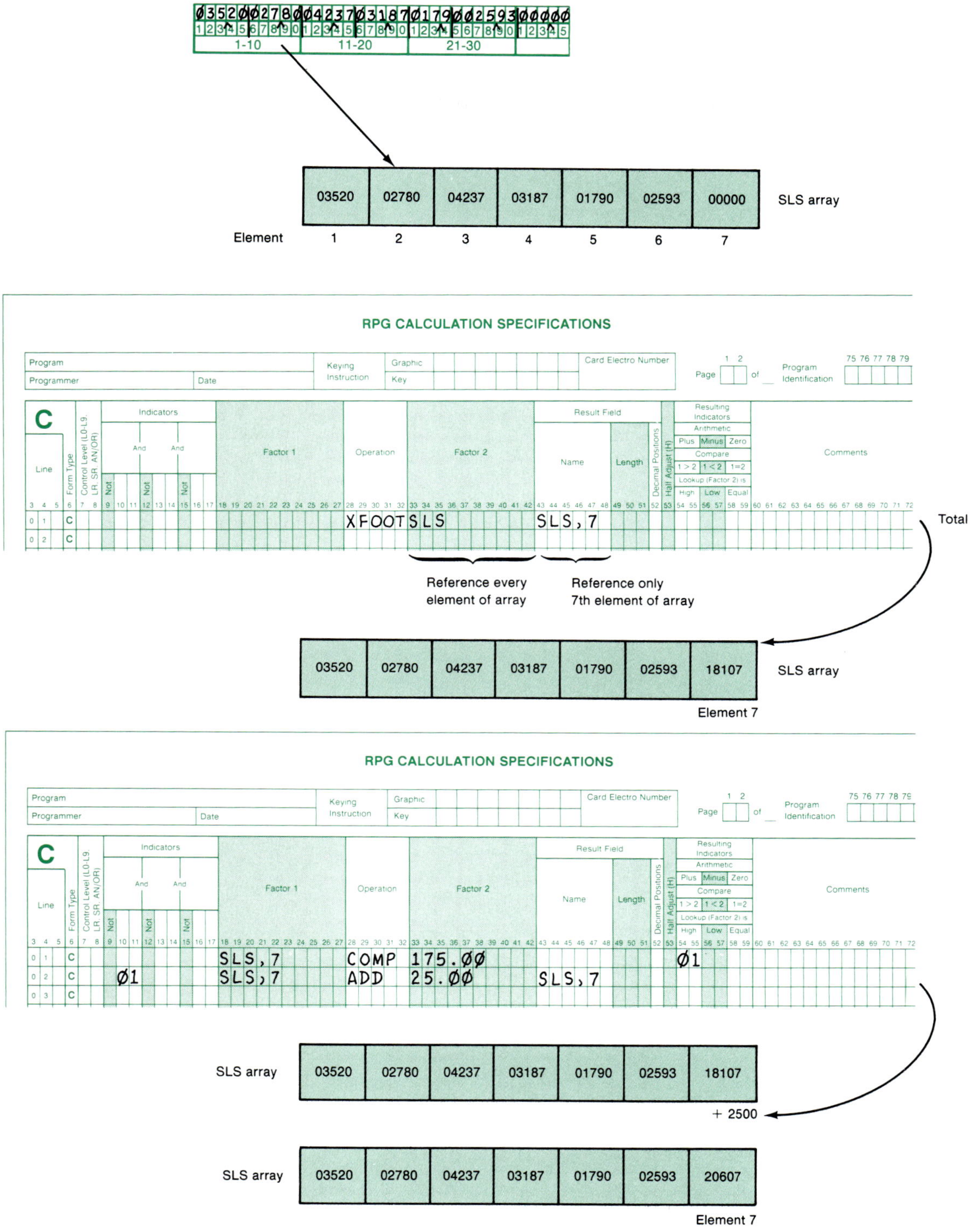

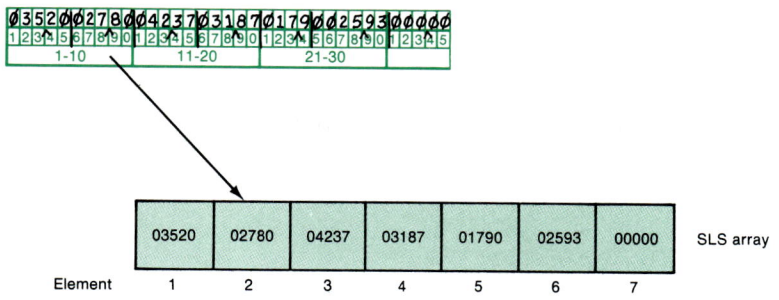

example, consider a case of address printing where the zip code falls within the same field as the city and state on an input record, but must be printed on a separate line.

The indexing capability of arrays can enable the programmer to reference specific characters from an input field. This is accomplished by setting up two arrays—one to contain the entire field of data and one to hold only the specific characters that are to be referenced.

Arrays 319

Figure 7.32 Specifying the name of a field as an index—example

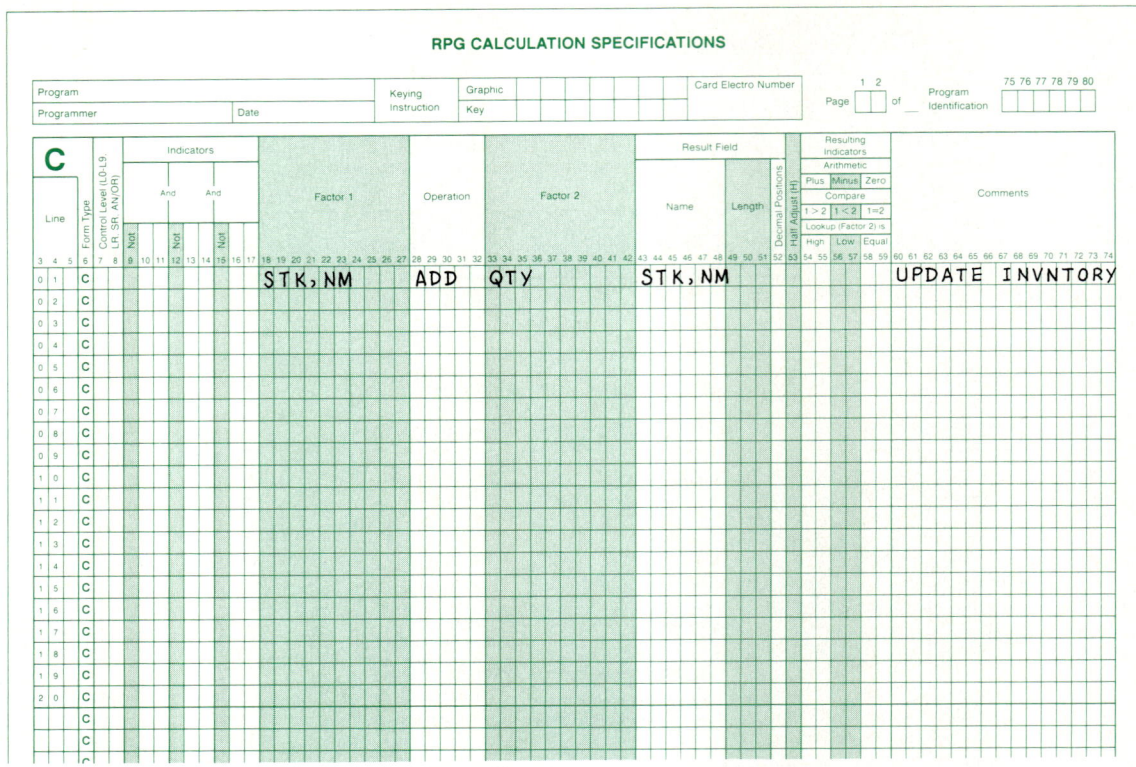

Figure 7.33 Output of individual array elements—example

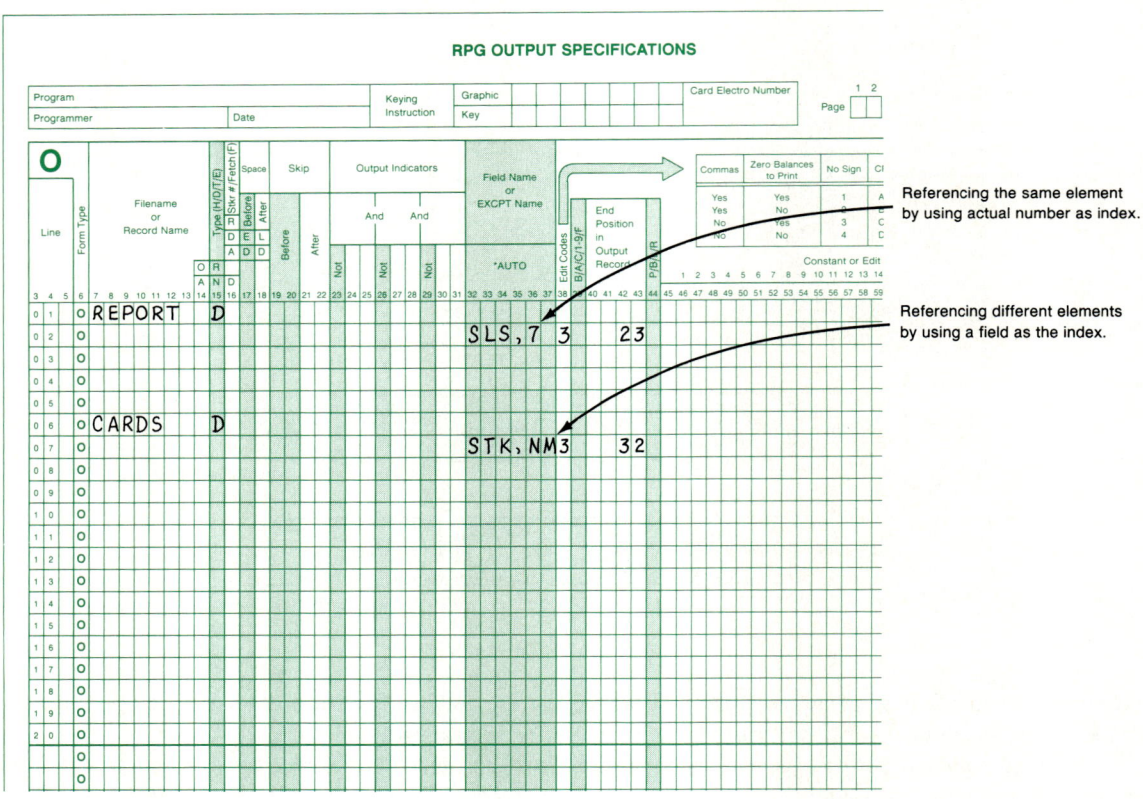

First, the entire field from which the programmer wishes to use the data is stored in an array of the same name. This array has been previously defined as containing as many single-character sizes as there are characters in the field to be referenced. Thus, each character of the entire field is actually stored in a separate element of the array. The array elements can then be referenced one at a time (using an index) until an element containing a specific character is located. This process of checking the elements of an array for particular data is referred to as field scanning.

After scanning the elements and locating a specific character, that character and any characters (elements) on either side of it can be moved to a smaller array. This array will then contain the portion of the original input field that the programmer wishes to reference separately in calculations or output. (See Figure 7.34.)

Figure 7.34 Field scanning—arrays—example

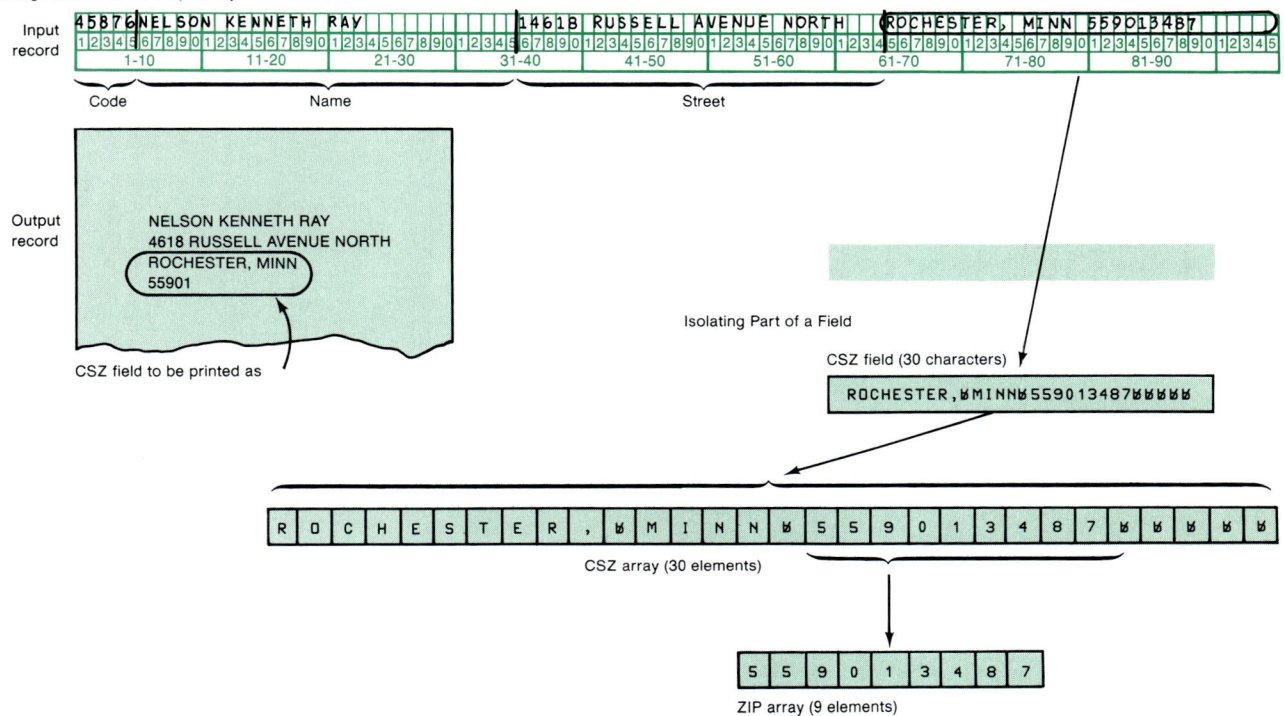

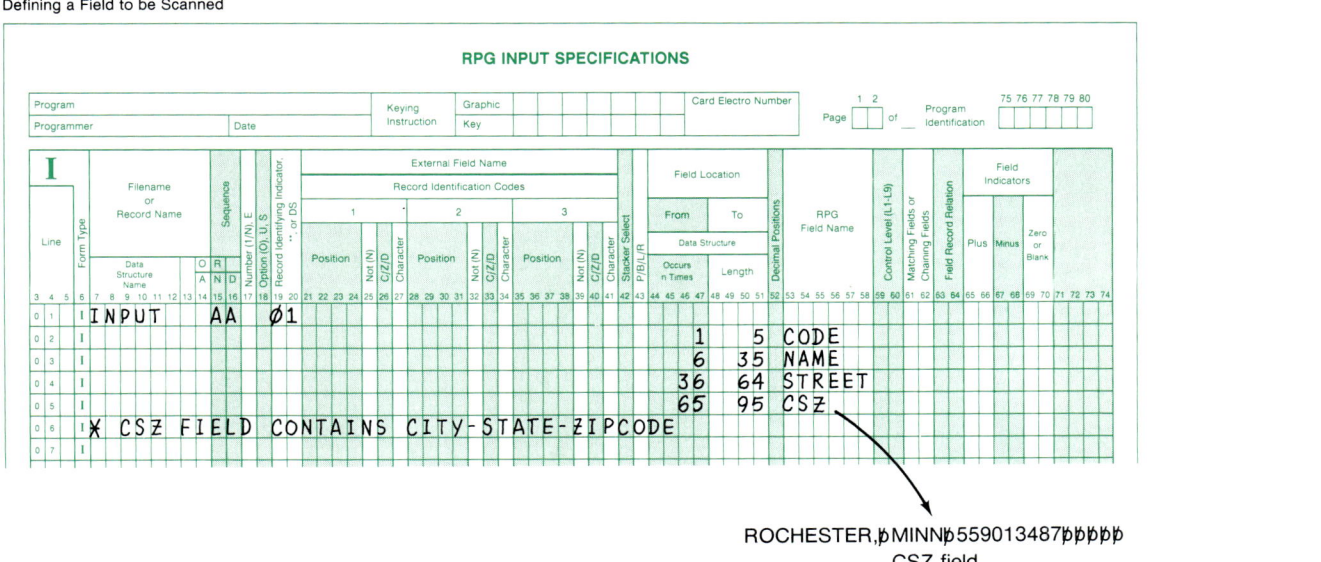

Arrays   321

Figure 7.34 continued

Defining Arrays for Field Scanning

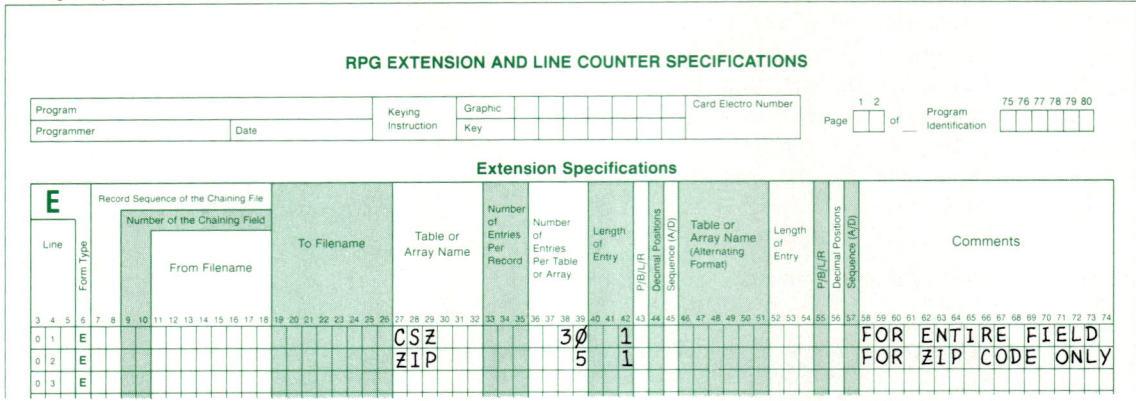

Field Scanning

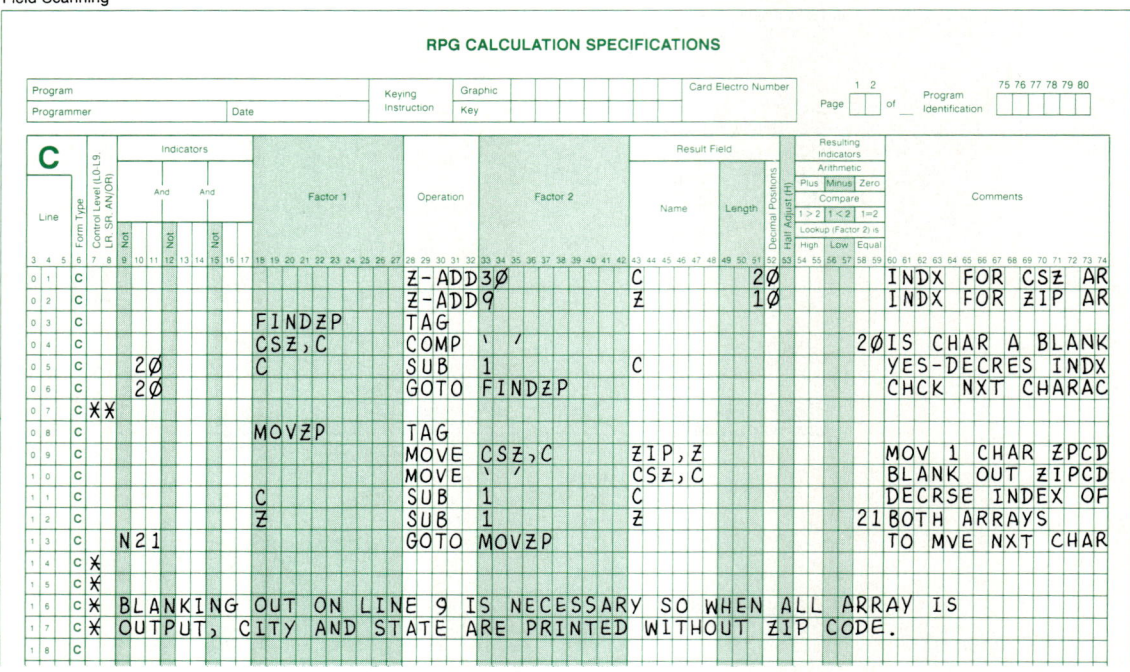

Output of Part of a Field

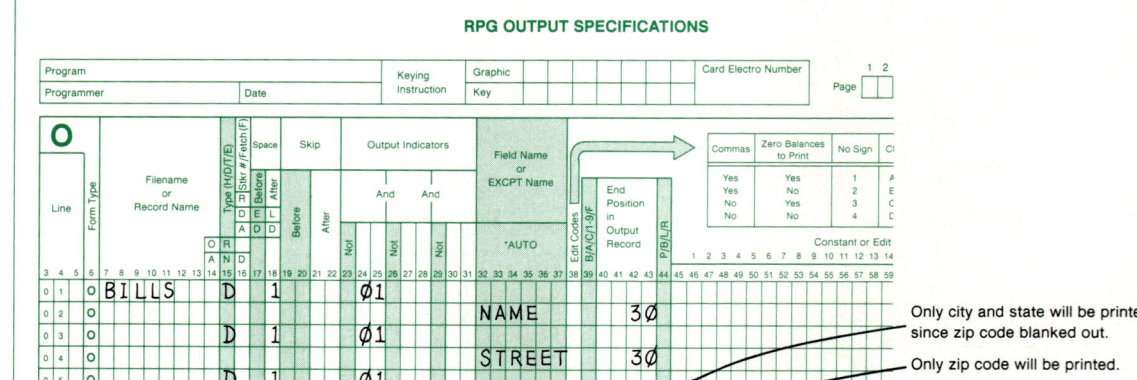

322 RPG II and RPG III Programming

Move Array (MOVEA)

The MOVEA operation moves the data starting from the leftmost position of factor 2 to the leftmost position of the result field. The shorter field (factor 2 or the result field) determines the length of the move. If factor 2 is longer than the result field, the excess rightmost characters of factor 2 will not be moved. If the result field is longer than factor 2, the characters to the right of the data moved in the result field will remain unchanged. Factor 2 and/or the result field must reference an alphameric array. Any field used with the MOVEA operation must be defined as alphameric. (See Figure 7.35.)

The MOVEA operation makes it possible to move any of the following:

1. Several contiguous array elements to a single field
2. A single field to several contiguous array elements
3. Contiguous elements of one array to contiguous elements of another array (See Figure 7.36.)

The movement of data starts with the first element of an array or field. If the array is indexed, the move starts with the element referenced. The movement of data is terminated when the last array element has been moved or filled, or when the number of characters moved equals the length of the shorter field specified in factor 2 or the result field. This may cause the move to terminate in the middle of an array element. (See Figure 7.37.)

Note: Factor 2 and the result field cannot both reference the same array. (See Figure 7.38.)

Figure 7.35 Move array—examples

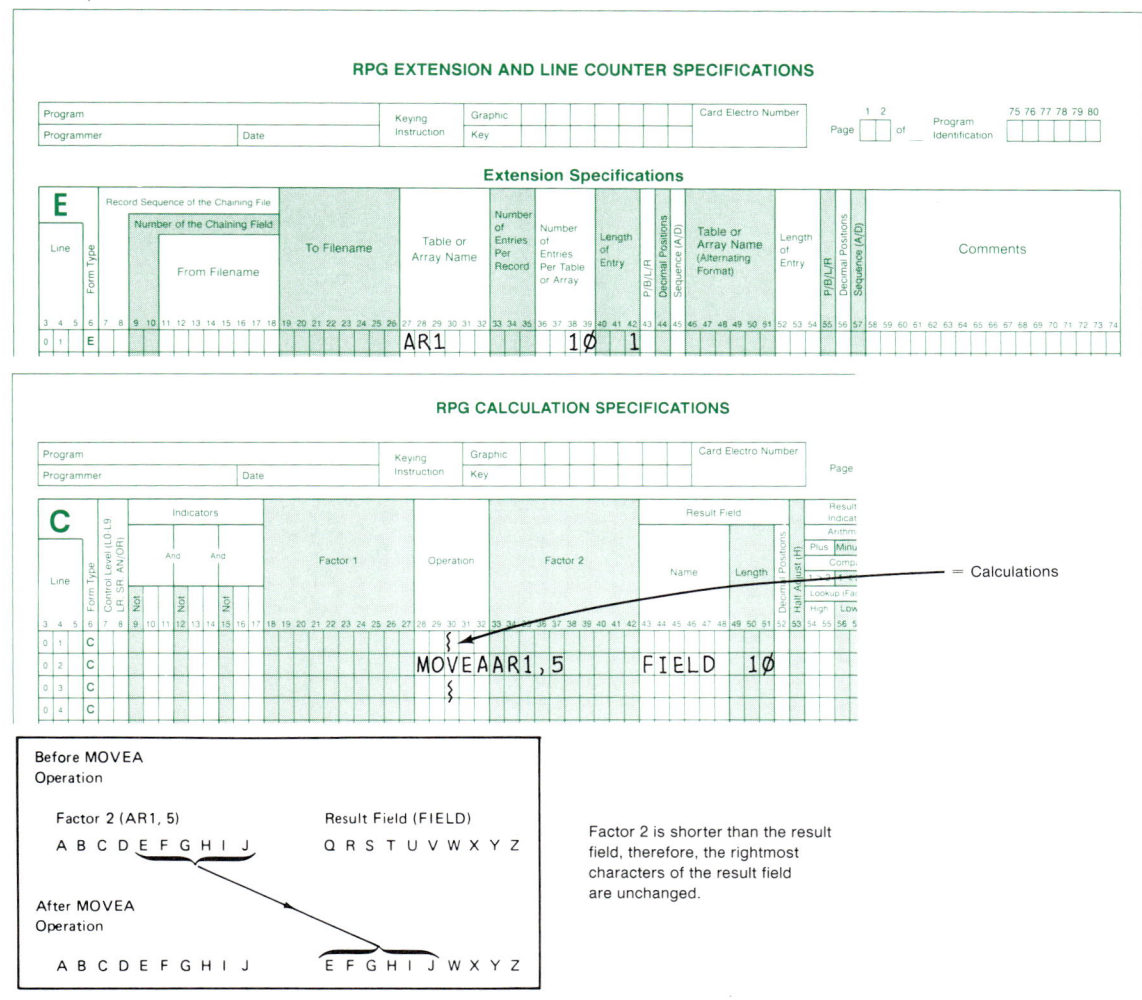

Arrays 323

Figure 7.35 continued

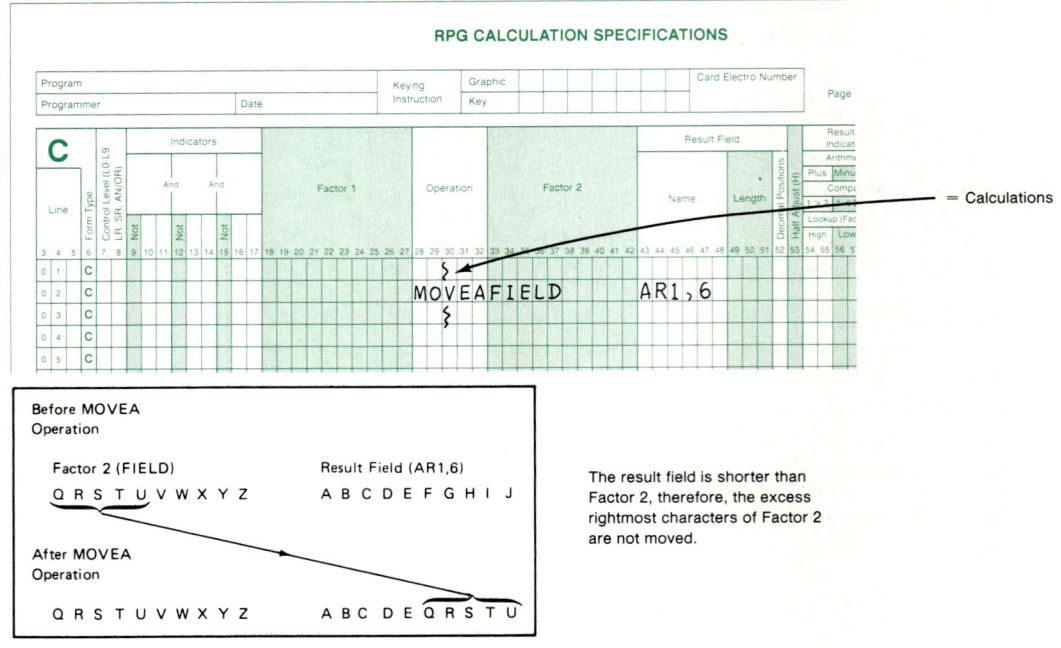

Figure 7.36 Move array—examples

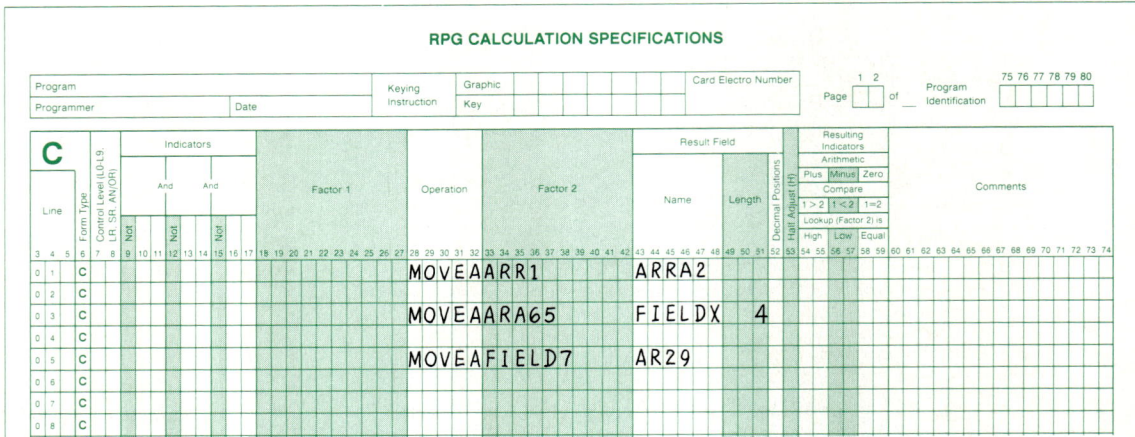

Notes on the Coding

Line meaning

01 Data in one array is moved to replace data in another array.

03 Part or all of the data in an array is moved into a field.

05 Part or all of the data in a field is moved into an array.

Figure 7.37 MOVEA operation—example

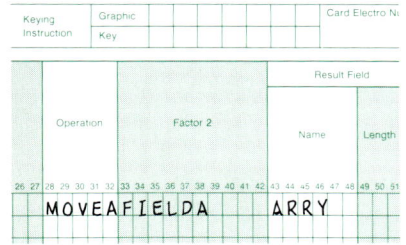

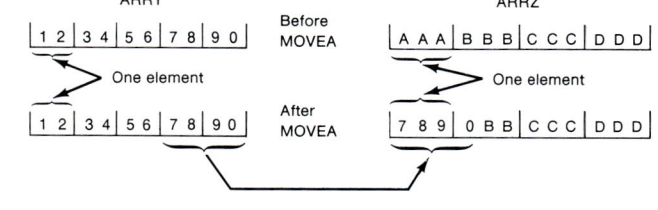

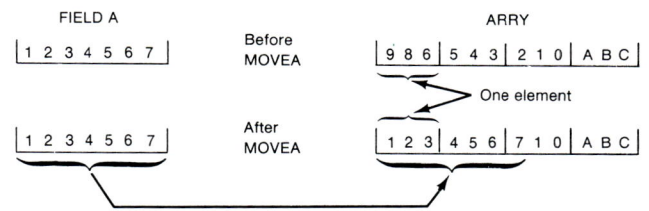

Arrays 325

Figure 7.37 continued

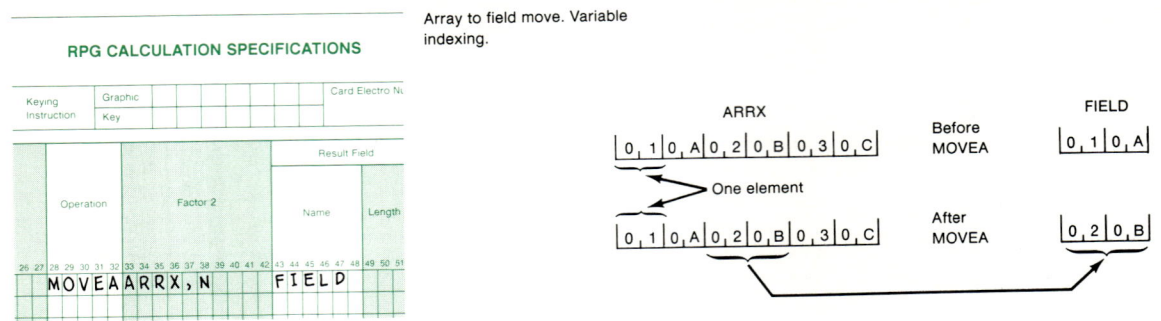

Array to field move. Variable indexing.

Figure 7.38 Table and array functions—summary

The following illustrations deal with the operations that may be used with table data (LOKUP) or array data (LOKUP, XFOOT, MOVEA).

1. Lookup (LOKUP)

   Use a known value

   to search a table or array having similar values

   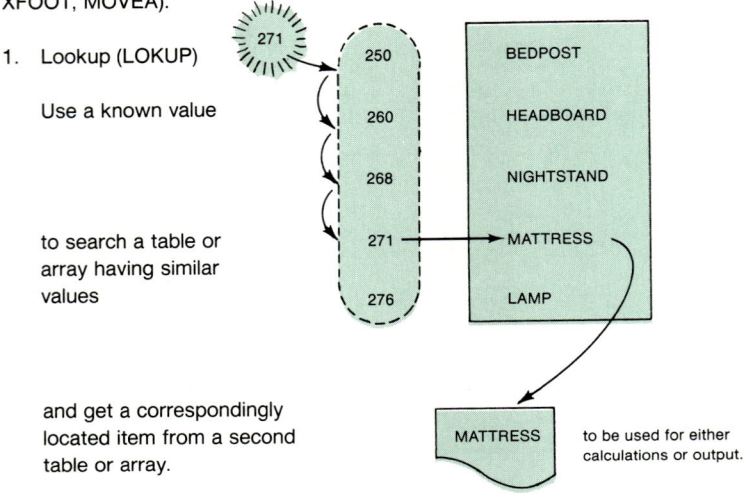

   and get a correspondingly located item from a second table or array.

2. Crossfoot (XFOOT)

   Add the value in each array element to find the total.

   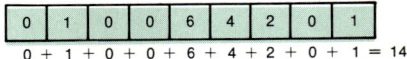

   0 + 1 + 0 + 0 + 6 + 4 + 2 + 0 + 1 = 14

3. Move an array (MOVEA)

   a. Move the contents of an array to a field or to another array.

   b. Move the contents of a field to an array.

   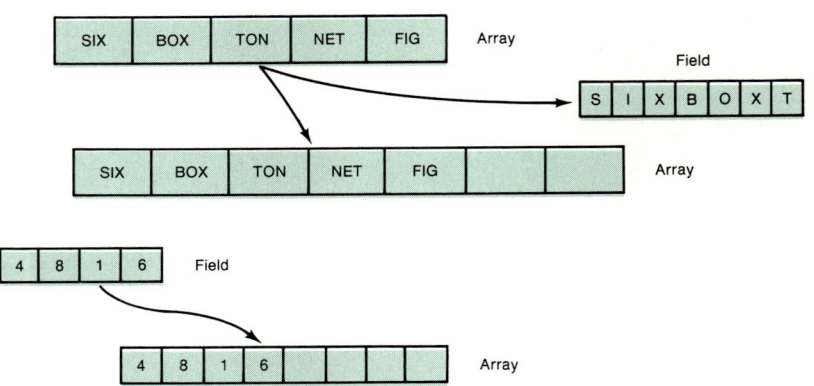

RPG III Enhancements

Several operations referred to in this chapter have been modified in RPG III. Some related features such as *IN have been added.

Move Array (MOVEA)

MOVEA, like MOVE and MOVEL (see chapter 5, RPG III Enhancements), is permitted to have resulting indicators in RPG III. RPG III permits resulting indicators to be set during the MOVEA operation. Thus blank or missing alphameric fields can be detected during their manipulation.

The result field determines which indicator is set on in move operations. Since the MOVEA operation may only be used on alphameric data, the result field is alphameric and only one resulting indicator (positions 58–59) can be specified. This indicator is set on if the result field is all blanks.

Resulting indicators cannot be specified if the result field is an array.

Sort Array (SORTA)

In RPG III, operation SORTA sorts an array according to the sequence specified in the extension specifications for the array.

The operation SORTA is coded in positions 28–32 of the calculation specifications. Factor 2 contains the name of the array to be sorted. That array is sorted into the sequence (ascending or descending) specified in position 45 of the extension specifications. (See Figure 7.39.) If no sequence is specified, the array is sorted into ascending sequence.

The array *IN cannot be specified in factor 2 of a SORTA operation.

Figure 7.39 SORTA operation

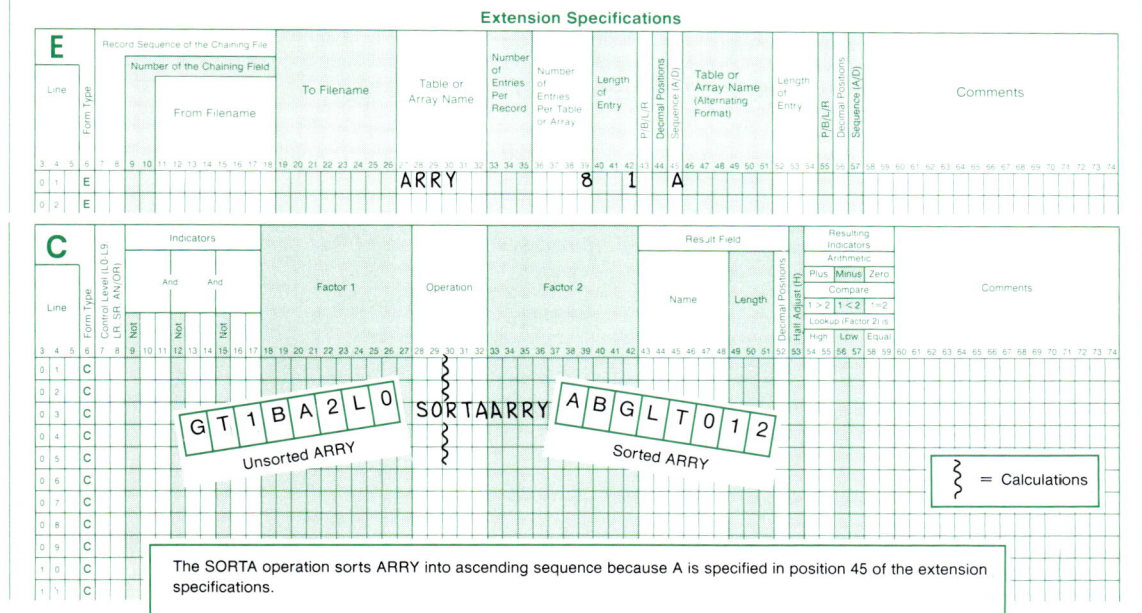

Figure 7.40 Array *IN—example

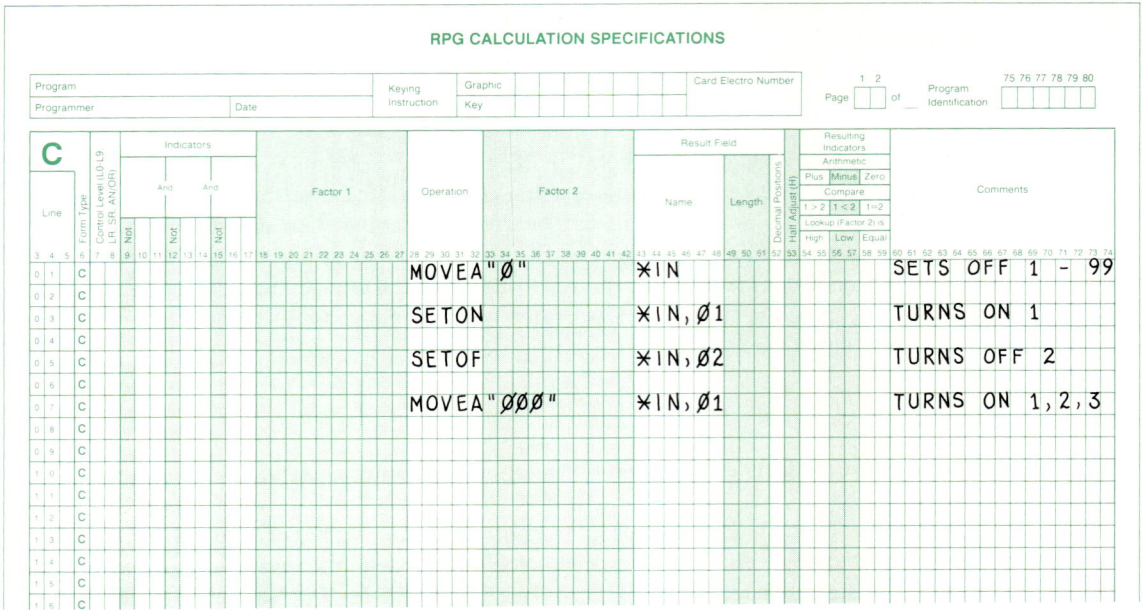

*IN

RPG III provides a predefined array of ninety-nine one-character alphameric elements representing the indicators 01–99. The elements of this array can contain only the alphameric values 0 or 1. The array *IN can be manipulated in that the individual bits, or indicators, can be turned on or off. A *1* represents on; a *0* represents off. Thus the use of the MOVEA operation with the array name *IN and the constant *0* could be used to SETOF indicators 01–99 (or any logical combination thereof). Likewise, the constant *1* could be used to SETON any number of indicators. (See Figure 7.40.)

The valid operations or references for an array of single-character elements are valid also with the array *IN, except that the array *IN cannot be specified as a subfield in a data structure (see chapter 12) or be referenced in a SORTA operation. Thus *IN,01 represents the first element of the array *IN, is indicator 01, and contains the value *0* or *1*. Each of the designations *IN,01–*IN,99 represents the indicators 01–99, contains the values *1* or *0,* and comprises the array *IN.

*INxx

The field *INxx is a predefined one-character alphameric field where xx represents any one of the RPG indicators except 1P. The field *INxx can be specified whenever a one-byte character field is valid except that the field *INxx cannot be specified as a subfield in a data structure (see chapter 12) or be referenced in a SORTA operation.

To summarize for the array *IN, the array element *INxx, or the field *INxx:

Moving an alphameric zero (*0*) to any of these fields sets off the corresponding indicator.
    Moving *0* to IN03 sets off indicator 03.
    Moving *0* to IN,05 sets off indicator 05.
    Moving *00000* to IN,09 sets off indicators 09, 10, 11, 12, and 13.
    Moving *0* to *IN sets off indicators 01–99.
Moving a *1* to any of these fields sets on the corresponding indicator.
    Moving *1* to *IN01 sets on indicator 01.
    Moving *1* to *IN,07 sets on indicator 07.
    Moving *1111* to *IN,12 sets on indicators 12, 13, 14, and 15.
    Moving *1* to *IN sets on indicators 01–99.

If the array *IN or the field *INxx is used to assign a value other than an alphameric *0* or *1* to an indicator, any subsequent normal RPG indicator tests may yield undesirable results.

Illustrative Program

Multiple Arrays—XFOOT: Product Report

Job Definition
A report is to be printed showing the total of the company's twelve products by day. The individual products are totaled and a monthly total is made. The percentages of each product in relation to the total sales of all products are to be calculated.

Input
A record with the following fields is input for each day's sales (units) of the company's twelve products:

Positions	Field Description
1–05	Product 1
6–10	Product 2
11–15	Product 3
16–20	Product 4
21–25	Product 5
26–30	Product 6
31–35	Product 7
36–40	Product 8
41–45	Product 9
46–50	Product 10
51–55	Product 11
56–60	Product 12

Processing
    Create an array using the input data.
    Add all sales for each day to arrive at a daily total.
    Print all daily sales including daily total.
    Print all individual product sales for the month.
    Calculate (for each product) the percentage that its monthly sales is of total monthly sales.
    Print the total product sales for the month and percentage of total for each product.

Output
The Printer Spacing Chart shows how the report is formatted:

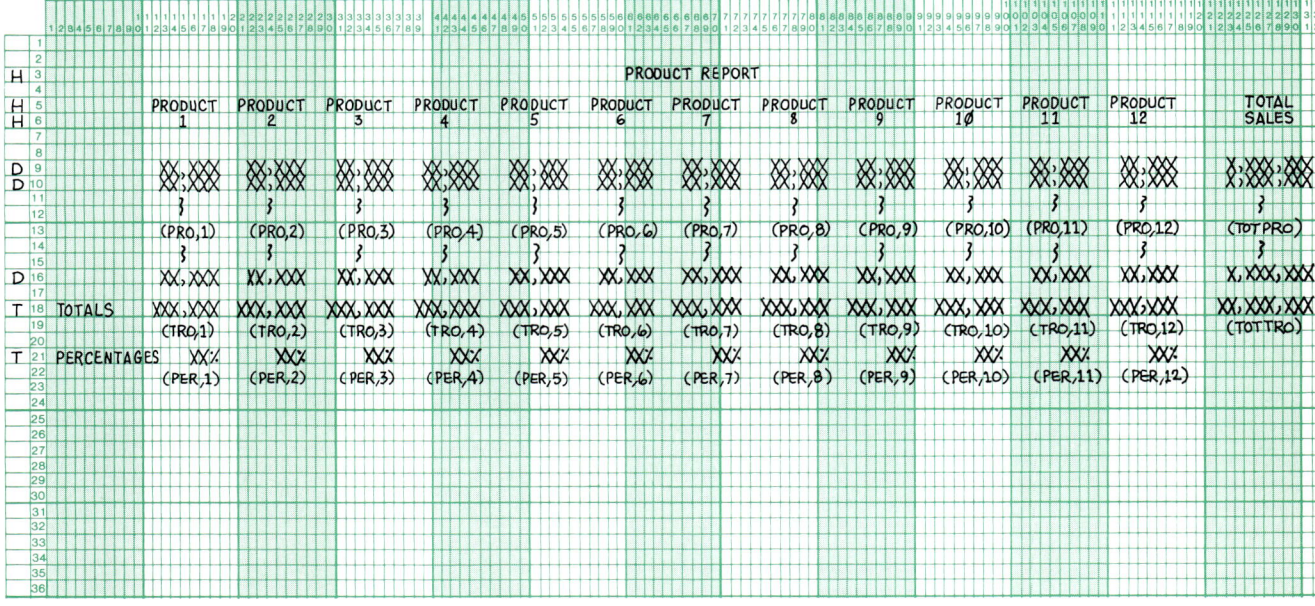

Coding sheets for the Product Report problem:

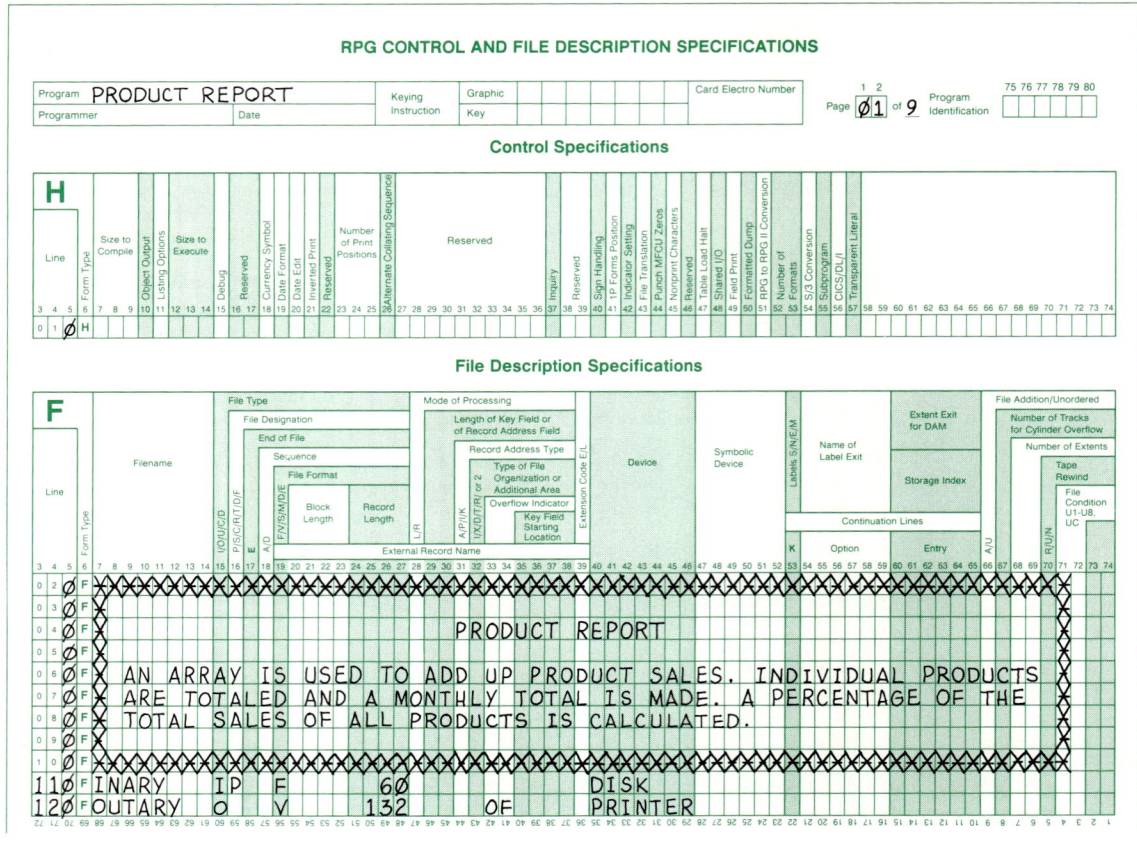

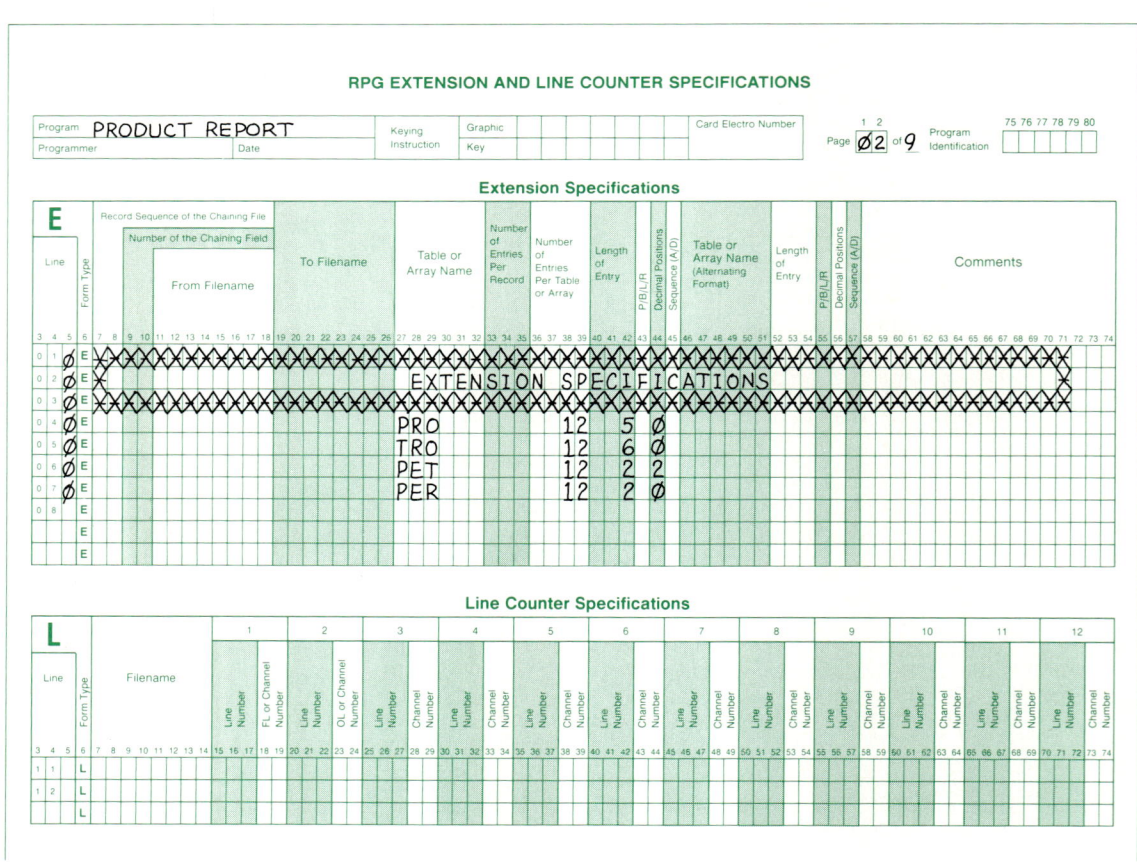

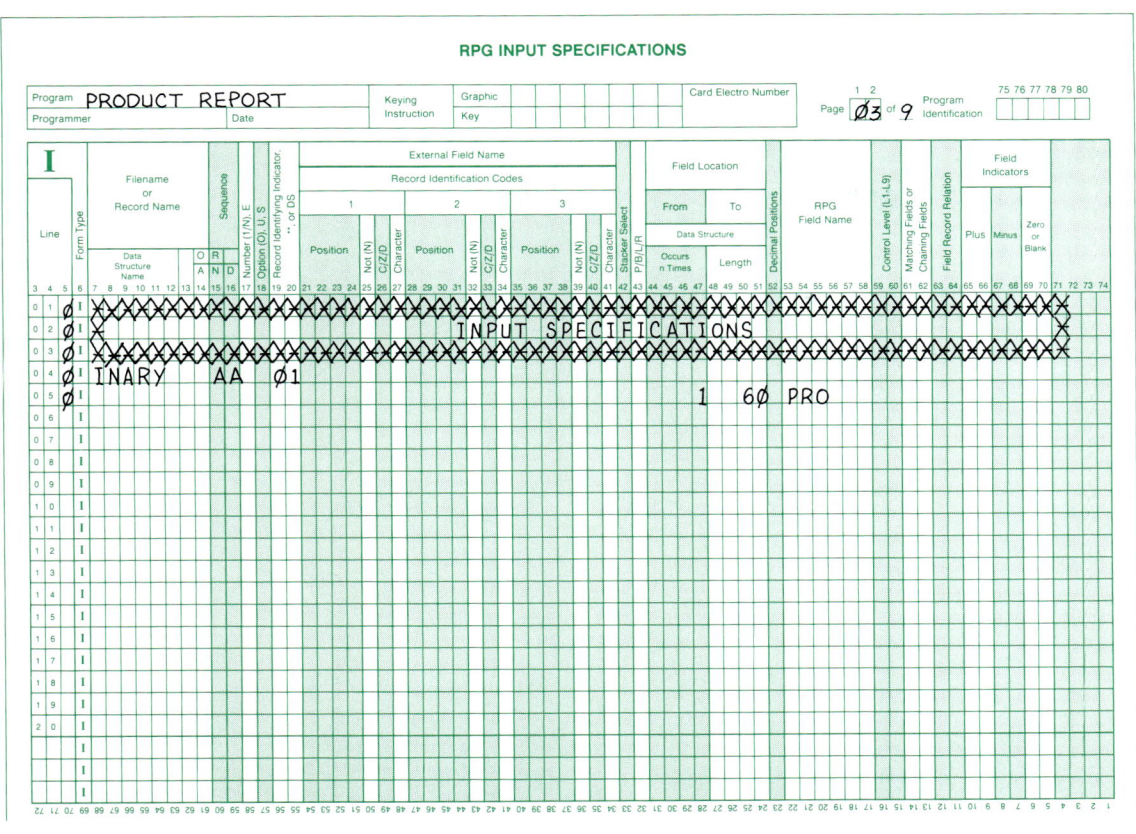

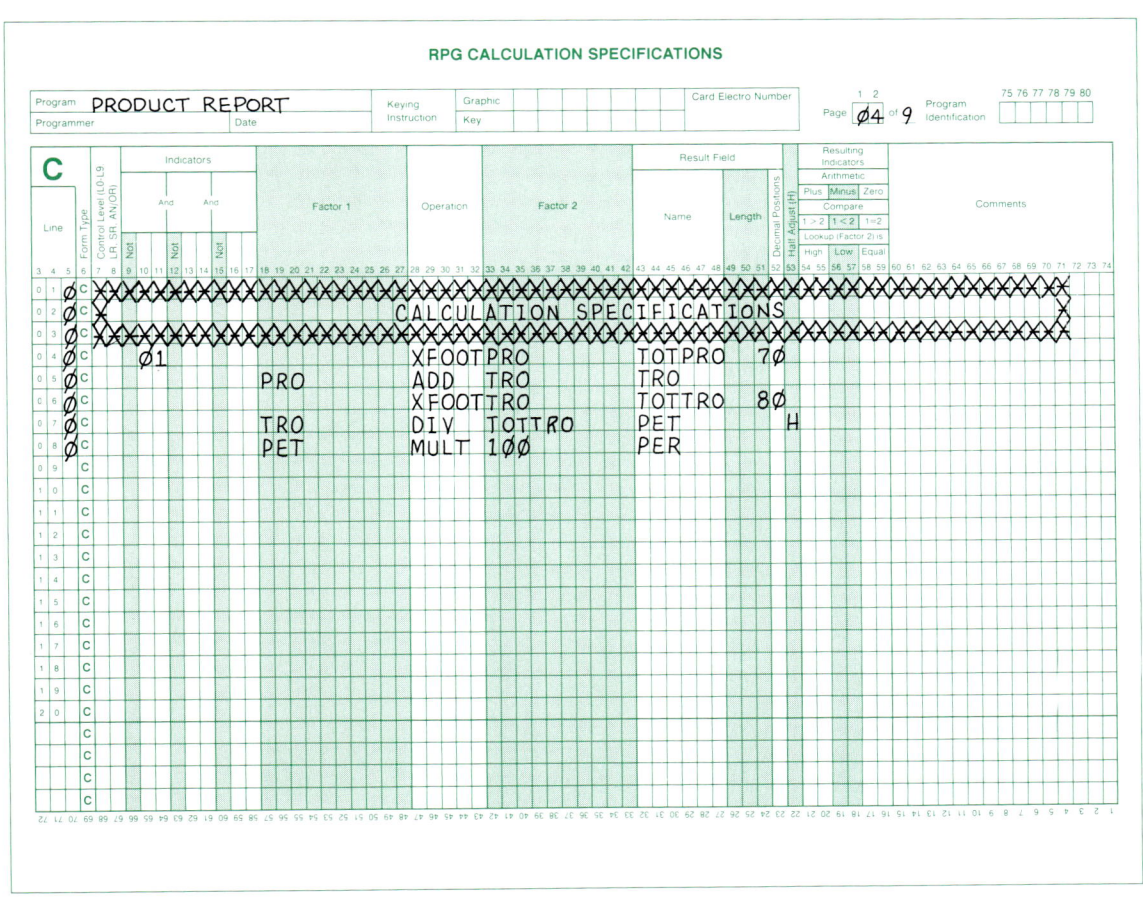

Arrays

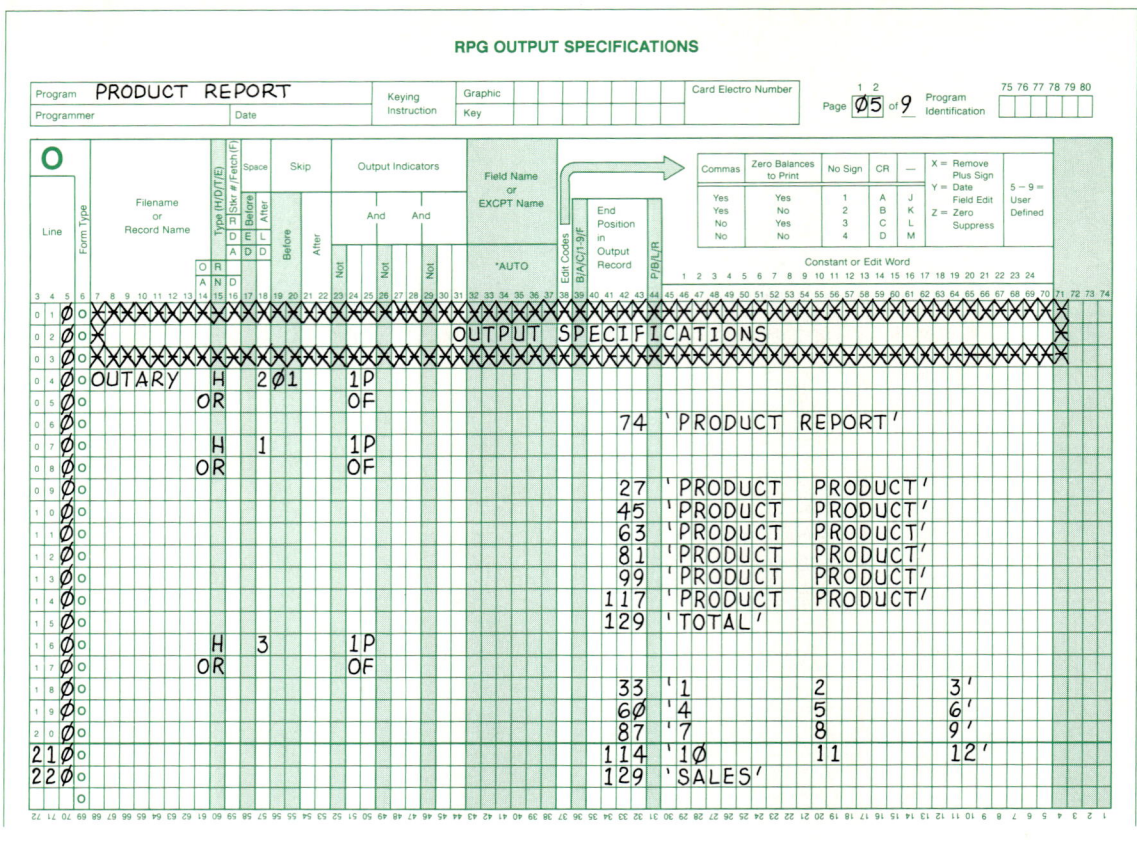
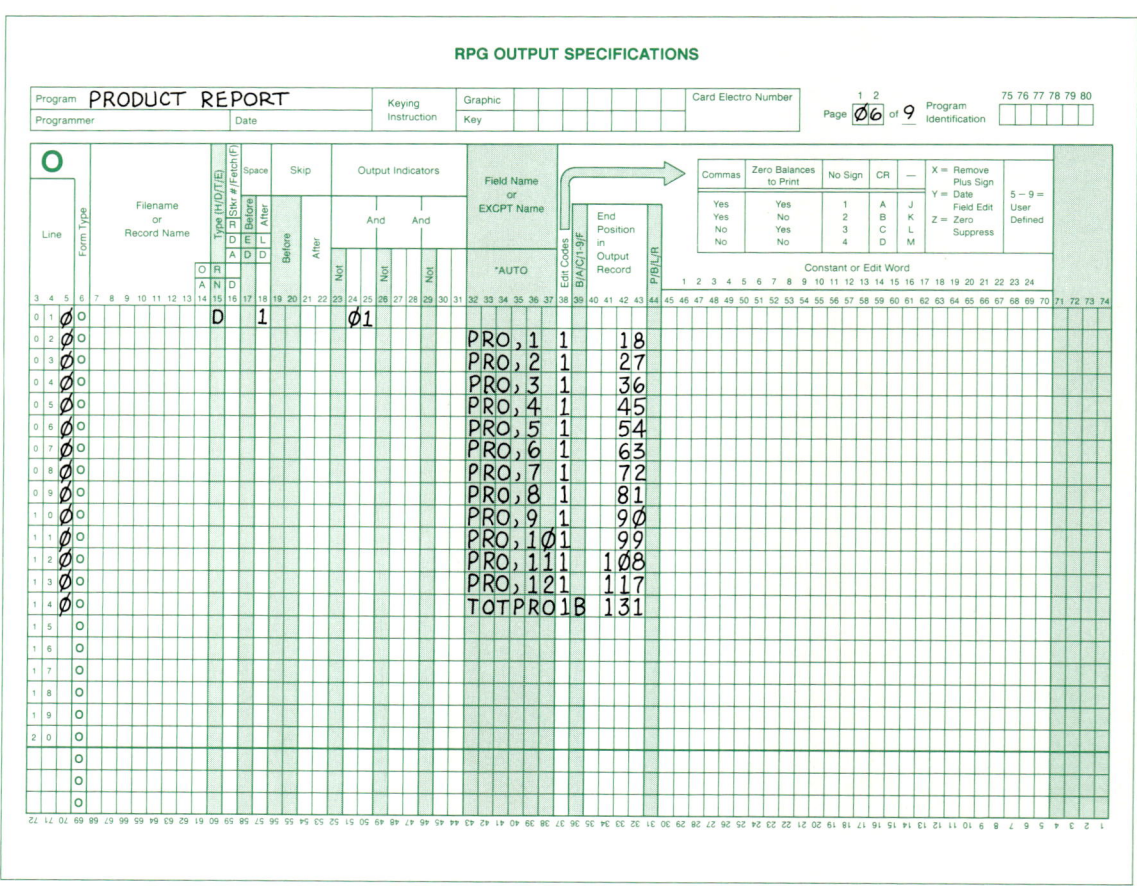

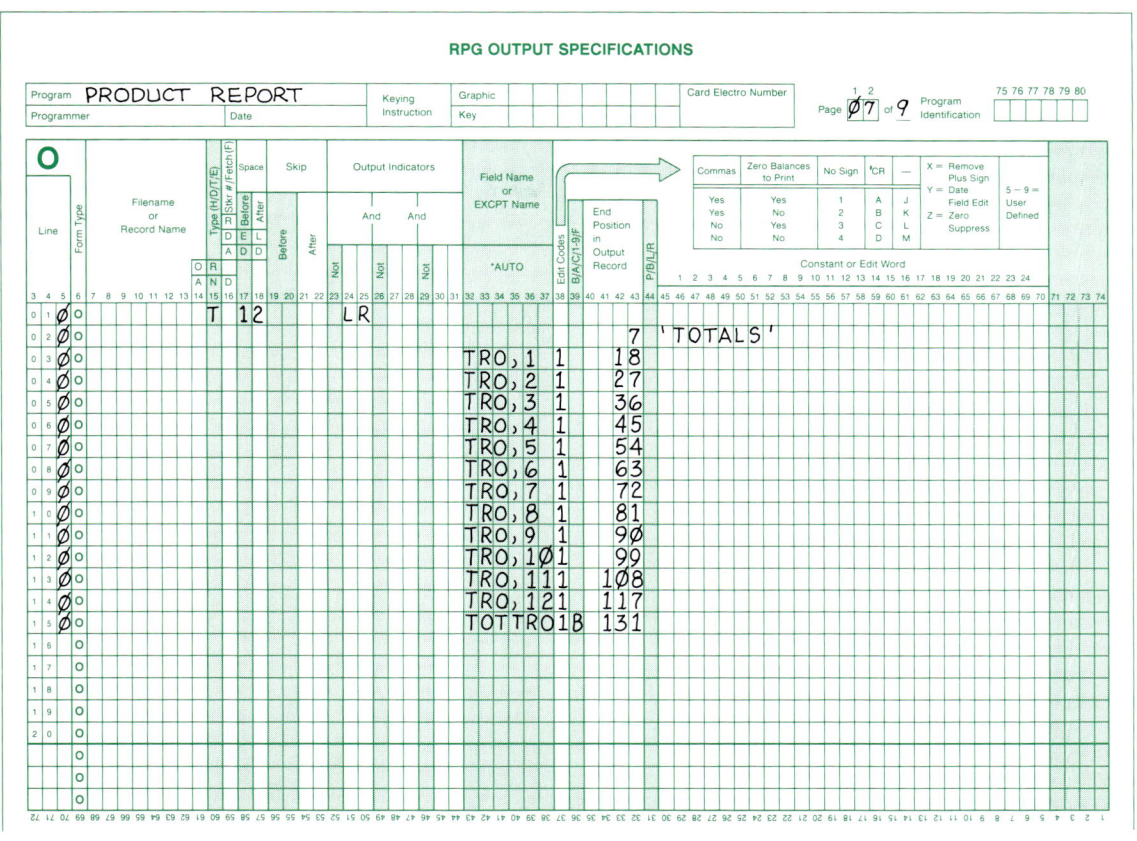
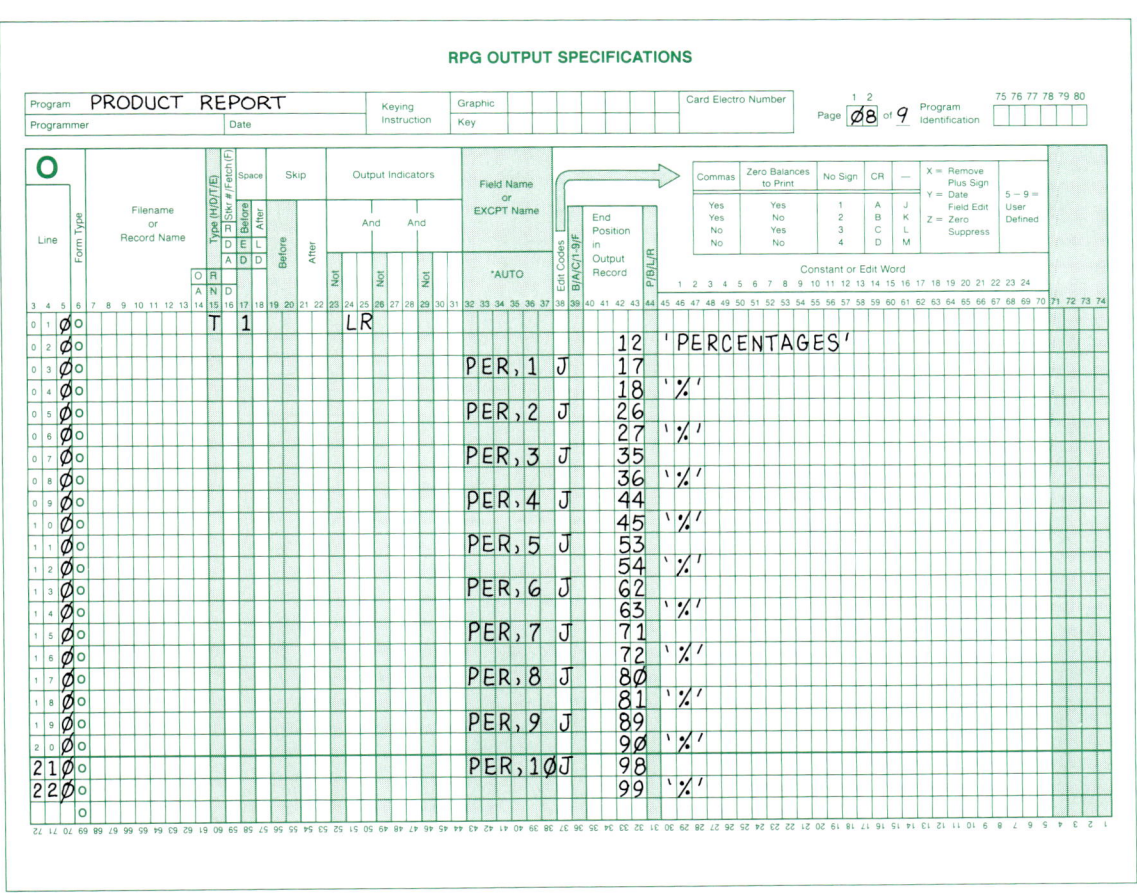

Arrays 333

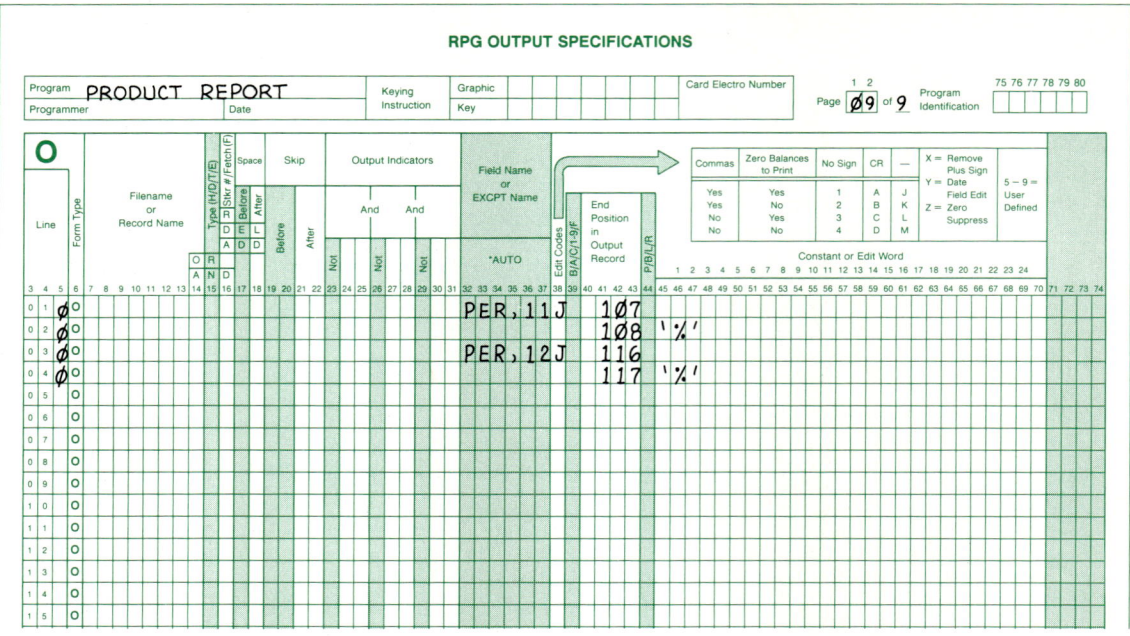

The source listing is as follows:

```
 1   01010H
 2  *01020F****************************************************************
 3  *01030F*                                                               *
 4  *01040F*                   PRODUCT REPORT                              *
 5  *01050F*                                                               *
 6  *01060F* AN ARRAY IS USED TO ADD UP PRODUCT SALES. INDIVIDUAL PRODUCTS *
 7  *01070F* ARE TOTALED AND A MONTHLY TOTAL IS MADE. A PERCENTAGE OF THE  *
 8  *01080F* TOTAL SALES OF ALL PRODUCTS IS CALCULATED.                    *
 9  *01090F*                                                               *
10  *01100F****************************************************************
11   01110FINARY    IP  F       60            DISK
12   01120FOUTARY   O   V      132       OF   PRINTER
13  *02010E****************************************************************
14  *02020E*                EXTENSION SPECIFICATIONS                       *
15  *02030E****************************************************************
16   02040E                   PRO      12   5 0
17   02050E                   TRO      12   6 0
18   02060E                   PET      12   2 2
19   02070E                   PER      12   2 0
20  *03010I****************************************************************
21  *03020I*                  INPUT SPECIFICATIONS                         *
22  *03030I****************************************************************
23   03040IINARY    AA  01
24   03050I                                        1  60 PRO
25  *04010C****************************************************************
26  *04020C*                CALCULATION SPECIFICATIONS                     *
27  *04030C****************************************************************
28   04040C   01           XFOOTPRO     TOTPRO   70
29   04050C           PRO  ADD  TRO     TRO
30   04060C                XFOOTTRO     TOTTRO   80
31   04070C           TRO  DIV  TOTTRO  PET        H
32   04080C           PET  MULT 100     PER
33  *050100****************************************************************
34  *050200*                 OUTPUT SPECIFICATIONS                         *
35  *050300****************************************************************
36   050400OUTARY   H  201   1P
37   050500 OR                OF
38   050600                              74 'PRODUCT REPORT'
39   050700         H  1     1P
40   050800 OR                OF
41   050900                              27 'PRODUCT     PRODUCT'
42   051000                              45 'PRODUCT     PRODUCT'
43   051100                              63 'PRODUCT     PRODUCT'
44   051200                              81 'PRODUCT     PRODUCT'
45   051300                              99 'PRODUCT     PRODUCT'
46   051400                             117 'PRODUCT     PRODUCT'
47   051500                             129 'TOTAL'
48   051600         H  3     1P
49   051700 OR                OF
50   051800                              33 '1        2          3'
51   051900                              60 '4        5          6'
52   052000                              87 '7        8          9'
53   052100                             114 '10       11         12'
54   052200                             129 'SALES'
55   060100         D  1     01
```

```
56     060200                          PRO,1 1     18
57     060300                          PRO,2 1     27
58     060400                          PRO,3 1     36
59     060500                          PRO,4 1     45
60     060600                          PRO,5 1     54
61     060700                          PRO,6 1     63
62     060800                          PRO,7 1     72
63     060900                          PRO,8 1     81
64     061000                          PRO,9 1     90
65     061100                          PRO,101     99
66     061200                          PRO,111    108
67     061300                          PRO,121    117
68     061400                          TOTPRO1B   131
69     070100          T 12     LR
70     070200                                       7 'TOTALS'
71     070300                          TRO,1 1     18
72     070400                          TRO,2 1     27
73     070500                          TRO,3 1     36
74     070600                          TRO,4 1     45
75     070700                          TRO,5 1     54
76     070800                          TRO,6 1     63
77     070900                          TRO,7 1     72
78     071000                          TRO,8 1     81
79     071100                          TRO,9 1     90
80     071200                          TRO,101     99
81     071300                          TRO,111    108
82     071400                          TRO,121    117
83     071500                          TOTTRO1B   131
84     080100          T  1     LR
85     080200                                      12 'PERCENTAGES'
86     080300                          PER,1 J     17
87     080400                                      18 '%'
88     080500                          PER,2 J     26
89     080600                                      27 '%'
90     080700                          PER,3 J     35
91     080800                                      36 '%'
92     080900                          PER,4 J     44
93     081000                                      45 '%'
94     081100                          PER,5 J     53
95     081200                                      54 '%'
96     081300                          PER,6 J     62
97     081400                                      63 '%'
98     081500                          PER,7 J     71
99     081600                                      72 '%'
100    081700                          PER,8 J     80
101    081800                                      81 '%'
102    081900                          PER,9 J     89
103    082000                                      90 '%'
104    082100                          PER,10J     98
105    082200                                      99 '%'
106    090100                          PER,11J    107
107    090200                                     108 '%'
108    090300                          PER,12J    116
109    090400                                     117 '%'
```

The Product Report is to be printed as follows:

PRODUCT REPORT

PRODUCT 1	PRODUCT 2	PRODUCT 3	PRODUCT 4	PRODUCT 5	PRODUCT 6	PRODUCT 7	PRODUCT 8	PRODUCT 9	PRODUCT 10	PRODUCT 11	PRODUCT 12	TOTAL SALES
1,111	1,222	1,333	1,444	1,555	1,666	1,777	1,888	1,999	1,000	2,111	2,222	19,328
3,111	3,222	3,333	3,444	3,555	3,666	3,777	3,888	3,999	3,000	4,111	4,222	43,328
5,111	5,222	5,333	5,444	5,555	5,666	5,777	5,888	5,999	5,000	6,111	6,222	67,328
7,111	7,222	7,333	7,444	7,555	7,666	7,777	7,888	7,999	7,000	8,111	8,222	91,328
9,111	9,222	9,333	9,444	9,555	9,666	9,777	9,888	9,999	9,000	10,111	10,222	115,328
12,111	12,222	12,333	12,444	12,555	12,666	12,777	12,888	12,999	12,000	13,111	13,222	151,328
14,111	14,222	14,333	14,444	14,555	14,666	14,777	14,888	14,999	14,000	15,111	15,222	175,328
16,111	16,222	16,333	16,444	16,555	16,666	16,777	16,888	16,999	16,000	17,111	17,222	199,328
18,111	18,222	18,333	18,444	18,555	18,666	18,777	18,888	18,999	18,000	19,111	19,222	223,328
20,111	20,222	20,333	20,444	20,555	20,666	20,777	20,888	20,999	20,000	21,111	21,222	247,328
22,111	22,222	22,333	22,444	22,555	22,666	22,777	22,888	22,999	22,000	23,111	23,222	271,328
24,111	24,222	24,333	24,444	24,555	24,666	24,777	24,888	24,999	24,000	25,111	5,222	275,328
26,111	26,222	26,333	26,444	26,555	26,666	26,777	26,888	26,999	26,000	27,111	27,222	319,328
28,111	28,222	28,333	28,444	28,555	28,666	28,777	28,888	28,999	28,000	29,111	9,222	323,328
30,111	30,222	30,333	30,444	30,555	30,666	30,777	30,888	30,999	30,000	31,111	31,222	367,328
32,111	32,222	32,333	32,444	32,555	32,666	32,777	32,888	32,999	32,000	33,111	33,222	391,328
34,111	34,222	34,333	34,444	34,555	34,666	34,777	34,888	34,999	34,000	35,111	35,222	415,328
36,111	36,222	36,333	36,444	36,555	36,666	36,777	36,888	36,999	36,000	37,111	37,222	439,328
38,111	38,222	38,333	38,444	38,555	38,666	38,777	38,888	38,999	38,000	9,111	39,222	433,328
40,111	40,222	40,333	40,444	30,555	40,666	40,777	40,888	40,999	40,000	41,111	41,222	477,328
42,111	42,222	42,333	42,444	42,555	42,666	42,777	42,888	42,999	42,000	43,111	43,222	511,328
44,111	44,222	44,333	44,444	44,555	44,666	44,777	44,888	44,999	44,000	45,111	45,222	535,328

	PRODUCT 1	PRODUCT 2	PRODUCT 3	PRODUCT 4	PRODUCT 5	PRODUCT 6	PRODUCT 7	PRODUCT 8	PRODUCT 9	PRODUCT 10	PRODUCT 11	PRODUCT 12	TOTAL
TOTALS	503,442	505,884	508,326	510,768	503,210	515,652	518,094	520,536	522,978	501,000	495,442	487,884	6,093,216
PERCENTAGES	8 %	8 %	8 %	8 %	8 %	8 %	9 %	9 %	9 %	8 %	8 %	8 %	

Illustrative Program

Array Loading with Input Specifications—Array XYZ

Job Definition

An array PRO contains previous totals and is specified as having eighteen elements (entries), each five characters long. The array is read in from a table file (*T* in column 16 of the file specification). On the first record type, array elements of array PRO are consecutive and, therefore, are loaded into the array by means of a single input specification line. Since array elements from the second record type are not consecutive or else are defined on several records, these elements are loaded individually and specified by field, location, array name, and index.

Input

Record 1 has the character *X* in position 46 and contains the following fields:

Positions	Field Description
1–45	XYZ elements 1–9

Record 2 has the character *Y* in position 46 and contains the following fields:

Positions	Field Description
1–05	XYZ element 10
6–10	XYZ element 11
11–15	XYZ element 12
16–20	XYZ element 13
21–25	XYZ element 14
26–30	XYZ element 15
31–35	XYZ element 16
36–40	XYZ element 17
41–45	XYZ element 18

Processing

Load an array from the file.
Print out the entire array as it was loaded.

Output

The Printer Spacing Chart shows how the report is formatted:

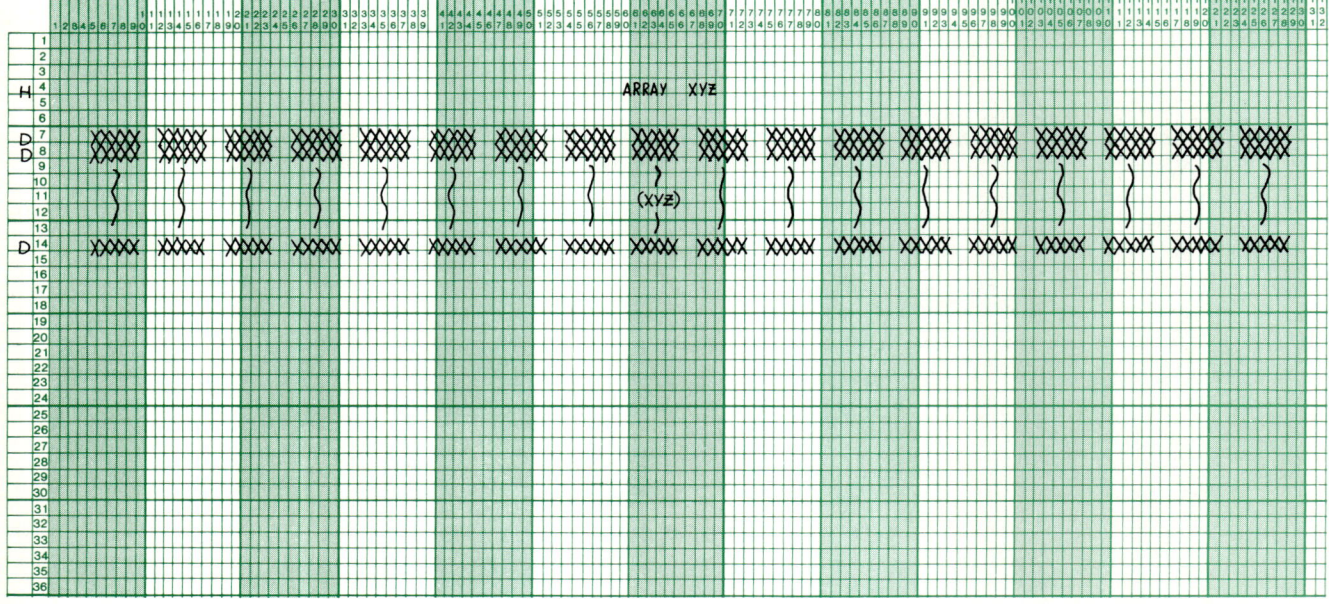

336   RPG II and RPG III Programming

Coding sheets for array XYZ problem:

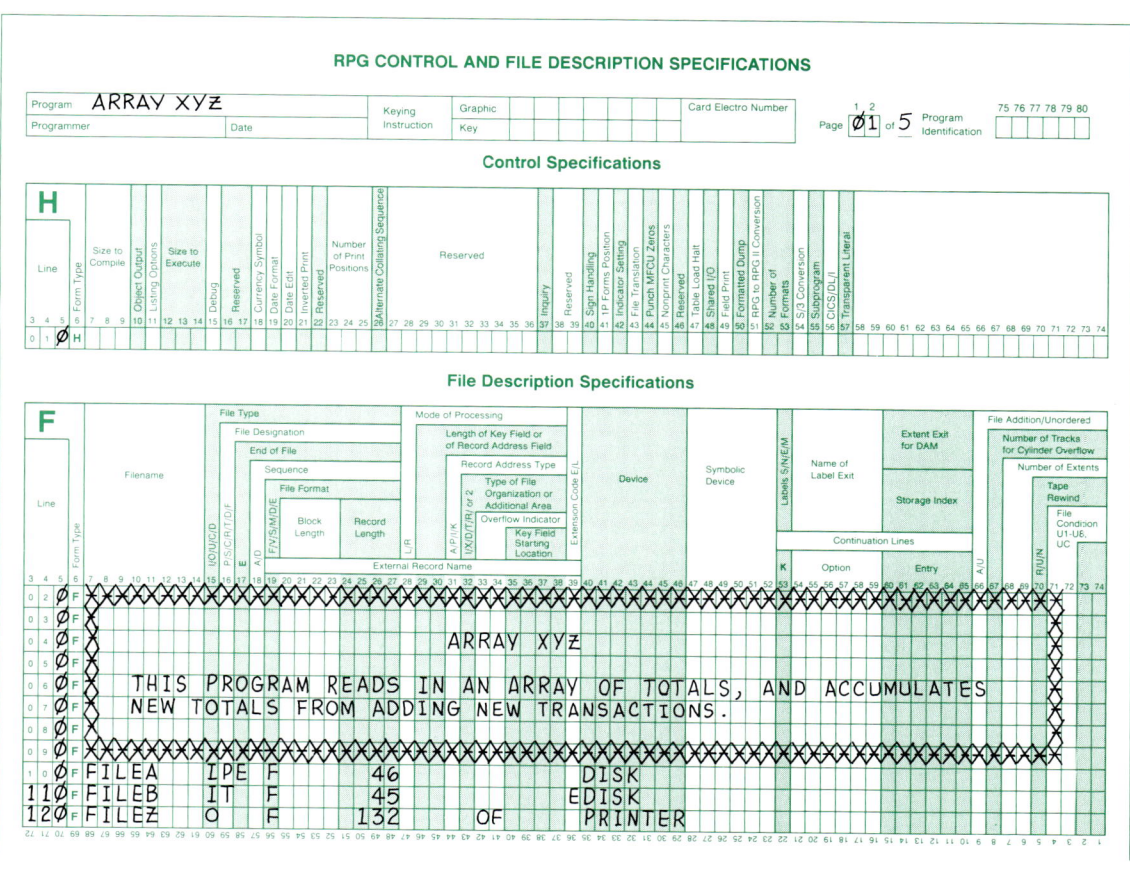

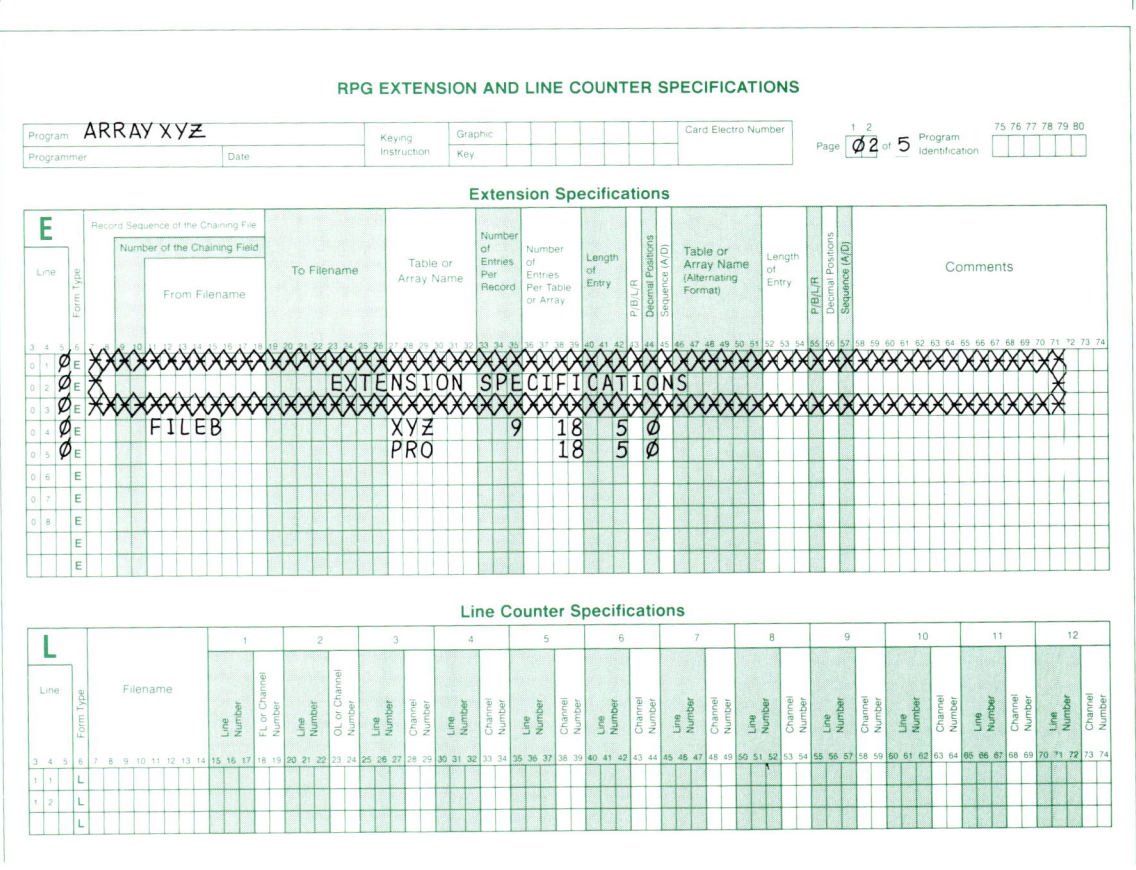

Arrays 337

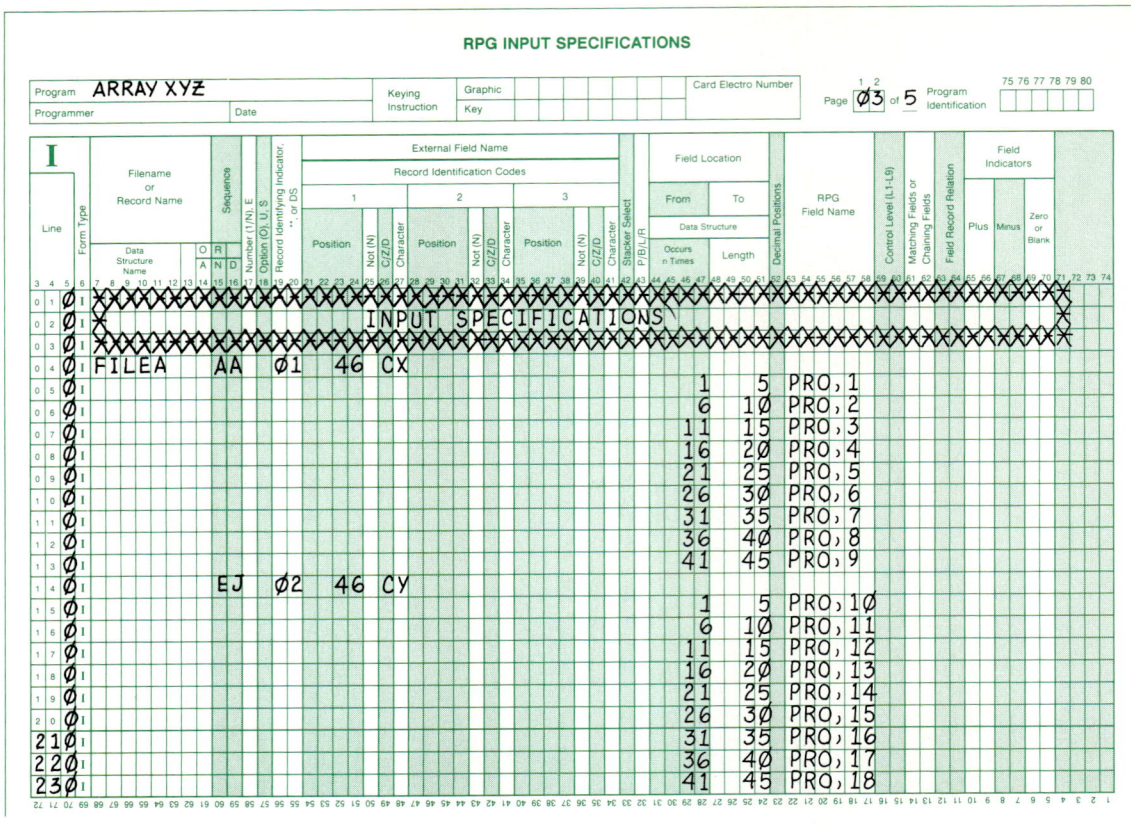
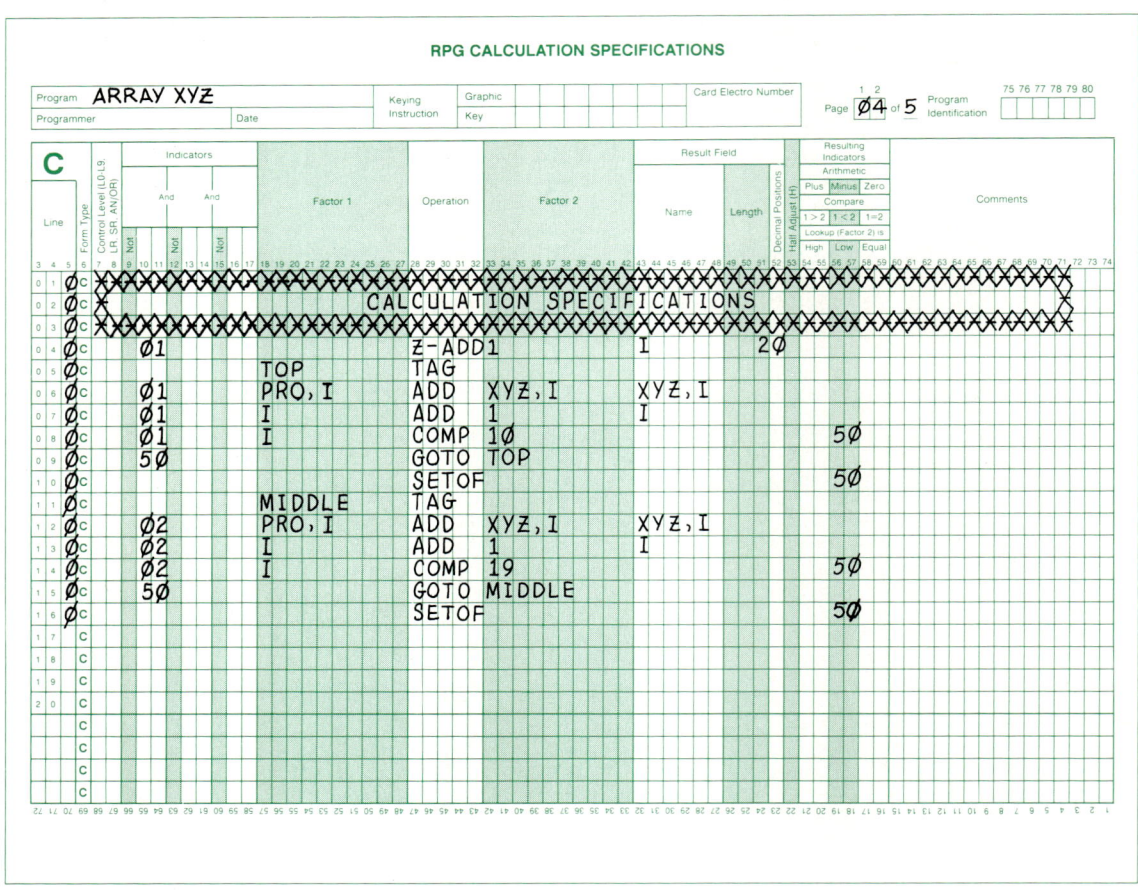

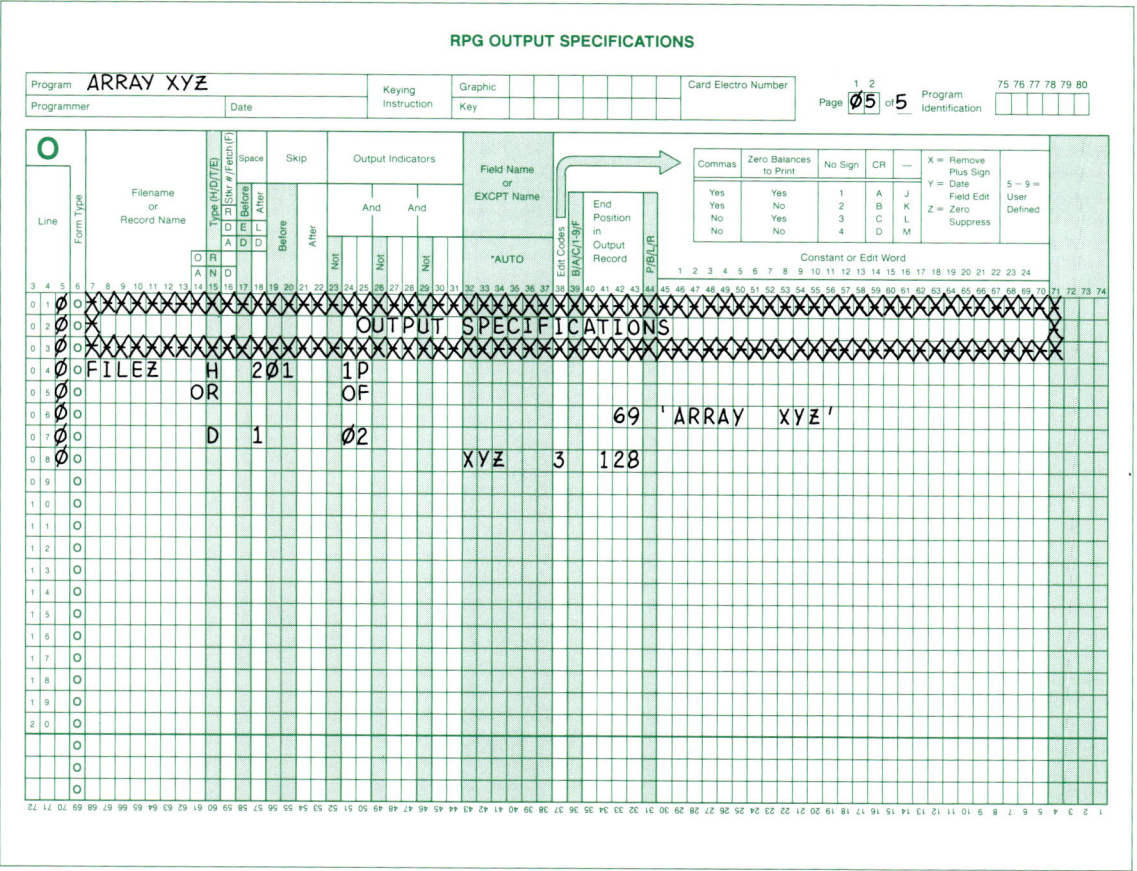

The source listing is as follows:

```
 1    01010H
 2  * 01020F***************************************************************
 3  * 01030F*                                                              *
 4  * 01040F*                      ARRAY XYZ                               *
 5  * 01050F*                                                              *
 6  * 01060F*   THIS PROGRAM READS IN AN ARRAY OF TOTALS, AND ACCUMULATES  *
 7  * 01070F*   NEW TOTALS FROM ADDING NEW TRANSACTIONS.                   *
 8  * 01080F*                                                              *
 9  * 01090F***************************************************************
10    01100FFILEA    IPE F      46           DISK
11    01110FFILEB    IT  F      45           EDISK
12    01120FFILEZ    O   F     132       OF  PRINTER
13  * 02010E***************************************************************
14  * 02020E*               EXTENSION SPECIFICATIONS                       *
15  * 02030E***************************************************************
16    02040E     FILEB         XYZ    9  18 5 0
17    02050E                   PRO       18 5 0
18  * 03010I***************************************************************
19  * 03020I*                 INPUT SPECIFICATIONS                         *
20  * 03030I***************************************************************
21    03040IFILEA   AA  01   46 CX
22    03050I                                         1    5 PRO,1
23    03060I                                         6   10 PRO,2
24    03070I                                        11   15 PRO,3
25    03080I                                        16   20 PRO,4
26    03090I                                        21   25 PRO,5
27    03100I                                        26   30 PRO,6
28    03110I                                        31   35 PRO,7
29    03120I                                        36   40 PRO,8
30    03130I                                        41   45 PRO,9
31    03140I        EJ  02   46 CY
32    03150I                                         1    5 PRO,10
33    03160I                                         6   10 PRO,11
34    03170I                                        11   15 PRO,12
35    03180I                                        16   20 PRO,13
36    03190I                                        21   25 PRO,14
37    03200I                                        26   30 PRO,15
38    03210I                                        31   35 PRO,16
39    03220I                                        36   40 PRO,17
40    03230I                                        41   45 PRO,18
41  * 04010C***************************************************************
42  * 04020C*               CALCULATION SPECIFICATIONS                     *
43  * 04030C***************************************************************
```

```
44    04040C   01                    Z-ADD1        I         20
45    04050C            TOP          TAG
46    04060C   01       PRO,I        ADD  XYZ,I   XYZ,I
47    04070C   01       I            ADD  1       I
48    04080C   01       I            COMP 10                       50
49    04090C   50                    GOTO TOP
50    04100C                         SETOF                         50
51    04110C            MIDDLE       TAG
52    04120C   02       PRO,I        ADD  XYZ,I   XYZ,I
53    04130C   02       I            ADD  1       I
54    04140C   02       I            COMP 19                       50
55    04150C   50                    GOTO MIDDLE
56    04160C                         SETOF                         50
57  * 050100***************************************************************
58  * 050200*                OUTPUT SPECIFICATIONS                        *
59  * 050300***************************************************************
60    050400OFILEZ    H   201      1P
61    050500       OR        OF
62    050600                                    69 'ARRAY   XYZ'
63    050700           D   1       02
64    050800                          XYZ    3  128
```

The array XYZ is to be printed as follows:

ARRAY XYZ

```
  211    422    633    844   1055   1266   1477   1688   1899   1011   1122   1233   1344   1455   1566   1677   1788   1899
20322    644   2966   1288  21610   1932  22254   4576   2898   2022   1144   1266  11388   2510   1632   2754   1876  31998
20433    866   3299   1732  22165   2598  23031   5464   3897   2433   1166   5299  11432   6565   1698   6831   5964  36097
20957   1218   9088  14270  43221  35087  44333  18716   4110   2854  57511  87451  41646  59202  84149  26954  62206  46350
21435  53353  71500  70594   2173  47587  65865  74961  79321   3311  42640  50707  82876  84625  49277   6496  30658  56670
99947  89002  57123  85596  53420  32800  97886    287  21473  48637  97512  61032  52721   5855  72845  81017  52888  79691
12405  45323  79144  40381  23376  55925  39988  32829  45127  49890  43199  56664   6933  35878  29099   2569  89409  38436
```

Questions for Review

1. What is an array and how is it similar to a table?
2. When should arrays be used instead of tables?
3. What are the four requirements for specifying an array?
4. Define the term 'array'.
5. How are arrays described on Extension Specifications forms?
6. How are arrays loaded at compile/preexecution time?
7. How are arrays loaded at execution time?
8. How is array information loaded from one record? From more than one record?
9. How may arrays be modified?
10. How may arrays be updated?
11. What is an index and how is it used with arrays?
12. What are the rules for using array names without an index in calculations?
13. What is the end use of an array?
14. How is an array referenced?
15. What operation does an XFOOT instruction perform?
16. What should be specified on the Calculation Specifications form to search an array for a particular element?
17. What is the difference between a table search and an array search?
18. What is the difference between tables and arrays in terms of beginning a search?
19. How is the success of a search determined?
20. How may an element that satisfied a search be referenced?
21. How can an array be searched for more than one element?
22. How is information outputted during the array search?
23. How may an entire array be outputted?
24. How may editing be used with the output of an entire array?
25. What is meant by the phrase 'rolling of totals'?
26. How are individual items referenced in an array?
27. How is an index specified that does not change? How is one specified that can be changed?
28. How may individual elements of an array be outputted?
29. How may only part of an item be referenced?
30. What operation does the move array perform?

Problems

Problem 1

Employees of a manufacturing company have been assigned a grade of one through nine according to the skills and knowledge required by their jobs. Recently the company approved pay rate increases for all employees. The increases vary with employee grade, as shown in the table below. A program is to be written to update the pay rate portion of each employee master record.

Input

Positions	Field Description
1–06	Employee number
7–27	Employee name
28–36	Social security number
37–37	Grade
38–41	Pay rate (XX.XX)

Calculation

The current pay rate is to be multiplied by the applicable increase percentage to arrive at the new pay rate.

Output

A report is to be prepared that includes all the input fields plus the new pay rate. Include the necessary headings and assign your own data names.

Required

Code the necessary file description specifications, extension specifications, input specifications, calculation specifications, and output specifications on the appropriate forms to accomplish the above.

Set up an array for the following:

GRADE	INCREASE
1	3%
2	3%
3	3%
4	5%
5	5%
6	8%
7	8%
8	8%
9	10%

Output is as follows:

```
                        PAY RATE INCREASE REPORT
EMPLOYEE        EMPLOYEE            SOC. SEC.                OLD PAY     NEW PAY
 NUMBER           NAME               NUMBER       GRADE       RATE        RATE

 184106       ROSA DELGADO          469871431       9          9.82       10.80

 198653       JEFF MCKEE            469871431       9          9.82       10.80

 378843       MELTON BROOKS         560891422       1          2.09        2.15

 216467       MICHAEL BOLTON        562121489       5          5.46        5.73

 221844       JAIME HOGAN           490809912       3          6.30        6.49
```

Problem 2

The BG Company sells three of its products in different geographical areas throughout the United States. A report is to be prepared showing the total sales of each product; the total sales for each product by salesperson, territory, and area; and a final total for all fields.

Arrays are to be used for the three products as well as for the different levels of totals. Totals are to be "rolled" into other totals at each level.

Input

Positions	Field Description	
1–06	Date	
7–10	Salesman number	
11–14	Territory number	
15–16	Area number	
30–36	Product 1 sales	(XX,XXX.XX)
37–43	Product 2 sales	(XX,XXX.XX)
44–50	Product 3 sales	(XX,XXX.XX)

Calculations

The sales for each salesperson are to be totaled. The sales for each product as well as for each salesperson are to be totaled by salesperson number, territory number, area number; a final total for all fields is to be given.

Output

Print necessary headings.

The input fields are to be outputted in the same sequence. The total field is to be outputted, as well.

Level totals for salesperson, territory, area, and final are to be outputted.

Required

Code the necessary file description specifications, extension specifications, input specifications, calculation specifications, and output specifications on the appropriate forms to accomplish the above.

Output is as follows:

TERRITORY SALES REPORT

DATE	SALESMAN NUMBER	TERRITORY NUMBER	AREA NUMBER	PRODUCT 1 SALES	PRODUCT 2 SALES	PRODUCT 3 SALES	TOTAL SALES
7/11/87	7104	30	21	3,500.00	4,500.00	3,200.50	11,200.50
7/22/87	7104	30	21	2,950.50	3,598.55	1,110.10	7,659.15
7/24/87	7104	30	21	590.30	1,000.00	2,000.08	3,590.38
	SALESMAN TOTALS			7,040.80	9,098.55	6,310.68	22,450.03
7/26/87	2134	30	21	1,953.00	2,553.30	3,280.50	7,786.80
7/28/87	2134	30	21	591.10	5,410.03	6,028.00	12,029.13
	SALESMAN TOTALS			2,544.10	7,963.33	9,308.50	19,815.93
	TERRITORY TOTALS			9,584.90	17,061.88	15,619.18	42,265.96
	AREA TOTALS			9,584.90	17,061.88	15,619.18	42,265.96
8/13/87	3007	60	22	555.55	6,532.10	7,755.00	14,842.65
8/19/87	3007	60	22	98.00	1,014.44	444.47	1,556.91
	SALESMAN TOTALS			653.55	7,546.54	8,199.47	16,399.56
8/27/87	1510	60	22	888.33	100.52	1,875.00	2,863.85
8/27/87	1510	60	22	97.50	1,500.00	2,350.00	3,947.50
	SALESMAN TOTALS			985.83	1,600.52	4,225.00	6,811.35
	TERRITORY TOTALS			1,639.38	9,147.06	12,424.47	23,210.91
8/17/87	1980	80	22	7,000.00	9,000.00	4,500.00	20,500.00
8/20/87	1980	80	22	175.00	1,950.00	8,510.00	10,635.00
8/22/87	1980	80	22	5,777.00	594.40	819.40	7,190.80
	SALESMAN TOTALS			12,952.00	11,544.40	13,829.40	38,325.80
	TERRITORY TOTALS			12,952.00	11,544.40	13,829.40	38,325.80
	AREA TOTALS			14,591.38	20,691.46	26,253.87	61,536.71
	FINAL TOTALS			24,176.28	37,753.34	41,873.05	103,802.67

Problem 3

The EZ Money Corporation manufactures the five products listed in the following table:

Product Number	Field Description
1	Soap
2	Bleach
3	Detergent
4	Cleanser
5	Powder

The unit cost price and unit selling price for each product is as follows:

Product Number	Unit Cost	Unit Selling Price
1	3.75	5.25
2	2.38	4.25
3	5.67	7.25
4	3.19	5.00
5	2.76	4.55

A report is to be prepared giving information under the following headings:

Product Report

Product Number	Description	Units	Cost	Sales	Profit

Input

Positions	Field Description
1–06	Date
7–07	Product number
8–12	Units sold

Calculations

Set up two arrays—one alternating array for the description and cost, and one array for the selling price. The following tasks are to be accomplished:

> The product number is to serve as the index.
> The description of the product is to be looked up in the array.
> The units sold are to be multiplied by the unit cost to arrive at the cost.
> The units sold are to be multiplied by the unit selling price to arrive at sales.
> The cost is to be subtracted from the sales, to give the profit.

Required

All arrays are to be loaded at compile time.
 Code the necessary file description specifications, extension specifications, input specifications, calculation specifications, and output specifications on the appropriate forms to accomplish the above.

Output
Output is as follows:

```
                            PRODUCT REPORT
PRODUCT
NUMBER     DESCRIPTION    UNITS       COST        SALES       PROFIT

   1          SOAP          250      937.50     1,312.50      375.00

   5          POWDER         30       82.80       136.50       53.70

   3          DETERGENT     100      567.00       725.00      158.00

   4          CLEANSER       20       63.80       100.00       36.20

   2          BLEACH         15       35.70        63.75       28.05

   3          DETERGENT     157      890.19     1,138.25      248.06

   1          SOAP           79      296.25       414.75      118.50

   4          CLEANSER      524    1,671.56     2,620.00      948.44

   5          POWDER         17       46.92        77.35       30.43
```

Problem 4

The records of the Himargin Department Stores contain the following information:

Store No	Department No	1st SALE	2nd SALE	3rd SALE	4th SALE	5th SALE
123	1359	001293	029160	200015	025037	010035
	1530	013000	000250	304000	002519	023410
	2400	002459	002947	012044	002830	016625
	3594	000248	001590	002300	000122	003520
530	1280	002510	020050	001257	011120	025910
	3320	100245	001945	027933	123450	300020
	7730	002460	001024	003913	029433	002930
	9250	002200	001050	023910	000200	000391

(1st STORE: 123; 2nd STORE: 530)

A report is to be prepared showing the total sales for each day, the total for each department for each day, and the total for all days for all stores. There are two stores and four departments in each store.

Input

Positions	Field Description	
1–03	Store number	
4–07	Department number	
8–13	Sales 1st day	(XXXX.XX)
14–19	Sales 2nd day	(XXXX.XX)
20–25	Sales 3rd day	(XXXX.XX)
26–31	Sales 4th day	(XXXX.XX)
32–37	Sales 5th day	(XXXX.XX)

Calculations

Add all sales for each department. Determine the totals for each store by day and the five-day totals.

Arrays are to be set up for the five days' sales. Arrays are to be set up for the two stores. Department totals are to be added to store totals. The records are in sequence by department number within store number.

Output

A report is to be prepared showing the sales for each of five days within each department within each store. The report should provide grand totals, store totals, and department totals for all days as well as the five-day total for each.

Required

Code the necessary file description specifications, extension specifications, input specifications, calculation specifications, and output specifications on the appropriate forms to accomplish the above.

Output is as follows:

STORE NUMBER	DEPARTMENT NUMBER	SALES 1ST DAY	SALES 2ND DAY	SALES 3RD DAY	SALES 4TH DAY	SALES 5TH DAY	TOTAL SALES
123	1359	12.93	291.60	2,000.15	250.37	111.35	2,666.40
123	1530	130.00	2.50	3,040.00	25.19	234.10	3,431.79
123	2400	24.59	29.47	120.44	28.30	166.25	369.05
123	3594	2.48	15.90	23.00	1.22	35.20	77.80
	STORE TOTALS	170.00	339.47	5,183.59	305.08	546.90	6,545.04
530	1280	25.10	200.50	12.57	111.20	259.10	608.47
530	3320	1,002.45	19.45	279.33	1,234.50	3,000.20	5,535.93
530	7730	24.60	10.24	39.13	294.33	29.30	397.60
530	9250	22.00	10.50	239.10	22.00	3.91	297.51
	STORE TOTALS	1,074.15	240.69	570.13	1,662.03	3,292.51	6,839.51

Disk Processing

8

Outline

Direct Access (Mass Storage
    Devices)
Terminology
    Direct Access Storage Device
        (DASD)
    File
    Record
    Key
    Volume
Data Files
    Sequential Files
    Indexed Files
    Direct Files
Processing Techniques
    Sequential Processing
    Random Processing
Data File Organization
    Sequential Organization
    Indexed Organization
    Direct Organization
    Disk File Organization—Summary
        Sequential Organization
        Indexed Organization
        Direct Organization
Sequential File Organization
    Creating a Sequential File
    Maintaining a Sequential File
        Adding Records
        Adding Records at the End
        of Records in the File
        Merging Records
        between Records in the File
        Tagging Records for Deletion
        Updating Records
        Reorganizing a File
Indexed File Organization
    Creating an Indexed File
        Creating an Ordered Indexed
            File
        Creating an Unordered Indexed
            File

Maintaining an Indexed File
    Updating Records
        Updating Records Sequentially
            by Key
        Updating Records Randomly
            by Key
    CHAIN Operation
    Adding Records
        Adding Records Randomly
            by Key Using Chaining
        Adding Records Randomly
            by Key without Chaining
        Adding Records Sequentially
            by Key
    Tagging Records for Deletion
    Reorganizing a File
Other Ways to Process Indexed Files
    Processing an Indexed File
        Consecutively
    Processing an Indexed File
        Randomly by Relative
        Record Number
    Direct File Organization
    Creating a Direct File
Record Address Files (RAF)
    Processing within Limits
    Processing Using Record Address
        File Key
    Files Containing Record Key
        Limits
    Creating a File with Record Key
        Limits
    Processing Sequentially within
        Limits
    File Description Specifications
    Extension Specifications

Direct Access (Mass Storage Devices)

Direct access mass storage devices enable the programmer to maintain current records of diversified applications and to process nonsequential and intermixed data for multiple application areas. Direct access implies access at random by multiple users of data (files, programs, subroutines, and programming aids) involving mass storage devices. Physically, these storage devices differ in appearance, capacity, and speed; functionally, they are similar in terms of data recording, checking, and programming. The direct access devices used for mass memory storage are disk, drum, and data cells. (See Figure 8.1.) Disk storage is the most popular of the mass storage devices in use today and will be the only one discussed in this section. (See Figures 8.2 and 8.3.)

Figure 8.1 Mass storage devices—types

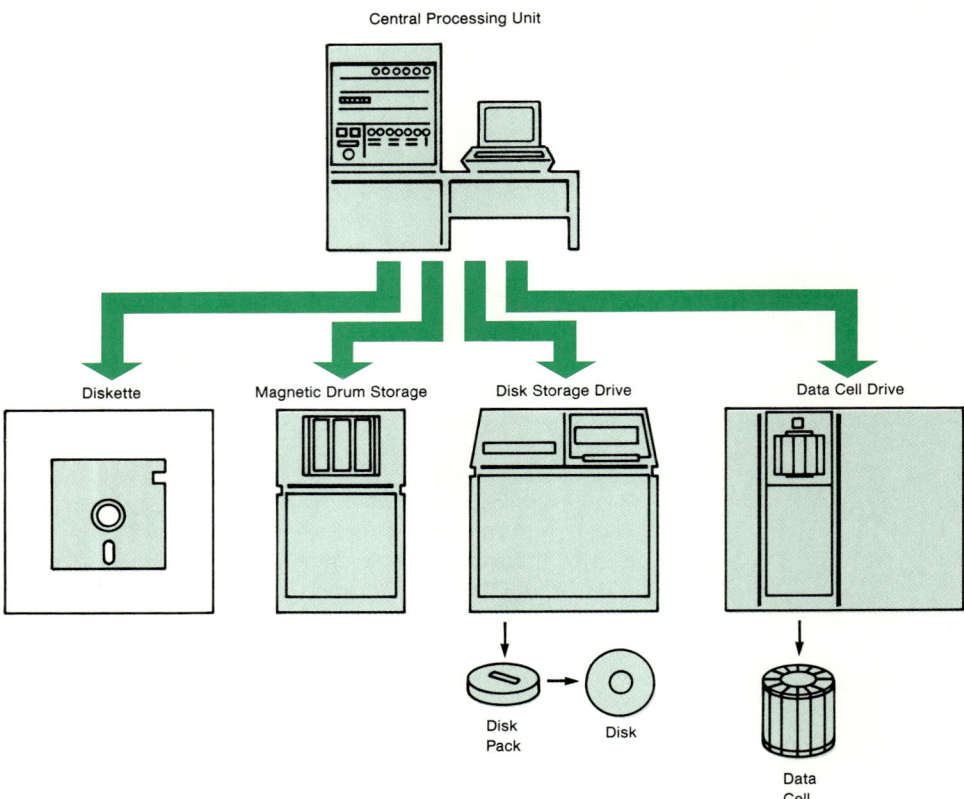

Figure 8.2 Mass storage devices

348   RPG II and RPG III Programming

Figure 8.3 Schematic of disk

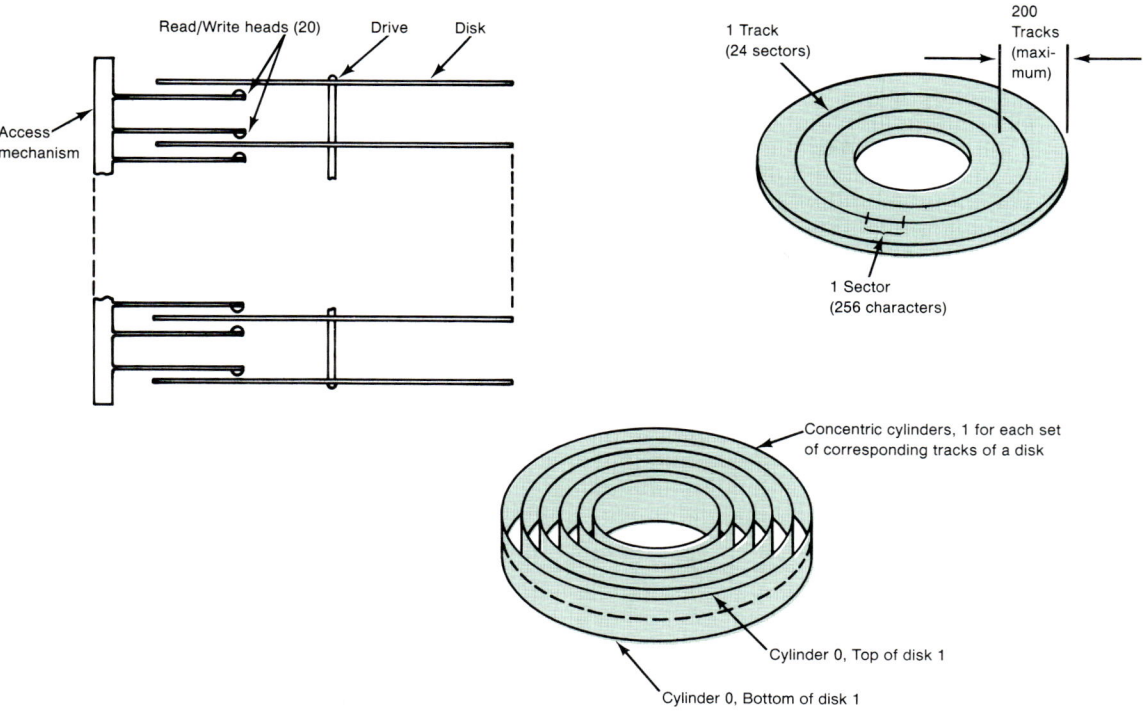

Terminology

Direct access terminology and concepts are prerequisite to understanding the use of direct access devices in programming.

Direct Access Storage Device (DASD)

A direct access storage device is one in which each physical record has a discrete location and a unique address. Records can be stored on a DASD in such a way that the location of any record can be determined without extensive searching. Records can be accessed directly as well as serially.

File

A file can be either a physical unit (a DASD, for instance) or an organized collection of related information. This text applies the latter definition. An inventory file, for example, contains all of the data concerning a particular inventory. It may occupy several physical units or part of one physical unit.

Record

The term record can refer to a physical unit or a logical unit. (See Figure 8.4.) A **logical record** may be defined as a collection of data related to a common identifier. An inventory file, for example, contains a logical record for each part number in the inventory. A **physical record** consists of one or more logical records. (See Figure 8.5.) The term **block** is equivalent to the term physical record. On a DASD, certain "nondata" information required by the control unit of the device is recorded in the same record area as the physical record. The nondata information and the physical record may be referred to as a whole by the term data record.

Disk Processing

Figure 8.4 File, logical record, field—example

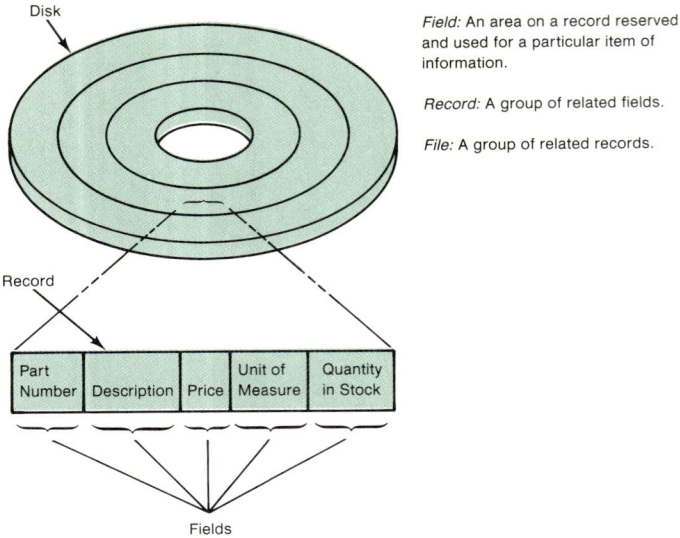

Figure 8.5 Physical records

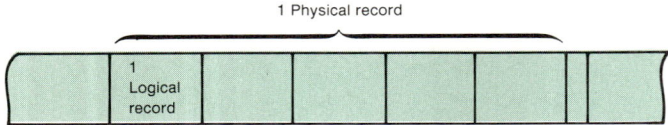

Key

Each logical record contains a control field or key that uniquely identifies it. The key of the inventory record, for example, would probably be the part number. The key of employees is usually their employee number or their social security number.

Volume

Volume is a generic term used to refer to a standard (physical) unit of auxiliary storage. A volume may be a reel of magnetic tape, a disk pack, or a drum. Direct access storage volumes are used to store executable programs including the operating system itself. Direct access storage is also used for data and for temporary working storage. One direct access volume may be used for many different data sets; space on it may be relocated and reused.

Data Files

Data files may be organized in several ways. Some of the more popular data organizations are outlined below.

Sequential Files

Records in sequentially organized files are placed in physical rather than logical sequence. Given one record, the location of the next record is determined by its physical position in the data files. Sequential organization is used for all magnetic tape devices, and may be selected for direct access devices. Punched cards and printed output are sequentially organized. (See Figure 8.6.)

Figure 8.6 Sequentially organized data file—example

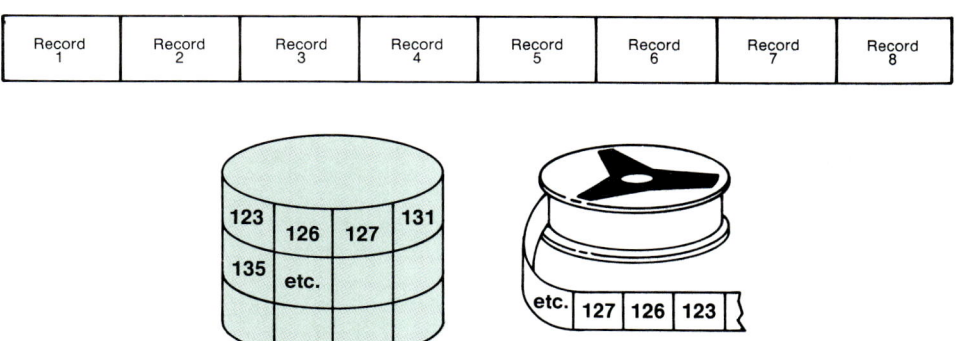

Indexed Files

Records in files that are index organized are arranged according to a key that is part of every record on the tracks of the direct access volume. The records may be ordered (in sequence by key) or unordered (in random sequence). An index or set of indexes maintained in sequence by the system gives the location of the records. This permits direct as well as sequential access to the records of the data file. (See Figure 8.7.)

Direct Files

The record within a directly organized data file that must be on a direct access volume may be organized in any manner that the programmer chooses. All space attached to the data file is available for data records. No space is required for indexes. The programmer specifies addresses by which records are stored and retrieved directly. (See Figure 8.8.)

Processing Techniques

Sequential Processing

In sequential processing input transactions are grouped together, sorted into a predetermined sequence, and processed against a master file. When information is recorded on magnetic tape or in punched cards, the only method of processing that can be used is the sequential method. Direct access storage devices are also efficient sequential processors, especially when the percentage of activity involving processing against the master file is high. (See Figure 8.9.)

Random Processing

The processing of detail transactions against a master file, regardless of the sequence of the input documents, is called random processing. With direct access storage devices it can be a very efficient processing technique, especially if the files are organized in such a manner that each record can be located quickly. (See Figure 8.10.) It is possible to process input transactions against more than one file in a single run. This saves time in both setup and sorting, and minimizes the control problems since the transactions are handled less frequently.

    The use of mass storage devices makes it possible to select the processing technique that will best suit the application. Some applications may be processed sequentially; others, in which the time required to sort or the delay with the batching process are material factors, can be processed randomly. Real savings can be made in overall processing time for a job by combining runs in which the same input data affects several files. The detail items can be processed sequentially against a primary file and randomly against the secondary files, all in one run.

Figure 8.7 Indexed organized data file—example

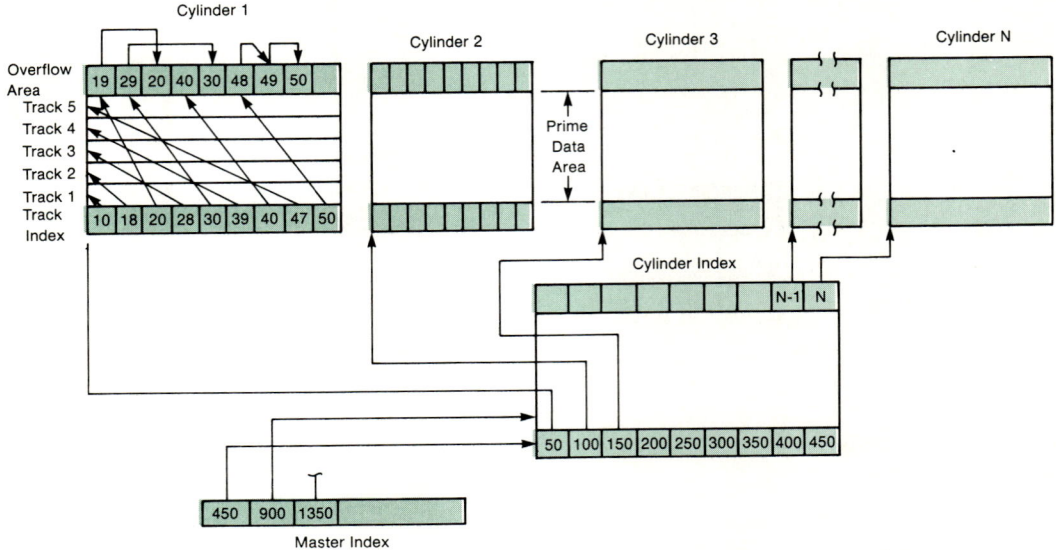

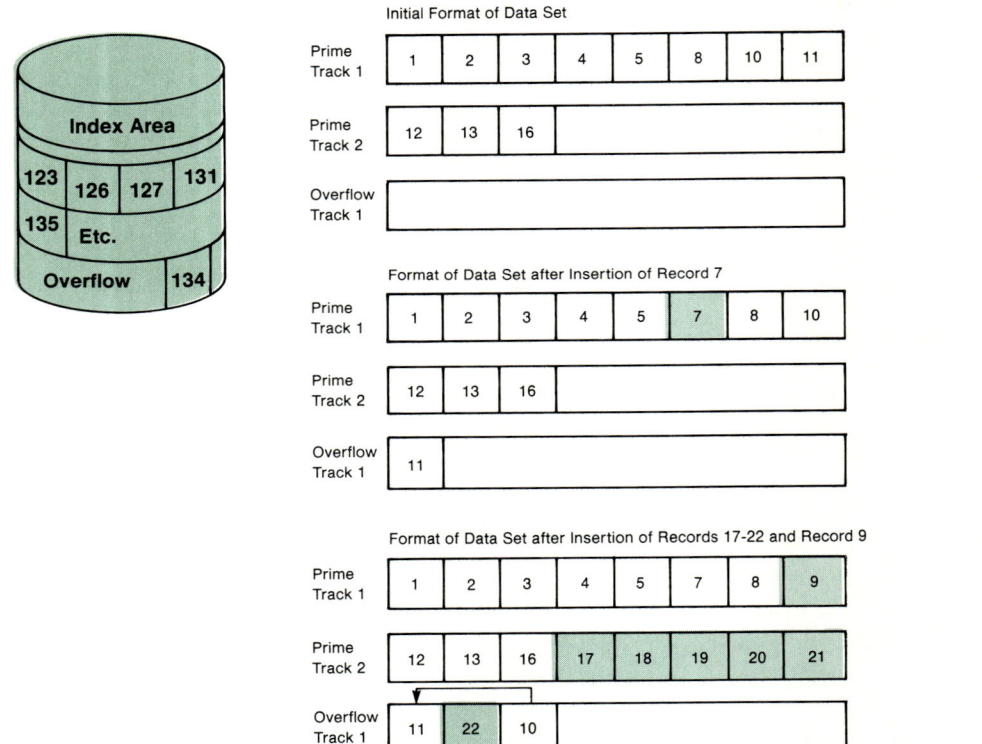

Figure 8.8 Direct organized data file—example

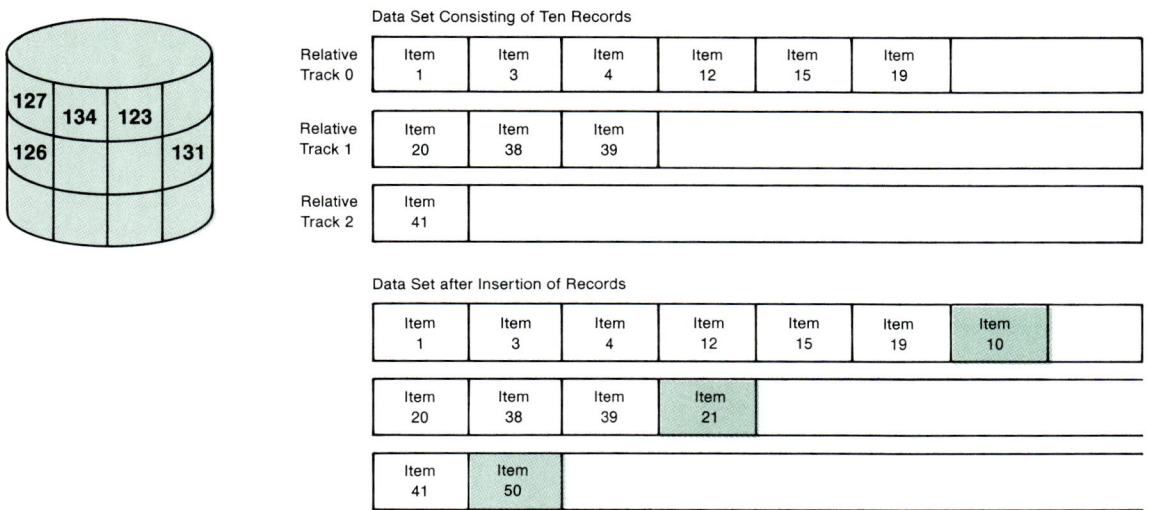

Figure 8.9 Sequential processing—example

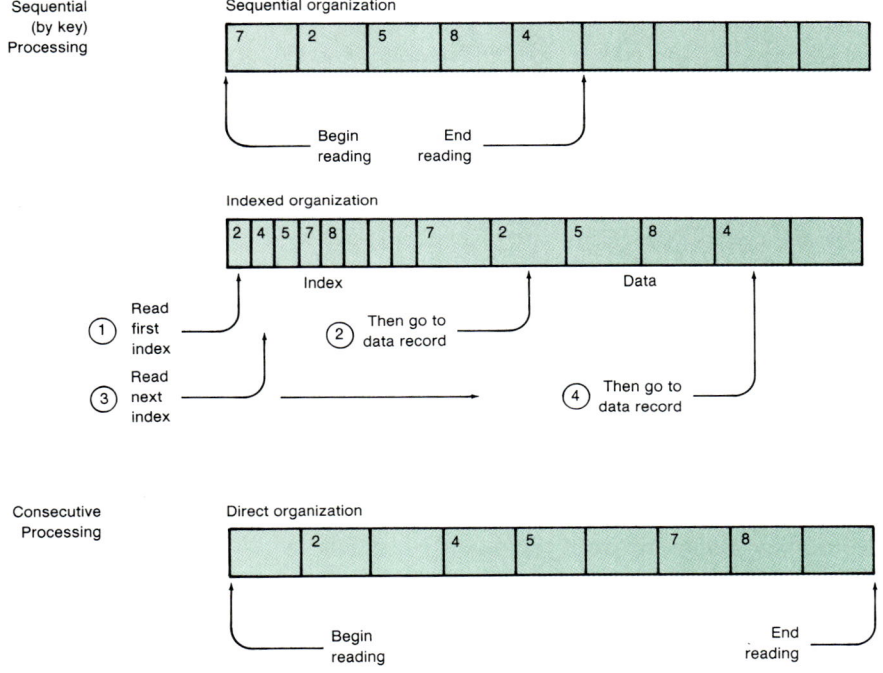

Figure 8.10 Random processing—example

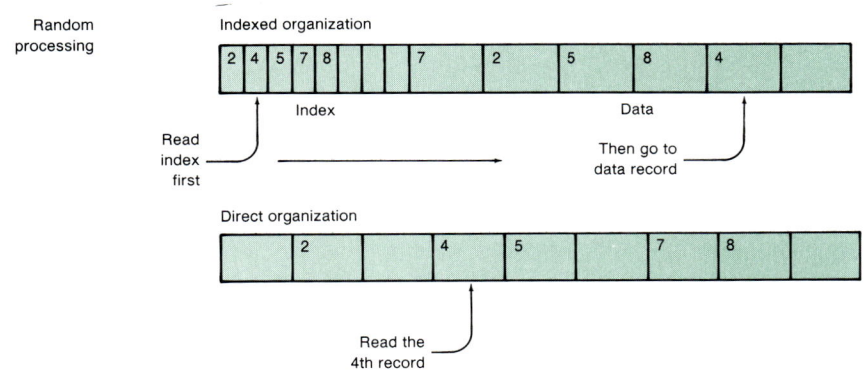

Disk Processing 353

Data File Organization

Data file organization refers to the physical arrangement of data records within a file. To give the programmer maximum flexibility in reading and writing data sets from mass storage devices, the following methods of data organization are most commonly used for disk operations: sequential, indexed, and direct.

Sequential Organization

In a sequential file, records are organized solely on the basis of their successive physical locations in the file. The records are written one after the other—track by track, cylinder by cylinder—at successively higher locations. The records are usually, but not necessarily, in sequence according to their keys (control numbers). The records are usually read or updated in the same sequence as that in which they appear. (See Appendix H.)

Updating a sequential file located on a mass storage device is more efficient than updating a file located on a magnetic tape. The record can be read, updated, and written back in the same location in the file without creating a new file. Thus, the file can be used for both input and output activities.

A file on a mass storage device may have the same standard sequential data file organization as any of the magnetic tape files. The mass storage file, however, may be differently organized so that any record may be accessed merely by specifying the **key field,** the unique field that tells the system where the desired record is located. This differs from standard sequential organization in that the desired records can be accessed at random without accessing all previous records.

Nonsequential processing of a sequential file is, at best, inefficient. If it is done infrequently, the time required to locate the records may not matter. There are several ways to program nonsequential processing, with significant differences in time required for each. The slowest way is to read the records sequentially until the desired one is located. On the average, half of the files would have to be read. A sequential search takes less time if the records are formatted with keys. The search is performed with the search key high or equal at the speed of one revolution per track. When the search condition is satisfied, the corresponding record is read.

Additions and deletions require a complete rewrite of a sequential file. Therefore, sequential organization is used in direct access storage primarily for tables and intermediate storage and less often for master files. Sequential organization is recommended for master files only if there is a high percentage of activity and if virtually all processing is sequential.

Indexed Organization

An indexed file is a file with indexes that permit rapid access to individual records as well as rapid sequential processing. The indexes are created in sequence by the system as the file is created or organized. The key provided by the programmer precedes each block of data and is used to specify the index. By referring to the indexes maintained with the file, it is possible to quickly locate individual records for random processing.

Moreover, a separate area can be set aside for additions making it unnecessary to rewrite the entire file, a process that would be required if the sequential processing method were being used. Although the records are not maintained in key sequence, the indexes are referred to in order. This way, the added records are retrieved in key sequence, thus making rapid sequential processing possible. (See Appendix H.)

The programming system has control over the location of the individual records in this method of organization. The programmer need do very little input or output programming; the programming system does most of it because the characteristics of the file are known.

Indexed organization gives the programmer greater flexibility in the operations that can be performed on the data file. The programmer is provided with the facilities for reading or writing records in a manner similar to that for sequential organization. The programmer can also read and write individual records whose keys may be in any order, and can add logical records with new keys. The system locates the proper position in the data file for the new record and makes all the necessary adjustments to the indexes.

The indexed file must be stored on a direct access device. The indexed files must be created with identifying data called keys (control fields of the record). As the records are written into the file, the system creates the indexes in ascending sequence based on the key. Thus, any record in an indexed file may be accessed by specifying the appropriate key.

In addition to the quick access of any record, an advantage of indexed files is that the records may be added to any part of the file after it has been created. The system will keep all records in a logical sequence, although some records may technically be in a special overflow area. In accessing the file sequentially, the system will access records in logical sequence by key, rather than in physical sequence by position on the device.

Direct Organization

A file organized in a direct manner is characterized by the presence of some predictable relationship between the key of the record and the address of that record in a direct access storage device. The relationship is established by the programmer and permits rapid access to any record of the file, provided the file has been carefully organized. It should be noted that indexed file organization is far more prevalent than direct organization. Using the social security number as an index obviates the necessity of translating the social security number through some algorithm into a relative record number. The records will probably be distributed nonsequentially throughout the file. If so, processing the record in key sequence requires a preliminary sort for the use of a finder file. (See Appendix H.)

Disk File Organization—Summary

File organization is the arrangement of records in a file. Three types of file organization may be described in the RPG language. When a file is created, it must be organized as one of the following:

1. A sequential file
2. An indexed file
3. A direct file

A **sequential file** is one in which the records are stored in the order in which they are read. An **indexed file** is a disk file in which the location of the records is stored in a separate portion of the file known as the index. A direct file is a disk file in which records are assigned specific record positions within the area reserved for storing that file. Relative record numbers identify the relative position of each record within the file. Regardless of the order in which these records are arranged prior to being put into the file, they always occupy their assigned (relative) record position within the file.

Indexed and direct files are always stored on disk. Sequential files may be stored on disk or on some other storage medium.

Disk file organization is planned prior to the coding of RPG programs that create the files.

Sequential Organization
1. Records are stored in the order that they are loaded.
2. Normally, records are sorted for convenience in processing, but sorting is not required.
3. No spaces appear between records, but space may be left at the end of the file so that new records may be added at some later date.

Indexed Organization
1. Data records are stored in sequence as they are loaded.
2. Index entries are stored in ascending key sequence.
3. No spaces appear between data records or between index entries.
4. Additional space called overflow is usually reserved so that new records and their index entries may be stored at a later time.

Direct Organization
1. Records are stored in a preassigned relative record position.
2. Unused record positions are reserved. During future processing a new record can be placed into its reserved space.

The best file organization method to use when creating disk file records depends upon the way in which the records will be processed in the future.

Figure 8.11 File description specifications in a sequentially organized file—example

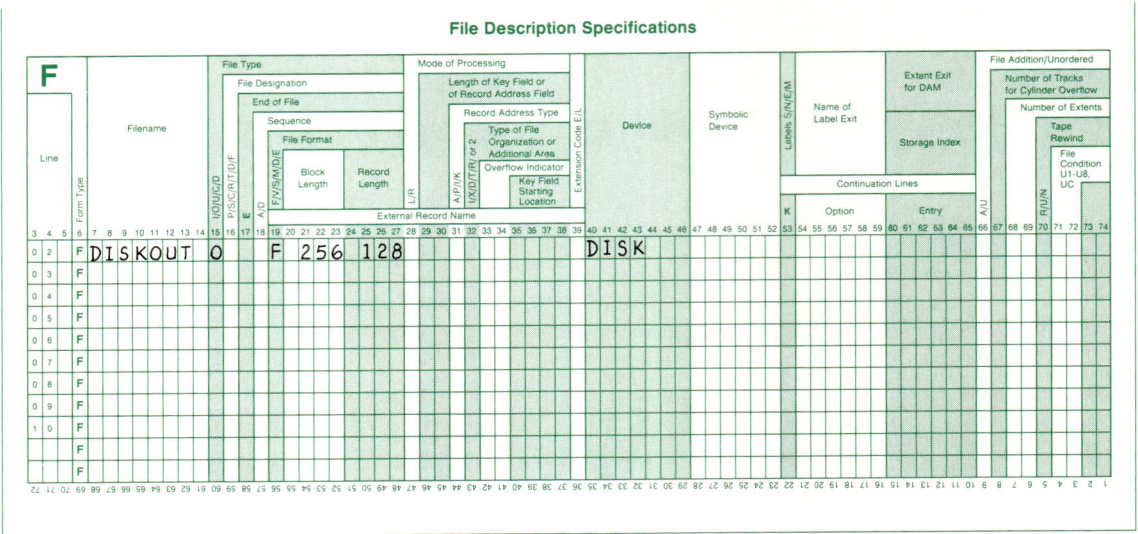

Sequential File Organization

Sequential organization refers to records on the disk that are arranged in the same physical order as that in which they were entered. Sequential organization does not necessarily mean ascending order. There are no gaps for missing records. The records are written onto the disk one after another as they occur. Any new records are added at the end of the file, rather than inserted between other records.

Creating a Sequential File

To create a sequential file, certain entries have to be made on the File Description Specifications form. The following entries are required for describing various characteristics of the disk files:

1. The disk file name must be entered in positions 7–14.

2. Position 15 must contain an *O* to indicate that the file is an output file.

3. All records in a file must be the same length. Thus, position 19 must contain an *F* to specify that the record length is fixed. (See Figure 8.11.)

4. A number that is equal to or a multiple of the logical record length must be entered in positions 20–23. This entry determines the size of the input/output area allocated by RPG. If the programmer wants unblocked records, the block length positions are left blank and the compiler assigns a block length. By blocking logical records, the input/output efficiency of the program is increased by reducing the number of accesses. However, enough main storage must be available in the input/output area. If positions 20–23 are blank, a fatal error may result on some compilers.

5. Positions 24–27 must contain the length of the logical record (the record described on the Input Specifications form).

6. Whenever a disk file is described, the device name is required in the device positions 40–46. (See Figures 8.12, 8.13, 8.14, and 8.15.)

Figure 8.12 Creating a sequential disk file—example

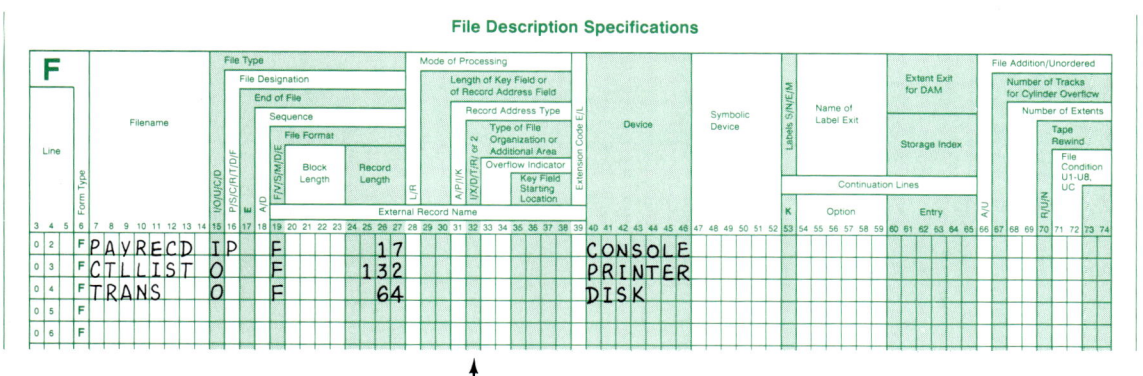

Notes on the Coding

Since there are a variety of ways that disk records can be arranged, this must be indicated to RPG on the File Description Specifications.

Position 32 is used to code "Type of File Organization." The entry for a sequential file is easy—a blank. By not coding an entry in position 32, RPG will know that the TRANS file is sequential.

The load program will then read records from the input device and place them on the file in the same "sequence" in which they are read.

Figure 8.13 Creating a sequential file coding—example

Problem

It is necessary to create a customer file on disk. Customer numbers are to be assigned on a sequential basis; new customers are assigned the next higher number. The file will be used to produce monthly reports of each customer's status. Thus, a sequential file will serve the needs of the organization.

To create the sequential file, the input record format and the output record format must be determined first. The file is created by writing the customer data from the input records onto disk. Notice that space is provided on the output record so that additional information can be added to the record later if necessary. Basic information about each customer in the file is also printed in the report.

The following shows the basic input record and output record formats as well as the necessary coding to create the sequential customer file and print the report.

Input Record and Output Record Formats

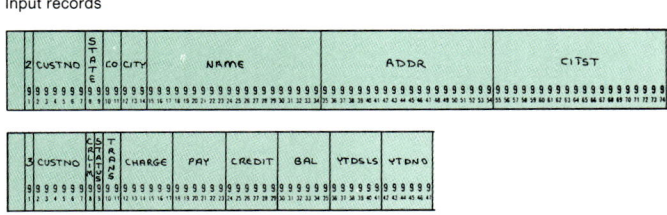

Key	
CODE	= Output code (CM)
CUSTNO	= Customer number
STATE	= State
CO	= County
CITY	= City
NAME	= Customer name
ADDR	= Customer street address
CITST	= City and state
CRLIM	= Credit limit
STATUS	= Status
TRANS	= Number of transactions this month
CHARGE	= Current month charges
PAY	= Current month payments
CREDIT	= Current month credits
BAL	= Balance
YTDSLS	= Year-to-date sales amount
YTDNO	= Year-to-date number of sales
DELETE	= Output record code

Disk Processing

Figure 8.13 continued

Output record

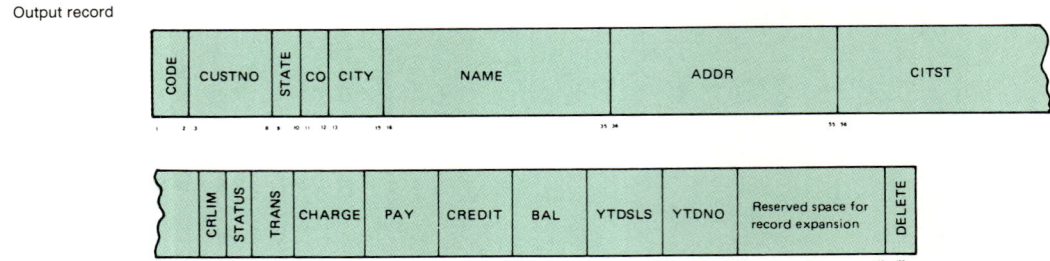

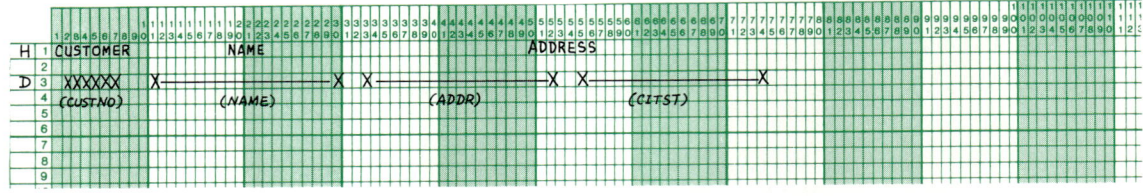

Customer Address Report

CUSTOMER	NAME	ADDRESS	
136728	JONES VARIETY	14 S MAIN	BEDROCK, TEX
301628	JIM'S 5 AND 10	1103 FRANKLIN ST	GLENCOE, MINN
795246	SCHMIDT HARDWARE	600 1ST ST NW	HILL CITY, MD

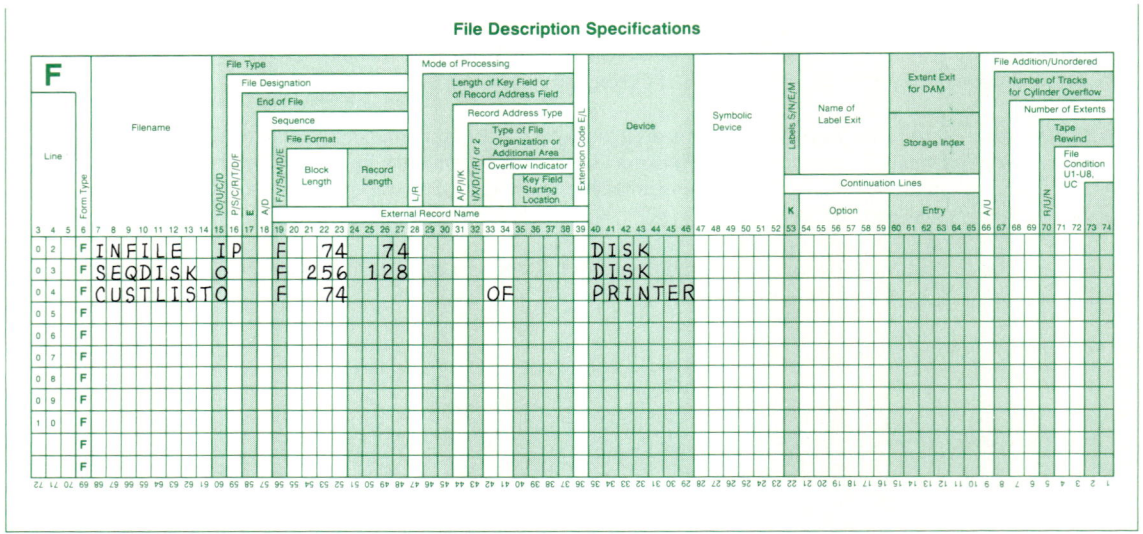

Note on the Coding

Records are blocked (128 x 2 = 256).

Figure 8.13 continued

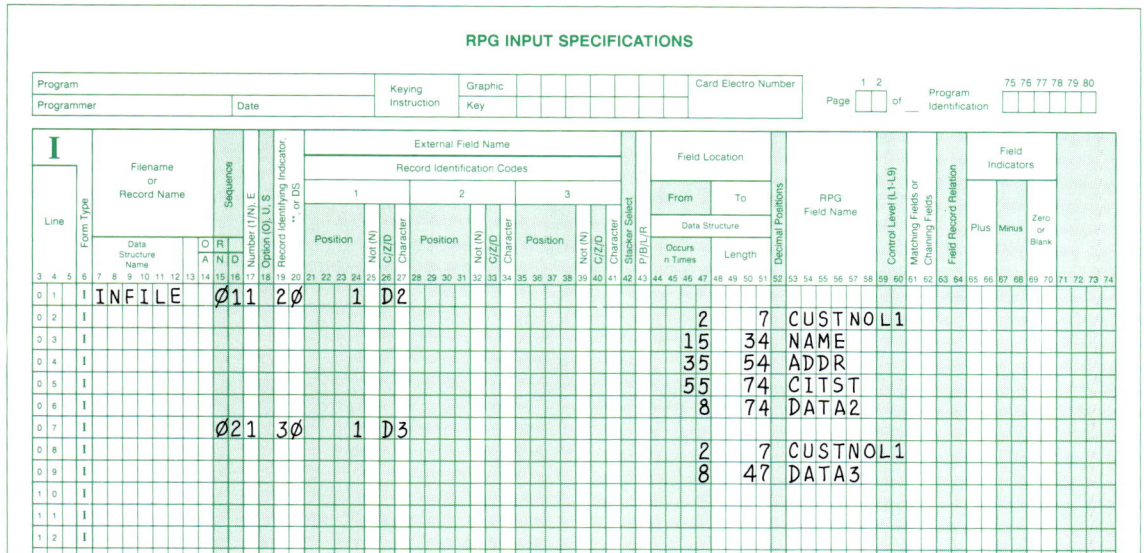

Notes on the Coding

On lines 01 and 07, positions 15-17 contain information used to sequence check the input record.

In positions 15 and 16, 01 means that record type 2 must be first followed by type 3 (identified by 02 sequence).

The 1 in position 17 means that one record type 2 and one record type 3 exist.

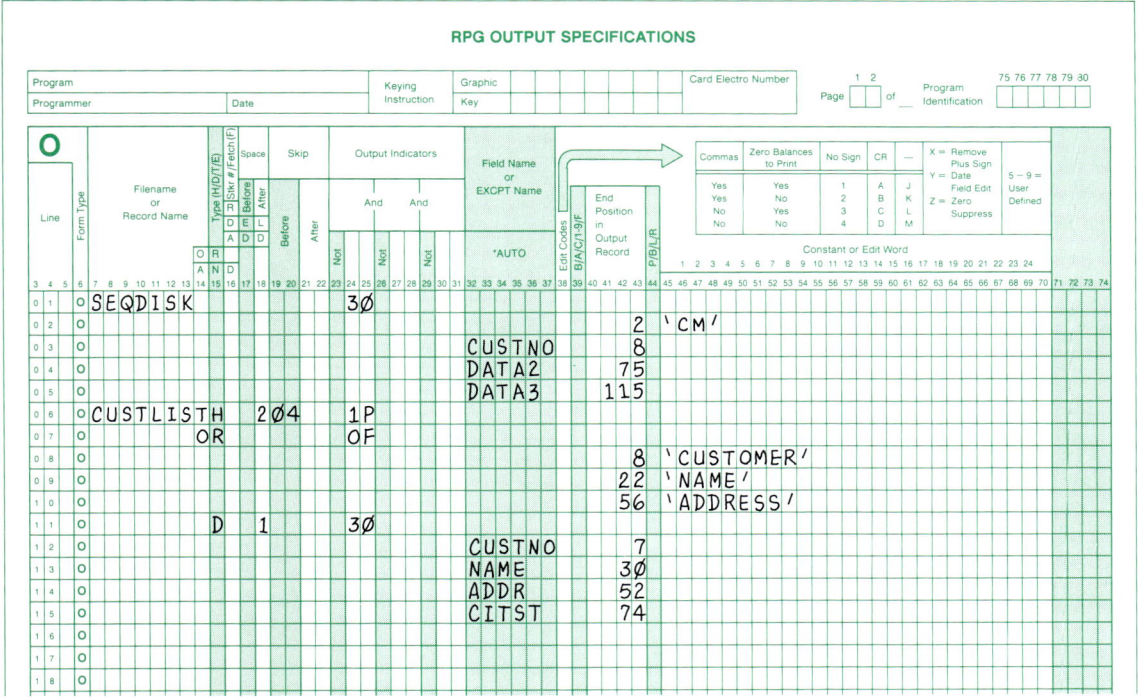

Notes on the Coding

On line 01, indicator 30 specifies that the disk record be written after input record type 3 is processed. Since both input record types are needed to write a disk record, we don't want to write it until the input record type 3 is processed.

On line 02, CM is added to the disk record. This code is a record code that can be used to identify a customer master record in other programs.

Disk Processing

Figure 8.14 Creating a sequential file—example

Create a file of disk records. These disk records are to be organized sequentially. The disk records shall each be sixty-seven positions long and contain the following fields. Input records contain this data in a different order, also shown.

Disk Output Fields

Positions	Fields
1-1	Code M
2-7	Customer number
8-27	Customer name
28-47	Street address
48-67	City/State address

Keyed Input Fields

Positions	Fields
1-1	Code M
2-21	Customer name
22-41	Street address
42-61	City/State address
62-67	Customer number

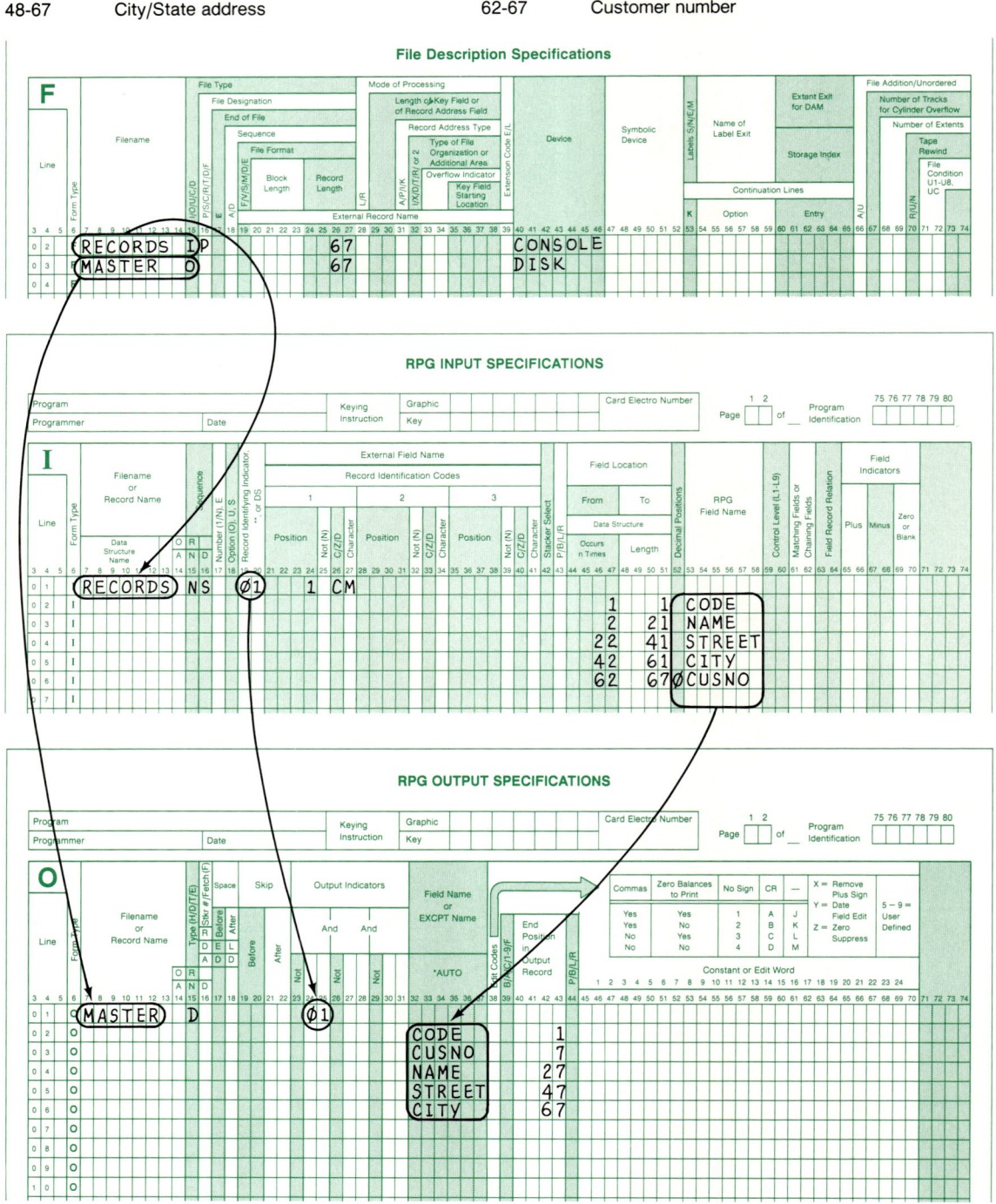

Figure 8.15 Printing a listing of a created sequential file coding—example

Print a list of the created disk records (fig. 8.14) in the following format:

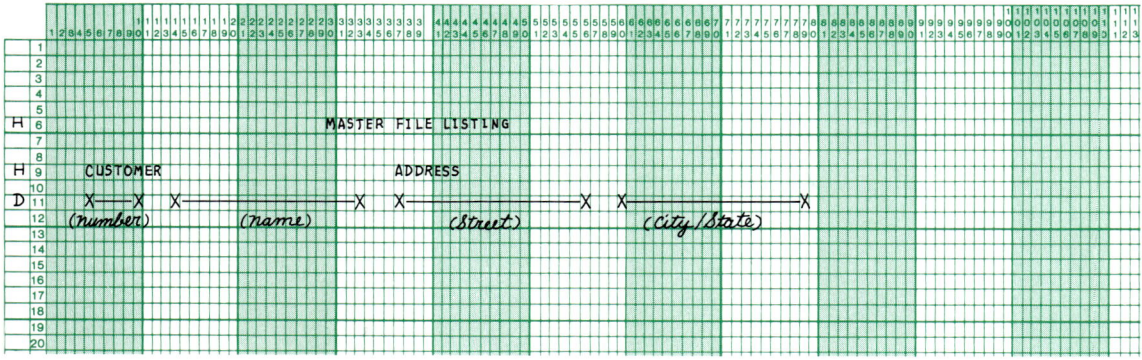

Master File Listing

Disk Processing

Figure 8.15 continued

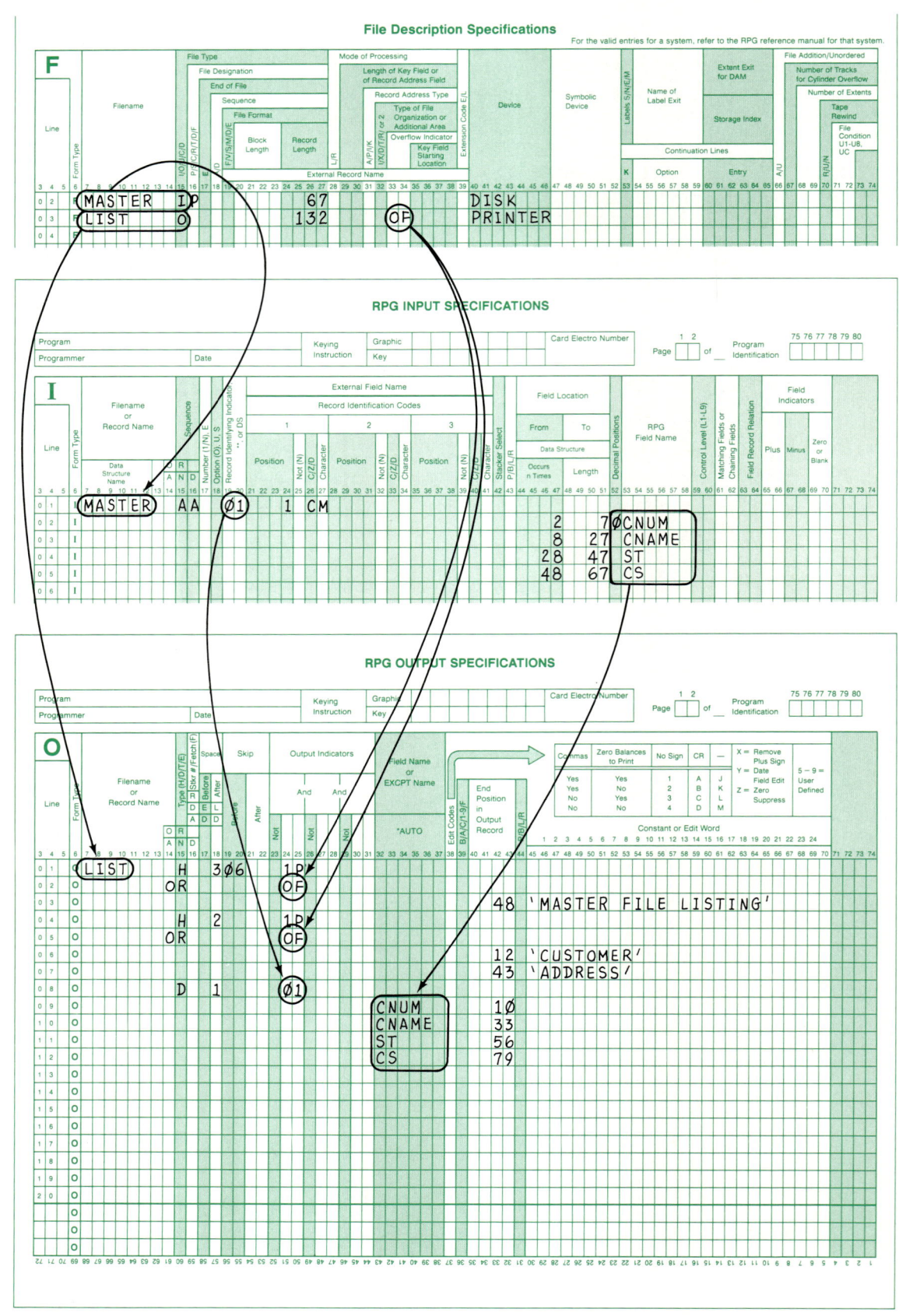

362 RPG II and RPG III Programming

Figure 8.16 Adding records to an existing sequential file at end of records in file—schematic

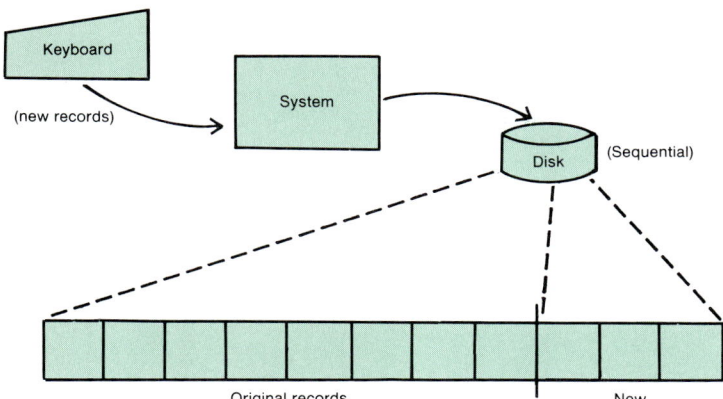

Maintaining a Sequential File

Once a file has been created, it usually needs to be maintained. File maintenance is performing those functions necessary to keep a file current for daily processing needs. Four file maintenance functions apply to sequential files:

1. Adding records
2. Tagging records for deletion
3. Updating records
4. Reorganizing a file

Adding Records

After a file is created, records can be added to it. Records can be added to a sequential file in either of two ways: by adding them to the end of the file or by merging them between the existing records of the file.

Adding Records at the End of Records in the File

Adding records at the end of the file (see Figure 8.16) requires certain entries on the File Description and Output Specifications forms. Some of the entries of the File Description form are the same ones needed to create a sequential file. Following are the additional entries needed:

1. An *A* in position 66 on the File Description form tells the system that records will be added to the file described on this line.

2. The ADD entry in positions 16–18 of the Output Specifications form tells the system that the fields defined on the following lines constitute the record to be added to the file specified in positions 7–14. (See Figures 8.17 and 8.18.)

Disk Processing

Figure 8.17 Coding for adding records to a disk file—example

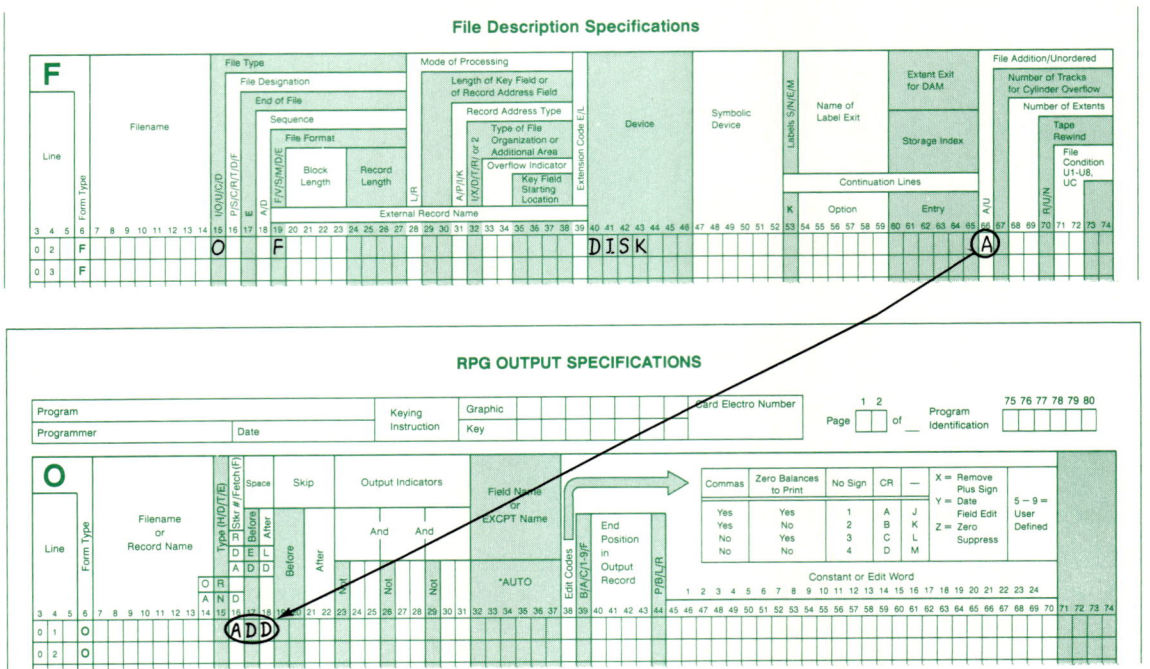

Notes on the Coding

An A in position 66 tells the system that records will be added to the file described on this line.

The ADD in positions 16-18 tells the system that the fields defined on the following lines constitute the record to be added to the file specified in positions 7-14.

Figure 8.18 Adding records to the end of a sequential file—example

Problem

As you get new customers, you will want to add them to the sequential customer file that was created in figure 8.13. Since customer numbers are assigned sequentially, each new customer record can be added following the records now in the file.

The input records and output records will be in the same format as the records used to create the file. A report can be printed like the one shown below to ensure that the new records have been added to the file.

The necessary coding for the problem follows.

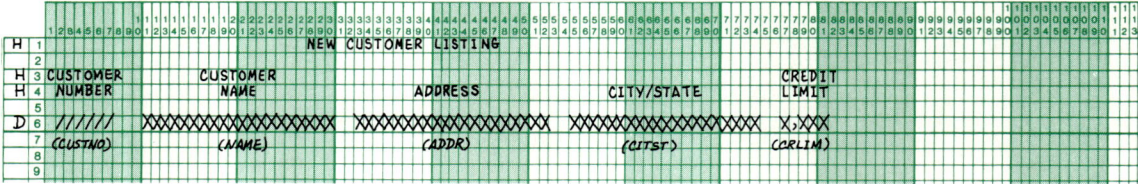

Report of New Customers Added to the Customer File

```
                      NEW CUSTOMER LISTING

        CUSTOMER    CUSTOMER                                              CREDIT
        NUMBER      NAME              ADDRESS            CITY/STATE       LIMIT

        136728      JONES VARIETY     14 S MAIN          BEDROCK, TEX     1,000
        301628      JIM'S 5 AND 10    1103 FRANKLIN ST   GLENCOE, MINN      250
        795246      SCHMIDT HARDWARE  600 1ST ST NW      HILL CITY, MD    2,000
```

364   RPG II and RPG III Programming

Figure 8.18 continued

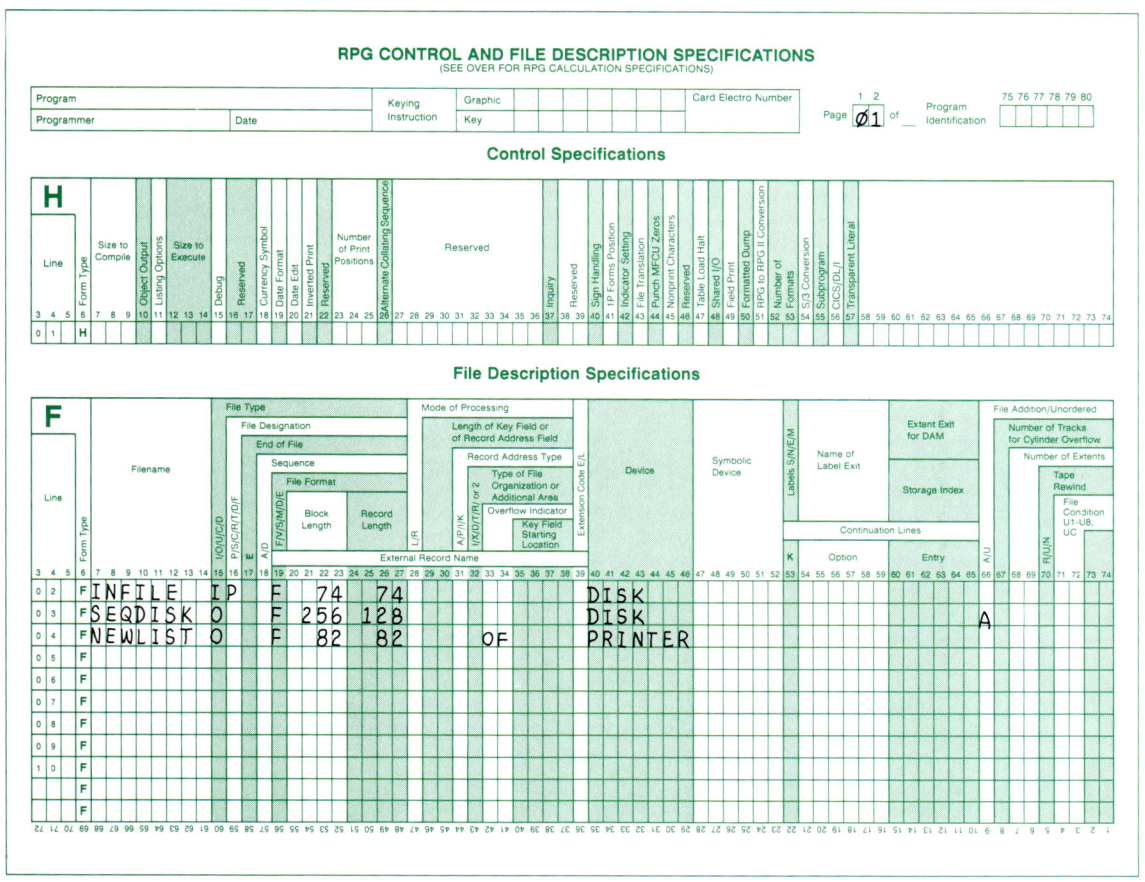

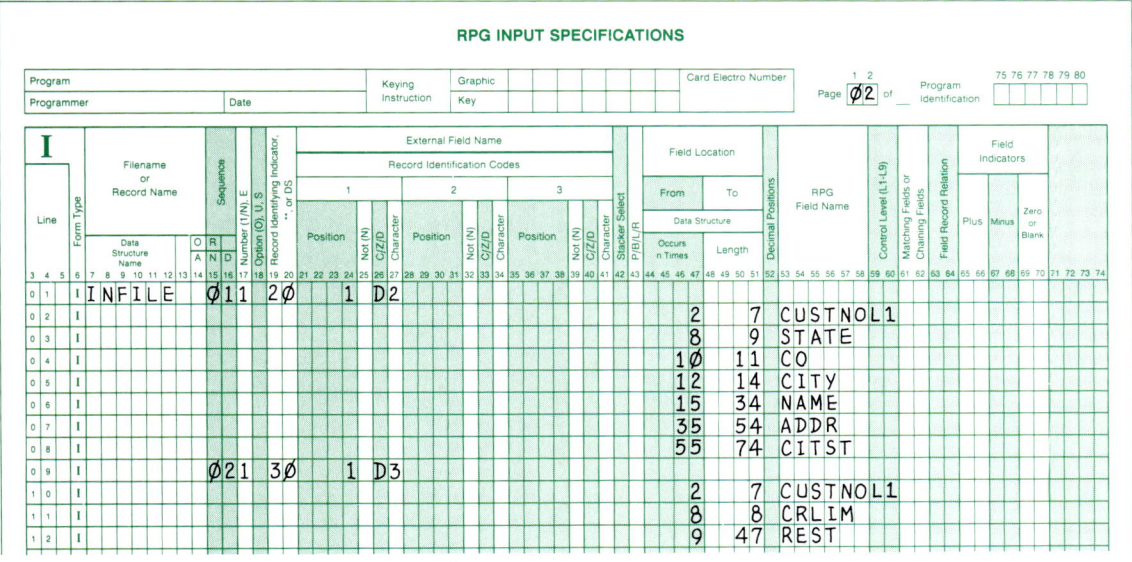

Figure 8.18 continued

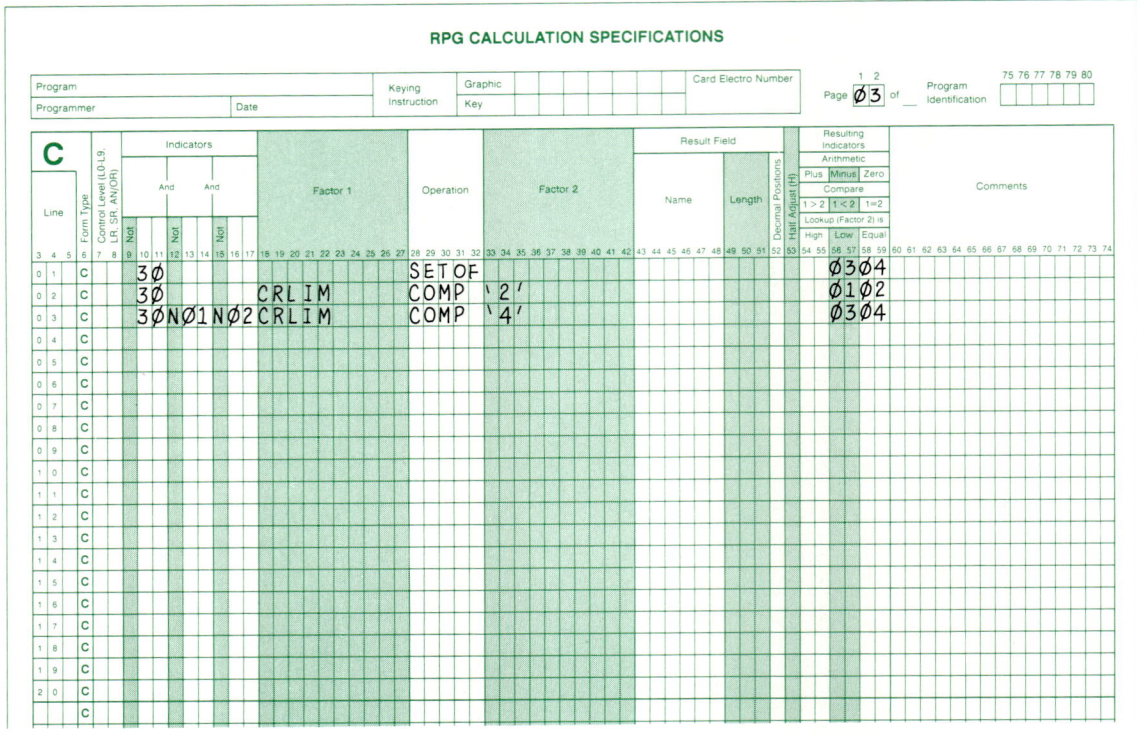

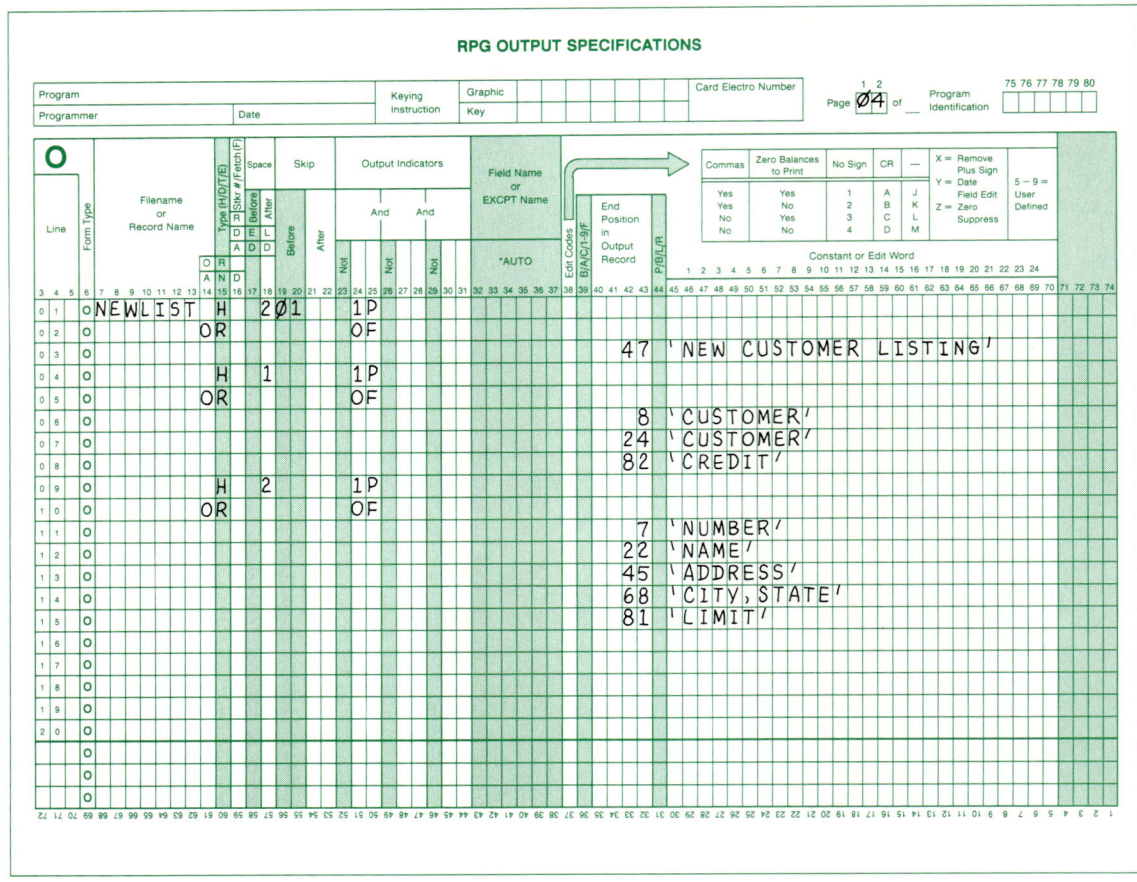

Figure 8.18 continued

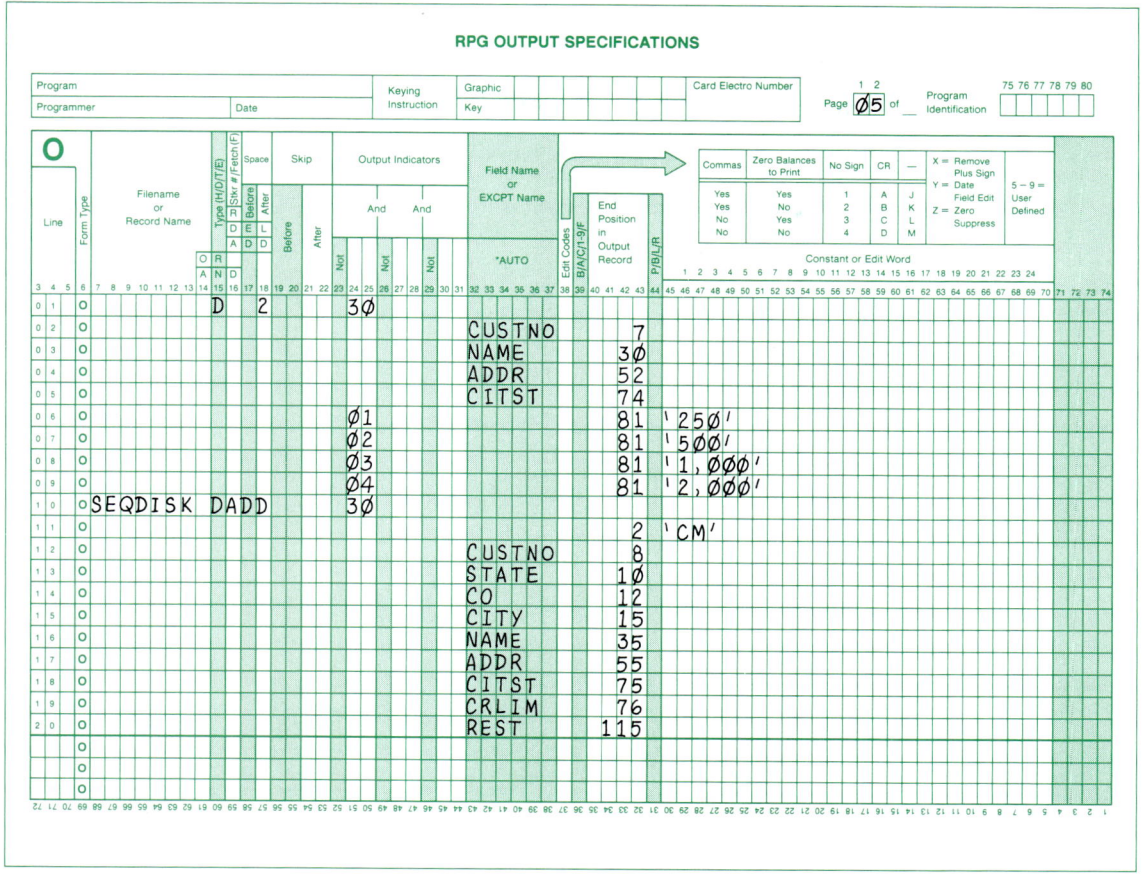

Disk Processing 367

Merging Records between Records in the File

Often records must be added between existing records in a sequential disk file. When records are to be added in this manner, the new records must be sorted into a predetermined sequence in another program and a new file re-created. This new file contains the added records merged in correct order with the records from the original file. (See Figures 8.19 and 8.20.)

Figure 8.19 Adding records to the end of a sequential file—example

Add records to a sequential file named INTER. Records in this disk file are 46 characters long and have code I in position 1. The keyed input records (NEW) contain the fields shown below.

The output records contain the same fields in different positions. Also, today's date (UDATE) is to be included so we know the creation date. This special field is provided for your use in any RPG program where today's date is needed.

The disk file to which records shall be added is to be described as an output file.

Keyed Input Records		Output Records	
Position	Input Field	Position	Output Field
1-1	Code N	1-1	Code I
2-7	Item number	2-7	Today's date
8-28	Item description	8-13	Item number
29-31	Unit code	14-34	Item description
32-36	Unit cost, 2 decimals	35-37	Unit code
37-40	Units in stock	38-42	Unit cost, 2 decimals
		43-46	Units in stock

Figure 8.19 continued

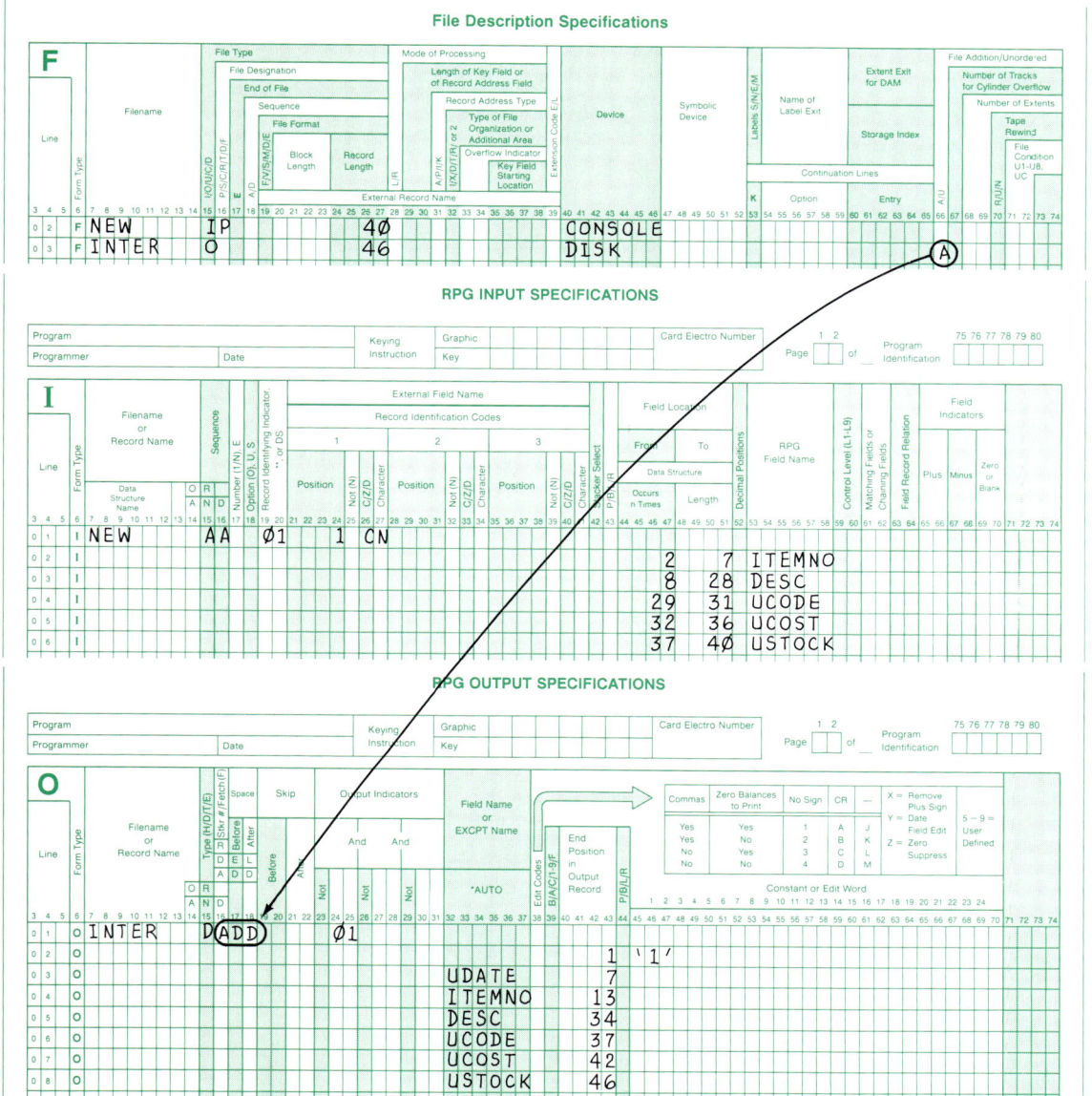

Figure 8.20 Merging records between records in a sequential file—example

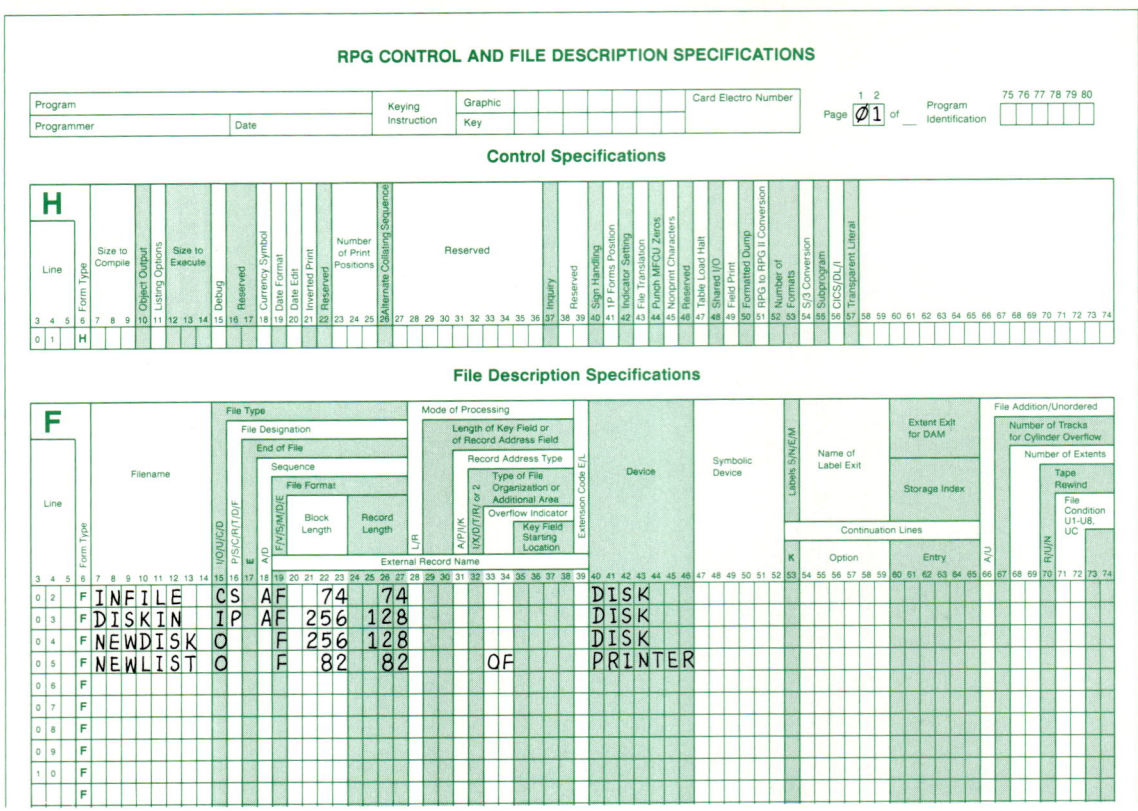

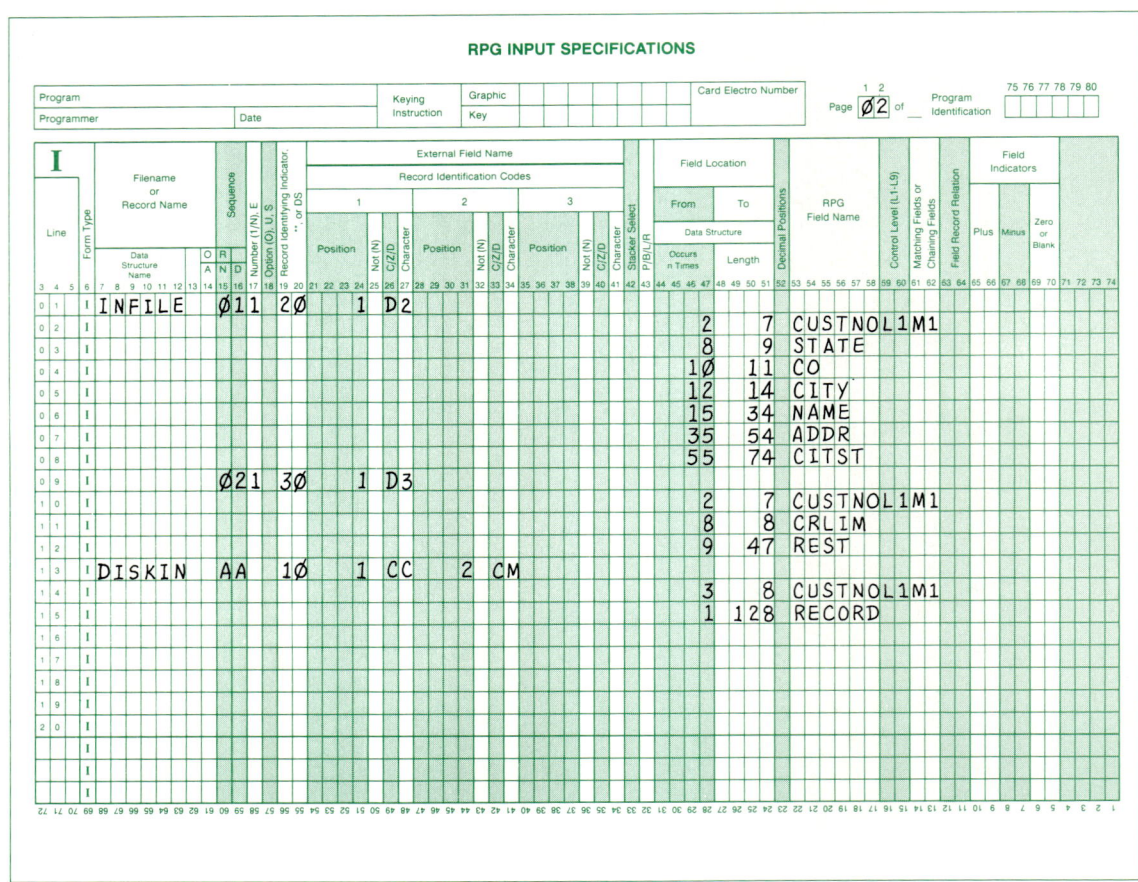

370 RPG II and RPG III Programming

Figure 8.20 continued

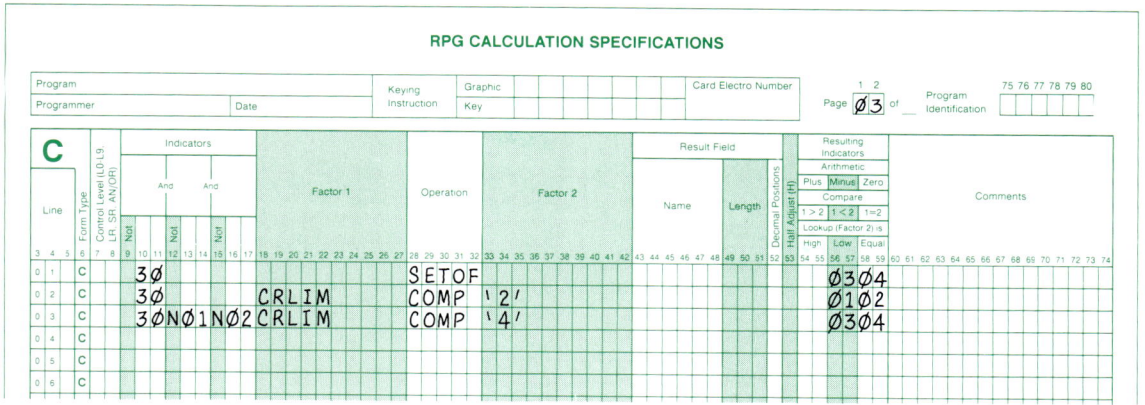

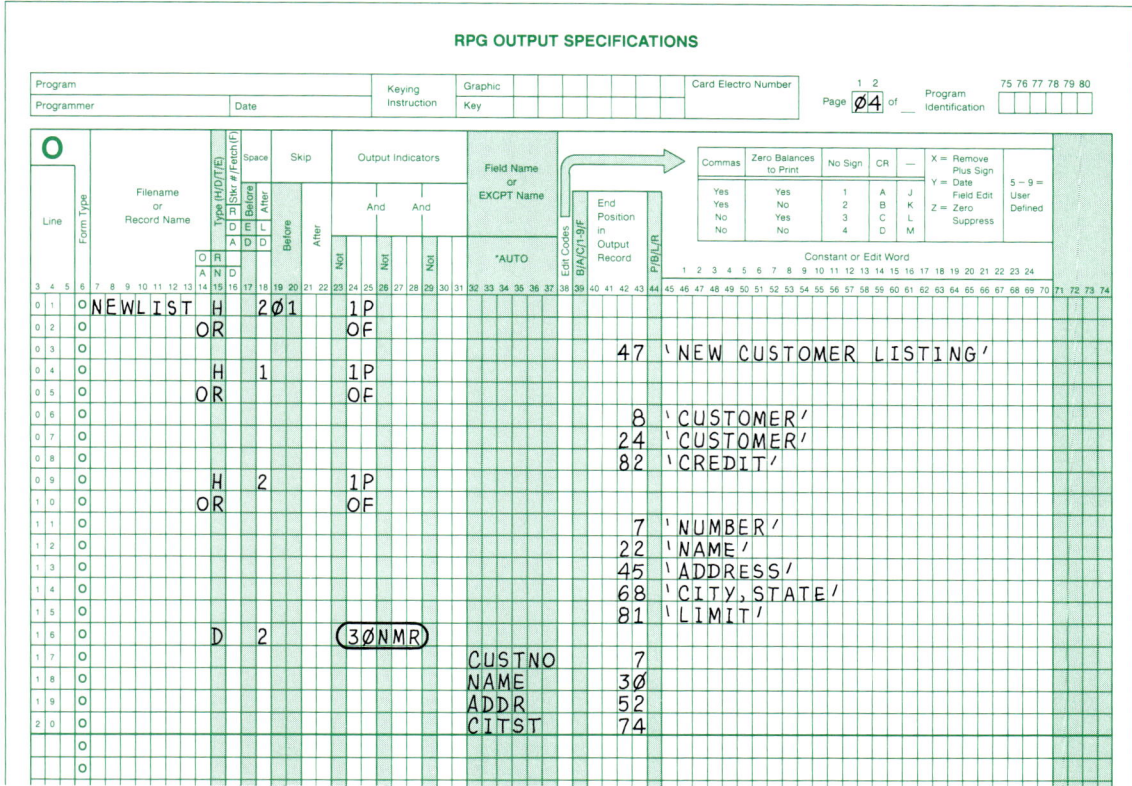

Notes on the Coding

Line Meaning
16   Records are added to the output disk file when there is no match between the customer number in the input records and the disk file. The added records are listed.

Disk Processing 371

Figure 8.20 continued

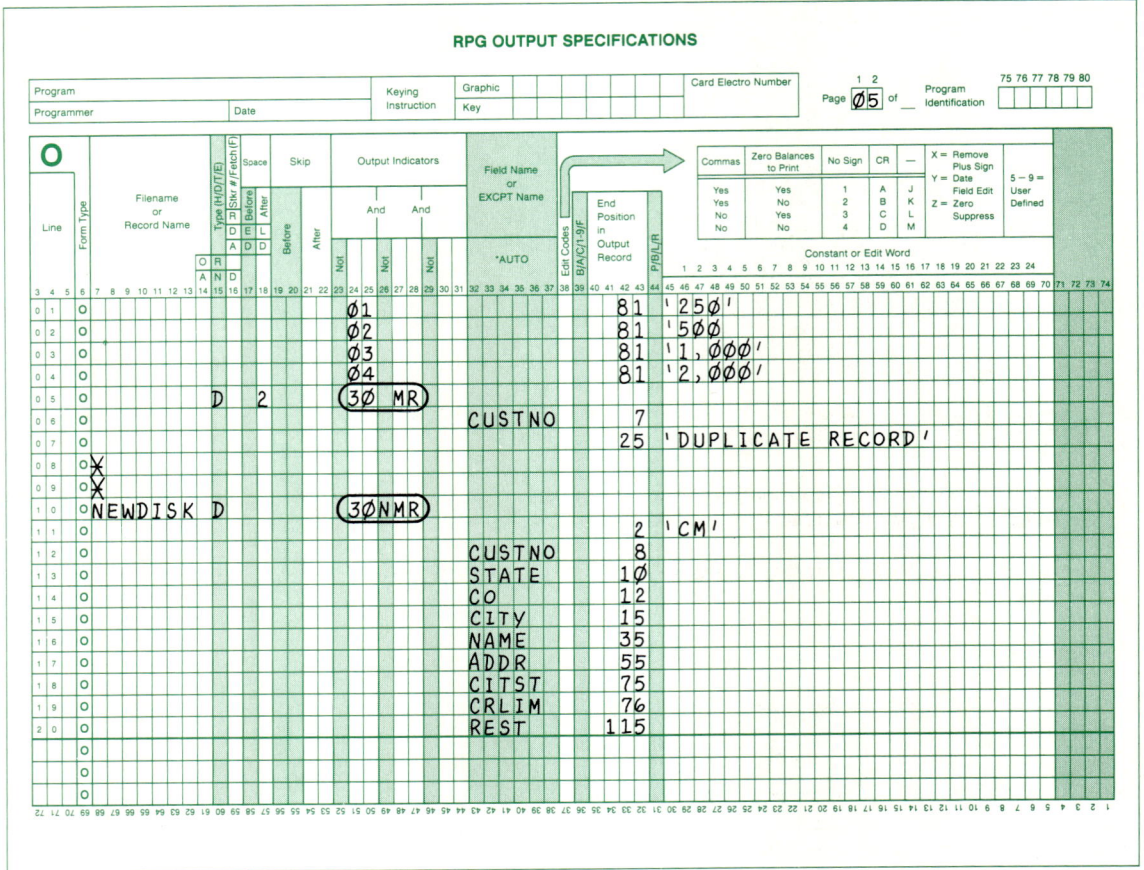

Notes on the Coding

Line	Meaning
05	The input records that match the disk file on customer number are in error. They should not match because they are new records.
10	Copy the new record.

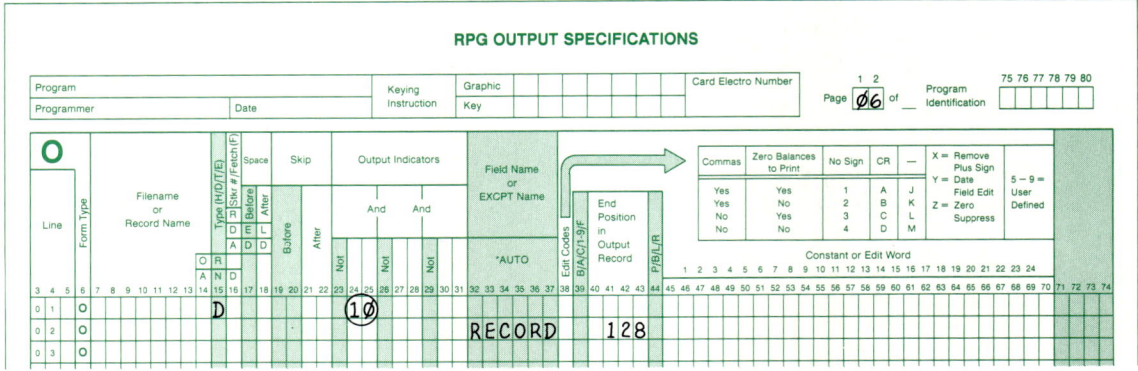

Notes on the Coding

Line	Meaning
01	Copy the record from the original file.

Figure 8.21 Updating coding—example

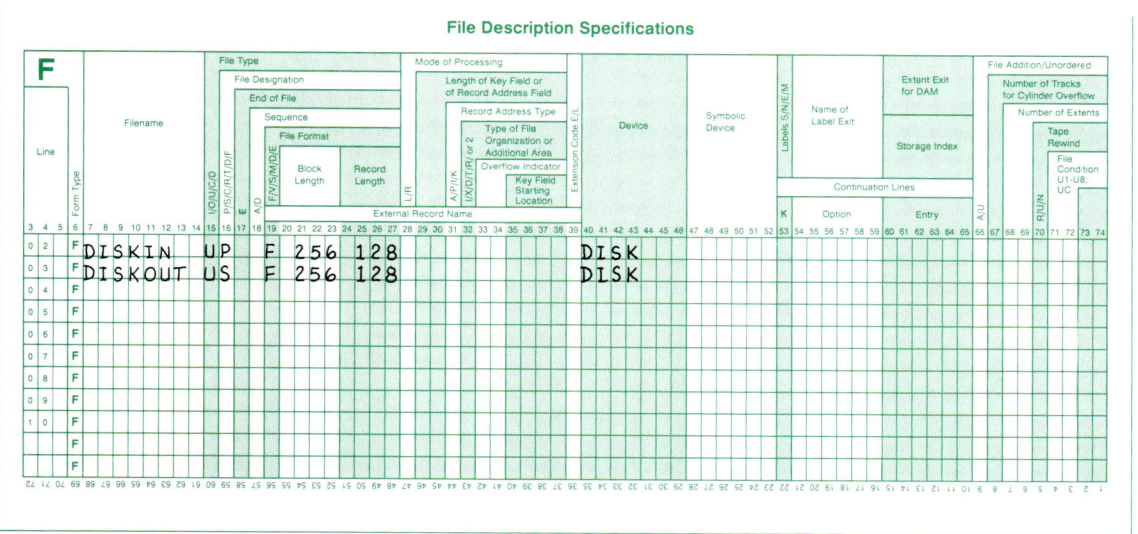

Tagging Records for Deletion

When a record becomes inactive, it may be no longer necessary to process it with other records. Since the record is not physically removed from that file, it must be identified so that it can be bypassed. One way to do this is for the programmer to put a delete code in a particular location in the record. The program can check for this code to determine whether or not to process records that are to be deleted. If the delete code is present, the program can bypass the tagged record until that record can be physically removed at the time the file is reorganized.

Updating Records

Many jobs require changes to certain data in a record. This function is called updating. Some of the entries required for updating disk files are the same as those needed for creating sequential files. Following are the additional entries needed on the file description for updating files:

1. Position 25 must contain a *U* to indicate that the file is an update file.

2. Position 16 can contain either a *P* or an *S*, depending on whether the file is a primary file or a secondary file. (See Figure 8.21.)

Since updating means getting a record from a disk file, changing some data, and putting the record back into its original location, an update file is like a combination input/output file. For this reason, the file to be updated must be specified on both the Input and Output Specifications forms, with each of the field locations defined in the same manner. (See Figure 8.22.) Field names may vary depending on the updating being done, but field lengths must agree. (See Figure 8.23.)

Reorganizing a File

The space reserved for a file often becomes filled as additions to it are made. Reorganizing is a means of freeing space by physically removing inactive records (those with a delete code) from a file. (See Figure 8.24.)

Disk Processing 373

Figure 8.22 Updating sequentially organized files using matching records technique—example

This problem is an example of file maintenance. Values will be updated in a field by either adding values to it or by subtracting values from it. Also, the activity will be done with two sequentially organized disk files. Because the matching records technique is applied, the following coding relationships need to be remembered.

File Description
1. File Designation (16) — one file must be specified as primary (P) and the other file(s) as secondary (S).

2. Sequence (18) — the sequence of the records must be specified as either A for ascending sequence or D for descending sequence.

Input
1. Describe the field or fields that are to be assigned for matching purposes for each file.

2. Matching fields (61–62) — if one field is used to control the matching of records, specify M1 for that field in each file; if two or more fields are used, specify appropriate entries (use M2-M9).

Calculation
1. Indicators (9-17) — calculations to be performed when a match occurs should include the matching records indicator (MR) along with the desired record identifying indicator. Calculations may be desired when a match does not occur. To describe this condition, include the letter N (for Not) in front of MR.

Output
1. Output indicators (23-31) — include the matching records indicator (MR) with the appropriate record identifying indicator. Again, if output is desired when a match does not occur, include the letter N (for Not).

Problem
Update customer records in a sequentially organized disk file by calculating a new account balance for each matched record. Transaction records are in a sequentially organized disk file. Both files are in ascending sequence by account number. To calculate the new balance, add the deposit value and subtract the withdrawal value.

The records in each file contain the following fields of data.

Transaction File

Each record has eighteen characters.

Position	Field
1-1	Code T
2-6	Account number
7-12	Deposit amount, 2 decimals
13-18	Withdrawal amount, 2 decimals

Customer Accounts File

Each record has seventy-five characters.

Position	Field
1-1	Code A
2-6	Account number
53-59	Account balance, 2 decimals

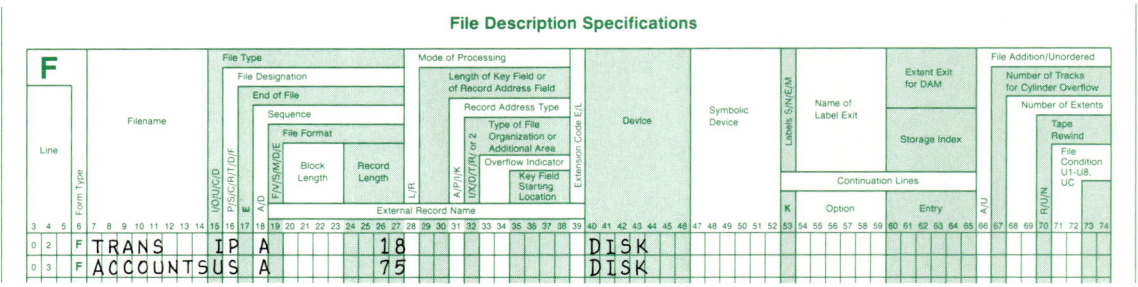

Figure 8.22 continued

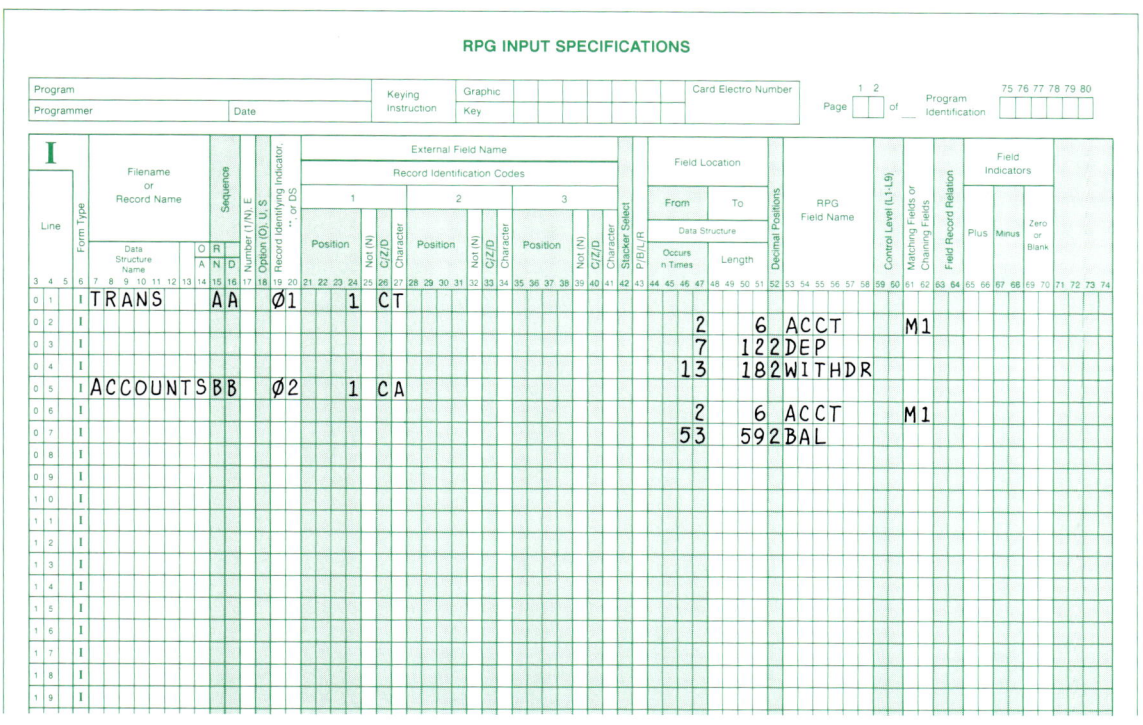

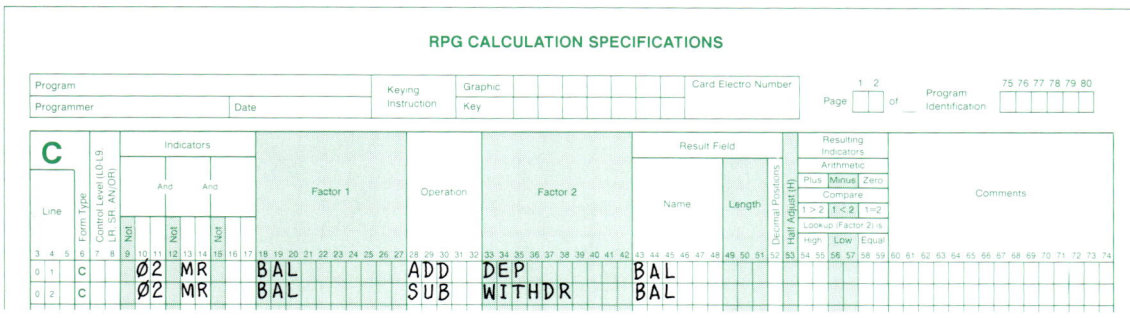

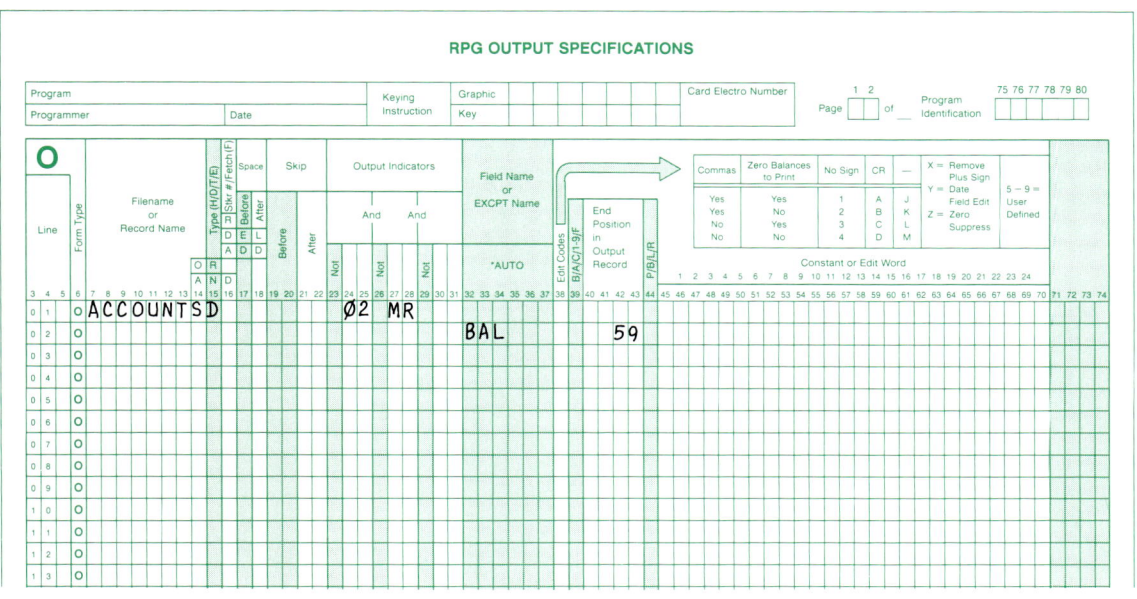

Disk Processing

Figure 8.23 Updating and deleting records in sequential files—example

Problem

Periodically, the programmer might want to update the accounting information for each customer in the customer file. The programmer might also want to tag some customer records for deletion. A printed report, like the one shown below, lists the updated information and the records tagged for deletion.

The TRANS file contains two input record types. One type identifies disk records to be deleted (D in position 1); the other type contains information needed to update the MASTER file (3 in column 1). The following shows the necessary RPG coding to update records and to tag records for deletion.

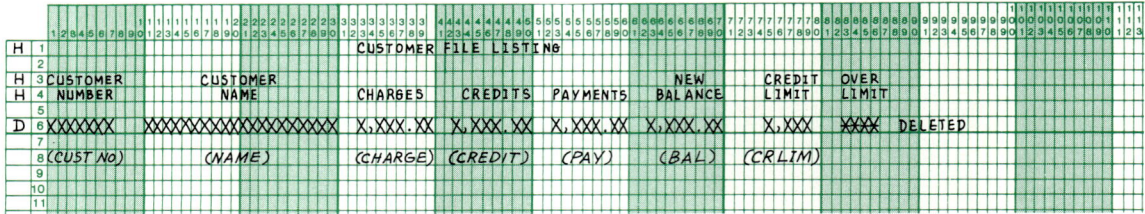

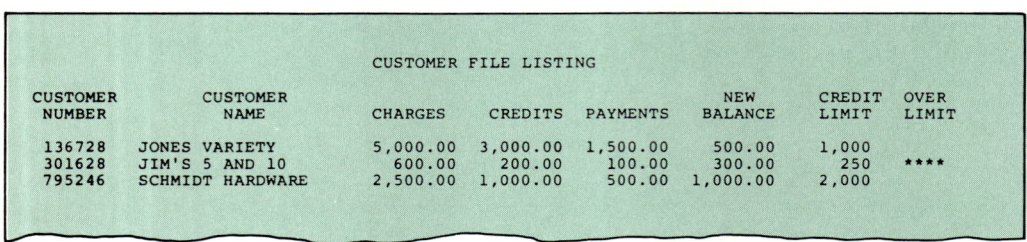

Report of Updated Customer Records and Deleted Customer Records

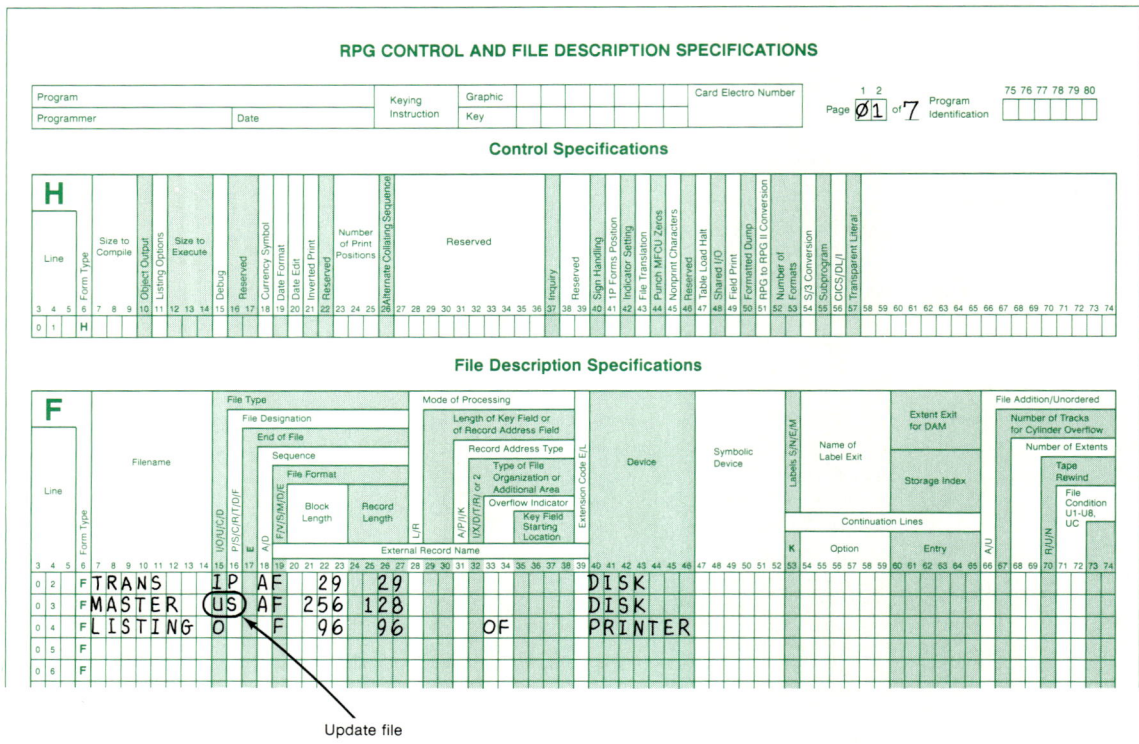

Figure 8.23 continued

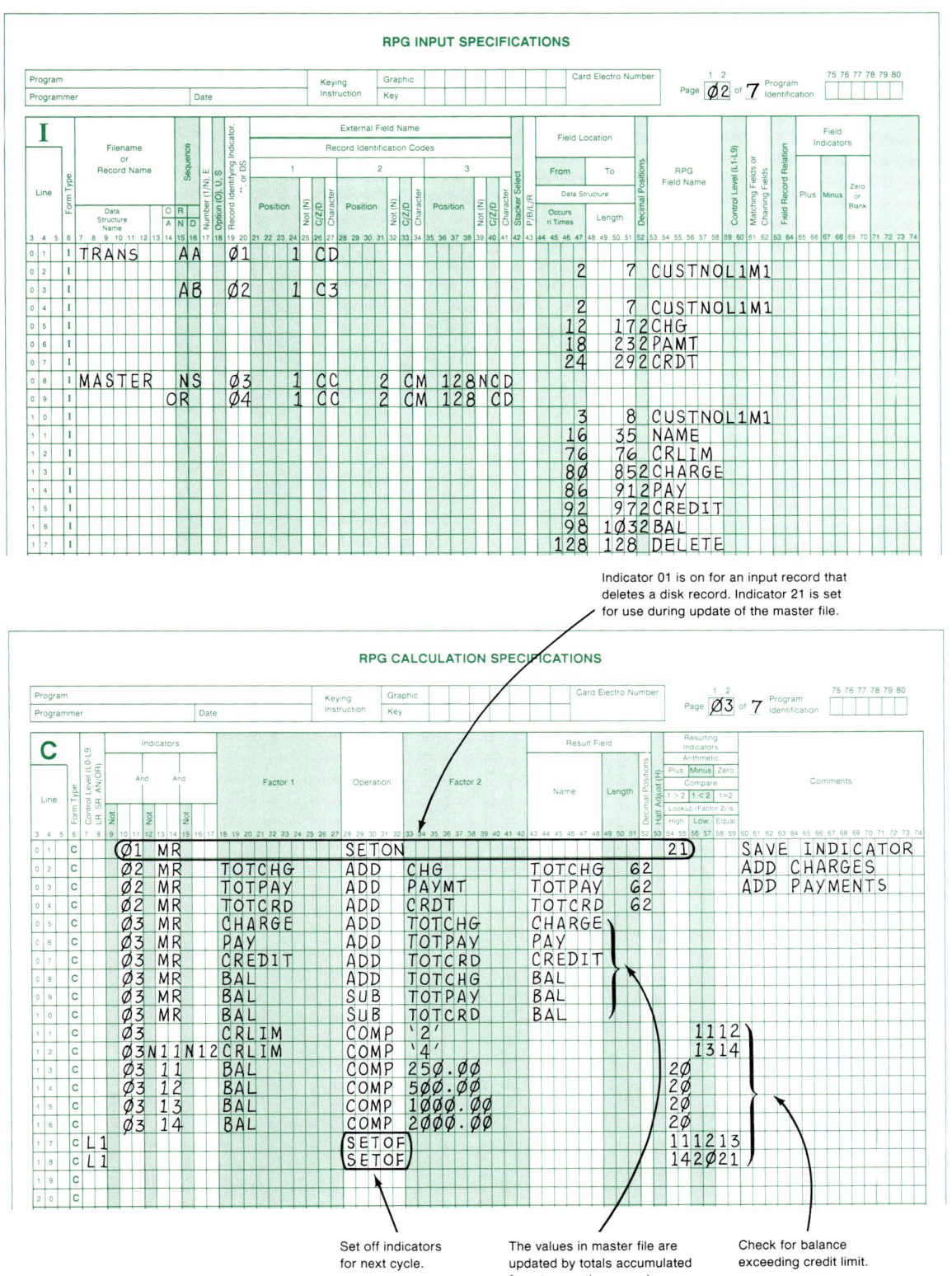

Disk Processing

Figure 8.23 continued

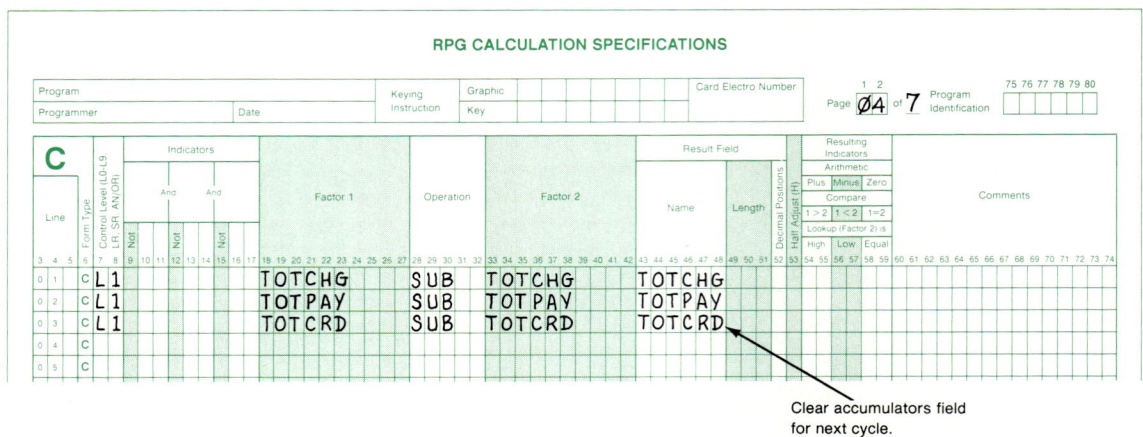

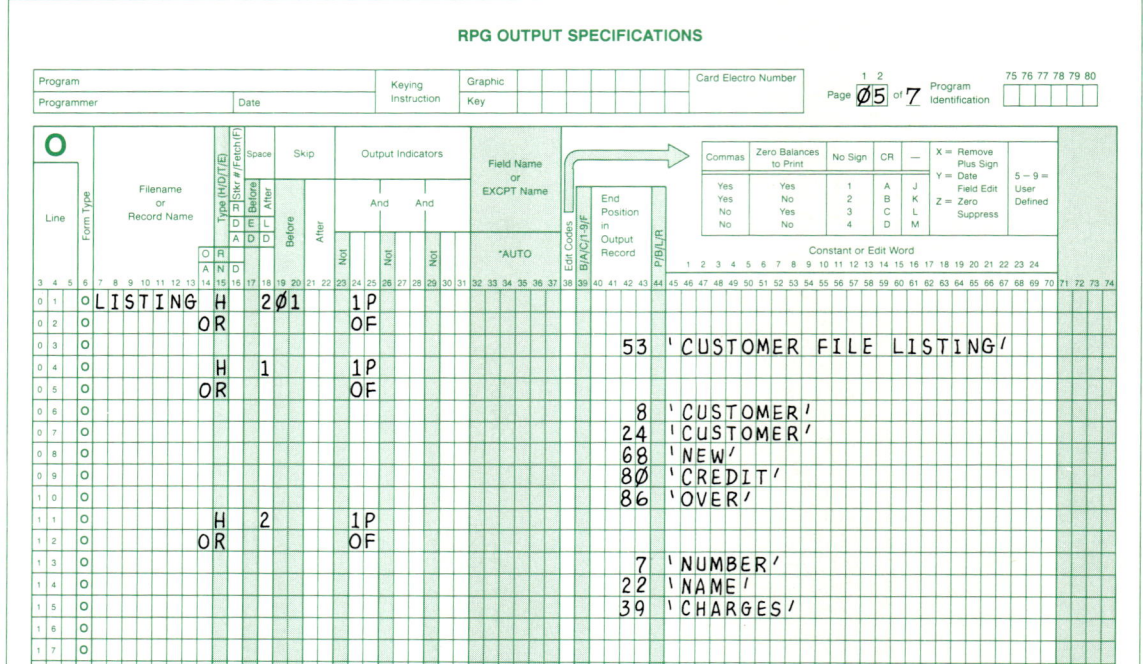

Figure 8.23 continued

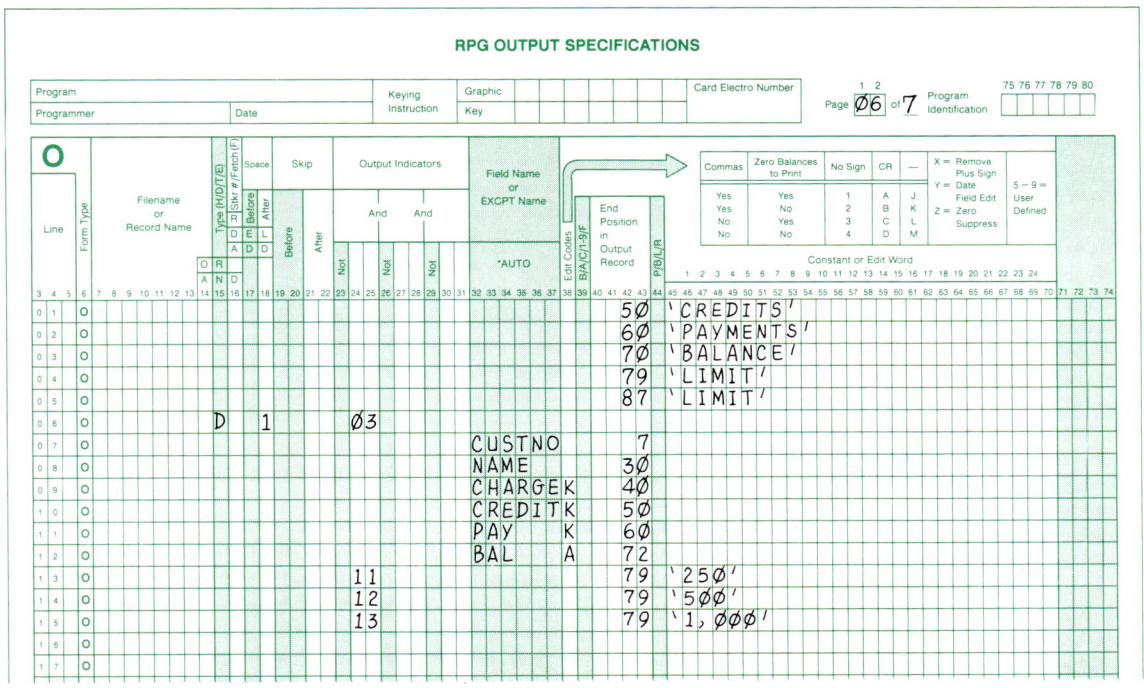

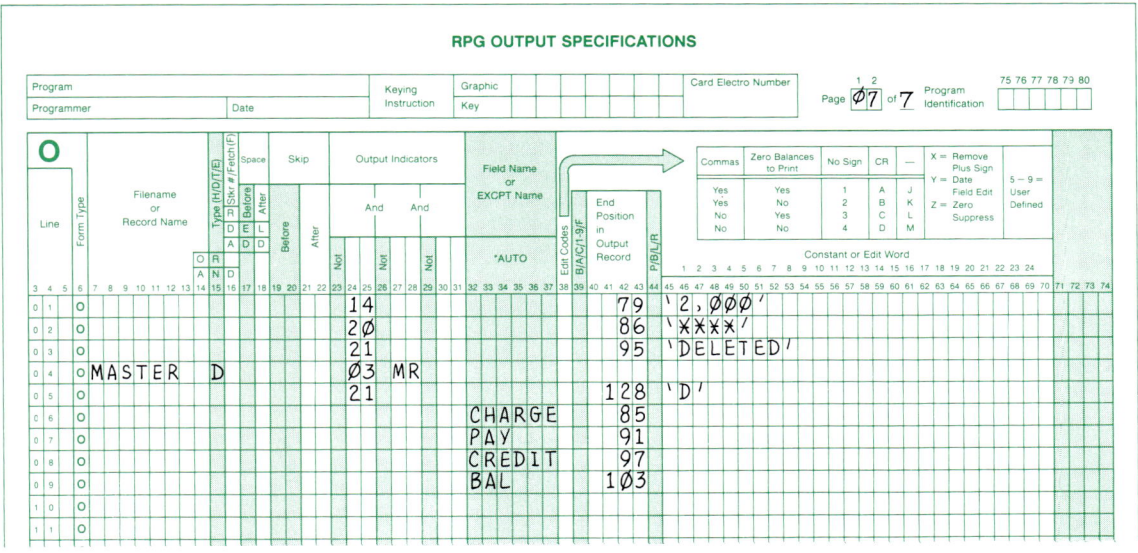

Figure 8.24 Reorganizing a sequential file to remove deleted records—example

Problem

In figure 8.23, records were tagged for deletion by placing a D in position 128. Now, suppose the programmer wants to reorganize the customer file to physically remove these records from the file. The programmer also wants to print a report listing the customer records deleted.

To delete these records, the programmer wants to copy all records that do not have a D in position 128.

The following shows the necessary RPG coding to reorganize the file.

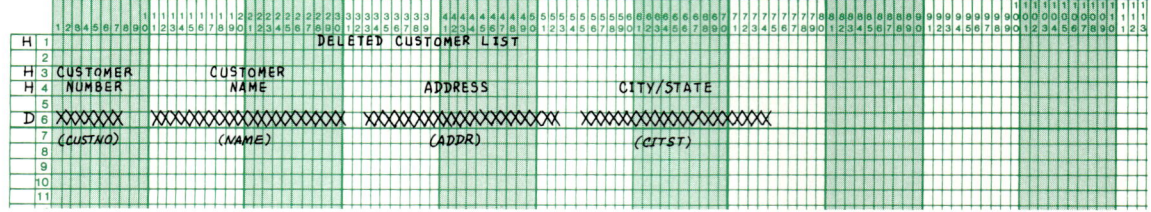

Report of Deleted Customer Records

```
                    DELETED CUSTOMER LIST

    CUSTOMER    CUSTOMER
    NUMBER      NAME              ADDRESS             CITY/STATE

    652791      GREEN GROCERY, INC   1739-6TH ST SW   BIG CITY, CALIF
    576290      STAR MARKET          3278 ADAMS ST    GOODTOWN, GA
```

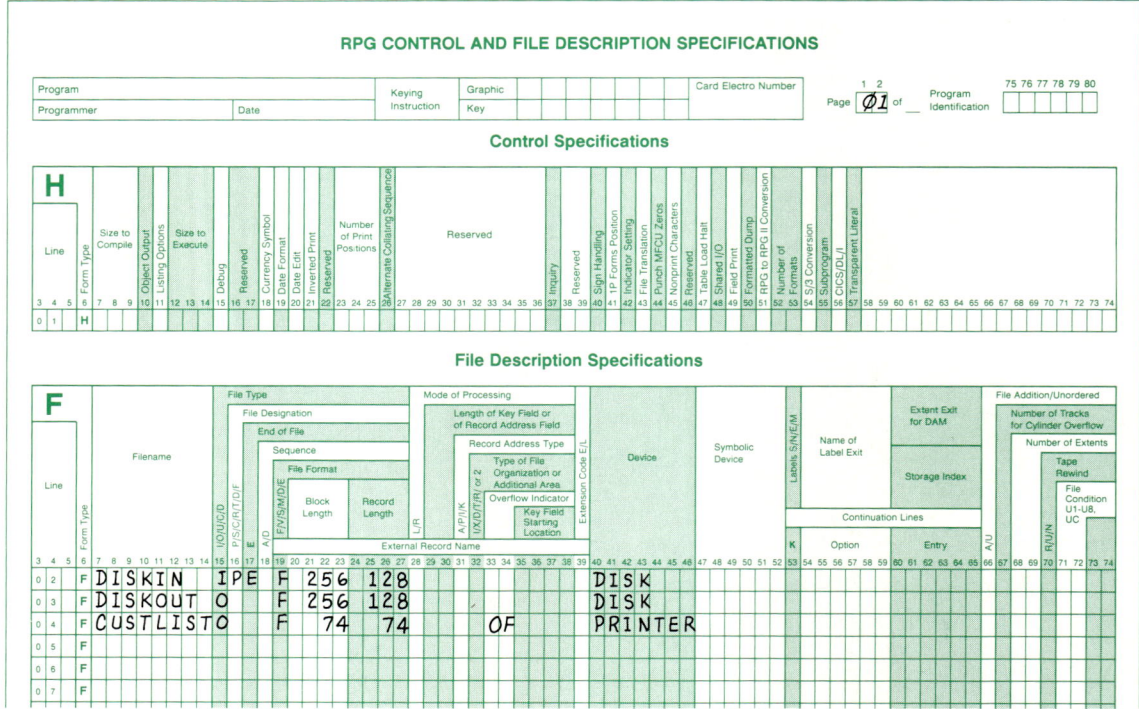

380 RPG II and RPG III Programming

Figure 8.24 continued

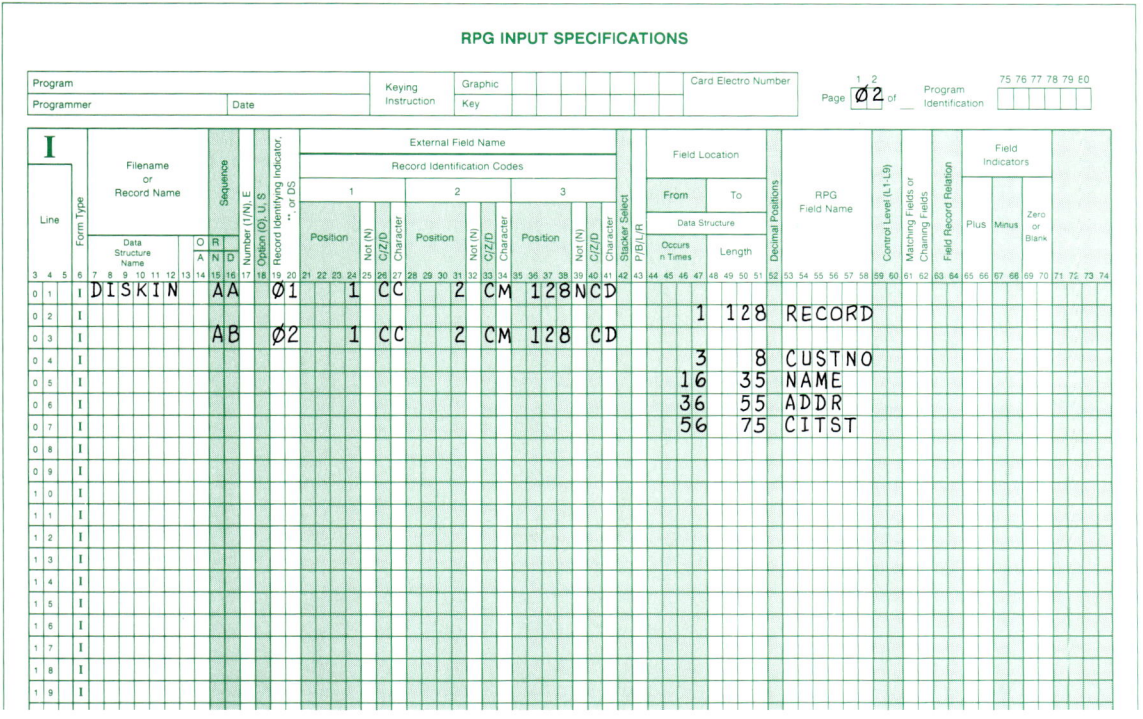

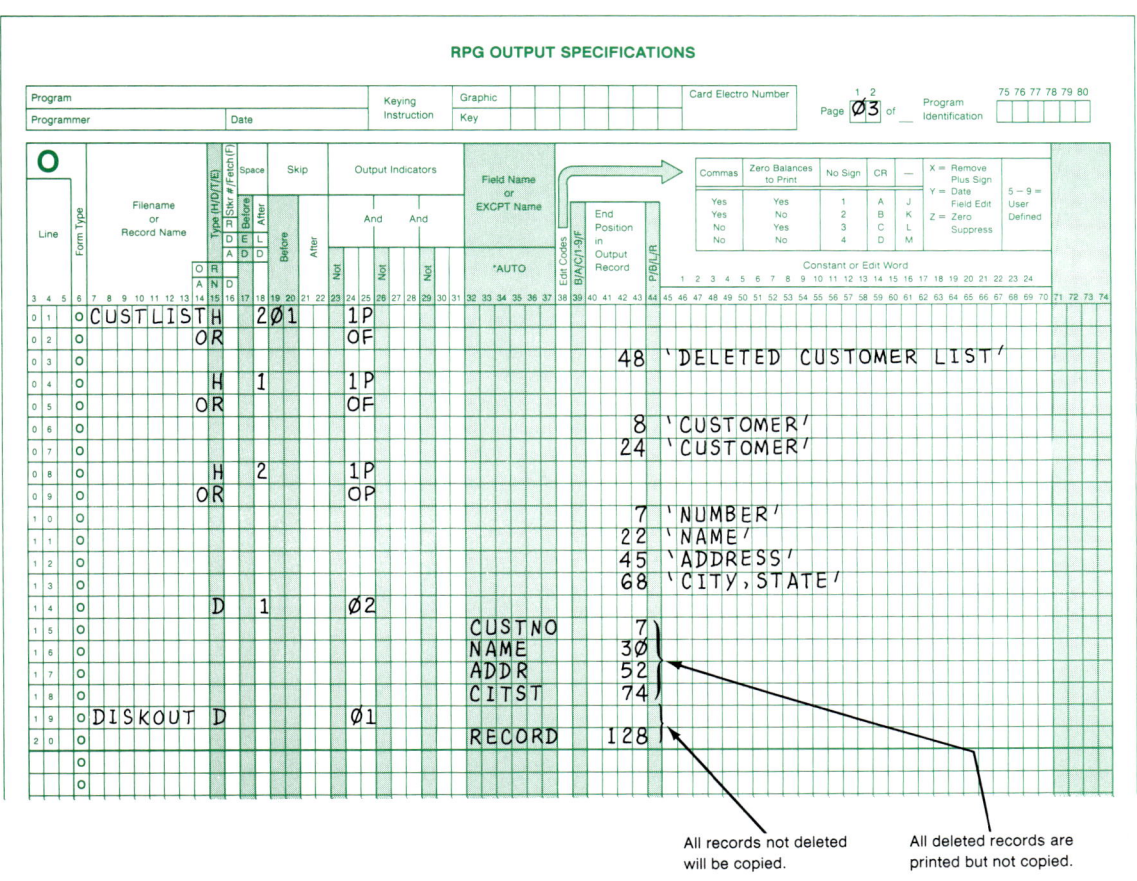

All records not deleted will be copied.

All deleted records are printed but not copied.

Disk Processing

Indexed File Organization

The indexed method of file organization builds the data records in the same way they are built in sequential organization but adds a locator or index at the front of the data record portion of the file. The data records are written in the order they are read—much as they are for sequential files. If the records are not in any specific order, the data portion of the file will not be in order. The index portion is a different matter; whatever the order of the original records when they were read in, that is the order of the index or locator portion of the file. This index is built automatically for the programmer in front of the data portion of the file. It contains a unique field called the key field and gives the location of the data associated with that unique field. It can be compared to an index of a book, which directs the reader to the desired page.

Since the key field can be anywhere within the record, it must be identified for RPG on the File Description form so that the proper index can be built for the programmer language specifications. (See Figures 8.25 and 8.26.)

As in sequential organization, no gaps are left for any new records; these will be added at the end of the data portion. When a record is added, the new key field is incorporated into the index area.

Creating an Indexed File

The programmer can create a single-volume indexed file with records that are in either ordered or unordered sequence. An ordered sequence means that the records are arranged in order according to the major control field that will be used as the key of the file. An unordered sequence means that the records are in no particular order. (Some systems do not permit an unordered sequence.) For example, in an inventory file organized by frequency of use, records are in an unordered sequence with the most active items at the beginning of the file. The index of an unordered file is sorted into ascending sequence after all the records have been loaded.

Creating an Ordered Indexed File

To create an indexed file in an ordered sequence, the following entries must be made on the File Description form:

1. The disk file name must be entered in positions 7–14.

2. Position 15 must contain an *O* to indicate that the file is an output file.

3. Because all records in a file must be the same length, position 19 must contain an *F* to specify that the record length is fixed.

4. A number equal to or a multiple of the logical record length must be entered in positions 20–23 to determine the size of the input/output area. (Refer to section on creating a sequential file, step 4.)

5. Positions 24–27 must contain the length of the logical record.

6. Whenever a disk file is being described, a device name is required in positions 40–46.

7. The key length entered in positions 29–30 must be the same for all records in a file.

8. Entries in positions 31–32 indicate that an indexed file is to be created. An *A* in position 31 specifies that a key field exists; an *I* in position 32 specifies an indexed file.

9. The location of the first character of the key is specified in positions 35–38. Thus, if a six-character key field is located in positions 73–78 of a disk record, the programmer will enter *73* in positions 37–38 of the File Description form and a *6* in position 30. (See Figure 8.27.)

Creating an Unordered Indexed File

To create an indexed file in an unordered sequence, one entry is needed on the File Description form in addition to the entries needed to create an ordered indexed file. This entry is a *U* in position 66, indicating that the records are to be loaded in an unordered sequence. (See Figures 8.28 and 8.29.)

Figure 8.25 Indexed organization creation—example

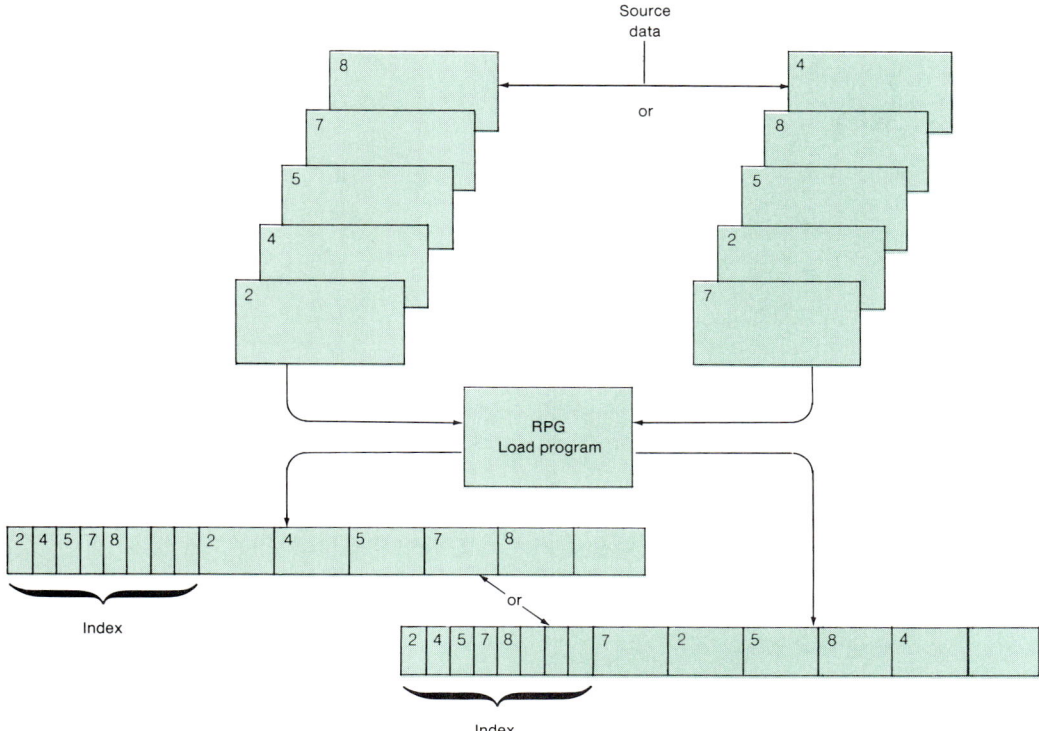

Figure 8.26 File description specifications—indexed file—example

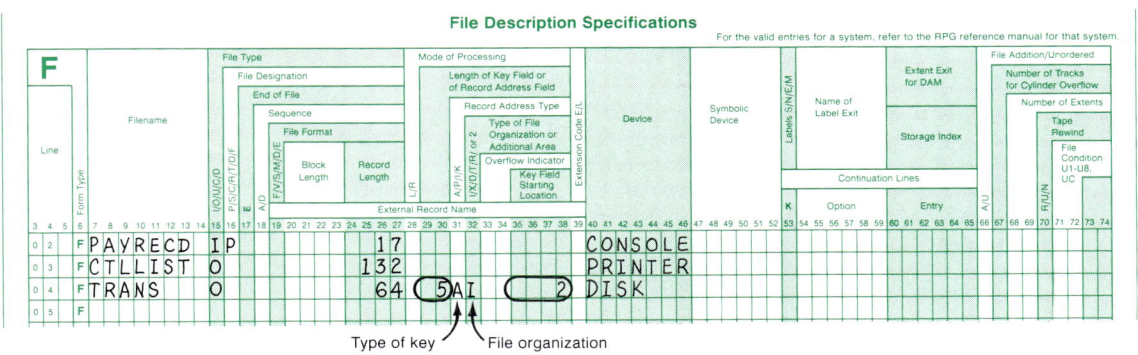

Notes on the Coding

Since the indexed file uses the "key" field both in creating the file and in its processing, the File Description entries must identify its length and location in the record. If you were to create the file TRANS as an indexed file, the coding would be as above:

Position 32 has an I for indexed file.

Positions 29 and 30 will be coded with the length of the key field. This may be determined from the record layout.

In addition, positions 35 to 38 will tell RPG the starting location of the key field.

Position 31 is coded with a A, which stands for alphameric keys—your key field must be comprised of numbers and/or letters.

Disk Processing 383

Figure 8.27 File description entries for an indexed file in an ordered sequence—example

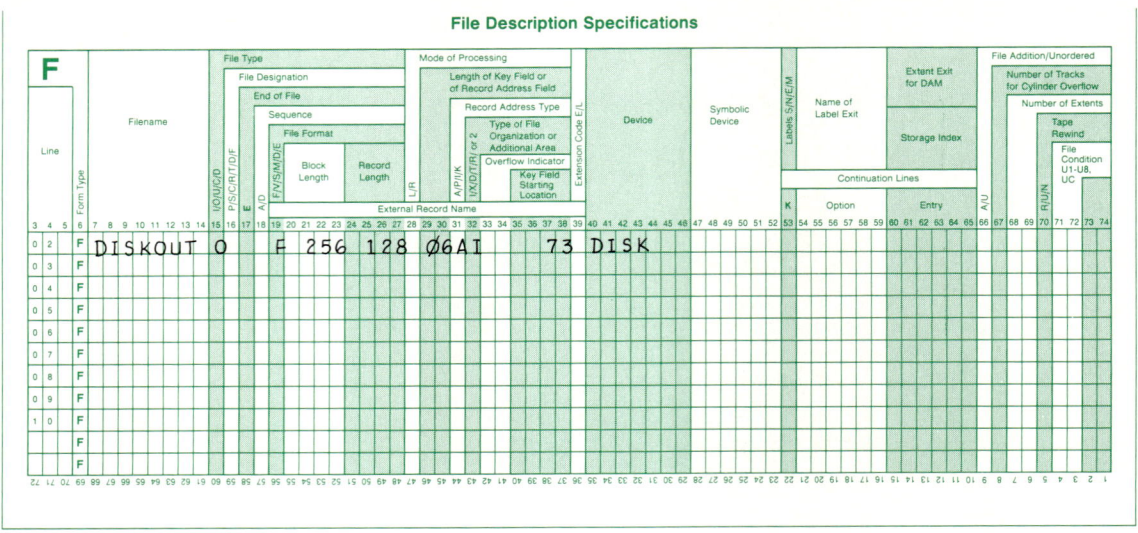

Figure 8.28 Additional entry for file description form for an indexed file in an unordered sequence—example

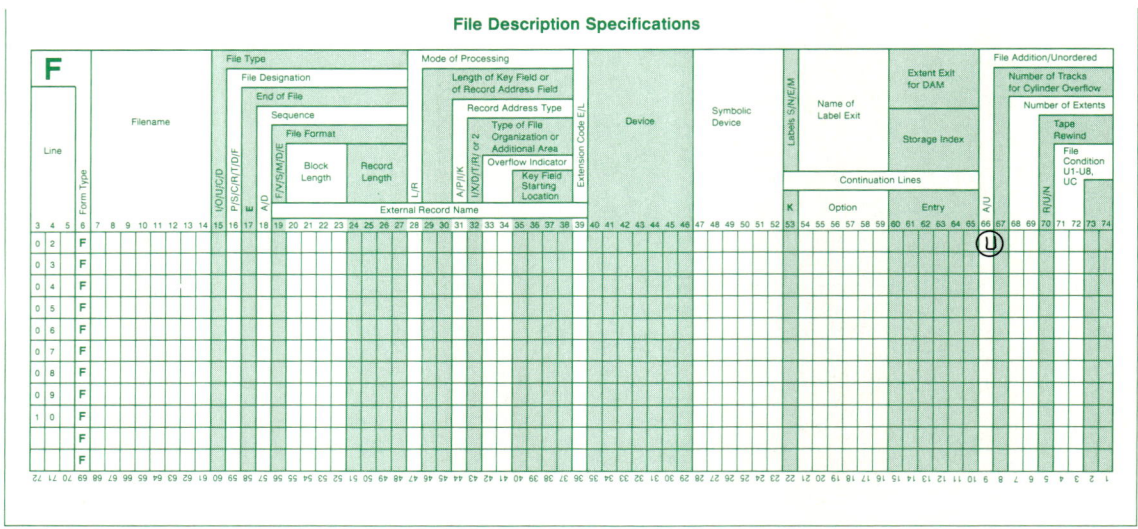

Figure 8.29 Creating an indexed file—example

Problem

Suppose the programmer wants to create an inventory file on disk and wants to process the records in various ways (sequentially, randomly, within limits). An indexed file provides this processing flexibility. Whether the programmer loads the records in ordered or unordered sequence depends on which sequence gives the most processing efficiency.

To create an indexed file, the programmer must first determine the input record format and the output record format. The file is created by writing the inventory item data from the input records onto disk. Notice that the output record format provides space so that additional information can be added to the records later if necessary.

The following shows the RPG coding necessary to create the indexed inventory file. The program will count the number of records and print the total after the file has been created.

Input Record and Output Record Formats

Input record
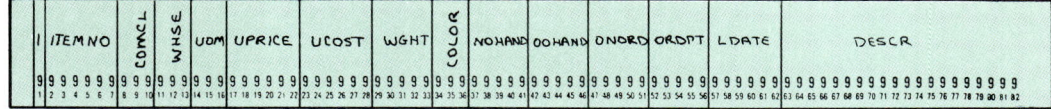

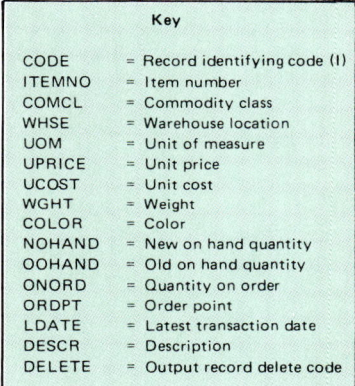

Output record
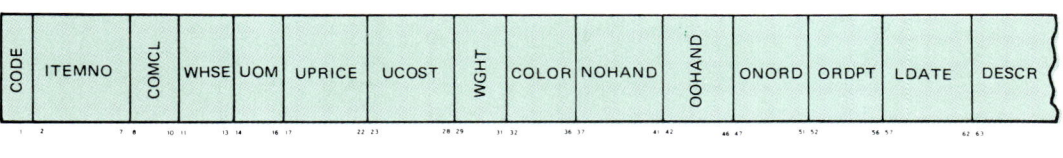

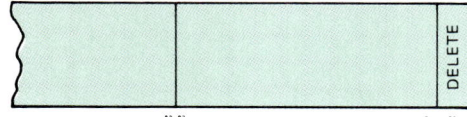

Disk Processing

Figure 8.29 continued

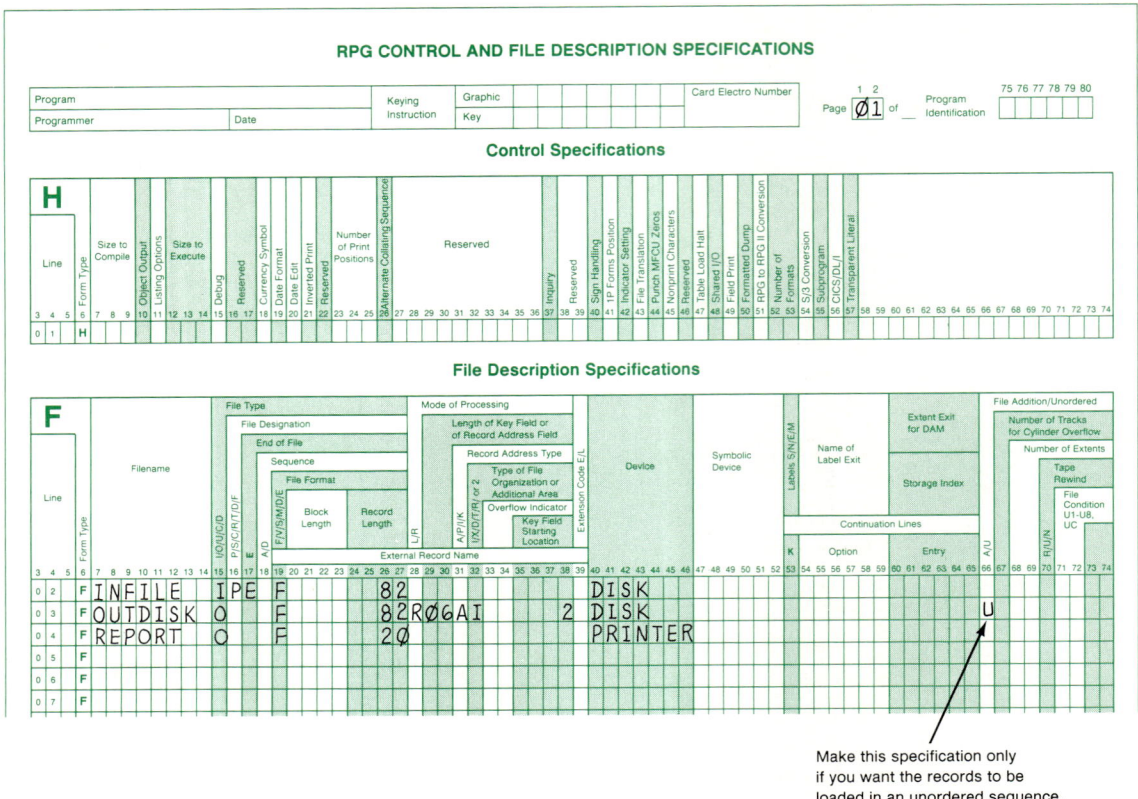

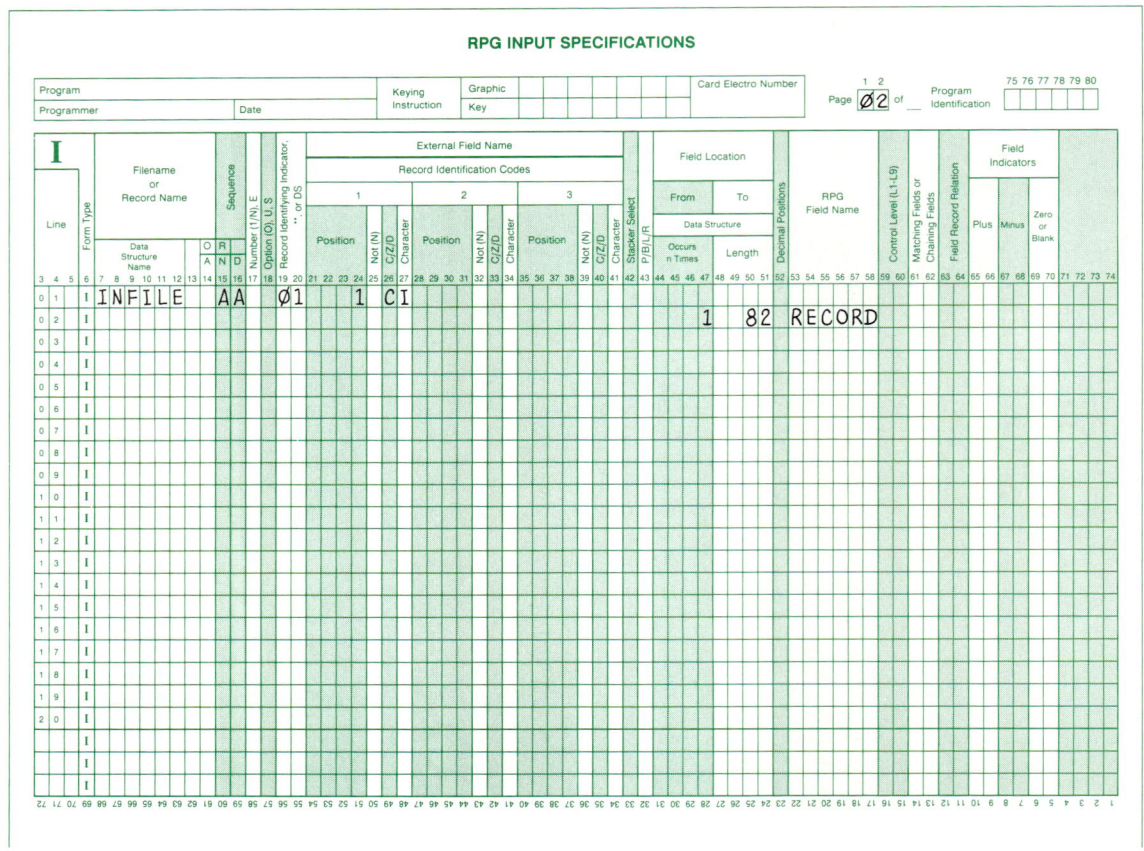

386 RPG II and RPG III Programming

Figure 8.29 continued

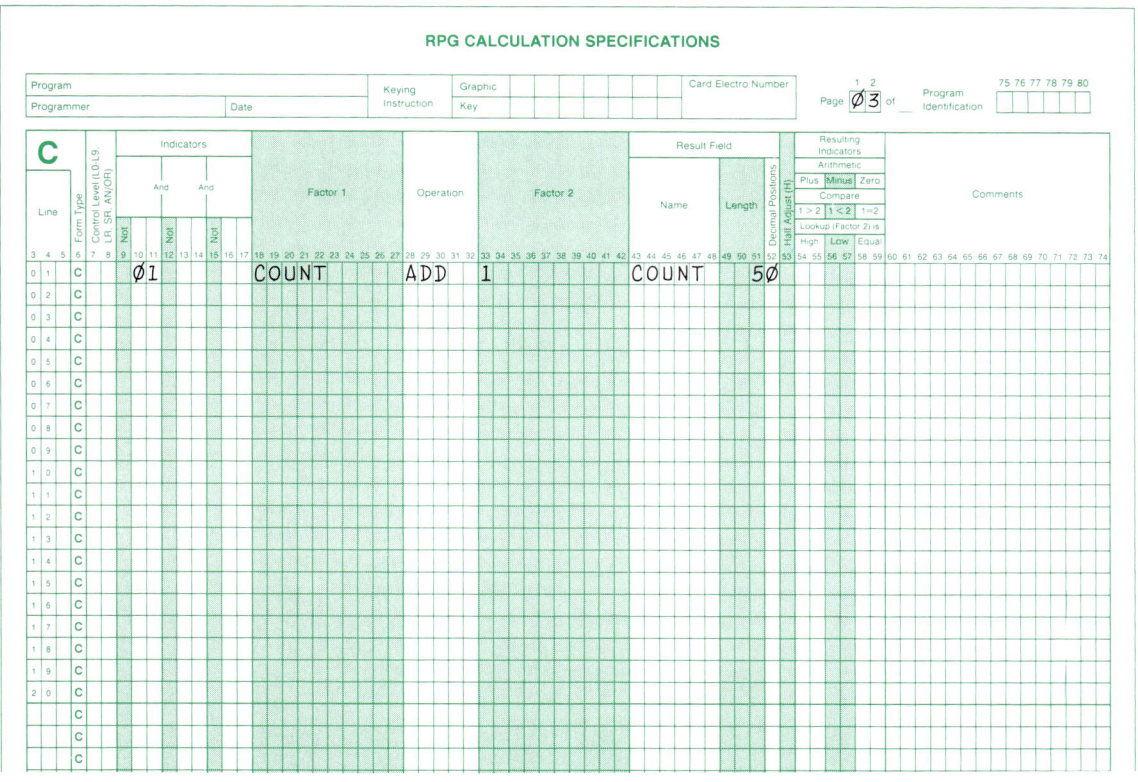

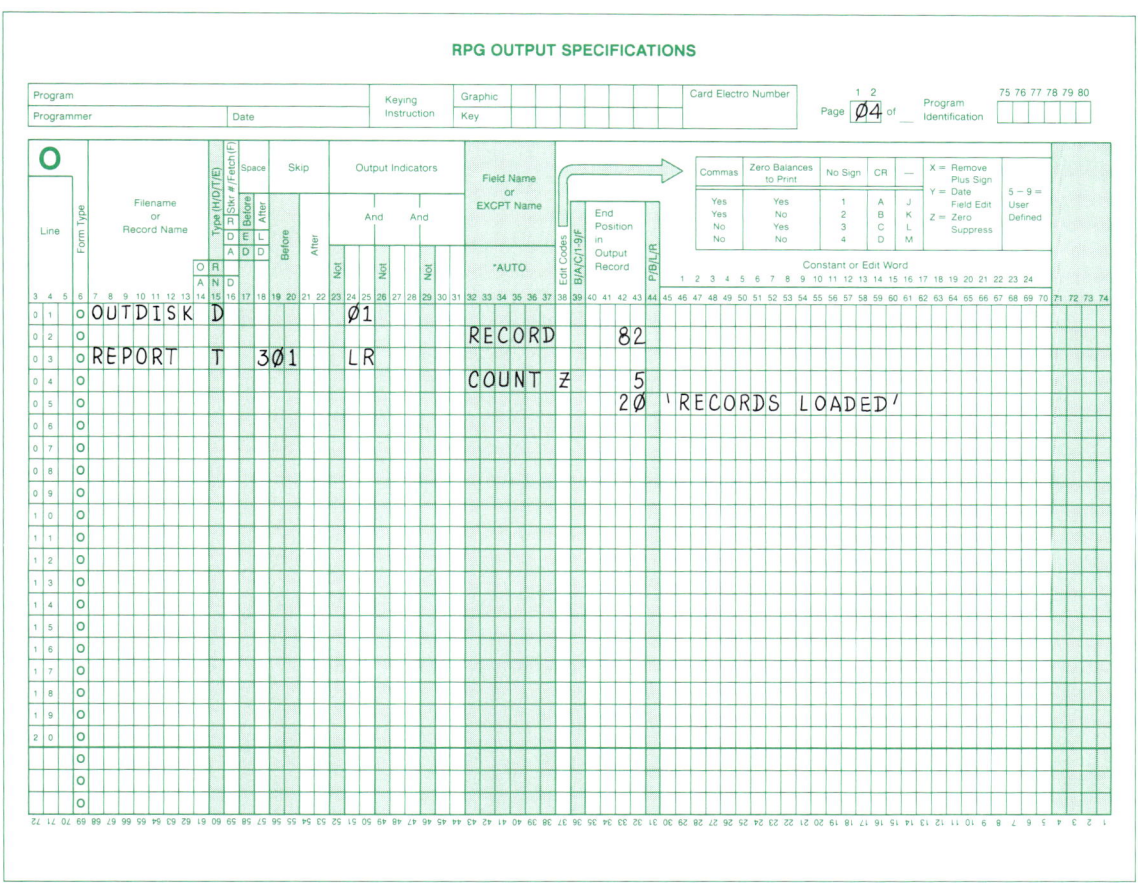

Maintaining an Indexed File

Once a file has been created, it usually needs to be maintained. File maintenance is performing those functions necessary to keep a file current for daily processing needs. Four file maintenance functions apply to indexed files:

1. Adding records
2. Updating records
3. Tagging records for deletion
4. Reorganizing a file

Updating Records

Many jobs require the programmer to change certain data in a record. This function is called updating. A file can be updated in one of three ways.

1. Sequentially by key
2. Randomly by key
3. Sequentially within limits

Updating requirements are the same as those for sequential file updating.

Updating Records Sequentially by Key

Records are usually updated sequentially by key when the programmer wants to update a large part of the file. Some of the File Description form entries needed to update records sequentially by key are the same entries needed to create an indexed file. Following are the additional entries required:

1. Position 15 must contain a *U* to indicate that the file is an update file.
2. Position 16 can contain either a *P* or an *S*, depending on whether the file is a primary or a secondary file. (See Figure 8.30.)

Updating Records Randomly by Key

When an indexed file is updated randomly by key, input records are chained to the indexed file. **Chaining** means comparing the record key with the key in the index. If the keys are equal, the corresponding data record is made available. The data used as a record key in the chain operation can be a field in an input record or it can be created in the program.

CHAIN Operation

The CHAIN operation allows the programmer flexibility in determining when a record is to be retrieved. For all other methods of accessing, records are read at fixed points in the processing cycle. Consider the value of added flexibility, using the example of customer order processing. The dollar amount of the order is calculated and added to the outstanding credit balance in the customer's accounts receivable record. The new balance is checked against a credit limit also contained in the customer record. If the new balance exceeds the limit, a credit exception file must be checked for an entry that may allow override of the limit for this customer.

Records are read from the indexed file during the calculation phase of the program. Fields of records read from chained update files can either be read during total calculation and updated during total output, or read during detail calculations from chained update files and updated during total output.

When records are updated randomly by key, entries must be made on the File Description and Calculation Specifications forms. This procedure requires one additional entry to those needed on the File Description form for updating sequentially by key. The new entry is an *R* in position 28, indicating that the file is to be processed randomly by key. (See Figure 8.31.)

Figure 8.30   Updating sequentially by key—additional file description entries—example

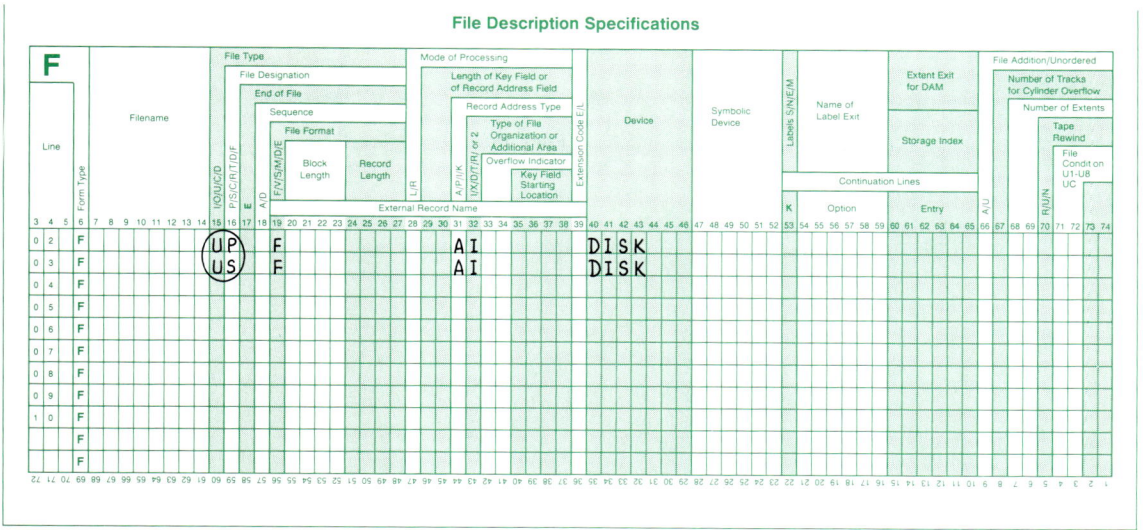

Figure 8.31   Updating randomly by key—additional file description entries—example

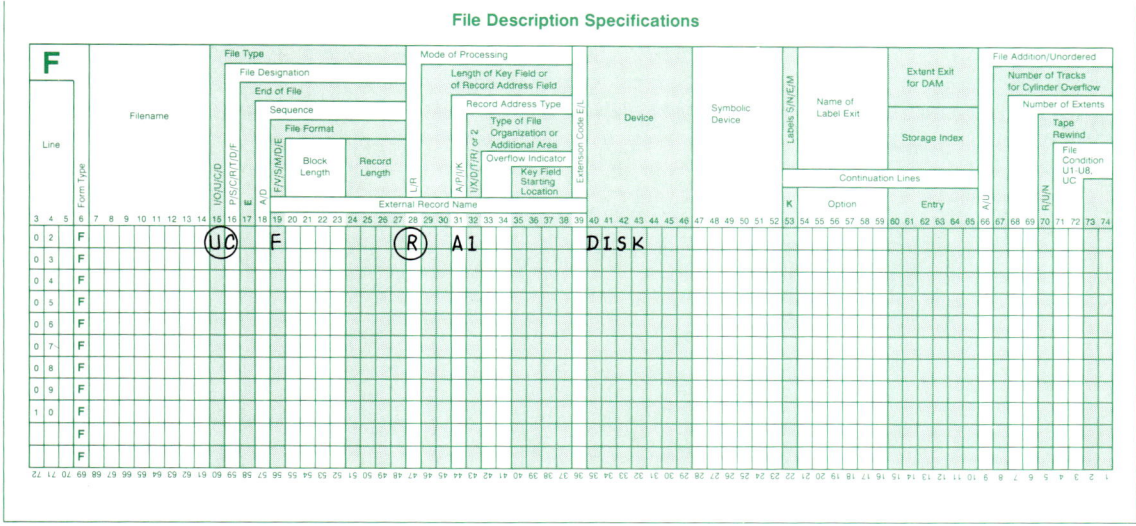

One of the previous entries also must be changed. The changed entry is a *C* in position 16, which identifies the file as a chained file.

The following entries are needed on the Calculation Specifications form to describe the chain operation:

1. Factor 1 must contain the name of the field to be used during the search for a match in the index. CHAIN must be entered as the operation, and factor 2 must contain the name of the update file.

2. A resulting indicator should be specified in positions 54–55 to indicate whether the record to be updated is in the index. If the indicator is omitted, an error will occur during compilation. When a match is found in the index, the disk address of the corresponding record is available. The desired record can then be located and read into storage. At that time the record can be updated. The program can look to see if the required record is in the file by checking the specified resulting indicator. When the indicator is off, the record is found and it can be updated; when the indicator is on, the record is not found. (See Figures 8.32 and 8.33.)

Disk Processing   389

Figure 8.32 Use of chaining technique to update indexed records and flag records for deletion— example

Input Records

Use the chaining technique to inquire about selected records in an indexed file. Print the desired information when found.

File	Record Type	Position	Field
Changes	Address Change	1-1	Code A
		2-7	Subscriber number
		8-47	New address
	Deletion	1-1	Code D
		2-7	Subscriber number
Master		1-1	Code M or D
		2-7	Subscriber number (key field)
		8-47	Address
		48-53	Expiration date

Update

Key points about updating records and flagging for deletion are as follows:

1. The record to be updated must be found in the file.
2. The file to be updated acts as both an input and output file.
3. The file is described on a File Description, Input and Output Specification forms.
4. Only the field or fields to be updated are described, not the entire record.
5. If a field is to be replace by substituting a new field value or constant, the field does not need to be described on the Input form.

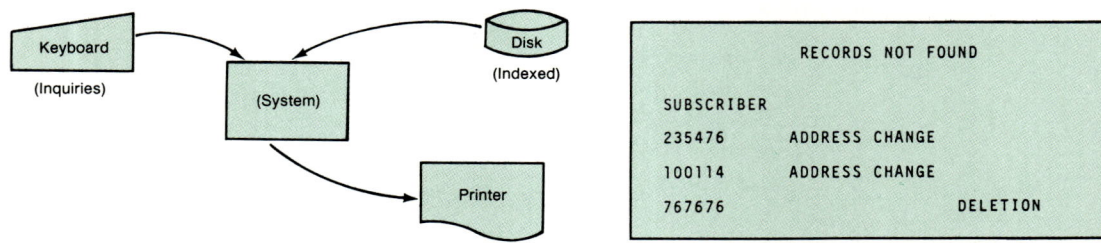

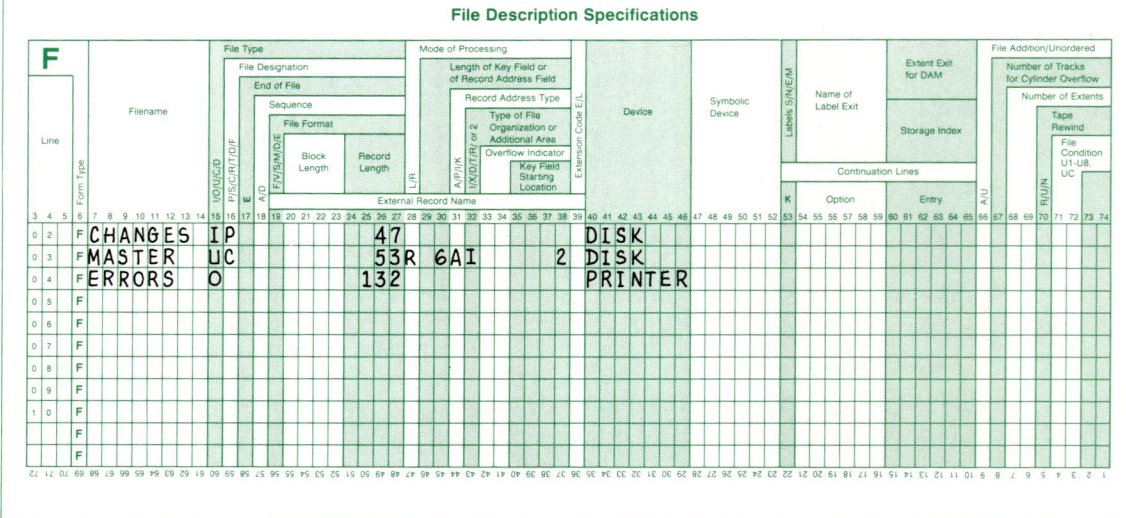

390   RPG II and RPG III Programming

Figure 8.32 continued

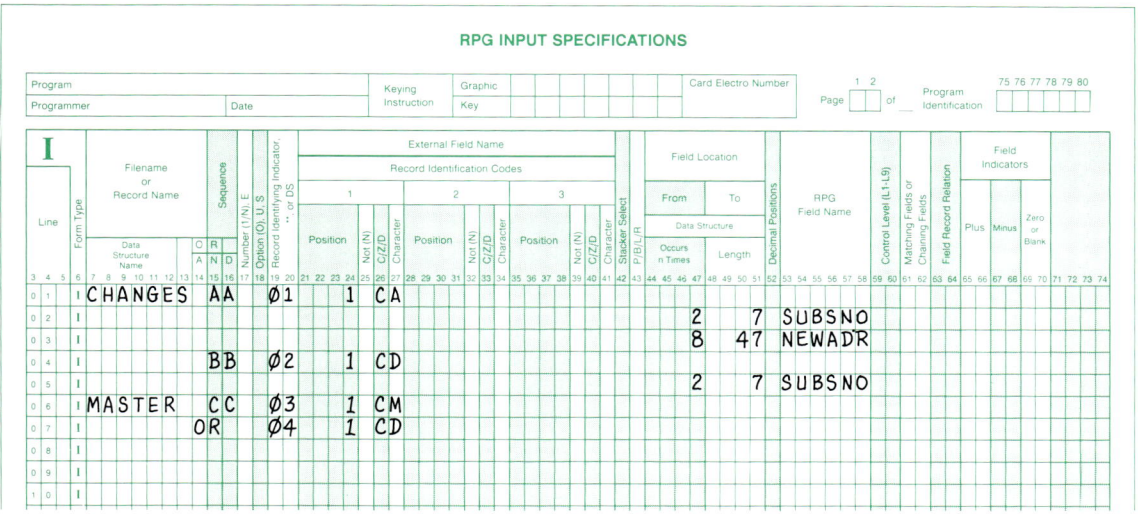

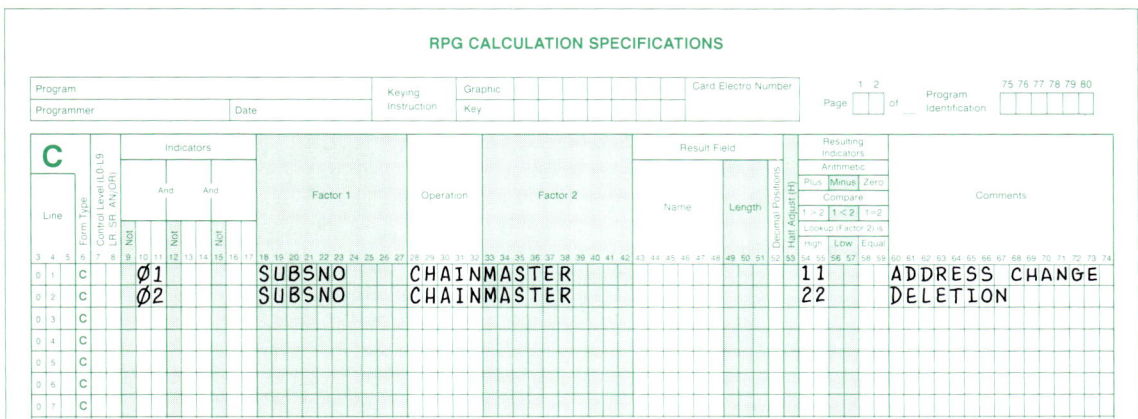

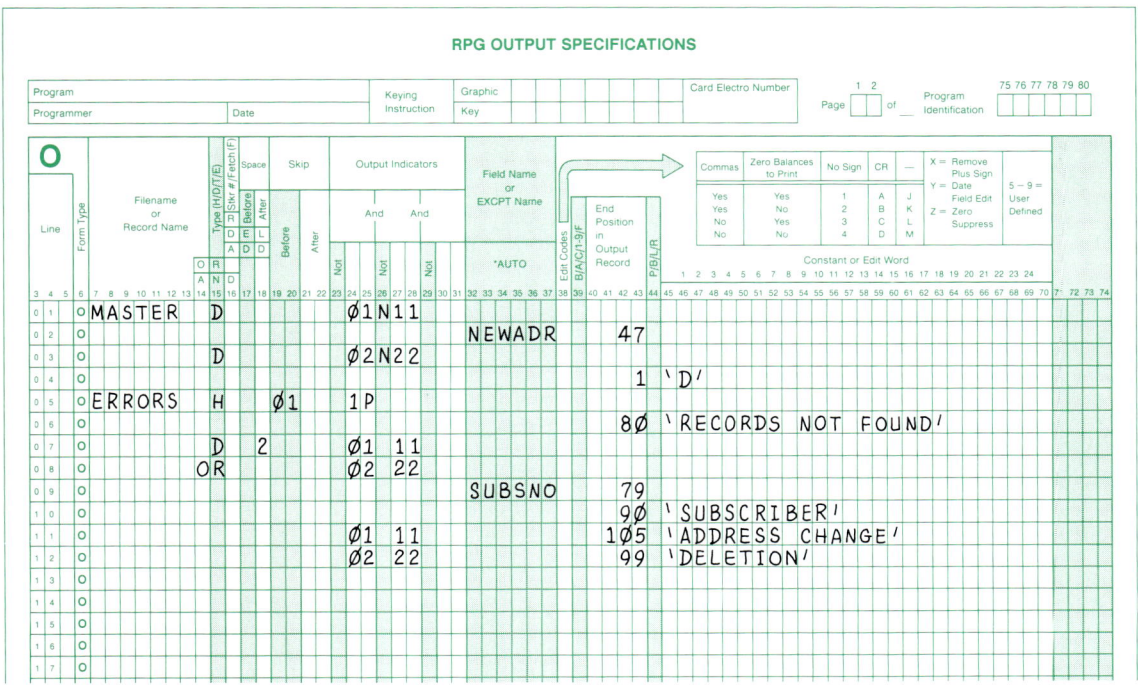

Disk Processing

Figure 8.33 Updating records randomly by key—example

Problem

Suppose that whenever a transaction is made the programmer wants to update the item record in the inventory file. Since the transaction records are not in sequence, the programmer will process the file randomly by key. The programmer might also want to tag some records for deletion while the file is being processed.

The following is the necessary coding to accomplish this.

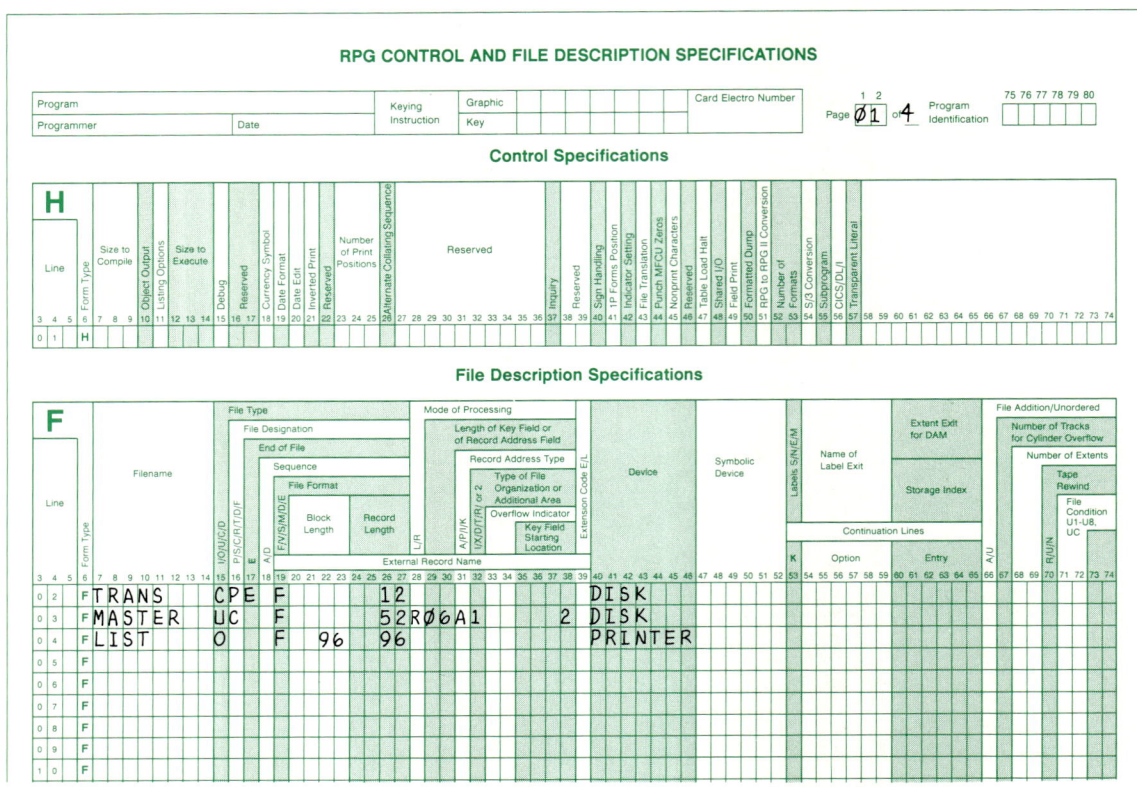

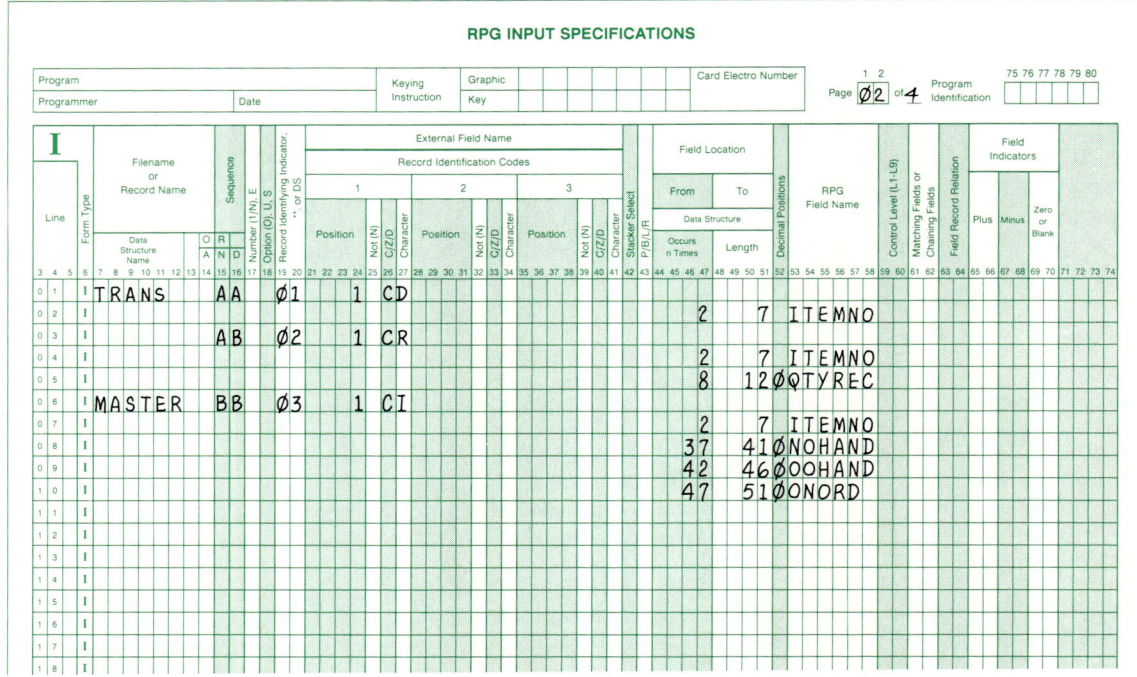

Figure 8.33 continued

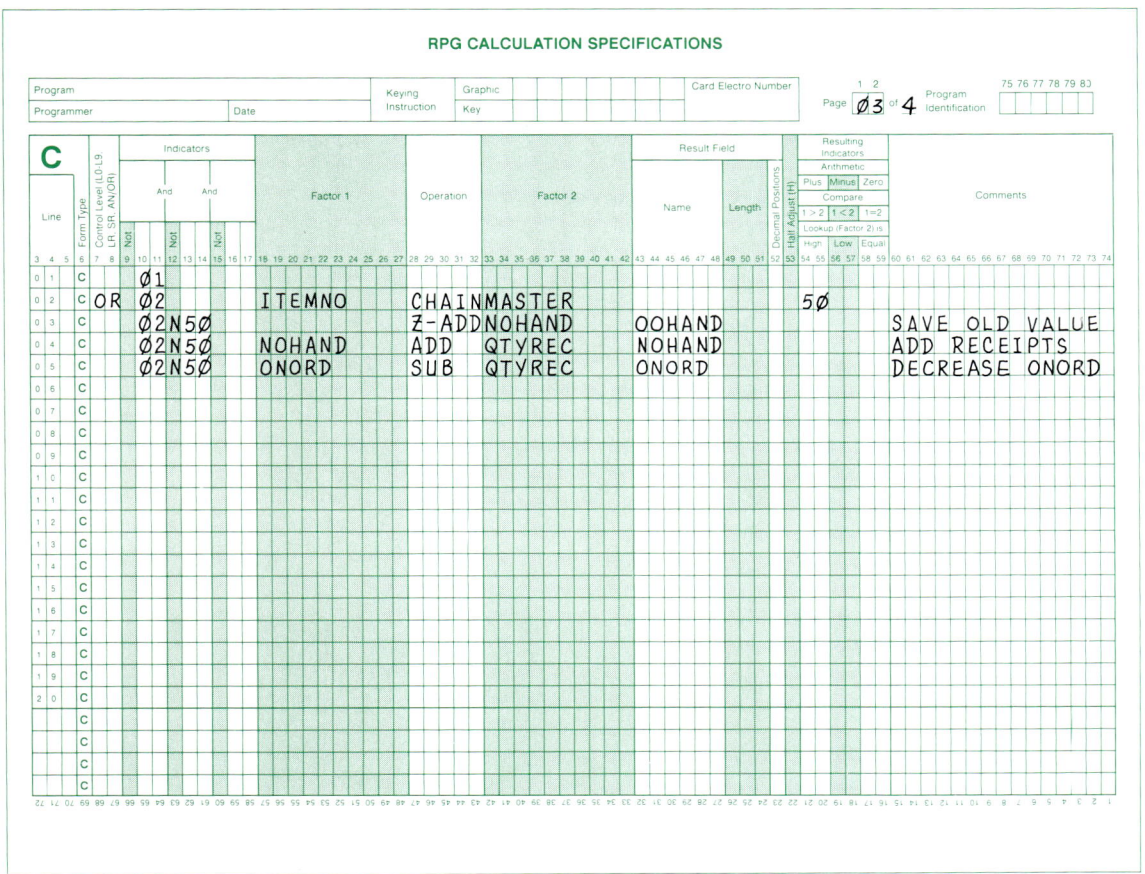

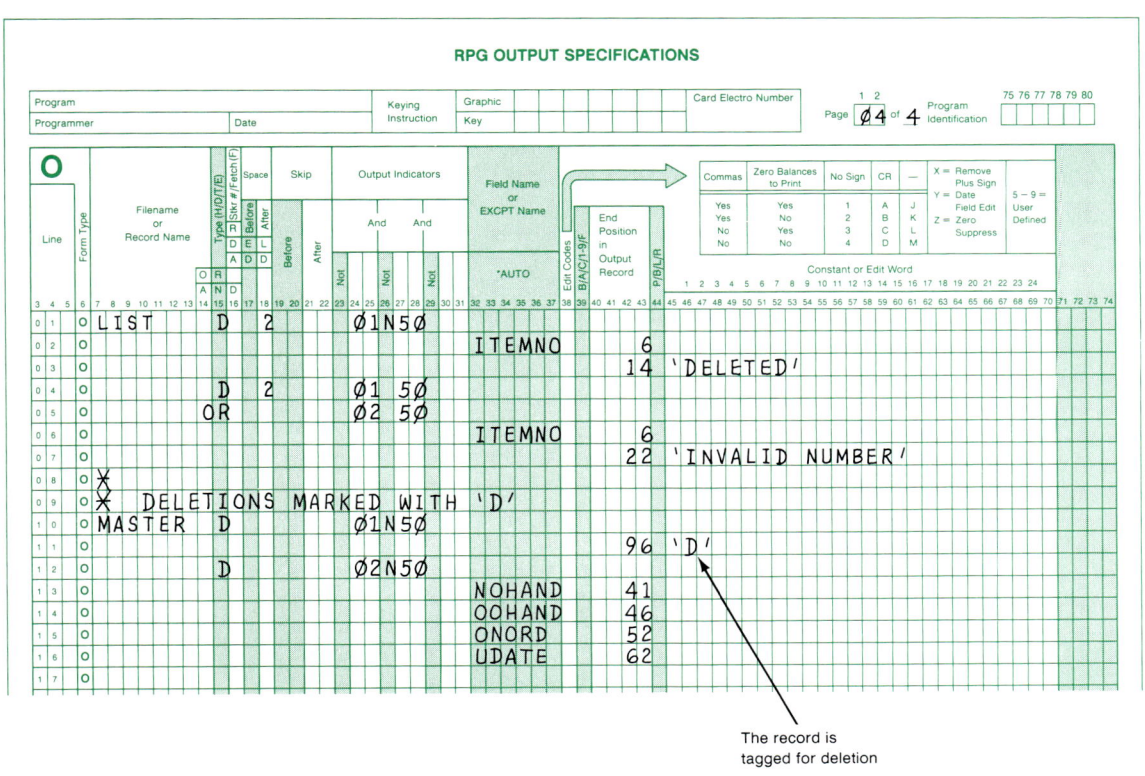

Adding Records

It is often necessary to add records to a file after it has been created. If it is an indexed file, records can be added that contain keys which are either above the highest key presently in the file, below the lowest key presently in the file, or between keys presently in the file. In any case, the added records are placed at the end of the records presently in the file. The index entry for each added record is written in the index area at the end of the current entries. (See Figure 8.34.) After all records are added, the system automatically sorts the index.

Records can be added to a file in one of two ways:

1. Randomly by key
2. Sequentially by key

Figure 8.34 Adding records to an existing indexed file—example

The existing records are sixty characters long with a key field in positions 2-8. The code character "$" is in position 1 of each disk record. The keyed-in records are to contain:

Position	Input Field
1-1	Code "$"
2-8	Identification (key field)
9-21	Transaction data
22-26	Start value
27-31	Last value

Disk record data is to be arranged like this:

Position	Output field
1-1	Code "$"
2-8	Identification (key field)
28-32	Start value
33-37	Last value
48-60	Transaction data

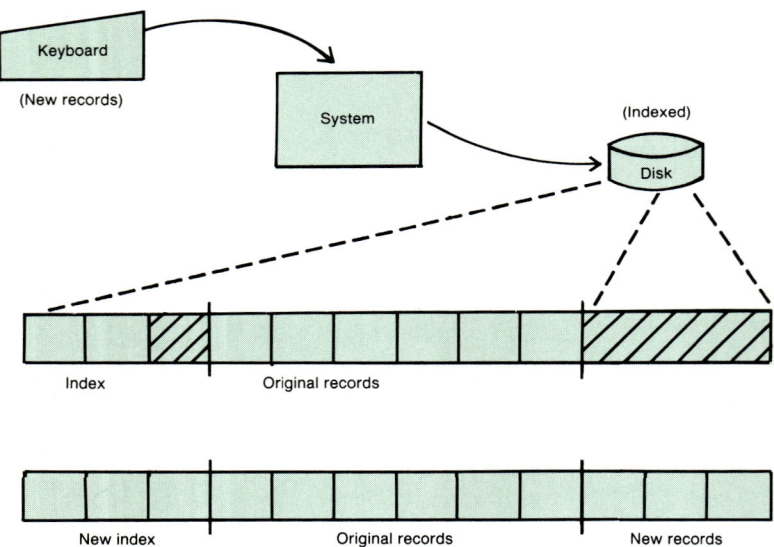

394 RPG II and RPG III Programming

Figure 8.34 continued

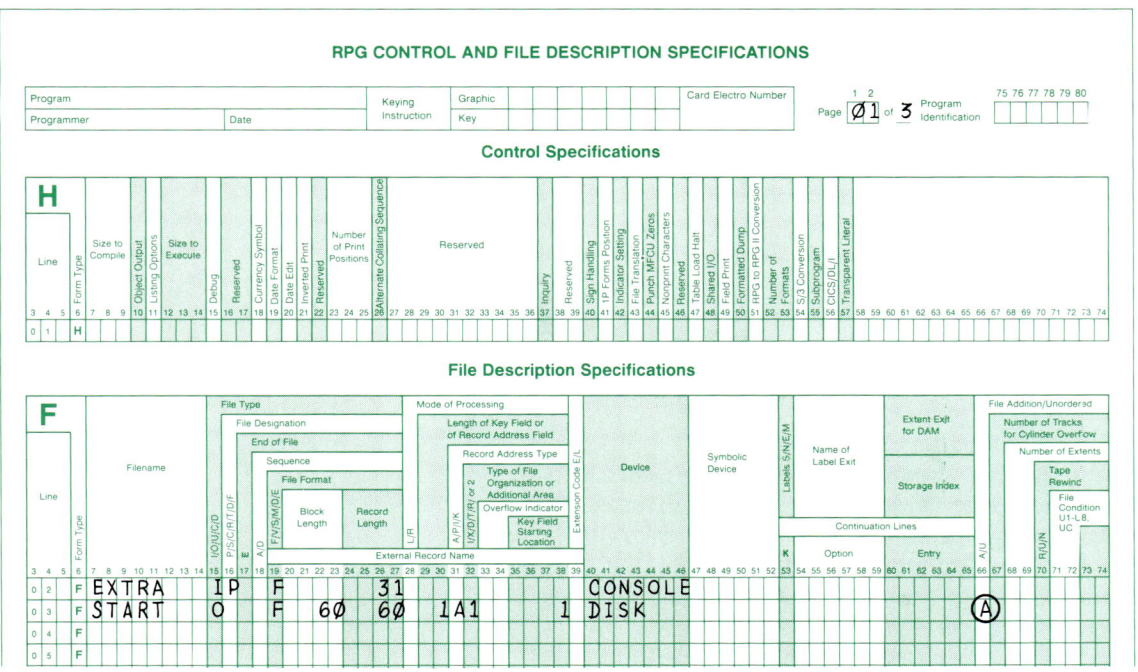

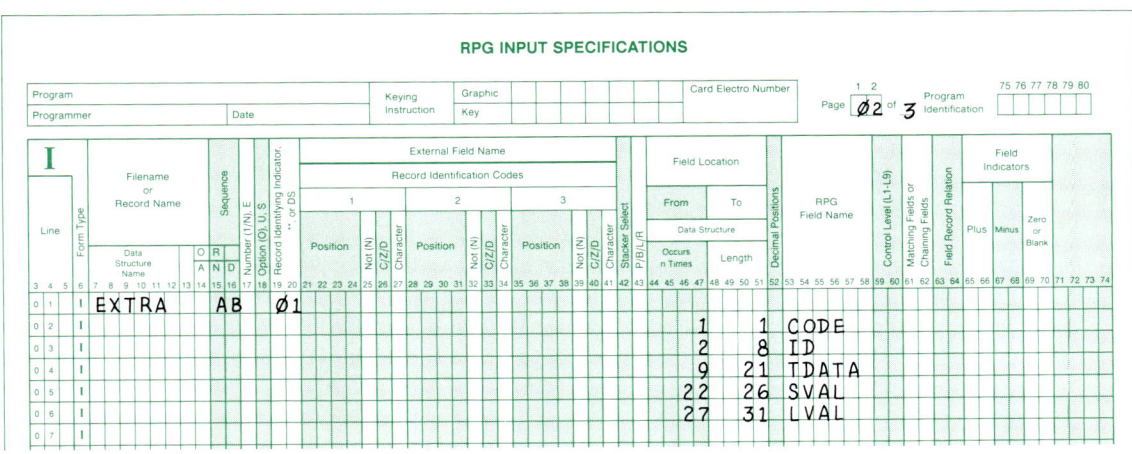

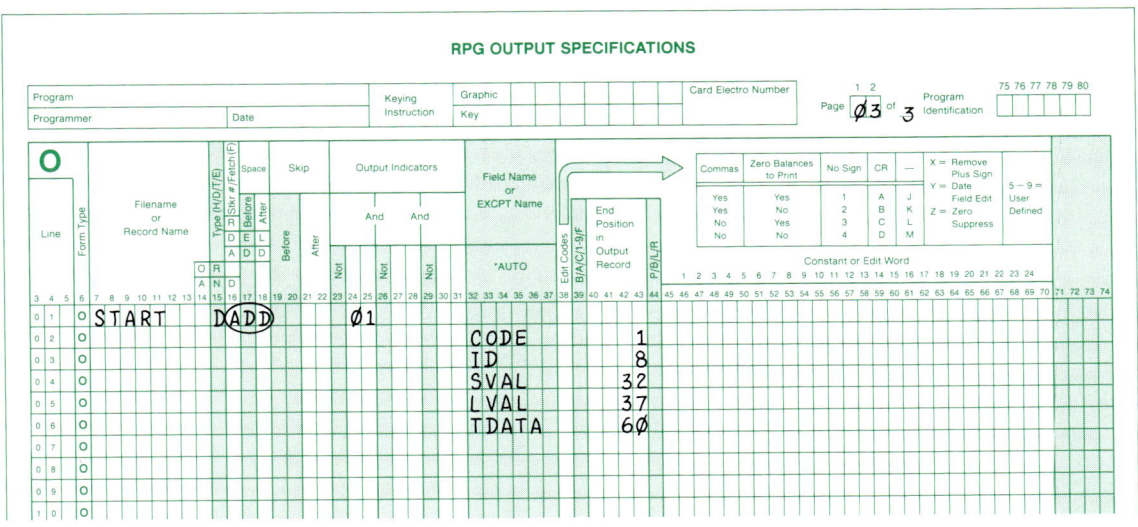

Figure 8.35 File description special entries for adding indexed records randomly by key using the chaining method

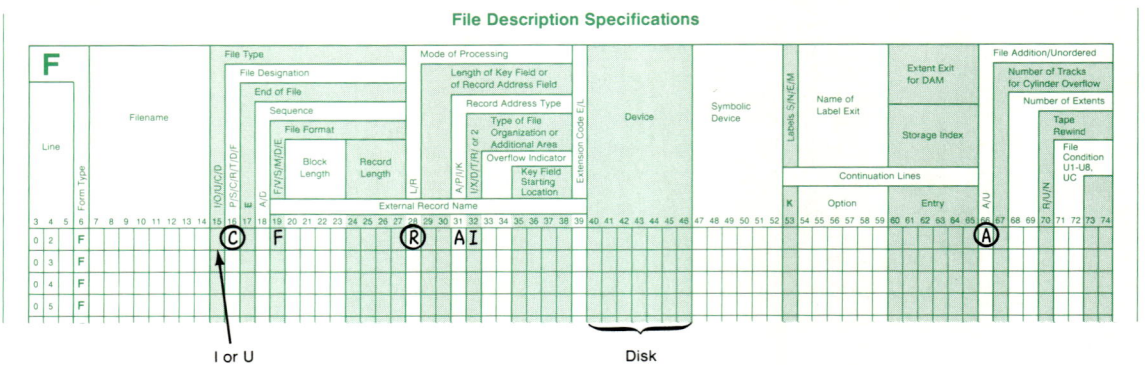

Adding Records Randomly by Key Using Chaining

Records can be added randomly by key to an indexed file in two ways: with chaining or without chaining.

Chaining means matching the record key of the record to be added with the keys of the index. This matching is done as a check to ensure that the record to be added is not a duplicate of a record already in the file. The data used as a record key in the chain operation can be either a field in an input record or it can be created in the program.

When adding records randomly by key using the chaining method, entries must be made on the File Description, Calculation Specifications, and Output Specifications forms.

The following special file description entries must be made:

1. Position 16 must contain a *C* to indicate that the file is a chained file.

2. An *R* in position 28 indicates the file is processed randomly by key.

3. Position 66 contains an *A* to indicate that records are to be added to the file.

4. The file type entry (position 15) contains an *I* or a *U*.

An *I* entry indicates the file will be read, but that the file will not be updated. A *U* entry indicates that the file will be read and that existing records will be updated. An *I* in position 15 and an *A* in position 66 will generate an error because records cannot be added to files designated as *I*. Likewise, a *U* in position 15 and a blank in position 66 will be flagged as a file designated because *U* must have an entry in position 66. (See Figure 8.35.)

The following entries are needed on the Calculation Specifications form to describe the chain operation:

1. Factor 1 must be the name of the field to be used in the search for a match in the index. CHAIN must be entered as the operation and factor 2 must contain the name of the file.

2. A resulting indicator should be specified in positions 54–55 to indicate whether the record to be added is a duplicate of a record already in the file. The record key is used to find the index entry that contains the same key. If a duplicate is not found, the record can be added to the file. The program can check for duplicates by checking the specified resulting indicator. If the indicator is off, the record is not added because it is a duplicate; if the indicator is on, the record can be added. (See Figure 8.36.)

The entry on the Output form is an ADD in positions 16–18. This entry tells the system that the fields defined on the following specification lines constitute the record to be added to the file specified in positions 7–14. (See Figures 8.37 and 8.38.)

Figure 8.36 Calculation entries for adding indexed records randomly by key using the chaining method

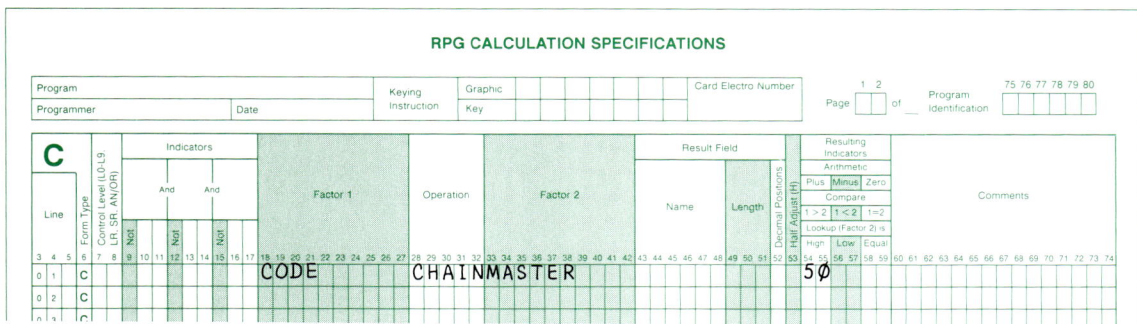

Figure 8.37 Output entries for adding indexed records

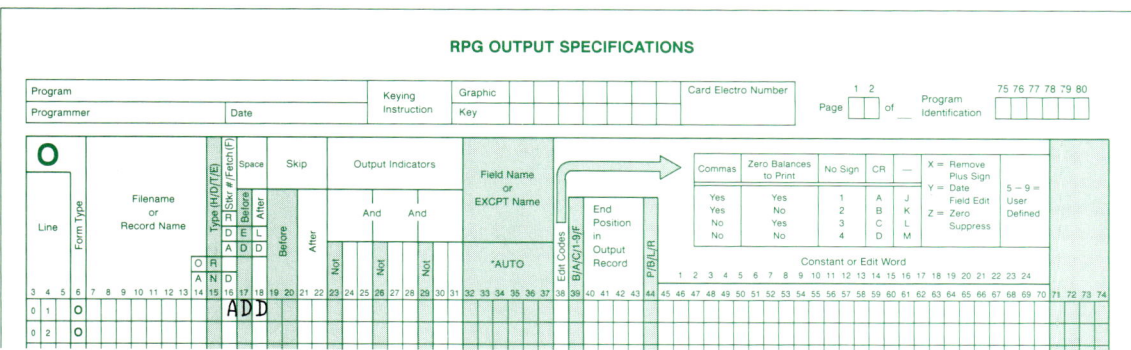

Figure 8.38 Adding indexed records randomly by key using chaining—example

Problem

Suppose you want to add new inventory items to the indexed inventory file created in the example in figure 8.29. The new records are not in sequence. New record keys may be lower, between, or higher than keys presently in the file.

Input and output records will be in the same format as the new records used to create the file. A printed report will list all the new records added to the file.

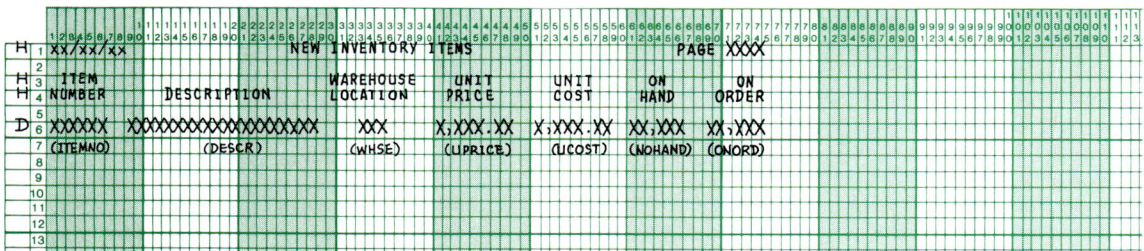

Report of New Items Added to the Inventory File

```
06/18/87              NEW INVENTORY ITEMS                    PAGE    1

ITEM                           WAREHOUSE   UNIT      UNIT     ON      ON
NUMBER      DESCRIPTION        LOCATION    PRICE     COST     HAND    ORDER

413010      CH001 BOX 100A FLUSH   768      4.90     4.00      10       6
412146      CH143 BREAKER 15A      913       .89      .59     100      75
411126      1500 TWIN SOCKET B     493      1.12      .97     500     325
```

Disk Processing 397

Figure 8.38 continued

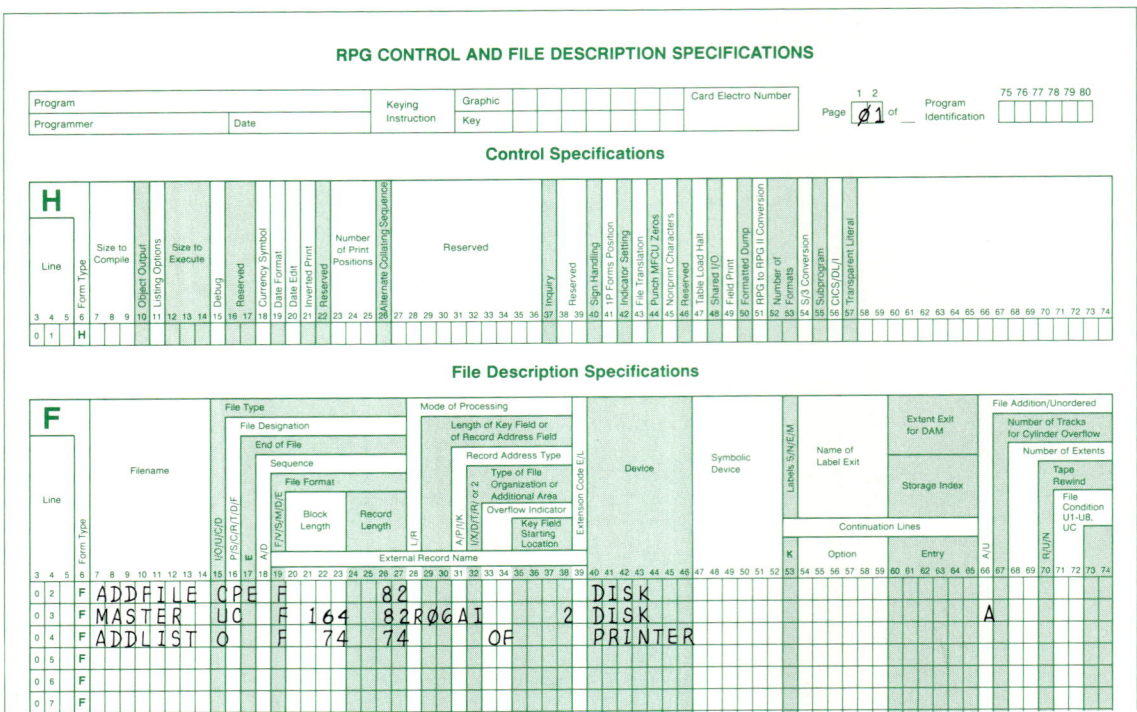

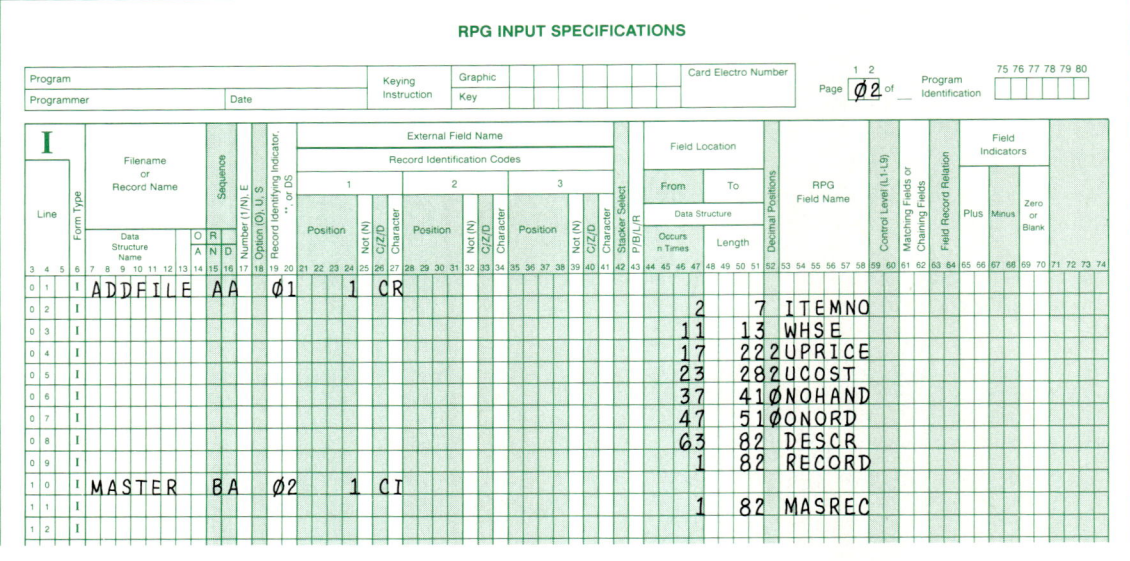

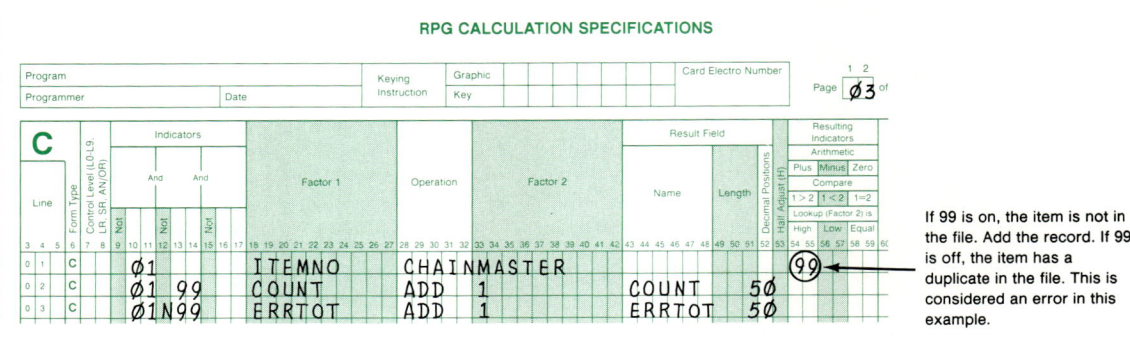

398 RPG II and RPG III Programming

Figure 8.38 continued

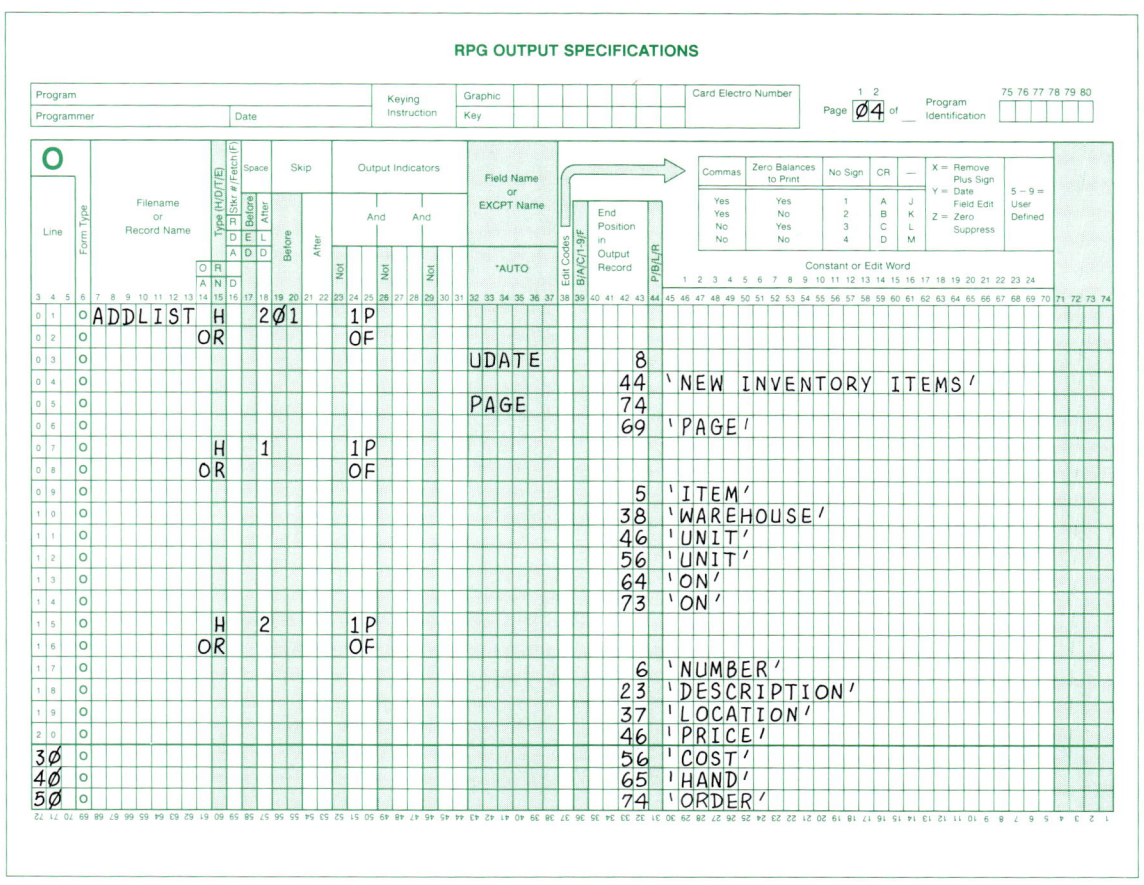

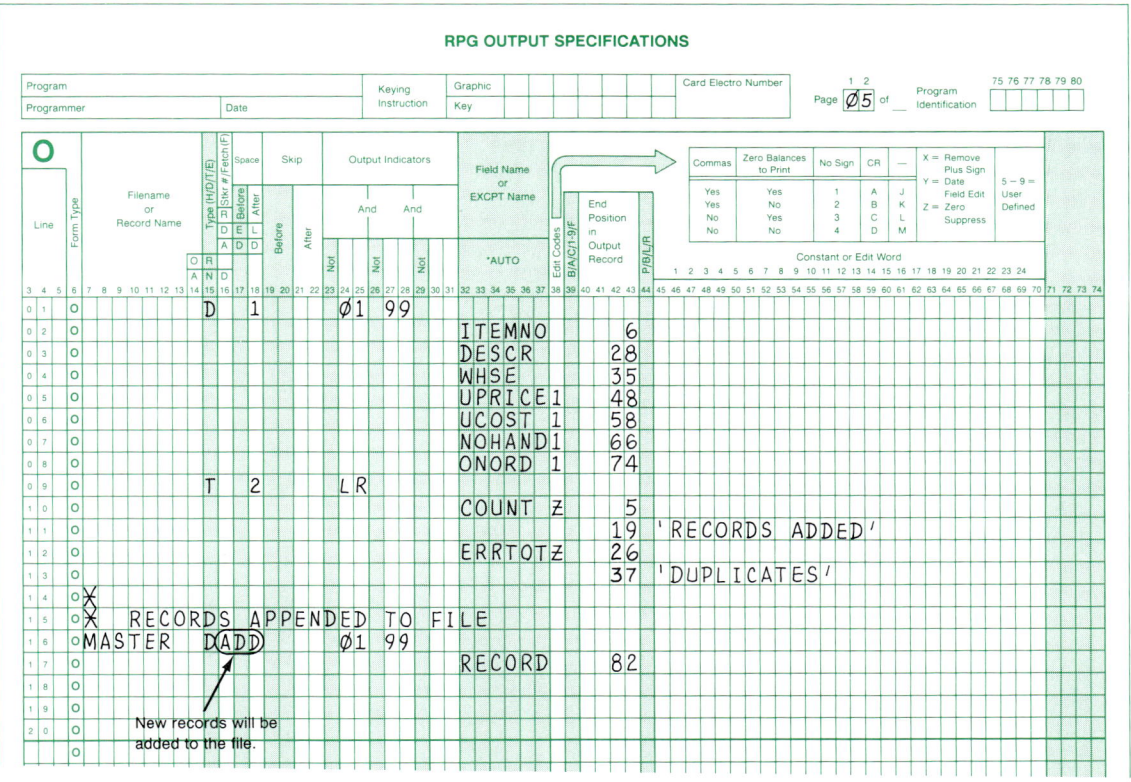

Disk Processing

Figure 8.39 File describing special entries for adding indexed records without chaining

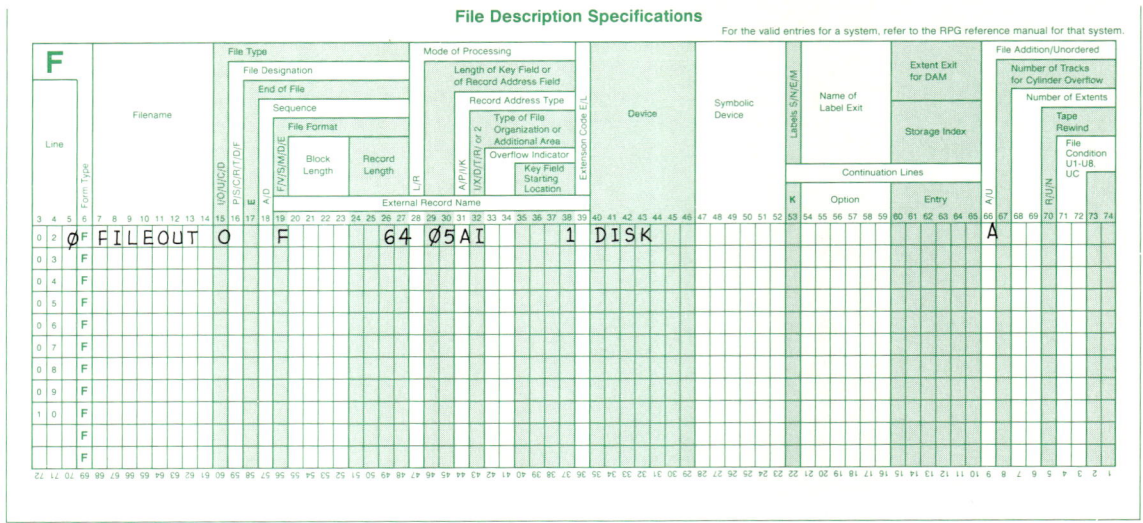

Adding Records Randomly by Key without Chaining
Chaining is not necessary if no checking for duplicate records is to be done by the program and if the file is not being read or updated. (The system will check for duplicate records and return a halt if duplicates exist even if chaining is not done.) Under this method, the indexed file is defined as an output file and records to be added are read from a separate file (or generated in the program) and are written out to the indexed file. The added records are placed at the end of the file. (In some systems the records are physically inserted sequentially in the prime area and current indexes are maintained with each record.) After the program has finished, the index is sorted into the key field sequence. Records added in this manner may

1. Contain keys that are above the highest key presently in the file. In this case, the records constitute an extension of the file.

2. Contain keys that are either lower than the lowest key presently in the file or that are somewhere between.

The following are the file description entries characteristic of this method of adding records to an indexed file:

1. An *O* for output file in position 15

2. An *F* for fixed records in position 19

3. An *A* specifying that a key field exists in position 31

4. An *I* specifying that the file is an indexed file in position 32

5. Remaining entries same as those for creating an indexed file

6. Position 66 must contain an *A* (See Figure 8.39.)

For an example of this kind of add, see Figure 8.18.

400 RPG II and RPG III Programming

Figure 8.40 File description and output specifications special entries for adding indexed records sequentially by key

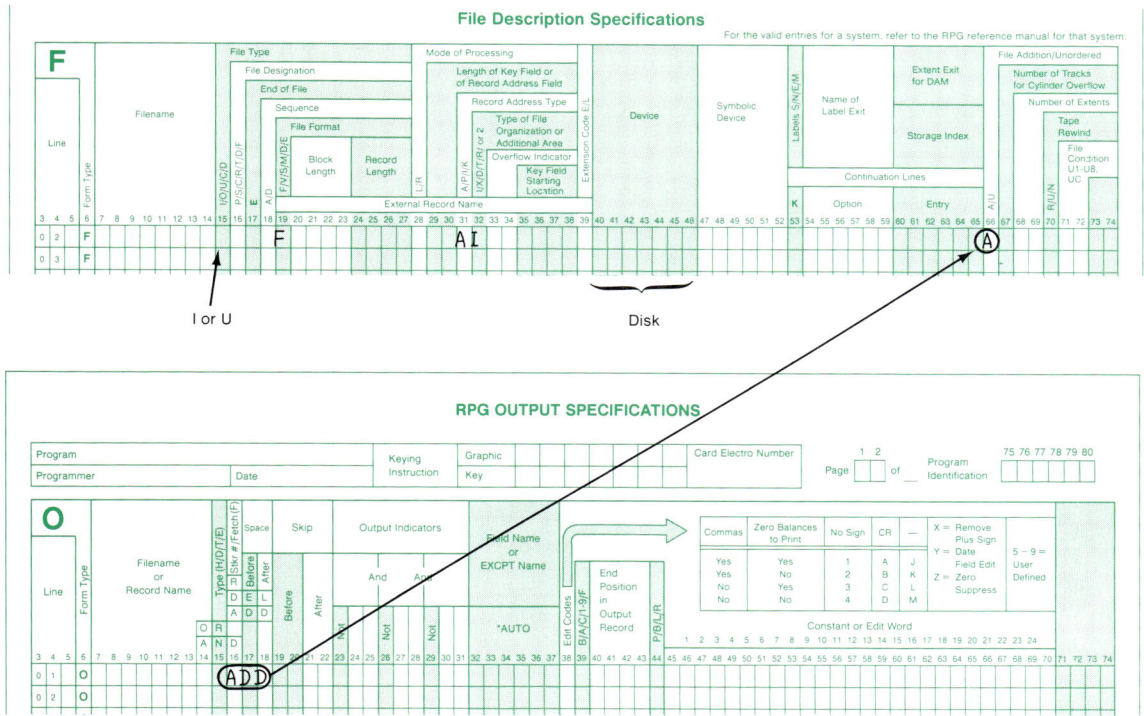

Adding Records Sequentially by Key

Records added to an indexed file sequentially by key (either by single volume or multiple volumes) must meet one or the other of the following sets of criteria:

1. Records must be added between existing records (i.e., the key of the record being added must be lower than the last key retrieved and higher than the preceding key).

2. Records must have keys that are higher than existing keys in the file (i.e., the indexed file must be at end of file).

The following items describes the appropriate entries for the File Description form:

1. The same entries used to create an indexed file are used to add records sequentially by key.

2. The file type entry (position 15) can contain either an *I* or a *U*.

3. An *A* in position 66 tells the system that records will be added to the file described on this line, unless the file was specified as *I* in position 15.

The entry on the Output Specifications form is an ADD in positions 16–18. (See Figure 8.40.)

Records might be added sequentially to an indexed file in situations where the activity of the file is high and where the records to be added have been previously sorted into ascending sequence by key fields. Adding sequentially in such a situation may produce a better performance than adding records randomly with chaining allowing large blocking factors. (See Figure 8.41.)

Disk Processing 401

Figure 8.41 Adding indexed records sequentially by key—example

Problem

Suppose you want to add new inventory items to the indexed inventory file created previously. The new items are merged with records of receipts of existing items; thus existing inventory records are updated and new records are added during the same program run. The activity of the inventory file (number of transactions against the file) is high, so the transaction file, containing new items and receipts, is organized into ascending sequence by item number (key field), enabling the file to be processed sequentially by key. Input records for new items are in the same format as the inventory records.

The program below shows the coding to update the inventory file to add new item records to the file. At the same time, a list of new inventory items is printed, similar to the list produced in the example of adding records randomly to the inventory file (fig. 8.33).

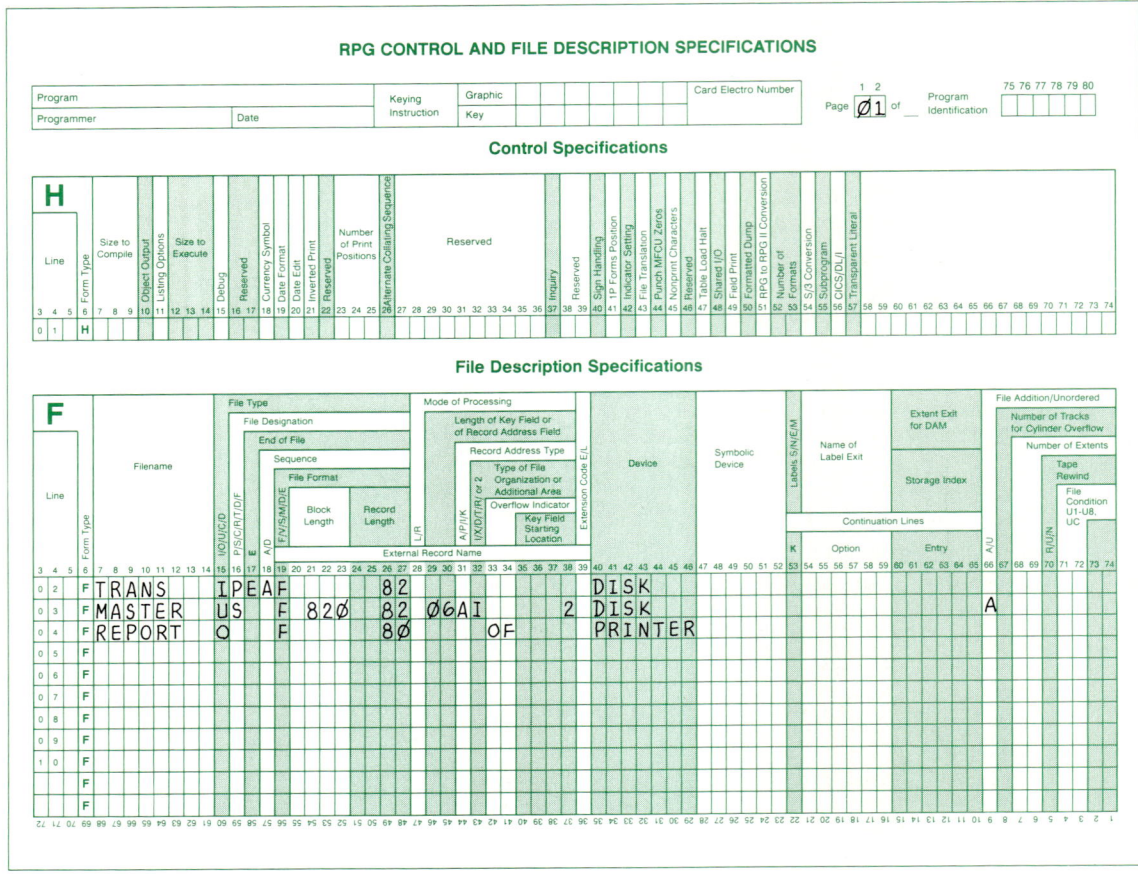

Figure 8.41 continued

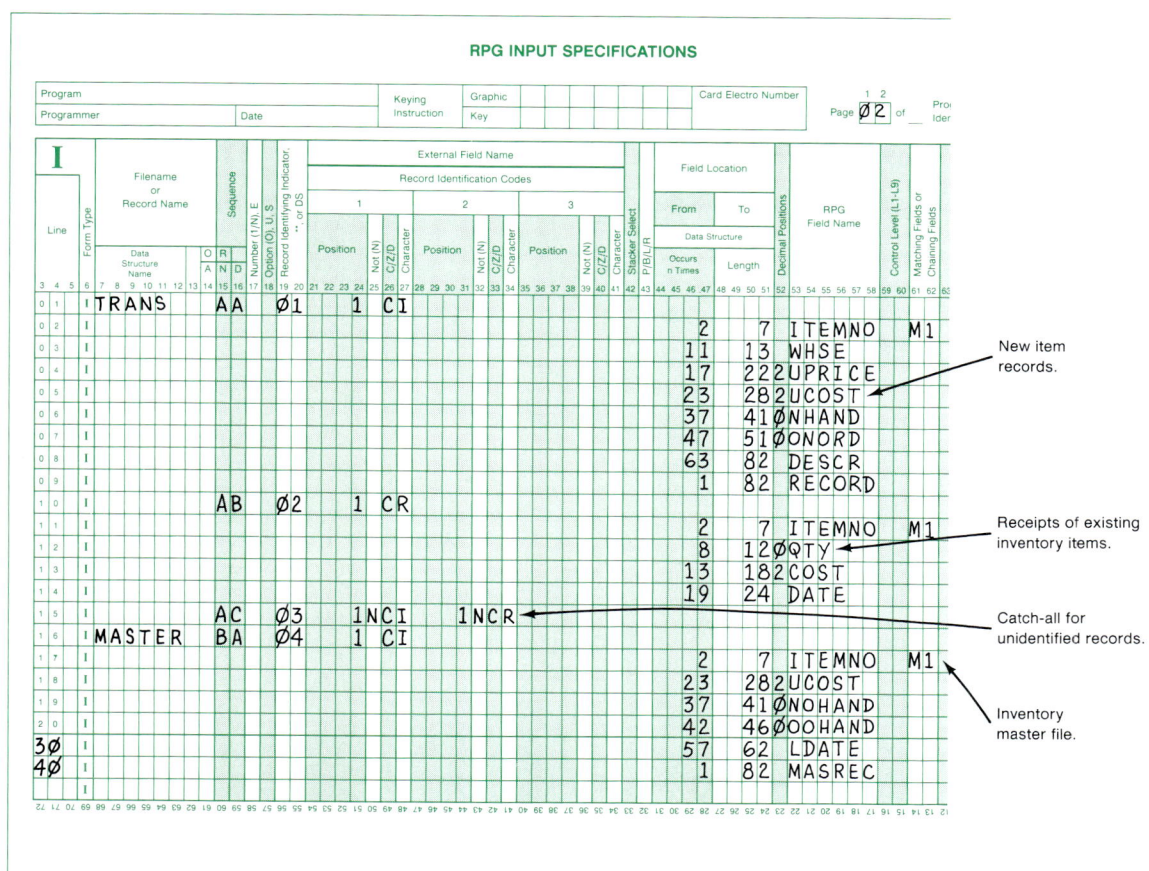

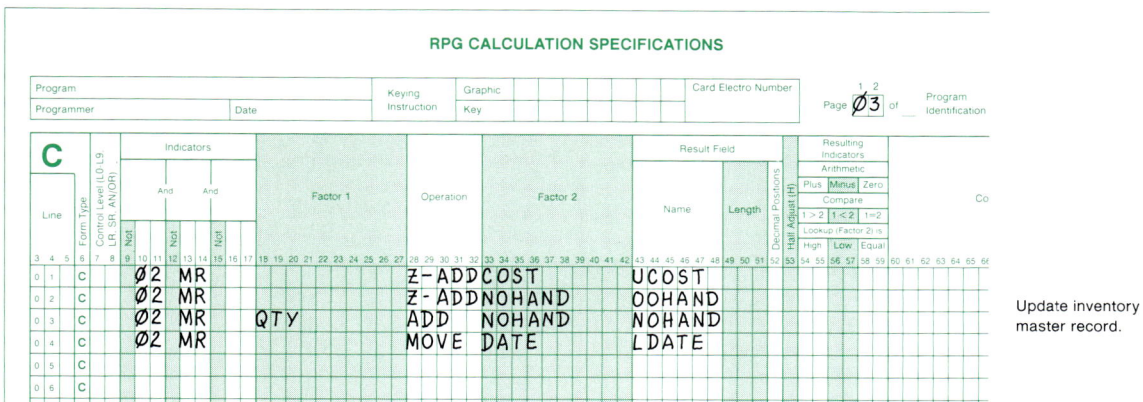

Disk Processing

Figure 8.41 continued

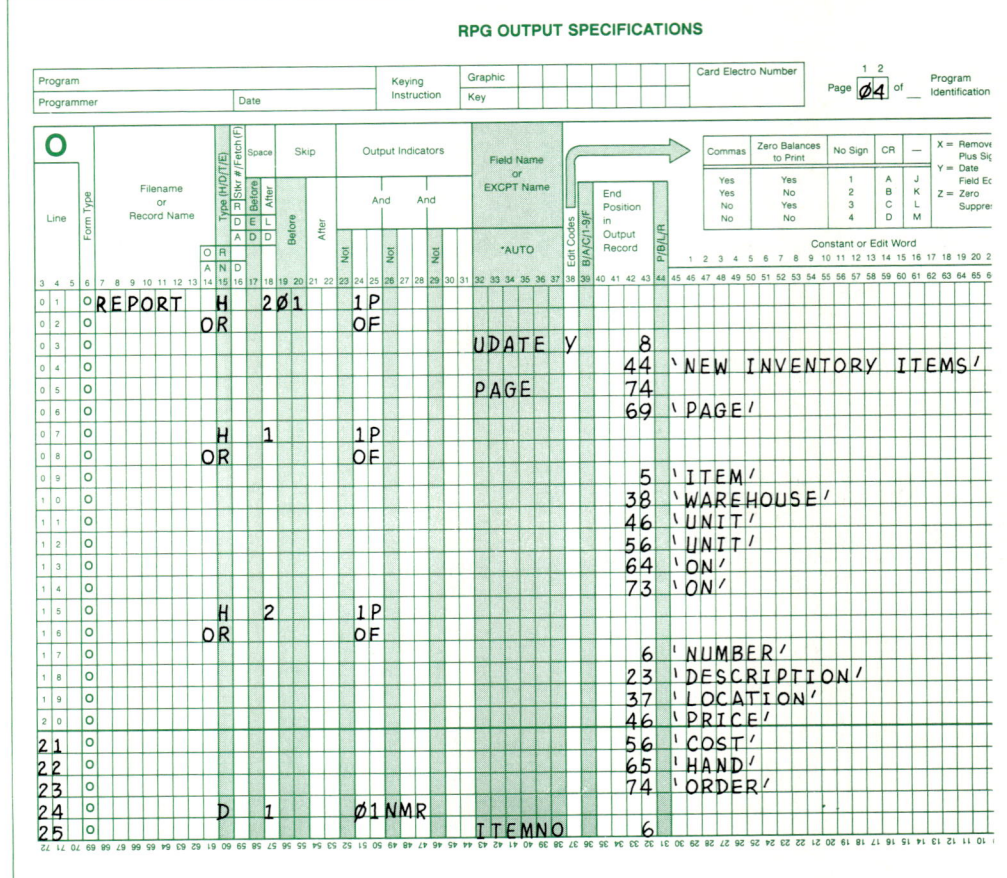

Printed report is shown under example of adding records randomly by key using chaining (fig. 8.38).

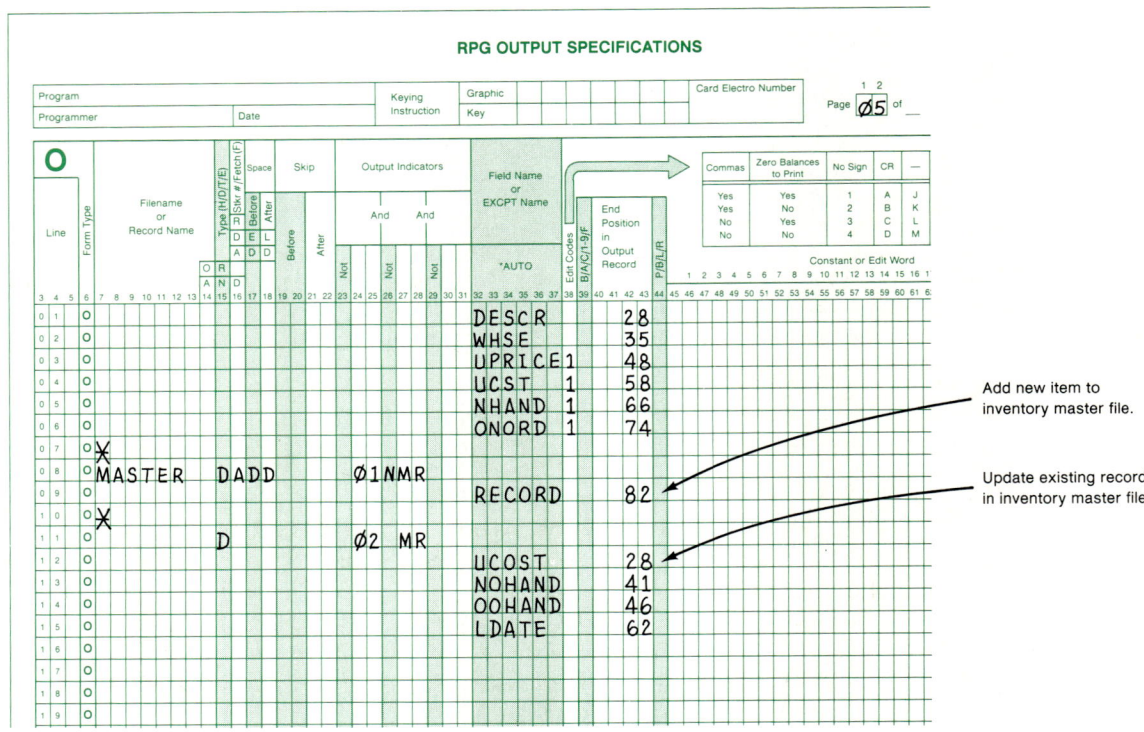

Add new item to inventory master file.

Update existing record in inventory master file.

Tagging Records for Deletion

When a record becomes inactive, the programmer probably will not want to process it with the other records. Since the record is not physically removed from the file, however, the programmer must identify it so it can be bypassed. One way to identify the record is to put in a code called a delete code. The delete code can be any character placed in a particular location in the record. A program can check for this code; if the code is present, the program will bypass the record. The deleted records can be physically removed from the file by reorganizing the file. For an example of tagging records for deletion see Figure 8.33.

Reorganizing a File

Reorganizing a file is similar to creating the file. Reorganization may be necessary for two reasons:
1. To increase processing efficiency
2. To free disk space, especially in the overflow areas

The programmer can increase processing efficiency by restoring the file to its original sequence. As records are added to a file, they are added at the end of the records already in the file; however, the keys are always in order in the index. When the file is processed sequentially by key, the disk access arm moves back and forth between the sequenced records (those originally created) and the added records. This back-and-forth movement increases processing time.

Disk space can be made available by removing inactive records during a file copy routine. All records with a delete code can be physically deleted from the file.

Other Ways to Process Indexed Files

Indexed files may be processed in a variety of ways depending upon the functionality desired.

Processing an Indexed File Consecutively

An indexed file may be processed consecutively (read only) by defining the indexed file as a sequential input file in the File Description form. When an indexed file is processed consecutively, the file index is bypassed and data records are read consecutively from the beginning of the file to the end, exactly as a sequential file is read. Indexed files may not be created, added to, or updated consecutively.

Consecutive processing of an indexed file is useful, for example, for reading records from an indexed file when the index is unusable for some reason.

Processing an Indexed File Randomly by Relative Record Number

An indexed file may be processed randomly by relative record number if the file is an input file. The file must be described as a sequential file (i.e., positions 31–32 must be blank) and must be described as a chained file (*C* in position 16 of the File Description form). The CHAIN operation must be used in calculations to read records from the file. Records may not be updated, added, or written out to an indexed file using this method.

Random processing of an indexed file by relative record number can provide improved performance over random processing by key because the file index need not be read. However, it is the programmer's responsibility to ensure that records in the indexed file are properly sequenced for this type of processing.

Direct File Organization

Another method of arranging the records on the disk is called direct organization. A direct file is one in which records are assigned specific record locations on disk. Direct file organization enables the program to access any record in the file without examining other records or searching an index. (See Figure 8.42.)

Figure 8.42 Direct organization creation—example

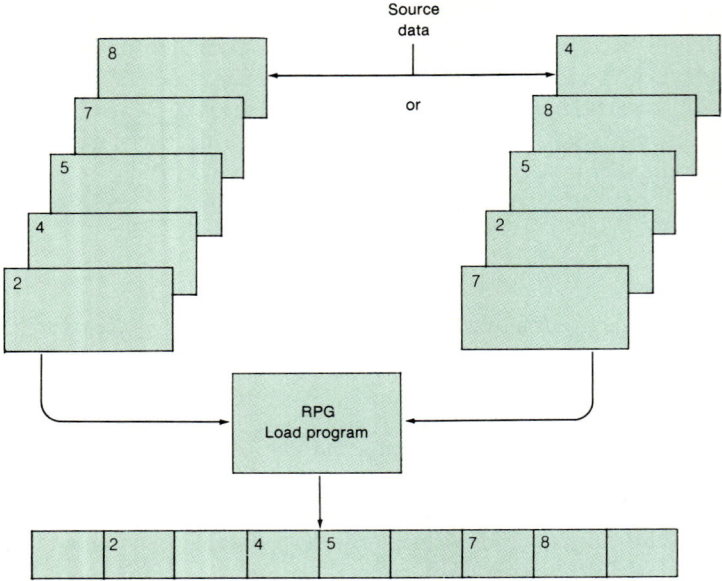

Instead of writing the records one after another as they are entered, each record is placed in a specific location according to a unique field (key). In this type of organization, gaps for missing records are left. The position of the record in the file is located using what is known as the relative record number. The **relative record number** is the location of the record relative to the beginning of the file.

Creating a Direct File

To create a direct file, the disk file must be defined as a chained output file. Certain entries are needed on the File Description form to describe various characteristics of the disk file. Direct file creation is discussed in Appendix H.

Relative record numbers are always used in the program along with the CHAIN operation code to make the corresponding record locations in a direct file available for loading.

Record Address Files (RAF)

A **record address file** is an input file that indicates which records are to be read from a disk file and the order in which the records are to be read from the disk file.

Processing within Limits

Processing of an indexed file that is ordered within limits can save time and simplify programming. A case in point is the generation of an inventory balance report for only certain inventory classes from a stock balance file, sequenced by stock number within inventory class. Another case is the printing of a list of employees having certain skills, using as input a skills inventory file that is sequenced by employee within skill category.

The processing-within-limits technique is applicable for any indexed sequential file that has a record key sequence by which logical subdivisions relative to processing may be identified. Consider an indexed sequential payment history file sequenced simply by customer number. A credit department function is to review each customer's payment experience monthly. To reduce the size of the listing used by the credit department and to provide most current data, only a fourth of the file is printed each week. This is easily done with a record address file (RAF) entry that defines the limits of processing. (See Figure 8.43.)

Figure 8.43 Processing within limits—example

Week	Record Address File	
	Lower Limit	Upper Limit
First	1	2500
Second	2501	5000
Third	5001	7500
Fourth	7501	10000

The customer numbers fall between 1 and 10,000.

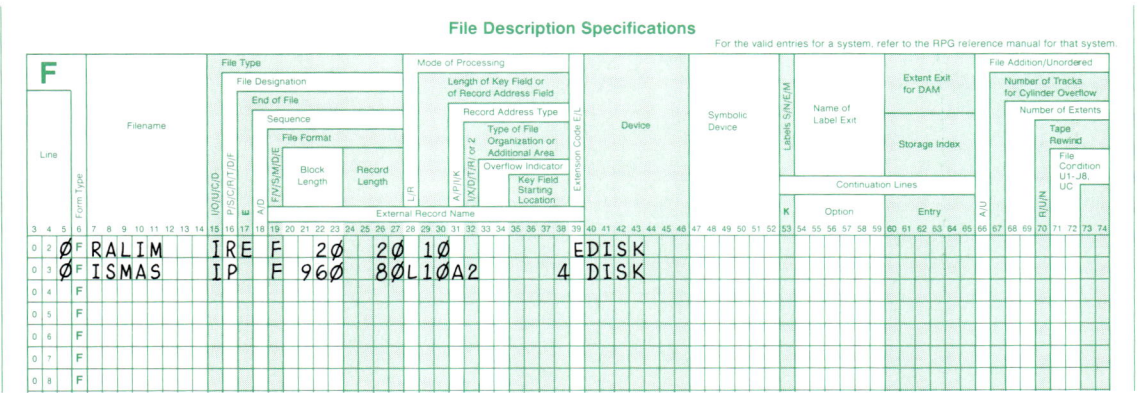

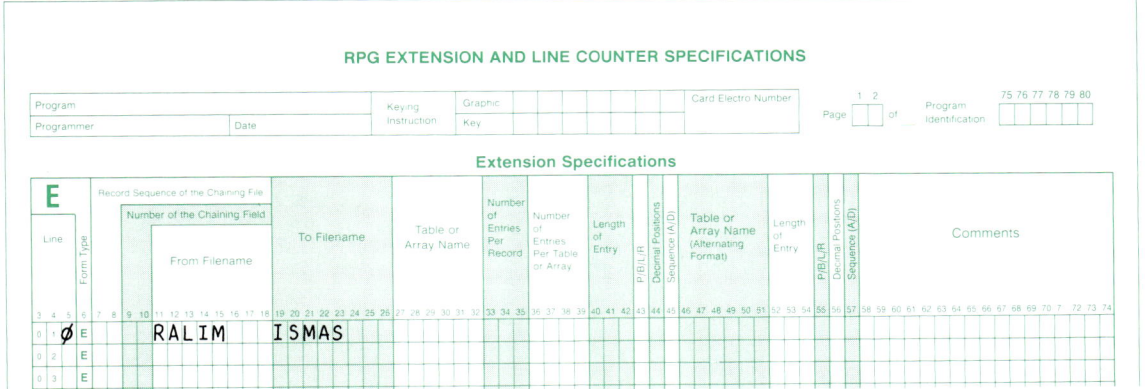

Notes on the Coding

File Description Specifications

Line   Meaning

020   The filename RALIM is a record address limit file. Each record contains up to four sets of ten-character keys. (A set is defined as two keys that indicate the limit boundaries.) A record may contain less than four sets of keys if the rest of the record contains blanks. The R in position 16 defines the file as a record address file. The length of the record address file is described in positions 29-30. The E in position 39 means that an extension specification (form E) will define the target file.

030   This line defines the Indexed file. The records are eighty bytes, blocked 12. It is processed via limit file, as indicated by the L in position 28. The keys are alphameric, and each key is ten bytes long. The I in position 32 defines the file as an indexed file. The key starts in position 4.

Extension Specifications

010   The record address limit file is specified in positions 11-18 and the target file in positions 19-20.

Disk Processing

Processing Using Record Address File Key

Processing an indexed file with the specific keys for accessing supplied by the record address file allows greater selectivity than does processing within limits. Furthermore, while processing within limits reduces the number of records to be handled, it still requires sequential accessing within those limits. Using keys supplied by the record address file, the order of processing is controlled by the order of the record address file entries.

This method of accessing is convenient for handling inquiries about specific information in the file. For example, an inventory manager may be concerned about the balances of certain critical stock items. These stock item numbers can be entered on a record address file to affect the printout of the stock position of those items by retrieval from an indexed inventory file ordered by stock number. Similarly, this method is suitable for retrieving the payment histories of specific customers with overdue accounts. (See Figure 8.44.)

Figure 8.44 Using record address keys to access indexed files—example

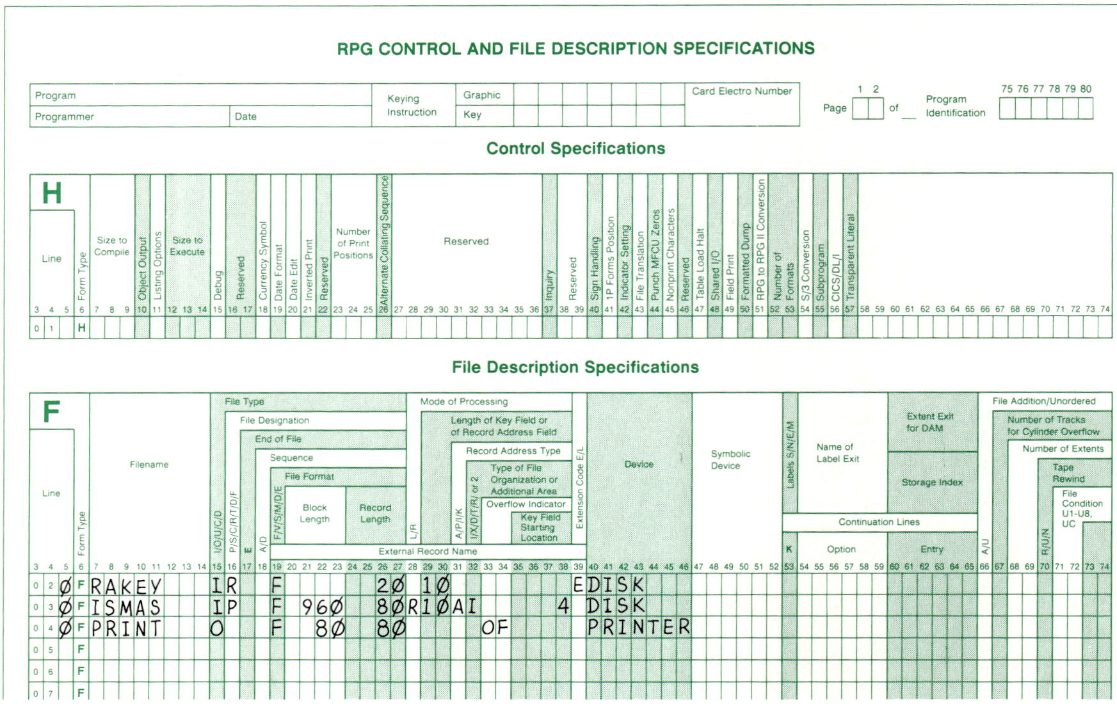

```
02 F RAKEY    IR  F      20 10         E   DISK
03 F ISMAS    IP  F     960 80R10AI  4     DISK
04 F PRINT    O   F      80 80     OF      PRINTER
```

Figure 8.44 continued

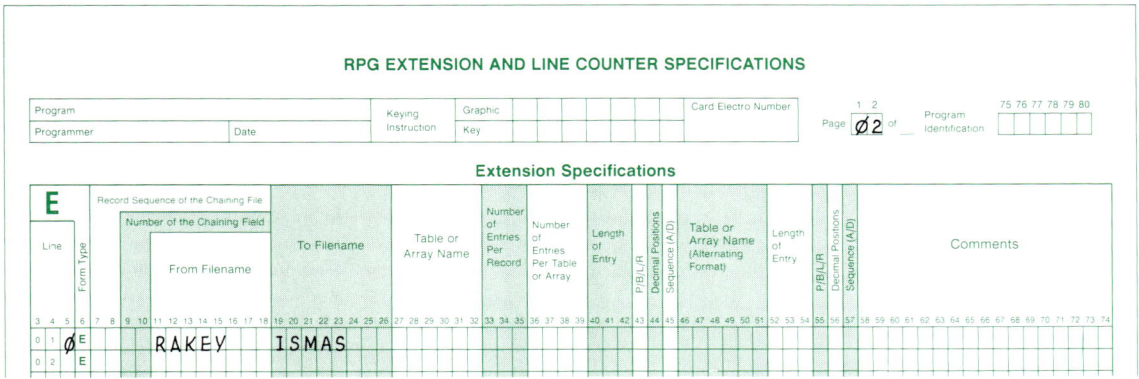

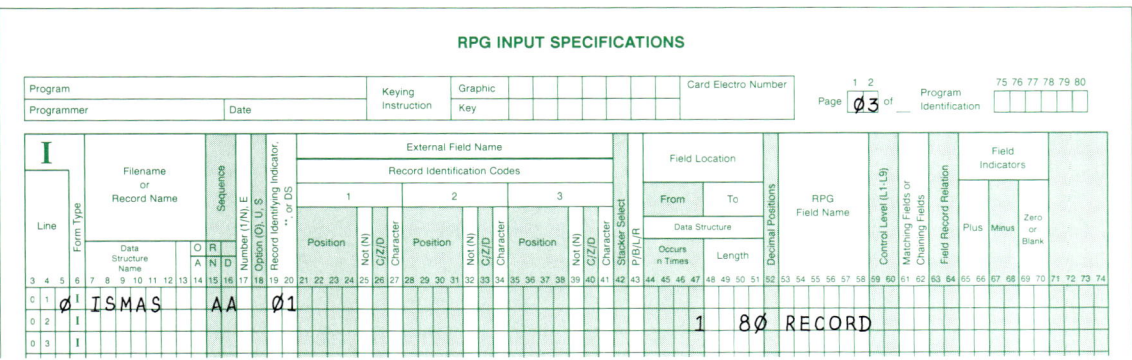

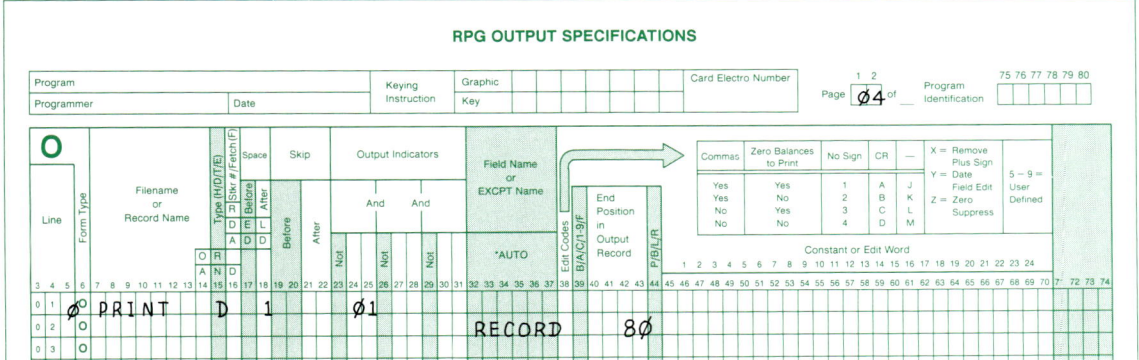

Notes on the Coding

The above coding shows how to access an indexed file via record address keys. The example retrieves selected records and lists them on the printer.

Files Containing Record Key Limits

A record address file with record key limits contains the lowest and the highest key fields for a specified section of an indexed file. Record address files containing record key limits can be entered from work station to disk using source entry utility (SEU) or a word processor. They are used to process indexed files only. When a section of an indexed file is processed using record key limits, it is known as sequential within limits processing.

Disk Processing 409

Creating a File with Record Key Limits

The following rules must be observed when creating a record address file with key limits:

1. Only one record address file can be used for each RPG program, but the record address file can contain several sets of limits.

2. Only one set of limits is allowed on each record in a record address file. Since a set of limits contains two keys, the length of each record in a record address file is twice as long as the length of the record key.

3. The low record key must begin in position 1 of the record.

4. The high record key must immediately follow the low record key. No spaces are allowed between the two keys. If the key field were four bytes long, the lowest record key were 2000, and the high record key 3000, the record would look like this:

    20003000

5. Each record key can be from one to twenty-nine characters long.

6. An alphameric key can contain blanks.

7. The length of the key must equal the length of the key field in the indexed file. To make the length of the keys equal, leading zeros may have to be placed in a numeric record key or blanks in an alphameric record key. For example, if the low record key were three positions (e.g., 200), the high record key four positions (e.g., 2999), and the length of the key field in the indexed file four positions, a zero must be placed before the 200 to make it a four-position number. The record would look like this:

    02002999

    Each key length must also equal the key field length specified in positions 29–30 of the File Description form.

8. The same set of limits can appear on more than one record in a record address file. Therefore, records within a set of limits can be processed as many times as needed.

9. The two record keys in a set of limits can be identical. For example, the low and high record keys may both be 2999, but only one record would be processed.

Processing Sequentially within Limits

Processing a section of an indexed file sequentially by record keys is known as sequential within limits processing. The RPG program uses one set of limits (one record in a record address file) at a time. Records are read from the section of the indexed file specified by the limits. When the records specified by one set of limits have been read, the program reads another set of limits from the record address file. The program continues reading records in this manner until the end of the record address file is reached.

To process an indexed file using a record address file in RPG, entries must be made on the File Description and Extension Specifications forms. Input specifications are not required.

File Description Specifications

The File Description form must describe both the indexed file to be processed and the record address file. The description of the indexed file to be processed must contain the following entries in addition to the others generally necessary for file description:

1. Position 28 must contain an *L* to indicate that the records are to be read sequentially within limits from this file.

2. Enter an *A* in position 31 to indicate that record keys are used in processing the file.

3. Enter an *I* in position 32 to indicate an indexed file. (See Figure 8.45.)

Figure 8.45 File description special entries for a file to be read sequentially between limits

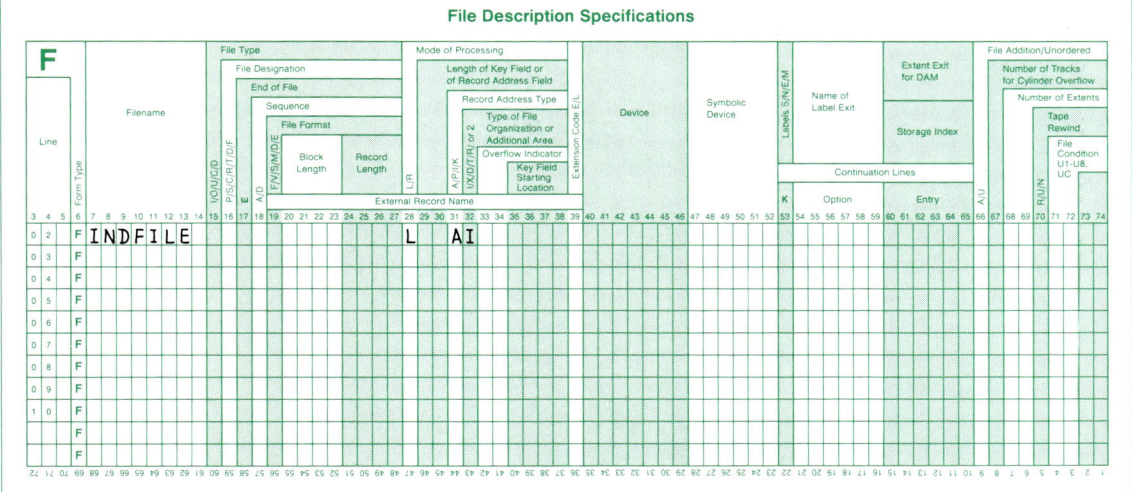

The record address file must be described with the following entries:

1. The name of the record address file must be entered in positions 7–14.
2. Position 15 must contain an *I* to indicate that the file is an input file.
3. Enter an *R* in position 16 to indicate that the file is a record address file.
4. All records must be the same length. Thus position 19 should contain an *F* to indicate that the record length is fixed.
5. A number equal to or a multiple of the disk record length must be entered in positions 20–23.
6. Positions 24–27 must contain the length of the disk record.
7. The key length entered in positions 29–30 must be the same length for all records in the file.
8. Whenever a disk is described, the name is required in the device (positions 40–46).
9. Since additional information is given on the Extension form, position 39 must contain an *E*. (See Figure 8.46.)

Figure 8.46 File description special entries for a record address file

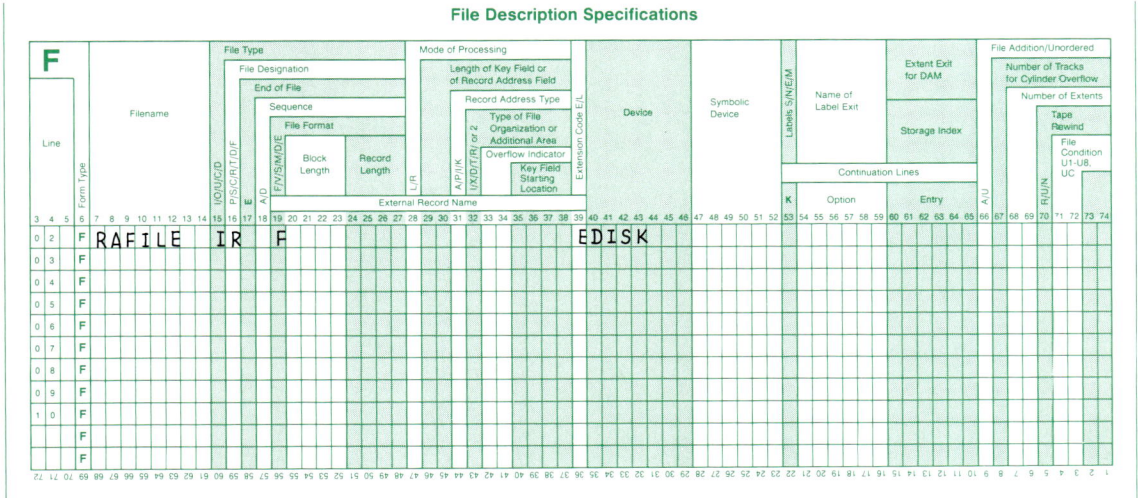

Disk Processing 411

Extension Specifications

To process a file using a record address file, two entries must be made on the Extension form:

1. Positions 11–18 must contain the name of the record address file. The name must be the same as the record address file described on the File Description form.

2. Positions 19–26 must contain the name of the file to be processed. This name must be the same filename defined on the File Description form. This entry indicates that the file is to be processed by the record address file coded in positions 11–18. (See Figures 8.47 and 8.48.)

Figure 8.47 Extension special entries for record address file to indexed file

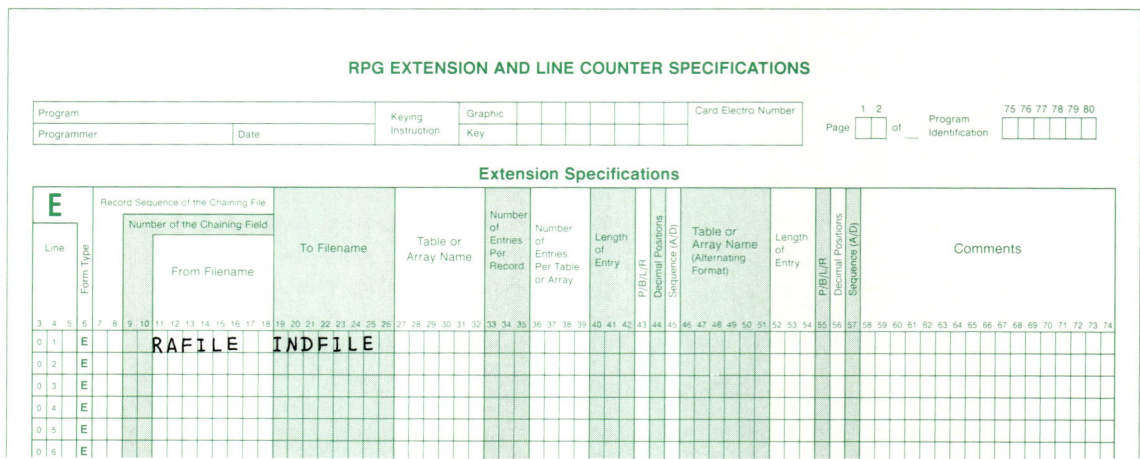

Figure 8.48 Processing sequentially within limits—example

Problem

You have a master customer file on disk consisting of 128-character records. The file is organized by customer number within customer class. Customers are separated into such classes as wholesalers or retailers. Together the customer number and class form a composite customer account number (key) in the form: ccnnnnn.

The customer class is cc and the customer number nnnnn. Customer classes begin at 01 and are in ascending order. Within each customer class, customer numbers range from 00000-99999.

You must prepare separate reports for each customer class for sales analysis purposes. A record address file can be used to supply the particular class categories and customer ranges as shown below. The key in each disk record begins in position 2, and the record address file contains the limits for processing.

Files for Processing Sequentially within Limits

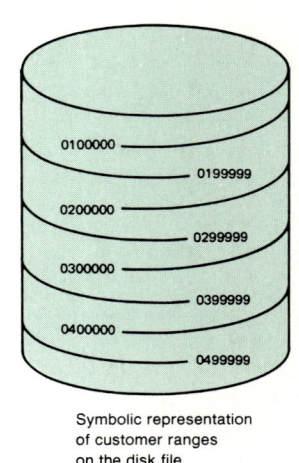

Figure 8.48 continued

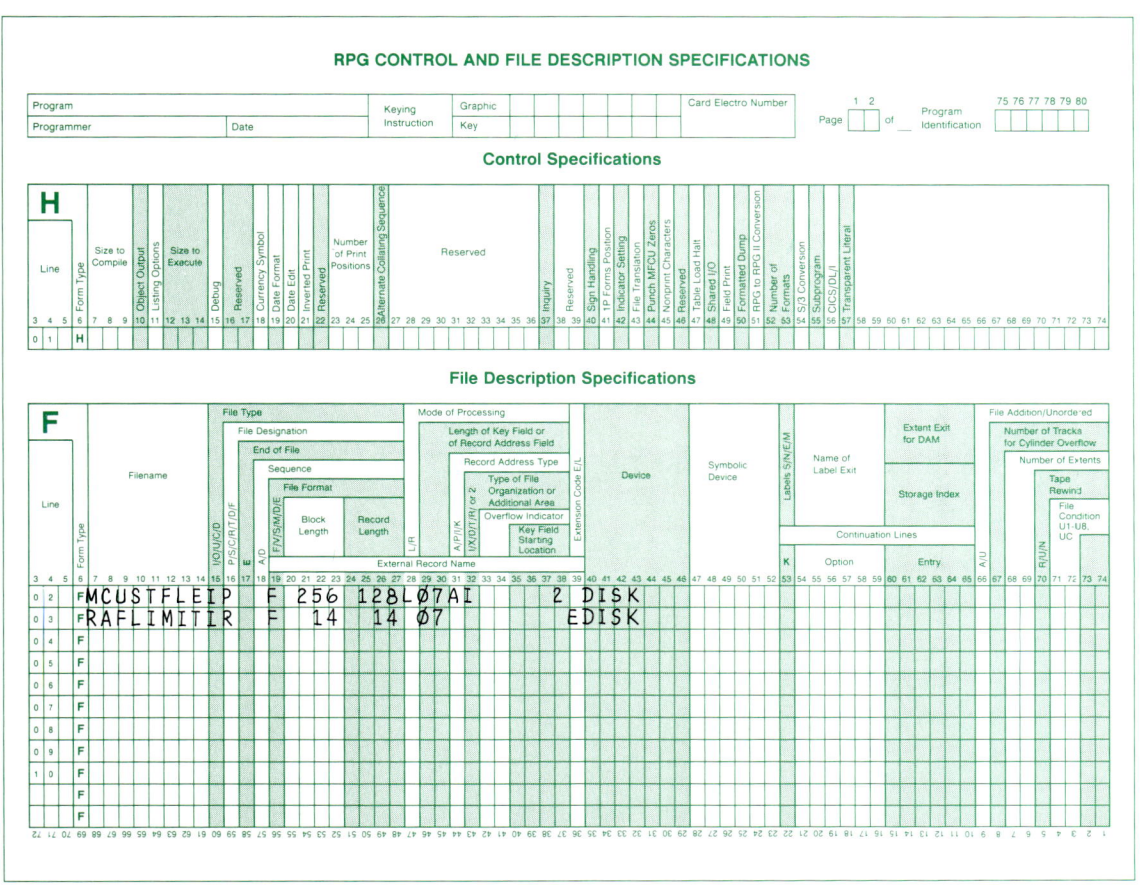

Illustrative Program

Creating an Indexed Disk File

Job Definition
An indexed disk file is to be created from a 52-position disk record.

Input
A 52-position disk record is to be used as input.

Processing
A 52-position indexed disk record is to be created.

Output
The created indexed disk file record is to have the same format as the input record.

Coding sheets for Creating an Indexed Disk File problem:

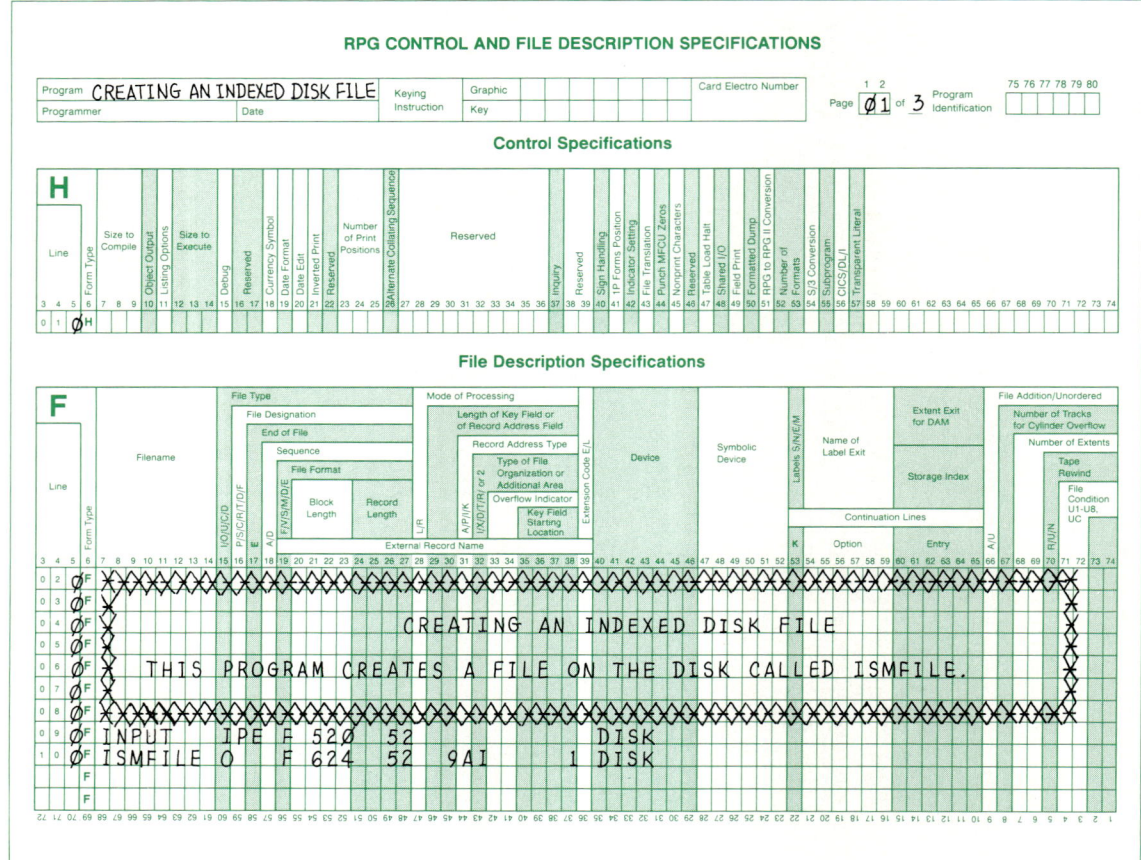

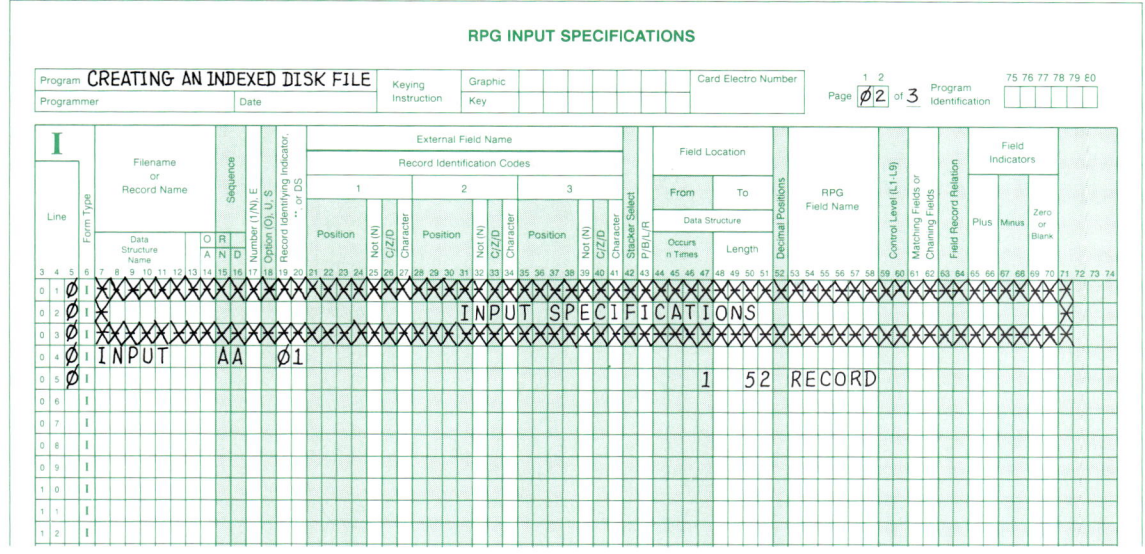

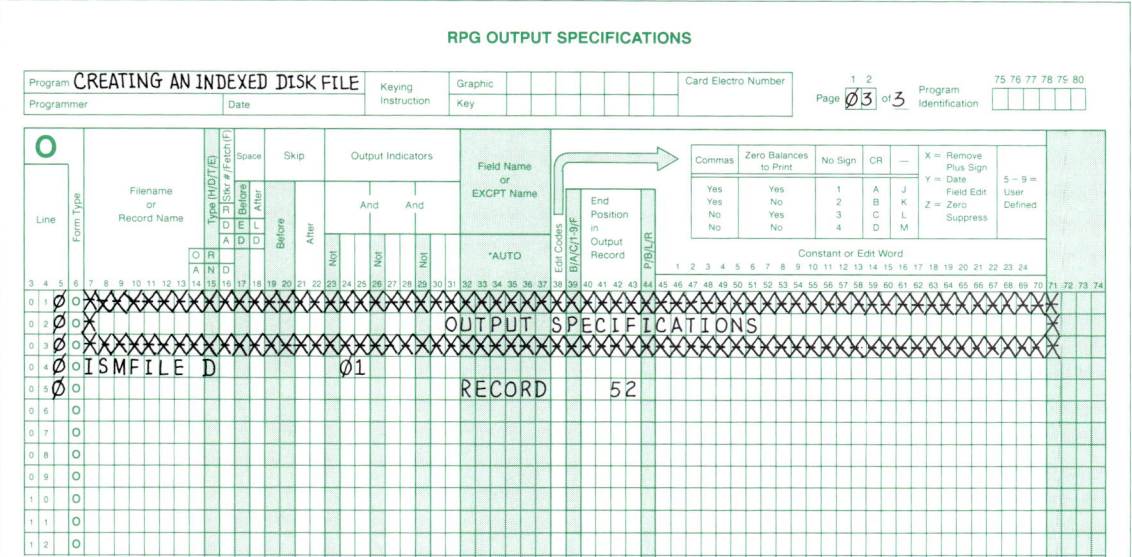

The source listing is as follows:

```
 1     01010H
 2   * 01020F******************************************************************
 3   * 01030F*                                                                 *
 4   * 01040F*              CREATING AN INDEXED DISK FILE                      *
 5   * 01050F*                                                                 *
 6   * 01060F*    THIS PROGRAM CREATES A FILE ON THE DISK CALLED ISMFILE.      *
 7   * 01070F*                                                                 *
 8   * 01080F******************************************************************
 9     01090FINPUT    IPE F 520    52                  DISK
10     01100FISMFILE O   F 624    52      9AI       1 DISK
11   * 02010I******************************************************************
12   * 02020I*                INPUT SPECIFICATIONS                             *
13   * 02030I******************************************************************
14     02040IINPUT    AA  01
15     02050I                                     1  52 RECORD
16   * 03010O******************************************************************
17   * 03020O*                OUTPUT SPECIFICATIONS                            *
18   * 03030O******************************************************************
19     03040OISMFILE D           01
20     03050O                         RECORD     52
```

Disk Processing 415

Illustrative Program

List Indexed Disk Records

Job Definition
List the data of the record stored on disk in the previous program to assure that the record was stored properly.

Input
A 52-position record is to be used.

Processing
Print out the contents of a 52-position indexed disk record.

Output
The Printer Spacing Chart shows how the report is formatted:

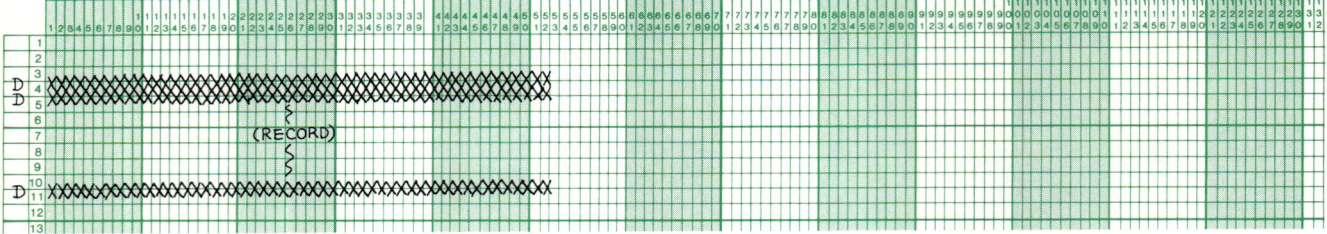

Coding sheets for the Listing Indexed Disk Records problem:

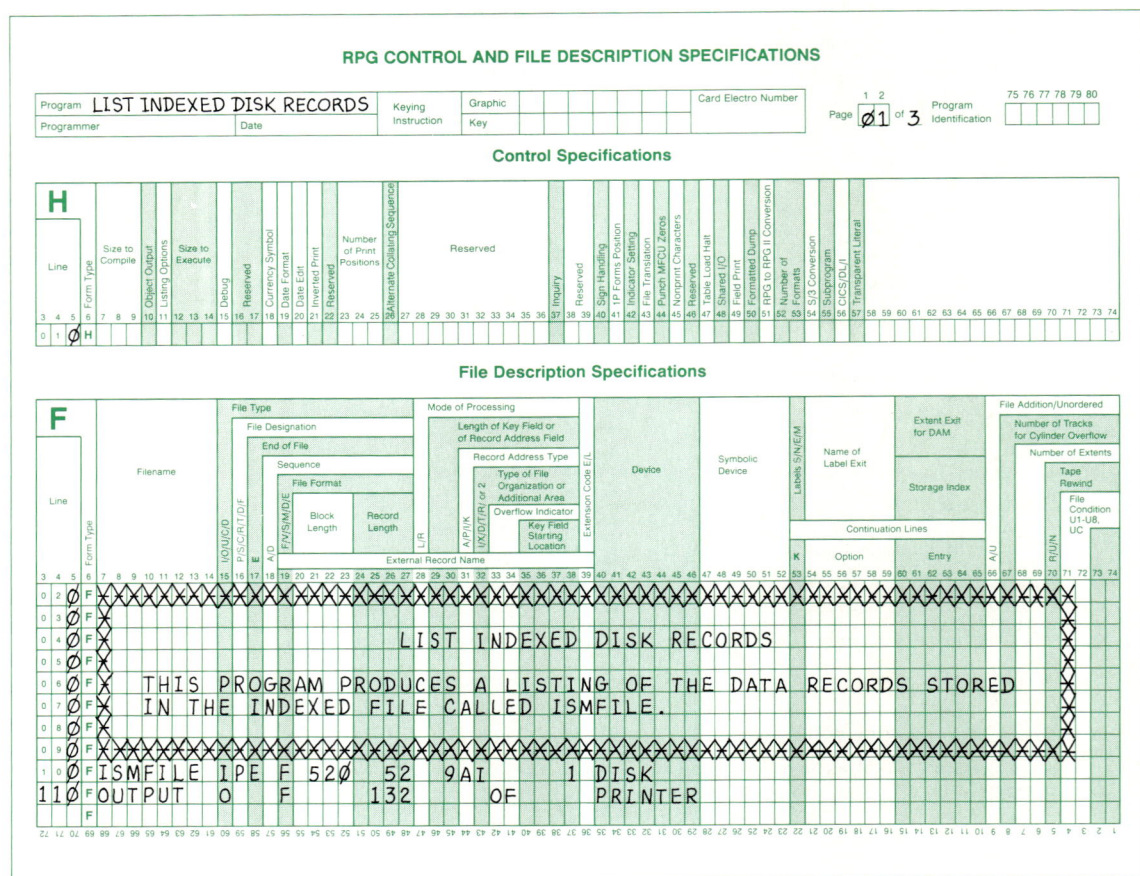

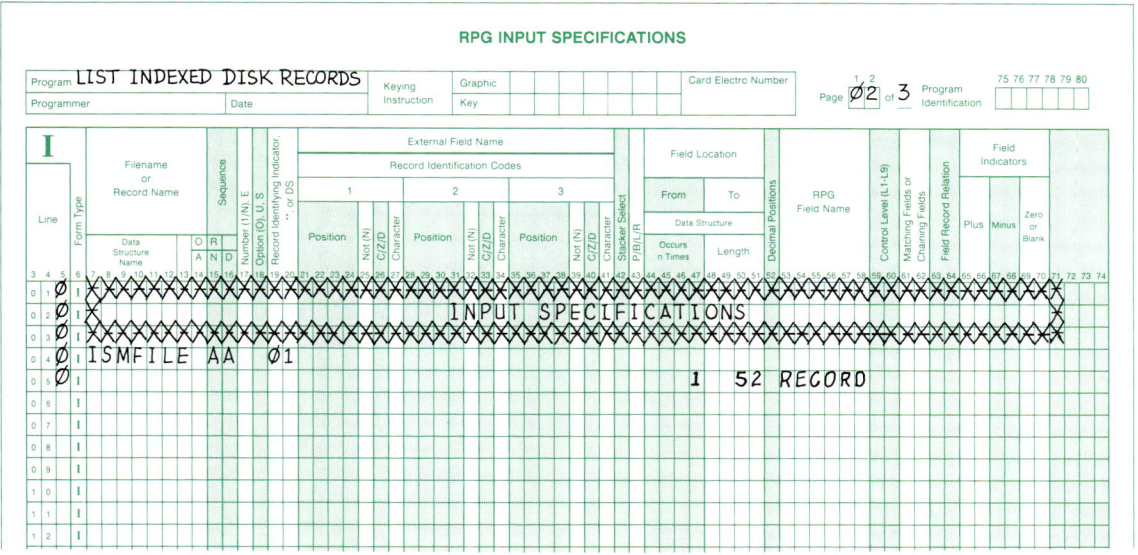

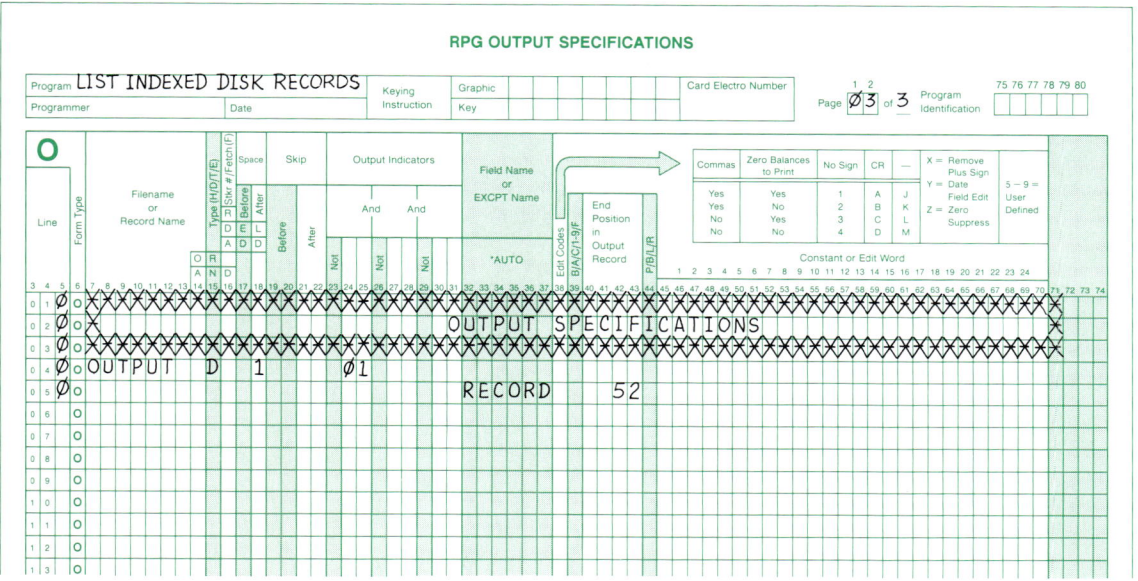

Source listing is as follows:

```
 1    01010H
 2  * 01020F*****************************************************************
 3  * 01030F*                                                                *
 4  * 01040F*              LIST INDEXED DISK RECORDS                         *
 5  * 01050F*                                                                *
 6  * 01060F*   THIS PROGRAM PRODUCES A LISTING OF THE DATA RECORDS STORED   *
 7  * 01070F*   IN THE INDEXED FILE CALLED ISMFILE.                          *
 8  * 01080F*                                                                *
 9  * 01090F*****************************************************************
10    01100FISMFILE IPE  F  520    52       9AI        1 DISK
11    01110FOUTPUT   O    F  132                         PRINTER
12  * 02010I**********************************************************
13  * 02020I*                INPUT SPECIFICATIONS                     *
14  * 02030I**********************************************************
15    02040IISMFILE AA   01
16    02050I                                    1   52 RECORD
17  * 03010O**********************************************************
18  * 03020O*               OUTPUT SPECIFICATIONS                     *
19  * 03030O**********************************************************
20    03040OOUTPUT   D  1      01
21    03050O                        RECORD     52
```

Disk Processing 417

The 52-position indexed disk record is to be printed as follows:

```
13009529475925FOX      WILLIAM       484636365530091845
36420884143785PHILLIPS ROBERT        559342463949171659
54301222242252JOHNSON  BEN           373333337033326733
54301222321663LEWIS    RITA          040669903766633791
54301222421074MONTGOMERY ALEX        041336703833324182
54301222537185SMITH    JOSEPH        819781081677732349
54301222615296BROWN    WALLACE       709336670633631628
54301222742307DUNIGAN  HENRY         932223892922334239
54301222837418JONES    WILLIAM       157777815477828411
54301222963529DELANY   JERRY         048666704566728470
54301223042630HALLECK  FRANCES       040003303700023402
54301223163741REID     PATRICIA      928958892595532329
54301223215375JACKSON  KENNETH       556327762345169896
54301223363852ALEXANDER CHARLES      049333304633328860
54301224037963HALL     GEORGE        501111150044437594
54301224121074SIPLE    CHARLES       167777816744434261
54301224215185GOODMAN  HENRY         949222194922144183
54301224312345CAMM     FRED  J       063333306333337050
54301224887307DENTON   TERRENCE      854444485444452627
54301224915141GOODSALL PHILLIP       531111153111155144
55632020142902SAWYER   DAVID         576596566381181753
55716778221472YOUNG    SAMUEL        566763268586476000
55910929987524HEPNER   ELMER         911159404263785805
57820114163708HORNE    ALBERT        779478979165972661
```

Illustrative Program

Disk Updating—Matching Records: Updated Records

Job Definition

An indexed disk record is to be updated from a sequential disk file. Both files are in social security number sequence. A report is to be printed showing the new updated record and, at the same time, the indexed disk file is to be updated.

If no matching record is found, it should be so indicated.

Input

The indexed disk file contains the following fields:

Positions	Field Description	
1–09	Social Security number	
10–11	Department number	
12–14	Clock number	
15–34	Name	
35–41	Old year-to-date gross earnings	(XXXXX.XX)
42–47	Old year-to-date withholding tax	(XXXX.XX)
48–52	Old year-to-date FICA	(XXX.XX)

The input disk record contains the following fields:

Positions	Field Description	
1–09	Social security number	
10–11	Department number	
12–14	Clock number	
62–68	Current gross earnings	(XXXXX.XX)
69–74	Current withholding tax	(XXXX.XX)
75–78	Current FICA	(XX.XX)
80–80	Code 1	

Processing

On matching fields (social security number) the following operations are to be performed:

1. The current gross earning is to be added to the old year-to-date gross earnings to find the updated year-to-date gross earnings.

2. The current withholding tax is to be added to the old year-to-date withholding tax to find the updated year-to-date withholding tax.

3. The current FICA tax is to be added to the old year-to-date FICA tax.

If the input record does not match the indexed disk record, a message is to be printed.

The indexed disk file will be updated.

Output
The Printer Spacing Chart shows how the report is formatted:

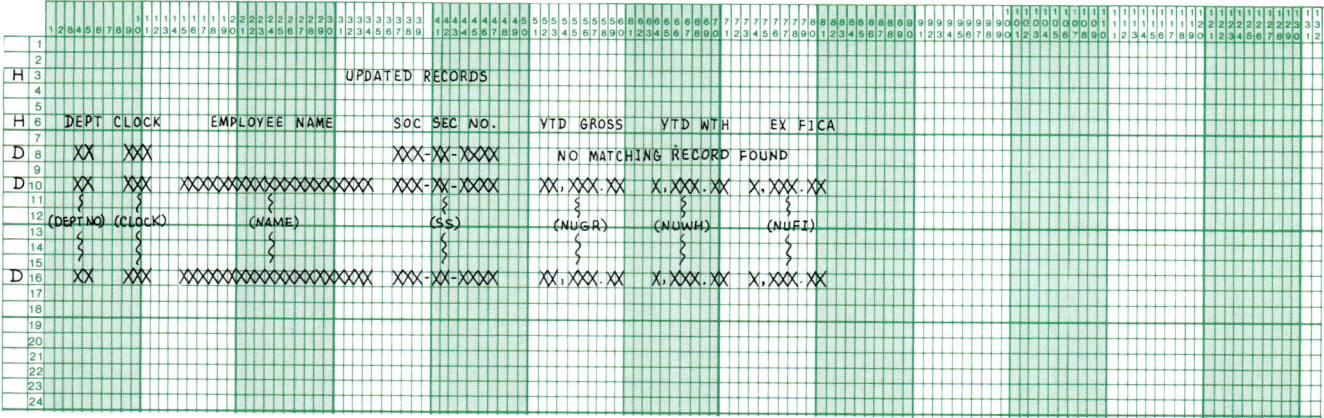

Coding sheets for Updated Records problem:

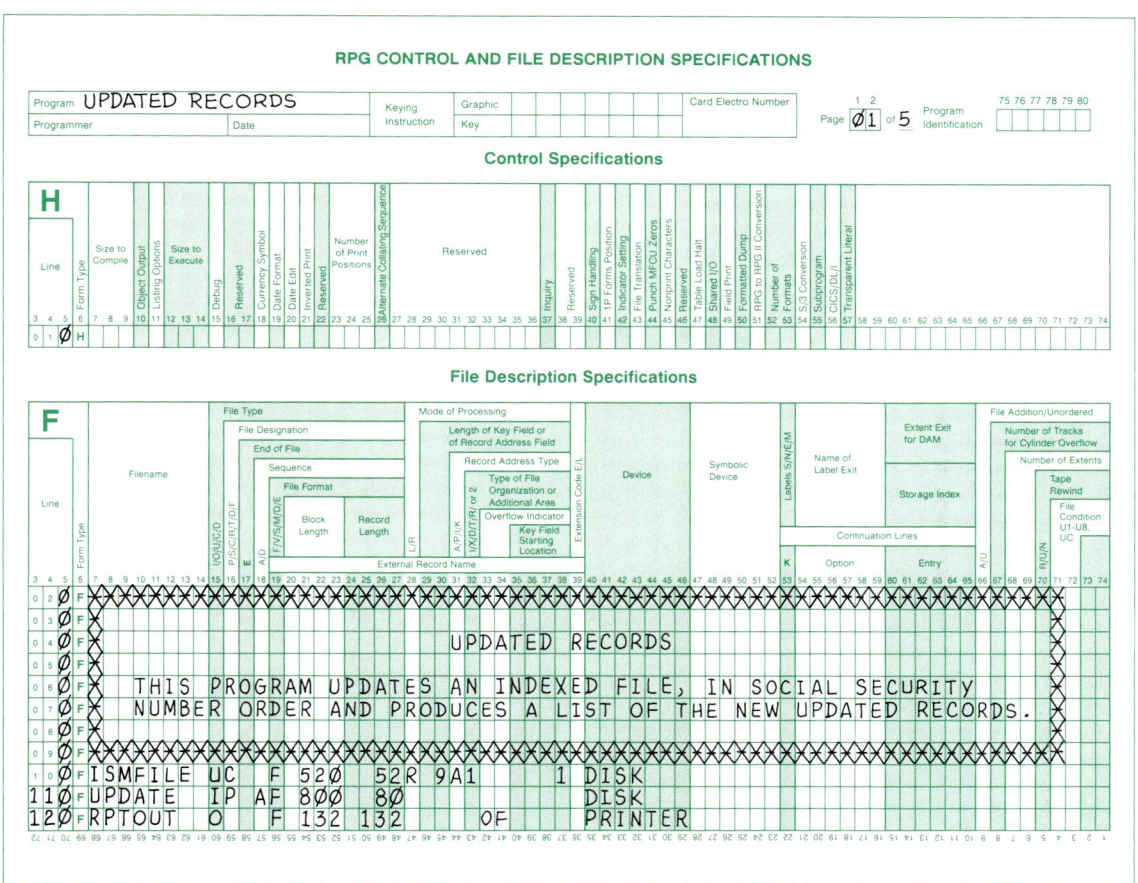

Disk Processing

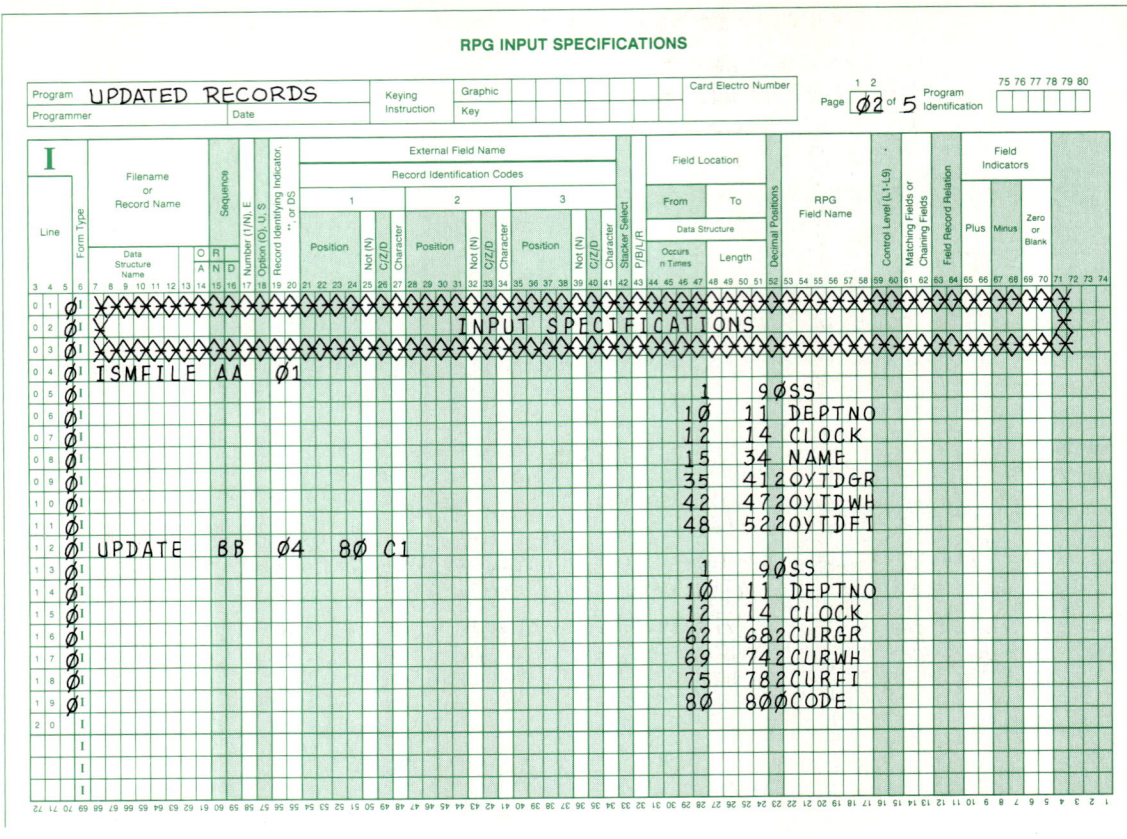
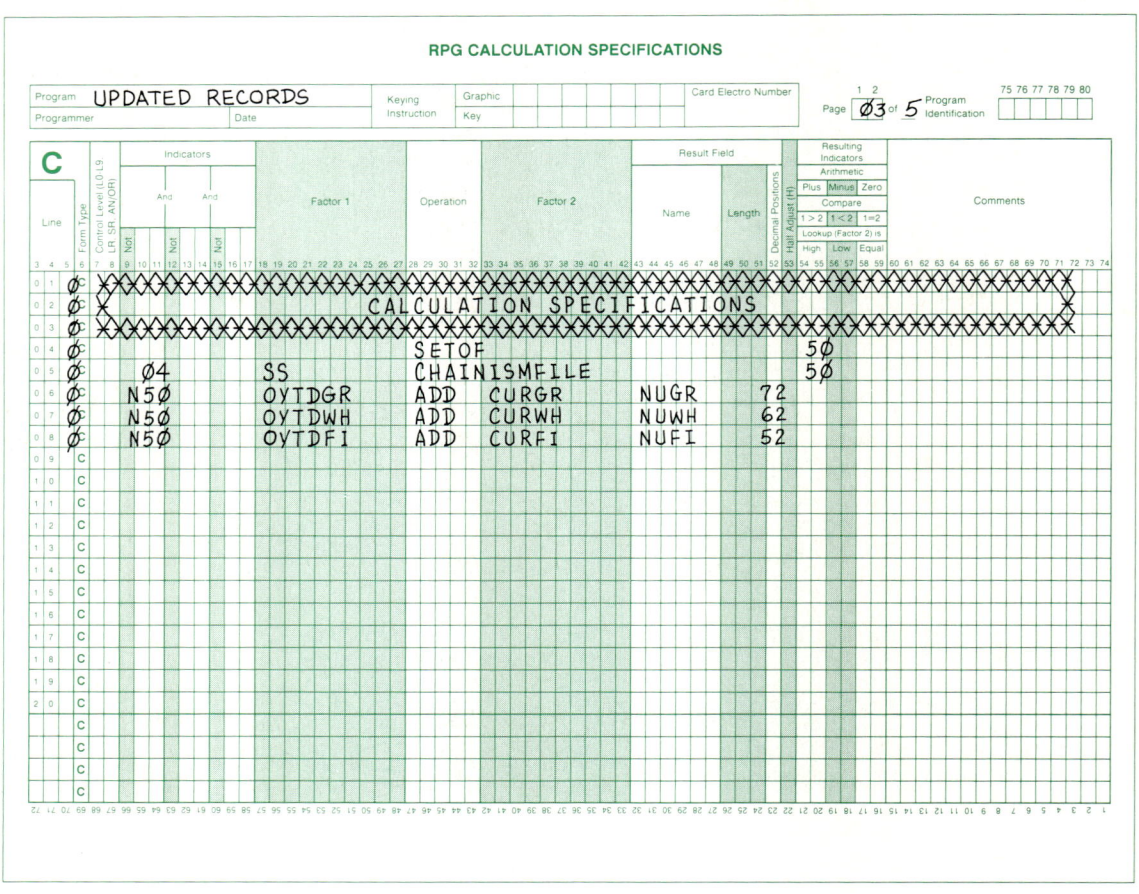

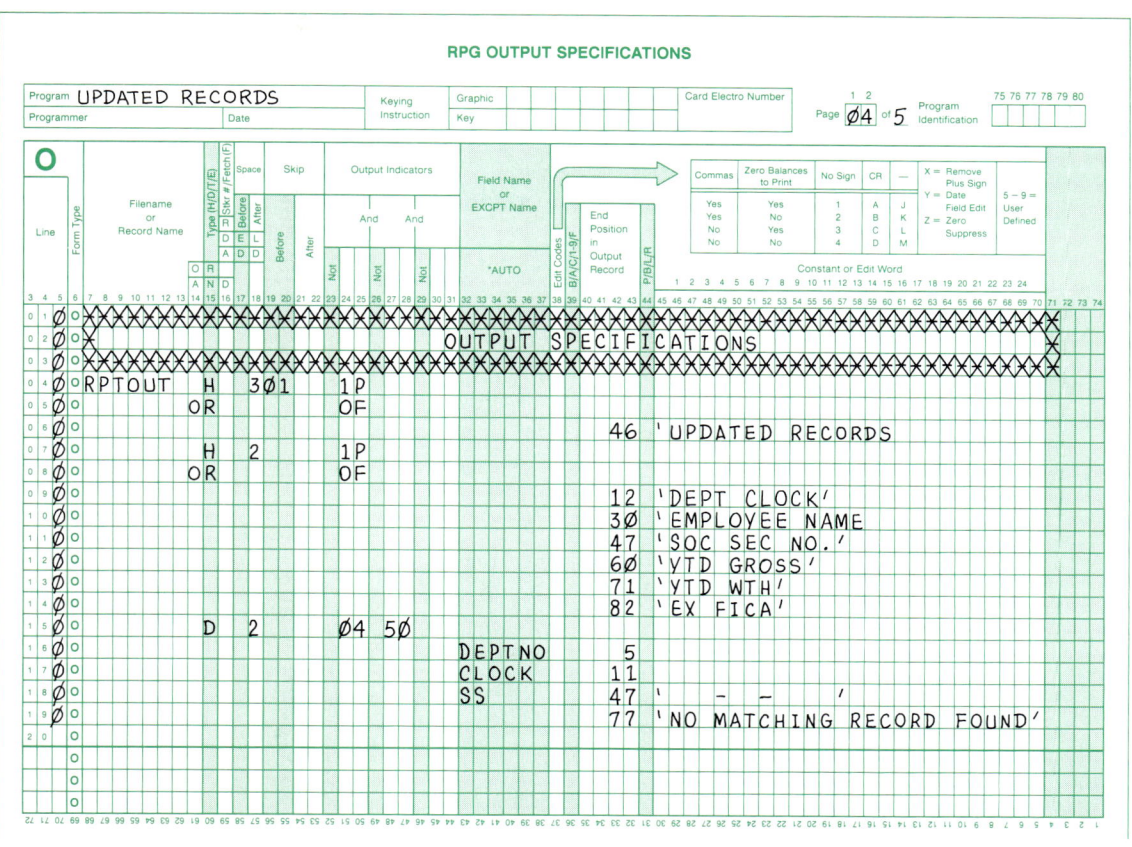
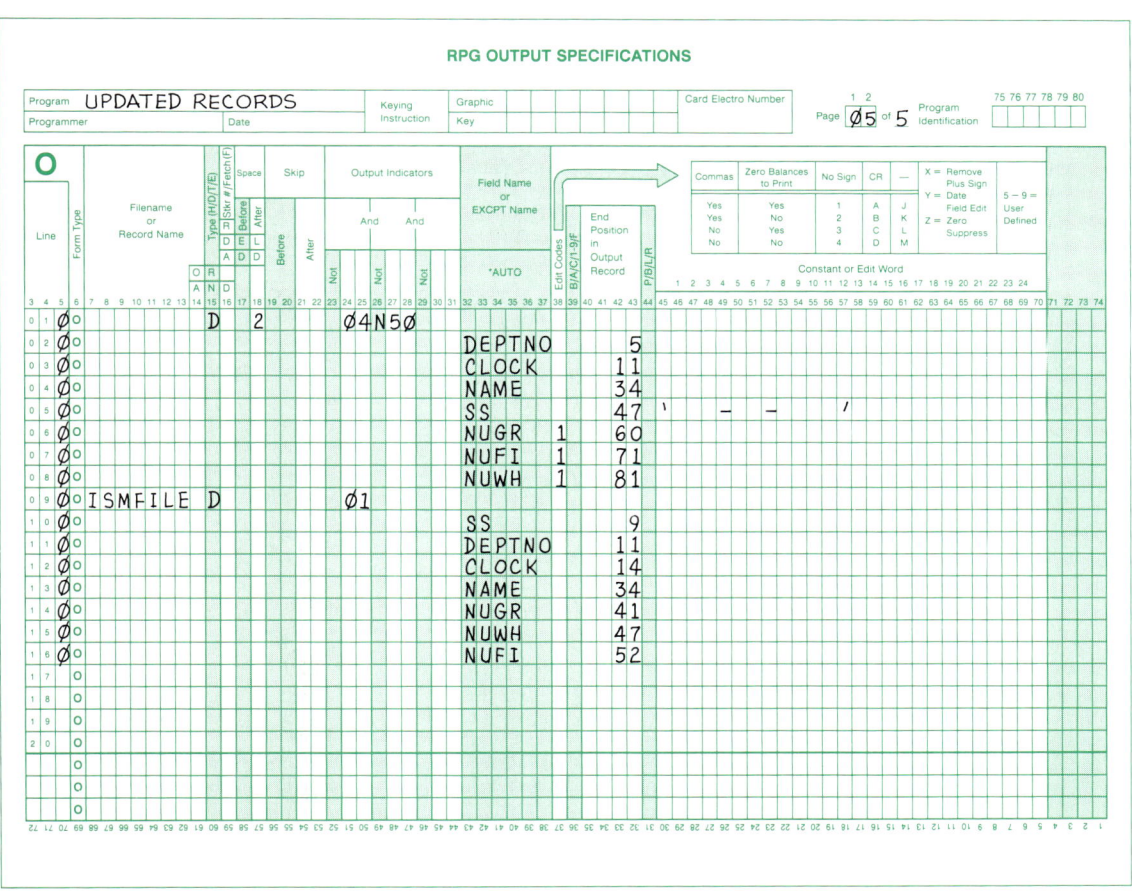

Disk Processing

The source listing is as follows:

```
1    01010H
2  * 01020F***************************************************************
3  * 01030F*                                                              *
4  * 01040F*                     UPDATED RECORDS                          *
5  * 01050F*                                                              *
6  * 01060F*   THIS PROGRAM UPDATES AN INDEXED FILE, IN SOCIAL SECURITY   *
7  * 01070F*   NUMBER ORDER AND PRODUCES A LIST OF THE NEW UPDATED RECORDS.*
8  * 01080F*                                                              *
9  * 01090F***************************************************************
10   01100FISMFILE UC  F  520    52R 9AI       1 DISK
11   01110FUPDATE   IP AF 800     80             DISK
12   01120FRPTOUT   O  F  132    132      OF     PRINTER
13 * 02010I***************************************************************
14 * 02020I*                    INPUT SPECIFICATIONS                      *
15 * 02030I***************************************************************
16   02040IISMFILE AA  01
17   02050I                                         1   90SS
18   02060I                                        10   11 DEPTNO
19   02070I                                        12   14 CLOCK
20   02080I                                        15   34 NAME
21   02090I                                        35   412OYTDGR
22   02100I                                        42   472OYTDWH
23   02110I                                        48   522OYTDFI
24   02120IUPDATE   BB  04   80 C1
25   02130I                                         1   90SS
26   02140I                                        10   11 DEPTNO
27   02150I                                        12   14 CLOCK
28   02160I                                        62   682CURGR
29   02170I                                        69   742CURWH
30   02180I                                        75   782CURFI
31   02190I                                        80   800CODE
32 * 03010C***************************************************************
33 * 03020C*                 CALCULATIONS SPECIFICATIONS                  *
34 * 03030C***************************************************************
35   03040C                    SETOF                          50
36   03050C           04    SS  CHAINISMFILE                  50
37   03060C    N50        OYTDGR  ADD  CURGR     NUGR    72
38   03070C    N50        OYTDWH  ADD  CURWH     NUWH    62
39   03080C    N50        OYTDFI  ADD  CURFI     NUFI    52
40 * 040100***************************************************************
41 * 040200*                   OUTPUT SPECIFICATIONS                      *
42 * 040300***************************************************************
43   040400ORPTOUT  H  301     1P
44   040500  OR              OF
45   040600                                    46 'UPDATED RECORDS'
46   040700         H   2     1P
47   040800  OR              OF
48   040900                                    12 'DEPT CLOCK'
49   041000                                    30 'EMPLOYEE NAME'
50   041100                                    47 'SOC SEC NO.'
51   041200                                    60 'YTD GROSS'
52   041300                                    71 'YTD WTH'
53   041400                                    82 'EX FICA'
54   041500         D   2    04 50
55   041600                          DEPTNO     5
56   041700                          CLOCK     11
57   041800                          SS        47 '  -  -  '
58   041900                                    77 'NO MATCHING RECORD FOUND'
59   050100         D   2    04N50
60   050200                          DEPTNO     5
61   050300                          CLOCK     11
62   050400                          NAME      34
63   050500                          SS        47 '  -  -  '
64   050600                          NUGR   1  60
65   050700                          NUWH   1  81
66   050800                          NUFI   1  71
67   050900OISMFILE D         01
68   051000                          SS         9
69   051100                          DEPTNO    11
70   051200                          CLOCK     25
71   051300                          NAME      34
72   051400                          NUGR      41
73   051500                          NUWH      47
74   051600                          NUFI      52
```

The updated records will be printed as follows:

```
                            UPDATED RECORDS

DEPT CLOCK    EMPLOYEE NAME    SOC SEC NO.    YTD GROSS    YTD WTH    EX FICA

 75   925   FOX     WILLIAM    130-09-5294    48,463.63    918.45   6,553.00

 43   785   7PHILLIPS ROBERT   364-20-8841    55,934.24    716.59   6,394.91

 42   252   JOHNSON  BEN       543-01-2222    37,333.33    267.33   3,703.33

 21   663   LEWIS   RITA       543-01-2223     4,066.99    337.91     376.66

 37   185   SMITH   JOSEPH     543-01-2225    81,978.10    323.49   8,167.77

 15   296   BROWN   WALLACE    543-01-2226    70,933.66    316.28   7,063.36

 42   307   DUNIGAN HENRY      543-01-2227    93,222.38    342.39   9,292.23

 37   418   JONES   WILLIAM    543-01-2228    15,777.78    284.11   1,547.78

 22   222                      543-01-2292    NO MATCHING RECORD FOUND

 77   777                      543-02-2230    NO MATCHING RECORD FOUND

 63   741   REID    PATRICIA   543-01-2231    92,895.88    323.29   9,259.55

 15   375   JACKSON KENNETH    543-01-2232    55,632.77    698.96   6,234.51

 37   963   HALL    GEORGE     543-01-2240    50,111.11    375.94   5,004.44

 22   222                      543-01-2412    NO MATCHING RECORD FOUND

 15   185   GOODMAN HENRY      543-01-2242    94,922.21    441.83   9,492.21

 87   307   DENTON  TERRENCE   543-01-2248    85,444.44    526.27   8,544.44

 15   141   GOODSALL PHILLIP   543-01-2249    53,111.11    551.44   5,311.11

 42   902   SAWYER  DAVID      556-32-0201    57,659.65    817.53   6,638.11

 21   472   YOUNG   SAMUEL     557-16-7782    56,676.32    760.00   6,858.64

 87   524   HEPNER  ELMER      559-10-9299    91,115.94    858.05     426.37

 63   708   HORNE   ALBERT     578-20-1141    77,947.89    726.61   7,916.59

 21   074   SIPLE   CHARLES    543-01-2241    16,777.78    342.61   1,674.44

 22   222                      543-01-2422    NO MATCHING RECORD FOUND
```

Questions for Review

1. What is meant by the term 'direct access'?
2. What is a direct access storage device?
3. What is a file? A record? A key? A volume?
4. Briefly describe sequential, indexed, and direct methods of data organization.
5. What is the difference between sequential and random processing?
6. How do mass storage devices make it possible to select the processing technique that will best suit the application?
7. How are records updated for a sequentially organized file on a mass storage device?
8. How does accessing a sequential mass storage file differ from accessing magnetic tape?
9. What are the major uses of sequential organization?
10. How are records retrieved in an indexed file?
11. What are the principal advantages of indexed organization?
12. How are records accessed in a direct organization file?
13. For what is a direct organization file used?
14. What are the entries used to create a sequential file?
15. Briefly describe the common functions necessary for maintenance of sequential files.
16. How is an indexed file created?
17. Briefly describe the ways an indexed file may be updated.
18. Briefly describe the use of the CHAIN operation for randomly updating records in an indexed file.
19. What entries are needed on the File Description and Calculation Specifications forms to update records in an indexed file randomly by key?
20. How may records be added to an indexed file?
21. What are the necessary entries on the File Description, Calculation Specifications, and Output Specifications forms for adding records randomly by key in an indexed file using chaining?
22. How are records added randomly by key to an indexed file without chaining?
23. How may records be added sequentially by key to an indexed file?
24. Why is it necessary to reorganize an indexed file?
25. What are some of the other ways to process indexed files?
26. What are relative record numbers and how are they used in direct file processing?
27. How does record insertion in a direct file differ from sequential or indexed file insertion?
28. What is a record address file?
29. What is meant by processing within limits?
30. How is processing performed using record address file keys?
31. What is a record address file containing record key limits and how is it created?
32. What is meant by processing sequentially within limits?
33. What are the necessary entries for a record address file?

Problems

Problem 1

Create a file of disk records. These disk file records are to be organized sequentially. The disk records shall be 72 positions long and contain the following fields. (Records are to be in blocks of 720 characters.)

Positions	Field Description
1–01	Code M
2–21	Customer name
22–41	Street address
42–61	City/State address
62–66	Zip code
67–72	Customer number

The information used to create these disk records is to be keyed from the terminal. The input fields are identical in name but have been rearranged as follows:

Positions	Field Description
1–01	Code M
2–07	Customer number
8–27	Customer name
28–47	Street address
48–67	City/State address
68–72	Zip code

Code the necessary file description, input specifications, and output specifications on the appropriate forms. Create your own names for input and output devices and any other information needed.

Output
Print the number of records loaded. This is the only printed output. Other output is a disk file.

Problem 2

Create a file of indexed records. Input records are to be read in from a sequential file of disk records.
The input file DISKIN contains the following fields:

Positions	Field Description	
1–02	Code characters X6	
3–06	Account number	(key field)
7–25	Name	
26–31	Beginning balance	(XXXX.XX)

The output file records MASTACCT are to contain the following fields:

Positions	Field Description	
1–04	Account number	(key field)
6–11	Beginning balance	(XXXX.XX)
12–17	Creation date	(UDATE)
31–49	Name	
50–50	Character B	

Code the necessary file description, input specifications, and output specifications on the appropriate forms. Create your own names for input and output devices and any other information needed.

DISKIN	RECORD LENGTH	31 CHARACTERS
	BLOCK LENGTH	310 CHARACTERS
MASTACCT	RECORD LENGTH	50 CHARACTERS
	BLOCK LENGTH	500 CHARACTERS

Output
There is no printed output; output is on disk.

Disk Processing

Problem 3

Print the contents of the indexed file created in problem 2. As part of the report, print the total amount of all the beginning balance fields in the entire file.

The output on the printer is to look like this:

REPORT OF MASTER ACCOUNTS

ACCOUNT	BALANCE	NAME
1002	$ 100.00	MONEMATERS
2116	$2,160.00	CASHINFLOW
2249	$1,728.50	BANKCREDIT
2367	$ 750.60	CASHIN
	$4,739.10	

Code the necessary file description, input specifications, calculations specifications, and output specifications on the appropriate forms. Create your own names for input and output devices and any other information needed.

The Printer Spacing Chart is as follows:

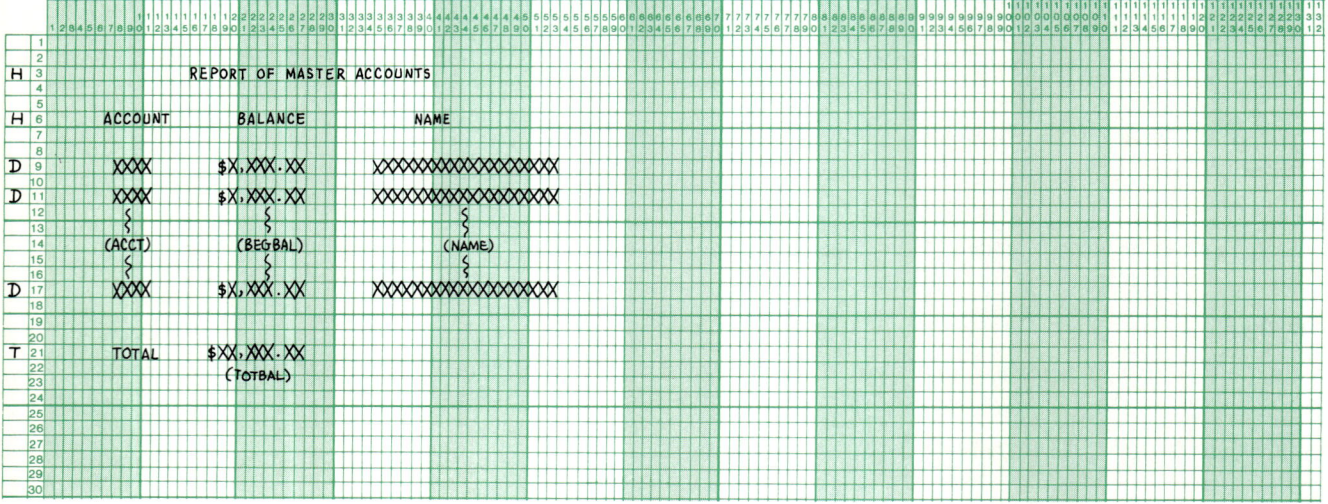

Output

Output is as follows:

```
        REPORT OF MASTER ACCOUNTS

    ACCOUNT      BALANCE         NAME

     1002        $100.00         MONEMATERS

     2116        $2,160.00       CASHINFLOW

     2249        $1,728.50       BANKCREDIT

     2367        $750.60         CASHIN


                $4,739.10
```

Problem 4

NAMEFILE, described as a chained output file on the File Description form, is to be loaded with records read from NAMES, a sequential disk file.

As each record is read from NAMES, the employee number is used as the relative record number to chain to NAMEFILE during calculations. The entire input record RECORD is written out on NAMEFILE in the relative record location corresponding to employee number.

The input record contains the employee number in positions 1–5.

Code the necessary file description, input specifications, calculations, and output specifications on the appropriate forms to random load the direct file on disk. Create your own names where necessary.

> RECORD LENGTH   80 CHARACTERS
> BLOCK LENGTH   80 CHARACTERS

Output

Print the number of records loaded. This is the only printed output. Other output is a disk file.

9 Multifile Batch Processing

Outline

Application Design Considerations
Primary Files
Secondary Files
   Processing Multiple Sequential
      Files
Multifile Processing
   Match Fields
Checking Sequence of Records
      within a File
   File Containing Only One
      Record Type
   File Containing More Than One
      Record Type
   Same Match Fields for All
      Record Types
Matching Records
   Matching Record Technique
   Matching Record Indicator
   Matching Comparisons
   Order of Processing Multiple File
      Records
   Processing Matching Records—
      Two or More Files
   Rules for Specifying Matching
      Records on Input
      Specifications
   Matching Fields
   Matching Record Entries
      on Calculation Specifications
   Matching Field Entries
      on Output Specifications
   One Record Type in Each File
   When All Records in One File
      Have Been Processed
   Use of Match Fields and Control
      Fields in the Same File

End-of-File Processing
Alternating the Order of Processing
   Files (FORCE)
   Specifying the Next File
      to Process
Read (READ)
   Processing Full Procedural
      or Demand Files (READ)
   Chaining
   Chain (CHAIN)
   Random Processing
Field Record Relation
OR Relationship
   Use with Control Fields
   Use with Matching Fields
   Use with Chaining Fields
   Use with External Indicators
      and Selective Processing

RPG incorporates powerful and convenient means of dealing with multiple, logically related input files on diverse physical media. Output files can be input files that have been updated; or, output files can be given new formats for printing or filing on appropriate media for further processing.

In order to take full advantage of RPG capabilities, the programmer must face a number of important considerations. Among these are issues of application design, and of the techniques of coordinating and controlling (collating) multiple files for both the sequential and indexed files.

Application Design Considerations

When designing and programming a minor listing application or a major multiple-file application, RPG programmers must begin with a clear conception of what they wish to achieve and what data resources are available. When dealing with existing files as inputs, the designer may be constrained by the existing file formats and the sequences in which the files are available. To avoid these constraints and to allow efficiency in the major processing, it is sometimes expedient to perform a preliminary run on an existing file for purposes of restructuring it, sorting it to a different order, or both. For new applications involving frequent processing and substantial amounts of computer time, it may be desirable to redesign existing applications to promote efficiency in the new processing of existing file data.

The immediate requirements alone should not form the entire basis for any new design. The programmer should make every effort to anticipate future requirements in terms of record expansion, file size changes, processing frequencies, and additional reports. Attention to the current and future place of the particular application within the entire data-processing system will minimize the amount of reprogramming and expensive data base modification needed over time.

Often, the RPG programmer must make trade-off decisions. For instance, a file assigned to a disk pack may be fast and easy to process. Magnetic tape, on the other hand, is a less expensive file storage medium and offers fewer problems if the file size expands significantly. Similarly, by combining several file processes in one program, some operational efficiencies may result. Factors such as these must enter into design decisions.

RPG provides a powerful set of tools to the programmer and incorporates many safeguards against oversights. Nevertheless, good application design decisions, apart from RPG itself, contribute heavily to overall efficiency.

Primary Files

In multifile batch processing, a primary file may be used to control the order in which records are selected for processing. A primary file can be an input, update, or combined file. If a program reads records from only one file, that file is the primary file. There can never be more than one primary file.

Secondary Files

Secondary files apply to programs that do multifile batch processing. A secondary file can be an input, update, or combined file. Secondary files are processed in the order in which they are written in the File Description Specifications form.

Processing Multiple Sequential Files

Within multiple sequential files, one file may be designated as primary and the other(s) as secondary. If no relationship exists between the processing of the two types of files, the primary file is completely processed before the secondary file(s). For two or more secondary files, processing occurs in the order in which the files are described on the File Description form. (See Figure 9.1.)

Figure 9.1 End-of-file processing

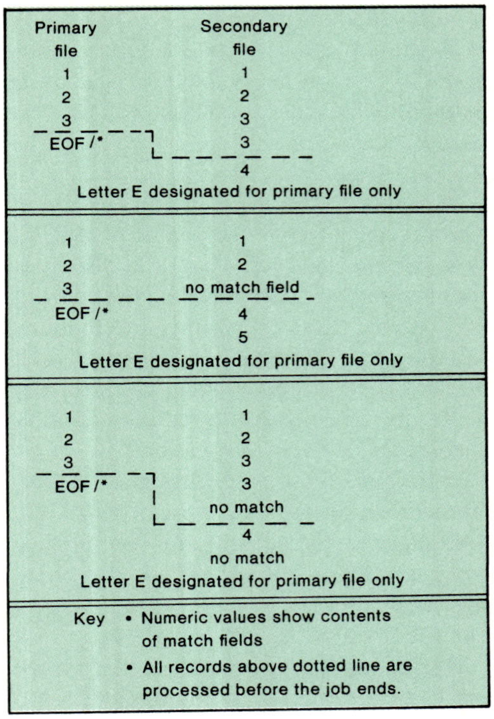

```
Primary         Secondary
 file             file
  1                1
  2                2
  3                3
 EOF/*    ┐ ┌ ─ ─ 3 ─ ─
          └ ─ ─ ─ 4
 Letter E designated for primary file only

  1                1
  2                2
  3      ─ ─ ─ no match field
 EOF/*             4
                   5
 Letter E designated for primary file only

  1                1
  2                2
  3                3
 EOF/*    ┐ ┌ ─ ─ 3
          │        no match
          └ ─ ─ ─  4
                   no match
 Letter E designated for primary file only

 Key  • Numeric values show contents
         of match fields
      • All records above dotted line are
         processed before the job ends.
```

When information (fields) from more than one file is needed to process a record, the file that controls processing is designated as primary and the others as secondary. Using the example of mailing bills, the billing transaction input file would be primary and the billing address file would be secondary. In designating a file as primary or secondary, the programmer must consider the kind of processing to be performed. For example, in a file updating that involves posting, posting occurs to the current record being processed. Other records containing values to be posted must be present by this time. The presence of the necessary records is assured by designating the file to be posted as secondary. When its matching record is present, the transactions to be posted already have been read and are available.

Multifile Processing

Multifile processing applies to programs that read records from a primary file and one or more secondary files. It is the name given to the methods by which programs select records for processing. The method used depends upon whether or not match fields are used in the records.

Match Fields

Match fields are data fields on separate records that are compared to establish a relationship between the records. Match fields perform two functions, sequence checking or matching file records, depending on whether the related records are in the same input file or in separate input type files. (An input type file can be an input, update, or combined file.)

When a primary sequential file is designated with one or more secondary sequential files, the matching fields are used for obtaining those records from secondary files that have values in their matching fields equaling values in the primary file record. When a match is found, the matching record indicator (MR) is turned on. This indicator may be used to condition calculations operations and output functions. If a sequential file record is encountered for which no matching record is found, an error may be present in the order of a file or the contents of the record. In many cases, the failure to find a matching record is a valid possibility. However, when a failure to match constitutes an error, the MR indicator is in an off state and may be used to condition such program functions as suspending the run, printing the unmatched record as an error, or initiating recovery procedures.

Figure 9.2 Sequenced files—examples

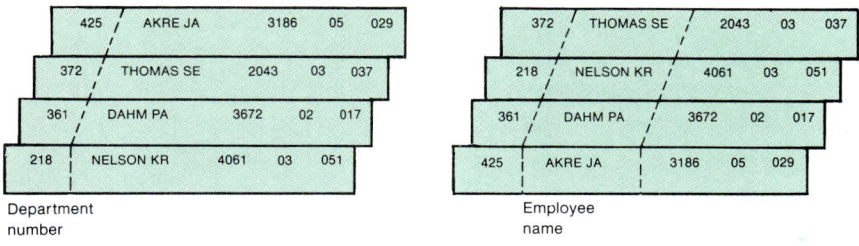

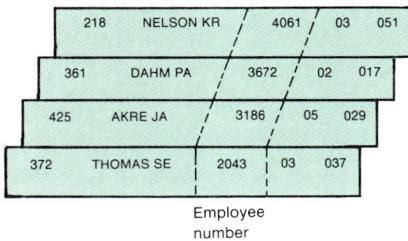

For example, suppose that in the posting of stock issue transactions to an inventory balance file an issue record is found for which there is no corresponding record in the balance file. The probable error is an improperly recorded stock number in the issue transaction. An appropriate action would be to print out the issue transaction as an exception record with a notation indicating that the record could not be processed. A balance record with no matching issue record is valid and error processing is unnecessary.

Within a file, match fields are used to check the sequence of records on which they appear. (See Figure 9.2.) The sequence checking is accomplished by comparing match fields in one record with the match fields in the next record of the same file. When two or more input files are used by a program, the sequence of each file can be checked just as sequence is checked for a single file. All files that are sequence checked by match fields must be in the same sequence, either ascending or descending.

In addition to sequence checking records within a file, match fields can also be used to establish a relationship between records in separate files. That is, match fields can be used to match records from two or more input type files to determine which record is to be processed on the current cycle. If two files are used in the same job and the programmer does not wish to specify the order of processing, the primary file is completely processed first. Only then are records from secondary files processed. If the programmer specifies that the order of processing is to be determined by comparing the contents of match fields, those records from secondary files that are related to a record in the primary file will be processed before the next primary record.

Processing more than one input type file, with or without match fields, is termed multifile processing. Selecting records from more than one file based on the contents of match fields is known as multifile processing by matching records.

Multifile processing is commonly used for jobs in which data files are set up to contain only a certain type of information. For example, a master payroll file might contain data that does not change often, such as an employee's pay rate. Another payroll file could contain records that change each week; the number of hours worked in the week is such an example. To produce a paycheck or other report, information from both files must be read. Furthermore, the records from the two files must be processed in a particular order. Matching records can be used both to determine which record to process on each program cycle and to sequence check the records within each file.

Figure 9.3 Assigning a match field for sequence checking—example

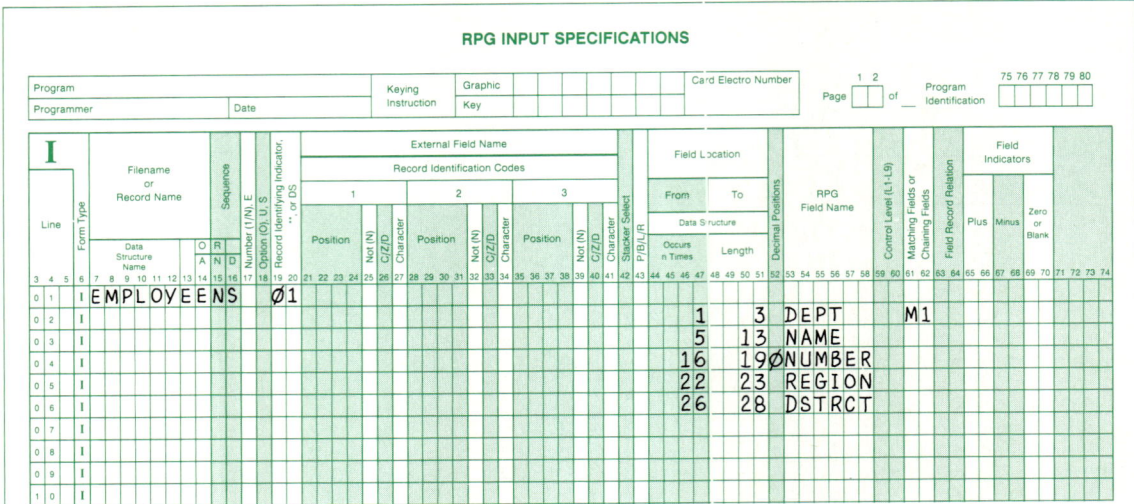

Checking Sequence of Records within a File

Two situations are possible in the sequence checking of records within a file: the file may contain only one record type, or the file may contain more than one record type.

File Containing Only One Record Type

An *A* or a *D* entry position 18 of a File Description form indicates that the records in the file described are to be in sequence. Before the program can check the sequence of records in a file, the field(s) that are to determine the order must be specified. The fields on which the sequence is to be checked (the match fields) are identified on the Input Specifications form by coding one of the entries M1–M9 in positions 61–62. (See Figure 9.3.)

Processing halts when the first record out of sequence is read. The order of the records can then be corrected to continue processing. Note, however, that only an error in the direction of sequence is detected. When sequence checking a file with match fields, RPG does not cause the processing to stop when a duplicate match field is read. This can be accomplished, however, by coding the sequence check using calculation specifications.

Records within a file may be sequenced on the basis of one or more data fields. Up to nine fields may be used by assigning one of the entries M1–M9 to each match field.

When more than one match field to check sequence is specified, the program considers all the match fields to be one continuous field, even though the fields may not be adjacent in a record. For this reason, all match fields assigned to a particular record type are considered to have the same type of data (alphameric or numeric). The individual fields are checked in order according to the level of the match field entry assigned to the field. M1 is the lowest level; M9 is the highest and is considered the most important. (See Figure 9.4.)

File Containing More Than One Record Type

A particular match field may not always be in the same record position in two different record types. The program must be told where to locate match fields for each record type.

Fields from different record types that have been assigned the same match value may have the same name.

If match fields are assigned to more than one record type in a job, all of the records (with match fields) must be assigned the same number of match fields. Furthermore, all match fields (on different record types) that are given the same value (M1–M9) must be the same length. Thus, all M1 fields must be the same length, all M2 fields must be the same length, and so on. This, of course, means that the total length of the match fields must be the same for each of the records. (See Figure 9.5.)

Figure 9.4 Sequence checking on more than one match field—example

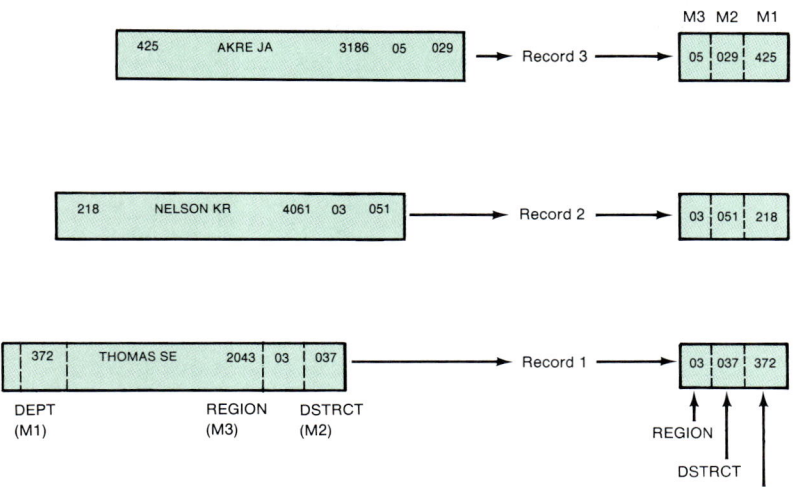

Assigning More than One Match Field for Sequence Checking

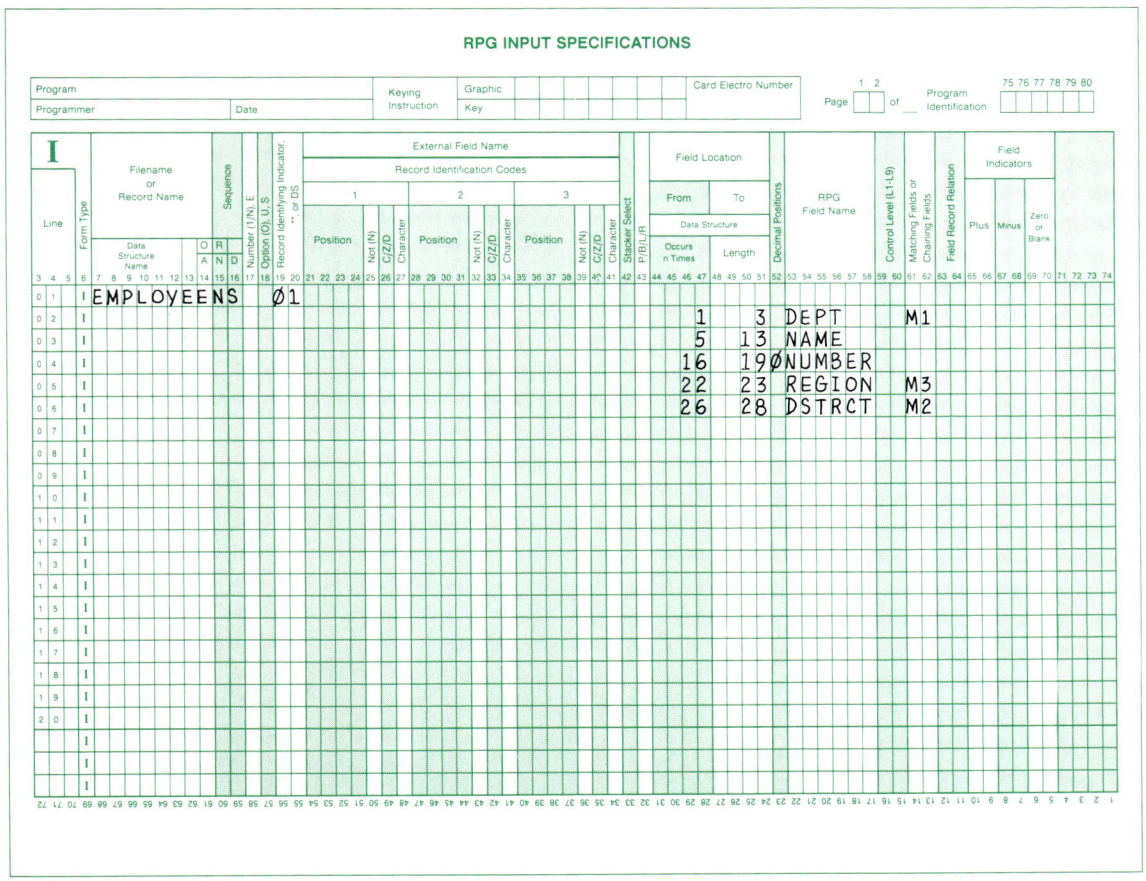

Multiple Batch Processing   433

Figure 9.5 Assigning match fields to different record types—example

Match Fields in Different Locations on Two Records

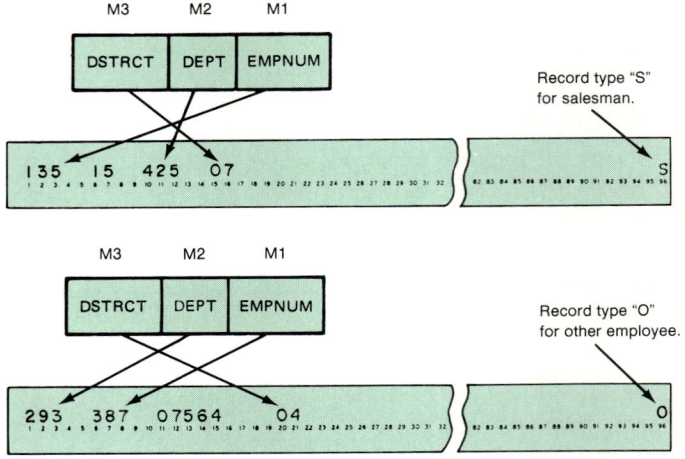

Assigning Match Fields to Different Record Types

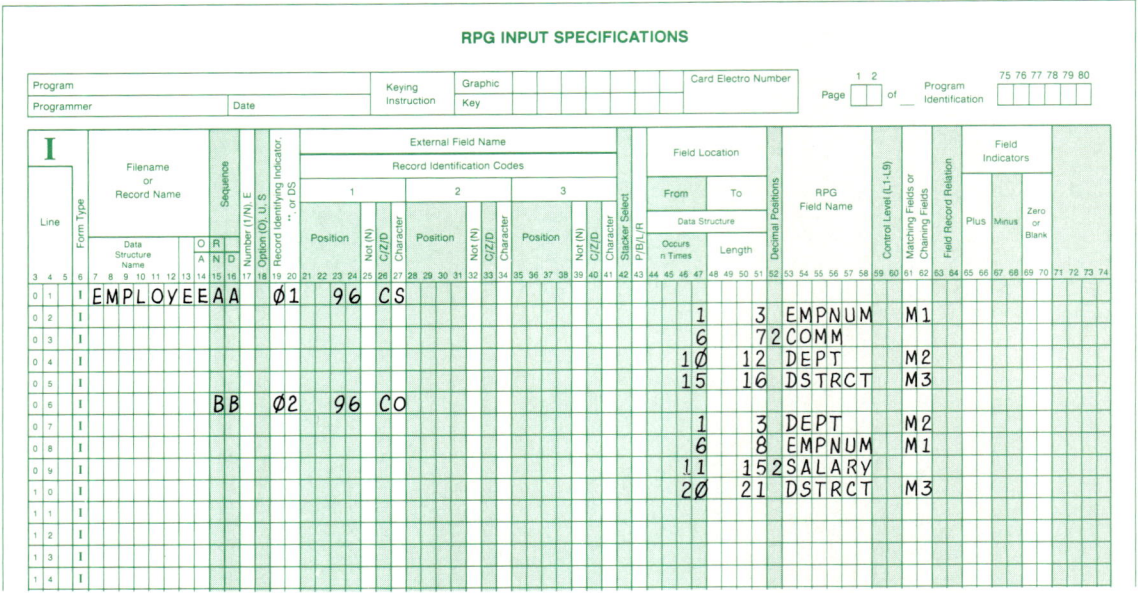

Same Match Fields for All Record Types

Often, however, the programmer may find that although there are different record types in a file, many of the fields are the same for all record types. That is, many fields have the same name, contain the same type of data, and are found in the same positions in all record types in the file.

When only a few fields differ, record types can be described on the Input Specifications form in an OR relationship. Instead of using separate sets of input specifications, common fields need to be described only once. Entries under field record relation (positions 63–64) can then identify records that are unique to a particular record type. All fields that are the same for all record types are described first. Next, all fields related to a particular record type are described. Finally, fields related to one or the other record type are specified.

Since they are described only once on the Input Specifications form without any field record relation entries, the match field entries need be assigned only once. When record types are described in an OR relationship and a match field entry is assigned to a field without any field record relation entry, the match field will be used for all record types. (See Figure 9.6.)

Figure 9.6 Assigning match fields once for two record types—example

Same Match Fields for Both Record Types

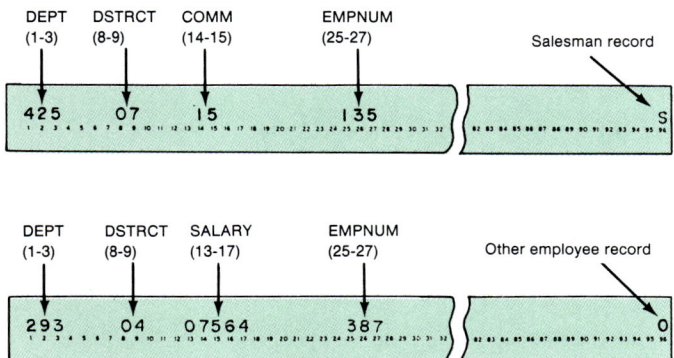

Assigning Match Fields Once for Two Record Types

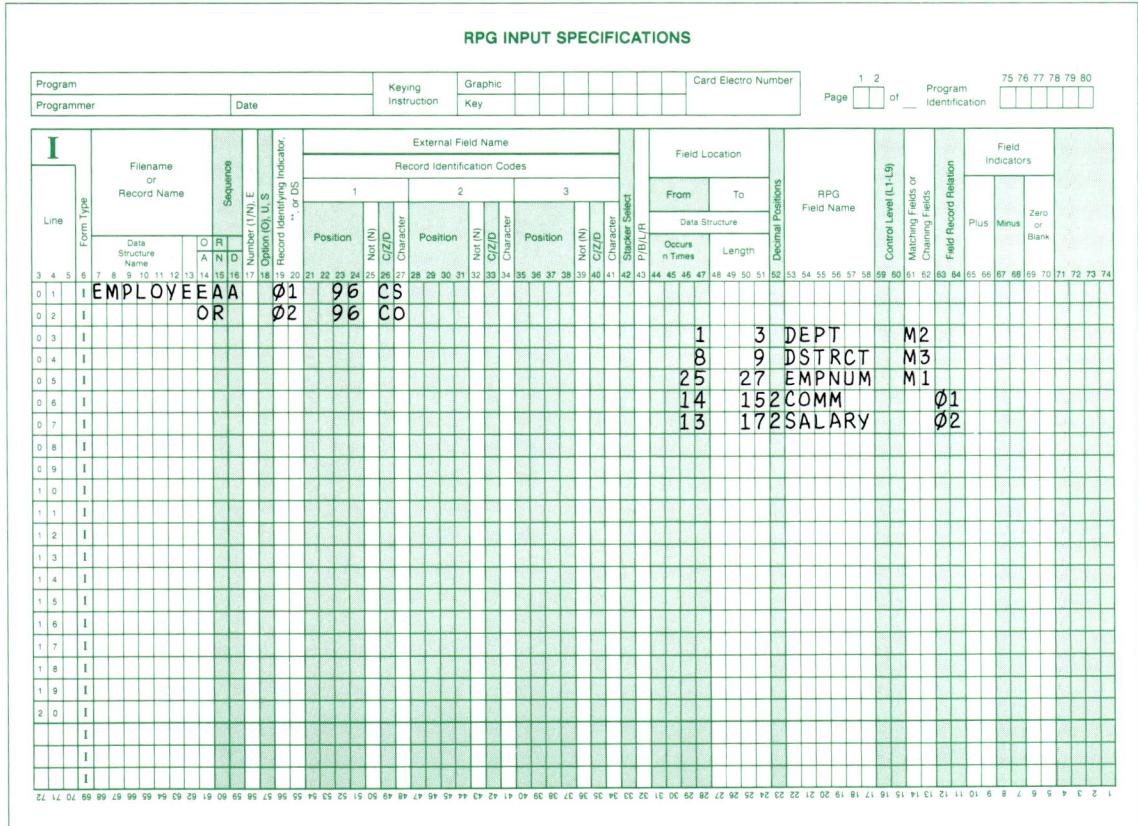

Matching Records

Many jobs require the use of two related input files. For example, invoices may be prepared using data from a name and address file to print headings while data from a transactions file may be used to print detail lines.

There must be a method of matching the name and address records for a customer with the transaction records. Part of the data in each record in each file will be some form of customer identification, usually a customer number. When the customer number from a record in the name and address file matches (is the same as) that from a record in the transactions file, the matching record indicator (MR) is turned on automatically. This indicator is then used to control calculations and output for the records that match. (See Figure 9.7.)

Multiple Batch Processing   435

Figure 9.7 Matching SALES records with related ITEM records to produce a printed report—example

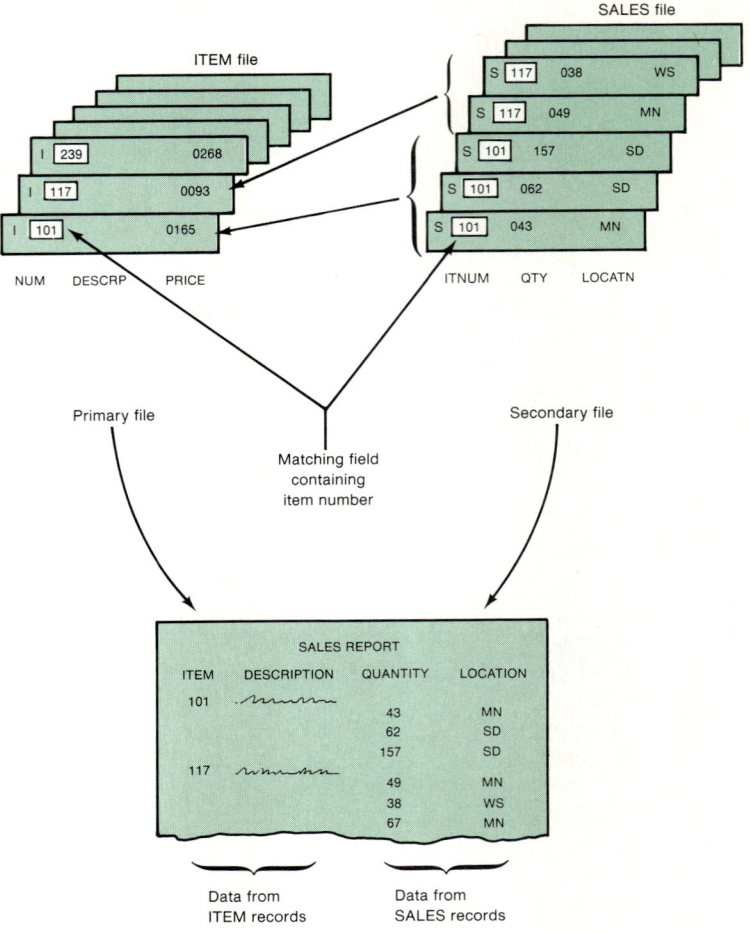

Notes on the Illustration

The above figure shows a weekly sales report to be printed, which is used to determine which items are selling best at which location. A SALES file contains records of individual items sold, giving quantity and location.

The description of each item, however, must be obtained from an ITEM master file. The ITEM master file consists of one ITEM record for each item in stock.

All ITEM records are in one format and are identified by the character I in position 1. All records in the SALES file are identified by an S in position 1 and are also in one format.

The SALES record for a particular item can be associated with the related ITEM master record by a common match field containing the item number.

In order to code for matching record jobs, the files and the fields in the records involved must be analyzed. It is also important to understand the logic RPG uses to select the records from each file for processing and how the matching record indicator is used to control calculations and output. (See Figure 9.8.)

Both input files in a two-file job must be described on the File Description form.

There are occasions when one of the matched files may be exhausted before the other. An invoicing situation is one example. If all of the transaction records have been processed, it would be convenient to stop the job even though there may be some name and address records left. This can be done by entering *E* in position 17 (end-of-file) on the File Description form for the transaction file. (See Figure 9.9.)

If files are to be matched, they must be arranged so that the data in the matching fields are in either ascending or descending order. Both files must be in the same order.

Figure 9.8 Logic of matching records

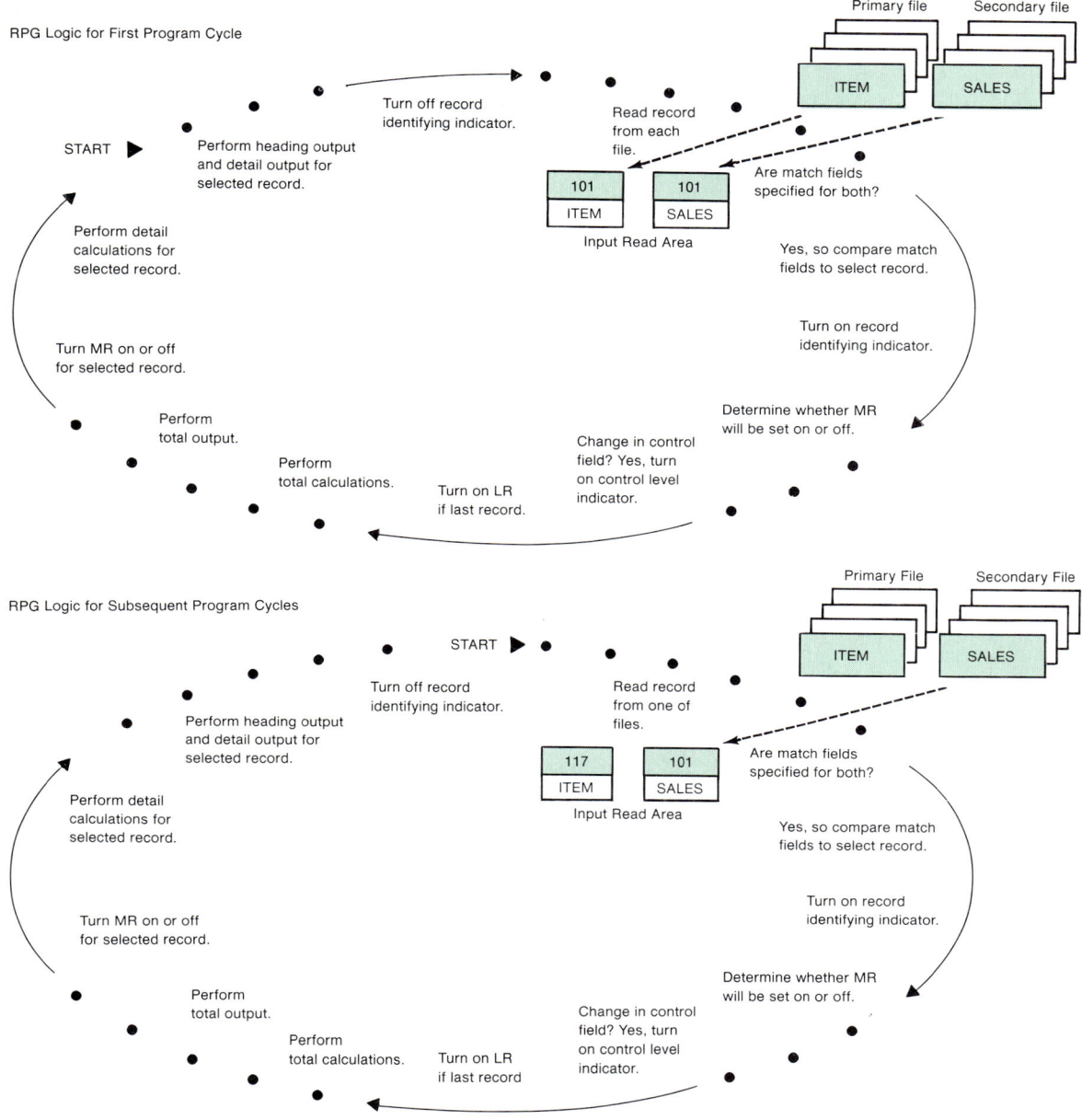

Notes on the Illustration

At the beginning of the first program cycle, a record is read from each file. The first step is to determine which record to process. The program determines if match fields are specified for both record types. In this case, both the ITEM record and the SALES record contain an M1 field.

The match fields from each file are then compared to see which is lower in sequence. (If the files had been in descending sequence, the program would check for the highest field match field.) In this case, neither field is lower, as the match fields on the primary and secondary records are both 101. When match fields from the two files are the same, the record from the primary file is always selected for processing.

The MR indicator is turned on to indicate that the matching record condition exists. The program knows which operations are to be performed depending on the status of the indicators.

Once the processing is completed for the record, the record identifying indicator is turned off, and the entire cycle will be repeated for each record processed.

Multiple Batch Processing

Figure 9.9 End-of-file indication

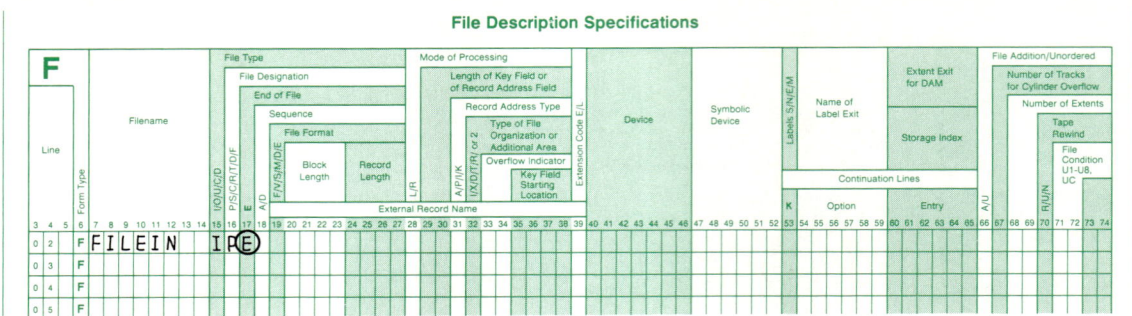

Matching Record Technique

Interrelated multiple files are processed by means of the matching record technique. The matching field entries (positions 61–62 on the Input Specifications form) determine when records of a secondary file are to be processed. (See Figure 9.10.) The following rules apply to matching field entries:

1. There can be from one to nine matching field specification entries (M1–M9) per record.

2. The locations of the matching fields within a record type of a file must be the same for all records of that type.

Figure 9.10 Specifications for matching records job—example

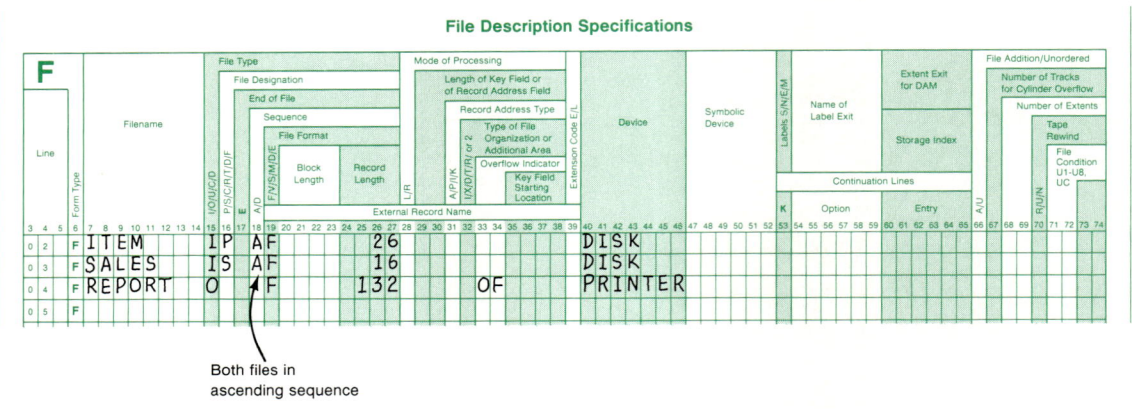

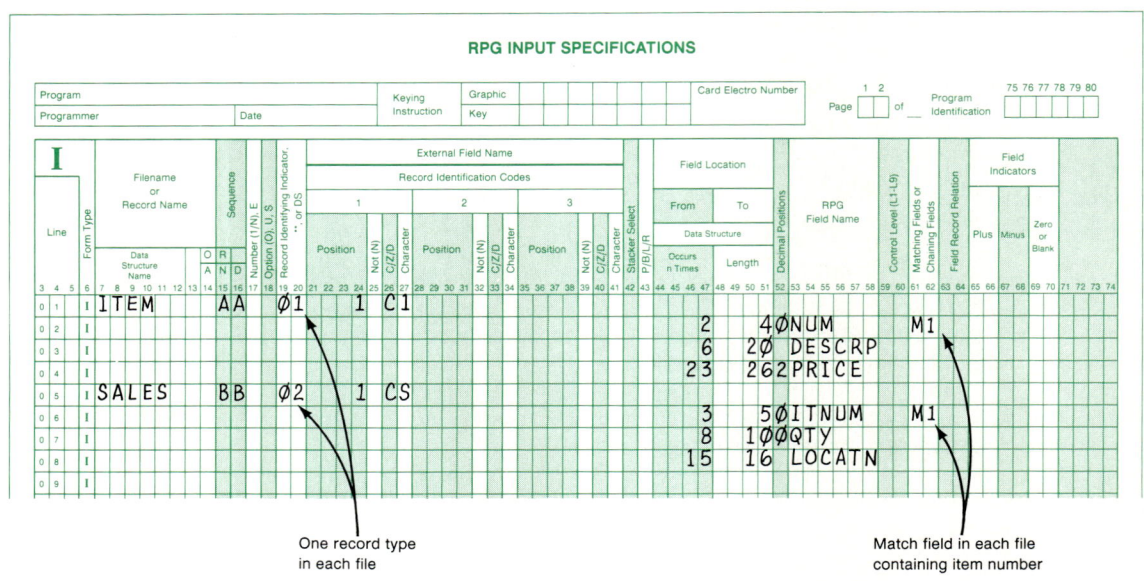

Figure 9.10 continued

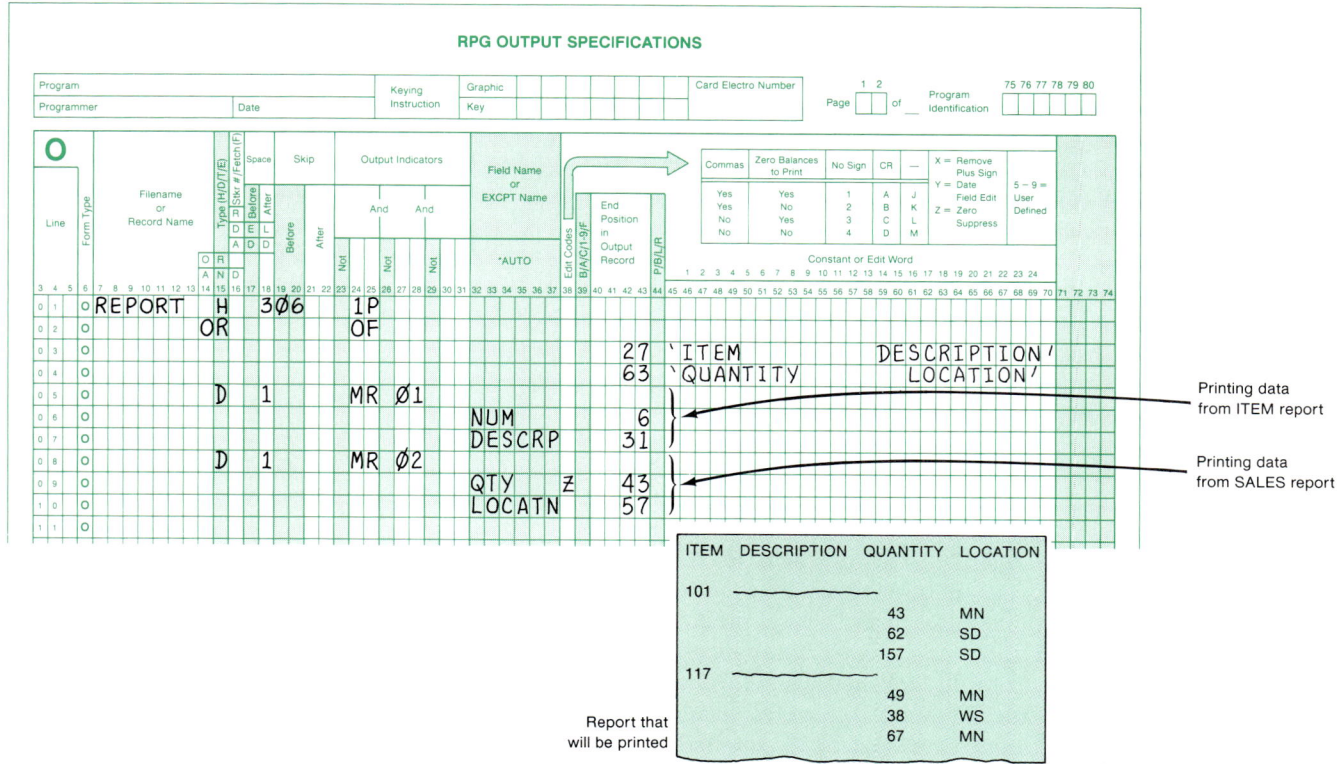

Notes on the Coding

Since the data from the two input files is only to be printed, calculation specifications are not necessary.

The File Description form defines the two input files to be used in matching, as well as the printer file on which the report is to be printed. Notice that the two input files must be specified as being the same sequence (A in position 18). The P and S in position 16 indicate to the system whether an input type file is to be considered as a primary or secondary file. The File Description specifications also associate each input file with a particular device.

The contents of the two input files are described in the Input form, with a separate set of specifications for each file. Record identifying 01 will turn on if an ITEM record is selected for processing; indicator 02 will turn on if a SALES record is selected. The single match field in each file is specified by assigning the M1 entry in positions 61-62.

Lines 01-04 of the Output form specify the headings to be printed at the top of each page of the report. The 01 record identifying indicator is on whenever an ITEM record is being processed. Furthermore, ITEM records are processed only if a matching record condition exists (MR on). Therefore, conditioning and the printing of the item number and description by MR and 01 ensures that the information is coming from the ITEM record.

The quantity and location are to be printed only when a SALES record is being processed. Because the MR indicator is on during the processing of both ITEM records and SALES records, it isn't sufficient to condition this output line only on the basis of MR. Therefore, the printing of quantity and location is conditioned by both the MR indicator and the 02 record identifying indicator.

In this case, calculation specifications are not required. However, if calculations are required and are to be performed only if a matching (or not matching) record condition exists, calculations must also be conditioned by the MR (or NMR) indicator.

Multiple Batch Processing

3. The locations of the matching fields in different record types may be different.
4. Not all record types in a file must have a matching field.
5. The same number of matching field entries must be specified for records of two or more files being matched.
6. The combined lengths of the matching fields for a given record must equal the combined lengths for any record to be matched.
7. The combined length must not exceed 256 bytes.
8. If matching fields are specified for a single input file, they are used in sequence checking the file.

Matching Record Indicator

The matching record indicator (MR) is turned on when a match occurs among records of a primary file and secondary file(s). This indicator may be used to condition calculation operations and output functions specified on the Calculation Specifications form and Output Specifications form. The MR indicator remains on during the complete processing of the record and is turned off after all calculations and output specified for this record are completed.

If no matching occurs among records of a primary file and secondary file(s), the MR indicator is not turned on. Its off status may condition calculations upon unmatched records and may condition selection of unmatched records for output.

The matching fields entry can be used even though not all of the record types in the file are to be matched. Record types that are not to be matched have no matching fields entry on the Input Specifications form. The object program makes no matching check against these records. These records are processed immediately after all records matched previously have been processed.

Matching Comparisons

If there is more than one matching fields entry for a record, the codes M1–M9 must be assigned in the order of the significance of the match fields. M1 is assigned to the least significant field and M2–M9 are assigned in turn to the fields of increasing significance. If a matching field in any record is defined as numeric, the fields at that same level (i.e., having the same value as Mn) will be treated as numeric in all records to be matched. If all fields at a given level are defined as alphameric, they will be compared logically.

Order of Processing Multiple File Records

Four possibilities may result from the processing of records in primary and secondary files:

1. A matching primary record
2. A matching secondary record
3. An unmatched primary record
4. An unmatched secondary record

Figure 9.11 illustrates the order of processing that the object program follows for two files in ascending sequence. For files in descending sequence the order is inverted.

The rule for the order of processing is that when records match, the primary file record is processed first. When the records do not match, the first record in sequence is processed first. Matching records of additional secondary files are processed in the order of specification of the files on the File Description form. Records having no designated matching fields are processed before those with matching fields.

As specifications for multiple-file processing applications are prepared the programmer should reference the RPG standard object program logic and the place of the program within it. A flowchart in appendix B shows the main logic flow patterns. Familiarity with the logical flow will permit proper designation of fields as primary and secondary and will help in determining the correct order of specification secondaries. Familiarity with object program logical flow also helps in preparing specifications for nonsequential processing of files on disk, both alone and together with sequentially processed files.

Figure 9.11 Processing two files by matching fields—example

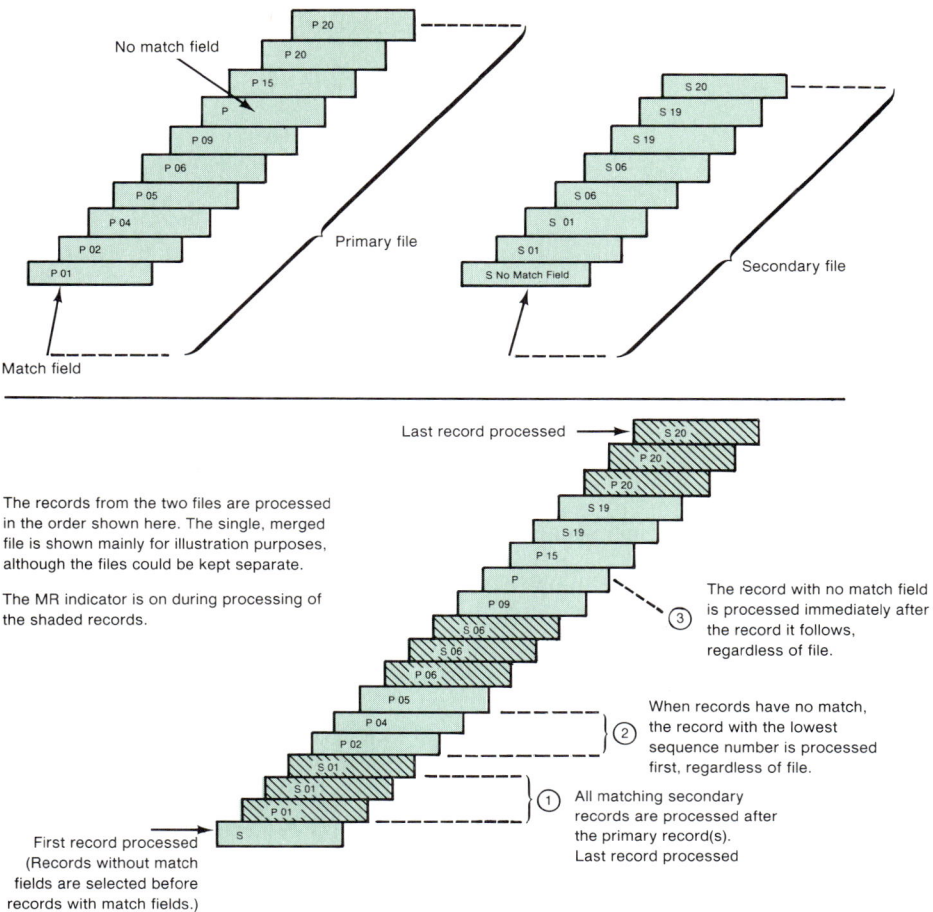

Processing Matching Records—Two or More Files

1. Whenever a record from the primary file matches a record from the secondary file, the primary file record is processed first. The matching secondary file record is then processed unless another file is forced. The record identifying indicator, which identifies the record type just selected, is on at the time the record is processed. This indicator is often used to control the type of processing that takes place.

2. Whenever records from ascending files do not match, the record with the lowest match field content is processed first. Whenever records from descending files do not match, the record with the highest match field content is processed first.

3. A record type with no matching field specification is processed immediately after the record it follows. The MR indicator is turned off. If this record type is first in the file, it is processed first even if it is not in the primary file.

4. The matching of records makes it possible to enter data from primary records into their matching secondary records since the primary record is processed before the matching secondary. However, the transfer of data from secondary records into matching primary records can only be done through look ahead fields.

Multiple Batch Processing

Rules for Specifying Matching Records on Input Specifications

1. The same number of matching fields must be specified for each record.
2. The same matching fields entries must be used for each record.
3. Fields given the same matching fields entry must be the same length.
4. Because field names are ignored in matching, matching fields may have the same name in each record.
5. Matching fields may be either alphameric or numeric.

Matching Fields (Positions 61–62)

1. Entries are M1–M9.
2. Up to nine fields in each record may be specified for matching.
3. The highest number must be assigned to the most significant field.

Matching Record Entries on Calculation Specifications

MR (matching record indicator) is the only new entry required on the Calculation Specifications form for matching record operations in which calculations are to be performed for matching records only. MR is the special indicator that is switched on when records match. Therefore, all detail calculations that are to be done for matching records only must be controlled by MR. MR may be used alone or in combination with other indicators.

Once a primary record and a secondary record have been processed, the storage areas will contain data from both a primary record and a secondary record. Data from both records are available for processing even though the records may not match each other. To avoid performing calculations with the wrong data or performing the same calculation twice, a simple rule must be followed when assigning indicators to calculations with matched records.

Rule: If all data required for calculations are available on one record, assign MR and the record identifying indicator for that record. If data are required from both a primary and a secondary record (or from result fields) assign MR and the record identifying indicator for the secondary record.

Matching Field Entries on Output Specifications

The coding of matching record output is similar to that for matching record calculations. The special indicator MR is entered under the heading Output Indicators when output is to be produced for matching records only. If all data required for an output record are available on one record, assign MR and the record identifying indicator for that record. If data are required from both a primary and a secondary record (or from result fields), assign MR and the record identifying indicator for the secondary record. (See Figure 9.12.)

Figure 9.12 Matching record—example

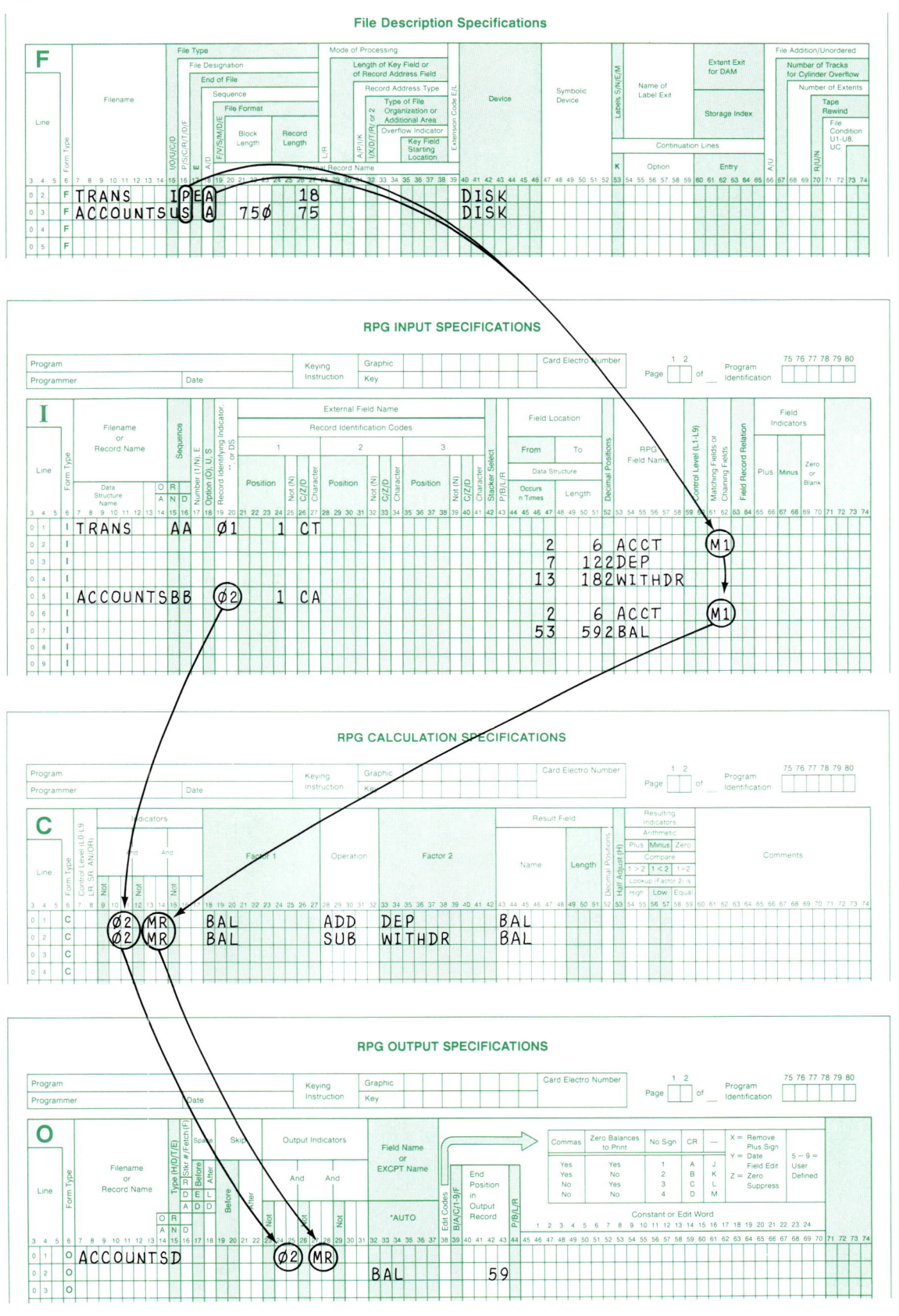

Multiple Batch Processing 443

Figure 9.12 continued

Notes on the coding

The problem is to update customer records in a sequentially organized file by calculating a new account balance for each matching record. Transaction records are in a sequentially organized file. Both files are in ascending sequence by account number.

To calculate the new balance, add the deposit value and subtract the withdrawal value.

The TRANS file contains eighteen characters, including the code T, account number, deposit amount, and withdrawal account. (Both amounts include two decimal positions).

The accounts file contains seventy-five characters, including the code A, account number, and accounts balance, including two decimal positions.

One Record Type in Each File

One of the most common forms of multifile processing involves using one file to obtain data from another file. At the beginning of the first program cycle, a record is read from each file. The first step is to determine which record to process. The program determines if match fields are specified for both record types. When match fields from the two files are the same, the record from the primary file is always selected for processing.

Once a record is selected for processing and the record identifying indicator is turned on, the program determines whether the MR should be turned on during processing of the record. If the match fields are equal, a matching record condition exists. The MR indicator is not turned on yet because the selected record is not yet ready to be processed.

First, the program checks to see if any total operations are to be performed for previously processed records. Total calculations and total output are performed only if control fields change or if the last record indicator in the file has already been processed (LR on). If neither condition exists, the MR indicator is turned on to indicate that the matching record condition exists. Now the program is ready to perform the detail operations for the record that was selected for processing.

When the primary file contains more than one matching record, all matched primary file records are processed first followed by all matched secondary file records. (See Figure 9.13.)

When All Records in One File Have Been Processed

When using two or more input type data files in a job, end-of-file is always reached in one file before all the records in the other file have been processed. This is because the matching record function can only select one record at a time for processing. Furthermore, files often contain unequal numbers of records.

In multifile processing, the programmer usually wishes the job to continue until all records from all files have been processed. RPG logic will do this.

The last record indicator (LR) is not turned on until the last record in the last file is read. In multifile processing, however, reading a last record indicator record from one file does not necessarily mean that all records from all files have been processed. Thus the program must determine if the end of that file has previously been reached in the other file(s).

In other multifile jobs, the programmer may want the job ended when a certain file has been completely processed, even if records remain in another file. By entering an *E* in position 17 of the File Description Specifications form, the programmer can specify which file is to end the job. (See Figure 9.14.)

In a matching records job, specifying the end-of-file entry for a particular file will not always cause processing to end as soon as the last record of that file is processed. If the file that has not been completely processed contains records that match the last record processed from the completed file, the matching records will be processed before the job is ended. Furthermore, processing will continue for any records without match fields until the next record with a match field is read.

Figure 9.13 More than one primary file record with same match field—example

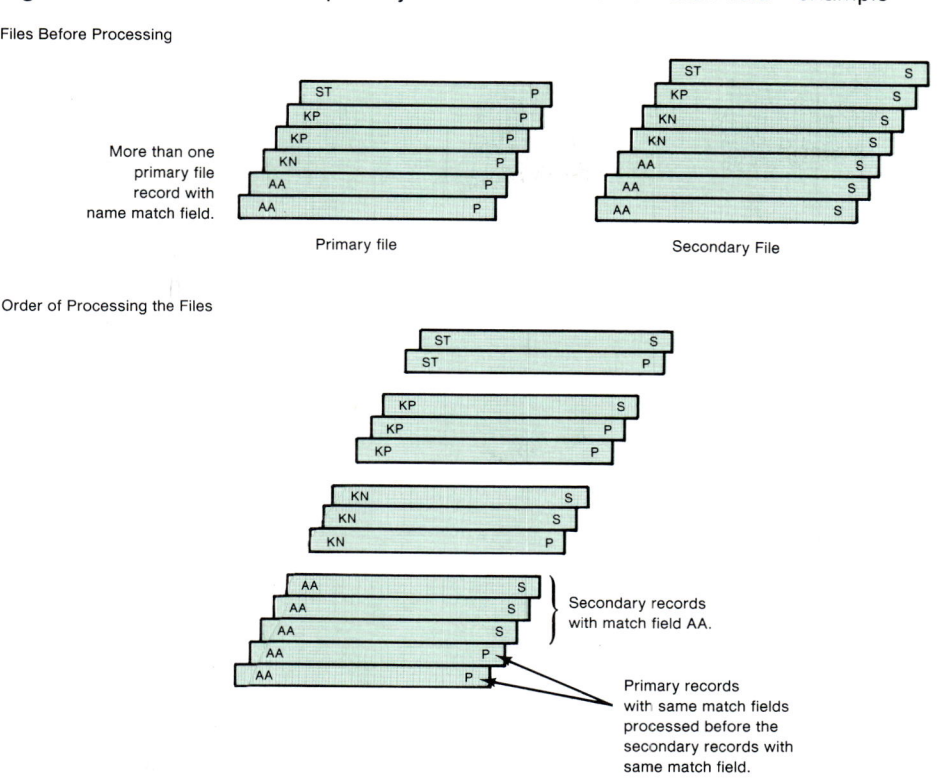

Figure 9.14 Specifying when processing is to stop in a matching records job—example

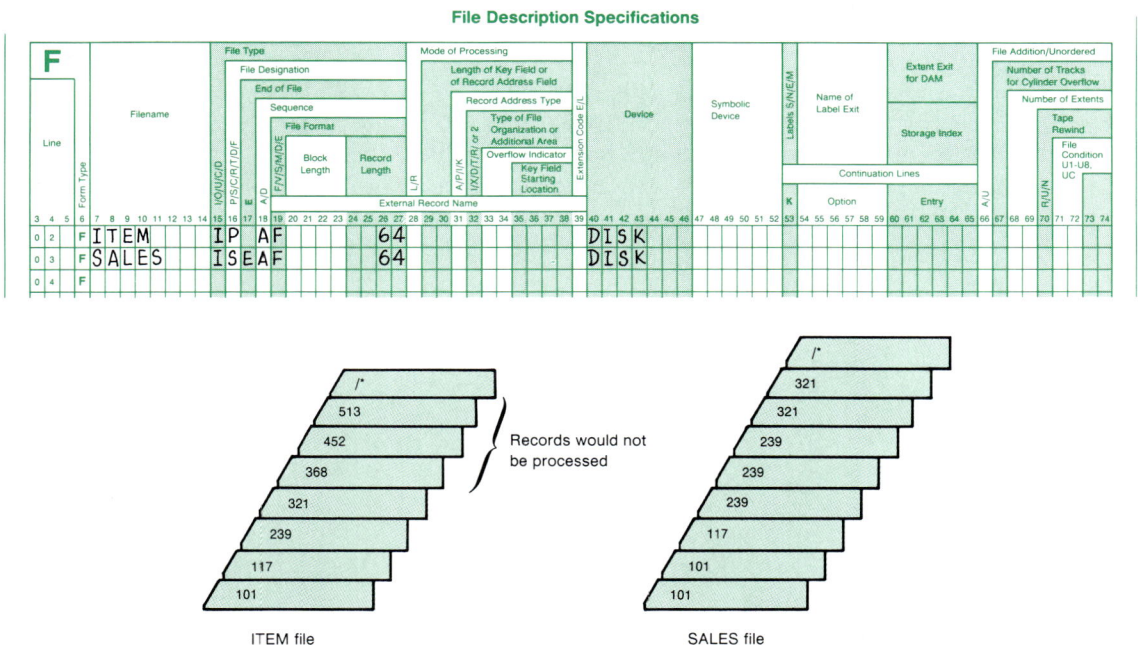

Notes on the Coding

In the above example, both files are in ascending order.

Once all SALES records have been processed, there wouldn't be much point in processing the remaining ITEM master records for which no sales were made. Thus, an E (end-of-file) entry could be specified for the SALES file.

Multiple Batch Processing   445

Figure 9.15 RPG logic of obtaining totals for matching records

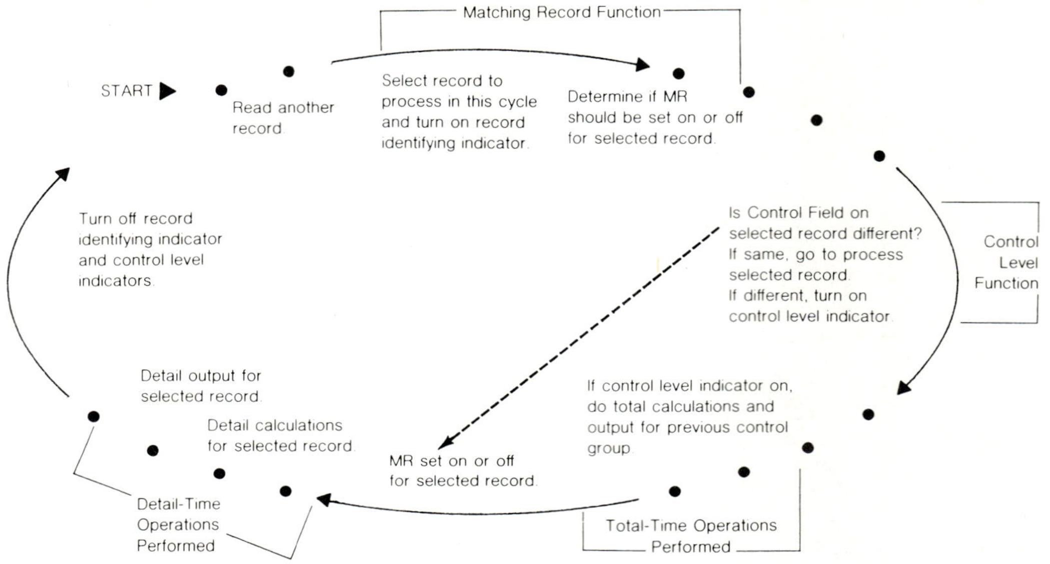

Use of Match Fields and Control Fields in the Same File

In order to perform total operations on a group of records, it is necessary that control fields be assigned to distinguish one group from the next. Although the files may contain both match fields and control fields, the two functions have no relationship. Even if the same fields on a record are used as both match and control fields, the only similarity between the operations is that the same data will be used in performing each.

Match fields are checked first to determine from which file the next record is to be processed. In effect, the matching record function is creating one file for processing by merging the data from the two files. (See Figure 9.15.)

In addition, comparison of the match fields determines whether the MR indicator will be turned on or off for processing of the selected record. The MR indicator is to be on for processing of a primary file record only if there is a matching record in the secondary file. Likewise, if a secondary file record is selected, MR is to be on for its processing only if a matching record from the primary file has already been processed. If an unmatched record is selected, MR is set off, of course. At this point, however, the matching record function only determines how the MR indicator is to be set; the status of MR is not actually changed yet. (See Figure 9.16.)

Figure 9.16 Use of match fields and control fields in the same file—example

Assigning the Same Field as a Match Field and as a Control Field

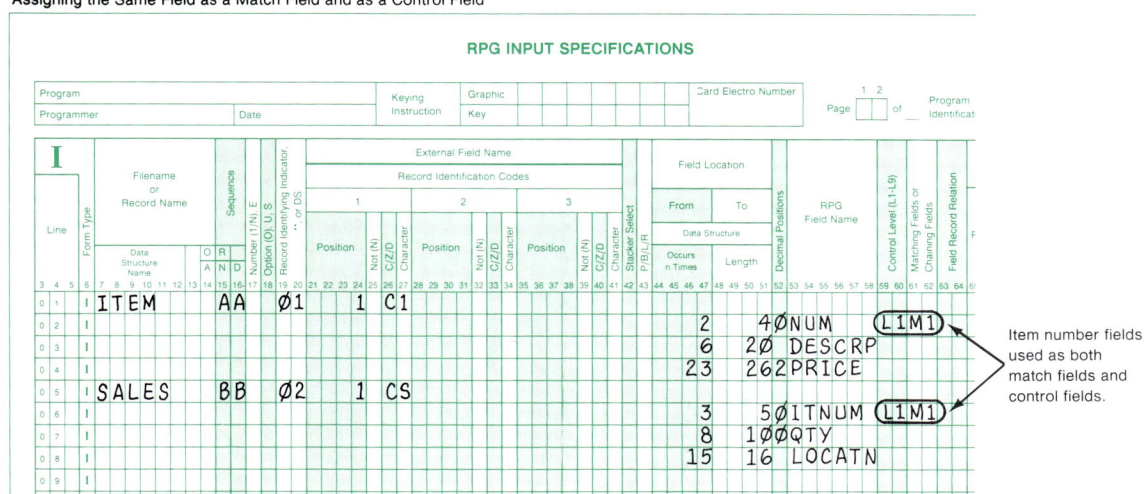

Controlling Performance of Total Operations in a Matching Records Job

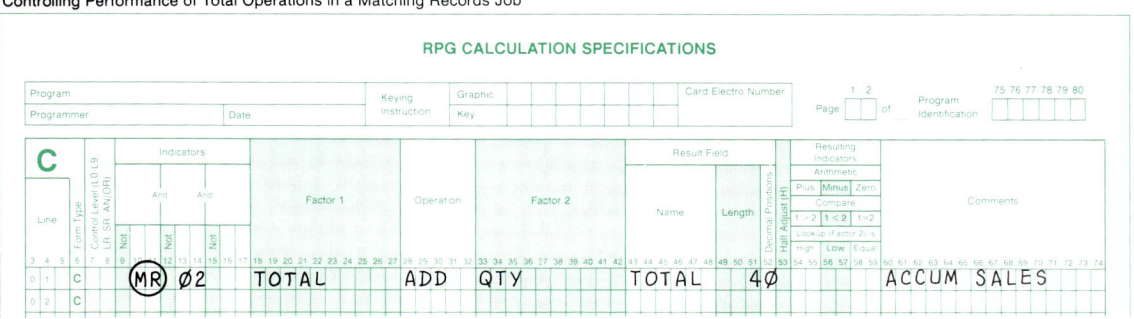

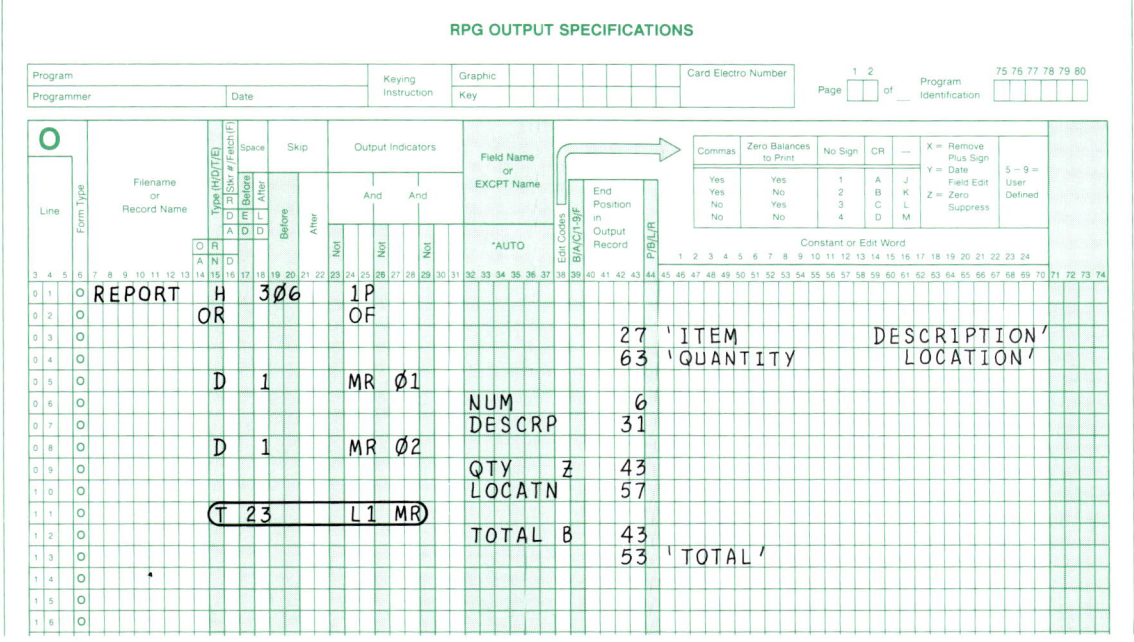

Multiple Batch Processing 447

Figure 9.16 continued

Printing Totals for Matching Records

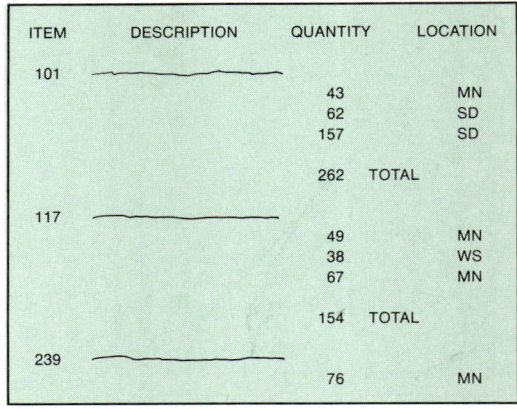

Notes on the Coding

In the previous example, the ITEM and SALES files were matched according to an item number field so that individual sales could be printed under the item description. Suppose you also wish to have the sales for each item totaled and printed.

To perform total operations on a group of records it is necessary that control fields be assigned to distinguish one group from the next.

For this job, the same item number field used for matching the records would be specified as a control field on the Input form. Although the files may contain both match fields and control fields, there is no relationship between the two functions performed. Even if the same fields on a record are used as both match and control fields, the only similarity is that the same data will be used in performing each function.

Match fields are checked first to determine from which file the next record is to be processed. In effect, the matching record function is creating one file for processing by merging the data from two files.

In addition, comparison of the match fields determine whether the MR indicator will be turned on or off for the processing of the selected record. As discussed previously, the MR indicator is to be on for processing of a primary file only if there is a matching record in the secondary file. Likewise, if a secondary file record is selected, MR is to be on for its processing only if a matching record from the primary file has already been processed.

For this job, sales are to be added and the total printed only if there is an ITEM master record with matching SALES records for that item. In such a case, MR would have been set on for the last SALES record of the group. MR would still be on, then, when the control break occurs. Thus, detail operations to accumulate sales should be performed whenever MR is on, and the total operations to print the TOTAL should be conditioned to be performed only with L1 and MR.

Once the matching record function has selected the next record to be processed, the control level function then considers the records as one file in determining if a control break has occurred. This check is made before the selected record is processed and, thus, before the MR indicator is set for the record just selected. The control field on the selected record is checked to see if it is different from that on the previously processed record. If it is the same, no totals are printed and the MR indicator is set. However, if the record control is different from that on the previously processed record, all functions of the previous group must be performed.

When total operations are performed, the selected record has not yet been processed. Therefore, during total time MR is still set for the previously processed record. Once total operations are complete, MR is then set for the selected record (the first record in the next control group) so it can be processed.

Whenever a control field changes (control break), a control level indicator is automatically turned on. Furthermore, whenever a control level indicator is on, total operations are performed. In a matching record job, however, there may be times when a control break occurs and the programmer does not want total operations to be done. Thus, the programmer must specify that total operations are to be performed only under certain conditions. (See Figure 9.17.)

Figure 9.17 Use of MR indicator to determine whether total operations are to be performed—example

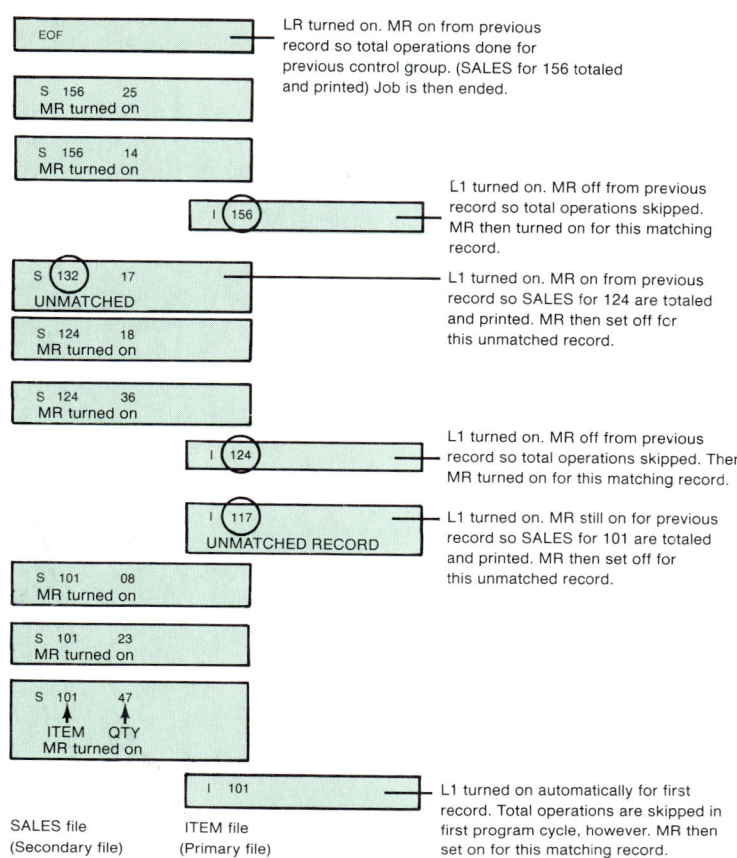

End-of-File Processing

By specifying an *E* in position 17 of the File Description form, the user indicates that the job is to end after all records are processed from the file for which the *E* was specified. In most cases, the job will end at the time all records from the file are processed. However, under certain conditions additional records may be processed after all records from the file designated with an *E* are processed. The exceptional situation is in matching records when an *E* is designated for the primary file and all records from that file have been processed. This job will end either after all secondary records that match the last primary record have been processed or after the first secondary record without a match field has been encountered. (See Figure 9.18.)

Alternating the Order of Processing Files (FORCE)

Normally records are read, identified, selected for processing, and output according to the fixed logic of the RPG object program. Sometimes, however, it is necessary to have direct control over the input and output of the program. RPG provides several operation codes that provide this control. By using the FORCE operation in the calculation routine, the normal RPG multifile logic for selecting input records for processing may be overridden. Recall that multifile processing applies to programs that read records from a primary file and one or more secondary files. It is the name given to the methods by which programs select records for processing. The method used depends upon whether or not match fields are used in the records.

The FORCE statement enables the user to select the file from which the next record is to be taken for processing. The selection applies to primary or secondary, input, update, or combined files.

Factor 2 in a FORCE statement identifies the file from which the next record is to be selected. (See Figure 9.19.) If the statement is executed, the record is selected at the start of the next program cycle. If more than one FORCE statement is executed during the same program cycle, all but the last is ignored. FORCE should not be specified at total time.

Multiple Batch Processing 449

Figure 9.18 Processing a matching records job after end-of-file

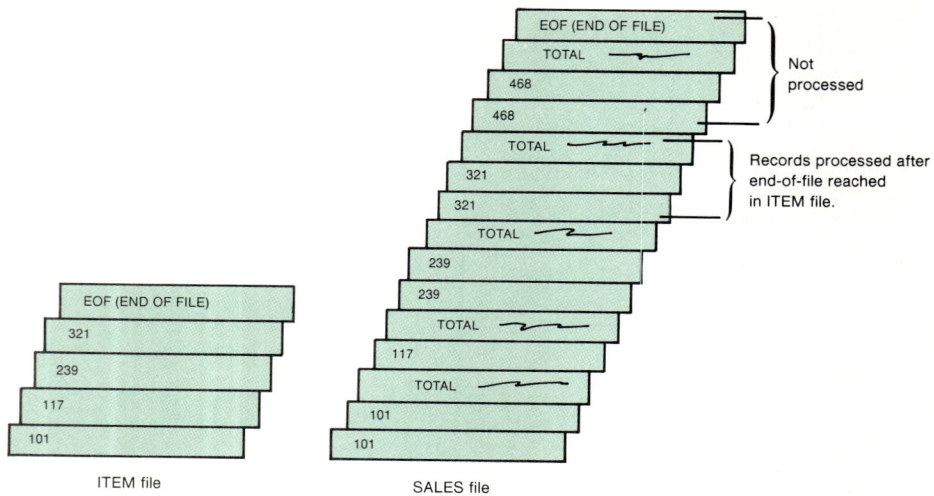

Figure 9.19 Specifying the file to be processed in the next program cycle

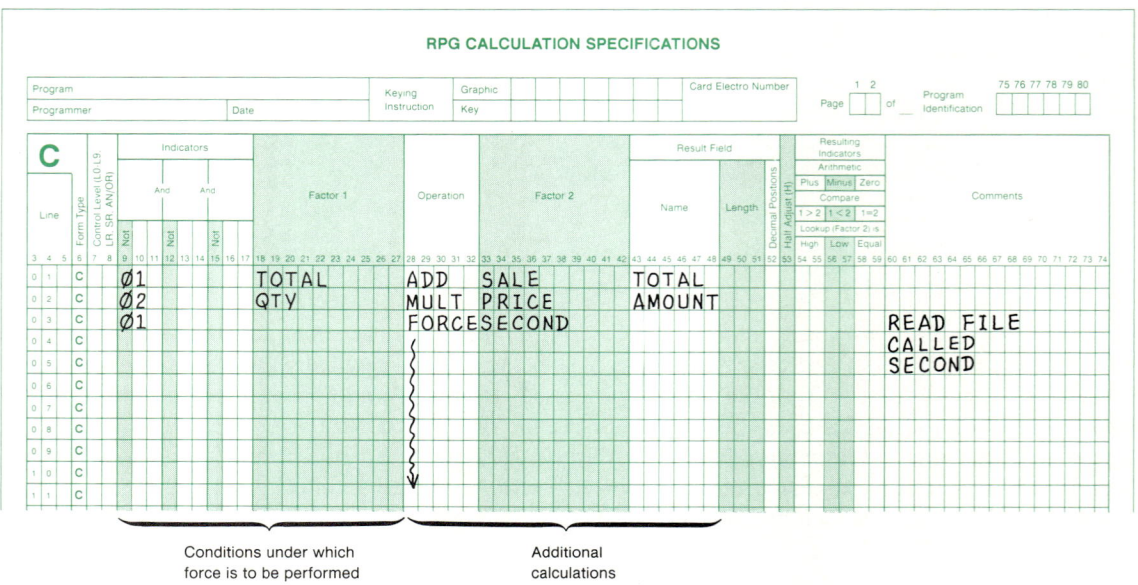

FORCE statements override the multifile processing method by which the program normally selects records. However, the first record to be processed is always selected by the normal method. The remaining records can be selected by FORCE statements. When end-of-file is encountered on a forced file, a record will not be retrieved from the file; normal record selection will determine which record is to be processed.

RPG uses two methods to determine the order in which records are processed in a multifile job.

1. If match fields are not specified for either file, all records in the primary file are processed followed by those in the secondary files in the order defined on the File Description forms.

2. When match fields are assigned (positions 61–62 on the Input Specifications form), the RPG logic of matching records determines from which file the next record is to be processed.

450   RPG II and RPG III Programming

The order of processing determined by RPG logic is appropriate for most of the multifile jobs. However, for certain jobs it may be necessary to have some of the records in the two files processed in an order other than that in which RPG logic would select the records.

A record can be processed out of order only if some indication is given to the program that the file containing that record is to be forced. To do this, additional specifications must be coded to override normal RPG multifile logic.

Regardless of how the files are organized, the following situations require that the order of processing be altered:

1. Match fields cannot be assigned to the files and an alternative must be chosen:
    a. Alternate processing between two files. (See Figures 9.20, 9.21, and 9.22.)
    b. Process a primary file record followed by a particular number of secondary file records.
    c. Process a secondary file record only when it matches a primary file record.
2. Match fields are assigned to both input files. The programmer may wish to process one primary file record, followed by the matching secondary file record, and then the rest of the matching primary records.

To alter the order of processing, the file to be processed—when and under which conditions—must be determined. After the order is determined, the next step is to establish for a particular programming cycle whether the RPG logic will select the appropriate record or the programming of that record must be forced.

The first record to be processed in any job can only be selected by RPG logic in the usual way. Thereafter, to alter the order of processing the program must be told to force a record from a file that would not ordinarily be processed next. Once the forced record is processed, and provided another record is not forced, the RPG logic selects the next record in the usual way. This is the record that would have ordinarily been processed if the other file had not been forced.

Specifying the Next File to Process

To process a record out of its normal sequence, the Calculation Specifications must specify the FORCE operation code and the name of the file that is to be forced in the next program cycle.

At the beginning of a normal program cycle, RPG logic looks at the two available records in order to select the one to process during that cycle. However, if the record from the file that would not normally be selected is the one that is to be processed, this must be indicated to the program before the beginning of the cycle. If a file is to be forced, there is no need for RPG logic to compare the records and make a selection. This is why, if a file is to be forced, the FORCE must be indicated during the program cycle immediately before the cycle in which the FORCE is to occur.

Depending on the job, a record may have to be forced in every program cycle. When the FORCE is to be done in such a situation it must be indicated by specifying conditioning indicators in positions 9–17 of the Calculation Specifications form. Whether or not the FORCE is to be performed in the next cycle may depend on any of several conditions:

The type of file or record type being processed at the time
The number of records that have been processed
The result of calculation performed
The contents of a field on the record being processed
The contents of a field on a record that has not yet been processed

Figure 9.20 Files to be alternately processed—example

Files to be Alternately Processed

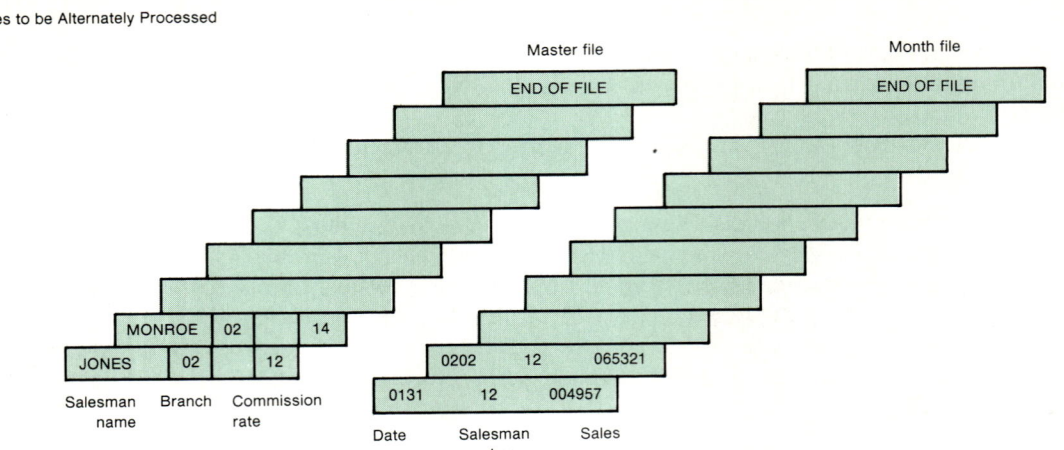

Specifications to Define and Describe Files to be Alternately Processed

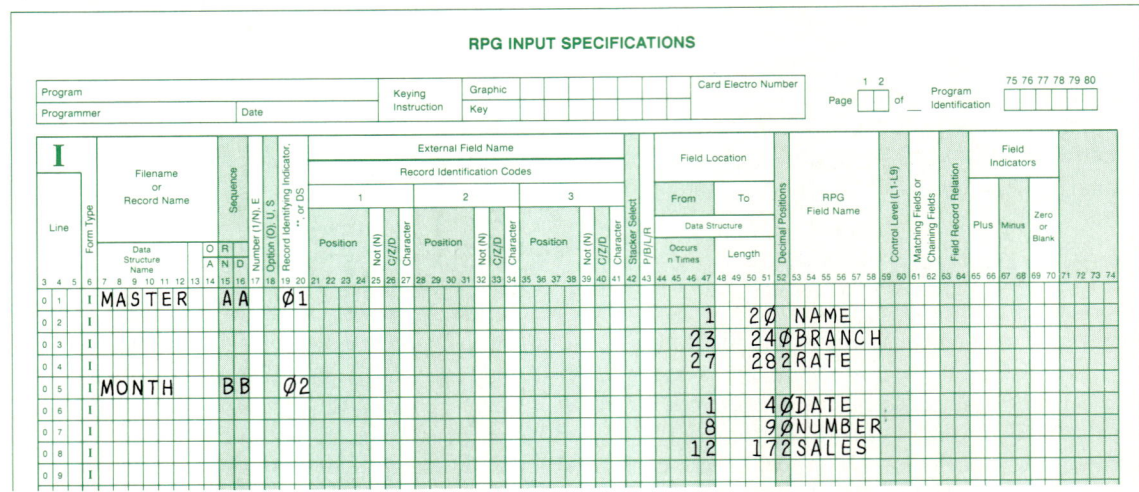

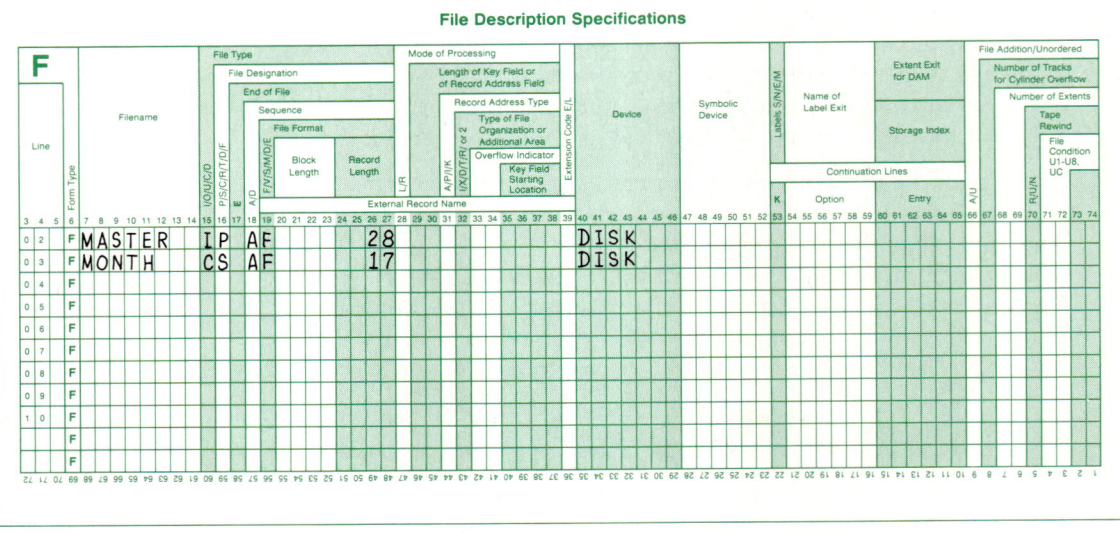

Figure 9.20 continued

Conditioning Operations on Basis of Record Type

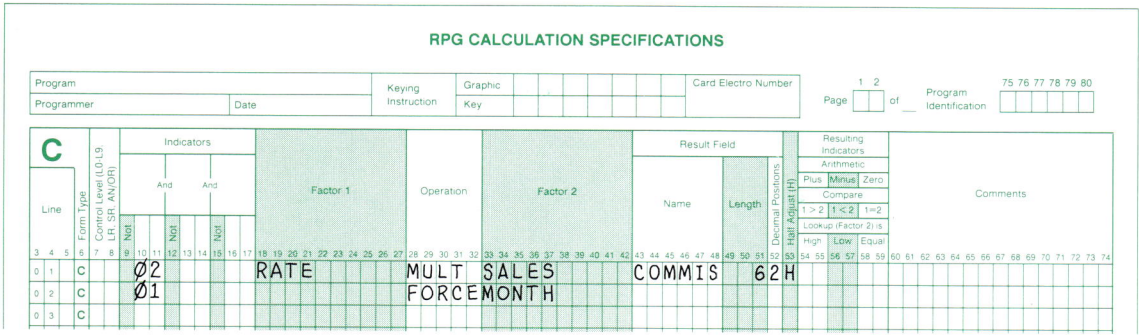

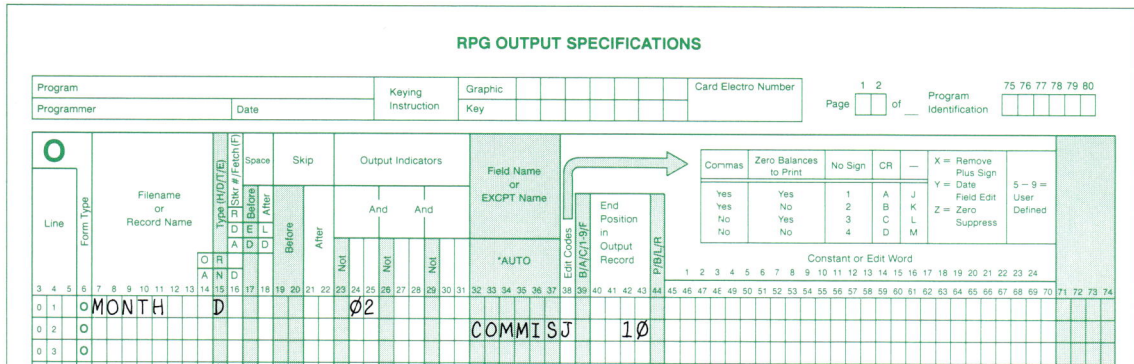

Notes on the Coding

In the above figure, each file contains one record for every salesman in a company.

The MASTER records are arranged in alphabetical order by salesman name; the MONTH file is arranged in ascending sequence by salesman number.

Although there is no common match field, the records in the two files are, nevertheless, in a one-to-one correspondence.

Salesman numbers have been assigned so that they correspond to the order of the salesman names. Thus, the first record in each file is for Baker (salesman #10); the second record in each file is for Costello (salesman #20), and so on.

The two files are to be processed to determine the amount of commission earned by each salesman. To do this, a salesman's commission rate from his MASTER record must be multiplied by the amount of his sales contained on his MONTH record. The calculated commission is recorded in the salesman's MONTH record.

Multiple Batch Processing   453

Figure 9.21 Using a FORCE statement to process a primary file followed by a particular number of secondary file records

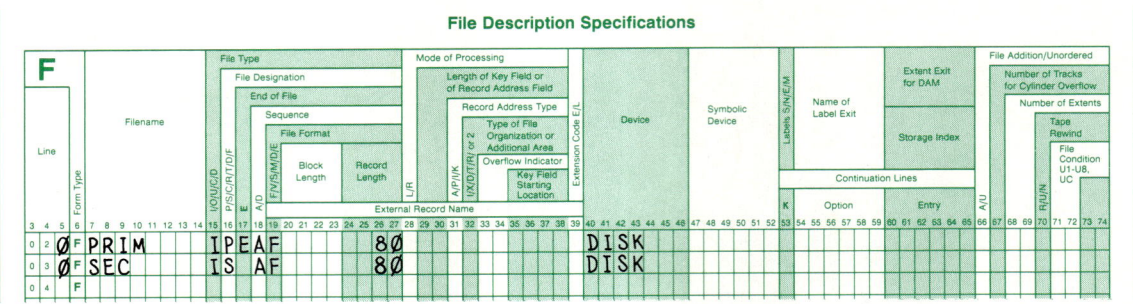

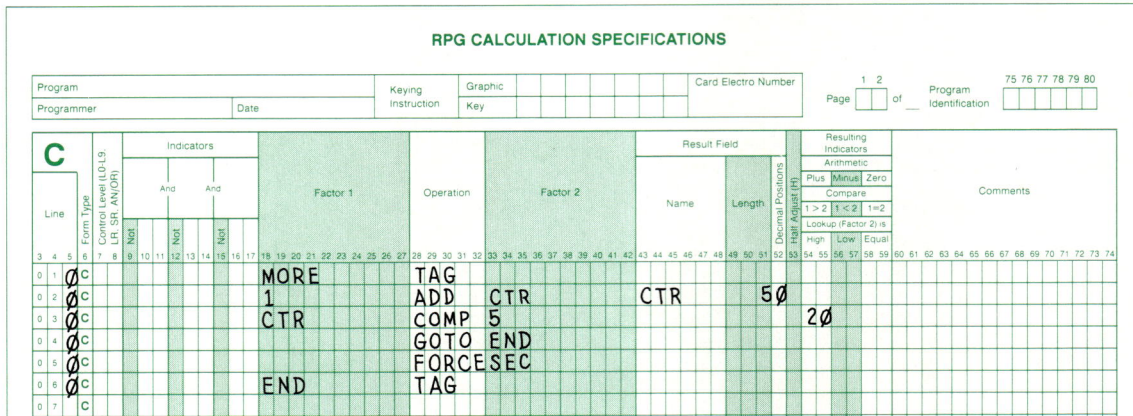

Notes on the Coding

The above figure shows the processing of a primary file and a secondary file.

The FORCE operation causes the secondary file to be read five times.

If the secondary file is forced and is at end of file, the FORCE operation will not take effect.

When CTR is greater than 5, the normal matching record logic determines which record is to be processed next.

Figure 9.22 Controlling the number of times FORCE is performed—example

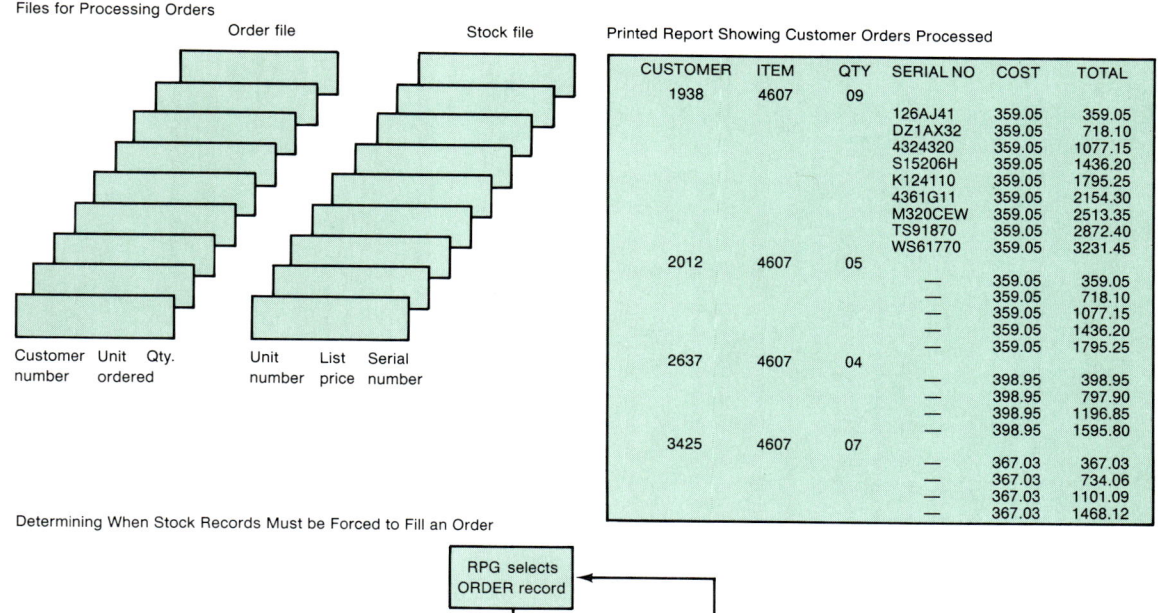

Determining When Stock Records Must be Forced to Fill an Order

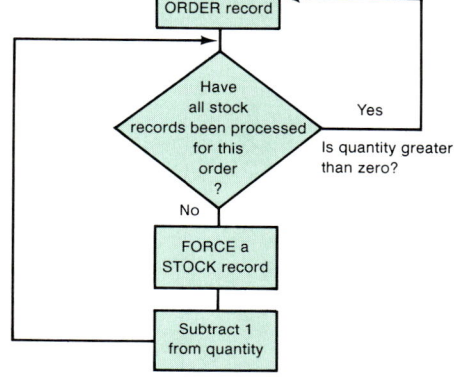

Controlling the Number of Times a File is Forced

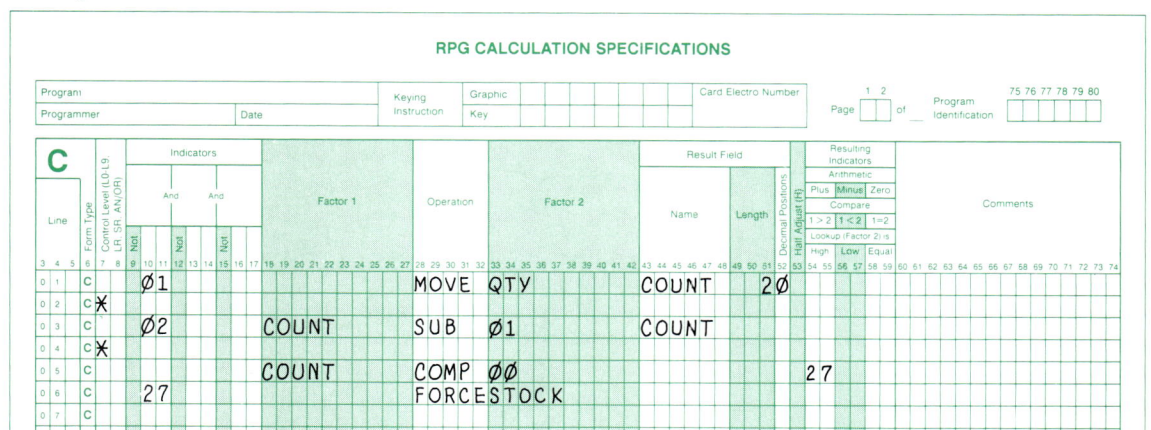

Multiple Batch Processing 455

Figure 9.22 continued

Specifications to Process Customer Orders

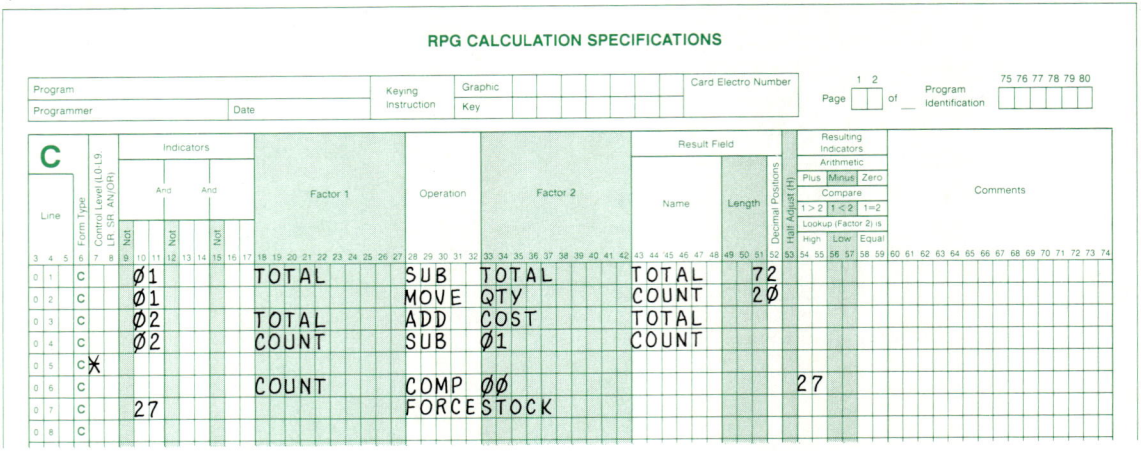

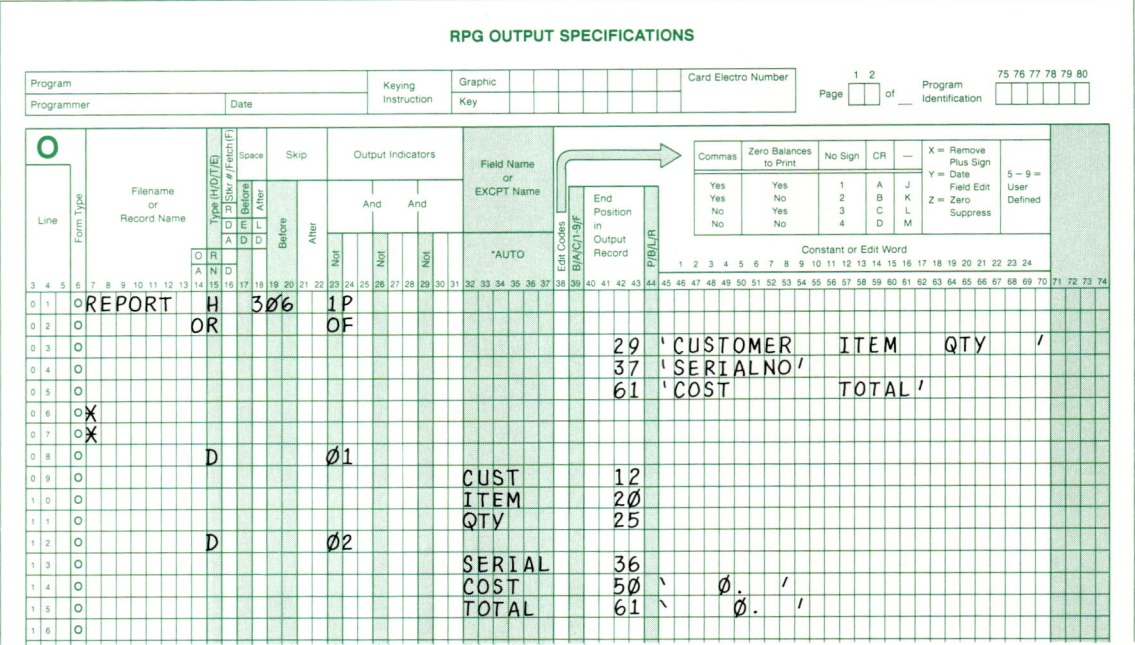

Notes on the Coding

Suppose that there are a number of customers who periodically order items to be delivered from a central warehouse. One record is kept for each unit in stock in the warehouse and another record for each customer's order of a particular unit.

Orders are processed according to the type of unit ordered. Therefore, for a particular run, the primary file (ORDER) contains all order records for only one type of unit, and the secondary file (STOCK) contains all in-stock records for that type of unit.

For this run, the ORDER file contains the week's order records for television sets, unit number 4607. The records show which customer placed the order and the quantity of televisions wanted.

The STOCK file consists of a separate record for each television set (unit 4607) in stock. Each record provides the unit number, list price, and serial number of the item.

There are two purposes for processing the files. First, it is necessary to get an indication of which orders can be filled and which orders cannot be filled. Secondly, the STOCK file is to be kept up to date so it only contains as many records as there are television sets available.

Read (READ)

The READ operation is used to call for immediate input from a demand file during the calculations in the program cycle. This operation differs from the FORCE operation because FORCE specifies input on the next program cycle, not the present one.

The operation code READ must appear in positions 28–32. Factor 2 contains the name of the file from which a record will be read immediately. An indicator should be used in positions 58–59. An indicator specified in these positions will turn on after each READ operation if an end-of-file condition is reached. If positions 58–59 are blank, a halt will occur on an end-of-file condition and on subsequent READ operations after the end-of-file condition is reached. Indicators may be specified in positions 7–17.

All field references by the READ operation must be designated either as demand files with a *D* in position 16 of the File Description form, or as full procedural files with an *F* in position 16 of the File Description form.

Processing Full Procedural or Demand Files (READ)

A file for which the input operations are controlled by calculation operation codes rather than the program cycle is called a **full procedural file.** The increased emphasis upon interactive, work station applications makes full procedural files increasingly important in RPG II as well as RPG III.

Using the FORCE operation (with demand files), normal RPG logic can be overridden for selecting records on the next program cycle. If, however, it is necessary to select records to be processed during the current program cycle, a READ operation may be used. (See Figures 9.23 and 9.24.)

Figure 9.23 READ operation and DEMAND or full procedural file—example

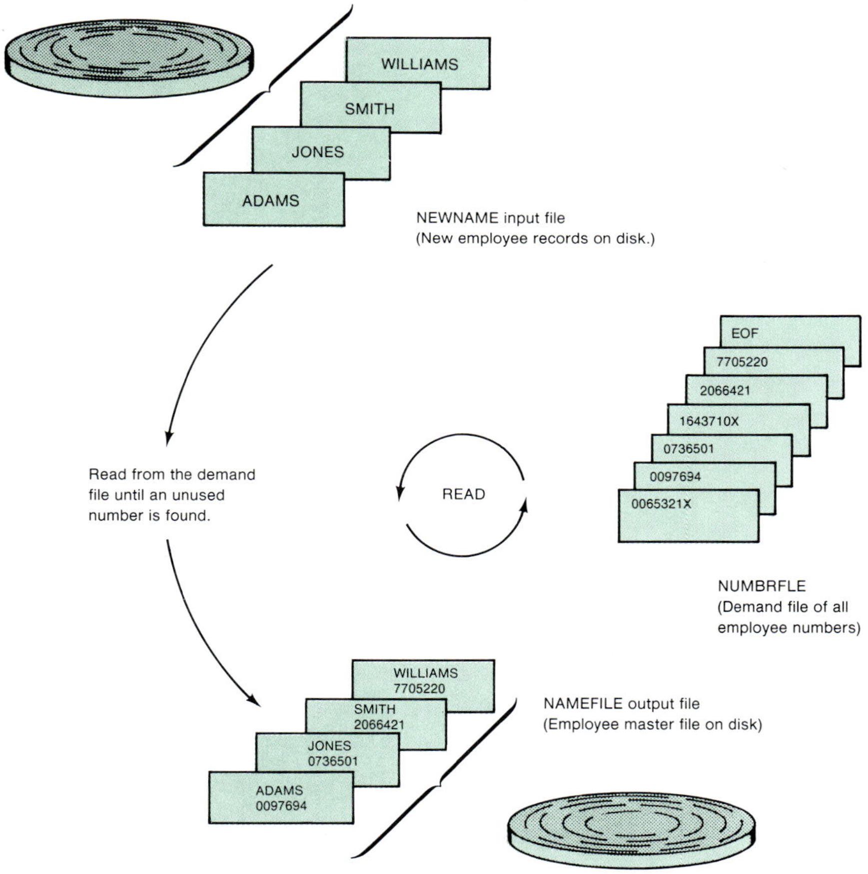

Using the READ Operation and a Demand File to Assign Man Numbers to New Employees

Multiple Batch Processing 457

Figure 9.23 continued

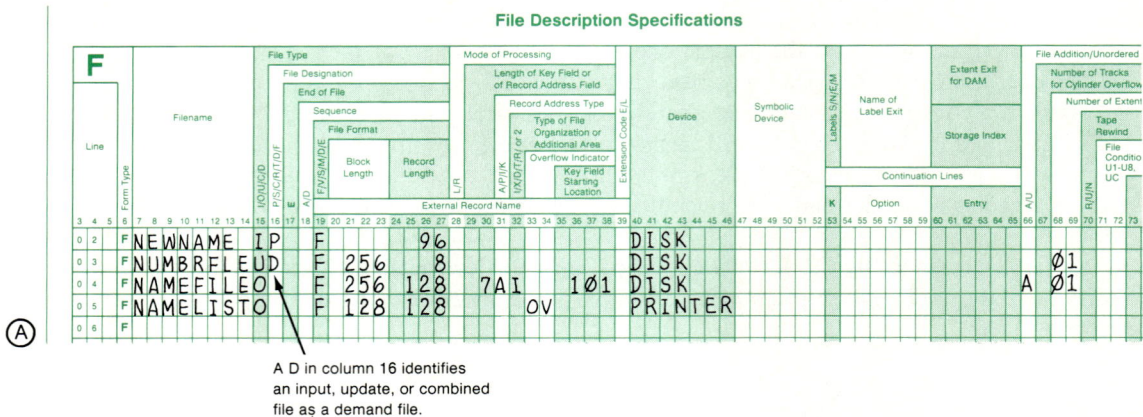

A D in column 16 identifies an input, update, or combined file as a demand file.

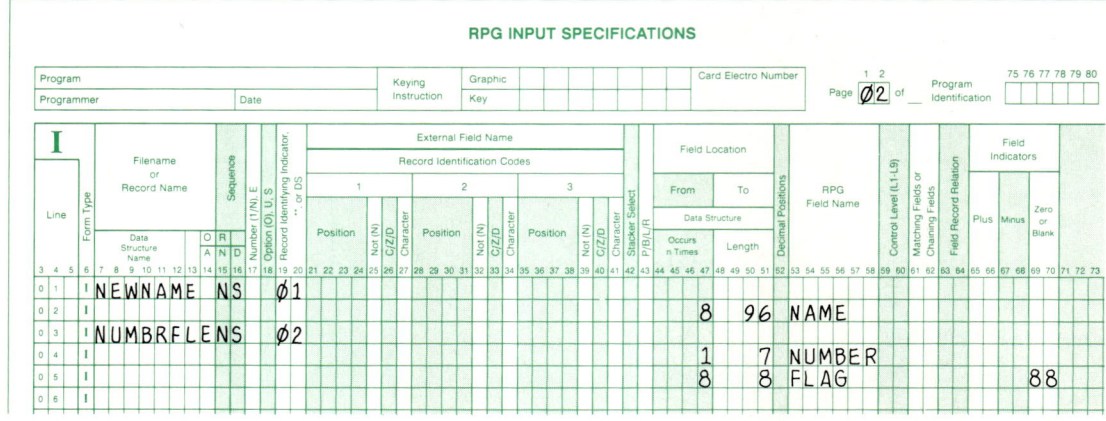

The indicator in columns 58-59 of a READ specification will turn on each time READ encounters an end-of-file condition in the demand file. If no indicator is used, the program halts each time end-of-file is encountered.

458 RPG II and RPG III Programming

Figure 9.23 continued

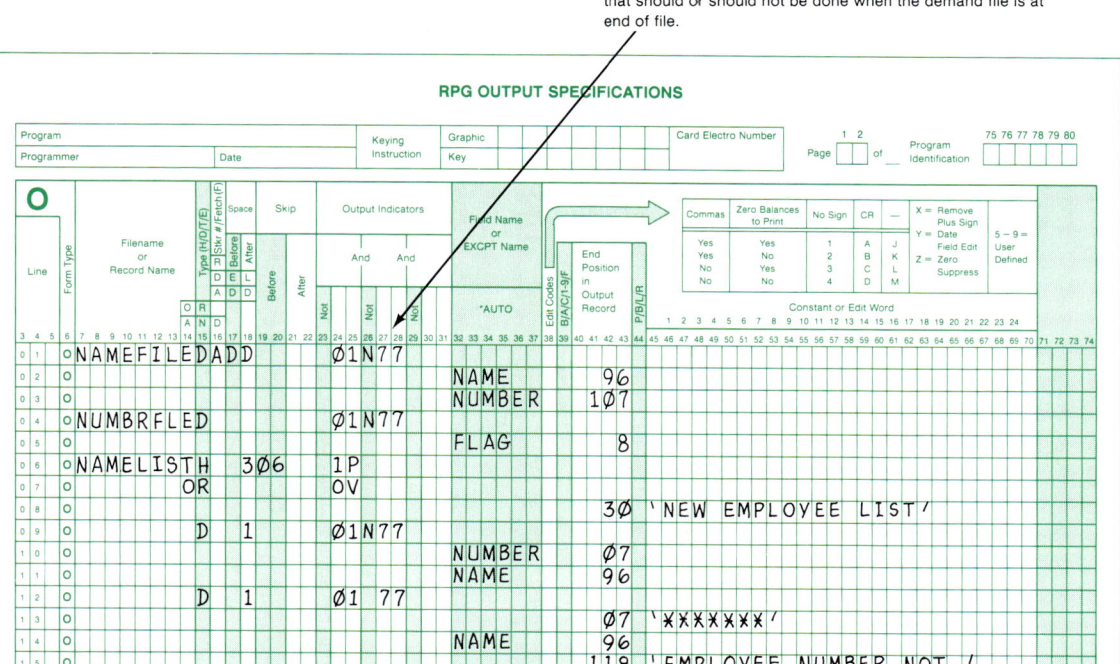

Notes on the Coding

Using the FORCE operation, normal RPG logic for selecting records on the next program cycle can be overridden. In this example, it is necessary to select records to be processed during the current program cycle.

A company maintains a file of employee numbers, NUMBRFLE. Each number is on a separate record. Those records containing numbers that are already assigned to employees are identified by a flag (character X in position 8 of the record). If the number has not been assigned to an employee, the record does not have a flag.

For each record that is read from the file of new employee records, NEWNAME, one or more records must be read from NUMBRFLE to find a number that can be assigned to the new employee. The new number must be found during the current cycle, since the new employee record is added to the employee master file, NAMEFILE, after a number is assigned.

By designating NUMBRFLE as a demand file (insert A), the programmer can request input from the file as many times as necessary during a single program cycle.

In order to request input, the programmer must use the READ operation code in the calculation portion of the program (insert C). Each time a READ operation is done, a record is read from NUMBRFLE.

It is possible that end of file for the demand file could be reached during the program cycle. Two options are available to handle this situation. In the example (insert C), an indicator that has been entered in positions 58-59 of the specification line containing the READ operation will turn on after each READ operation if an end-of-file condition is reached. In the example, new employee records are listed on the printer as they are added to NAMEFILE.

If end of file is reached on NUMBRFLE before numbers have been assigned to all new employees, indicator 77 is turned on and the new employee records to which numbers have not been assigned are listed with an appropriate identification.

If an end-of-file indicator is not entered in positions 58-59, the program will halt when end of file is reached on the demand file and each time READ is executed thereafter.

Multiple Batch Processing

Figure 9.24 READ operation and DEMAND file—example

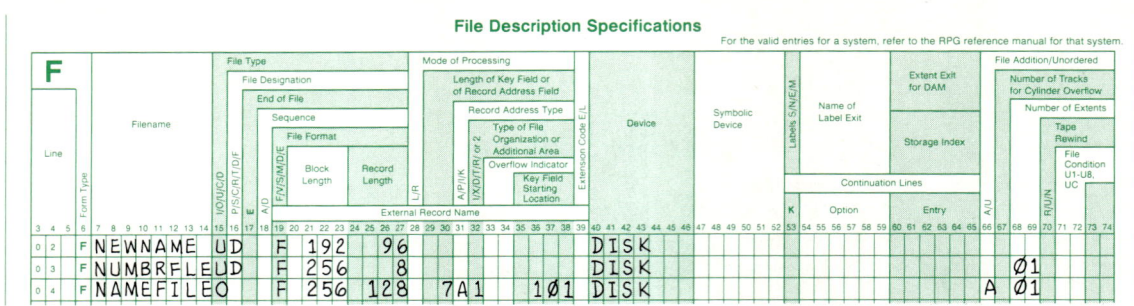
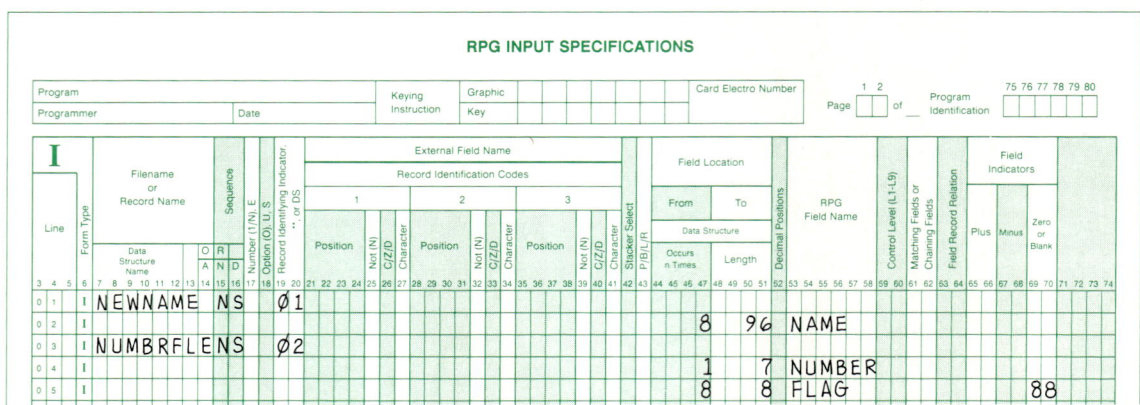
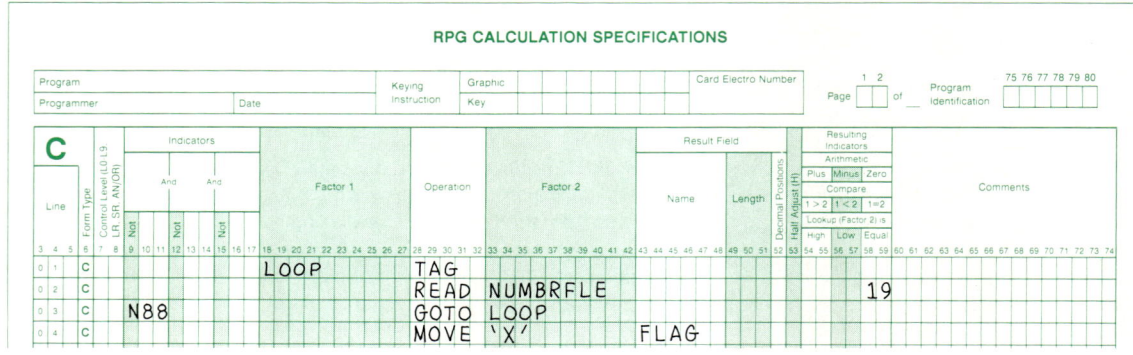
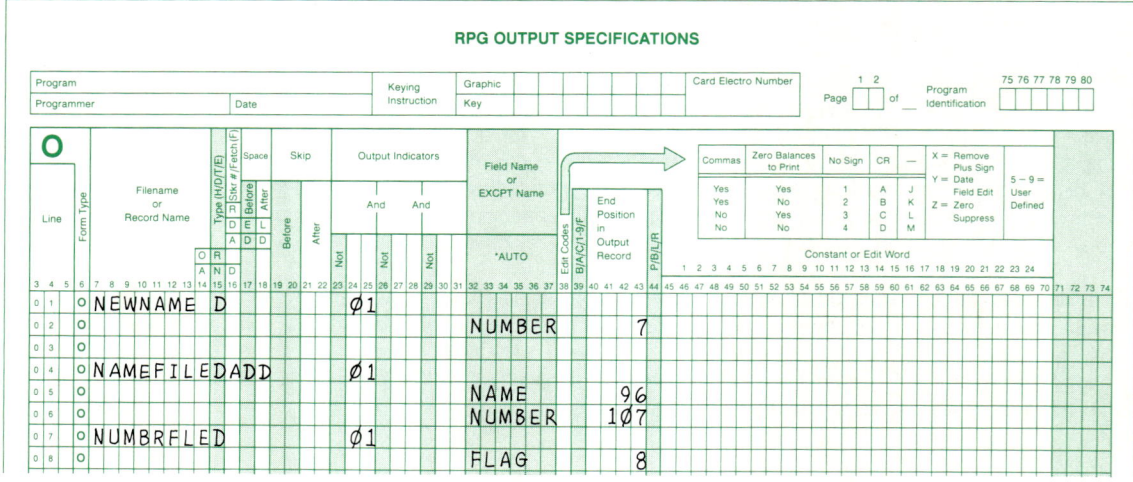

460 RPG II and RPG III Programming

Figure 9.24 continued

Notes on the Coding

The above example shows the coding necessary to process a demand file with the READ operation code.

The combined input and output tape file NEWNAME, consisting of a name field in positions 8-96.

The disk file NUMBRFLE, specified as an update demand file, consists of records containing a seven-digit number and a flag mark.

For each record read from NEWNAME, a record is also read from NUMBRFLE during the calculation phase by means of the READ operation code.

If the record from the demand file contains a flag (field indicator 88 is off), another record is immediately read. This loop is repeated until a record without a flag has been read from the NUMBRFLE; a flag of X is then moved into the flag field.

When the end of the file has been reached on the demand file and each time READ is encountered thereafter, resulting indicator 19 is turned on.

At detail output time, the flagged number from the record in NUMBRFLE is written on a tape called NEWNAME. The record from NUMBRFLE, which now contains a flag, is returned to its original location on the disk.

The disk file, NAMEFLE, is then written containing the name from the NEWNAME tape file and the number from the demand file, NUMBRFLE.

Chaining

Random processing through the chaining operation can add significant flexibility to programming. After one record is read, auxiliary information from many other files as determined by the calculation specifications may be retrieved by the program.

Generally, two input files are required when some additional data are needed in the program and are already available in the other file(s). By using the CHAIN operation in a program, the input for the chained file actually occurs at the time the calculation takes place. The information for that file is then immediately available for processing.

In the file description the chained file must be described as input chained (*I* in position 15 and *C* in position 16 of the input specifications) or update chained (*U* in position 15 and *C* in position 16 of the input specifications) and the mode of processing is random (*R* in position 28 of file description specifications). The other files are described as before.

In the input specifications each file is described separately with the file name, record codes, and appropriate fields.

In calculation specifications the CHAIN operation must be coded to actually get the data from the second file. Factor 2 is the name of the file, not a field name. The CHAIN operation uses the field from the input primary file to link to the other file. The resulting indicator will turn on if the corresponding record cannot be found.

The resulting indicator used with the CHAIN operation code tests for a "not found" condition. Since it is a resulting indicator, it is not turned off at the end of the cycle; rather, it is reset (on or off) the next time the CHAIN takes place. (See Figure 9.25.)

Figure 9.25 CHAIN operation

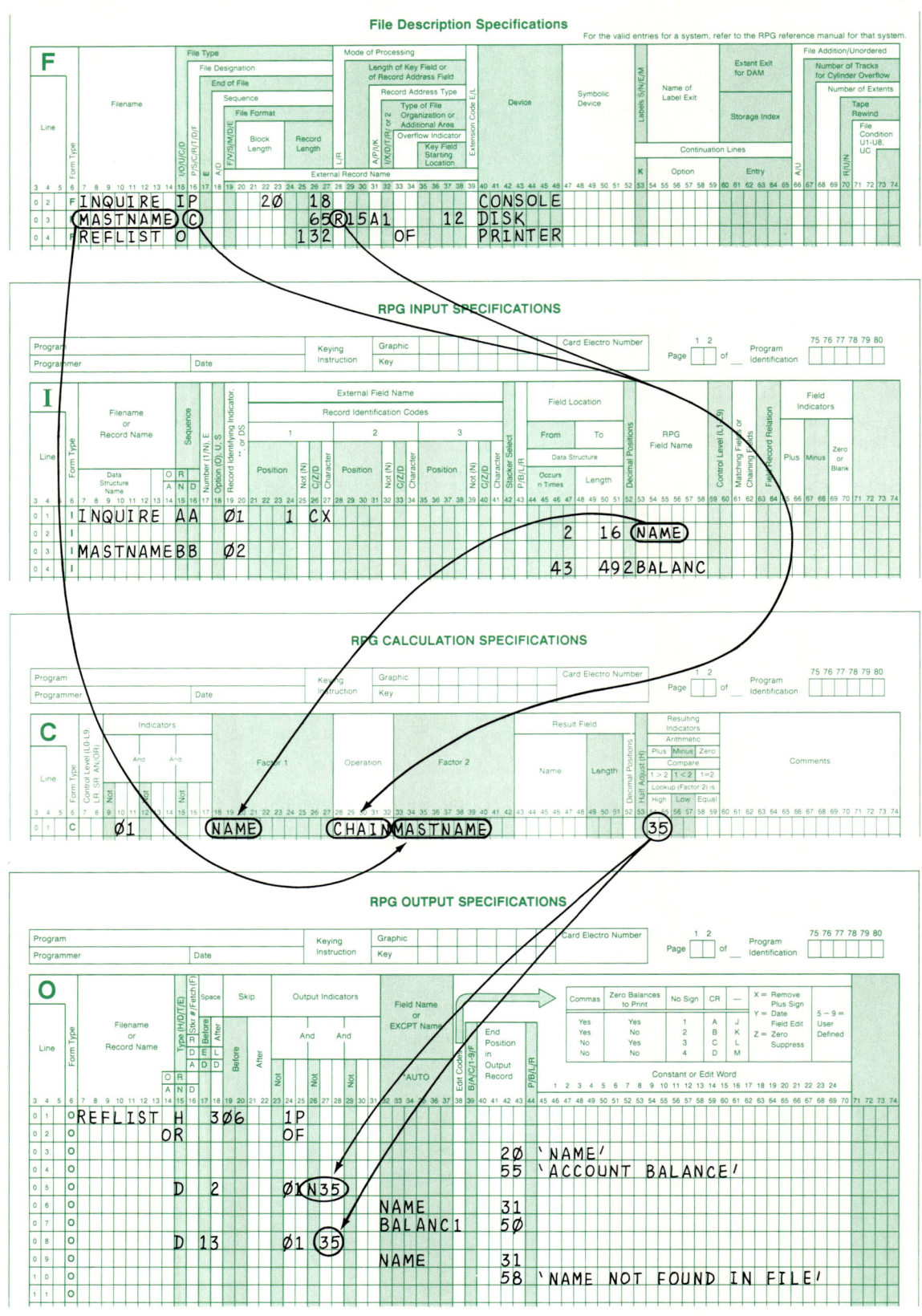

Figure 9.25 continued

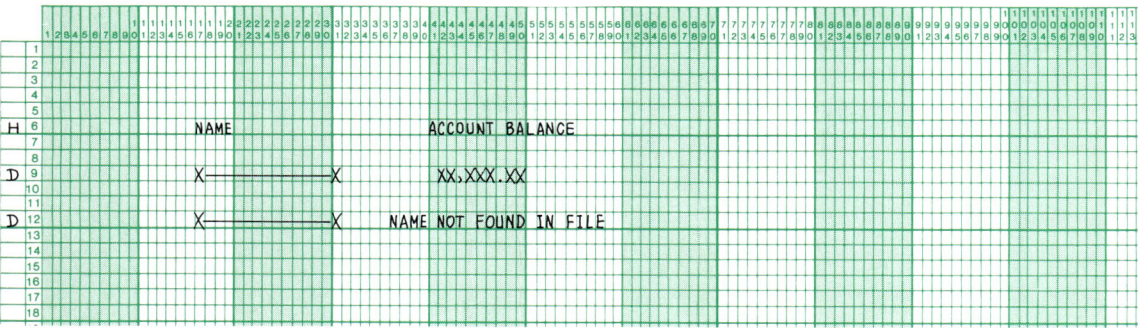

Notes on the Coding

The problem is to use the chaining technique to inquire about selected records in an indexed file and to print the desired information when found.

When the chaining technique is used to search a file, a number of new entries have to be specified, such as the following.

File Description

1. File designation (16)—enter code C for the input file to designate it as the chained file.

2. Mode of processing (28)—enter code R for the input file to denote that its records are to be processed randomly.

Calculation

1. Factor 1 (18-27)—enter the name of the field in the file that contains the search field.

2. Operation (28-32)—enter CHAIN to do the search.

3. Factor 2 (33-42)—enter the name of the chained file.

4. Resulting indicators (54-55)—assign an unused indicator.
   a. If no corresponding record is found, this indicator turns ON.
   b. If a desired record is found, this indicator stays OFF.

Output

Output indicators (23-31)—include the letter N (for NOT) along with the resulting indicator assigned to the CHAIN operation in 54-55 on the Calculations form when the search is successful.

The output list is to include a message, NAME NOT FOUND IN FILE, if the search is not successful.

NAME	ACCOUNT BALANCE
SMITH	307.16
LAWRENCE	1,000.00
JONS	NAME NOT FOUND IN FILE
MILLER	500.00
ADDAMS	17,560.60

Refer to the print chart for end positions when coding output sheet entries.

Multiple Batch Processing 463

Figure 9.26 CHAIN operation—example

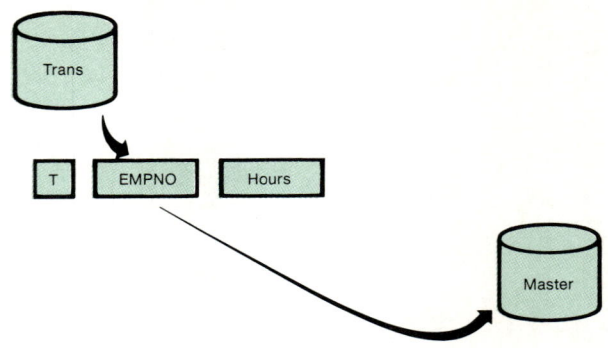

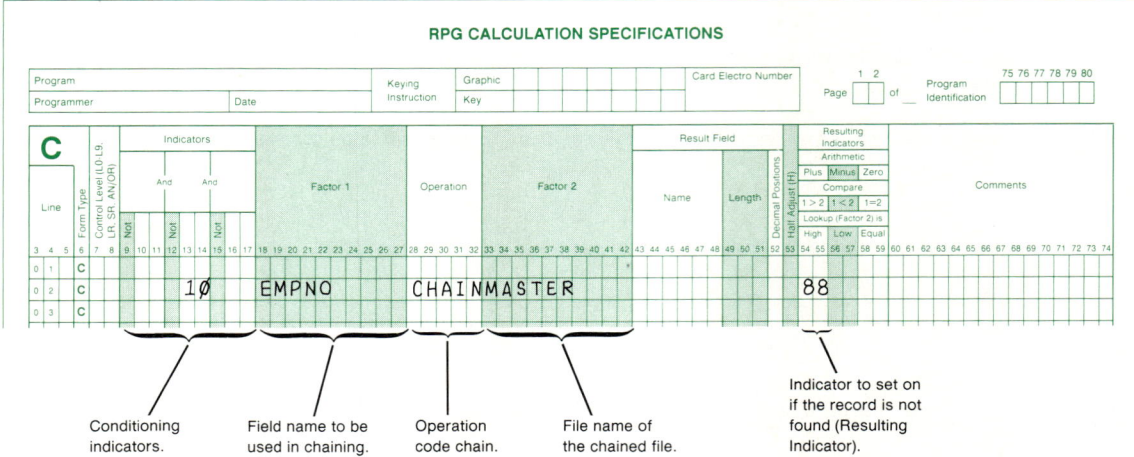

Chain (CHAIN)

The CHAIN operation causes a record to be read from a file during calculations. This operation allows one record to be read in when the operation code CHAIN appears in positions 28–32 of the Calculation Specifications form. (See Figure 9.26.)

The CHAIN operation is used for two purposes:

1. Random processing of a sequential, indexed, or direct file
2. Loading a direct file

Note: When chaining to one or more files during the same RPG cycle, record identifying indicators assigned to the chained file(s) remain on throughout the cycle if the previous operations were executed successfully. When chaining to the same file more than once during the RPG cycle, only the last record processed will be updated during output time unless an exception output is associated with each chain operation.

Indicators in positions 7–17 may be used, but result field, field length, decimal position, and half-adjust (positions 43–53 of the Calculation Specifications form) must be left blank.

Positions 54–55 should contain an entry. If the record is not found, the indicator specified in these positions will turn on. No update to a chained update file is permitted when the specified record is not found. However, addition to a file is allowed when the specified record is not found. Positions 56–59 must always be blank for chain operations.

If an indicator is not specified in positions 54–55 on the Calculation Specifications form and the record is not found, the H0 indicator will turn on and the program will stop. The options given are to end the job or to bypass the remainder of the current cycle and begin a new cycle. If LR processing has already been initiated, the bypass-and-begin-new-cycle option is not allowed. If the controlled cancel option is taken, files are closed, but the rest of the LR processing does not occur. (See Figure 9.27.)

Figure 9.27 CHAIN operation—example

Problem Statement

Code the specifications necessary to read the payroll transactions from the file TRANS and chain to the file MASTER for the additional employee data. The calculations should use the HOURS from the transaction file and the RATE from the MASTER file to produce the gross pay. Fields from both of these files should then be written to the printer.

The system flowchart is shown below. The record layout is diagrammed with the Input Specifications.

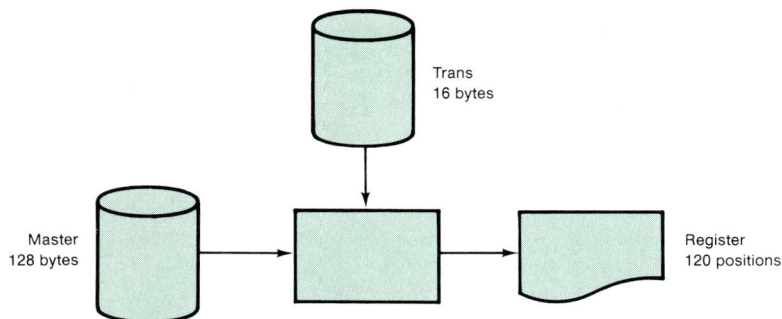

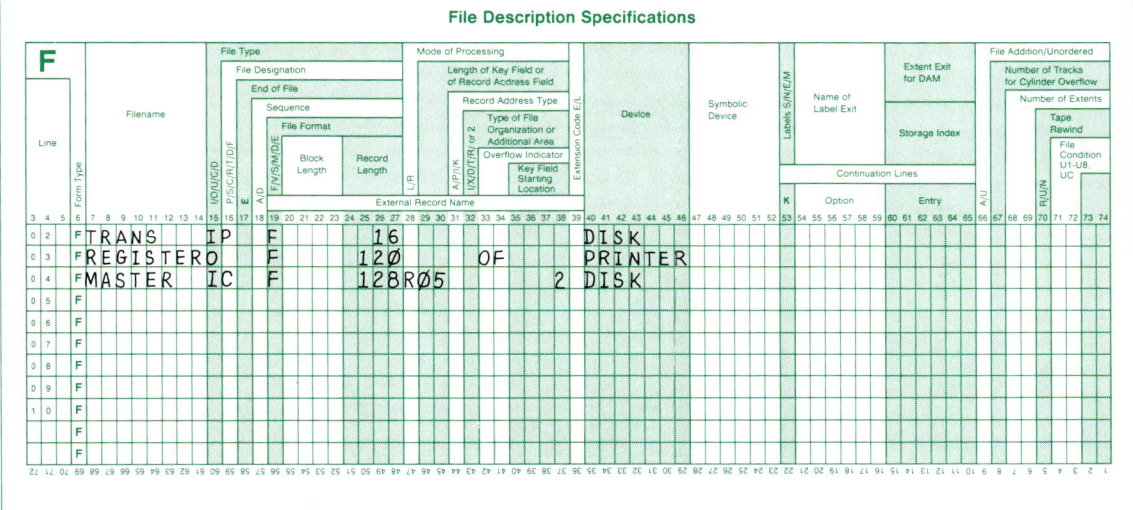

Notes on the Coding

Since there are multiple input files, both of them will have to be defined on the File Description Specifications.

The TRANS file is defined as the input primary file.

The printer file has the OF to indicate that the programmer will control the overflow.

MASTER is also determined as an input file on disk, but there are two new entries for this file:

1. The C in position 16 is for a "chained" file—you will chain to this file on the Calculation Specifications. TRANS is read by RPG automatically; MASTER will be read by the operation code chain.

2. Since the record wanted in MASTER could be anywhere in the file, the method of processing is random. The File Description entry in position 28 has an R to indicate this type of access to the records.

The entry in position 28 for TRANS is blank. This means that the records will be read consecutively as they occur in the file. As each record is read from the TRANS file, another record will be read from the MASTER file. Both fields from both files will be available for processing.

Multiple Batch Processing   465

Figure 9.27 continued

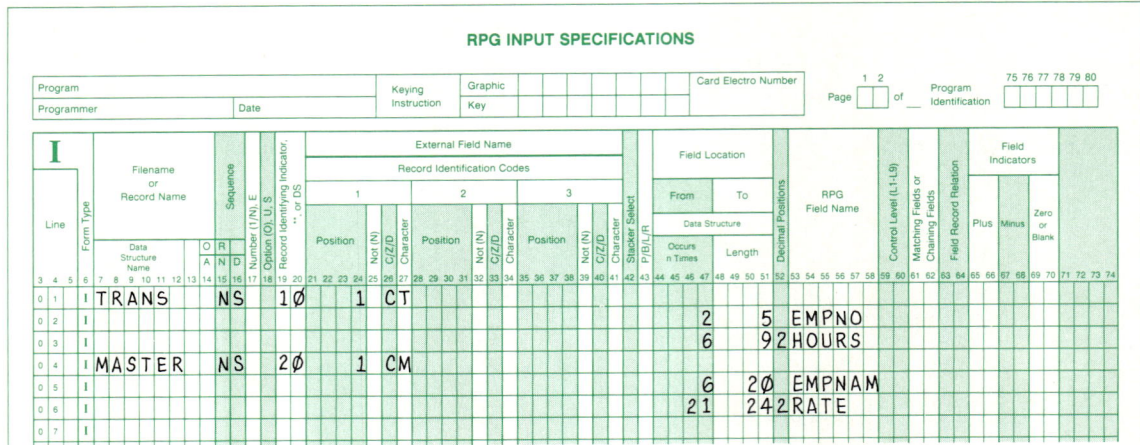

Notes on the Coding

Since there are two files described as Input on the File Description Specifications, both must be further defined.

TRANS is described as the Input file. If there could be other types of records in this file, a catchall indicator could be coded.

The second file, MASTER, is separately defined with its file name, the record code, and fields. Note the field EMP is not defined on the Input Specifications. This field will be read from the TRANS file, so there is no reason to define it again from the MASTER file.

There are two different record identifying indicators for the different types of records.

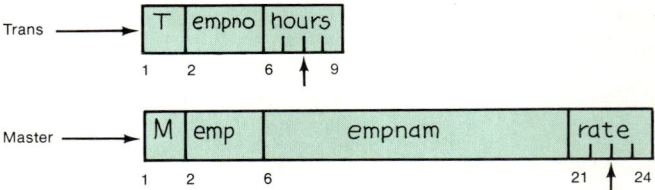

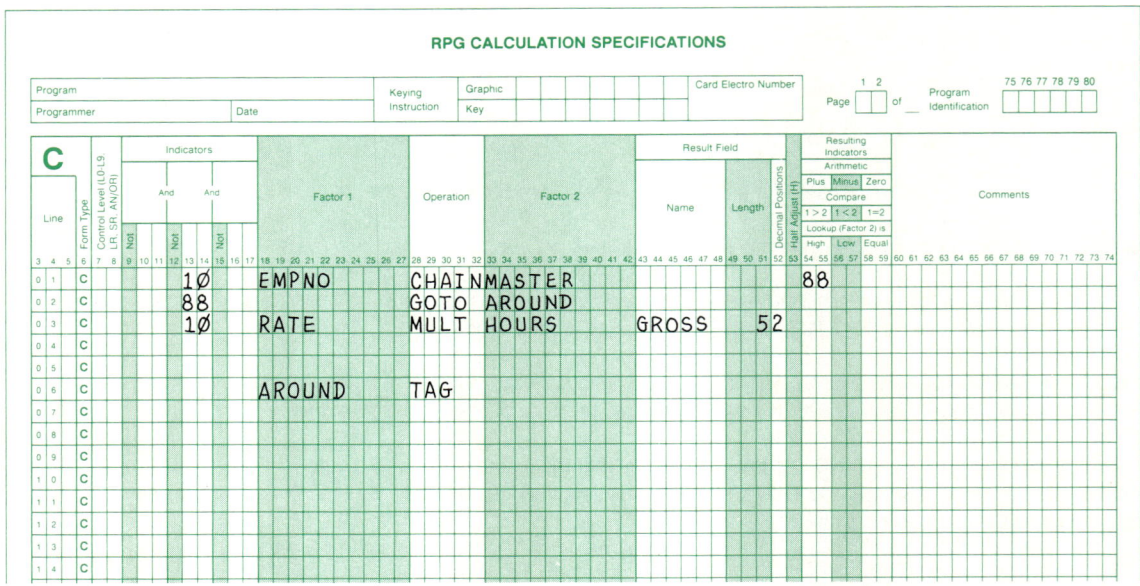

466 RPG II and RPG III Programming

Figure 9.27 continued

Notes on the Coding

The File Description Specifications indicated that the file MASTER would be a "chained file," so the Calculation Specifications must have a CHAIN operation code.

If indicator 10 is on, at detail calculation time of the cycle use the field EMPNO, which was read from the TRANS file and read from the MASTER file. The operation code for the reading is CHAIN. Factor 2 must be the name of the file to be read, the chained file, in this case MASTER. Since there is a chance that the record may not be on the MASTER file, an indicator is defined in 54 and 55 to turn on if the employee cannot be found in the file. Use any indicator not previously defined.

If 88 is on (a not found condition) then bypass any calculations for this record. The GOTO allows this branching to occur. If 88 is not on, then the payroll calculations for GROSS are done plus any other operations for this program.

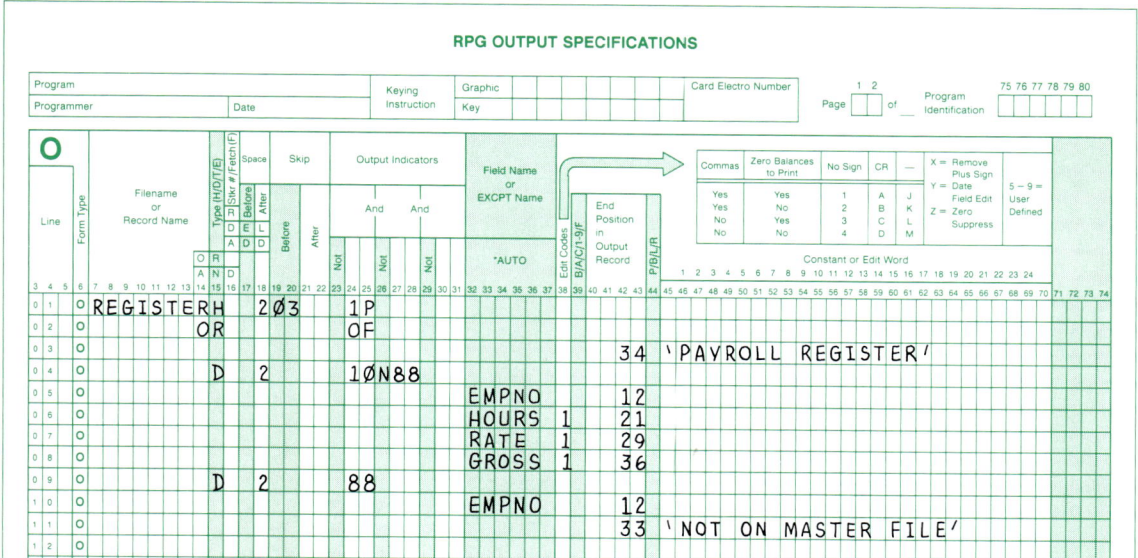

Notes on the Coding

The heading, detail, and total output entries will not change for the chaining operation, but there may be some additional controls or messages using the "not found" indicator.

The detail lines are conditioned by the record identifying indicator, as before. Since there will be no calculations if there is no master data, it is not necessary to print that detail line. The N88 will only allow the detail line to print if 88 is off—the record was found.

If 88 is on—a not found condition—then the employee number and the constant will print.

Random Processing

In order to read a record from a sequential file or a direct file, the record must be identified by a relative record number. The CHAIN operation requires that factor 1 be a relative record number or key. Relative record numbers must be numeric. Factor 2 must contain the name of the file from which the record will be read. This file is the file that is chained to, and it is called the chained file. (See Figures 9.28 and 9.29.)

Figure 9.28 CHAIN operation—example

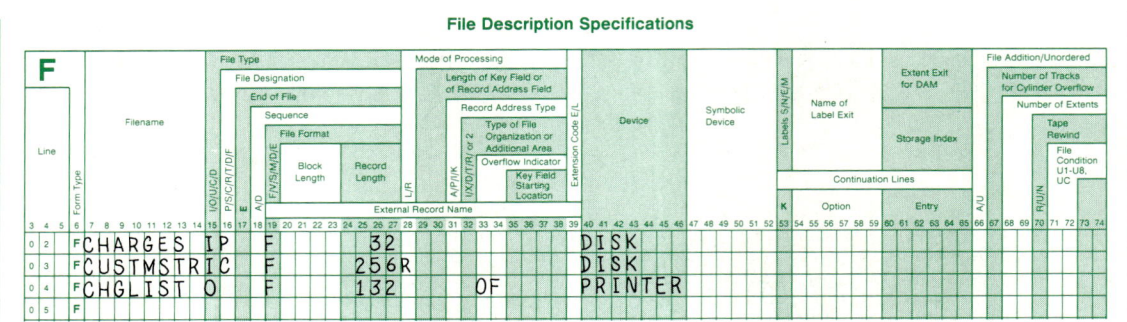

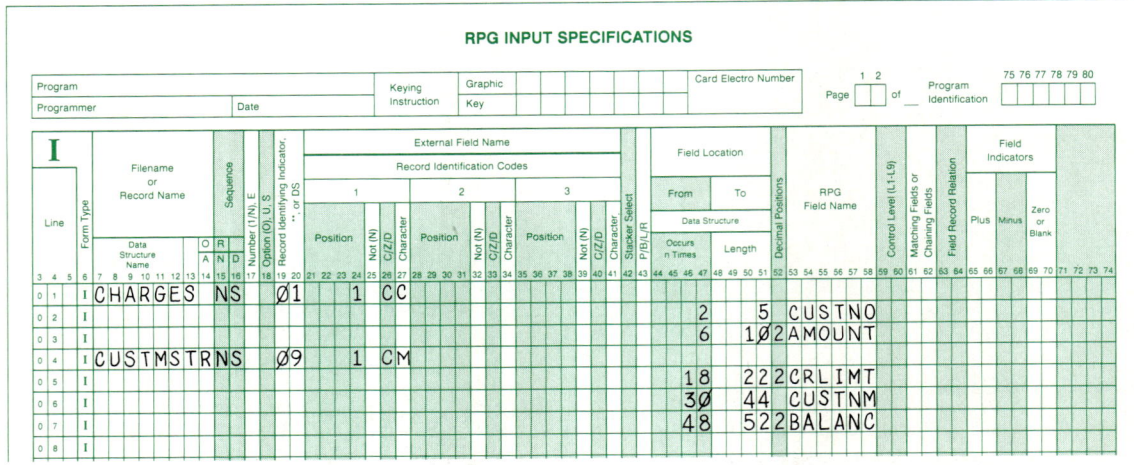

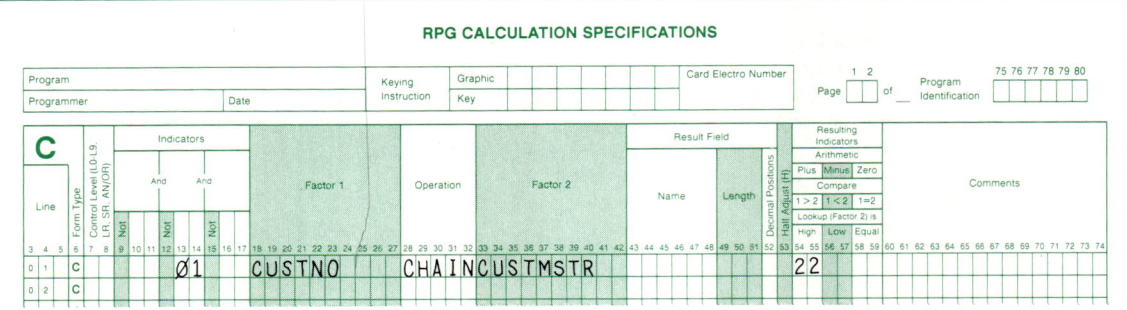

Figure 9.28 continued

Notes on the Coding

The record identifying indicator 01 is used to condition the operation.

CUSTNO is the field to be used in chaining. The field is a special field sometimes referred to as the "key field," which enables RPG to find the corresponding record in the other file.

The operation code is CHAIN.

Factor 2 must be the name of the file designated as IC on the File Description Specifications.

Indicator 22 is assigned to turn on if the record is not found in the CUSTMSTR file.

When the CHAIN operation is successful, the fields described on the Input Specifications are immediately available for processing. For this reason, the CHAIN is usually done early in the calculations so it may use the fields from both Input files; adding AMOUNT to the BALANC, comparing the AMOUNT to the CRLIMT.

Remember: The CHAIN calculation is really performing an INPUT function in the program.

Figure 9.29 CHAIN operation—example

Problem Statement

The SALES file has the amount of the sale, the customer's number, and the salesman's number. It will be necessary to CHAIN to the SLSMSTR file to get the salesman's name, the commission rate, and the year-to-date figures to complete the processing for this program. Code only the File Description, Input, and CHAIN operation for this program.

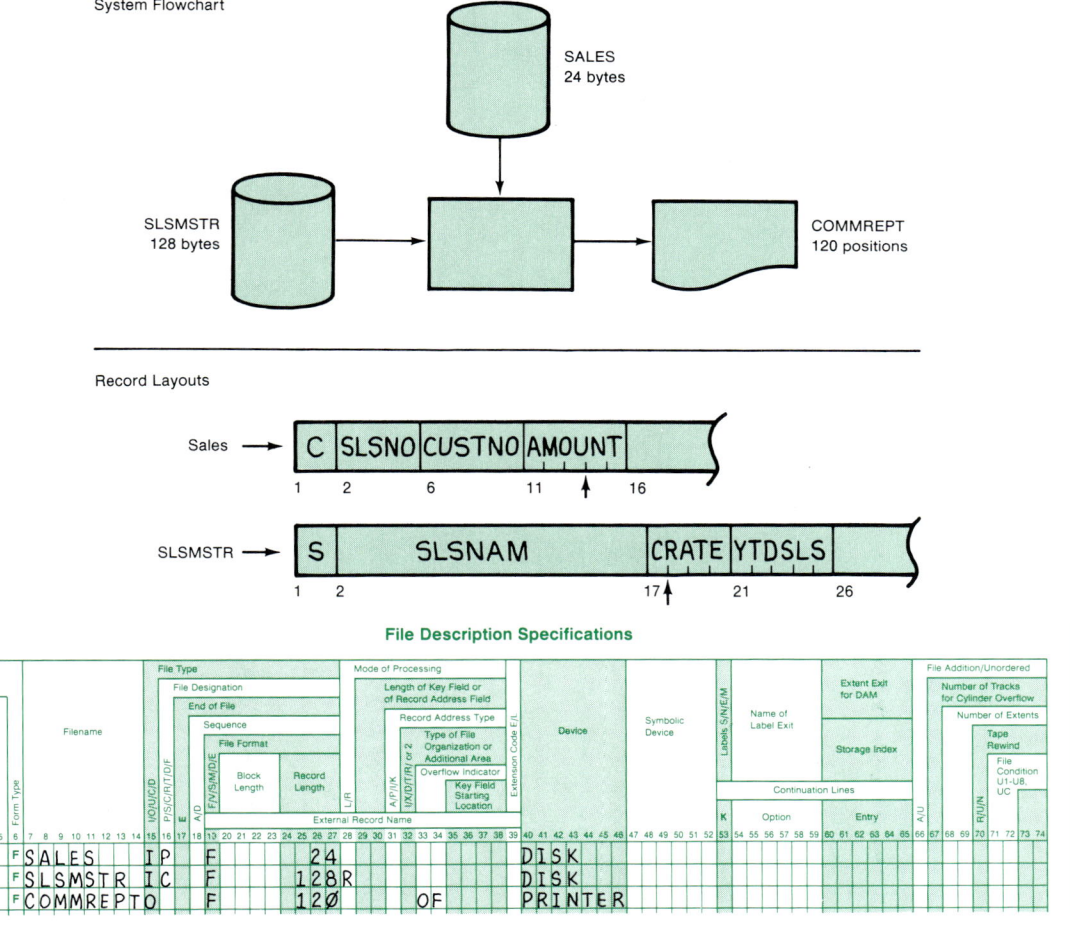

Multiple Batch Processing

Figure 9.29 continued

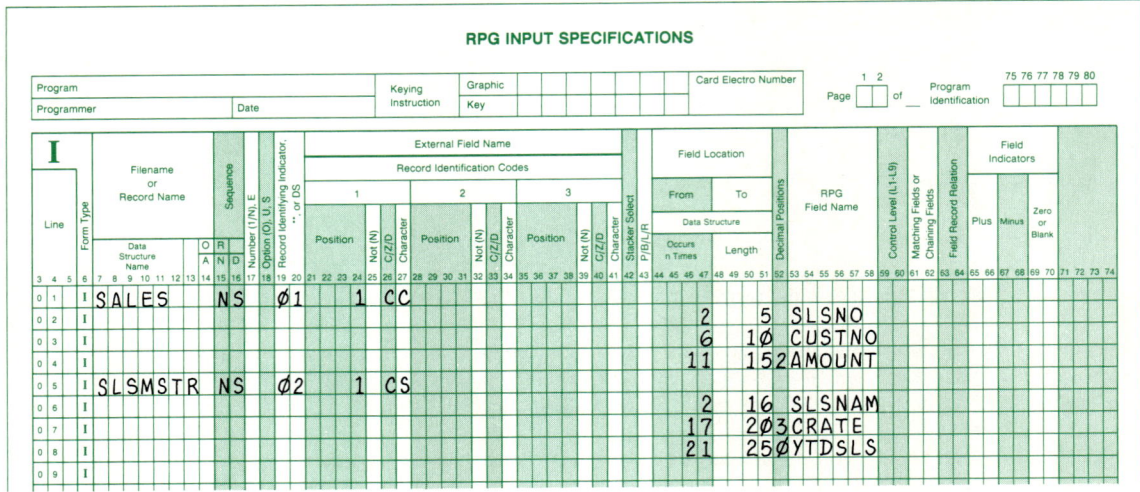

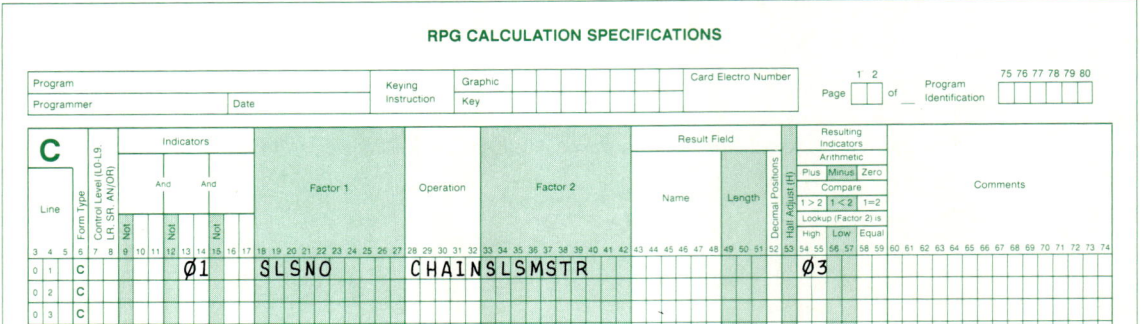

Notes on the Coding

SLSMSTR is the input chained file, since that is the one to search for the additional data. The R in position 28 indicates that the processing will be random.

Both files must be defined on the Input Specifications. If this was a complete program, naturally more fields would be used.

The CHAIN operation uses the field SLSNO from the input primary file to link to the other file SLSMSTR. Resulting indicator 03 will turn on if the corresponding salesman's record cannot be found.

Figure 9.30 Field record relation—example

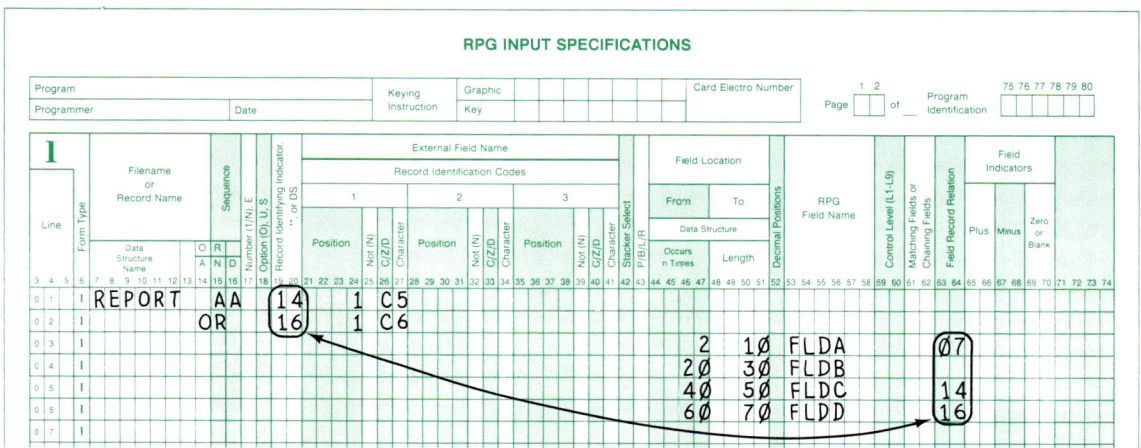

Notes on the Coding

The above illustration shows how record identifying indicators are used to relate a field to a record. The file contains two different types of records, one identified by a 5 in position 1 and the other by a 6 in position 1.

FLDC is related by record identifying indicator 14 to the record type that is identified by a 5 in position 1.

FLDD is related to a record type having a 6 in position 1 by record identifying indicator 16. This means that FLDC is found on only one type of record (that identified by 5 in position 1) and FLDD is found only on the other type.

FLDA is conditioned by indicator 07, which had been previously defined in the program elsewhere.

FLDB is found on both types, since it is not related by any one type by a record identifying indicator.

Field Record Relation

There are programs that process several different record types. Two or more record types might contain identical fields. To eliminate coding these identical fields for every record type the OR relationship, which indicates that certain fields are found in all record types, may be used. Not all fields are identical in different record types, however. There must be some way of specifying in the OR relationship those fields found only in specific record types. **Field record relation indicators** are used to indicate those fields found only on specific record types. (See Figure 9.30.)

Field record relation indicators will relate the following:

1. A field to a specific record type in the OR relationship
2. Control fields to a specific record type in an OR relationship
3. Matching chaining fields for more than one record type
4. External indicator definition and selective processing

The use of field record relation indicators is a means of reducing the number of lines to be coded. It also provides a convenient means of selective control of processing. This is particularly the case with records in an OR relationship (OR in positions 14–15 of the Input Specifications form) when the record fields are in different locations.

The presence of one of these indicators in positions 63–64 means that the field described on that line will be used only when that indicator is on. A field record relation indicator can be used in conjunction with control level field (positions 59–60), and with a matching record field or chaining field (positions 61–62).

Multiple Batch Processing

Figure 9.31 Using the OR relationship to describe identical record types—example

RPG INPUT SPECIFICATIONS

Line	Form Type	Filename or Record Name	Sequence	Record Identifying Indicator	Position	C/Z/D	Character	From	To	Decimal Positions	RPG Field Name
01	I	INVENTRY	AA	Ø1	96	C	N				
02	I	OR		Ø2	96	C	D				
03	I	OR		Ø3	96	C	O				
04	I							1	5		CLASS
05	I							6	12		ITEMNO
06	I							13	32		DESC
07	I							33	38	Ø	ONHAND
08	I							39	44	Ø	DATE

OR Relationship

Suppose there are several record types in OR relationship with record fields in different locations. The record type indicators specified in positions 19–20 on the Input Specifications form can be used as the indicators in positions 63–64 to designate with which record types the fields are to be used. As an example, notice the record identifying indicators (positions 19–20) for the file named INVENTRY. (See Figure 9.31.) These same indicators are used in positions 63–64 to designate with which record type the machine fields are to be used. In this case, 01, 02, and 03 are the only valid entries for positions 63–64.

When using the OR relationship, it is necessary to write the names of identical fields from more than one type of record only once on the Input Specifications form. OR relationship specifications indicate that the fields named may be found on all of the record types. The following input specifications are necessary to set up the OR relationship:

1. Record identifying indicators (01–99) for each record type
2. The letters OR in positions 14–15 for all record types other than the first
3. Entries describing the record identification code of each record type (positions 21–41)

The record identifying codes must be described for all record types in the file before any fields are described. The letters OR placed before the description of each record type except the first indicates that the fields listed may be found in all record types.

Figure 9.32 Field record relation—example

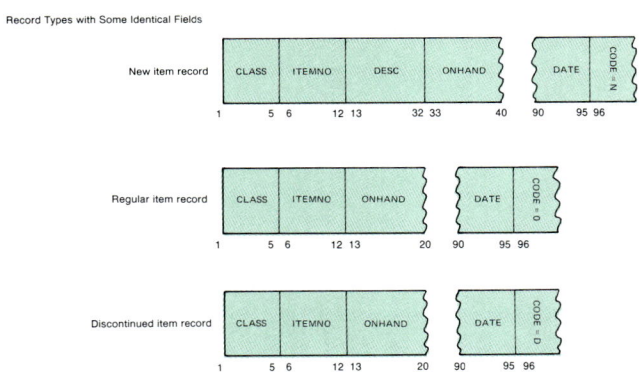

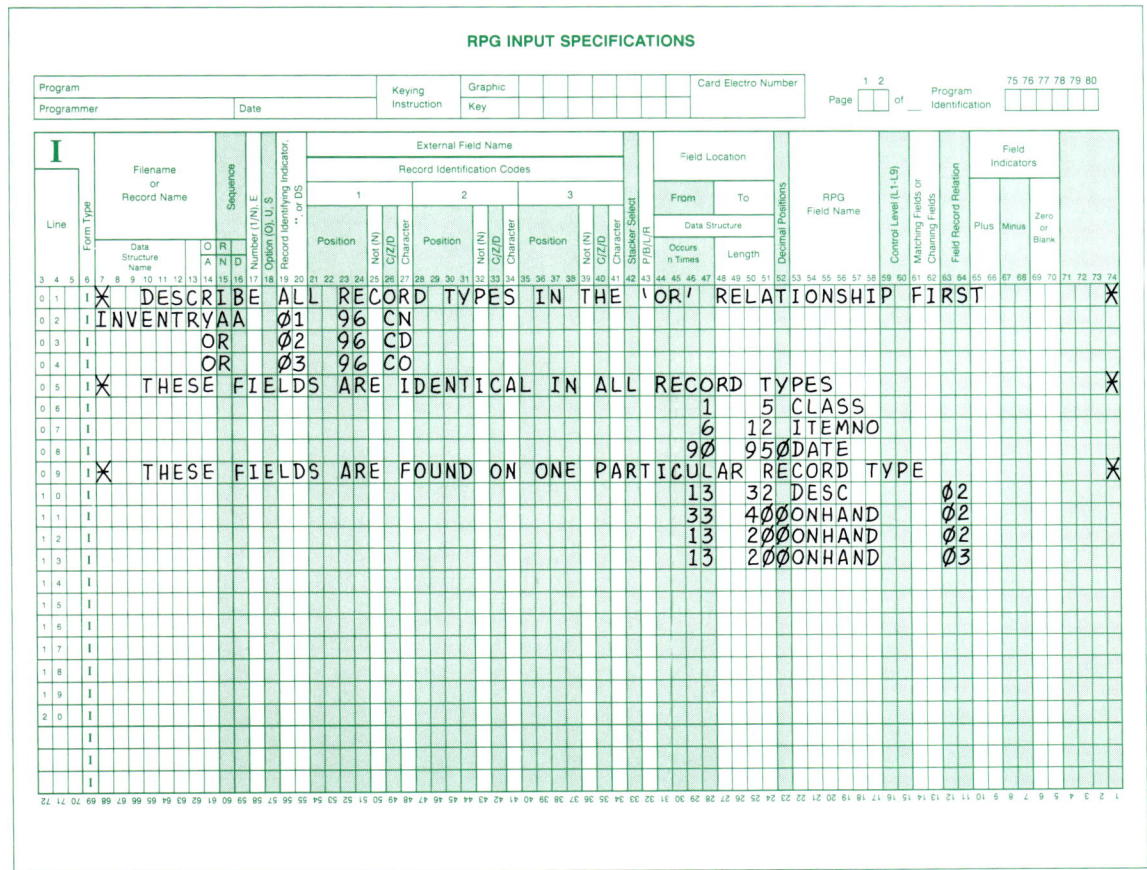

When positions 63–64 are left blank, the fields listed are assumed to be found in the positions specified in all records in the OR relationship. When an entry is specified in positions 63–64, the field is found only in the record type having that record identifying indicator.

Remember that when fields on all record types are not identical, the field must be described and related to all record types on which it is found. All fields relating to only one record type should be entered as a group, and must be given the same record identifying indicators in positions 63–64.

If most fields are common, describing the record type with field record relationship usually reduces the number of specifications that must be written and the amount of storage necessary to hold the instructions. (See Figure 9.32.)

Multiple Batch Processing   473

Figure 9.33 Field record relation used with control fields—example

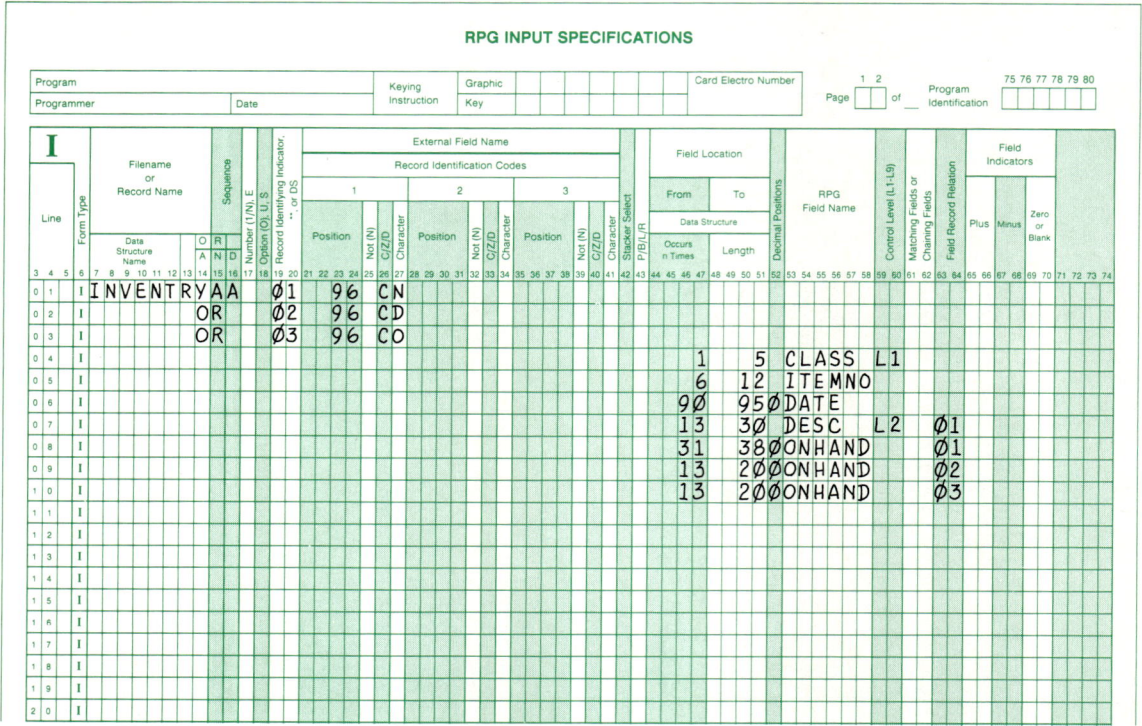

Use with Control Fields

Another situation in which the programmer may use field record relation indicators is one in which it is necessary to accept and use data from a particular field only when a control break (L1–L9) occurs. Control fields can also be related to a specific record type in an OR relationship by the use of field record relation entries. Blanks in positions 63–64 indicate that a control field is found on all record types. If a control field is found only in one record type, however, the control field must be related to the record type in which it is found by an entry in positions 63–64. The number of control fields need not be the same for every record in the OR relationship. Regardless of the number of control fields per record type, all control fields and all other fields related to the same record type should be entered as a group. (See Figure 9.33.)

Use with Matching Fields

A field record relation entry may be used with a field also designated as a matching field (Mn in positions 61–62) when (a) input is on two or more files, (b) records on one or more files are in an OR relationship, and (c) the matching fields are in different locations within the records. For each record type, the field encoded with a value of Mn constitutes a control set. Within a control set, either all fields must have the same value encoded in positions 63–64 or the positions must be left blank.

An MR field record relation indicator may be used to accept data from the field named in positions 53–58 when the indicator is on. (See Figure 9.34.)

Use with Chaining Fields

The field record relation coding is used to selectively control the chaining function, which is otherwise indicated by the entry of C1–C9 in positions 61–62. The desired indicator value is entered in positions 63–64 on the same line(s) in which Cn (where n is a digit between one and nine) has been encoded. Automatic chaining occurs only if the field record relation indicator specified is on when the record is read.

Figure 9.34 Field record relation used with match fields—example

Assigning Match Fields Once for Two Record Types

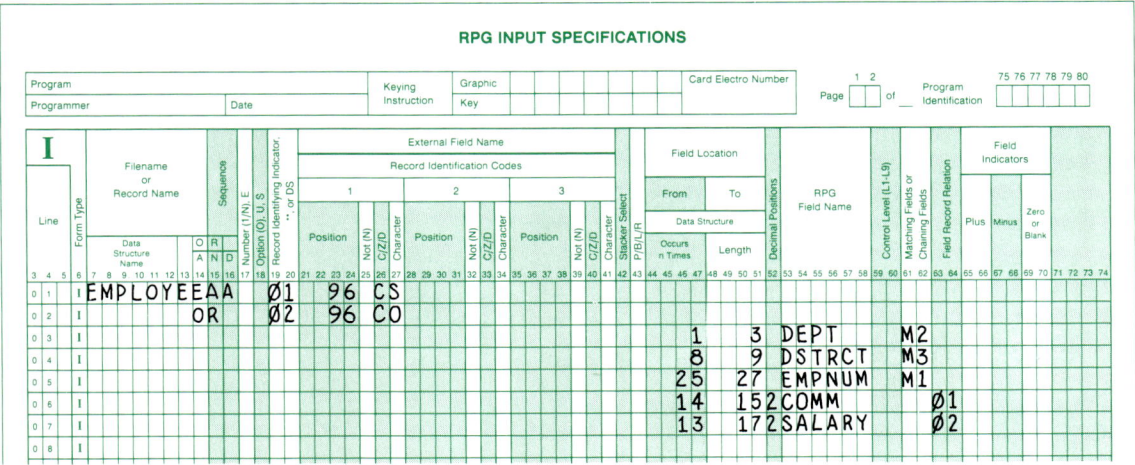

Notes on the Coding

When only a few fields differ, record types can be described on the Input form in an OR relationship. Instead of using separate sets of input specifications, common fields need to be described only once.

Entries under field record relation (positions 63-64) can then identify the fields that are unique to a particular record type.

Notice that the fields that are the same for all record types are then described before specifying the fields related to one of the other record types.

DSTRCT, DEPT, and EMPNUM are the three match fields to be used in sequence-checking the EMPLOYEE file.

Since they are described only once on the input form without any field record relation entries, the match field entries also need be assigned only once. When record types are described in an OR relationship and a match field entry is assigned to a field without any field record relation entry, the match field will be used for all record types.

Use with External Indicators and Selective Processing

Often the programmer may find it desirable to allow for options in record processing. These options may be selected at the time of execution. The facility for this is provided through the external indicators U1–U8 (sometimes referred to as user indicators) set on at run time by job control commands. These external indicators may be used within the object program to condition operations and functions, permitting a program to be written to perform multiple functions depending upon run parameters. Specifically, if U1–U8 has been encoded in positions 63–64, the normal processing for that field is carried out if the specified external indicator has been set on by a job control command. If the indicator is off, all input processing of the field in this record is bypassed. (Similarly, any calculation or output operation conditioned by a given indicator is bypassed unless the specified on or off status exists.) This feature is useful for external control of the object program, such as directing one kind of processing in a daily run and another at the end of a week, month, or quarter. Another use is in selecting only certain classes of records (e.g., summarizing only salaried employee pay records from a combined hourly/salaried employee pay file). The external indicators must not be used for fields defined as matching or control level fields (positions 61–62).

Entries in the field record relation positions relate particular fields to particular records.

Illustrative Program

Compare—GOTO: Aged Trial Balance Report

Job Definition

An Aged Trial Balance Report is to be prepared showing the customers' accounts with their credit limits, total charges, and the charges broken down into time periods of overdue accounts. Various percentages are to be calculated showing what percentage of the total charges are the various current charges and what are delinquency charges. This report will be used by the credit department to evaluate the customers' accounts.

Input

There are two record types in the customer file: master record and invoice record. The formats for the two records are as follows:

Master Record

Positions	Field Description	
1–01	Code	(letter *M*)
2–06	Customer number	
7–30	Customer name	
37–43	Credit limit	(XXXXX.XX)

Invoice Record

Positions	Field Description	
1–01	Code	(letter *I*)
2–06	Customer number	
44–49	Invoice date	(mm/dd/yy)
50–56	Invoice amount	(XXXXX.XX)

There is one record for each customer invoice.

Processing

Total charges—all invoice amounts will be added here.

Current charges—only the current month invoice amounts will be added here.

Overdue accounts (30 days)—only the previous month's invoice amounts will be added here.

Overdue accounts (60 days)—only the second previous month's invoice amounts will be added here.

Overdue accounts (90 days)—All past due accounts beyond 60 days will be added here.

Final totals—total charges, current charges, and overdue accounts (30, 60, and 90 days, and more than 90 days).

Percentages for current charges and overdue accounts for each column—each total divided by total charges.

Output
The Printer Spacing Chart shows how the report is formatted:

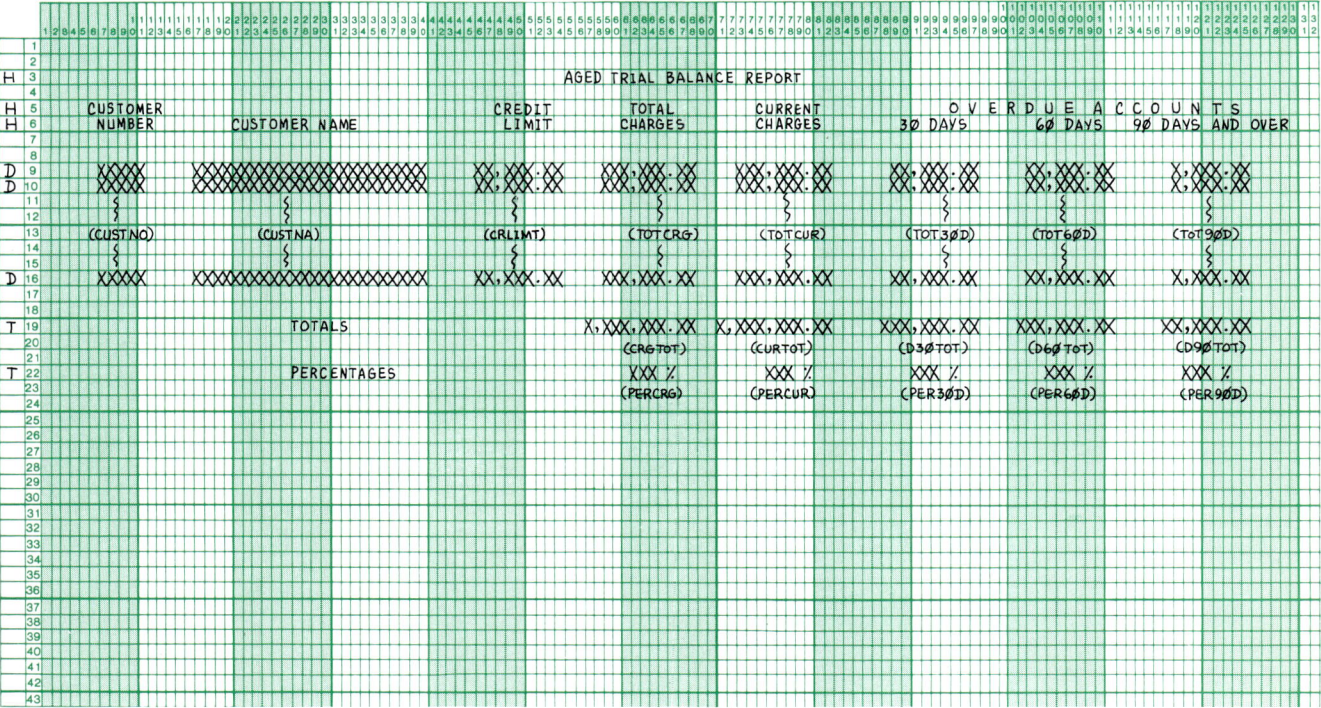

Coding sheets for the Aged Trial Balance problem:

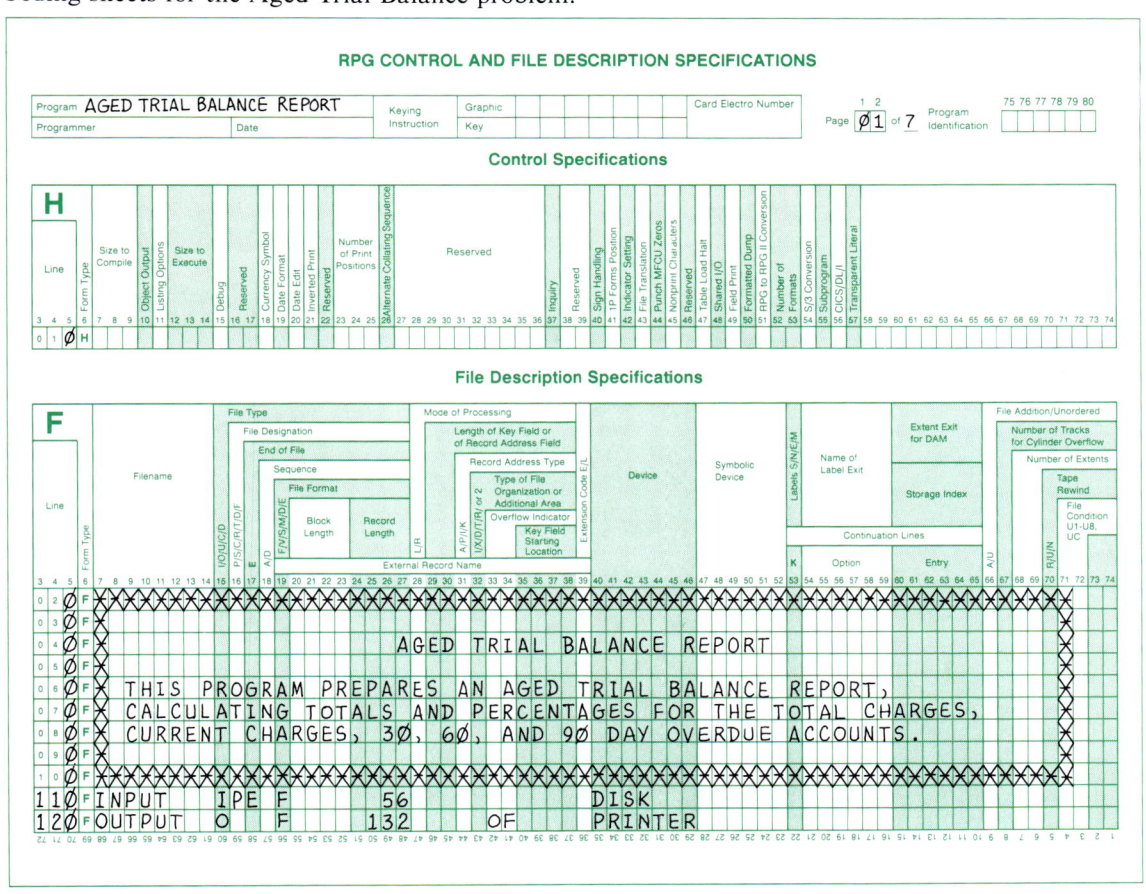

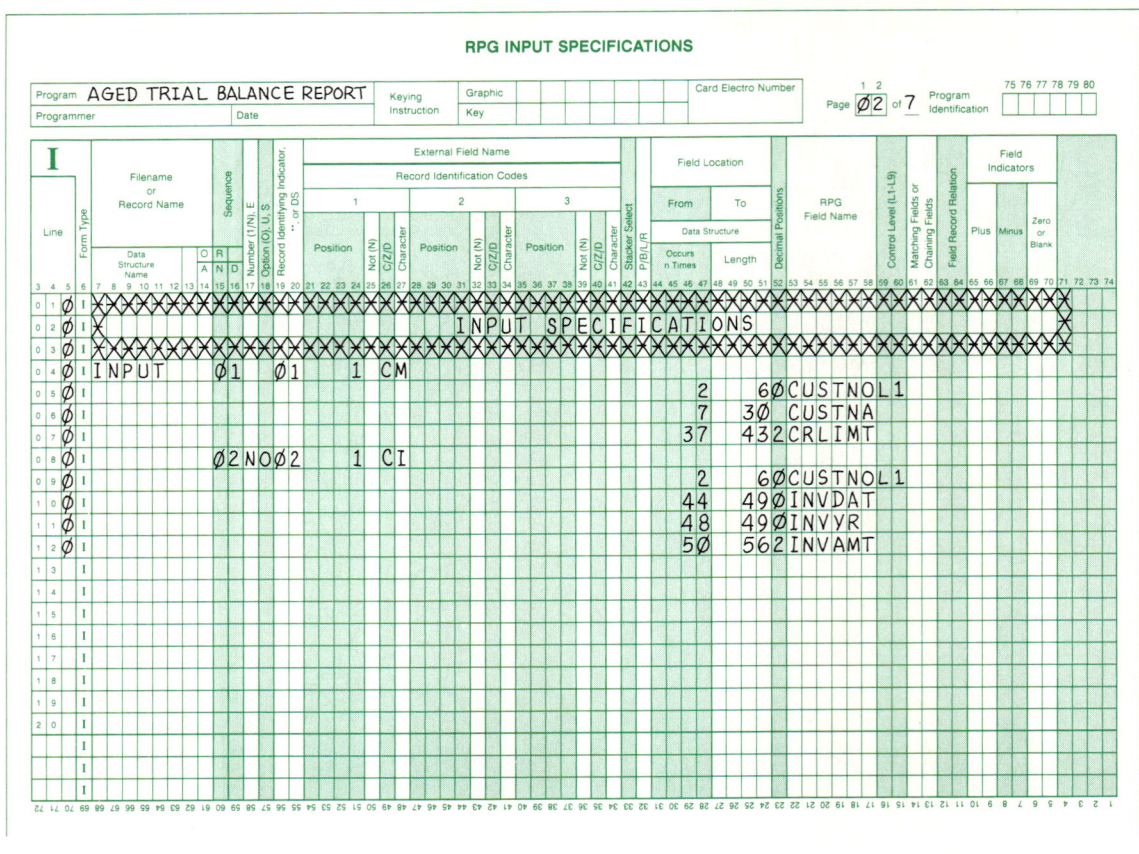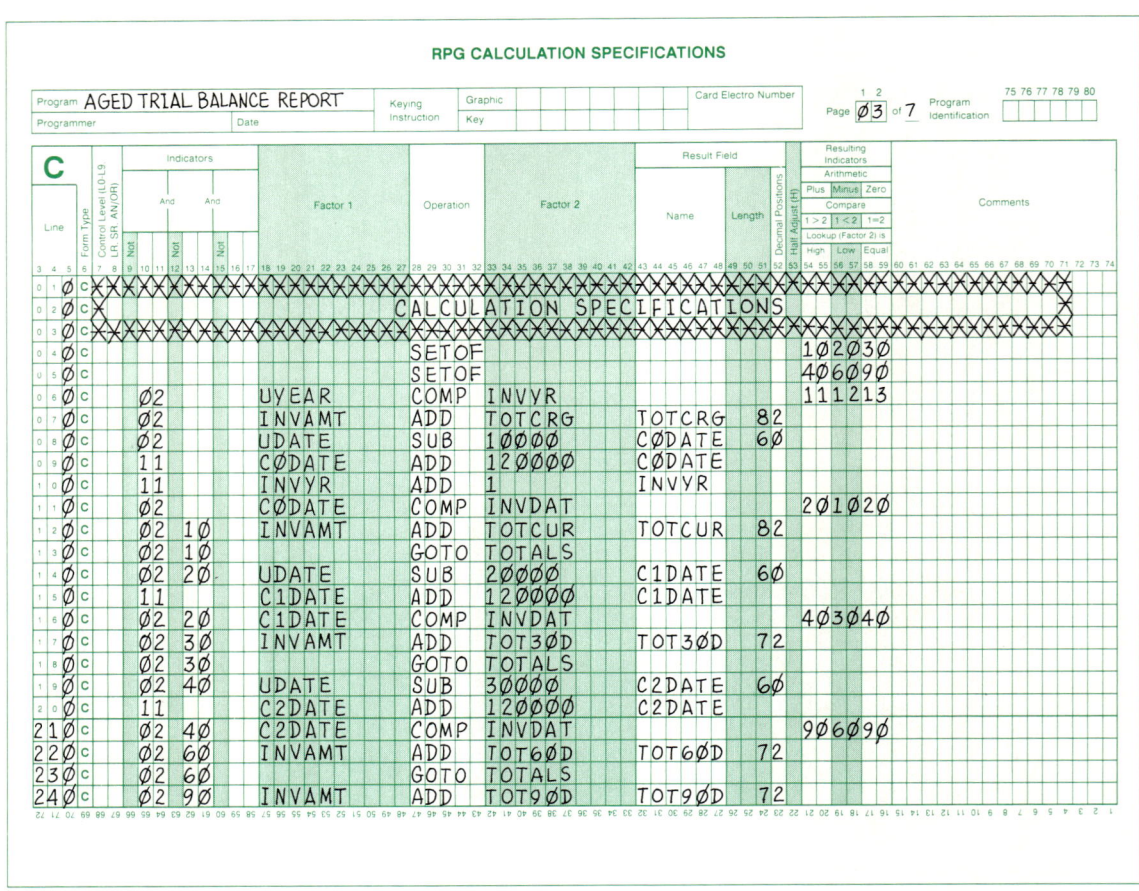

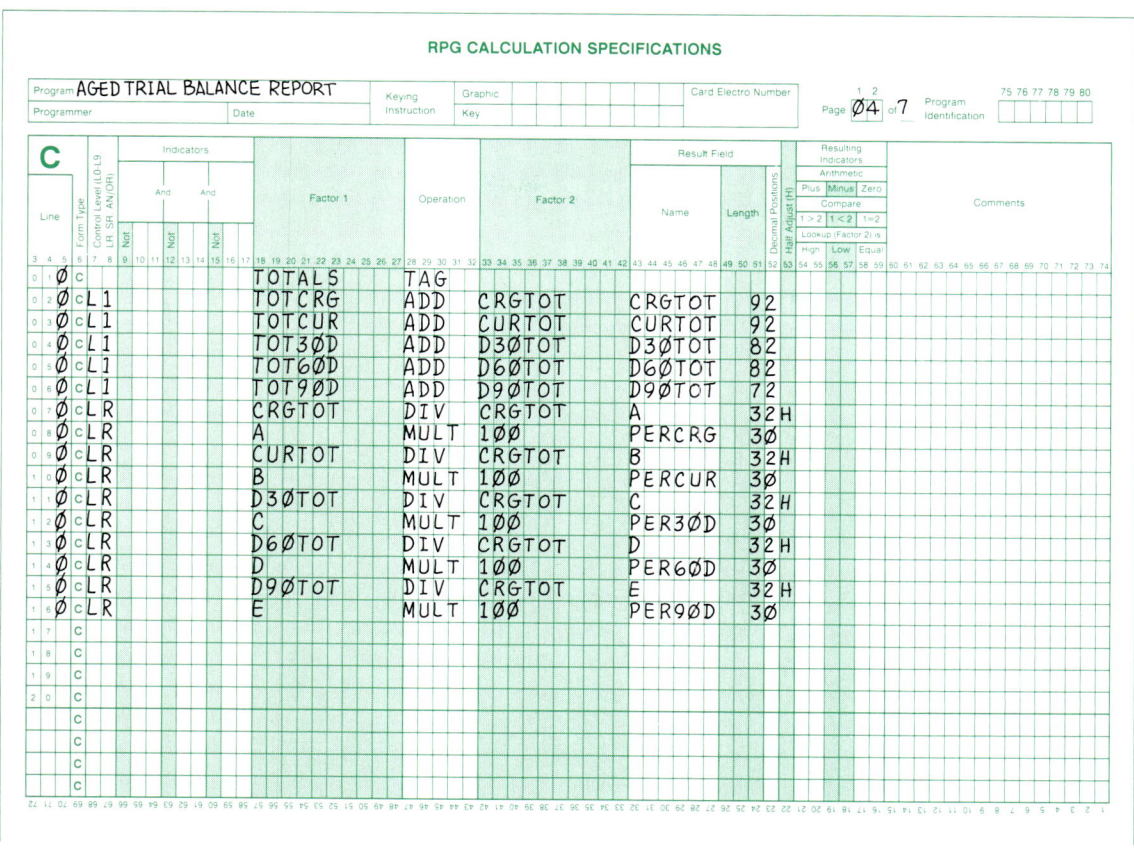

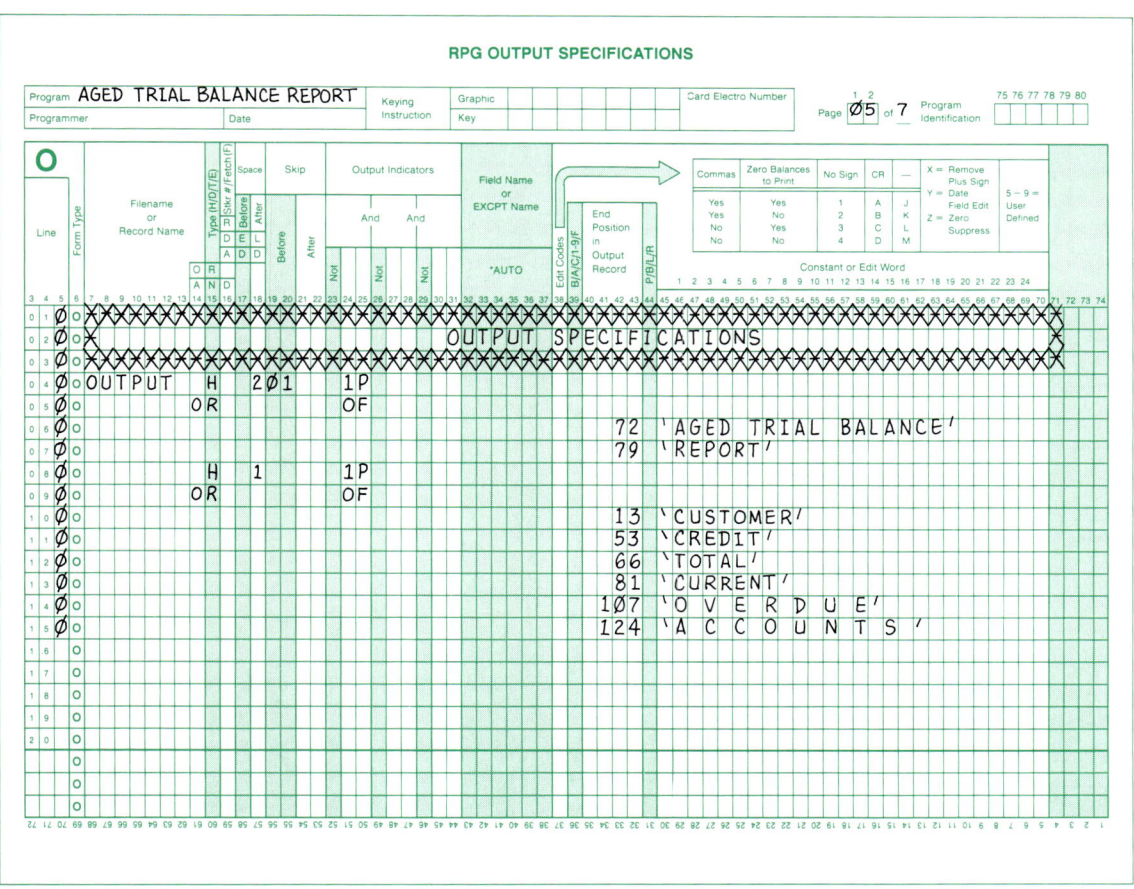

Multiple Batch Processing

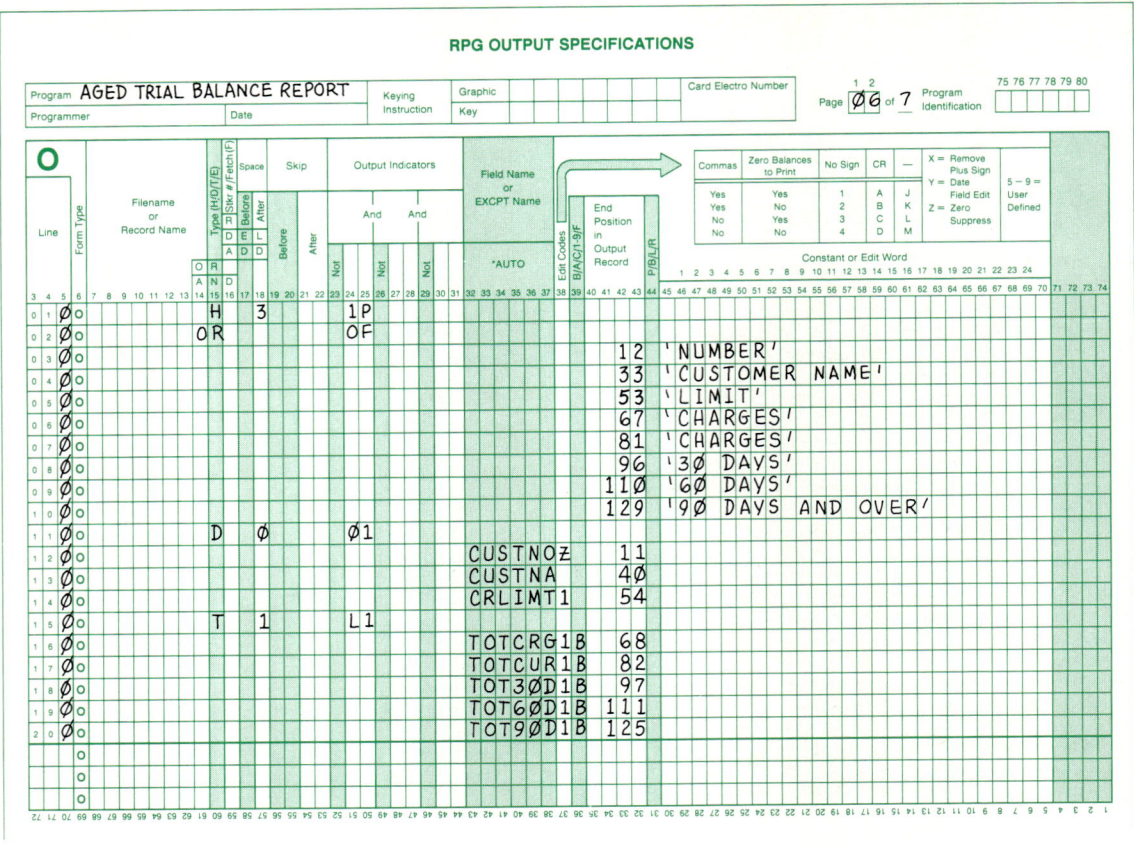
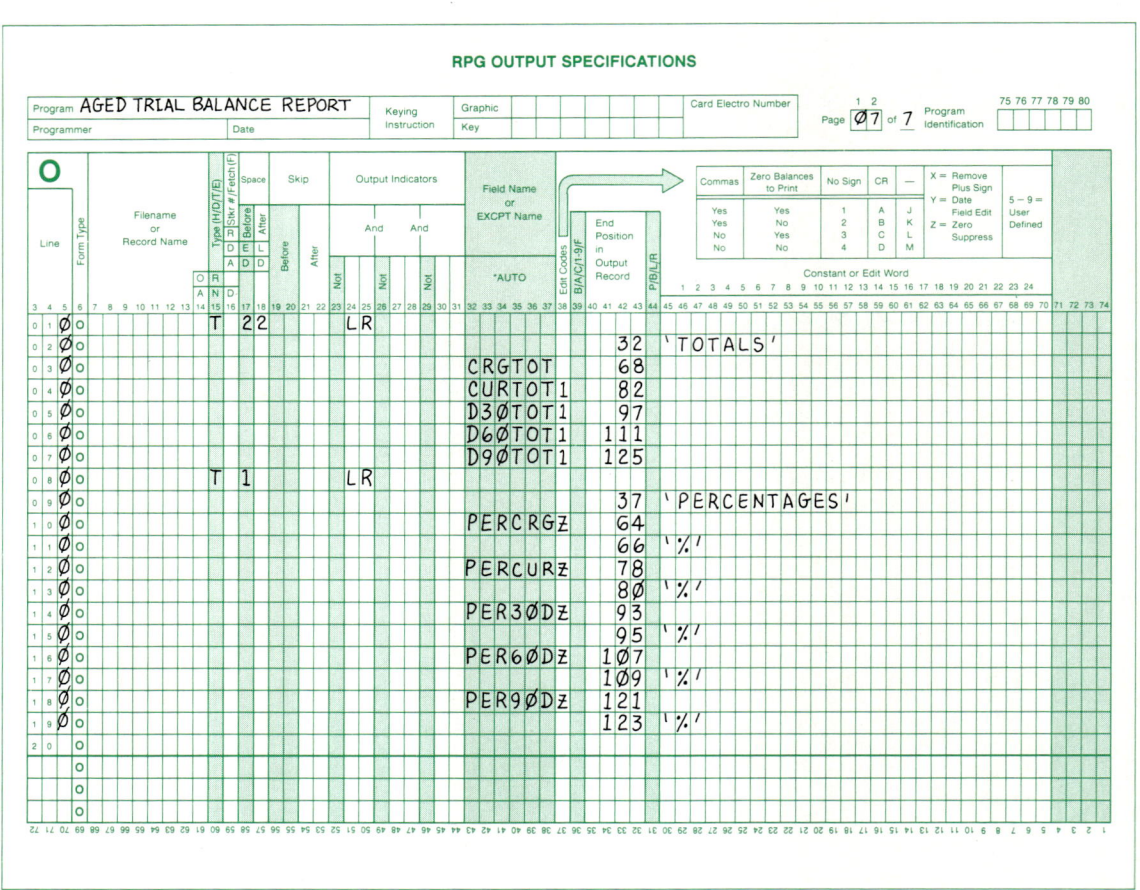

The source listing for the Aged Trial Balance problem:

```
 1    01010H
 2  * 01020F****************************************************************
 3  * 01030F*                                                               *
 4  * 01040F*               AGED TRIAL BALANCE REPORT                       *
 5  * 01050F*                                                               *
 6  * 01060F* THIS PROGRAM PREPARES AN AGED TRIAL BALANCE REPORT,           *
 7  * 01070F* CALCULATING TOTALS AND PERCENTAGES FOR THE TOTAL CHARGES,     *
 8  * 01080F* CURRENT CHARGES, 30, 60, AND 90 DAY OVERDUE ACCOUNTS.         *
 9  * 01090F*                                                               *
10  * 01100F****************************************************************
11    01110FINPUT   IPE F      56           DISK
12    01120FOUTPUT  O   F     132       OF  PRINTER
13  * 02010I****************************************************************
14  * 02020I*                    INPUT SPECIFICATIONS                       *
15  * 02030I****************************************************************
16    02040IINPUT    01   01    1 CM
17    02050I                                           2   60CUSTNOL1
18    02060I                                           7   30 CUSTNA
19    02070I                                          37  432CRLIMT
20    02080I         02NO02    1 CI
21    02090I                                           2   60CUSTNOL1
22    02100I                                          44  490INVDAT
23    02110I                                          48  490INVYR
24    02120I                                          50  562INVAMT
25  * 03010C****************************************************************
26  * 03020C*                 CALCULATION SPECIFICATIONS                    *
27  * 03030C****************************************************************
28    03040C                   SETOF                           102030
29    03050C                   SETOF                           406090
30    03060C   02      UYEAR   COMP  INVYR                     111213
31    03070C   02      INVAMT  ADD   TOTCRG   TOTCRG   82
32    03080C   02      UDATE   SUB   10000    C0DATE   60
33    03090C   11      C0DATE  ADD   120000   C0DATE
34    03100C   11      INVYR   ADD   1        INVYR
35    03110C   02      C0DATE  COMP  INVDAT                    201020
36    03120C   02 10   INVAMT  ADD   TOTCUR   TOTCUR   82
37    03130C   02 10           GOTO  TOTALS
38    03140C   02 20   UDATE   SUB   20000    C1DATE   60
39    03150C   11      C1DATE  ADD   120000   C1DATE
40    03160C   02 20   C1DATE  COMP  INVDAT                    403040
41    03170C   02 30   INVAMT  ADD   TOT30D   TOT30D   72
42    03180C   02 30           GOTO  TOTALS
43    03190C   02 40   UDATE   SUB   30000    C2DATE   60
44    03200C   11      C2DATE  ADD   120000   C2DATE
45    03210C   02 40   C2DATE  COMP  INVDAT                    906090
46    03220C   02 60   INVAMT  ADD   TOT60D   TOT60D   72
47    03230C   02 60           GOTO  TOTALS
48    03240C   02 90   INVAMT  ADD   TOT90D   TOT90D   72
49    04010C          TOTALS   TAG
50    04020CL1        TOTCRG   ADD   CRGTOT   CRGTOT   92
51    04030CL1        TOTCUR   ADD   CURTOT   CURTOT   92
52    04040CL1        TOT30D   ADD   D30TOT   D30TOT   82
53    04050CL1        TOT60D   ADD   D60TOT   D60TOT   82
54    04060CL1        TOT90D   ADD   D90TOT   D90TOT   72
55    04070CLR        CRGTOT   DIV   CRGTOT   A        32H
56    04080CLR        A        MULT  100      PERCRG   30
57    04090CLR        CURTOT   DIV   CRGTOT   B        32H
58    04100CLR        B        MULT  100      PERCUR   30
59    04110CLR        D30TOT   DIV   CRGTOT   C        32H
60    04120CLR        C        MULT  100      PER30D   30
61    04130CLR        D60TOT   DIV   CRGTOT   D        32H
62    04140CLR        D        MULT  100      PER60D   30
63    04150CLR        D90TOT   DIV   CRGTOT   E        32H
64    04160CLR        E        MULT  100      PER90D   30
65  * 05010O****************************************************************
66  * 05020O*                   OUTPUT SPECIFICATIONS                       *
67  * 05030O****************************************************************
68    05040OOUTPUT  H  201     1P
69    05050O          OR       OF
70    05060O                                     72 'AGED TRIAL BALANCE'
71    05070O                                     79 'REPORT'
72    05080O        H  1       1P
73    05090O          OR       OF
74    05100O                                     13 'CUSTOMER'
75    05110O                                     53 'CREDIT'
76    05120O                                     66 'TOTAL'
77    05130O                                     81 'CURRENT'
78    05140O                                    107 'O V E R D U E'
79    05150O                                    124 'A C C O U N T S'
80    06010O        H  3       1P
81    06020O          OR       OF
82    06030O                                     12 'NUMBER'
83    06040O                                     33 'CUSTOMER NAME'
84    06050O                                     53 'LIMIT'
85    06060O                                     67 'CHARGES'
86    06070O                                     81 'CHARGES'
87    06080O                                     96 '30 DAYS'
88    06090O                                    110 '60 DAYS'
89    06100O                                    129 '90 DAYS AND OVER'
```

```
 90   061100        D  0      01
 91   061200                      CUSTNOZ   11
 92   061300                      CUSTNA    40
 93   061400                      CRLIMT1   54
 94   061500        T  1      L1
 95   061600                      TOTCRG1B  68
 96   061700                      TOTCUR1B  82
 97   061800                      TOT30D1B  97
 98   061900                      TOT60D1B 111
 99   062000                      TOT90D1B 125
100   070100        T 22      LR
101   070200                                32 'TOTALS'
102   070300                      CRGTOT1   68
103   070400                      CURTOT1   82
104   070500                      D30TOT1   97
105   070600                      D60TOT1  111
106   070700                      D90TOT1  125
107   070800        T  1      LR
108   070900                                37 'PERCENTAGES'
109   071000                      PERCRGZ   64
110   071100                                66 '%'
111   071200                      PERCURZ   78
112   071300                                80 '%'
113   071400                      PER30DZ   93
114   071500                                95 '%'
115   071600                      PER60DZ  107
116   071700                               109 '%'
117   071800                      PER90DZ  121
118   071900                               123 '%'
```

The Aged Trial Balance Report is to be printed as follows:

AGED TRIAL BALANCE REPORT

CUSTOMER NUMBER	CUSTOMER NAME	CREDIT LIMIT	TOTAL CHARGES	CURRENT CHARGES	OVERDUE ACCOUNTS		
					30 DAYS	60 DAYS	90 DAYS AND OVER
10867	ALLEN & CO.	15,000.00	7,296.35	6,919.77	376.58	.00	.00
16535	ANDERSON AUTO SUPPLY	2,500.00	1,665.49	1,665.49	.00	.00	.00
17849	ANDREWS AND SONS INC.	750.00	146.64	.00	.00	146.64	.00
18978	ARGONAUT ENGINEERING	2,000.00	3,458.41	3,055.84	.00	312.13	90.44
24743	BERKLEY PAPER CO.	6,300.00	5,289.00	3,837.95	.00	1,400.05	51.00
25271	BEST DISTRIBUTING CO.	1,000.00	765.44	3.25	.00	.00	762.19
	TOTALS		18,621.33	15,482.30	376.58	1,858.82	903.63
	PERCENTAGES		100 %	83 %	2 %	10 %	5 %

Illustrative Program

Compare—Record Relation Indicators: Stock Status Report

Job Definition

Print a Stock Status Report. This report is printed whenever inventory is updated. It gives detailed information on all active merchandise. The first line for each item in the report shows standard descriptive data for the item—item number, item description, quantity on hand, and quantity on order. This information is taken directly from the input record.

Subsequent lines give the detail on current transactions involving the item—sales to customers and receipts from suppliers. This information is also taken directly from input records.

Quantity remaining on hand and on order are calculated for each item and printed after all transactions for the item are listed.

Input

An inventory file consists of three different types of records. Following are the formats of the three record types:

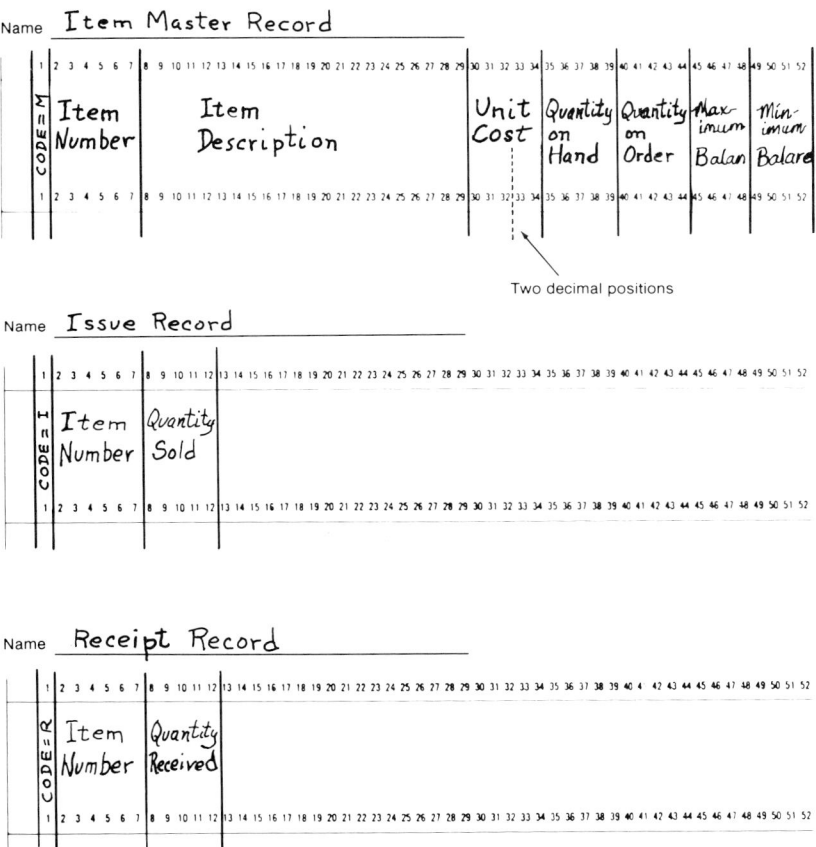

The file is organized in ascending order by item number. One master record is required for each item. Issue and receipt records are optional; when present, however, there may be any number of each. Records for each item are to be in the following order:

1. Item master
2. Issue(s)
3. Receipt(s)

Processing

Find total number of each item sold. To do this, perform the calculation ISSUE + TOTAL ISSUE = TOTAL ISSUE for each issue record.

Find total number of each item received. Perform the calculation RECEIPT + TOTAL RECEIPT = TOTAL RECEIPT for each record.

When all transaction records for one item have been read, find new quantity on hand (ON HAND + TOTAL RECEIPT − TOTAL ISSUE = NEW ON HAND) and new quantity on order (ON ORDER − TOTAL RECEIPT = NEW ON ORDER).

Output

The Printer Spacing Chart shows how the report is formatted:

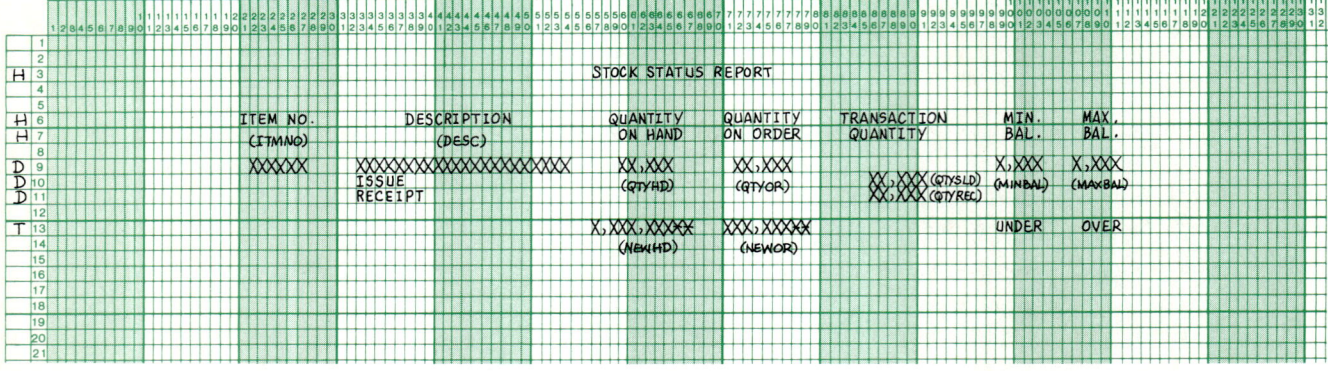

Coding sheets for the Stock Status Report problem:

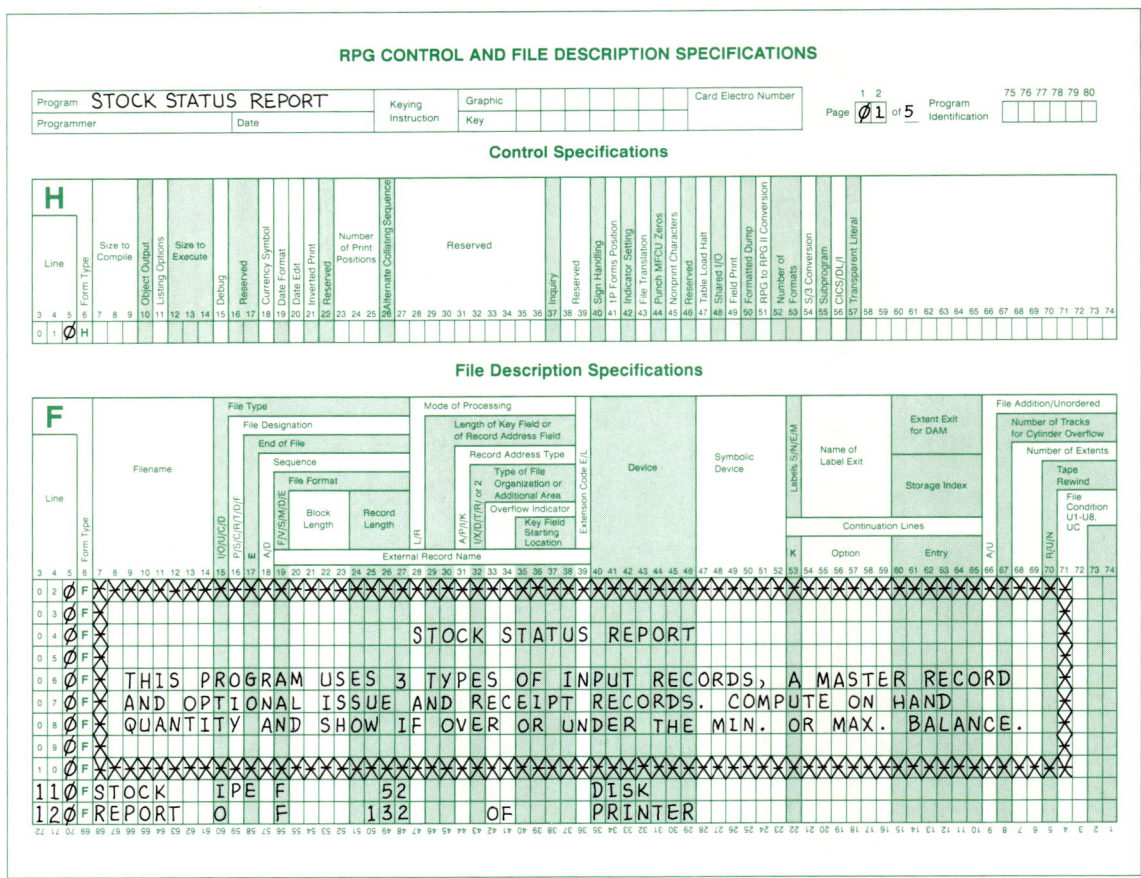

484   RPG II and RPG III Programming

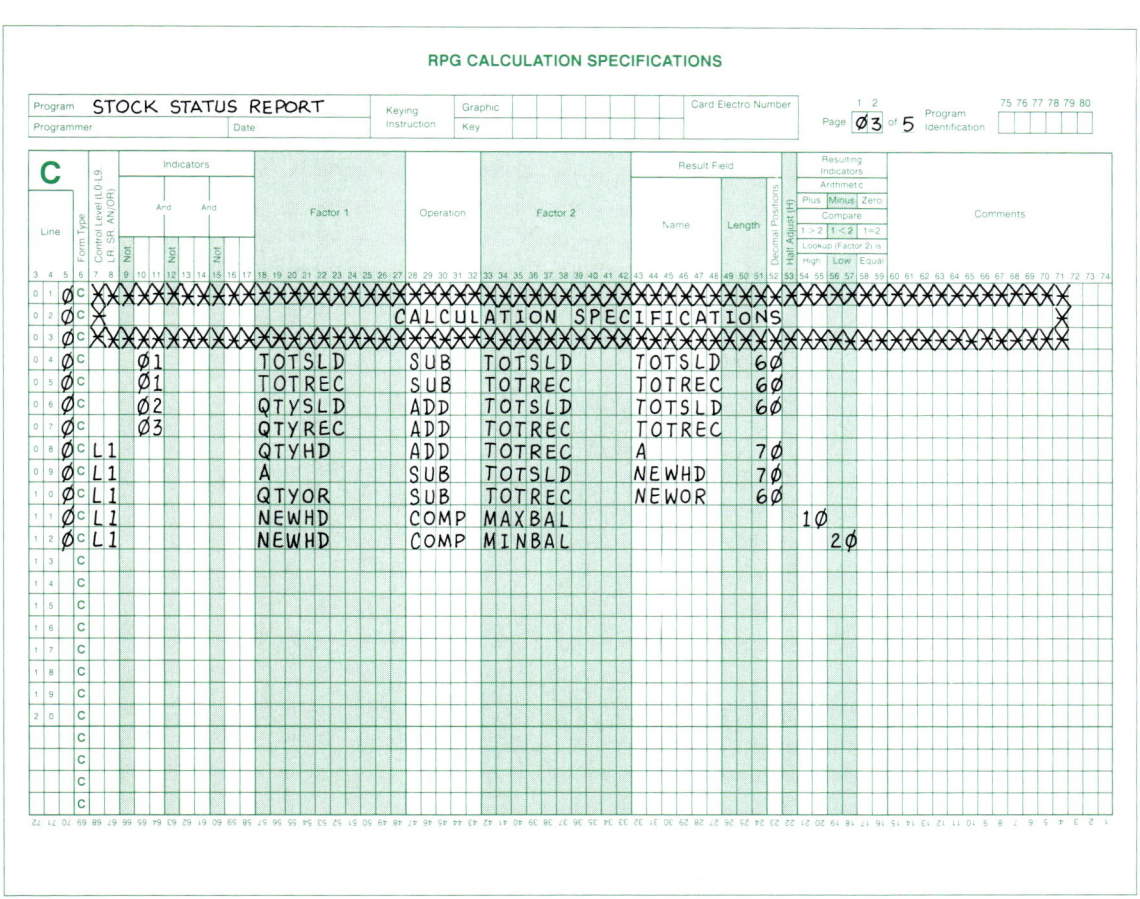

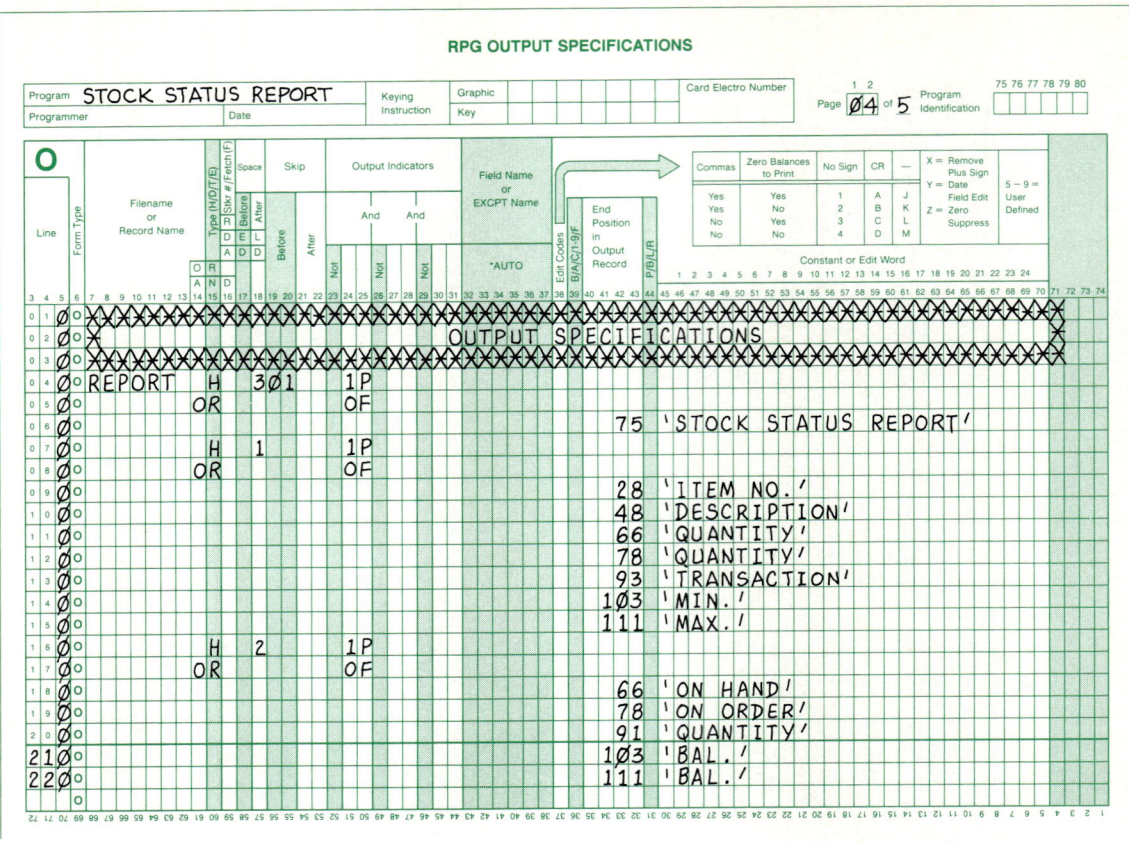
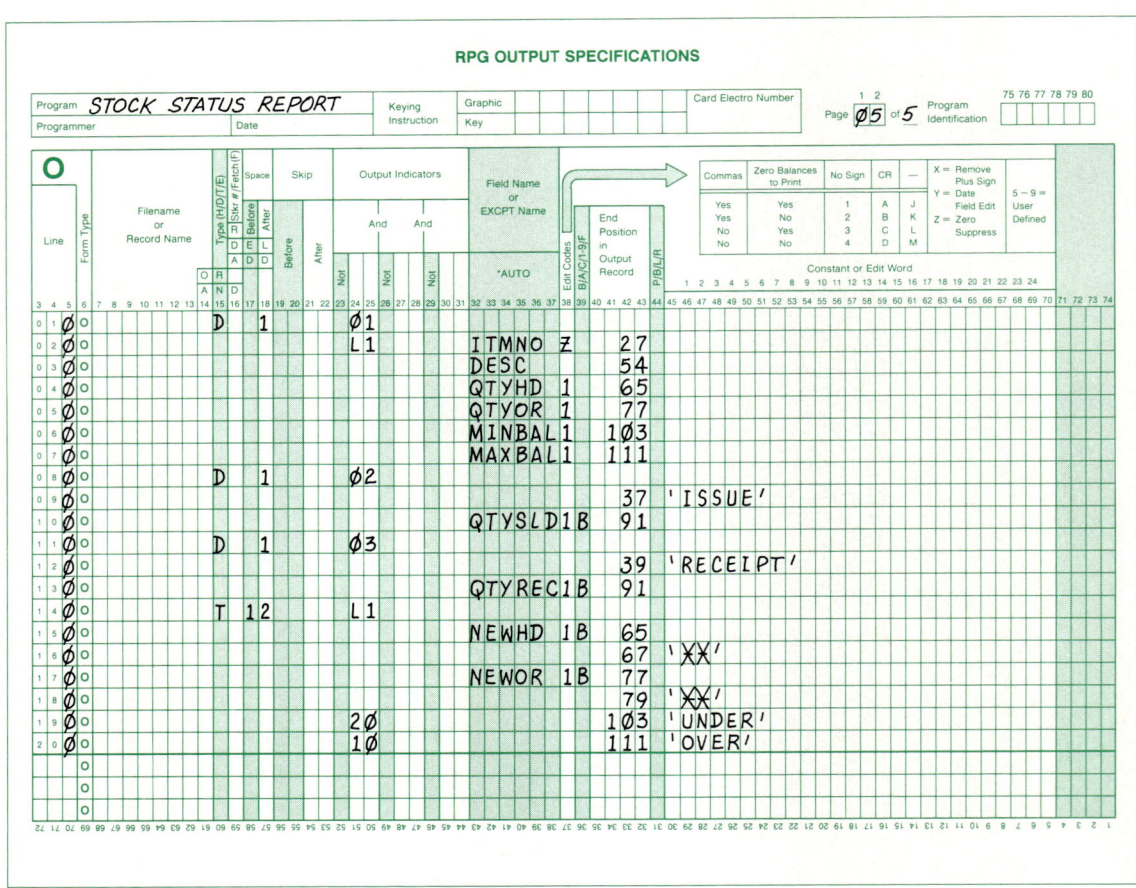

The source listing for the Stock Status Report problem:

```
1     01010H
2   * 01020F****************************************************************
3   * 01030F*                                                                *
4   * 01040F*                   STOCK STATUS REPORT                          *
5   * 01050F*                                                                *
6   * 01060F* THIS PROGRAM USES 3 TYPES OF INPUT RECORDS, A MASTER RECORD    *
7   * 01070F* AND OPTIONAL ISSUE AND RECEIPT RECORDS. COMPUTE ON HAND        *
8   * 01080F* QUANTITY AND SHOW IF OVER OR UNDER THE MIN. OR MAX. BALANCE.   *
9   * 01090F*                                                                *
10  * 01100F****************************************************************
11    01110FSTOCK    IPE F      52           DISK
12    01120FREPORT   O   F     132     OF    PRINTER
13  * 02010I****************************************************************
14  * 02020I*                   INPUT SPECIFICATIONS                         *
15  * 02030I****************************************************************
16    02040ISTOCK       011 01   1 CM
17    02050I                                              2   70ITMNO   L1
18    02060I                                              8   29 DESC
19    02070I                                             30   342UTCOST
20    02080I                                             35   390QTYHD
21    02090I                                             40   440QTYOR
22    02100I                                             45   480MAXBAL
23    02110I                                             49   520MINBAL
24    02120I           02N002   1 CI
25    02130I           OR  03   1 CR
26    02140I                                              2   70ITMNO   L1
27    02150I                                              8   120QTYSLD      02
28    02160I                                              8   120QTYREC      03
29  * 03010C****************************************************************
30  * 03020C*                  CALCULATION SPECIFICATIONS                    *
31  * 03030C****************************************************************
32    03040C   01        TOTSLD    SUB  TOTSLD   TOTSLD    60
33    03050C   01        TOTREC    SUB  TOTREC   TOTREC    60
34    03060C , 02        QTYSLD    ADD  TOTSLD   TOTSLD    60
35    03070C   03        QTYREC    ADD  TOTREC   TOTREC
36    03080CL1           QTYHD     ADD  TOTREC   A         70
37    03090CL1           A         SUB  TOTSLD   NEWHD     70
38    03100CL1           QTYOR     SUB  TOTREC   NEWOR     60
39    03110CL1           NEWHD     COMP MAXBAL             10
40    03120CL1           NEWHD     COMP MINBAL             20
41  * 04010O****************************************************************
42  * 04020O*                    OUTPUT SPECIFICATIONS                       *
43  * 04030O****************************************************************
44    04040OREPORT   H  301      1P
45    04050O         OR          OF
46    04060O                                         75 'STOCK STATUS REPORT'
47    04070O         H    1      1P
48    04080O         OR          OF
49    04090O                                         28 'ITEM NO.'
50    04100O                                         48 'DESCRIPTION'
51    04110O                                         66 'QUANTITY'
52    04120O                                         78 'QUANTITY'
53    04130O                                         93 'RANSACTION'
54    04140O                                        103 'MIN.'
55    04150O                                        111 'MAX.'
56    04160O         H    2      1P
57    04170O         OR          OF
58    04180O                                         66 'ON HAND'
59    04190O                                         78 'ON ORDER'
60    04200O                                         91 'QUANTITY'
61    04210O                                        103 'BAL.'
62    04220O                                        111 'BAL.'
63    05010O         D    1       01
64    05020O                      L1      ITMNO Z   27
65    05030O                              DESC      54
66    05040O                              QTYHD 1   65
67    05050O                              QTYOR 1   77
68    05060O                              MINBAL1  103
69    05070O                              MAXBAL1  111
70    05080O         D    1       02
71    05090O                                         37 'ISSUE'
72    05100O                              QTYSLD1B  91
73    05110O         D    1       03
74    05120O                                         39 'RECEIPT'
75    05130O                              QTYREC1B  91
76    05140O         T   12      L1
77    05150O                              NEWHD 1B  65
78    05160O                                         67 '**'
79    05170O                              NEWOR 1B  77
80    05180O                                         79 '**'
81    05190O                      20                103 'UNDER'
82    05200O                      10                111 'OVER'
```

Multiple Batch Processing

A Stock Status Report is to be printed as follows:

```
                            STOCK STATUS REPORT

ITEM NO.      DESCRIPTION        QUANTITY   QUANTITY   RANSACTION    MIN.    MAX.
                                 ON HAND    ON ORDER   QUANTITY      BAL.    BAL.

411116     B500 TWIN SOCKET BLUE   458        500                     800   1,600
           ISSUE                                           50
           RECEIPT                                        500

                                   908**       0**

411122     B506 SOCKET ADAPT BRN   325        100                     300    800
           ISSUE                                           20
           ISSUE                                           38
           ISSUE                                           10

                                   257**      100**                  UNDER

411173     C151C SIL SWITCH IVORY  150        100                     100    200
           RECEIPT                                        150

                                   300**       50**                          OVER
```

Questions for Review

1. What are the considerations in designing applications?
2. What is a primary file? A secondary file?
3. What is a sequential file and how may it be in logical sequence?
4. Does RPG require sequential files to be in logical sequence?
5. How does RPG process records of sequential files?
6. How is a single sequential file processed?
7. How are multiple sequential files processed?
8. What is meant by multifile processing?
9. What are match fields and what are their functions?
10. How can match field processing change the sequence of normal RPG programs?
11. How is sequence checking indicated for records within a single file?
12. How is sequence checking indicated in files containing more than one record type?
13. How may match fields that are the same for all record types be described on the Input Specifications form?
14. What is the matching record technique?
15. What rules apply to matching field entries?
16. When is the matching record indicator (MR) turned on, and how is it used in multifile processing?
17. What are the four possible outcomes of processing in a primary and secondary field?
18. How are matching records processed in two or more files?
19. How are matching record entries used on Calculation Specifications forms?
20. How may the programmer avoid performing calculations on the wrong data or programming the same calculation twice?

21. What are the steps involved in multifile processing using one file to obtain data from another file?
22. What are the considerations in determining the kind of processing to be done after all the records in one file have been processed?
23. How may match fields be used with control fields in the same file?
24. How is end-of-file processing specified for a particular file and under what conditions does end-of-file processing take place?
25. What is the main purpose of chaining?
26. How is the CHAIN operation specified?
27. What does the CHAIN operation do and how is it used?
28. What are some of the problems involved in chaining files during the same RPG cycle?
29. What indicators and entries on the Calculation Specifications form are used with the CHAIN operation?
30. How is random processing accomplished with the CHAIN operation?
31. When are field record relationships used?
32. What do field record indicators relate?
33. What are the necessary entries on the Input Specifications form for setting up the OR relationship?
34. How are field record relation indicators used with control fields?
35. How are field record relation indicators used with matching fields?
36. How are field record relation indicators used with chaining fields?
37. How are field record relation indicators used with external indicators in selective processing?
38. How are records normally read and processed, and how is FORCE used to change this sequence?
39. What are two methods used by RPG in which records are processed in a multifile job?
40. How may a record be processed out of order?
41. What situations require that the order of processing be altered?
42. How is the order of processing altered?
43. How is the next file to be processed specified?
44. Under what conditions may a record be forced?
45. What is the main function of the READ statement, and how does it differ from the FORCE statement?
46. How is a READ operation coded?

Problems

Problem 1

Using the following documentation, code the RPG solution for printing a proof listing of customer balances. The TRANS file contains charge and payment records. Consider only one type of transaction for any customer. The CUSTMSTR will be a chained file.

Your calculations should include:

1. Chaining to the CUSTMSTR file
2. Saving the original balance due so it may be listed with the new balance
3. Adding gas charges to the balance
4. Subtracting any payments.

Do not perform any of the calculations if the customer is not on the master file.

The output coding should include:

1. Headings on all pages
2. Writing both the new balance and the original balance
3. Customer number and a message printed as a detail line for customers not on the CUSTMSTR file.

Code the necessary file description, input specifications, calculation specifications, and output specifications on the appropriate forms.

Create a disk file (see CUSTMSTR) in a separate program before processing TRANS records.

System Flowchart

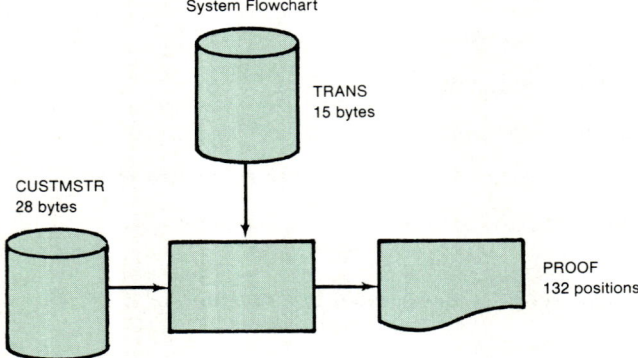

Record Layouts

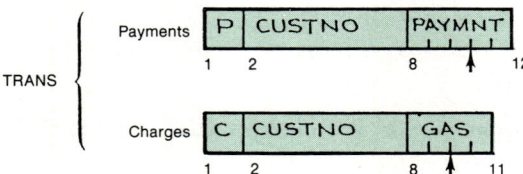

Disk

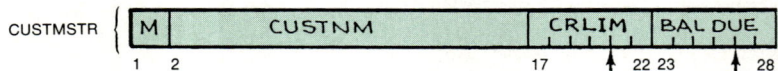

RPG II and RPG III Programming

The Printer Spacing Chart is as follows:

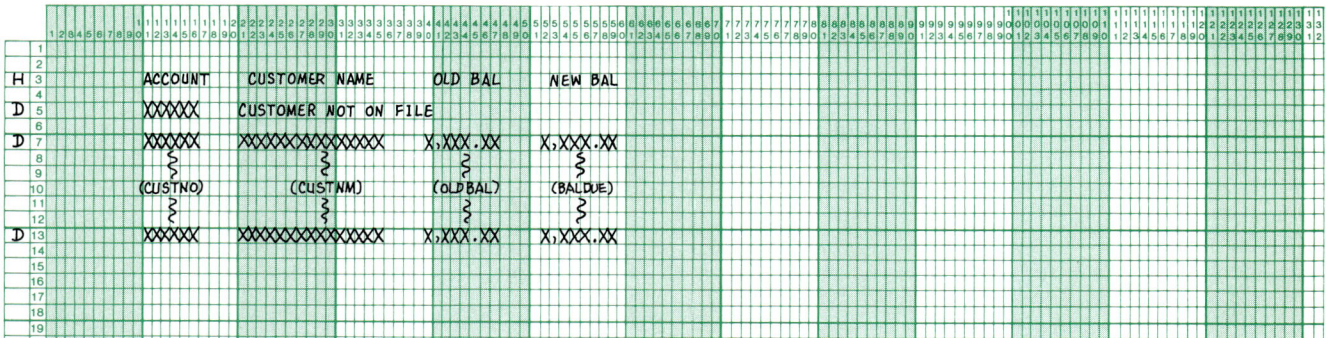

Output is as follows:

```
ACCOUNT    CUSTOMER NAME      OLD BAL      NEW BAL

147258     JONES ELEC CO       123.64        66.48

258635     BYRAN FURN CO       165.41        89.78

528636     MASON FLOUR CO    2,458.95     3,113.82

852321     HIBLER CO           856.98       361.33

852324     CUSTOMER NOT ON FILE
```

Problem 2

Using the information provided, code an RPG solution for the following problem.

General Description
Before running a payroll job, two files are run through a computer producing an exceptions listing. This shows how many employees there are, how many of each kind of record are missing, and so forth. A sample listing is shown.

Input
There are two files: RATECDS and TIMECDS. Both files are matched on the ascending field employee number. The record layouts are shown.

Calculations
The following totals are to be accumulated:

1. Number of rate records for matching records
   1 + MATCH = MATCH

2. Number of rate records without matching time cards
   1 + UMRATE = UMRATE

3. Number of time cards without matching rate records
   1 + UMTIME = UMTIME

4. Total number of employees (calculate at the end of the run)
   MATCH + UMRATE + UMTIME = TOTEMP

Output
A printed report called EXCPLIST is to be outputted on the printer. When a rate record has no matching time card, print employee name, employee number, and the message: MISSING TIMECARD. When a time card has no matching rate record, print employee number and the message: MISSING RATE CARD. The Printer Spacing Chart for EXCPLIST is shown.

Code the necessary file description, input specifications, calculation specifications, and output specifications on the appropriate forms.

Create a disk file RATECDS in a separate program before processing TIMECDS records.

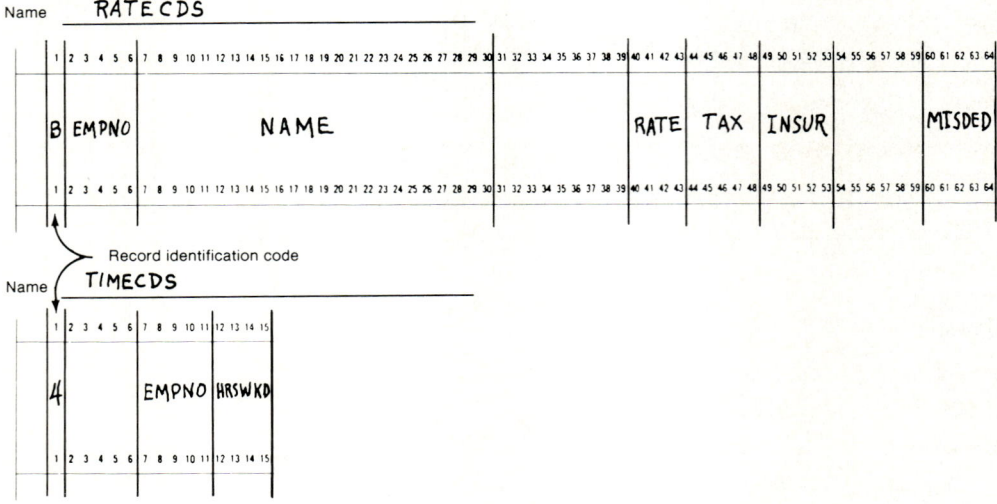

The Printer Spacing Chart is as follows:

Output is as follows:

```
                       EXCEPTION LISTING

    NUMBER            NAME                  EXCEPTION


    39264      WILLIAMSON,JAMES P      MISSING TIMECARD

    39627      HARVEY,ELVIN J          MISSING TIMECARD

    40039                              MISSING RATECARD

    40101      SMITH, JOHN             MISSING TIMECARD



                                       MISSING TIMECARDS      3

                                       MISSING RATECARDS      1

                                       TOTAL PAYROLL          7
```

492   RPG II and RPG III Programming

Problem 3

Using the documentation provided, code the RPG solution for the following problem.

General Description
A Job Cost to Date report is to be prepared. A sample of this report is shown.

Input
There are two disk files: JOBFILE and ITEMFILE. Their record layouts are provided. JOBFILE is in ascending order by job number, and ITEMFILE is arranged in ascending order by item number within job number. They are to be matched by job number.

Calculations
For matching records, a total job cost is to be accumulated from individual item costs. The final total is to be an accumulation of total job costs.

1. ITECST + CSTJOB = CSTJOB
2. CSTJOB + FINTOT = FINTOT

Output
A printed report called JOBCOST is to be outputted on the printer. Printed information should come only from matching records. The report is to be group indicated by job number and description. The Printer Spacing Chart is shown.

Code the necessary file description, input specifications, calculation specifications, and output specifications on the appropriate forms.

Record Layouts

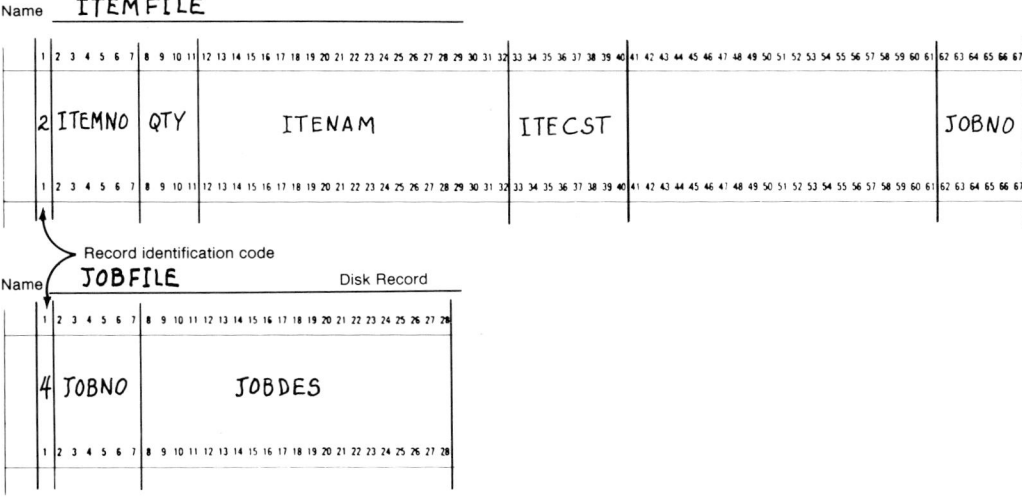

The Printer Spacing Chart is as follows:

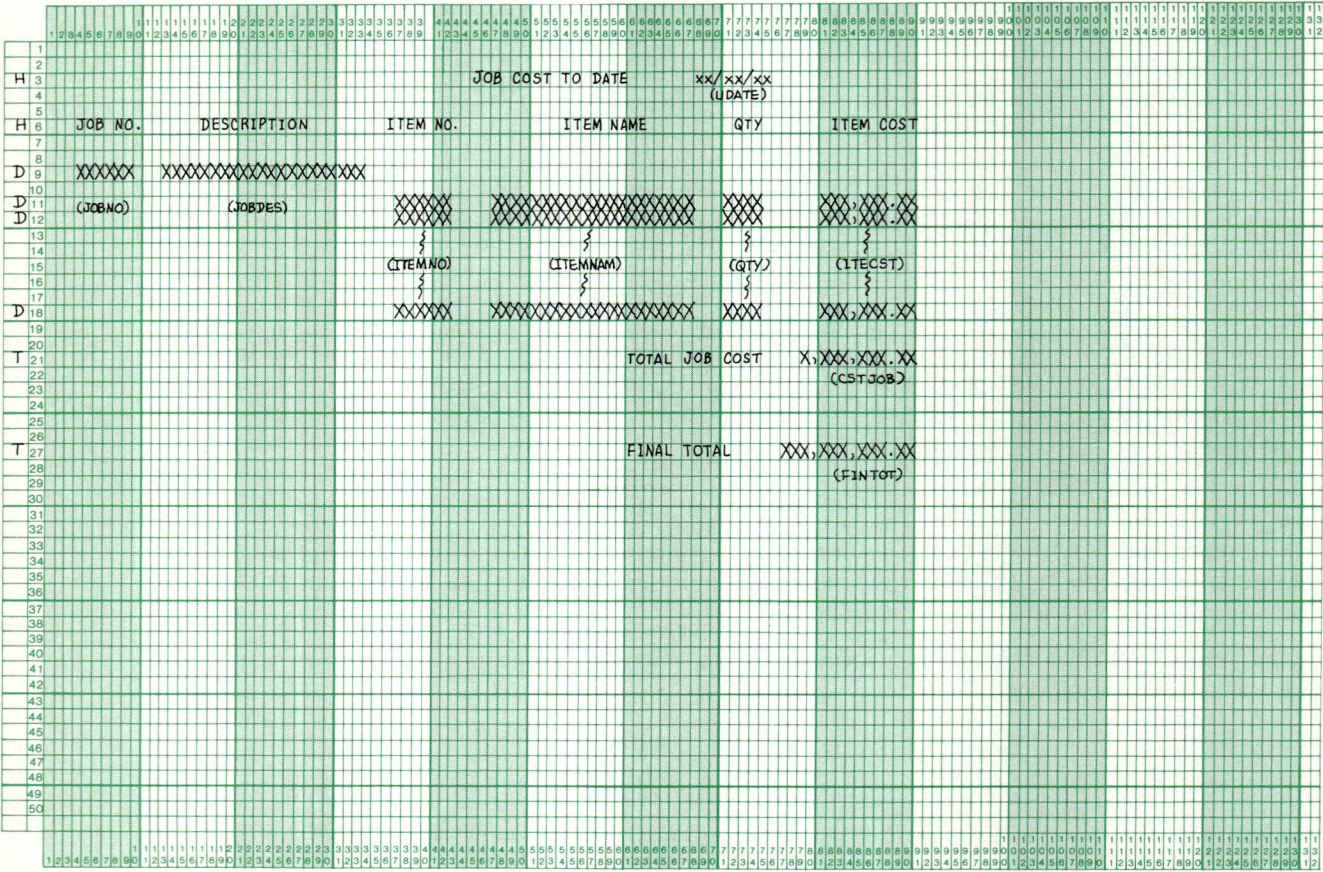

Output is as follows:

```
                              JOB COST TO DATE      5/18/87

JOB NO.     DESCRIPTION      ITEM NO.          ITEM NAME           QTY        ITEM COST

203962      MECHANICAL LINK
                              396001       3/4 IN. SPROCKET         9            396.27
                              396059       2 IN. COTTER            53          6,103.96
                              420006       1/2 IN. GROMET RUBBER  350              9.60
                              501201       PAINT. BLUE/GREEN       10             35.00

                                                           TOTAL JOB COST     6,544.83

203990      ASSEMBLY #49
                              207059       16 IN. GAS TURBINES      2         26,347.01
                              639027       13 IN. DRIVE SHAFT       1             27.00
                              747142       1/4 IN. FILE ROUND     137            973.20

                                                           TOTAL JOB COST    27,347.21


                                                              FINAL TOTAL    33,892.04
```

Problem 4

Using the information provided, code the RPG solution for the following problem.

General Description

The data-processing department is to prepare a weekly labor distribution report showing the total number of hours worked by each employee, as well as the total number of hours worked by all employees within a department. Therefore, the report must be organized by department number and by man number within a department.

Input

Two input files provide the necessary data for the report.

1. PMSTER is a master payroll file containing three types of records:
   a. Date record—first record in file
   b. Department name records
   c. Employee master records

   The employee records are in ascending sequence by department number and by number within a department. A department name record appears within the file immediately before the group of employee records for that particular department.

2. LABOR is a file of daily records containing the number of hours an employee worked. Since each employee's daily hours (two decimal positions) are recorded on a separate record, there will be more than one LABOR record for each employee. The LABOR file is also in ascending sequence by department number and by man number within a department.

Calculations

In processing the two files, there should be an employee master record related to all LABOR records. In fact, more than one LABOR record will match the same employee master record from the PMSTER file. However, it is possible that the LABOR file contains the following unmatched records:

1. Records with errors in match fields
2. Records for new employees for whom employee master records have not yet been created

Processing should end when the last record from the LABOR file has been processed.

Hours are to be accumulated for each employee and the total hours are to be accumulated for each department. A final total of the hours worked is to be accumulated for all departments.

Output

Prepare the necessary Printer Spacing Chart showing the department number, department name, manager's name, man number, name, and hours worked. Include the necessary totals for each control level. The report should contain all necessary headings.

Code the necessary file description, input specifications, calculation specifications, and output specifications on the appropriate forms.

PMSTER File — 3 Record Types

Date record layout
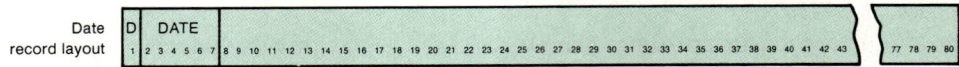

Department name record layout
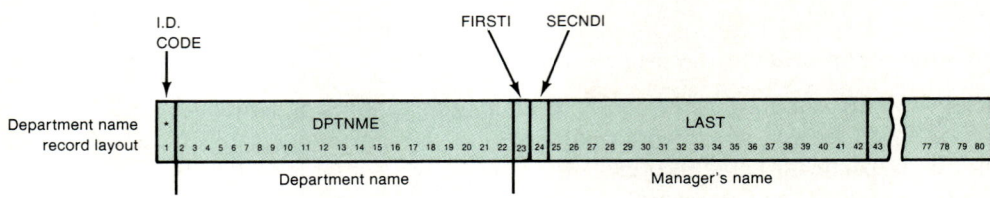

Employee master record layout
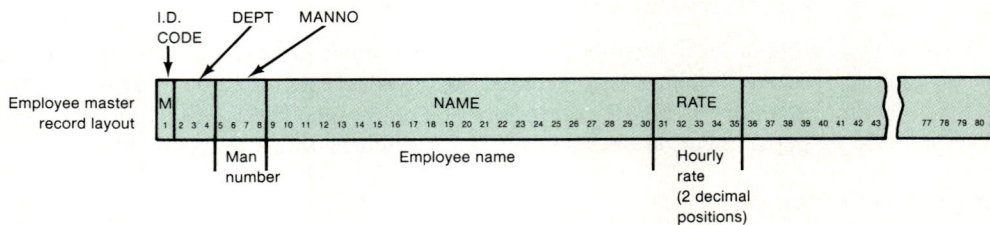

LABOR File — 1 Record Type
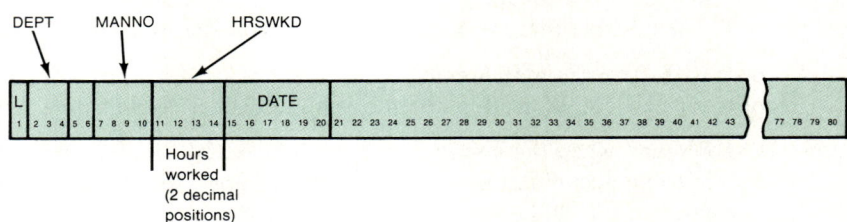

Output is as follows:

```
                    WEEKLY LABOR DISTRIBUTION REPORT

          DEPARTMENT          MANAGER          MAN          EMPLOYEE         HOURS
DEPT.       NAME               NAME          NUMBER           NAME          WORKED


  12    SHIPPING/RECEIVING   S N MASON        1111       ROBERT  MORGAN

                                                                             8.25
                                                                             8.00
                                                                             8.50
                                                    SALESMAN TOTAL HOURS    24.75
                                                    DEPARTMENT TOTAL HOURS  24.75


  22    RETAIL SALES         W L BROWN        1223       JAMES ERLICH

                                                                             7.50
                                                                             7.50
                                                                             7.50
                                                                             8.50
                                                    SALESMAN TOTAL HOURS    31.00
                                                    DEPARTMENT TOTAL HOURS  31.00

  35    SECURITY             F J JACKSON      9900       EDWARD PANGBORN

                                                                             8.00
                                                                             8.00
                                                                             8.00
                                                                             8.00
                                                                             8.00
                                                                             8.00
                                                    SALESMAN TOTAL HOURS    48.00
                                                    DEPARTMENT TOTAL HOURS  48.00
                                                    FINAL TOTAL HOURS      103.75
```

10 Other RPG II Statements

Outline

Move Zone Operations
    Altering the Structure
        of Characters
    How Move Zone Operations Work
    Coding a Move Zone Operation
    Differences in the Move Zone
        Operations
        Move from High-Order Zone
           to High-Order Zone
           (MHHZO)
        Move from Low-Order Zone
           to High-Order Zone
           (MLHZO)
        Move from High-Order Zone
           to Low-Order Zone
           (MHLZO)
        Move from Low-Order Zone
           to Low-Order Zone (MLLZO)

Test Numeric (TESTN)
Test Zone (TESTZ)
Bit Operations
    Set Bit On (BITON)
    Set Bit Off (BITOF)
    Test Bit (TESTB)
Look Ahead
Writing Specifications for Look Ahead
Look Ahead Fields—Summary
Display Information (DSPLY)
Zoned, Packed, and Binary Formats
    Zoned (Unpacked) Format
    Packed Decimal Format
    Binary Format

Figure 10.1 Changing zones changes characters

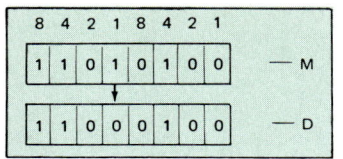

In this example, if the *A* bit of the letter *M* is changed from on to off, the letter *M* becomes the letter *D*.

The preceding chapters have illustrated and demonstrated most of the statements commonly used in RPG programming. Other statements are not used as often but aid the programmer in programming certain data-processing problems. This chapter presents some of those more particular problems.

Move Zone Operations

An assortment of move zone operations perform sophisticated modifications to data. An explanation of their operation and benefits follows.

Altering the Structure of Characters

Each character of data is represented in the machine by a unique setting of eight bits—four zone bits and four digit bits. If any change is made to either the zone or digit bits, the entire character is changed. (See Figure 10.1.)

A character can, of course, be changed before it is read into the computer by putting different zone bits into the input record. But a character can also be changed after it has been read. This is done by changing the zones of characters using move zone operation codes.

Why might the programmer ever want to change the zone of a character after it has been read? One common reason for changing zones is to deliberately change the sign of a field from positive to negative, or vice versa.

Changing the sign of a field becomes necessary when a numeric field is read in from a special file with its sign in the high-order (leftmost) position of the field. The sign of numeric fields must be placed in the low-order (rightmost) position of the field. Thus, a numeric input field having its sign in the high-order position must have it moved to the low-order position. The move zone operation accomplishes this task.

How Move Zone Operations Work

Move zone operations involve only the zone portion of characters. The computer does not actually move the zone of one character to the zone portion of another. Rather, it changes a character by making its zone identical to the zone of the character that the programmer has indicated should serve as a model. The character serving as a model is not changed by the operation.

In order to use the move zone operations, the programmer must have

1. A character that needs to be changed
2. A character with the zone necessary to change the character

The function of the move zone instruction is to move the zone part of a single character. For example, a numeric field in storage includes a digit and a sign in the rightmost position. The sign may be either plus or minus. The rightmost character in a numeric field, if printed without editing, will show up as a letter or a special character.

Field	Rightmost Character	Printed
+	+	
1234	4 or D	123D
−	−	
707	7 or P	70P

Other RPG II Statements 499

Figure 10.2 Function of move zone operations

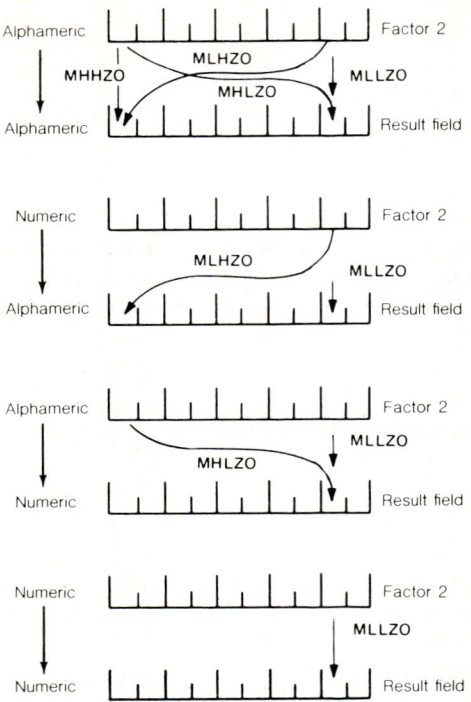

Using a minus (−) sign in a move operation will not yield a negative character in the result field. Minus is represented by a X'60' internally and a D zone is required for a negative character. Characters J–R have a D zone representation in the internal representation of the EBCDIC system and can be used to obtain a negative value (J−X'D1', . . . R−X'D9').

If for any reason the programmer needs to manipulate the zone portion of a numeric character with a sign, the move zone operation can be used because the sign is the zone portion of the rightmost character.

Note: Generally, when the word 'high' is used, the field involved must be alphameric; whenever 'low' is used, the field involved may be either alphameric or numeric. (See Figure 10.2.)

Coding a Move Zone Operation

The name of the field containing the character to be changed must be entered in the result field. Either a constant or the name of the field that contains the model character must be entered as factor 2. The move zone operation is specified in the operations positions (28–32). Conditioning indicators can be specified, but resulting indicators cannot be used. (See Figure 10.3.)

Differences in the Move Zone Operations

Four different move operation codes are available. Each code involves the zone of characters located in different positions. Those positions are

1. High-order positions in both factor 2 and the result field
2. High-order positions in factor 2 and low-order positions in the result field
3. Low-order positions in both factor 2 and the result field
4. Low-order position in factor 2 and high-order position in the result field

Since only the zones of high-order and low-order characters in a field or constant are involved in the move zone operations, only the high-order or low-order positions of a field can be changed. (See Figure 10.4.)

Figure 10.3 Coding for a move zone instruction—examples

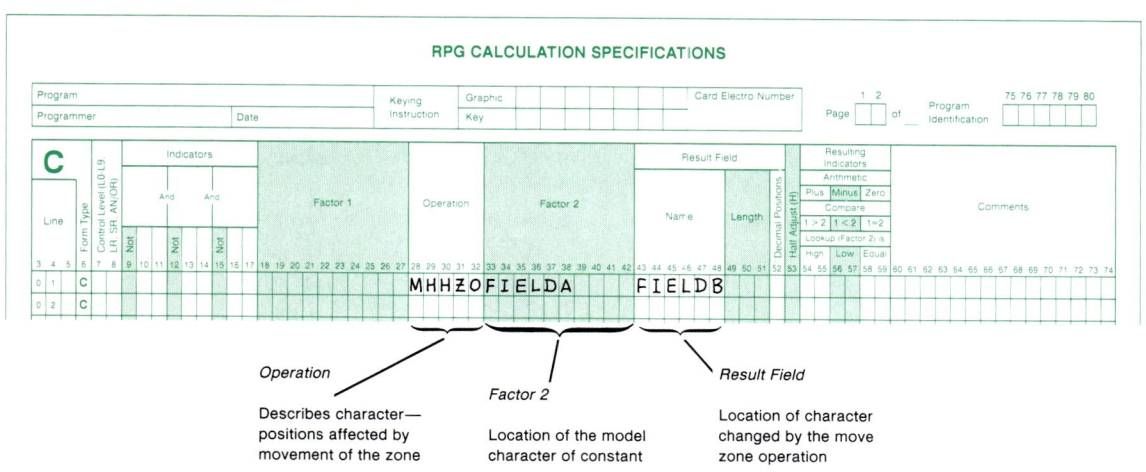

Figure 10.4 Move zone operations—examples

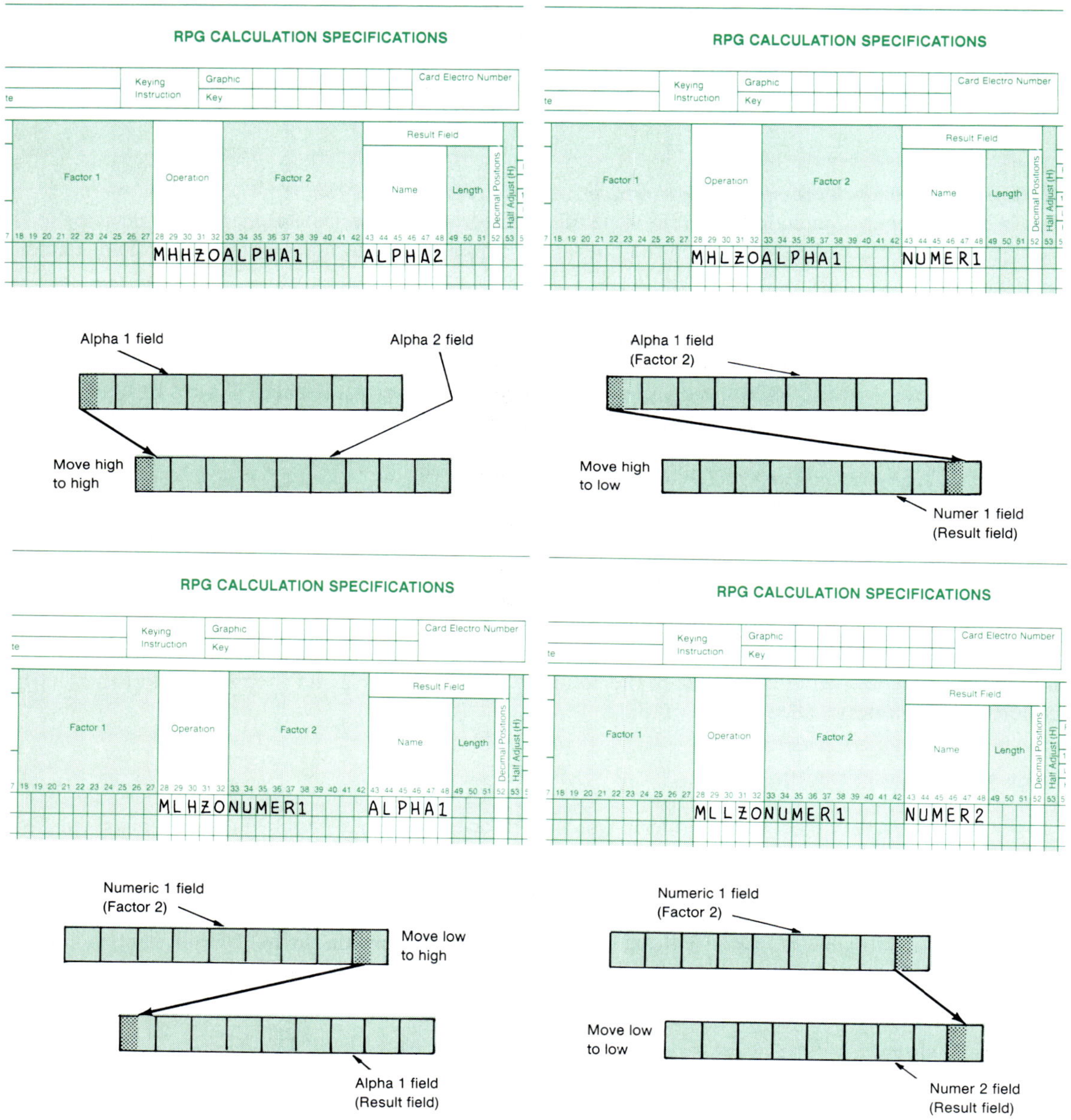

Other RPG II Statements

Figure 10.5 Move zone operations—summary

Move zone operation	Factor 2	Result field	Description
MLLZO	Alphanumeric	Alphanumeric	Bits 0-3 of rightmost byte of Factor 2 are moved to bits 0-3 of rightmost byte of result field.
	Alphanumeric	Numeric	Bits 0-3 of rightmost byte of Factor 2 are moved to bits 0-3 of rightmost byte of result field.
	Numeric	Alphanumeric	Bits 0-3 of rightmost byte of Factor 2 are moved to bits 0-3 of rightmost byte of result field.
	Numeric	Numeric	Bits 0-3 of rightmost byte of Factor 2 are moved to bits 0-3 of rightmost byte of result field.
MHLZO	Alphanumeric	Numeric	Bits 0-3 of leftmost byte of Factor 2 are moved to bits 0-3 of rightmost byte of result field.
	Alphanumeric	Alphanumeric	Bits 0-3 of leftmost byte of Factor 2 are moved to bits 0-3 of rightmost byte of the result field.
MLHZO	Alphanumeric	Alphanumeric	Bits 0-3 of rightmost byte of Factor 2 are moved to bits 0-3 of leftmost byte of result field.
	Numeric	Alphanumeric	Bits 0-3 of rightmost byte of Factor 2 are moved to bits 0-3 of leftmost byte of result field.
MHHZO	Alphanumeric	Alphanumeric	Bits 0-3 of leftmost byte of Factor 2 are moved to bits 0-3 of leftmost byte of result field.

Move from High-Order Zone to High-Order Zone (MHHZO)

The MHHZO operation code moves the zone of the high-order (leftmost) alphameric character in the constant or field entered in factor 2 to the high-order alphameric character in the result field. Factor 2 and the result field must both be alphameric.

Move from Low-Order Zone to High-Order Zone (MLHZO)

The MLHZO operation moves the zone of the low-order (rightmost) character in the field or constant entered in factor 2 to the high-order alphameric character in the result field. The result field must be alphameric; factor 2 can be either numeric or alphameric.

Move from High-Order Zone to Low-Order Zone (MHLZO)

The MHLZO operation code moves the zone of the high-order alphameric character in the constant or field entered in factor 2 to the low-order rightmost character in the result field. The result field must be alphameric; factor 2 can be either numeric or alphameric.

Move from Low-Order Zone to Low-Order Zone (MLLZO)

The MLLZO operation code moves the zone of the low-order character in the field or constant entered in factor 2 to the low-order character in the result field. Both factor 2 and the result field can be either numeric or alphameric. (See Figure 10.5.)

Test Numeric (TESTN)

The TESTN operation tests an alphameric result field for the presence of zoned decimal characters and blanks. This operation is used to perform data validation on numeric zoned decimal data. The result field must be alphameric.

To prevent undesirable results or an abnormal termination of a program, the TESTN operation validates fields before arithmetic or editing operations are performed on the fields. Following validation, the field must be moved to a numeric field to perform the arithmetic and editing operations.

Figure 10.6 Test numeric operations—examples

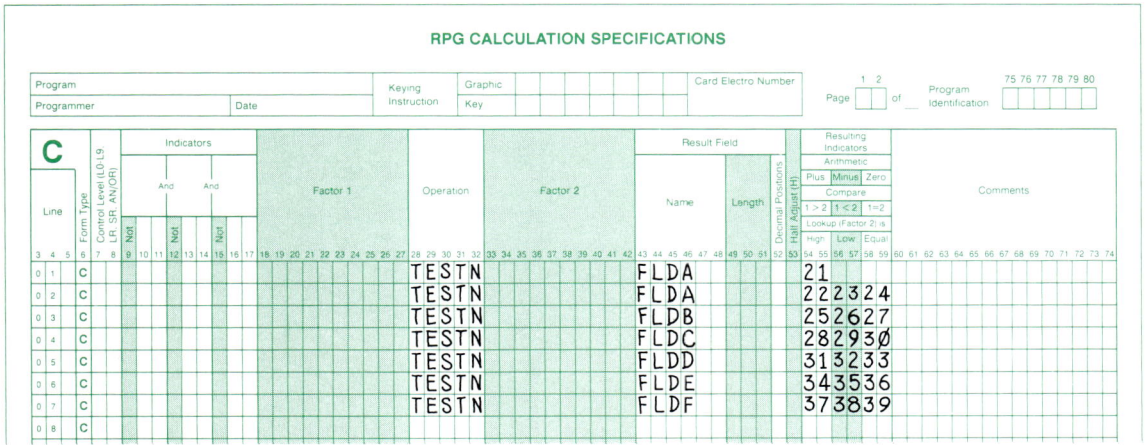

Notes on the Coding

The field values are:

FLDA = 123 FLDD = bbb (b denotes blank character)
FLDB = 1X4 FLDE = b1b3
FLDC = 004 FLDF = b12

As a result of the TESTN operations:

Line   Meaning

01   Indicator 21 is set on because FLDA contains all numeric characters.

02   Indicator 22 is set on because FLDA contains numeric characters. Indicators 23 and 24 are off.

03   All indicators are off because FLDB does not contain valid numeric data.

04   Indicator 28 is set on because FLDC contains valid numeric data. Indicators 29 and 30 are off.

05   Indicator 33 is set on because FLDD contains all blanks. Indicators 31 and 32 are set off.

06   Indicators 34, 35, and 36 are all off. Indicator 35 is off because FLDE contains a blank after a digit.

07   Indicator 38 is set on because FLDF contains leading blanks and low-order digits. Indicators 37 and 39 are off.

As a result of the TESTN operation the resulting indicators are set as follows:

Positions 54–55. All of the characters in the result field must be numeric. To be considered numeric, each character in the field except the low-order character must contain a hex F zone and a digit (0–9).

Positions 56–57. The result field contains both numeric characters and at least one blank. For example, the values b123 or bb123 (*b* denotes blank character) set on this indicator. However, the value b1b23 is an invalid numeric field and does not set this indicator on. *Note:* An indicator in these positions cannot be specified when a field length of one is tested because the alphameric field must contain at least one numeric character and one leading blank.

Positions 58–59. The result field contains all blanks. The same indicator can be used for more than one condition. If any of the conditions exist, the indicator is set on.

Each character in the field except the low-order character must contain a hex F zone and a digit (0–9) to be considered numeric. (See Figure 10.6.) The low-order character is numeric if it contains a hex C, hex D, or hex F zone and a digit (0–9).

Figure 10.7 Conditioning a calculation by the result of a TESTZ operation

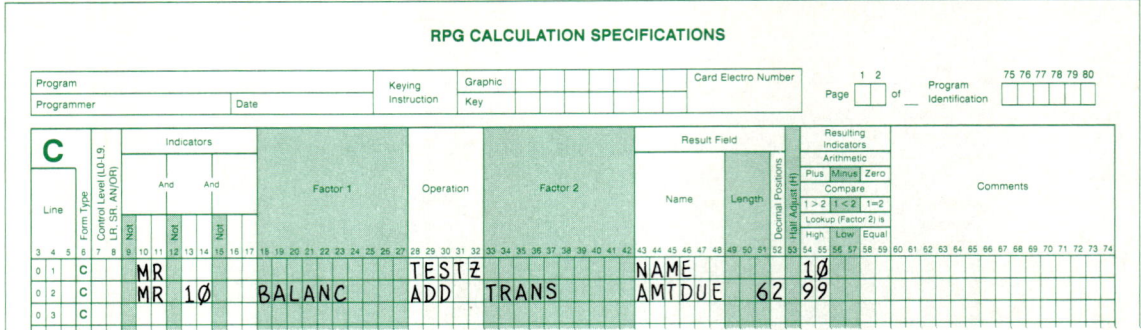

Notes on the Coding

The above figure shows the calculation specifications necessary to bill customers whose last names fall into category A–I.

Test Zone (TESTZ)

Test zone (TESTZ) is available to test data during calculations so that the programmer can determine which calculation to do next. TESTZ tests only the zone portion of the leftmost character of an alphameric field. TESTZ does not specifically test for plus, minus, or zero. Rather, it tells the programmer into which group of zones the tested zone falls.

The TESTZ operation code tests the zone of the leftmost character in the result field. The result field must be alphameric since this operation can be done only on alphameric characters. Resulting indicators are used to determine the results of the test.

The zones of the characters & (ampersand) and A–I cause the plus indicator entered in positions 54–55 to be turned on.

The zone of the characters − (minus) and J–R cause the minus indicator entered in positions 56–57 to be turned on.

The zones of all other characters cause the indicator entered in positions 58–59 to be turned on.

Factor 1 and factor 2 are not used in this operation.

The test zone operation could prove very useful in a large billing job. Consider the case of a company that has so many accounts that the billing job must be divided. Customers whose last names are in the first part of the alphabet are billed on the fifteenth of the month; all others are billed at the end of the month. The master file used in the billing job is organized in ascending order according to account number.

The records in this file could be sorted by name so that the file could be divided for the billing job. However, the file is used for so many other purposes that it would be a waste of time to keep sorting it according to name for billing and sorting it again according to account number for other jobs.

A better way to set up the billing job is to test the name file in each record to see in which part of the alphabet the name falls. During the first of the month, the amount due will have to be found for all names beginning with the letters A–I. TESTZ will test the first letter in the field to determine in which part of the alphabet the names fall. (See Figure 10.7.)

At the end of the month, the rest of the customers will be billed. It will not be necessary to write another program for the end-of-month billing. One program will do both jobs by using external indicators to condition the specifications for each job. (See Figures 10.8, 10.9, and 10.10.)

Figure 10.8 Using TESTZ and external indicators—example

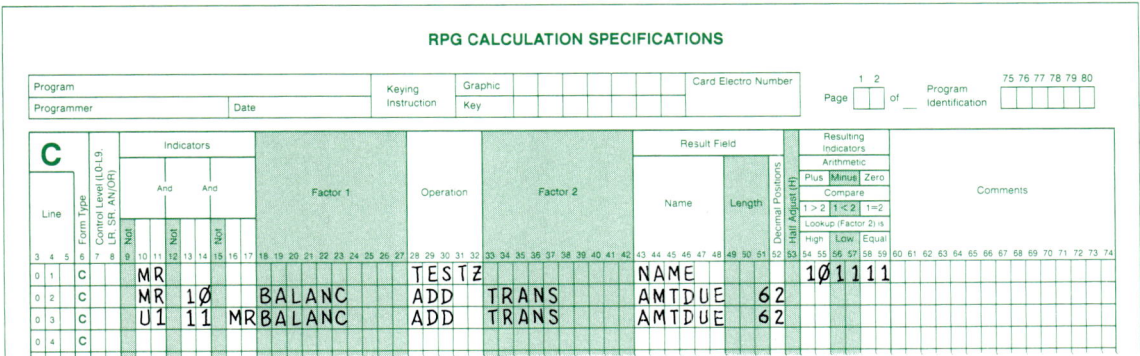

Notes on the Coding

The above figure shows the calculations necessary to do both jobs using external indicators to condition the specifications for each job.

Figure 10.9 TESTZ operation code—example

Testing a Field to Determine a Code

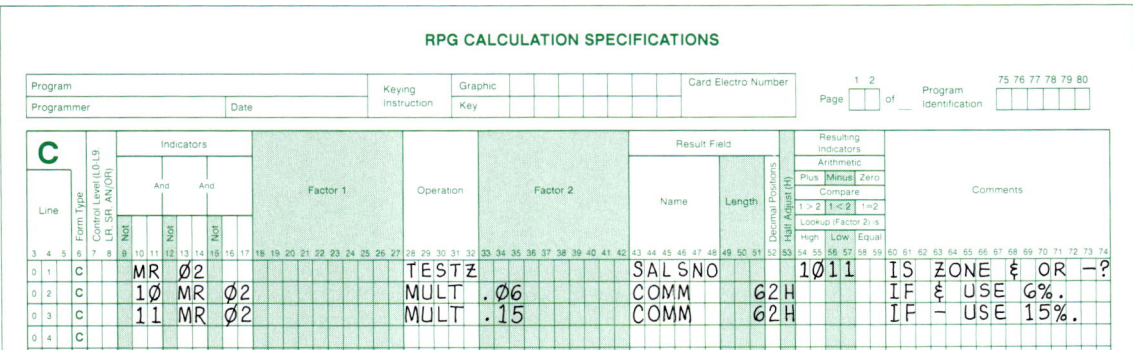

Notes on the Coding

The TESTZ code can be used for any special code set up by using the zone of a character.

For example, in the above illustration, a code is established for the percentage of commission received by each salesman.

Any of the letters A-I are used to indicate 6 percent and any of the letters J-R are used to indicate 15 percent.

The code is placed in the leftmost position of the numeric field because this is the position tested by the TESTZ operation.

The above figure shows how the code is placed in the field containing salesman number. However, the field must be defined as alphameric, since the TESTZ operation can only be performed on an alphameric field.

The Calculation Specifications coding shows the TESTZ used on the SALSNO (salesman number) field, which contains the commission code in order to find rate of commission. The results of the test determine what other calculations will be done.

Other RPG II Statements   505

Figure 10.10 Using move zone operations to change the sign of a field—example

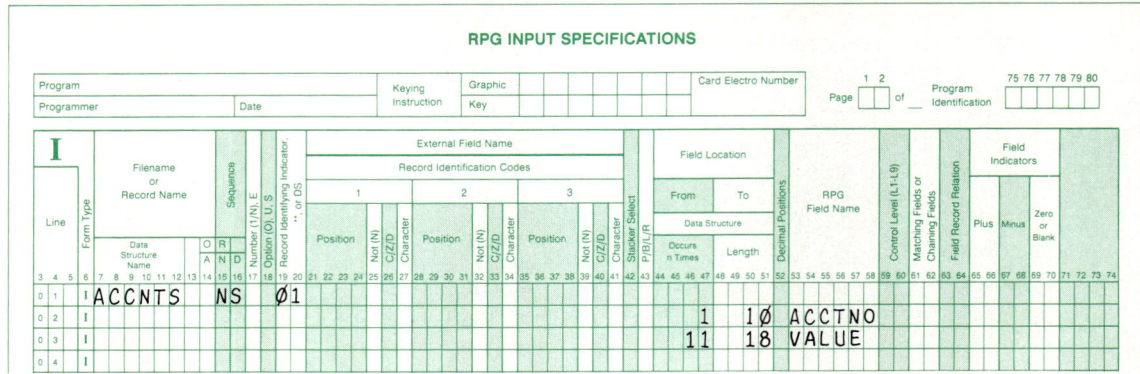

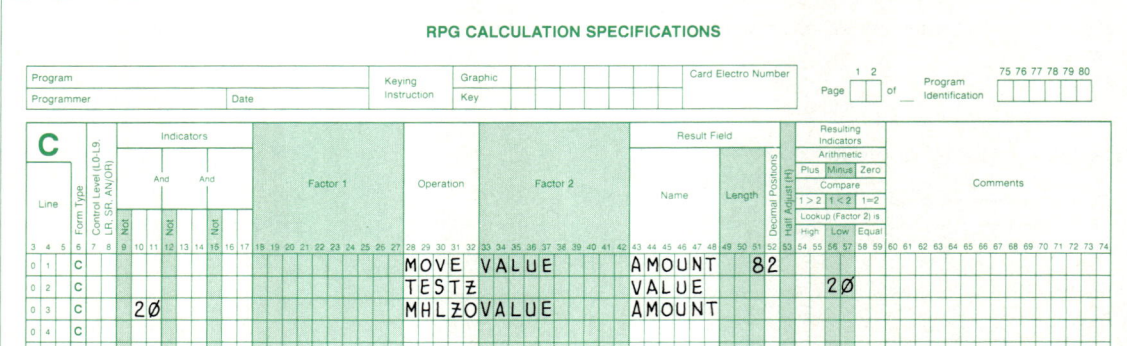

Notes on the Coding

In the above example, the move zone operation code is used to change the sign of the field, VALUE, from the high-order to the low-order position.

Naturally, any field that has zones other than in the low-order position must be defined as alphameric if those zones are to be used by the computer. But if the field is to be involved in an arithmetic operation, it must be numeric.

To allow for both possibilities, the field should be defined twice, once as alphameric and once as numeric. (Two unique field names are needed.) Another possibility is to define the field once as alphameric and then change it into a numeric field by moving it into a numeric field. This is what is done in the above example.

Before any arithmetic operations can be performed, the sign must be put in the low-order position of a numeric field. First, the programmer must determine what the sign is. This is done by the TESTZ operation. Remember that TESTZ turns on the minus indicator when it finds the characters -, or J through R in the high-order position of the tested field.

The specification in the Calculation Specifications form on line 20 causes indicator 20 to turn on if the sign of the field is minus.

If indicator 20 is on, the zone of VALUE, which is the minus sign to the computer, is moved to the low-order position of the AMOUNT field.

If the field tested is plus, no zone is moved, because a numeric field having no minus sign is automatically assumed to be positive.

Notice that the MHLZO (Move High to Low Zone) operation code was used to change the zone of the low-order position of the AMOUNT field by giving it the same zone as the high-order position of VALUE.

Bit Operations

RPG provides certain operation codes that set and test individual bits in storage. These individual bits can be set and tested to allow further control over processing. In these testing situations the bits are called switches and their functions are similar to those of RPG indicators. The operation codes that set and test the bits are known as binary field operations. A binary field is a one-byte field containing eight bits identified left to right by the digits 0–7. The bits can be set on, set off, and tested. Since each bit can be utilized, there are eight indicators in every byte.

When using binary field operations, it is important to remember how data fields are initialized by the system:

1. Alphameric fields are initialized to hexadecimal '40'.

2. Numeric fields are initialized to hexadecimal 'F0'.

The binary field containing the bits to be tested should be initialized to binary zero (hexadecimal '00') at the beginning of the program.

Three operation codes, BITON, BITOF, and TESTB, are provided to set and test individual bits. The individual bits can be used as switches in a program. In binary field operations, the operation codes BITON, BITOF, or TESTB must appear in positions 28–32 of the Calculations Specifications form.

Factor 2 can contain:

1. *Bit numbers 0–7.* One or more bits (a maximum of eight) may be set on, set off, or tested. The bits are numbered from left to right and are enclosed in apostrophes. The order of specification of bits is not restricted. For example, to specify the first bit of a field, enter *'0'* in factor 2 (positions 33–35). To specify bits 0, 2, and 5, enter *'025'* in factor 2 (positions 33–37). Bits not specified in factor 2 are not changed.

2. *Field name.* The name of a one-position, alphameric field or table, or array element can be entered. In this case, the bits that are on in the field or array element are set on, set off, or tested in the result field; bits that are not on are not affected.

Any field named in factor 2 or the result field must be a one-position, alphameric field (no entries in the decimal positions on the Input or Calculations forms).

Set Bit On (BITON)

The BITON operation code causes specified bits in factor 2 to turn on (set to 1) in the field named in the result field. The field named in the result field must be a one-position alphameric field. Since it is one position in length, a *'1'* must be entered in position 51 of field length. One or more of the eight bits can be turned on. To turn on the first bit in a field, enter *'0'* in factor 2. (These bit numbers must be enclosed by apostrophes.)

The operation may be conditioned with indicators in positions 7–17. A bit in an array element may be turned on, but that array element must be one position in length.

Factor 1, decimal positions, half-adjust, and resulting indicators are not used with the BITON operation. (See Figures 10.11 and 10.12.)

Figure 10.11 BITON operation code—example

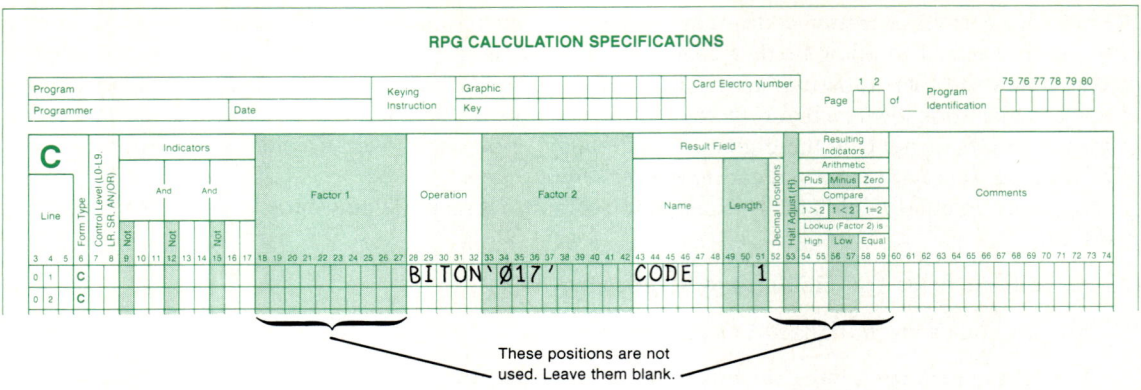

Notes on the Coding

In the above illustration, bits 0, 1, and 7 are set to 1 in the binary field labeled CODE.

Figure 10.12 BITON operation code—examples

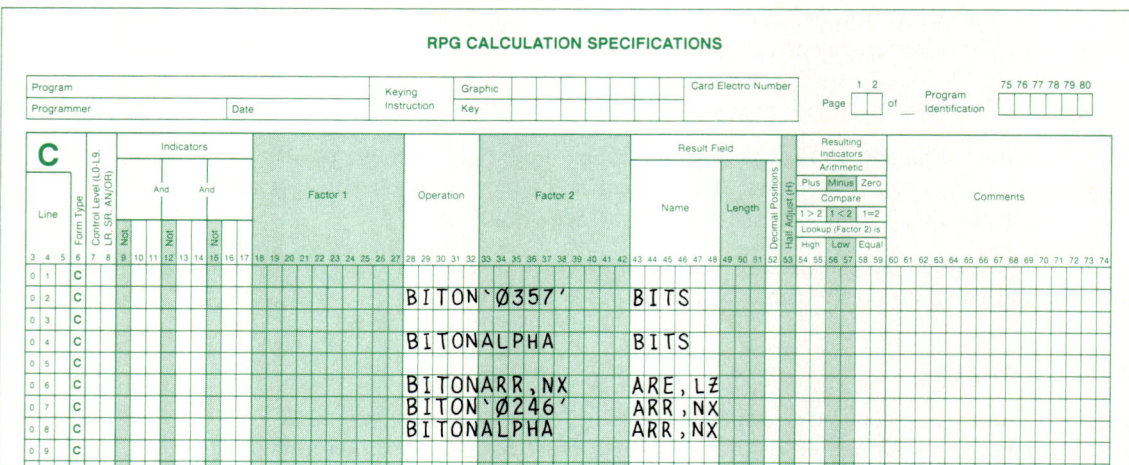

Notes on the Coding

Line   Meaning

02   This operation sets bits 0, 3, 5, and 7 on in the field named BITS. Assume that the one-position field has been previously defined.

04   This operation uses a one-position alphameric field as a source of bits. Any bits that are on in the field named ALPHA will cause corresponding bits to be set on in the field named BITS. If bits 5 and 7 are on in the field named ALPHA, the BITON operation will set bits 5 and 7 on in the field named BITS.

06-08   The operations in these lines use a one-position alphameric array element as either a source of bits, as a result field, or both. In the first operation, any bits on in the array element, ARR,NX, will cause corresponding bits to be set on in the array element ARE,LZ.

508   RPG II and RPG III Programming

Set Bit Off (BITOF)

The BITOF operation causes specified bits identified in factor 2 to turn off (set to 0) in a field named in the result field. All other specifications are the same as those specified under the BITON operation code. (See Figures 10.13 and 10.14.)

Figure 10.13 BITOF operation code—example

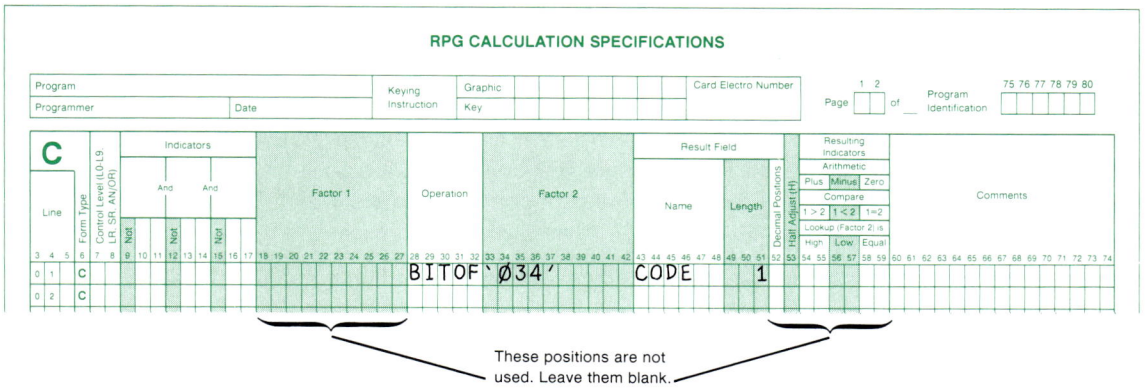

Notes on the Coding

In the above illustration, bits 0, 3, and 4 are turned off (set to 0) in the binary field labeled CODE.

Figure 10.14 BITOF operation code—examples

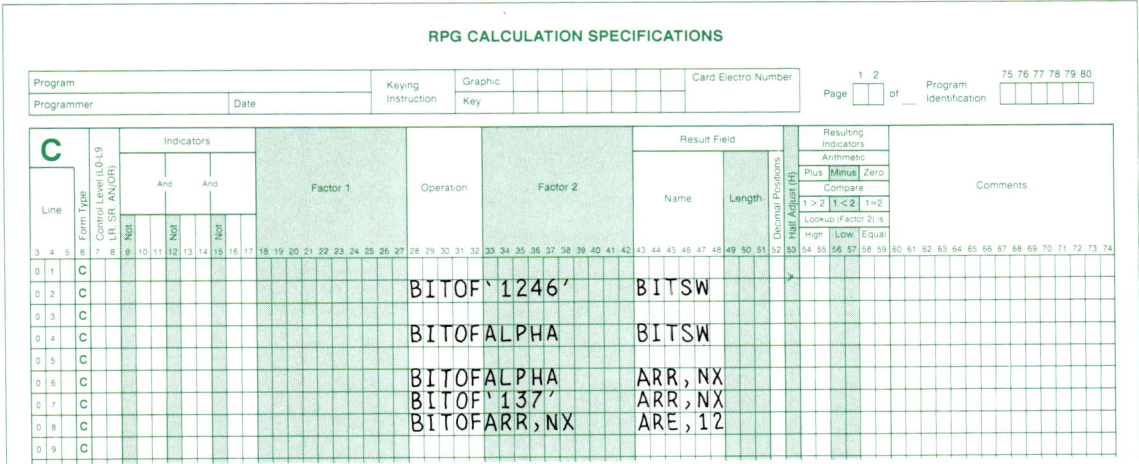

Notes on the Coding

Line   Meaning

02   This operation sets bits 1, 2, 4, and 6 off in the field named BITSW. Assume that the one-position field has been previously defined.

04   This operation uses a one-position alphameric field as a source of bits. Any bits that are on in the field named ALPHA will cause corresponding bits to be set off in the field named BITSW. If bits 5 and 7 are on in the field named ALPHA, the BITOF operation will set 5 and 7 off in the field named BITSW.

06-08   The operations in these lines use a one-position alphameric array element as either a source of bits, as a result field, or both. In the first operation, any bits that are on in the field named ALPHA will cause corresponding bits to be set off in the array element, ARR,NX.

Other RPG II Statements   509

Test Bit (TESTB)

The TESTB operation code causes bits identified in factor 2 to be tested for an on or off condition in the field named as the result field. The condition of the bits can be determined by looking at the resulting indicators in positions 54–59. All other specifications are the same as those for BITON and BITOF.

At least one resulting indicator must be used with the TESTB operation; as many as three can be named for one operation. Two indicators, but not all three, may be the same for one TESTB operation. If a field specified in factor 2 contains bits that are all off (binary 0), no resulting indicators are turned on. A resulting indicator has different meanings depending upon the positions in which it appears.

Positions 54–55. An indicator in these positions is turned on if each bit specified in factor 2 is off (0) in the result field.

Positions 56–57. An indicator in these positions is turned on if two or more bits are tested and found to be of mixed status (i.e., some bits on, other bits off). It is the programmer's responsibility to ensure that the field named in factor 2 contains more than one bit, which is set on if an indicator appears in positions 56–57.

Positions 58–59. An indicator in these positions is turned on if each bit specified in factor 2 is on (1) in the result field. (See Figures 10.15, 10.16, 10.17, and 10.18.)

Figure 10.15 TESTB operation code—example

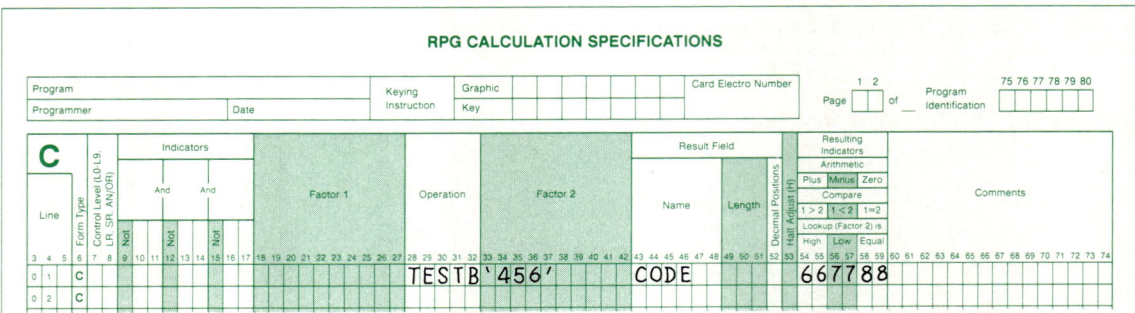

Notes on the Coding

In the above illustration, bits 4, 5, and 6 in the binary field named CODE are tested.

Resulting indicator 66 is turned on if bits 4, 5, and 6 are off.

If some are on and others off, resulting indicator 77 is turned on.

If they are all on, resulting indicator 88 is turned on.

Figure 10.16 TESTB operation code—example

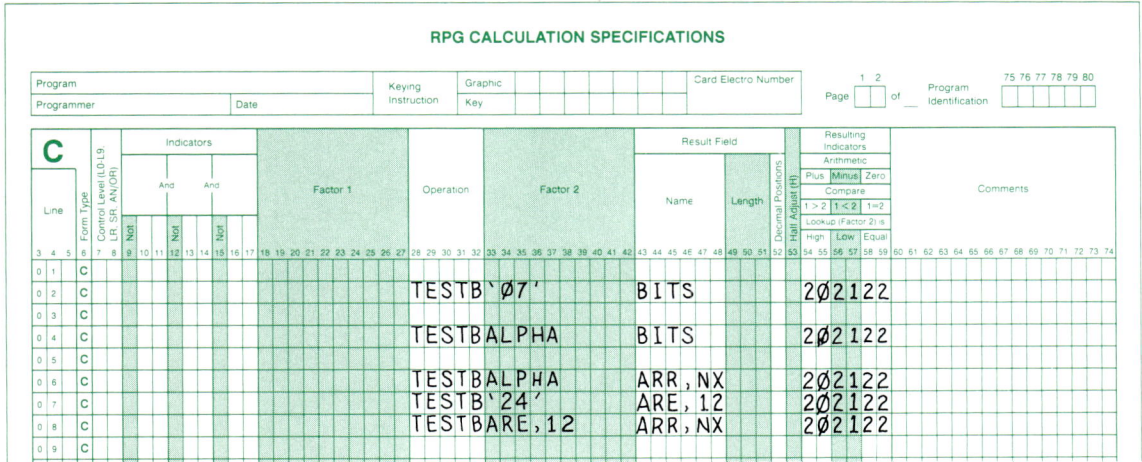

Notes on the Coding

Line   Meaning

02   The TESTB operation on this line will compare bits 0 and 7 with corresponding bits in the field named BITS.

      a. If bits 0 and 7 are off in the field named BITS, indicator 20 will turn on.

      b. If bits 0 and 7 are of mixed status (one on, one off) in the field named BITS, indicator 21 will turn on.

      c. If bits 0 and 7 are on in the field named BITS, indicator 22 will turn on.

04   The TESTB operation on this line will compare the bits that are on in the field named ALPHA with corresponding bits in the field named BITS.

      a. If the bits are on in the field named ALPHA and are off in the field named BITS, indicator 20 will turn on.

      b. If the bits are on in the field named ALPHA and are of mixed status (some on, some off) in the field named BITS, indicator 21 will turn on.

      c. If the bits are on in the field named ALPHA and are on in the field named BITS, indicator 22 will turn on.

06-08   The TESTB operation on these lines uses a one-position array element as either a source of bits, as a result field, or both. In the first operation, the bits that are on in the field named ALPHA are compared to corresponding bits in the array element, ARR,NX. For example, assume that bits 1 and 4 are on in the field named ALPHA.

      a. If bits 1 and 4 are off in the array element ARR,NX, indicator 20 will turn on.

      b. If bits 1 and 4 are of mixed status (one on, one off) in array element ARR,NX, indicator 21 turns on.

      c. If bits 1 and 4 are on in array element ARR,NX, indicator 22 will turn on.

Figure 10.17 Test bit operations—examples

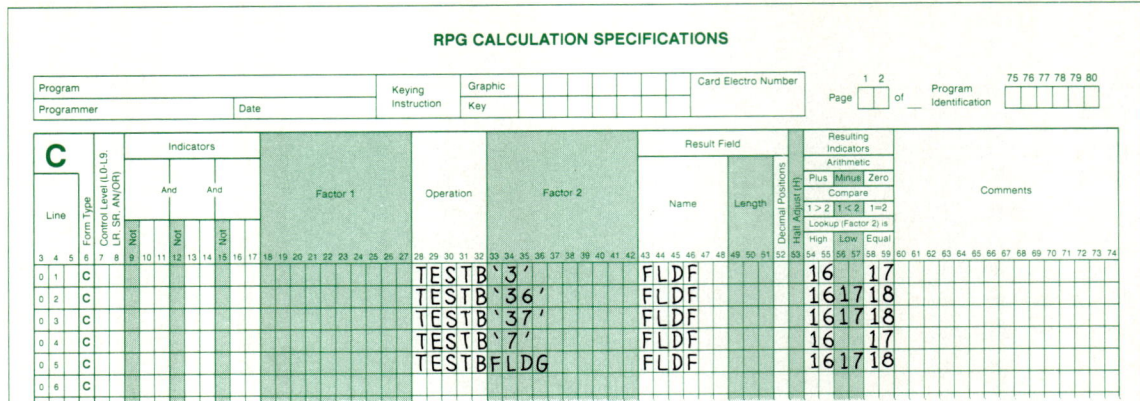

Notes on the Coding

The field bit settings are:

FLDF = 00000001

FLDG = 11110001

The following indicators are set on or remain off as a result of the TESTB operations.

Line	Meaning
01	Indicator 16 is set on because bit 3 is off (0) in FLDF. Indicator 17 is off.
02	Indicator 16 is set on because both bits 3 and 6 are off (0) in FLDF. Indicators 17 and 18 are off.
03	Indicator 17 set on because bit 3 is off (0) and bit 7 is on (1) in FLDF. Indicators 16 and 18 are off.
04	Indicator 17 is set on because bit 7 is on (1) in FLDF. Indicator 16 is off.
05	Indicator 17 is set on because bits 0, 1, 2, and 3 are off (0) and bit 7 is on (1). Indicators 16 and 18 are off.

Figure 10.18 Binary field operations—example

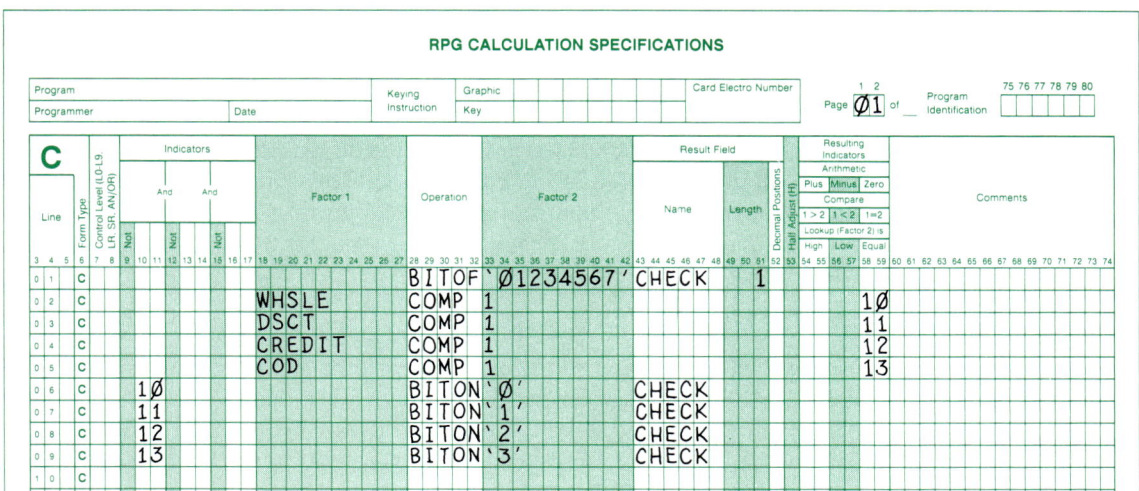

Notes on the Coding

Fields are sometimes present in customer master files to indicate particular types of customers. When such a master file is created, each of the conditions indicating a particular customer type is represented in a record by a one-position field. Since each position occupies one byte of storage, four positions indicating customer types will be stored in four bytes of storage. Binary field operations can be used to convert each one-byte record position to one bit of information on disk. Therefore, four bytes of information can be reduced to four bits of information on disk.

For example, there is a customer master file on disk. They have four positions containing the following information:

1. Whether the customer is a wholesaler or retailer.

2. If the customer is entitled to a discount.

3. If orders should be checked by the credit department.

4. If due to a bad payment history, the shipment should be sent cash on delivery.

The disk file of compressed data consisting of the information from the four fields in four bits in a binary field labeled CHECK. The four columns will be labeled WHSLE, DSCT, CREDIT, and COD respectively. The following operations should be performed.

1. If WHSLE is equal to 1, turn on bit 0 in CHECK.

2. If DSCT is equal to 1, turn on bit 1 in CHECK.

3. If CREDIT is equal to 1, turn on bit 2 in CHECK.

4. If COD is equal to 1, turn on bit 3 in CHECK.

The above shows the correct coding for this problem. Remember that before setting up data in a binary field, the binary field should be set to binary zero. This can be done by the BITOF instruction (line 01).

Other RPG II Statements

Look Ahead

Sometimes calculations to be performed may depend upon the information in the next record to be processed. For example, in a certain kind of job, calculations for the current record may be bypassed if the contents of the next record in the file are identical to the current record.

The RPG language has a special feature that extends the basic RPG logic called look ahead. **Look ahead** allows the computer to look at information in the next record to be processed while it is processing the current record. This means that information in record *B* can be used while record *A* is being processed. By using this feature, a program can be written that uses information from the next record available for processing.

Writing Specifications for Look Ahead

Any field that the programmer wishes to look at in the next record to be processed must be defined as a look ahead field. If that field is being used in normal processing (other than a look ahead field), it must also be defined in the normal way. Thus, most look ahead fields will be specified twice.

All look ahead fields must be defined as a different record type than the others defined. This is done by using a unique alphabetic sequence entry in positions 15–16 on the Input Specifications form. No record identifying indicator (01–99) may be used. A double asterisk (**) is placed in positions 19–20 of the Input Specifications form to specify that the fields described in the following lines are look ahead fields. Field location is also specified for look ahead fields.

Every look ahead field must be named, but the name given must be different from the description it was given as a normal input field. The same field is given two names so that a distinction can be made between the field on the record being processed and the same field on the record that is to be processed next (the look ahead field). (See Figure 10.19.)

Once the look ahead record has been specified, it can be used by any other field. The only exceptions are that it cannot be used as a result field in calculations nor can it be blanked after output.

Only one look ahead record type may be used for a file. There may be several fields listed under that record type specification, however.

Look Ahead Fields—Summary

A look ahead field allows the programmer to look at information in a field on the next record of any input file that is available for processing.

1. Asterisks are used in positions 19–20 to indicate that the fields named in positions 53–58 of the Input Specifications form are look ahead fields.
2. In update and combined files, the look ahead field is for the record currently in process.
3. Two of the uses for look ahead fields are
   a. To determine when the last record of control group is being processed
   b. To extend the RPG matching record capability.
4. One set of look ahead fields per file may be described.
5. The field description applies to all records in the file, regardless of their type.
6. Look ahead fields cannot be altered in the program.
7. If it is necessary to use information before and after the record is selected for processing, the fields must be described twice—once as a look ahead field and once as a normal field. (See Figure 10.20.)

Figure 10.19 Look ahead feature—example

Look Ahead Specifications

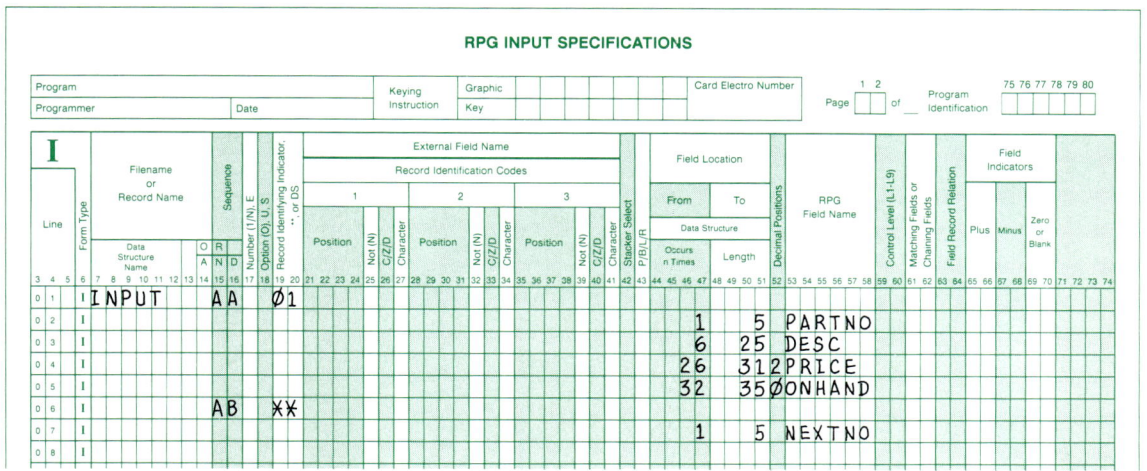

Look Ahead Field: A Field with Two Names

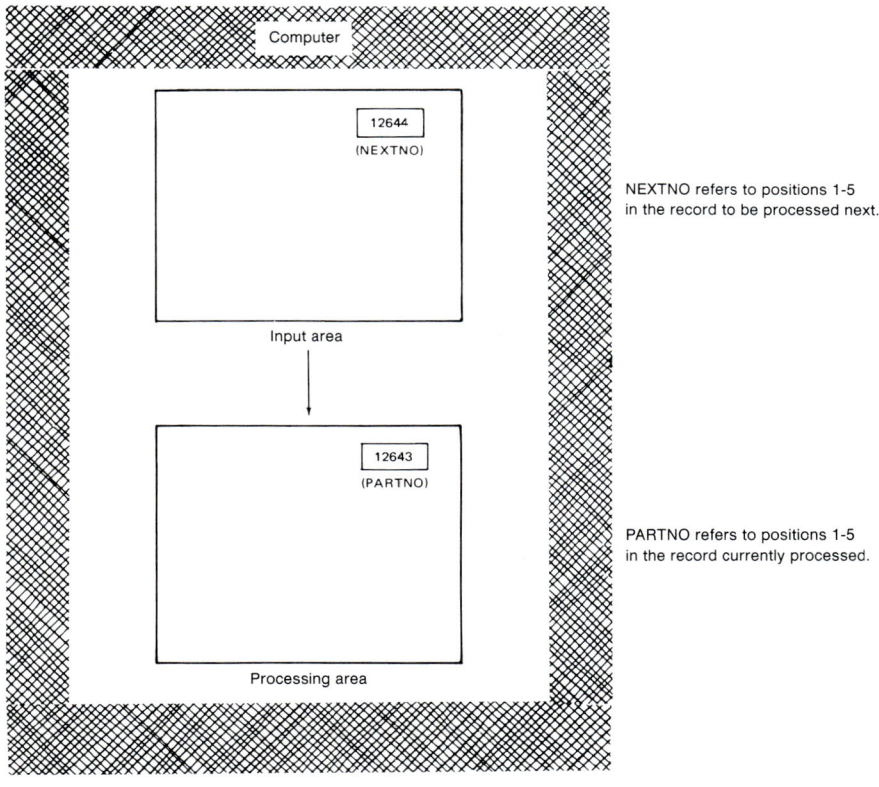

NEXTNO refers to positions 1-5 in the record to be processed next.

PARTNO refers to positions 1-5 in the record currently processed.

Other RPG II Statements

Figure 10.19 continued

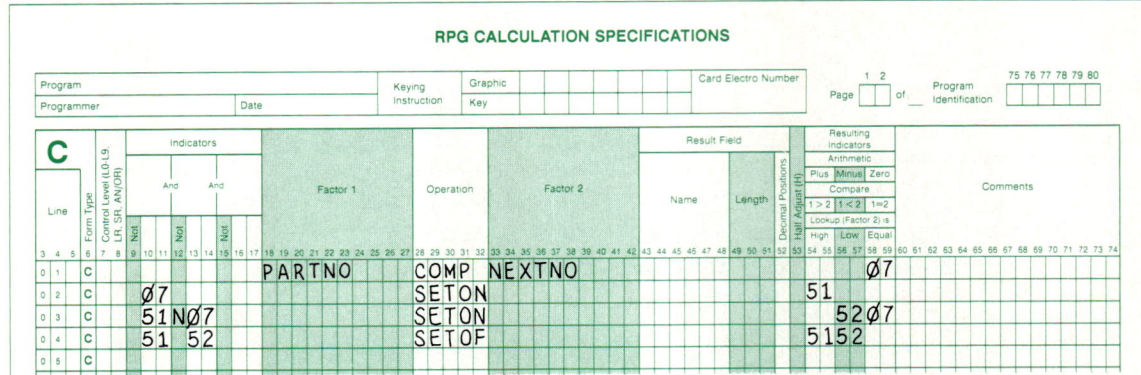

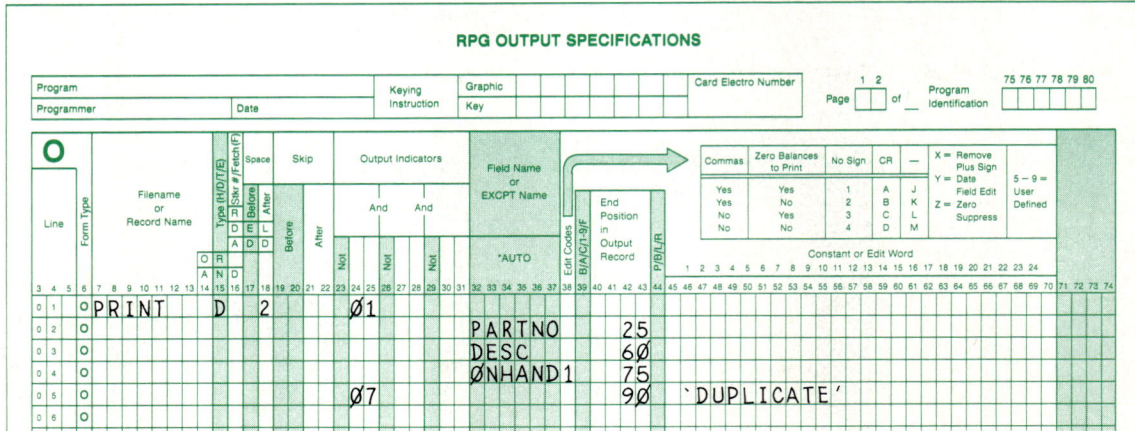

Notes on the Coding

When PARTNO equals NEXTNO, 07 turns on. This in turn causes indicator 51, which is used to indicate that a duplicate record is processed, to turn on.

During the next program cycle, the compare does not indicate duplicates, therefore 07 is not on. But 51 is on, meaning that the record being processed is a duplicate, since the part number on it matched the part number on the previous record. Therefore, 07 is set on. Remember 07 conditions are those output operations that are to be done for duplicates.

Indicator 52 is set on in line 03 to indicate that the last duplicate record is being processed. Indicator 52 then conditions line 04 so that indicator 51 will be set off and not indicate duplicates in the following cycle.

Figure 10.20 Look ahead feature—example

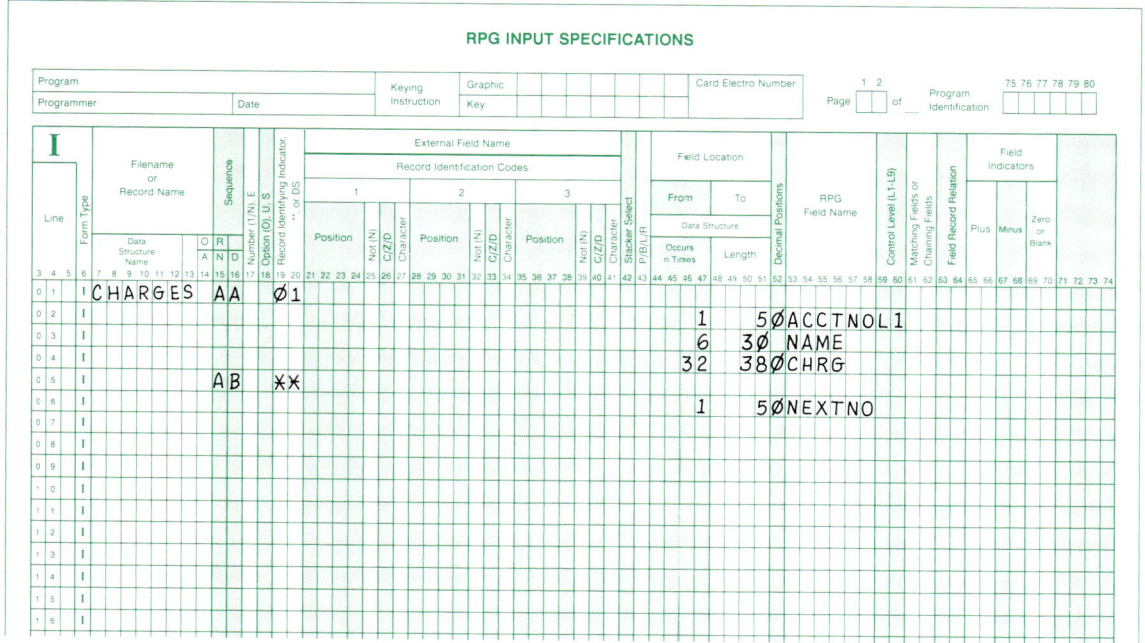

Using Look Ahead to Find the First and Only Record in a Group

Other RPG II Statements

Figure 10.20 continued

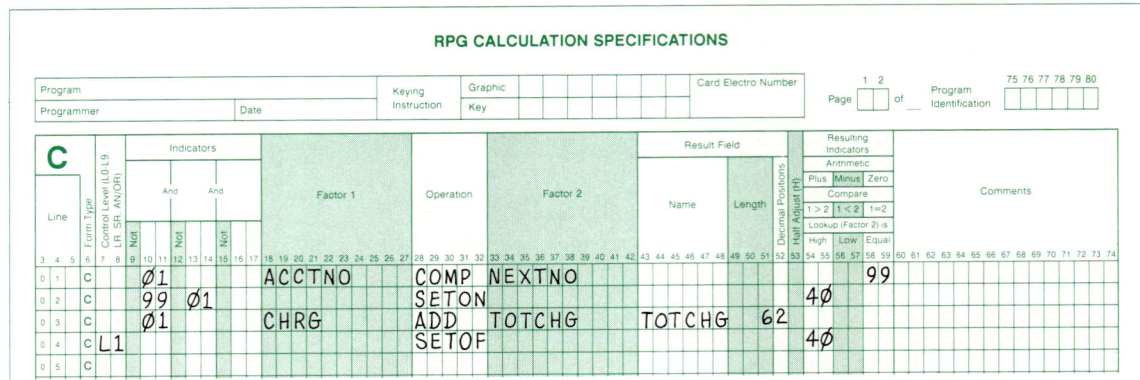

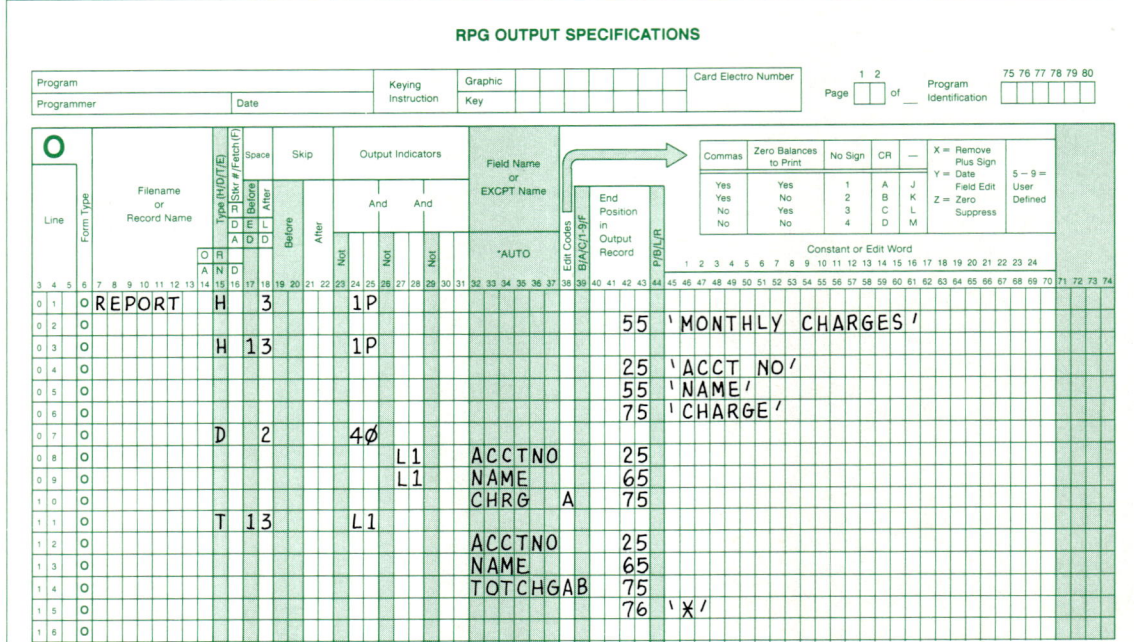

Notes on the Coding

It is often important to know if and when one is processing the only record in a group. The job described above is such a case.

A report is prepared showing charges made by customers during the month. The input file is organized in ascending order by customer number. During the month some customers will have made one charge; others several.

When only one charge is made per customer, the total line is nearly a duplicate of the only detail line. In this case, there is no need to print both the detail line and total line, because only the total line will do.

Account number is established as a look ahead field in this job. Any look ahead field specified applies to all record types. Thus, each record contains information that will be looked at before the record itself is processed. By looking ahead into this field, the programmer will know whether or not the next record to be processed is part of a new group.

Display Information (DSPLY)

The DSPLY operation allows the programmer to do either of the following:

1. Display information at a system console or display work station during program execution and the program continues execution.

2. Display information at a system console or display work station during program execution and the program execution halts so that information can be changed.

In either case, certain common entries must be made and certain positions must be left blank. The letters DSPLY must be entered in positions 28–32 and the filename of the console device must be entered in factor 2. Indicators (positions 7–17) can be specified for a display operation, but positions 49–59 must be left blank.

If information is to be displayed but not changed, factors 1 and 2 must be specified and the result field left blank. Factor 1 specifies the information to be displayed (i.e., a field, an array element, a table, or a literal). Factor 2 specifies the filename of the console device.

If information is to be displayed and then changed, factor 1 must be left blank; factor 2 and the result field must be specified. Factor 2 specifies the filename of the console device, and the result field specifies the information to be displayed and changed (i.e., a field, an array element, a table, or a literal). After information is displayed a wait occurs. To resume processing the programmer can enter new data followed by a carriage return, or can indicate no change by pressing carriage return.

The DSPLY operation allows either or both of the following to occur:

1. Print a field, table element, array element, or literal during program execution without a program halt.

2. Print a field, table element, array element, or literal and the program halts, allowing that field to be changed.

Or

1. Display a field, table element, array element, or literal on the CRT during program execution without a program halt.

2. Display a field, table element, array element, or literal on the CRT and the program halts, allowing that field to be changed. A literal may not be changed with DSPLY.

There are several points to remember if the programmer wishes to enter data during program execution:

1. Numeric data need not be entered with leading zeros; numeric data is right-justified after all characters are keyed.

2. To key a negative field, the field is keyed followed by a minus sign. The length of the field does not need to accommodate the minus sign.

3. Alphameric fields are left-justified after all characters are displayed.

4. Alphameric fields are blanked out and numeric fields are zeroed out.

5. If no characters are entered or the space bar is not pressed, the result field will not be changed. (See Figure 10.21.)

Figure 10.21 Display entry—example

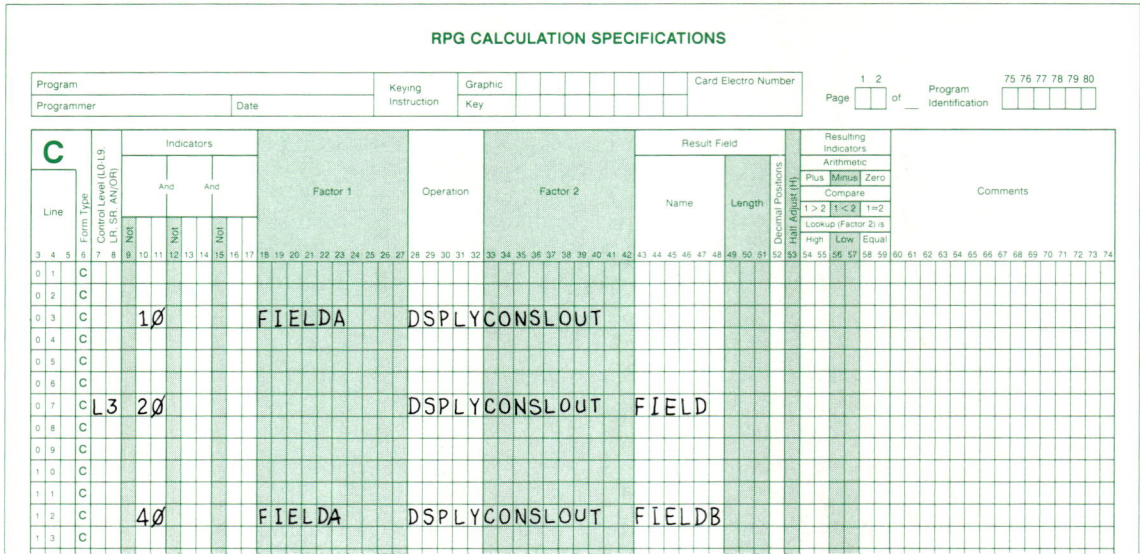

Notes on the Coding

Results

Line   Meaning
03   1. FIELDA is printed as shown.
       2. FIELDA does not change.
       3. Program does not halt.

07   1. FIELDB is printed as shown.
       2. Program halts.
       3. FIELDB is blanked out if data is entered or the space bar is pressed.
       4. Data can be entered in FIELDB.

12   1. FIELDA and FIELDB are printed as shown.
       2. FIELDA does not change.
       3. FIELDB is blanked out if data is entered or the space bar is pressed.
       4. Program halts.
       5. Data can be entered in FIELDB.

Notes

Factor 1 cannot be the name of a whole array.

Fields A and B can be up to 125 characters.

Zoned, Packed, and Binary Formats

Zoned (Unpacked) Format

Each byte of storage, whether on disk or in the computer, can contain one character. That character can be a decimal number or an alphabetic or special character. The format of the characters is known as unpacked decimal format. Each byte of storage is divided into a four-bit zone and a four-bit digit part. (See Figure 10.22.)

The zone part of the low-order (rightmost) byte indicates whether the decimal number is positive or negative. In unpacked decimal format, the zone part is included for each digit in a decimal number; however, only the zone over the low-order digit serves as the sign. The low-order digit is the only digit that makes use of the zone portion. (See Figures 10.23 and 10.24.)

Figure 10.22 An example of a byte

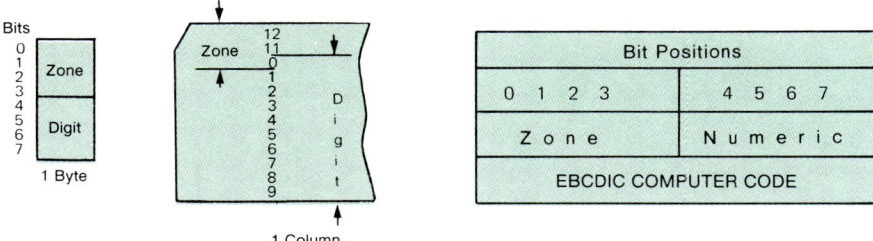

Figure 10.23 Zoned format—examples

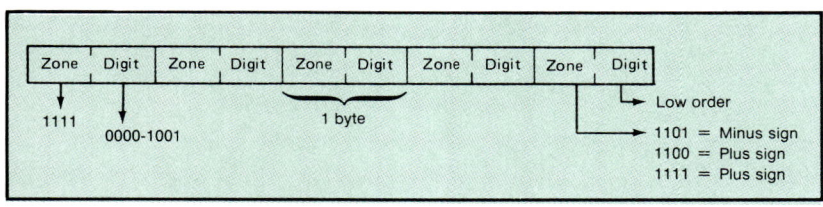

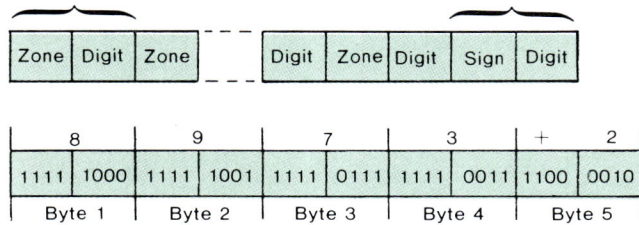

Figure 10.24 Unpacked (zoned) format—examples

Unpacked Decimal Format

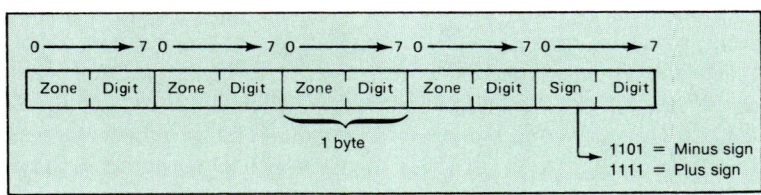

Unpacked Format of Decimal Number 9,269

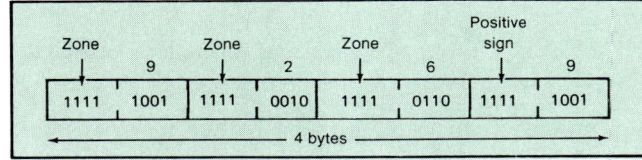

Other RPG II Statements 521

Figure 10.25 Packed format—example

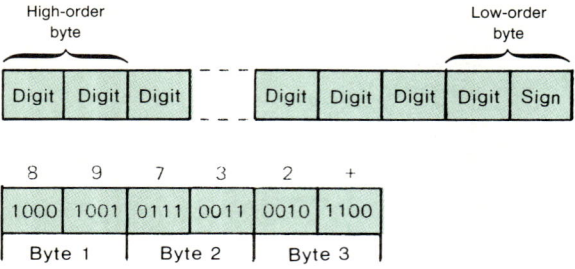

Figure 10.26 Packed decimal format—example

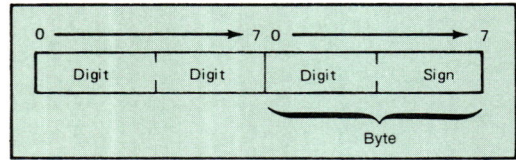

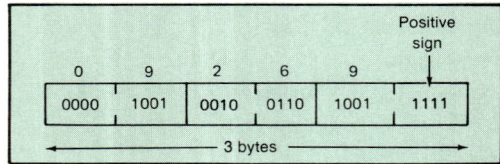

Packed Decimal Format

In **packed decimal format,** each byte of storage can contain two decimal numbers. A decimal number will occupy the unused zone portion in unpacked decimal format. This allows the programmer to put almost twice as much data into a byte as would be possible using unpacked decimal format.

The low-order byte in packed decimal format is also divided into two four-bit parts. Each byte, except the low-order byte, contains one decimal digit in each four-bit part. The low-order byte contains a decimal digit in the leftmost four-bit part (bits 0–3) and the sign of the decimal field in the rightmost four-bit part (bits 4–7). The sign of the low-order byte is used to indicate whether the numeric value represented in the digit part is positive or negative. (See Figures 10.25 and 10.26.) For example, a packed length of 3 in the Input Specifications form will need a length code of 5 when used in calculations.

Packed input, output, table, or array fields can be specified in the following manner:

Packed input fields. Enter a *P* in position 43 of the Input Specifications form. This causes the data to unpack before it is stored.

Packed output fields. Enter a *P* in position 44 of the Output Specifications form. This causes the data to be packed before it is output. (See Figure 10.27.)

Packed table or array fields. Enter a *P* in position 43 and/or 55 of the Extension form. The data will be unpacked before being stored. Packed tables or arrays are not allowed at compile time.

Since data must be represented in unpacked decimal form once inside the computer, the programmer must give the RPG program an indication when input fields are in a different format.

Because data must be represented in unpacked decimal format before being processed, unpacked decimal fields may be stored on disk to eliminate converting from packed to unpacked format during input. However, storing unpacked fields on disk requires more space than storing packed fields. Data must be in the unpacked format to be printed.

Figure 10.27 Output specifications—packed format coding—example

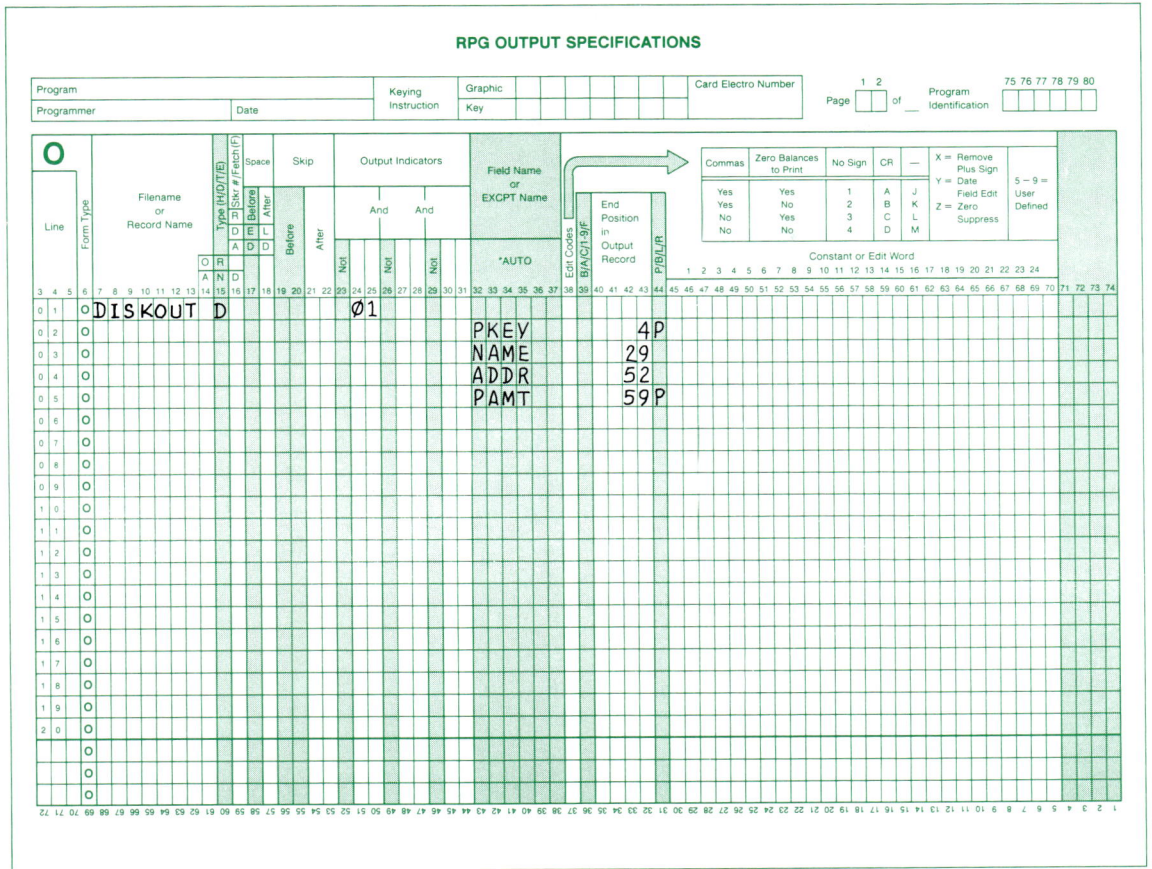

Binary Format

More storage space can be saved than in packed decimal format by storing numeric data in binary format. In **binary format,** each numeric field in storage must be either two or four bytes long. Each two-byte binary field can contain a value equivalent to four decimal places; each four-byte binary field can contain a value equivalent to nine decimal places. In other words, a numeric value in binary format occupies approximately half as many bytes of storage as the equivalent value in unpacked decimal format.

Each two-byte binary field consists of a sign bit followed by a fifteen-bit numeric value. This value can be as large as 9,999. When a two-byte binary field from storage is read into the computer, the RPG program converts it to a four-byte unpacked decimal field.

Each four-byte binary field consists of a sign bit followed by a thirty-one-bit numeric value. This value can be as large as 999,999,999. When a four-byte binary field from storage is read into the computer, the RPG program converts it to a nine-byte unpacked decimal field.

In each case, the sign portion of the high-order byte (leftmost) is used to indicate whether the numeric value is positive or negative. Notice that in binary format the zone portion of the decimal number is not given. (See Figures 10.28 and 10.29.)

Other RPG II Statements 523

Figure 10.28 Binary format—examples

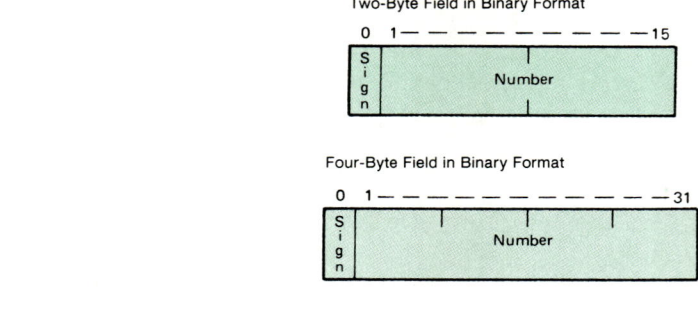

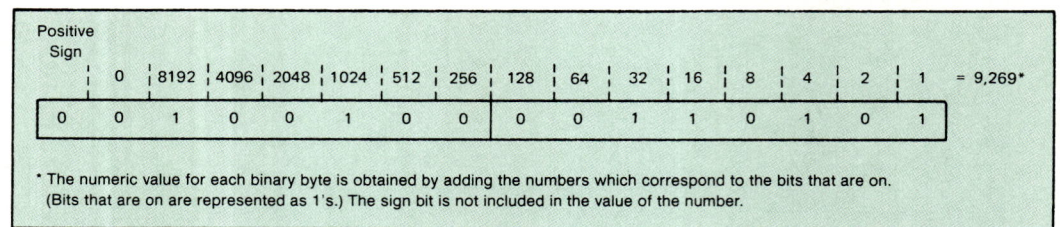

Figure 10.29 Input specifications—binary format coding—examples

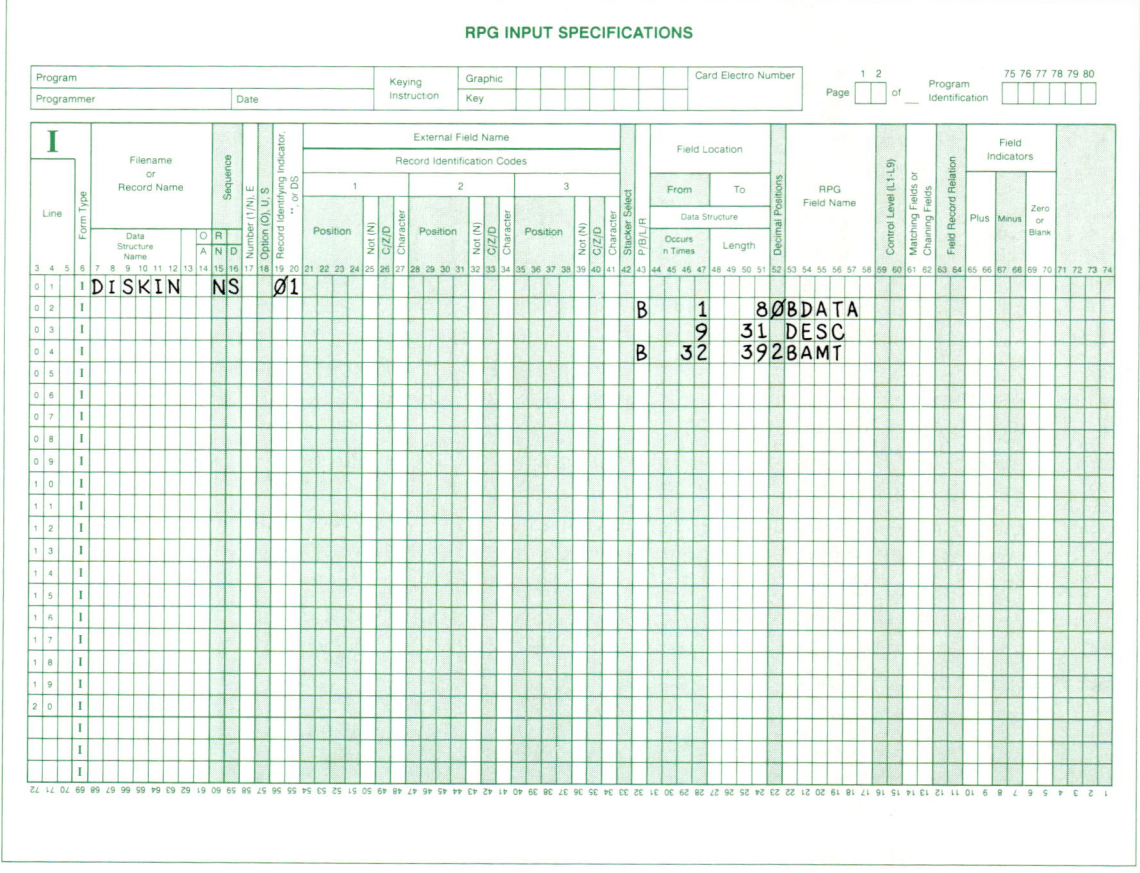

524 RPG II and RPG III Programming

Illustrative Program

Compare—Arithmetic/Test Numeric: Weekly Payroll Register

Job Definition

A Weekly Payroll Register is to be printed. The program should calculate the FICA taxes and the UCI taxes at the current rates. The net pay for each employee is to be calculated, as well as totals for all positions for each department, as well as an overall total. The GROSS field is validated to guarantee numeric data; an error message is printed, if non-numeric data is detected. An error is to be indicated if the net earnings value is zero or negative.

Input

The input consists of an eighty-byte record:

Positions	Field Descriptions	
1–03	Month	
4–05	Day	
6–07	Year	
14–16	Department number	
17–21	Serial number	
57–61	Gross earnings	
62–65	Insurance	(XX.XX)
69–72	Withholding tax	(XX.XX)
76–79	Miscellaneous	(XX.XX)
80–80	Code 'E'	

Processing

The FICA tax is to be computed by multiplying the gross earnings by the current rate (6.13 percent).

The UCI tax is to be computed by multiplying the gross earnings by the current rate (1 percent).

All the deductions are to be subtracted from the gross earnings to arrive at the net pay.

A test of the net pay is to be made to see if it is zero or negative. If net pay is zero or negative, a message is to be printed.

All fields are to be accumulated and printed at department control break.

TESTN is to be used to test GROSS field for nonnumeric data. A message is to be printed and data from the record excluded from processing.

Final totals are to be printed for each field.

Output

This Printer Spacing Chart shows how the report is formatted:

Coding sheets for the Weekly Payroll Register problem:

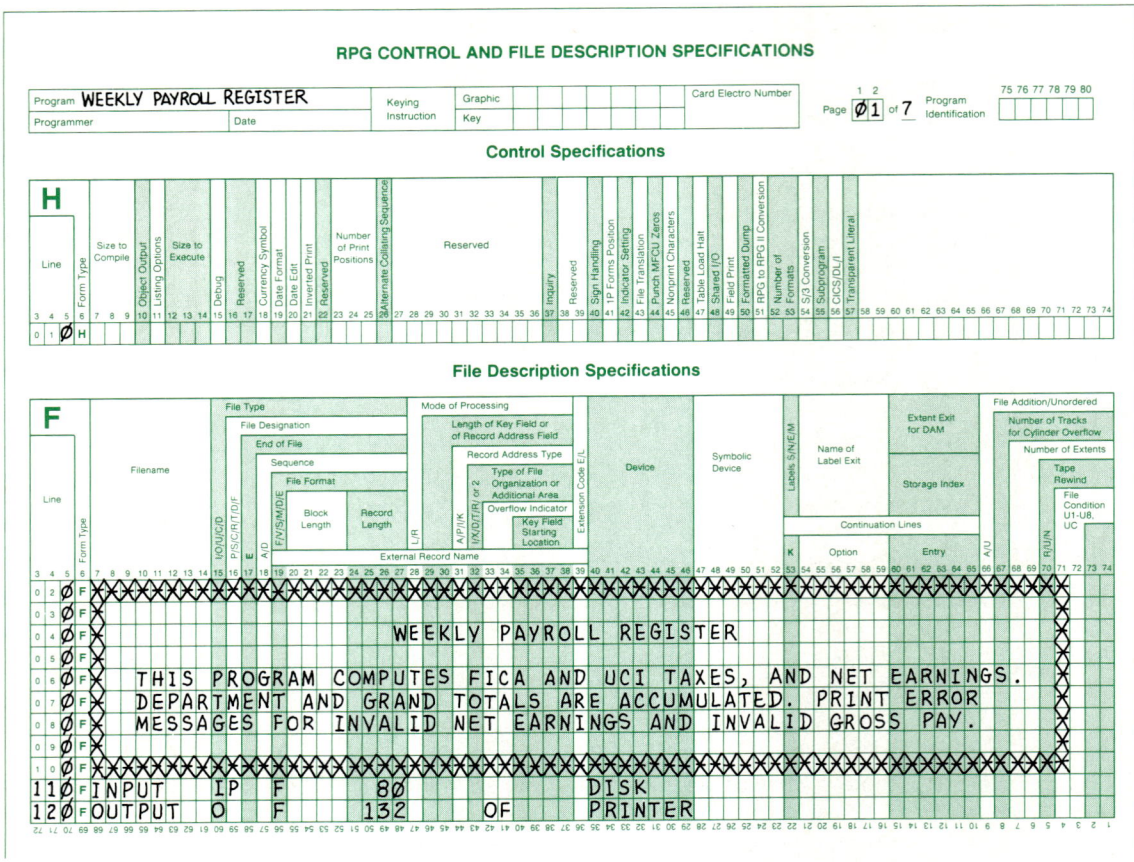

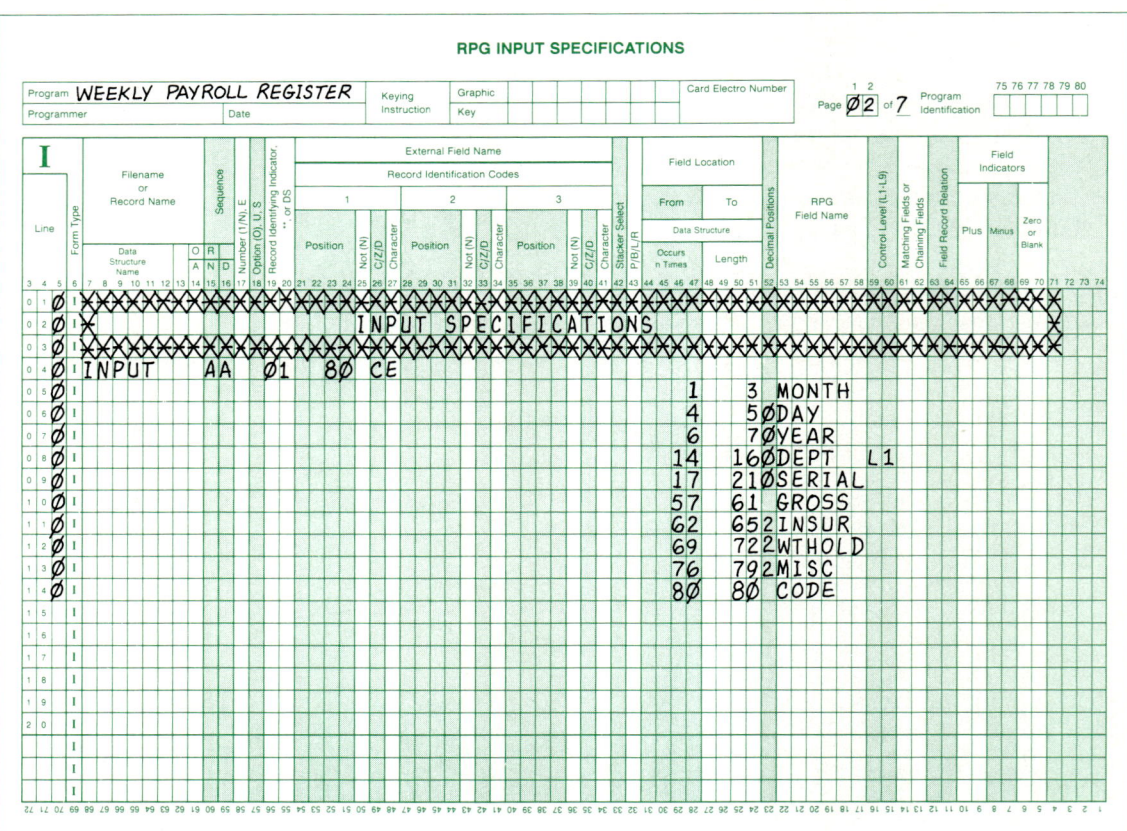

526 RPG II and RPG III Programming

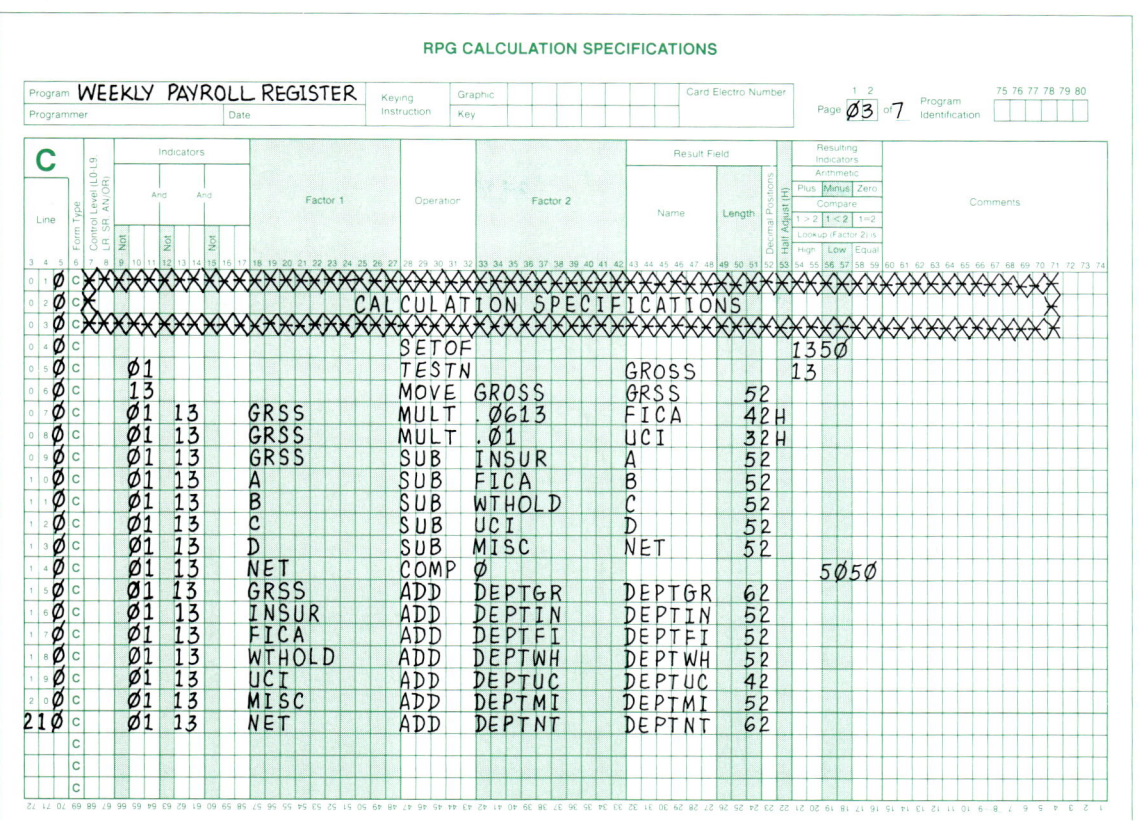

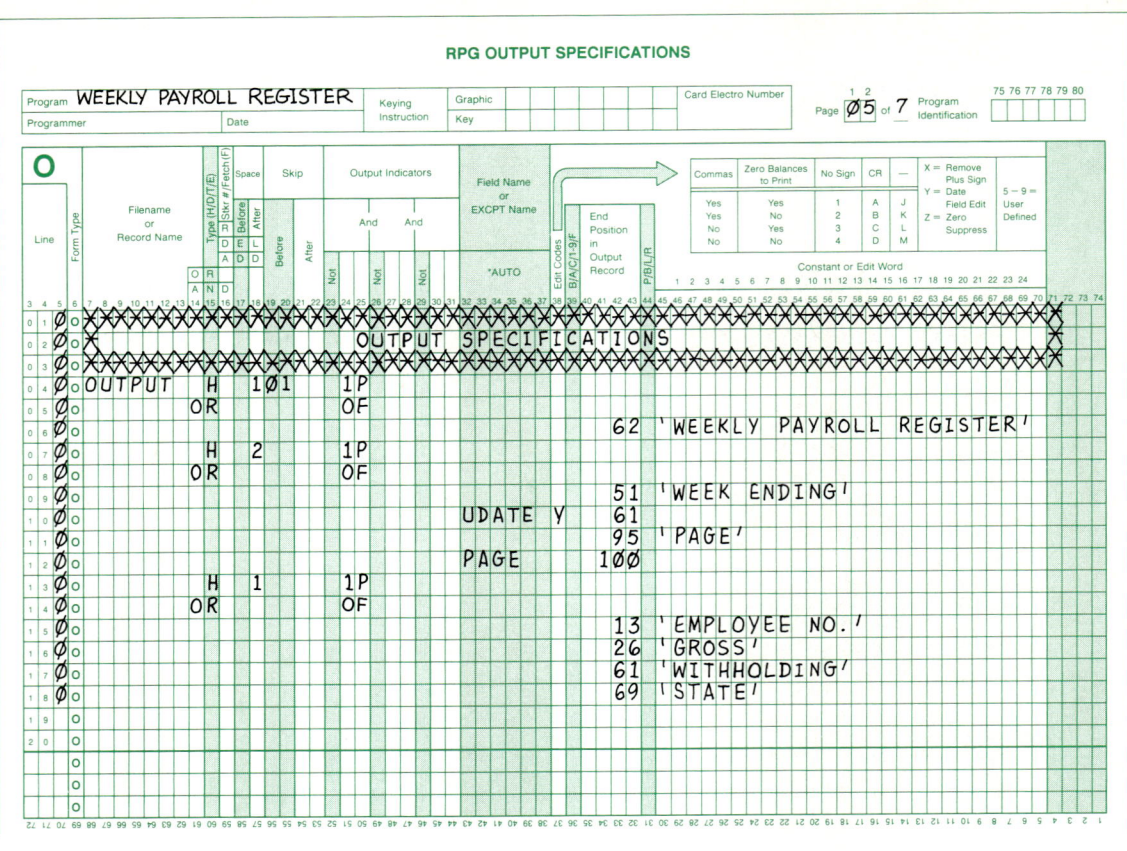
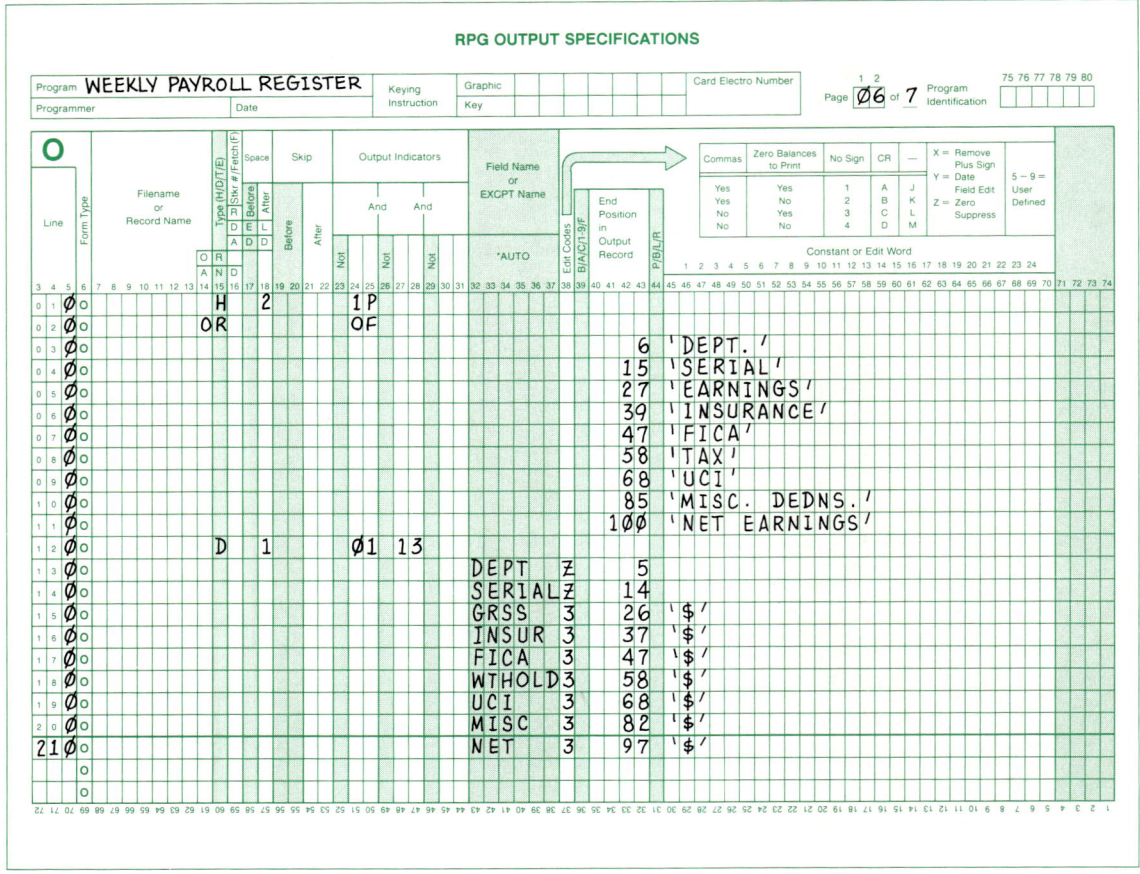

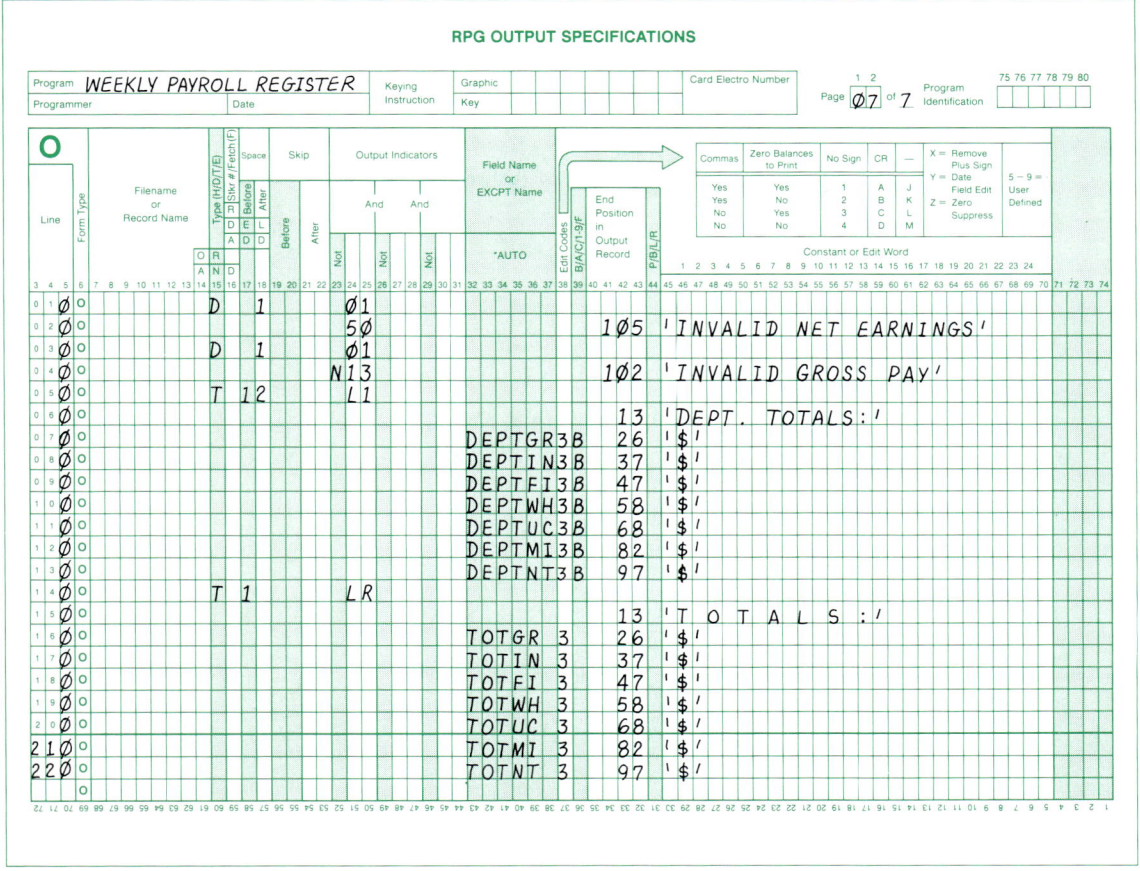

The source listing for the Weekly Payroll Register:

```
 1     01010H
 2   * 01020F********************************************************
 3   * 01030F*                                                       *
 4   * 01040F*            WEEKLY PAYROLL REGISTER                    *
 5   * 01050F*                                                       *
 6   * 01060F*   THIS PROGRAM COMPUTES FICA AND UCI TAXES, AND NET EARNINGS. *
 7   * 01070F*   DEPARTMENT AND GRAND TOTALS ARE ACCUMULATED. PRINT ERROR    *
 8   * 01080F*   MESSAGES FOR INVALID NET EARNINGS AND INVALID GROSS PAY.    *
 9   * 01090F*                                                       *
10   * 01100F********************************************************
11     01110FINPUT    IP  F      80           DISK
12     01120FOUTPUT   O   F     132      OF   PRINTER
13   * 02010I********************************************************
14   * 02020I*              INPUT SPECIFICATIONS                     *
15   * 02030I********************************************************
16     02040IINPUT    AA  01   80 CE
17     02050I                                       1    3 MONTH
18     02060I                                       4   50DAY
19     02070I                                       6   70YEAR
20     02080I                                      14  160DEPT    L1
21     02090I                                      17  210SERIAL
22     02100I                                      57   61 GROSS
23     02110I                                      62  652INSUR
24     02120I                                      69  722WTHOLD
25     02130I                                      76  792MISC
26     02140I                                      80   80 CODE
27   * 03010C********************************************************
28   * 03020C*            CALCULATION SPECIFICATIONS                *
29   * 03030C********************************************************
30     03040C                   SETOF                     1350
31     03050C   01              TESTN     GROSS           13
32     03060C   13              MOVE GROSS GRSS    52
33     03070C   01 13   GRSS    MULT .0613 FICA    42H
34     03080C   01 13   GRSS    MULT .01   UCI     32H
35     03090C   01 13   GRSS    SUB  INSUR A       52
36     03100C   01 13   A       SUB  FICA  B       52
37     03110C   01 13   B       SUB  WTHOLD C      52
38     03120C   01 13   C       SUB  UCI   D       52
39     03130C   01 13   D       SUB  MISC  NET     52
40     03140C   01 13   NET     COMP 0                    5050
```

```
 41    03150C   01 13   GRSS      ADD   DEPTGR    DEPTGR  62
 42    03160C   01 13   INSUR     ADD   DEPTIN    DEPTIN  52
 43    03170C   01 13   FICA      ADD   DEPTFI    DEPTFI  52
 44    03180C   01 13   WTHOLD    ADD   DEPTWH    DEPTWH  52
 45    03190C   01 13   UCI       ADD   DEPTUC    DEPTUC  42
 46    03200C   01 13   MISC      ADD   DEPTMI    DEPTMI  52
 47    03210C   01 13   NET       ADD   DEPTNT    DEPTNT  62
 48    04010CL1         DEPTGR    ADD   TOTGR     TOTGR   72
 49    04020CL1         DEPTIN    ADD   TOTIN     TOTIN   62
 50    04030CL1         DEPTFI    ADD   TOTFI     TOTFI   62
 51    04040CL1         DEPTWH    ADD   TOTWH     TOTWH   62
 52    04050CL1         DEPTUC    ADD   TOTUC     TOTUC   52
 53    04060CL1         DEPTMI    ADD   TOTMI     TOTMI   62
 54    04070CL1         DEPTNT    ADD   TOTNT     TOTNT   72
 55  * 05010O***********************************************************
 56  * 05020O*                OUTPUT SPECIFICATIONS                    *
 57  * 05030O***********************************************************
 58    05040OOUTPUT   H 101     1P
 59    05050O         OR        OF
 60    05060O                                   62 'WEEKLY PAYROLL REGISTER'
 61    05070O         H 2       1P
 62    05080O         OR        OF
 63    05090O                                   51 'WEEK ENDING'
 64    05100O                           UDATE Y 61
 65    05110O                                   95 'PAGE'
 66    05120O                           PAGE   100
 67    05130O         H 1       1P
 68    05140O         OR        OF
 69    05150O                                   13 'EMPLOYEE NO.'
 70    05160O                                   26 'GROSS'
 71    05170O                                   61 'WITHHOLDING'
 72    05180O                                   69 'STATE'
 73    06010O         H 2       1P
 74    06020O         OR        OF
 75    06030O                                    6 'DEPT.'
 76    06040O                                   15 'SERIAL'
 77    06050O                                   27 'EARNINGS'
 78    06060O                                   39 'INSURANCE'
 79    06070O                                   47 'FICA'
 80    06080O                                   58 'TAX'
 81    06090O                                   68 'UCI'
 82    06100O                                   85 'MISC. DEDNS.'
 83    06110O                                  100 'NET EARNINGS'
 84    06120O         D 1       01 13
 85    06130O                           DEPT  Z   5
 86    06140O                           SERIALZ  14
 87    06150O                           GRSS  3  26 '$'
 88    06160O                           INSUR 3  37 '$'
 89    06170O                           FICA  3  47 '$'
 90    06180O                           WTHOLD3  58 '$'
 91    06190O                           UCI   3  68 '$'
 92    06200O                           MISC  3  82 '$'
 93    06210O                           NET   3  97 '$'
 94    07010O         D 1       01
 95    07020O                    50             105 'INVALID NET EARNINGS'
 96    07030O         D 1       01
 97    07040O                    N13            102 'INVALID GROSS PAY'
 98    07050O         T 12      L1
 99    07060O                                   13 'DEPT. TOTALS:'
100    07070O                           DEPTGR3B 26 '$'
101    07080O                           DEPTIN3B 37 '$'
102    07090O                           DEPTFI3B 47 '$'
103    07100O                           DEPTWH3B 58 '$'
104    07110O                           DEPTUC3B 68 '$'
105    07120O                           DEPTMI3B 82 '$'
106    07130O                           DEPTNT3B 97 '$'
107    07140O         T 1       LR
108    07150O                                   13 'T O T A L S :'
109    07160O                           TOTGR 3  26 '$'
110    07170O                           TOTIN 3  37 '$'
111    07180O                           TOTFI 3  47 '$'
112    07190O                           TOTWH 3  58 '$'
113    07200O                           TOTUC 3  68 '$'
114    07210O                           TOTMI 3  82 '$'
115    07220O                           TOTNT 3  97 '$'
```

A Weekly Payroll Register is to be printed as follows:

```
                              WEEKLY PAYROLL REGISTER
                              WEEK ENDING   6/07/87                              PAGE  0001

  EMPLOYEE NO.      GROSS                              WITHHOLDING    STATE
 DEPT.   SERIAL    EARNINGS    INSURANCE    FICA          TAX          UCI      MISC. DEDNS.   NET EARNINGS

  200    10670     $202.00       $3.10     $12.12       $28.00        $2.02        $.00          $156.76

  200    10695     $203.00       $3.10     $12.18       $28.00        $2.03       $5.00          $152.69

  200    10700     $204.00       $3.10     $12.24       $28.00        $2.04        $.00          $158.62

  200    10703     $205.00       $3.10     $12.30       $28.00        $2.05        $.00          $159.55

  200    10725     $207.00       $3.10     $12.42       $28.00        $2.07       $5.00          $156.41

  200    10730     $208.00       $3.10     $12.48       $28.00        $2.08        $.00          $162.34

  200    10742     $209.00       $3.10     $12.54       $28.00        $2.09        $.00          $163.27

  200    10800     $210.00       $3.10     $12.60       $28.00        $2.10       $5.00          $159.20

  200    10890     $211.00       $3.10     $12.66       $28.00        $2.11       $1.00          $164.13

 DEPT. TOTALS:    $1859.00      $27.90    $111.54      $252.00       $18.59      $16.00         $1432.97

  300    10904     $212.00       $3.10     $12.72       $28.00        $2.12       $5.00          $161.06

  300    10905     $213.00       $3.10     $12.78       $28.00        $2.13        $.00          $166.99

  300    10906     $214.00       $3.10     $12.84       $28.00        $2.14        $.00          $167.92

  300    10907     $215.00       $3.10     $12.90       $28.00        $2.15        $.00          $168.85

 DEPT. TOTALS:     $854.00      $12.40     $51.24      $112.00        $8.54       $5.00          $664.82

  400    11215     $218.00       $3.10     $13.08       $28.00        $2.18        $.00          $171.64

  400    11225     $219.00       $3.10     $13.14       $28.00        $2.19        $.00          $172.57

  400    11240     $220.00       $3.15     $13.20       $28.50        $2.20        $.00          $172.95

  400    11250     $221.00       $3.15     $13.26       $28.50        $2.21        $.00          $173.88

 DEPT. TOTALS:     $878.00      $12.50     $52.68      $113.00        $8.78        $.00          $691.04

  600    12330     $225.00       $3.15     $13.50       $28.50        $2.25       $2.00          $175.60

  600    12340     $226.00       $3.15     $13.56       $28.50        $2.26       $2.00          $176.53

  600    12350     $227.00       $3.15     $13.62       $28.50        $2.27        $.00          $179.46

  600    12366     $229.00       $3.15     $13.74       $28.50        $2.29        $.00          $181.32

  600    12400     $229.00       $3.15     $13.74       $28.50        $2.29        $.00          $181.32

 DEPT. TOTALS:    $1136.00      $15.75     $68.16      $142.50       $11.36       $4.00          $894.23


  T O T A L S :   $4727.00      $68.55    $283.62      $619.50       $47.27      $25.00         $3683.06
```

Illustrative Program

Line Counter Specifications: Invoice

Job Definition

An invoice is to be prepared like the one shown in the following sample. There are two types of records: name/address records for all customers who made purchases on credit during the month, and transaction records for each item purchased by customers during the month.

Input

The input file consists of two types of records: name/address records and transaction records.

The name/address records have the following fields:

Positions	Field Description
1–01	Code 'N'
2–06	Account number
7–26	Name of customer
27–44	Address line 1
45–62	Address line 2
63–80	Address line 3

The transaction records have the following fields:

Positions	Field Description	
1–01	Code 'T'	
2–06	Account number	
9–14	Item number	
15–29	Description	
30–34	Quantity	
35–39	Unit price	(XXX.XX)

The input file is organized so that all transaction records for a customer follow the customer's name/address record.

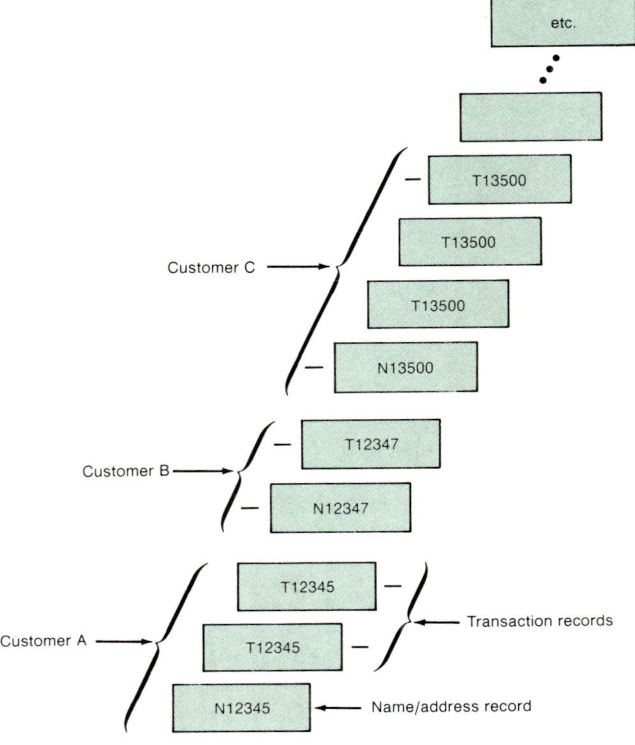

There will always be one name/address record for each customer, but there may be one or more transactions per customer.

Processing

The invoice is to be printed under line counter specifications control with the proper spacing between all heading items and body items.

The quantity is to be multiplied by the unit price to find the amount.

The amounts are to be accumulated and the total is to be printed on the invoice.

Each customer's invoice is to be printed on a separate page.

Output

This Printer Spacing Chart shows how the report is to be formatted:

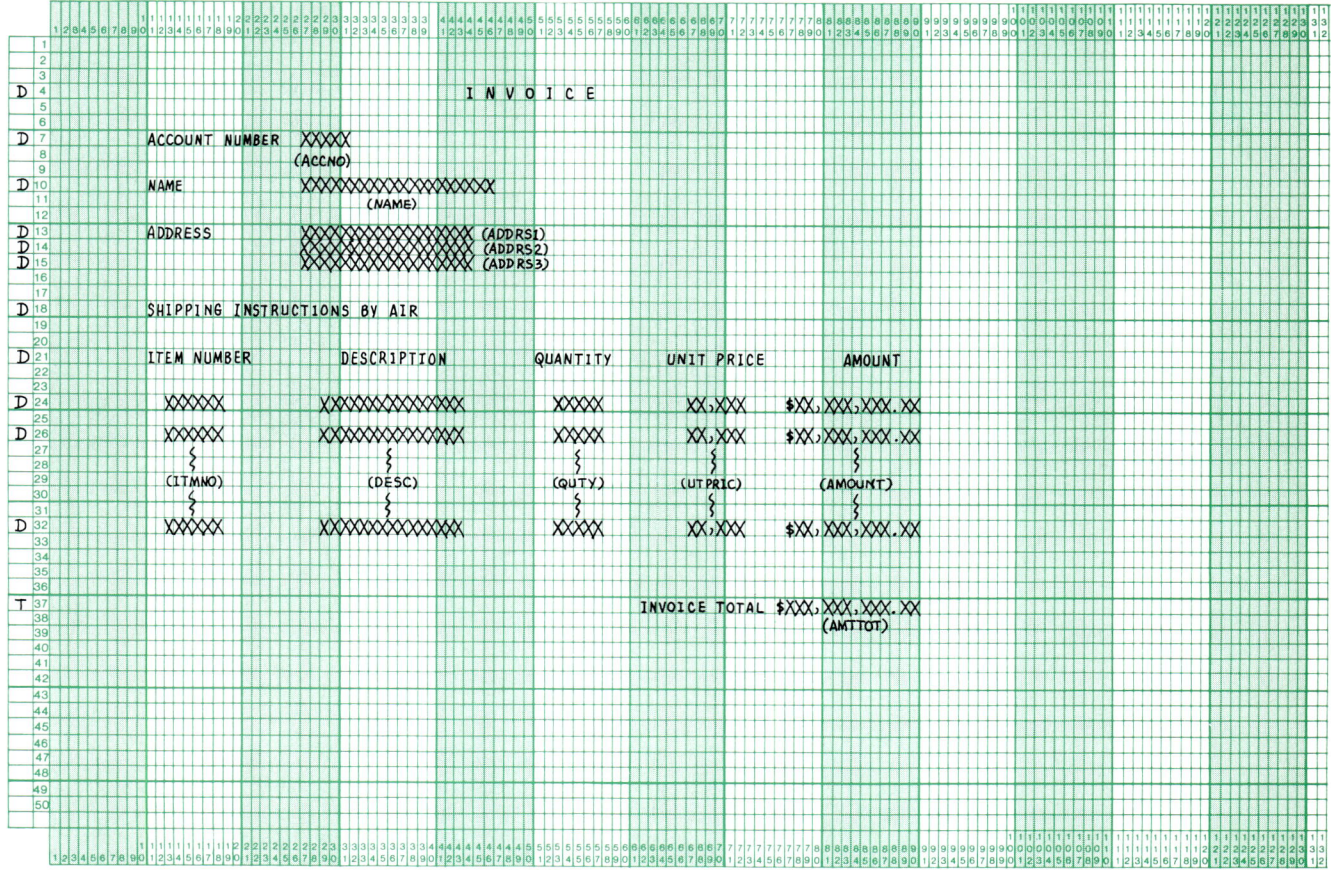

Coding sheet for the Invoice Report problem:

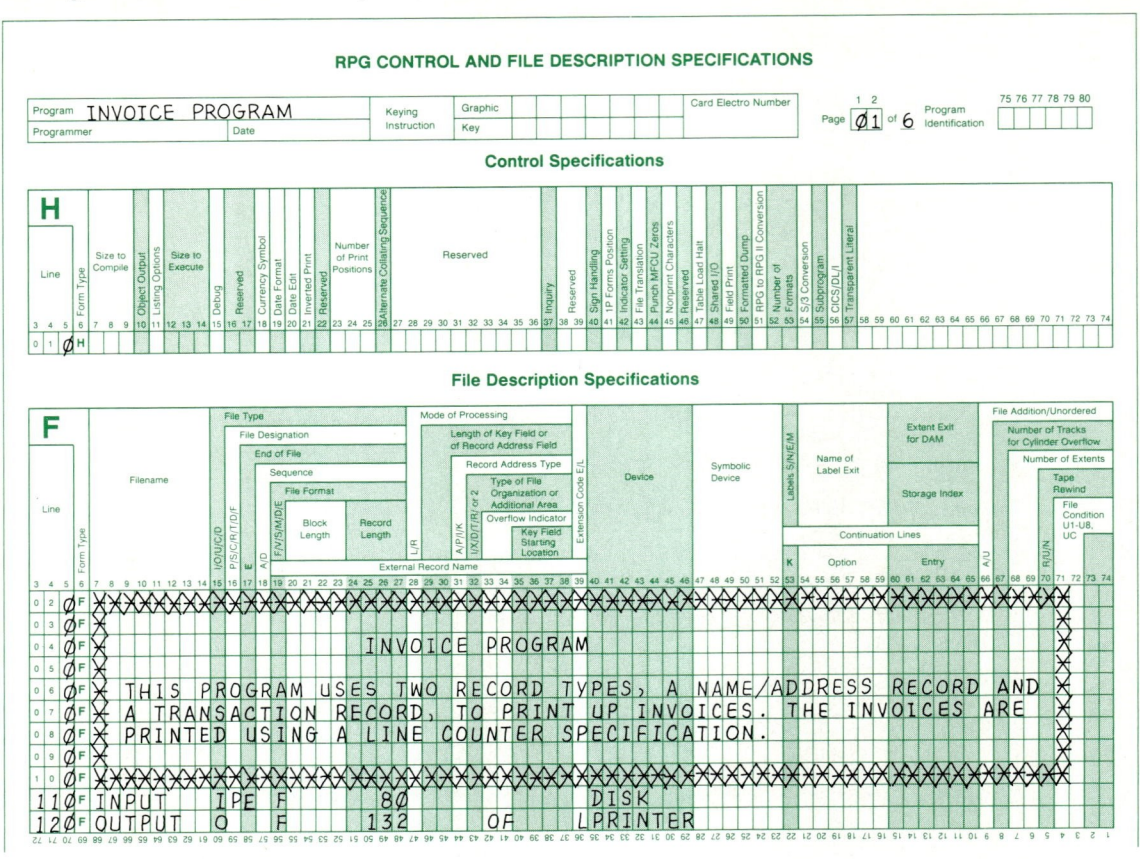

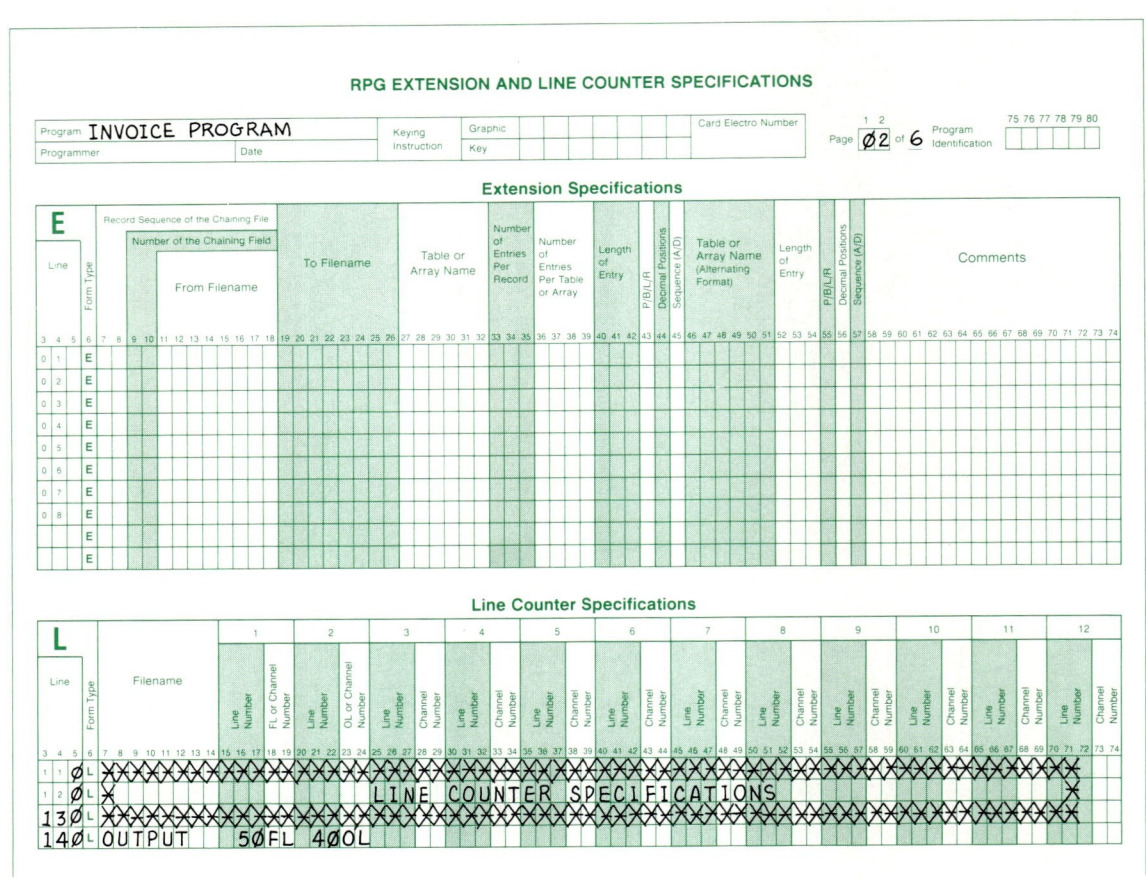

534 RPG II and RPG III Programming

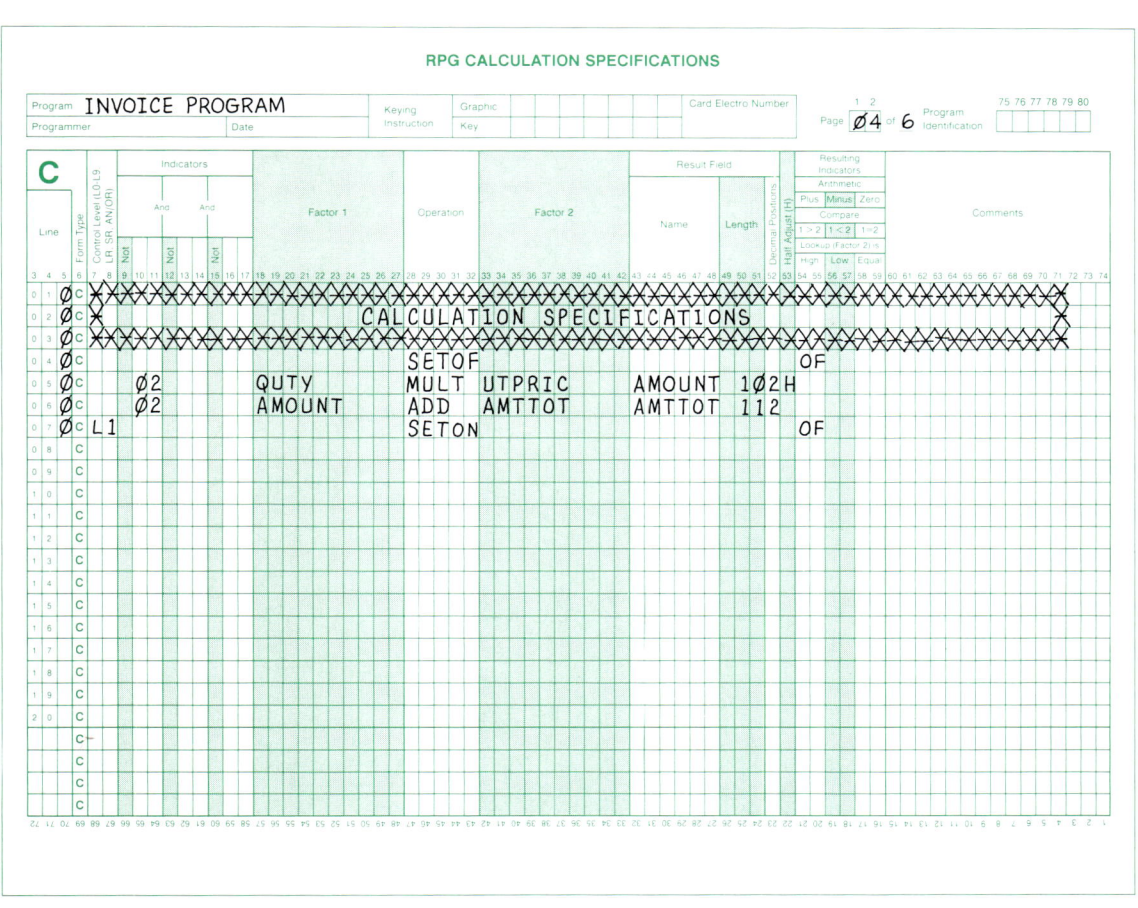

Other RPG II Statements

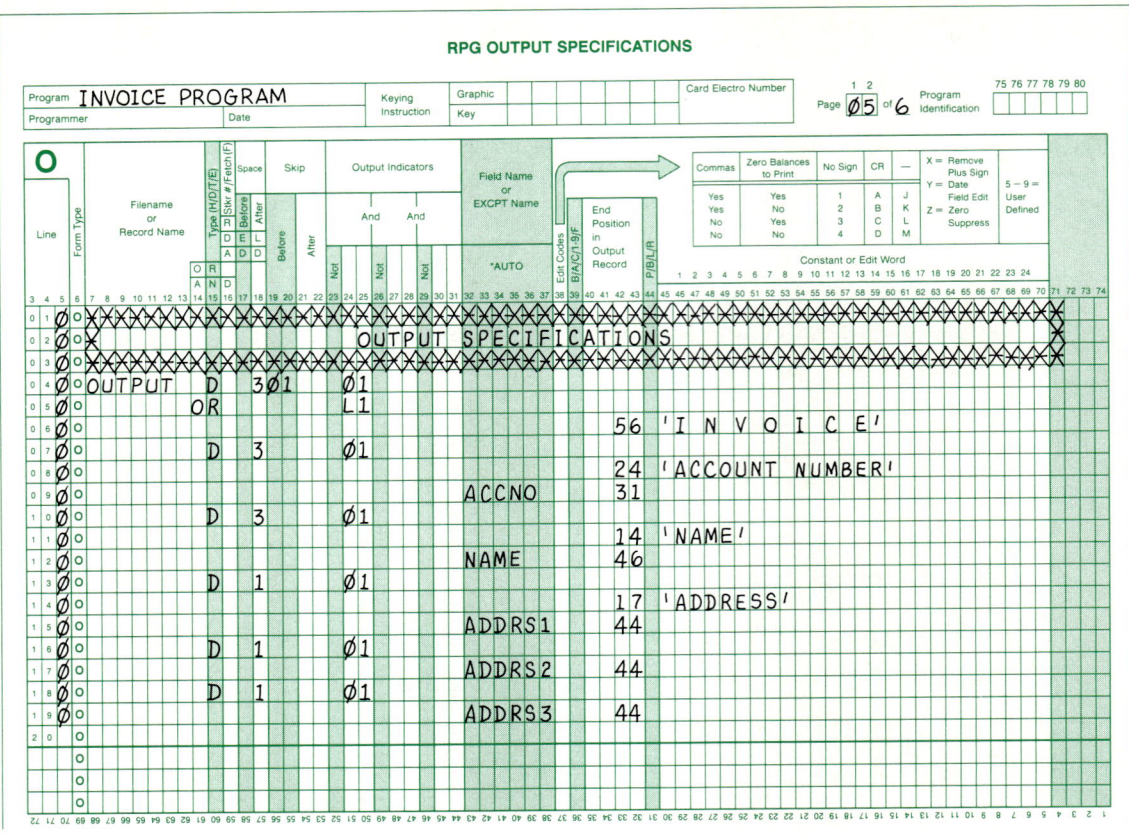
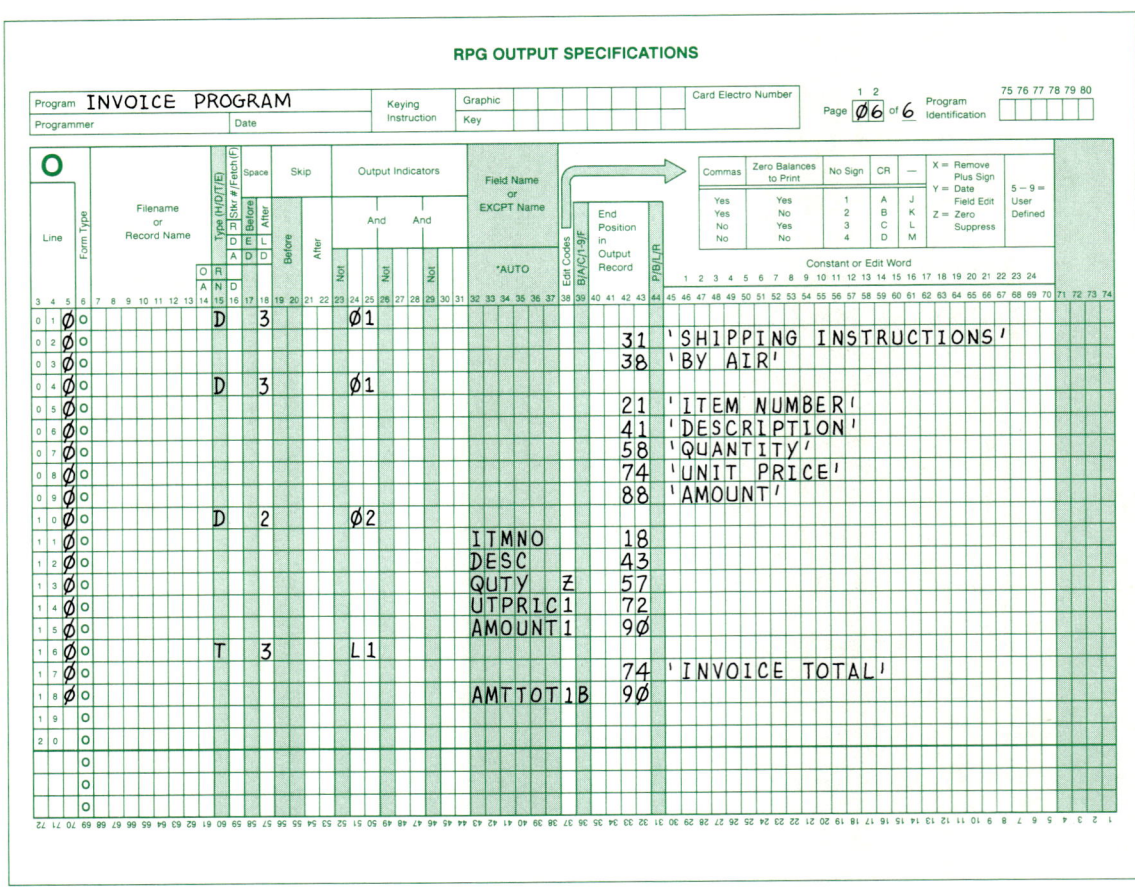

The source listing for the Inventory Report problem:

```
1     01010H
2   * 01020F***************************************************************
3   * 01030F*                                                              *
4   * 01040F*                   INVOICE PROGRAM                            *
5   * 01050F*                                                              *
6   * 01060F* THIS PROGRAM USES TWO RECORD TYPES, A NAME/ADDRESS RECORD AND *
7   * 01070F* A TRANSACTION RECORD, TO PRINT UP INVOICES. THE INVOICES ARE  *
8   * 01080F* PRINTED USING A LINE COUNTER SPECIFICATION.                  *
9   * 01090F*                                                              *
10  * 01100F***************************************************************
11    01110FINPUT    IPE  F      80           DISK
12    01120FOUTPUT   O    F     132        OF LPRINTER
13  * 02110L***************************************************************
14  * 02120L*              LINE COUNTER SPECIFICATIONS                     *
15  * 02130L***************************************************************
16    02140LOUTPUT   50FL 40OL
17  * 03010I***************************************************************
18  * 03020I*                 INPUT SPECIFICATIONS                         *
19  * 03030I***************************************************************
20    03040IINPUT    011 01   1 CN
21    03050I                                          2  60ACCNO  L1
22    03060I                                          7  26 NAME
23    03070I                                         27  44 ADDRS1
24    03080I                                         45  62 ADDRS2
25    03090I                                         63  80 ADDRS3
26    03100I         02NO02  1 CT
27    03110I                                          2  60ACCNO  L1
28    03120I                                          9  14 0ITMNO
29    03130I                                         15  29 DESC
30    03140I                                         30  34 0QUTY
31    03150I                                         35  39 2UTPRIC
32  * 04010C***************************************************************
33  * 04020C*              CALCULATION SPECIFICATIONS                      *
34  * 04030C***************************************************************
35    04040C                    SETOF                              OF
36    04050C           02   QUTY      MULT UTPRIC    AMOUNT  102H
37    04060C           02   AMOUNT    ADD  AMTTOT    AMTTOT  112
38    04070CL1                   SETON                              OF
39  * 05010O***************************************************************
40  * 05020O*                OUTPUT SPECIFICATIONS                         *
41  * 05030O***************************************************************
42    05040OOUTPUT   D  301    01
43    05050O         OR        L1
44    05060O                                     56 'I N V O I C E'
45    05070O         D    3    01
46    05080O                                     24 'ACCOUNT NUMBER'
47    05090O                            ACCNO    31
48    05100O         D    3    01
49    05110O                                     14 'NAME'
50    05120O                            NAME     46
51    05130O         D    1    01
52    05140O                                     17 'ADDRESS'
53    05150O                            ADDRS1   44
54    05160O         D    1    01
55    05170O                            ADDRS2   44
56    05180O         D    3    01
57    05190O                            ADDRS3   44
58    06010O         D    3    01
59    06020O                                     31 'SHIPPING INSTRUCTIONS'
60    06030O                                     38 'BY AIR'
61    06040O         D    3    01
62    06050O                                     21 'ITEM NUMBER'
63    06060O                                     41 'DESCRIPTION'
64    06070O                                     58 'QUANTITY'
65    06080O                                     74 'UNIT PRICE'
66    06090O                                     88 'AMOUNT'
67    06100O         D    2    02
68    06110O                            ITMNO    18
69    06120O                            DESC     43
70    06130O                            QUTY   Z 57
71    06140O                            UTPRIC1  72
72    06150O                            AMOUNT1  90
73    06160O         T    3    L1
74    06170O                                     74 'INVOICE TOTAL'
75    06180O                            AMTTOT1B 90
```

An invoice is to be printed as follows:

```
                              I N V O I C E

   ACCOUNT NUMBER  68252


   NAME          JUDGE STORES INC.


   ADDRESS       210 SO MAIN ST
                 LOS ANGELES
                 CALIF      90006


   SHIPPING INSTRUCTIONS BY AIR


   ITEM NUMBER      DESCRIPTION     QUANTITY    UNIT PRICE      AMOUNT


      167242        GAS STOVES         4          15,075       60,300.00

      267415        TABLES             7          15,055      105,385.00

      672637        TOP CHAIRS        15           1,000       15,000.00

      786424        BLACK DECKS        5          11,100       55,500.00



                                             INVOICE TOTAL    236,185.00
```

Questions for Review

1. How may a character be changed after it is read, and why might the programmer want to change a character?
2. How does the move operation work and what elements must be present for the programmer to use move zones?
3. How is a move zone operation coded?
4. Briefly describe the four move zone operations.
5. What is the function of the test numeric operation and what is its main use?
6. How are the resulting indicators used in a TESTN operation?
7. What is the function of the TESTZ operation and what is its main use?
8. How are the resulting indicators used in a TESTZ operation?
9. What is the purpose of bit operations?
10. What is a binary field and what are binary field operations?
11. Briefly explain the coding of binary field operations.
12. Briefly explain the functions of BITON, BITOF, and TESTB operations.
13. How are the resulting indicators used with TESTB?
14. What is the main function of the DSPLY operation?
15. What are the different codings for the DSPLY operations?
16. What are zoned, packed, and binary formats?

Problems

Problem 1

Using the following documentation, code the RPG solution for printing of an order proof listing and creating a transaction file of the orders for further processing. Choose an input device appropriate to your particular system.

Your calculations should include the following:

1. Counting the number of orders processed.
2. Accumulating all order numbers for a control "Hash" total to be printed at the end of the report.
3. Output is both printer and disk.
4. Disk output is one record for each order processed; the record layout is shown.
5. Printer output according to the Printer Spacing Chart as shown.

Required

Code the necessary file description, input specifications, calculation specifications, and output specifications on the appropriate forms.

System Flowchart

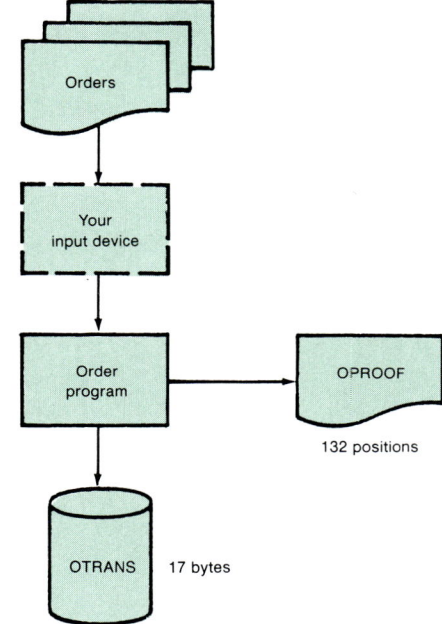

Record Layouts

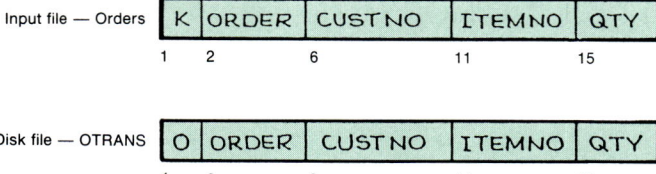

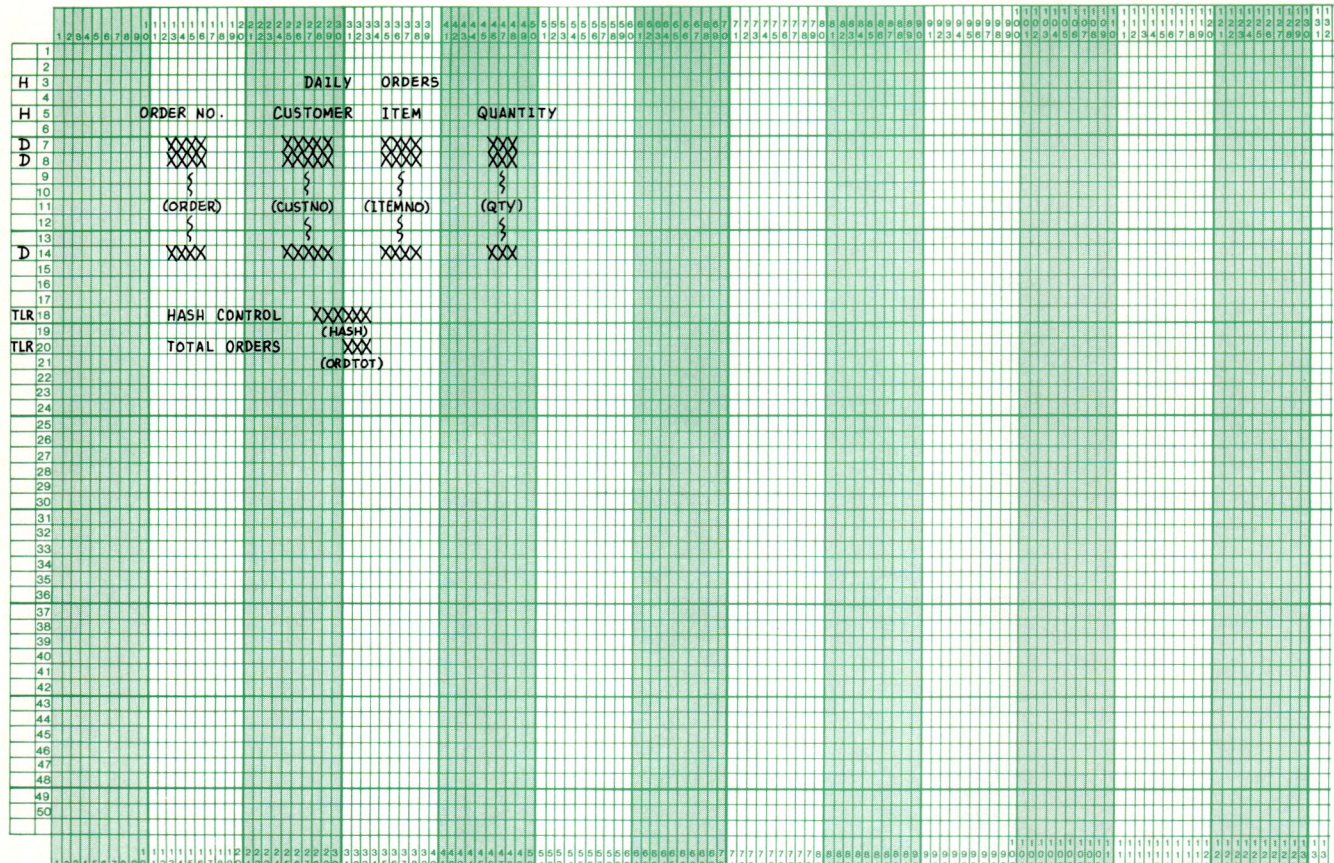

Output is as follows:

```
                DAILY    ORDERS
     ORDER NO.   CUSTOMER    ITEM     QUANTITY

        1234      51634      9414        10
        1321      49943      5102         5
        1479      73194      8634       105
        1498      41712       502         1
        2143      52348       703         3

     HASH   CONTROL     7675

        TOTAL ORDERS      5
```

Problem 2

Using the following documentation, code the RPG solution for printing of payroll checks and producing a summary disk file of the check records.

1. Output is both printer and disk.
2. Check output should have two detail lines according to the Printer Spacing Chart. All numeric fields should be edited; the check amount should have a floating $ for protection.
3. The disk output should be one record for each check written with the fields as shown on the record layout.
4. The payroll checks are eighteen lines long. Assume the overflow line is line 18.
5. The constants *Date* and *Pay to the order of* are preprinted on the checks.

Required

Code the entries on the file description, line counter specifications, input specifications, calculation specifications, and output specifications on the appropriate forms.

System Flowchart

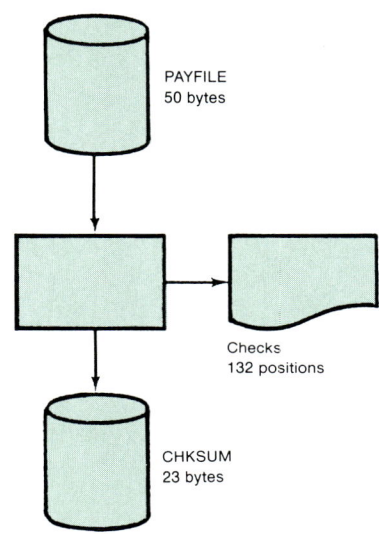

Record Layouts

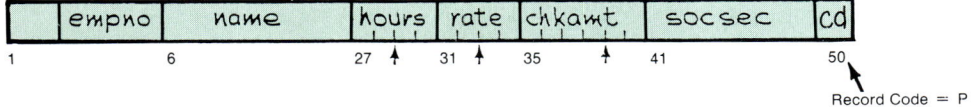

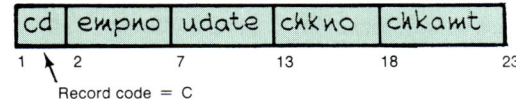

```
        Date    xx/xx/xx              XXXXX                    XXXXX
D                (UDATE)             (EMPNO)                  (CHKNO)


D       Pay to the order of  XXXXXXXXXXXXXXXXX         $X,XXX.XX
                                 (NAME)                 (CHKAMT)



        A. B. Company
```

Output is as follows:

```
1/18/87              68832                     150

              JOHN  P  SMITH              $400.00

1/18/87              68948                     151

              DAVID  S  JONES             $177.80

1/18/87              69041                     152

              JEFFREY  H  HICKS           $140.00

1/18/87              71248                     153

              STEVEN  J  STEVENS          $334.00
```

Problem 3

Prepare a statement of account for each customer. A sample report is provided.

Input

The input file RECORDS contains four types of records. The record layouts are shown. The sequence and number of the input records is as follows:

Name and address record
    One record for each account number
    Must be only one record
    Must be the first record of each account

Balance forward record
    One record for each account number
    Must be only one record
    If present, must be the second record of each account

Payment record
    May be several records for each account
    If present, must be the third record of each account

Current charges record
    May be several for each account
    If present, must be the fourth record of each account

Calculations

Compute the amount of each customer.

1. Z-ADD OLDBAL for NEWBAL
2. NEWBAL SUB PAYMT for NEWBAL
3. NEWBAL ADD SURCHG for NEWBAL

Output

A statement for each customer is called REPORT. Use a 132-position printer. Print on a preprinted form. The spacing is described on the Printer Spacing Chart.
    Use the reserved word UDATE to date the report.
    Use the edit code that will reflect a credit balance (payments greater than charges) by printing CR.
    For balance forward and payment, print the constant BALANCE FORWARD or PAYMENT in the description field.
    Assume that overflow will not be required on any statement.
    The form length is 50; the overflow line is 40.

Required

Code the necessary file description, line counter specifications, input specifications, calculation specifications, and output specifications on the appropriate forms.

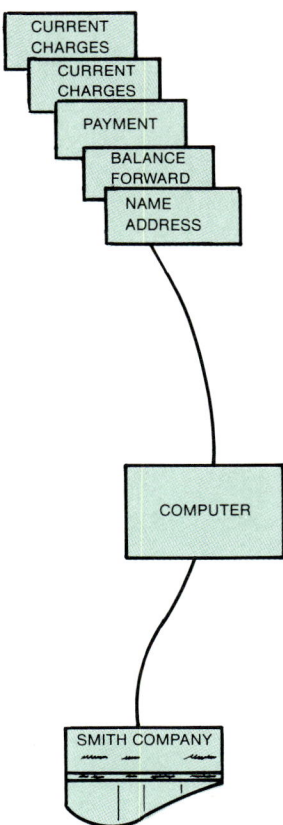

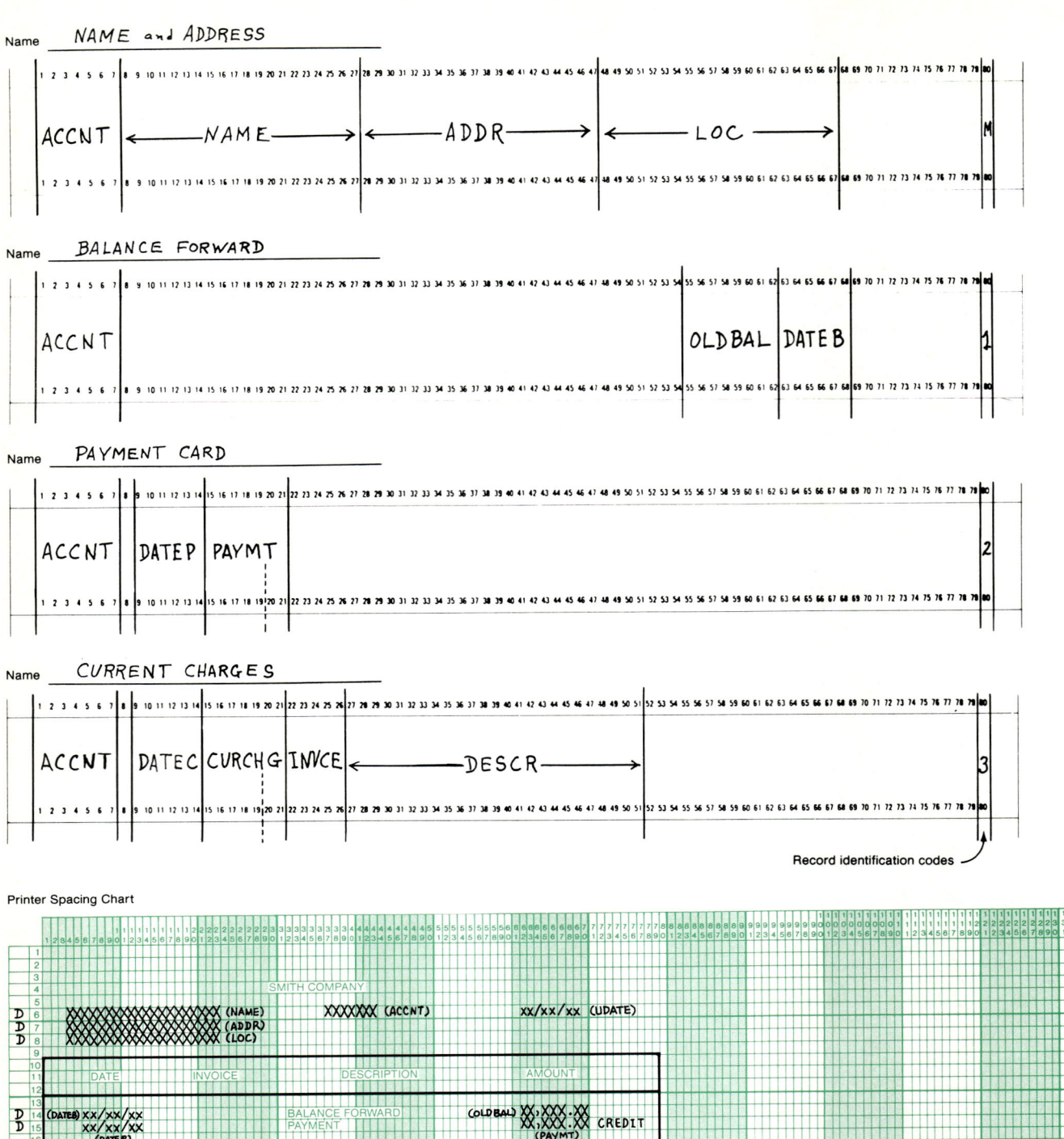

Sample Report

	SMITH COMPANY		
customer		account	today's date
name			
street address			
city/state			

DATE	INVOICE	DESCRIPTION	AMOUNT
4/21/87		BALANCE FORWARD	200.00
5/10/87		PAYMENT	175.00 CREDIT
5/04/87	64765	King Size Bed	500.00
5/04/87	64765	Easy Chair	75.00
5/25/87	80000	Floor Lamp	8.75
5/25/87	80000	End Table	15.00
		TOTAL AMOUNT DUE	$623.75

Output is as follows:

```
JONES & JONES CO.            1234493                 6/12/87
131 WEST EAST ST.
VAN NUYS, CALIFORNIA



  4/21/87              BALANCE FORWARD         200.00
  5/01/87              PAYMENT                 175.00 CREDIT

  5/04/87     64765    KING SIZE BED           500.00

  5/04/87     64765    EASY CHAIR               75.00

  5/25/87     80000    FLOOR LAMP                8.75

  5/25/87     80000    END TABLE                15.00


                                              $623.75
```

Problem 4

Prepare monthly statements of account, one for each customer. A sample statement is provided.

Input
An input file called TRANSACT contains three types of records. The record layouts are shown.

Customer master record
- One record for each customer
- Must be only one record
- Must be the first record of each account

Customer credit record
- One record for each customer
- Must be only one record
- Must be the second record of each account

Amount due record
- May be more than one record for each account
- If present, must be the third record of each account

Tables
Related tables show account balance and minimum payment required. The record layout is shown.

Calculations

Compute the new balance for the customer. Look up the new balance in the table TABBAL to find the minimum payment required as listed in the related table TABMIN. For balances $50.00 or less, the entire amount is due.

> PREBAL SUB CREDIT = NEWBAL
> NEWBAL ADD CHARGE = NEWBAL
> NEWBAL COMP 50.00
> NEWBAL LOKUP TABBAL to find TABMIN

Output

A statement for each customer is called STATMENT. Use a 132-position printer. Print on a preprinted form. The spacing is described on the Printer Spacing Chart.

The page is 40 lines long; the overflow line is line 34. Assume that overflow will not be required on any statement.

Required

Code the necessary file description, extension specifications, line counter specifications, input specifications, calculation specifications, and output specifications on the appropriate forms.

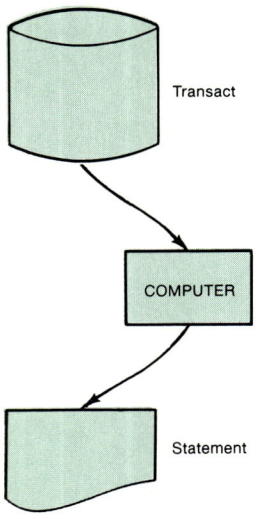

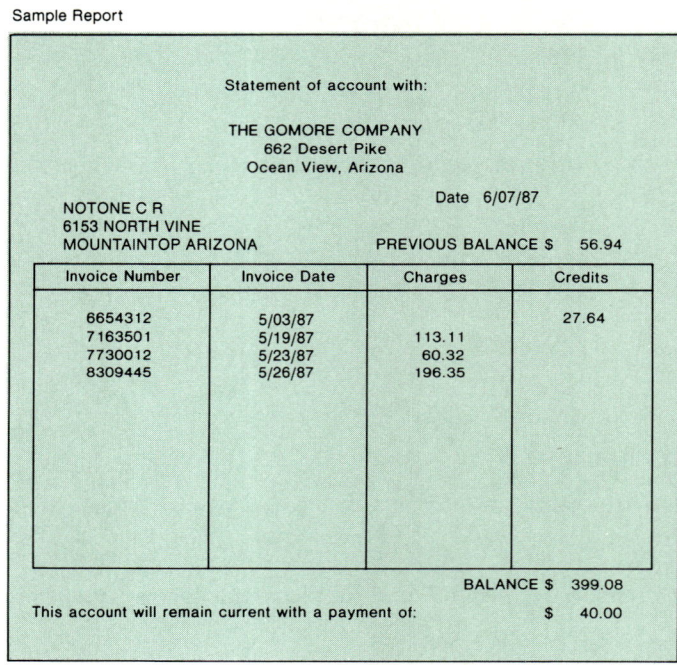

Input File Layouts

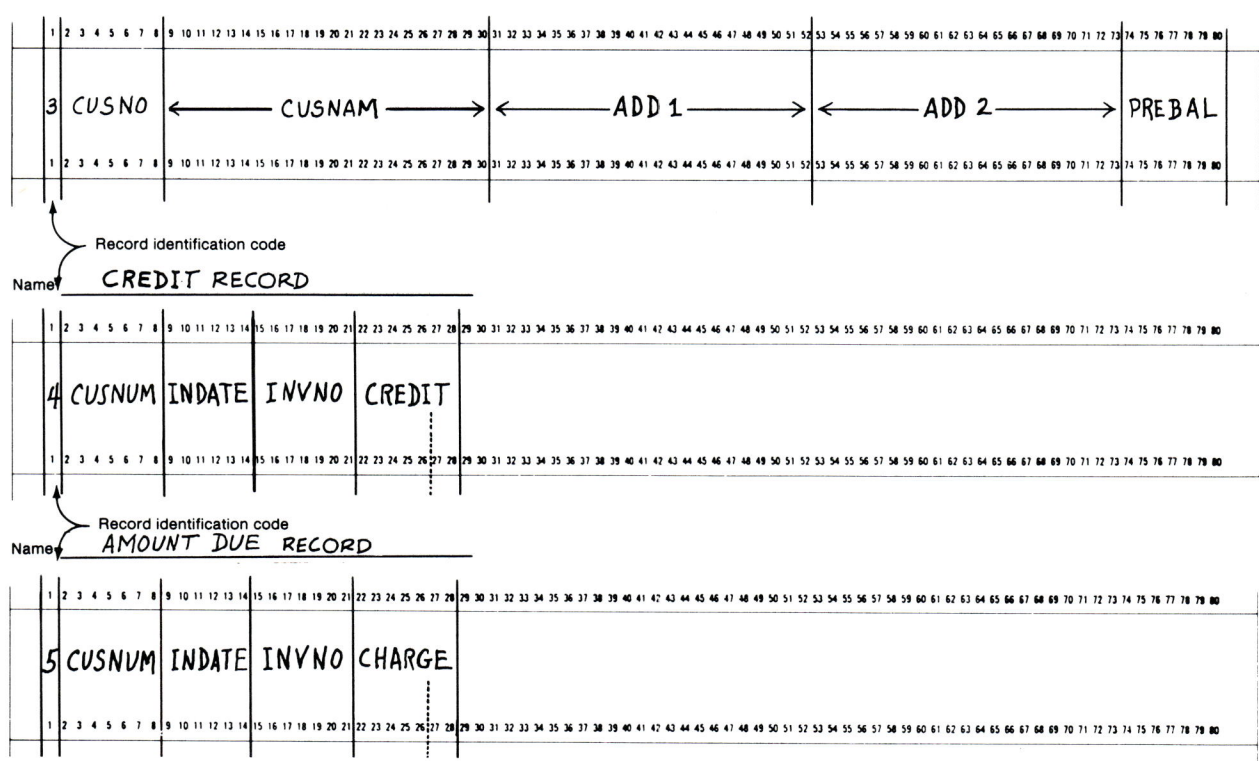

Other RPG II Statements

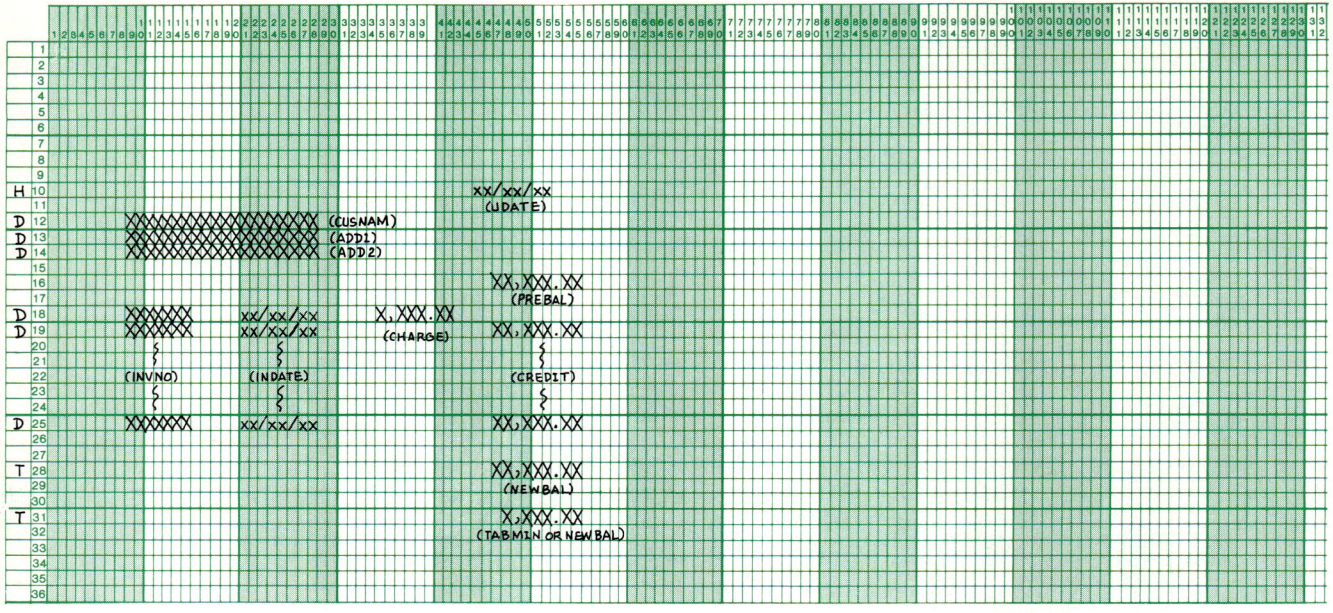

Output is as follows:

```
                                            6/07/87


NOTONE C R
6153 NORTH VINE
MOUNTAINTOP ARIZONA

                                              56.94
    6654312      5/03/87                      27.64
    7163501      5/19/87         113.11
    7730012      5/23/87          60.32
    8309445      5/25/87         196.35



                                             399.08


                                              40.00
```

Problem 5

Prepare gas bills on preprinted forms. A sample gas bill is provided.

Input

An input file called CUSTFILE contains two types of records. The record layouts are shown.

Name and address record
    One record for each customer
    Must be only one record
    Must be the first record of each account

Units of gas used record
    Record indicates number of units of gas used by the customer that month
    One record for each account
    Must be the second record of each account

Tables

Related tables show the number of units of gas used and the cost per unit. The record layout is shown.

Calculations

Use the table below to find the appropriate cost per unit according to the number of units used (NOUNIT). If the number of units exceeds 1200 (i.e., is not found in the table), the rate will be .095 per unit.

Calculate the charge for each customer. Prepare a final total to be printed out after all records have been processed.

NOUNIT	LOKUP	TABUNT		to find TABCST
TABCST	×	NOUNIT	=	CHARGE
.095	×	NOUNIT	=	CHARGE
CHARGE	+	STDCHG	=	TOTAL
TOTAL	+	FINTOT	=	FINTOT

Output

A statement for each customer is called GASBILL. Use a 132-position printer. Use a preprinted form that is 50 lines long; this is considered a page. The last line on which printing is to occur is line 40.

The spacing is described on the Printer Spacing Chart.

Required

Code the necessary file description, extension specifications, line counter specifications, input specifications, calculation specifications, and output specifications on the appropriate forms.

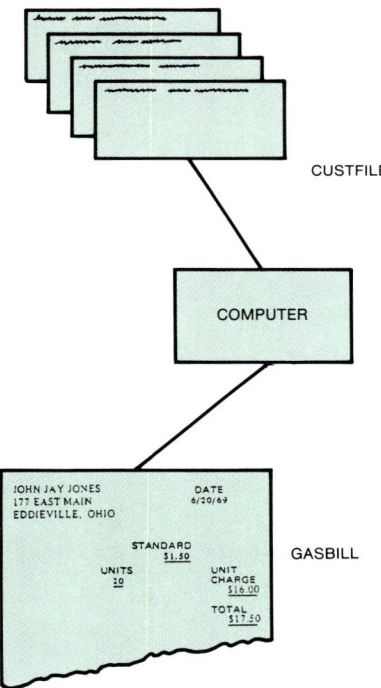

Other RPG II Statements

Sample Gas Bill

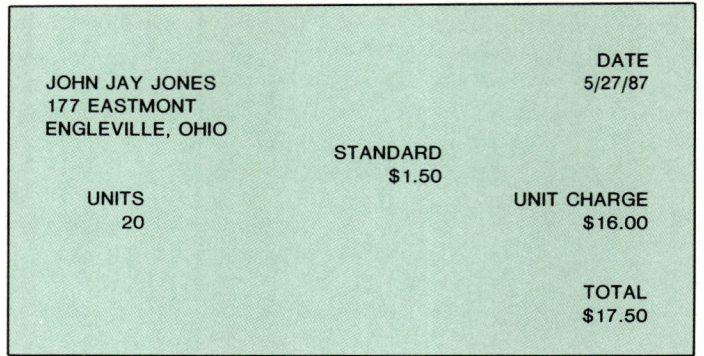

Related Tables

	TABUNT	TABCST
(0-5)	0050	.800
(51-100)	0100	.725
(101-200)	0200	.700
(201-300)	0300	.650
(301-450)	0450	.550
(451-600)	0600	.400
(601-800)	0800	.300
(801-1000)	1000	.225
(1001-1200)	1200	.175

Ranges covered by corresponding entries in the table TABCST

Compile Time Table

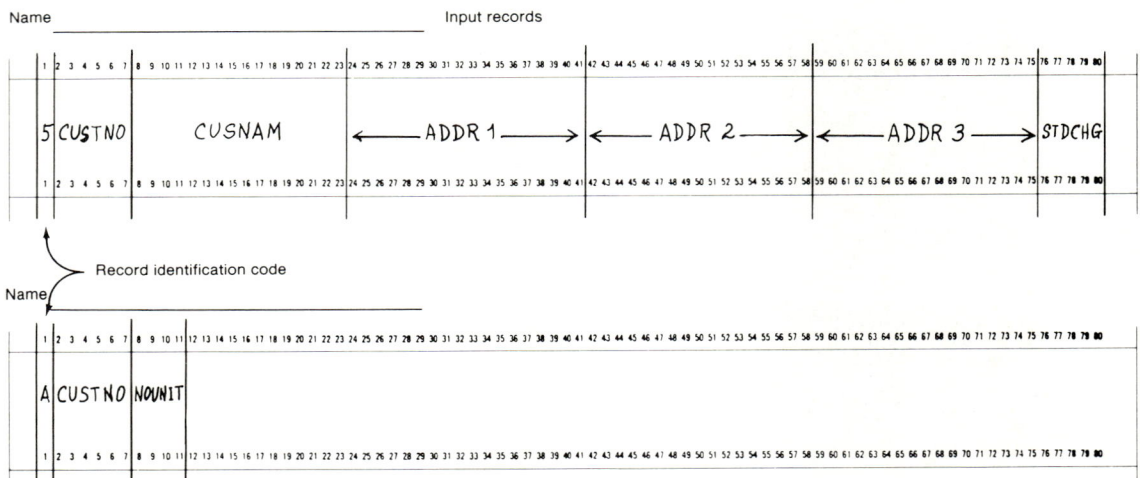

Record Layouts

550   RPG II and RPG III Programming

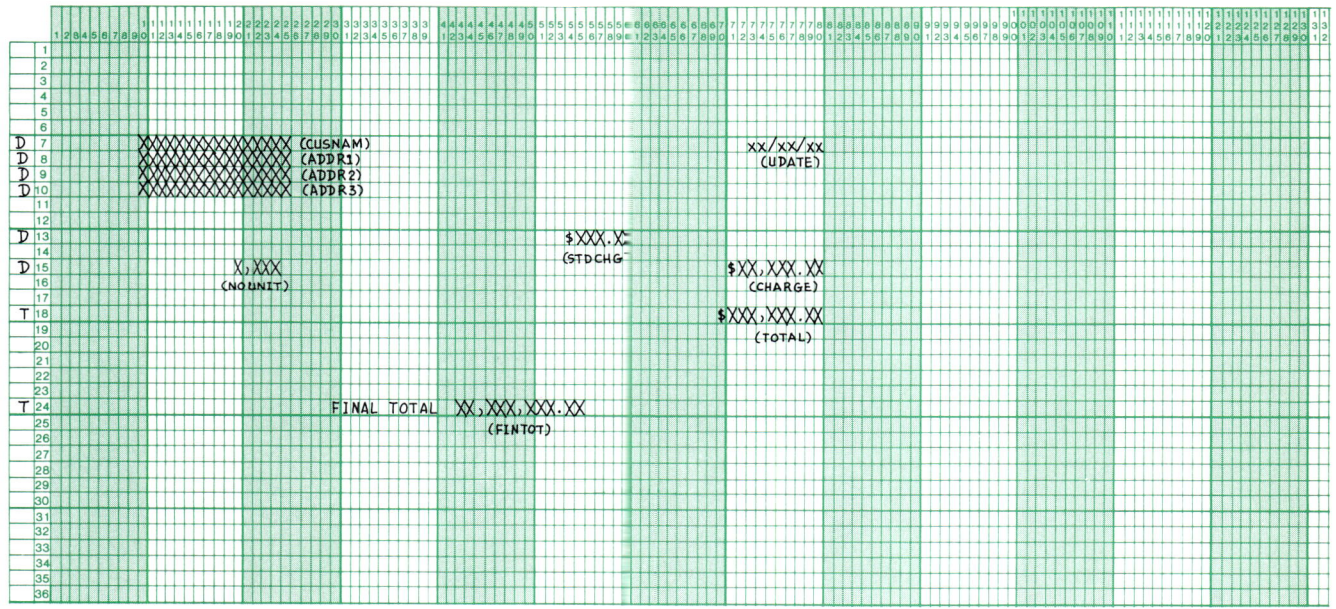

Output is as follows:

```
JOHN JAY JONES                                              5/27/87
177 EASTMONT
ENGLEVILLE, OHIO



                                      $1.50
           20                                          16.00


                                                       $17.50



           FINAL TOTAL      17.50
```

Other RPG II Statements

11 RPG III and the IBM System/38

Outline

RPG III Rationale
RPG III Improvements
    (IBM System/38)
  Hardware
  Software
  Technique
RPG III Language Enhancements
  Source Entry Utility (SEU)
    SEU Sequence Number
    Source Diagnostic Error
      Notation
    SEU Summary
  Externally Described Data (CPF)
  Data Description Specification
    (DDS)
  Full Procedural File Specifications
  File Operations
    Random Retrieval from a File
      Based on RECNO or Key
      Value (CHAIN)
    Delete Record (DELET)
    Execute Format (EXFMT)
    Read a Record (READ)
    Read Next Modified Record
      (READC)
    Read Equal Key (READE)
    Read Prior Key (READP)
    Set Greater Than (SETGT)
    Set Greater Than or Equal To
      (SETLL)
    Modify Existing Record
      (UPDAT)
    Create New Records (WRITE)
  File Control Operations
    Force End of Data (FEOD)
    Open File for Processing
      (OPEN)
    Close File for Processing
      (CLOSE)

Work Station Support
  Externally Described WORKSTN
    Files
  Processing an Externally
    Described WORKSTN File
  Command Key Indicators
  Work Station Subfile Operations
Processing WORKSTN Files
  Program Described WORKSTN
    Files
    Input Files
    Output Files
    Combined Files

RPG III is an enhancement to RPG II that was first introduced in 1980. RPG III adds numerous capabilities to RPG II but at this point in time, is limited in its availability to the IBM System/36 and the IBM System/38. RPG II is a subset of RPG III, meaning that RPG II language statements are valid in RPG III. (The converse of that statement—that RPG III language statements are valid in RPG II—is not always true.) Thus, all computers capable of executing RPG III are capable of executing RPG II, as well.

RPG III Rationale

RPG III is a programming development designed to deal with the more advanced environments recently introduced to computers and data processing. The term 'environment' is not restricted to physical environment alone. The environment includes machines, programming languages, file structures, systems analysis methodologies, programming techniques, and workplace. The majority of microcomputers now in use have at least 640K bytes of memory. Languages are still being developed (e.g., Pascal, Modula-2, C, and dBase III+), all of which emphasize structured technologies, as the marketplace requires. File structures are coming to be maintained more by operating systems than by programmers; data base technology continues to evolve. RPG III addresses externalization of data, structured programming, data base technology, and the usage of the CRT as the input/output (I/O) device of primary use.

RPG III Improvements (IBM system/38)

For this discussion of RPG III, the IBM System/38 will be the environment used in all examples. Environmental modifications can be discussed in three categories: hardware, software, and programming technique.

Hardware There has been increased emphasis placed upon the CRT (WORKSTN), and a deemphasis upon (if not elimination of) punched cards.

Software The concepts of externally described data, screen formats, and data base technology (with associated systems control) are implemented in the IBM System/38 control program facility (CPF).

Technique The advent of structured programming has worked to improve programmer throughput. IF/ELSE, DOWxx, and other structured constructs are provided; commands are simplified and coding is lessened.

Following are listed the distinguishing features of each version of RPG within the three categories of environmental modification.

Hardware

RPG I   The original RPG using the card reader and the line printer.

RPG II   Introduced disk drives.

RPG III   Makes extensive use of the CRT as the primary input/output device.

Software

RPG I   Uses sequential files and is batch oriented.

RPG II   Introduced direct access (indexed) files, but remains batch oriented.

RPG III   Provides data base technology support (e.g., record positioning op-codes); uses data described externally to the CPF; stresses interactivity (WORKSTN).

Technique

RPG I Makes extensive use of the GOTO and of the RPG logic cycle.

RPG II Introduced subroutines (a modularity still heavily encouraged); still relies heavily upon the RPG logic cycle.

RPG III Provides verbs permitting structured programming (if/then, else, do whiles, do untils, etc.) to deemphasize the popular GOTOs of previous RPG versions. The ability of structured programming to increase programmer productivity was a major reason for the introduction of RPG III; simplifies the coding of numerous instructions; simplifies and standardizes programming control through extensive use of the control program facility (CPF) with externally described data, and formats.

RPG III Language Enhancements

A number of language enhancements have been added to RPG III. These include source entry utility (SEU); externally described data (CPF); data description specification (DDS); full procedural file specifications; work station support (WORKSTN); and work station subfile operations. Each of these forms of language enhancement is discussed in turn in the following sections.

Source Entry Utility (SEU)

The source entry utility is part of the interactive data base utilities licensed program (IDU) that allows online source entry and maintenance. On any computer a programmer uses an editor to create and modify source code. Various forms of editors available—from line editors requiring one editing technique to full-screen editors (e.g., word processors). Either editing method is a powerful tool for the simplification of program production.

SEU, however, is an RPG-specific editor. When the RPG source is identified, SEU provides special display screen formats (corresponding to the RPG specifications) that simplify keying. The programmer can enter the specifications position-by-position or field-by-field.

SEU can also call an RPG syntax checker to check each specification line entered for errors. This syntax checker eliminates careless mistakes and helps minimize the number of compilations required for creating and maintaining a program. The syntax checker skips over fields inappropriate to a particular specification line or operation. It guarantees the entry of required fields, and prohibits the entry of prohibited fields.

SEU permits the entry of source programs by issuing the CRTSRC (create source) command. This command invokes SEU (the APP parameter invokes the RPG syntax checker). The control program permits entry of source through other media such as diskette copying or spooling.

SEU Sequence Number

The SEU provides source sequence numbers used as the default numbering method for statements and diagnostics. Thus, the conventions of source line numbering have been automated. Using SEU in this way allows the programmer to proceed directly from a diagnostic that discusses a source statement in error, to the specified statement.

Source Diagnostic Error Notation

The feature of source diagnostic error notation allows errors to be seen on the compiler listing by the use of an asterisk (*) in position 1. The *, followed by an error message number, indicates that a syntax error has been noted. Asterisks are also placed immediately under each field in error for easy identification. This correlation of source line numbers with compiler listing greatly facilitates programmer productivity.

SEU Summary

RPG III, the IBM System/38, and SEU together create an efficient toolkit for programmers. It works in a variety of ways to improve programmer productivity and throughput. SEU provides an interactive syntax-checking data entry tool which prompts for required fields and skips past unnecessary ones. The compiler provides simple diagnostic tools for repair of the source through SEU, and so contributes to this productive environment.

Externally Described Data (CPF)

The advantages of copylibraries (libraries of data descriptions, etc., stored on disk) have long been known to data processors. Copylibraries offer control and program consistency to a programming system. RPG III and its control program facility (CPF) provides the kind of programming systems support that permits externally described data. The IBM System/38 offers SEU as a programming tool and CPF as a programming tool/systems control environment.

Record descriptions for a file are stored externally to the RPG program on the IBM Systems/38 using CPF. The advantage of externally described data is that the file need be described to the control program facility only once and need not be described for each program that uses the file. If the file description changes, the programmer can change its description in one place, and then recompile the programs that use it. This ability is extremely important to the concept information management and the associated effort to gain systematic control of data and the programs that process such data.

All files in the IBM System/38 data base must be described to CPF at a field or record level. That description then becomes available (in a common format) to programs accessing that data. The description of a file to the field level contains the following information:

1. Where the data originates
2. The name and position of each field within the record
3. The attributes (size in bytes, type, and decimal positions, if numeric) of each field within the record

The description of a file to the record level tells the following:

1. Where the data originates
2. The length of the records within the file

To use a file that has been defined to the CPF at the field level, that file must be named on the file specifications (positions 7–14). Input and output specifications are not required to further define a file which has been defined to the CPF. The CPF will copy those descriptions into the RPG program. Files used in this manner are called externally described files. (For purposes of illustration, compare this procedure to that of copylib in COBOL. The RPG operation is similar, but more integrated.) A change to a file in RPG will result in a change to the record descriptions supplied by the CPF to other programs; a change to a copylib in COBOL cannot produce a change in a file. Files can only be changed by human intervention.

Externally described files offer a number of advantages.

1. Externally described files require less coding by programmers. In many programs, the definition of a file to the CPF, in effect, provides that definition to all programs using the file. Naturally, the more programs accessing a file, the greater the resultant benefit in productivity because it eliminates the need to code input and output specifications for RPG programs using files defined to the field level. It further eliminates that element of "creativity" that has permitted programmers to assign one name field in one program and use a different name in a succeeding program, even though the same data was being accessed. Accuracy (fewer errors) is the major benefit to be gained by reducing the amount of coding. Provide less opportunity for error, and less error will occur. Reduction in the amount of labor required is another advantage.

2. Externally described files demand less and simplified maintenance when the format of a file is changed. This permits better production control for such individuals as quality assurance groups in monitoring a system's maintenance. Programs can be updated to a change in a file's format by recompiling the programs that use that file. Note that if programs accessing the file are not recompiled, they will use the record description that was read into the object program when compiled prior to the file's format change. The new file description will be read in from the CPF at compilation time.

3. Externally described files result in improved documentation. The CPF provides information about files with consistent format and field names. Fields are never forgotten, misspelled, or accidentally redefined. Thus all programs use the same names with the same field attributes.

These advantages of standardization can be overridden to meet particular demands of immediacy and flexibility. An RPG program making use of an externally described file (one described to the CPF at the field level) can make modifications to that file's description for the particular program execution. Such a modification would constitute an override of the description rather than a redefinition of the description. A redefinition would require a new data description definition to the CPF. For example, fields can be renamed, field indicators can be assigned, and certain fields be written or omitted. The RPG program must, of course, include the input and output specifications that specify modifications to the CPF definitions of the file.

An RPG program can use files described to the CPF at the record level. Such a file is called a **program described file** and must be described by input and output specifications in the RPG program.

Data Description Specification (DDS)

All data base files are created by the CPF create file commands. The external description of the disk file results from the record format description on the data description specification (DDS) submitted to the CPF create file command.

The record format specifications describe the characteristics (size, type, and decimal position length, if numeric) and locations of fields within a record. The fields in the record are located in the order specified upon the DDS. The field description generally includes the field name, the field type (alphameric, binary, zoned decimal, or packed decimal), and the field length (including the number of decimal positions in a numeric field). These decimal positions are implicit (i.e., not made explicit through the use of such punctuation as decimal points or commas). Only the output (print image) files of externally described files can contain punctuation (edit codes and words). Instead of being specified in the record format for a physical or logical file, the field attributes can be defined in a field reference file. (See Figure 11.1 and Figure 11.2.)

Figure 11.1 Data description specifications (DDS)

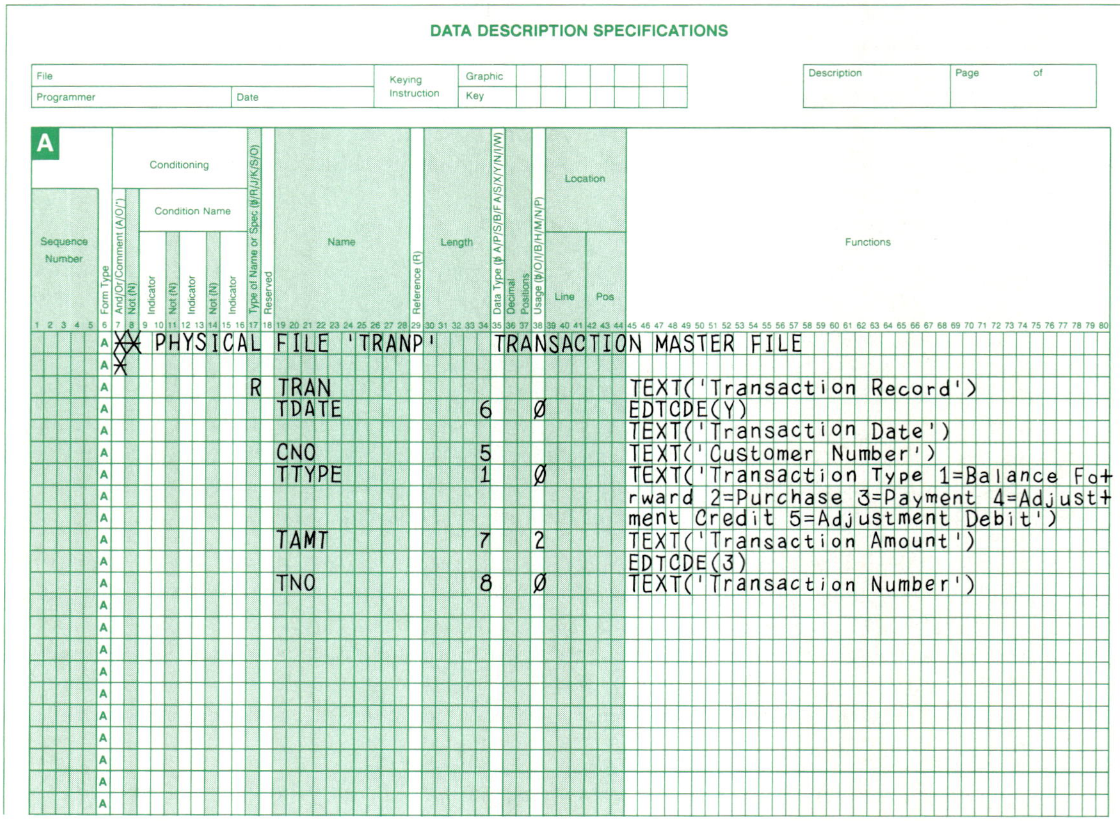

```
A** PHYSICAL FILE 'TRANP'   TRANSACTION MASTER FILE
A**
A      R TRAN                         TEXT('Transaction Record')
A        TDATE      6  0              EDTCDE(Y)
A                                     TEXT('Transaction Date')
A        CNO        5                 TEXT('Customer Number')
A        TTYPE      1  0              TEXT('Transaction Type 1=Balance Fo+
A                                     rward 2=Purchase 3=Payment 4=Adjust+
A                                     ment Credit 5=Adjustment Debit')
A        TAMT       7  2              TEXT('Transaction Amount')
A                                     EDTCDE(3)
A        TNO        8  0              TEXT('Transaction Number')
```

Physical File TRANP describes transaction record in terms of field names, types, sizes, decimal positions, relative displacement (by order of specification), using keywords like EDTCDE to specify edit codes and TEXT to associate text with fields.

Figure 11.2 DDS for a logical file

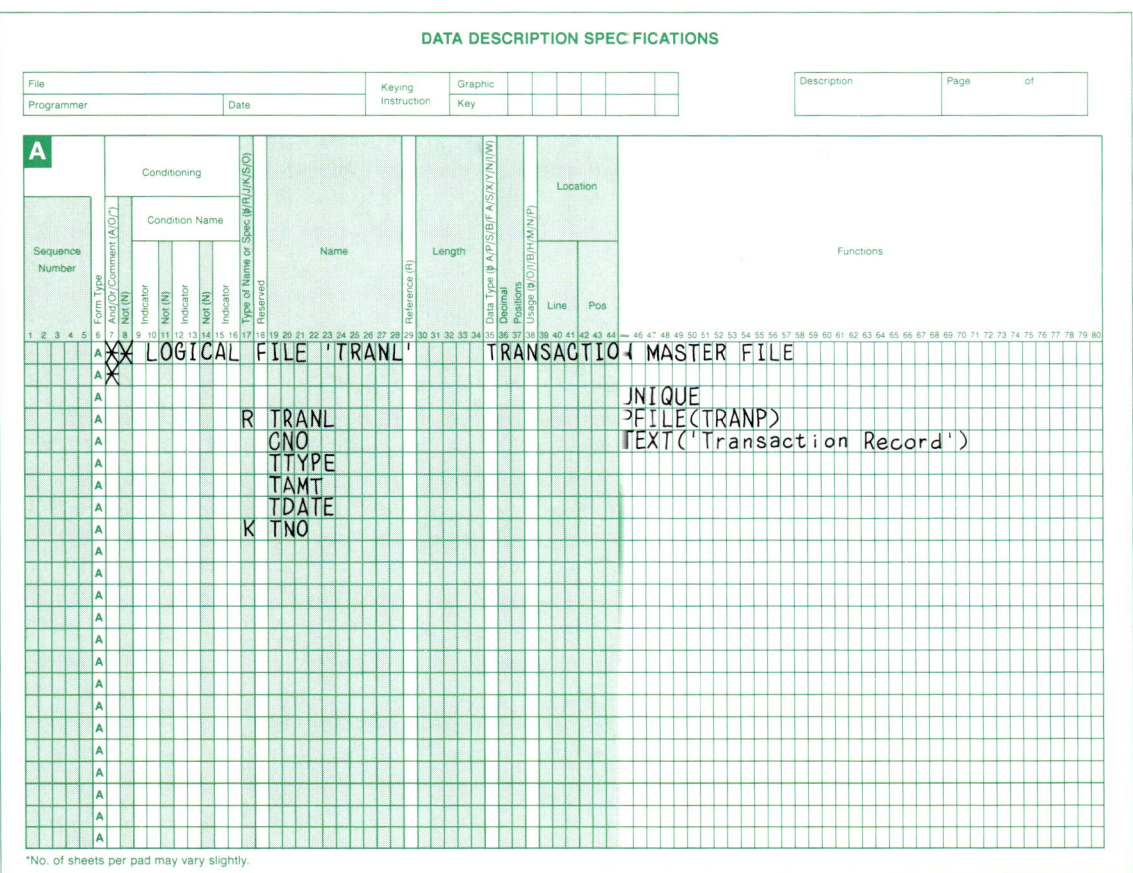

Logical File TRANL refers to the physical file TRANP through the PFILE keyword; describes TNO (transaction number) as the key field on which there are no duplicates, as specified by the keyword UNIQUE.

In addition, special DDS keywords can be used to

1. Specify edit codes for a field (EDTCDE)
2. Specify edit words for a field (EDTWRD)
3. Specify that duplicate key values are not allowed for the record format (UNIQUE)
4. Specify a text description for a record format or a field (TEXT).

Any editing to be performed on externally described output files (decimal points, commas, dollar signs, or edit word-supplied hyphens) is specified in the DDS. An edit code or edit word cannot be specified on the output specifications for an externally described output file. (Such a specification is interpreted as redundant and produces no overriding effect.) Only conditioning indicators (positions 23–31), field name (positions 32–37), and blank after (position 39) can be specified on an output field specification line for an externally described file.

Figures 11.1 and 11.2 are examples of the DDS for a data base file, and for a field reference file that defines the attributes for the fields in the data base file.

Full Procedural File Specifications

The specification of a full procedural file in the file specification indicates to the compiler that the file is processed by programmer-specified calculation operations (e.g., READ, CHAIN). A primary file specification is not mandatory. This is consistent with the shift of emphasis away from the RPG logic cycle toward the interactivity of CRT (WORKSTN) input and its "on demand" requests.

To specify a full procedural file, place an *F* in position 16 of the file specification. When both full procedural files and a primary file (*P* in position 16 of the file description specifications) are specified in a program, some of the input (the full procedural file) is controlled by the programmer and some of the input (the primary file) is controlled by the cycle. Secondary files (*S* in position 16 of the file specifications) maintain their usual relationships to the primary file. The program cycle exists at the time a full procedural file is specified; however, processing occurs at both detail and total calculation time.

Although the cycle retains its importance in batch processing, full procedural file specifications are becoming prevalent. Major examples are the WORKSTN applications. (See Figure 11.3.)

File Operations

Following is a discussion of the valid file operation codes for RPG III.

Random Retrieval from a File Based on RECNO or Key Value (CHAIN)
The CHAIN operation code has been enhanced and its use intensified in RPG III due to increased dependence upon programmer-controlled input/output (i.e., full procedural files).

The CHAIN operation retrieves a record from a full procedural file (F in position 16 of the file description specifications). This sets on a record identifying indicator, if one is specified on the input specifications. Data from the record are placed into the input fields.

Delete Record (DELET)
The DELET operation code, new to RPG III, deletes a record from a data base file. The file must be an update file (*U* in position 15 of the file description specifications). The deleted record can never be retrieved. DELET performs a physical rather than a logical deletion. Note the difference between this concept of physical deletion and that of logical deletion (records marked for deletion and later removed by a batch utility run). DELET deletes records by key, relative record number, or last record read.

Execute Format (EXFMT)
The EXFMT operation is a combination of a WRITE followed by a READ to the same record format. EXFMT is valid only for a WORKSTN file defined as a full procedural (*F* in position 16 of the file description specifications) combined file (*C* in position 15 of the file description specifications) that is externally described (*E* in position 19 of the file description specifications). EXFMT is RPG III in style and content. A CRT work station support instruction can exist only when a DDS is described to the CPF.

Factor 2 must contain the name of the record format to be written and then read. A resulting indicator can be specified in positions 56–57 to be set on if the EXFMT operation does not complete successfully.

Read a Record (READ)
The READ operation is a verb enhanced in RPG III to meet the challenge of increased emphasis upon this and all other operation codes which are noncyclical by nature.

The READ operation reads the next record from a full procedural file (*F* in position 16 of the file description specifications). If a READ operation is successful, the file is positioned at the next record that satisfies the read. If a READ operation is not successful, the file must be repositioned (using a CHAIN, SETLL, or SETGT operation). An indicator can be specified in positions 56–57 of the calculation specifications to be set on if the READ operation does not complete successfully.

An indicator must be specified in position 58–59 to signal whether end-of-file occurred in the READ operation. This indicator is set on or off every time READ executes.

Read Next Modified Record (READC)
The READC operation can be used only with an externally described WORKSTN file to obtain the next changed record in a subfile. Factor 2 is required and must be the name of a record format defined as a subfile by the SFILE keyword on the file description specifications.

A resulting indicator can be specified in positions 56–57 to be set on if an error occurs during execution of the operation. A resulting indicator in positions 58–59 is required; it is set on when there are no more changed records in the subfile.

Figure 11.3 Random processing of an externally described file

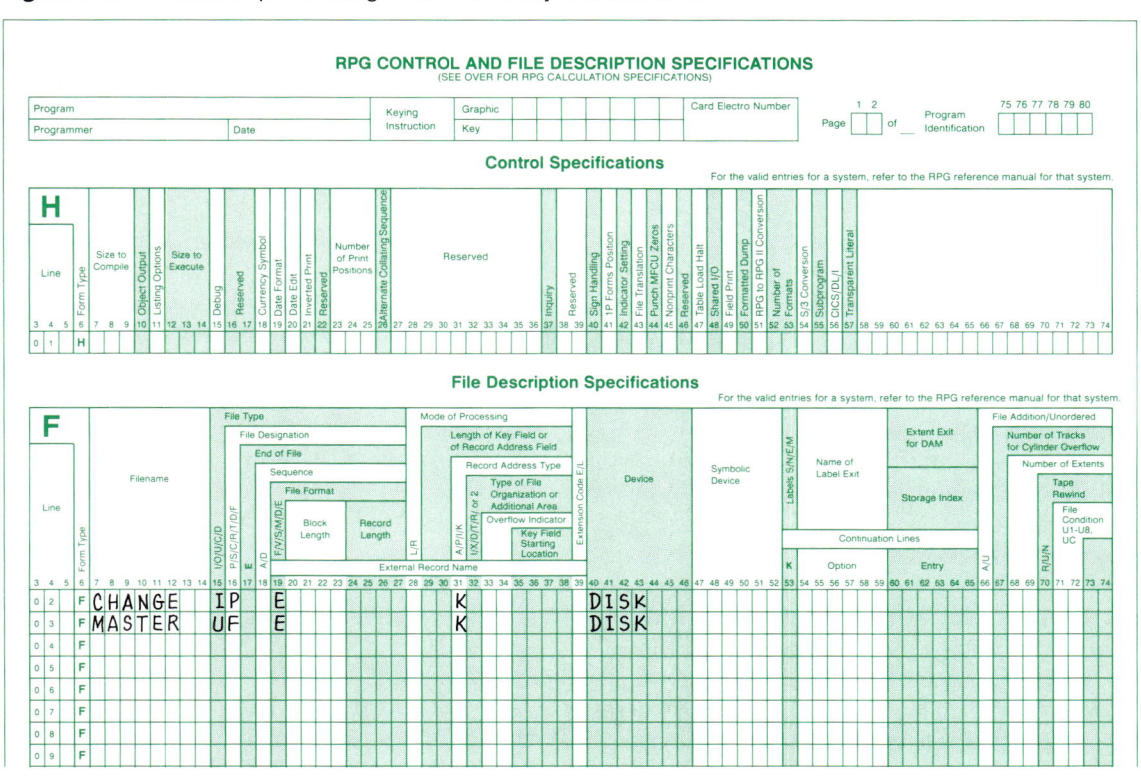

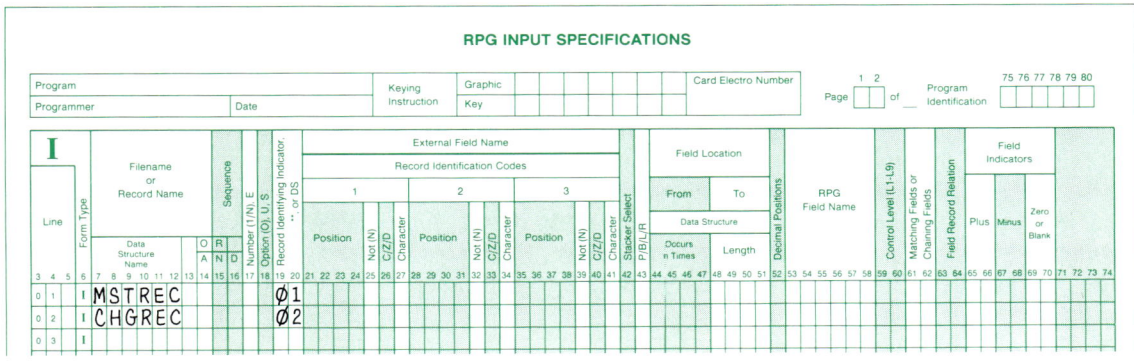

The update file MASTER is to be processed by keys. The data description specifications (DDS) for each of the externally described files (MASTER and CHANGE) identify the ACCT field as the key field. As each field is read from the primary input file, CHANGE, the account number (ACCT) is used as the key to chain the corresponding record in the MASTER file. Input specifications are used to assign record identifying indicators to the records in the CHANGE and MASTER files. The MASTER file contains one record format MSTREC that contains two fields, ACCT and NEW. The data in the NEW field must be moved into the NAMADR field before the MSTREC can be updated.

Read Equal Key (READE)

READE is another operation code new with RPG III. This code retrieves the next sequential record from a full procedural file (*F* in position 16 of the file description specifications) if the key of the record matches the search argument specified in factor 1. If the key of the record does not match the search argument, the indicator specified in positions 58–59 is set on, and the record is not returned to the program. If a READE operation is not successful, the file must be repositioned (using SETGT, SETLL, or CHAIN).

Read Prior Key (READP)

Another new operation, READP, reads the prior record from a full procedural file (*F* in position 16 of the file description specifications).

If a READP operation is successful, the file is positioned at the next record that satisfies the read. If a READP operation is not successful, the programmer must reposition the file (e.g., using a CHAIN or SETLL operation). An indicator can be specified in positions 56–57 to be set on if the READP operation does not complete successfully.

An indicator must be specified in positions 58–59 to be set on when no prior record exists in the file (the record pointer is at the beginning of the file).

Set Greater Than (SETGT)

The SETGT operation positions a file at the next record having a key or a relative record number greater than the key or relative record number specified by factor 1. The file must be a full procedural file (*F* in position 16 of the file description specifications).

Figurative constants can be used to position the file. They can be used in files with composite keys. *LOVAL (COBOL's low values, hexadecimal zeros, a byte of '00000000') positions the file so that the first read retrieves the record with the lowest key. *HIVAL (COBOL's high values, hexadecimal FF, a byte of '11111111') positions the file so that a READP operation senses end-of-file and, therefore, reads the last record; subsequent READP operations read the file in reverse order.

Set Greater Than or Equal To (SETLL)

The SETLL operation positions a file at the next record having a key or a relative record number greater than or equal to the key or relative record number specified by factor 1. The file must be a full procedural file (*F* in position 16 of the file description specifications).

As with SETGT, figurative constants can be used to position the file. They can be used in files with composite keys. If the programmer uses *LOVAL (COBOL's low values, hexadecimal zeros, a byte of '00000000') to position the file, the first read retrieves the record with the lowest key. Positioning the file with *HIVAL (COBOL's high values, hexadecimal FF, a byte of '11111111') positions the file so that a READP operation senses end-of-file and, therefore, reads the last record; subsequent READP operations read the file in reverse order.

Modify Existing Record (UPDAT)

UPDAT is another operation new with RPG III. UPDAT modifies the last record retrieved from an update file (*U* in position 15 of the file description specifications). Factor 2 must contain the name of a file or record format to be updated. If a record format name is specified as factor 2, the operation is only valid with an externally described file. The record format name must be the name of the last record read from the file; otherwise an error occurs. A file name is permitted as factor 2 only with a program described file.

The result field must contain a data structure name from which the updated record is directly written if factor 2 contains a file name. The result field must be blank if factor 2 contains a record format name.

A resulting indicator can be specified in positions 56–57; this indicator will be set on if the UPDAT operation is not successful.

Create New Records (WRITE)

The WRITE operation writes new records to a file. Factor 2 must contain the name of a file or record format. A record format name is required in factor 2 with an externally described file. A file name in factor 2 is permitted only with a program described file.

Positions 56–57 can contain an indicator to be set on if the WRITE operation is not successful. Positions 58–59 can specify an indicator on a WRITE to a subfile (SFILE) record name to indicate when the subfile is filled.

When records using relative record numbers are written, the RECNO (relative record number) field must be set to the appropriate number.

When writing records to a file other than an output file, an *A* must be specified in position 66 of the file description specifications.

File Control Operations

Following is a discussion of the file control operations that have been added with RPG III.

Force End of Data (FEOD)

The FEOD operation, new with RPG III, characterizes the trend toward programmer-controlled input/output. The FEOD operation signals the logical end of data for a primary, secondary, or full procedural file. The FEOD function differs depending on the file type and device.

FEOD differs from the CLOSE operation in that the program is not disconnected from the device or file. The device can be used again for subsequent file operations without an explicit open being issued upon the file.

Conditioning indicators can be specified. Factor 2 names the file to which the FEOD is specified. A resulting indicator can be specified in positions 56–57 to be set on if the operation does not complete successfully.

Open File for Processing (OPEN)

The OPEN operation, also new with RPG III, follows the full procedural philosophy of RPG III, just as do the FEOD and CLOSE.

The explicit OPEN statement opens the file named in factor 2. The factor 2 entry cannot be designated as a primary, secondary, or table file (because they are dependent upon the RPG logic cycle rather than programmer dependent). A resulting indicator can be specified in positions 56–57 to be set on if the OPEN operation is not completed successfully.

To open the file specified in factor 2 for the first time in a program with an explicit OPEN statement, specify *UC* (user control) in positions 71–72 of the file description specifications.

Multiple OPEN statements to the same file in a program are valid as long as the file is closed when the OPEN is issued to it. If an OPEN operation is specified for a file that is already open, an error occurs and the RPG exception/error handling routine receives control.

Close File for Processing (CLOSE)

As with OPEN, the CLOSE operation goes with FEOD, and is in the full procedural philosophy of RPG III. The CLOSE operation is new with RPG III.

The explicit CLOSE statement closes a file and disconnects the file or device from the program. The factor 2 entry cannot be designated as a table file (*T* in position 16 of the file description specifications). A resulting indicator can be specified in positions 56–57 to be set on if the CLOSE operation is not completed successfully. Positions 54, 55, 58, and 59 must be blank.

The keyword *ALL can be specified as factor 2 to close all files at once.

Multiple CLOSE statements to the same file in a program are valid. No operation will be performed on the files already closed.

Work Station Support

The WORKSTN file allows an RPG program to interactively communicate with a work station user. A WORKSTN file is the representation of a CRT screen. The CRT is now the primary input/output device. The required CRT support with the documentation control of the DDS within the CPF makes RPG III a leader in modern programming environments. WORKSTN files (as with all files and the CPF) can be either externally described or program described.

Externally Described WORKSTN Files

An RPG WORKSTN file using an externally described display device file contains file information and a description of the fields in the records.

In addition to the field descriptions (such as field names, positions, type, length, and decimal positions, if numeric), the data description specifications (DDS) for a display device file are used to

1. Format the placement of the record on the screen by specifying the line number and position number entries for each field and constant.

2. Specify attention functions such as underlining and highlighting fields, reverse image, or a blinking cursor.

3. Specify validity checking for data entered at the display work station (CRT). Validity checking functions include detecting fields where data are required, detecting mandatory fill fields, detecting incorrect data types, range checking input values, detecting data for a valid entry, and performing modulus 10 or 11 check-digit verification.

4. Control screen management functions such as when fields are to be erased, overlaid, or retained when new data is displayed.

5. Associate indicators 01–99 with command attention or command function keys. If a command key is described as a command function key (CF), both the data record and the indication that the key was pressed are returned to the processing unit. If a command key is described as a command attention key (CA), the indication that the key was pressed is passed to the processing unit and no data are transferred. In the case of the IBM System/38, however, a full data record is always returned to the program whether or not a CF or CA key is pressed. If a CA key is pressed, the record contains blanks or zeros for those fields normally keyed by the work station user.

6. Assign an edit code (EDTCDE) or edit word (EDTWRD) keyword to a field to specify how the values of the field are to be displayed.

7. Specify subfiles.

A display device record format contains three types of fields: input fields, output fields, and output/input fields.

Input fields. Input fields are passed from the device to the program when the program reads a record. Input fields can be initialized with a default value; if the default value is not changed, that value is passed to the program. Input fields that are not initialized are displayed as blanks into which the work station user can enter data.

Output fields. Output fields are passed from the program to the device when the program writes a record to a display. Output fields can be provided by the program or by the record format in the device file.

Output/input fields. An output/input field is an output field that can be changed and, in being changed, becomes an input field. Output/input fields are passed from the program when the program writes a record to the display; they are passed to the program when the program reads a record from the display. Output/input fields are used when the data written to the display from the program are to be changed or updated.

Processing an Externally Described WORKSTN File

When an externally described WORKSTN file is processed, the CPF first transforms data from the program to the format specified for the file, and then displays the data. When passed to the program, the data are transformed to the format used by the program.

CPF provides device control information for performing input/output operations from the device. When an input record is requested from the device CPF issues the request, then removes device control information from the data before passing the data to the program. CPF can also pass indicators to the program indicating whether or not any of the fields have been changed and which fields have been changed.

When the program requests an output operation, it passes the output record to the CPF. The CPF provides the necessary device control information to display the record. CPF also adds any constant information (e.g., prompts, headings) specified for the record format when the record is displayed.

When a record is passed to the program, the fields are arranged in the order in which they were specified in the DDS. The order in which the fields are displayed is based on the display positions (line numbers and position) assigned to the fields in the DDS. Therefore, the order in which the fields are specified in the DDS and the order in which the same fields appear on the screen need not be the same.

Command Key Indicators

The command key indicators KA–KN and KP–KY are valid for a program that contains a WORKSTN file if the associated command key is specified in the DDS.

The command key indicators relate to the command keys as follows:

Indicator	Command Key	Indicator	Command Key
KA	Command key 1	KN	Command key 13
KB	Command key 2	KO	Command key 14
KC	Command key 3	KP	Command key 15
KD	Command key 4	KQ	Command key 16
KE	Command key 5	KR	Command key 17
KF	Command key 6	KS	Command key 18
KG	Command key 7	KT	Command key 19
KH	Command key 8	KU	Command key 20
KI	Command key 9	KV	Command key 21
KJ	Command key 10	KW	Command key 22
KK	Command key 11	KX	Command key 23
KL	Command key 12	KY	Command key 24

Command keys are specified in the DDS with the CFxx (command function) or CAxx (command attention) keyword. For example, CF01 allows command function key 1 to be used. When command function key 1 is pressed, command key indicator KA is set on in the RPG program. If the command function key is specified as CF01 (77), both command key indicator KA and indicator 77 are set on in the RPG program. If a workstation user presses a command key that is not specified in the DDS, CPF informs the user that an invalid key was pressed.

If the work station user presses a specified command key, the associated command key indicator in RPG is set on when fields extracted from the record (move fields logic) and all other command key indicators are set off. If a command key is not pressed, all command key indicators are set off at move fields time. The command key indicators are set off if the user presses the Enter key.

Work Station Subfile Operations

Subfiles can be specified for a display device file in the DDS to allow the programmer to handle multiple records of the same type on the display. (See Figure 11.4.) A subfile is a group of records that is read from or written to a display device file. For example, a program reads records from a data base and creates a subfile of output records. When the entire subfile has been written, the program sends the entire subfile to the display device in one write operation. The work station user can change data or enter additional data into the subfile. The program then reads the entire subfile from the display device into the program and processes each record in the subfile individually as if it were a relative file.

Records to be included in a subfile are specified in the DDS for the file. The number of records that can be included in a subfile must also be specified in the DDS. One file can contain more than one subfile; however, only two subfiles can be active concurrently. Two subfiles can be displayed at the same time.

The DDS for a subfile consists of two record formats: a subfile record format and a subfile control record format. The subfile record format contains the field information that is transferred to or from the display file under control of the subfile control format. The subfile control format causes the physical read, write, or setup operations of a subfile to take place. (See Figures 11.5 and 11.6.)

Figure 11.4 DDS for a WORKSTN file

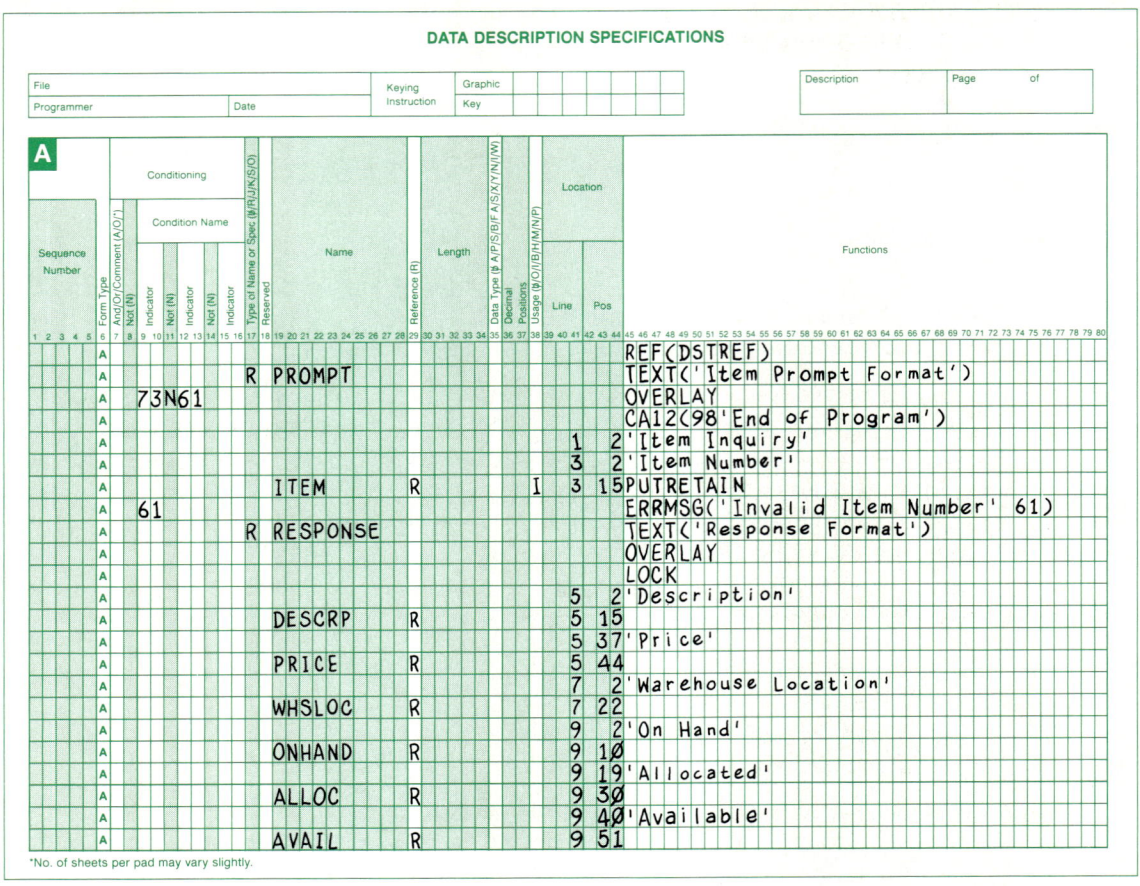

Figure 11.5 DDS for a subfile record format

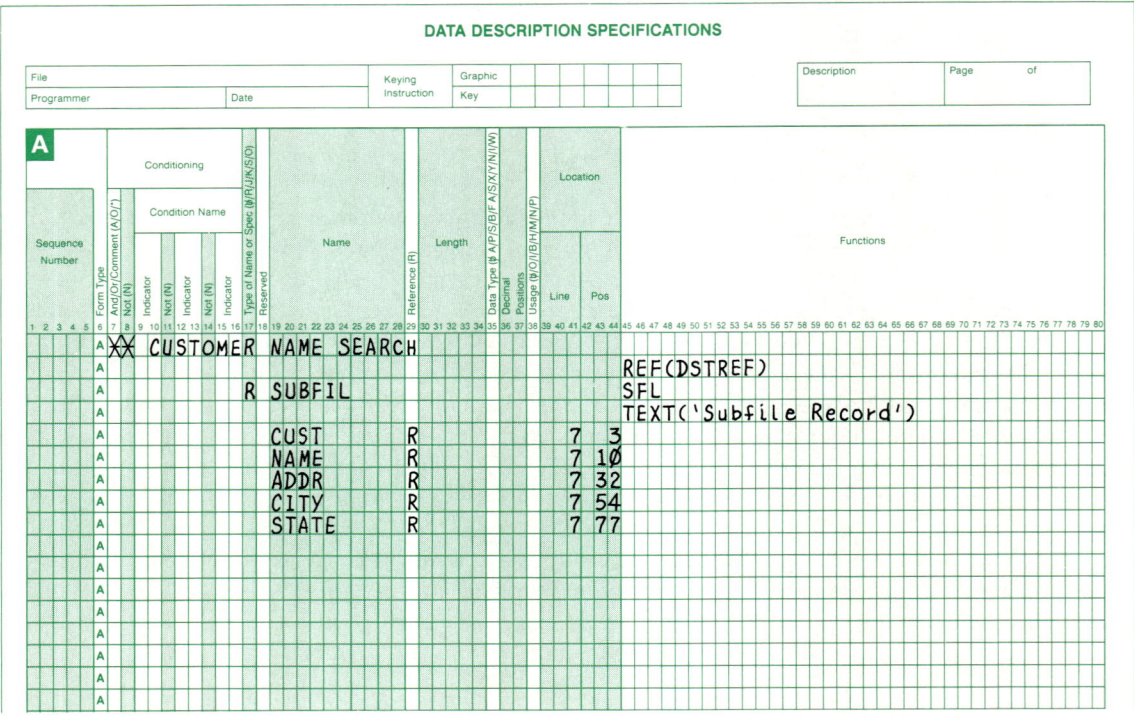

Figure 11.6 DDS for a subfile control record format

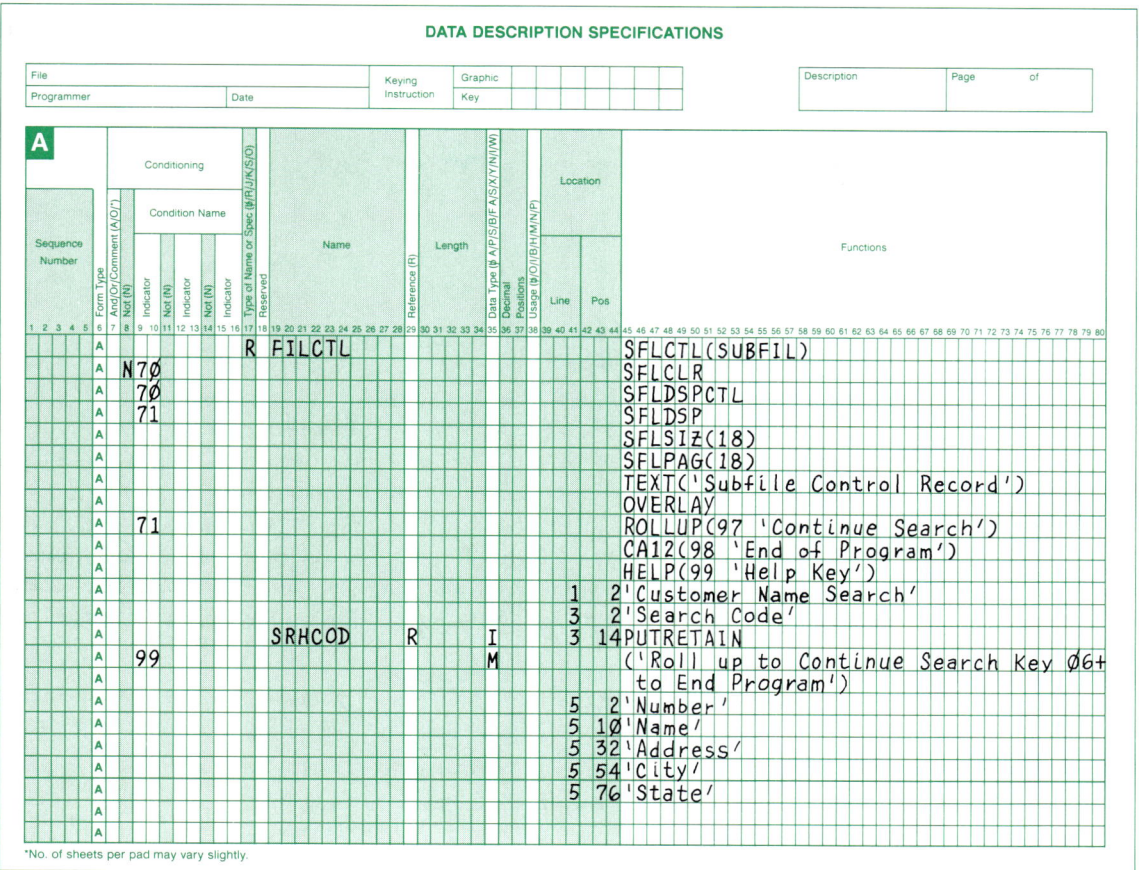

To use a subfile for a display device in an RPG program, the SFILE keyword must be specified in positions 54–59 on a file description specifications continuation line for the WORKSTN file. The SFILE keyword must be specified on a separate continuation line. The WORKSTN file must be an externally described file (*E* in position 19 of the file description specifications).

Positions 60–67 of the continuation line must specify the name of the record format to be processed as the subfile. Positions 47–52 must specify the name of the field that contains the relative record number to be used in processing the subfile.

In RPG III, relative record number processing is defined as part of the SFILE definition. The SFILE definition implies a full procedural update file with ADD for the subfile. Therefore, the file operations that are valid for the subfile are not dependent on the definition of the main WORKSTN file. That is, the WORKSTN file can be defined as a primary file or a full procedural file. Valid file operations for the subfile are: CHAIN, READC, UPDAT, and WRITE.

Subfile processing follows the rules for relative record number processing. The WRITE operation code and the ADD specification on the output specifications requires that a relative record number field be specified in positions 47–52 of the file description specifications SFILE continuation line.

If a WORKSTN file has an associated subfile, all implicit input operations and explicit calculation operations referring to the file name are performed against the main WORKSTN file. Any operations that reference a record format name not designated as a subfile are performed on the main WORKSTN file.

Processing WORKSTN Files

If a WORKSTN file is described as full procedural (*F* in position 16 of the file specifications) combined file (*C* in position 15) that uses externally described data (*E* in position 19), the EXFMT (execute format) operation code can be used to write and read from the display. The EXFMT operation is a combination of a WRITE followed by a READ to the same record format.

The READ operation is valid for a full procedural combined file or a full procedural input file that uses externally described data or program described data. The READ operation that specifies a record format name in factor 2 retrieves the next sequential record of the specified type. The WRITE operation writes a new record to a file and is valid for a combined file or an output file. Output specifications and the EXCPT operation can also be used to write to a WORKSTN file.

Following are valid operations codes for a WORKSTN file:

File Specifications Positions 15	16	Calculation Specifications Positions 28–32
I	P or S	CLOSE, FEOD (cycle controlled processing)
C	P or S	WRITE, CLOSE, FEOD
I	F	READ, OPEN, CLOSE, FEOD
C	F	READ, WRITE, EXFMT, OPEN, CLOSE, FEOD
O	blank	WRITE, OPEN, CLOSE, FEOD

Program Described WORKSTN Files

A program described display device file describes a file containing one record format description with one field. The fields in the record must be described within the program that uses the file.

When the display file is created by the CPF using the create display file command, the file has the following attributes:

1. A variable record length can be specified; therefore, the actual record length must be specified in the using program. (The maximum record length allowed is the screen size minus one; for example, $80 \times 24 = 1920 - 1$.)

2. No indicators are passed to or from the program.

3. No command key indicators are defined.

4. The record is written to the display beginning in position 2 of the first available line.

Input Files

For an input file, the CPF device support treats the input record as a single input field. The input record is initialized to blanks when the file is opened. The cursor is positioned at the beginning of the field, which is position 2 of the display.

Output Files

For an output file, the CPF device support treats the output record as a string of characters to be sent to the display. Each output record is written as the next sequential record in the file; that is, each record displayed overlays the previous record displayed.

Combined Files

For a combined file, the record is treated by CPF device support as a single field. The record appears on the screen as both the output and the input record. Device support initializes the input record to blanks and the cursor is placed in position 2.

Illustrative Program

The following is an example of an RPG III program which updates a parts inventory. The Data Description Specifications for the program's files are described in the following figures.

In this example, the shipping department needs to review the items on an order to post the changes to the quantity shipped, if there is a sufficient stock to fill the order. The clerk is first prompted to enter the order number to be reviewed. The program then displays the order, using data from the order detail record, as well as the customer number from the order header record and the customer name from the customer master record. After updating the appropriate items on the order, the clerk can either review additional orders or end the program. See the following flow chart for the program flow.

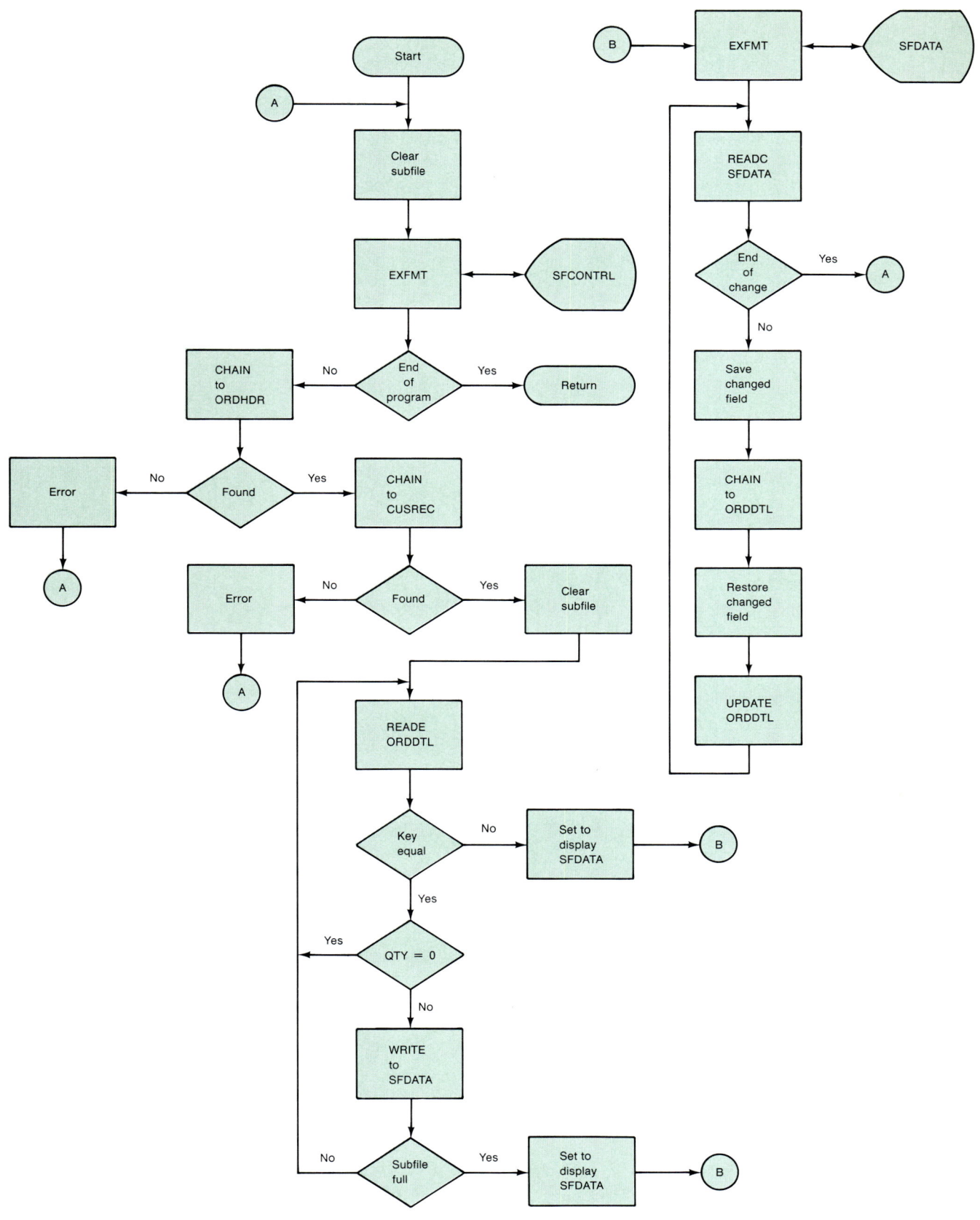

This layout shows the display that the clerk views. The clerk is prompted for the order number, and the program displays the order, using data from the order detail record, as well as the customer number from the order header record and the customer name from the customer master record.

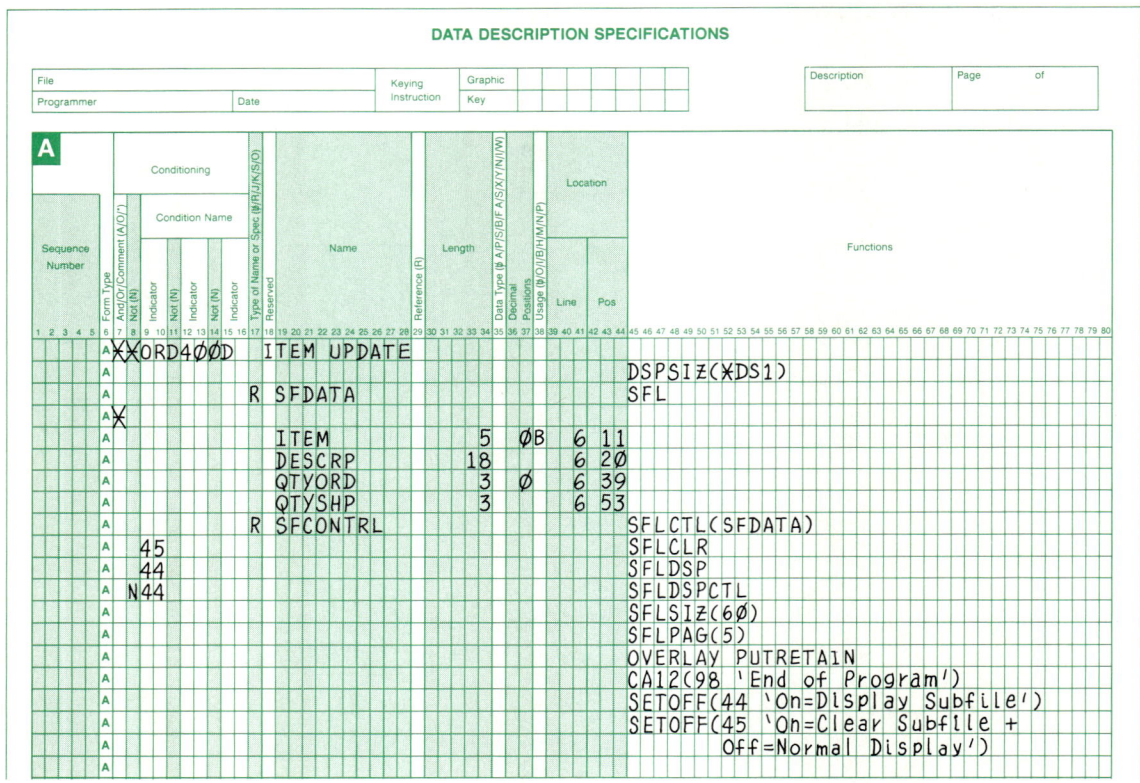

Subfiles are used in this program to illustrate how to handle multiple records of the same type on the display. The data description specifications for the ORD400D display file are shown here. Two display formats are used: SFDATA (the subfile record format) and SFCONTRL (the subfile control record format).

The subfile record format SFDATA describes the fields used by the subfile. It is necessary only to describe the location of the first record in the display format. The subfile control record format specifies how many records are to be written to the display. The subfile record format description (SFDATA) must immediately precede the subfile control record format (SFCONTRL).

The SFCONTRL is used as:

    A subfile control record format

    A normal format to display customer name and number

    A prompt for the user to enter the order number

DATA DESCRIPTION SPECIFICATIONS

Description: ORD400D

```
     A                                                    2  6'ITEM UPDATE'
     A                                                    2 21'Order'
     A              ORDER           5   0I                2 27
     A   91                                                  ERRMSG('Order Number Not Found' 91)
     A   92                                                  ERRMSG('No Customer Record Found +
     A                                                        for this Order' 92)
     A   93                                                  ERRMSG('# Lines in Order Exceeds +
     A                                                        60' 93)
     A   94                                                  ERRMSG('No Lines for this Order' 94)
     A   95                                                  ERRMSG('Update Failed - - Reenter +
     A                                                        Order #, Don't Change Item Field, +
     A                                                        Any Changes after this Record Were+
     A                                                        not Made to ORDFILL' 95)
     A                                                    2 36'Customer'
     A              CUST            5   O                 2 45
     A                                                    2 51'Name'
     A              NAME           20   O                 2 56
     A                                                    4 11'Item'
     A                                                    4 20'Description'
     A                                                    4 39'Qty'
     A                                                    4 46'Ship'
     A                                                    4 53'Loc'
     A
```

The subfile data is displayed (SFLDSP keyword) only if indicator 44 is on. If indicator 45 is on, the subfile is cleared (SFLCLR keyword) to allow the user to review additional orders before ending the program. If indicator 44 is not on, the data in the SFCONTRL format is displayed (SFLDSPCTL keyword).

A limit of 60 line items for a particular order is specified by the SFLSIZ keyword, and a page size of 5 line items is specified by the SFLPAG keyword. Subfile support has paging capability that allows the program to first fill the subfile and then allows the display station user to roll pages up and down in the subfile without any program control.

The OVERLAY keyword eliminates the need to retransmit the constants to the display with each additional request.

```
A**  LOGICAL    CUSMSTL         CUSTOMER MASTER FILE
A                                                   UNIQUE
A            R  CUSREC                              PFILE(CUSMSTP)
A                                                   TEXT('Customer Master Record')
A               CUST
A               NAME
A               ADDR
A               CITY
A               STATE
A               ZIP
A               SRHCOD
A               CUSTYP
A               ARBAL
A               ORDBAL
A               LSTAMT
A               LSTDAT
A               CRDLMT
A               SLSYR
A               SLSLYR
A            K  CUST
```

The data description for the data base files used by this program are shown on the following pages. Included here are the data description specifications for the logical CUSMSTL (customer master) file, for the physical CUSMSTP (customer master) file, for the logical ORDFILL file (order file that contains the order header and order detail records), for the physical ORDHDRP (order header) file, and for the physical ORDDTLP (order detail) file. The physical file CUSMSTP is referenced by the logical file CUSMSTL. The physical files ORDHDRP and ORDDTLP are referenced by the logical file ORDFILL.

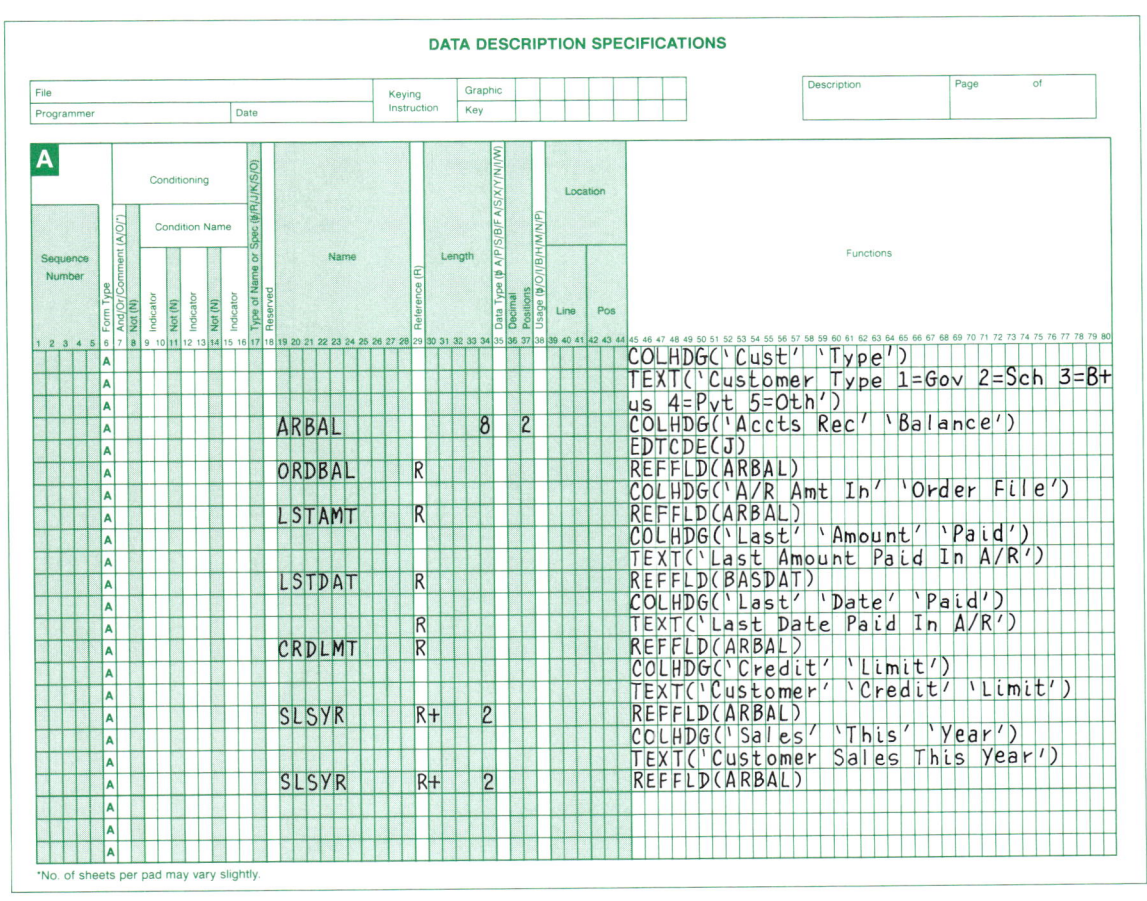

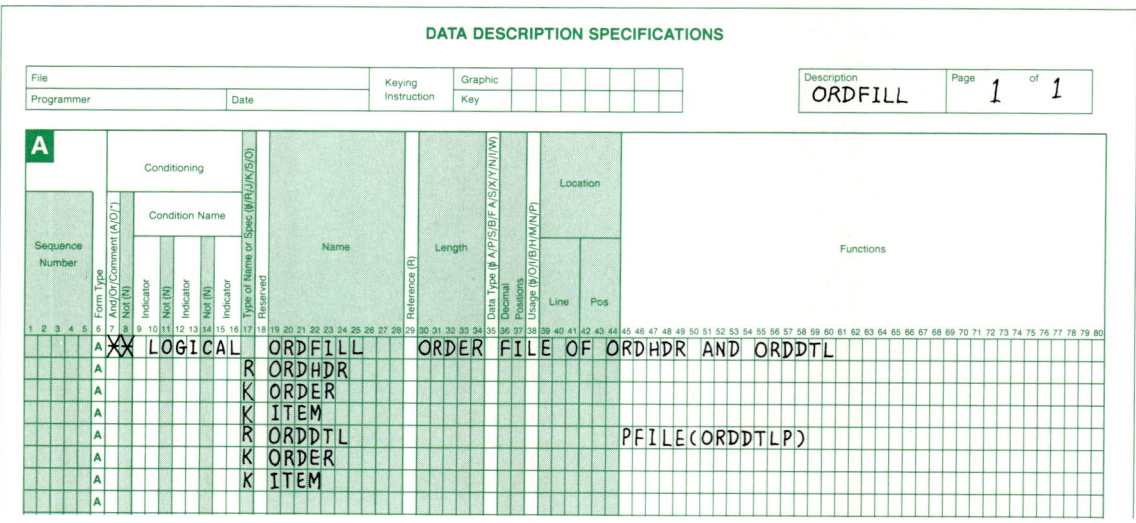

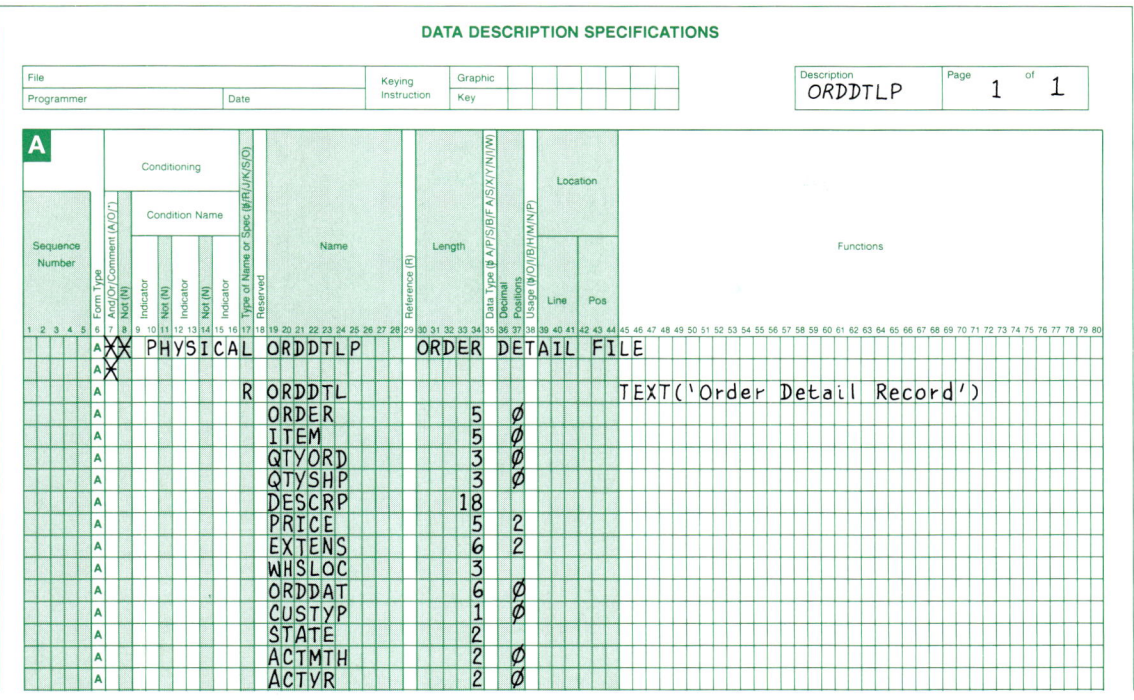

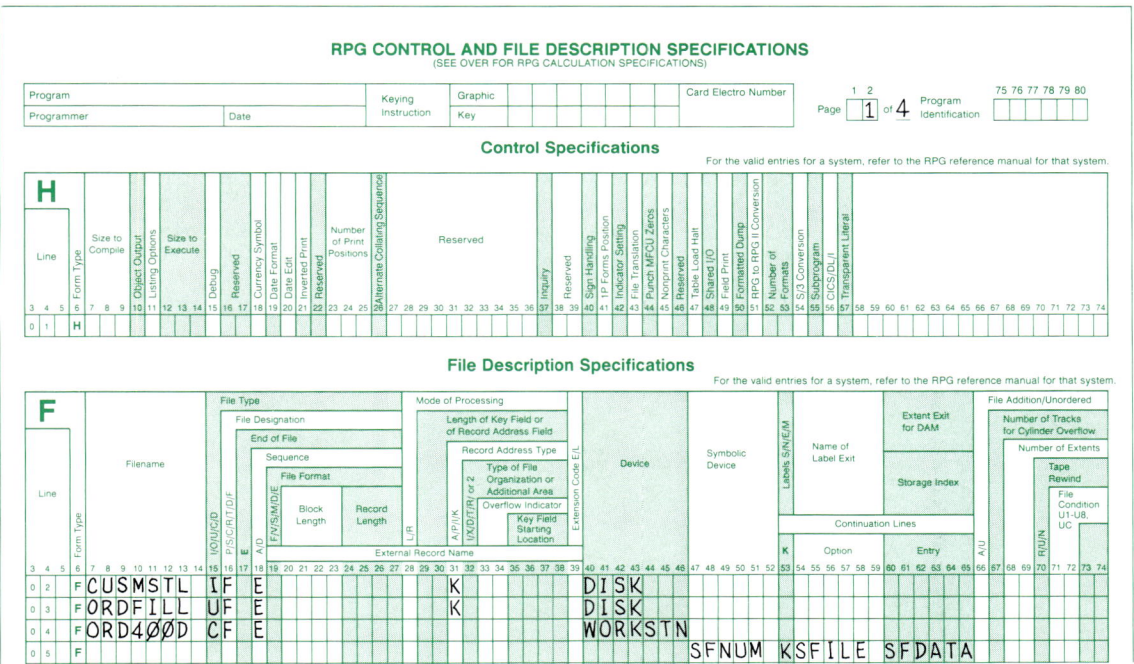

The RPG program uses the following three files:

The CUSMSTL file (customer master logical file). The CUSTMSTL file is a data base file (DISK in positions 40 through 46) that is processed as a full procedural file (F in position 16) with input only (I in position 15). This file is described externally (E in position 19) and is accessed by keys.

The ORDFILL (order logical) file. The ORDFILL file is also described as a full procedural, data base file with a keyed access. The file is externally described. The ORDFILL file is defined as an update file (U in position 15). This logical file uses data from two physical files, ORDHDRP (order header file) and ORDDTLP (order detail file).

The ORD400D display file. The ORD400D file is a display file (WORKSTN in positions 40 through 46) that is processed as a full procedural file and is described as a combined file (C in position 15). This file is externally described and contains the subfile SFDATA. A relative record number field (SFNUM) is defined for the SFDATA subfile.

RPG III and the IBM System/38

```
                                    RPG CALCULATION SPECIFICATIONS

Line  C  Indicators      Factor 1    Operation    Factor 2    Result Field         Resulting      Comments
                                                              Name    Length       Indicators
01    C                  START       TAG
02    C                              Z-ADD0                   ITEM
03    C       10                     SETON                                         45             45=CLEAR SUBFIL
04    C      N10                     SETON                                         10
05    C                              EXFMT SFCONTRL                                                WRITE/READ
06    C       98                     SETON                                         LR             98=END OF PROG
07    C       98                     RETRN
08    C                  ORDKEY      CHAIN ORDHDR                                  91             91=NOT FOUND
09    C       91                     GOTO  START
10    C                  CUST        CHAIN CUSREC                                  92             92=NOT FOUND
11    C       92                     GOTO  START
12    C                              Z-ADD0                   SFNUM                                INTL REL REL#
13    C
```

The Z-ADD operation on line 2 sets the ITEM field to zero so that it is always zero when the field is used in the ORDKEY composite field for chaining to the ORDHDR record.

The SETON operations on lines 3 and 4 establish when the subfile is cleared. The first time through the START routine, the subfile is not cleared because indicator 45 is not on. After the first time through the START routine, the subfile is cleared because indicator 45 is on when the SFCONTRL format is written to the display by the EXFMT operation.

The program then sends the SFCONTRL format to the display station in the shipping department. The user responds by entering the order number to be reviewed and pressing the Enter key. If the user presses the command key 12, indicator 98 is set on through the data description specifications for the SFCONTRL format, and the prcgram ends.

If the user presses the Enter key, the program performs the CHAIN operation to the order header record to retrieve the customer number. If there is no record, an error occurs (indicator 91, which is specified in positions 54 and 55, is set on). The CHAIN operation on line 8 uses a KLIST name (ORDKEY) in factor 1 for the key field. This field is required whenever the key for the logical file is a composite key (multiple key fields). In this example, the value in the ITEM field is always zero when the ORDKEY is used to chain to ORDHDR.

The program performs another CHAIN operation to the customer record (CUSREC) to retrieve the customer name.

The Z-ADD operation on line 12 initializes the SFNUM field, which is used as the relative record number (RECNO) field for the subfile.

```
                                    RPG CALCULATION SPECIFICATIONS

         Indicators                                      Result Field    Resulting Indicators
 Line  And  And    Factor 1    Operation    Factor 2    Name    Length   Plus Minus Zero         Comments
                                                                         1>2  1<2  1=2
01  C              BLDSF       TAG                                                          BUILD SUBFILE
02  C                          READE ORDDTL                                      55         55=END OF ORDER
03  C       55                 GOTO  DSPSF
04  C              QTYORD      IFNE  0                                                      IF ORD NOT CANC
05  C                          ADD   1          SFNUM                                       NEXT REL REC
06  C                          WRITE SFDATA                                     93          93=FULL SUBFIL
07  C                          END
08  C       N93                GOTO  BLDSF
09  C              DSPSF       TAG
10  C              SFNUM       COMP  0                                               94     94=NO ITEMS
11  C                          SETON                                            44          44=DSP SUBFILE
12  C                          EXFMT SFCONTRL
13  C
```

The BLDSF routine reads the order detail records sequentially and fills the subfile with successive READ and WRITE operations. (Remember, in the logical file ORDFILL, records are accessed in order sequence so header records are logically intermixed with detail records and can be accessed sequentially by key—even though they are in different physical files.) If the quantity on order is zero, the record is bypassed.

If there are no more line items for this order (indicator 55 is on) or if the subfile is now full (indicator 93 is now on), the BLDSF routine ends. Indicator 44 is set on to cause the subfile to be displayed, and the program continues with the UPDATE routine.

```
                                    RPG CALCULATION SPECIFICATIONS                          Page 4 of 4

         Indicators                                      Result Field    Resulting Indicators
 Line  And  And    Factor 1    Operation    Factor 2    Name    Length   Plus Minus Zero         Comments
01  C              UPDATE      TAG                                                          UPDATE FILES
02  C                          READC SFDATA                                      65         65=END OF CHG
03  C       65                 GOTO  START
04  C                          Z-ADD QTYSHP    SAVE
05  C              ORDKEY      CHAIN ORDDTL                                          95
06  C                          Z-ADD 0         SFNUM     30                                 INIT REL REC#
07  C              XLIKE       DEFN  QTYSHP    SAVE                                         DEFINE: SAVE
08  C       N95                UPDAT ORDDTL                                                 UPDATE ORDDTL
09  C       N95                Z-ADD SAVE      QTYSHP
10  C       N95                GOTO  UPDATE
11  C       95                 GOTO  START
12  C              ORDKEY      KLIST
13  C                          KFLD            ORDER                                        DEFINE: ORDKEY
14  C                          KFLD            ITEM                                         (COMPOSITE KEY)
15  C
```

The READC operation in the UPDATE routine returns to the program only those records in the subfile that were changed by the user. The changed field is temporarily saved while the old ORDDTL record is read into the program by the CHAIN operation. The ORDDTL record is then updated with the changed field.

If there are no more changed items for this order (indicator 65 in on), the program branches back to START.

If no record is found on the CHAIN (indicator 95 is on), the program branches back to the START. An error message is then displayed, indicating that the update failed and requesting the user to reenter the ORDER key.

No input or output specifications are required by this program.

RPG III and the IBM System/38

Questions for Review

1. What are the advantages of the SEU?
2. How does the DDS assist the programmer?
3. What is an externally defined file?
4. What are the main advantages in describing files externally?
5. How does the CPF assist in systems control?
6. Explain the relationship between compilation listing diagnostics and SEU sequence numbers.
7. What is a full procedural file?
8. Why is an explicit open or explicit close statement disallowed with table files?
9. How does the EXFMT operation work?
10. What does the WRITE operation do?
11. What is a logically deleted record?
12. Why is the RPG logic cycle being deemphasized?
13. What is the difference between the FEOD and CLOSE operations?
14. What is a WORKSTN file?
15. How does one describe a WORKSTN file?
16. What is a subfile?
17. How are subfiles processed?
18. What is a physically deleted record?
19. How does the DELET operation work?
20. Explain the READP operation.

RPG III Features

12

Outline

Interprogram Functions
   CALL/RETRN Function
   SPECIAL File
      with PLIST Operation
Data Structures
   Multiple Occurrence
      Data Structures
   File Information Data Structures
      (INFDS)
Calculation Modifications
   Compare and Branch (CABxx)
   Short Form of Arithmetic
      Operations
   Calculation Time Output (EXCPT)
   Sort Array (SORTA)
   Indicators Referenced as Data
      (*IN, *INxx, *IN,xx)
   Field Definition (DEFN)
   Relative End-Positions (40–43)
      on Output Specifications
   Figurative Constants
   Time (TIME)
   Shutdown (SHTDN)
   User-Defined Edit Codes (5–9)
   Dynamic Space/Skip Function
      (PRTCTL)
   Display Function (DSPLY)
   Improved Relative File Support
   Table File Replacement
   Default Control Specification

New Compilation Listing Functions
   Cross-Reference Listing
   Text Descriptions from Data
      Description Specifications
   Resulting Indicator Usage
   /EJECT Specifications
   /SPACE Specifications
   Nesting Indication
   Last Update Indication
Enhanced Debug Facilities
   System Debug Facility
   Formatted Dump
   Debug Function (DEBUG)
   Program Dump (DUMP)
   Create RPG Program
      (CRTRPGPGM)
   Check Reconciliation System

Chapter 11 discussed the primary differences between RPG III and RPG II, particularly within the IBM System/38 environment. To summarize, RPG III departs from RPG II primarily in the externalization of data files through CPF; the deemphasis of the RPG logic cycle with increased control of reading and writing coming from calculation operations; the use of the CRT as the primary input/output device; and the provision of an environment lending itself to greater programmer productivity. A number of innovations to RPG III have been introduced in sections of earlier chapters under discussions of modified or improved operation codes. This chapter introduces a few more operation codes and makes reference back to earlier chapters where that information will aid understanding of the new material.

An interactive check reconciliation system written for the IBM System/38 using externally described WORKSTN files and full procedural file logic is also discussed in this chapter.

Interprogram Functions

CALL/RETRN Function

RPG III provides communication support allowing one RPG program to call any other program. An RPG program can consist of any group of RPG specifications that can exist by themselves. (See Figure 12.1.) Data in a parameter list can be accessed by both the calling and called programs. The CALL (call a program) operation code with PLIST (identify a parameter list), and the PARM (identify parameters) operation codes and RETRN (return to caller) operation code allow an RPG program to call and be called by other programs. The PLIST and PARM operations permit the same data to be accessed by a calling and a called program. (See Figure 12.2.)

RPG does not provide automatic storage allocation. When an RPG program is called for the first time the program is located, the fields are set up, and the program is given control. If the called program has not terminated all fields, indicators, and files in the called program on each succeeding call will be the same as they were when the program did a return on the preceding call. If the called program has terminated or if FREE was specified, a fresh copy of the program is made available on each succeeding call.

Figure 12.1 Calling and freeing RPG programs

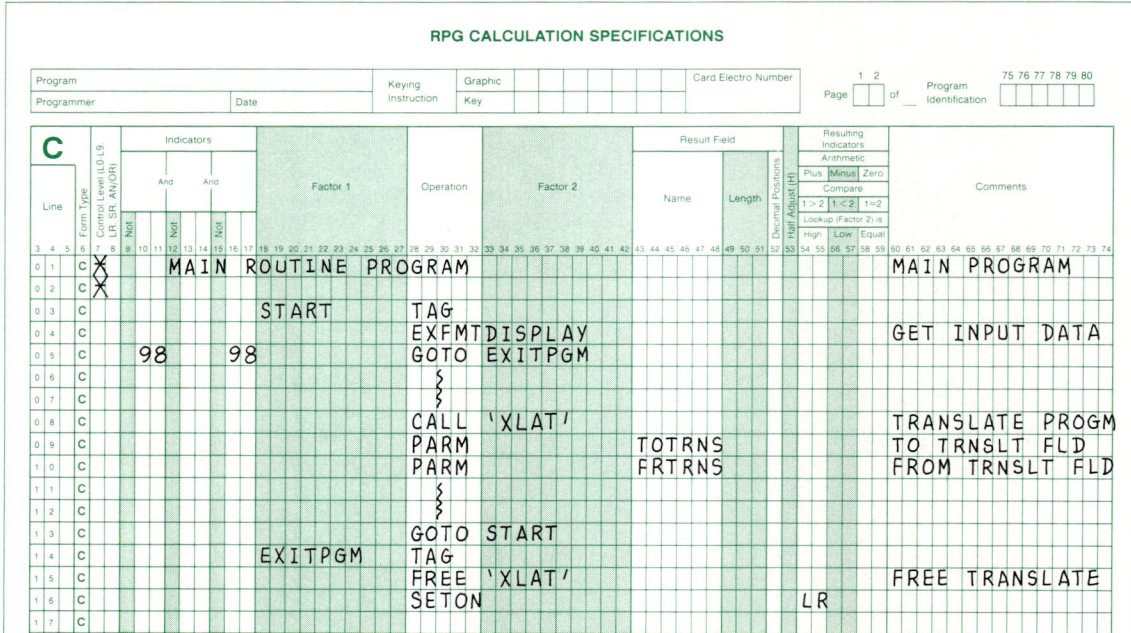

This example shows an RPG program (MAIN) using the CALL/RETURN function to call another RPG program (XLAT). The EXFMT operation in MAIN (line 03) writes the DSPLY record to the display screen. TOTRNS and FRTRNS are fields in the record. The work station user can key data into the record, which is placed in the TOTRNS field (line 09). The key information in the TOTRNS field is to be translated by the TRANS program.

Figure 12.2 CALL/RETRN function

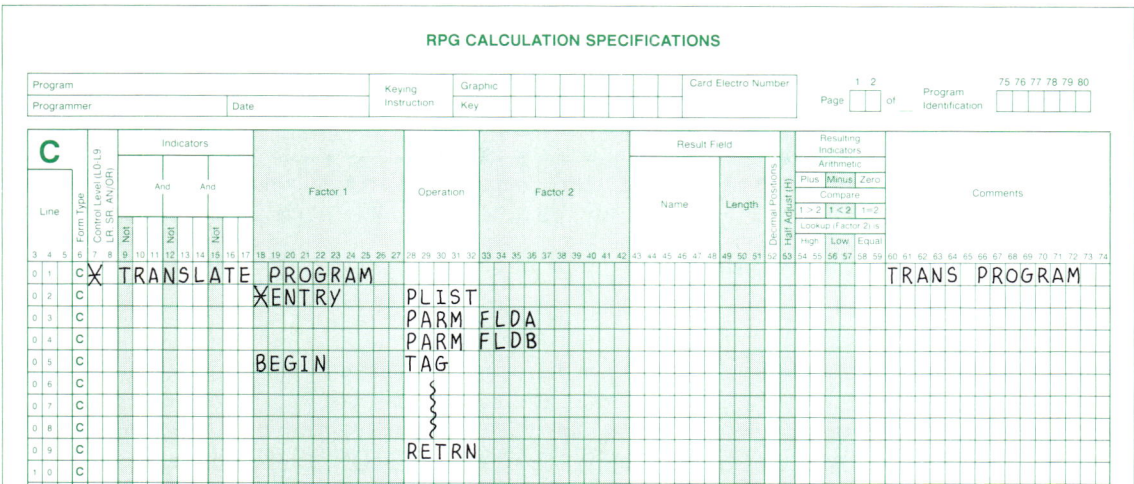

When the CALL 'XLAT' statement in MAIN executes (line 08), the FLDA and FLDB names in XLAT are used to access the data in the TOTRNS and FRTRNS fields in the PARMs in MAIN. Using this data, XLAT translates the TOTRNS field, the result of the operation is placed in the FRTRNS field in MAIN (line 09), and the RETRN operation in XLAT executes (line 09). A RETRN without LR is specified in order to keep the program and all its work areas intact.

Return from XLAT is to the statement immediately following the last PARM statement in MAIN (line 11). The MAIN program completes the transaction (lines 11 and 12). When the GOTO operation is executed (line 13), the program branches back to the beginning of calculations. This loop continues until the work station user presses a command attention key that sets on indicator 98 to end the program. (In the Data Description Specification for the record format DSPLY, a command attention key would be associated with indicator 98.)

When indicator 98 is on, the program branches to the ENDPGM TAG statement and the FREE operation (line 14) frees the XLAT program. The MAIN program ends when LR is set on (line 15).

The concept of reentrancy is gaining importance as environments of multiple work stations invoke multiple copies of the same program at varying points in time. A program is said to be reentrant if initialization routines dynamically reinitialize data areas altered by previous runs of the program. By providing a new copy, the FREE command achieves the same objective. (See Figure 12.1.)

Calls can be dynamic. The name of the program to be called may be specified at execution time. An explicit return is provided with the RETRN operation code. Implicit returns are provided through the passage of indicators such as LR, H1–H9, and the new RT indicator.

The new operation codes associated with the CALL/RETRN function are

1. CALL (Call a program)
2. FREE (Remove a program)
3. PARM (Identify parameters)
4. PLIST (Identify a parameter list)
5. RETRN (Return to caller)

The new indicator RT indicates to the internal RPG logic that control should be returned immediately to the calling program.

SPECIAL File with PLIST Operation

The SPECIAL file feature allows the programmer to specify an input/output device not directly supported by RPG. The input and output operations for the file are controlled by a user-written routine. SPECIAL permits only fixed, unblocked records. RPG uses the user-written routine to open the file, read and write the records, and close the file. RPG creates a parameter list to be used by the user-written routine. The parameter list (PLIST) contains the option code parameter (option), a return status parameter (status), an error-found parameter (error), and a record area parameter (area). This parameter list is accessed by RPG and by the user-written routine; it cannot be accessed by the RPG program containing the SPECIAL file.

Data Structures

RPG III incorporates a feature allowing an internal area to be redefined (one or more times), noncontiguous data to be grouped into contiguous internal storage locations, contents of a field to be changed, and a field to be subdivided into subfields. These capabilities simplify many application approaches and can be used to eliminate the coding and execution of MOVE and MOVEL operations. A common application is the creation of mailing labels from noncontiguous fields of names and addresses.

Data structures can be program described or externally described. A data structure statement has *DS* in positions 19–20 of an input specification. Externally described data structures have an *E* in position 17 of the data structure statement. Externalization of data structures offers the usual benefits: less coding, greater consistency, fewer errors, letter documentation, and easier maintenance.

Multiple Occurrence Data Structures

A multiple occurrence data structure is one whose definition is repeated *n* times within a program to form a series of data structures with identical formats. The number of occurrences of a data structure is specified in positions 44–47 of a data structure statement. (See Figure 12.3.) When positions 44–47 do not contain an entry, the data structure is not a multiple occurrence data structure. All occurrences of a data structure have the same attributes and can be referenced individually.

The OCUR operation code can be used only with a multiple occurrence data structure; this code allows the programmer to specify which occurrence of a data structure is to be referenced for subsequent operations within the program. Thus data structures can be manipulated in a manner similar to arrays. (See Figure 12.4.)

Figure 12.3 Specification of a multiple occurrence data structure

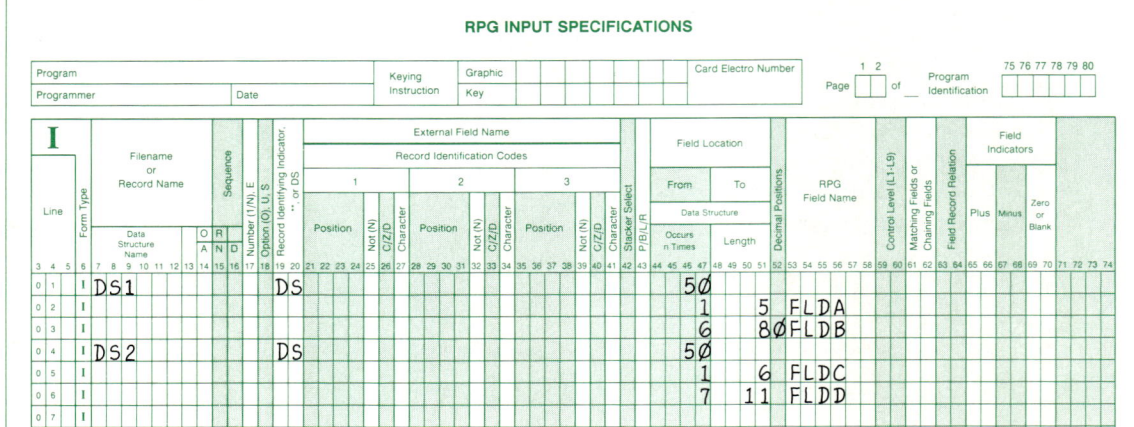

DS1 and DS2 are multiple occurrence data structures specified in lines 01 and 05 of the input specification. Each data structure has 50 occurrences.

Figure 12.4 Uses of the OCUR operation

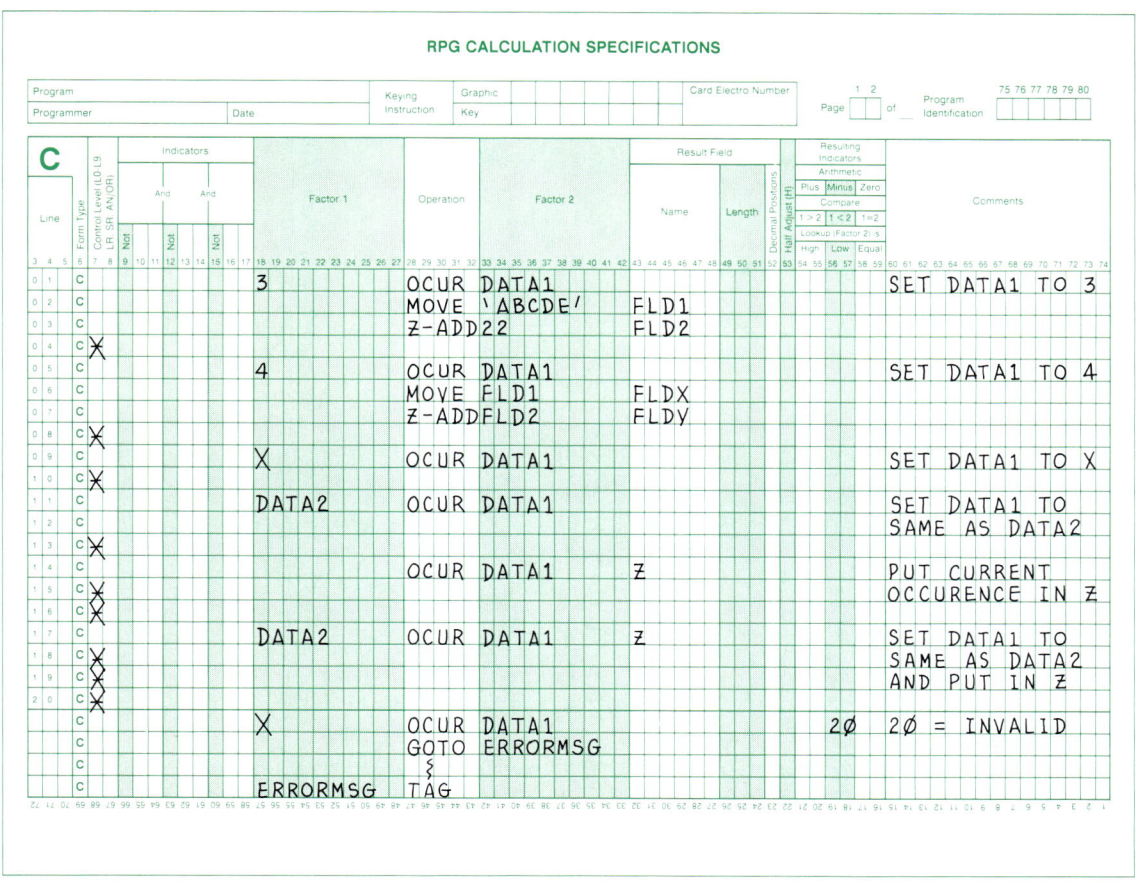

line 01   DS1 is set to the third occurrence. The subfields FLDA and FLDB of the third occurrence can now be used. The MOVE and Z-ADD operations respectively change the contents of FLDA and FLDB in the third occurrence of DS1.
line 05   DS1 is set to the fourth occurrence. MOVEs and Z-ADDs use the fourth occurrence of FLDA and FLDB fields.
line 09   DS1 is set to the occurrence specified in field X.
line 11   DS1 is set to the current occurrence of DS2.
line 13   The value of the current occurrence of DS1 is placed in the result field Z, which must be numeric with zero decimal positions.
line 15   DS1 is set to the current occurrence of DS2. The value of the current occurrence of DS1 is then moved to the result field, Z.
line 17   DS1 is set to the current occurrence of X. If X is less than or equal to zero, or X is greater than 50, an error occurs and indicator 20 is set on. The program then branches to an error routine.

File Information Data Structures (INFDS)

A file information data structure, defined by the keyword INFDS on a file description specifications continuation line (positions 54–59), allows the programmer to receive file exception/error information from various data management functions. A file information data structure can be defined by specifying its name in positions 60–65 and INFDS in position 54 through position 59 of file description specifications. These specifications must be made for each file to make file exception/error information available to the program. (See Figure 12.5.) The file information data structure must be unique for each file. A file information data structure contains predefined subfields that identify

> The name of the file for which the error occurred.
> The record being processed when the error occurred.
> The operation being performed when the error occurred.
> The status code.

RPG III Features

Figure 12.5 File exception/error handling (INFDS)

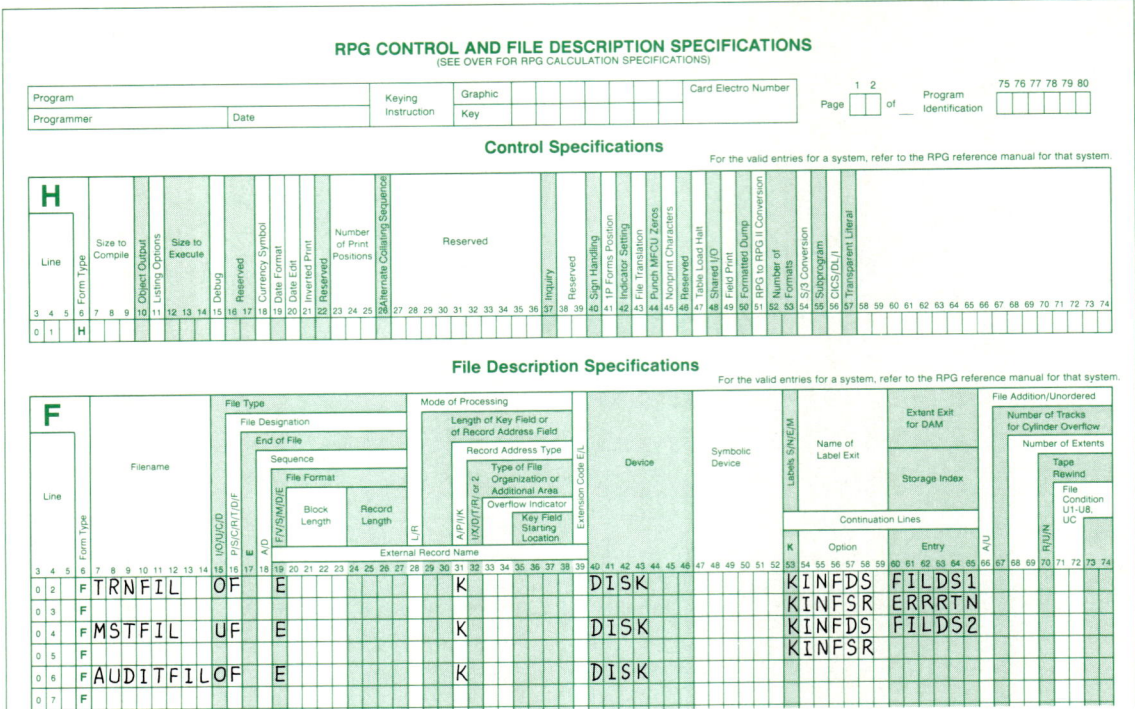

Three files are defined on the file description specifications. The programmer wants to control the program logic if an exception occurs on the TRNFIL file or on the MSTFIL file. For this reason, a unique file information data structure (INFDS) and a file error subroutine (INFSR) are defined for each file. No INFDS or INFSR is defined for the AUDITFIL file.

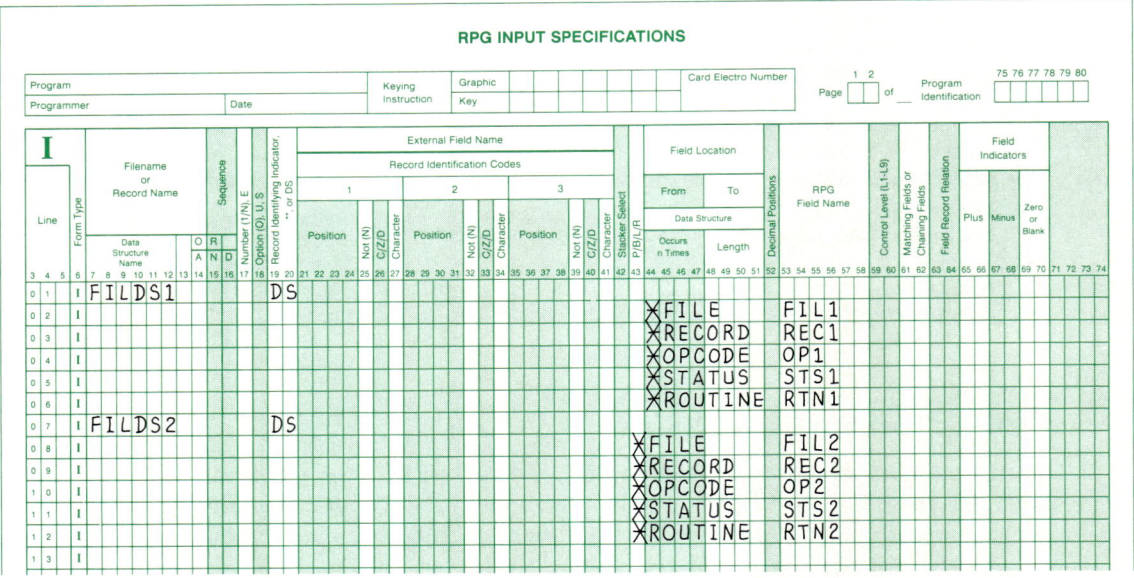

The location of the subfields in the file information data structures is defined by special keywords in positions 44 through 51. To reference these predefined subfields, a name must be assigned to each subfield in positions 53 through 58. If an error occurs, the programmer can test the information in the data structure to determine, for example, what exception occurred (*STATUS) and on which operation it occurred (*OPCODE), etc.

Certain keywords in positions 44–51 and field names in positions 53–58 must be specified to receive certain error handling/exception information. Following are those keywords and their descriptions.

Keyword	Description
*FILE	Eight-character alphameric field identifying the name of the file (as specified in positions 7–14 of the file description specifications).
*RECORD	Externally described file: Eight-character alphameric field containing the RPG name of the record being processed when the error occurred.
	Program described file: Eight-character alphameric field containing the record identifying indicator left-justified with blanks in the remaining six positions.
*OPCODE	Six-character alphameric field containing the operation code left-justified in the leftmost five bytes. The sixth byte contains one of the following: F The last operation was specified for a file name. R The last operation was specified for a record. I The last operation was an implicit file operation.
*STATUS	Five-digit numeric field with no decimal positions and containing the status code.

Normal Codes

Code	Condition
00000	No exception/error
00011	End-of-File on input
00012	No record found on CHAIN operation
00013	Subfile full

Exception/Error Conditions

Code	Condition
01011	Undefined record type
01031	Match field out of sequence
01041	Array/Table load sequence error
01051	Excess entries in array/table file
01071	Numeric sequence error
01211	I/O operation to closed file
01215	Open issued to file already opened
01216	Error on implicit OPEN/CLOSE statement
01217	Error on explicit OPEN/CLOSE statement
01221	Update operation attempted without prior read
01231	Error on SPECIAL file
01235	Error in PRTCTL space or skip entries
01241	Record number not found (record number specified in record address file is not present in file being processed)
01299	Other I/O error detected

*ROUTINE   Eight-character alphameric field containing the name of the RPG routine in which the error occurred. This subfield is updated only when the location *STATUS is updated with a value of nonzeros. The following names identify the routines:

*INIT	Program initialization
*DETL	Detail lines
*GETIN	Get input record
*TOTC	Total calculations
*TOTL	Total lines
*DETC	Detail calculations
*OFL	Overflow lines
*TERM	Program termination
srname	Name of BEGSR
pgmname	Name of the program called (first eight characters)

The *ROUTINE capability allows the programmer to code for unusual events and permits a more sophisticated approach to many applications. This results in the intelligent "trapping" of error conditions to permit recovery and/or restart of jobs. The process of debugging abnormal terminations is facilitated by the tools provided in the file information data structure (INFDS).

Calculation Modifications

Compare and Branch (CABxx)

The compare and branch operation allows the programmer to do a compare and branch in a single operation and eliminates the need to set and test indicators. See the RPG III enhancements section of chapter 5 for further information about CABxx.

Short Form of Arithmetic Operations

RPG III allows the use of add, subtract, multiply, and divide operations for which factor 1 need not be specified. For example:

	Factor 1	Operation	Factor 2	Result Field
RPG II statement	QTY	ADD	TOTQTY	TOTQTY
RPG III statement		ADD	QTY	TOTQTY

This capability reduces coding and makes a program easier to read. See the RPG III enhancements section of chapter 3 for further information about the short form of arithmetic operations in RPG III.

Calculation Time Output (EXCPT)

RPG III has expanded the effectiveness of the EXCPT operation by allowing simplified control of one or more EXCPT output lines. This eliminates the coding of several indicators and provides better logic control of output. See the RPG III enhancements section of chapter 5 for further information about changes to the EXCPT operation.

Sort Array (SORTA)

SORTA allows an array to be sorted into sequence (ascending or descending). See the RPG III enhancements section of chapter 7 for further information about the SORTA operation.

Indicators Referenced as Data (*IN, *INxx, *IN,xx)

The ability to reference indicators as data is a feature that gives the programmer an alternative method of referencing and manipulating indicators. Referencing the array of indicators 01–99 as data reduces coding and provides a simplified approach to many program processing requirements, such as the ability to set (on or off) a block of indicators. See the RPG III enhancements section of chapter 7 for further information about *IN, *INxx, and *IN,xx.

Field Definition (DEFN)

The nonexecutable DEFN statement can do either of the following depending on the factor 1 entry:

Define a field based on the attributes (length and decimal positions) of another field
Define a field as a data area

The DEFN operation can be specified anywhere in calculations. Indicators of timing (L0–L9, LR) are permitted but conditioning indicators (positions 9–17) are not.

The DEFN operation with *LIKE in factor 1 defines a field (specified as the result field) based upon the attributes of another field (specified as factor 2). The length of the factor 2 field can be modified

Figure 12.6 DEFN operations

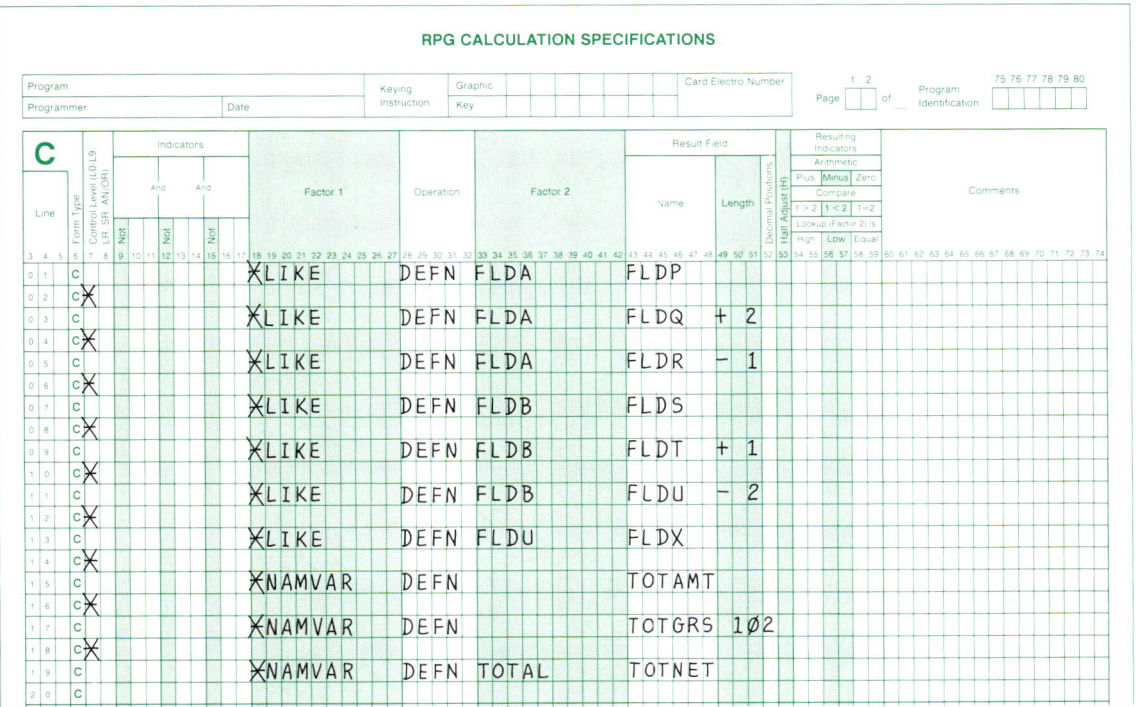

FLDA is 7 positions alphameric.
FLDB is 5 digits long with 2 decimal positions.

line 01	FLDP is 7 positions alphameric.
line 03	FLDQ is 9 positions alphameric.
line 05	FLDR is 6 positions alphameric.
line 07	FLDS is 5 positions numeric with 2 decimal positions.
line 09	FLDT is 6 positions numeric with 2 decimal positions.
line 11	FLDU is 3 positions numeric with 2 decimal positions.
line 13	FLDX is 3 positions numeric with 2 decimal positions.
line 15	The attributes (length and decimal positions) of the data area are retrieved by the program from the external description of the data area.
line 17	If specified, the attributes of the data area (length and decimal positions) must be the same as those of the external description of the data area.
line 19	The result field entry (TOTNET) is the name of the data area to be used within the RPG program. The factor 2 entry (TOTAL) is the name of the data area defined to the program.

upward or downward during this operation by placing a plus sign (+) or a minus sign (−) in position 49. The sign indicates a length increase or decrease, respectively; the amount of the increase or decrease is specified in positions 50–51. Decimal positions may not be changed. (See Figure 12.6.)

The DEFN operation with *NAMVAR in factor 1 defines a field as a data area.

Relative End-Positions (40–43) on Output Specifications

To specify the output position based upon the end-position of another field allows the programmer to develop programs more rapidly (i.e., in an interactive mode). RPG III allows the programmer to specify the output of a field based upon relative end-position from the previously described field. Thus the programmer may specify a relative field address in positions 40–43 provided the sign is specified in position 40 and the increment/decrement is right-justified. (See Figure 12.7.) If a negative relative end-position is specified, overprinting occurs.

RPG III Features

Figure 12.7 Relative end-positions for fields specified on output specifications

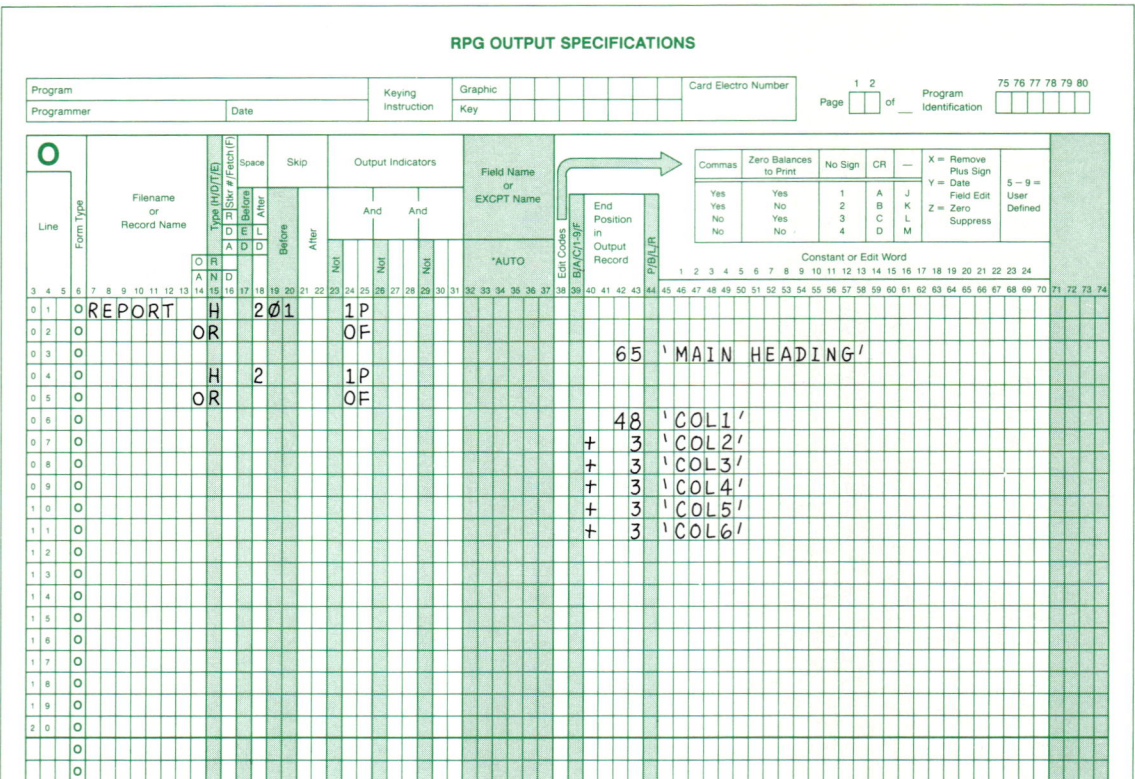

Figurative Constants

The use of figurative constants allows RPG-defined names to eliminate initialization statements and provide an easier solution for many program requirements. To RPG, a **figurative constant** is an implied literal specified in the calculation specifications without reference to length. The implied length and decimal positions are the same as that of the field with which the figurative constant is associated. (See Figure 12.8.) The figurative constant names and implied values are described in the following:

Figurative Constant	Implied Value
*BLANK/*BLANKS	A field of blanks (spaces); valid for alphameric fields only.
*ZERO/*ZEROS	A field of all zeros; valid for alphameric or numeric fields.
*HIVAL	A field with the highest collating value in the collating sequence (hexadecimal *FF*s, binary *1*s); valid for alphameric fields only.
*LOVAL	A field with the lowest collating value in the collating sequence (hexadecimal or binary zeros) when used with alphameric fields. When used with a numeric field, *LOVAL is all nines with a negative sign.
*ALL'X'	A field of alphameric characters with string '*X*' repeated cyclically to a length equal to the receiving field. If a field is a numeric field, all characters within the string must be numeric (0–9). No sign or decimal point can be specified when ALL'X' is used as a numeric constant.

Time (TIME)

TIME (in a manner similar to the UDATE treatment of date) allows the program to retrieve the system time of day and, if specified, the system date at any time during program execution. This simplifies a number of functions such as the time stamping of transaction.

Figure 12.8 Figurative constants

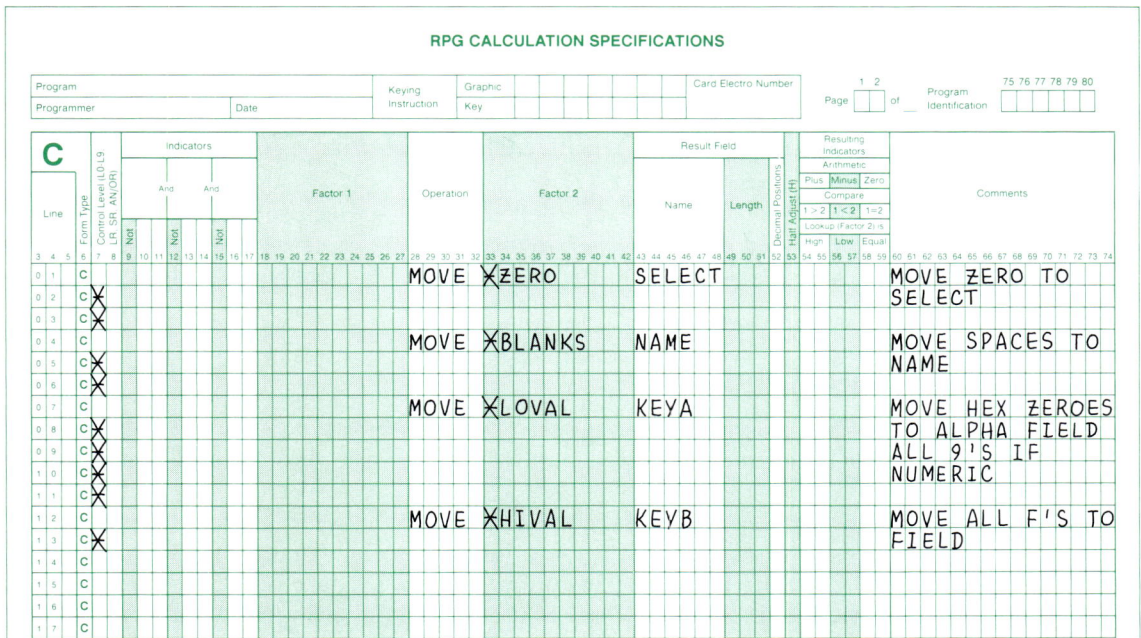

TIME is an operation code; it should not be confused with UDATE, which is a field. Thus, TIME can be invoked repeatedly during program execution while UDATE is static.

The required result field of the TIME operation code contains six numeric characters; zero decimal positions provided the system time in the format hhmmss (where hh = hours, mm = minutes, and ss = seconds). When the required result field is twelve numeric characters, the system time is provided in the first six positions as before, but the system date is also included in positions 7–12 of the result field. The date format depends on the system date format (positions 19–21 of the control specification) and can be mmddyy, ddmmyy, or yymmdd (mmddyy is the default). (See Figure 12.9.)

Figure 12.9 TIME operation

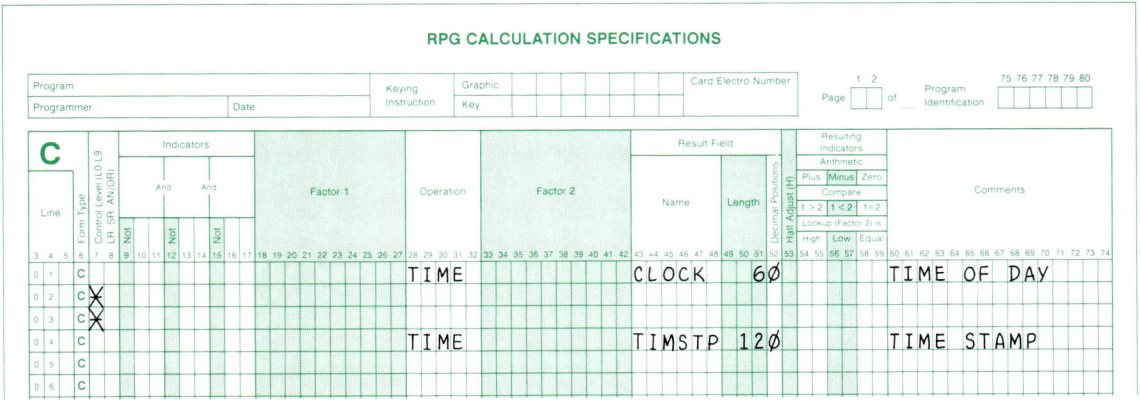

When the TIME operation in line 01 is executed (with a 6-digit numeric field), the current time (in the form hhmmss) is placed in the result field CLOCK. The TIME operation is based on the 24-hour system. For example, 132710, (in the twelve hour system 132710 is 1:27:10 p.m.) CLOCK can then be specified in the output specifications.

When the time operation in line 4 is executed (with a twelve digit numeric field), the current time and date is placed in the result field TIMSTP. The first six digits are the time and the last six digits are the date. The TIME operation is based on the 24-hour system. For example, 093315121579, (in the twelve hour system 093315 is 9:33:15 a.m.) TIMSTP can then be specified in the output specifications.

Shutdown (SHTDN)

The SHTDN operation allows a resulting indicator to be set on if shutdown was requested by the system operator. If a shutdown is requested, certain programming housekeeping functions will be performed in an automated manner.

User-Defined Edit Codes (5–9)

The user-defined edit codes (5–9) allow the user to handle common editing problems that would otherwise require the use of an edit word. Instead of repeatedly coding the same edit word, a user-defined edit code is created. These codes are defined to the system by the CPF command CRTEDTD (create edit description).

Dynamic Space/Skip Function (PRTCTL)

The PRTCTL option allows the program to specify space/skip operations on the output specifications instead of using literals. In addition, the current line number is made available to the program for better control of overflow.

Specifying PRTCTL in positions 54–59 of the continuation lines of a file description specification along with the name of the data structure containing the printer control and line count information gives the programmer the ability to modify forms control information. (See Figure 12.10.)

The data structure specified in positions 60–65 of the file description specifications continuation line must be specified on the input specifications, and must contain the following subfields specified in the following order:

Data Structure Positions	Subfield Contents
1	A one-character alphameric field containing the space-before value
2	A one-character alphameric field containing the space-after value
3–4	A two-character alphameric field containing the skip-before value
5–6	A two-character alphameric field containing the skip-after value
7–9	A three-digit numeric field with zero decimal positions containing the current line count value

Display Function (DSPLY)

The DSPLY operation permits access to the display device without the use of a data description file. Interaction can take place through the use of control keys and display system messages from the message file QUSERMSG (if present). If there is no message file, the DSPLY operation is used. If factor 1 contains an entry and the result field is blank, factor 1 is displayed. When factor 1 is blank and the result field contains an entry, the result field is displayed and the program waits for a reply that is then placed in the result field. When both factor 1 and the result field contain entries, the fields are combined and displayed; the program waits for a reply that is then placed in the result field.

Improved Relative File Support

The improved relative file support of RPG III allows the programmer easier access and more control of files processed by relative record number. The RECNO field defined in the file description specifications allows for easier control and feedback.

The RECNO keyword is entered in positions 54–59 of the continuation lines of the file description specifications. RECNO is only one of a series of powerful keywords that may be specified in this position (e.g., INFDS, INFSR, PLIST, PRTCTL, RENAME, and SFILE), all of which are new to RPG III. Positions 60–65 of the file description specification continuation lines contain the name of the RPG field that will contain the RECNO value.

Figure 12.10 PRTCTL option

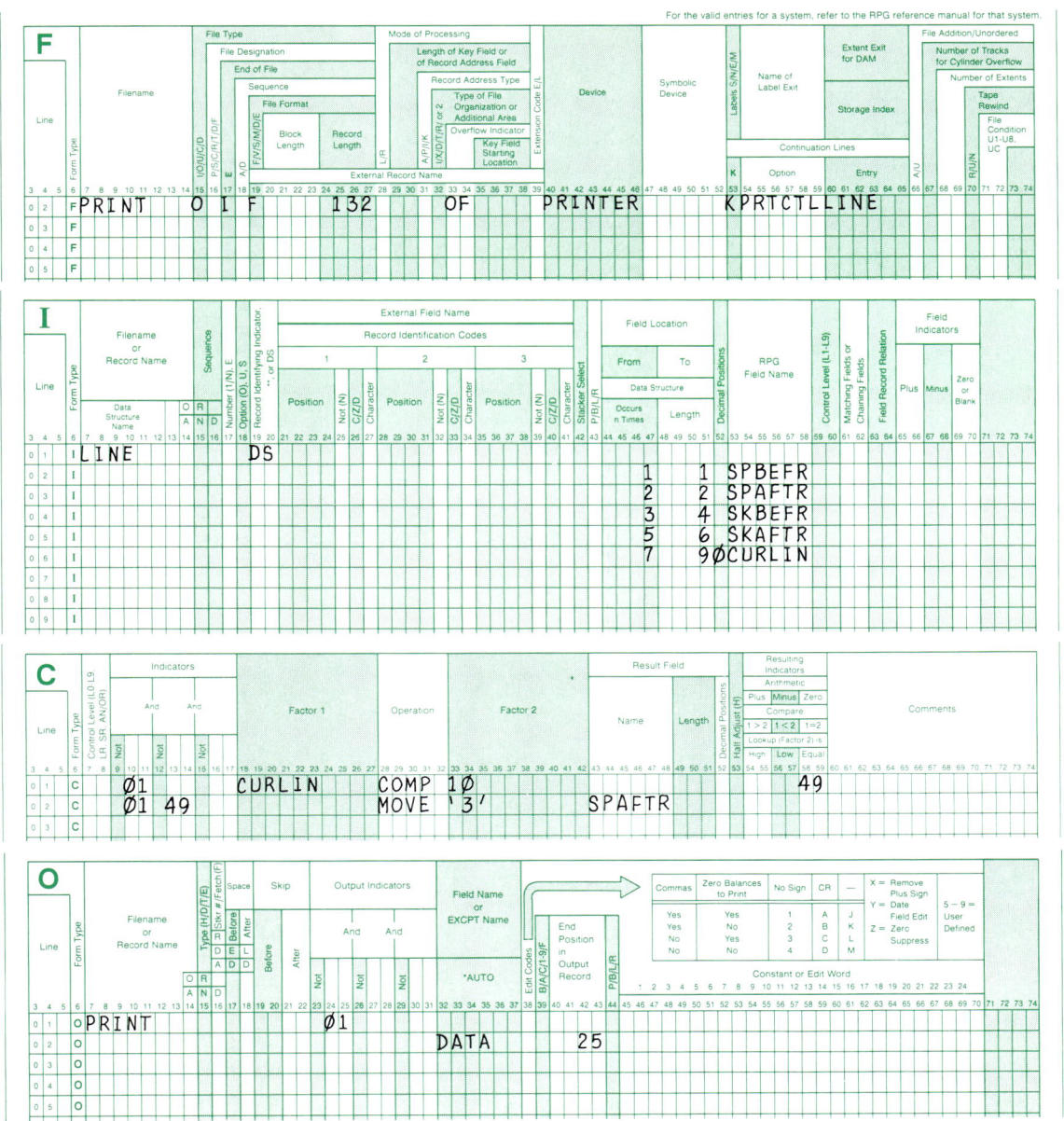

On the file description specifications, the PRTCTL option is specified for the PRINT file. The name of the associated data structure is LINE.

The LINE data structure is defined on the input specifications as having only those subfields that are predefined for the PRTCTL data structure. The first four subfields in position 1 through position 6 are used to supply space and skip information that is generally specified in positions 17 through 22 of the output specifications. The PRTCTL option allows the programmer to change these specifications within the program.

In this example, the value in the SPAFTR subfield is changed to 3 when the value in the CURLIN (current line value) subfield is equal to 10. Indicator 01 was the record identifying indicator.

    This entry is optional for files to be processed by relative record number. A RECNO field *must* be specified for output files (*a*) that are processed by relative record numbers, (*b*) that are referenced by a random WRITE operation, or (*c*) that are used with an ADD on output specifications.
    The RECNO option can be specified for input and update files. The field name specified in positions 60–65 of the file description specification continuation lines must be defined as numeric with zero

RPG III Features   589

decimal positions and as having sufficient length to accommodate the largest record number for the file (i.e., a file of 10,000 records cannot have a field RECNO with 4.0 decimal positions).

Table File Replacement

RPG III allows the programmer, at end of program, to write an array or table back to the same file from which it was input. In previous versions of RPG, table files were read-only files. In order to write a table or array back to the same file from which it was read, the file must be specified as a combined file. This capability permits externalization of data with controlled program modification. For example, a program could read in yesterday's totals as a table file; modify that table file by adding today's sales; and rewrite the totals to the same table file for tomorrow's run.

Default Control Specification

A control specification may be specified as a data area. Such a specification eliminates the need for control specifications in every program and allows standardization of various functions (e.g., editing and date format).

RPG uses the control specification that is present in the program. If no control specification is present, RPG checks for the data area (QRPGHSPEC); if the data area is not found, RPG creates an all-blank control specification except for the program name. Thus the control specification is optional for programs without a specific need for it. Since the standardization of control specification externalization, few programs use H specifications.

New Compilation Listing Functions

Cross-Reference Listing

A thorough cross-reference listing allows easy determination of where files, fields, and indicators are defined, referenced, and modified for both program described files and externally described files. Cross-referencing simplifies corrections and improves program documentation.

Text Descriptions from Data Description Specifications

Text descriptions are provided for fields and indicators and are specified in data description specifications. These appear on the listing to help document the program.

Resulting Indicator Usage

Including indicator usage in compilation listings allows quick determination of which resulting indicators have been specified in calculation specifications. This eliminates confusion and helps document the program. (See Figure 12.11.)

/EJECT Specifications

Including /EJECT in source files allows lines in the source listing to be skipped for easier reading of major program functions. The compiler directive /EJECT is found in positions 7–12 of a record; position 6 can contain any valid RPG form type. If all other positions except positions 1–6 are blank, the /EJECT specification will cause a page eject in the compilation listing. This is useful for organizing a source program into increasingly readable modules.

/SPACE Specifications

The compiler directive /SPACE (also placed in positions 7–12 with a valid form type in position 6) contains a positive, left-justified, integer value from 1–112 in positions 14–16. This value specifies the number of lines to be skipped in the compilation listing.

Figure 12.11 Compilation listing

```
5714RG1 RPG   R07M00  850913        PGM12.TOMLIB     01/14/87  16:35:46  PAGE    2
SEQUENCE        1         2         3         4         5         6         7      IND  DO   LAST       PA
NUMBER    6789012345678901234567890123456789012345678901234567890123456789012345678901234  USE  NUM  UPDATE    LI

     100  F*****************************************************************
     200  F* PROGRAM:          PGM12                                       *
     300  F* TITLE:            UPDATE SEQUENTIAL FILE USING CRT AS INPUT DEVICE *              01/09/87
     400  F* DATE WRITTEN      01/12/87                                    *              01/12/87
     500  F* WRITTEN BY:       THOMAS HOOPER                               *
     600  F* DESCRIPTION:      UPDATES FIELDS ON-LINE                      *              01/12/87
     700  *
     800  *

NAME OF PROGRAM WILL BE PGM12 IN LIBRARY TOMLIB
                                                                                                        **
          H
     900  FCRT     CF  E                       WORKSTN                                    01/06/87
              RECORD FORMAT(S):  FILE CRT LIB TOMLIB
                        EXTERNAL FORMAT MENU RPG NAME MENU
    1000  FISAMEX  UF  E           K           DISK                                       01/08/87
```

Nesting Indication

RPG indicates the nested level of a statement in do-groups and IFxx/ELSE groups; this adds clarification to the nesting of embedded statements. As structured programming develops, the ability of the system to properly indent nested IFs and DOs makes rapid modification of programs possible without adversely affecting the clarity of nested loop indication. (The compiler will repair any damage caused by the insertion or deletion of IF or DO structures.) (See Figure 12.12.)

Last Update Indication

RPG III indicates on the extreme right of the source file the date the source statement was last changed. Last update is a valuable control feature that permits a programmer to keep track of modifications; it is the *only* accurate way of keeping track of line changes during maintenance. (See Figure 12.11.)

Figure 12.12 Compilation listing

```
    1100  C*****************************************************************
    1200  C*   CALCULATIONS                                                *
    1300  C*****************************************************************
          RECORD FORMAT(S):   FILE ISAMEX LIB TOMLIB
                  EXTERNAL FORMAT ISAM RPG NAME ISAM
 1000000  INPUT   FIELDS FOR RECORD MENU FILE CRT FORMAT MENU
 1000001                                     1    1 *IN01              RETURN
 1000002                                     2   60 FLD001
 1000003                                     7   70 FLD002
 2000000  INPUT   FIELDS FOR RECORD ISAM FILE ISAMEX FORMAT ISAM
 2000001                                     1   10 TYPE
 2000002                                     2    3 FIL1
 2000003                                     4   80 CUST#
 2000004                                     9   80 FIL2
    1400  C           START     TAG                                                       01/09/87
    1500  C                     MOVE *BLANK   FLD001                                      01/02/87
    1600  C                     MOVE *BLANK   FLD002                                      01/07/87
    1700  C                     EXFMTMENU                                                 01/07/87
    1800  C           *IN01     IFEQ '1'                                     B001         01/14/87
    1900  C                     GOTO END                                      001         01/14/87
    2000  C                     END                                          E001         01/12/87
    2100  C           FLD001    CHAINISAMEX               13             1                01/14/87
    2200  C                     MOVE FLD002   TYPE                                        01/14/87
    2300  C                     UPDATISAM                                                 01/14/87
    2400  C                     GOTO START                                                01/14/87
    2500  C           END       TAG                                                       01/14/87
    2600  C                     MOVE '1'      *INLR                                       01/14/87
 3000000  OUTPUT  FIELDS FOR RECORD MENU FILE CRT FORMAT MENU
 3000001                                FLD001    5  ZONE  5,0
 3000002                                FLD002    6  ZONE  1,0
 4000000  OUTPUT  FIELDS FOR RECORD ISAM FILE ISAMEX FORMAT ISAM
 4000001                                TYPE      1  ZONE  1,0
```

Enhanced Debug Facilities

System Debug Facility

RPG III allows online debugging of every RPG program without any special source statements. Debugging functions include the following:

1. Stopping at specific statement numbers or RPG major functions (e.g., first detail calculation)
2. Display and changing of fields, indicators, and arrays
3. Tracing of specific ranges of statements and the output of changed fields

Formatted Dump

A formatted dump allows the programmer to pinpoint the occurrence of specific execution errors and the status of the program at the time the errors occurred. The formatted dump provides a text description of the cause of error and names the RPG statement number on which the error occurred. Field values are displayed at the time of termination. This is a significant aid both in determining the source of problems and in correcting them.

Debug Function (DEBUG)

The DEBUG operation functions as it does in RPG II to allow either one or two records to be written that contain information helpful for finding programming errors. Output goes to a file or a printer.

Program Dump (DUMP)

The DUMP controls the time that a formatted dump is provided.

Create RPG Program (CRTRPGPGM)

The CRTRPGPGM (create RPG program) command becomes of greater interest as users come to compile in an online rather than a batch mode.

The CRTRPGPGM command invokes the RPG compiler, which loads the source program into main storage and creates an executable program. The command includes options to control the source listing and security functions.

Check Reconciliation System

A check reconciliation system is one in which the operator invokes, through a menu screen, the checking account to be reconciled. The check numbers are entered to screen D$ZCK11A. (See Figure 12.16.) Records are chained from the check history file for the data entry screen D$ZCK11B, which either updates or adds the record to the check history file. Figure 12.16 contains the data description specification for the $ZCK11.SOURCE file describing the screen (record format) from which to choose the account to reconcile.

Figure 12.13 shows the menu program source file CKMENU.SOURCE. When compiled the source file invokes the screen D$ZCKMNA (see Figure 12.16) through the use of the EXFMT operation. The EXFMT operation is a write of the screen record followed by a read of that screen. In this screen one of three programs is selected to reconcile the bank account of a particular branch of the company.

CKOL11.SOURCE reads the check history file for the chosen branch by chaining the check history with check number keys supplied through the execution of the EXFMT operation with D$ZCK11B. (See Figures 12.18, 12.19, and 12.20.)

This system includes externally described files and records; full procedural file specifications; data structures; PLISTs with PARMs; IFxx structures with resultant nesting indication shown on the compilation listing; EXFMT operations; MOVEA used with '00' and *IN,84; a CABEQ operation with *IN01 as factor 1; the use of the figurative constants; and *ZERO, *BLANK, and ALL'0'.

Figure 12.13 Source file CKMENU.SOURCE

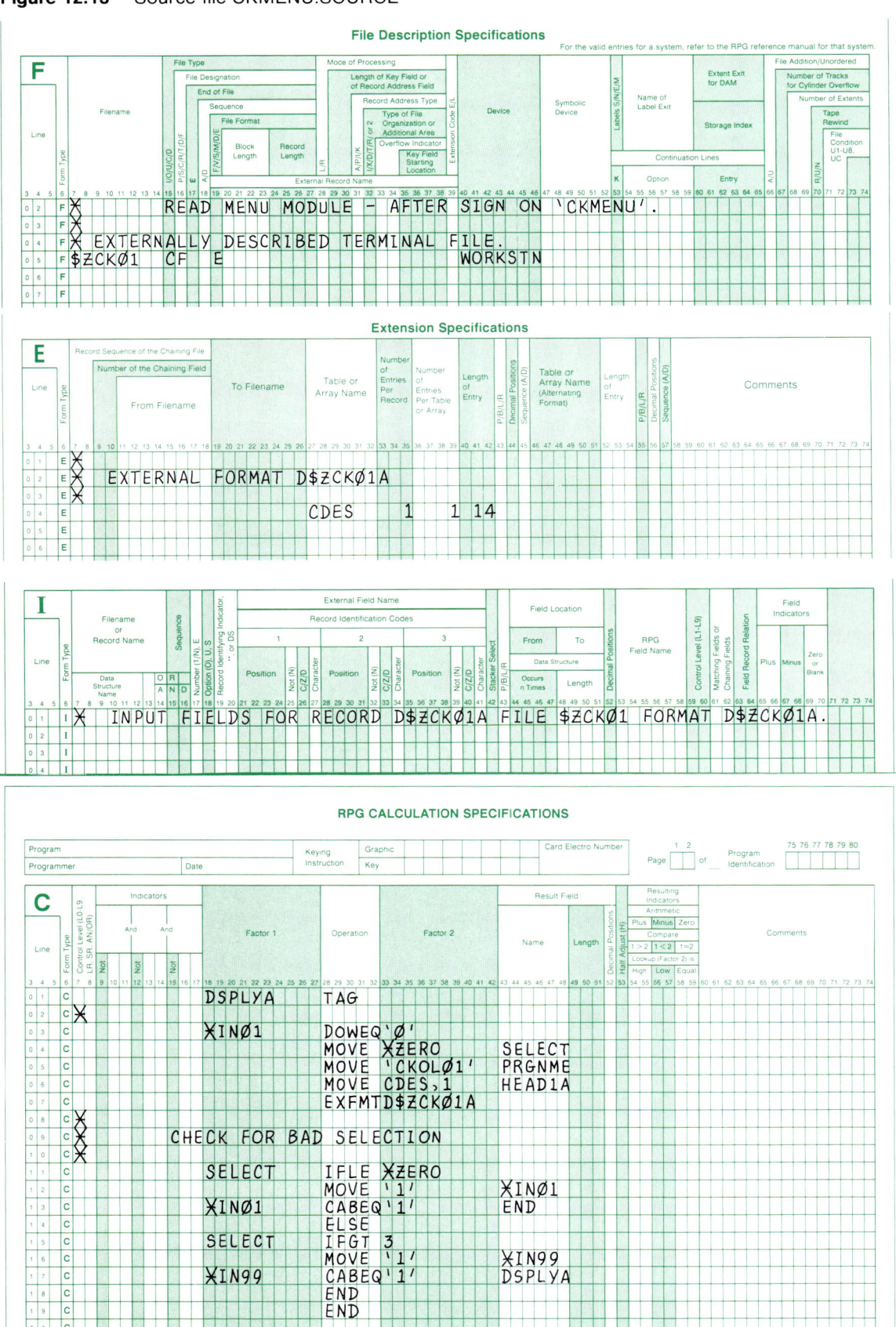

RPG III Features

Figure 12.14 Data description specifications D$ZCKO1A

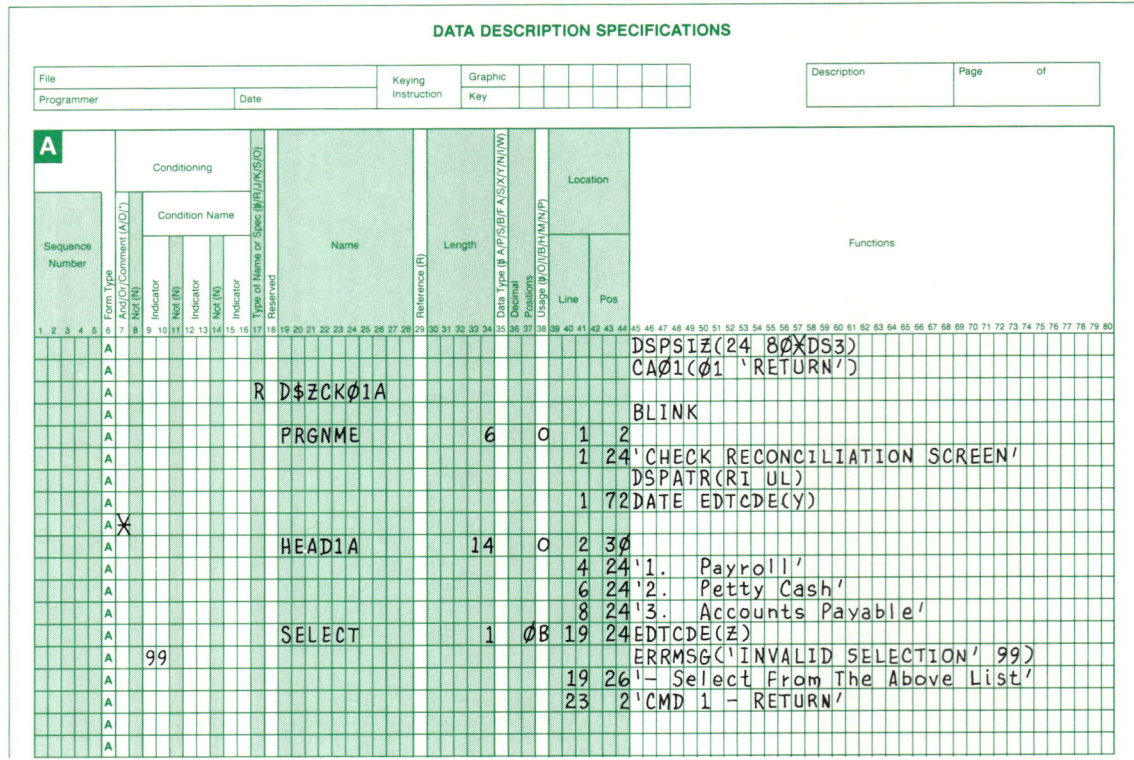

Figure 12.15 Data description specifications D$ZCK11A and D$ZCK11B

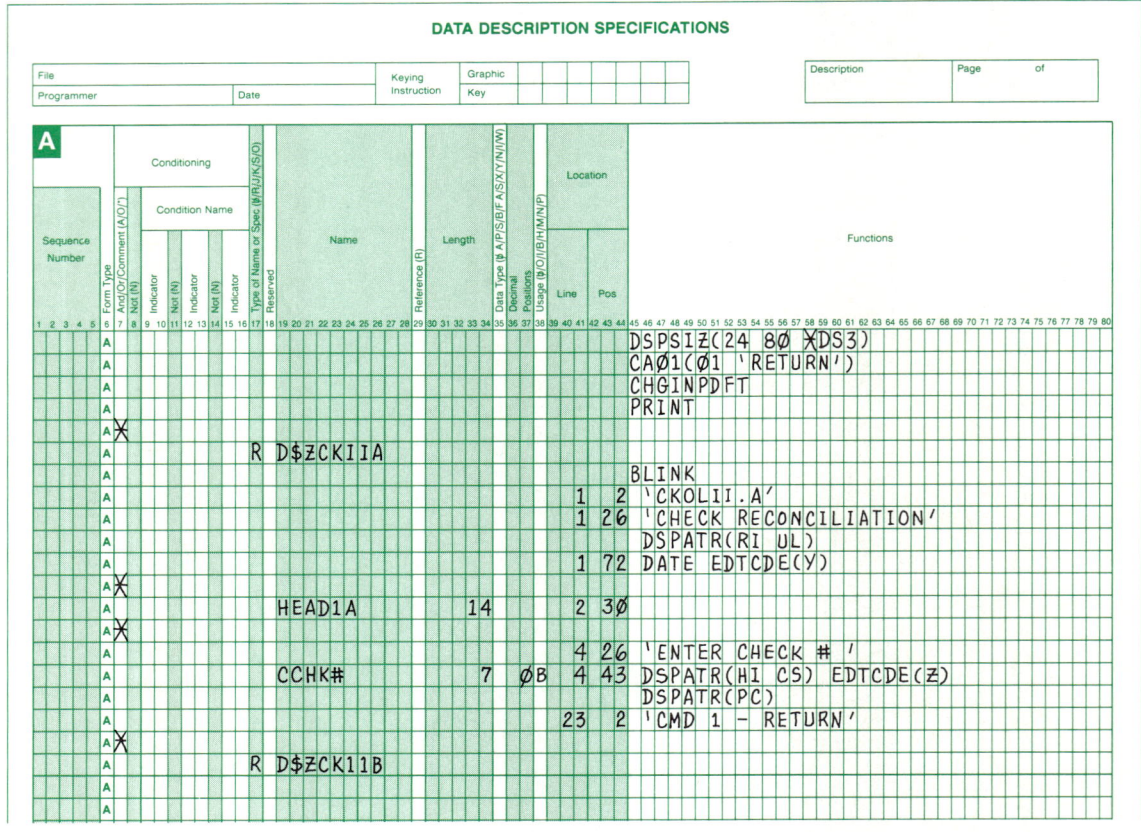

594 RPG II and RPG III Programming

Figure 12.15 continued

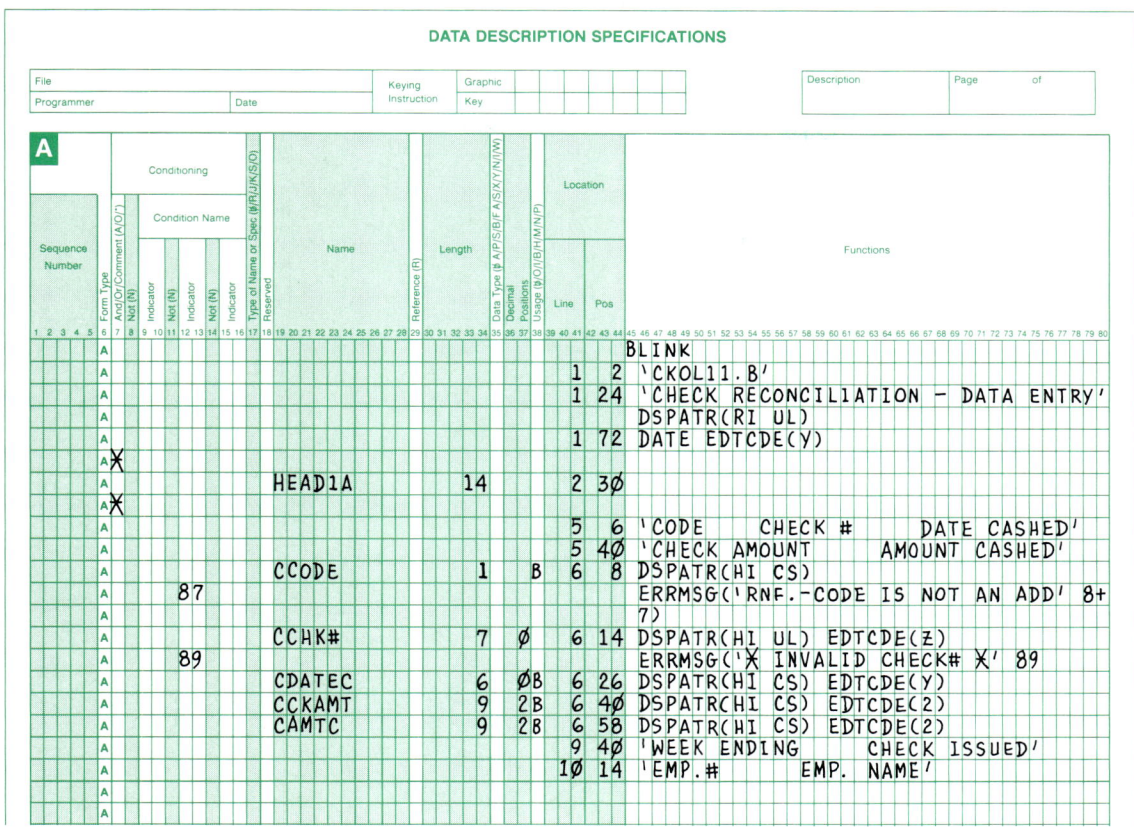

Figure 12.16 Data description specifications D$ZCKMNA

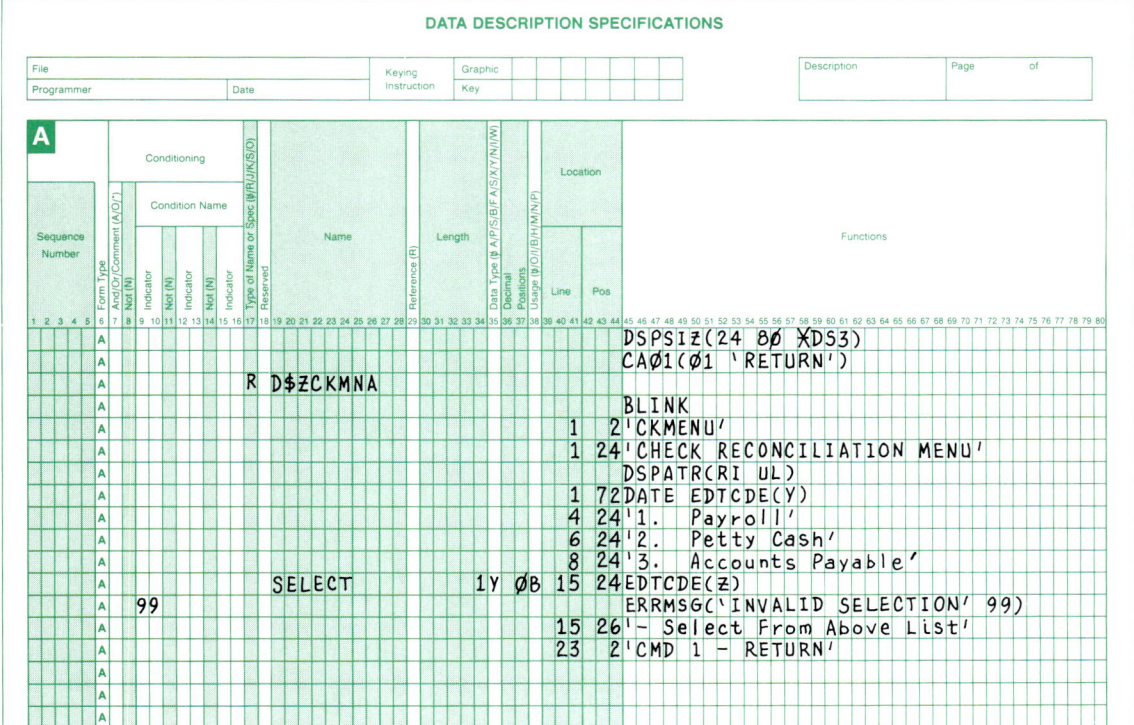

Figure 12.17 CKOL11.SOURCE file specifications

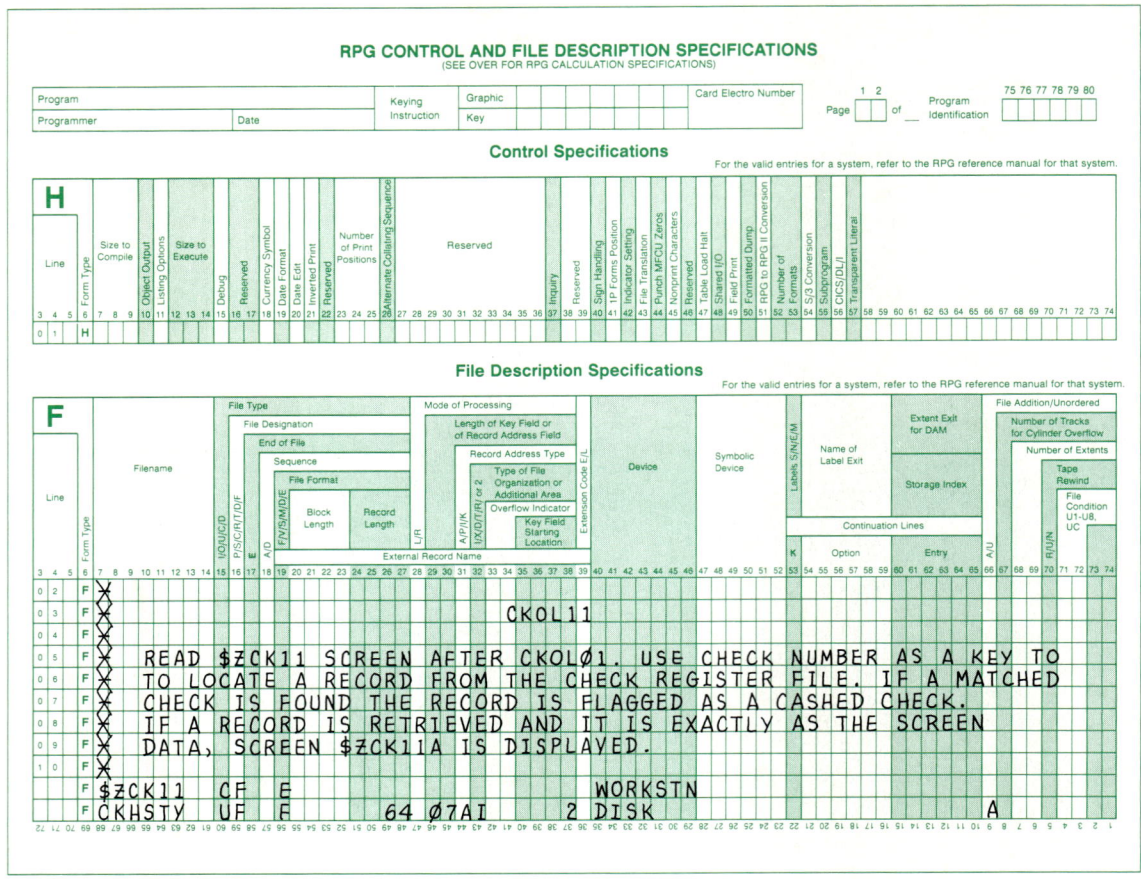

Figure 12.18 CKOL11.SOURCE extension specifications

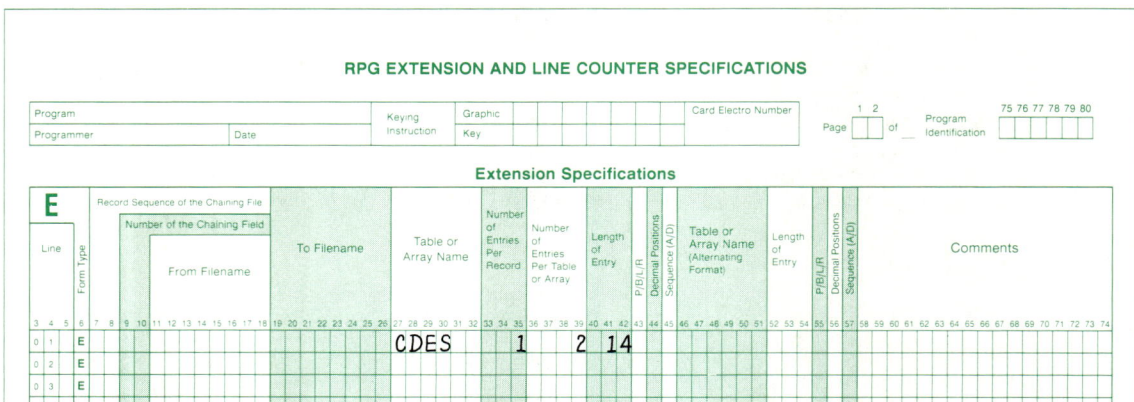

Figure 12.19 CKOL11.SOURCE input specifications

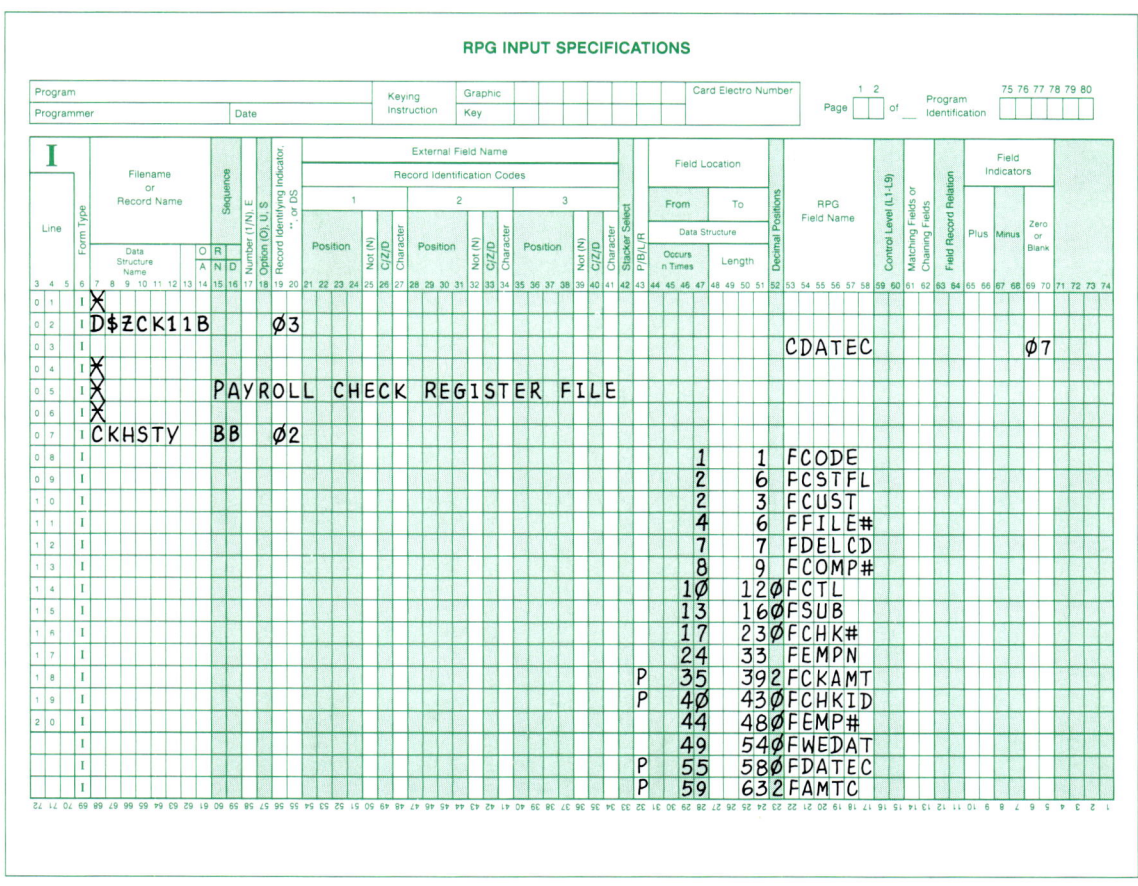

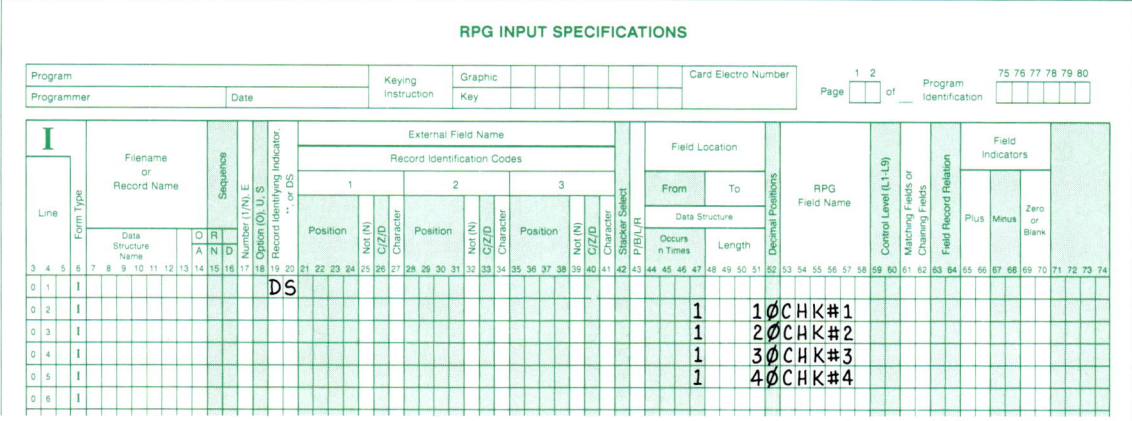

Figure 12.20 CKOL11.SOURCE calculation specifications

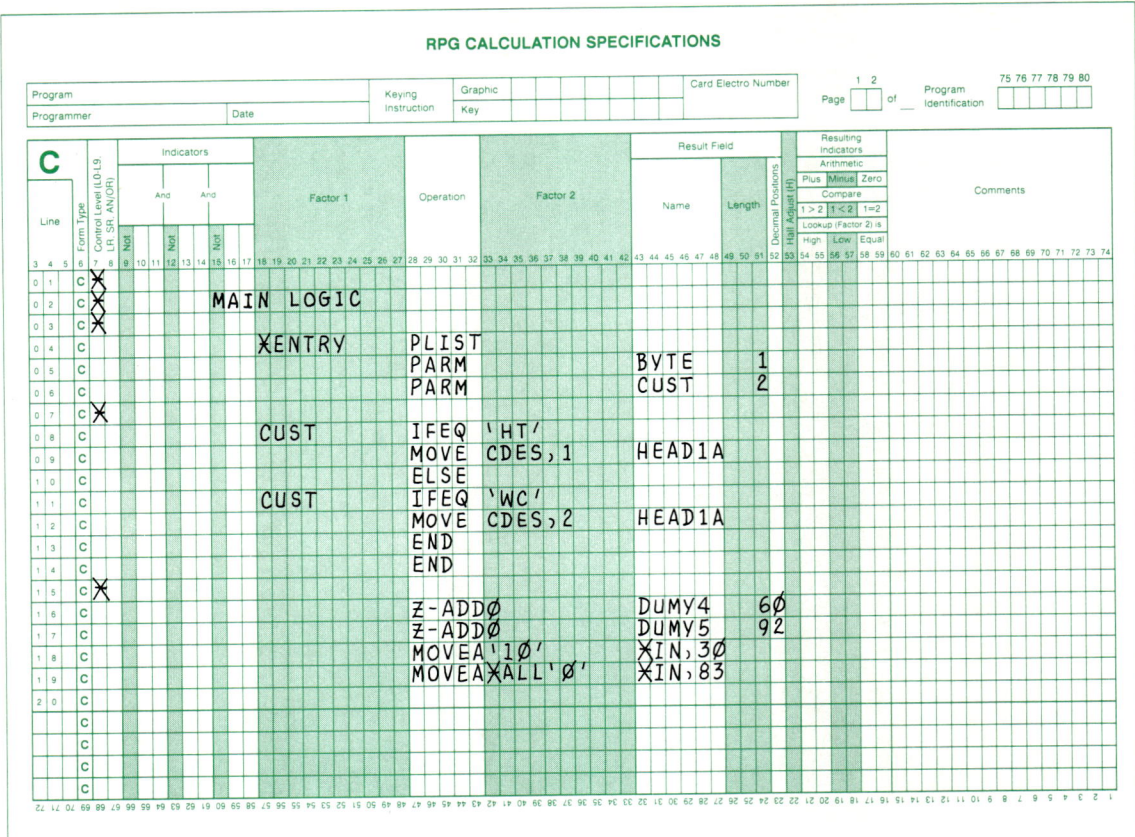
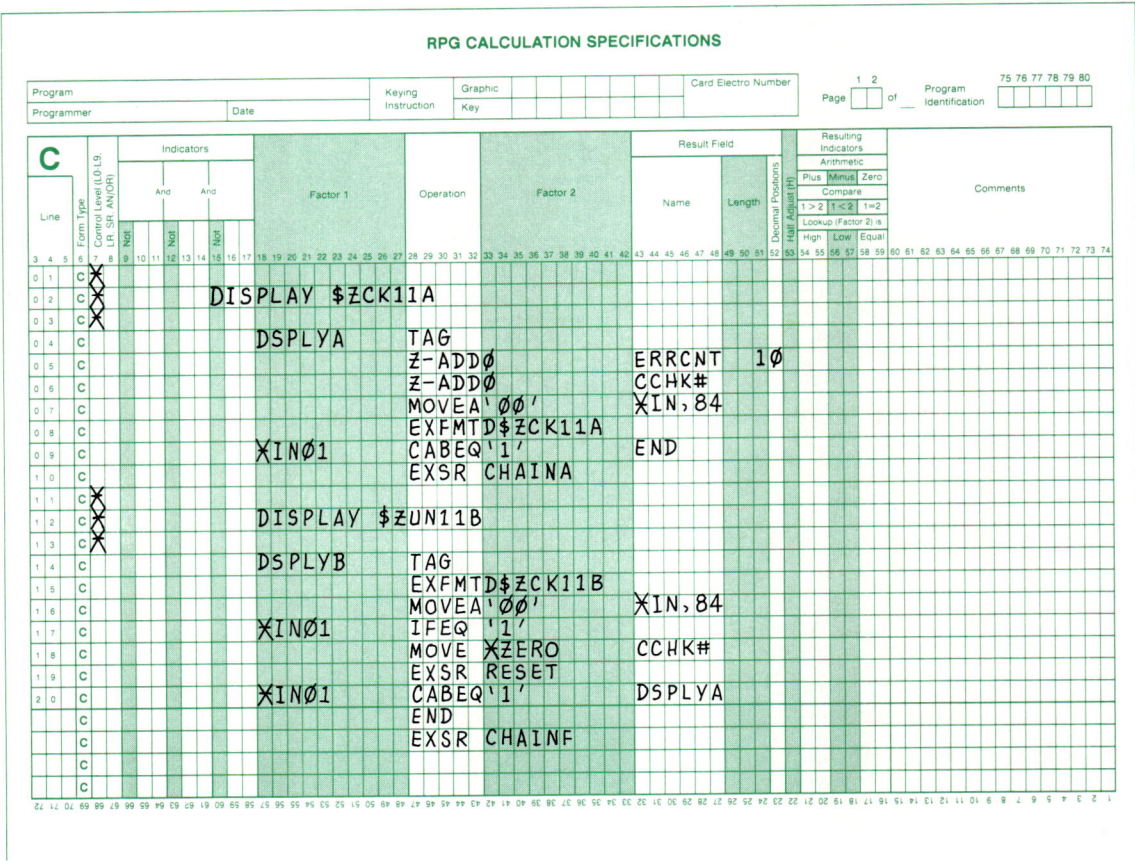

598   RPG II and RPG III Programming

Figure 12.20 continued

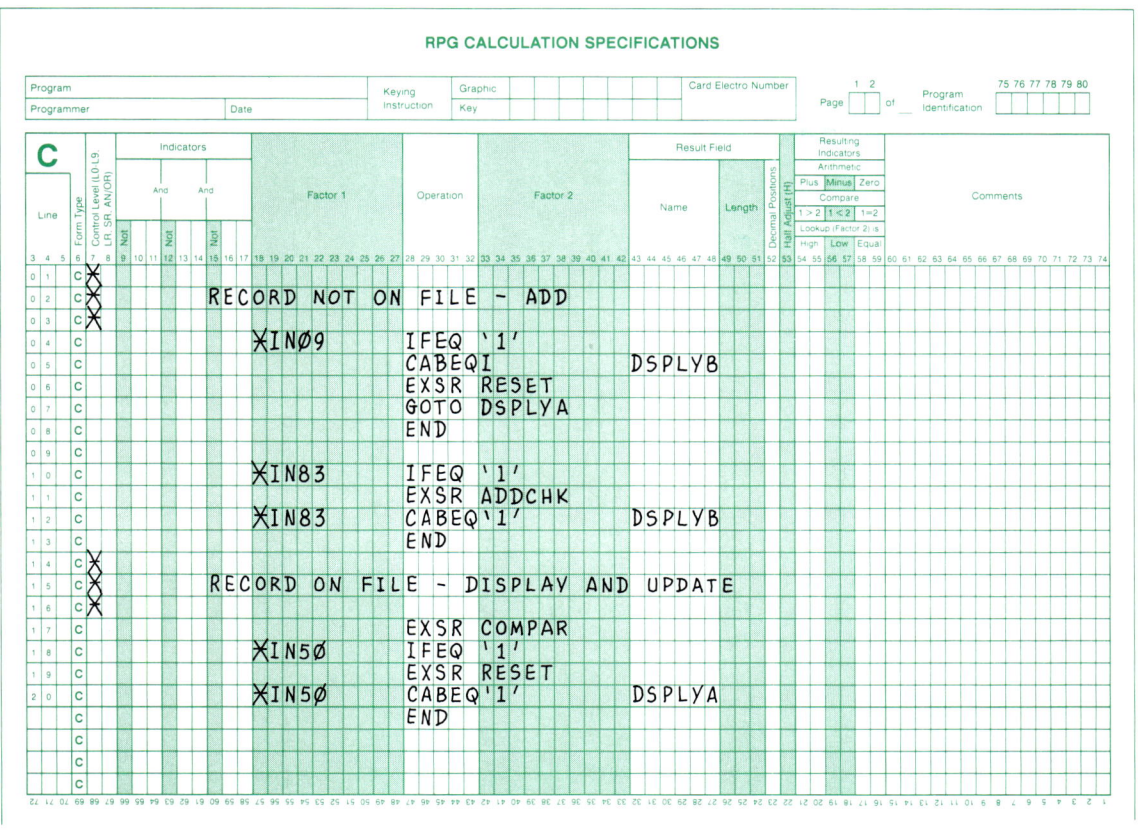

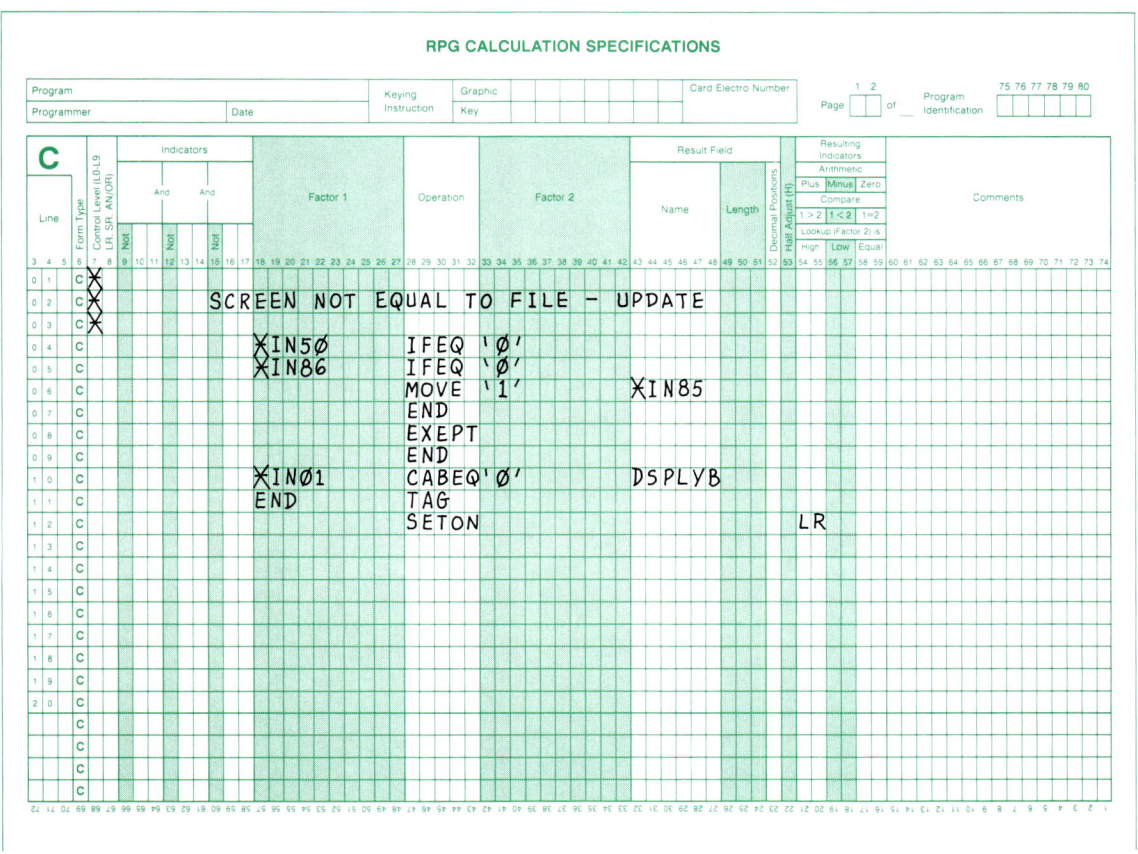

RPG III Features 599

Figure 12.20 continued

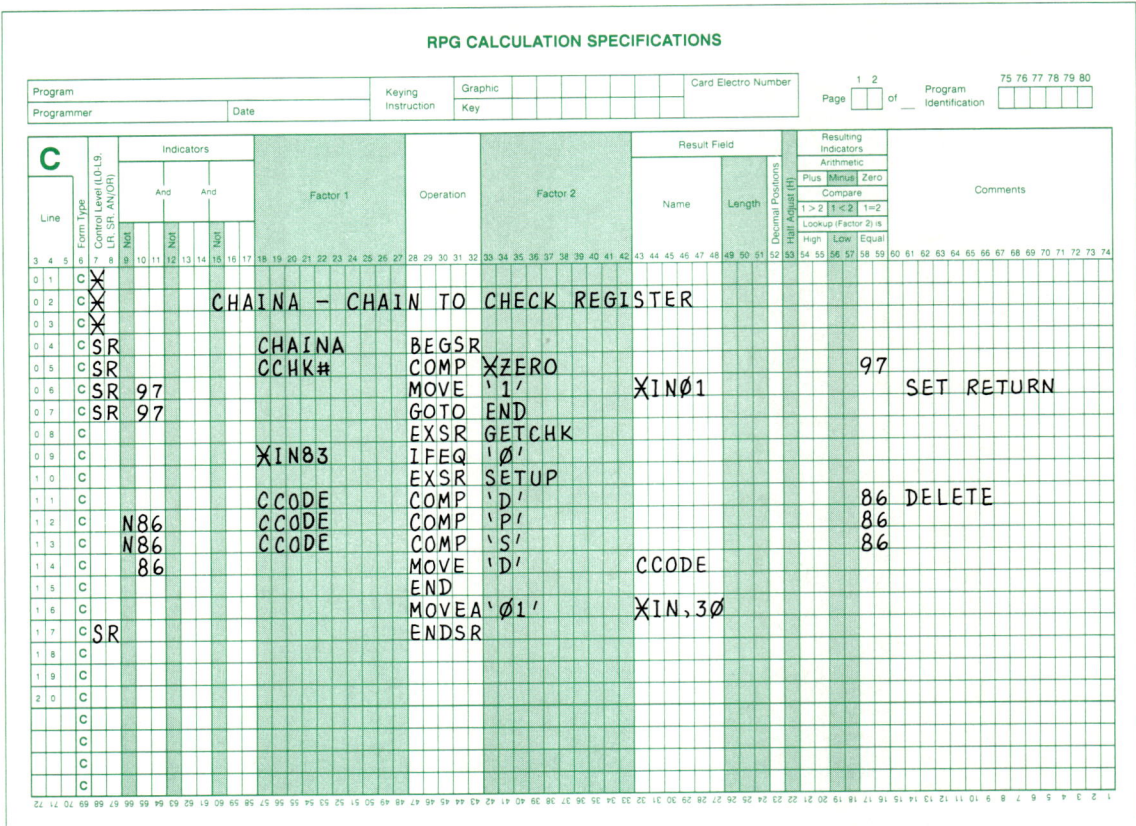

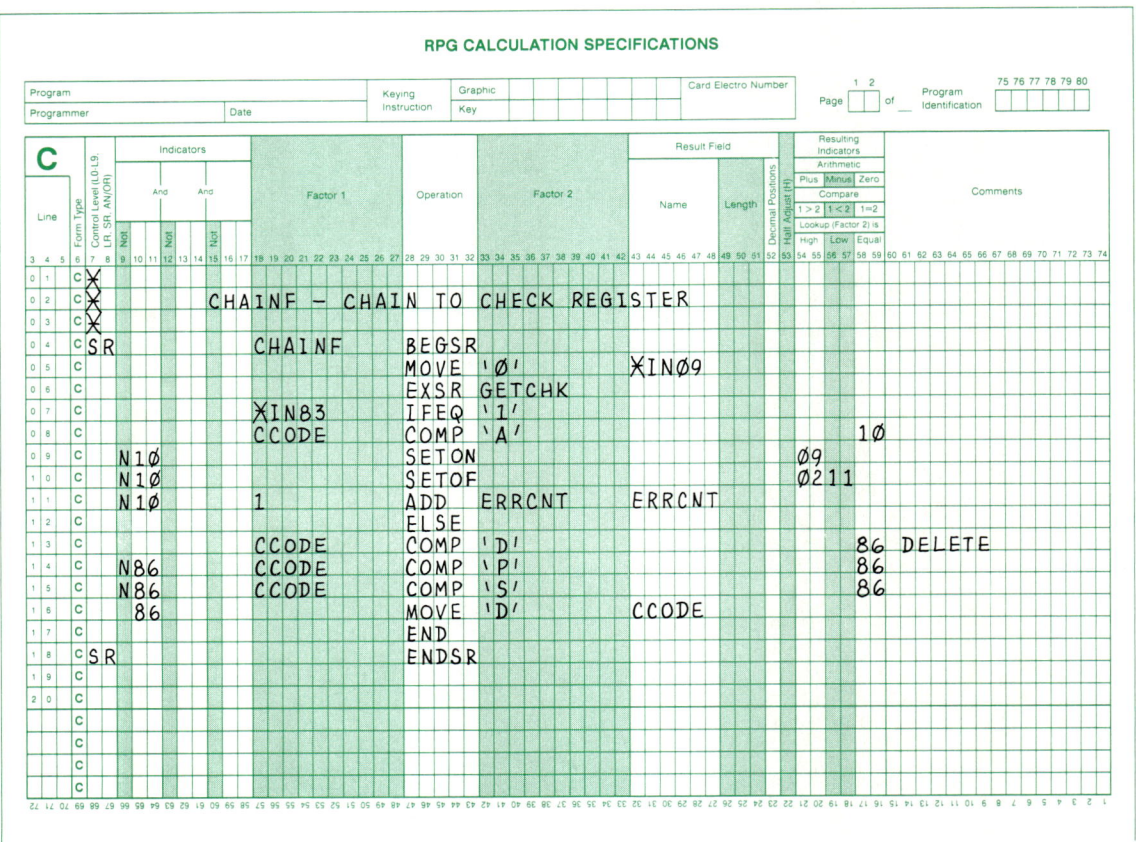

Figure 12.20 continued

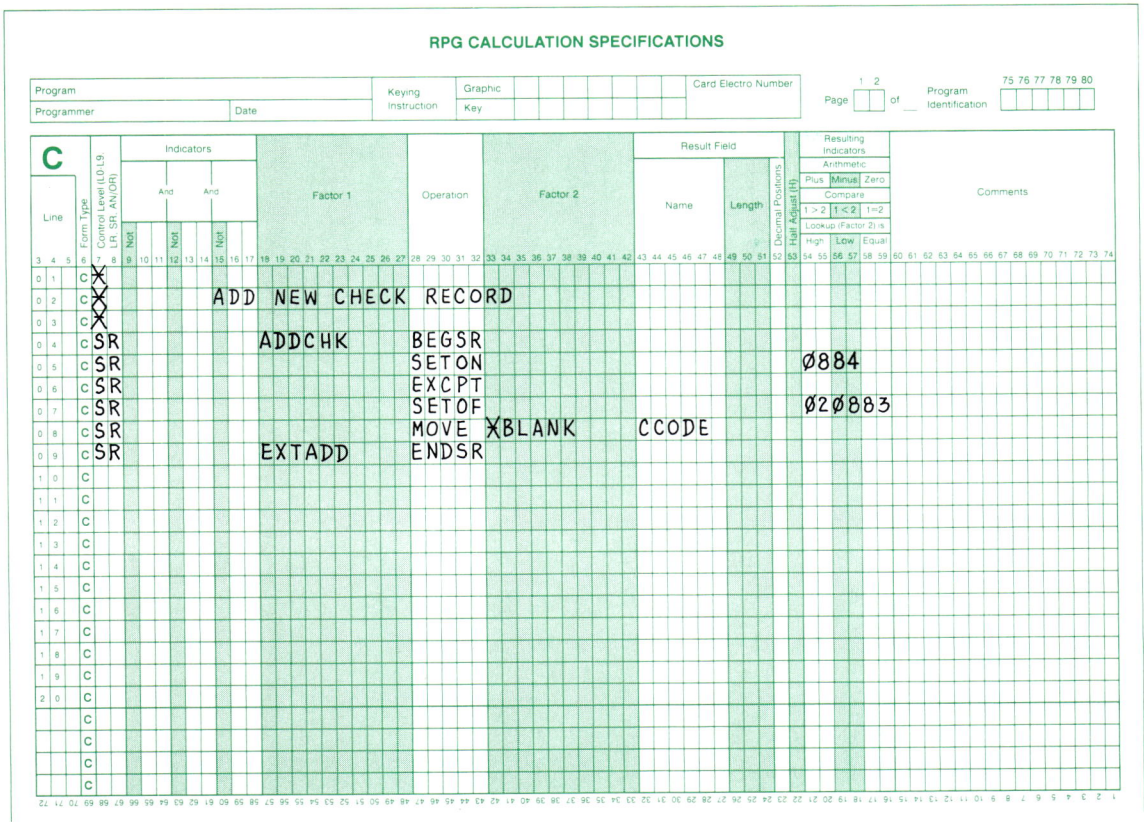

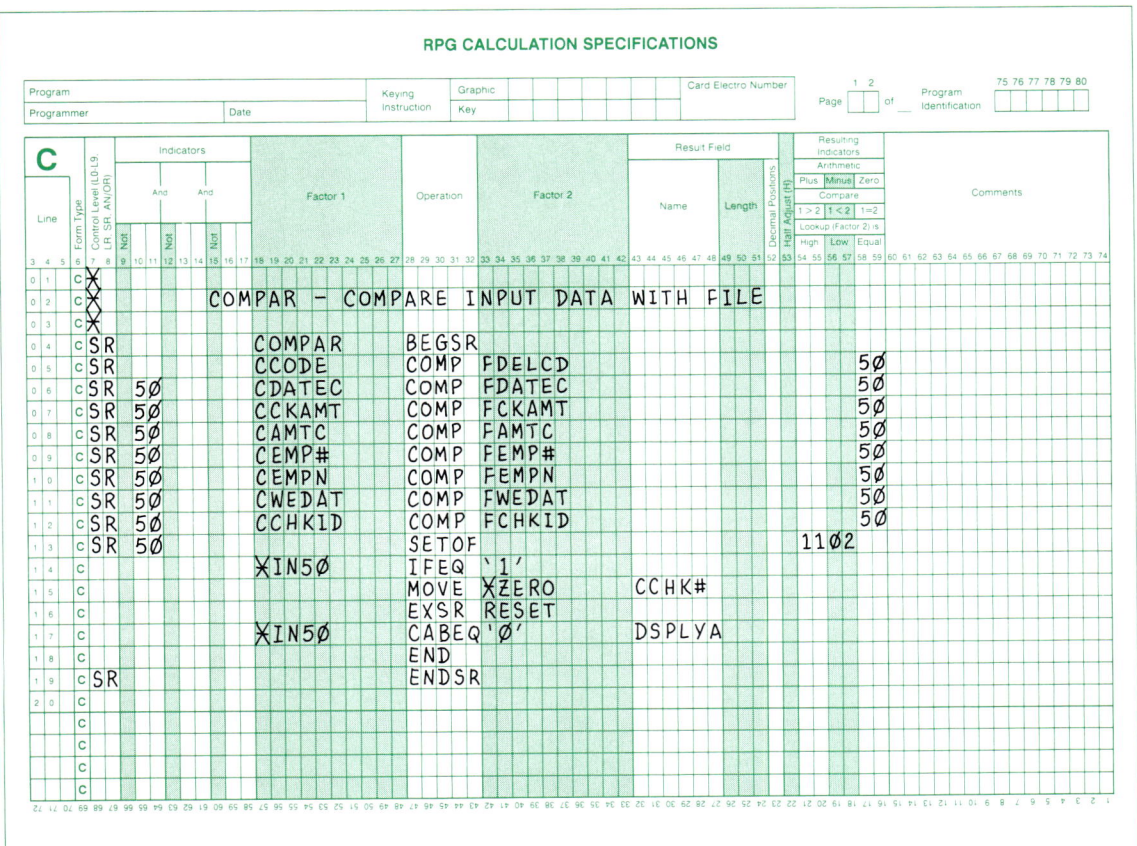

RPG III Features

Figure 12.20 continued

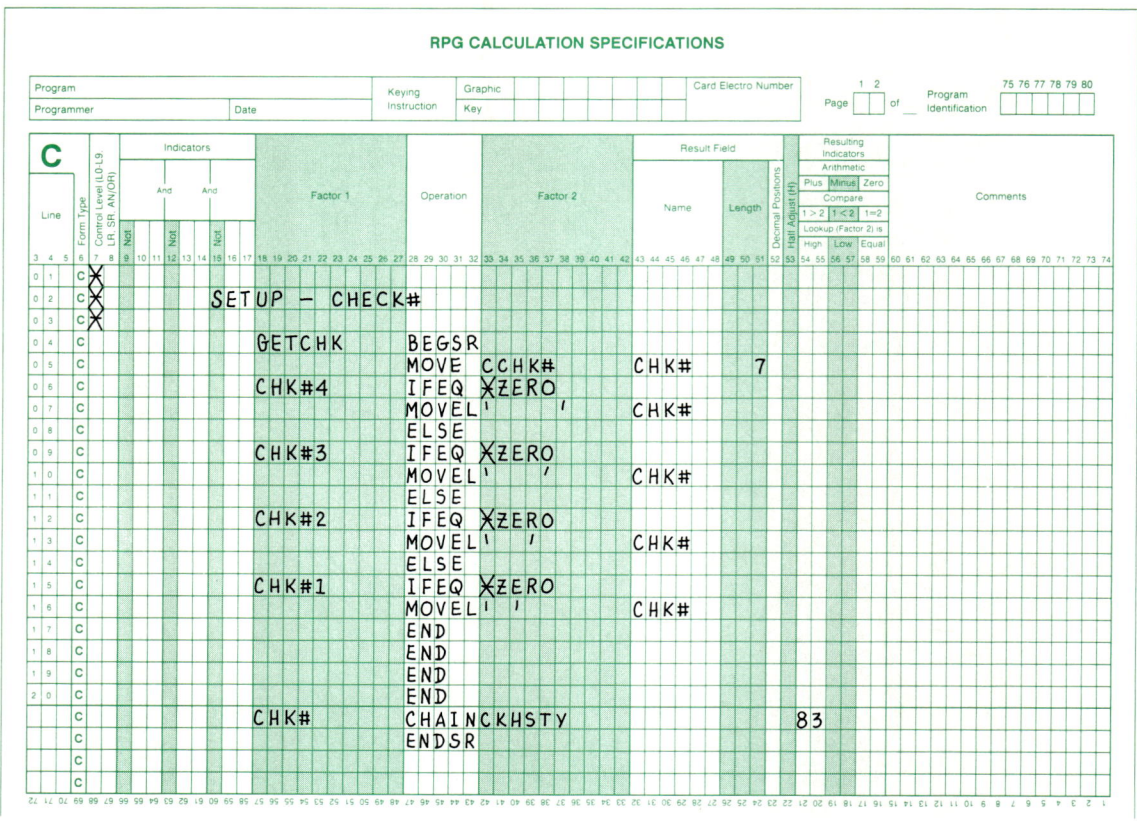

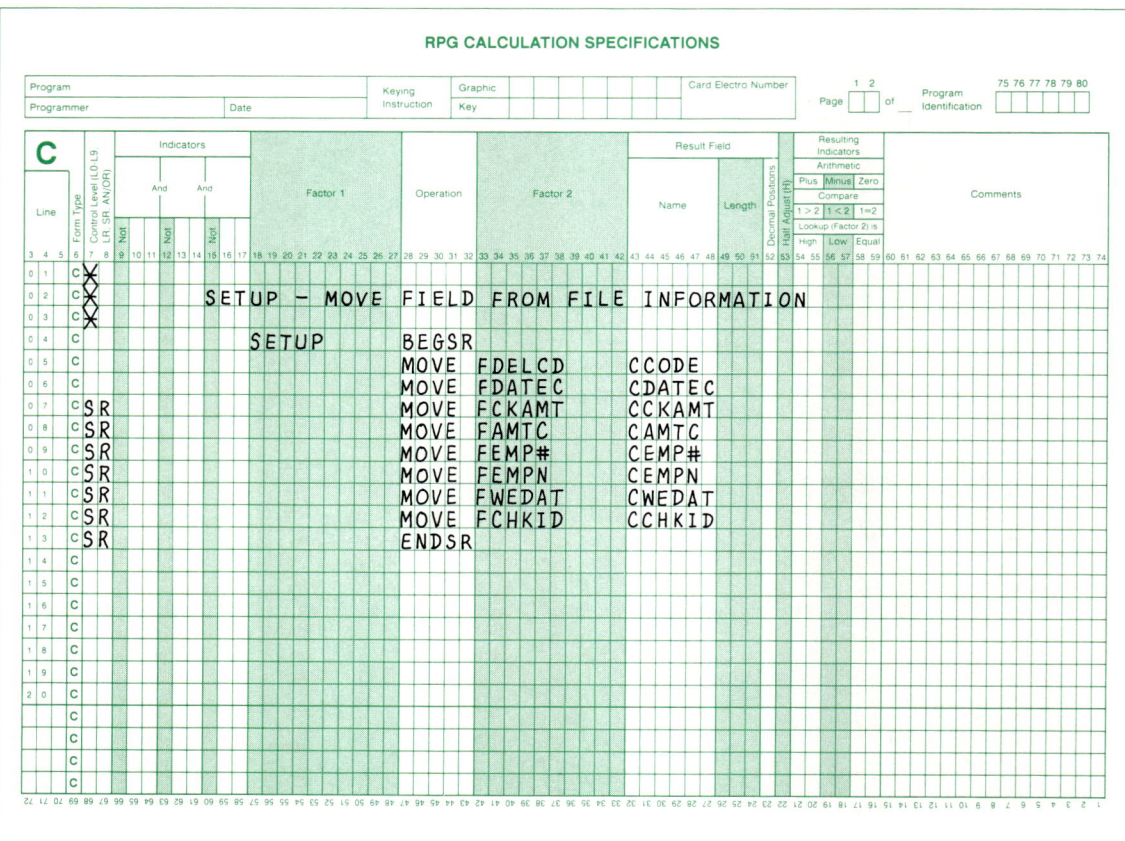

Figure 12.20 continued

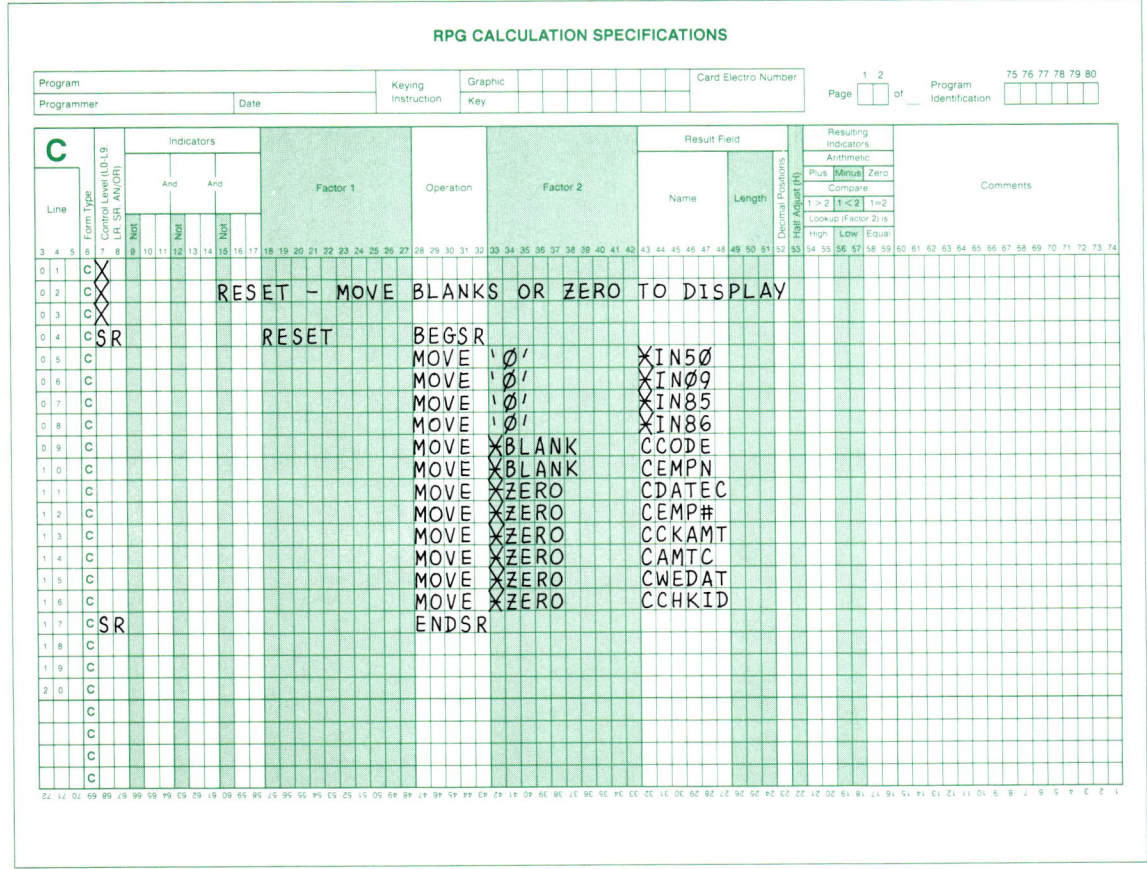

Questions for Review

1. How is another program invoked from within an RPG III program?
2. What methods (operation codes) are provided to pass information from program to program?
3. How do the PARM and PLIST operations interrelate?
4. To what or whom does the RETRN operation apply?
5. What are the implications of dynamic allocation with respect to the data integrity of called/calling programs?
6. What steps need to be taken to ensure consistent results among core-resident programs?
7. What is the purpose of the FREE operation?
8. What is the name of the indicator associated with interprogram communications?
9. On which specification form is a data structure specified?
10. Name two benefits of data structures.
11. How do data structures achieve data redefinition?
12. What are the benefits of the externalization of data structures?
13. How can an internal data structure be differentiated from an external data structure?
14. What is a multiple-occurrence data structure?

15. How might the number of elements in a multiple-occurrence data structure be specified?
16. What is the operation associated with multiple-occurrence data structures?
17. What is the operation associated with multiple-occurrence data structures and how is it used?
18. What is an INFDS?
19. For what are the continuation lines of the file description specification used?
20. What information can be provided by the inclusion of an INFDS?
21. Name three keywords that can be specified in an INFDS.
22. What are the benefits of the CABxx operation?
23. What RPG II operations are supplanted by CABxx?
24. How are CABxx indicators specified?
25. What are the possible interpretations of xx in the instruction CABxx?
26. What are the advantages of shortening the syntax of certain arithmetic operation codes?
27. What new capability is provided by SORTA?
28. What are the advantages to the removal of the requirement to specify *SR* in positions 7–8 of a subroutine?
29. What are the benefits of referencing indicators as data?
30. Describe the format of the three references to indicators as data.
31. How are multiple indicators set on or off using *IN?
32. How is the DEFN operation used?
33. What is meant by a nonexecutable instruction?
34. Name three methods of data redefinition in RPG III.
35. What is a figurative constant?
36. What is the hexadecimal value of *HIVAL?
37. What is the hexadecimal value of *LOVAL?
38. How are relative end-positions specified on fields of a report?
39. What are the contents of the receiving field of a TIME operation?
40. How does PRTCTL affect line spacing?
41. How should PRTCTL be specified to take advantage of the benefits it offers?
42. What is RECNO?
43. How is RECNO used?
44. What is the relation of RECNO to the file specification?
45. What do INFDS, PRTCTL, and PLIST have in common?
46. How has exception time output become more important in RPG III?
47. What is the meaning of EXCPT name?
48. What are the benefits of multiple EXCPT name records?
49. Why might a table file be replaced?
50. What new features have been provided in RPG III compilation?

Appendixes

- **A** DEBUG Function
- **B** Detailed RPG II Object Program Logic
- **C** Reference Tables—RPG II
- **D** The Programmer's Job
- **E** Summary Charts—RPG III
- **F** RPG III Enhancements
- **G** Problems for Term Assignment
- **H** Indexed and Direct Files
- **I** Input Data for Chapter 2-10 Problems
- **J** Input Data for Appendix G Problems

Appendix A

DEBUG Function

A program that you write may not always work perfectly the first time or even the first few times it is run. The reason for this is that the program contains errors—errors that you were not aware you were making when you wrote the program. Some of the errors you make are easy to find; others may be very difficult to find. Nevertheless, they all have to be corrected. But how do you do this? Where do you start?

Just knowing the types of errors that are commonly made can give you a hint as to what you should check. Most of the errors fall into one of the following categories:

1. Incorrect use of RPG entries on the specifications sheets
2. Errors in describing input data or the format of output data
3. Errors in specifying the kind of calculation operations needed to do the job
4. Specifying calculation operations in the wrong sequence

The RPG compiler, when compiling your program, will diagnose the specifications to see if they contain errors. If they do, the compiler will print messages telling you the errors made. In this way, you can find errors made in the specifications.

Using the DEBUG Function

Suppose you have made all correct entries on the sheets and still get the wrong results. What can you do then? You can, of course, check through your work. But this does not always show you where the error(s) lies.

Sometimes the specifications you write will not cause the computer to do what you think they will. It is often possible to miss an error because you assumed that a statement or group of statements needed to perform a certain task worked correctly when, in fact, they did not. For example, you may pass statement 06 believing it to be correct when it is not, and then spend hours looking for errors in statements that are really correct.

It would be helpful to find just how far along in your program everything is working correctly. But how can you find out with what information your program is working at various points in your program?

The RPG language has a special operation code that shows you some of the information the computer is working with. This code is known as the DEBUG code. The code received its name from the slang term *bugs,* a term referring to errors in a program. To debug a program, therefore, is to get all errors out of it. This is what the DEBUG code helps you do.

The DEBUG code will cause a maximum of two different types of records to be printed out showing you

What data are contained in a specified field
What indicators are on

One of the most common errors found in a program is the incorrect use of indicators. Without a thorough understanding of RPG logic, the programmer may condition an operation using an indicator thinking it is on when it really is not. Thus the program does not work properly.

If at any point in your calculations you want to check to see if you are using indicators properly, you can specify DEBUG. This code will cause a record to be put out showing what indicators are on at the point DEBUG is specified. If you wish to know the contents of a field as well as what indicators are on, you can specify that in the DEBUG statement. A second record type will then be put out showing the contents of the field.

Specifications for DEBUG

When using DEBUG, the first specification you must make is on the control card. A *1* in column 15 indicates that DEBUG is going to be used. If this column is left blank, all DEBUG statements will be treated as comments.

Figure A.1 Specifications for DEBUG statement

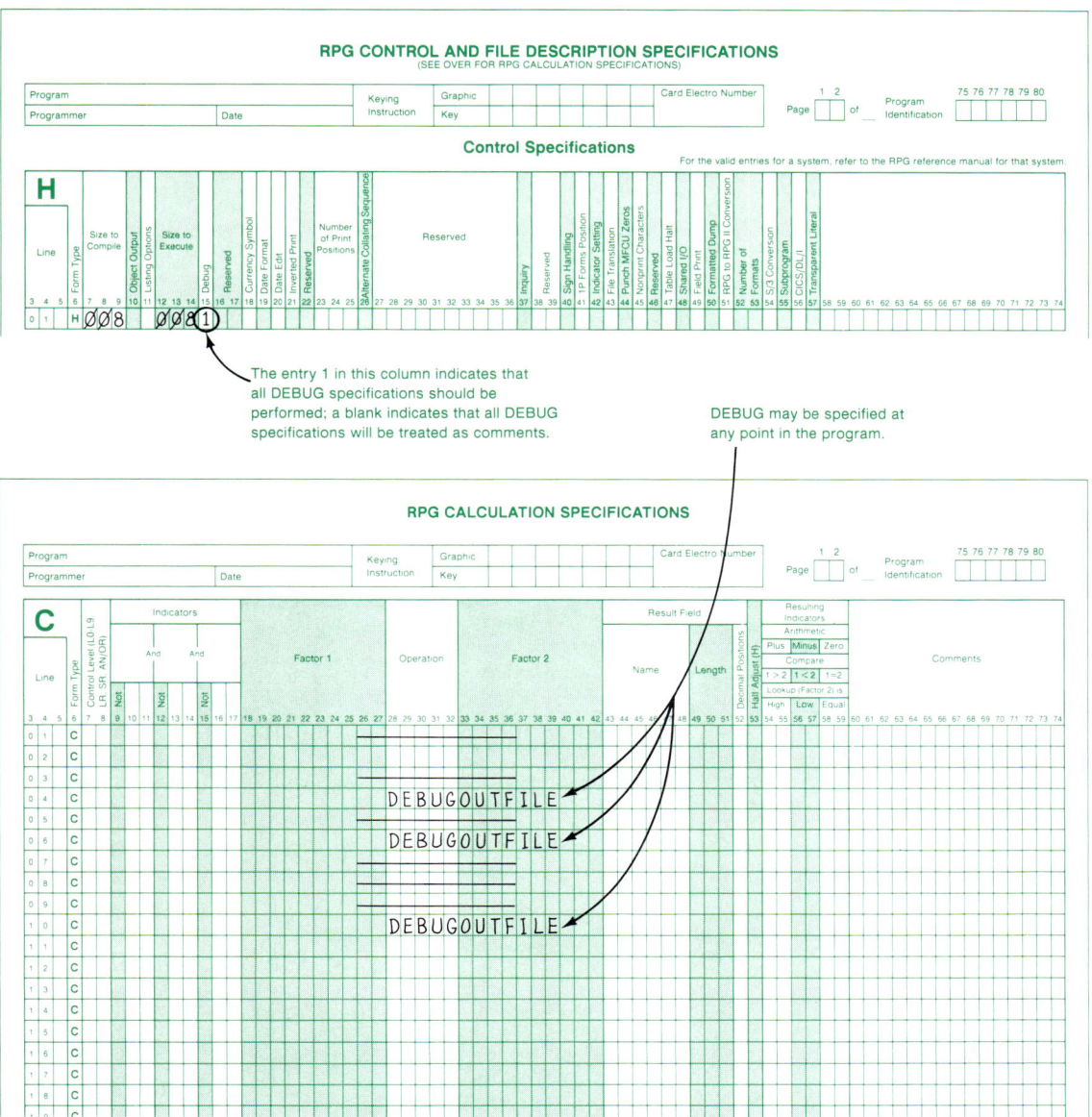

In positions 28–32 (operation) on the calculations sheet, specify the code DEBUG. You may specify it at any point in the calculations and as many times as you want.

For each DEBUG statement, enter in positions 33–42 (factor 2) the name of the file on which DEBUG records will be written. Use the filename previously assigned on the File Description form. The same output file must be used for all DEBUG operations in a program. (See Figure A.1.)

The entries just described will give you a record showing what indicators are on. If you also want to know the contents of a field, you must make another entry—the name of the field whose value you wish to know must be entered as the result field in positions 43–48.

Positions 18–27 (factor 1) are optional. If you have several DEBUG statements, you may wish to know which records were caused by a particular DEBUG statement. You can name the DEBUG statement by entering a literal in positions 18–27. This name will then be included in the records the statement causes to be put out. (See Figure A.2.)

Positions 7–17 may contain any valid conditioning indicator. The external indicators U1–U8 are most often used here. They make the DEBUG statement optional. Through their use you can establish, prior to a run, whether or not you wish to use DEBUG. Positions 53–59 cannot be used for the DEBUG statement.

Appendix A

Figure A.2 Additional entries for DEBUG statement

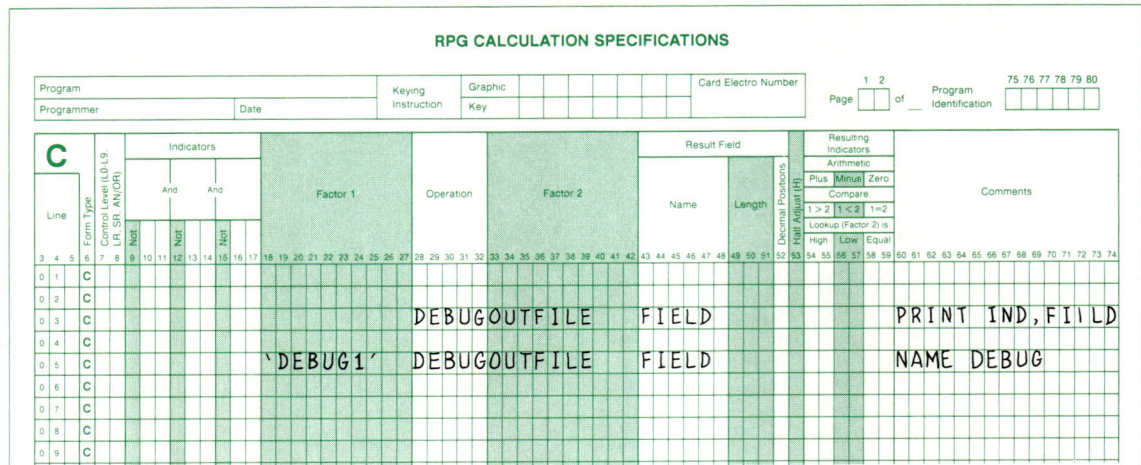

Figure A.3 Printer output format of DEBUG records

Record 1

| DEBUG = DEBUG 1   INDICATORS ON = 20 42 02 11   MR |

Record 2

| FIELD VALUE = 005648219R |

Format of Records Created by DEBUG

Two records may be created by the DEBUG operation. Record 1 is required; record 2 is optional. (See Figure A.3.)

Record 1 will look like this:

Position	Entry
1–8	DEBUG =
9–16	The name entered in factor 1 of the debug statement. These columns will be blank if no entry is found in factor 1.
17–18	Blank
19–33	INDICATORS ON =
34	Blank
35–37	Name of the indicators that are on.
38–40	Each indicator is followed by a blank.
etc.	If a large number of indicators are on, more than one record may be required to show all indicators.

Record 2 will look like this:

1–14	FIELD VALUE =
15–	The contents of the field named as the result field in the debug statement. If the field is rather large, only eighty of the rightmost characters are displayed.

Getting Results from DEBUG

DEBUG will not automatically provide you with the specific reason your program is in error. But by showing the indicator setting and contents of fields at various points, it can give you a clue as to where the error lies. From there you will have to work through the logic of sections in your program to find specific bugs.

Figure A.4 DEBUG statement—example—coding to examine the contents of the field total twice within the detail calculation cycle

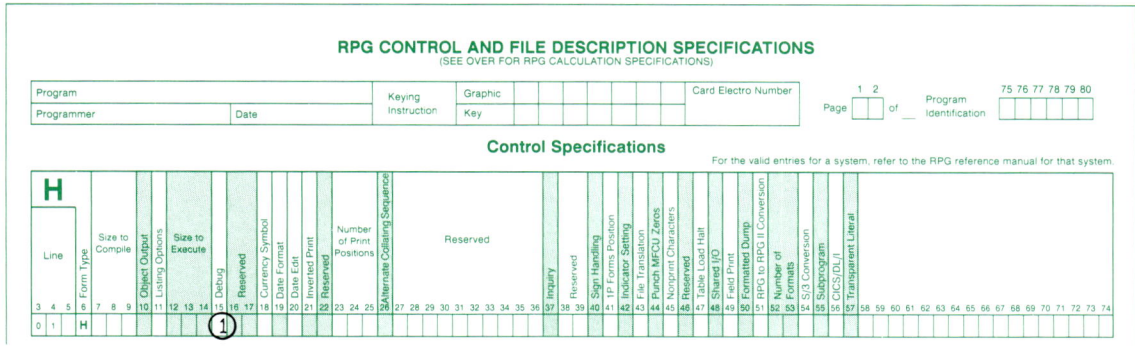

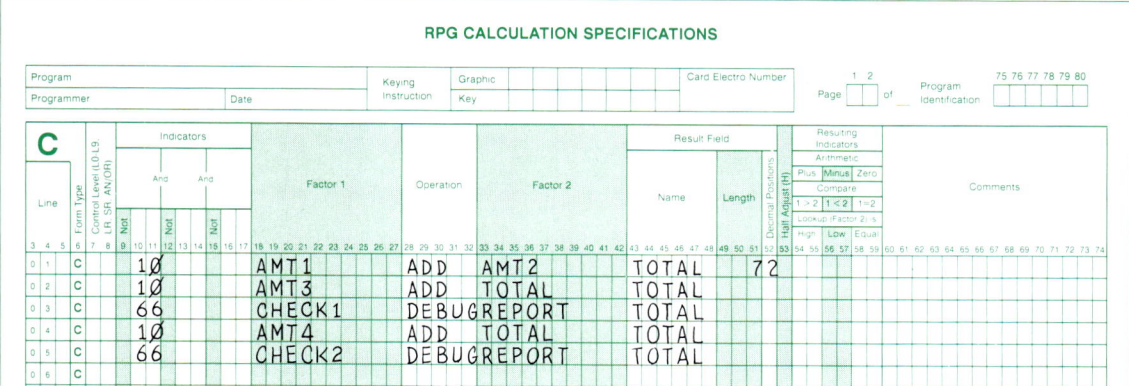

Placement of DEBUG

DEBUG statements can be placed anywhere in the calculations. However, much thought should be given to their position. If they are not placed in proper positions, they may give misleading information and be of no help at all. For example, if you are concerned about the status of an indicator at a certain point in your program, be sure to position DEBUG so that the indicator has no chance to change before it is displayed.

If you want to find if a statement or group of statements is working correctly, you must know what is in the field immediately *before* and *after* the statement(s). This means placing DEBUG before and after the statement(s) you are checking. In order to determine if the results obtained from these statements are correct, you will have to make the same calculations manually and compare the two results. In this case, however, you must make certain your own calculations are correct. Much time can be wasted trying to make the computer arrive at the same wrong answer that you have calculated. (See Figure A.4.)

Making Your Program Work for All Cases

Be certain that you test your program to see that it will correctly handle all possible situations that might arise when doing an actual job. If you test for only one or two situations, you can be sure your program works only for those situations. This means that the data you use to test your program must be *complete* and valid so that it tests all possible situations. In this way, when doing an actual job, you can be sure your program can handle all situations in an actual job without encountering hidden bugs.

Summary—DEBUG Feature

A special feature operation named DEBUG is a part of the RPG language. It is used to help locate program errors during test data runs so that corrections can be made prior to the use of the program

Figure A.5 DEBUG statement—example—testing data before and after loops

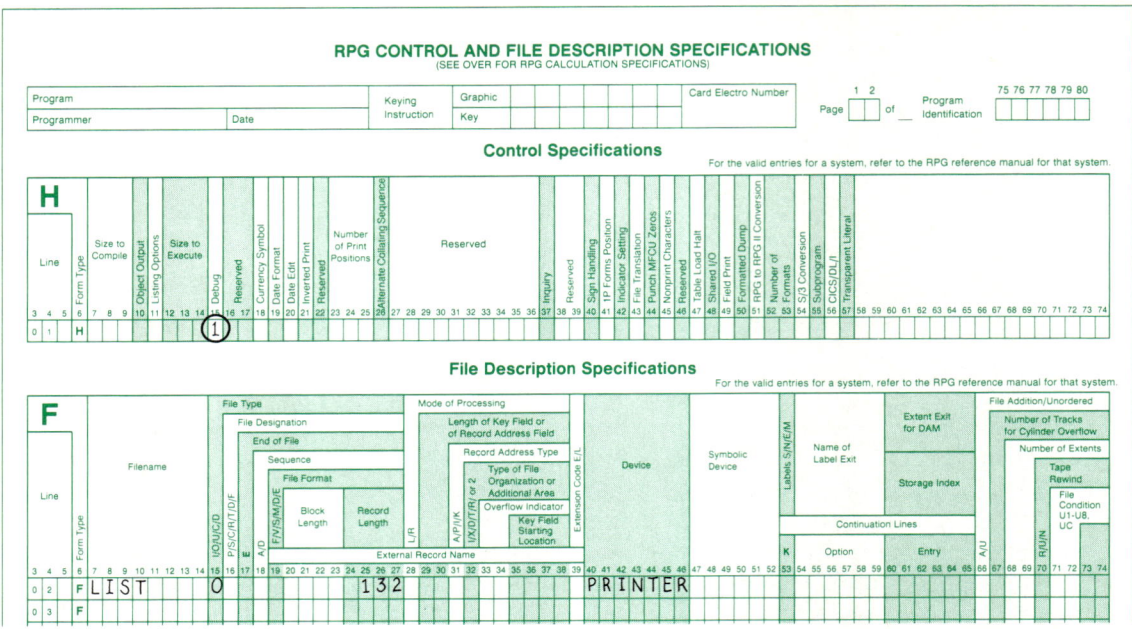

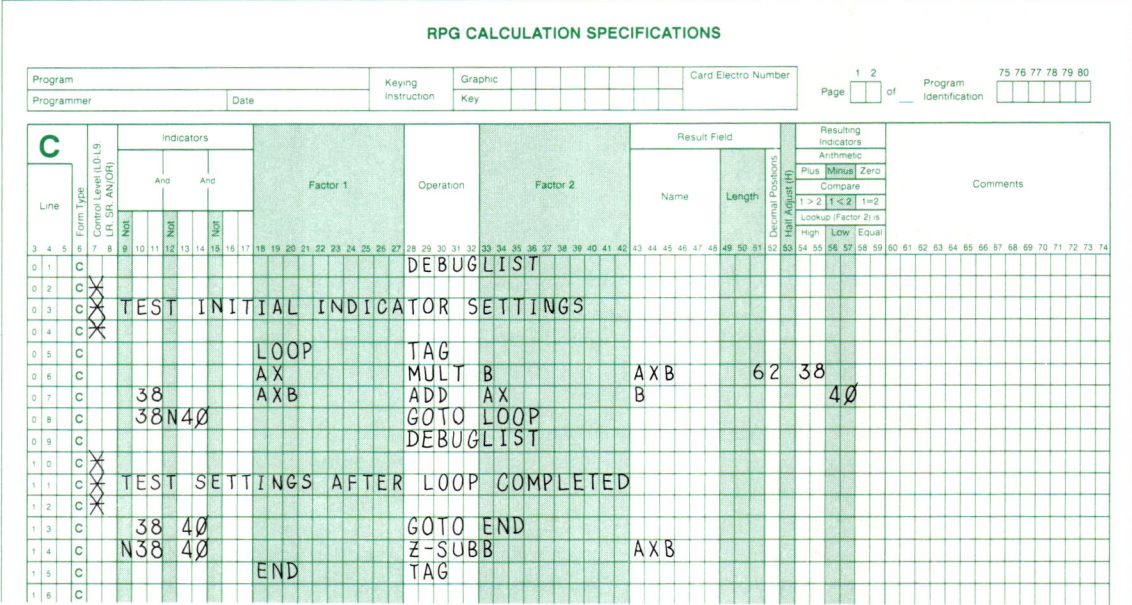

with real data. You can specify its use on any line on a Calculation Specifications form. When encountered, it temporarily stops the data run in order to print a list of all indicators that are on at that time as well as the value stored in any one field, if desired. When this information has been recorded, the test run continues. Any number of DEBUG statements may be included in a program, but they are generally placed at strategic points such as before a GOTO or TAG operand.

Insert the special operation DEBUG for use when running test data to check the accuracy of your program before it is released for general use in your installation. We use it during test runs to verify indicator settings where we suspect that improper coding exists. Since the computer can run at high speed, it is a very nice way to trace data through calculations as opposed to desk checking by hand.

Notice in the example shown that the operation DEBUG must include the filename in factor 2. This directs RPG to write out to the specified file a list of all indicators that are on when the DEBUG operation is encountered during a test run. Every DEBUG statement must refer to the same output file. (See Figure A.5.)

Figure A.6 DEBUG statement—example—identifying printer output and contents of a field

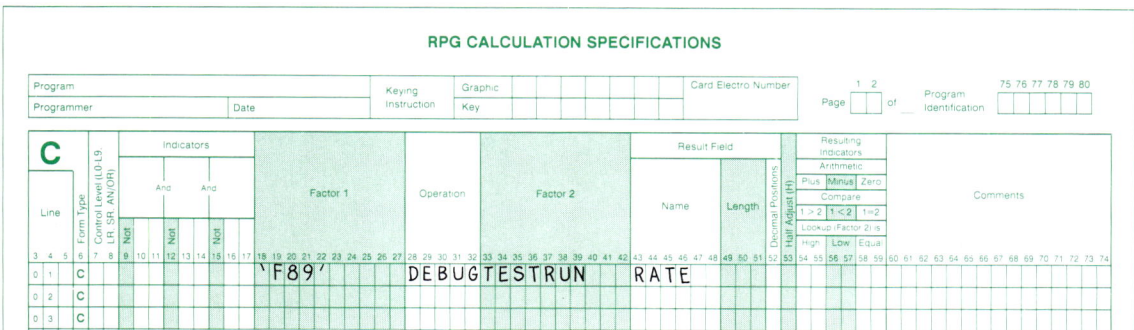

If an alphameric literal is entered in factor 1, that literal will identify the particular DEBUG statement when it is printed. If a field is specified as a result field, the contents of that field will also be printed. So a DEBUG statement could be specified as shown in Figure A.6.

As a result the printed output will be identified by F89 and the contents of the field named RATE will also be printed along with the list of indicators that are on at that time.

To eliminate the use of the DEBUG statements after a successful run, the programmer does not change them. Instead, a special entry in the control card in position 15 is left blank and all DEBUG statements are treated as comments. (See Figure A.7.)

Figure A.7 Sample program using DEBUG statement option

```
•11 TEST PROGRAM   STANDARD DEBUG OPTION      XEROX RPG II C00       11/20/   16:53  PAGE    1

  1            H*TITLE  •11 TEST PROGRAM  STANDARD DEBUG OPTION
  2     S      H            1
  3         02 FDUMMYIN IPEAF   80   80          READER SYS105
  4         03 FD11TEST O       F00800080         PRINTER
  5     S   01 IDUMMYIN AA   01
  6     S      C L0           START         TAG
  7         01 C L0           CTR           ADD   1         CTR       30
  8         02 C L0           CTR           COMP  10                        02
  9         03 C L0      N02                EXCPT
 10         04 C L0      N02CTR             ADD   TOTCTR    TOTCTR    30
 11     S      C L0           'DBGTST'      DEBUGD11TEST    TOTCTR
 12     S      C L0      N02                GOTO  START
 13         01 OD11TEST H  2         1P
 14     S       O                                 27 'TEST RELEASE MASTER,'
 15         03 O                                  48 'ADD NUMBERS 1-10 AND'
 16         04 O                                  60 'PRINT TOTAL'
 17         05 O                      UDATE  Y    70
 18         06 O                                  75 'PAGE'
 19         07 O                      PAGE   Z    79
 20         08 O        E  1
 21         09 O                      CTR    Z    20
 22         10 O        T  1     LR
 23         11 O                                  17 'TOTAL= '
 24         12 O                      TOTCTRZ     20

CALLED SUBPROGRAMS
    RIRAD         RIRCPA        RIDEBUG       RIRTIND       RIROAN        RIROEW        RIRPPT        RIROFS
    RIGXPO        RIRPRT        RIRIPG

INDICATORS
    1P   01EA     H0   01EB     L0   01F5     L1   01F6     L2   01F7     L3   01F8     L4   01F9     L5   01FA
    L6   01FB     L7   01FC     L8   01FD     L9   01FE     LR   01FF     01   0211     02   0212

FILE CONTROL BLOCKS




             •11 TEST PROGRAM   STANDARD DEBUG OPTION      XEROX RPG II C00       11/20/   16:53  PAGE    2

    DUMMYIN  007C      D11TEST  009E
FIELDS
    PAGE     01CE     PAGE1    01D1     PAGE2    01D4     UDATE    01D7     UDAY     01DB     UMONTH   01DD
    UYEAR    01DF     *ERROR   01E1     CTR      01E3     TOTCTR   01E6

PROGRAM LENGTH   02E9

NO ERRORS
```

Appendix A

Figure A.7 continued

```
       LOC       NAME     CROSS REFERENCE          XEROX RPG II C00        11/20/      16:53   PAGE    3
       X'01FF'   LR         22
       X'01F5'   L0          6        7        8         9        10         11        12
       X'0211'   01          5
       X'0212'   02          8        9       10        12
       X'01EA'   1P         13
       X'01E3'   CTR         7        7        8        10        21
       X'007C'   DUMMYIN     3        5
       X'009E'   D11TEST     4       11       13
       X'01CE'   PAGE       19
       X'00D3'   START       6       12
       X'01E6'   TOTCTR     10       10       11        24
       X'01D7'   UDATE      17

ET.000.13

  @LOAD
  @ROOT ,,GO
  @END
```

```
            TEST RELEASE MASTER, ADD NUMBERS 1-10 AND PRINT TOTAL  11/20/    PAGE   1
                         1
DEBUG.  0C11   DBGTST      INDICATORS ON=  L0  L1  L2  L3  L4  L5  L6  L7  L8  L9
                                           LR
FIELD VALUE = 001
                         2
DEBUG.  0C11   DBGTST      INDICATORS ON=  L0  L1  L2  L3  L4  L5  L6  L7  L8  L9
                                           LR
FIELD VALUE = 003
                         3
DEBUG.  0011   DBGTST      INDICATORS ON=  L0  L1  L2  L3  L4  L5  L6  L7  L8  L9
                                           LR
FIELD VALUE = 006
                         4
DEBUG.  0011   DBGTST      INDICATORS ON=  L0  L1  L2  L3  L4  L5  L6  L7  L8  L9
                                           LR
FIELD VALUE = 010
                         5
DEBUG.  0C11   DBGTST      INDICATORS ON=  L0  L1  L2  L3  L4  L5  L6  L7  L8  L9
                                           LR
FIELD VALUE = 015
                         6
DEBUG.  0C11   DBGTST      INDICATORS ON=  L0  L1  L2  L3  L4  L5  L6  L7  L8  L9
                                           LR
FIELD VALUE = 021
                         7
DEBUG.  0011   DBGTST      INDICATORS ON=  L0  L1  L2  L3  L4  L5  L6  L7  L8  L9
                                           LR
FIELD VALUE = 028
                         8
DEBUG.  0011   DBGTST      INDICATORS ON=  L0  L1  L2  L3  L4  L5  L6  L7  L8  L9
                                           LR
FIELD VALUE = 036
                         9
DEBUG.  0011   DBGTST      INDICATORS ON=  L0  L1  L2  L3  L4  L5  L6  L7  L8  L9
                                           LR
FIELD VALUE = 045
                        10
DEBUG.  0011   DBGTST      INDICATORS ON=  L0  L1  L2  L3  L4  L5  L6  L7  L8  L9
                                           LR
FIELD VALUE = 055
DEBUG.  0011   DBGTST      INDICATORS ON=  L0  L1  L2  L3  L4  L5  L6  L7  L8  L9
                                           LR  02
FIELD VALUE = 055
           TOTAL= 55

ET.000.45
```

Appendix B

Detailed RPG II Object Program Logic

Detailed RPG II Object Program Logic—Explanatory Notes

For each record that is processed, the RPG II object program goes through the same general cycle of operations. After a record is read, there are two different instances when calculation operations are performed and records are written out. These instances in time are called total time and detail time. During total time, all total calculation operations (those conditioned by control level indicators in positions 7–8 of the Calculation Specifications form) and all total output operations (those conditioned by control level indicators) are done. During detail time, all detail calculation operations (those not conditioned by control level indicators in positions 7–8) and all detail operations are done. Total time includes steps 18 and 19 of the RPG II object program cycle; detail time includes steps 25 and 3 of the cycle.

Total calculations are performed before the information on the record selected for processing is made available. Detail calculations are performed after the information on the selected records is available. The following discussion describes this concept in more detail.

Whenever a record is read, a check is made to determine if the information in a control field (when one has been specified) is different from the control field information on the previous record. A change in the control field information indicates that all records from a particular control group have been read and that a new group is starting. When all records from a group have been read (indicated by control level indicators being turned on), operations may be done using information accumulated from all records in that group. At this time, all calculations conditioned by control level indicators in positions 7–8 are done. Total output operations are performed immediately after all total calculation operations are completed. Remember that information on the record being read at the beginning of the program cycle is not used in these operations; only information from records in the previous control group is used.

Detail calculations (all calculations not conditioned by control level indicators in positions 7–8) occur after the information on the selected record has been made available. Detail calculations are used to calculate values needed each time a record is processed. They are also used to calculate totals for the current control group (if control fields are specified). Immediately after detail calculation operations are completed, detail output operations are performed.

The specific steps taken in the program cycle are shown in the flowchart. The item numbers in the following description refer to the numbers in the figure. A program cycle begins with step 3 and continues through step 25. (See Figure B.1.)

1. All data files to be used by the RPG II object program are opened (prepared to be processed) by the object program. Preexecution time tables and arrays are loaded before the first program cycle.

2. The object program performs all output conditioned by the 1P indicator. This output is performed only once per job and does not fall within the program cycle (steps 3–25).

3. The object program performs all specified heading and detail output operations whose conditions are satisfied. This includes specifications that are conditioned by the overflow indicator if the overflow routine has been fetched.

4. The object program performs a test to determine if the overflow line was encountered during detail calculations in the previous cycle or when heading and detail records were written in the current cycle. If it was, the overflow indicator turns on. Otherwise the indicator turns off unless the overflow routine was fetched in step 3.

5. The object program tests the halt indicators. If the halt indicators are off, the program branches to step 6.
    a. The execution of the program is stopped once for each halt indicator that is on. The operator selects one of three options: continue, controlled cancel, or immediate cancel.
    b. If the operator desires to continue the job, the program returns to step 5 to test for other halt indicators. If the operator selects one of the cancel options, a branch is taken to step 34.

6. All record identifying indicators and indicators 1P, L1–L9, and H1–H9 are turned off.

7. The program tests to see if the LR indicator is on. If it is, the program branches to step 26.

8. The program reads (and translates, if necessary) the next input record. At the beginning of processing, one record from each input file (except forced files and demand files) is read. If the file has look ahead fields, it is read only on the first cycle. After that, records with look ahead fields only are identified.

9. The program performs a test to determine if the record is an end-of-file record. If an end-of-file condition has occurred, the program branches to step 11.

10. If an end-of-file has not occurred, the program performs a test to determine if the input records are in the sequence specified for them on the Input Specifications form. If the sequence is incorrect, the program branches to step 32.

11. If end-of-job conditions have been met, a branch is taken to step 26. All files for which an *E* has been specified in position 17 of the File Description form must be at end-of-file.

12. When multiple input files are used, it is necessary to select the next record to process. A branch to step 27 is made.

13. If there is only one input file, no record selection is needed. A test is made to determine if sequence checking has been requested. If so, a branch is taken to step 30.

14. The record identifying indicator specified for the current record type turns on. Data from the current record type are not available for processing until step 24.

15. If the record contains control fields, the object program performs a test to determine if a control break has occurred (the contents of the control fields are not equal to the contents of a previously stored field). If a control break has not occurred or control fields are not specified, the program branches to step 17.

16. If a control break has occurred, the control level indicator reflecting the condition is turned on. All lower-level indicators are turned on also.

17. If this is the first program cycle, the program bypasses all total calculations and output operations and branches to step 20.

18. All calculations conditioned by control level indicators (positions 7–8 of the Calculation Specifications form) are performed and resulting indicators are turned on or off as specified. If the LR indicator is on, calculations conditioned by LR are done after other total calculations. File translation, if specified, is done for exception output, chain, and read operations. Fetch overflow is performed if it is required by exception output. If the overflow line has been reached because of exception output, the overflow indicator is turned on.

19. All total output that is not conditioned by an overflow indicator is performed. The program performs a test to determine if an overflow condition has occurred. If an overflow condition has occurred at any time during this cycle, the overflow indicator turns on. If the LR indicator is on, output conditioned by LR is done after other total output. File translation, if specified, is done for total output. Fetch overflow is performed if required.

20. The program performs a test to determine if the last record indicator (LR) is on. If the indicator is on, the program branches to step 37.

21. The program performs a test to determine if any overflow indicators are on. If no overflow indicators are on, the program branches to step 23.

22. All output operations conditioned by a positive (no *N* preceding the indicator) overflow indicator are performed. File translation, if specified, is done for overflow output.

23. The MR indicator turns on if this is a multifile job and the record to be processed is a matching record. Otherwise, the MR indicator turns off.

24. Field indicators are turned on or off as specified. Data from the last record read and from specified look ahead fields are made available for processing.

Figure B.1 Detailed RPG II object program logic

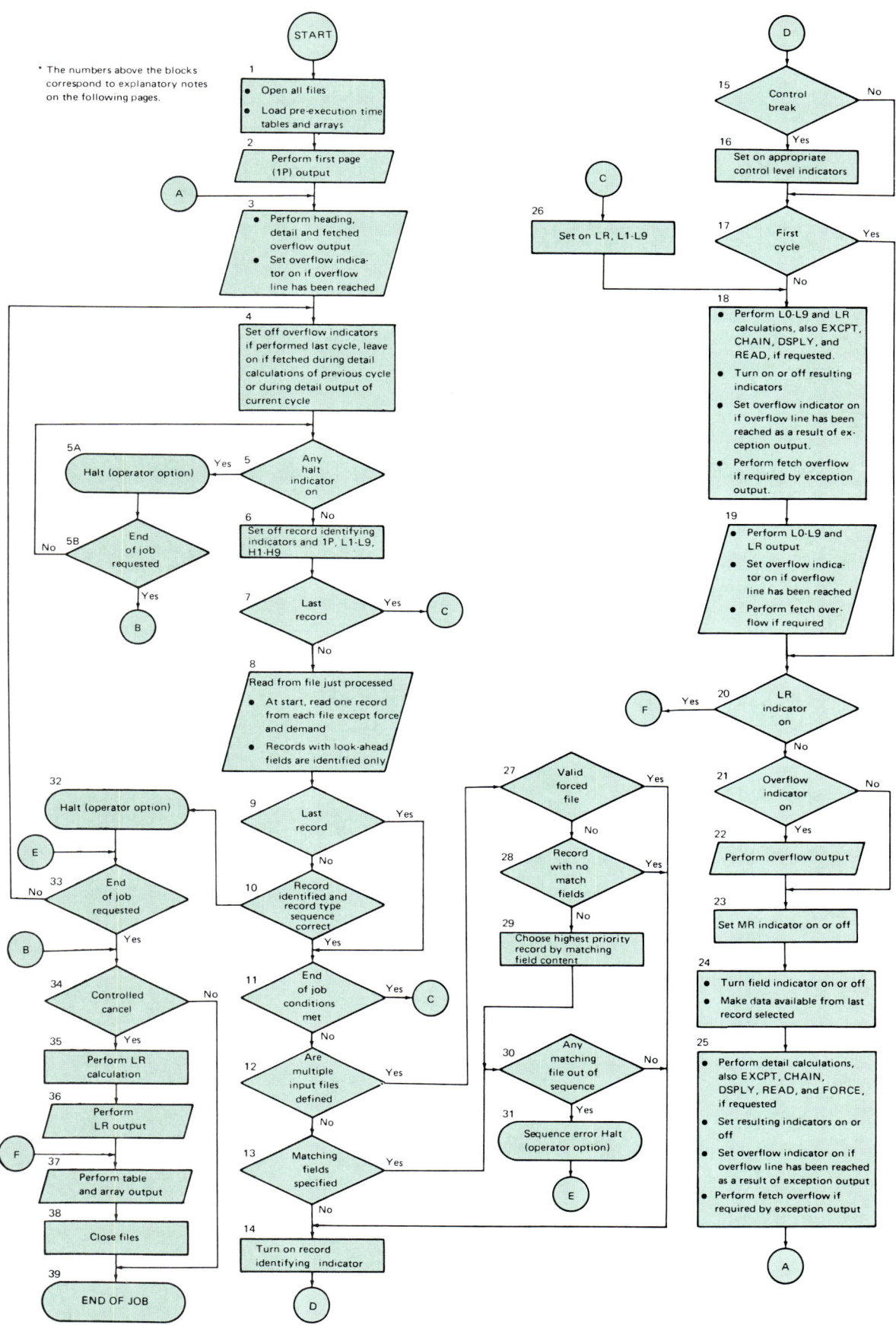

Appendix B 615

25. Any calculations not conditioned by control level indicators (positions 7–8 of the Calculation Specifications form) are performed, and resulting indicators are turned on or off as specified. File translation, if specified, is done for exception output, chain, and read operations. Fetch overflow is performed if it is required by exception output. If the overflow line has been reached because of exception output, the overflow indicator is turned on. Processing continues with step 3.

26. The last record indicator (LR) and all control level indicators (L1–L9) are turned on and processing continues with step 18.

27. If a file has been forced, the next record in that file is selected for processing and a branch is taken to step 14.

28. If a record with no matching fields is found in a normal input file that is not at end-of-file, it is selected.

29. When matching fields are specified, the normal file with the highest priority matching record field is selected. If two or more files have the equal and highest priority matching record fields, the file of highest priority is selected. (The primary file has the highest priority, the first specified secondary file is next, and so forth.)

30. The match field is compared to the match field value of the last record. If it is in sequence, the record is accepted and processing continues with step 14. If the record is out of sequence, processing goes to step 31.

31. The execution of the program is stopped because a file with matching fields is out of sequence. The operator's option, indicated in step 33, is to bypass (read the next record from the same file) or cancel the job.

32. The execution of the program is stopped because of a record type sequence error or an unidentified record.

33. Step 33 tests the operator's decision either to bypass the record that causes the error condition (branch to step 4) or to cancel the job.

34. If the operator elects to terminate the job by means of a controlled cancel, steps 35–39 are performed. If the operator selects an immediate cancel, the job is terminated.

35. All operations conditioned by the LR indicator are done.

36. Same as 35.

37. The program writes out tables or arrays for which a *to filename* is specified on the Extension Specifications form. Output tables or arrays are translated, if necessary.

38. All files used by the program are closed (final termination functions are done).

39. End of job occurs.

Appendix C

Reference Tables—RPG II

Figure C.1 Program indicators—summary

Indicator	Where specified	Where used	Turned on	Turned off	Notes

Field Indicators 01-99
  Zero and Blank
  Plus
  Minus
	Input form	Indicator (calc), Output Indicators	By Blank or Zero in specified field
			By Plus in specified field
			By Minus in specified field
				Before this field status is to be tested the next time	Note 1

H1 through H9	Input form Calculation form	Indicator (calc), Output	Whenever the specified field status or record identification condition is satisfied	Internal, at the end of the detail cycle	Note 1
LR	Internal	Control Level (calc), Output Indicators	After processing the last record of the last file (see column 17 of File Descr)	At the beginning of processing	Note 1 (Cannot be SETOF) Note 2
L0 (Level Zero)	Internal	Control Level (calc), Output Indicators	At beginning of the program	Is never turned off by RPG	Cannot be SETON or SETOF
Control Level Indicators L1 through L9	Input form Columns 59-60	Control Level (calc), Indicators (calc), Output Indicators	When the value in a control field changes All indicators of the lower levels are also turned on	At end of following detail cycle	Note 1
MR (Matching)	Internal	Indicators (calc), Output Indicators	If the matching-field contents of the record of a secondary file match the matching-field contents of a record in the primary file	When all total calculations and output are completed for the last record of the matching group	
OA, OB, OC, OD, OE, OF, OG, OV	File Description form	Indicators (calc), Output Indicators	If the destination of a space, skip, or print operation falls within the forms overflow area	At the end of the detail cycle	Note 3
Record Identifying Indicator 01-99	Input form Columns 19-20	Indicators (calc), Output Indicators Field Record Relation	When specified record has been read and before total calculations are executed	Before the next record is read during the next processing cycle	Note 1

Resulting Indicators 01-99
  Plus
  Minus
  Zero
Compare operation
  High
  Low
  Equal
	Calculation form	Indicators (calc), Output Indicators	By a positive balance in field, by a negative balance in field, by zero balance in field
			
			if Factor 1>Factor 2
			if Factor 1<Factor 2
			if Factor 1=Factor 2
				The next time a calculation is performed for which the program specifies the indicator as a resulting indicator and the specified condition is not satisfied	Note 1

Look-up operation
  High
  Low
  Equal
TESTZ operation
  High
  Low
  Equal
Chain operation
	Calculation form	Indicators (calc) Output indicators	if table >Factor 1
			if table<Factor 1
			if table=Factor 1
			if a C zone or & is present
			if a D zone or minus(−) is present
			C or D zone is not present
			By a no record found condition
					Note 1

1P (First Page)	Internal	Output Indicators	At beginning of processing before any input records are read	Before the first detail record is read	Note 4

Note 1 Turning indicators on or off can also be accomplished by using SETON and SETOF operation codes
Note 2 All control level indicators (L1-9) are also turned on when LR is turned on
Note 3 The overflow indicator remains on during the following detail calculations and output cycles
Note 4 This indicator is used to condition printing of the first page of the report

Note

When a program is doing multiple reads from one or several demand files during the same RPG II cycle, the record identifying indicators assigned to the file(s) remain on throughout the cycle if the previous READ operations were executed successfully

When chaining to one or more files during the same RPG II cycle, record identifying indicators assigned to the chained file(s) remain on throughout the cycle if the previous operations were executed successfully

Figure C.2 Operation codes—summary

Type of operation	Function of operation	Operation code (columns 28-32)	Control level	Indicators	Factor 1	Factor 2	Result field	Field length	Decimal position	Half adjust	Resulting indicators
Arithmetic operations	Add Factor 2 to Factor 1	ADD	O	O	R	R	R	O	O	O	O
	Clear Result Field and add Factor 2	Z-ADD	O	O	B	R	R	O	O	O	O
	Subtract Factor 2 from Factor 1	SUB	O	O	R	R	R	O	O	O	O
	Clear Result Field and subtract Factor 2	Z-SUB	O	O	B	R	R	O	O	O	O
	Multiply Factor 1 by Factor 2	MULT	O	O	R	R	R	O	O	O	O
	Divide Factor 1 by Factor 2	DIV	O	O	R	R	R	O	O	O	O
	Move remainder of preceding division to a Result Field	MVR	O	O	B	B	R	O	O	B	O
	Sum elements of an array and put sum in Result Field	XFOOT	O	O	B	R	R	O	O	O	O
	Derive the square root of Factor 2	SQRT	O	O	B	R	R	O	O	O	B
Move operation	Move Factor 2 into Result Field, right justified	MOVE	O	O	B	R	R	O	O	B	B
	Move Factor 2 into Result Field, left justified	MOVEA	O	O	B	R	R	O	B	B	B
	Move Factor 2 into Result Field, left justified	MOVEL	O	O	B	R	R	O	O	B	B
Move zone operation	Move zone from low-order position of Factor 2 to low-order position of Result Field	MLLZO	O	O	B	R	R	O	O	B	B
	Move zone from high-order position of alphameric Factor 2 to high-order of alphameric Result Field	MHHZO	O	O	B	R	R	O	B	B	B
	Move zone from low-order position of Factor 2 to high-order position of alphameric Result Field	MLHZO	O	O	B	R	R	O	B	B	B
	Move zone from high-order position of alphameric Factor 2 to low-order position of Result Field	MHLZO	O	O	B	R	R	O	O	B	B
Compare and zone testing operations	Compare Factor 1 to Factor 2	COMP	O	O	R	R	B	B	B	B	R
	Identify the zone in the leftmost position of an alphameric Result Field	TESTZ	O	O	B	B	R	O	B	B	R
Bit operations	Set on specified bits	BITON	O	O	B	R	R	O	B	B	B
	Set off specified bits	BITOF	O	O	B	R	R	O	B	B	B
	Test specified bits	TESTB	O	O	B	R	R	O	B	B	R
Setting indicators	Set one, two, or three specific indicators on	SETON	O	O	B	B	B	B	B	B	R
	Set one, two, or three specific indicators off	SETOF	O	O	B	B	B	B	B	B	R
Branching within RPG II	Branch to another RPG II calculation specification line	GOTO	O	O	B	B	B	B	B	B	B
	Identify the name in Factor 1 as a destination label to which GOTO may branch	TAG	O	B	R	B	B	B	B	B	B
Lookup operations	Table Lookup	LOKUP	O	O	R	R	O	O	O	B	R
	Array Lookup	LOKUP	O	O	R	R	B	B	B	B	R
Subroutine	Beginning of the subroutine	BEGSR	*	B	R	B	B	B	B	B	B
	End of the subroutine	ENDSR	*	B	O	B	B	B	B	B	B
	Call to execute the subroutine	EXSR	O	O	B	R	B	B	B	B	B
Program control	Forcing record to be read next	FORCE	B	O	B	R	B	B	B	B	B
	Forcing output printing	EXCPT	O	O	B	B	B	B	B	B	B
	A field is printed on the printer-keyboard and/or data is entered via the printer-keyboard into a field	DSPLY	O	O	O	R	O	B	B	B	B
	A record is read from a demand file	READ	O	O	B	R	B	B	B	B	O
	A record is read from a disk file	CHAIN	O	O	R	R	B	B	B	B	O
Debug function	Aid in finding programming errors	DEBUG	O	O	O	R	O	B	B	B	B

O - Optional
R - Required
B - Blank

* Columns 7-8 must have an SR entry for all subroutine lines.
*** The control level entry can be given for any operation code if it is an AN or OR line

Figure C.3 Valid indicators

Indicators	File Description Specifications		Input Specifications				Calculation Specifications			Output-Format Specifications
	Overflow indicator (33-34)	File conditioning (71-72)	[1]Record identifying indicator (19-20)	Control level (59-60)	[1]Field record relation (63-64)	Field Indicator (65-70)	Control level indicator (7-8)	Conditioning indicator (9-17)	Resulting indicator (54-59)	Conditioning indicator (23-31)
01-99			X	X	X	X		X	X	X
H1-H9			X		X	X		X	X	X
1P										X[3]
MR					X[2]			X		X
OA-OG, OV	X							X	X	X[4]
L0							X			X
L1-L9			X	X	X[2]		X	X	X	X
LR			X				X	X	X	X
U1-U8		X[5]			X			X		X

Note

X denotes the indicators that may be used.

[1]Not valid on look-ahead fields

[2]When field named is not a match field or a control field

[3]Only for detail or heading line

[4]Cannot condition an exception line, but may condition fields within the exception record

[5]Not valid for table input files

Appendix D

The Programmer's Job

Your responsibilities as a programmer include

    Determining the job requirements
    Determining what RPG II specifications and program cycle operations are needed for the job
    Writing the specifications
    Documenting the program
    Preparing your source program for compilation
    Compiling the source program
    Testing the program

Determining the Job Requirements

The requirements for a job are generally described in terms of the input provided and the output required. The following paragraphs and illustrations describe the job requirements.

An invoice is to be prepared like that shown below:

```
                        INVOICE

ACCOUNT NUMBER 09621

NAME      SMITH MANUFACTURING

ADDRESS   13620 9TH ST NE
          BERNALILLO
          NEW MEXICO 96120

SHIPPING INSTRUCTIONS     BY AIR

ITEM NUMBER  DESCRIPTION       QUANTITY   UNIT PRICE    AMOUNT

  439167     SHEARS              100        27.56       2,756.00
  629408     GASKET CORK        3000         1.15       3,450.00
  102139     SPRIDGET WHITE       50       750.00      37,500.00


                                           INVOICE TOTAL   212,157.92
```

The input file contains two types of records—name/address records for all customers who made purchases on credit during the month, and transaction records for each item purchased by the customers during the month. The name/address and transaction records look like this:

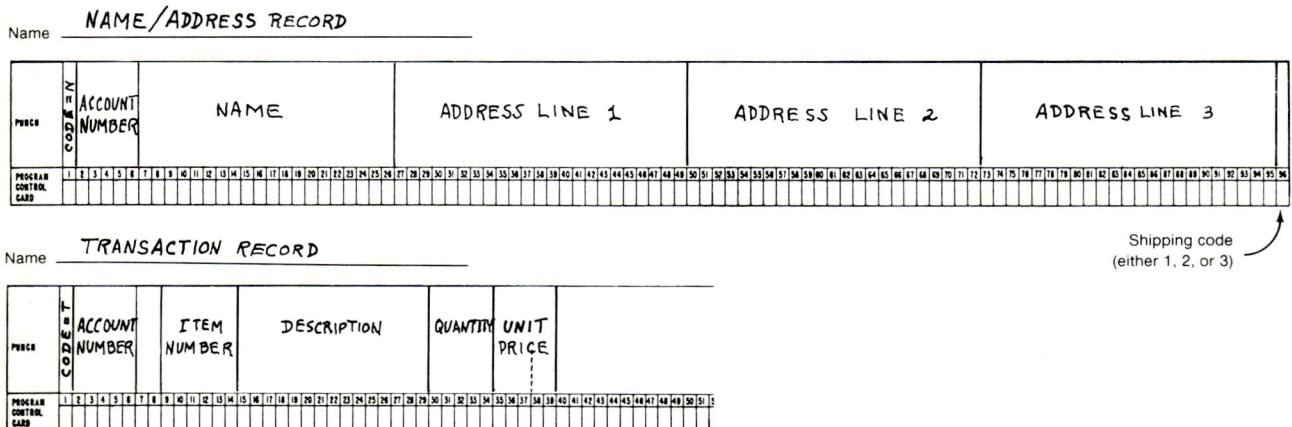

Shipping code (either 1, 2, or 3)

The input file is organized so that all transaction records for a customer follow the customer's name/address record. Each customer has one name/address record, but might have one or more transaction records.

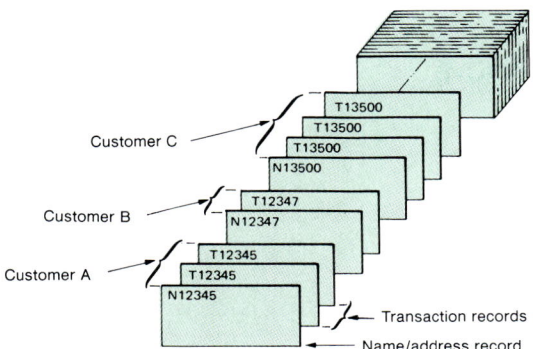

Standard computer paper is to be used for printing the invoices. Each invoice should be formatted like this:

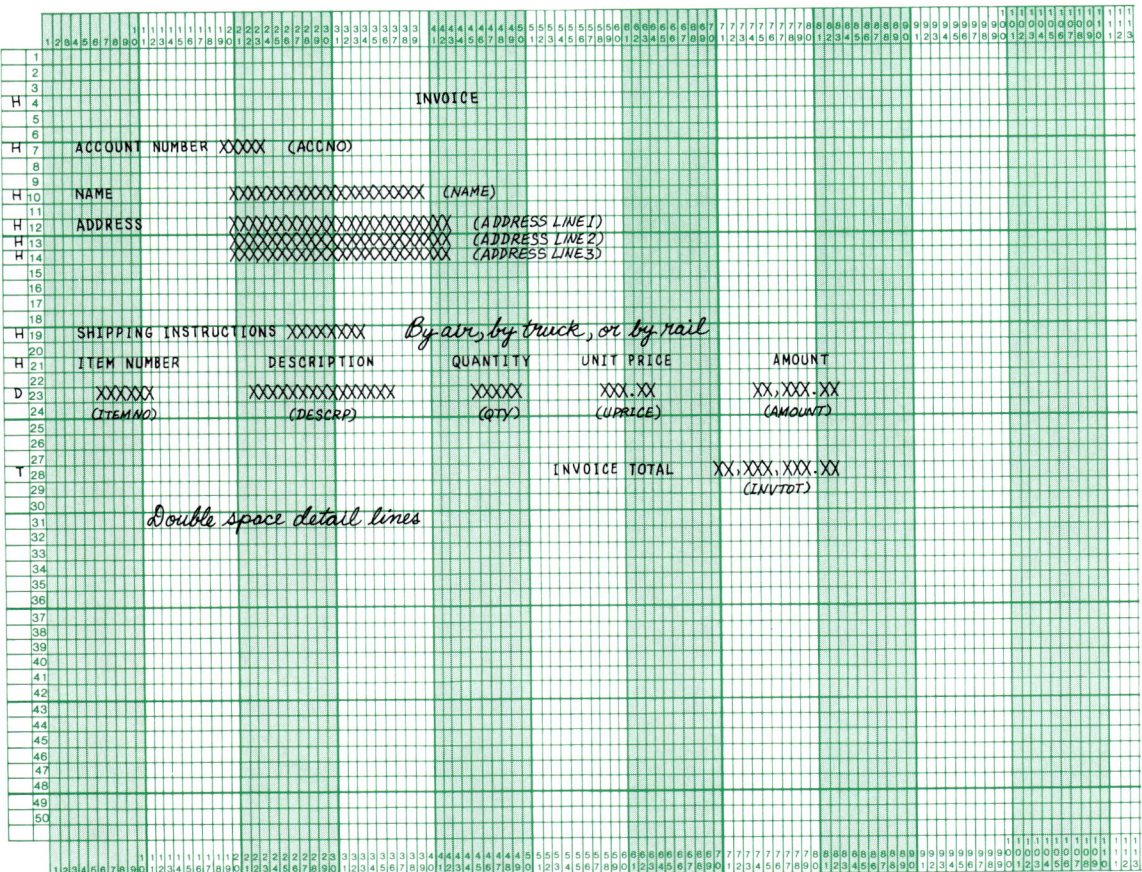

Your first step is to analyze the problem and decide what processing must be done to get the desired results. Always keep in mind how things are done using RPG II. In your analysis of the job, you would probably think of these points:

Information for the first part of the invoice is taken from the name/address record. Information for the second part (list of transactions) is taken from transaction records.

In order to print shipping instructions, the shipping code must be determined:

1 = By truck
2 = By rail
3 = By air

AMOUNT and INVTOT (invoice total) must be calculated because this information is not in the input records. These calculations must be done for all transaction records:

QTY × PRICE = AMOUNT
AMOUNT + INVTOT = INVTOT

INVTOT should be printed only after all transaction records for one account have been processed. The invoice for each customer must be on a separate page. This means that forms must advance each time a new customer name/address record is found. It is possible that one customer has purchased so many items that they cannot all be listed on one page. In this case, forms should advance when the end of a page is reached. When an invoice includes more than one page, headings should be printed on all pages.

Determine RPG II Specifications Needed for the Job

After you have carefully analyzed the job, determine what RPG II specifications and program cycle operations you need. For example, consider the following:

1. Different record types are used. This means that record identifying indicators must be specified to tell what to do for each record.

2. The shipping code must be determined. One way to do this is to compare the shipping code to 2. Through the use of resulting indicators, you can determine if the code is less than 2 (1), greater than 2 (3), or equal to 2.

3. INVAMT is printed only after all transaction records for one account have been processed. This is a total operation, done only after a group of records has been processed. Therefore, control fields and control level indicators must be used to do a total operation. The account number field can be used as the control field.

4. Forms should advance each time a different name/address record is encountered or whenever overflow occurs. Thus, heading lines must be conditioned by a record identifying indicator and the OV indicator.

If the indicators and steps just listed are used, the RPG II cycle would include the steps shown below.

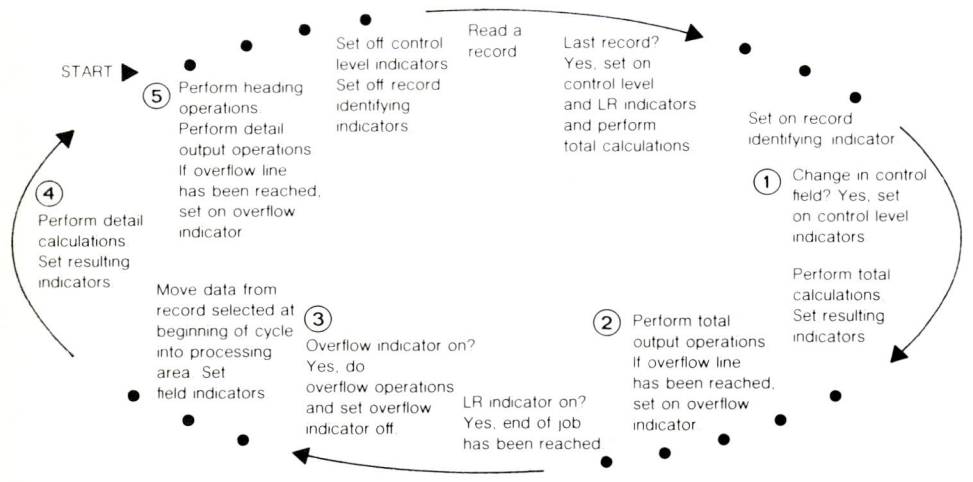

Write the Specifications

After you have analyzed the problem and determined how to solve it using RPG II, you can write the specifications. The program below shows the specifications for the job:

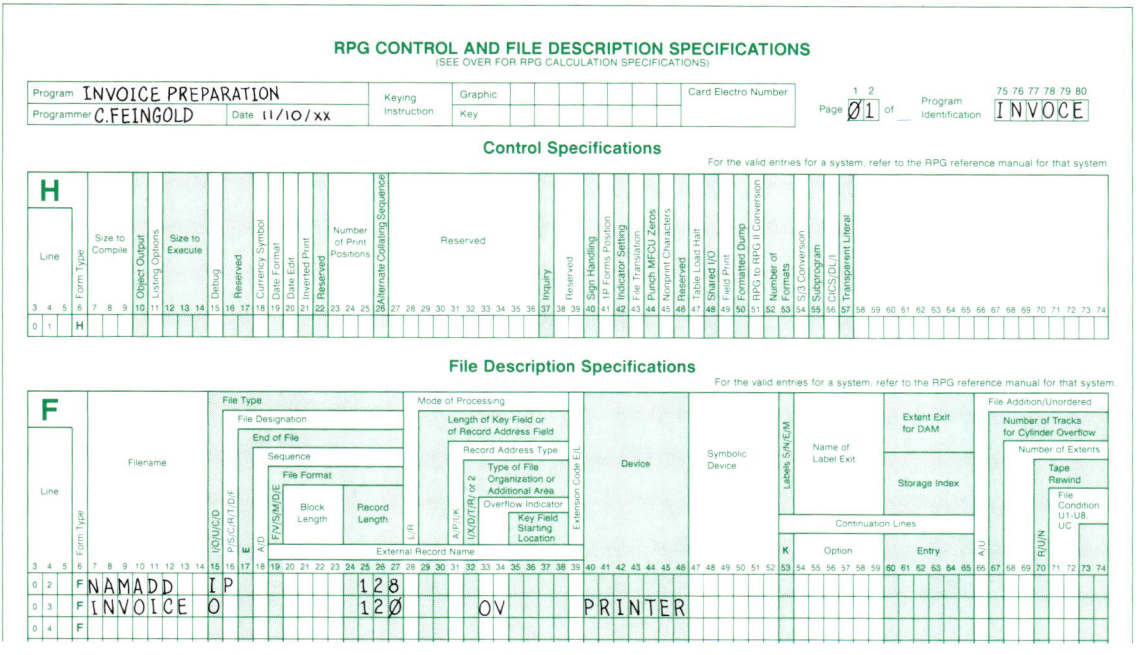

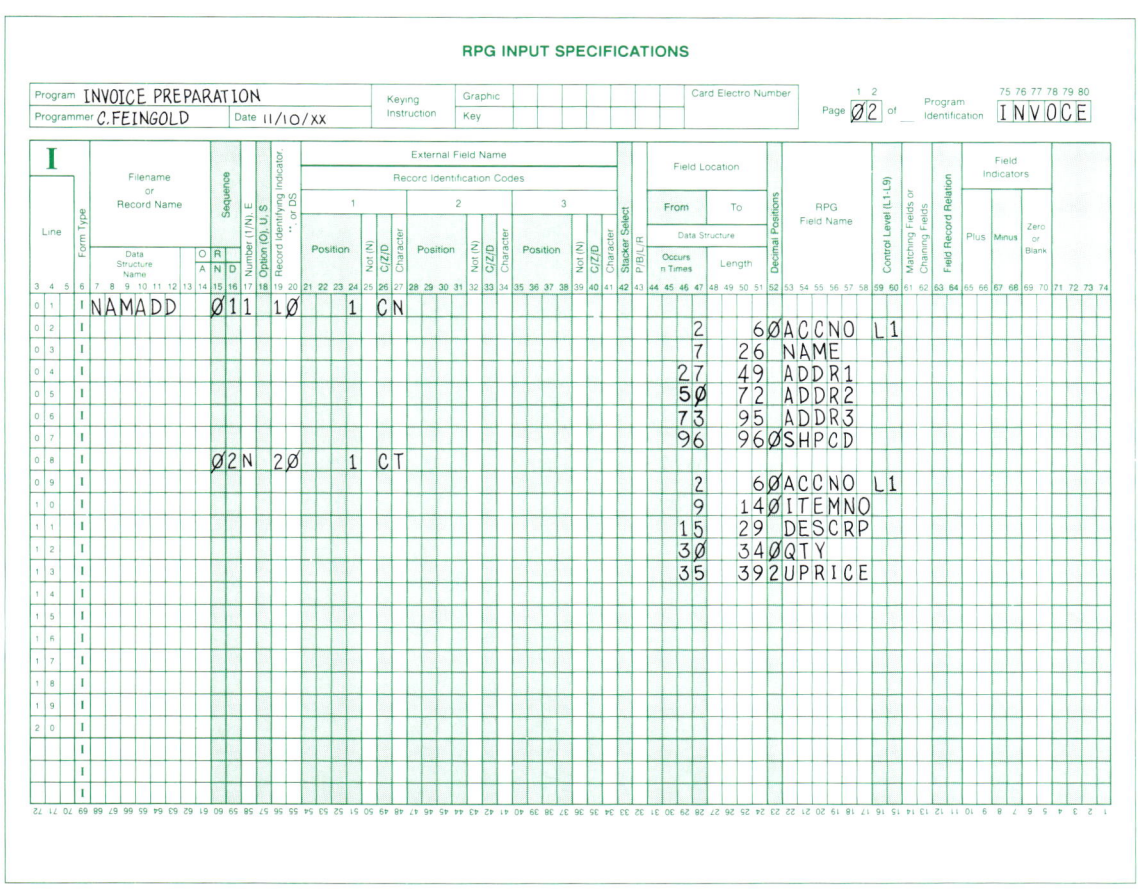

Appendix D

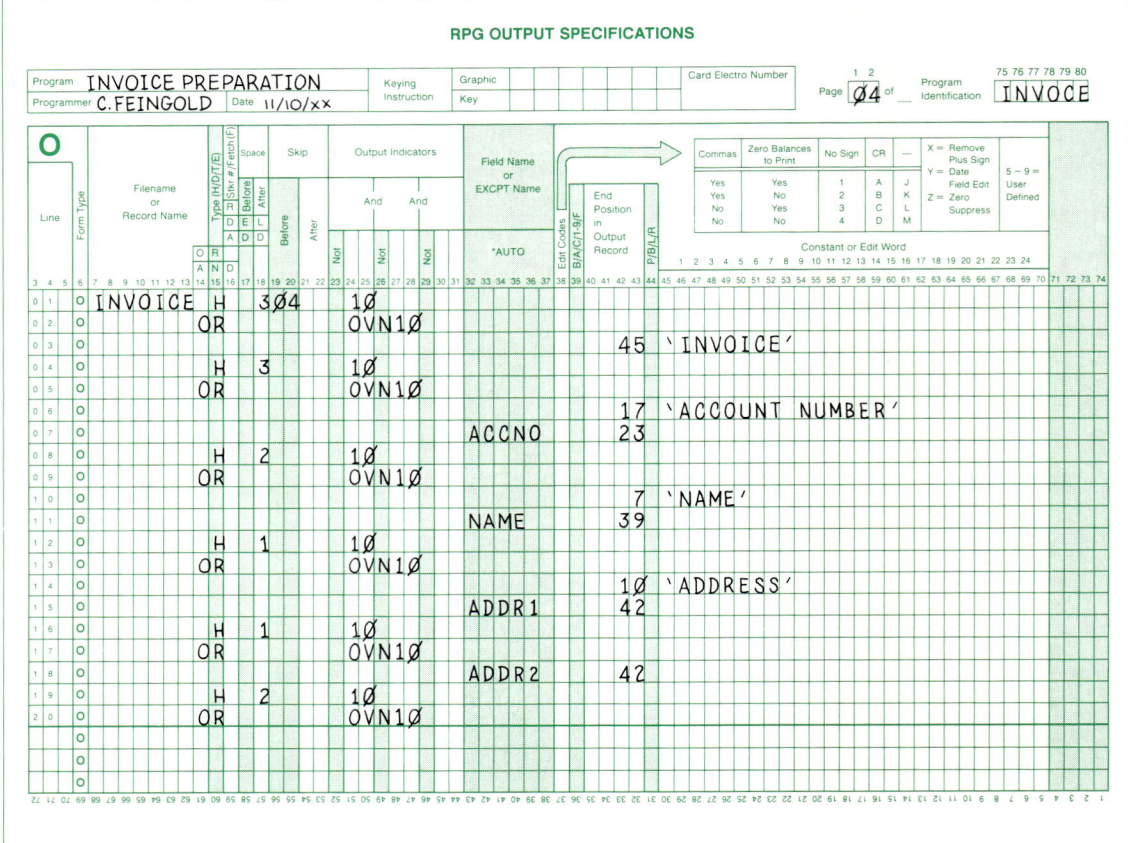

RPG OUTPUT SPECIFICATIONS

Program: **INVOICE PREPARATION**
Programmer: **C. FEINGOLD** Date: **11/10/XX**
Page: **05** Program Identification: **INVOICE**

Line	Form Type	Filename or Record Name	Type (H/D/T/E)	Stkr#/Fetch(F)	Space Before	Space After	Skip Before	Skip After	Output Indicators (And/And/And)	Field Name or EXCPT Name	Edit Codes	End Position in Output Record	Constant or Edit Word
01	O									ADDR3		42	
02	O		H		32		10						
03	O	OR					OVN10						
04	O											24	'SHIPPING INSTRUCTIONS'
05	O								97			33	'BY AIR'
06	O								98			33	'BY TRUCK'
07	O								99			33	'BY RAIL'
08	O		H		2		10						
09	O	OR					OVN10						
10	O											14	'ITEM NUMBER'
11	O											34	'DESCRIPTION'
12	O											50	'QUANTITY'
13	O											65	'UNIT PRICE'
14	O											81	'AMOUNT'
15	O		D		2		20						
16	O									ITEMNO Z		11	
17	O									DESCRP		36	
18	O									QTY Z		49	
19	O									UPRICE 1		63	
20	O									AMOUNT 1		82	

RPG OUTPUT SPECIFICATIONS

Program: **INVOICE PREPARATION**
Programmer: **C. FEINGOLD** Date: **11/10/XX**
Page: **06** Program Identification: **INVOICE**

Line	Form Type	Filename or Record Name	Type	Space Before	Skip Before	Output Indicators	Field Name or EXCPT Name	Edit Codes	End Position	Constant or Edit Word
01	O		T	32		L1				
02	O								65	'INVOICE TOTAL'
03	O						INVTOT 1	B	82	

Appendix D

Documenting the Program

An important part of every programmer's job is to explain the program. This documentation provides information for people who will run the program and for programmers who may later need to alter or update it. Documentation is also useful to you. It is not always easy to remember specific characteristics of every program you write. Reading the documentation is a much easier way to recall the program than figuring out each instruction.

Documentation

1. Tells generally what the program does.

2. Describes input and output. (Record Layout forms and Printer Spacing Charts are an excellent means of describing input and output.) Filenames and field names should be meaningful.

3. Explains the coding.

4. Tells the operator how to run the program, what to do if the system stops because of an error, and what to do when the job is completed.

All documentation cannot be done at the time you write specifications. However, when writing your specifications, you can also write an explanation for a line or lines of coding on the specifications forms. You have probably noticed positions labeled *Comments* on the specifications sheets. This is where you write an explanation for your coding.

In addition to using the comment positions on the coding forms, you can use comment lines. A comment line is indicated by an * (asterisk) in position 7 of the coding form.

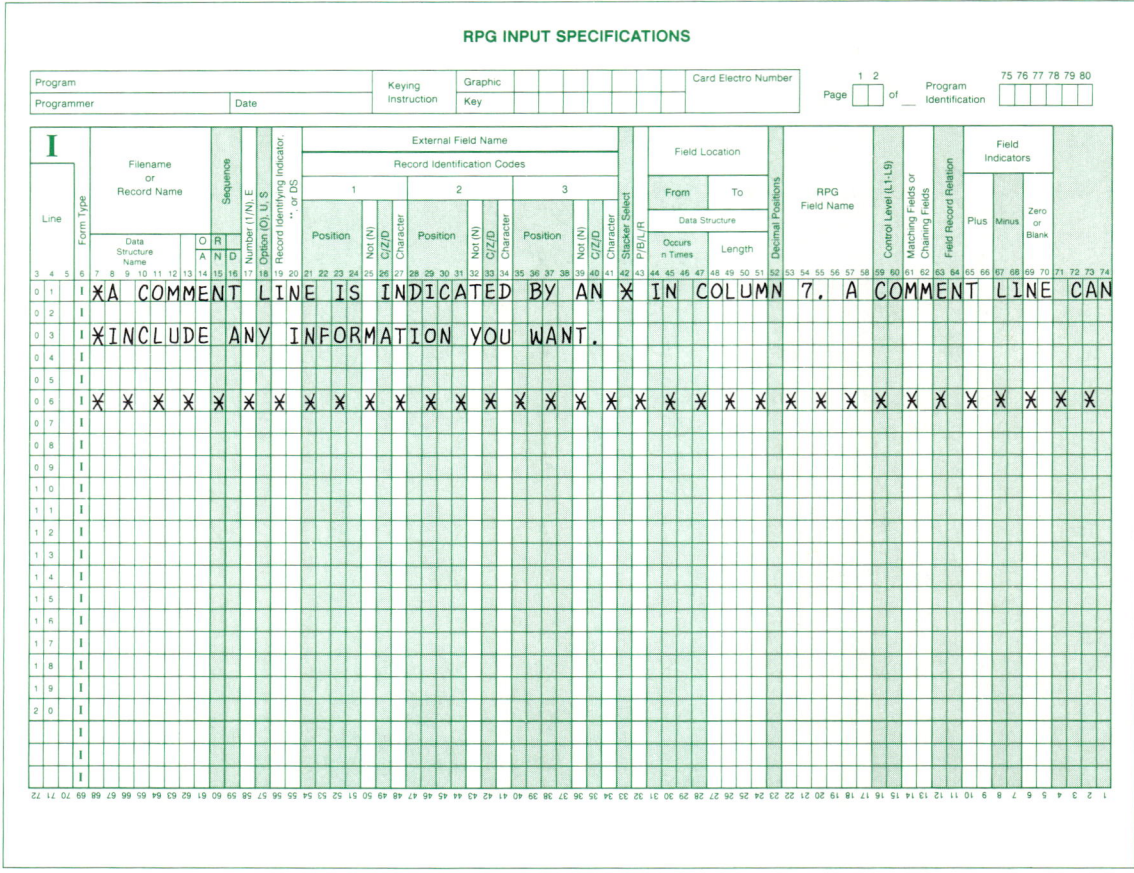

Comment lines can be used anywhere on any specifications form. There is no limit to the number you can use. The RPG II compiler does not regard comments or comment lines as part of the program. Therefore, the compiler does not translate the comments into instructions; however, the lines are printed as part of the source program listing.

Prepare for Compilation

After completing your source program, you must prepare it for compilation.

Specifications Form Order

Your specifications forms must be in this order:

1. Control and File Description Specifications form
2. Input Specifications form
3. Calculation Specifications form
4. Output Specifications form

Number the forms in positions 1 and 2. At this time, you might also check to see that the top part of each form is completely filled in.

If you are planning to have someone key these specifications, it is a good idea to fill in the box labeled *Keying Instructions*. Indicate what graphic symbols you are using and the meaning of those symbols in this box. Some printed letters and numbers are easily confused. For example, it is sometimes difficult to differentiate between the number *0* and the letter *O*, and the number *2* and the letter *Z*. You may, therefore, devise a graphic symbol that you use for certain letters. Some people use ∅ for zero, and Ƶ for the letter Z. Explain your symbols so that the operator will know what to key when the symbol appears on the coding forms.

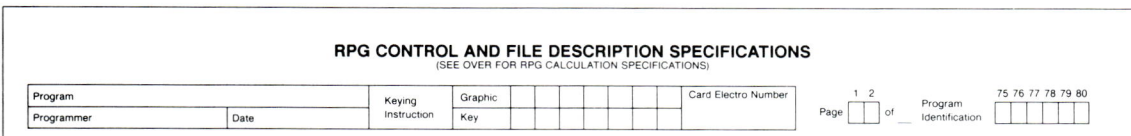

Control Specifications Preparation

Some systems require control specifications. If yours does, you will have to fill out the control specifications at the top of the Control and File Description Specifications form.

Control specifications give the compiler information about the system and tell whether any special RPG II functions are used in the program. The entries are such things as are shown in the following example:

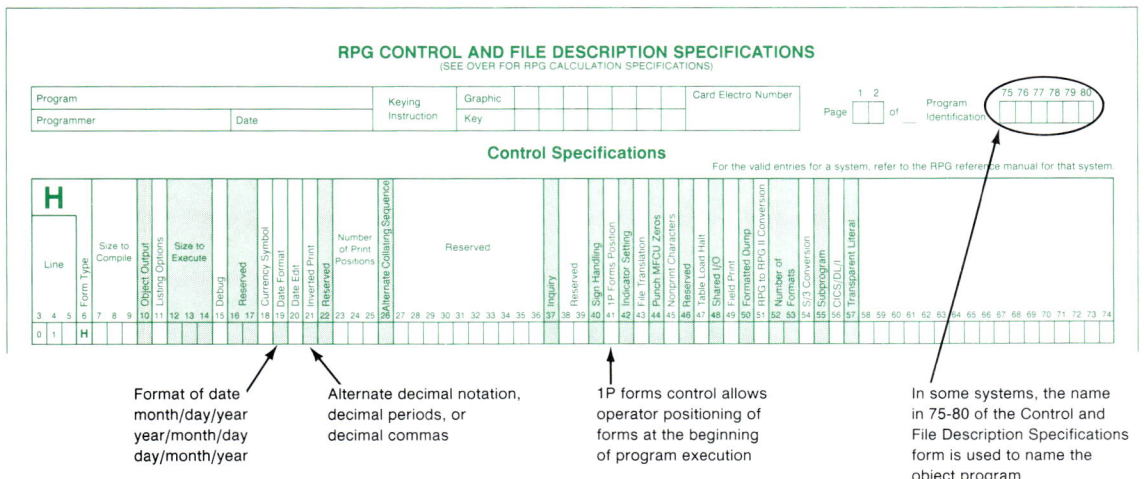

Appendix D 627

Checking the Specifications

Desk checking is a good way to reduce the number of potential program errors. Desk checking means carefully checking through your specifications to see whether you have

Placed entries in appropriate positions
Used correct entries in positions
Spelled the same field names and filenames identically throughout your program
Used your indicators correctly

If you should find that you have omitted a specification (did not name an input field or an output field or did not enter a calculation), you can enter it on a line following line 20 (line 10 on the Control and File Description Specifications form under the heading *File Description*).

Notice that no line numbers have been entered in positions 3–5 of the specification lines located below line 20. You can place numbers in these positions to tell where the missing specification belongs.

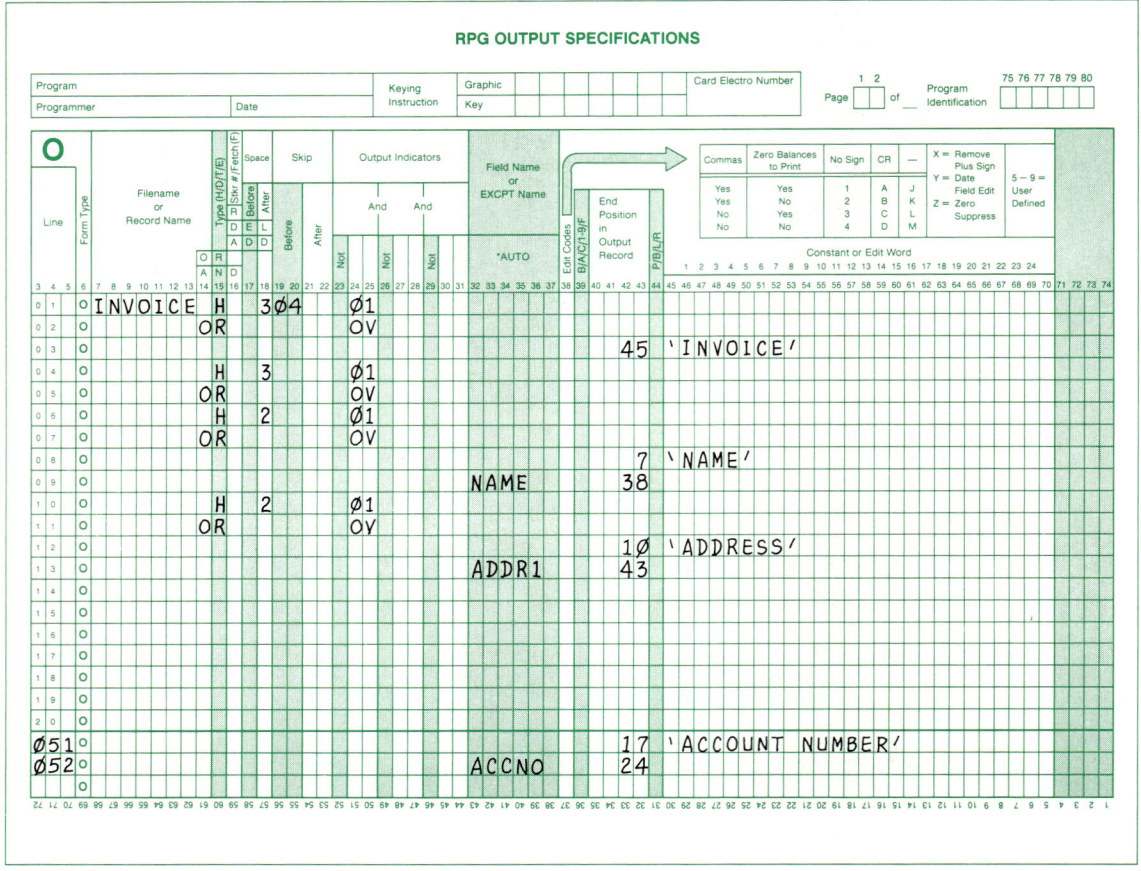

In this example, the programmer did not specify information to be included on the second heading line. On the line following line 20, the missing specifications were specified. Notice that positions 3–5 tell where the specifications belong. The line numbers 051 and 052 indicate that the specifications belong between lines 05 and 06.

If your specifications are being keypunched, the out-of-order cards must be inserted in the appropriate place. If the source program is being entered directly into the system through a keyboard, the missing specifications will have to be inserted in the appropriate place when the specifications are keyed.

Compile the Source Program

When you think your source program is free of errors, it can be keyed according to the source entry method for your system. You can then compile your source program. The important part of compilation is, of course, translating the source program into machine language. But in addition to this, the compiler also produces the following program listing:

```
         0001 H    014                                                    INVOCE

    0001 0002 FNAMADD   IP    128 128            DSIK                     INVOCE
RG 025
    0002 0003 FINVOICE  O     120 120     OV     PRINTER                  INVOCE


    0003 0004 INAMADD   011 10   1 CN                                     INVOCE
    0004 0005 I                                  2   60ACCNO L1           INVOCE
    0005 0006 I                                  7   26 NAME              INVOCE
    0006 0007 I                                 27   49 ADDR1             INVOCE
    0007 0008 I                                 50   72 ADDR2             INVOCE
    0008 0009 I                                 73   95 ADDR3             INVOCE
    0009 0010 I                                 96   96 SHPCD             INVOCE
    0010 0011 I            02N 20   1 CT                                  INVOCE
    0011 0012 I                                  2   60ACCNO L1           INVOCE
    0012 0013 I                                  9   14 ITEMNO            INVOCE
    0013 0014 I                                 15   29 DESCRP            INVOCE
    0014 0015 I                                 30   34 0QTY              INVOCE
    0015 0016 I                                 35   392UPRICE            INVOCE


    0016 0017 C     10    SHPCD      COMP 2              979899IS CODE 1,2,3,? INVOCE
    0017 0018 C     20    QTY        MULT UPRICE   AMOUNT  52    FIND ITEM TOTAL INVOCE
    0018 0019 C     20    AMOUNT     ADD  INVTOT   INVTOT 102    FIND INV TOTAL  INVOCE


    0019 0020 OINVOICE  H   304   10                                      INVOCE
    0020 0021 O         OR        OVN10                                   INVOCE
    0021 0022 O                                 45 'INVOICE'              INVOCE
    0022 0023 O         H   3     10                                      INVOCE
    0023 0024 O         OR        OVN10                                   INVOCE
    0024 0025 O                                 17 'ACCOUNT NUMBER'       INVOCE
    0025 0026 O                            ACCNO   23                     INVOCE
    0026 0027 O         H   2     10                                      INVOCE
    0027 0028 O         OR        OVN10                                   INVOCE
    0028 0029 O                                  7 'NAME'                 INVOCE
    0029 0030 O                            NAME    39                     INVOCE
    0030 0031 O         H   1     10                                      INVOCE
    0031 0032 O         OR        OVN10                                   INVOCE
    0032 0033 O                                 10 'ADDRESS'              INVOCE
    0033 0034 O                            ADDR1   42                     INVOCE
    0034 0035 O         H   1     10                                      INVOCE
    0035 0036 O         OR        OVN10                                   INVOCE
    0036 0037 O                            ADDR2   42                     INVOCE
    0037 0038 O         H   2     10                                      INVOCE


    0038 0039 O         OR        OVN10                                   INVOCE
    0039 0040 O                            ADDR3   42                     INVOCE
    0040 0041 O         H   32    10                                      INVOCE
    0041 0042 O         OR        OVN10                                   INVOCE
    0042 0043 O                                 24 'SHIPPING INSTRUCTIONS' INVOCE
    0043 0044 O                         97      33 'BY AIR'               INVOCE
    0044 0045 O                         98      33 'BY TRUCK'             INVOCE
    0045 0046 O                         99      33 'BY RAIL'              INVOCE
    0046 0047 O         H   2     10                                      INVOCE
    0047 0048 O         OR        OVN10                                   INVOCE
    0048 0049 O                                 14 'ITEM NUMBER'          INVOCE
    0049 0050 O                                 34 'DESCRIPTION'          INVOCE
    0050 0051 O                                 50 'QUANTITY'             INVOCE
    0051 0052 O                                 65 'UNIT PRICE'           INVOCE
    0052 0053 O                                 81 'AMOUNT'               INVOCE
    0053 0054 O         D   2     20                                      INVOCE
    0054 0055 O                            ITEMNOZ  11                    INVOCE
    0055 0056 O                            DESCRP   36                    INVOCE
    0056 0057 O                            QTY    Z 49                    INVOCE
    0057 0058 O                            UPRICE1  63                    INVOCE
    0058 0059 O                            AMOUNT1  82                    INVOCE
    0059 0060 O         T   32    L1                                      INVOCE
    0060 0061 O                                 65 'INVOICE TOTAL'        INVOCE
    0061 0062 O                            INVTOT1B 82                    INVOCE

INDICATORS USED
     L1 OV 10 20 97 98 99
```

Appendix D

```
        FIELD NAMES USED
       STMT#  NAME  DEC  LNG   DISP
        0004  ACCNO  0   0005  016C
        0005  NAME       0020  0113
        0006  ADDR1      0023  012A
        0007  ADDR2      0023  0141
C       0008  ADDR3      0023  015B
        0009  SHPCD  0   0001  016D
        0012  ITEMNO 0   0006  0173
        0013  DESCRP     0015  0167
        0014  QTY    0   0005  0178
        0015  UPRICE 2   0005  0170
        0017  AMOUNT 2   0005  0182
        0018  INVTOT 2   0010  018C

        ERROR NUMBER   STATEMENT NUMBER
          RPG-0221          0017
D
        ERROR SEVERITY                              TEXT
        RPG-0025    T    INVALID DEVICE NAME IN COLUMNS 40-46, ASSUME DISK.
        RPG-0221    W    RESULT FIELD LENGTH MAY NOT BE LARGE ENOUGH.
```

The most important parts of the program listing[1] are:

(A) A printout of source specifications including comment lines. Notice the number at the left of each line. This is the sequence number the compiler assigns to the specification.

(B) A list of all indicators used in the program.

(C) A list of all fields used in the program. Included in the list is the storage location assigned to each field and a description of each field as indicated in your specifications. Some compilers also provide this information for constants used in the program.

(D) Diagnostic messages indicating the types of errors made and the statement in which they occur.

[1] Note that the sample listing shown is the program listing for the invoice job (INVOCE).

If the compiler finds any errors in your source specifications, it will print diagnostic messages telling you what errors were made. You will find that different types of messages are printed—warning, terminal, or informative. A warning message is an indication that something may be wrong. If you check the questioned specification and find that it is all right for your program, you need not make changes. If you get a terminal message, however, something is wrong with your coding. You must fix the specification and recompile the program before the compiler will actually translate your specifications.

The diagnostic message section of the program listing contains two basic parts: (1) a list of messages (X) and (2) an explanation of each message (Y).

```
              ①              ②
        ERROR NUMBER  STATEMENT NUMBER
X {       RPG-0221         0017

        ERROR SEVERITY   ④    ③                    TEXT
Y {     RPG-0025    T     INVALID DEVICE NAME IN COLUMNS 40-46, ASSUME DISK.
        RPG-0221    W     RESULT FIELD LENGTH MAY NOT BE LARGE ENOUGH.
```

Each error message in the list is identified by a three-digit number ①. Next to the message number is either a statement number identifying the specification in which the error appears or a field name or constant associated with the error ②. Following the list of messages is an explanation of each error ③ and an indication of the severity of each error (W = warning; T = terminal) ④.

The sample above shows diagnostic messages printed for the invoice job. Note that message 221 is a warning. A warning is an indication that something may be wrong. If you check the specification noted and find that it will work for the job, you need not change it.

Checking the message in the listing, you would find that the warning points to the AMOUNT field in statement 0017:

```
0017 0018 C    20      QTY      MULT UPRICE     AMOUNT   52      FIND ITEM TOTALINVOCE
```

The AMOUNT field is specified as five characters with two decimal positions. In checking your specifications, you will find that the amount shown should have been seven digits with two decimals, and it was incorrectly keyed in the source data.

Message 0025 is a terminal error. This error number appears below the statement at which the error occurred. Checking the listing where it appears at statement 1, the device entry DISK was mis-keyed as DSIK. You must correct this error. (Check the RPG II reference manual for your system for the correct entries for the device positions.)

Test the Program

It is a good practice to test your program before using it for an actual job. To do this, make up test data representing all possible situations that could arise during an actual job. Run your program using that data to see if your program will really handle the situations you think it will. If you get the wrong results when testing, you know your program is not doing what you thought it would. You can usually find your errors by using actual input data and doing the operations specified yourself, step-by-step, in the order the system would do them. When doing this, you have to closely follow your specifications and the program cycle operations taken by your program. After you test your program and the results show it can handle all situations, your job is complete.

Appendix E

Summary Charts—RPG III

Figure E.1 Operation codes—summary

Operation Code	Factor 1	Factor 2	Result Field	Resulting Indicators Positions 54–55	56–57	58–59
ADD[1]	O	R	R	O: +	O: −	O: Z
BEGSR	R					
BITOF		R	R			
BITON		R	R			
CABxx	R	R	R	O: HI	O: LO	O: EQ
CALL		R	O		O: ER	O
CHAIN	R	R	O	R: NR	O: ER	
CLOSE		R			O: ER	
COMP	R	R		O: HI[2]	O: LO[2]	O: EQ[2]
DEBUG	O	O	O			
DEFN	R	O	R			
DELET	O	R		O: NR	O: ER	
DIV[1]	O	R	R	O: +	O: −	O: Z
DO	O	O	O			
DOUxx	R	R				
DOWxx	R	R				
DSPLY	O	O	O			
DUMP	O					
ELSE						
END		O				
ENDSR	O	O				
EXCPT		O				
EXFMT		R			O: ER	
EXSR		R				
FEOD		R			O: ER	
FORCE		R				
FREE		R			O: ER	
GOTO		R				
IFxx	R	R				
IN	O	R			O: ER	
KFLD			R			
KLIST	R					
LOKUP (Array)	R	R		O: HI[2]	O: LO[2]	O: EQ[2]
LOKUP (Table)	R	R	O	O: HI[2]	O: LO[2]	O: EQ[2]
MHHZO		R	R			
MHLZO		R	R			
MLHZO		R	R			

Operation Code	Factor 1	Factor 2	Result Field	Resulting Indicators Positions 54–55	56–57	58–59
MLLZO		R	R			
MOVE		R	R	O: +	O: −	O: ZB
MOVEA		R	R	O: +	O: −	O: ZB
MOVEL		R	R	O: +	O: −	O: ZB
MULT[1]	O	R	R	O: +	O: −	O: Z
MVR			R	O: +	O: −	O: Z
OCUR	O	R	O		O: ER	
OPEN		R			O: ER	
OUT	O	R			O: ER	
PARM	O	O	R			
PLIST	R					
READ		R	O		O: ER	R: EOF
READC		R			O: ER	R: EOF
READE	R	R	O		O: ER	R: EOF
READP		R	O		O: ER	R: BOF
RETRN						
SETGT	R	R		O: NR	O: ER	
SETLL	R	R		O: NR	O: ER	O: EQ
SETOF				O[2]	O[2]	O[2]
SETON				O[2]	O[2]	O[2]
SHTDN				R		
SORTA		R				
SQRT[1]		R	R			
SUB[1]	O	R	R	O: +	O: −	O: Z
TAG	R					
TESTB		R	R	O[2]	O[2]	O[2]
TESTN			R	O[2]	O[2]	O[2]
TESTZ			R	O[2]	O[2]	O[2]
TIME			R			
UNLCK	R				O: ER	
UPDAT		R	O		O: ER	
WRITE		R	O		O: ER	O: EOF
XFOOT[1]		R	R	O: +	O: −	O: Z
Z-ADD[1]		R	R	O: +	O: −	O: Z
Z-SUB[1]		R	R	O: +	O: −	O: Z

[1] Half adjust (position 53) can be specified for this operation.
[2] At least one resulting indicator must be specified in positions 54 through 59.

Fields without entries must be blank.

+ = Plus EQ = Equal R = Required
− = Minus ER = Error Z = Zero
BOF = Beginning of file NR = No record found ZB = Zero or blank
EOF = End of file O = Optional

Figure E.2 RPG III restrictions—summary

Function	Restriction
AN/OR lines (positions 7 and 8 of calculation specifications)	Maximum of seven per operation.
Arrays and tables	Maximum of 200 per program.
Array/table input record length for compile time	Maximum length is 80.
Control fields (positions 59 and 60 of input specifications) length	Maximum length is 256.
Data structure length	Maximum of 9999.
Data structure occurrences (number of)	Maximum of 9999 per data structure.
Do-groups (nested)	Maximum of 100 per program.
Elements in an array/table (positions 36 through 39 of extension specifications)	Maximum of 9999 per array/table.
File	Maximum of 50 per program.
Look-ahead	Can be specified only once for a file. Can be specified only for primary and secondary files.
Overflow indicator	Only one unique overflow indicator can be specified per file.
Primary file (P in position 16 of file description specifications)	Maximum of one per program.
Printer file (PRINTER in positions 40 through 46 of file description specifications)	Maximum of eight per program.
Printing lines per page	Minimum of 18; maximum of 112.
Program status data structure	Only one allowed per program.
Record address file (R in position 16 of file description specifications)	Only one allowed per program.
Record length for program described file (positions 24 through 27 of file description specifications)	Maximum length is 9999.[1]
Subroutines	Maximum of 254 per program.
Tables (see arrays)	

[1] Any device record size restraints override this value.

Appendix F

RPG III Enhancements

Language Enhancements

The RPG language enhancements in RPG III are listed below.

Externally described data: Record descriptions for a file are stored external to the RPG program. The advantage of externally described data is that the file need be described only once to the control program facility and need not be described for each program that uses the file; if the file description changes, the programmer can change its description in one place, and then recompile the programs that use it.

Full procedural file specifications: Indicate to the compiler that the file is processed by programmer-specified calculation operations. A primary file specification is not mandatory.

File operations: The following file processing operation codes have been enhanced in RPG III:

1. CHAIN (Random Retrieval from a File Based on RECNO or Key Value)
2. READ (Read a Record)
3. SETLL (Set Greater Than or Equal To)

The following file processing operation codes are new to RPG III:

1. DELET (Delete Record)
2. READE (Read Equal Key)
3. READP (Read Prior Key)
4. SETGT (Set Greater Than)
5. UPDAT (Modify Existing Record)
6. WRITE (Create New Records)

The following control operation codes are new to RPG III:

1. CLOSE (Close Files)
2. FEOD (Force End of Data)
3. OPEN (Open File for Processing)

Work station support: Allows the specification of a WORKSTN device for input and output of an RPG program. The operation codes that support direct control over specific work station formats include the following:

1. EXFMT (Write Followed by Read)
2. READ (Read a Record)
3. WRITE (Create New Records)

In addition, RPG supports the subfile capacity in WORKSTN support with the following operation codes:

1. CHAIN (Random Retrieval from a File Based on RECNO or Key Value)
2. READC (Read Next Modified Record)
3. UPDAT (Modify Existing Record)
4. WRITE (Create New Records)

Program structure: An RPG program can consist of any group of RPG specifications that can exist by themselves.

CALL/RETRN function: Allows any RPG program to call any other program. Data in a parameter list can be accessed by both the calling and called programs. The new operation codes associated with the CALL/RETRN function are the following:

1. CALL (Call a Program)
2. FREE (Remove a Program)
3. PARM (Identify Parameters)

4. PLIST (Identify a Parameter List)
5. RETRN (Return to Caller)

A new indicator, RT, indicates to the internal RPG logic that control should be returned immediately to the calling program.

Data structures: Allow the capability to redefine (one or more times) an internal area, group noncontiguous data into contiguous internal storage locations, change the contents of a field, and divide a field into subfields. This capability simplifies many application approaches and eliminates the coding and execution of MOVE and MOVEL operations. A data structure can also link to data that are external to a program.

File information data structure (INFDS): Allows the programmer to receive file exception/error information from various data management functions. This capability allows the programmer to code for unusual events and permits a more straightforward approach to many applications.

Multiple occurrence data structures: Allow a data structure to appear many times in a program.

CABxx (Compare and Branch) operation: Allows the programmer to do a compare and branch in one operation and eliminates the need to set and test indicators.

Short form of arithmetic operations: Allows the use of an ADD, SUB, MULT, and DIV operation where factor 1 does not have to be specified. For example:

Factor 1	**Operation**	**Factor 2**	**Result Field**	
QTY	ADD	TOTQTY	TOTQTY	Traditional statement
	ADD	QTY	TOTATY	New function

This capability reduces coding and makes your program easier to read.

EXCPT (Calculation Time Output) operation: Allows simplified control of one or more EXCPT output lines, eliminates the coding of several indicators, and provides better logic control of output.

Simplified subroutine specifications: An SR entry (positions 7–8 of the calculation specifications) for a subroutine is optional.

*Indicators referenced as data (*IN, *INxx, *IN,xx):* Allow the programmer an alternative method of referencing and manipulating indicators. The array of indicators 01–99 reduces coding and provides a simplified approach to many program processing requirements such as the ability to set (on or off) a block of indicators.

Do-groups: The DO (Do), DOUxx (Do Until), and DOWxx (Do While) operations allow for coding loops. Do-groups simplify coding where repetitive functions are required and provide a structured programming approach.

IFxx (If/Then)/ELSE (Else) operations: Allow the execution of a series of RPG operations without the use of branching or indicator control. The operations can be used for a structured programming approach.

Exception/error handling: Allows the programmer to control the program logic if the program exception/errors occur during program execution.

TESTN (Test Numeric) operation: Allows the programmer to validity check an alphameric field to ensure that it contains zoned decimal characters and blanks.

DEFN (Field Definition) operation: Allows a field to be defined based on the attributes (length and decimal positions) of another field. The other field can be defined in the program or in data description specifications. Fewer source code changes and considerations are required during program creation and maintenance.

Improved use of U1–U8 indicators: The U1–U8 indicators can be set (on or off) during program execution and returned to the caller. U1–U8 indicators can condition the execution of a following program or pass switches for use by a following program.

Relative end positions (40–43) on output specifications: Allow the programmer to specify the output of a field based upon relative end position from the previously described field.

Resulting indicators with MOVE and MOVEL operations: Resulting indicators can be specified on MOVE and MOVEL statements. This eliminates the need for additional operations to check for blank, zero, or plus/minus conditions.

Figurative constants: Allow the use of RPG-defined names to eliminate initialization statements and provide an easier solution for many program requirements. The figurative constant names and implied values are the following:

Figurative Constant	Implied Value
*BLANK/*BLANKS	A field of blanks
*ZERO/*ZEROS	A field of all zeros
*HIVAL	A field with the highest collating value
*LOVAL	A field with the lowest collating value
*ALL'..'	A field of an alphameric character string used for cylical functions

TIME (Time) operation: Allows the program to retrieve the system time of day and, if specified, the system date at any time during the program execution. This simplifies the time stamping of transaction and other functions.

SHTDN (Shutdown) operation: Allows a resulting indicator to be set on if shutdown was requested.

SORTA (Sort an Array) operation: Allows an array to be sorted into sequence (ascending or descending).

KLIST (Define a Composite Key)/KFLD (Define Parts of a Key) operations: Allow the programmer to indicate the name by which a composite key may be referenced and the fields that comprise the composite key.

SPECIAL file with PLIST operation: Allows the programmer to specify an input/output device that is not directly supported by RPG. The input and output operations for the file are controlled by a user-written routine.

User-defined edit codes (5–9): Allow for unique customer- or national-oriented editing.

Alternate currency symbol: Allows a currency symbol other than a $ to be specified for edit codes and edit words that use a floating currency symbol.

Dynamic space/skip function (PRTCTL) option: Allows the program to dynamically specify space/skip operations on the output specifications instead of using literals. In addition, the current line number is made available to the program for better control of overflow.

Default control specification: Allows a control specification to be specified as a data area. This eliminates the need for control specifications in every program and allows standardization of various functions (for example, editing and date format).

Table file replacement: Allows the programmer, at end of program, to write an array or table back to the same file from which it was input.

BITON (Bit On)/BITOF (Bit Off) operations with arrays: Allow the use of bit settings on whole arrays.

DSPLY (Display Function)/SET (Setnn)/KEY (Keynn) operations: Allow access to the display device without the use of a data description file. With SET/KEY operations, you can specify the KA–KN and KP–KY indicators and access a message file defined to the system.

Improved file support: Allows the programmer easier access and control of files that are processed by relative record number. The RECNO field defined in the file description specifications allows for easier control and feedback.

New Compilation Listing Functions

The new RPG compilation listing functions on RPG III are listed below.

Cross-reference listing: Allows easy determination of where files, fields, and indicators are defined, referenced, and modified for both program described and externally described files. This simplifies corrections and improves program documentation.

Text description from data description specifications: Text description provided for fields and indicators specified in data description specifications appear on the listing to help document the program.

Resulting indicator usage: Allows quick determination of which resulting indicator has been specified in calculation specifications (for example, positions 54–55, 56–57, and 58–59). This eliminates confusion and helps document the program.

Consecutive position rule: Allows the programmer to determine the position of any character in the source record.

SEU sequence number: Used as the default numbering method for statements and diagnostics if SEU is used to enter the source program. This allows the programmer to go directly from a diagnostic that discusses a source statement in error to the specified statement using SEU.

Source diagnostic error notation: Allows errors to be seen on the compiler listing by the use of an * in position 1. The *, followed by an error message number, indicates that a syntax error has been noted. Asterisks are also placed immediately under each field in error for easy identification.

/EJECT and /SPACE specifications: Allow the skipping of lines in the source listing for easier reading of major program functions.

Nesting indication: Indicates the nested level of a statement in do-groups and IFxx/ELSE groups.

Last update indication: Indicates the date the source statement was last changed.

Auto Report

Auto report is a component of RPG III. RPG invokes auto report through CRTRPTPGM (Create Auto Report Program) command. Auto report accepts special simplified specifications and standard RPG source specifications, and uses them to generate a complete RPG source program. Auto report has automatic formatting functions and the /COPY function that simplify programming requirements.

Enhanced DEBUG Facilities

The enhanced RPG debug facilities in RPG III are the following:

Support of the system debug facility: Allows online debugging of the program. Without any special source statements, every RPG program is available for debugging purposes. This includes such functions as

1. Stopping at specific statement numbers or RPG major functions (for example, first detail calculation)
2. Display and changing of fields, indicators, and arrays
3. Tracing of specific ranges of statements and the output of changed fields

Formatted dump: Allows the programmer to easily determine specific execution errors and the status of the program at the time of the error. The formatted dump provides a text description of the cause of error and the RPG statement number on which the error occurred. Field values are displayed with their values at the time of termination. This is a significant aid in pinpointing and correcting problems.

DEBUG (Debug Function) operation: Allows either one or two records to be written containing information helpful for finding programming errors. Output goes to a file or a requester.

DUMP (Program Dump) operation: Allows control of when a formatted dump is provided.

Other Support

Source Entry Utility (SEU): SEU is part of the Interactive Data Base Utilities Program Product (IDU) that allows online source entry and maintenance. When the RPG source is identified, SEU provides special display screen formats (corresponding to the RPG specifications) that simplify keying. SEU can also call an RPG syntax checker that checks each specification line entered for errors. This syntax checker eliminates careless errors and helps minimize the number of compilations required to create and maintain a program.

CRTRPGPGM (Create RPG Program) command: Invokes the RPG compiler, which loads the source program into main storage and creates an executable program. The command includes options to control the source listing and security functions.

For further discussion and more information on the operations of RPG III, consult the reference manuals for RPG III.

Appendix G

Problems for Term Assignment

Problem 1

Accounts Receivable Register

Job Definition

An Accounts Receivable Register is to be printed each quarter showing the transactions for the period. A final total is to be printed at the end of the report.

Input

The Accounts Receivable file consists of 61-byte records as follows:

Positions	Field Description
8–29	Customer name
34–38	Invoice number
39–43	Customer number
44–45	State code
46–48	City code
49–54	Invoice date
55–61	Invoice amount (XXXXX.XX)

Processing

1. The individual detail records are to be printed with proper headings and editing.

2. A final total, the sum of all invoice amounts, is to be printed on the last page of the report.

Output

An Accounts Receivable Register is to be printed as follows:

```
                        ACCOUNTS  RECEIVABLE  REGISTER

CUSTOMER                          LOCATION     INVOICE   INVOICE   INVOICE
NUMBER      CUSTOMER NAME        STATE CITY    NUMBER     DATE     AMOUNT

01201     AMERICAN STEEL CO        36   49      11666    4/23/87    640.31

01281     AMERICAN STEEL CO        36   49      12336    5/30/87    909.04

02179     APALACHIN LUMBER CO       4  227      09852    6/15/87    469.20

02183     B J E SERVICE CORP       22   37      12332    6/29/87  1,474.78

11905     CHALLIS ALMERS           47   77      10901    9/18/87     27.63

29031     DENNIS MFG CO             6   63      11615    9/14/87    440.12



                                                         $3,961.08 **
```

The Printer Spacing Chart shows how the report is formatted:

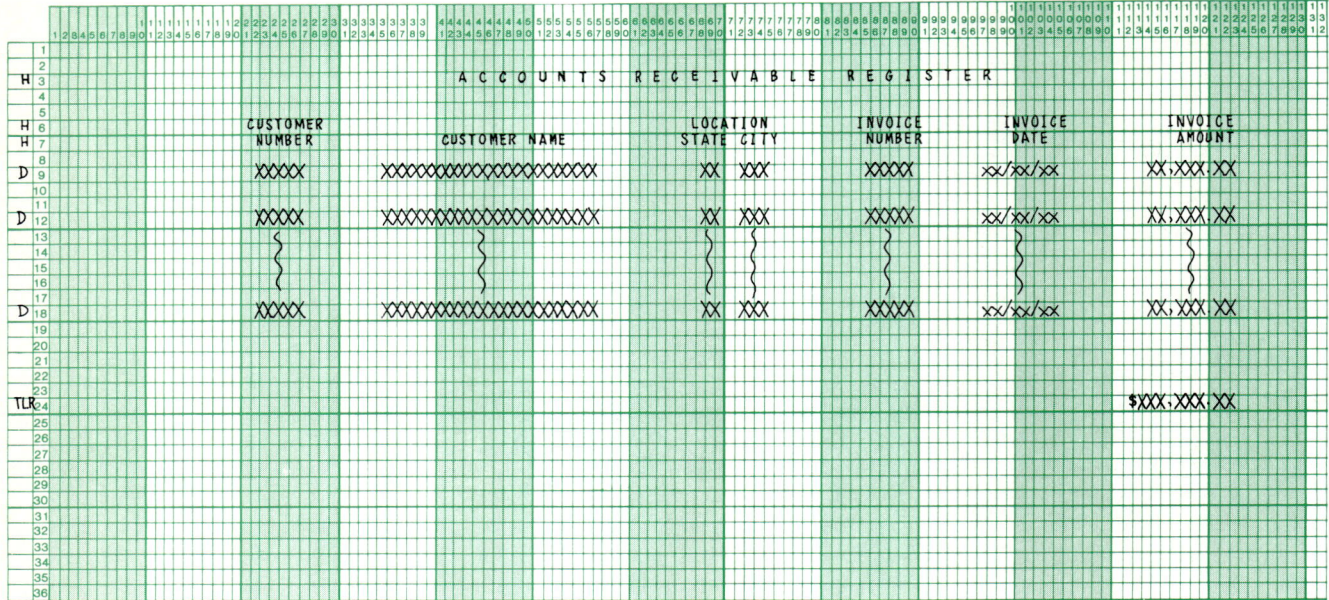

Problem 2

Stock Inventory Report

Job Definition
A detail printed report titled Stock Inventory Report is to be produced from a file of records arranged in ascending numerical order (by the material number field). Totals of on-hand cost are to be printed for each type of material.

Input
The input file consists of two 75-byte records.

	Date Record
Positions	**Field Description**
1–06	Date
75–75	Code: Letter *D*
	Stock Record
Positions	**Field Description**
7–09	Material number
12–16	Stock number
19–22	Unit cost (XXX.XX)
26–29	Item description
70–73	Quantity on hand
75–75	Code: Letter *M*

Processing

1. The individual detail records are to be printed with proper headings and editing.

2. The total lines are to be printed with proper headings and editing.

3. For each detail record, the quantity on hand is to be multiplied by the unit cost to calculate the on-hand cost. This cost is to be rounded to the nearest whole dollar.

4. A total on-hand cost is to be calculated for each group of records with the same material number.

5. A date record precedes the file of records.

Output

A Stock Inventory Report is to be printed as follows:

```
                         STOCK INVENTORY REPORT
                               1/16/86


MATERIAL    STOCK         DESCRIPTION         UNIT       QUANTITY      ON HAND
  NO.        NO.                              COST       ON HAND        COST

  025       96543      CARBORUNDUM WHEELS     102.50       4646        476,215

            THE TOTAL ON HAND COST IN DOLLARS FOR MATERIAL NUMBER 025 IS    $476,215  **

  111       00986      STAINLESS SET SCREWS NSP  4.20      5986         25,141
  111       01598      STAINLESS RODS            85.90      934         80,231
  111       09346      HI GRADE CARBON           48.20       52          2,506
  111       11632      CARBON STEEL              59.60     1598         95,241
  111       11723      STAINLESS PINS            91.70       52          4,768
  111       11725      STAINLESS TUBING          11.50      915         10,523

            THE TOTAL ON HAND COST IN DOLLARS FOR MATERIAL NUMBER 111 IS    $218,410  **
```

The Printer Spacing Chart shows how the report is formatted:

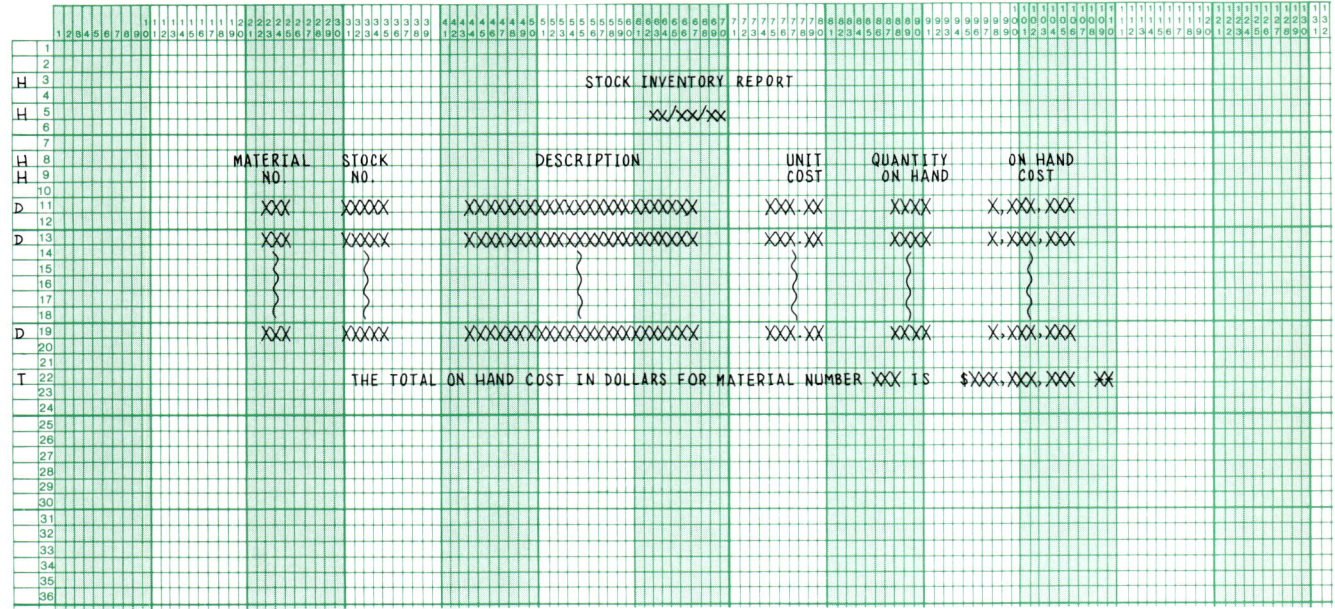

Problem 3

Weekly Payroll Register

Job Definition

A detailed printed report titled Weekly Payroll Register is to be prepared weekly from a file of records arranged by employee numbers within departments. The report should show the various payroll calculations as well as totals by department for net earnings. A final total of all net earnings should be printed.

Input

The input file consists of detail records for each employee with the following information:

Positions	Field Description	
1–03	Department number	
4–08	Week-ending date	(XX/XX/XX)
9–14	Employee number	
15–34	Employee name	
39–43	Hours worked	(XXX.XX)
44–48	Hourly rate	(XX.XXX)
52–53	Number of exemptions	
54–58	Insurance	(XXX.XX)
59–63	Miscellaneous deductions	(XXX.XX)
67–73	Year-to-date earnings	(XXXXX.XX)

Processing

The following computations are to be performed on the input data:

1. Gross earnings = hours worked × hourly rate (round to two decimal places)
2. FICA = gross earnings (up to $16,500 of year-to-date earnings only) × .0585 (round to two decimal places)
3. Withholding tax = gross earnings (number of exemptions × $15.00) × 16 percent (round to two decimal places)
4. State UCI = gross earnings (up to $9,000 of year-to-date earnings only) × 1 percent (round to two decimal places)
5. Net earnings = gross earnings (insurance, FICA, withholding tax, state UCI, miscellaneous deductions)
6. YTD gross = YTD gross + gross earnings
7. Department earnings total = the sum of net earnings for each employee in the department
8. Final earnings total = the sum of all net earnings for employees

Output

A Weekly Payroll Register is to be printed as follows:

```
                              WEEKLY PAYROLL REGISTER

DEPT.  EMPLOYEE                    GROSS                        WITH.   STATE  MISC.    NET       Y-T-D
NO.    NUMBER    EMPLOYEE NAME     EARNINGS  INSURANCE  FICA    TAX     UCI    DEDNS.   EARNINGS  EARNINGS


014    045867    J D ROBINSON      190.00    12.00      11.11   20.80   1.90   5.60     138.59    8,942.64
014    078546    G S HAYES         325.95    175.10     19.06   44.95   .00    36.75    50.09     16,172.12
014    146978    C M MICHOLESON    500.08    80.10      .00     68.01   .00    7.50     344.47    19,000.25
014    385692    C J MEYERSHMIDT   217.44    5.00       12.72   25.19   2.17   .00      172.36    1,074.39

                                                                                        705.51 *


125    069574    T R HENDERSON     311.24    6.50       18.20   45.00   .00    8.25     233.29    10,986.09
125    148562    B S CAMIRILLO     540.35    50.10      .00     76.86   .00    15.00    398.39    21,144.50
125    897054    S M WATTERS       475.00    140.50     27.78   66.40   .00    135.64   104.68    16,327.94

                                                                                        736.36 *



                                                                                        1,441.87 **
```

The Printer Spacing Chart shows how the report is formatted:

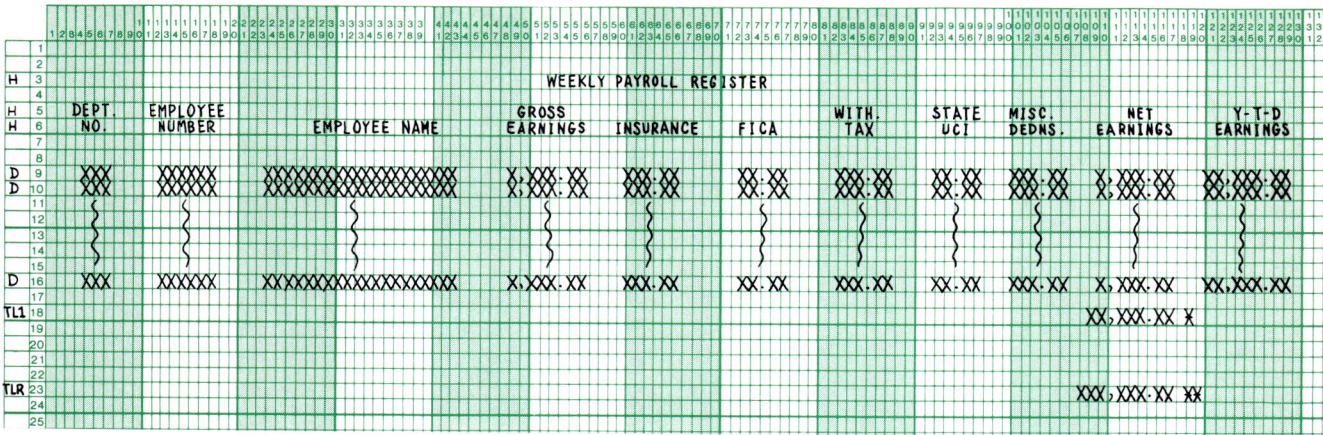

Problem 4

Salesman District Report

Job Definition

A summary printed report is to be prepared showing the totals by salesman and district as well as an overall sales total for all salesmen. The file is in sequence by salesman number within each district.

Input

The input file consists of detail records for each sale of each product by salesman. The file is arranged in ascending sequence of salesman number within each district. The file consists of the following:

Positions	Field Description
1–02	Product number
3–07	Quantity amount (XXX.XX)
8–09	Salesman number
10–10	District number

Processing

1. *Minor Control:* The quantity amount is to be accumulated for each salesman number.
2. *Intermediate Control:* The salesman totals are to be accumulated for a district total.
3. A final total is to be accumulated for all salesmen.

Output

A Salesman District Report is to be printed as follows:

```
        SALESMAN              DISTRICT         TOTAL
        --------              --------         -----

   10    $241.80
   20    $148.08
                                 1           $389.88
   41    $457.50
   60    $117.40
                                 2           $574.90
   31    $145.70
   32    $404.48
   61    $189.12
                                 3           $739.30
                                             $1,704.08
```

Appendix G 643

The Printer Spacing Chart shows how the report is formatted:

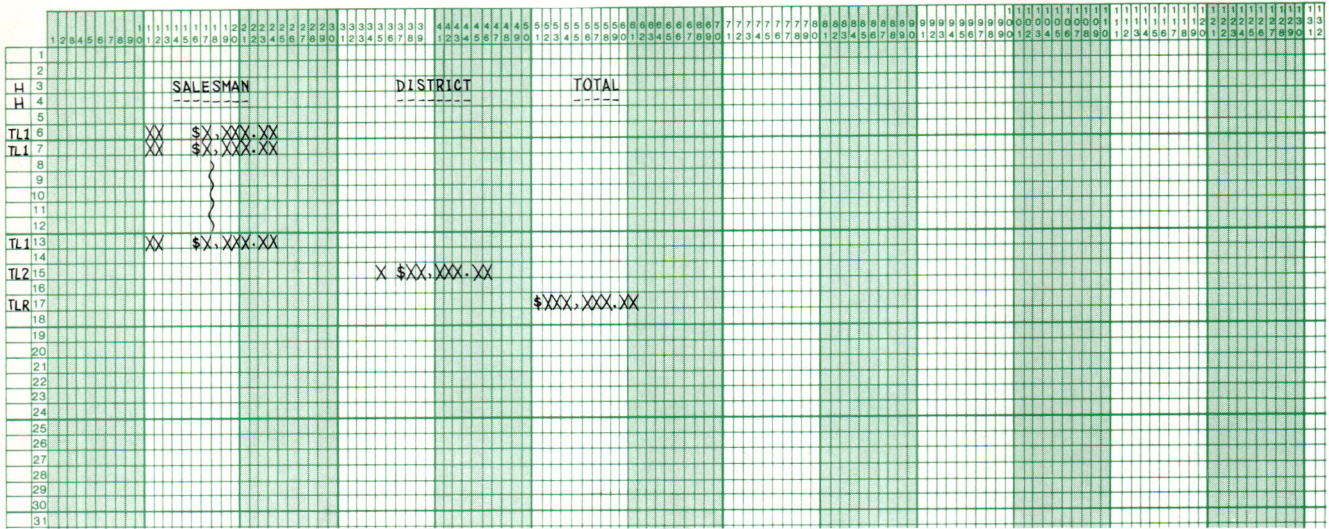

Problem 5

Bank Balance Report

Job Definition

A quarterly report of the depositors' balances is to be prepared. Each account number, whether checking or savings, has an identification code. The new depositor balances are to be computed. The savings accounts receive 5.75 percent interest on the new balance.

Input

The input file consists of 32-byte records with the following information:

Positions	Field Description	
1–05	Account number	
6–06	Type code:	1 indicates a checking account
		2 indicates a savings account
9–16	Deposits	(XXXXXX.XX)
17–24	Withdrawals	(XXXXXX.XX)
25–32	Last balance	(XXXXXX.XX)

Processing

1. The interest earned on a savings account is calculated as follows:

    INTEREST EARNED = RATE (.0575) × LAST BALANCE (WITHDRAWALS + DEPOSITS)

2. The new balance is calculated as follows:

    NEW BALANCE = LAST BALANCE (WITHDRAWALS + DEPOSITS + INTEREST, if any).

Output
A Bank Balance Report is to be printed as follows:

```
ACCOUNT NO.        NEW BALANCE

   61788             7,666.88
   61003            11,103.75
   58440           103,589.92
   57905            38,872.38
   60756            37,656.25
   61880            26,061.43
   59425            51,404.28
   63740            45,587.50
   65500            11,103.75
   62711             5,551.88
   60912            11,103.75
   57280             7,931.25
   59014            20,150.00
   60545            51,456.63
```

The Printer Spacing Chart shows how the report is to be formatted:

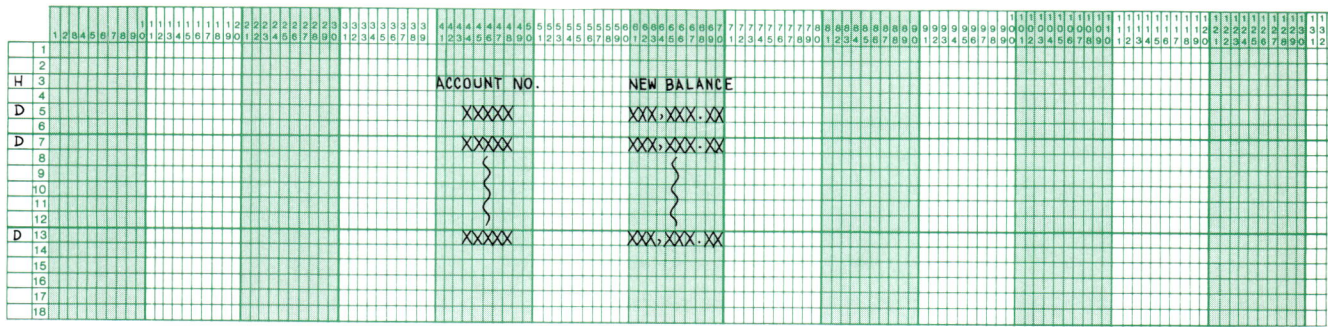

Problem 6

Department Store Report

Job Definition
A department store prepares a monthly listing of its credit record customers. The purchases and payments for the month are posted to the accounts and a 1 percent service charge is added to the new balance. The report lists all charges, sales, payments, service charges, and amount due.

Input
The input file consists of a 70-byte record containing the following information:

Positions	Field Description	
1–15	Customer name	
16–50	Customer address	
51–55	Account number	
56–60	Last balance	(XXX.XX)
61–65	Month's sales	(XXX.XX)
66–70	Payments	(XXX.XX)

Appendix G 645

Processing

1. The service charge is to be computed as follows:

   SERVICE CHARGE = .015 × LAST BALANCE (PAYMENTS). The answer is to be rounded to two decimal positions.

2. The amount due is to be computed as follows:

   AMOUNT DUE = LAST BALANCE (PAYMENTS) + SERVICE CHARGE + MONTH'S SALES

Output

A Department Store Report is to be printed as follows:

DEPARTMENT STORE REPORT

NAME OF CUSTOMER	ADDRESS OF CUSTOMER	ACCOUNT	PREVIOUS BALANCE	SALES	PAYMENT	SERVICE CHARGE	AMT DUE
DAVID ANDERSON	18745 MOBILE ST., RESEDA, CA	62986	$100.00	$100.00	$20.00	$1.20	$181.20
BETTY L. BREWER	10321 LUNDY DR., INGLEWOOD, CA	61477	$350.25	$50.00	$30.00	$4.80	$375.05
ARTHUR BROWN	12145 MADISON ST., LA, CA	38940	$450.00	$30.00	$50.00	$6.00	$436.00
THOMAS CASSIDY	3726 HOPE AVE., LYNWOOD, CA	62180	$121.50	$40.00	$20.00	$1.52	$143.02
BOB CHAMBERS	3840 HOPE AVE., LYNWOOD, CA	58920	$320.00	$15.50	$35.00	$4.28	$304.78
JACK T. CROSS	6421 BELMAR ST., RESEDA, CA	43313	$105.80	$150.85	$20.00	$1.29	$237.94
KENT B. DAVIS	11621 PENN DRIVE, ENCINO, CA	84082	$320.75	$75.75	$35.00	$4.29	$365.79
SAMUAL FELLOWS	10732 LINDLEY AVE., ENCINO, CA	41750	$290.60	$40.37	$30.00	$3.91	$304.88
MICHAEL FISHER	6345 TAMPA AVE., TARZANA, CA	30040	$444.35	$65.25	$50.00	$5.92	$465.52
GLADYS BUTTONS	3701 BALBOA AVE., VAN NUYS, CA	67542	$375.00	$89.30	$45.00	$4.95	$424.25
PATRICK HANEY	4218 VICTORY ST., LA, CA	72111	$450.10	$27.95	$55.00	$5.93	$428.98
LYNN HUBBARD	13245 VENTURA BLVD., RESEDA, CA	64375	$195.75	$36.45	$25.00	$2.56	$209.76
MARVIN JACOBS	13211 VENTURA BLVD., READEA, CA	62550	$225.95	$44.95	$30.00	$2.94	$243.84
LINDA JOHNSON	20715 VAN NUYS BLVD., ENCINO, CA	58214	$300.00	$87.50	$35.00	$3.98	$356.48
HOWARD KEYES	2181 SHERMAN WAY, RESEDA, CA	46615	$279.80	$101.75	$30.00	$3.75	$355.30
HAZEL J. MEYER	2188 ROSCOE BLVD., LYNWOOD, CA	30881	$380.50	$30.00	$40.00	$5.11	$375.61
DONALD OLSON	11650 ROSCOE BLVD., LYNWOOD, CA	43779	$277.60	$15.95	$30.00	$3.71	$267.26
IAN SWIFT	17521 LINDLEY AVE., ENCINO, CA	58090	$251.75	$85.50	$35.00	$3.25	$305.50
SHARON WATTERS	13155 MADISON STREET, LA, CA	60070	$355.25	$47.95	$40.00	$4.73	$367.93

The Printer Spacing Chart shows how the report is to be formatted:

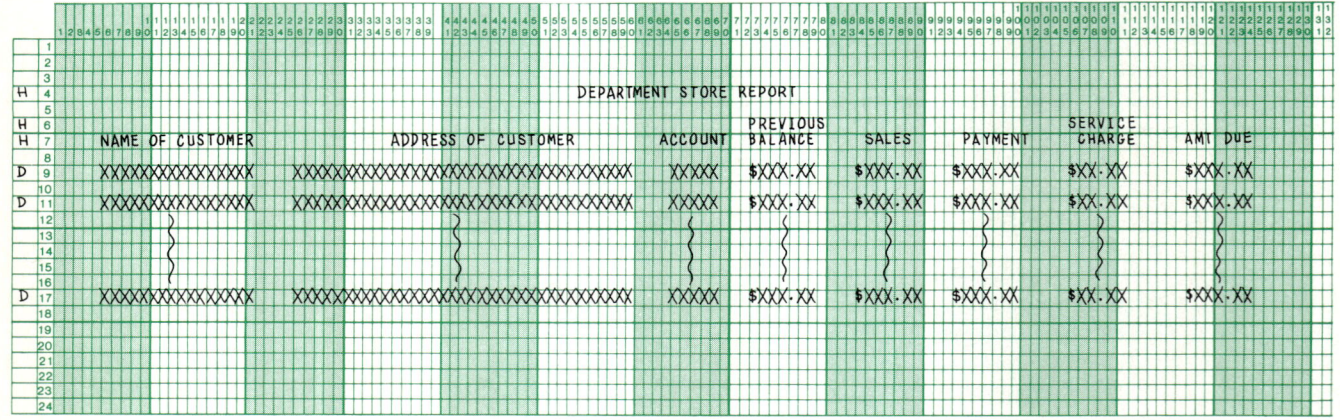

Problem 7

"Africa" Payroll Report

Job Definition
Each month a payroll is processed in order to print checks. The company has a subsidiary in Africa whose employees, though U.S. citizens, are not required to pay income tax. These employees have the characters *As* in front of their numbers; other employees have spaces in these character positions.

A record file contains a master record for every employee in the company. Each record contains the employee's name, number, the regular and overtime hours worked during the month, the wages earned so far this year, the rate of pay, and the number of dependents. The payroll is processed in the usual manner, computing gross pay, FICA, withholding tax, and net pay. The results are used to print checks and to create new master records. These new records contain the new year-to-date gross earnings and zeros in the hours field (both regular and overtime). These new records create an output file that will be used next month as input. (During the month the regular hours and overtime hours are added in by another program.)

Input
The input file consists of a 62-byte record containing the following information:

Positions	Field Description	
1–19	Employee name	
30–39	Employee number	
41–43	Rate	(X.XX)
44–45	Dependents	
46–50	Regular hours	(XXX.XX)
51–55	Overtime hours	(XXX.XX)
56–62	Year-to-date gross earnings	(XXXXX.XX)

Processing
The program will use a table of income tax exemptions according to the number of dependents. The table looks like this:

0	1	2	3	4	5	6	7	8	9	10
$0	$56	$112	$168	$224	$280	$336	$392	$448	$504	$560

The following computations will be used in the program:

In America
1. GROSS PAY = (REGULAR HOURS × RATE) + (OVERTIME HOURS × 1½ RATE)
2. FICA = .0613 × GROSS PAY (if year-to-date gross earnings is less than $16,500)
3. WITHHOLDING TAX × .18 = (GROSS PAY − SUB). SUB is the exemption according to dependents chart.
4. NET PAY = GROSS PAY − FICA − WITHHOLDING TAX

In Africa
1. GROSS PAY = (REGULAR HOURS × RATE) + (OVERTIME HOURS × 1½ RATE)
2. WITHHOLDING TAX = 0
3. FICA = .0613 × GROSS PAY (if year-to-date gross earnings is less than $16,500)
4. NET PAY = GROSS PAY − FICA

Output

The checks for the Monthly Payroll Report are printed on three lines as follows:

NAME	EMP. NO.	GROSS	WH-TAX	FICA	NET PAY	NET PAY	DATE
PAUL A. EVANS							8/23/87
						$338.81	
PAUL A. EVANS	053487	$420.00	$55.44	$25.75	$338.81		
MARY DIXON							8/23/87
						$433.33	
MARY DIXON	A062986	$461.63	$.00	$28.30	$433.33		
GUY T GOODWIN							8/25/87
						$433.05	
GUY T GOODWIN	020981	$504.35	$40.38	$30.92	$433.05		
JAMES F KING							9/01/87
						$57.50	
JAMES F KING	A053219	$61.26	$.00	$3.76	$57.50		
MILTON C MORGAN							9/05/87
						$422.60	
MILTON C MORGAN	064378	$464.00	$12.96	$28.44	$422.60		
JOHN L REED							9/06/87
						$452.00	
JOHN L REED	052887	$569.18	$82.29	$34.89	$452.00		
JACK L SHAFFER							9/07/87
						$473.64	
JACK L SHAFFER	061758	$571.13	$62.48	$35.01	$473.64		

The Printer Spacing Chart shows how the report is to be formatted:

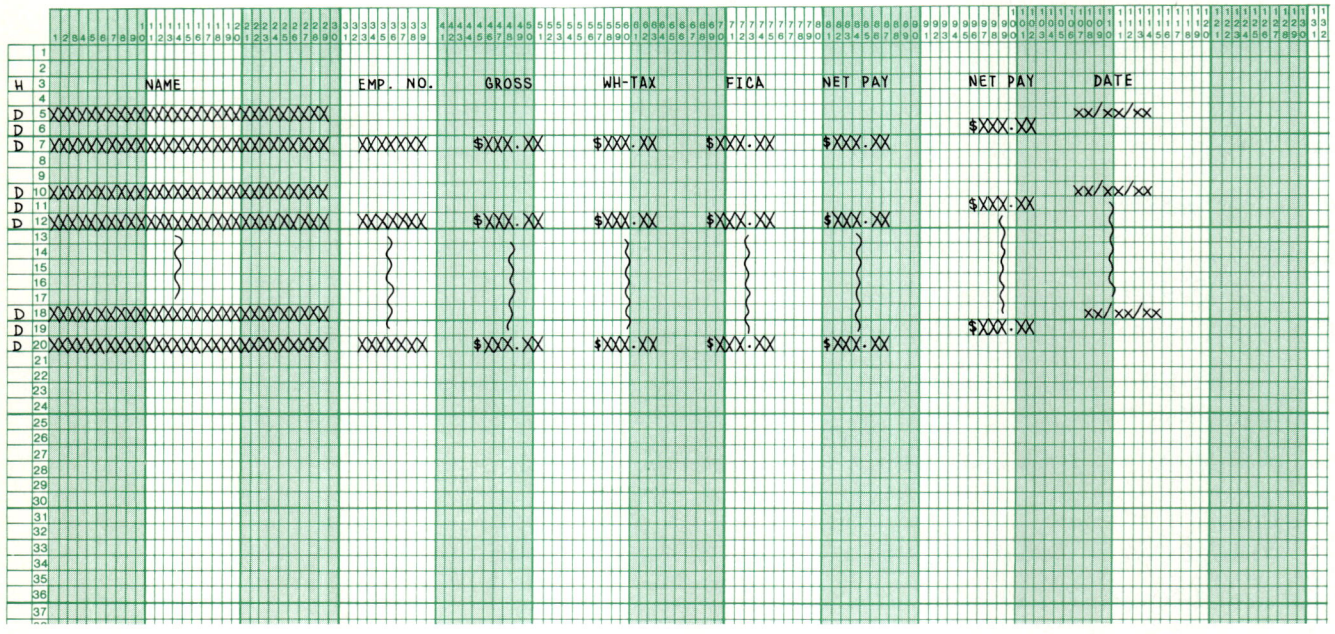

RPG II and RPG III Programming

Problem 8

Shampoo Report

Job Definition

In a beauty salon, operators are paid by the amount and type of work they do. The shampoo operators receive $4.00 per customer; the hair cutters receive $5.50 per customer; the hair setters receive $6.00 per customer; the stylists receive $8.00 per customer; and the permanent wave operators receive $10.00 per customer.

The earnings for each operator are to be computed based on the number of customers in each rate category served.

Input

The input file consists of a 29-byte record containing the following information:

Positions	Field Description
1–25	Customer name
26–26	Type:
	1 = Shampoo
	2 = Hair cutters
	3 = Hair setters
	4 = Stylists
	5 = Permanent wave
27–29	Number of customers

Processing

To find gross pay, the number of customers is to be multiplied by the appropriate rate based on the type.

Output

The report of salon operations is to be printed as follows:

```
TYPE OF OPERATION.
     SHAMPOO - - - - - - 1
     HAIR CUTTERS- - - - 2
     HAIR SETTERS- - - - 3
     STYLISTS- - - - - - 4
     PERMANENT WAVE- - - 5
```

NAME OF OPERATOR	TYPE	NO. OF CUSTOMERS	GROSS PAY
SUSAN CALDWELL	1	100	400.00
BETTY JANE CLANCY	1	120	480.00
RUTH ANN CORBETT	1	150	600.00
MARGARET CUSHING	2	100	550.00
ROSEMARY DUPUIS	2	75	412.50
MAURICE ERICKSON	2	50	275.00
LILLIAN FELLING	3	100	600.00
NANCY HAMILTON	3	125	750.00
BARBARA HICKMAN	3	110	660.00
JOSEPHINE HOUSTON	4	50	400.00
LORETTA JOHNSON	4	40	320.00
ELAINE LEONARD	4	30	240.00
LORRAINE CLARK	5	30	300.00
TERRY MCDONNELL	5	35	350.00
MARY ANN PALMER	5	40	400.00

The Printer Spacing Chart shows how the report is formatted:

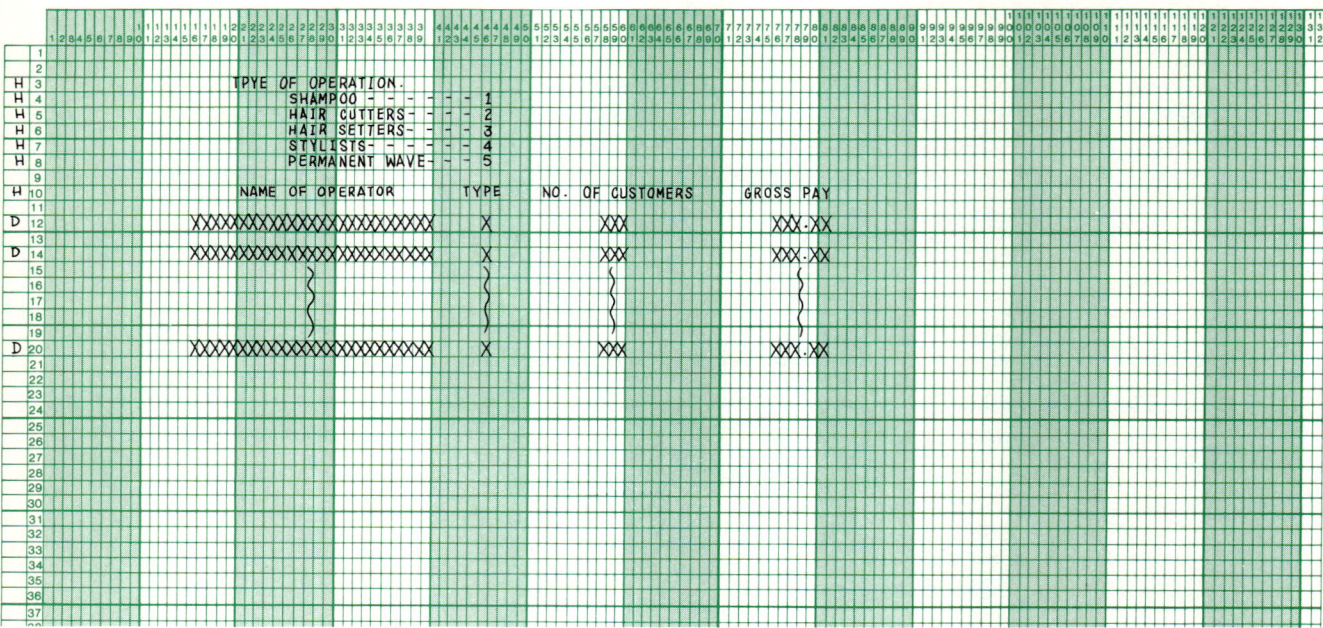

Problem 9

Customer Discount Report

Job Definition

The TNW Company grants discounts to its customers based on a certain code. A report is prepared showing the customer number, item number, list price, quantity, code, gross amount, discount amount, and net due.

Input

The input file consists of a 22-byte record containing the following fields:

Positions	Field Description	
1–05	Customer number	
6–09	Item number	
12–16	List price	(XXX.XX)
17–20	Quantity	
21–22	Class code	

Processing

1. The gross amount is computed by multiplying the quantity by the list price. The discount allowed is based on the following codes:

    Class code 1 receives a 15 percent discount.
    Class code 2 receives a 10 percent discount.
    Class code 3 receives a 5 percent discount.
    Class code 4 receives no discount.

2. The net amount is computed by subtracting the discount allowed from the gross amount.

Output

The Customer Discount Report is printed as follows:

```
                        CUSTOMER DISCOUNT REPORT

CUSTOMER    ITEM      LIST
NUMBER      NUMBER    PRICE     QUANTITY    CODE    GROSS       DISCOUNT      NET

 45321      5000      450.00        20        3     9,000.00       450.00     8,550.00
 45678      5000      450.00        30        1    13,500.00     2,025.00    11,475.00
 12345      3012       30.00       150        2     4,500.00       450.00     4,050.00
 03567      4126       12.50        50        2       625.00        62.50       562.50
 14075      2115       35.60      2162        1    76,967.20    11,545.08    65,422.12
 75709      7654      125.75       564        1    70,923.00    10,638.45    60,284.55
 89705      3624       75.12      3645        4   273,812.40          .00   273,812.40
 39876      4255      102.34       365        3    37,354.10     1,867.70    35,486.40
```

The Printer Spacing Chart shows how the report is formatted:

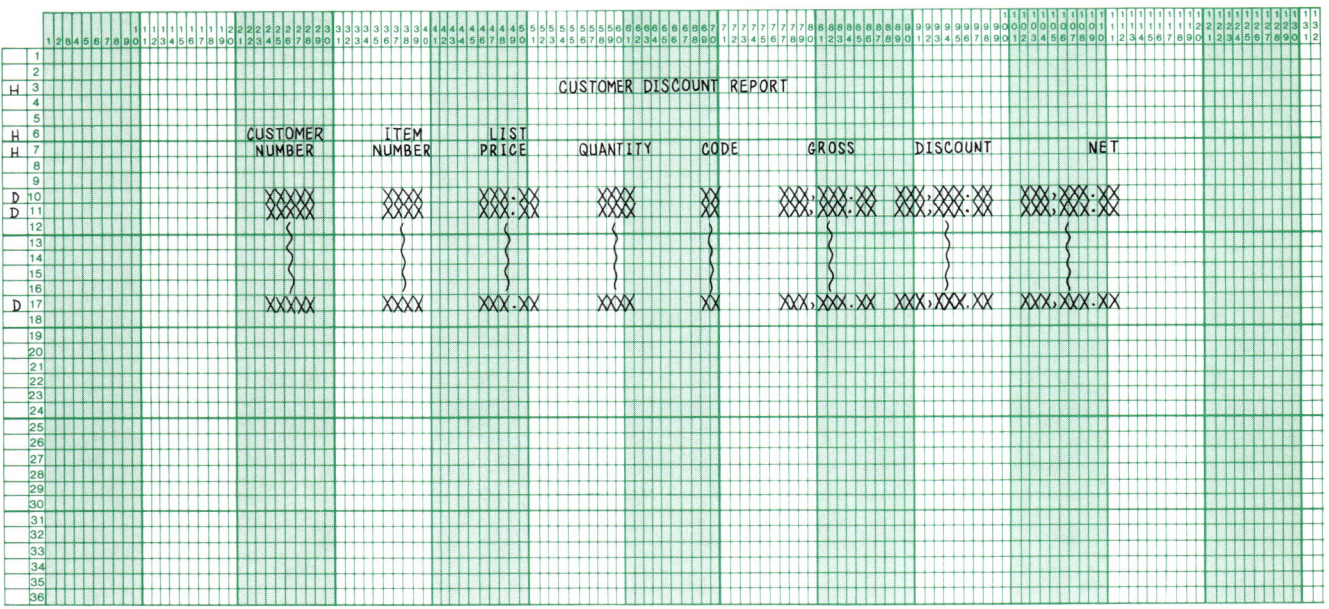

Problem 10

State Report

Job Definition

The program is to be designed to calculate the average of a set of numbers. The calculation is to be written into a subroutine. The main program will read in the specific data, call the subroutine, and print out the results. The data (population, size, and road mileage of each of fifty states) is to be read in, and the average population, size, and road mileage calculated.

Input

The input file consists of a 46-byte record with the following information:

Positions	Field Description
1–16	State name
21–38	Population
31–36	Size
41–46	Road mileage

Processing

1. The average for population, size, and road mileage is to be calculated.
2. A subroutine is to be used to calculate the various averages.
3. The averages are to be printed at the end of the report.

Output

The State Report is to be printed as follows:

```
                            STATE REPORT

                                        SIZE       ROAD
            STATE NAME    POPULATION   SQ. MILES  MILEAGE

            ALABAMA        3,444,165     51,609    85,845
            ALASKA           302,173    586,412     9,043
            ARIZONA        1,772,482    113,909    51,415
            ARKANSAS       1,923,295     53,104    78,088
            CALIFORNIA    19,953,134    158,693   169,564
            COLORADO       2,207,259    104,247    83,586
            CONNECTICUT    3,032,217      5,009    13,734
            DELAWARE         548,104      2,057     5,150
            FLORIDA        6,789,443     58,560    98,129
            GEORGIA        4,589,575     58,876   100,335
            HAWAII           769,913      6,450     3,666
            IDAHO            713,008     83,557    55,910
            ILLINOIS      11,113,976     56,540   130,494
            INDIANA        5,193,689     36,291    91,111
            IOWA           2,825,041     56,290   112,944
            KANSAS         2,249,071     82,264   134,770
            KENTUCKY       3,219,311     40,395    69,791
            LOUISIANA      3,643,180     48,523    54,124
            MAINE            993,663     33,215    21,499
            MARYLAND       3,922,399     10,577    26,859
            MASSACHUSETTS  5,689,170      8,257    29,811
            MICHIGAN       8,875,083     58,016   118,310
            MINNESOTA      3,805,069     84,068   128,235
            MISSISSIPPI    2,216,912     47,716    66,686
            MISSOURI       4,677,399     69,686   114,966
            MONTANA          694,409    147,138    77,932
            NEBRASKA       1,483,791     77,227    98,017
            NEVADA           488,738    110,540    49,659
            NEW HAMPSHIRE    737,681      9,304    15,024
            NEW JERSEY     7,168,164      7,836    32,422
            NEW MEXICO     1,016,000    121,666    70,307
            NEW YORK      18,241,266     49,576   107,776
            NORTH CAROLINA 5,082,059     52,586    87,922
            NORTH DAKOTA     617,761     70,665   106,247
            OHIO          10,652,017     41,222   109,965
            OKLAHOMA       2,559,253     69,919   108,509
            OREGON         2,091,385     96,981   101,397
            PENNSYLVANIA  11,793,909     45,333   114,497
            RHODE ISLAND     949,723      1,214     5,540
            SOUTH CAROLINA 2,509,516     31,055    60,295
            SOUTH DAKOTA     666,257     77,047    82,720
            TENNESSEE      3,924,164     42,244    80,656
            TEXAS         11,196,730    267,338   251,489
            UTAH           1,059,273     84,916    47,653
            VERMONT          444,732      9,609    13,924
            VIRGINIA       4,648,494     40,817    62,351
            WASHINGTON     3,409,169     68,192    81,202
            WEST VIRGINIA  1,744,237     24,181    36,323
            WISCONSIN      4,417,933     56,154   104,290
            WYOMING          332,416     97,914    40,602

THE AVERAGE POPULATION IS    4,047,956

THE AVERAGE SIZE IS             72,300

THE AVERAGE ROAD MILEAGE IS     76,016
```

The Printer Spacing Chart shows how the report is formatted:

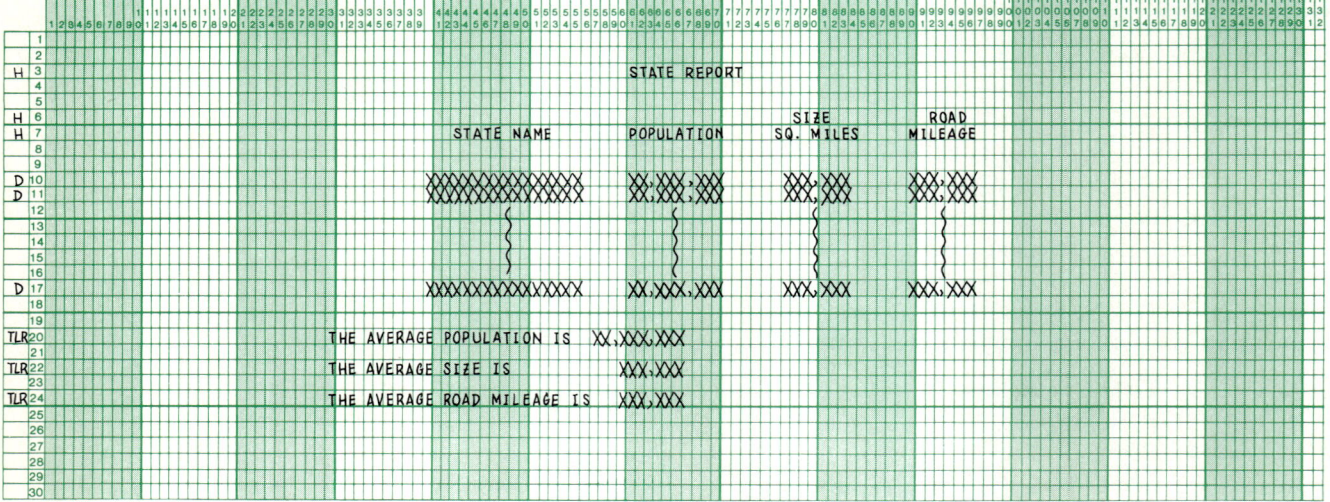

Problem 11

Insurance Premiums

Job Definition

In an insurance premium run, monthly rates are determined by the risk class. In this situation a wide and irregular gap exists between the argument assigned to one table value and the argument assigned to the table value that follows. The premium rate assigned should correspond either to the table value that matches or to the next higher table value.

Input

The input file consists of a 43-byte record with the following information:

Positions	Field Description
1–10	Policy number
11–31	Name
32–37	Date
40–43	Risk class

Processing

An alternating compile time table is to be set up as follows:

Risk Class	Premium Rate
210	$17.50
273	15.50
370	12.30
420	11.95
465	14.60
481	15.25
900	19.45
950	20.01
988	18.10
1030	8.55
1245	14.03
1366	19.99
1505	20.33
1666	12.22
1899	10.00

Search the table for the appropriate (or near appropriate) risk class and record the premium rate. If the appropriate risk class cannot be found, the premium rate for the next higher risk class must be used.

Output

The Insurance Premiums Report is to be printed as follows:

```
                      INSURANCE PREMIUMS

POLICY NUMBER         NAME               DATE       RISK CLASS

  563 781 532    ROBERT PALMER         8/25/87         536

 5310 562 386    SUZIE WILSON          8/25/87        1302

 7802 619 435    DAVE LEWIS            8/25/87        1723

 4530 789 138    BONNIE SELWOOD        8/25/87         798

  400 831 562    GISELLE AGERGAARD     8/25/87         639

 7319 530 088    DEAN HOPKINS          8/25/87        1699

 7066 238 009    DOUG KEANS            8/25/87         901

 4308 615 398    MIKE COOPER           8/25/87        1086

 8023 614 528    RONNIE SALTZER        8/25/87        1630
```

The Printer Spacing Chart shows how the report is formatted:

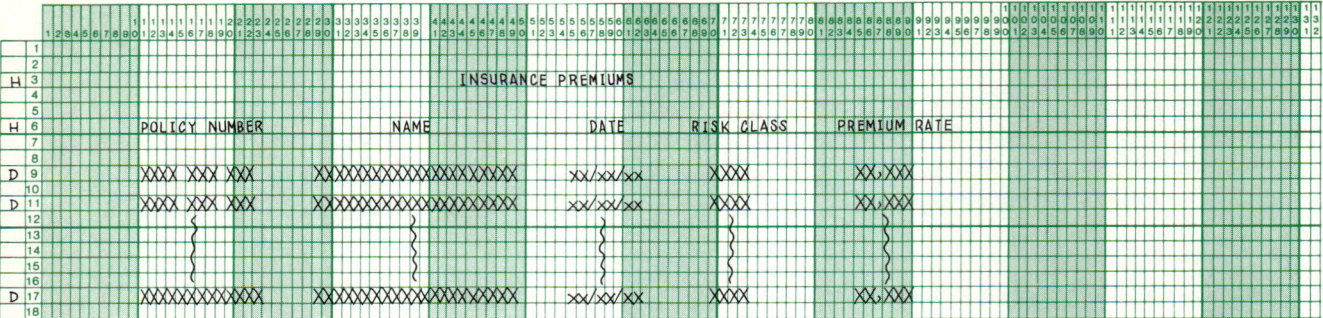

Problem 12

Daily Sales Report

Job Definition

The Duron Corporation maintains various departments in its stores. A Daily Sales Report is to be printed showing the daily sales of each department as well as a weekly total of daily sales. A daily sales total and a weekly total is to be shown for each store; an overall total for all days and totals is also to be provided.

Input

The input file consists of a 39-byte record with the following information:

Positions	Field Description
1–03	Store number
4–07	Department number
10–39	A five-element array of daily sales (each day's sales consists of six positions with the format) (XXXX.XX)

Processing

1. Three arrays are to be set up for the department, store, and overall totals.
2. Each array should be added to the other arrays to arrive at daily totals for stores as well as overall totals.
3. Each array should be crossfooted to arrive at weekly totals.

Output

The Daily Sales Report is to be printed as follows:

```
                              DAILY SALES REPORT

STORE   DEPARTMENT   FIRST      SECOND     THIRD      FOURTH     FIFTH      TOTALS
NO.     NO.          SALE       SALE       SALE       SALE       SALE

123     1359         12.93      291.60     2,000.15   250.37     100.35     2,655.40
        1530        130.00        2.50     3,040.00    25.19     234.10     3,431.79
        2400         24.59       29.47       120.44    28.30     166.25       369.05
        3594          2.48       15.90        23.00     1.22      35.20        77.80

                    170.00      339.47     5,183.59   305.08     535.90     6,534.04

530     1280         25.10      200.50        12.57   111.20     259.10       608.47
        3320      1,002.45       19.45       279.33 1,234.50   3,000.20     5,535.93
        7730         24.60       10.24        39.13   294.33      29.30       397.60

                  1,052.15      230.19       331.03 1,640.03   3,288.60     6,542.00


        TOTALS    1,222.15      569.66     5,514.62 1,945.11   3,824.50    13,076.04
```

The Printer Spacing Chart shows how the report is to be formatted:

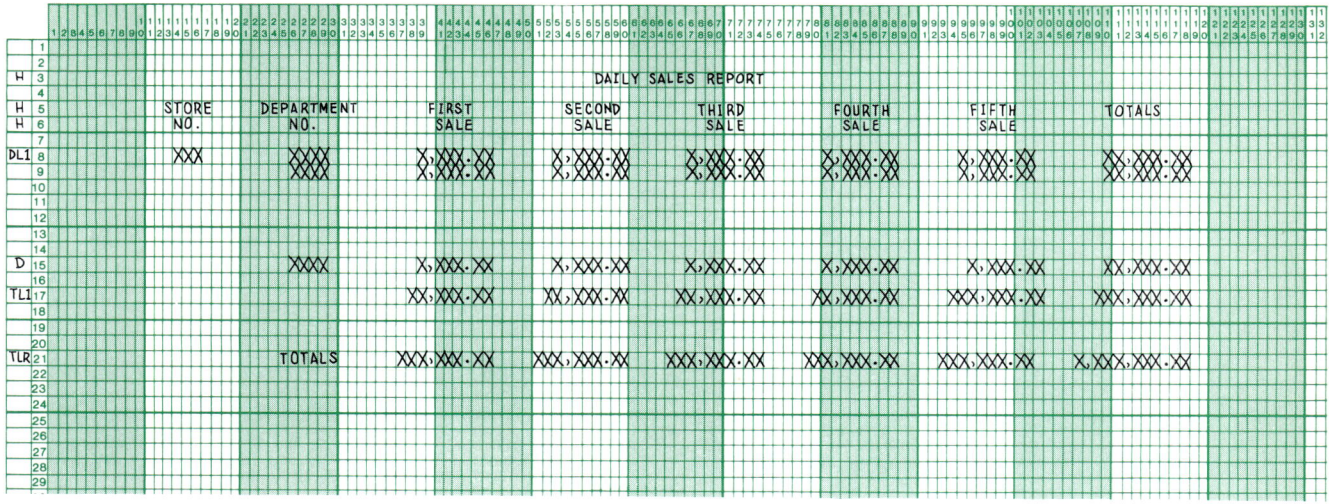

Problem 13

Creating an Indexed Disk File

Job Definition
The Toluca Community College has a problem keeping track of students who move frequently and needs a program to update addresses in its indexed disk file. This program will create the indexed disk file that will be updated subsequently in another program.

Input
The input file will consist of 66-byte records with the following information:

Positions	Field Description
1–09	Social security number
10–31	Student name
35–55	Street address
60–62	City
65–66	State

Processing
Create an indexed disk file containing the information listed above.

Output
The output will be the indexed disk record containing the above information.

Problem 14

Output an Indexed Disk File

Job Definition
The indexed disk file created in problem 13 is to be outputted on the printer to check the accuracy of the created records.

Input
No data will be inputted.

Processing
Print out the contents of the indexed disk records created in problem 13.

Output

The output of the indexed disk records will be printed as follows:

```
420689235STEVE  JENSON              3740  OVERLAND ST.           LA    CA
555096862WILLIAM  FOSTER            10816 SLAUSON AVE.           LA    CA
559236156DAN  SCHOENECKER           10814 KINGSLAND ST.          LS    CA
750236999TOM  WILLIAMS              4500  WEST 57 TH ST.         LA    CA
755423306KATHY BUTLER               4240  WEST WASHINGTON PL.    BH    CA
800263349TONY SCHOENECKER           83556 WILSHIRE BLVD.         WLA   CA
808612377ROBERT  PALMER             2465  MADISON AVE.           NY    NY
836205691MARY SCHOENECKER           99304 CHATSWORTH BLVD.       SE    ILL
838562008JANETTE  SPORTCOLEMAN      83566 COMMUNITY LN.          CH    ILL
850315663JIM COLEMAN                88302 SEPULVEDA BLVD.        LA    CA
850324961JANE COLEMAN               832   DON MILLS RD.          SM    CA
862034856JOEY  SCHOENECKER          9604  JEFFERSON BLVD.        CC    CA
```

The Printer Spacing Chart shows how the report is formatted:

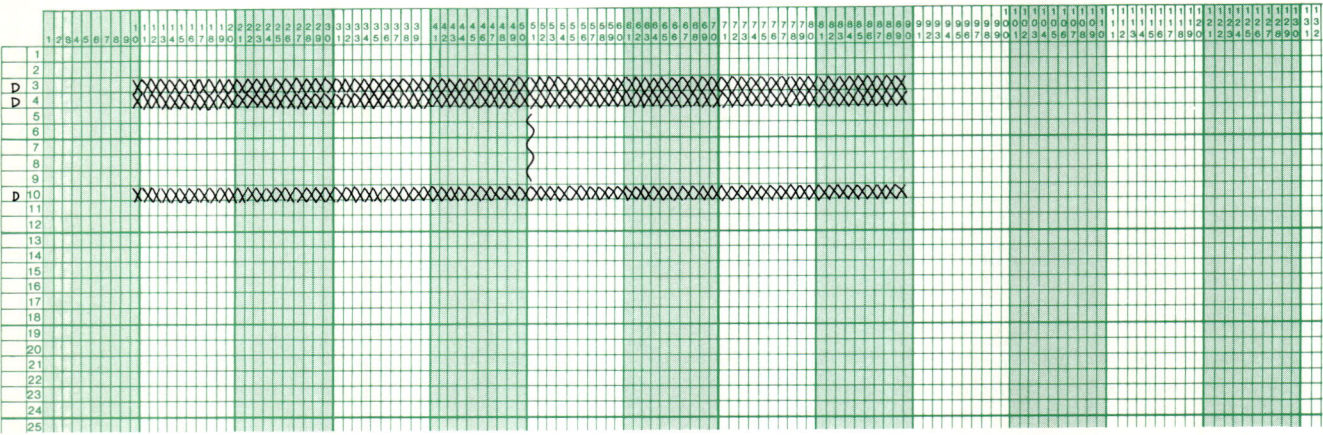

Problem 15

Student Status Report

Job Definition

This program updates the indexed disk records created in problem 13. Change transactions are submitted and are to be processed with the master indexed disk file to update addresses. If no match is found, this should be properly indicated with a message.

Input

There will be two input files: the indexed disk file and the change transactions.

	Indexed Disk File
Positions	**Field Description**
1–09	Social security number
10–31	Name
35–55	Street address
60–62	City
65–66	State

	Change Records
Positions	**Field Description**
1–09	Social security number
10–31	Name
35–55	New street address
60–62	New city
65–66	New state

Processing

1. Change records are to be matched against the indexed disk file on social security number.
2. If a match occurs, the new address is to be written on the indexed disk file.
3. If no match occurs, the message "NO MATCHING RECORD" is to be written on the printer output report.
4. A report is to be prepared on the printer showing the various changes.

Output

The indexed disk record is to be updated. The Student Status Report will be printed as follows:

```
                            STUDENT STATUS
    SOC. SEC.         NAME              STREET              CITY     STATE

    420-68-9235    NO MATCHING RECORD

    555-09-6862    WILLIAM FOSTER    7881 BRADDOCK STREET    CC       CA

    559-23-6156    SCHOENECKER DAN   5950 SUNNYBROOK WAY     WLA      CA

    750-23-6999    TOM WILLIAMS      80261 VAN NESS AVENUE   VN       CA

    755-42-3306    KATHY BUTLER      7509 CULVER BLVD        CC       CA

    800-26-3349    CATHY GORING      83250 STUBBS LANE       CC       CA

    802-35-9185    NO MATCHING RECORD

    808-61-2377    ROBERT PALMER     8385 GREENFIELD STREE   WLA      CA

    836-20-5691    STELLA MARGARITIS 12354 LIFESAVER STREE   WLA      CA

    838-56-2008    LORRAINE PEREZ    85320 SOUTH BROADWAY    LA       CA

    850-23-9455    NO MATCHING RECORD

    850-31-5663    JEFF LANDSBERG    80361 MONTANA AVENUE    LA       CA

    850-32-4961    SCHOENECKER JOEY  80265 LUCILLE STREET    CC       CA

    862-03-4856    NO MATCHING RECORD
```

The Printer Spacing Chart shows how the report is to be formatted:

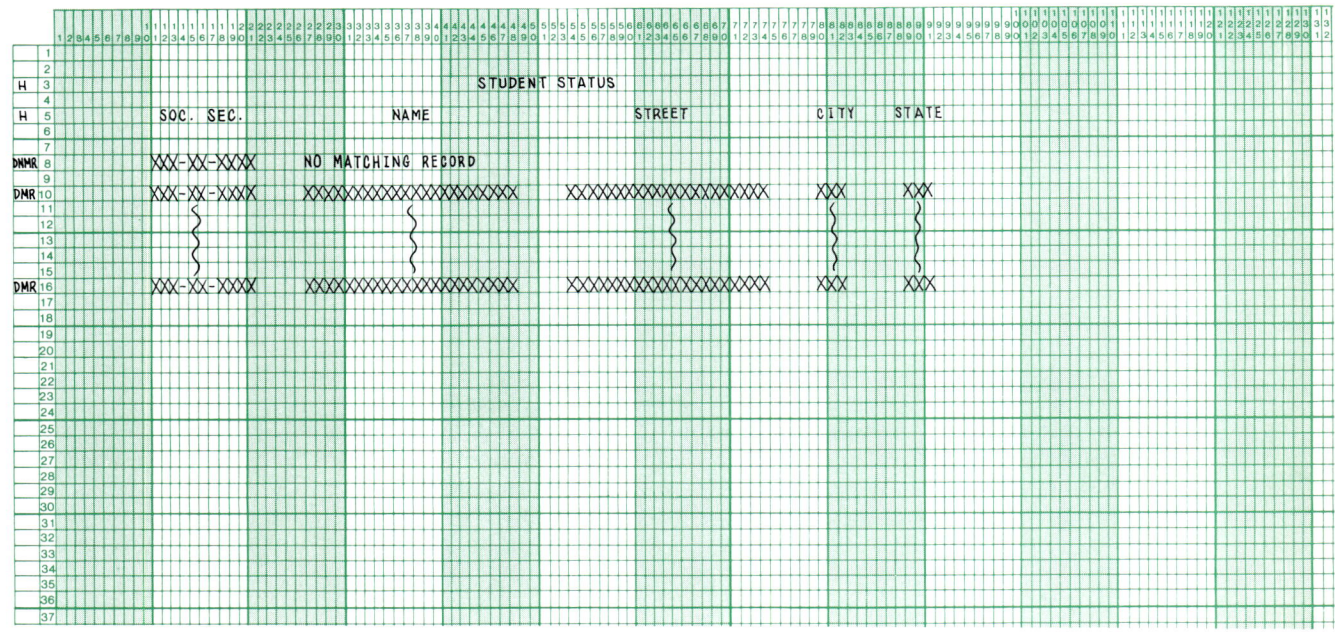

Appendix G

Appendix H

Indexed and Direct Files

Indexed Files

An indexed file is a file with indexes that permit both rapid access to individual records and rapid sequential processing. An indexed file has three distinct areas—a prime area, indexes, and an overflow area.

Prime Area

The prime area is the area in which records are written when the file is created or is subsequently reorganized. Additions to the file may also be written in the prime area. The prime area may span multiple volumes and consist of several noncontiguous areas. The records in the prime area must be formatted with keys. The records may be blocked or unblocked. If the records are blocked, each logical record contains its key; the key area contains the key of the highest record in the block.

Indexes

Indexed files contain two or more indexes of different levels. These indexes are created and written by the operating system at the time the file is created or reorganized.

Track Index

The **track index** is the lowest level of index and is always present. Its entries point to data records. There is one track address for each cylinder in the prime area. (A **cylinder** consists of the tracks of a disk storage device that can be accessed without repositioning the access mechanism.) The track index is always written on the first track(s) of the cylinder that it indexes. There is a pair of entries for each prime data track in the cylinder. These entries contain the home addresses of the prime track and the key of the highest record in the track (normal entry), and the overflow area. The last entry of each track index is a dummy entry indicating the end of the index. The remainder of the track index contains prime records if there is enough room for them.

Cylinder Index

The **cylinder index** is the highest level of index and is always present. Its entries point to track indexes. There is one cylinder index for the file; it may reside on a different type of DASD than the rest of the file. It consists of one entry for each cylinder in the prime area, followed by a dummy entry. The entries are formatted in the same fashion as the track index entries. The key area contains the key of the highest record in the cylinder to which the entry points. The data area contains the home address of the track index for that cylinder.

Overflow Area

A certain number of whole tracks, as specified by the programmer, are reserved in each cylinder for overflow data from prime tracks in that cylinder.

Direct Files

When requesting that a record be stored or retrieved, an address relative to the beginning of the file or an actual address (i.e., cylinder, track, or record position) must be furnished. The address specified may be the actual address of the desired record or it may be a starting point within the file where the search for the record is to begin. When a record search is specified, the programmer must also furnish the key (i.e., the part number or customer number) associated with the record. With direct addressing, every key in the file converts to a unique address; this makes it possible to locate any record in the file with one search and one read.

The programmer has complete freedom in deciding where records are to be located in a direct organized file. When creating or making additions to the file, the programmer may specify the location

Figure H.1 Direct organization creation—example

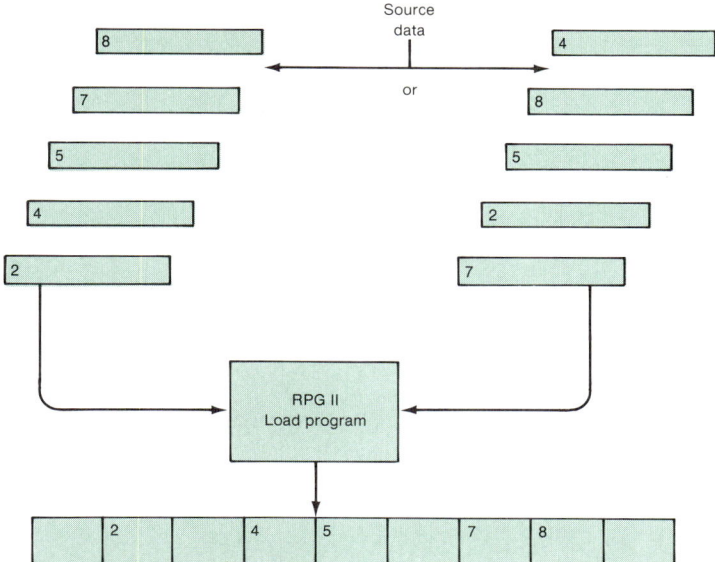

for a record key by supplying either the track address and identifier, or the track address, alone; the system finds the location for the record. The record is written in the first available location on the track specified. If the specified track is full, the system continues to search successive tracks until a location is found.

Use of Direct File Organization

Direct organization is generally used (*a*) for files whose characteristics do not permit the use of sequential or indexed files or (*b*) for situations in which the time required to locate individual records must be kept at a minimum. The direct file organization method has considerable flexibility, but has a serious disadvantage in that the programming system must provide the routines for reading a file organized in this way. The programmer holds primary responsibility for the logic and programming of locating records since it is the programmer who establishes the relationship between the key of the record and the addresses in the direct access storage device. (See Figure H.1.)

In a direct organization file, the records will probably be distributed nonsequentially throughout the file. If so, processing the records in key sequence requires a preliminary sort or the use of a finder file.

The disk is a device that may be used as either an input or an output device. In fact, there are many applications in which it serves both functions during the same job. When used in this manner, a disk file is called an **update file.** After an update file record is processed, the new output record replaces the original disk record. In this way an update file is used both as an input file and as an output file.

Creating a Direct File

To create a direct file the disk file must be defined as a chained output file. The following entries are needed on the File Description form for defining particular characteristics of the disk file:

1. The disk filename must be entered in positions 7–14.

2. Position 15 must contain an *O*.

3. Position 16 must contain a *C* to indicate that the file is a chained output file.

4. All records in the file must be of the same length; position 19 must contain an *F* to specify that the record length is fixed.

Figure H.2 File description special entries—direct files

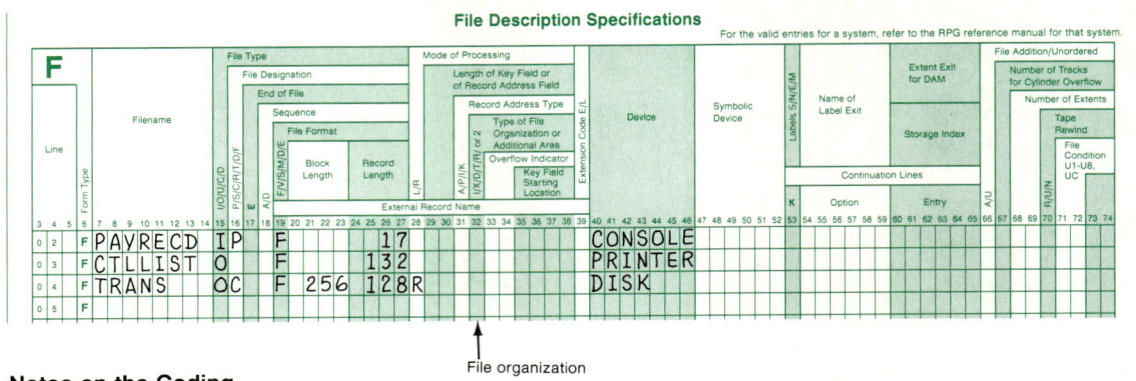

Notes on the Coding

Position 28 has an R for random. The records will be placed on the file according to a unique sequence. These will not be necessarily in 1, 2, 3 order, so the creation will be random.

Position 16 has a C for chained. The method of performing this random operation will be through the CHAIN operation code on the calculations.

5. A number equal to or a multiple of the disk record length must be entered in positions 20–23.

6. Positions 24–27 must contain the length of the disk record.

7. Position 28 contains an *R* to indicate that random processing is to take place.

8. A DASD device name must be entered in positions 40–46. (See Figure H.2.)

Relative record numbers are always used with the CHAIN operation code in the program to make the corresponding record locations in a direct file available for loading. The data used as a relative record number in the chain operation can be a field in an input record; or, it can be created in the program. To use the chain operation, the following entries must be made on the Calculation Specifications form.

1. Factor 1 must contain either the name of the field containing the relative record number or the relative record number, itself.

2. CHAIN must be entered as the operation.

3. Factor 2 must contain the name of the file to be loaded.

4. A resulting indicator should be specified in positions 54–55 with the CHAIN operation. If the record is not found (i.e., if the record location does not exist in the file), the indicator specified in positions 54–55 is turned on. This situation can occur either when the relative record number is higher than the highest record location in the file, or when the relative record number is invalid for some reason. If an indicator is not specified in positions 54–55 and the record is not found, the program halts.

When a direct file is loaded as a chained output file, the disk management system clears the entire file area to blanks before records are loaded. Thus, if a record is not loaded the space reserved for it remains blank. Programs written to access records in the direct file should check each record for blanks before attempting to process it since the record may not have been previously loaded.

Relative record numbers define the record position for each record in the direct file. The relative number can be all or part of a field in input records or it can be generated by an RPG program. Relative record numbers are used for record identification on the disk records after the disk file is loaded. The relative record number is used to chain to the corresponding relative record number in the disk file. The information is then written on disk and blanks are replaced with data. (See Figure H.3.) If a record is not loaded, the space reserved for that record in the disk file remains blank (until the proper record is loaded at a later time).

Once the direct file is loaded, records are inserted or changed in the file by defining the direct file as an update file processed consecutively or by the CHAIN operation.

Inserting records in a direct file is quite a different procedure from adding records to sequential or indexed files. The new record in a sequential file is added in at the first available position at the end of the file. The same process occurs for an indexed file except that the record key and disk address are added to the file index. Any new records inserted in a direct file have space reserved for them already. Hence, the record is inserted in its proper place, not merely added to the physical end of the file.

Figure H.3 Creating a direct file—example

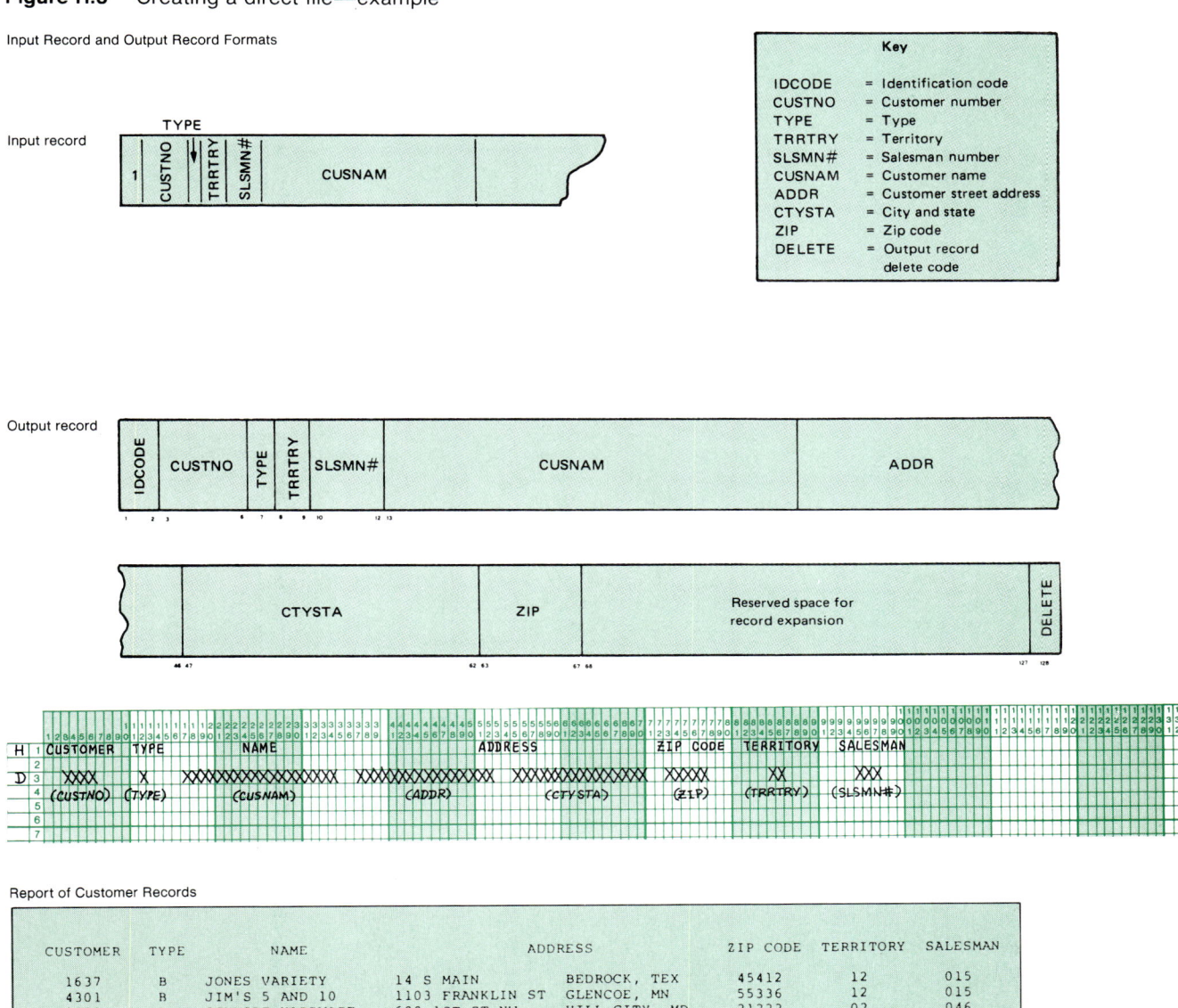

Appendix H

Figure H.3 continued

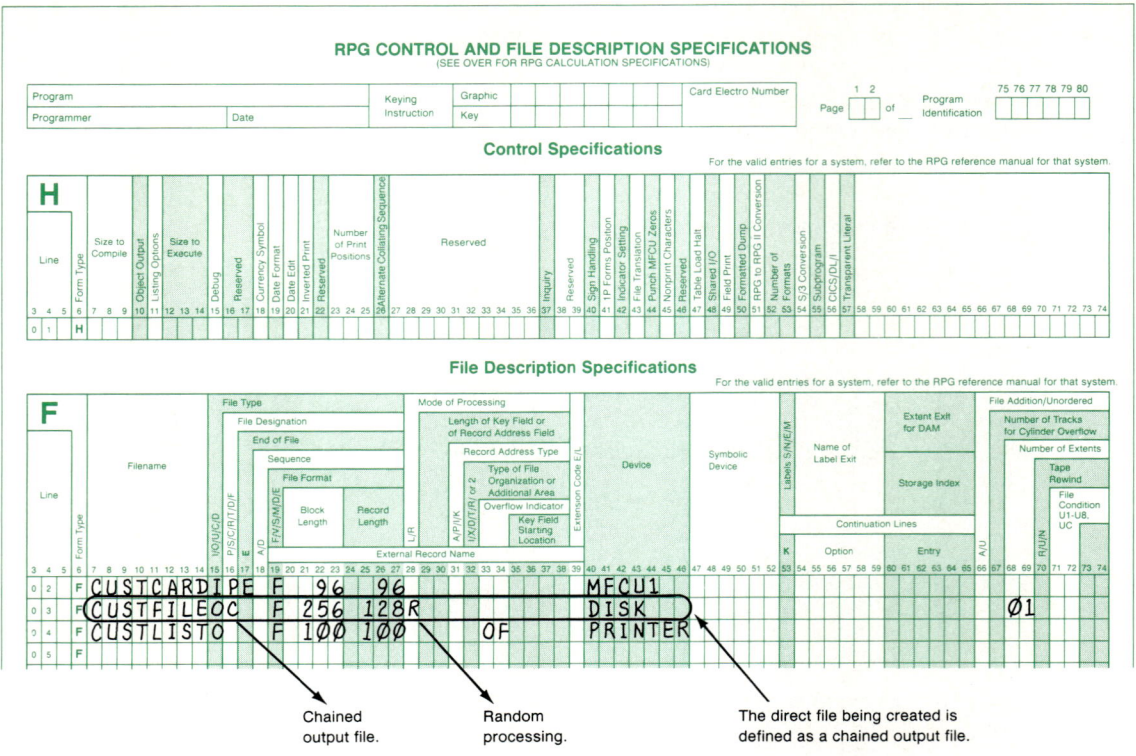

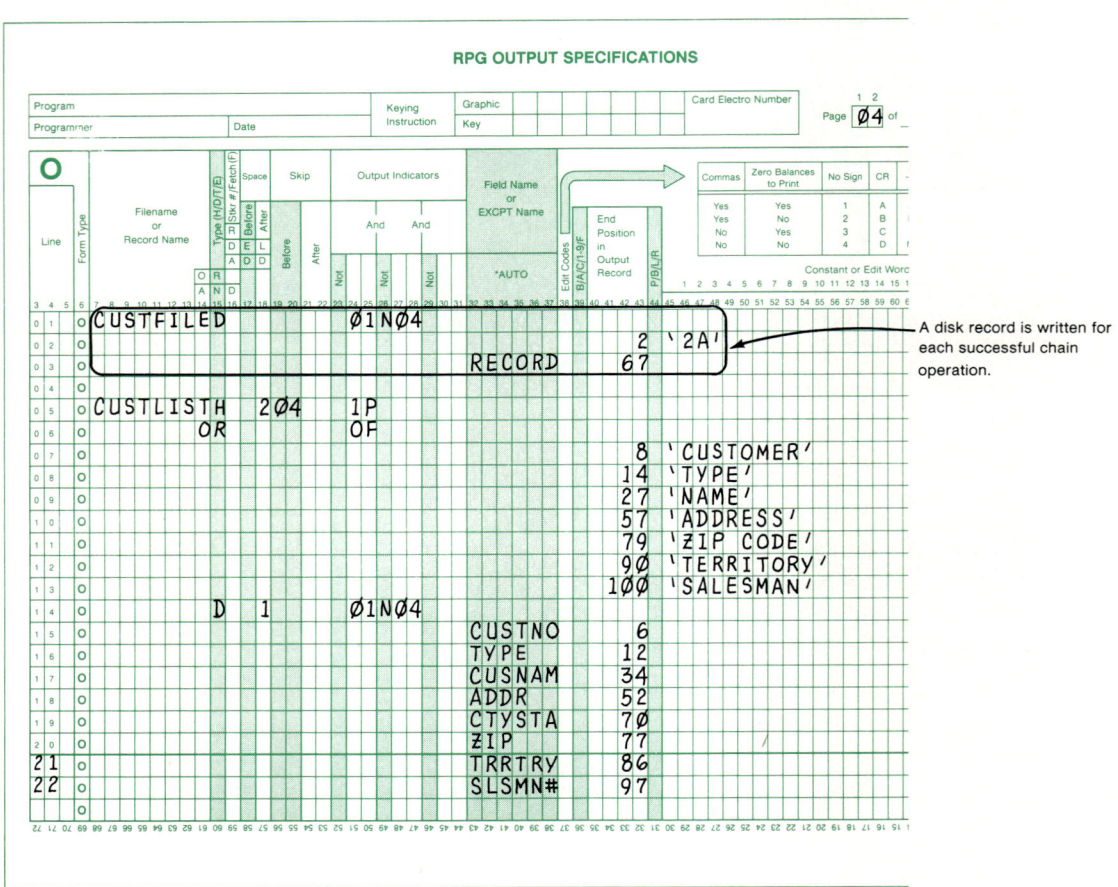

662 RPG II and RPG III Programming

Figure H.3 continued

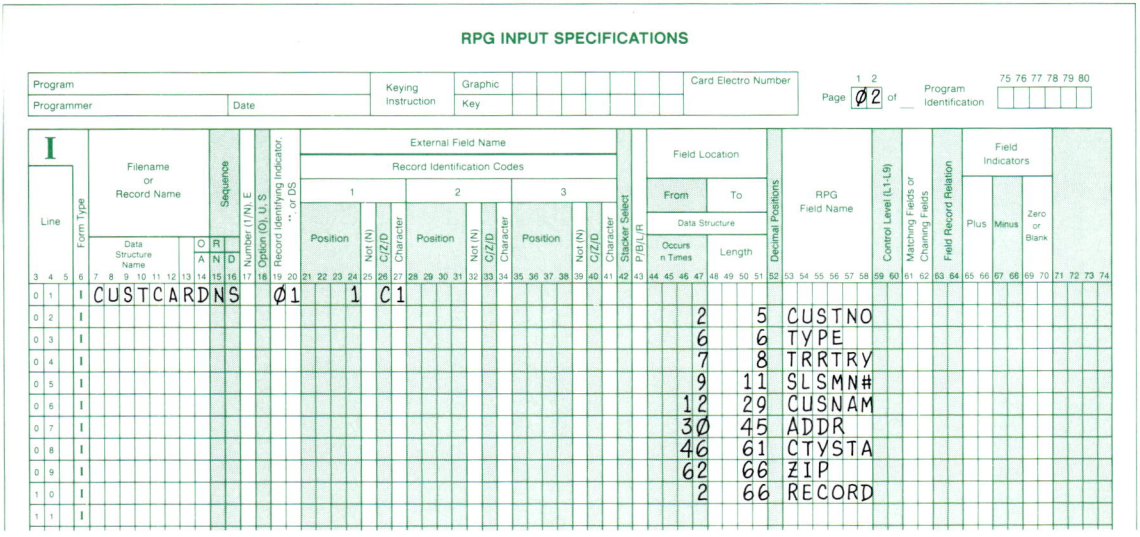

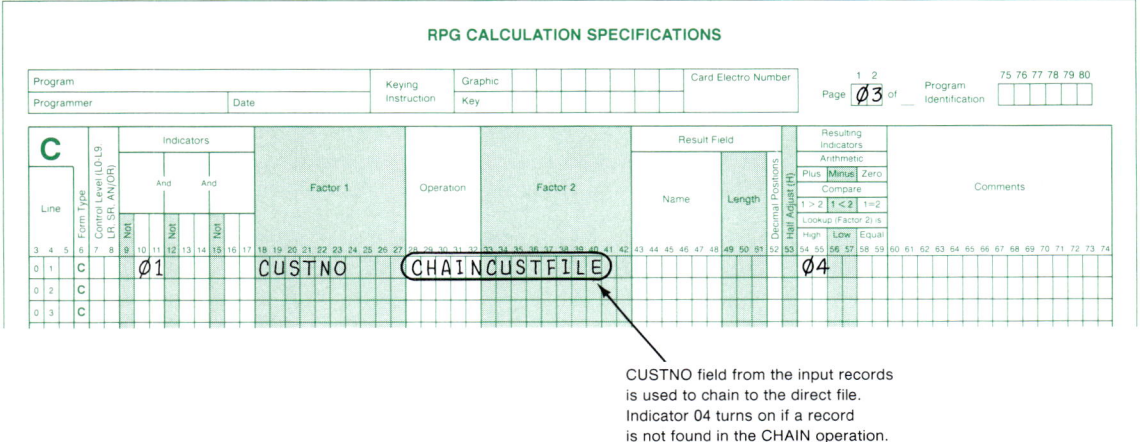

CUSTNO field from the input records is used to chain to the direct file. Indicator 04 turns on if a record is not found in the CHAIN operation.

Retrieval of Records in a Direct File

Record retrieval is used when the programmer wants to obtain information from a record but does not want to modify the record. This method would normally be used when the programmer needs data from a record to produce a report. Record retrieval can be either consecutive or random by relative record number.

Consecutive Retrieval

Consecutive retrieval of records from a direct file requires particular entries on the File Description form. Some of the entries are the same as those needed to create a direct file. Additional entries required include the following:

1. An *I* in position 15 to indicate that the file is an input file
2. Either a *P* or an *S* in position 16, depending on whether the file is a primary or secondary file (see Figure H.4)

Because the file is an input file, it must also be defined on the Input Specifications form. (See Figure H.5.)

Appendix H 663

Figure H.4 File description special entries for consecutive retrieval of records from a direct file

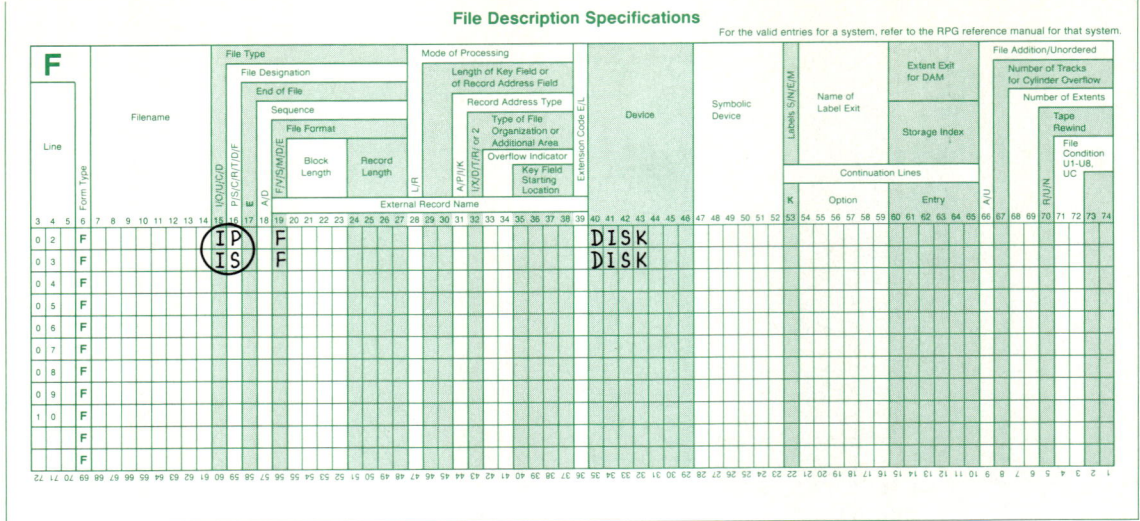

Figure H.5 Consecutive retrieval of a direct file—example

Problem

Suppose you wish to process the direct customer file, CUSTFILE created in figure H.3, to produce a monthly report. This report lists all customers who have had no sales activity during the period. This report is analyzed by sales personnel, who then make follow-up calls. Since all the customer records will be checked and since the file is in sequence by customer number, the report is produced by consecutive processing of the direct file.

The format of the disk records in the CUSTFILE is shown below. The report to be produced by the consecutive processing is also shown. The report consists of fields selected from CUSTFILE and an accumulated total for accounts receivable (TOTAR).

The following program shows the specification sheets necessary to consecutively retrieve records from CUSTFILE to produce REPORT1, which is a list of recently inactive customers.

Since the direct file probably contains blank record locations and inactive records, a technique is employed on the Input form to bypass such records. If a method is not used to bypass unidentified records, the program halts when they are encountered.

Disk Record Format for the Direct Customer File

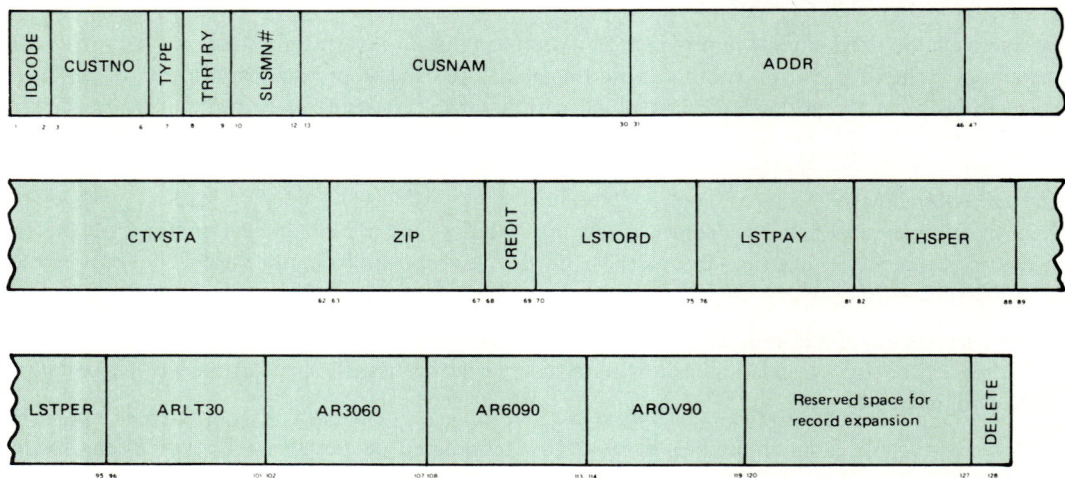

664 RPG II and RPG III Programming

Figure H.5 continued

Key			
IDCODE	= Identification code	LSTORD	= Last order date
CUSTNO	= Customer number	LSTPAY	= Last pay date
TYPE	= Type	THSPER	= Charges for this period (month)
TRRTRY	= Territory	LSTPER	= Charges for last period (month)
SLSMN#	= Salesman number	ARLT30	= Accounts receivable for less than 30 days
CUSNAM	= Customer name	AR3060	= Accounts receivable for 30 to 60 days
ADDR	= Customer street address	AR6090	= Accounts receivable for 60 to 90 days
CTYSTA	= City and state	AROV90	= Accounts receivable for over 90 days
ZIP	= Zip code	DELETE	= Delete code
CREDIT	= Credit code		

Report of Inactive Customers in the Direct Customer File

CUSTOMER	NAME	CITY, STATE	SALESMAN	LAST ORDER	SLS PREV PER	CRDT	TOT A/R
1637	JONES VARIETY	BEDROCK, TEX	15	4/13/71	240.07	01	.00
2279	GREEN GROCERY, INC	BIG CITY, CALIF	102	4/27/71	1,200.00	01	600.00
2331	STAR MARKET	GOODTOWN, GA	74	4/01/71	31.95	03	937.16

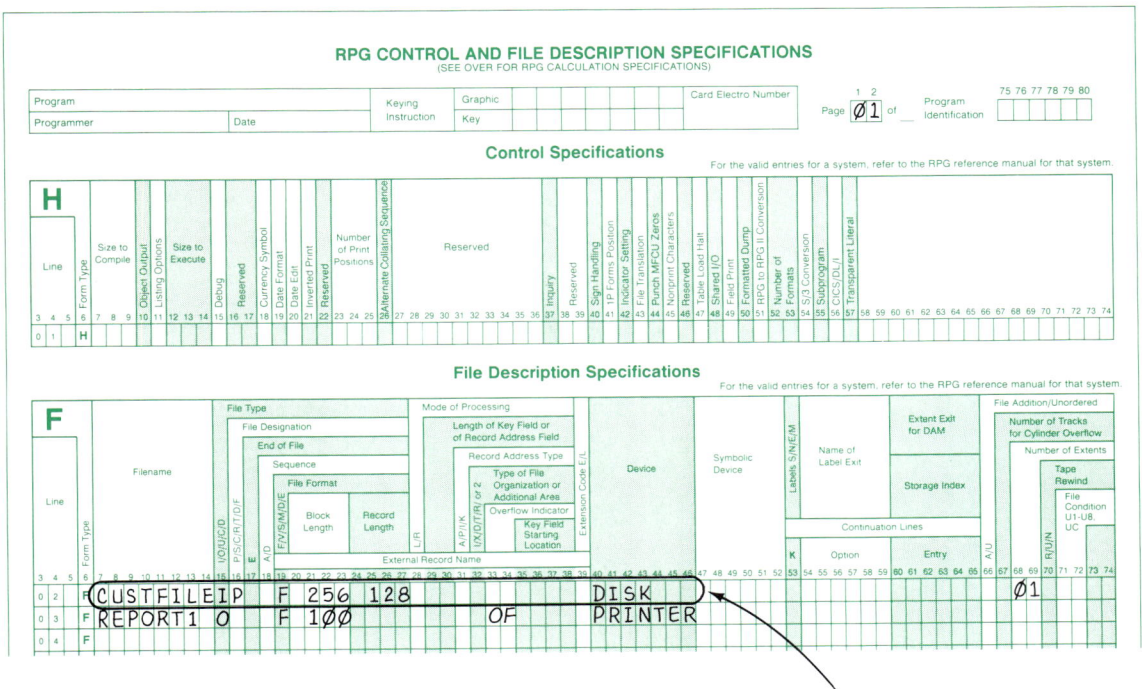

The direct file is described as a disk file to be processed consecutively (identical to the description of a sequential disk file).

Appendix H   665

Figure H.5 continued

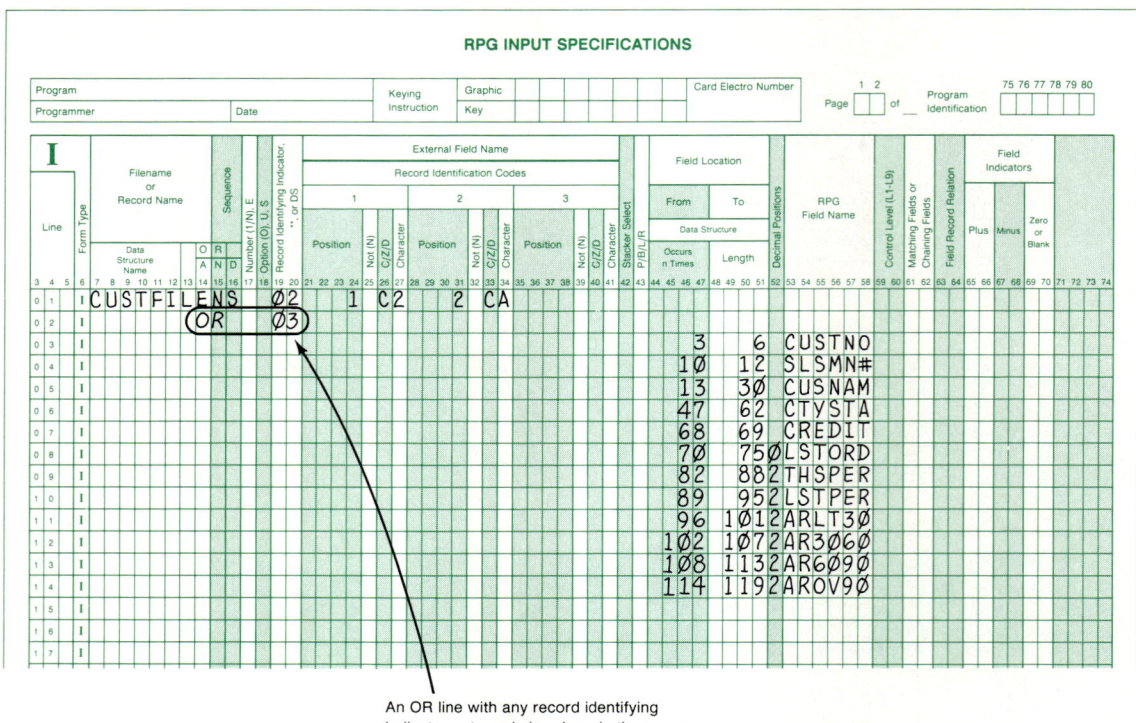

An OR line with any record identifying indicator not used elsewhere in the program causes unwanted records to be bypassed, including blank records.

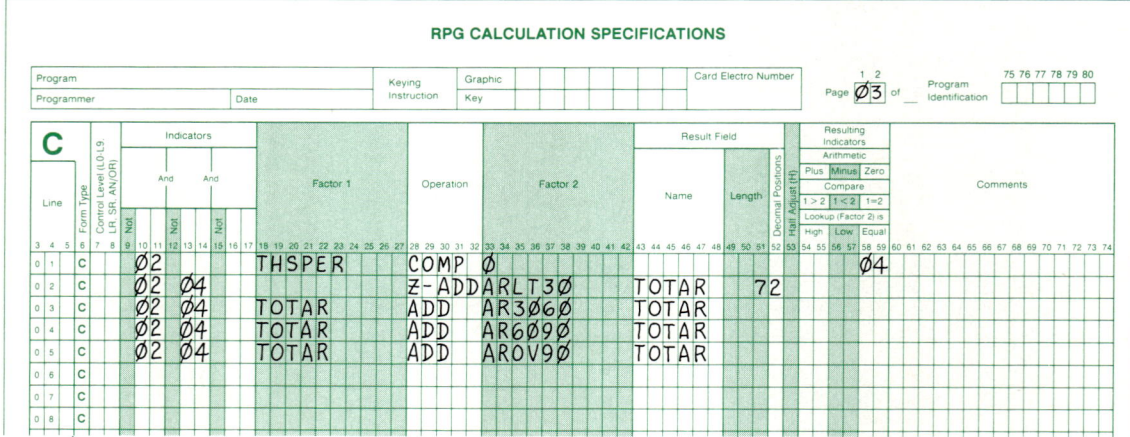

Figure H.5 continued

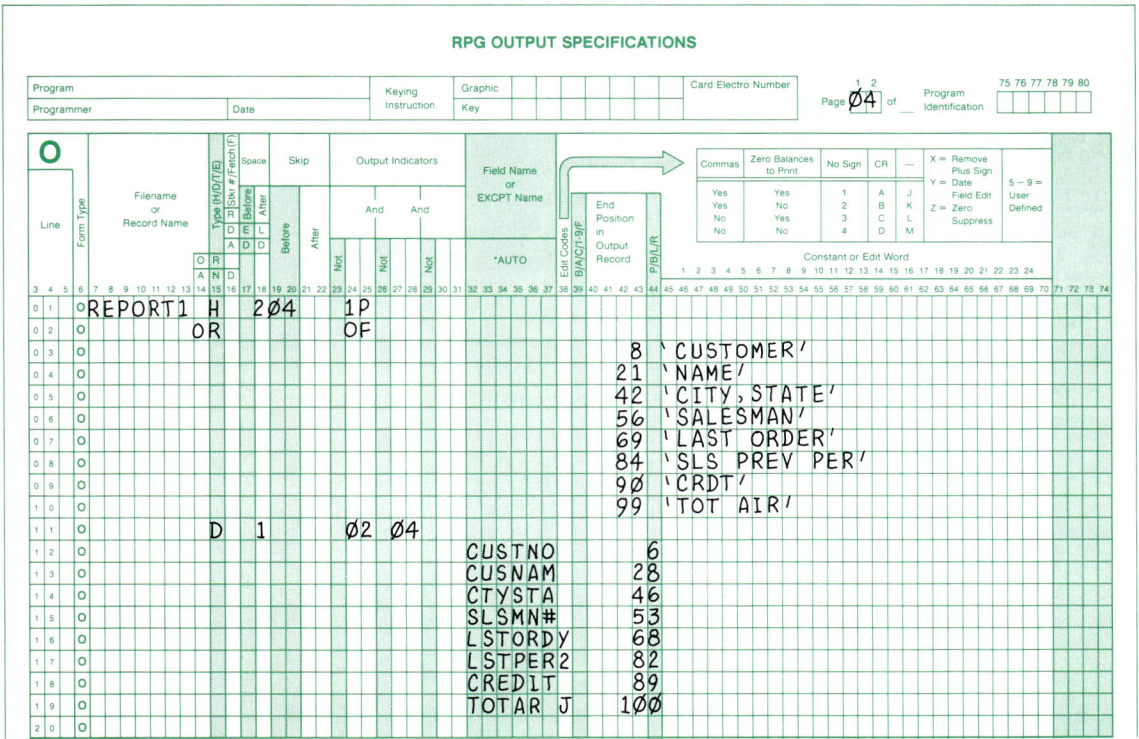

Random Retrieval

Random retrieval of records from a direct file requires particular entries on the File Description form. Some of the entries are the same as those needed to create a direct file. Additional entries required include the following:

1. An *I* in position 15 to indicate that the file is an input file
2. An *R* in position 28 to indicate that random processing is to take place (see Figure H.6)

Figure H.6 File description special entries for random retrieval of records from a direct file

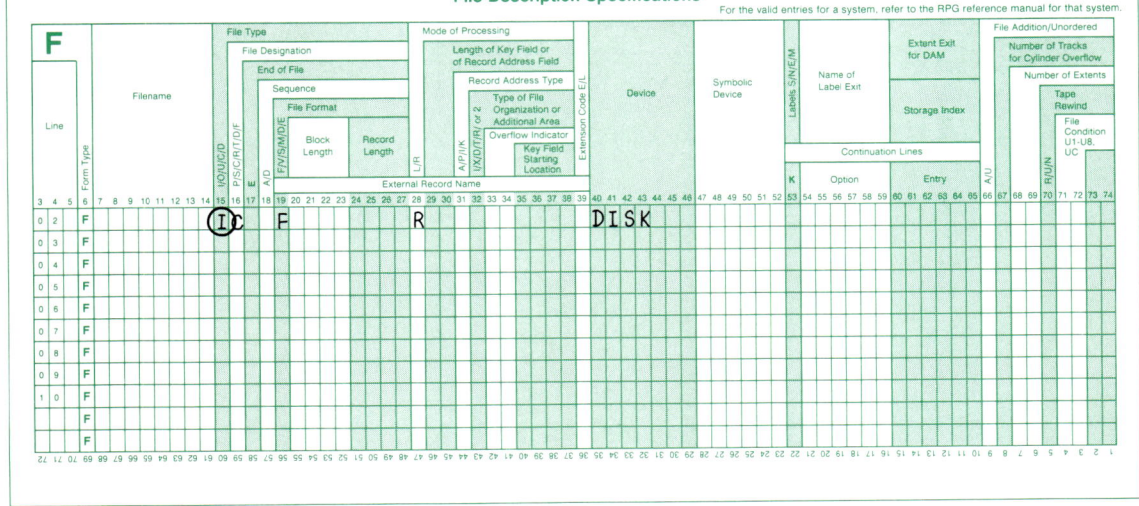

The records in the direct file to be retrieved must be further described on the Input Specifications form. A direct file being retrieved must have an alphabetic sequence entry on the input specifications (positions 15–16) because sequence-checking cannot be done for chained files.

The CHAIN operation code must be specified on the Calculation Specifications form to randomly retrieve records from a direct file. The entries are the same as those listed in the section on creating a direct file. (See Figure H.7.)

Figure H.7 Random retrieval of a direct file—example

Problem

Suppose the direct customer file CUSTFILE, created in figure H.3 and processed consecutively in figure H.5 is to be retrieved randomly. You want to make demand inquiries each day concerning customer sales and account information. Inquiries are received for records containing an I in position 1 followed by the customer number of the record to be retrieved. Inquiry records are read from the primary MFCU hopper in this example; substitute devices, such as the console/keyboard devices, can also be used. When an inquiry is read, the customer number (CSTMER) is used as the relative record number to chain the CUSTFILE.

The format of the disk records in CUSTFILE is the same as the disk record format used in the consecutive retrieval example.

If a record corresponding to the number on the inquiry record is found in CUSTFILE, a response is printed. This response lists pertinent sales information and the total accounts receivable amount.

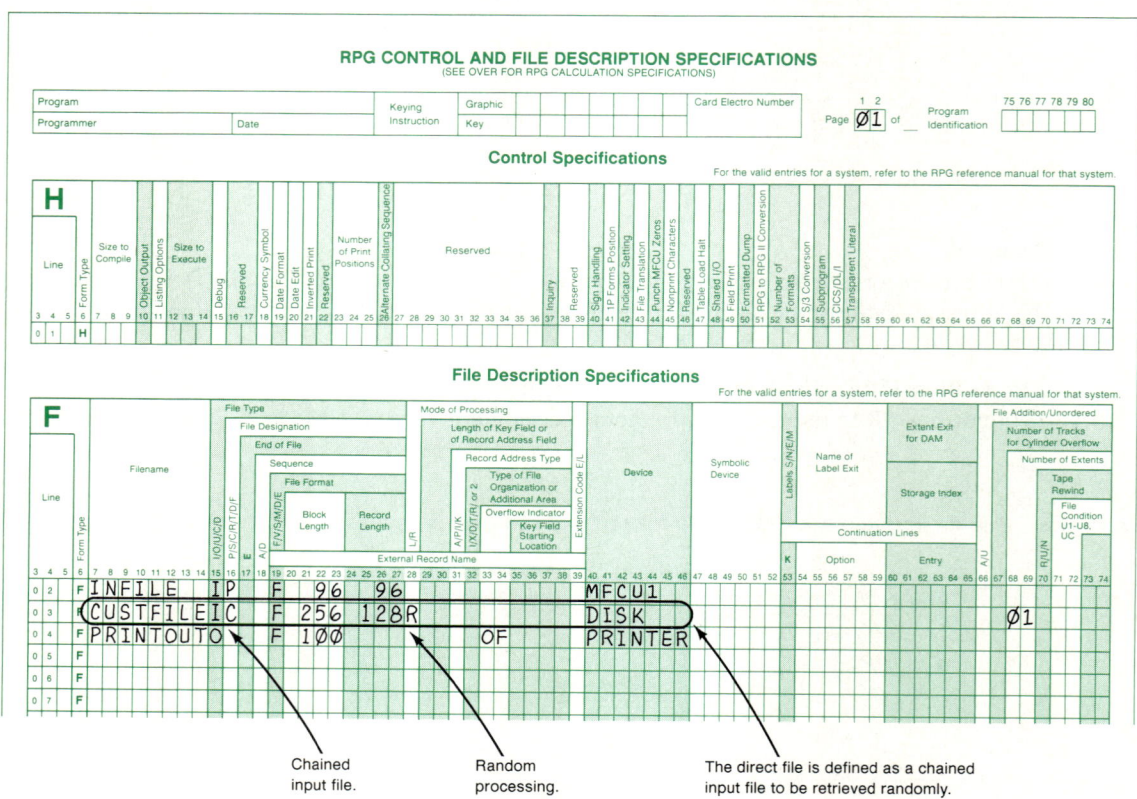

Figure H.7 continued

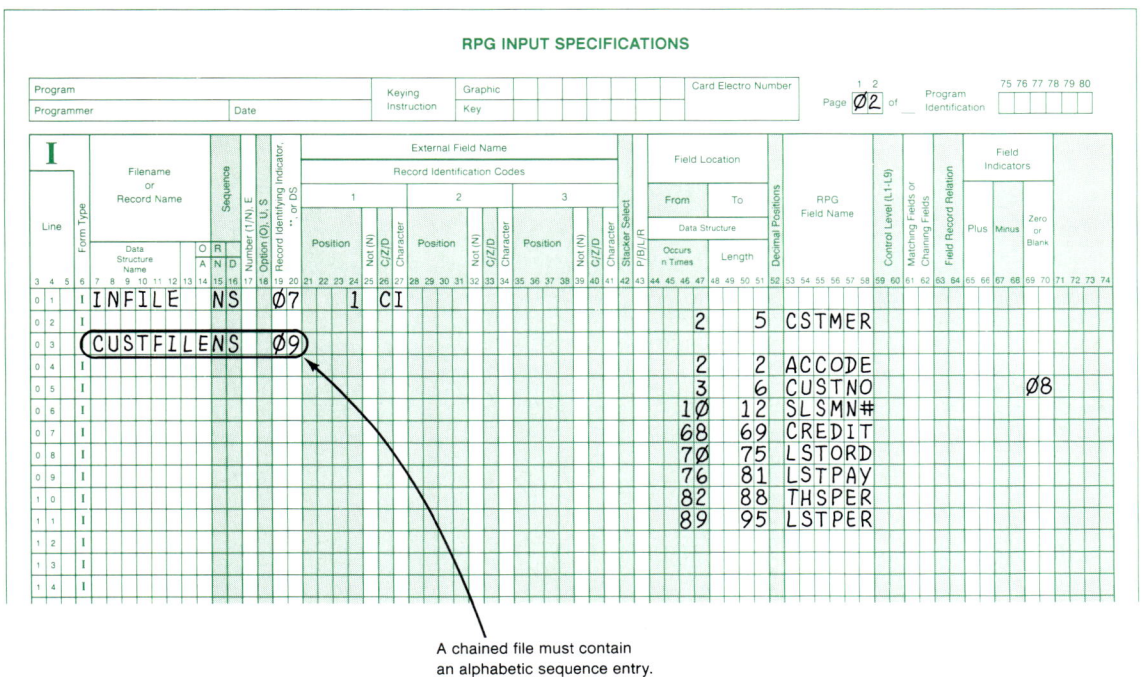

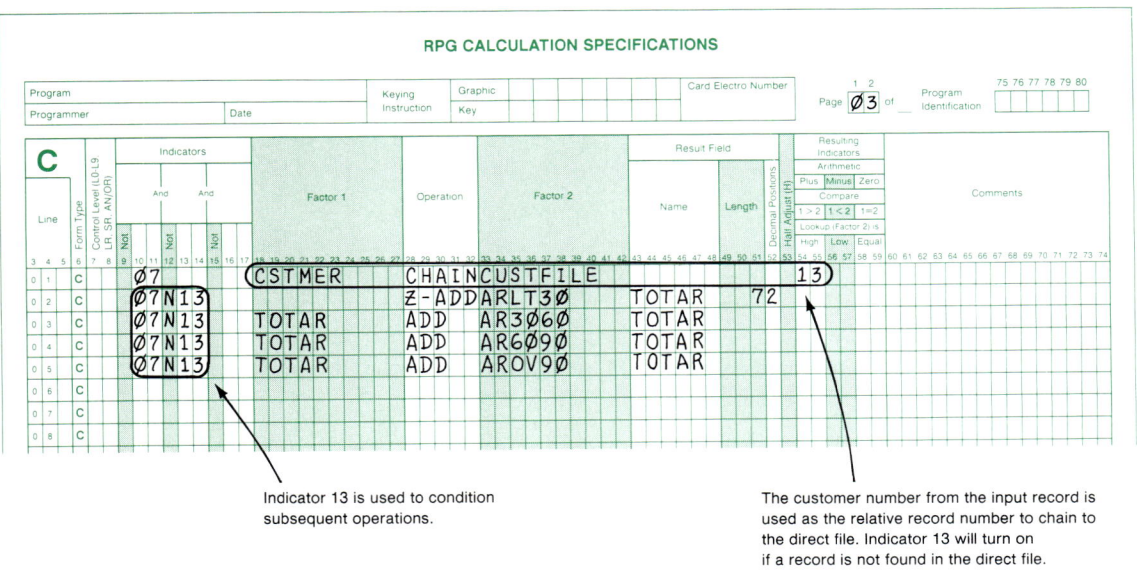

Appendix H

Figure H.7 continued

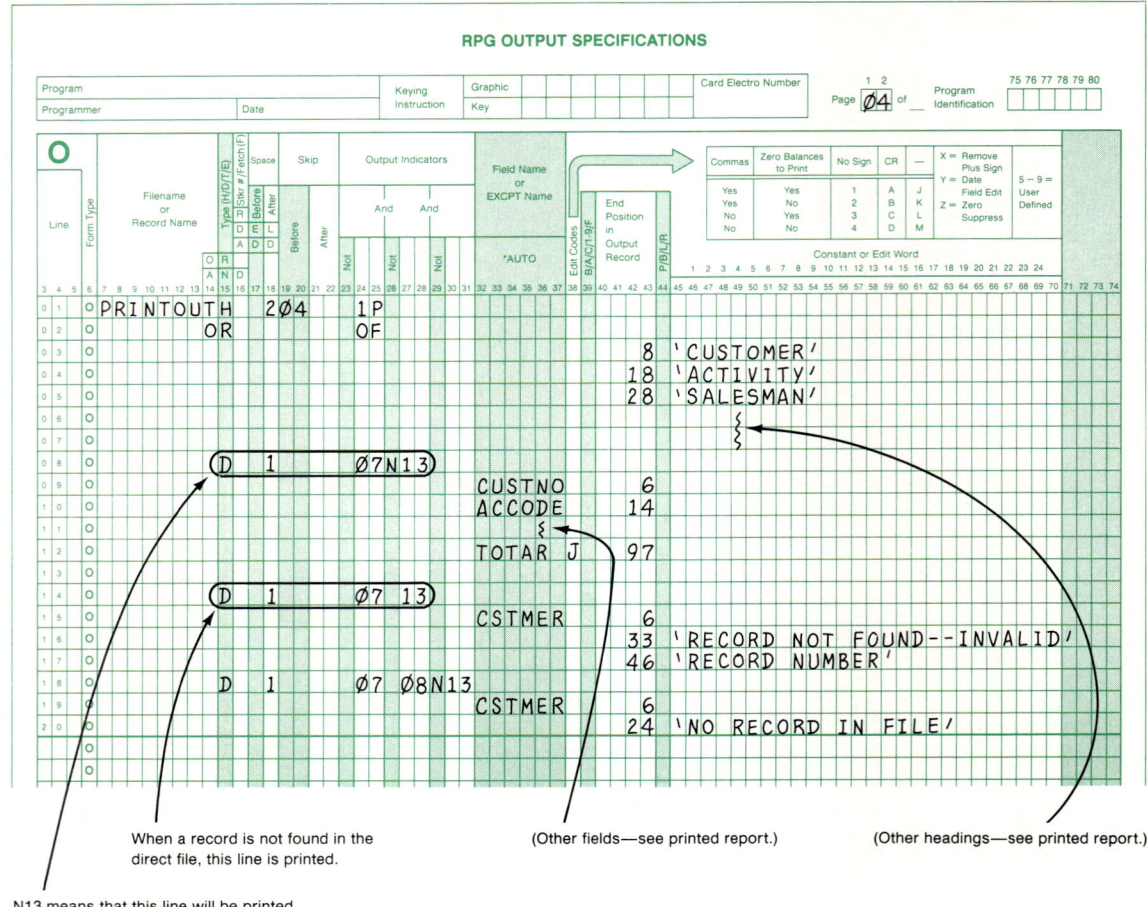

Maintaining a Direct File

After a file is created, file maintenance is usually necessary to keep the file current. The following three file maintenance functions apply to direct files:

1. Adding records
2. Tagging records for deletion
3. Updating records

Adding Records

Unlike sequential and indexed files, direct files can have space available between records for new records to be added. Records are added to a direct file by normal update operation (either sequential or random processing) as follows:

1. The relative record number is developed for the record to be added.
2. The location is read into main storage.
3. If the location is blank, the new record can be stored.

For a discussion of the entries needed to add records sequentially, see the sections of this appendix that discuss updating records and the sequential updating of records. For a discussion of the entries needed to add records randomly, see the sections discussing updating records and the random updating of records.

If the records must be added but the allotted space is full, the total space available for the file must be increased. In the meantime the program aborts, the file is not closed, and it is likely that the entire file will have to be re-created.

Tagging Records for Deletion

Like sequential and indexed file records, direct file records are identified for deletion code. If the code is present, the record can be bypassed.

Another method of deleting records which may sometimes be preferable to using a delete code is to restore the record location to blanks. A blank record in a direct file is an available record.

Updating Records

To modify certain data in the disk records, the update function must be used. Updating means getting a record from a disk file, changing some data, and putting the record back in its original location. Thus, an update file is like a combination input/output file.

The file to be updated must be specified on both the Input and Output Specifications forms. Field locations should agree between the two forms. Field names may vary depending on the kind of updating to be performed; field lengths must agree.

Consecutive Updating of Records

If all or most of the records in a direct file are to be processed, the programmer may want to update the file consecutively.

Consecutive updating of records in a direct file requires the same file description entries as a consecutive retrieval of records with one exception: position 15 must contain a *U* to indicate that the file is an update file. (See Figures H.8 and H.9.)

Figure H.8 File description special entries for consecutive updating of records in a direct file

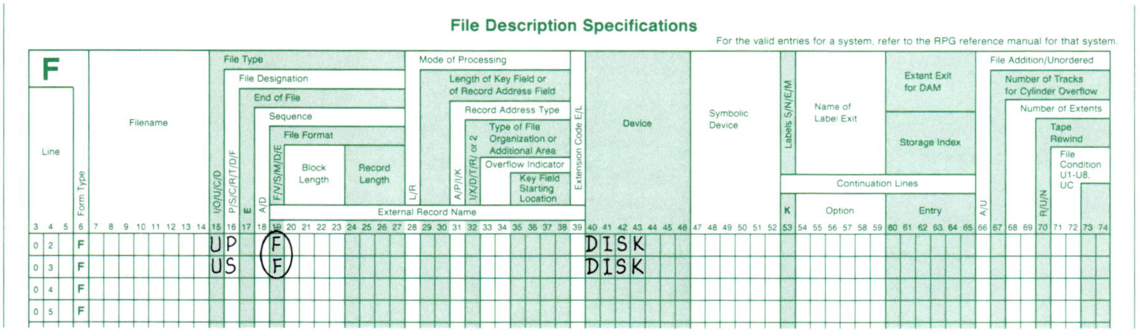

Figure H.9 Consecutive updating of records in a direct file—example

Problem

Suppose the direct customer file created in figure H.3 and retrieved consecutively in figure H.5 is to be updated. At the end of each sales period, when all reports are completed, the sales figures for that period must be adjusted. Sales amounts for the last period (LSTPER) are replaced by sales amounts from the current period (THSPER). The field containing the current sales amount is reset to zero, ready to accumulate the sales amount for the next selling period. Fields containing overdue amounts will be updated when the monthly accounts receivable statements are written.

The coding below shows the necessary program to consecutively update CUSTFILE. As an update file, CUSTFILE must be defined by File Description Specifications, and the fields to be updated must be described by Input and Output Specifications. Customer records are read, updated, and written out in the order in which they are stored in the direct file.

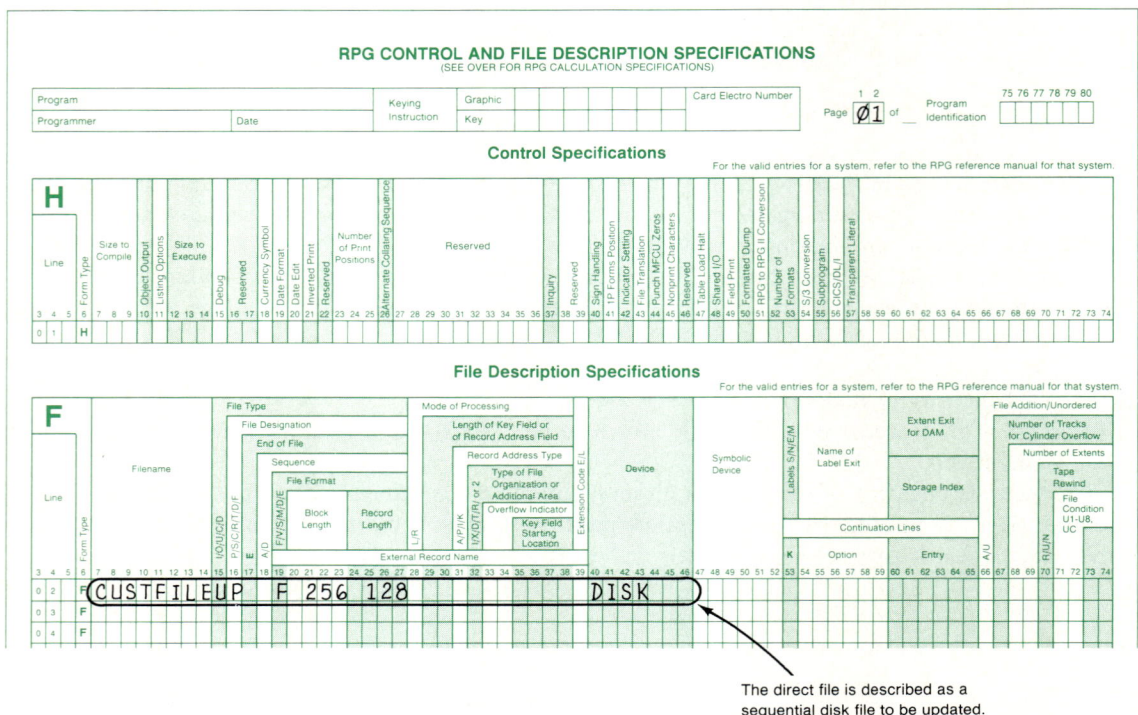

The direct file is described as a sequential disk file to be updated.

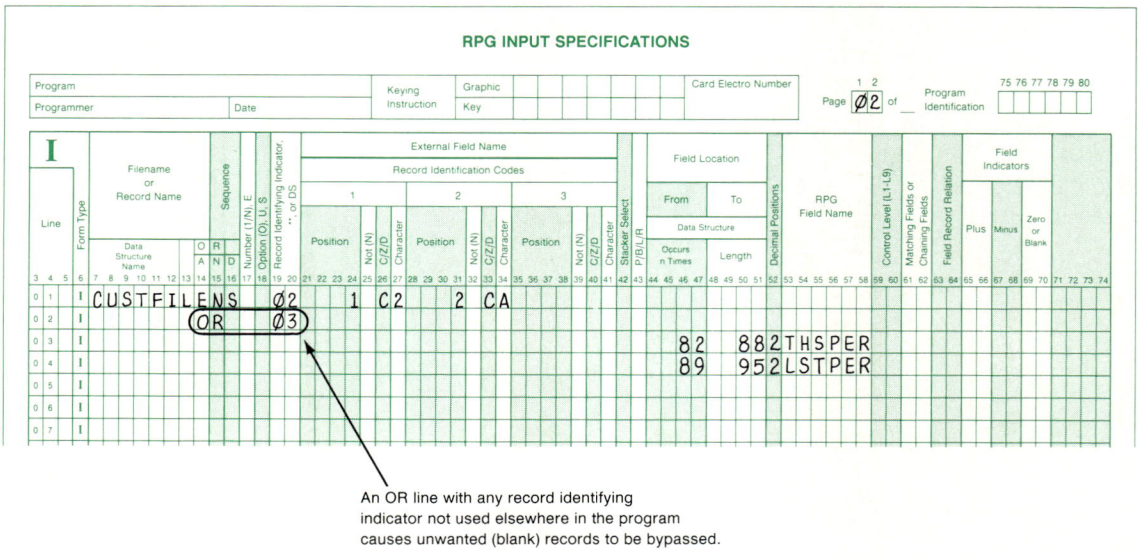

An OR line with any record identifying indicator not used elsewhere in the program causes unwanted (blank) records to be bypassed.

Figure H.9 continued

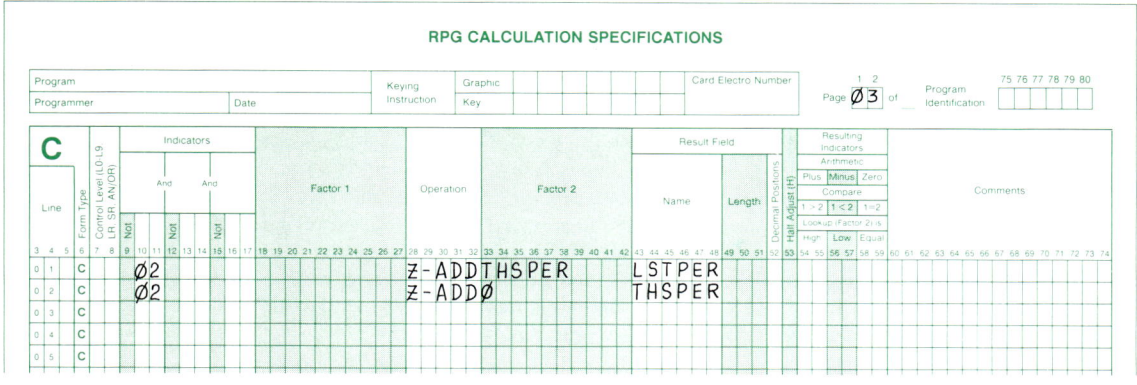

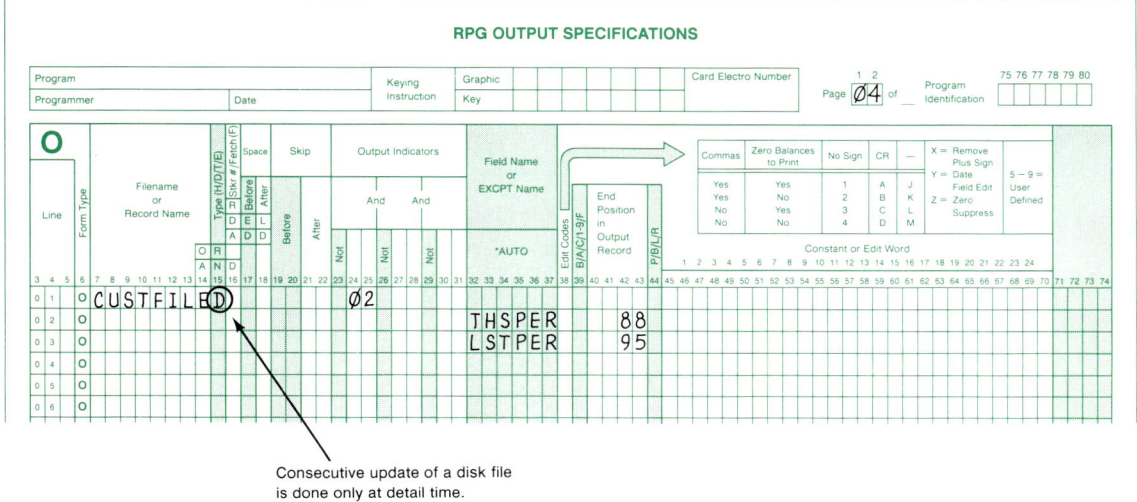

Consecutive update of a disk file is done only at detail time.

Random Updating of Records

Random updating of records in a direct file requires the same file description entries as random retrieval of a record with one exception: position 15 must contain a *U* to indicate that the file is an update file. (See Figures H.10 and H.11.)

Figure H.10 File description special entries for random updating of records in a direct file

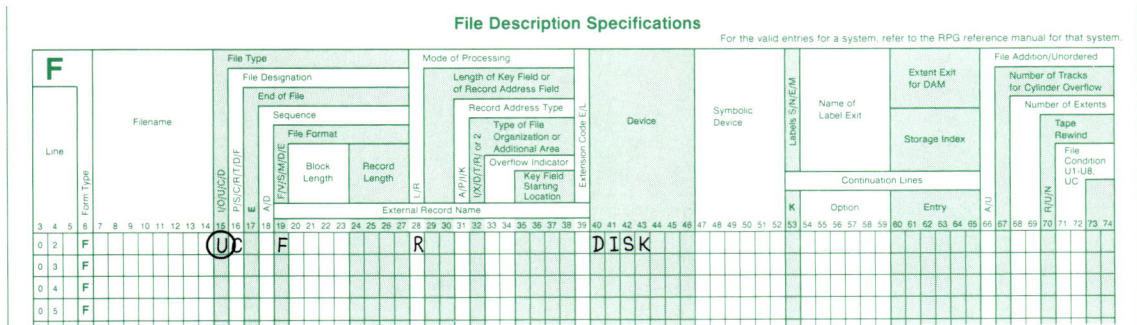

Appendix H   673

Figure H.11 Random updating of records in a direct file—example

Problem

Each day you want to prepare invoices for customer orders for the file described in figure H.5. Information from the invoices is used to update the customer file, CUSTFILE. Since the information is read from records in an unordered manner, a random update is required.

The input records contain the date and total amount of the transactions for each customer. New addresses are also on this record when required. As each record is read, the customer number (CUSTMR) is used to chain to the direct file. The amount of the transaction is added to the total sales for the period (THSPER) and to the accounts receivable amount (ARLT30). The transaction date is placed in the date of last order (LSTORD) in the customer record.

If an address change is indicated (an X in position 18 of the input record), the new customer address replaces the old. If a record is not found in CUSTFILE because of an invalid relative record number, the input record is printed, followed by the statement, "Above record not found—invalid customer number."

CUSTFILE, described as a chained update file, must be described on both Input and Output Specifications forms because data is read from and written on the file.

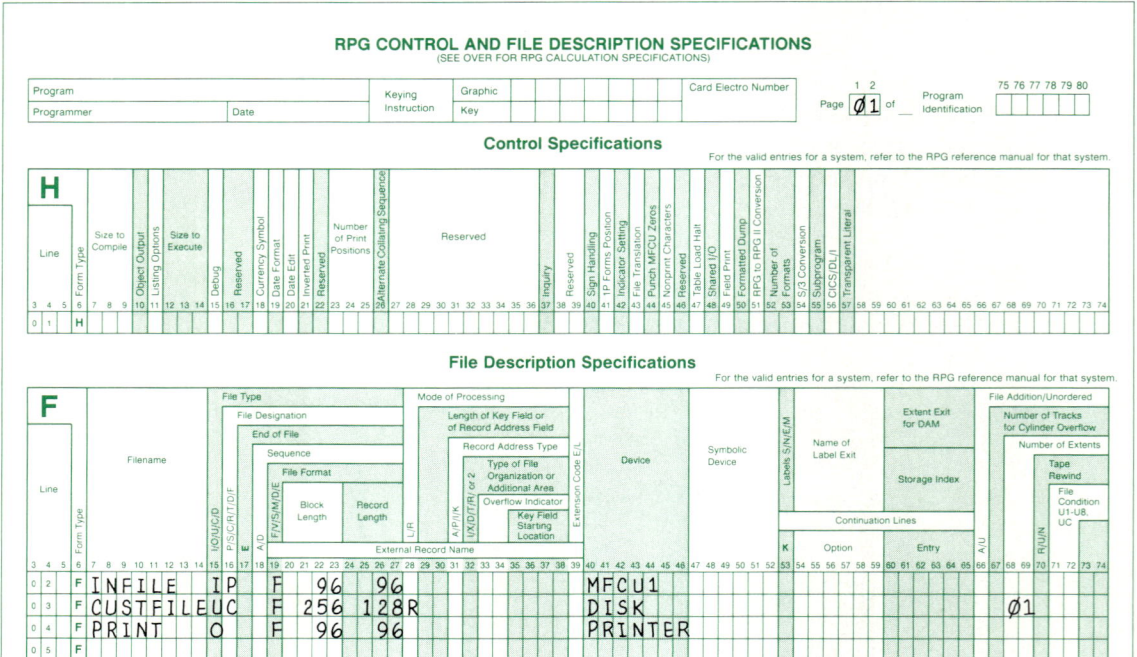

Figure H.11 continued

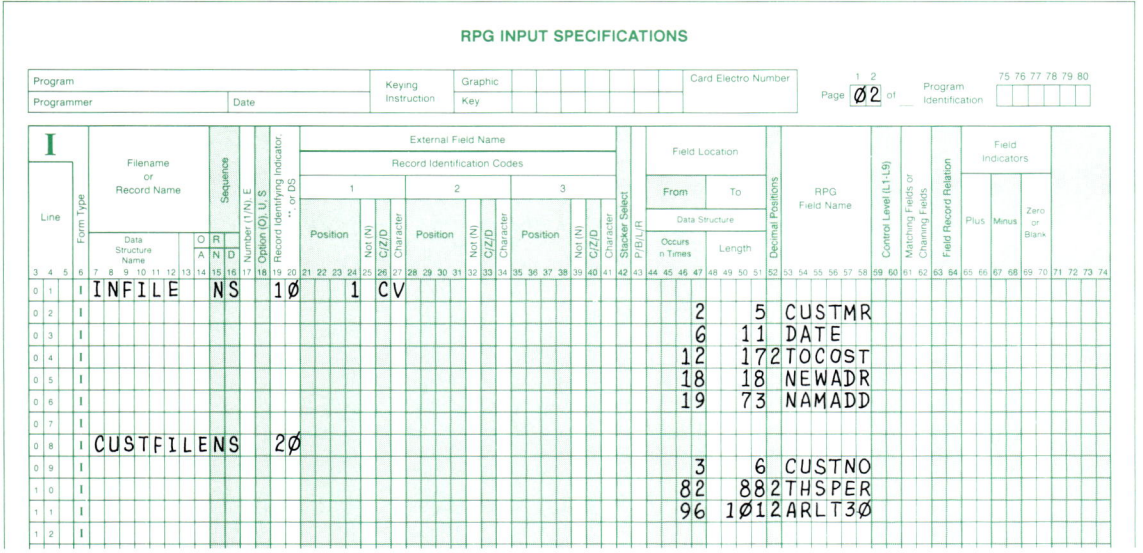

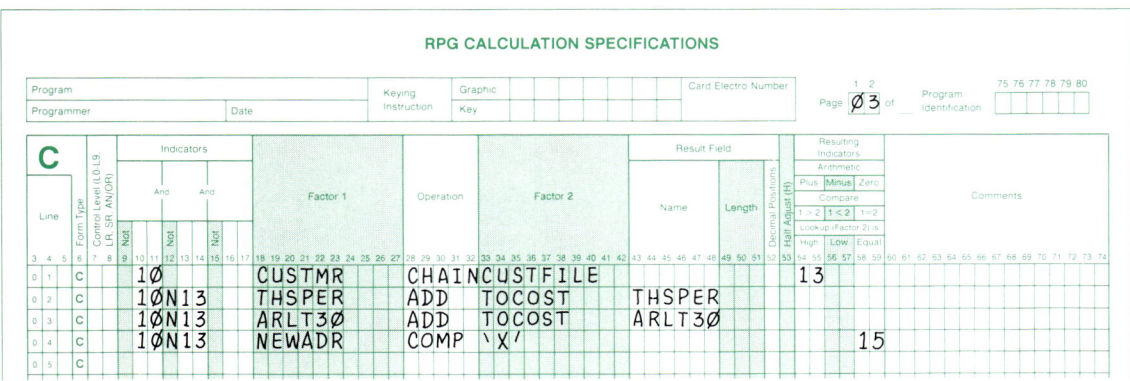

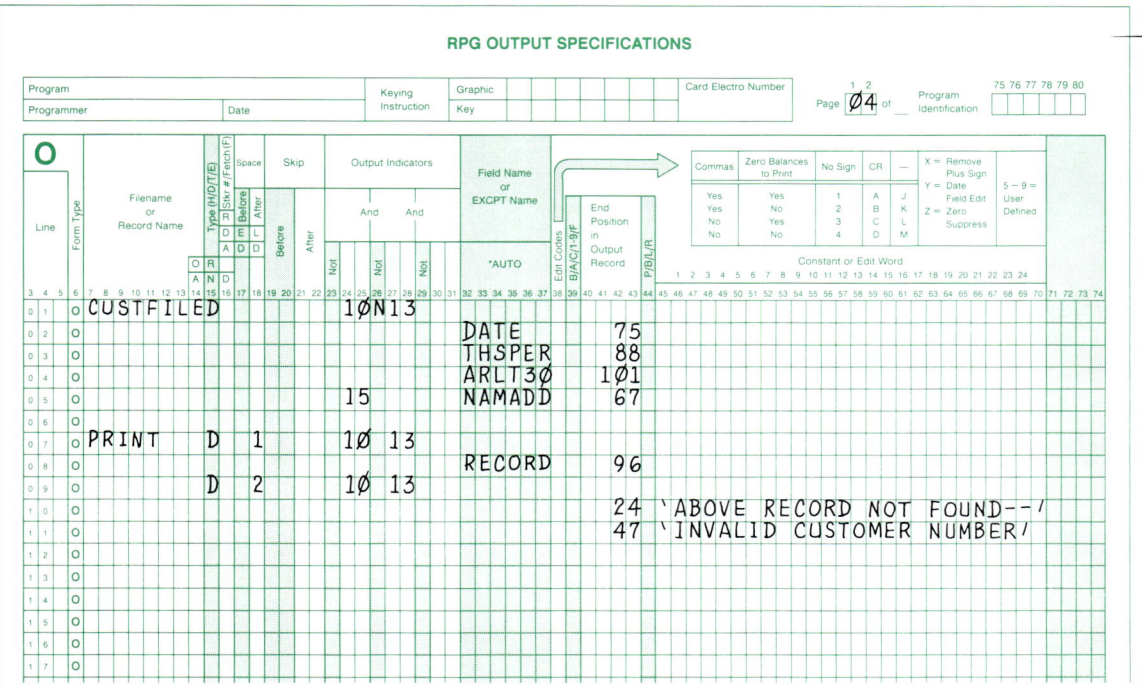

Appendix I

Input Data for Chapter 2-10 Problems

Chapter 2

Problem 1
```
                                                            6
.........1.........2.........3.........4.........5.........6...4
GOLDMAN             STEVEN       J1445 MAIN ST VAN NUYS  CA914010001
ANDONAEGUI          NICOLA       X425 HARVARD   L. A.    CA900380010
LEWIS               VICTORIA     Q3444 VICTORY BURBANK   CA914110004
SHERMAN             HAROLD       R777 SUNSET STRIP L. A. CA900270003
/*
```

Problem 2
```
                             2
.........1.........2..3
68832SWAROBERT JONES
68322SWAJACK SMITH
78832STHHENRY KAHN
79876TTHMARGARET KAISER
68325STHJUSTIN KRAMER
/*
```

Problem 3
```
                                 3
.........1.........2.........0
01 39864STEVEN LEWIS         A
02  2491DAVID MAIN           A
03964111MICHAEL MELTON       C
04 49923JEAN MYERS           D
05123941HAROLD OWENS         F
/*
```

Problem 4
```
                                           4
.........1.........2.........3..........1
502126934RON PATTERSON       31367 62734
419638319THOMAS PATRICK      12346 24692
214906184MARIA PEREZ          6243 12486
436704125LEE RICHARDSON        979  1958
383807581JOHN SANDERS         4774  9548
/*
```

Chapter 3

Problem 1
```
                                                    4
.........1.........2.........9.........4.........8
245231  53042                                40000
246194 500001                               400000
251416  46667                                50000
319874 250025                                50000
4319425050050                              7500000
/*
```

Problem 2
```
                  1
.........1....6
55047214400 40T
55047392355 00T
55097419400105T
74094193150000T
74153284205 00T
99151272400150T
99151438350 00T
99305277400 00T
/*
```

Problem 3

```
         .........1.........2.........3.........4.........5.........6.........7       9
                                                                                7
         S1552JOHN HOFFMAN      005238164041987PAUL FRIEDMAN                      305004
         S1631RICHARD KING      014374719092387BARBARA SMITH                      305004
         S1679LARRY HAM    N    056554257011087JOSEPH BURK                       1946832
         S1741PAULA LONDONRD    103261906082087HERBERT HOWARD                       3419
         S1832ED GRIFFEN        239472393093087RON MARTINEZ                        72734
         /*
```

Problem 4

```
                          2
         .........1.........2....5
         132550  1200  1400  02002
         141625  1450  1530    802
         145105  1605  1732   1302
         167830  1800  2350   5502
         185320  2400  3005  05102
         /*
```

Chapter 4

Problem 1

```
                  1
         .........1..3
         J028168312125
         J028159478300
         J028367129155
         J028370049423
         J028571312403
         /*
```

Problem 2

```
                                              4
         .........1.........2.........3.........0
         LOAN DEPARTMENT2701BILL BROOKS         X
         LOAN DEPARTMENT2680JOHN CALDWELL       X
         LOAN DEPARTMENT2712DAVID HAMILTON      X
         PAYROLL SECTION4014BENNY BROWN         X
         PAYROLL SECTION4238ROBERT CARLSON      X
         PAYROLL SECTION4115LARRY HOOPER        X
         PAYROLL SECTION4229JOHN JOHNSON        X
         /*
```

Problem 3

```
                           2
         .........1.........2....5
         S    1002791245    196280
         S    1002791245    253105
         S    1002791245    082271
         S    1002789449    348849
         S    1002789449    090152
         S    1050691248    039923
         S    1050691248    105398
         S    1050691248    002075
         S    1050729231    653114
         S    1050729231    860152
         S    1050729231    085320
         S    1050729231    008501
         S    1050798882    514980
         /*
```

Problem 4

```
                                                                      8
         .........1.........2.........3.........4.........5.........6....5
         12345    651   4751HAMMER-BALL PEEN    EA2468100246ACME HDWE CO., INC
         24762        13246953BOILER-STEAM      EA2468100246ACMECO., INC
         47672        11189752WASHING MACHINE   EA2468100246ACMECO., INC
         67302    821   4875NAILS-STEEL WIRE    LB2468100246ACME HDWE CO., INC
         15762    671    752LAG SCREWS          DZ2468212481E.C. MORGAN CO.
         38576     76   1065CLIPS-FILE          GR2468212481E.C. MORGAN CO.
         69251     52   6521PAINT               GL2468212481E.C. MORGAN CO.
         07603   1105    151NUTS HEX 1/8        DZ2468328762WILLIAMS TOOL CO.
         07603   1105    151NUTS HEX 1/8        DZ2468328762WILLIAMS TOOL CO.
         39827        37264721GRADERS           EA2468328762WILLIAMS TOOL CO.
         /*
```

Chapter 5

Problem 1
```
         1
.........1....5
  800 1200   50
/*
```

Problem 2
```
                  2
.........1........0
   50     5000    1
  750     2500    4
 1500     1530    3
12000      963    2
  500      120    2
/*
```

Problem 3
```
                                                                    8
.........1.........2.........3.........4.........5.........6.......8
05001600564491212941625941621941              92119748 000 000
05018951562128436900003500020000              5000350025002500
06202300581010334877775877  5897              819994197514 928
06204400495149142094820482 8148   824          519 2431411 519
07502196591804330870503750012500              8300750035005000
/*
```

Problem 4
```
                                           4
.........1.........2.........3.........4.....6
JANE DOE                  95050 600000    000
HENRY HINES              120000  55555 750000
JOSEPH LEWIS              46000    000  42000
WALTER REID              159260 172036 917940
JACK SMITH               792911826291 6512300
/*
```

Chapter 6

Problem 1A
```
                                                                    7
.........1.........2.........3.........4.........5.........6.........7.2
**
BAKER T V   5120374FRANKS R E 8963201GRANT W E   4520312GUNTHER K L7860021
JOHNSON T P2363210JONSON M    8865632JUGGERS Z T2770296JUSTICE P   3062981
KRAMER F R 2345123LEARNER R T4432423
/*
```

Problem 1B
```
           1
..........1
JOHNSON T P
JONSON M
JUGGERS Z T
JUSTICE P
KAMBERLEIN W
/*
```

Problem 2A
```
                                                                    7
.........1.........2.........3.........4.........5.........6.........0
**
10625251063625106454010654501066550106747510686501069450107050010 71800
/*
```

Problem 2B
```
                                        3
.........1.........2.........3......8
1062                              155
1065                              325
1066                              400
1068                              050
1071                              250
/*
```

Problem 3A
```
          0
.....6
**
019001
039002
059003
079004
099005
/*
```

Problem 3B
```
              1
.........1...4
10865       149
12850       052
22560       168
25647       121
26841       185
36875     12356
47250     25863
7825      65324
/*
```

Problem 4A
```
                                                                                              8
.........1.........2.........3.........4.........5.........6.........7.........0
**
010450205003050040550505506055070600806009065100651106512070130701407515075160 75
170801808019085200852108522090230902409525095260952710028100291053 0105
/*
```

Problem 4B
```
                                                          6
.........1.........2.........3.........4.........5......6...4
0174
0195
2105
2109
0169
2733
0596
0456
1100
1157
1366
0290
1475
0377
1977
/*
```

Problem 4C
```
                    2
.........1..........1
  210555741242 2500
  01005788210070 3000
  02902450219157 9542
  050286512350 2304
  1977512021484500
/*
```

Chapter 7

Problem 1A
```
         1
....1....8
**
030303050508080810
/*
```

Problem 1B
```
                                   4
....1....2....3....1
184106ROSA DELGADO      4698714319 982
198653JEFF MCKEE        4698714319 982
378843MELTON BROOKS     5608914221 209
216467MICMAEL BOLTON    5621214895 546
221844JAIME HOGAN       4908099123 630
/*
```

Problem 2A
```
                3
....1....2....0
**
000000000000000000
**
00000000000000000000
**
0000000000000000000000
**
000000000000000000000000
**
00000000000000000000000000
/*
```

Problem 2B
```
                                            5
....1....2....3....4....0
0711877104003021        350000 450000 320050
0722877104003021        295050 359855 111010
0724877104003021         59030 100000 200008
0726872134003021        195300 255330 328050
0728872134003021         59110 541003 602800
0813873007006022         55555 653210 775500
0819873007006022          9800 101444  44447
0827871510006022         88833  10052 187500
0827871510006022          9750 150000 235000
0817871980008022        700000 900000 450000
0820871980008022         17500 195000 851000
0822871980008022        577700  59440  81940
/*
```

Problem 3A
```
                                                  6
....1....2....3....4....5....0
**
SOAP      375BLEACH   238DETERGENT567CLEANSER 319POWDER    276
/*
```

Problem 3B
```
         1
....1....5
**
525425725500455
/*
```

Problem 3C
```
                    1
         .........1.2
0115871     250
0115875      30
0115813     100
0115814     200
0115872      15
0115873     157
0115871      79
0115874     524
0115875      17
/*
```

Problem 4
```
                                          3
         .........1.........2.........3......7
1231359001293029160200015025037011135
1231530013000000250304000002519023410
1232400002459002947012044002830016625
1233594000248001590002300000122003520
5301280002510020050001257011120025910
5303320100245001945027933123450300020
5307730002460001024003913029433002930
5309250002200001050023910002200000391
/*
```

Chapter 8

Problem 1
```
                                                                    7
         .........1.........2.........3.........4.........5.........6.........7.2
MJOHNSON MFG. CO.     27 S. MAIN ST.     BILOXI, MISS.         14765249501
MCOLE PRODUCTS INC.   395 HARRISON ST.   DES MOINES, IOWA      52675350795
MSAVOY ELECTRONICS    1425 S. PACIFIC ST. SAN FRANCISCO, CALI  96317409523
MHENSHEY PUBLISHING   399 RIVERDALE AVE. BROOKLYN, N. Y.       12795510704
MSTAR FURNISHINGS CO.4070 BLANKE AVE.    CHIC4GO, ILL.         30562935247
/*
```

Problem 2
```
                          3
         .........1.........2.........31
X61002MONEMATERS          010000
X62116CASHINFLOW          216000
X62249BANKCREDIT          172850
X62367CASHIN              075060
/*
```

Problem 3   NO DATA

Problem 4
```
                                                         6
         .........1.........2.........3.........4.........5.........6.2
13762JOHN R. MASON        325 CULVER ST.    JAMESTOWN, N. Y.
34965SIMON T. FRASER      695 AMES AVE.     TERRE HAUTE, INDIANA
43925MORTON M. WOLFF      3751 LOCKE RD.    DAVIE, FLORIDA
53862HELEN Z. MALKIND     6947 TORRENT AVE. HEMPSTEAD, N. Y.
97541JOSEPH ANDREWS       14162 S. LAKE ST. ST. ALBANS, VERMONT
```

Chapter 9

Problem 1
```
         1
.........1.2
P14725805716
P25863507563
C52863665487
P85232149565
C85232465851
```

Problem 2
```
         1
.........1....5
4    200000400
4    400390200
4    400950355
4    751240382
/*
```

Problem 3
```
                                                              6
.........1.........2.........3.........4.........5.........6.7
239600100093/4 IN. SPROCKET        00039827           203962
239605900592 IN. COTTER            00610396           203962
242000609501/2 IN. GROMET,RUBBER00000960              203962
25012010010PAINT, BLUE/GREEN       00003500           203962
2207059000216 IN. GAS TURBINES     02634701           203990
2639027000113 IN. DRIVE SHAFT      00002700           203990
274714201871/4 IN. FILE ROUND      00097320           203990
\*
```

Problem 4
```
              2
.........1....0
L012   11110825012186
L012   11110800012287
L012   11110850012387
L022   12230750020187
L022   12230950020287
L022   12290750020387
L022   12230850020587
L035   99000800030187
L035   99000800030287
L035   99000800030387
L035   99000800030487
L035   99000800030587
L035   99000800030687
/*
```

Chapter 10

Problem 1
```
         1
.........1......7
K1234516349414010
K1321499435102005
K1479731948634105
K1498417120502001
K2143523480703003
/*
```

Problem 2
```
                    2
.........1.........2..3
C68832011881001500400000
C68948011881001510177500
C69041011881001520140000
C71248011881001530334000
C72148011881001540234000
/*
```

682 RPG II and RPG III Programming

Problem 3

```
                                                                8
         .........1.........2.........3.........4.........5.........6.........7.........0
         1234493JONES & JONES CO.   131 WEST EAST ST.   VAN NUYS, CALIFORNIA            M
         1234493                                            0020000042167               1
         1234493 050167   17500                                                         2
         1234493 050467   5000064765KING SIZE BED                                       3
         1234493 050467    750064765EASY CHAIR                                          3
         1234493 052567     87580000FLOOR LAMP                                          3
         1234493 052567    150080000END TABLE                                           3
         /*
```

Problem 4A

```
                                                          6
         .........1.........2.........3.........4.........5......6....5
         **
           10000   1000   15000   1500   20000   2000   25000   2500   30000   3000
           35000   9500   40000   4000   45000   4500   50000   5000   55000   5500
           60000   6000   65000   6500   70000   7000   75000   7500   80000   8000
           85000   8500   90000   9000   92000   9200   94000   9400   99000   9900
         /*
```

Problem 4B

```
                                                                                8
         ........ .1.........2.........3.........4.........5.........6.........7.........0
         33459876NOTONE C R          6153 NORTH VINE     MOUNTAINTOP ARIZONA   0005694
         4345987607038766548L2    2764
         5345987607198771635O1   11311
         5345987607238777300L2    6032
         5345987607308783094A5   19635
         /*
```

Problem 5A

```
                                                          6
         .........1.........2.........9.........4.........5.........6..3
         **
         005080001009250200700030065004505500600400080030010002251200175
         /*
```

Problem 5B

```
                                                                                8
         .........1.........2.........3.........4.........5.........6.........7.........0
         5612578JOHN JAY JONES   177 EASTMONT      ENGLEVILLE, OHIO             00150
         A6125780020
         /*
```

Appendix J

Input Data for Appendix G Problems

Problem 1
```
                                                                6
.........1.........2.........3.........4.........5.........1
         AMERICAN STEEL CO       11666 120136 49042387  64031
         AMERICAN STEEL CO       12336 128136 49053087  90904
         APALACHIN LUMBER CO      9852   2179 4227061587 46920
         B J E SERVICE CORP      12332 218322 37062987 147478
         CHALLIS ALMERS         109011190547 77091887   2763
         DENNIS MFG CO         1161529031 6 63091487   44012
/*
```

Problem 2
```
.........1.........2.........3.........4.........5.........6.........7....5
011686                                                                     D
        025 96543    1025  CARBORUNDUM WHEELS                         4646 M
        111 00986      42  STAINLESS SET SCREWS NSP                   5986 M
        111 01598     859  STAINLESS RODS                              934 M
        111 09346     482  HI GRADE CARBON                              52 M
        111 11632     596  CARBON STEEL                               1598 M
        111 11723     917  STAINLESS PINS                               52 M
        111 11725     115  STAINLESS TUBING                            915 M
        159 11899    1567  STAINLESS FITTINGS                         1792 M
        159 55292      14  STEEL SHANK 4X9X1                          4138 M
        159 62549   10048  HEX STOCK TITANIUM                           89 M
        159 65342    9589  TITANIUM BARS                                85 M
        231 72359    1186  STEEL PLATE                                  98 M
        231 81192    1592  FLAT ROLLED STEEL SHEETS                   1139 M
        291 81536     480  STEEL FLANGE                               1985 M
        231 45678   96543  ALLIIGTOR PUMPS                            9999 M
/*
```

Problem 3
```
.........1.........2.........3.........4.........5.........6.......7..3
01412176045867J D ROBINSON          0400004750    040120000560   0875264
01412176078546G S HAYES             0395008252    031751003675    1584617
01412176146978C M MICHOLESON        0400012502    050801000750    1850017
01412176385962C J MEYERSHMIDT       0355006125    040050000000    0085695
12512176069574T R HENDERSON         0365308520    020065000825    1067485
12512176148562B S CAMIRILLO         1010005350    040501001500    2060415
12512176897054S M WATTERS           0380012500    041405013564    1585294
/*
```

Problem 4
```
          1
.........0
1004000101
0100100101
0020080101
1200800201
0014008201
0005750412
0400000412
1040000412
1001705602
0300035602
0010000602
0310035313
1200030313
0004005313
0000500313
1340045323
0300403323
0000912613
1708000613
0010000613
/*
```

Problem 5

```
                              3
         .........1.........2.........3.2
617882   009500000040000000175000
610031   032000000365000001500000
584401   050000000041310005681650
579051   000650000405265007852650
607561   012500000250000005000000
618801   000520000000900002516000
594251   001000000007890005028950
637401   002500000001000004260000
655001   000000000009000001140000
627111   000275000000755000505050
609121   001275000072250001645000
572801   000250000010000000825000
590141   000100000100000002990000
605451   000675000000000004987500
/*
```

Problem 6

```
                                                                        7
         .........1.........2.........3.........4.........5.........6.........0
DAVID   ANDERSON  18745 MOBILE ST., RESEDA, CA       629861000010000002000
BETTY L. BREWER10321 LUNDY DR., INGLEWOOD, CA        614773502505000003000
ARTHUR  BROWN     12145 MADISON ST., LA, CA          389404500003000005000
THOMAS  CASSIDY   3726 HOPE AVE., LYNWOOD, CA        621801215004000002000
BOB     CHAMBERS  3840 HOPE AVE., LYNWOOD, CA        589203200001550003500
JACK T. CROSS     6421 BELMAR ST., RESEDA, CA        433131058015085020000
KENT B. DAVIS     11621 PENN DRIVE, ENCINO, CA       840823207507575035000
SAMUAL  FELLOWS   10782 LINDLEY AVE., ENCINO, CA     417502906004037030000
MICHAEL FISHER    8345 TAMPA AVE., TARZANA, CA       304004443506525050000
GLADYS  BUTTONS   3701 BALBOA AVE., VAN NUYS, CA     675423750008930045000
PATRICK HANEY     4218 VICTORY ST., LA, CA           721114501002795055000
LYNN    HUBBARD   13245 VENTURA BLVD., RESEDA, CA    643751957503645025000
MARVIN  JACOBS    13211 VENTURA BLVD., RESEDA, CA    625502259504495030000
LINDA   JOHNSON   20715 VAN NUYS BLVD., ENCINO, CA   582143000008750035000
HOWARD  KEYES     2181 SHERMAN WAY, RESEDA, CA       466152798010175030000
HAZEL J. MEYER    2188 ROSCOE BLVD., LYNWOOD, CA     308813805003000040000
DONALD  OLSON     11650 ROSCOE BLVD., LYNWOOD, CA    437792776001595030000
IAN     SWIFT     17521 LINDLEY AVE., ENCINO, CA     580902517508550035000
SHARON  WATTERS   13155 MADISON STREET, LA, CA       600703552504795040000
/*
```

Problem 7

```
                                                                      5
         .........1.........2.........3.........4.........5.........6....5
PAUL A. EVANS                    000053487 300021400000000751060487
MARY DIXON                       A000062986 275031600000525077502018 7
GUY T GOODWIN                    000020981 287051600001050095007108 7
JAMES F KING                     A000053219 312041600001201010470909 87
MILTON C MORGAN                  000064378 290071600000000064508208 7
JOHN L REED                      000052887 350021600000175052206048 7
JACK L SHAFFER                   000061758 325041600001050096007908 7
/*
```

Problem 8

```
                    2
         .........1.........2.........9
SUSAN CALDWELL          1100
BETTY JANE CLANCY       1120
RUTH ANN CORBETT        1150
MARGARET CUSHING        2100
ROSEMARY DUPUIS         2075
MAURICE ERICKSON        2050
LILLIAN FELLING         3100
NANCY HAMILTON          3125
BARBARA HICKMAN         3110
JOSEPHINE HOUSTON       4050
LORETTA JOHNSON         4040
ELAINE LEONARD          4030
LORRAINE CLARK          5030
TERRY MCDONNELL         5035
MARY ANN PALMER         5040
/*
```

Problem 9

```
                             2
        .........1.........2..2
        453215000  45000002003
        456785000  45000003001
        123453012  03000015002
        035674126  01250005002
        140752115  03560216201
        757097654  12575056401
        897053624  07512364504
        398764255  10234 36503
        /*
```

Problem 10

```
                                                        4
        .........1.........2.........3.........4.....6
        ALABAMA          03444165   051609   085845
        ALASKA           00302173   586412   009043
        ARIZONA          01772482   113909   051415
        ARKANSAS         01923295   053104   078088
        CALIFORNIA       19953134   158693   169564
        COLORADO         02207259   104247   083586
        CONNECTICUT      03032217   005009   013734
        DELAWARE         00548104   002057   005150
        FLORIDA          06789443   058560   098129
        GEORGIA          04589575   058876   100335
        HAWAII           00769913   006450   003666
        IDAHO            00713008   083557   055910
        ILLINOIS         11113976   056540   130494
        INDIANA          05193689   036291   091111
        IOWA             02825041   056290   112944
        KANSAS           02249071   082264   134770
        KENTUCKY         03219311   040395   069791
        LOUISIANA        03643180   048523   054124
        MAINE            00993663   033215   021499
        MARYLAND         03922399   010577   026859
        MASSACHUSETTS    05689170   008257   029811
        MICHIGAN         08875083   058016   118310
        MINNESOTA        03805069   084068   128235
        MISSISSIPPI      02216912   047716   066686
        MISSOURI         04677399   069686   114966
        MONTANA          00694409   147138   077932
        NEBRASKA         01483791   077227   098017
        NEVADA           00488738   110540   049659
        NEW HAMPSHIRE    00737681   009304   015024
        NEW JERSEY       07168164   007836   032422
        NEW MEXICO       01016000   121666   070307
        NEW YORK         18241266   049576   107776
        NORTH CAROLINA   05082059   052586   087922
        NORTH DAKOTA     00617761   070665   106247
        OHIO             10652017   041222   109965
        OKLAHOMA         02559259   069919   108509
        OREGON           02091385   096981   101397
        PENNSYLVANIA     11793909   045333   114497
        RHODE ISLAND     00949723   001214   005540
        SOUTH CAROLINA   02509516   081055   060295
        SOUTH DAKOTA     00666257   077047   082720
        TENNESSEE        03924164   042244   080656
        TEXAS            11196730   267338   251489
        UTAH             01059273   084916   047653
        VERMONT          00444732   009609   013924
        VIRGINIA         04648494   040817   062351
        WASHINGTON       03409169   068192   081202
        WEST VIRGINIA    01744237   024181   036323
        WISCONSIN        04417933   056154   104290
        WYOMING          00332416   097914   040602
        /*
```

Problem 11

```
            .........1.........2.........3.........4..3
                                          4
0563781532ROBERT PALMER         082587   0536
5310562386SUZIE WILSON          082587   1302
7802619435DAVE LEWIS            082587   1723
4530789138BONNIE SELWOOD        082587   0798
0400831562GISELLE AGERGAARD     082587   0639
7319530088DEAN HOPKINS          082587   1699
7066238009DOUG KEANS            082587   0901
4308615398MIKE COOPER           082587   1086
8023614528RONNIE SALTZER        082587   1630
/*
```

Problem 12

```
            .........1.........2.........3........9
                                         3
1231359    001293029160200015025037010035
1231530    013000000250304000002519023410
1232400    002459002947012044002830016625
1233594    000248001590002300000122003520
5301280    002510020050001257011120025910
5303320    100245001945027933123450300020
5307730    002400001024003913029433002930
5309250    002200001050023910000200000391
/*
```

Problem 13

```
            .........1.........2.........3.........4.........5......6.....6
                                                                       6
420689235STEVE JENSON         3740 OVERLAND ST.          LA    CA
555096862WILLIAM FOSTER       10816 SLAUSON AVE.         LA    CA
559236156DAN SCHOENECKER      10814 KINGSLAND ST.        LS    CA
750236999TOM WILLIAMS         4500 WEST 57 TH ST.        LA    CA
755423306KATHY BUTLER         4240 WEST WASHINGTON PL.   BH    CA
800263349TONY SCHOENECKER     83556 WILSHIRE BLVD.       WLA   CA
808612377ROBERT PALMER        2465 MADISON AVE.          NY    NY
836205691MARY SCHOENECKER     99304 CHATSWORTH BLVD.     SE    ILL
838582008JANETTE SPORTCOLEMAN 83566 COMMUNITY LN.        CH    ILL
850315663JIM COLEMAN          88302 SEPULVEDA BLVD.      LA    CA
850324961JANE COLEMAN         832 DON MILLS RD.          SM    CA
862034856JOEY SCHOENECKER     9604 JEFFERSON BLVD.       CC    CA
/*
```

Problem 14

NO DATA

Problem 15

```
            .........1.........2.........3.........4.........5......6.....6
555096862WILLIAM FOSTER       7881 BRADDOCK STREET       CC    CA
559236156SCHOENECKER DAN      5950 SUNNYBROOK WAY        WLA   CA
750236999TOM WILLIAMS         80261 VAN NESS AVENUE      VN    CA
755423306KATHY BUTLER         7509 CULVER BLVD           CC    CA
800263349CATHY GORING         83250 STUBBS LANE          CC    CA
802359185SCHOENECKER TONY     75196 GRAY DRIVE           CC    CA
808612377ROBERT PALMER        8385 GREENFIELD STREET     WLA   CA
836205691STELLA MARGARITIS    12354 LIFESAVER STREET     WLA   CA
838562008LORRAINE PEREZ       85320 SOUTH BROADWAY AVE   LA    CA
850239455SCHOENECKER MARY     75582 EAST 19TH STREET     SM    CA
850315663JEFF LANDSBERG       80361 MONTANA AVENUE       LA    CA
850324961SCHOENECKER JOEY     80265 LUCILLE STREET       CC    CA
/*
```

Glossary

Access path
The means by which the control program facility provides a logical sequence to the data records in a data base file so that they can be processed by a program.

Access time
The time it takes to read a disk record into storage or write a record from storage.

Accumulating
The process of totaling the values of a particular field as records are processed.

Address
A number identifying a location in storage.

Alphabetic character
Any one of the letters A–Z, or one of the special characters #, $, and @.

Alphameric character
Any alphabetic character or one of the digits 0–9.

Alphameric field
An area on a record that is reserved for a particular unit of information and that can contain any of the characters in the data character set.

Alphameric literal
A symbol, quantity, or constant in a source program that is itself data rather than a reference to data. An alphameric literal can contain any of the characters in the data character set. The characters used in an alphameric literal must be enclosed in apostrophes (e.g., 'TOTALS').

Alternate collating sequence
A function that alters the normal collating sequence or allows two or more characters to be considered equal. See Collating sequence.

Alternating array or table
Two arrays or two tables that are loaded together.

AND relationship
Specification of conditioning indicators to cause an operation to be performed only when all conditions are met.

Application program
A program used to perform a particular data-processing task (e.g., inventory control or payroll).

Arithmetic/logic unit
An area inside the processing unit where calculations are performed.

Arithmetic operation
An operation such as addition, subtraction, multiplication, or division that is performed only on numeric fields in the processing unit.

Array
A series of elements with like characteristics. Each element can be treated as a unique field. The elements can be accessed using an index.

Array element
A data item in an array.

Array file
An input file containing array entries.

Array index
The number of an element to be referenced in an array or the name of a field containing the number of an element to be referenced in an array.

Arrival sequence access path
An access path that is based on the order in which records are stored in a physical file.

Ascending sequence
The arrangement of data in order from low to high based on the contents of a specific field in each record.

Auto report
A function of the RPG licensed program that simplifies the defining of formats for printed reports and that allows previously written statements to be included in new programs. Auto report uses simplified specifications and standard RPG specifications to generate a complete RPG source program.

Auto Report Option Specifications form
An RPG coding form used to specify options for an auto report program.

Auto report program
A set of instructions using the RPG auto report function. See Auto report.

Batch processing
A method of running a program or a series of programs in which one or more records (a batch) is processed with minimal or no interaction with the user or operator. See Interactive processing for contrast.

Binary
Relating to, being, or belonging to a system of numbers with a base of two (e.g., the binary digits 0 and 1).

Binary format
Format in which each field has a length of two or four bytes. The sign (+ or −) is in the leftmost bit of the field and the integer value is in the remaining bits of the field. Positive numbers have a 0 (zero) in the sign bit; negative numbers have a 1 (one) in the sign bit and are in twos complement form.

Blank after
An output specification that changes the content of a field to contain only zeros (if it is a numeric field) or blanks (if it is an alphameric field) after that field has been output.

Block
A group of logical records that together form a physical record.

Branching
The technique of bypassing specific calculation operations by using certain operation codes (e.g., GOTO and TAG).

Breakpoint
A place in a program (specified by a command or a condition) where the system halts execution so that the user can display or modify variables, modify the execution sequence of the program, or test the program.

Byte
The representation of a character by eight binary bits; the amount of storage required for one EBCDIC character.

Calculation specifications
A description of the type and order of processing to be performed by the program found on the Calculation Specifications form.

Called program
A program that is invoked by another program, a calling program. *See* Calling program.

Calling program
A program that invokes another program, a called program. *See* Called program.

Card
In data processing, an obsolescent data medium containing combinations of holes representing data.

Card file
A group of related punched-card records.

Card layout form
A chart for planning the design and format of cards.

Card punch
A device that records information on a card in the form of combinations of holes representing characters.

Card reader
A device that electronically senses information on punched cards and transfers that information to the processing unit.

Character
Any individual data item that can be represented in printed form—as a letter, digit, or special character.

Coding
Making entries on RPG specification forms.

Collating sequence
The order of each character in relation to other characters according to the bit structure.

Combined file
A data file used as both an input file and an output file. The output file contains only those fields described for the output file (i.e., the output record does not necessarily contain the same fields as the input file).

Comments
Words or statements in a program that serve as documentation rather than as instructions to the compiler.

Compilation
The translation of a source program (such as RPG specifications) into an executable program.

Compile
To translate a source program (such as RPG specifications) into an object program (machine language) using the compiler.

Compiler
A program that translates a source program and/or data description specifications into an executable program.

Compile time array or table
An array or table in which the data are compiled with the source program to become a permanent part of the object program. *See also* Execution time array and Preexecution time array or table.

Computer
An electronic device or group of interrelated devices capable of processing data either separately or in conjunction with other interrelated devices.

Conditioning
The use of indicators in an RPG program to control when calculation or output operations are to be done.

Consecutive processing
File processing that reads records in the order in which they exist in the file.

Constant
The actual data to be used in processing rather than a field name containing the data. A constant does not change during the execution of a program, but the contents of a field can. A constant can contain any of the characters in the data character set. For example, COST is a name representing a field containing data that change, whereas the constant *100* is an actual piece of data that does not change. *See also* Literal.

Continuation lines
Additional lines specified on the file description specifications to provide information about the file being defined.

Control break
A change in the content of a control field indicating that all records from a particular control group have been read and that a new control group is starting.

Control and File Description form
An RPG coding form that gives information needed for control of the system and a description of the files used for a particular job.

Control field
One or more fields that are compared from record to record to determine when the information in the fields changes. When the information changes, the control level indicator (L1–L9) assigned to the field(s) is set on.

Control group
A set of records all having the same control field information.

Control level indicator
An indicator (L1–L9) used to specify certain fields as control fields and subsequently used to condition which operations are to be performed at detail or total calculation time, or output time.

Control specifications
Information provided on the RPG Control Specifications form that affects program generation and execution.

Control unit
An area inside the processing unit that determines from instructions what has to be done. It directs other units or devices to perform the required functions.

Create
The function used to bring an object (e.g., a file) into existence in the program.

Cross-reference listing
The portion of the compiler listing that contains information on the location in the program in which files, fields, and indicators are defined, referenced, and modified.

CRT
A (C)athode (R)ay (T)ube; the television monitor which is the primary input/output peripheral.

Currency symbol
A character used to identify monetary values.

Cursor
A movable, visible underscore mark used to indicate a position on a display screen.

Cylinder
A set of tracks on a magnetic disk that can be accessed by one positioning of the access arm.

Cylinder index
An index used to determine in which cylinder a record is located.

Data
A collection of facts, numbers, letters, and symbols that can be processed or produced by a system.

Data area
An object used to communicate data between programs within a job and between jobs.

Data area data structure
A data structure used to pass data between programs within a job and between jobs.

Data base
The collection of all data files stored in the system. Files in the data base are called data base files.

Data base file
An organized collection of related records in the data base.

Data character set
All of the 256 EBCDIC characters.

Data Description Specifications form
A system coding form using a fixed-form syntax that describes the data base or device file of the user.

Data structure
An area in storage that is composed of one or more subfields. A data structure can be either program described or externally described.

Data structure name
A name used to identify a data structure. A data structure name is composed of alphameric characters, the first of which must be alphabetic. The maximum length of a data structure name is six characters.

Default error handler
The portion of the RPG logic cycle that handles program or file exception/errors when program or file exception/errors are not controlled by the programmer.

Descending sequence
The arrangement of data in an order from high to low based on the content of specific fields in each record.

Detail line
See Detail record.

Detail record
An output record produced during detail output time of the RPG program cycle.

Detail time
An operation in the RPG program cycle in which calculation and output operations are performed for each record read.

Diagnostic message
An output message that identifies RPG specification errors and their severity.

Digit
One of the characters 0–9.

Disk
A flat, circular plate with a magnetic surface on which data can be stored.

Disk drive
A device that reads data from or writes data on a disk.

Diskette
A thin, flexible magnetic disk permanently enclosed in a semirigid protective jacket.

Disk file
A group of related records stored on a DASD device. A written explanation of a program and its use, function, and operations.

Do-group
A group of calculations that are executed one or more times based on the results of comparing factor 1 and factor 2 of certain calculation operations (e.g., DOUxx). A DO operation with an END operation forms a do-group.

Dump
To write the contents of storage or part of storage, usually from an internal storage medium, for a specific purpose (e.g., to allow other use of storage to safeguard against faults or errors, or in connection with debugging.

Dynamic
Occurring at execution time.

EBCDIC
Extended binary coded decimal interchange code.

Edit
To punctuate a field by suppressing zeros and inserting commas, periods, currency symbols, sign status, or other constant information.

Edit code
A number or letter indicating that editing should be done on a numeric output field according to a predefined pattern. This includes zero suppression and punctuation.

Edit word
A word (with a specific format) indicating that editing should be done on a numeric output field according to a predefined pattern. This includes zero suppression, punctuation, and constant information.

Eighty-column card
A punch card with eighty vertical columns representing eighty characters.

Element
The smallest addressable unit of an array or table.

End-of-file
The end of records in a file.

End of program
The point at which a program ends and returns control to the calling program.

End-position
An entry in the output specifications that indicates where the end-position of a field or constant is to be placed in the output record.

Error handling
Programmer-written coding that handles program or file exception/errors. If program or file exception/errors are not controlled by the programmer, the RPG default error handler receives control.

Error message
See Diagnostic message.

Exception handling
See Error handling.

Execution
The processing of input data files according to instructions to produce the specified output.

Execution time array
An array loaded or created by input or calculation specifications after actual execution begins. *See* Compile time array or table and Preexecution time array or table.

Extension and Line Counter Specifications form
An RPG coding form used to provide information about record address, array, and table files used by the program and the number of lines to be printed on the forms that are used.

External indicators (U1–U8)
Indicators that can be defined by a control language command or as a resulting or field indicator in the calculation or input specifications. The indicators can be altered by the job during execution. External indicators can be used to condition the opening of files for a program.

Externally described data
File data of records whose fields are described through the control program facility when the file is created using data description specifications. The field descriptions can be used by the program when the file is processed.

Externally described file
A file containing externally described data.

Factor
A value (e.g., a field or data structure) used in an operation on a Calculation Specifications form.

Fetch overflow
A routine that allows the user (*a*) to alter the basic RPG overflow logic to prevent printing over the perforation and (*b*) to use as much of the page as possible. When fetch overflow is specified, RPG checks overflow on each line for which fetch overflow is specified.

Field
An area of a record that is reserved and used for a particular item of information. One or more adjacent record positions containing related information constitute a field.

Field indicator
An indicator signifying whether the value of a given field in an input record is plus, minus, zero, or blank.

Field length
The number of positions allowed for a given field, determined by the maximum length of information that will be entered in the field. A numeric field can be a maximum of 15 digits and an alphameric field can be a maximum of 256 characters.

Field name
In RPG programming, a combination of no more than six alphabetic or numeric characters that identify a field. The first character must be alphabetic; no blanks can appear between characters.

Field record relation indicator
An indicator used to associate fields in an input record with a particular record type. The field record relation indicator is normally used when the record type is one of several in an OR relationship.

Figurative constant
An implied literal that is specified (in the calculation specifications) without reference to length because the implied length and decimal positions are the same as that of the receiver field (e.g., *BLANK/*BLANKS, *ZERO/*ZEROS, *HIVAL/*LOVAL, *ALL'X..').

File
An organized set of related records treated as a unit that includes descriptive information about the record. See Input file, Output file, Primary file, and Secondary file. For types of file organization, see Sequential file and Indexed file. For types of file processing, see Consecutive processing, Sequential by key processing, and Random by relative record number processing. See also Logical file.

File description
Information in a file that describes the file and its contents. The data in the file can be described to the record level (*see* Program described data) or to the field level (*see* Externally described data).

File description specifications
Information on the File Description Specifications form that identifies all files used in a program.

Filename
The name associated with a file. A filename can be from one to eight characters long. The first character must be alphabetic and the remaining characters can be any combination of alphabetic or numeric characters. Blanks cannot appear between characters in a filename.

File operation code
An operation code (e.g., CHAIN) that allows the user to control the access method of a file.

File translation
A function used to change any of the 256 EBCDIC characters into another EBCDIC character.

First-page (1P) indicator
An indicator used to specify which lines should be printed on the first page only (e.g., headings).

Floating dollar sign
A currency symbol that changes positions depending upon the number of zero suppressed positions.

Flowchart
A pictorial representation of either program logic (program flowchart) or systems architecture (system flowchart).

Full procedural file
A file for which the input operations are controlled by calculation operation codes rather than the program cycle.

Half-adjust
A method of rounding off a number by adjusting the last digit to be kept. When the number to the right of the last digit to be retained is five or greater, one is added to the last retained digit. For example, 2.475 half-adjusted to two decimal places becomes 2.48, but 2.474 becomes 2.47.

Halt indicators (H1–H9)
An indicator used to terminate the program when an unacceptable condition occurs.

Heading record
A constant, usually printed at the top of the page, identifying the information or report on that page.

Hexadecimal
Pertaining to a number system with a base of sixteen; valid digits range from 0–9 and letters A–F.

Indexed file
A program described data base file whose access path is built on key values. Each record in the file is identified by a key field.

Indicator
(1) A two-character entry on the specification forms used to test a field or record or to tell when certain operations are to be performed. (2) An internal switch used by the program to remember when a certain event occurs

and telling what to do when the event occurs. *See* Control level indicator, Field indicator, Field record relation indicator, First page (1P) indicator, Last record (LR) indicator, Matching record (MR) indicator, Overflow indicator (OA–OG, OV), Record identifying indicator, Resulting indicator, and Return (RT) indicator.

Initialize
To set counters, switches, addresses, or contents of storage to zero or other starting values at the beginning or at prescribed points during the operation of a computer routine.

Input
Information (or data) to be processed by the system.

Input file
A set of records a program uses as source information.

Input specifications
Information contained on the Input Specifications form on which records and their fields or the data structure for a program described data file are specified; the input specifications are also used to add RPG functions to an externally described input data file.

Inquiry
A request for information in storage entered from the system console or a display work station. *See also* Inquiry program.

Inquiry file
The file into which an inquiry is made using the inquiry function of the customer program.

Inquiry program
A program that enables the user to access information from a disk file. *See* Inquiry.

Instruction
A statement specifying an operation to be performed by the system and identifying the data, if any, involved in that operation.

Integer
A whole number, positive or negative, without a decimal point.

Interactive processing
A method of processing a program in which each operator action causes a response from the program. *Contrast with* Batch processing.

Job control specification (JCL)
A specification relating to the work a computer should do: what programs to run, the order in which to run them, and the data to be used by each program.

Keyboard
A systematic arrangement of keys by which commands, control statements, and data are entered into a computer.

Keyed sequence access path
An access path based on the contents of key fields contained in the records.

Key field
A field contained in every record in a file, the contents of which function to sequence the records when the file is used.

Keypunch
A device, similar to a typewriter, used for punching information into cards. *Synonymous with* Card punch.

Label
A name defined in factor 1 of a TAG or ENDSR operation to identify the destination of the operations.

Last record (LR) indicator
An indicator that signifies when the last data record is processed. This indicator can be used to condition the calculation and output operations to be done at end of program.

Left-justified
The movement of the contents of a field or entry on a specification form so that the first character of the entry is in the leftmost position of the field.

Level zero (L0) entry
An entry on the Calculation Specifications form indicating operations that are to be done during total time for each program cycle when no control break has occurred.

Library
An object that serves as a directory to other objects. A library is used to group objects and to find objects by name.

Library list
An ordered list of library names indicating which libraries are to be searched and the order in which they are to be searched to find an object.

Logical record
A group of related fields that comprises a unit of information. Several logical records are usually combined to form a block or physical record.

Limits file
A record address file containing limits records when the sequential within limits processing method is used.

Limits record
A record consisting of the lowest record key and the highest record key of the records in the keyed file that are to be read.

Line counter specifications
Information on the Line Counter Specifications form used to indicate or to override the system defaults of the length of the printer form and the number of lines to print on a page. Line counter specifications may be used for each printer file in a program.

Literal
The actual data to be used in processing rather than the name of a field containing the data. A literal does not change during the execution of a program, but the contents of a field can. A literal can contain any of the characters in the data character set. *See also* Alphameric literal, Constant, and Numeric literal.

Logical file
A data base file through which data stored in one or more physical fields can be accessed by means of record formats and/or access paths.

Logic error
An execution time error that does not violate any syntactical rules. A logic error indicates that an instruction or instructions have executed correctly but have produced undesirable results (i.e., the programmer asked the program to do the wrong thing or the right thing at the wrong time).

Look ahead
A feature that allows the program to look at information in a field on the next record available for processing in any input or update file.

LR indicator
See Last record (LR) indicator.

L0 entry
See Level zero (L0) entry.

Machine language
A language that can be interpreted and used by a system.

Match fields
Fields within a record type in primary or secondary multifile processing; these files are used for sequence checking a single file or matching the records of one file with those of another file.

Matching record (MR) indicator
An indicator used in calculation or output specifications to indicate the operations to be performed only when records match in primary and secondary files.

Match level
The level assigned to the match field (M1–M9). The match level identifies fields by which records are matched during primary or secondary multifile processing.

Message file
A file containing all RPG compile time and message definitions.

Message identification code
A two-digit number identifying a record in a message file. This number can be part of the message identifier.

Mnemonic
Memory assisting (e.g., the operation code MULT is mnemonic for multiply).

Modular program design
A design in which multiple programs perform a function (normally one program per function). Modular program design applies to both batch and interactive processing.

MR indicator
See Matching record (MR) indicator.

Multiple occurrence data structure
A data structure occurring more than one time in a program.

Nested do-group
A do-group contained entirely within another do-group.

Ninety-six column card
A punch card with ninety-six vertical columns representing ninety-six characters. The columns are divided horizontally into thirds; the columns in the upper third are numbered 1–32; those in the middle third, 33–64; and those in the lower third, 65–96.

Numeric
Any combination of the digits 0–9.

Numeric characters
The digits 0–9.

Numeric constant
A constant used to represent a number; the constant may consist of a decimal point, a sign, and the digits 0–9.

Numeric field
An area of a record reserved for a particular unit of information containing only the numeric digits 0–9.

Numeric literal
The actual numerical value to be used in processing rather than the name of a field containing the data. A numeric literal can contain any of the numeric digits 0–9, a sign (plus or minus), and a decimal point.

Object
A named unit consisting of data and a set of attributes describing the object. The term 'object' is used to refer to anything that exists in and occupies space in storage on which operations can be performed. Examples of objects are programs, files, and libraries.

Object program
A set of instructions in machine language. The object program is produced from the source program by the compiler.

Operation
A defined action performed on one or more data items (e.g., adding, multiplying, comparing, or moving information).

Operation code
A word or abbreviation specified in the Calculation Specifications form used to identify an operation (e.g., SUB for subtract, ADD for add, or COMP for compare).

OR relationship
The specification of conditioning indicators to cause the operation conditioned to be performed when any one of the conditions is met.

Output
Data transferred from storage to an output device.

Output file
A file on which information (the results of processing) is to be written.

Output indicator
An indicator used in the output specifications to define the conditions under which an output record or an output field is to be written. An output indicator must be previously defined before it is used in the output specifications.

Output specifications
Information on the Output Specifications form describing the format of fields in the output record and indicating when the record is to be written out.

Overflow
The condition occurring when the line specified as the overflow line to be printed on a page has been passed.

Overflow indicator (OA–OG, OV)
An indicator signalling when the overflow line on a page has been printed or passed. The indicator can be used to specify which lines are to be printed on the next page.

Overflow line
The line specified as the last line to be printed on a page.

Overflow page
The new page advanced when overflow occurs.

Packed decimal format
Format in which each byte within a field represents two numeric digits except the rightmost byte, which contains one digit in bits 0–3 and the sign in bits 4–7. For all other bytes, bits 0–3 represent one digit; bits 4–7 represent one digit (e.g., the decimal value +123 is represented as 0001 0010 0011 1111). *Contrast with* Zoned decimal format.

Packed field
A field containing data in the packed decimal format.

Packed key
A key in the packed decimal format.

Parameter
Within RPG, data passed to or received from another program.

Parameter list
A list of values that provides a means of associating addressability of data defined in a called program to data in the calling program. The list contains parameter names and the order in which they are to be associated in the calling and called programs.

Physical file
A data base file containing data records. All records have the same format (i.e., a physical file contains fixed-length records, all of which contain the same fields in the same order.

*PLACE
A special RPG function used to duplicate printing with less coding.

Preexecution time array or table
An array or table that is loaded at the same time as the source program before execution of the program begins. *See also* Compile time array or table and Execution time array.

Physical record
See Block.

Primary file
If specified, the main file from which a program first reads records. In multifile processing, the primary file is used to determine whether the matching record indicator is set on.

Printer
The output device that records information on paper in the form of printed characters.

Printer/Display Layout form
A coding form that can be used to determine the format for a printed report or a display file.

Printer Spacing Chart
A form used to plan the location of data in the printer output file.

Processing
The action of performing operations on data as specified in the program.

Processing unit
The part of a system controlling the system and its attached devices; it provides storage area for the programs and data, and performs the operations specified in the program.

Program
(1) A sequence of instructions to a computer written in a special form the computer can interpret. A program tells the computer where to get input, how to process it, and where to put the results. (2) A set of instructions telling the computer which operations are to be done and how to do them.

Program cycle
A series of steps performed in a specific order for each record read by the compiled RPG program.

Program described file
File for which the fields must be described in the program that processed the file.

Program listing
A printout giving information about the source program (e.g., source statements, diagnostic messages, indicators used, storage addresses of fields, constants used).

Prompt
A message issued by a program requesting either information or action on the part of an operator or user action to continue processing.

*PSSR
Program exception/error subroutine.

Random by key processing
A method of processing a full procedural file using the CHAIN operation code. Records to be processed are identified by record keys.

Random by relative record number processing
A method of processing a full procedural file using the CHAIN operation code. Records to be processed are identified by relative record numbers.

Record
A group of related fields; also the basic unit of data transferred between a file and a program. Records are made up of fields defined in the user's program (e.g., RPG input specifications) or outside the user's program on data description specifications for the file.

Record address file
An input file indicating which records are to be read from another file and the order in which the records are to be read from that file.

Record format
The definition of the way data is structured in the records of a file. The definition includes the record name and field descriptions for the fields contained in the record. The record formats used in a file are contained in the file description. Each record format in a file is identified by a unique name and cannot be the same as the filename.

Record identifying code
Characters placed in a record to identify that record type. A code placed in a record when it is created to identify that record type.

Record identifying indicator
An indicator identifying the type of record being processed during the current program cycle.

Record key
See Key field.

Record length
The total number of characters (bytes) in a record.

Record type
The classification of records in a file. Records are classified according to a specific field or fields within each record. Records of the same type have the same fields in the same order and identical record identification codes.

Relational checking
(1) Diagnostics performed against two statements to ensure that the statements are valid (e.g., a GOTO operation must have an associated TAG operation). This type of checking is only done by the compiler as opposed to single-statement syntax checking. (2) Operations performed against a field value to ensure that the field value contains appropriate data if validation requires evaluation of more than one field. *See* Validity checking.

Relative end-position
An entry on the Output Specifications form indicating the number of blank positions to appear between one field or constant and the field or constant defined in the preceding specification line.

Relative record number
A number specifying the location of a record in relation to the beginning of the file.

Reserved word
A special word in the RPG language allowing access to a particular function in the system.

Result field
A field designated on the calculation specifications for placement of the outcome of an operation.

Resulting indicator
An indicator that signals the result of a calculation (e.g., whether the result is plus, minus, or zero; whether a given field is greater than, less than, or equal to another field; whether an operation was successfully completed).

Glossary

Return (RT) indicator
An indicator used to indicate to the internal RPG logic that control should be returned to the calling program.

Right-adjust
The placement of an entry in a field so that the rightmost character of the entry is in the rightmost position of the field.

RT indicator
See Return (RT) indicator.

Search word
Data for which a match, or a greater than or less than quantity in a table or array, is to be found. The search word is specified in the lookup statement.

Secondary file
Any file other than the primary file used in multifile processing.

Sequence checking
An RPG function that checks the sequence of records in input, update, or combined files used as primary and secondary files.

Sequential by key processing
A method of file processing that reads records from a keyed sequence file in the order in which the keys are arranged in the access path.

Sequential file
A file into which records are entered one after the other. If the file is keyed, the records are processed in the sequence of the access path.

Single-program design
A design in which all functions are done within one program.

Source file
A file created to contain source statements for such items as high-level language programs and data description specifications.

Source listing
The portion of the compiler listing that contains the source statements and diagnostics.

Source program
A set of instructions written in a programming language such as RPG that represent a particular job as defined by a programmer.

Special character
A character other than a digit, a letter, or #, $, @ (e.g., *, +, and %).

Specifications forms
Forms on which an RPG program is coded and described. *See* Calculation Specifications form, Control and File Description Specifications form, Extension and Line Counter Specifications form, Input Specifications form, and Output Specifications form.

Storage unit
An area inside the processing unit where instructions and data are stored.

Subfield
A field within a data structure.

Subfile
A group of records read from or written to a display device in one operation.

Subroutine
A group of calculation specification statements in a program that can be executed several times in that program.

Symbolic name
A name used to define a program, file, or reference within the RPG program. Symbolic names are composed of alphameric characters, the first of which must be alphabetic. The maximum length of a filename is eight characters. All other symbolic names have a maximum length of six characters.

Table
A collection of data in which each item is uniquely identified by a label, by its position relative to the other items, or by some other means.

Table file
A file containing table entries.

Total operations
Operations (calculation or output) performed only at end of program or after a control group of records has been processed.

Total records
Output records written after a group of detail records. Total records generally contain data produced as the result of calculations performed on the information in a group of detail records.

Total time
The part of the RPG program cycle in which operations (calculation or output) specified for a group of records are done. Total time operations are conditioned by control level indicators (L1–L9 or LR).

Track index
An index that is used to determine in which track a record is located.

Update file
A file that is used as both an input file and an output file. If the program alters the data in one or more fields of an input record and then writes the altered field and the unaltered fields back to the same positions in the same record, the file is an update file.

User-defined edit code
A number (5–9) indicating that editing should be done on a numeric output field according to a pattern predefined to the control program facility. User-defined edit codes can take the place of edit words making unnecessary the repetitive coding of the same edit word.

Validity checking
Operations performed against a field value to ensure that the field contains appropriate data. Checking may be done on a single field (e.g., if FIELDA contains a *1,* FIELDB can only contain a *2* or *3*).

Variable
A named entity used to refer to data and to which values can be assigned. Its attributes remain constant, but it can refer to different values at different times. Variables fall into three categories, applicable to any data type: element, array, and structure.

Volume
A complete physical unit such as a reel of tape, a cartridge, a diskette, or a disk pack.

Work station file
A file used to process a work station device.

WORKSTN
The device name specified for a combined file used to communicate with a display station.

Zero suppression
The elimination of leading zeros in a number (e.g., 00057 becomes 57 and represents one blank space when zero suppressed).

Zoned decimal format
Representation of a decimal value by one byte per digit. Bits 0–3 of the rightmost byte represent the sign; bits 0–3 of all other bytes represent the zone portion; bits 4–7 of all bytes represent the numeric portion (e.g., in zoned decimal format, the decimal value +123 is represented as 1111 0001 1111 0010 1111 0011). *Contrast with* Packed decimal format.

Zoned field
A field containing data in the zoned decimal format.

Index

ADD add operation code, 85
Alphabetic, 6
Alphabetic literal, 84
Alphameric, 6
ANDxx, 205, 208
Application design considerations, 429
Argument, 230, 233–234
Arithmetic operators, 84–92
Array, 286
Arrays
   accumulating groups of totals, 315–317
   calculations, 302–304
   compile time, 287
   defining, 286–288
   determining if a search is successful, 308
   element, 286
   execution time, 287
   Extension Specifications, 287–288
      alternating arrays, 288
      array name, 287
      decimal positions, 288
      from filename, 287
      length of entry, 288
      number of entries per array, 287
      number of entries per record, 287
      packed/binary, 288
      sequence, 288
      to filename, 287
   indexing, 318–322
   loading, 288–293
      at compile/preexecution time, 288–290
      during execution time, 290–293
      execution time—information in more than one record, 293
      execution time—information in one record, 290
      execution time—modifying the contents of arrays, 293
   lookup (LOKUP), 304–311
   name and index, 299
   output during an array search, 311–315
   output of an entire array, 311–313
      Extension Specifications, 311–312
      Output Specifications, 312–315
   output of individual elements of an array, 318
   preexecution time, 287
   references in calculations, 299–300
   referencing an element that satisfies a search, 308–309
   referencing individual elements, 318–322
   referencing only part of a field, 318–322
   searching an array for more than one element, 309–310
   searching an array for a particular element, 304–305
   specifying, 286–288
   specifying an index that can be changed, 318
   specifying an index that does not change, 318
   starting the search at a particular element, 305
   to array calculations, 301–302
   updating, 293–294
   using, 299–304
   when to use an array instead of a table, 286
Ascending, 252
Asterisk fill, 108–109

Basic data processing logic, 16
Basic RPG logic, 136
BEGSR begin subroutine operation code, 195–198, 200
Binary format, 523–524
BITOF set bit off operation code, 509
BITON set bit on operation code, 507–508
Bit operations, 507–513
Blank After
   array, 293
   specifications, 145–146
Block, 349
Branching, 182
Branching and looping, 190

C, 553
CABxx (Compare and Branch), 204, 584
Calculation operations, 82–84
   conditions, 83
   data, 83
   field length, 87
   logic cycle, 81
   operators, 82–83
   purpose of calculations, 82–84
   RPG III, shorter format, 116–117, 588
   writing specification forms, 84–116
Calculations
   bypassing, 183–184
Calculation Specifications, 12
   decimal positions, 88
   describing use of data, 85
   describing result field, 87–88
   describing type of operations, 85
   half-adjusting results (rounding), 88
   order, 84
   result field length, 87
   resulting indicators, 88–89
   testing results of arithmetic operations, 88–89
   tests, 84
CALL/RETRN Function, 579
Chaining, 461–470
CHAIN operation code, 388–393, 464–467, 558, 565, 583
   random processing, 468–471
   RPG III, 558
Chapter 1 problem 1, 24
Chapter 1 problem 2, 24
Chapter 1 problem 3, 25
Chapter 1 problem 4, 25
Chapter 2 problem 1, 77
Chapter 2 problem 2, 77–78
Chapter 2 problem 3, 78
Chapter 2 problem 4, 79
Chapter 3 problem 1, 128
Chapter 3 problem 2, 129
Chapter 3 problem 3, 129–130
Chapter 3 problem 4, 130–131
Chapter 4 problem 1, 165–166
Chapter 4 problem 2, 167
Chapter 4 problem 3, 168–169
Chapter 4 problem 4, 169–170
Chapter 5 problem 1, 225
Chapter 5 problem 2, 226–227

Chapter 5 problem 3, 227
Chapter 5 problem 4, 228
Chapter 6 problem 1, 280–281
Chapter 6 problem 2, 281
Chapter 6 problem 3, 282
Chapter 6 problem 4, 283–284
Chapter 7 problem 1, 342
Chapter 7 problem 2, 343
Chapter 7 problem 3, 344–345
Chapter 7 problem 4, 345–346
Chapter 8 problem 1, 425
Chapter 8 problem 2, 425
Chapter 8 problem 3, 426
Chapter 8 problem 4, 427
Chapter 9 problem 1, 489–490
Chapter 9 problem 2, 491–492
Chapter 9 problem 3, 493–494
Chapter 9 problem 4, 495–497
Chapter 10 problem 1, 539–540
Chapter 10 problem 2, 541–542
Chapter 10 problem 3, 542–545
Chapter 10 problem 4, 545–548
Chapter 10 problem 5, 549
Checking the specifications, 628
CLOSE (Close File for Processing), 561
COBOL, 555
Coding, 2
Command Key Indicators, 563
Comments, 67
Common entries, 66–68
COMP compare operation code, 92–95
Compilation, 4
Compiler, 2, 4
Constant, 10
Constants, 116
    alphameric, rules, 93
    numeric, rules, 93
Control breaks, 133–134, 137–139
Control field, 137, 139
Control group, 137
Control level
    coding, 140–145
    indicators, 139–145
        assignment, 140–143
        output coding, 144–145
    RPG II specifications, 140–141
    RPG logic, 139
    terminology, 137
Control levels and indicators, 133–136
Controlling operations in RPG program, 172
Control of calculations, 180–201
Control of output, 172–179
Control Specifications, 12, 28–29
Control specification preparation, 627
    Default control specifications, 590
Copylib, 555
CPF, 554–558, 561–563, 566, 578
CRT, 553, 557, 558, 561, 578
CRTRPGPGM, 592
Cylinder index, 658

Data, describing, 27
Data blocks, 6–7
Data Description Specification (DDS), 556, 557
Data file organizations, 354–355
Data files, 350–351
Data Processing, 2
Data processing logic, basic, 16
Data Structures, 580–584
dBASE III+, 553
DDS, 556, 557
DEBUG function, 606–612
    format of records created, 608
    getting results, 608
    introduction, 606
    making your program work for all cases, 609
    placement, 609
    RPG III, 592
    specifications, 606–607
    using, 606
Default Control Specification, 590
DEFN (Field Definition), 584–585
DELET, (Delete Record) 558
Demand file, Chapter 9
Descending, 252, 254
Detail lines, 10
Detail operations, 136
Detail output, 116
    constants, 116
    indicators, 113
Detail records, 54
Detail time, 16, 136
Determine RPG specifications needed for the job, 622
Determining the job requirements, 620–622
Direct Access (mass storage devices), 348
Direct access storage devices (DASD), 349
Direct file organization, 405, 658–662
Direct files, 351, 658–675
    consecutive retrieval, 663–666
    consecutive updating of records, 671–672
    creation, 406, 659–662
    maintenance, 670–675
    random retrieval, 667–669
    random updating of records, 673–675
    retrieval of records, 663–669
    tagging records for deletion, 671
    updating records, 671–675
Direct organization, 355, 658–675
DIV divide operation code, 85
DO, 205–206
DOUxx, 205, 207
DOWxx, 205, 207–208
Documenting the program, 626

DSPLY display information operation code, 519–520
    OR option, 519
    RPG III, 588
DUMP, 592

Edit, 116
Edit codes, 104–106
Edit code Y (date field edit), 105–106
Edit code Z (zero suppress), 105
Editing, 104–113
Edit words, 107
EDTCDE, 557
EDTWRD, 557
Element, 286
End-of-file processing, 449–450
ENDSR end subroutine operation code, 195–198, 200
EXCPT calculation time output operation code, 200
    condition the use of, 174
    overflow printing, 175
    RPG III, 201–203, 584
EXCPT Name, 201–203
Execute, 4
EXFMT (Execute Format), 558
EXSR execute subroutine operation code, 195–197, 200
Extension Specifications, 12, 135–140
    comments, 240
    decimal positions, 240
    length of an entry, 238
    number of table entries per table, 238
    number of table entries per table-input record, 236
    packed binary fields, 239
    positions 240
    program identification, 240
    table entries sequence, 240
    table names, 236

FEOD (Force End Of Data), 561
Fetch overflow, 174, 178–179
Field, 6
Field record relation, 471–475
    use with chaining fields, 474–475
    use with control fields, 474–475
    use with external indicators and selective processing, 474–475
Figurative Constants, 586
File, 11, 349
File Description Specifications, 12, 31–36
    device designation, 36
    file designation, 32
    filenames, 31
    file use, 32
    overflow indicators, 33–34
    program cycle operations, 34
    RPG specifications, 34–35

using overflow and 1P indicators together, 35
record size, 33
File Information Data Structure (INFDS), 581–584
Files describing, 29–31
First program, writing the, 66–68
Floating $, 107–108
FORCE selects file during calculations operation code
   alternating the order of processing files, 449–456
   specifying the next file to be processed, 451
Formatted Dump, 592
Full procedural file, 457, 554. 557–562
Full Procedural File Specifications, 554, 557–562
Function, 230, 233–234

Glossary, 689–697
GOTO branching operation code, 184–189
Group indication, 146–147, 150

Heading
   1P indicator and type, 65
   lines, 10
   output, 65, 116
   records, 54
   spacing and skipping, 65

IBM System/36, 553
IBM System/38, 553–555, 578
IFxx, 205, 208
Illustrative programs
   Accumulating final totals-Deduction Register, 118–122
   Alternating tables-multiple control levels-Monthly Sales and Commission Report, 272–278
   Alternating tables-table lookup-Tax Deduction Report, 267–272
   Array loading with input specifications-Array XYZ, 336–340
   Compare arithmetic-test numeric-Weekly Payroll Register, 525–531
   Compare-GOTO-Aged Trial Balance Report, 476–482
   Compare-record relation indicators-Stock Status Report, 483–487
   Control levels-group indication-Daily Sales Register, 154–159
   Control levels-group indication-Transaction Register, 150–154
   Creating an Indexed Disk File, 414–415
   Disk updating-matching records-Updating Records, 418–423

Line Counter Specifications-Invoice, 532–538
Line Counter Specifications-Transaction Register, 72–75
List indexed disk records, 416–417
Multiple arrays-XFOOT-Product Report, 329–335
Multiple control levels-Hospital Patient Report, 160–164
Simple Calculation-accumulating final totals-Transaction Register, 122–126
Simple listing-Returned Check Register, 68–71
Simple listing-Transaction Register, 72–75
Stock Inventory Report, 18–22
Subroutines-Compare Class Grades, 211–216
Subroutines-EXCPT-Depreciation Schedule, 216–223
*IN, 327, 584
Index, 299, 318
Indexed file organization, 382–405
Indexed files, 351
   adding records, 394–405
   adding records randomly by key using chaining, 396–399
   adding records randomly by key without chaining, 400
   adding records sequentially by key, 401–404
   creating an ordered file, 382
   creating an unordered file, 382
   creation, 382, 384–387
   maintenance, 388–405
   other ways to process, 405
   processing consecutively, 405
   processing randomly by relative record number, 405
   reorganizing a file, 405
   tagging records for deletion, 405
   updating records, 388
   updating records randomly by key, 388
   updating records sequentially by key, 388
Indexed organization, 354–355, 658
Indexes, 658
INFDS, 581–584
Indicators, 17, 113
   control calculations and output, 97
   L1-L9, 147
   RPG logic related to, 17
   valid, 619
   referenced as data (*IN, *INxx, *IN,xx), RPG III, 327, 584
Input, 2
Input and output operations-writing specifications, 27–65

Input data for end-of-chapter problems, 676–683
Input data for term assignments, 684–687
Input records describing, 39–50
Input Specifications, 12, 40–50
   describing fields, 47
   describing fields within records, 47
   field description entries, 40
   field location, 47
   field names, 48–49
   file and record type identification, 40
   filenames, 40
   record identifying indicators, 34
   specifying record identification codes, 45–46
   specifying record identifying indicators, 41
   specifying record type sequence, 40
   type of data, 47–48
Interprogram Functions, 578–579

Key, 350
Key field, 354

Last record indicator (LR), 100–103
   program cycle operations, 100, 102
   RPG specifications, 102–104
Line Counter Specifications, 12, 36–38
   filename, 38
   specifications, 38
Line number, 66–67
Literal, 83
Load
   member, 4
   program, 4
LOKUP look up operation code, 299–300
   single table, 243–245
   two table search, 246–247
Look ahead, 514–518
   specifications, 514–518
Loop, 182

Machine language, 2
Mass storage device. See Direct access storage devices
Match fields, 430–431, 442
   output specifications, 442
   use of match fields and control fields in the same file, 446–448
Matching comparisons, 440
Matching record entries
   Calculation Specifications, 442
Matching record indicator (MR), 430, 440
Matching records, 435–448
   processing two or more files, 441
   rules for specifying Input Specifications, 442

Matching record technique, 438–440
Modula-2, 553
MOVEA move array operation code, 323–326
    RPG III, 327
MOVEL move left operation code, 191–194
    RPG III, 203
MOVE move operation code, 191–194
    RPG III, 203
Move from high-order zone to high-order zone (MHHZO), 502
Move from high-order zone to low-order zone (MHLZO), 502
Move from low-order zone to high-order zone (MLHZO), 502
Move from low-order zone to low-order zone (MLLZO), 502
Movement of data calculations, 189–194
Move zones operations, 499–502
    coding, 501–502
    differences, 500–501
    how they work, 499–500
Moving data, 191
    specifications, 192–193
Multifile processing, 449–450
    one record type in each file, 444
    when all records in one file have been processed, 445
Multifile records
    order of processing, 440
Multiple Occurrence Data Structures, 580–581
MULT multiply operation code, 85
MVR move remainder operation code, 98

Notations, 10
Numeric, 6
Numeric constants, 93
Numeric literal, 83

Object program, 2, 3, 4
OPEN (Open File for Processing), 561
Operation codes-summary RPG II, 618
Operation codes-summary RPG III, 632
OR relationship, 472–473
ORxx, 205, 210
Output, 2
Output records, describing, 50–65
Output Specifications, 12, 52–65
    editing, 58
    field location, 56
    field name, 55–56
    filename, 53
    first page indicator, 60, 62
    headings, 61, 63
    program cycle operations, 60
    record description entries, 53
    record type, 54
    skipping, 57
    spacing, 56

Overflow area, 658
Overflow indicators (OA-OG, OV), 33

Packed decimal format, 522
PAGE, 110
Page number, 60
Pascal, 553
*PLACE operation code, 58–60
Prepare for compilation, 627
Primary files, 429
Prime area, 658
Printed reports, 56–65
Printer spacing chart, 9–11
PRTCTL (Dynamic Space/Skip Function), 588
Problem 1—Accounts Receivable Register, 639
Problem 2—Stock Inventory Report, 640–641
Problem 3—Weekly Payroll Register, 642–643
Problem 4—Salesman District Report, 643–644
Problem 5—Bank Balance Report, 644–645
Problem 6—Department Store Report, 645–646
Problem 7—"Africa" Payroll Report, 647–648
Problem 8—Shampoo Report, 649–650
Problem 9—Customer Discount Report, 650–651
Problem 10—State Report, 651–652
Problem 11—Insurance Premiums, 653–654
Problem 12—Daily Sales Report, 654–655
Problem 13—Creating An Indexed Disk File, 655
Problem 14—Output An Indexed Disk File, 655–656
Problem 15—Student Status, 656–657
Processing, 2
Processing techniques, 351
Program, 2
Program cycle, 16
    operations, 136–137
Program identification, 68
Program indicators-summary, 617
Programmer's job, 620–631
Programming languages, 2
Programs, 2
punched cards, 553

Random processing, 351
READ read a record operation code, 457–460
    processing demand files, 457–460
    RPG III, 558
READ (Read a Record), RPG III, 558

READC (Read Next Modified Record), 558
READE (Read Equal Key), 559
READP (Read Prior Key), 559
Record, 6, 11, 349–350
Record Address Files (RAF), 406–413
    creating a file with record key limits, 410
    files containing record key limits, 409
    processing sequentially within limits, 410
        Extension Specifications, 412–413
        File Description Specifications, 410–411
    processing using record address file key, 408–409
    processing within limits, 406–408
Record data, 349
Record layout, 7
Record logical, 349
Record physical, 349
Records within a file
    checking sequence, 432–435
    Files containing more than one record type, 432–433
    files containing only one record type, 432
    same match fields for all record types, 434–435
Relative End Positions (40 through 43) on Output Specifications, 585
Relative record number, 406
Reserved fields. 110–112
    PAGE, 110
    Userdate, 110–112
    UDATE, 110–111
        UDAY, 110–111
        UMONTH, 110–111
        UYEAR, 110–111
Resulting indicators, 112–114
RPG specifications, 99–101
RPG
    basic cycle, 12
    basic logic cycle, 27
    compiler, basic operations, 3–4
    data movement within logic cycle, 27
    logic, 139
    logic cycle, 12, 15–16, 81–82, 147
    logic related to indicators, 17
    object program logic-detailed, 613–616
        explanatory notes, 613–616
    reference tables, 617–619
RPG III
    ANDxx, 205, 208
    CABxx (Compare and Branch), 204, 584
    Calculation Modifications, 584
    CALL/RETRN Function, 579

CHAIN (Random Retrieval from a File on RECNO or Key Value), 558
CLOSE (Close File for Processing), 561
Command Key Indicators, 563
CPF, 554–558, 561–563, 566, 578
CRTRPGPGM, 592
Data Description Specification (DDS), 556, 557
Data Structures, 580–584
Default Control Specification, 590
DDS, 556, 557
DEBUG, 592
DEFN (Field Definition), 584–585
DELET, (Delete Record), 558
DO, 205–206
DOUxx, 205, 207
DOWxx, 205, 207–208
DSPLY, (Display), 588
DUMP, 592
EDTCDE, 557
EDTWRD, 557
ELSE, 205, 210
END, 205, 210
Enhanced Debug Facilities, 592
EXCPT (Calculation Time Output), 201–203, 584
EXCPT Name, 201–203
EXFMT (Execute Format), 558
FEOD (Force End Of Data), 561
Figurative Constants, 586
File Information Data Structure (INFDS), 581–584
Formatted Dump, 592
Full Procedural File Specifications, 554, 557–562
IBM System/36, 553
IBM System/38, 553–555, 578
IFxx, 205, 208
Improvements, 553
INFDS, 581–584
Indicators Referenced as Data (*IN, *INxx, *IN,xx), 327, 584
Interprogram Functions, 578–579
Multiple Occurrence Data Structures, 580–581
New Compilation Listing Functions, 590–591
/EJECT and /SPACE Specifications, 590
Cross Reference Listing, 590
Last Update Indication, 590
Nesting Indication, 591
Resulting Indicator Usage, 590
Text Description From Data Description Specifications, 590
OPEN (Open File for Processing), 561
ORxx, 205, 210

PRTCTL (Dynamic Space/Skip Function), 588
Rationale, 553
READ (Read a Record), 558
READC (Read Next Modified Record), 558
READE (Read Equal Key), 559
READP (Read Prior Key), 559
Relative End Positions (40 through 43) on Output Specifications, 585
SETGT (Set Greater Than), 559
SETLL (Set Greater Than or Equal To), 559
SEU, 554
Sequence Number, 554
Short Form of Arithmetic Operations, 116–117, 584
SHTDN (Shutdown), 588
SORTA (Sort Array), 327, 584
Source Diagnostic Error Notation, 554
Source Entry Unit (SEU), 554
System Debug Facility, 592
Table File Replacement, 590
TEXT, 557
TIME (Time), 586–587
UNIQUE, 557
UPDAT (Modify Existing Record), 559
User-defined Edit Codes (5 through 9), 588
Work Station Subfile Operations, 563
Work Station Support, 561–563
WORKSTN File, Externally Described, 561–562
Processing, 565–566
Processing an Externally Described, 562–563
Program Described, 566
WRITE (Create New Records), 560–561

Secondary files, 429
Sequence
ordered, 382
unordered, 382
Sequential file, 350, 355, 429
Sequential file organization, 356–382
adding records, 364–367
adding records at the end of records in the file, 364
creation, 356–365
maintenance, 364–381
merging records between records in the file, 368–372
processing multiple files, 429–430
reorganizing a file, 373
tagging records for deletion, 373
updating records, 373–379
Sequential organization, 354

Sequential processing, 351
SETGT (Set Greater Than), 559
SETLL (Set Greater Than or Equal To), 559
SETOF setting indicators off operation code, 180–182
SETON setting indicators on operation code, 180–182
Setting indicators on and off, 180–182
SEU, 554
Sequence Number, 554
SHTDN (Shutdown), 588
SORTA (Sort Array), 327, 584
Source code, 4
Source Diagnostic Error Notation, 554
Source Entry Unit (SEU), 554
Source program, 2, 3, 4
compile, 644–46
Specification forms, 11–12
Specifications, 2, 12, 147
Structure of characters altering, 499
Structured programming, 201
Subroutines, 194–201
coding, 195–201
RPG III, simplified, 203
SUB subtraction operation code, 85
Subtotals and totals, 136
System Debug Facility, 592

Table, 230
data in calculations and output, 249–266
element, 230
files, 234–235
input records
describing, 235–240
Extension Specifications, 235–240
number of entries, 236
two tables design, 247–249
Table File Replacement, 590
Table lookup operation
coding-single table, 243–245
coding-two tables, 249
conditioning indicators, 249–254
searching for low, high, or equal conditions, 251
single table, 243–245
Table records and entries, 234
Tables, 232–235
alternating entries on one record, 247
changing, 241
compile time, 241–242
forming, 234
loading, 240–242
making permanent changes to table data, 257
making temporary changes to table data, 255
modifying contents, 255–257
moving data, 254–255

output of an entire table, 258–260
preexecution time, 242
    changing, 242
    loading, 242
    specifications, 242
related, 245–249
    retrieving entries, 235
    searching, 230
    sequence, 234–235, 252–254
    short, 238
    short tables for adding new table entries, 257
two tables
    Extension Specifications, 248–249
    search, 246–247
    updating, 235
TAG providing a label for GOTO operation code, 184–189
TESTB test bit operation code, 510–513
TESTN test numeric operation code, 502–503
Test the program, 631
TESTZ test zone operation code, 504–506

TEXT, 557
TIME (Time), 586–587
Total lines, 10
Total output, 116
Total time, 16
Track index, 658

UDATE, 111
UDAY, 111
UMONTH, 111
UNIQUE, 557
Unpacked decimal format, 320
UPDAT (Modify Existing Record), 559
Userdate
    UDAY, 111
    UMONTH, 111
    UYEAR, 111
User-defined Edit Codes (5 through 9), 588
UYEAR, 111

Volume, 350

WORKSTN File, Externally Described, 561–562
    Processing, 565–566
    Processing an Externally Described, 562–563
    Program Described, 566
Work Station Subfile Operations, 563
Work Station Support, 561–563
WRITE (Create New Records), 560–561
Write the specifications, 623–625

XFOOT sum array elements operation code, 299–300
    adding all elements within an array, 304

Z-ADD zero and add operation code, 189, 191, 193
Z-SUB zero and subtract operation code, 191–192
Zoned (unpacked) format, 520–521